THIRTEENTH EDITION

REASON AND RESPONSIBILITY

Readings in Some Basic Problems of Philosophy

JOEL FEINBERG
Late of University of Arizona

RUSS SHAFER-LANDAU
University of Wisconsin

THOMSON
™
WADSWORTH

AUSTRALIA • BRAZIL • CANADA • MEXICO • SINGAPORE
SPAIN • UNITED KINGDOM • UNITED STATES

THOMSON

✦

WADSWORTH

Philosophy Editor: *Worth Hawes*
Assistant Editor: *Barbara Hillaker*
Editorial Assistant: *Patrick Stockstill*
Technology Project Manager: *Julie Aguilar*
Marketing Manager: *Christina Shea*
Marketing Assistant: *Mary Anne Payumo*
Marketing Communications Manager:
  Stacey Purviance
Creative Director: *Rob Hugel*
Executive Art Director: *Maria Epes*

Print Buyer: *Doreen Suruki*
Permissions Editor: *Bobbie Broyer*
Production Service: *Matrix Productions Inc.*
Text Designer: *Lisa Henry*
Copy Editor: *Cheryl Smith*
Cover Designer: *Yvo Riezebos Design/Matt Calkins*
Cover Image: *SuperStock, Inc.*
Compositor: *International Typesetting
  and Composition*
Text and Cover Printer: *West Group*

Thomson Higher Education
10 Davis Drive
Belmont, CA 94002-3098
USA

Library of Congress Control Number: 2006935585

Paper Edition: ISBN-13: 978-0-495-09492-0
           ISBN-10: 0-495-09492-7
Case Edition: ISBN-13: 978-0-495-09605-4
           ISBN-10: 0-495-09605-9

For more information about our products,
contact us at:
Thomson Learning Academic Resource Center
1-800-423-0563
For permission to use material from this text or
product, submit a request online at
http://www.thomsonrights.com.
Any additional questions about permissions
can be submitted by e-mail to
thomsonrights@thomson.com.

CONTENTS

PART FOUR

Determinism, Free Will, and Responsibility   407

PART FIVE

Morality and Its Critics   513

PROPOSED STANDARDS OF RIGHT CONDUCT   555

ETHICAL PROBLEMS   661

JOEL FEINBERG
IN MEMORIAM

JOEL FEINBERG (1926–2004) was a brilliant philosopher, certainly one of the most important social and political philosophers of the last half century. He was also a very kind, humble man. And he was an extremely conscientious teacher. The great care and preparation that he devoted to his teaching is evident here, in the plan and format of *Reason and Responsibility*. Joel developed the first edition of this textbook about forty years ago, dissatisfied with existing options, and intent on providing coverage of those areas of philosophy that struck him as deeply important and deserving of every student's careful study.

Most of you reading this will know Joel Feinberg only as the editor of a book you've been assigned to read. If you have a chance, you ought to seek out one of the many exciting works that Joel penned during his prolific career. He was a philosophical writer of rare talent. He wrote about things that matter, and did so in a way that everyone could understand. He was clear, he was elegant, always ready with the telling example, the well-chosen reference to literature or history, dropped into place with a light touch. Open any one of his many books and read at random—you can't help but be impressed by the humanism, the clarity, the originality and, certainly, the wisdom of the views that receive expression there.

Joel was also a man of great common sense and discernment. One of the most desirable things in life is to have a person of integrity and genuinely sound judgment to rely on for advice, companionship, and, if one is especially fortunate, for friendship. I was lucky enough to study with Joel for five years, to write a dissertation under his direction, and later to work with him as a collaborator on this book over the past decade. His suggestions during our collaboration, both about substantive matters of content and about the more mundane, practical matters of the publishing world, epitomized his practical wisdom. He was a man whose judgment you could trust.

Joel was curious, interested in the whole range of human experience, attentive to relevant detail, appreciative of salient distinctions, a lover of taxonomies and, at the same time, able to resist the pressure that such taxonomies impose—pressure to falsify the phenomena and straitjacket it into categories that generate misunderstanding. It is a very rare talent, to be so analytically minded and yet so broad in one's outlook, to appreciate system and yet to be sensitive to the fine detail that must constrain its development. Joel possessed such talent, to a degree that was almost unrivalled. There were very few in his league.

Joel died after a long struggle with Parkinson's disease and its complications. He left us a great and valuable legacy, both personal and professional. It was a true honor to have known him, to have learned from him, and to have counted him a friend.

R. S. L.
Madison 2007

PREFACE

THE CONVICTION UNDERLYING this volume is that introducing the college student to philosophy by means of a few representative problems examined in great detail is far preferable to offering a "little bit of everything," with each "branch" of philosophy, each major "ism," and each major historical period represented with scrupulous impartiality, even though the articles may have little relevance to one another. Accordingly, articles have been selected from both classical and contemporary sources on such topics as religion, mind, personal identity, death, freedom, responsibility, duty, justice, and selfishness. The problems that concern philosophers under these headings are not mere idle riddles, but rather questions of vital interest to any reflective person. Each set of problems is plumbed in considerable depth in essays expressing different, often opposing, views. The hope is that exposure to this argumentative give-and-take will encourage students to take part in the process themselves, and through this practice to develop their powers of philosophical reasoning.

This thirteenth edition of *Reason and Responsibility* has been strengthened by the addition of thirteen new selections. The policy of securing the very best available English translations for foreign works has been retained. We have tried to strike a good balance between classic works and relatively new material on these subjects of enduring philosophical interest.

I encourage readers to have a look at our website, located at www.thomsonedu.com/philosophy/feinberg. Once there, you will see a substantial introduction, study questions, and relevant philosophical internet links associated with each of the 77 selections included in this latest edition. Research assistants Alan Rubel and David Killoren have prepared these materials under my supervision. I would like to thank Wadsworth for absorbing the costs associated with this project. I am proud of the site and think that it will be a terrific aid to student learning.

The following major parts of this work have been updated and expanded. Part 1, "Reason and Religious Belief," reinstates, by popular demand, J. L. Mackie's now-classic argument from evil, one that seeks to show that the presence of avoidable suffering demonstrates that a perfect God does not exist. Also on offer is a reply by philosopher George Schlesinger, one that seeks to show that the existence of evil is no threat at all to the existence of God.

Part 2 ("Human Knowledge: Its Grounds and Limits") is strengthened by a new defense of radical skepticism, by Peter Unger, and a generous selection from Bertrand Russell's *Problems of Philosophy*, in which Russell presents and analyzes the worries surrounding skepticism in his characteristically instructive and lucid way.

Part 3 ("Mind and Its Place in Nature") now includes a piece by Brie Gertler, written especially for this edition of *Reason and Responsibility*. Gertler defends mind–body dualism, and does so with verve. This view, once the default position in this area of philosophy, has become the subject of widespread doubt. Gertler does an excellent job of resuscitating it in the face of criticisms, and presenting challenges of her own to the views of her opponents. Also new to this part is a pair of readings on animal minds, one by John Searle, defending their existence, and the other by Peter Carruthers, who denies that animals are conscious, and rejects the claim that animals have feelings (of pain, pleasure, etc.) that give them any claim to our moral attention.

Part 4 ("Determinism, Free Will and Responsibility") includes three new selections. Derk Pereboom adds his defense of "hard incompatibilism," a view that is agnostic about the truth of determinism, but strongly affirms the view that we lack freedom, and that freedom and determinism are incompatible. John Martin Fischer is enlisted in support of compatibilism, the view that we can have our cake and eat it, too: freedom can, after all, peacefully co-exist with determinism. There is also a new selection on freedom and moral responsibility by the late philosopher James Rachels, who carefully and engagingly surveys the territory in this area, and comes up with some surprising results.

This volume currently contains seven major classics: two that are complete (Descartes' *Meditations* and Plato's *Crito*); one that is presented in virtual totality (Hume's *Dialogues*); and four that appear in very substantial sections (Berkeley's *Principles*, Hume's *Inquiry*, Mill's *Utilitarianism*, and Kant's *Groundwork*). In addition, we have included shorter selections from sixteen more classic texts: those authored by Anselm, Gaunilo, Aquinas, Clarke, Paley, Pascal, William James, G. E. Moore, Locke, Reid, Hume, Plato, Nietzsche, Aristotle and Hobbes. This book can be used to teach an introductory course based solidly on a reading of these classics; more recent articles can be seen as a kind of dividend. The book contains many articles by contemporary philosophers, including eight that are addressed specifically to beginning students and that were written expressly for this book by William Rowe, Wesley Salmon, John Perry, Robert Kane, Brie Gertler, Philip Quinn, and both editors.

There is no single "necessary and natural" order or sequence in which to read these materials. The book begins with the philosophy of religion because many beginners are familiar with its problems. But it is just as "natural" to begin with Part 2, because the question of our knowledge of God presupposes the question of the "grounds and limits of human knowledge" generally. Similarly, there is no reason why one could not begin with the mind–body problem (Part 3) or the problem of determinism and free will (Part 4). Indeed, many professors have said that they prefer to begin with ethics (Part 5) and work their way toward the front of the book.

I am grateful for advice on how to improve the format and content of subsequent editions of *Reason and Responsibility*. Those with such advice are very welcome to email me at shaferlandau@wisc.edu with their suggestions.

I'd like to thank Andrew Johnson (SMU), Kihyeon Kim (Seoul National University), Jonny Anomaly (Ithaca College), and my colleagues Eric Margolis and Claudia Card for their very helpful advice on materials for this new edition. And a special note of thanks to my research assistant, David Killoren, who offered invaluable help and advice over the course of the many months that this new edition was being prepared.

Russ Shafer-Landau

Reason and Religious Belief

WHAT CAN REASON TELL US about such vast topics as the origin of the universe and the existence and nature of God? Most of us have beliefs about these matters—beliefs derived from religious authorities or based on faith; but is there any way to demonstrate that these beliefs are reasonable or unreasonable? This question provides the unifying theme for the readings in Part 1.

Traditional arguments for the existence of God are often divided into two groups: those whose premises are justified **a posteriori** (based on experience), and those whose premises are known **a priori** (independently of experience). In fact, however, only one mode of argument has ever purported to be wholly independent of experience, namely, the **ontological argument,** invented by St. Anselm in the eleventh century and defended in one form or another by Descartes, Spinoza, and Leibniz in the seventeenth century. (For Descartes' version of the argument, see his fifth Meditation.) According to this argument, the very concept of God (or definition of the word *God*) entails that God must exist. If the argument is correct, anyone who has an idea of God—even if that person has no knowledge whatever of the kind derived from sense experience—has conclusive rational grounds for believing that God exists. The ontological argument still has defenders among philosophers of religion today, but among those who reject it, there is little agreement over precisely what is wrong with the argument. One classic and one recent discussion of the argument are included here. The brief but famous reply of Gaunilo, a monk who was a contemporary of Anselm's, appears here, and is complemented by an article that reflects some current thinking regarding the famous argument. William L. Rowe's essay sets forth Anselm's argument clearly, step-by-step (including steps that are only implicit in Anselm's own formulation), summarizes the three most important objections to the argument, and then presents his own criticism. Rowe concludes that the ontological argument is defective but that it is nevertheless a "work of genius," which, despite its apparent simplicity, raises philosophical questions about the nature of existence that are subtle and fascinating in their own right.

Other arguments for God's existence are often called a priori, but these always contain at least one premise that asserts some simple experiential fact. Factual premises summarizing some facet of our experience are found in the various versions of the **cosmological argument**—illustrated in this section by the selections from St. Thomas Aquinas and Samuel Clarke. For the first three of his "Five Ways," Aquinas begins each argument by citing a familiar fact of experience: Some things are in motion; there are causes and effects; things are generated and corrupted. He then tries to show that this fact can be explained only by the existence of God, because alternative explanations lead to logical absurdities. In his second article in this section, Rowe examines the cosmological argument in the form given it by Samuel Clarke and other seventeenth- and eighteenth-century philosophers. Put simply, the argument goes as follows:

1. Every being (that exists or ever did exist) is either a dependent being or self-existent being.
2. Not every being can be a dependent being.
3. Therefore, there exists a self-existent being.

The argument clearly is valid; that is, *if* its premises are true, then its conclusion is true. But the premises, especially the second, are highly controversial. Rowe reviews the dialectic of the debate, pro and con, over the truth of the second premise, before cautiously concluding that the premise has not yet been conclusively shown to be true.

Both the ontological and the cosmological arguments are **deductive** in form; that is, they purport to demonstrate that if their premises are true, then their conclusions must necessarily be true. It is logically impossible for a valid deductive argument to have both true premises and false conclusion. The **teleological argument** (more commonly called "the argument from design") for God's existence is more modest. It argues not that its conclusion follows necessarily from its premises, but only that its premises establish a probability that the conclusion is true. It is therefore what logicians call an **inductive argument.** The famous argument from design, which is given classic formulations in William Paley's *Natural Theology* (1802), and by Cleanthes, a character in David Hume's *Dialogues Concerning Natural Religion* (1779), has the **inductive** form. More precisely, it is an argument by analogy, with the following form:

1. *a, b, c,* and *d* all have properties *P* and *Q.*
2. *a, b,* and *c* all have property *R* as well.
3. Therefore, *d* has property *R* too (probably).

The closer the similarity between *d* and *a, b,* and *c,* the more probable is the conclusion. Cleanthes' argument can be rendered as follows:

1. Boats, houses, watches, and the whole experienced world have such properties as "mutual adjustment of parts to whole" and "curious adapting of means to ends."
2. Boats, houses, and watches have the further property of having been produced by design.
3. Therefore, it is probable that the universe also has this further property, that it too was produced by design.

The conclusion of this argument, that a designer of the world exists, has the same logical role as a scientific hypothesis designed to explain the facts of experience, and must be accepted or rejected according to whether it meets the criteria of adequacy by which hypotheses are appraised in science and in everyday life.

In Hume's *Dialogues,* the case against the argument from design is stated with great force and ingenuity by Philo, probably speaking for Hume himself. The analogies cited by the argument, he claims, are weak, partly because we know only one small part of the universe and cannot with confidence infer from it the nature of the whole. Moreover, he argues, there are other equally plausible ways of accounting for the observed order in the world. One of these alternative explanations, called "The Epicurean Hypothesis" by Philo in Part 7 of the *Dialogues,* bears striking resemblance to the Darwinian theory that biological adaptations are the result of chance variations and the survival of the fittest.

After canvassing some classic arguments for God's existence, and some replies, we come to what is perhaps the strongest of the arguments of the other side, namely, the **problem of evil.** Parts X and XI of Hume's *Dialogues* contain one of the most famous discussions of this problem, so central to religious belief. Here Philo concedes that if the existence of God has already been established by some a priori argument, then perhaps one can account for the appearance of evil in the world. But, he goes on to argue, one cannot infer the existence of an all-good and all-powerful being from the appearance of evil; that is, the former can hardly be an *explanation* of the latter.

In the subsection devoted entirely to the problem of evil, the great Russian novelist Fyodor Dostoevsky dramatically sets the stage for the philosophical discussion that follows by showing how the problem can arise in human experience. Dostoevsky's excerpt (from his novel, *The Brothers Karamazov*) is complemented by two sets of contemporary discussions of this problem.

The first pair of readings is focused on the so-called *logical problem of evil*. John Mackie's now-classic critique of theism is perhaps the best-known presentation of this problem. Mackie claims that the idea of an all-powerful, all-knowing and all-good God is logically incoherent, given the existence of evil in our world. Logically speaking, claims Mackie, a perfect God is one who is (among other things) able and willing to eradicate evil. Since evil exists, God either does not exist, or does, but is not perfect. In short, the very idea of an omnipotent, omniscient and perfectly good God logically requires that any such being eliminate evil. So it is logically incoherent to suppose that a perfect God can co-exist with evil.

George Schlesinger rejects this line of thought, arguing that the existence of evil poses no threat at all to the existence of a perfect God. True, says Schlesinger, God cannot create the greatest possible happiness. But this does not signal any limitation on His part, because the greatest possible happiness is like the greatest possible integer—a logically incoherent notion. Asking that God make us infinitely happy is demanding what is logically impossible, and, as almost everyone agrees, no one (not even God) can be asked to do what is logically impossible.

Richard Swinburne next offers his theodicy—his effort to demonstrate the justice of God in the face of the world's ills. He approaches the problem from the Christian standpoint, but he does not underestimate the difficulty for Christian belief posed by the undeniable fact of human suffering. **Moral evil** (wickedness), according to a predominant strain of Christian teaching, is a necessary concomitant of human free will, indeed the price we pay for freedom; and it is logically impossible, in this line of thought, for God to have created perfectly free creatures who always behave in a perfectly good way. God is a just and loving God, for He cared enough about us to endow us with something of very great value–free will. Being free, we sometimes make mistakes. The misery in this world is properly charged to our misdeeds, rather than God's culpability. A world with free will, and the suffering it sometimes engenders, is a better world than one in which human beings are mere automata.

Numerous philosophers, on both sides of the issue, agree that the coherence of the crucial description—"created so as always to freely choose what is right"—is at the root of the problem of evil. It may be useful to the student who is especially interested in the problem of evil to read the materials on free will in Part 4.

B. C. Johnson takes direct aim at Swinburne's kind of theodicy, finding no contradiction in the thought of beings perfectly free and perfectly virtuous. In a nutshell, Johnson's argument is that God could have created a world inhabited by such people. That world would have been far better than ours. Therefore if God were perfect, He'd have created such a world. He didn't. Therefore the perfect God of classical monotheism doesn't exist.

Some of Johnson's many critical arguments echo Mackie's skepticism, and seek to show that it is logically impossible for evil and a perfect God to co-exist. But Johnson also develops a variety of *evidential arguments from evil*. These do not assert that the idea of a perfect God is logically incoherent. There could be such a being. But, given the vast evidence we have of avoidable suffering, the odds are very good that God does not exist. This is thus an inductive argument; it seeks to establish that the probability of atheism is very high, given our evidence. On this skeptical view, God might yet exist, though our best evidence says that He doesn't.

What if it should turn out (as many philosophers now believe) that all traditional arguments for the existence of God are defective, or at least inconclusive? Would it follow that religious belief is unreasonable? Not necessarily. Some believers have claimed that the grounds of their belief have nothing to do with argument, but rather derive from a direct experience of deity (a "mystic experience"). These believers cannot prove that God exists, but they cannot prove that *they themselves* exist either. In both cases, they claim to know directly, by immediate experience, that something exists, and further proof is unnecessary.

Although they have nothing to do with argument, mystical experiences might nevertheless be considered a kind of "evidence" for their attendant beliefs. The question posed by the final subsection of this chapter, however, is whether beliefs based on no evidence at all can nonetheless be, in some circumstances, reasonable. In his selection here, Kelly James Clark defends an affirmative answer to this question. He argues that we already accept the credibility of certain non-religious beliefs on the basis of no evidence at all, and are quite reasonable to do so. If we criticize the religious believer for lack of evidence, then, to be consistent, we must abandon many eminently reasonable beliefs. Since, in the end, it would not be rational to abandon them, it wouldn't be rational for the theist to abandon her religious beliefs, either.

W. K. Clifford argues emphatically for the negative and affirms his own rationalistic "ethic of belief," namely, that "it is wrong always, everywhere, and for anyone to believe anything upon insufficient evidence." The seventeenth-century mathematician-philosopher Blaise Pascal had argued for the reasonableness of a kind of "bet" on God's existence even in the absence of all evidence, urging that it costs little to believe in God and act accordingly even if God in fact does not exist, whereas there is an infinite amount to lose by not believing if in fact God exists. Many Christian **fideists** (those whose belief is based on faith rather than argument), including William James, have found the unveiled appeal to self-interest in Pascal's "wager" to be a kind of embarrassment. James, in his famous "The Will to Believe," disowns Pascal but goes on to explain in his own way why belief in the absence of evidence can in some circumstances be reasonable. (Careful readers might well ask themselves, however, whether James's strict conditions for the proper exercise of "the will to believe" are in fact ever satisfied.) If there is one thing that James, the nineteenth-century Protestant, has in common with Pascal, the seventeenth-century Catholic, it is the conviction that the primary function of religious belief is not simply to allay philosophical curiosity about things. Both writers are aware that, to many, religious belief is a vital practical need, and each in his own way urges this to be taken into account when the reasonableness of belief is assessed.

The last of our offerings in the philosophy of religion sounds a decidedly skeptical note. Central to many religions is the idea of literally miraculous divine intervention. Many think that religious faith can receive rational support from warranted belief in miracles. Simon Blackburn explains what miracles are and must be if they are to play this central role. He sides with Hume and others in claiming that we never have better evidence for thinking that what we have experienced is a genuine miracle, as opposed to some phenomenon subject to scientific or psychological explanation. To the extent that our religious beliefs are grounded in the view that we (or others we know) have experienced miracles, our religious beliefs are unjustified. The world we live in, hints Blackburn, is a wholly material world, governed solely by the laws of nature.

This sort of skepticism about miracles, and more generally about the sorts of things that escape scientific confirmation, has implications for many other areas of philosophy. Students interested in exploring the consequences of such a "naturalistic" or "materialistic" world view can find articles that address these implications in every one of the remaining parts of this book. Those so minded are encouraged to have a look at works in Part 2 ("The Methods of Science"), Part 3 ("The Mind-Body Problem"), Part 4 ("Hard Determinism"), and Part 5 ("Challenges to Morality").

THE EXISTENCE AND NATURE OF GOD

The Ontological Argument, from *Proslogion*

ANSELM OF CANTERBURY

Anselm of Canterbury (1033–1109) was Archbishop of Canterbury.

CHAPTER 2. THAT GOD TRULY EXISTS

Well then, Lord, You who give understanding to faith, grant me that I may understand, as much as You see fit, that You exist as we believe You to exist, and that You are what we believe You to be. Now we believe that You are something than which nothing greater can be thought. Or can it be that a thing of such a nature does not exist, since 'the Fool has said in his heart, there is no God' [Ps. 13: I; 52: I]? But surely, when this same Fool hears what I am speaking about, namely, 'something-than-which-nothing-greater-can-be-thought', he understands what he hears, and what he understands is in his mind, even if he does not understand that it actually exists. For it is one thing for an object to exist in the mind, and another thing to understand that an object actually exists. Thus, when a painter plans beforehand what he is going to execute, he has [the picture] in his mind, but he does not yet think that it actually exists because he has not yet executed it. However, when he has actually painted it, then he both has it in his mind and understands that it exists because he has now made it. Even the Fool, then, is forced to agree that something-than-which-nothing-greater-can-

be-thought exists in the mind, since he understands this when he hears it, and whatever is understood is in the mind. And surely that-than-which-a-greater-cannot-be-thought cannot exist in the mind alone. For if it exists solely in the mind, it can be thought to exist in reality also, which is greater. If then that-than-which-a-greater-cannot-be-thought exists in the mind alone, this same that-than-which-a-greater-*cannot*-be-thought is that-than-which-a-greater-*can*-be-thought. But this is obviously impossible. Therefore there is absolutely no doubt that something-than-which-a-greater-cannot-be-thought exists both in the mind and in reality.

CHAPTER 3. THAT GOD CANNOT BE THOUGHT NOT TO EXIST

And certainly this being so truly exists that it cannot be even thought not to exist. For something can be thought to exist that cannot be thought not to exist, and this is greater than that which can be thought not to exist. Hence, if that-than-which-a-greater-cannot-be-thought can be thought not to exist, then that-than-which-a-greater-cannot-be-thought is not the same as that-than-which-a-greater-cannot-be-thought, which is absurd. Something-than-which-a-greater-cannot-be-thought

From *Anselm's Proslogion*, trans. M. J. Charlesworth.

exists so truly then, that it cannot be even thought not to exist.

And You, Lord our God, are this being. You exist so truly, Lord my God, that You cannot even be thought not to exist. And this is as it should be, for if some intelligence could think of something better than You, the creature would be above its Creator and would judge its Creator—and that is completely absurd. In fact, everything else there is, except You alone, can be thought of as not existing. You alone, then, of all things most truly exist and therefore of all things possess existence to the highest degree; for anything else does not exist as truly, and so possesses existence to a lesser degree. Why then did 'the Fool say in his heart, there is no God' [Ps. 14: 1; 53: 1] when it is so evident to any rational mind that You of all things exist to the highest degree? Why indeed, unless because he was stupid and a fool?

CHAPTER 4. HOW 'THE FOOL SAID IN HIS HEART' WHAT CANNOT BE THOUGHT

How indeed has he 'said in his heart' what he could not think; or how could he not think what he 'said in his heart', since to 'say in one's heart' and to 'think' are the same? But if he really (indeed, since he really) both thought because he 'said in his heart' and did not 'say in his heart' because he could not think, there is not only one sense in which something is 'said in one's heart' or thought. For in one sense a thing is thought when the word signifying it is thought; in another sense when the very object which the thing is understood. In the first sense, then, God can be thought not to exist, but not at all in the second sense. No one, indeed,

understanding what God is can think that God does not exist, even though he may say these words in his heart either without any [objective] signification or with some peculiar signification. For God is that-than-which-nothing-greater-can-be-thought. Whoever really understands this understands clearly that this same being so exists that not even in thought can it not exist. Thus whoever understands that God exists in such a way cannot think of Him as not existing.

I give thanks, good Lord, I give thanks to You, since what I believed before through Your free gift I now so understand through Your illumination, that if I did not want to *believe* that You existed, I should nevertheless be unable not to *understand* it.

CHAPTER 5. THAT GOD IS WHATEVER IT IS BETTER TO BE THAN NOT TO BE AND THAT, EXISTING THROUGH HIMSELF ALONE, HE MAKES ALL OTHER BEINGS FROM NOTHING

What then are You, Lord God, You than whom nothing greater can be thought? But what are You save that supreme being, existing through Yourself alone, who made everything else from nothing? For whatever is not this is less than that which can be thought of; but this cannot be thought about You. What goodness, then, could be wanting to the supreme good, through which every good exists? Thus You are just, truthful, happy, and whatever it is better to be than not to be—for it is better to be just rather than unjust, and happy rather than unhappy.

On Behalf of the Fool

GAUNILO OF MARMOUTIERS

Gaunilo was an eleventh-century Benedictine monk whose fame rests on his critique of Anselm's ontological argument.

From *Anselm's Proslogion,* trans. M. J. Charlesworth.

1

To one doubting whether there is, or denying that there is, something of such a nature than which nothing greater can be thought, it is said here [in the *Proslogion*] that its existence is proved, first because the very one who denies or doubts it already has it in his mind, since when he hears it spoken of he understands what is said; and further, because what he understands is necessarily such that it exists not only in the mind but also in reality. And this is proved by the fact that it is greater to exist both in the mind and in reality than in the mind alone. For if this same being exists in the mind alone, anything that existed also in reality would be greater than this being, and thus that which is greater than everything would be less than some thing and would not be greater than everything, which is obviously contradictory. Therefore, it is necessarily the case that which is greater than everything, being already proved to exist in the mind, should exist not only in the mind but also in reality, since otherwise it would not be greater than everything.

2

But he [the Fool] can perhaps reply that this thing is said already to exist in the mind only in the sense that I understand what is said. For could I not say that all kinds of unreal things, not existing in themselves in any way at all, are equally in the mind since if anyone speaks about them I understand whatever he says? Unless perhaps it is manifest that this being is such that it can be entertained in the mind in a different way from unreal or doubtfully real things, so that I am not said to think of or have in thought what is heard, but to understand and have it in mind, in that I cannot really think of this being in any other way save by understanding it, that is to say, by grasping by certain knowledge that the thing itself actually exists. But if this is the case, first, there will be no difference between having an object in mind (taken as preceding in time), and understanding that the object actually exists (taken as following in time), as in the case of the picture which exists first in the mind of

the painter and then in the completed work. And thus it would be scarcely conceivable that, when this object had been spoken of and heard, it could not be thought not to exist in the same way in which God can [be thought] not to exist. For if He cannot, why put forward this whole argument against anyone denying or doubting that there is something of this kind? Finally, that it is such a thing that, as soon as it is thought of, it cannot but be certainly perceived by the mind as indubitably existing, must be proved to me by some indisputable argument and not by that proposed, namely, that it must already be in my mind when I understand what I hear. For this is in my view like [arguing that] any things doubtfully real or even unreal are capable of existing if these things are mentioned by someone whose spoken words I might understand, and, even more, that [they exist] if, though deceived about them as often happens, I should believe them [to exist]—which argument I still do not believe!

3

Hence, the example of the painter having the picture he is about to make already in his mind cannot support this argument. For this picture, before it is actually made, is contained in the very art of the painter and such a thing in the art of any artist is nothing but a certain part of his very understanding, since as St Augustine says [*In Iohannem,* tract. 1, n. 16], 'when the artisan is about actually to make a box he has it beforehand in his art. The box which is actually made is not a living thing, but the box which is in his art is a living thing since the soul of the artist, in which these things exist before their actual realization, is a living thing.' Now how are these things living in the living soul of the artist unless they are identical with the knowledge or understanding of the soul itself? But, apart from those things which are known to belong to the very nature of the mind itself, in the case of any truth perceived by the mind by being either heard or understood, then it cannot be doubted that this truth is one thing and that the understanding which grasps it is another. Therefore even if it were true that there was something than which nothing greater could be thought, this thing, heard and understood, would not, however, be the same as the not-yet-made picture is in the mind of the painter.

4

To this we may add something that has already been mentioned, namely, that upon hearing it spoken of I can so little think of or entertain in my mind this being (that which is greater than all those others that are able to be thought of, and which it is said can be none other than God Himself) in terms of an object known to me either by species or genus, as I can think of God Himself, whom indeed for this very reason I can even think does not exist. For neither do I know the reality itself, nor can I form an idea from some other things like it since, as you say yourself, it is such that nothing could be like it. For if I heard something said about a man who was completely unknown to me so that I did not even know whether he existed, I could nevertheless think about him in his very reality as a man by means of that specific or generic notion by which I know what a man is or men are. However, it could happen that, because of a falsehood on the part of the speaker, the man I thought of did not actually exist, although I thought of him nevertheless as a truly existing object—not this particular man but any man in general. It is not, then, in the way that I have this unreal thing in thought or in mind that I can have that object in my mind when I hear 'God' or 'something greater than everything' spoken of. For while I was able to think of the former in terms of a truly existing thing which was known to me, I know nothing at all of the latter save for the verbal formula, and on the basis of this alone one can scarcely or never think of any truth. For when one thinks in this way, one thinks not so much of the word itself, which is indeed a real thing (that is to say, the sound of the letters or syllables), as of the meaning of the word which is heard. However, it [that which is greater than everything] is not thought of in the way of one who knows what is meant by that expression—thought of, that is, in terms of the thing [signified] or as true in

thought alone. It is rather in the way of one who does not really know this object but thinks of it in terms of an affection of his mind produced by hearing the spoken words, and who tries to imagine what the words he has heard might mean. However, it would be astonishing if he could ever [attain to] the truth of the thing. Therefore, when I hear and understand someone saying that there is something greater than everything that can be thought of, it is agreed that it is in this latter sense that it is in my mind and not in any other sense. So much for the claim that that supreme nature exists already in my mind.

5

That, however, [this nature] necessarily exists in reality is demonstrated to me from the fact that, unless it existed, whatever exists in reality would be greater than it and consequently it would not be that which is greater than everything that undoubtedly had already been proved to exist in the mind. To this I reply as follows: if something that cannot even be thought in the true and real sense must be said to exist in the mind, then I do not deny that this also exists in my mind in the same way. But since from this one cannot in any way conclude that it exists also in reality, I certainly do not yet concede that it actually exists, until this is proved to me by an indubitable argument. For he who claims that it actually exists because otherwise it would not be that which is greater than everything does not consider carefully enough whom he is addressing. For I certainly do not yet admit this greater [than everything] to be any truly existing thing; indeed I doubt or even deny it. And I do not concede that it exists in a different way from that—if one ought to speak of 'existence' here—when the mind tries to imagine a completely unknown thing on the basis of the spoken words alone. How then can it be proved to me on that basis that which is greater than everything truly exists in reality (because it is evident that it is greater than all others) if I keep on denying and also doubting that this is evident and do not admit that this greater [than everything] is either in my mind or thought, not even in the sense in which many doubtfully real and unreal things are? It must first of all be proved to me then that this same greater than everything truly exists in reality somewhere, and then only will the fact that it is greater than everything make it clear that it also subsists in itself.

6

For example: they say that there is in the ocean somewhere an island which, because of the difficulty (or rather the impossibility) of finding that which does not exist, some have called the 'Lost Island'. And the story goes that it is blessed with all manner of priceless riches and delights in abundance, much more even than the Happy Isles, and, having no owner or inhabitant, it is superior everywhere in abundance of riches to all those other lands that men inhabit. Now, if anyone tell me that it is like this, I shall easily understand what is said, since nothing is difficult about it. But if he should then go on to say, as though it were a logical consequence of this: You cannot any more doubt that this island that is more excellent than all other lands truly exists somewhere in reality than you can doubt that it is in your mind; and since it is more excellent to exist not only in the mind alone but also in reality, therefore it must needs be that it exists. For if it did not exist, any other land existing in reality would be more excellent than it, and so this island, already conceived by you to be more excellent than others, will not be more excellent. If, I say, someone wishes thus to persuade me that this island really exists beyond all doubt, I should either think that he was joking, or I should find it hard to decide which of us I ought to judge the bigger fool—I, if I agreed with him, or he, if he thought that he had proved the existence of this island with any certainty, unless he had first convinced me that its very excellence exists in my mind precisely as a thing existing truly and indubitably and not just as something unreal or doubtfully real.

7

Thus first of all might the Fool reply to objections. And if then someone should assert that this greater [than everything] is such that it cannot be thought not to exist (again without any other proof than that otherwise it would not be greater than everything), then he could make this same reply and say: When have I said that there truly existed some being that is 'greater than everything', such that from this it could be proved to me that this same being really existed to such a degree that it could not be thought not to exist? That is why it must first be conclusively proved by argument that there is some higher nature, namely that which is greater and better than all the things that are, so that from this we can also infer everything else which necessarily cannot be wanting to what is greater and better than everything. When, however, it is said that this supreme being cannot be *thought* not to exist, it would perhaps be better to say that it cannot be *understood* not to exist nor even to be able not to exist. For, strictly speaking, unreal things cannot be *understood*, though certainly they can be *thought* of in the same way as the Fool *thought* that God does not exist. I know with complete certainty that I exist, but I also know at the same time nevertheless that I can not-exist. And I *understand* without any doubt that that which exists to the highest degree, namely God, both exists and cannot not exist. I do not know, however, whether I can *think* of myself as not existing while I know with absolute certainty that I do exist; but if I can, why cannot [I do the same] with regard to anything else I know with the same certainty? If however I cannot, this will not be the distinguishing characteristic of God [namely, to be such that He cannot be thought not to exist].

The Ontological Argument

WILLIAM L. ROWE

William L. Rowe teaches philosophy at Purdue University. He is a distinguished authority in the philosophy of religion.

Arguments for the existence of God are commonly divided into a posteriori and a priori arguments. An a posteriori argument depends on a principle or premise that can be known only by means of our experience of the world. An a priori argument, on the other hand, purports to rest on principles which can be known independently of our experience of the world, just by reflecting on and understanding them. Of the three major arguments for the existence of God—the Cosmological, Teleological, and Ontological—only the last is entirely a priori. In the Cosmological argument one starts from some simple fact about the world, such as the fact that it contains things which are caused to exist by other things. In the Teleological argument a somewhat more complicated fact about the world serves as a starting point: the fact that the world exhibits order and design. In the Ontological argument, however, one begins simply with a concept of God.

I

It is perhaps best to think of the Ontological argument as a family of arguments, each member of which begins with a concept of God, and by appealing only to a priori principles, endeavors to establish that God actually exists. Within this family of arguments the most important historically is the argument set forth by Anselm in the second chapter of his *Proslogium* (A Discourse).[1] Indeed, the Ontological argument begins with chapter II of Anselm's *Proslogium*. In an earlier work, *Monologium* (A Soliloquy), Anselm had endeavored to establish the existence and nature

of God by weaving together several versions of the Cosmological argument. In the Preface to *Proslogium* Anselm remarks that after the publication of *Monologium* he began to search for a single argument which alone would establish the existence and nature of God. After much strenuous but unsuccessful effort, he reports that he sought to put the project out of his mind in order to turn to more fruitful tasks. The idea, however, continued to haunt him until one day the proof he had so strenuously sought became clear to his mind. Anselm sets forth this proof in the second chapter of *Proslogium*.

Before discussing Anselm's argument in step-by-step fashion, there are certain concepts that will help us understand some of the central ideas of the argument. Suppose we draw a vertical line in our imagination and agree that on the left side of our line are all the things which exist, while on the right side of the line are all the things which don't exist. We might then begin to make a list of some of the things on both sides of our imaginary line, as follows:

Things Which Exist	Things Which Don't Exist
The Empire State Building	The Fountain of Youth
	Unicorns
Dogs	The Abominable
The planet Mars	Snowman

Now each of the things (or sorts of things) listed thus far has (have) the following feature: it (they) logically might have been on the other side of the line. The Fountain of Youth, for example, is on the right side of the line, but *logically* there is no absurdity in the idea that it might have been on the left side of the line. Similarly, although dogs do exist, we surely can imagine without logical absurdity that they might not have existed, that they might have been on the right side of the line. Let us then record this feature of the things thus far listed by introducing the idea of a *contingent thing* as a thing that logically might have been on the other side of the line from the side it actually is on. The planet Mars and the Abominable Snowman are contingent things, even though the former happens to exist and the latter does not.

Suppose we add to our list the phrase "the object which is completely round and completely square at the same time" on the right side of our line. The round square, however, unlike the other things thus far listed on the right side of our line, is something that *logically could not* have been on the left side of the line. Noting this, let us introduce the idea of an *impossible thing* as a thing that is on the right side of the line and logically could not have been on the left side of the line.

Looking again at our list, we wonder if there is anything on the left side of our imaginary line which, unlike the things thus far listed on the left side, *logically could not* have been on the right side of the line. At this point we don't have to answer this question, but it is useful to have a concept to apply to any such things, should there be any. Accordingly, let us say that a *necessary thing* is a thing on the left side of our imaginary line and logically could not have been on the right side of the line.

Finally, a *possible thing* is any thing that is either on the left side of our imaginary line or logically might have been on the left side of the line. Possible things, then, will be all those things that are not impossible things—that is, all those things that are either contingent or necessary. If there are no necessary things, then all possible things will be contingent and all contingent things will be possible. If there is a necessary thing, however, then there will be a possible thing which is not contingent.

Armed with these concepts, we can clarify certain important distinctions and ideas in Anselm's thought. The first of these is his distinction between *existence in the understanding* and *existence in reality*. Anselm's notion of existence in reality is the same as our notion of existence; that is, being on the left side of our imaginary line. Since the Fountain of Youth is on the right side of the line, it does not exist in reality. The things which exist are, to use Anselm's phrase, the things which exist in reality. Anselm's notion of existence in the understanding, however, is not the same as any idea we normally employ. When we think of a certain thing, say the Fountain of Youth, then that thing, on Anselm's view, exists in the understanding. Also, when we think of an existing thing like the Empire State Building, it, too, exists in the understanding. So some of the things on both sides of our imaginary line exist in the understanding, but only those on the left side of our line exist in reality. Are there any things that don't exist in the understanding? Undoubtedly there are, for there are things, both existing and non-existing, of which we have not really thought. Now suppose I assert that the Fountain of Youth does not exist. Since to meaningfully deny the existence of something I have to have that thing in mind, I have to think of it, it follows on Anselm's view that whenever someone asserts that some thing does not exist, that thing *does* exist in the understanding.[2] So in asserting that the Fountain of Youth does not exist, I imply that the Fountain of Youth does exist in the understanding. And in asserting that it does not exist I have asserted (on Anselm's view) that it does not exist in reality. This means that my simple assertion amounts to the somewhat more complex claim that the Fountain of Youth exists in the understanding but does not exist in reality—in short, that the Fountain of Youth exists *only* in the understanding.

We can now understand why Anselm insists that anyone who hears of God, thinks about God, or even denies the existence of God is, nevertheless, committed to the view that God exists in the understanding. Also, we can understand why Anselm treats what he calls "the fool's claim" that God does not exist as the claim that God exists *only* in the understanding—that is, that God exists in the understanding but does not exist in reality.

In *Monologium* Anselm sought to prove that among those beings which do exist there is one which is the greatest, highest, and the best. But in *Proslogium* he undertakes to prove that among those beings which exist there is one which is not just the greatest among existing beings, but is such that no conceivable being is greater. We need to distinguish these two ideas: (1) a being than which *no existing being* is greater, and (2) a being than which *no conceivable being* is greater. If the only things in existence were a stone, a frog, and a man, the last of these would satisfy our first idea but not our second—for we can conceive of a being (an angel or God) greater than a man. Anselm's idea of God, as he expresses it in *Proslogium* II, is the same as (2) above; it is the idea of "a being than which nothing greater can be conceived." It will facilitate our understanding of Anselm's argument if we make two slight changes in the way he has expressed his idea of God. For his phrase I shall substitute the following: "*the* being than which none greater *is possible*."[3] This idea says that if a certain being is God then no *possible being* can be greater than it, or conversely, if a certain being is such that it is even *possible* for there to be a being greater than it, then that being is not God. What Anselm proposes to prove, then, is that the being than which none greater is possible exists in reality. If he proves this he will have proved that God, as he conceives of Him, exists in reality.

But what does Anselm mean by "greatness"? Is a building, for example, greater than a man? In *Monologium*, chapter II, Anselm remarks: "But I do not mean physically great, as a material object is great, but that which, the greater it is, is the better or the more worthy—wisdom, for instance." Contrast wisdom with size. Anselm is saying that wisdom is something that contributes to the greatness of a thing. If a thing comes to have more wisdom than it did before then (given that its other characteristics remain the same), that thing has become a greater, better, more worthy thing than it was. Wisdom, Anselm is saying, is a great-making quality. However, the mere fact that something increases in size (physical greatness) does not make that thing a better thing than it was before, so size is not a great-making quality. By "greater than" Anselm means "better than," "superior to," or "more worthy than," and he believes that some characteristics, like wisdom and moral goodness, are great-making characteristics in that anything which has them is a *better thing* than it would be (other characteristics of it remaining the same) were it to lack them.

We come now to what we may call the *key idea* in Anselm's Ontological argument. Anselm believes that *existence in reality is a great-making quality*. Does Anselm mean that anything that exists is a greater thing than anything that doesn't? Although he does not ask or answer the question, it is perhaps reasonable to believe that Anselm did not mean this. When he discusses wisdom as a great-making quality he is careful not to say that any wise thing is better than any unwise thing—for he recognizes that a just but unwise man might be a better being than a wise but unjust man.[4] I suggest that what Anselm means is that anything that doesn't exist but might have existed (is on the right side of our line but might have been on the left) would have been a greater thing if it had existed (if it had been on the left side of our line). He is not comparing two different things (one existing and one not existing) and saying that the first is therefore greater than the second. Rather, he is talking about *one* thing and pointing out that if it does not exist but might have existed, then *it* would have been a greater thing if it had existed. Using Anselm's distinction between existence in the understanding and existence in reality, we may express the key idea in Anselm's reasoning as follows: If something exists only in the understanding but might have existed in reality, then it might have been greater than it is. Since the Fountain of Youth, for example, exists only in the understanding but (unlike the round square) might have existed in reality, it follows by Anselm's principle that the Fountain of Youth might have been a greater thing than it is.

II

We can now consider the step-by-step development of Anselm's Ontological argument. I shall use the term "God" in place of the longer phrase "the being than which none greater is possible"—wherever the term "God" appears we are to think of it as simply an abbreviation of the longer phrase.

1. God exists in the understanding.

As we have noted, anyone who hears of the being than which none greater is possible is, on Anselm's view, committed to premise (1).

2. God might have existed in reality (God is a possible being).

Anselm, I think, assumes the truth of (2) without making it explicit in his reasoning. By asserting (2) I do not mean to imply that God does not exist in reality, but that, unlike the round square, God is a possible being.

3. If something exists only in the understanding and might have existed in reality, then it might have been greater than it is.

As we noted, this is the key idea in Anselm's Ontological argument. It is intended as a general principle, true of anything whatever.

Steps (1)–(3) constitute the basic premises of Anselm's Ontological argument. From these three items, Anselm believes, it follows that God exists in reality. But how does Anselm propose to convince us that if we accept (1)–(3) we are committed by the rules of logic to accept his conclusion that God exists in reality? Anselm's procedure is to offer what is called a *reductio ad absurdum* proof of his conclusion. Instead of showing directly that the existence of God follows from steps (1)–(3), Anselm invites us to *suppose* that God does not exist (i.e., that the conclusion he wants to establish is false) and then shows how this supposition, when conjoined with steps (1)–(3), leads to an absurd result, a result that couldn't possibly be true because it is contradictory. Since the supposition that God does not exist leads to an absurdity, that supposition must be rejected in favor of the conclusion that God does exist.

Does Anselm succeed in reducing the "fool's belief" that God does not exist to an absurdity? The best way to answer this question is to follow the steps of his argument.

4. Suppose God exists only in the understanding.

This supposition, as we saw earlier, is Anselm's way of expressing the belief that God does not exist.

5. God might have been greater than He is. (2, 4, and 3)[5]

Step (5) follows from steps (2), (4), and (3). Since (3), if true, is true of anything whatever, it will be true of God. Therefore, (3) implies that if God exists only in the understanding and might have existed in reality, then God might have been greater than He is. If so, then given (2) and (4), (5) must be true. For what (3) says when applied to God is that given (2) and (4), it follows that (5).

6. God is a being than which a greater is possible. (5)

Surely if God is such that He logically might have been greater, then He is such than which a greater is possible.

We can now appreciate Anselm's *reductio* argument. He has shown that if we accept steps (1)–(4), we must accept step (6). But (6) is unacceptable; it is the absurdity Anselm was after. By replacing "God" in (6) with the longer phrase it abbreviates, we see that (6) amounts to the absurd assertion:

7. The being than which none greater is possible is a being than which a greater is possible. Now since steps (1)–(4) have led us to an obviously false conclusion, and if we accept Anselm's basic premises (1)–(3) as true, then (4), the supposition that God exists only in the understanding, must be rejected as false. Thus we have shown that:

8. It is false that God exists only in the understanding.

But since premise (1) tells us that God does exist in the understanding and (8) tells us that God does not exist only there, we may infer that

9. God exists in reality as well as in the understanding. (1, 8)

III

Most of the philosophers who have considered this argument have rejected it because of a basic conviction that from the logical analysis of a certain idea or concept we can never determine that there exists in reality anything answering to that idea or concept. We may examine and analyse, for example, the idea of an elephant or the idea of a unicorn, but it is only by our experience of the world that we can determine that there exist things answering to our first idea and not to the second. Anselm, however, believes that the concept of God is utterly unique—from an analysis of this concept he believes that it can be determined that there exists in reality a being which answers to it. Moreover, he presents us with an argument to show that it can be done in the case of the idea of God. We can, of course, simply reject Anselm's argument on the grounds that it violates the basic conviction noted above. Many critics, however, have sought to prove more directly that it is a bad argument and to point out the particular step that is mistaken. Next we shall examine the three major objections that have been advanced by the argument's critics.

The first criticism was advanced by a contemporary of Anselm's, a monk named "Gaunilo," who wrote a response to Anselm entitled, "On Behalf of the Fool."[6] Gaunilo sought to prove that Anselm's reasoning is mistaken by applying it to things other than God, things which we know don't exist. He took as his example the island than which none greater is possible. No such island really exists. But, argues Gaunilo, if Anselm's reasoning were correct we could show that such an island really does exist. For since it is greater to exist than not to exist, if the island than which none greater is possible doesn't exist then it is an island than which a greater is possible. But it is impossible for the island than which none greater is possible to be an island than which a greater is possible. Therefore, the island than which none greater is possible must exist. About this argument Gaunilo remarks:

> If a man should try to prove to me by such reasoning that this island truly exists, and that its existence should no longer be doubted, either I should believe that he was jesting, or I know not which I ought to regard as the greater fool: myself, supposing I should allow this proof; or him, if he should suppose that he had established with any certainty the existence of this island.[7]

Gaunilo's strategy is clear: by using the very same reasoning Anselm employs in his argument, we can prove the existence of things we know don't exist. Therefore, Anselm's reasoning in his proof of the existence of God must be mistaken. In reply to Gaunilo, Anselm insisted that his reasoning applies only to God and cannot be used to establish the existence of things other than God. Unfortunately, Anselm did not explain just why his reasoning cannot be applied to things like Gaunilo's island.

In defense of Anselm against Gaunilo's objection, there are two difficulties in applying Anselm's reasoning to things like Gaunilo's island. The first derives from the fact that Anselm's principle that existence is a great-making quality was taken to mean that if something does not exist then it is not as great *a thing* (being) as it would have been had it existed. Now if we use precisely this principle in Gaunilo's argument, all we will prove is that if Gaunilo's island does not exist then the island than which none greater is possible is an island than which *a greater thing* is possible. But this statement is not an absurdity. For the island than which no greater *island* is possible can be something than which *a greater thing* is possible—an unsurpassable island may be a surpassable thing. (A perfect man might be a greater thing than a perfect island.) Consequently, if we follow Anselm's reasoning exactly, it does not appear that we can derive an absurdity from the supposition that the island than which none greater is possible does not exist.

A second difficulty in applying Anselm's reasoning to Gaunilo's island is that we must accept the premise that Gaunilo's island is a possible thing. But this seems to require us to believe that some finite, limited thing (an island) might have unlimited perfections. It is not at all clear that this is possible. Try to think, for example, of a hockey player than which none greater is possible. How fast would he have to skate? How many goals would he have to score in a game? How fast would he have to shoot the puck? Could he ever fall down, be checked, or receive a penalty? Although the phrase, "the hockey player than which none greater is possible," seems meaningful, as soon as we try to get a clear idea of what such a being would be like we discover that we can't form a coherent idea of it all. For we are being invited to think of some limited, finite thing—a hockey player or an island—and then to think of it as exhibiting unlimited, infinite perfections. Perhaps, then, since Anselm's reasoning applies only to possible things, Anselm can reject its application to Gaunilo's island on the grounds that the island than which none greater is possible is, like the round square, an impossible thing.

By far the most famous objection to the Ontological argument was set forth by Immanuel Kant in the eighteenth century. According to this objection the mistake in the argument is its claim, implicit in premise (3), that existence is a quality or predicate that adds to the greatness of a thing. There are two parts to this claim: (1) existence is a quality or predicate, and (2) existence, like wisdom and unlike physical size, is a great-making quality or predicate. Someone might accept (1) but object to (2); the objection made famous by Kant, however, is directed at (1). According to this objection, existence is not a predicate at all. Therefore, since in its third premise Anselm's argument implies that existence *is* a predicate, the argument must be rejected.

The central point in the philosophical doctrine that existence is not a predicate concerns what we do when we ascribe a certain quality or predicate to something: for example, when we say of a man next door that he is intelligent, six feet tall, or fat. In each case *we* seem to assert or presuppose that there *exists* a man next door and then go on to ascribe to him a certain predicate—"intelligent," "six feet tall," or "fat." And many proponents of the doctrine that existence is not a predicate claim that this is a *general feature* of predication. They hold that when we ascribe a quality or predicate to anything we assert or presuppose that the thing exists and then ascribe the predicate to it. Now if this is so, then it is clear that existence cannot be a predicate which we may ascribe to or deny of something. For if it were a predicate, then when we assert of some thing (things) that it (they) exists (exist) we would be asserting or presupposing that it (they) exists (exist) and then going on to predicate existence of it

(them). For example, if existence were a predicate, then in asserting "tigers exist" we would be asserting or presupposing that tigers exist and then going on to predicate existence of them. Furthermore, in asserting "dragons do not exist" we would be asserting or presupposing, if existence were a predicate, that dragons do exist and then going on to deny that existence attaches to them. In short, if existence were a predicate, the affirmative existential statement "tigers exist" would be a redundancy and the negative existential statement "dragons do not exist" would be contradictory. But clearly "tigers exist" is not a redundancy; and "dragons do not exist" is true and, therefore, not contradictory. What this shows, according to the proponents of Kant's objection, is that existence is not a genuine predicate.

According to the proponents of the above objection, when we assert that tigers exist and that dragons do not we are not saying that certain things (tigers) have and certain other things (dragons) do not have a peculiar predicate, *existence*; rather, we are saying something about the *concept* of a tiger and the *concept* of a dragon. We are saying that the concept of a tiger applies to something in the world and that the concept of a dragon does not apply to anything in the world.

Although this objection to the Ontological argument has been widely accepted, it is doubtful that it provides us with a conclusive refutation of the argument. It may be true that existence is not a predicate, that in asserting the existence of something we are not ascribing a certain predicate or attribute to that thing. But the arguments presented for this view seem to rest on mistaken or incomplete claims about the nature of predication. For example, the argument which we stated earlier rests on the claim that when we ascribe a predicate to anything we assert or presuppose that that thing exists. But this claim appears to be mistaken. In asserting that Dr. Doolittle is an animal lover I seem to be ascribing the predicate "animal lover" to Dr. Doolittle, but in doing so I certainly am not asserting or presupposing that Dr. Doolittle actually exists. Dr. Doolittle doesn't exist, but it is nevertheless true that he is an animal lover. The plain fact is that we can talk about and ascribe predicates to many things which do not exist and never did. Merlin, for example, no less than Houdini, was a magician, although Houdini existed but Merlin did not. If, as these examples suggest, the claim that whenever we ascribe a predicate to something we assert or presuppose that the thing exists is a false claim, then we will need a better argument for the doctrine that existence is not a predicate. There is some question, however, whether anyone has succeeded in giving a really conclusive argument for this doctrine.[8]

A third objection against the Ontological argument calls into question the premise that God might have existed in reality (God is a possible being). As we saw, this premise claims that the being than which none greater is possible is not an impossible object. But is this true? Consider the series of positive integers: 1, 2, 3, 4, etc. We know that any integer in this series, no matter how large, is such that a larger integer than it is possible. Therefore, the positive integer than which none larger is possible is an impossible object. Perhaps this is also true of the being than which none greater is possible. That is, perhaps no matter how great a being may be, it is possible for there to be a being greater than it. If this were so, then, like the integer than which none larger is possible, Anselm's God would not be a possible object. The mere fact that there are degrees of greatness, however, does not entitle us to conclude that Anselm's God is like the integer than which none larger is possible. There are, for example, degrees of size in angles—one angle is larger than another—but it is not true that no matter how large an angle is it is possible for there to be an angle larger than it. It is logically impossible for an angle to exceed four right angles. The notion of an angle, unlike the notion of a positive integer, implies a degree of size beyond which it is impossible to go. Is Anselm's God like a largest integer, and therefore impossible, or like a largest angle, and therefore possible? Some philosophers have argued that Anselm's God is impossible,[9] but the arguments for this conclusion are not very compelling. Perhaps, then, this objection is best construed not as proving that Anselm's God is impossible, but as raising the question whether any of us is in a

position to know that the being than which none greater is possible is a possible object. For Anselm's argument cannot be a successful proof of the existence of God unless its premises aren't just true but are really *known* to be true. Therefore, if we do not know that Anselm's God is a possible object, then his argument cannot prove the existence of God to us, cannot enable us to know that God exists.

IV

Finally, I want to present a somewhat different critique of Anselm's argument, a critique suggested by the basic conviction noted earlier; namely that from the mere logical analysis of a certain idea or concept we can never determine that there exists in reality anything answering to that idea or concept.

Suppose someone comes to us and says:

> I propose to define the term "God" as *an existing, wholly perfect being.* Now since it can't be true that an existing, wholly perfect being does not exist, it can't be true that God, as I've defined Him, does not exist. Therefore, God must exist.

His argument appears to be a very simple Ontological argument. It begins with a particular idea or concept of God and ends by concluding that God, so conceived, must exist. What can we say in response? We might start by objecting to his definition, claiming: (1) that only predicates can be used to define a term, and (2) that existence is not a predicate. But suppose he is not impressed by this response—either because he thinks that no one has fully explained what a predicate is or proved that existence isn't one, or because he thinks that anyone can define a word in whatever way he pleases. Can we allow him to define the word "God" in any way he pleases and still hope to convince him that it will not follow from that definition that there actually exists something to which his concept of God applies? I think we can. Let us first invite him, however, to consider some concepts other than his peculiar concept of God.

Earlier we noted that the term "magician" may be applied both to Houdini and Merlin, even though the former existed and the latter did not. Noting that our friend has used "existing" as part of his definition of "God," suppose we agree with him that we can define a word in any way we please, and, accordingly, introduce the following definitions:

A "magican" is defined as *an existing magician.*

A "magico" is defined as a *non-existing magician.*

Here we have introduced two words and used "existing" or "non-existing" in their definitions. Now something of interest follows from the fact that "existing" is part of our definition of a "magican." For while it is true that Merlin was a *magician,* it is not true that Merlin was a *magican.* And something of interest follows from our including "non-existing" in the definition of a "magico"—it is true that Houdini was a *magician,* but it is not true that Houdini was a *magico.* Houdini was a *magician* and a *magican . . . ,* but not a *magico;* Merlin was a *magician* and a *magico,* but not a *magican.*

We have just seen that introducing "existing" or "non-existing" into the definition of a concept has a very important implication. If we introduce "existing" into the definition of a concept, it follows that no non-existing thing can exemplify that concept. And if we introduce "non-existing" into the definition of a concept, it follows that no existing thing can exemplify that concept. No non-existing thing can be a *magican,* and no existing thing can be a *magico.*

But must some existing thing exemplify the concept "magican"? No! From the fact that "existing" is included in the definition of "magican" it does not follow that some existing thing is a magican—all that follows is that no non-existing thing is a magican. If there were no magicans in existence there would be nothing to which the term "magican" would apply. This being so, it clearly does not follow merely from our definition of "magican" that some existing thing is a magican. Only if magicians exist will it be true that some existing thing is a magican.

We are now in a position to help our friend see that the mere fact that "God" is defined as an existing, wholly perfect being it will not follow that some existing being is God. Something of interest does follow from his definition; namely that no non-existing being can be God. But whether some existing thing is God will depend entirely on whether some existing thing is a wholly perfect being. If no wholly perfect being exists there will be nothing to which his concept of God can apply. This being so, it clearly does not follow merely from his definition of "God" that some existing thing is God. Only if a wholly perfect being exists will it be true that God, as he conceives of Him, exists.

The implications of these considerations for Anselm's ingenious argument can now be traced. Anselm conceives of God as a being than which none greater is possible. He then claims that existence is a great-making quality and something that has it is greater than it would have been had it lacked existence. Clearly then, no non-existing thing can exemplify Anselm's concept of God. For if we suppose that some non-existing thing exemplifies Anselm's concept of God and also suppose that that non-existing thing might have existed in reality (is a possible thing) then we are supposing that that non-existing thing (1) might have been a greater thing, and (2) is, nevertheless, a thing than which a greater is not possible. Thus far Anselm's reasoning is, I believe, impeccable. But what follows from it? All that follows from it is that no non-existing thing can be God (as Anselm conceives of God). All that follows is that given Anselm's concept of God, the proposition, "Some non-existing thing is God," cannot be true. But, as we saw earlier, this is also the case with the proposition, "Some non-existing thing is a magican." What remains to be shown is that some existing thing exemplifies Anselm's concept of God. What really does follow from his reasoning is that the only thing that logically could exemplify his concept of God is something which actually exists. And this conclusion is not without interest. But from the mere fact that nothing but an existing thing could exemplify Anselm's concept of God, it does not follow that some existing thing actually does exemplify his concept of God—no more than it follows from the mere fact that no non-existing thing can be a magican that some existing thing is a magican.[10]

There is, however, one major difficulty in this critique of Anselm's argument. This difficulty arises when we take into account Anselm's implicit claim that God is a possible thing. To see just what this difficulty is, let us return to the idea of a possible thing, which is any thing that either is on the left side of our imaginary line or logically might have been on the left side of the line. Possible things, then, will be all those things that, unlike the round square, are not impossible things. Suppose we concede to Anselm that God, as he conceives of Him, is a possible thing. Now, of course, the mere knowledge that something is a possible thing does not enable us to conclude that that thing is an existing thing. Many possible things, like the Fountain of Youth, do not exist. But if something is a possible thing then it is either an existing thing or a non-existing thing. The set of possible things can be exhaustively divided into those possible things which actually exist and those possible things which do not exist. Therefore, if Anselm's God is a possible thing it is either an existing thing or a non-existing thing. We have concluded, however, that no non-existing thing can be Anselm's God; therefore, it seems we must conclude with Anselm that some actually existing thing does exemplify his concept of God.

To see the solution to this major difficulty we need to return to an earlier example. Let us consider again the idea of a "magican," an existing magician. It so happens that some magicians have existed—Houdini, the Great Blackstone, etc. But, of course, it might have been otherwise. Suppose, for the moment that no magicians have ever existed. The concept "magician" would still have application, for it would still be true that Merlin was a magician. But would any possible object be picked out by the concept of a "magican"? No, for no non-existing thing could exemplify the concept "magican." And on the supposition that no magicians ever existed, no existing thing would exemplify the concept "magican."[11] We then would have a coherent concept "magican" which would not be exemplified by any possible object at all. For if all the possible objects which are magicians are non-existing things, none of them would be a magican and, since no possible objects which exist are magicians, none of them would be a

magican. Put in this way, our result seems paradoxical. We are inclined to think that only contradictory concepts like "the round square" are not exemplified by any possible things. The truth is, however, that when "existing" is included in or implied by a certain concept, it may be the case that no possible object does in fact exemplify that concept. For no possible object that doesn't exist will exemplify a concept like "magican" in which "existing" is included; and if there are no existing things which exemplify the other features included in the concept—for example, "being a magician" in the case of the concept "magican"—then no possible object that exists will exemplify the concept. Put in its simplest terms, if we ask whether any possible thing is a magican the answer will depend entirely on whether any existing thing is a magician. If no existing things are magicians then no possible things are magicans. Some possible object is a magican just in the case some actually existing thing is a magician.

Applying these considerations to Anselm's argument, we can find the solution to our major difficulty. Given Anselm's concept of God and his principle that existence is a great-making quality, it really does follow that the only thing that logically could exemplify his concept of God is something which actually exists. But, we argued, it doesn't follow from these considerations alone that God actually exists, that some existing thing exemplifies Anselm's concept of God. The difficulty we fell into, however, is that when we add the premise that God is a possible thing, that some possible object exemplifies his concept of God, it really does follow that God actually exists, that some actually existing thing exemplifies Anselm's concept of God. For if some possible object exemplifies his concept of God, that object is either an existing thing or a non-existing thing. But since no non-existing thing could exemplify Anselm's concept of God, it follows that the possible object which exemplifies his concept of God must be a possible object that actually exists. Therefore, given (1) Anselm's concept of God, (2) his principle that existence is a great-making quality, and (3) the premise that God, as conceived by Anselm, is a possible thing, it really does follow that Anselm's God actually exists. But we now can see that in granting Anselm the premise that God is a possible thing we have granted far more than we intended. All we thought we were conceding is that Anselm's concept of God, unlike the concept of a round square, is not contradictory or incoherent. But without realizing it we were in fact granting much more than this, as became apparent when we considered the idea of a magican. There is nothing contradictory in the idea of a magican, an existing magician. But in asserting that a magican is a possible thing we are, as we saw, directly implying that some existing thing is a magician. For if no existing thing is a magician, the concept of a magician will apply to no possible object whatever. The same point holds with respect to Anselm's God. Since Anselm's concept of God logically cannot apply to some non-existing thing, the only possible objects to which it could apply are possible objects which actually exist. Therefore, in granting that Anselm's God is a possible thing we are conceding far more than that his idea of God isn't incoherent or contradictory. Suppose, for example, that every existing being has some defect which it might not have had. Without realizing it we were denying this when we granted that Anselm's God is a possible being. If every existing being has a defect it might not have had, then every existing being might have been greater. But if every existing being might have been greater, then Anselm's concept of God will apply to no possible object whatever. Therefore, if we allow Anselm his concept of God and his principle that existence is a great-making quality, then in granting that God, as Anselm conceives of Him, is a possible being we will be granting much more than that his concept of God is not contradictory. We will be conceding, for example, that some existing thing is as perfect as it can be. The fact is that Anselm's God is a possible thing only if some *existing* thing is as perfect as it can be.

Our final critique of Anselm's argument is simply this. In granting that Anselm's God is a possible thing we are in fact granting that Anselm's God actually exists. But since the purpose of the argument is to prove to us that Anselm's God exists, we cannot be asked to grant as a premise a statement which is virtually equivalent to the conclusion that is to be proved. Anselm's concept of God may be coherent and his principle that existence is a great-making quality may be true. But all that

follows from this is that no non-existing thing can be Anselm's God. If we add to all of this the premise that God is a possible thing it will follow that God actually exists. But the additional premise claims more than that Anselm's concept of God isn't incoherent or contradictory. It amounts to the assertion that some existing being is supremely great. And since this is, in part, the point the argument endeavors to prove, the argument begs the question: it assumes the point it is supposed to prove.

If the above critique is correct, Anselm's argument fails as a proof of the existence of God. This is not to say, however, that the argument is not a work of genius. Perhaps no other argument in the history of thought has raised so many basic philosophical questions and stimulated so much hard thought. Even if it fails as a proof of the existence of God, it will remain as one of the high achievements of the human intellect.

NOTES

1. Some philosophers believe that Anselm sets forth a different and more cogent argument in chapter III of his *Proslogium*. For this viewpoint see Charles Hartshorne, *Anselm's Discovery* (LaSalle, Ill.: Open Court Publishing Co., 1965); and Norman Malcolm, "Anselm's Ontological Arguments," *The Philosophical Review* LXIX, No. 1 (January 1960): pp. 41–62. For an illuminating account both of Anselm's intentions in *Proslogium II* and *III* and of recent interpretations of Anselm see Arthur C. McGill's essay "Recent Discussions of Anselm's Argument" in *The Many-faced Argument*, ed. John Hick and Arthur C. McGill (New York: The Macmillan Co., 1967), pp. 33–110.

2. Anselm does allow that someone may assert the sentence "God does not exist" without having in his understanding the object or idea for which the word 'God' stands (see *Proslogium*, chapter IV). But when a person does understand the object for which a word stands, then when he uses that word in a sentence denying the existence of that object he must have that object in his understanding. It is doubtful, however, that Anselm thought that incoherent or contradictory expressions like "the round square" stand for objects which may exist in the understanding.

3. Anselm speaks of "a being" rather than "the being" than which none greater can be conceived. His argument is easier to present if we express his

idea of God in terms of "the being." Secondly, to avoid the psychological connotations of "can be conceived" I have substituted "possible."

4. See Anselm, *Monologium*, chapter XV.

5. The numbers in parentheses refer to the earlier steps in the argument from which the present step is derived.

6. Gaunilo's brief essay, Anselm's reply, and several of Anselm's major works, as translated by S. N. Deane, are collected in *Saint Anselm: Basic Writings* (LaSalle, Ill.: Open Court Publishing Co., 1962).

7. *Saint Anselm, Basic Writings,* p. 151.

8. Perhaps the most sophisticated presentation of the objection that existence is not a predicate is William P. Alston's "The Ontological Argument Revisited" in *The Philosophical Review* 69 (1960): pp. 452–474.

9. See, for example, C. D. road's discussion of the Ontological Argument in *Religion, Philosophy, and Psychical Research* (New York: Harcourt, Brace & World, 1953).

10. An argument along the lines just presented may be found in J. Shaffer's illuminating essay "Existence, Predication and the Ontological Argument," *Mind* 71 (1962): pp. 307–325.

11. I am indebted to Professor William Wainwright for bringing this point to my attention.

The Five Ways, from *Summa Theologica*

SAINT THOMAS AQUINAS

Saint Thomas Aquinas (1225–1274) is the philosopher whose teachings are most favored by the Roman Catholic Church.

There are five ways in which one can prove that there is a God.

The first and most obvious way is based on change. Some things in the world are certainly in process of change: this we plainly see. Now anything in process of change is being changed by something else. This is so because it is characteristic of things in process of change that they do not yet have the perfection towards which they move, though able to have it; whereas it is characteristic of something causing change to have that perfection already. For to cause change is to bring into being what was previously only able to be, and this can only be done by something that already is: thus fire, which is actually hot, causes wood, which is able to be hot, to become actually hot, and in this way causes change in the wood. Now the same thing cannot at the same time be both actually *x* and potentially *x*, though it can be actually *x* and potentially *y*: the actually hot cannot at the same time be potentially hot, though it can be potentially cold. Consequently, a thing in process of change cannot itself cause that same change; it cannot change itself. Of necessity therefore anything in process of change is being changed by something else. Moreover, this something else, if in process of change, is itself being changed by yet another thing; and this last by another. Now we must stop somewhere, otherwise there will be no first cause of the change, and, as a result, no subsequent causes. For it is only when acted upon by the first cause that the intermediate causes will produce the change: if the hand does not move the stick, the stick will not move anything else. Hence one is bound to arrive at some first cause of change not itself being changed by anything, and this is what everybody understands by God.

The second way is based on the nature of causation. In the observable world causes are found to be ordered in series; we never observe, nor ever could, something causing itself, for this

From *Summa Theologica* by St. Thomas Aquinas; translated by the Fathers of the English Dominican Province. (Westminster, MD: Christian Classics, 1981, © 1948), vol. I, pp. 13–14 (pt. I, q. II, art. III).

would mean it preceded itself, and this is not possible. Such a series of causes must however stop somewhere; for in it an earlier member causes an intermediate and the intermediate a last (whether the intermediate be one or many). Now if you eliminate a cause you also eliminate its effects, so that you cannot have a last cause, nor an intermediate one, unless you have a first. Given therefore no stop in the series of causes, and hence no first cause, there would be no intermediate causes either, and no last effect, and this would be an open mistake. One is therefore forced to suppose some first cause, to which everyone gives the name 'God'.

The third way is based on what need not be and on what must be, and runs as follows. Some of the things we come across can be but need not be, for we find them springing up and dying away, thus sometimes in being and sometimes not. Now everything cannot be like this, for a thing that need not be, once was not; and if everything need not be, once upon a time there was nothing. But if that were true there would be nothing even now, because something that does not exist can only be brought into being by something already existing. So that if nothing was in being nothing could be brought into being, and nothing would be in being now, which contradicts observation. Not everything therefore is the sort of thing that need not be; there has got to be something that must be. Now a thing that must be, may or may not owe this necessity to something else. But just as we must stop somewhere in a series of causes, so also in the series of things which must be and owe this to other things. One is forced

therefore to suppose something which must be, and owes this to no other thing than itself; indeed it itself is the cause that other things must be.

The fourth way is based on the gradation observed in things. Some things are found to be more good, more true, more noble, and so on, and other things less. But such comparative terms describe varying degrees of approximation to a superlative; for example, things are hotter and hotter the nearer they approach what is hottest. Something therefore is the truest and best and most noble of things, and hence the most fully in being; for Aristotle says that the truest things are the things most fully in being. Now *when many things possess some property in common, the one most fully possessing it causes it in the others: fire,* to use Aristotle's example, *the hottest of all things, causes all other things to be hot.* There is something therefore which causes in all other things their being, their goodness, and whatever other perfection they have. And this we call 'God'.

The fifth way is based on the guidedness of nature. An orderedness of actions to an end is observed in all bodies obeying natural laws, even when they lack awareness. For their behaviour hardly ever varies, and will practically always turn out well; which shows that they truly tend to a goal, and do not merely hit it by accident. Nothing however that lacks awareness tends to a goal, except under the direction of someone with awareness and with understanding; the arrow, for example, requires an archer. Everything in nature, therefore, is directed to its goal by someone with understanding, and this we call 'God'.

A Modern Formulation of the Cosmological Argument

SAMUEL CLARKE

Samuel Clarke (1675–1729), English theologian and philosopher, was one of the first to be greatly influenced by Isaac Newton's physics.

From Samuel Clarke, *A Demonstration of the Being and Attributes of God* (1705), Part II.

There has existed from eternity some one unchangeable and independent being. For since something must needs have been from eternity; as hath been already proved, and is granted on all hands: either there has always existed one unchangeable and *independent* Being, from which all other beings that are or ever were in the universe, have received their original; or else there has been an infinite succession of changeable and *dependent* beings, produced one from another in an endless progression, without any original cause at all: which latter supposition is so very absurd, that tho' all atheism must in its account of most things (as shall be shown hereafter) terminate in it, yet I think very few atheists ever were so weak as openly and directly to defend it. For it is plainly impossible and contradictory to itself. I shall not argue against it from the supposed impossibility of infinite succession, *barely and absolutely considered in itself;* for a reason which shall be mentioned hereafter: but, if we consider such an infinite progression, as *one* entire endless *series* of *dependent* beings; 'tis plain this whole *series* of beings can have no cause *from without,* of its existence; because in it are supposed to be included *all things* that are or ever were in the universe: and 'tis plain it can have no reason *within itself,* of its existence; because no one being in this infinite succession is supposed to be self-existent or *necessary* (which is the only ground or reason of existence of any thing, that can be imagined *within the thing itself,* as will presently more fully appear), but every one *dependent* on the foregoing; and where *no part* is necessary, 'tis manifest *the whole* cannot be necessary; absolute necessity of existence, not being an outward, relative, and accidental determination; but an inward and essential property of the nature of the thing which so exists. An infinite succession therefore of merely *dependent* beings, without any original independent cause; is a *series* of beings, that has neither necessity nor cause, nor any reason *at all* of its existence, neither *within itself* nor *from without:* that is, 'tis an express contradiction and impossibility; 'tis a supposing *something* to be *caused,* (because it's granted in every one of its stages of succession, not to be necessary and from itself); and yet that in the whole it is caused *absolutely by nothing:* Which every man knows is a contradiction to be done *in time;* and because duration in this case makes no difference, 'tis equally a contradiction to suppose it done from eternity: And consequently there must *on the contrary,* of necessity have existed from eternity, *some one* immutable and *independent* Being: Which, what it is, remains in the next place to be inquired.

The Cosmological Argument

WILLIAM L. ROWE

Since ancient times thoughtful people have sought to justify their religious beliefs. Perhaps the most basic belief for which justification has been sought is the belief that there is a God. The effort to justify belief in the existence of God has generally started either from facts available to believers and nonbelievers alike or from facts, such as the experience of God, normally available only to believers. . . . We shall consider some major attempts to justify belief in God by appealing to facts supposedly available to any rational person, whether religious or not. By starting from such facts theologians and philosophers have developed arguments for the

From William L. Rowe, *Philosophy of Religion* (Belmont, Calif.: Wadsworth Publishing Co., 1978), pp. 16–30. Reprinted by permission of the publisher and the author.

existence of God, arguments which, they have claimed, prove beyond reasonable doubt that there is a God.

STATING THE ARGUMENT

Arguments for the existence of God are commonly divided into *a posteriori* arguments and *a priori* arguments. An *a posteriori* argument depends on a principle or premise that can be known only by means of our experience of the world. An *a priori* argument, on the other hand, purports to rest on principles all of which can be known independently of our experience of the world, by just reflecting on and understanding them. Of the three major arguments for the existence of God—the Cosmological, the Teleological, and the Ontological—only the last of these is entirely *a priori*. In the Cosmological Argument one starts from some simple fact about the world, such as that it contains things which are caused to exist by other things. In the Teleological Argument a somewhat more complicated fact about the world serves as a starting point, the fact that the world exhibits order and design. In the Ontological Argument, however, one begins simply with a concept of God. In this chapter we shall consider the Cosmological Argument....

Before we state the Cosmological Argument itself, we shall consider some rather general points about the argument. Historically, it can be traced to the writings of the Greek philosophers, Plato and Aristotle, but the major developments in the argument took place in the thirteenth and in the eighteenth centuries. In the thirteenth century, Aquinas put forth five distinct arguments for the existence of God, and of these, the first three are versions of the Cosmological Argument.[1] In the first of these he started from the fact that there are things in the world undergoing change and reasoned to the conclusion that there must be some ultimate cause of change that is itself unchanging. In the second he started from the fact that there are things in the world that clearly are caused to exist by other things and reasoned to the conclusion that there must be some ultimate cause of existence whose own existence is itself uncaused.

And in the third argument he started from the fact that there are things in the world which need not have existed at all, things which do exist but which we can easily imagine might not, and reasoned to the conclusion that there must be some being that had to be, that exists and could not have failed to exist. Now it might be objected that even if Aquinas' arguments do prove beyond doubt the existence of an unchanging changer, an uncaused cause, and a being that could not have failed to exist, the arguments fail to prove the existence of the theistic God. For the theistic God, as we saw, is supremely good, omnipotent, omniscient, and creator of but separate from and independent of the world. How do we know, for example, that the unchanging changer isn't evil or slightly ignorant? The answer to this objection is that the Cosmological Argument has two parts. In the first part the effort is to prove the existence of a special sort of being, for example, a being that could not have failed to exist, or a being that causes change in other things but is itself unchanging. In the second part of the argument the effort is to prove that the special sort of being whose existence has been established in the first part has, and must have, the features—perfect goodness, omnipotence, omniscience, and so on—which go together to make up the theistic idea of God. What this means, then, is that Aquinas' three arguments are different versions of only the first part of the Cosmological Argument. Indeed, in later sections of his *Summa Theologica* Aquinas undertakes to show that the unchanging changer, the uncaused cause of existence, and the being which had to exist are one and the same being and that this single being has all of the attributes of the theistic God.

We noted above that a second major development in the Cosmological Argument took place in the eighteenth century, a development reflected in the writings of the German philosopher, Gottfried Leibniz (1646–1716), and especially in the writings of the English theologian and philosopher, Samuel Clarke (1675–1729). In 1704 Clarke gave a series of lectures, later published under the title *A Demonstration of the Being and Attributes of God*. These lectures constitute, perhaps, the most complete, forceful, and cogent presentation of the Cosmological Argument we possess. The lectures were read by the major skeptical philosopher of the century, David Hume (1711–1776), and in his brilliant attack on the attempt to justify religion in the court of reason, his *Dialogues Concerning Natural Religion,* Hume advanced several penetrating criticisms of Clarke's arguments, criticisms which have persuaded many philosophers in the modern period to reject the Cosmological Argument. In our study of the argument we shall concentrate our attention largely on its eighteenth-century form and try to assess its strengths and weaknesses in the light of the criticisms which Hume and others have advanced against it.

The first part of the eighteenth-century form of the Cosmological Argument seeks to establish the existence of a self-existent being. The second part of the argument attempts to prove that the self-existent being is the theistic God, that is, has the features which we have noted to be basic elements in the theistic idea of God. We shall consider mainly the first part of the argument, for it is against the first part that philosophers from Hume to Russell have advanced very important objections.

In stating the first part of the Cosmological Argument we shall make use of two important concepts, the concept of a *dependent being* and the concept of a *self-existent being*. By "a dependent being" we mean a *being whose existence is accounted for by the causal activity of other things.* Recalling Anselm's division into the three cases: "explained by another," "explained by nothing," and "explained by itself," it's clear that a dependent being is a being whose existence is explained by another. By "a self-existent being" we mean *a being whose existence is accounted for by its own nature.* This idea . . . is an essential element in the theistic concept of God. Again, in terms of Anselm's three cases, a self-existent being is a being whose existence is explained by itself. Armed with these two concepts, the concept of a dependent being and the concept of a self-existent being, we can now state the first part of the Cosmological Argument.

1. Every being (that exists or ever did exist) is either a dependent being or a self-existent being.

2. Not every being can be a dependent being.

Therefore,

3. There exists a self-existent being.

Deductive Validity

Before we look critically at each of the premises of this argument, we should note that this argument is, to use an expression from the logician's vocabulary, *deductively valid*. To find out whether an argument is deductively valid we need only ask the question: If its premises were true would its conclusion have to be true? If the answer is yes, the argument is deductively valid. If the answer is no, the argument is deductively invalid. Notice that the question of the validity of an argument is entirely different from the question of whether its premises are in fact true. The following argument is made up entirely of false statements, but it is deductively valid.

1. Babe Ruth is the President of the U.S.
2. The President of the U.S. is from Indiana.

Therefore,

3. Babe Ruth is from Indiana.

The argument is deductively valid because even though its premises are false, if they were true its conclusion would have to be true. Even God, Aquinas would say, cannot bring it about that the premises of this argument are true and yet its conclusion is false, for God's power extends only to what is possible, and it is an absolute impossibility that Babe Ruth be the President, the President be from Indiana, and yet Babe Ruth not be from Indiana.

The Cosmological Argument (that is, its first part) is a deductively valid argument. If its premises are or were true its conclusion would have to be true. It's clear from our example about Babe Ruth, however, that the fact that an argument is deductively valid is insufficient to establish the truth of its conclusion. What else is required? Clearly that we know or have rational grounds for believing that the premises are true. If we know that the Cosmological Argument is deductively valid and can establish that its premises are true, we shall thereby have proved that its conclusion is true. Are, then, the premises of the Cosmological Argument true? To this more difficult question we must now turn.

PSR and the First Premise

At first glance the first premise might appear to be an obvious or even trivial truth. But it is neither obvious nor trivial. And if it appears to be obvious or trivial, we must be confusing the idea of a self-existent being with the idea of a being that is not a dependent being. Clearly, it is obviously true that any being is either a dependent being (explained by other things) or it is not a dependent being (not explained by other things). But what our premise says is that any being is either a dependent being (explained by other things) or it is a self-existent being (explained by itself). Consider again Anselm's three cases.

a. explained by another
b. explained by nothing
c. explained by itself

What our first premise asserts is that each being that exists (or ever did exist) is either of sort *a* or of sort *c*. It denies that any being is of sort *b*. And it is this denial that makes the first premise both significant and controversial. The obvious truth we must not confuse it with is the truth that any being is either of sort *a* or not of sort *a*. While this is true it is neither very significant nor controversial.

Earlier we saw that Anselm accepted as a basic principle that whatever exists has an explanation of its existence. Since this basic principle denies that any thing of sort *b* exists or ever did exist, it's clear that Anselm would believe the first premise of our Cosmological Argument. The eighteenth-century proponents of the argument also were convinced of the truth of the basic principle we attributed to Anselm. And because they were convinced of its truth, they readily accepted the first premise of the Cosmological Argument. But by the eighteenth century, Anselm's basic principle had been more fully elaborated and had received a name, "the Principle of Sufficient Reason." Since this principle (PSR, as we shall call it) plays such an important role in justifying the premises of the Cosmological Argument, it will help us to consider it for a

moment before we continue our enquiry into the truth or falsity of the premises of the Cosmological Argument.

The Principle of Sufficient Reason (PSR), as it was expressed by both Leibniz and Samuel Clarke, is a very general principle and is best understood as having two parts. In its first part it is simply a restatement of Anselm's principle that there must be an explanation of the *existence* of any being whatever. Thus if we come upon a man in a room, PSR implies that there must be an explanation of the fact that that particular man exists. A moment's reflection, however, reveals that there are many facts about the man other than the mere fact that he exists. There is the fact that the man in question is in the room he's in, rather than somewhere else, the fact that he is in good health, and the fact that he is at the moment thinking of Paris, rather than, say, London. Now the purpose of the second part of PSR is to require an explanation of these facts as well. We may state PSR, therefore, as the principle that *there must be an explanation (a) of the existence of any being, and (b) of any positive fact whatever*. We are now in a position to study the role this very important principle plays in the Cosmological Argument.

Since the proponent of the Cosmological Argument accepts PSR in both its parts, it is clear that he will appeal to its first part, PSRa, as justification for the first premise of the Cosmological Argument. Of course, we can and should enquire into the deeper question of whether the proponent of the argument is rationally justified in accepting PSR itself. But we shall put this question aside for the moment. What we need to see first is whether he is correct in thinking that *if* PSR is true then both of the premises of the Cosmological Argument are true. And what we have just seen is that if only the first part of PSR, that is, PSRa, is true, the first premise of the Cosmological Argument will be true. But what of the second premise of the Argument? For what reasons does the proponent think that it must be true?

The Second Premise

According to the second premise, not every being that exists can be a dependent being, that is, can have the explanation of its existence in some other being or beings. Presumably, the proponent of the argument thinks there is something fundamentally wrong with the idea that every being that exists is dependent, that each existing being was caused by some other being which in turn was caused by some other being, and so on. But just what does he think is wrong with it? To help us in understanding his thinking, let's simplify things by supposing that there exists only one thing now, A_1, a living thing perhaps, that was brought into existence by something else A_2, which perished shortly after it brought A_1 into existence. Suppose further that A_2 was brought into existence in similar fashion some time ago by A_3, and A_3 by A_4, and so forth back into the past. Each of these beings is a *dependent* being, it owes its existence to the preceding thing in the series. Now if nothing else ever existed but these beings, then what the second premise says would not be true. For if every being that exists or ever did exist is an A and was produced by a preceding A, then every being that exists or ever did exist would be dependent and, accordingly, premise two of the Cosmological Argument would be false. If the proponent of the Cosmological Argument is correct there must, then, be something wrong with the idea that every being that exists or did exist is an A and that they form a causal series, A_1 caused by A_2, A_2 caused by A_3, A_3 caused by $A_4, \ldots A_n$ caused by A_{n+1}. How does the proponent of the Cosmological Argument propose to show us that there is something wrong with this view?

A popular but mistaken idea of how the proponent tries to show that something is wrong with the view that every being might be dependent is that he uses the following argument to reject it.

1. There must be a *first being* to start any causal series.
2. If every being were dependent there would be no *first being* to start the causal series.

Therefore,

3. Not every being can be a dependent being.

Although this argument is deductively valid and its second premise is true, its first premise overlooks the distinct possibility that a causal series might be *infinite,* with no first member at all. Thus if we go back to our series of A beings, where each A is dependent, having been produced by the preceding A in the causal series, it's clear that if the series existed it would have no first member, for every A in the series there would be a preceding A which produced it, *ad infinitum*. The first premise of the argument just given assumes that a causal series must stop with a first member somewhere in the distant past. But there seems to be no good reason for making that assumption.

The eighteenth-century proponents of the Cosmological Argument recognized that the causal series of dependent beings could be infinite, without a first member to start the series. They rejected the idea that every being that is or ever was is dependent not because there would then be no first member to the series of dependent beings, but because there would then be no explanation for the fact that there are and have always been dependent beings. To see their reasoning let's return to our simplification of the supposition that the only things that exist or ever did exist are dependent beings. In our simplification of that supposition only one of the dependent beings exists at a time, each one perishing as it produces the next in the series. Perhaps the first thing to note about this supposition is that there is no individual A in the causal series of dependent beings whose existence is unexplained—A_1 is explained by A_2, A_2 by A_3, and A_n by A_{n+1}. So the first part of PSR, PSRa, appears to be satisfied. There is no particular being whose existence lacks an explanation. What, then, is it that lacks an explanation, if every particular A in the causal series of dependent beings has an explanation? It is the *series itself* that lacks an explanation. Or, as I've chosen to express it, *the fact that there are and have always been dependent beings.* For suppose we ask why it is that there are and have always been As in existence. It won't do to say that As have always been producing other As—we can't explain why there have always been As by saying there always have been As. Nor, on the supposition that only As have ever existed, can we explain the fact that there have always been As by appealing to something other than an A—for no such thing would have existed. Thus the supposition that the only things that exist or ever existed are dependent things leaves us with a fact for which there can be no explanation; namely, the fact that there are and have always been dependent beings.

Questioning the Justification of the Second Premise

Critics of the Cosmological Argument have raised several important objections against the claim that if every being is dependent the series or collection of those beings would have no explanation. Our understanding of the Cosmological Argument, as well as of its strengths and weaknesses, will be deepened by a careful consideration of these criticisms.

The first criticism is that the proponent of the Cosmological Argument makes the mistake of treating the collection or series of dependent beings as though it were itself a dependent being, and, therefore, requires an explanation of its existence. But, so the objection goes, the collection of dependent beings is not itself a dependent being any more than a collection of stamps is itself a stamp.

A second criticism is that the proponent makes the mistake of inferring that because each member of the collection of dependent beings has a cause the collection itself must have a cause. But, as Bertrand Russell noted, such reasoning is as fallacious as to infer that the human race (that is, the collection of human beings) must have a mother because each member of the collection (each human being) has a mother.

A third criticism is that the proponent of the argument fails to realize that for there to be an explanation of a collection of things is nothing more than for there to be an explanation of each of the things making up the collection. Since in the infinite collection (or series) of dependent beings, each being in the collection does have an explanation—by virtue of having been caused by some preceding member of the collection—the explanation of the collection, so the criticism goes, has already been given. As David Hume remarked, "Did I show you the particular causes of each individual in a collection of twenty particles of matter, I should think it very unreasonable, should you afterwards ask me, what was the cause of the whole twenty. This is sufficiently explained in explaining the cause of the parts."[2]

Finally, even if the proponent of the Cosmological Argument can satisfactorily answer these objections, he must face one last objection to his ingenious attempt to justify premise two of the Cosmological Argument. For someone may agree that if nothing exists but an infinite collection of dependent beings, . . . the infinite collection will have no explanation of its existence, and still refuse to conclude from this that there is something wrong with the idea that every being is a dependent being. Why, he might ask, should we think that everything has to have an explanation? What's wrong with admitting that the fact that there are and have always been dependent beings is a *brute fact*, a fact having no explanation whatever? Why does everything have to have an explanation anyway? We must now see what can be said in response to these several objections.

Responses to Criticism

It is certainly a mistake to think that a collection of stamps is itself a stamp, and very likely a mistake to think that the collection of dependent beings is itself a dependent being. But the mere fact that the proponent of the argument thinks that there must be an explanation not only for each member of the collection of dependent beings but for the collection itself is not sufficient grounds for concluding that he must view the collection as itself a dependent being. The collection of human beings, for example, is certainly not itself a human being. Admitting this, however, we might still seek an explanation of why there is a collection of human beings, of why there are such things as human beings at all. So the mere fact that an explanation is demanded for the collection of dependent beings is no proof that the person who demands the explanation must be supposing that the collection itself is just another dependent being.

The second criticism attributes to the proponent of the Cosmological Argument the following bit of reasoning:

1. Every member of the collection of dependent beings has a cause or explanation.

Therefore,

2. The collection of dependent beings has a cause or explanation.

As we noted in setting forth this criticism, arguments of this sort are often unreliable. It would be a mistake to conclude that a collection of objects is light in weight simply because each object in the collection is light in weight, for if there were many objects in the collection it might be quite heavy. On the other hand, if we know that each marble weighs more than one ounce we could infer validly that the collection of marbles weighs more than an ounce. Fortunately, however, we don't need to decide whether the inference from (1.) to (2.) is valid or invalid. We need not decide this question because the proponent of the Cosmological Argument need not use this inference to establish that there must be an explanation of the collection of dependent beings. He need not use this inference because he has in PSR a principle from which it follows immediately that the collection of dependent beings has a cause or explanation. For according to PSR every positive fact must have an explanation. If it is a fact that there exists a collection of dependent beings then, according to PSR, that fact too must have an explanation. So it is PSR that the proponent of the Cosmological Argument appeals to in concluding that there must be an explanation of the collection of dependent beings, and not some dubious inference from the premise that each member of the collection has an explanation. It seems, then, that neither of the first two criticisms is strong enough to do any serious damage to the reasoning used to support the second premise of the Cosmological Argument.

The third objection contends that to explain the existence of a collection of things is the same thing as to explain the existence of each of its members. If we consider a collection of dependent beings where each being in the collection is explained by the preceding member which caused it, it's clear that no member of the collection will lack an explanation of its existence. But, so the criticism goes, if we've explained the existence of every member of a collection we've explained the existence of the collection—there's nothing left over to be explained. This forceful criticism, originally advanced by David Hume, has gained considerable support in the modern period. But the criticism rests on an assumption that the proponent of the Cosmological Argument would not accept. The assumption is that to explain the existence of a collection of things it is *sufficient* to explain the existence of every member in the collection. To see what is wrong with this assumption is to understand the basic issue in the reasoning by which the proponent of the Cosmological Argument seeks to establish that not every being can be a dependent being.

In order for there to be an explanation of the existence of the collection of dependent beings, it's clear that the eighteenth-century proponents would require that the following two conditions be satisfied:

C1. There is an explanation of the existence of each of the members of the collection of dependent beings.
C2. There is an explanation of why there are *any* dependent beings.

According to the proponents of the Cosmological Argument if every being that exists or ever did exist is a dependent being—that is, if the whole of reality consists of nothing more than a collection of dependent beings—C1 will be satisfied, but C2 will not be satisfied. And since C2 won't be satisfied there will be no explanation of the collection of dependent beings. The third criticism, therefore, says in effect that if C1 is satisfied C2 will be satisfied, and, since in a collection of dependent beings each member will have an explanation in whatever it was that produced it, C1 will be satisfied. So, therefore, C2 will be satisfied and the collection of dependent beings will have an explanation.

Although the issue is a complicated one, I think it is possible to see that the third criticism rests on a mistake: the mistake of thinking that if C1 is satisfied C2 must also be satisfied. The mistake is a natural one to make for it is easy to imagine circumstances in which if C1 is satisfied C2 also will be satisfied. Suppose, for example, that the whole of reality includes not just a collection of dependent beings but also a self-existent being. Suppose further that instead of each dependent being having been produced by some other dependent being every dependent being was produced by the self-existent being. Finally, let us consider both the possibility that the collection of dependent beings is finite in time and has a first member and the possibility that the collection of dependent being is infinite in past time, having no first member. Using "G" for the self-existent being, the first possibility may be diagrammed as follows:

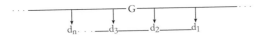

G, we shall say, has always existed and always will. We can think of d_1 as some presently existing dependent being, d_2, d_3, and so forth as dependent beings that existed at some time in the past, and d_n as the first dependent being to exist. The second possibility may be portrayed as follows:

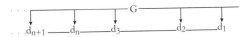

On this diagram there is no first member of the collection of dependent beings. Each member of the infinite collection, however, is explained by reference to the self-existing being G which produced it. Now the interesting point about both these cases is that the explanation that has been provided for the members of the collection of dependent beings carries with it, at least in part, an answer to the question of why there are any dependent beings at all. In both cases we may explain why there are dependent beings by pointing out that there exists a self-existent being that has been engaged in producing them. So once we have learned that the existence of each member of the collection of dependent beings has its existence explained by the fact that G produced it, we have already learned why there are dependent beings.

Someone might object that we haven't really learned why there are dependent beings until we also learn *why* G has been producing them. But, of course, we could also say that we haven't really explained the existence of a particular dependent being, say d_3, until we also learn not just that G produced it but *why* G produced it. The point we need to grasp, however, is that once we admit that every dependent being's existence is explained by G, we must admit that the fact that there are

dependent beings has also been explained. So it is not unnatural that someone should think that to explain the existence of the collection of dependent beings is nothing more than to explain the existence of its members. For, as we've seen, to explain the collection's existence is to explain each member's existence and to explain why there are any dependent beings at all. And in the examples we've considered, in doing the one (explaining why each dependent being exists) we've already done the other (explained why there are any dependent beings at all). We must now see, however, that on the supposition that the whole of reality consists *only* of a collection of dependent beings, to give an explanation of each member's existence is not to provide an explanation of why there are dependent beings.

In the examples we've considered we have gone *outside* of the collection of dependent beings in order to explain the members' existence. But if the only beings that exist or ever existed are dependent beings then each dependent being will be explained by some other dependent being, ad infinitum. This does not mean that there will be some particular dependent being whose existence is unaccounted for. Each dependent being has an explanation of its existence; namely, in the dependent being which preceded it and produced it. So C1 is satisfied: there is an explanation of the existence of each member of the collection of dependent beings. Turning to C2, however, we can see that it will not be satisfied. We cannot explain why there are (or have ever been) dependent beings by appealing to all the members of the infinite collection of dependent beings. For if the question to be answered is why there are (or have ever been) any dependent beings at all, we cannot answer that question by noting that there always have been dependent beings, each one accounting for the existence of some other dependent being. Thus on the supposition that every being is dependent it seems there will be no explanation of why there are dependent beings. C2 will not be satisfied. Therefore, on the supposition that every being is dependent there will be no explanation of the existence of the collection of dependent beings.

The Truth of PSR

We come now to the final criticism of the reasoning supporting the second premise of the Cosmological Argument. According to this criticism, it is admitted that the supposition that every being is dependent implies that there will be a *brute fact* in the universe, a fact, that is, for which there can be no explanation whatever. For there will be no explanation of the fact that dependent beings exist and have always been in existence. It is this brute fact that the proponents of the argument were describing when they pointed out that if every being is dependent the series or collection of dependent beings would lack an explanation of *its* existence. The final criticism asks what is wrong with admitting that the universe contains such a brute, unintelligible fact. In asking this question the critic challenges the fundamental principle, PSR, on which the Cosmological Argument rests. For, as we've seen, the first premise of the argument denies that there exists a being whose existence has no explanation. In support of this premise the proponent appeals to the first part of PSR. The second premise of the argument claims that not every being can be dependent. In support of this premise the proponent appeals to the second part of PSR, the part which states that there must be an explanation of any positive fact whatever.

The proponent reasons that if every being were a dependent being then although the first part of PSR would be satisfied—every being would have an explanation—the second part would be violated, there would be no explanation for the positive fact that there are and have always been dependent beings. For first, since every being is supposed to be dependent, there would be nothing outside of the collection of dependent beings to explain the collection's existence. Second, the fact that each member of the collection has an explanation in some other dependent being is insufficient to explain why there are and have always been dependent beings. And, finally, there is nothing about the collection of dependent beings that would suggest that it is a self-existent collection. Consequently, if every being were dependent, the fact that there are and have always been dependent

beings would have no explanation. But this violates the second part of PSR. So the second premise of the Cosmological Argument must be true, not every being can be a dependent being. This conclusion, however, is no better than the principle, PSR, on which it rests. And it is the point of the final criticism to question the truth of PSR. Why, after all, should we accept the idea that every being and every positive fact must have an explanation? Why, in short, should we believe PSR? These are important questions, and any final judgment of the Cosmological Argument depends on how they are answered.

Most of the theologians and philosophers who accept PSR have tried to defend it in either of two ways. Some have held that PSR is (or can be) known *intuitively* to be true. By this they mean that if we fully understand and reflect on what is said by PSR we can see that it must be true. Now, undoubtedly, there are statements which are known intuitively to be true. "Every triangle has exactly three angles" or "No physical object can be in two different places in space at one and the same time" are examples of statements whose truth we can apprehend just by understanding and reflecting on them. The difficulty with the claim that PSR is intuitively true, however, is that a number of very able philosophers fail to apprehend its truth, and some even claim that the principle is false. It is doubtful, therefore, that many of us, if any, know intuitively that PSR is true.

The second way philosophers and theologians who accept PSR have sought to defend it is by claiming that although it is not known to be true, it is, nevertheless, a presupposition of reason, a basic assumption that rational people make, whether or not they reflect sufficiently to become aware of the assumption. It's probably true that there are some assumptions we all make about our world, assumptions which are so basic that most of us are unaware of them. And, I suppose, it might be true that PSR is such an assumption. What bearing would this view of PSR have on the Cosmological Argument? Perhaps the main point to note is that even if PSR is a presupposition we all share, the premises of the Cosmological Argument could still be false. For PSR itself could still be false.

The fact, if it is a fact, that all of us *presuppose* that every existing being and every positive fact has an explanation does not imply that no being exists, and no positive fact obtains, without an explanation. Nature is not bound to satisfy our presuppositions. As the American philosopher, William James, once remarked in another connection, "In the great boarding house of nature, the cakes and the butter and the syrup seldom come out so even and leave the plates so clear."

Our study of the first part of the Cosmological Argument has led us to the fundamental principle on which its premises rest, the Principle of Sufficient Reason. Since we do not seem to know that PSR is true we cannot reasonably claim to know that the premises of the Cosmological Argument are true. They might be true. But unless we do know them to be true they cannot *establish* for us the conclusion that there exists a being that has the explanation of its existence within its own nature. If it were shown, however, that even though we do not *know* that PSR is true we all, nevertheless, *presuppose* PSR to be true, then, whether PSR is true or not, to be consistent we should accept the Cosmological Argument. For, as we've seen, its premises imply its conclusion and its premises do seem to follow from PSR. But no one has succeeded in *showing* that PSR is an assumption that most or all of us share. So our final conclusion must be that although the Cosmological Argument might be a *sound* argument (valid with true premises), it does not provide us with good rational grounds for believing that among those beings that exist there is one whose existence is accounted for by its own nature. Having come to this conclusion we may safely put aside the second part of the argument. For even if it succeeded in showing that a self-existent being would have the other attributes of the theistic God, the Cosmological Argument would still not provide us with good rational grounds for belief in God, having failed in its first part to provide us with good rational grounds for believing that there is a self-existent being.

NOTES

1. See St. Thomas Aquinas, *Summa Theologica,* 1a, 2, 3.
2. David Hume, *Dialogues Concerning Natural Religion,* Part IX, ed. H. D. Aiken (New York: Hafner Publishing Company, 1948), pp. 59–60

The Argument from Design

WILLIAM PALEY

William Paley (1743–1805) was an English philosopher of religion and ethics.

CHAPTER ONE: STATE OF THE ARGUMENT

In crossing a heath, suppose I pitched my foot against a *stone* and were asked how the stone came to be there, I might possibly answer that for anything I knew to the contrary it had lain there forever; nor would it, perhaps, be very easy to show the absurdity of this answer. But suppose I had found a *watch* upon the ground, and it should be inquired how the watch happened to be in that place. I should hardly think of the answer which I had before given, that for anything I knew the watch might have always been there. Yet why should not this answer serve for the watch as well as for the stone? Why is it not as admissible in the second case as in the first? For this reason, and for no other, namely, that when we come to inspect the watch, we perceive—what we could not discover

From *Natural Theology* (1800).

in the stone—that its several parts are framed and put together for a purpose, e.g., that they are so formed and adjusted as to produce motion, and that motion so regulated as to point out the hour of the day; that if the different parts had been differently shaped from what they are, of a different size from what they are, or placed after any other manner or in any other order than that in which they are placed, either no motion at all would have been carried on in the machine, or none which would have answered the use that is now served by it. To reckon up a few of the plainest of these parts and of their offices, all tending to one result; we see a cylindrical box containing a coiled elastic spring, which, by its endeavor to relax itself, turns round the box. We next observe a flexible chain—artificially wrought for the sake of flexure—communicating the action of the spring from the box to the fusee. We then find a series of wheels, the teeth of which catch in and apply to each other, conducting the motion from the fusee to the balance and from the balance to the pointer, and at the same time, by the size and shape of those wheels, so regulating that motion as to terminate in causing an index, by an equable and measured progression, to pass over a given space in a given time. We take notice that the wheels are made of brass, in order to keep them from rust; the springs of steel, no other metal being so elastic; that over the face of the watch there is placed a glass, a material employed in no other part of the work, but in the room of which, if there had been any other than a transparent substance, the hour could not be seen without opening the case. This mechanism being observed—it requires indeed an examination of the instrument, and perhaps some previous knowledge of the subject, to perceive and understand it; but being once, as we have said, observed and understood—the inference we think is inevitable, that the watch must have had a maker—that there must have existed, at some time and at some place or other, an artificer or artificers who formed it for the purpose which we find it actually to answer, who comprehended its construction and designed its use.

I. Nor would it, I apprehend, weaken the conclusion, that we had never seen a watch made—that we had never known an artist capable of making one—that we were altogether incapable of executing such a piece of workmanship ourselves, or of understanding in what manner it was performed; all this being no more than what is true of some exquisite remains of ancient art, of some lost arts, and, to the generality of mankind, of the more curious productions of modern manufacture. Does one man in a million know how oval frames are turned? Ignorance of this kind exalts our opinion of the unseen and unknown artist's skill, if he be unseen and unknown, but raises no doubt in our minds of the existence and agency of such an artist, at some former time and in some place or other. Nor can I perceive that it varies at all the inference, whether the question arise concerning a human agent or concerning an agent of a different species, or an agent possessing in some respects a different nature.

II. Neither, secondly, would it invalidate our conclusion, that the watch sometimes went wrong or that it seldom went exactly right. The purpose of the machinery, the design, and the designer might be evident, and in the case supposed, would be evident, in whatever way we accounted for the irregularity of the movement, or whether we could account for it or not. It is not necessary that a machine be perfect in order to show with what design it was made: still less necessary, where the only question is whether it were made with any design at all.

III. Nor, thirdly, would it bring any uncertainty into the argument, if there were a few parts of the watch, concerning which we could not discover or had not yet discovered in what manner they conduced to the general effect; or even some parts, concerning which we could not ascertain whether they conduced to that effect in any manner whatever. For, as to the first branch of the case, if by the loss, or disorder, or decay of the parts in question, the movement of the watch were found in fact to be stopped, or disturbed, or retarded, no doubt would remain in our minds as to the utility or intention of these parts, although we should be unable to investigate the manner according to which, or the connection by which, the ultimate effect depended upon their action or assistance; and the more complex is the machine, the more likely is this obscurity to arise. Then, as to the second thing supposed, namely, that there were parts which might be spared without prejudice to the movement of the watch, and that we had proved this by experiment, these superfluous parts, even if we were completely assured that they were such, would not vacate the reasoning which we had instituted concerning other parts. The indication of contrivance remained, with respect to them, nearly as it was before.

IV. Nor, fourthly, would any man in his senses think the existence of the watch with its various machinery accounted for, by being told that it was one out of possible combinations of material forms; that whatever he had found in the place where he found the watch, must have contained some internal configuration or other; and that this configuration might be the structure now exhibited, namely, of the works of a watch, as well as a different structure.

V. Nor, fifthly, would it yield his inquiry more satisfaction, to be answered that there existed in things a principle of order, which had disposed the parts of the watch into their present form and situation. He never knew a watch made by the principle of order; nor can he even form to himself an idea of what is meant by a principle of order distinct from the intelligence of the watchmaker.

VI. Sixthly, he would be surprised to hear that the mechanism of the watch was no proof of contrivance, only a motive to induce the mind to think so:

VII. And not less surprised to be informed that the watch in his hand was nothing more than the result of the laws of *metallic* nature. It is a perversion of language to assign any law as the efficient, operative cause of any thing. A law presupposes an agent, for it is only the mode according to which an agent proceeds; it implies a power, for it is the order according to which that power acts. Without this agent, without this power, which are both distinct from itself, the *law* does nothing, is nothing. The expression, "the law of metallic nature," may sound strange and harsh to a philosophic ear; but it seems quite as justifiable as some others which are more familiar to him, such as "the law of vegetable nature," "the law of animal nature," or, indeed, as "the law of nature" in general, when assigned as the cause of phenomena, in exclusion of agency and power, or when it is substituted into the place of these.

VIII. Neither, lastly, would our observer be driven out of his conclusion or from his confidence in its truth by being told that he knew nothing at all about the matter. He knows enough for his argument; he knows the utility of the end; he knows the subserviency and adaptation of the means to the end. These points being known, his ignorance of other points, his doubts concerning other points affect not the certainty of his reasoning. The consciousness of knowing little need not beget a distrust of that which he does know.

CHAPTER TWO: STATE OF THE ARGUMENT CONTINUED

Suppose, in the next place, that the person who found the watch should after some time discover that, in addition to all the properties which he had hitherto observed in it, it possessed the unexpected property of producing in the course of its movement another watch like itself—the thing is conceivable; that it contained within it a mechanism, a system of parts—a mold, for instance, or a complex adjustment of lathes, files, and other tools—evidently and separately calculated for this purpose; let us inquire what effect ought such a discovery to have upon his former conclusion.

I. The first effect would be to increase his admiration of the contrivance, and his conviction of the consummate skill of the contriver. Whether he regarded the object of the contrivance, the distinct apparatus, the intricate, yet in many parts intelligible mechanism by which it was carried on, he would perceive in this new observation nothing but an additional reason for doing what he had already done—for referring the construction of the watch to design and to supreme art. If that construction *without* this property, or, which is the same thing, before this property had been noticed, proved intention and art to have been employed about it, still more strong would the proof appear when he came to the knowledge of this further property, the crown and perfection of all the rest.

II. He would reflect, that though the watch before him were, *in some sense,* the maker of the watch, which, was fabricated in the course of its movements, yet it was in a very different sense from that in which a carpenter, for instance, is the maker of a chair—the author of its contrivance, the cause of the relation of its parts to their use. With respect to these, the first watch was no cause at all to the second; in no such sense as this was it the author of the constitution and order, either of the parts which the new watch contained, or of the parts by the aid and instrumentality of which it was produced. We might possibly say, but with great latitude of expression, that a stream of water ground corn; but no latitude of expression would allow us to say, no stretch of conjecture could lead us to think that the stream of water built the mill, though it were too ancient for us to know who the builder was. What the stream of water does in the affair is neither more nor less than this: by the application of an unintelligent impulse to a mechanism previously arranged, arranged independently of it and arranged by intelligence, an effect is produced, namely, the corn is ground. But the effect results from the arrangement. The force of the stream cannot be said to be the cause or author of the effect, still less of the arrangement. Understanding and plan in the formation of the mill were not the less necessary for any share which the water has in grinding the corn; yet is this share the same as that which the watch would have contributed to the production of the new watch, upon the supposition assumed in the last section. Therefore,

III. Though it be now no longer probable that the individual watch which our observer had found was made immediately by the hand of an artificer, yet does not this alteration in anyway affect the inference that an artificer had been originally employed and concerned in the production. The argument from design remains as it was. Marks of design and contrivance are no more accounted for now than they were before. In the same thing, we may ask for the cause of different properties. We may ask for the cause of the color of a body, of its hardness, of its heat; and these causes may be all different. We are now asking for the cause of that subserviency to a use, that relation to an end, which we have remarked in the watch before us. No answer is given to this question by telling us that a preceding watch produced it. There cannot be design without a designer; contrivance without a contriver; order without choice; arrangement without anything capable of arranging; subserviency and relation to a purpose without that which could intend a purpose; means suitable to an end, and executing their office in accomplishing that end, without the end ever having been contemplated or the means accommodated to it. Arrangement, disposition of parts, subserviency of means to an end, relation of instruments to a use imply the presence of intelligence and mind. No one, therefore, can rationally believe that the insensible, inanimate watch, from which the watch before us issued, was the proper cause of the mechanism we so much admire in it—could be truly said to have constructed the instrument, disposed its parts, assigned their office, determined their order, action, and mutual dependency, combined their several motions into one result, and that also a result connected with the utilities of other beings. All these properties, therefore, are as much unaccounted for as they were before.

IV. Nor is anything gained by running the difficulty farther back, that is, by supposing the watch before us to have been produced from another watch, that from a former, and so on indefinitely. Our going back ever so far brings us no nearer to the least degree of satisfaction upon the subject. Contrivance is still unaccounted for. We still want a contriver. A designing mind is neither supplied by this supposition nor dispensed with. If the difficulty were diminished the farther we went back, by going back indefinitely we might exhaust it. And this is the only case to which this sort of reasoning applies. Where there is a tendency, or, as we increase the number of terms, a continual approach toward a limit, *there,* by supposing the number of terms to be what is called infinite, we may conceive the limit to be attained; but where there is no such tendency or approach, nothing is effected by lengthening the series. There is no difference as to the point in question, whatever there may be as to many points, between one series and another—between a series which is finite and a series which is infinite. A chain composed of an infinite number of links, can no more support itself, than a chain composed of a finite number of links. And of this we are assured, though we never *can* have tried the experiment; because, by increasing the number of links, from ten, for instance, to a hundred, from a hundred to a thousand, etc., we make not the smallest approach, we observe not the smallest tendency toward self-support. There is no difference in this respect—yet there may be a great difference in several respects—between a chain of a greater or less length, between one chain and another, between one that is finite and one that is infinite. This very much resembles the case before us. The machine which we are inspecting demonstrates, by its construction, contrivance and design. Contrivance must have had a contriver, design a designer, whether the machine immediately proceeded from another machine or not. That circumstance alters not the case. That other machine may, in like manner, have proceeded from a former machine; nor does that alter the case; contrivance must have had a contriver. That former one from one preceding it: no alteration still; a contriver is still necessary. No tendency is perceived, no approach toward a diminution of this necessity. It is the same with any and every succession of these machines—a succession of ten, of a hundred, of a thousand; with one series, as with another—a series which is finite, as with a series which is infinite. In whatever other respects they may differ, in this they do not. In all equally, contrivance and design are unaccounted for.

The question is not simply, How came the first watch into existence? which question, it may be pretended, is done away by supposing the series of watches thus produced from one another to have been infinite, and consequently to have had no such *first* for which it was necessary to provide a cause. This, perhaps, would have been nearly the state of the question, if nothing had been before us but an unorganized, unmechanized substance, without mark or indication of contrivance. It might be difficult to show that such substance could not have existed from eternity, either in succession—if it were possible, which I think it is not, for unorganized bodies to spring from one another—or by individual perpetuity. But that is not the question now. To suppose it to be so is to suppose that it made no difference whether he had found a watch or a stone. As it is, the metaphysics of that question have no place; for, in the watch which we are examining are seen contrivance, design, an end, a purpose, means for the end, adaptation to the purpose. And the question which irresistibly presses upon our thoughts is, whence this contrivance and design? The thing required is the intending mind, the adapting hand, the intelligence by which that hand was directed. This question, this demand is not shaken off by increasing a number or succession of substances destitute of these properties; nor the more, by increasing that number to infinity. If it be said that, upon the supposition of one watch being produced from another in the course of that other's movements and by means of the mechanism within it, we have a cause for the watch in my hand, namely, the watch from which it proceeded; I deny that for the design, the contrivance, the suitableness of means to an end, the adaptation of instruments to a use, all of which we discover in the watch, we have any cause whatever. It is in vain, therefore, to assign a series of such causes or to allege that a series may be carried back to infinity; for I do not admit that we have yet any cause at all for the phenomena, still less any series of causes either finite or infinite. Here is contrivance but no contriver; proofs of design, but no designer.

V. Our observer would further also reflect that the maker of the watch before him was in truth and reality the maker of every watch produced from it; there being no difference, except that the latter manifests a more exquisite skill, between the making of another watch with his own hands, by the mediation of files, lathes, chisels, etc., and the disposing, fixing, and inserting of these instruments, or of others equivalent to them, in the body of the watch already made, in such a manner as to form a new watch in the course of the movements which he had given to the old one. It is only working by one set of tools instead of another.

The conclusion which the *first* examination of the watch, of its works, construction, and movement, suggested, was that it must have had, for cause and author of that construction, an artificer who understood its mechanism and designed its use. This conclusion is invincible. A *second* examination presents us with a new discovery. The watch is found, in the course of its movement, to produce another watch similar to itself; and not only so, but we perceive in it a system of organization separately calculated for that purpose. What effect would this discovery have or ought it to have upon our former inference? What, as has already been said, but to increase beyond measure our admiration of the skill which had been employed in the formation of such a machine? Or shall it, instead of this, all at once turn us round to an opposite conclusion, namely, that no art or skill whatever has been concerned in the business, although all other evidences of art and skill remain as they were, and this last and supreme piece of art be now added to the rest? Can this be maintained without absurdity? Yet this is atheism. . . .

CHAPTER FIVE: APPLICATION OF THE ARGUMENT CONTINUED

Every observation which was made in our first chapter concerning the watch may be repeated with strict propriety concerning the eye, concerning animals, concerning plants, concerning, indeed, all the organized parts of the works of nature. As,

I. When we are inquiring simply after the *existence* of an intelligent Creator, imperfection, inaccuracy, liability to disorder, occasional irregularities may subsist in a considerable degree without inducing any doubt into the question; just as a watch may frequently go wrong, seldom perhaps exactly right, may be faulty in some parts, defective in some, without the smallest ground of suspicion from thence arising that it was not a watch, not made, or not made for the purpose ascribed to it. When faults are

pointed out, and when a question is started concerning the skill of the artist or dexterity with which the work is executed, then, indeed, in order to defend these qualities from accusation, we must be able either to expose some intractableness and imperfection in the materials or point out some invincible difficulty in the execution, into which imperfection and difficulty the matter of complaint may be resolved; or, if we cannot do this, we must adduce such specimens of consummate art and contrivance proceeding from the same hand as may convince the inquirer of the existence, in the case before him, of impediments like those which we have mentioned, although, what from the nature of the case is very likely to happen, they be unknown and unperceived by him. This we must do in order to vindicate the artist's skill, or at least the perfection of it; as we must also judge of his intention and of the provisions employed in fulfilling that intention, not from an instance in which they fail but from the great plurality of instances in which they succeed. But, after all, these are different questions from the question of the artist's existence; or, which is the same, whether the thing before us be a work of art or not; and the questions ought always to be kept separate in the mind. So likewise it is in the works of nature. Irregularities and imperfections are of little or no weight in the consideration when that consideration relates simply to the existence of a Creator. When the argument respects His attributes, they are of weight; but are then to be taken in conjunction—the attention is not to rest upon them, but they are to be taken in conjunction with the unexceptionable evidence which we possess of skill, power, and benevolence displayed in other instances; which evidences may, in strength, number, and variety, be such and may so overpower apparent blemishes as to induce us, upon the most reasonable ground, to believe that these last ought to be referred to some cause, though we be ignorant of it, other than defect of knowledge or of benevolence in the author. . . .

Dialogues Concerning Natural Religion

DAVID HUME

David Hume (1711–1776) was a leading philosopher of the Enlightenment, the author of a famous history of England, and the tutor of Adam Smith in political economy. He spent most of his life in Edinburgh.

PART II

I must own, Cleanthes, said Demea, that nothing can more surprise me than the light in which you have all along put this argument. By the whole tenor of your discourse, one would imagine that you were maintaining the Being of a God against the cavils of atheists and infidels, and were necessitated to become a champion for that fundamental principle of all religion. But this, I hope, is not by any means a question among us. No man, no man at least of common sense, I am persuaded, ever entertained a serious doubt with regard to a truth so certain and self-evident. The question is not concerning the *being* but the *nature* of God. This I affirm, from the infirmities of human understanding, to be altogether incomprehensible and unknown to us. The essence of that supreme Mind, his attributes, the manner of his existence, the very nature of his duration—these and every particular which regards so divine a Being are mysterious to men. Finite, weak, and blind creatures, we ought to humble ourselves in his august presence, and, conscious of our frailties, adore in silence his infinite perfections which eye hath not seen, ear hath not heard, neither hath it entered into the heart of man to conceive. They are covered in a deep cloud from human curiosity; it is profaneness to attempt penetrating through these sacred obscurities, and, next to the impiety of denying his existence, is the temerity of prying into his nature and essence, decrees and attributes.

But lest you should think that my *piety* has here got the better of my *philosophy*, I shall support my opinion, if it needs any support, by a very great authority. I might cite all the divines, almost from the foundation of Christianity, who have ever treated of this or any other theological subject; but I shall confine myself, at present, to one equally celebrated for piety and philosophy. It is Father Malebranche who, I remember, thus expresses himself.[1] "One ought not so much," says he, "to call God a spirit in order to express positively what he is, as in order to signify that he is not matter. He is a Being infinitely perfect—of this we cannot doubt. But in the same manner as we ought not to imagine, even supposing him corporeal, that he is clothed with a human body, as the anthropomorphites asserted, under colour that that figure was the most perfect of any, so neither ought we to imagine that the spirit of God has human ideas or bears any resemblance to our spirit, under colour that we know nothing more perfect than a human mind. We ought rather to believe that as he comprehends the perfections of matter without being material . . . he comprehends also the perfections of created spirits without being spirit, in the manner we conceive spirit: that his true name is *He that is,* or, in other words, Being without restriction, All Being, the Being infinite and universal."

After so great an authority, Demea, replied Philo, as that which you have produced, and a thousand more which you might produce, it would appear ridiculous in me to add my sentiment or express my approbation of your doctrine. But surely, where reasonable men treat these subjects, the question can never be concerning the *being* but only the *nature* of the Deity. The former

First published in 1779.

truth, as you well observe, is unquestionable and self-evident. Nothing exists without a cause; and the original cause of this universe (whatever it be) we call God, and piously ascribe to him every species of perfection. Whoever scruples this fundamental truth deserves every punishment which can be inflicted among philosophers, to wit, the greatest ridicule, contempt, and disapprobation. But as all perfection is entirely relative, we ought never to imagine that we comprehend the attributes of this divine Being, or to suppose that his perfections have any analogy or likeness to the perfections of a human creature. Wisdom, thought, design, knowledge—these we justly ascribe to him because these words are honourable among men, and we have no other language or other conceptions by which we can express our adoration of him. But let us beware lest we think that our ideas anywise correspond to his perfections, or that his attributes have any resemblance to these qualities among men. He is infinitely superior to our limited view and comprehension, and is more the object of worship in the temple than of disputation in the schools.

In reality, Cleanthes, continued he, there is no need of having recourse to that affected scepticism so displeasing to you in order to come at this determination. Our ideas reach no further than our experience. We have no experience of divine attributes and operations. I need not conclude my syllogism, you can draw the inference yourself. And it is a pleasure to me (and I hope to you, too) that just reasoning and sound piety here concur in the same conclusion, and both of them establish the adorably mysterious and incomprehensible nature of the Supreme Being.

Not to lose any time in circumlocutions, said Cleanthes, addressing himself to Demea, much less in replying to the pious declamations of Philo, I shall briefly explain how I conceive this matter. Look round the world, contemplate the whole and every part of it: you will find it to be nothing but one great machine, subdivided into an infinite number of lesser machines, which again admit of subdivisions to a degree beyond what human senses and faculties can trace and explain. All these various machines, and even their most minute parts, are adjusted to each other with an accuracy which ravishes into admiration all men who have ever contemplated them. The curious adapting of means to ends, throughout all nature, resembles exactly, though it much exceeds, the productions of human contrivance—of human design, thought, wisdom, and intelligence. Since therefore the effects resemble each other, we are led to infer, by all the rules of analogy, that the causes also resemble, and that the Author of nature is somewhat similar to the mind of man, though possessed of much larger faculties, proportioned to the grandeur of the work which he has executed. By this argument *a posteriori,* and by this argument alone, do we prove at once the existence of a Deity and his similarity to human mind and intelligence.

I shall be so free, Cleanthes, said Demea, as to tell you that from the beginning I could not approve of your conclusion concerning the similarity of the Deity to men, still less can I approve of the mediums by which you endeavour to establish it. What! No demonstration of the Being of God! No abstract arguments! No proofs *a priori!* Are these which have hitherto been so much insisted on by philosophers all fallacy, all sophism? Can we reach no farther in this subject than experience and probability? I will not say that this is betraying the cause of a Deity; but surely, by this affected candour, you give advantages to atheists which they never could obtain by the mere dint of argument and reasoning.

What I chiefly scruple in this subject, said Philo, is not so much that all religious arguments are by Cleanthes reduced to experience, as that they appear not to be even the most certain and irrefragable of that inferior kind. That a stone will fall, that fire will burn, that the earth has solidity, we have observed a thousand and a thousand times; and when any new instance of this nature is presented, we draw without hesitation the accustomed inference. The exact similarity of the cases gives us a perfect assurance of a similar event, and a stronger evidence is never desired nor sought after. But wherever you depart, in the least, from the similarity of the cases, you diminish proportionably the evidence, and may at last bring it to a very weak *analogy,* which is confessedly liable to error and uncertainty. After having experienced the circulation of the blood in human creatures, we make no doubt that it takes place in Titius and Maevius; but from its circulation in frogs and fishes it is only a presumption, though a strong one, from analogy that it takes place in men and other animals. The analogical reasoning is much weaker when we infer the circulation of the sap in vegetables from our experience that the blood circulates in animals; and those who hastily followed that imperfect analogy are found, by more accurate experiments, to have been mistaken.

If we see a house, Cleanthes, we conclude, with the greatest certainty, that it had an architect or builder because this is precisely that species of effect which we have experienced to proceed from that species of cause. But surely you will not affirm that the universe bears such a resemblance to a house that we can with the same certainty infer a similar cause, or that the analogy is here entire and perfect. The dissimilitude is so striking that the utmost you can here pretend to is a guess, conjecture, a presumption concerning a similar cause; and how that pretension will be received in the world, I leave you to consider.

It would surely be very ill received, replied Cleanthes; and I should be deservedly blamed and detested did I allow that the proofs of Deity amounted to no more than a guess or conjecture. But is the whole adjustment of means to ends in a house and in the universe so slight a resemblance? the economy of final causes? the order, proportion, and arrangement of every part? Steps of a stair are plainly contrived that human legs may use them in mounting; and this inference is certain and infallible. Human legs are also contrived for walking and mounting; and this inference, I allow, is not altogether so certain because of the dissimilarity which you remark; but does it, therefore, deserve the name only of presumption or conjecture?

Good God! cried Demea, interrupting him, where are we? Zealous defenders of religion allow that the proofs of a Deity fall short of perfect evidence! And you, Philo, on whose assistance I depended in proving the adorable mysteriousness of the Divine Nature, do you assent to all these extravagant opinions of Cleanthes? For what other name can I give them? or, why spare my censure when such principles are advanced, supported by such an authority, before so young a man as Pamphilus?

You seem not to apprehend, replied Philo, that I argue with Cleanthes in his own way, and, by showing him the dangerous consequences of his tenets, hope at last to reduce him to our opinion. But what sticks most with you, I observe, is the representation which Cleanthes has made of the argument *a posteriori;* and, finding that the argument is likely to escape your hold and vanish into air, you think it so disguised that you can scarcely believe it to be set in its true light. Now, however much I may dissent, in other respects, from the dangerous principle of Cleanthes, I must allow that he has fairly represented that argument, and I shall endeavour so to state the matter to you that you will entertain no further scruples with regard to it.

Were a man to abstract from everything which he knows or has seen, he would be altogether incapable, merely from his own ideas, to determine what kind of scene the universe must be, or to give the preference to one state or situation of things above another. For as nothing which he clearly conceives could be esteemed impossible or implying a contradiction, every chimera of his fancy would be upon an equal footing; nor could he assign any just reason why he adheres to one idea or system, and rejects the others which are equally possible.

Again, after he opens his eyes and contemplates the world as it really is, it would be impossible for him at first to assign the cause of any one event, much less of the whole of things, or of the universe. He might set his fancy a rambling, and she might bring him in an infinite variety of reports and representations. These would all be possible, but, being all equally possible, he would never of himself give a satisfactory account for his preferring one of them to the rest. Experience alone can point out to him the true cause of any phenomenon.

Now, according to this method of reasoning, Demea, it follows (and is, indeed, tacitly allowed by Cleanthes himself) that order, arrangement, or the adjustment of final causes, is not of itself any proof of design, but only so far as it has been experienced to proceed from that principle. For aught we can know *a priori,* matter may contain the source or spring of order originally within itself, as well as mind does; and there is no more difficulty in conceiving that the several elements, from an internal unknown cause, may fall into the most exquisite arrangement, than to conceive that their ideas, in the great universal mind, from a like internal unknown cause, fall into that arrangement. The equal possibility of both these suppositions is allowed. But, by experience, we find (according to Cleanthes) that there is a difference between them. Throw several pieces of steel together, without shape or form, they will never arrange themselves so as to compose a watch. Stone and mortar and wood, without an architect, never erect a house. But the ideas in a human mind, we see, by an unknown, inexplicable economy, arrange themselves so as to form the plan of a watch or house. Experience, therefore, proves that there is an original principle of order in mind, not in matter. From similar effects we infer similar causes. The adjustment of means to ends is alike in the universe, as in a machine of human contrivance. The causes, therefore, must be resembling.

I was from the beginning scandalized, I must own, with this resemblance which is asserted between the Deity and human creatures, and must conceive it to imply such a degradation of the Supreme Being as no sound theist could endure. With your assistance, therefore, Demea, I shall endeavour to defend what you justly call the adorable mysteriousness of the Divine Nature, and shall refute this reasoning of Cleanthes, provided he allows that I have made a fair representation of it.

When Cleanthes had assented, Philo, after a short pause, proceeded in the following manner.

That all inferences, Cleanthes, concerning fact are founded on experience, and that all experimental reasonings are founded on the supposition that similar causes prove similar effects, and similar effects similar causes, I shall not at present much dispute with you. But observe, I entreat you, with what extreme caution all just reasoners proceed in the transferring of experiments to similar cases. Unless the cases be exactly similar, they repose no perfect confidence in applying their past observation to any particular phenomenon. Every alteration of circumstances occasions a doubt concerning the event; and it requires new experiments to prove certainly that the new circumstances are of no moment or importance. A change in bulk, situation, arrangement, age, disposition of the air, or surrounding bodies—any of these particulars may be attended with the most unexpected consequences. And unless the objects be quite familiar to us, it is the highest temerity to expect with assurance, after any of these changes, an event similar to that which before fell under our observation. The slow and deliberate steps of philosophers here, if anywhere, are distinguished from the precipitate march of the vulgar, who, hurried on by the smallest similitude, are incapable of all discernment or consideration.

But can you think, Cleanthes, that your usual phlegm and philosophy have been preserved in so wide a step as you have taken when you compared to the universe houses, ships, furniture, machines, and, from their similarity in some circumstances, inferred a similarity in their causes? Thought, design, intelligence, such as we discover in men and other animals, is no more than one of the springs and principles of the universe, as well as heat or cold, attraction or repulsion, and a hundred others which fall under daily observation. It is an active cause by which some particular parts of nature, we find, produce alterations on other parts. But can a conclusion, with any propriety, be transferred from parts to the whole? Does not the great disproportion bar all comparison and inference? From observing the growth of a hair, can we learn anything concerning the generation of a man? Would the manner of a leaf's blowing, even though perfectly known, afford us any instruction concerning the vegetation of a tree?

But allowing that we were to take the *operations* of one part of nature upon another for the foundation of our judgment concerning the *origin* of the whole (which never can be admitted), yet why select so minute, so weak, so bounded a principle as the reason and design of animals is found to be upon this planet? What peculiar privilege has this little agitation of the brain which we call *thought*, that we must thus make it the model of the whole universe? Our partiality in our own favour does indeed present it on all occasions, but sound philosophy ought carefully to guard against so natural an illusion.

So far from admitting, continued Philo, that the operations of a part can afford us any just conclusion concerning the origin of the whole, I will not allow any one part to form a rule for another part if the latter be very remote from the former. Is there any reasonable ground to conclude that the inhabitants of other planets possess thought, intelligence, reason, or anything similar to these faculties in men? When nature has so extremely diversified her manner of operation in this small globe, can we imagine that she incessantly copies herself throughout so immense a universe? And if thought, as we may well suppose, be confined merely to this narrow corner and has even there so limited a sphere of action, with what propriety can we assign it for the original cause of all things? The narrow views of a peasant who makes his domestic economy the rule for the government of kingdoms is in comparison a pardonable sophism.

But were we ever so much assured that a thought and reason resembling the human were to be found throughout the whole universe, and were its activity elsewhere vastly greater and more commanding than it appears in this globe, yet I cannot see why the operations of a world constituted, arranged, adjusted, can with any propriety be extended to a world which is in its embryo state, and is advancing towards that constitution and arrangement. By observation we know somewhat of the economy, action, and nourishment of a finished animal, but we must transfer with great caution that observation to the growth of a foetus in the womb, and still more to the formation of an animalcule in the loins of its male parent. Nature, we find, even from our limited experience, possesses an infinite number of springs and principles which incessantly discover themselves on every change of her position and situation. And what new and unknown principles would actuate her in so new and unknown a situation as that of the formation of a universe, we cannot, without the utmost temerity, pretend to determine.

A very small part of this great system, during a very short time, is very imperfectly discovered to us; and do we thence pronounce decisively concerning the origin of the whole?

Admirable conclusion! Stone, wood, brick, iron, brass, have not, at this time, in this minute globe of earth, an order or arrangement without human art and contrivance; therefore, the universe could not originally attain its order and arrangement without something similar to human art. But is a part of nature a rule for another part very wide of the former? Is it a rule for the whole? Is a very small part a rule for the universe? Is nature in one situation a certain rule for nature in another situation vastly different from the former?

And can you blame me, Cleanthes, if I here imitate the prudent reserve of Simonides, who, according to the noted story, being asked by Hiero, *What God was?* desired a day to think of it, and then two days more; and after that manner continually prolonged the term, without ever bringing in his definition or description? Could you even blame me if I had answered, at first, *that I did not know,* and was sensible that this subject lay vastly beyond the reach of my faculties? You might cry out sceptic and raillier, as much as you pleased; but, having found in so many other subjects much more familiar the imperfections and even contradictions of human reason, I never should expect any success from its feeble conjectures in a subject so sublime and so remote from the sphere of our observation. When two *species* of objects have always been observed to be conjoined together, I can *infer,* by custom, the existence of one wherever I *see* the existence of the other; and this I call an argument from experience. But how this argument can have place where the objects, as in the present case, are single, individual, without parallel or specific resemblance, may be difficult to explain. And will any man tell me with a serious countenance that an orderly universe must arise from some thought and art like the human because we have experience of it? To ascertain this reasoning it were requisite that we had experience of the origin of worlds; and it is not sufficient, surely, that we have seen ships and cities arise from human art and contrivance.

Philo was proceeding in this vehement manner, somewhat between jest and earnest, as it appeared to me, when he observed some signs of impatience in Cleanthes, and then immediately stopped short. What I had to suggest, said Cleanthes, is only that you would not abuse terms, or make use of popular expressions to subvert philosophical reasonings. You know that the vulgar often distinguish reason from experience, even where the question relates only to matter of fact and existence, though it is found, where that *reason* is properly analyzed, that it is nothing but a species of experience. To prove by experience the origin of the universe from mind is not more contrary to common speech than to prove the motion of the earth from the same principle. And a caviller might raise all the same objections to the Copernican system which you have urged against my reasonings. Have you other earths, might he say, which you have seen to move? Have. . .

Yes! cried Philo, interrupting him, we have other earths. Is not the moon another earth, which we see to turn around its centre? Is not Venus another earth, where we observe the same phenomenon? Are not the revolutions of the sun also a confirmation, from analogy, of the same theory? All the planets, are they not earths which revolve about the sun? Are not the satellites moons which move round Jupiter and Saturn, and along with these primary plnets round the sun? These analogies and resemblances, with others which I have not mentioned, are the sole proofs of the Copernican system; and to you it belongs to consider whether you have any analogies of the same kind to support your theory.

In reality, Cleanthes, continued he, the modern system of astronomy is now so much received by all inquirers, and has become so essential a part even of our earliest education, that we are not commonly very scrupulous in examining the reasons upon which it is founded. It is now become a matter of mere curiosity to study the first writers of that subject who had the full force of prejudice to encounter, and were obliged to turn their arguments on every side in order to render them popular and convincing. But if we peruse Galileo's famous *Dialogues* concerning the system of the world, we shall find that that great genius, one of the sublimest that ever existed, first bent all his endeavours to prove that there was no foundation for the distinction commonly made between elementary and celestial substances. The schools, proceeding from the illusions of sense, had carried this distinction very far; and had established the latter substances to be ingenerable, incorruptible, unalterable, impassible; and had assigned all the opposite qualities to the former. But Galileo, beginning with the moon, proved its similarity in every particular to the earth: its convex figure, its natural darkness when not illuminated, its density, its distinction into solid and liquid, the variations of its phases, the mutual illuminations of the earth and moon, their mutual eclipses, the inequalities of the lunar surface, etc. After many instances of this kind, with regard to all the planets, men plainly saw that these bodies became proper objects of experience, and that the similarity of their nature enabled us to extend the same arguments and phenomena from one to the other.

In this cautious proceeding of the astronomers you may read your own condemnation, Cleanthes, or rather may see that the subject in which you are engaged exceeds all human reason and inquiry. Can you pretend to show any such similarity between the fabric of a house and the generation of a universe? Have you ever seen nature in any such situation as resembles the first arrangement of the elements? Have worlds ever been formed under your eye, and have you had leisure to observe the whole progress of the phenomenon, from the first appearance of order to its final consummation? If you have, then cite your experience and deliver your theory.

PART III

How the most absurd argument, replied Cleanthes, in the hands of a man of ingenuity and invention, may acquire an air of probability! Are you not aware, Philo, that it became necessary for Copernicus and his first disciples to prove the similarity of the terrestrial and celestial matter because several philosophers, blinded by old systems and supported by some sensible appearances, had denied this similarity? But that it is by no means necessary that theists should prove the similarity of the works of *nature* to those of *art* because this similarity is self-evident and undeniable? The same matter, a like form;

what more is requisite to show an analogy between their causes, and to ascertain the origin of all things from a divine purpose and intention? Your objections, I must freely tell you, are no better than the abstruse cavils of those philosophers who denied motion, and ought to be refuted in the same manner—by illustrations, examples, and instances rather than by serious argument and philosophy.

Suppose, therefore, that an articulate voice were heard in the clouds, much louder and more melodious than any which human art could ever reach; suppose that this voice were extended in the same instant over all nations and spoke to each nation in its own language and dialect; suppose that the words delivered not only contain a just sense and meaning, but convey some instruction altogether worthy of a benevolent Being superior to mankind—could you possibly hesitate a moment concerning the cause of this voice, and must you not instantly ascribe it to some design or purpose? Yet I cannot see but all the same objections (if they merit that appellation) which lie against the system of theism may also be produced against this inference.

Might you not say that all conclusions concerning fact were founded on experience; that, when we hear an articulate voice in the dark and thence infer a man, it is only the resemblance of the effects which leads us to conclude that there is a like resemblance in the cause; but that this extraordinary voice, by its loudness, extent, and flexibility to all languages, bears so little analogy to any human voice that we have no reason to suppose any analogy in their causes; and, consequently, that a rational, wise, coherent speech proceeded, you know not whence, from some accidental whistling of the winds, not from any divine reason or intelligence? You see clearly your own objections in these cavils, and I hope too you see clearly that they cannot possibly have more force in the one case than in the other.

But to bring the case still nearer the present one of the universe, I shall make two suppositions which imply not any absurdity or impossibility. Suppose that there is a natural, universal, invariable language, common to every individual of human race, and that books are natural productions which perpetuate themselves in the same manner with animals and vegetables, by descent and propagation. Several expressions of our passions contain a universal language: all brute animals have a natural speech, which, however limited, is very intelligible to their own species. And as there are infinitely fewer parts and less contrivance in the finest composition of eloquence than in the coarsest organized body, the propagation of an *Iliad* or *Aeneid* is an easier supposition than that of any plant or animal.

Suppose, therefore, that you enter into your library thus peopled by natural volumes containing the most refined reason and most exquisite beauty; could you possibly open one of them and doubt that its original cause bore the strongest analogy to mind and intelligence? When it reasons and discourses; when it expostulates, argues, and enforces its views and topics; when it applies sometimes to the pure intellect, sometimes to the affections; when it collects, disposes, and adorns every consideration suited to the subject; could you persist in asserting that all this, at the bottom, had really no meaning, and that the first formation of this volume in the loins of its original parent proceeded not from thought and design? Your obstinacy, I know, reaches not that degree of firmness; even your sceptical play and wantonness would be abashed at so glaring an absurdity.

But if there be any difference, Philo, between this supposed case and the real one of the universe, it is all to the advantage of the latter. The anatomy of an animal affords many stronger instances of design than the perusal of Livy or Tacitus; and any objection which you start in the former case, by carrying me back to so unusual and extraordinary a scene as the first formation of worlds, the same objection has place on the supposition of our vegetating library. Choose, then, your party, Philo, without ambiguity or evasion; assert either that a rational volume is no proof of a rational cause or admit of a similar cause to all the works of nature.

Let me here observe, too, continued Cleanthes, that this religious argument, instead of being weakened by that scepticism so much affected by you, rather acquires force from it and becomes more firm and undisputed. To exclude all argument or reasoning of every kind is either affectation or madness. The declared profession of every reasonable sceptic is only to reject abstruse, remote, and refined arguments; to adhere to common sense and the plain instincts of nature; and to assent, wherever any reasons strike him with so full a force that he cannot, without the greatest violence, prevent it. Now the arguments for natural religion are plainly of this kind; and nothing but the most perverse, obstinate metaphysics can reject them. Consider, anatomize the eye, survey its structure and contrivance, and tell me, from your own feeling, if the idea of a contriver does not immediately flow in upon you with a force like that of sensation. The most obvious conclusion, surely, is in favour of design; and it requires time, reflection, and study, to summon up those frivolous though abstruse objections which can support infidelity. Who can behold the male and female of each species, the correspondence of their parts and instincts, their passions and whole course of life before and after generation, but must be sensible that the propagation of the species is intended by nature? Millions and millions of such instances present themselves through every part of the universe, and no language can convey a more intelligible irresistible meaning than the curious adjustment of final causes. To what degree, therefore, of blind dogmatism must one have attained to reject such natural and such convincing arguments?

Some beauties in writing we may meet with which seem contrary to rules, and which gain the affections and animate the imagination in opposition to all the precepts of criticism and to the authority of the established masters of art. And if the argument for theism be, as you pretend, contradictory to the principles of logic, its universal, its irresistible influence proves clearly that there may be arguments of a like irregular nature. Whatever cavils may be urged, an orderly world, as well as a coherent, articulate speech, will still be received as an incontestable proof of design and intention.

It sometimes happens, I own, that the religious arguments have not their due influence on an ignorant savage and barbarian, not because they are obscure and difficult, but because he never asks himself any question with regard to

them. Whence arises the curious structure of an animal? From the copulation of its parents. And these whence? From *their* parents? A few removes set the objects at such a distance that to him they are lost in darkness and confusion; nor is he actuated by any curiosity to trace them farther. But this is neither dogmatism nor scepticism, but stupidity: a state of mind very different from your sifting, inquisitive disposition, my ingenious friend. You can trace causes from effects; you can compare the most distant and remote objects; and your greatest errors proceed not from barrenness of thought and invention, but from too luxuriant a fertility which suppresses your natural good sense by a profusion of unnecessary scruples and objections.

Here I could observe, Hermippus, that Philo was a little embarrassed and confounded; but, while he hesitated in delivering an answer, luckily for him, Demea broke in upon the discourse and saved his countenance.

Your instance, Cleanthes, said he, drawn from books and language, being familiar, has, I confess, so much more force on that account; but is there not some danger, too, in this very circumstance, and may it not render us presumptuous, by making us imagine we comprehend the Deity and have some adequate idea of his nature and attributes? When I read a volume, I enter into the mind and intention of the author; I become him, in a manner, for the instant, and have an immediate feeling and conception of those ideas which revolved in his imagination while employed in that composition. But so near an approach we never surely can make to the Deity. His ways are not our ways, his attributes are perfect but incomprehensible. And this volume of nature contains a great and inexplicable riddle, more than any intelligible discourse or reasoning.

The ancient Platonists, you know, were the most religious and devout of all the pagan philosophers, yet many of them, particularly Plotinus, expressly declare that intellect or understanding is not to be ascribed to the Deity, and that our most perfect worship of him consists, not in acts of veneration, reverence, gratitude, or love, but in a certain mysterious self-annihilation or total extinction of all our faculties. These ideas are, perhaps, too far stretched, but still it must be acknowledged that, by representing the Deity as so intelligible and comprehensible, and so similar to a human mind, we are guilty of the grossest and most narrow partiality, and make ourselves the model of the whole universe.

All the *sentiments* of the human mind, gratitude, resentment, love, friendship, approbation, blame, pity, emulation, envy, have a plain reference to the state and situation of man, and are calculated for preserving the existence and promoting the activity of such a being in such circumstances. It seems, therefore, unreasonable to transfer such sentiments to a supreme existence or to suppose him actuated by them; and the phenomena, besides, of the universe will not support us in such a theory. All our *ideas* derived from the senses are confessedly false and illusive, and cannot therefore be supposed to have place in a supreme intelligence. And as the ideas of internal sentiment, added to those of the external senses, composed the whole furniture of human understanding, we may conclude that none of the *materials* of thought are in any respect similar in the human and in the divine intelligence. Now, as to the *manner* of thinking, how can we make any comparison between them or suppose them anywise resembling? Our thought is fluctuating, uncertain, fleeting, successive, and compounded; and were we to remove these circumstances, we absolutely annihilate its essence, and it would in such a case be an abuse of terms to apply to it the name of thought or reason. At least, if it appear more pious and respectful (as it really is) still to retain these terms when we mention the Supreme Being, we ought to acknowledge that their meaning, in that case, is totally incomprehensible, and that the infirmities of our nature do not permit us to reach any ideas which in the least correspond to the ineffable sublimity of the Divine attributes.

PART IV

It seems strange to me, said Cleanthes, that you, Demea, who are so sincere in the cause of religion, should still maintain the mysterious, incomprehensible nature of the Deity, and should insist so strenuously that he has no manner of likeness or resemblance to human creatures. The Deity, I can readily allow, possesses many powers and attributes of which we can have no comprehension; but, if our ideas, so far as they go, be not just and adequate and correspondent to his real nature, I know not what there is in this subject worth insisting on. Is the name, without any meaning, of such mighty importance? Or how do you mystics, who maintain the absolute incomprehensibility of the Deity, differ from sceptics or atheists, who assert that the first cause of all is unknown and unintelligible? Their temerity must be very great if, after rejecting the production by a mind—I mean a mind resembling the human (for I know of no other)—they pretend to assign, with certainty, any other specific intelligible cause; and their conscience must be very scrupulous, indeed, if they refuse to call the universal unknown cause a God or Deity, and to bestow on him as many sublime eulogies and unmeaning epithets as you shall please to require of them.

Who could imagine, replied Demea, that Cleanthes, the calm philosophical Cleanthes, would attempt to refute his antagonists by affixing a nickname to them, and, like the common bigots and inquisitors of the age, have recourse to invective and declamation instead of reasoning? Or does he not perceive that these topics are easily retorted, and that *anthropomorphite* is an appellation as invidious, and implies as dangerous consequences, as the epithet of *mystic* with which he has honoured us? In reality, Cleanthes, consider what it is you assert when you represent the Deity as similar to the human mind and understanding. What is the soul of man? A composition of various faculties, passions, sentiments, ideas—united, indeed, into one self or person, but still distinct from each other. When it reasons, the ideas which are the parts of its discourse arrange themselves in a certain form or order which is not preserved entire for a moment, immediately gives place to another arrangement. New opinions, new passions, new affections, new feelings arise which continually diversify the mental scene and produce in it the greatest variety and most rapid succession imaginable. How is this compatible with that perfect immutability and simplicity which all true theists ascribe to the Deity? By the same act, say they, he sees past, present, and future; his love and hatred, his mercy and justice, are one individual operation; he is entire in every point of space, and complete in every instant of duration. No succession, no change, no acquisition, no diminution. What he is implies not in it any shadow of distinction or diversity. And what he is this moment he ever has been and ever will be, without any new judgment, sentiment, or operation. He stands fixed in one simple, perfect state; nor can you ever say, with any propriety, that this act of his is different from that other, or that this judgment or idea has been lately formed and will give place, by succession, to any different judgment or idea.

I can readily allow, said Cleanthes, that those who maintain the perfect simplicity of the Supreme Being, to the extent in which you have explained it, are complete mystics, and chargeable with all the consequences which I have drawn from their opinion. They are, in a word, atheists, without knowing it. For though it be allowed that the Deity possesses attributes of which we have no comprehension, yet ought we never to ascribe to him any attributes which are absolutely incompatible with that intelligent nature essential to him. A mind whose acts and sentiments and ideas are not distinct and successive, one that is wholly simple and totally immutable, is a mind which has no thought, no reason, no will, no sentiment, no love, no hatred; or, in a word, is no mind at all. It is an abuse of terms to give it that appellation, and we may as well speak of limited extension without figure, or of number without composition.

Pray consider, said Philo, whom you are at present inveighing against. You are honouring with the appellation of *atheist* all the sound, orthodox divines, almost, who have treated of this subject; and you will at last be, yourself, found, according to your reckoning, the only sound theist in the world. But if idolaters be atheists, as, I think, may justly be asserted, and Christian theologians the same, what becomes of the argument, so much celebrated, derived from the universal consent of mankind?

But, because I know you are not much swayed by names and authorities, I shall endeavor to show you, a little more distinctly, the inconveniences of that anthropomorphism which you have embraced, and shall prove that there is no ground to suppose a plan of the world to be formed in the Divine mind, consisting of distinct ideas, differently arranged, in the same manner as an architect forms in his head the plan of a house which he intends to execute.

It is not easy, I own, to see what is gained by this supposition, whether we judge of the matter by *reason* or by *experience*. We are still obliged to mount higher in order to find the cause of this cause which you had assigned as satisfactory and conclusive.

If *reason* (I mean abstract reason derived from inquiries *a priori*) be not alike mute with regard to all questions concerning cause and effect, this sentence at least it will venture to pronounce: that a mental world or universe of ideas requires a cause as much as does a material world or universe of objects, and, if similar in its arrangement, must require a similar cause. For what is there in this subject which should occasion a different conclusion or inference? In an abstract view, they are entirely alike; and no difficulty attends the one supposition which is not common to both of them.

Again, when we will needs force *experience* to pronounce some sentence, even on these subjects which lie beyond her sphere, neither can she perceive any material difference in this particular between those two kinds of worlds, but finds them to be governed by similar principles, and to depend upon an equal variety of causes in their operations. We have specimens in miniature of both of them. Our own mind resembles the one; a vegetable or animal body the other. Let experience, therefore, judge from these samples. Nothing seems more delicate, with regard to its causes, than thought; and as these causes never operate in two persons after the same manner, so we never find two persons who think exactly alike. Nor indeed does the same person think exactly alike at any two different periods of time. A difference of age, of the disposition of his body, of weather, of food, of company, of books, of passions—any of these particulars, or others more minute, are sufficient to alter the curious machinery of thought and communicate to it very different movements and operations.

As far as we can judge, vegetables and animal bodies are not more delicate in their motions, nor depend upon a greater variety or more curious adjustment of springs and principles.

How, therefore, shall we satisfy ourselves concerning the cause of that Being whom you suppose the Author of nature, or, according to your system of anthropomorphism, the ideal world into which you trace the material? Have we not the same reason to trace that ideal world into another ideal world or new intelligent principle? But if we stop and go no farther, why go so far? Why not stop at the material world? How can we satisfy ourselves without going on *in infinitum*? And, after all, what satisfaction is there in that infinite progression? Let us remember the story of the Indian philosopher and his elephant. It was never more applicable than to the present subject. If the material world rests upon a similar ideal world, this ideal world must rest upon some other, and so on without end. It were better, therefore, never to look beyond the present material world. By supposing it to contain the principle of its order within itself, we really assert it to be God; and the sooner we arrive at that Divine Being, so much the better. When you go one step beyond the mundane system, you only excite an inquisitive humour which it is impossible ever to satisfy.

To say that the different ideas which compose the reason of the Supreme Being fall into order of themselves and by their own nature is really to talk without any precise meaning. If it has a meaning, I would fain know why it is not as good sense to say that the parts of the material world fall into order of themselves and by their own nature. Can the one opinion be intelligible, while the other is not so?

We have, indeed, experience of ideas which fall into order of themselves and without any *known* cause. But, I am sure, we have a much larger experience of matter which does the same, as in all instances of generation and vegetation where the accurate analysis of the cause exceeds all human comprehension. We have also experience of particular systems of thought and of matter which have no order; of the first in madness, of the second in corruption. Why, then, should we think that order is more essential

to one than the other? And if it requires a cause in both, what do we gain by your system, in tracing the universe of objects into a similar universe of ideas? The first step which we make leads us on for ever. It were, therefore, wise in us to limit all our inquiries to the present world, without looking farther. No satisfaction can ever be attained by these speculations which so far exceed the narrow bounds of human understanding.

It was usual with the Peripatetics, you know, Cleanthes, when the cause of any phenomenon was demanded, to have recourse to their *faculties* or *occult qualities,* and to say, for instance, that bread nourished by its nutritive faculty, and senna purged by its purgative. But it has been discovered that this subterfuge was nothing but the disguise of ignorance, and that these philosophers, though less ingenuous, really said the same thing with the sceptics or the vulgar who fairly confessed that they knew not the cause of these phenomena. In like manner, when it is asked, what cause produced order in the ideas of the Supreme Being, can any other reason be assigned by you, anthropomorphites, than that it is a *rational* faculty, and that such is the nature of the Deity? But why a similar answer will not be equally satisfactory in accounting for the order of the world, without having recourse to any such intelligent creator as you insist on, may be difficult to determine. It is only to say that *such* is the nature of material objects, and that they are all originally possessed of a *faculty* of order and proportion. These are only more learned and elaborate ways of confessing our ignorance; nor has the one hypothesis any real advantage above the other, except in its greater conformity to vulgar prejudices.

You have displayed this argument with great emphasis, replied Cleanthes: You seem not sensible how easy it is to answer it. Even in common life, if I assign a cause for any event, is it any objection, Philo, that I cannot assign the cause of that cause, and answer every new question which may incessantly be started? And what philosophers could possibly submit to so rigid a rule?—philosophers who confess ultimate causes to be totally unknown, and are sensible that the most refined principles into which they trace the phenomena are still to them as inexplicable as these phenomena themselves are to the vulgar. The order and arrangement of nature, the curious adjustment of final causes, the plain use and intention of every part and organ—all these bespeak in the clearest language an intelligent cause or author. The heavens and the earth join in the same testimony: The whole chorus of nature raises one hymn to the praises of its Creator. You alone, or almost alone, disturb this general harmony. You start abstruse doubts, cavils, and objections; you ask me what is the cause of this cause? I know not; I care not; that concerns not me. I have found a Deity; and here I stop my inquiry. Let those go farther who are wiser or more enterprising.

I pretend to be neither, replied Philo; and for that very reason I should never, perhaps, have attempted to go so far, especially when I am sensible that I must at last be contented to sit down with the same answer which, without further trouble, might have satisfied me from the beginning. If I am still to remain in utter ignorance of causes and can absolutely give an explication of nothing, I shall never esteem it any advantage to shove off for a moment a difficulty which you acknowledge must immediately, in its full force, recur upon me. Naturalists indeed very justly explain particular effects by more general causes, though these general causes themselves should remain in the end totally inexplicable, but they never surely thought it satisfactory to explain a particular effect by a particular cause which was no more to be accounted for than the effect itself. An ideal system, arranged of itself, without a precedent design, is not a whit more explicable than a material one which attains its order in a like manner; nor is there any more difficulty in the latter supposition than in the former.

PART V

But to show you still more inconveniences, continued Philo, in your anthropomorphism, please to take a new survey of your principles. *Like effects prove like causes.* This is the experimental argument; and this, you say too, is the sole theological argument. Now it is certain that the liker the effects are which are seen and the liker the causes

which are inferred, the stronger is the argument. Every departure on either side diminishes the probability and renders the experiment less conclusive. You cannot doubt of the principle; neither ought you to reject its consequences.

All the new discoveries in astronomy which prove the immense grandeur and magnificence of the works of nature are so many additional arguments for a Deity, according to the true system of theism; but, according to your hypothesis of experimental theism, they become so many objections, by removing the effect still farther from all resemblance to the effects of human art and contrivance. For if Lucretius, even following the old system of the world, could exclaim:

> Quis regere immensi summam, quis habere profundi
> Indu manu validas potis est moderanter habenas?
> Quis pariter coelos omnes convertere? et omnes
> Ignibus aetheriis terras suffire feraces?
> Omnibus inque locis esse omni tempore praesto?[2]
> [The English translation is in the end note.]

If Tully [Cicero] esteemed this reasoning so natural as to put it into the mouth of his Epicurean:

> Quibus enim oculis animi intueri potuit vester Plato fabricam illam tanti operis, qua construi a Deo atque aedificari mundum facit? quae molitio? quae ferramenta? qui vectes? quae machinae? qui ministri tanti muneris fuerunt? quemadmodum autem obedire et parere voluntati architecti aer, ignis, aqua, terra potuerunt?[3]
> [The English translation is in the end note.]

If this argument, I say, had any force in former ages, how much greater must it have at present when the bounds of Nature are so infinitely enlarged and such a magnificent scene is opened to us? It is still more unreasonable to form our idea of so unlimited a cause from our experience of the narrow productions of human design and invention.

The discoveries by microscopes, as they open a new universe in miniature, are still objections, according to you, arguments, according to me. The further we push our researches of this kind, we are still led to infer the universal cause of all to be vastly different from mankind, or from any object of human experience and observation.

And what say you to the discoveries in anatomy, chemistry, botany? . . . These surely are no objections, replied Cleanthes; they only discover new instances of art and contrivance, it is still the image of mind reflected on us from innumerable objects. Add a mind *like the human,* said Philo. I know of no other, replied Cleanthes. And the liker, the better, insisted Philo. To be sure, said Cleanthes.

Now, Cleanthes, said Philo, with an air of alacrity and triumph, mark the consequences. *First,* by this method of reasoning you renounce all claim to infinity in any of the attributes of the Deity. For, as the cause ought only to be proportioned to the effect, and the effect, so far as it falls under our cognizance, is not infinite, what pretensions have we, upon your suppositions, to ascribe that attribute to the Divine Being? You will still insist that, by removing him so much from all similarity to human creatures, we give in to the most arbitrary hypothesis, and at the same time weaken all proofs of his existence.

Secondly, you have no reason, on your theory, for ascribing perfection to the Deity, even in his finite capacity, or for supposing him free from every error, mistake, or incoherence, in his undertakings. There are many inexplicable difficulties in the works of nature which, if we allow a perfect author to be proved *a priori,* are easily solved, and become only seeming difficulties from the narrow capacity of man, who cannot trace infinite relations. But according to your method of reasoning, these difficulties become all real, and, perhaps, will be insisted on as new instances of likeness to human art and contrivance. At least, you must acknowledge that it is impossible for us to tell, from our limited views, whether this system contains any great faults or deserves any considerable praise if compared to other possible and even real systems. Could a peasant, if the *Aeneid* were read to him, pronounce that poem to be absolutely faultless, or even assign to it its proper rank among the productions of human wit, he who had never seen any other production?

But were this world ever so perfect a production, it must still remain uncertain whether all the excellences of the work can justly be ascribed to the workman. If we survey a ship, what an exalted idea must we form of the ingenuity of the carpenter who framed so complicated, useful, and beautiful a machine? And what surprise must we feel when we find him a stupid mechanic who imitated others, and copied an art which, through a long succession of ages, after multiplied trials, mistakes, corrections, deliberations, and controversies, had been gradually improving? Many worlds might have been botched and bungled, throughout an eternity, ere this system was struck out; much labour lost, many fruitless trials made, and a slow but continued improvement carried on during infinite ages in the art of world-making. In such subjects, who can determine where the truth, nay, who can conjecture where the probability lies, amidst a great number of hypotheses which may be proposed, and a still greater which may be imagined?

And what shadow of an argument, continued Philo, can you produce from your hypothesis to prove the unity of the Deity? A great number of men join in building a house or ship, in rearing a city, in framing a commonwealth; why may not several deities combine in contriving and framing a world? This is only so much greater similarity to human affairs. By sharing the work among several, we may so much further limit the attributes of each, and get rid of that extensive power and knowledge which must be supposed in one deity, and which, according to you, can only serve to weaken the proof of his existence. And if such foolish, such vicious creatures as man can yet often unite in framing and executing one plan, how much more those deities or demons, whom we may suppose several degrees more perfect!

To multiply causes without necessity is indeed contrary to true philosophy, but this principle applies not to the present case. Were one deity antecedently proved by your theory who were possessed of every attribute requisite to the production of the universe, it would be needless, I own (though not absurd) to suppose any other deity existent. But while it is still a question whether all these attributes are united in one subject or dispersed among several independent beings, by what phenomena in nature can we pretend to decide the controversy? Where we see a body raised in a scale, we are sure that there is in the opposite scale, however concealed from sight, some counterpoising weight equal to it; but it is still allowed to doubt whether that weight be an aggregate of several distinct bodies or one uniform united mass. And if the weight requisite very much exceeds anything which we have ever seen conjoined in any single body, the former supposition becomes still more probable and natural. An intelligent being of such vast power and capacity as is necessary to produce the universe, or, to speak in the language of ancient philosophy, so prodigious an animal exceeds all analogy and even comprehension.

But further, Cleanthes: Men are mortal, and renew their species by generation; and this is common to all living creatures. The two great sexes of male and female, says Milton, animate the world. Why must this circumstance, so universal, so essential, be excluded from those numerous and limited deities? Behold, then, the theogeny of ancient times brought back upon us.

And why not become a perfect anthropomorphite? Why not assert the deity or deities to be corporeal, and to have eyes, a nose, mouth, ears, etc.? Epicurus maintained that no man had ever seen reason but in a human figure; therefore, the gods must have a human figure. And this argument, which is deservedly so much ridiculed by Cicero, becomes, according to you, solid and philosophical.

In a word, Cleanthes, a man who follows your hypothesis is able, perhaps, to assert or conjecture that the universe sometime arose from something like design; but beyond that position he cannot ascertain one single circumstance, and is left afterwards to fix every point of his theology by the utmost license of fancy and hypothesis. This world, for aught he knows, is very faulty and imperfect, compared to a superior standard, and was only the first rude essay of some infant deity who afterwards abandoned it, ashamed of his lame performance; it is the work only of some dependent, inferior deity, and is the object of derision to his superiors; it is the production of old age and dotage in some superannuated deity, and ever since his death has run on at adventures, from the first impulse and active force which it received from him. You justly give signs of horror, Demea, at these strange suppositions; but these, and a thousand more of the same kind,

are Cleanthes' suppositions, not mine. From the moment the attributes of the Deity are supposed finite, all these have place. And I cannot, for my part, think that so wild and unsettled a system of theology is, in any respect, preferable to none at all.

These suppositions I absolutely disown, cried Cleanthes: they strike me, however, with no horror, especially when proposed in that rambling way in which they drop from you. On the contrary, they give me pleasure when I see that, by the utmost indulgence of your imagination, you never get rid of the hypothesis of design in the universe, but are obliged at every turn to have recourse to it. To this concession I adhere steadily; and this I regard as a sufficient foundation for religion.

PART VI

It must be a slight fabric, indeed, said Demea, which can be erected on so tottering a foundation. While we are uncertain whether there is one deity or many, whether the deity or deities, to whom we owe our existence, be perfect or imperfect, subordinate or supreme, dead or alive, what trust or confidence can we repose in them? What devotion or worship address to them? What veneration or obedience pay them? To all the purposes of life the theory of religion becomes altogether useless; and even with regard to speculative consequences its uncertainty, according to you, must render it totally precarious and unsatisfactory.

To render it still more unsatisfactory, said Philo, there occurs to me another hypothesis which must acquire an air of probability from the method of reasoning so much insisted on by Cleanthes. That like effects arise from like causes—this principle he supposes the foundation of all religion. But there is another principle of the same kind, no less certain and derived from the same source of experience, that, where several known circumstances are observed to be similar, the unknown will also be found similar. Thus, if we see the limbs of a human body, we conclude that it is also attended with a human head, though hid from us. Thus, if we see, through a chink in a wall, a small part of the sun, we conclude that were the wall removed we should see the whole body. In short, this method of reasoning is so obvious and familiar that no scruple can ever be made with regard to its solidity.

Now, if we survey the universe, so far as it falls under our knowledge, it bears a great resemblance to an animal or organized body, and seems actuated with a like principle of life and motion. A continual circulation of matter in it produces no disorder; a continual waste in every part is incessantly repaired; the closest sympathy is perceived throughout the entire system; and each part or member, in performing its proper offices, operates both to its own preservation and to that of the whole. The world, therefore, I infer, is an animal; and the Deity is the *soul* of the world, actuating it, and actuated by it.

You have too much learning, Cleanthes, to be at all surprised at this opinion which, you know, was maintained by almost all the theists of antiquity, and chiefly prevails in their discourses and reasonings. For though, sometimes, the ancient philosophers reason from final causes, as if they thought the world the workmanship of God, yet it appears rather their favourite notion to consider it as his body whose organization renders it subservient to him. And it must be confessed that, as the universe resembles more a human body than it does the works of human art and contrivance, if our limited analogy could ever, with any propriety, be extended to the whole of nature, the inference seems juster in favour of the ancient than the modern theory.

There are many other advantages, too, in the former theory which recommended it to the ancient theologians. Nothing more repugnant to all their notions because nothing more repugnant to common experience than mind without body, a mere spiritual substance which fell not under their senses nor comprehension, and of which they had not observed one single instance throughout all nature. Mind and body they knew because they felt both; an order, arrangement, organization, or internal machinery, in both they likewise knew, after the same manner; and it could not but seem reasonable to transfer this experience to the universe, and to suppose the divine mind and body to be also coeval and to have, both of them, order and arrangement naturally inherent in them and inseparable from them.

Here, therefore, is a new species of *anthropomorphism*, Cleanthes, on which you may deliberate, and a theory which seems not liable to any considerable difficulties. You are too much superior, surely, to *systematical prejudices* to find any more difficulty in supposing an animal body to be, originally, of itself or from unknown causes, possessed of order and organization, than in supposing a similar order to belong to mind. But the *vulgar prejudice* that body and mind ought always to accompany each other ought not, one should think, to be entirely neglected; since it is founded on *vulgar experience*, the only guide which you profess to follow in all these theological inquiries. And if you assert that our limited experience is an unequal standard by which to judge of the unlimited extent of nature, you entirely abandon your own hypothesis, and must thenceforward adopt our mysticism, as you call it, and admit of the absolute incomprehensibility of the Divine Nature.

This theory, I own, replied Cleanthes, has never before occurred to me, though a pretty natural one; and I cannot readily, upon so short an examination and reflection, deliver any opinion with regard to it. You are very scrupulous, indeed, said Philo. Were I to examine any system of yours, I should not have acted with half that caution and reserve in stating objections and difficulties to it. However, if anything occur to you, you will oblige us by proposing it.

Why then, replied Cleanthes, it seems to me that, though the world does, in many circumstances, resemble an animal body, yet is the analogy also defective in many circumstances the most material: no organs of sense; no seat of thought or reason; no one precise origin of motion and action. In short, it seems to bear a stronger resemblance to a vegetable than to an animal, and your inference would be so far inconclusive in favour of the soul of the world.

But, in the next place, your theory seems to imply the eternity of the world; and that is a principle which, I think, can be refuted by the strongest reasons and probabilities. I shall suggest an argument to this purpose which, I believe, has not been insisted on by any writer. Those who reason from the late origin of arts and sciences, though their inference wants not force, may perhaps be refuted by considerations derived from the nature of human society, which is in continual revolution between ignorance and knowledge, liberty and slavery, riches and poverty; so that it is impossible for us, from our limited experience, to foretell with assurance what events may or may not be expected. Ancient learning and history seem to have been in great danger of entirely perishing after the inundation of the barbarous nations; and had these convulsions continued a little longer or been a little more violent, we should not probably have now known what passed in the world a few centuries before us. Nay, were it not for the superstition of the popes, who preserved a little jargon of Latin in order to support the appearance of an ancient and universal church, that tongue must have been utterly lost; in which case the Western world, being totally barbarous, would not have been in a fit disposition for receiving the Greek language and learning, which was conveyed to them after the sacking of Constantinople. When learning and books had been extinguished, even the mechanical arts would have fallen considerably to decay; and it is easily imagined that fable or tradition might ascribe to them a much later origin than the true one. This vulgar argument, therefore, against the eternity of the world seems a little precarious.

But here appears to be the foundation of a better argument. Lucullus was the first that brought cherry-trees from Asia to Europe, though that tree thrives so well in many European climates that it grows in the woods without any culture. Is it possible that, throughout a whole eternity, no European had ever passed into Asia and thought of transplanting so delicious a fruit into his own country? Or if the tree was once transplanted and propagated, how could it ever afterwards perish? Empires may rise and fall, liberty and slavery succeed alternately, ignorance and knowledge give place to each other; but the cherry-tree will still remain in the woods of Greece, Spain, and Italy, and will never be affected by the revolutions of human society.

It is not two thousand years since vines were transplanted into France, though there is no climate in the world more favourable to them. It is not three centuries since horses, cows, sheep, swine, dogs, corn, were known in America. Is it possible that during the revolutions of a whole eternity there never arose a Columbus who might open the communication between Europe and that continent? We may as well imagine that all men would wear stockings for ten thousand years, and never have the sense to think of garters to tie them. All these seem convincing proofs of the youth or rather infancy of the world, as being founded on the operation of principles more constant and steady than those by which human society is governed and directed. Nothing less than a total convulsion of the elements will ever destroy all the European animals and vegetables which are now to be found in the Western world.

And what argument have you against such convulsions? replied Philo. Strong and almost incontestable proofs may be traced over the whole earth that every part of this globe has continued for many ages entirely covered with water. And though order were supposed inseparable from matter, and inherent in it, yet may matter be susceptible of many and great revolutions, through the endless periods of eternal duration. The incessant changes to which every part of it is subject seem to intimate some such general transformations; though, at the same time, it is observable that all the changes and corruptions of which we have ever had experience are but passages from one state of order to another; nor can matter ever rest in total deformity and confusion. What we see in the parts, we may infer in the whole; at least, that is the method of reasoning on which you rest your whole theory. And were I obliged to defend any particular system of this nature, which I never willingly should do, I esteem none more plausible than that which ascribes an eternal inherent principle of order to the world, though attended with great and continual revolutions and alterations. This at once solves all difficulties; and if the solution, by being so general, is not entirely complete and satisfactory, it is at least a theory that we must sooner or later have recourse to, whatever system we embrace. How could things have been as they are, were there not an original inherent principle of order somewhere, in thought or in matter? And it is very indifferent to which of these we give the preference. Chance has no place, on any hypothesis, sceptical or religious. Everything is surely governed by steady, inviolable laws. And were the inmost essence of things laid open to us, we should then discover a scene of which, at present, we can have no idea. Instead of admiring the order of natural beings, we should clearly see that it was absolutely impossible for them, in the smallest article, ever to admit of any other disposition.

Were anyone inclined to revive the ancient pagan theology which maintained, as we learned from Hesiod, that this globe was governed by 30,000 deities, who arose from the unknown powers of nature, you would naturally object, Cleanthes, that nothing is gained by this hypothesis; and that it is as easy to suppose all men animals, beings more numerous but less perfect, to have sprung immediately from a like origin. Push the same inference a step further, and you will find a numerous society of deities as explicable as one universal deity who possesses within himself the powers and perfections of the whole society. All these systems, then, of Scepticism, Polytheism, and Theism, you must allow, on your principles, to be on a like footing, and that no one of them has any advantage over the others. You may thence learn the fallacy of your principles.

PART VII

But here, continued Philo, in examining the ancient system on the soul of the world there strikes me, all of a sudden, a new idea which, if just, must go near to subvert all your reasoning, and destroy even your first inferences on which you repose such confidence. If the universe bears a greater likeness to animal bodies and to vegetables than to the works of human art, it is more probable that its cause resembles the cause of the former than that of the latter, and its origin ought rather to be ascribed to generation or vegetation than to reason or design. Your conclusion, even according to your own principles, is therefore lame and defective.

Pray open up this argument a little further, said Demea, for I do not rightly apprehend it in that concise manner in which you have expressed it.

Our friend Cleanthes, replied Philo, as you have heard, asserts that, since no question of fact can be proved otherwise than by experience, the existence of a Deity admits not of proof from any other medium. The world, says he, resembles the works of human contrivance; therefore its cause must also resemble that of the other. Here we may remark that the operation of one very small part of nature, to wit, man, upon another very small part, to wit, that inanimate matter lying within his reach, is the rule by which Cleanthes judges of the origin of the whole; and he measures objects, so widely disproportioned, by the same individual standard. But to waive all objections drawn from this topic, I affirm that there are other parts of the universe (besides the machines of human invention) which bear still a greater resemblance to the fabric of the world, and which, therefore, afford a better conjecture concerning the universal origin of this system. These parts are animals and vegetables. The world plainly resembles more an animal or a vegetable than it does a watch or a knitting-loom. Its cause, therefore, it is more probable, resembles the cause of the former. The cause of the former is generation or vegetation. The cause, therefore, of the world we may infer to be something similar or analogous to generation or vegetation.

But how is it conceivable, said Demea, that the world can arise from anything similar to vegetation or generation?

Very easily, replied Philo. In like manner as a tree sheds its seed into the neighboring fields and produces other trees, so the great vegetable, the world, or this planetary system, produces within itself certain seeds which, being scattered into the surrounding chaos, vegetate into new worlds. A comet, for instance, is the seed of a world; and after it has been fully ripened, by passing from sun to sun, and star to star, it is, at last, tossed into the unformed elements which everywhere surround this universe, and immediately sprouts up into a new system.

Or if, for the sake of variety (for I see no other advantage), we should suppose this world to be an animal: a comet is the egg of this animal;

and in like manner as an ostrich lays its egg in the sand, which, without any further care, hatches the egg and produces a new animal, so...I understand you, says Demea. But what wild, arbitrary suppositions are these! What *data* have you for such extraordinary conclusions? And is the slight, imaginary resemblance of the world to a vegetable or an animal sufficient to establish the same inference with regard to both? Objects which are in general so widely different, ought they to be a standard for each other?

Right, cries Philo: This is the topic on which I have all along insisted. I have still asserted that we have no *data* to establish any system of cosmogony. Our experience, so imperfect in itself and so limited both in extent and duration, can afford us no probable conjecture concerning the whole of things. But if we must needs fix on some hypothesis, by what rule, pray, ought we to determine our choice? Is there any other rule than the greater similarity of the objects compared? And does not a plant or an animal, which springs from vegetation or generation, bear a stronger resemblance to the world than does any artificial machine, which arises from reason and design?

But what is this vegetation and generation of which you talk? said Demea. Can you explain their operations, and anatomize that fine internal structure on which they depend?

As much, at least, replied Philo, as Cleanthes can explain the operations of reason, or anatomize that internal structure on which it depends. But without any such elaborate disquisitions, when I see an animal, I infer that it sprang from generation; and that with as great certainty as you conclude a house to have been reared by design. These words *generation, reason* mark only certain powers and energies in nature whose effects are known, but whose essence is incomprehensible; and one of these principles, more than the other, has no privilege for being made a standard to the whole of nature.

In reality, Demea, it may reasonably be expected that the larger the views are which we take of things, the better will they conduct us in our conclusions concerning such extraordinary and such magnificent subjects. In this little corner of the world alone, there are four principles, *reason, instinct, generation, vegetation,* which are similar to each other, and are the causes of similar effects. What a number of other principles may we naturally suppose in the immense extent and variety of the universe could we travel from planet to planet, and from system to system, in order to examine each part of this mighty fabric? Any one of these four principles above mentioned (and a hundred others which lie open to our conjecture) may afford us a theory by which to judge of the origin of the world; and it is a palpable and egregious partiality to confine our view entirely to that principle by which our own minds operate. Were this principle more intelligible on that account, such a partiality might be somewhat excusable; but reason, in its internal fabric and structure, is really as little known to us as instinct or vegetation; and, perhaps, even that vague, undeterminate word *nature,* to which the vulgar refer everything is not at the bottom more inexplicable. The effects of these principles are all known to us from experience; but the principles themselves and their manner of operation are totally unknown; nor is it less intelligible or less comfortable to experience to say that the world arose by vegetation, from a seed shed by another world, than to say that it arose from a divine reason or contrivance, according to the sense in which Cleanthes understands it.

But methinks, said Demea, if the world had a vegetative quality and could sow the seeds of new worlds into the infinite chaos, this power would be still an additional argument for design in its author. For whence could arise so wonderful a faculty but from design? Or how can order spring from anything which perceives not that order which it bestows?

You need only look around you, replied Philo, to satisfy yourself with regard to this question. A tree bestows order and organization on that tree which springs from it, without knowing the order; an animal in the same manner on its offspring; a bird on its nest; and instances of this kind are even more frequent in the world than those of order which arise from reason and contrivance. To say that all this order in animals and vegetables proceeds ultimately from design is begging the question; nor can that great point be ascertained otherwise than by proving, *a priori,* both that order is, from its nature, inseparably attached to thought and that it can never of itself or from original unknown principles belong to matter.

But further, Demea, this objection which you urge can never be made use of by Cleanthes, without renouncing a defense which he has already made against one of my objections. When I inquired concerning the cause of that supreme reason and intelligence into which he resolves everything, he told me that the impossibility of satisfying such inquiries could never be admitted as an objection in any species of philosophy. *We must stop somewhere, says he; nor is it ever within the reach of human capacity to explain ultimate causes or show the last connections of any objects. It is sufficient if any steps, as far as we go, are supported by experience and observation.* Now that vegetation and generation, as well as reason, are experienced to be principles of order in nature is undeniable. If I rest my system of cosmogony on the former, preferably to the latter, it is at my choice. The matter seems entirely arbitrary. And when Cleanthes asks me what is the cause of my great vegetative or generative faculty, I am equally entitled to ask him the cause of his great reasoning principle. These questions we have agreed to forbear on both sides; and it is chiefly his interest on the present occasion to stick to this agreement. Judging by our limited and imperfect experience, generation has some privileges above reason; for we see every day the latter arise from the former, never the former from the latter.

Compare, I beseech you, the consequences on both sides. The world, say I, resembles an animal; therefore it is an animal, therefore it arose from generation. The steps, I confess, are wide, yet there is some small appearance of analogy in each step. The world, says Cleanthes, resembles a machine; therefore it is a machine, therefore it arose from design. The steps are here equally wide, and the analogy less striking. And if he pretends to carry on *my* hypothesis a step further, and to infer design or reason from the great principle of generation on which I insist, I may, with better authority, use the same freedom to push further *his* hypothesis, and infer a divine generation or theogony from his principle of reason. I have at least some faint shadow of experience, which is the utmost that can ever be attained in the present

subject. Reason, in innumerable instances, is observed to arise from the principle of generation, and never to arise from any other principle.

Hesiod and all the ancient mythologists were so struck with this analogy that they universally explained the origin of nature from an animal birth, and copulation. Plato, too, so far as he is intelligible, seems to have adopted some such notion in his *Timaeus*.

The Brahmins assert that the world arose from an infinite spider, who spun this whole complicated mass from his bowels, and annihilates afterwards the whole or any part of it, by absorbing it again and resolving it into his own essence. Here is a species of cosmogony which appears to us ridiculous because a spider is a little contemptible animal whose operations we are never likely to take for a model of the whole universe. But still here is a new species of analogy, even in our globe. And were there a planet wholly inhabited by spiders (which is very possible), this inference would there appear as natural and irrefragable as that which in our planet ascribes the origin of all things to design and intelligence, as explained by Cleanthes. Why an orderly system may not be spun from the belly as well as from the brain, it will be difficult for him to give a satisfactory reason.

I must confess, Philo, replied Cleanthes, that, of all men living, the task which you have undertaken, of raising doubts and objections, suits you best and seems, in a manner, natural and unavoidable to you. So great is your fertility of invention than I am not ashamed to acknowledge myself unable, on a sudden, to solve regularly such out-of-the-way difficulties as you incessantly start upon me, though I clearly see, in general, their fallacy and error. And I question not, but you are yourself, at present, in the same case, and have not the solution so ready as the objection, while you must be sensible that common sense and reason are entirely against you, and that such whimsies as you have delivered may puzzle but never can convince us.

PART VIII

What you ascribe to the fertility of my invention, replied Philo, is entirely owing to the nature of the subject. In subjects adapted to the narrow compass of human reason there is commonly but one determination which carries probability or conviction with it; and to a man of sound judgment all other suppositions but that one appear entirely absurd and chimerical. But in such questions as the present, a hundred contradictory views may preserve a kind of imperfect analogy, and invention has here full scope to exert itself. Without any great effort of thought, I believe that I could, in an instant, propose other systems of cosmogony which would have some faint appearance of truth, though it is a thousand, a million to one if either yours or any one of mine be the true system.

For instance, what if I should revive the old Epicurean hypothesis? This is commonly, and I believe justly, esteemed the most absurd system that has yet been proposed; yet I know not whether, with a few alterations, it might not be brought to bear a faint appearance of probability. Instead of supposing matter infinite, as Epicurus did, let us suppose it finite. A finite number of particles is only susceptible of finite transpositions; and it must happen, in an eternal duration, that every possible order or position must be tried an infinite number of times. This world, therefore, with all its events, even the most minute, has before been produced and destroyed, and will again be produced and destroyed, without any bounds and limitations. No one who has a conception of the powers of infinite, in comparison of finite, will ever scruple this determination.

But this supposes, said Demea, that matter can acquire motion without any voluntary agent or first mover.

And where is the difficulty, replied Philo, of that supposition? Every event, before experience, is equally difficult and incomprehensible; and every event, after experience, is equally easy and intelligible. Motion, in many instances, from gravity, from elasticity, from electricity, begins in matter, without any known voluntary agent; and to suppose always, in these cases, an unknown voluntary agent is mere hypothesis and hypothesis attended with no advantages. The beginning of motion in matter itself is as conceivable *a priori* as its communication from mind and intelligence.

Besides, why may not motion have been propagated by impulse through all eternity, and the same stock of it, or nearly the same, be still upheld in the universe? As much is lost by the composition of motion, as much is gained by its resolution. And whatever the causes are, the fact is certain that matter is and always has been in continual agitation, as far as human experience or tradition reaches. There is not probably, at present, in the whole universe, one particle of matter at absolute rest.

And this very consideration, too, continued Philo, which we have stumbled on in the course of the argument, suggests a new hypothesis of cosmogony that is not absolutely absurd and improbable. Is there a system, an order, an economy of things, by which matter can preserve that perpetual agitation which seems essential to it, and yet maintain a constancy in the forms which it produces? There certainly is such an economy, for this is actually the case with the present world. The continual motion of matter, therefore, in less than infinite transpositions, must produce this economy or order, and by its very nature, that order, when once established, supports itself for many ages if not to eternity. But wherever matter is so poised, arranged, and adjusted, as to continue in perpetual motion, and yet preserve a constancy in the forms, its situation must, of necessity, have all the same appearance of art and contrivance which we observe at present. All the parts of each form must have a relation to each other and to the whole; and the whole itself must have a relation to the other parts of the universe, to the element in which the form subsists, to the materials with which it repairs its waste and decay, and to every other form which is hostile or friendly. A defect in any of these particulars destroys the form, and the matter of which it is composed is again set loose, and is thrown into irregular motions and fermentations till it unite itself to some other regular form. If no such form be prepared to receive it, and if there be a great quantity of this corrupted matter in the universe, the universe itself is entirely disordered, whether it be the feeble embryo of a world in its first beginnings that is thus destroyed or the rotten carcase of one languishing in old age and infirmity. In either case, a chaos ensues till finite though innumerable revolutions produce, at last, some forms whose parts and organs are so adjusted as to support the forms amidst a continued succession of matter.

Suppose (for we shall endeavour to vary the expression) that matter were thrown into any position by a blind, unguided force; it is evident that this first position must, in all probability, be the most confused and most disorderly imaginable, without any resemblance to those works of human contrivance which, along with a symmetry of parts, discover an adjustment of means to ends and a tendency to self-preservation. If the actuating force cease after this operation, matter must remain for ever in disorder and continue an immense chaos, without any proportion or activity. But suppose that the actuating force, whatever it be, still continues in matter, this first position will immediately give place to a second which will likewise, in all probability, be as disorderly as the first, and so on through many successions of changes and revolutions. No particular order or position ever continues a moment unaltered. The original force, still remaining in activity, gives a perpetual restlessness to matter. Every possible situation is produced and instantly destroyed. If a glimpse or dawn of order appears for a moment, it is instantly hurried away and confounded by that never-ceasing force which actuates every part of matter.

Thus the universe goes on for many ages in a continued succession of chaos and disorder. But is it not possible that it may settle at last, so as not to lose its motion and active force (for that we have supposed inherent in it), yet so as to preserve an uniformity of appearance, amidst the continual motion and fluctuation of its parts? This we find to be the case with the universe at present. Every individual is perpetually changing, and every part of every individual; and yet the whole remains, in appearance, the same. May we not hope for such a position or rather be assured of it from the eternal revolutions of unguided matter; and may not this account for all the appearing wisdom and contrivance which is in the universe? Let us contemplate the subject a little, and we shall find that this adjustment if attained by matter of a seeming stability in the forms, with a real and perpetual revolution or motion of parts, affords a plausible, if not a true, solution of the difficulty.

It is in vain, therefore, to insist upon the uses of the parts in animals or vegetables, and their curious adjustment to each other. I would fain know how an animal could subsist unless its parts were so adjusted? Do we not find that it immediately perishes whenever this adjustment ceases, and that its matter, corrupting, tries some new form? It happens indeed that the parts of the world are so well adjusted that some regular form immediately lays claim to this corrupted matter; and if it were not so, could the world subsist? Must it not dissolve, as well as the animal, and pass through new positions and situations till in great but finite succession it fall, at last, into the present or some such order?

It is well, replied Cleanthes, you told us that this hypothesis was suggested on a sudden, in the course of the argument. Had you had leisure to examine it, you would soon have perceived the insuperable objections to which it is exposed. No form, you say, can subsist unless it possess those powers and organs requisite for its subsistence; some new order or economy must be tried, and so on, without intermission, till at last some order which can support and maintain itself is fallen upon. But according to this hypothesis, whence arise the many conveniences and advantages which men and all animals possess? Two eyes, two ears are not absolutely necessary for the subsistence of the species. The human race might have been propagated and preserved without horses, dogs, cows, sheep, and those innumerable fruits and products which serve to our satisfaction and enjoyment. If no camels had been created for the use of man in the sandy deserts of Africa and Arabia, would the world have been dissolved? If no loadstone had been framed to give that wonderful and useful direction to the needle, would human society and the human kind have been immediately extinguished? Though the maxims of nature be in general very frugal, yet instances of this kind are far from being rare; and any one of them is a sufficient proof of design—and of a benevolent design—which gave rise to the order and arrangement of the universe.

At least, you may safely infer, said Philo, that the foregoing hypothesis is so far incomplete and imperfect, which I shall not scruple to allow. But can we ever reasonably expect greater success in any attempts of this nature? Or can we ever hope to erect a system of cosmogony that will be liable to no exceptions, and will contain no circumstance repugnant to our limited and imperfect experience of the analogy of nature? Your theory itself cannot surely pretend to any such advantage, even though you have run into *anthropomorphism,* the better to preserve a conformity to common experience. Let us once more put it to trial. In all instances which we have ever seen, ideas are copied from real objects, and are ectypal, not archetypal, to express myself in learned terms. You reverse this order and give thought the precedence. In all instances which we have ever seen, thought has no influence upon matter except where that matter is so conjoined with it as to have an equal reciprocal influence upon it. No animal can move immediately anything but the members of its own body; and, indeed, the equality of action and reaction seems to be an universal law of nature; but your theory implies a contradiction to this experience. These instances, with many more which it were easy to collect (particularly the supposition of a mind or system of thought that is eternal or, in other words, an animal ingenerable and immortal)—these instances, I say, may teach all of us sobriety in condemning each other, and let us see that as no system of this kind ought ever to be received from a slight analogy, so neither ought any to be rejected on account of a small incongruity. For that is an inconvenience from which we can justly pronounce no one to be exempted.

All religious systems, it is confessed, are subject to great and insuperable difficulties. Each disputant triumphs in his turn, while he carries on an offensive war, and exposes the absurdities, barbarities, and pernicious tenets of his antagonist. But all of them, on the whole, prepare a complete triumph for the *sceptic,* who tells them that no system ought ever to be embraced with regard to such subjects: for this plain reason that no absurdity ought ever to be assented to with regard to any subject. A total suspense of judgment is here our only reasonable resource. And if every attack, as is commonly observed, and no defence among theologians is successful, how complete must be *his* victory who remains always, with all mankind, on the offensive, and has himself no fixed station or abiding city which he is ever, on any occasion, obliged to defend?

PART IX

But if so many difficulties attend the argument *a posteriori,* said Demea, had we not better adhere to that simple and sublime argument *a priori* which, by offering to us infallible demonstration, cuts off at once all doubt and difficulty? By this argument, too, we may prove the *infinity* of the Divine attributes, which, I am afraid, can never be ascertained with certainty from any other topic. For how can an effect which either is finite or, for aught we know, may be so—how can such an effect, I say, prove an infinite cause? The unity, too, of the Divine Nature it is very difficult, if not absolutely impossible, to deduce merely from contemplating the works of nature; nor will the uniformity alone of the plan, even were it allowed, give us any assurance of that attribute. Whereas the argument *a priori....*

You seem to reason, Demea, interposed Cleanthes, as if those advantages and conveniences in the abstract argument were full proofs of its solidity. But it is first proper, in my opinion, to determine what argument of this nature you choose to insist on; and we shall afterwards, from itself, better than from its *useful* consequences, endeavour to determine what value we ought to put upon it.

The argument, replied Demea, which I would insist on is the common one. Whatever exists must have a cause or reason of its existence, it being absolutely impossible for anything to produce itself or be the cause of its own existence. In mounting up, therefore, from effects to causes, we must either go on in tracing an infinite succession, without any ultimate cause at all, or must at last have recourse to some ultimate cause that is *necessarily* existent. Now that the first supposition is absurd may be thus proved. In the infinite chain or succession of causes and effects, each single effect is determined to exist by the power and efficacy of that cause which immediately preceded; but the whole eternal chain or succession, taken together, is not determined or caused by anything, and yet it is evident that it requires a cause or reason, as much as any particular object which begins to exist in time. The question is still reasonable why this particular succession of causes existed from eternity, and not any other succession or no succession at all. If there be no necessarily existent being, any supposition which can be formed is equally possible; nor is there any more absurdity in *nothing's* having existed from eternity than there is in that succession of causes which constitutes the universe. What was it, then, which determined *something* to exist rather than *nothing,* and bestowed being on a particular possibility, exclusive of the rest? *External causes,* there are supposed to be none. *Chance* is a word without a meaning. Was it *nothing?* But that can never produce anything. We must, therefore, have recourse to a necessarily existent Being who carries the *reason* of his existence in himself, and who cannot be supposed not to exist, without an express contradiction. There is, consequently, such a Being—that is, there is a Deity.

I shall not leave it to Philo, said Cleanthes, though I know that the starting objections is his chief delight, to point out the weakness of this metaphysical reasoning. It seems to me so obviously ill-grounded, and at the same time of so little consequence to the cause of true piety and religion, that I shall myself venture to show the fallacy of it.

I shall begin with observing that there is an evident absurdity in pretending to demonstrate a matter of fact, or to prove it by arguments *a priori.* Nothing is demonstrable unless the contrary implies a contradiction. Nothing that is distinctly conceivable implies a contradiction. Whatever we conceive as existent, we can also conceive as nonexistent. There is no being, therefore, whose nonexistence implies a contradiction. Consequently there is no being whose existence is demonstrable. I propose this argument as entirely decisive, and am willing to rest the whole controversy upon it.

It is pretended that the Deity is a necessarily existent being; and this necessity of his existence is attempted to be explained by asserting that, if we knew his whole essence or nature, we should perceive it to be as impossible for him not to exist, as for twice two not to be four. But it is evident that this can never happen, while our faculties remain the same as at present. It will still be possible for us, at any time, to conceive the nonexistence of what we formerly conceived to exist; nor can the mind ever lie under a necessity of supposing any object to remain always in being; in the same manner as we lie under a necessity of always conceiving twice two to be four. The words, therefore, *necessary existence* have no meaning or, which is the same thing, none that is consistent.

But further, why may not the material universe be the necessarily existent Being, according to this pretended explication of necessity? We dare not affirm that we know all the qualities of matter; and, for aught we can determine, it may contain some qualities which, were they known, would make its nonexistence appear as great a contradiction as that twice two is five. I find only one argument employed to prove that the material world is not the necessarily existent Being; and this argument is derived from the contingency both of the matter and the form of the world. "Any particle of matter," it is said, "may be *conceived* to be annihilated, and any form may be *conceived* to be altered. Such an annihilation or alteration, therefore, is not impossible."[4] But it seems a great partiality not to perceive that the same argument extends equally to the Deity, so far as we have any conception of him, and that the mind can at least imagine him to be nonexistent or his attributes to be altered. It must be some unknown, inconceivable qualities which can make his nonexistence appear impossible or his attributes unalterable; and no reason can be assigned why these qualities may not belong to matter. As they are altogether unknown and inconceivable, they can never be proved incompatible with it.

Add to this that in tracing an eternal succession of objects it seems absurd to inquire for a general cause or first author. How can anything that exists from eternity have a cause, since that relation implies a priority in time and a beginning of existence?

In such a chain, too, or succession of objects, each part is caused by that which preceded it, and causes that which succeeds it. Where then is the difficulty? But the *whole,* you say, wants a cause. I answer that the uniting of these parts into a whole, like the uniting of several distinct countries into one kingdom, or several distinct members into one body is performed merely by an arbitrary act of the mind, and has no influence on the nature of things. Did I show you the particular causes of each individual in a collection of twenty particles of matter, I should think it very unreasonable should you afterwards ask me what was the cause of the whole twenty. This is sufficiently explained in explaining the cause of the parts.

Though the reasonings which you have urged, Cleanthes, may well excuse me, said Philo, from starting any further difficulties, yet I cannot forbear insisting still upon another topic. It is observed by arithmeticians that the products of 9 compose always either 9 or some lesser product of 9 if you add together all the characters of which any of the former products is composed. Thus, of 18, 27, 36, which are products of 9, you make 9 by adding 1 to 8, 2 to 7, 3 to 6. Thus 369 is a product also of 9; and if you add 3, 6, and 9, you make 18, a lesser product of 9.[5] To a superficial observer so wonderful a regularity may be admired as the effect either of chance or design; but a skillful algebraist immediately concludes it to be the work of necessity, and demonstrates that it must for ever result from the nature of these numbers. Is it not probable, I ask, that the whole economy of the universe is conducted by a like necessity, though no human algebra can furnish a key which solves the difficulty? And instead of admiring the order of natural beings, may it not happen that, could we penetrate into the intimate nature of bodies, we should clearly see why it was absolutely impossible they could ever admit of any other disposition? So dangerous is it to introduce this idea of necessity into the present question! and so naturally does it afford an inference directly opposite to the religious hypothesis!

But dropping all these abstractions, continued Philo, and confining ourselves to more familiar topics, I shall venture to add an observation that the argument *a priori* has seldom been found very convincing, except to people of a metaphysical head who have accustomed themselves to abstract reasoning, and who, finding from mathematics that the understanding frequently leads to truth through obscurity, and contrary to first appearances, have transferred the same habit of thinking to subjects where it ought not to have place. Other people, even of good sense and the best inclined to religion, feel always some deficiency in such arguments, though they are not perhaps able to explain distinctly where it lies—a certain proof that men ever did and ever will derive their religion from other sources than from this species of reasoning.

PART X

It is my opinion, I own, replied Demea, that each man feels, in a manner, the truth of religion within his own breast, and, from a consciousness of his imbecility and misery rather than from any reasoning, is led to seek protection from that Being on whom he and all nature is dependent. So anxious or so tedious are even the best scenes of life that futurity is still the object of all our hopes and fears. We incessantly look forward and endeavour, by prayers, adoration, and sacrifice, to appease those unknown powers whom we find, by experience, so able to afflict and oppress us. Wretched creatures that we are! What resource for us amidst the innumerable ills of life did not religion suggest some methods of atonement, and appease those terrors with which we are incessantly agitated and tormented?

I am indeed persuaded, said Philo, that the best and indeed the only method of bringing everyone to a due sense of religion is by just representations of the misery and wickedness of men. And for that purpose a talent of eloquence and strong imagery is more requisite than that of reasoning and argument. For is it necessary to prove what everyone feels within himself? It is only necessary to make us feel it, if possible, more intimately and sensibly.

The people, indeed, replied Demea, are sufficiently convinced of this great and melancholy truth. The miseries of life, the unhappiness of man, the general corruptions of our nature, the unsatisfactory enjoyment of pleasures, riches, honours—these phrases have become almost proverbial in all languages. And who can doubt of what all men declare from their own immediate feeling and experience?

In this point, said Philo, the learned are perfectly agreed with the vulgar; and in all letters, *sacred* and *profane,* the topic of human misery has been insisted on with the most pathetic eloquence that sorrow and melancholy could inspire. The poets, who speak from sentiment, without a system, and whose testimony has therefore the more authority, abound in images of this nature. From Homer down to Dr. Young, the whole inspired tribe have ever been sensible that no other representation of things would suit the feeling and observation of each individual.

As to authorities, replied Demea, you need not seek them. Look round this library of Cleanthes. I shall venture to affirm that, except authors of particular sciences, such as chemistry or botany, who have no occasion to treat of human life, there is scarce one of those innumerable writers from whom the sense of human misery has not, in some passage or other, extorted a complaint and confession of it. At least, the chance is entirely on that side; and no one author has ever, so far as I can recollect, been so extravagant as to deny it.

There you must excuse me, said Philo: Leibniz has denied it, and is perhaps the first[6] who ventured upon so bold and paradoxical an opinion; at least, the first who made it essential to his philosophical system.

And by being the first, replied Demea, might he not have been sensible of his error? For is this a subject in which philosophers can propose to make discoveries especially in so late an age? And can any man hope by a simple denial (for the subject scarcely admits of reasoning) to bear down the united testimony of mankind, founded on sense and consciousness?

And why should man, added he, pretend to an exemption from the lot of all other animals? The whole earth, believe me, Philo, is cursed and polluted. A perpetual war is kindled amongst all living creatures. Necessity, hunger, want stimulate the strong and courageous; fear, anxiety, terror agitate the weak and infirm. The first entrance into life gives anguish to the new-born infant and to its wretched parent; weakness, impotence, distress attend each stage of that life, and it is, at last finished in agony and horror.

Observe, too, says Philo, the curious artifices of nature in order to embitter the life of every living being. The stronger prey upon the weaker and keep them in perpetual terror and anxiety. The weaker, too, in their turn, often prey upon the stronger, and vex and molest them without relaxation. Consider that innumerable race of insects, which either are bred on the body of each animal or, flying about, infix their stings in him. These insects have others still less than themselves which torment them. And thus on each hand, before and behind, above and below, every animal is surrounded with enemies which incessantly seek his misery and destruction.

Man alone, said Demea, seems to be, in part, an exception to this rule. For by combination in society he can easily master lions, tigers, and bears, whose greater strength and agility naturally enable them to prey upon him.

On the contrary, it is here chiefly, cried Philo, that the uniform and equal maxims of nature are most apparent. Man, it is true, can, by combination, surmount all his *real* enemies and become master of the whole animal creation; but does he not immediately raise up to himself *imaginary* enemies, the demons of his fancy, who haunt him with superstitious terrors and blast every enjoyment of life? His pleasure, as he imagines, becomes in their eyes a crime; his food and repose give them umbrage and offence; his very sleep and dreams furnish new materials to anxious fear; and even death, his refuge from every other ill, presents only the dread of endless and innumerable woes. Nor does the wolf molest more the timid flock than superstition does the anxious breast of wretched mortals.

Besides, consider, Demea: This very society by which we surmount those wild beasts, our natural enemies, what new enemies does it not raise to us? What woe and misery does it not occasion? Man is the greatest enemy of man. Oppression, injustice, contempt, contumely, violence, sedition, war, calumny, treachery, fraud—by these they mutually torment each other, and they would soon dissolve that society which they had formed were it not for the dread of still greater ills which must attend their separation.

But though these external insults, said Demea, from animals, from men, from all the elements, which assault us from a frightful catalogue of woes, they are nothing in comparison of those which arise within ourselves, from the distempered condition of our mind and body. How many lie under the lingering torment of diseases? Hear the pathetic enumeration of the great poet.

> *Intestine stone and ulcer, colic-pangs,*
> *Demoniac frenzy, moping melancholy,*
> *And moon-struck madness, pining atrophy*
> *Marasmus, and wide-wasting pestilence.*
> *Dire was the tossing, deep the groans:* Despair
> *Tended the sick, busiest from couch to couch*
> *And over them triumphant* Death *his dart*
> *Shook: but delay'd to strike, though oft invok'd*
> *With vows, as their chief good and final hope.*[7]

The disorders of the mind, continued Demea, though more secret, are not perhaps less dismal and vexatious. Remorse, shame, anguish, rage, disappointment, anxiety, fear, dejection, despair—who has ever passed through life without cruel inroads from these tormentors? How many have scarcely ever felt any better sensations? Labour and poverty, so abhorred by everyone, are the certain lot of the far greater number; and those few privileged persons who enjoy ease and opulence never reach contentment or true felicity. All the goods of life united would not make a very happy man, but all the ills united would make a wretch indeed; and any one of them almost (and who can be free from every one?), nay, often the absence of one good (and who can possess all?) is sufficient to render life ineligible.

Were a stranger to drop on a sudden into this world, I would show him, as a specimen of its ills, an hospital full of diseases, a prison crowded with malefactors and debtors, a field of battle strewed with carcases, a fleet floundering in the ocean, a nation languishing under tyranny, famine, or pestilence. To turn the gay side of life to him and give him a notion of its pleasures—whither should I conduct him? To a ball, to an opera, to court? He might justly think that I was only showing him a diversity of distress and sorrow.

There is no evading such striking instances, said Philo, but by apologies which still further aggravate the charge. Why have all men, I ask, in all ages, complained incessantly of the miseries of life?...They have no just reason, says one: these complaints proceed only from their discontented, repining, anxious disposition....And can there possibly, I reply, be a more certain foundation of misery than such a wretched temper?

But if they were really as unhappy as they pretend, says my antagonist, why do they remain in life?...

Not satisfied with life, afraid of death—

This is the secret chain, say I, that holds us. We are terrified, not bribed to the continuance of our existence.

It is only a false delicacy, he may insist, which a few refined spirits indulge, and which has spread these complaints among the whole race of mankind....And what is this delicacy, I ask, which you blame? Is it anything but a greater sensibility to all the pleasures and pains of life? And if the man of a delicate, refined temper, by being so much more alive than the rest of the world, is only so much more unhappy, what judgment must we form in general of human life?

Let men remain at rest, says our adversary, and they will be easy. They are willing artificers of their own misery....No! reply I: an anxious languor follows their repose: disappointment, vexation, trouble, their activity and ambition.

I can observe something like what you mention in some others, replied Cleanthes, but I confess I feel little or nothing of it in myself, and hope that it is not so common as you represent it.

If you feel not human misery yourself, cried Demea, I congratulate you on so happy a singularity. Others, seemingly the most prosperous, have not been ashamed to vent their complaints in the most melancholy strains. Let us attend to the great, the fortunate emperor, Charles V, when tired with human grandeur, he resigned all his extensive dominions into the hands of his son. In the last harangue which he made on that memorable occasion, he publicly avowed *that the greatest prosperities which he had ever enjoyed had been mixed with so many adversities that he might truly say he had never enjoyed any satisfaction or contentment.* But did the retired life in which he sought for shelter afford him any greater happiness? If we may credit his son's account, his repentance commenced the very day of his resignation.

Cicero's fortune, from small beginnings, rose to the greatest lustre and renown; yet what pathetic complaints of the ills of life do his familiar letters, as well as philosophical discourses, contain? And suitably to his own experience, he introduces Cato, the great, the fortunate Cato protesting in his old age that had he a new life in his offer he would reject the present.

Ask yourself, ask any of your acquaintance, whether they would live over again the last ten or twenty years of their life. No! but the next twenty, they say, will be better:

And from the dregs of life, hope to receive What the first sprightly running could not give.[8]

Thus, at last, they find (such is the greatness of human misery, it reconciles even contradictions) that they complain at once of the shortness of life and of its vanity and sorrow.

And is it possible, Cleanthes, said Philo, that after all these reflections, and infinitely more which might be suggested, you can still persevere in your anthropomorphism, and assert the moral attributes of the Deity, his justice, benevolence, mercy, and rectitude, to be of the same nature with these virtues in human creatures? His power, we allow, is infinite; whatever he wills is executed; but neither man nor any other animal is happy; therefore, he does not will their happiness. His wisdom is infinite; he is never mistaken in choosing the means to any end; but the course of nature tends not to human or animal felicity; therefore, it is not established for that purpose. Through the whole compass of human knowledge there are no inferences more certain and infallible than these. In what respect, then, do his benevolence and mercy resemble the benevolence and mercy of men?

Epicurus' old questions are yet unanswered.

Is he willing to prevent evil, but not able? then is he impotent. Is he able, but not willing? then is he malevolent. Is he both able and willing? whence then is evil?

You ascribe, Cleanthes (and I believe justly), a purpose and intention to nature. But what, I beseech you, is the object of that curious artifice and machinery which she has displayed in all animals—the preservation alone of individuals, and propagation of the species? It seems enough for her purpose, if such a rank be barely upheld in the universe, without any care or concern for the happiness of the members that compose it. No resource for this purpose: no machinery in order merely to give pleasure or ease; no fund of pure joy and contentment; no indulgence without some want or necessity accompanying it. At least, the few phenomena of this nature are over-balanced by opposite phenomena of still greater importance.

Our sense of music, harmony, and indeed beauty of all kinds, gives satisfaction, without being absolutely necessary to the preservation and propagation of the species. But what racking pains, on the other hand, arise from gouts, gravels, megrims, toothaches, rheumatisms, where the injury to the animal machinery is either small or incurable? Mirth, laughter, play, frolic seem gratuitous satisfactions which have no further tendency; spleen, melancholy, discontent, superstition are pains of the same nature. How then does the Divine benevolence display itself, in the sense of you anthropomorphites? None but we mystics, as you were pleased to call us, can account for this strange mixture of phenomena, by deriving it from attributes infinitely perfect but incomprehensible.

And have you, at last, said Cleanthes smiling, betrayed your intentions, Philo? Your long agreement with Demea did indeed a little surprise me, but I find you were all the while erecting a concealed battery against me. And I must confess that you have now fallen upon a subject worthy of your noble spirit of opposition and controversy. If you can make out the present point, and prove mankind to be unhappy or corrupted, there is an end at once of all religion. For to what purpose establish the natural attributes of the Deity, while the moral are still doubtful and uncertain?

You take umbrage very easily, replied Demea, at opinions the most innocent and the most generally received, even amongst the religious and devout themselves; and nothing can be more surprising than to find a topic like this—concerning the wickedness and misery of man—charged with no less than atheism and profaneness. Have not all pious divines and preachers who have indulged their rhetoric on so fertile a subject, have they not easily, I say, given a solution of any difficulties which may attend it? This world is but a point in comparison of the universe; this life but a moment in comparison of eternity. The present evil phenomena, therefore, are rectified in other regions, and in some future period of existence. And the eyes of men, being then opened to larger views of things, see the whole connection of general laws, and trace, with adoration, the benevolence and rectitude of the Deity through all the mazes and intricacies of his providence.

No! replied Cleanthes, no! These arbitrary suppositions can never be admitted, contrary to matter of fact, visible and uncontroverted. Whence can any cause be known but from its known effects? Whence can any hypothesis be proved but from the apparent phenomena? To establish one hypothesis upon another is building entirely in the air; and the utmost we ever attain by these conjectures and fictions is to ascertain the bare possibility of our opinion, but never can we, upon such terms, establish its reality.

The only method of supporting Divine benevolence—and it is what I willingly embrace—is to deny absolutely the misery and wickedness of man. Your representations are exaggerated; your melancholy views mostly fictitious; your inferences contrary to fact and experience. Health is more common than sickness; pleasure than pain; happiness than misery. And for one vexation which we meet with, we attain, upon computation, a hundred enjoyments.

Admitting your position, replied Philo, which yet is extremely doubtful, you must at the same time allow that, if pain be less frequent than pleasure, it is infinitely more violent and durable. One hour of it is often able to outweigh a day, a week, a month of our common insipid enjoyments; and how many days, weeks, and months are passed by several in the most acute torments? Pleasure, scarcely in one instance, is ever able to reach ecstasy and rapture; and in no one instance can it continue for any time at its highest pitch and altitude. The spirits evaporate, the nerves relax, the fabric is disordered, and the enjoyment quickly degenerates into fatigue and uneasiness. But pain often, good God, how often! rises to torture and agony; and the longer it continues, it becomes still more genuine agony and torture. Patience is exhausted, courage languishes, melancholy seizes us, and nothing terminates our misery but the removal of its cause or another event which is the sole cure of all evil, but which, from our natural folly, we regard with still greater horror and consternation.

But not to insist upon these topics, continued Philo, though most obvious, certain, and important, I must use the freedom to admonish you, Cleanthes, that you have put the controversy upon a most dangerous issue, and are unawares introducing a total scepticism into the most essential articles of natural and revealed theology. What! no method of fixing a just foundation for religion unless we allow the happiness of human life, and maintain a continued existence even in this world, with all our present pains, infirmities, vexations, and follies, to be eligible and desirable! But this is contrary to everyone's feeling and experience; it is contrary to an authority so established as nothing can subvert. No decisive proofs can ever be produced against this authority; nor is it possible for you to compute, estimate, and compare all the pains and all the pleasures in the lives of all men and of all animals; and thus, by your resting the whole system of religion on a point which, from its very nature, must for ever be uncertain, you tacitly confess that that system is equally uncertain.

But allowing you what never will be believed, at least, what you never possibly can prove, that animal or, at least, human happiness in this life exceeds its misery, you have yet done nothing; for this is not, by any means, what we expect from infinite power, infinite wisdom, and infinite goodness. Why is there any misery at all in the world? Not by chance, surely. From some cause then. Is it from the intention of the Deity? But he is perfectly benevolent. Is it contrary to his intention? But he is almighty. Nothing can shake the solidity of this reasoning, so short, so clear, so decisive, except we assert that these subjects exceed all human capacity, and that our common measures of truth and falsehood are not applicable to them—a topic which I have all along insisted on, but which you have, from the beginning, rejected with scorn and indignation.

But I will be contented to retire still from this intrenchment, for I deny that you can ever force me in it. I will allow that pain or misery in man is *compatible* with infinite power and goodness in the Deity, even in your sense of these attributes: what are you advanced by all these concessions? A mere possible compatibility is not sufficient. You must *prove* these pure, unmixt, and uncontrollable attributes from the present mixt and confused phenomena, and from these alone. A hopeful undertaking! Were the phenomena ever so pure and unmixt, yet, being finite, they would be insufficient for that purpose. How much more, where they are also so jarring and discordant!

Here, Cleanthes, I find myself at ease in my argument. Here I triumph. Formerly, when we argued concerning the natural attributes of intelligence and design, I needed all my sceptical and metaphysical subtilty to elude your grasp. In many views of the universe and of its parts, particularly the latter, the beauty and fitness of final causes strike us with such irresistible force that all objections appear (what I believe they really are) mere cavils and sophisms; nor can we then imagine how it was ever possible for us to repose any weight on them. But there is no view of human life or of the condition of mankind from which, without the greatest violence, we can infer the moral attributes or learn that infinite benevolence, conjoined with infinite power and infinite wisdom, which we must discover by the eyes of faith alone. It is your turn now to tug the labouring oar, and to support your philosophical subtilties against the dictates of plain reason and experience

PART XI

I scruple not to allow, said Cleanthes, that I have been apt to suspect the frequent repetition of the word *infinite*, which we meet with in all theological writers, to savour more of panegyric than of philosophy, and that any purposes of reasoning, and even of religion, would be better served were we to rest contented with more accurate and more moderate expressions. The terms *admirable, excellent, superlatively great, wise,* and *holy*—these sufficiently fill the imaginations of

men, and anything beyond, besides that it leads into absurdities, has no influence on the affections or sentiments. Thus, in thy present subject, if we abandon all human analogy, as seems your intention, Demea, I am afraid we abandon all religion and retain no conception of the great object of our adoration. If we preserve human analogy, we must forever find it impossible to reconcile any mixture of evil in the universe with infinite attributes; much less can we ever prove the latter from the former. But supposing the Author of nature to be finitely perfect, though far exceeding mankind, a satisfactory account may then be given of natural and moral evil, and every untoward phenomenon be explained and adjusted. A less evil may then be chosen in order to avoid a greater; inconveniences be submitted to in order to reach a desirable end; and, in a word, benevolence, regulated by wisdom and limited by necessity, may produce just such a world as the present. You, Philo, who are so prompt at starting views and reflections and analogies, I would gladly hear, at length, without interruption, your opinion of this new theory; and if it deserve our attention, we may afterwards, at more leisure, reduce it into form.

My sentiments, replied Philo, are not worth being made a mystery of; and, therefore, without any ceremony, I shall deliver what occurs to me with regard to the present subject. It must, I think, be allowed that, if a very limited intelligence whom we shall suppose utterly unacquainted with the universe were assured that it were the production of a very good, wise, and powerful Being, however finite, he would, from his conjectures, form *beforehand* a different notion of it from what we find it to be by experience; nor would he ever imagine, merely from these attributes of the cause of which he is informed, that the effect could be so full of vice and misery and disorder, as it appears in this life. Supposing now that this person were brought into the world, still assured that it was the workmanship of such a sublime and benevolent Being, he might, perhaps, be surprised at the disappointment, but would never retract his former belief if founded on any very solid argument, since such a limited intelligence must be sensible of his own blindness and ignorance, and must allow that there may be many solutions of those phenomena which will for ever escape his comprehension. But supposing, which is the real case with regard to man, that this creature is not antecedently convinced of a supreme intelligence, benevolent, and powerful, but is left to gather such a belief from the appearances of things— this entirely alters the case, nor will he ever find any reason for such a conclusion. He may be fully convinced of the narrow limits of his understanding, but this will not help him in forming an inference concerning the goodness of superior powers, since he must form that inference from what he knows, not from what he is ignorant of. The more you exaggerate his weakness and ignorance, the more diffident you render him, and give him the greater suspicion that such subjects are beyond the reach of his faculties. You are obliged, therefore, to reason with him merely from the known phenomena, and to drop every aritrary supposition or conjecture.

Did I show you a house or palace where there was not one apartment convenient or agreeable, where the windows, doors, fires, passages, stairs, and the whole economy of the building were the source of noise, confusion, fatigue, darkness, and the extremes of heat and cold, you would certainly blame the contrivance, without any further examination. The architect would in vain display his subtilty, and prove to you that, if this door or that window were altered, greater ills would ensue. What he says may be strictly true: the alteration of one particular, while the other parts of the building remain, may only augment the inconveniences. But still you would assert in general that, if the architect had had skill and good intentions, he might have formed such a plan of the whole, and might have adjusted the parts in such a manner as would have remedied all or most of these inconveniences. His ignorance, or even your own ignorance of such a plan, will never convince you of the impossibility of it. If you find any inconveniences and deformities in the building, you will always, without entering into any detail, condemn the architect.

In short, I repeat the question: Is the world, considered in general and as it appears to us in this life, different from what a man or such a limited being would, *beforehand,* expect from a very

powerful, wise, and benevolent Deity? It must be strange prejudice to assert the contrary. And from thence I conclude that, however consistent the world may be, allowing certain suppositions and conjectures with the idea of such a Deity, it can never afford us an inference concerning his existence. The consistency is not absolutely denied, only the inference. Conjectures, especially where infinity is excluded from the Divine attributes, may perhaps be sufficient to prove a consistency, but can never be foundations for any inference.

There seem to be *four* circumstances on which depend all or the greatest part of the ills that molest sensible creatures; and it is not impossible but all these circumstances may be necessary and unavoidable. We know so little beyond common life, or even of common life, that, with regard to the economy of a universe, there is no conjecture, however wild, which may not be just, nor any one, however plausible, which may not be erroneous. All that belongs to human understanding, in this deep ignorance and obscurity, is to be sceptical or at least cautious, and not to admit of any hypothesis whatever, much less of any which is supported by no appearance of probability. Now this I assert to be the case with regard to all the causes of evil and the circumstances on which it depends. None of them appear to human reason in the least degree necessary or unavoidable, nor can we suppose them such, without the utmost licence of imagination.

The *first* circumstance which introduces evil is that contrivance or economy of the animal creation by which pains, as well as pleasures, are employed to excite all creatures to action, and make them vigilant in the great work of self-preservation. Now pleasure alone, in its various degrees, seems to human understanding sufficient for this purpose. All animals might be constantly in a state of enjoyment; but when urged by any of the necessities of nature, such as thirst, hunger, weariness, instead of pain, they might feel a diminution of pleasure by which they might be prompted to seek that object which is necessary to their subsistence. Men pursue pleasure as eagerly as they avoid pain; at least, they might have been so constituted. It seems, therefore, plainly possible to carry on the business of life without any pain. Why then is any animal ever rendered susceptible of such a sensation? If animals can be free from it an hour, they might enjoy a perpetual exemption from it, and it required as particular a contrivance of their organs to produce that feeling as to endow them with sight, hearing, or any of the senses. Shall we conjecture that such a contrivance was necessary, without any appearance of reason, and shall we build on that conjecture as on the most certain truth?

But a capacity of pain would not alone produce pain were it not for the *second* circumstance, viz., the conducting of the world by general laws; and this seems nowise necessary to a very perfect Being. It is true, if everything were conducted by particular volitions, the course of nature would be perpetually broken, and no man could employ his reason in the conduct of life. But might not other particular volitions remedy this inconvenience? In short, might not the Deity exterminate all ill, wherever it were to be found, and produce all good, without any preparation or long progress of causes and effects?

Besides, we must consider that, according to the present economy of the world, the course of nature, though supposed exactly regular, yet to us appears not so, and many events are uncertain, and many disappoint our expectations. Health and sickness, calm and tempest, with an infinite number of other accidents whose causes are unknown and variable, have a great influence both on the fortunes of particular persons and on the prosperity of public societies; and indeed all human life, in a manner, depends on such accidents. A being, therefore, who knows the secret springs of the universe might easily, by particular volitions, turn all these accidents to the good of mankind and render the whole world happy, without discovering himself in any operation. A fleet whose purposes were salutary to society might always meet with a fair wind. Good princes enjoy sound health and long life. Persons born to power and authority be framed with good tempers and virtuous dispositions. A few such events as these, regularly and wisely conducted, would change the face of the world, and yet would no more seem to disturb the course of nature or confound human conduct than the present economy of things where the causes are secret and variable

and compounded. Some small touches given to Caligula's brain in his infancy might have converted him into a Trajan. One wave, a little higher than the rest, by burying Caesar and his fortune in the bottom of the ocean, might have restored liberty to a considerable part of mankind. There may, for aught we know, be good reasons why Providence interposes not in this manner, but they are unknown to us; and, though the mere supposition that such reasons exist may be sufficient to *save* the conclusion concerning the Divine attributes, yet surely it can never be sufficient to *establish* that conclusion.

If everything in the universe be conducted by general laws, and if animals be rendered susceptible of pain, it scarcely seems possible but some ill must arise in the various shocks of matter and the various concurrence and opposition of general laws; but this ill would be very rare were it not for the *third* circumstance which I proposed to mention, viz., the great frugality with which all powers and faculties are distributed to every particular being. So well adjusted are the organs and capacities of all animals, and so well fitted to their preservation, that, as far as history or tradition reaches, there appears not to be any single species which has yet been extinguished in the universe. Every animal has the requisite endowments, but these endowments are bestowed with so scrupulous an economy that any considerable diminution must entirely destroy the creature. Wherever one power is increased, there is a proportional abatement in the others. Animals which excel in swiftness are commonly defective in force. Those which possess both are either imperfect in some of their senses or are oppressed with the most craving wants. The human species, whose chief excellence is reason and sagacity, is of all others the most necessitous, and the most deficient in bodily advantages, without clothes, without arms, without food, without lodging, without any convenience of life, except what they owe to their own skill and industry. In short, nature seems to have formed an exact calculation of the necessities of her creatures, and, like a *rigid master,* has afforded them little more powers or endowments than what are strictly sufficient to supply those necessities. An *indulgent parent* would have bestowed a large stock in order to guard against accidents, and secure the happiness and welfare of the creature in the most unfortunate concurrence of circumstances. Every course of life would not have been so surrounded with precipices that the least departure from the true path, by mistake or necessity must involve us in misery and ruin. Some reserve, some fund, would have been provided to ensure happiness, nor would the powers and the necessities have been adjusted with so rigid an economy. The Author of nature is inconceivably powerful; his force is supposed great, if not altogether inexhaustible, nor is there any reason, as far as we can judge, to make him observe this strict frugality in his dealings with his creatures. It would have been better, were his power extremely limited, to have created fewer animals, and to have endowed these with more faculties for their happiness and preservation. A builder is never esteemed prudent who undertakes a plan beyond what his stock will enable him to finish.

In order to cure most of the ills of human life, I require not that man should have the wings of the eagle, the swiftness of the stag, the force of the ox, the arms of the lion, the scales of the crocodile or rhinoceros; much less do I demand the sagacity of an angel or cherubim. I am contented to take an increase in one single power or faculty of his soul. Let him be endowed with a greater propensity to industry and labour, a more vigorous spring and activity of mind, a more constant bent to business and application. Let the whole species possess naturally an equal diligence with that which many individuals are able to attain by habit and reflection, and the most beneficial consequences, without any allay of ill, is the immediate and necessary result of this endowment. Almost all the moral as well as natural evils of human life arise from idleness; and were our species, by the original constitution of their frame, exempt from this vice or infirmity, the perfect cultivation of land, the improvement of arts and manufactures, the exact execution of every office and duty, immediately follow; and men at once may fully reach that state of society which is so imperfectly attained by the best regulated government. But as industry is a power, and

the most valuable of any, nature seems determined, suitably to her usual maxims, to bestow it on man with a very sparing hand, and rather to punish him severely for his deficiency in it than to reward him for his attainments. She has so contrived his frame that nothing but the most violent necessity can oblige him to labour; and she employs all his other wants to overcome, at least in part, the want of diligence, and to endow him with some share of a faculty of which she has thought fit naturally to bereave him. Here our demands may be allowed very humble, and therefore the more reasonable. If we required the endowments of superior penetration and judgment, of a more delicate taste of beauty, of a nicer sensibility to benevolence and friendship, we might be told that we impiously pretend to break the order of nature, that we want to exalt ourselves into a higher rank of being, that the presents which we require, not being suitable to our state and condition, would only be pernicious to us. But it is hard, I dare to repeat it, it is hard that, being placed in a world so full of wants and necessities, where almost every being and element is either our foe or refuses its assistance...we should also have our own temper to struggle with, and should be deprived of that faculty which can alone fence against these multiplied evils.

The *fourth* circumstance whence arises the misery and ill of the universe is the inaccurate workmanship of all the springs and principles of the great machine of nature. It must be acknowledged that there are few parts of the universe which seem not to serve some purpose, and whose removal would not produce a visible defect and disorder in the whole. The parts hang all together, nor can one be touched without affecting the rest, in a greater or less degree. But at the same time, it must be observed that none of these parts or principles, however useful, are so accurately adjusted as to keep precisely within those bounds in which their utility consists; but they are, all of them, apt, on every occasion, to run into the one extreme or the other. One would imagine that this grand production had not received the last hand of the maker—so little finished is every part, and so coarse are the strokes with which it is executed. Thus the winds are requisite to convey the vapours along the surface of the globe, and to assist men in navigation; but how often, rising up to tempests and hurricanes, do they become pernicious? Rains are necessary to nourish all the plants and animals of the earth; but how often are they defective? how often excessive? Heat is requisite to all life and vegetation, but is not always found in the due proportion. On the mixture and secretion of the humours and juices of the body depend the health and prosperity of the animal; but the parts perform not regularly their proper function. What more useful than all the passions of the mind, ambition, vanity, love, anger? But how often do they break their bounds and cause the greatest convulsions in society? There is nothing so advantageous in the universe but what frequently becomes pernicious, by its excess or defect; nor has nature guarded, with the requisite accuracy, against all disorder or confusion. The irregularity is never perhaps so great as to destroy any species, but is often sufficient to involve the individuals in ruin and misery.

On the concurrence, then, of these *four* circumstances does all or the greatest part of natural evil depend. Were all living creatures incapable of pain, or were the world administered by particular volitions, evil never could have found access into the universe; and were animals endowed with a large stock of powers and faculties, beyond what strict necessity requires, or were the several springs and principles of the universe so accurately framed as to preserve always the just temperament and medium, there must have been very little ill in comparison of what we feel at present. What then shall we pronounce on this occasion? Shall we say that these circumstances are not necessary, and that they might easily have been altered in the contrivance of the universe? This decision seems too presumptuous for creatures so blind and ignorant. Let us be more modest in our conclusions. Let us allow that, if the goodness of the Deity (I mean a goodness like the human) could be established on any tolerable reasons *a priori,* these phenomena, however untoward, would not be sufficient to subvert that principle, but might easily, in some unknown manner, be reconcilable to it. But let us still assert that, as this goodness is not antecedently established but

must be inferred from the phenomena, there can be no grounds for such an inference while there are so many ills in the universe, and while these ills might so easily have been remedied, as far as human understanding can be allowed to judge on such a subject. I am sceptic enough to allow that the bad appearances, notwithstanding all my reasonings, may be compatible with such attributes as you suppose, but surely they can never prove these attributes. Such a conclusion cannot result from scepticism, but must arise from the phenomena, and from our confidence in the reasonings which we deduce from these phenomena.

Look round this universe. What an immense profusion of beings, animated and organized, sensible and active! You admire this prodigious variety and fecundity. But inspect a little more narrowly these living existences, the only beings worth regarding. How hostile and destructive to each other! How insufficient all of them for their own happiness! How contemptible or odious to the spectator! The whole presents nothing but the idea of a blind nature, impregnated by a great vivifying principle, and pouring forth from her lap, without discernment or parental care, her maimed and abortive children!

Here the Manichaean system occurs as a proper hypothesis to solve the difficulty; and, no doubt, in some respects it is very specious and has more probability than the common hypothesis, by giving a plausible account of the strange mixture of good and ill which appears in life. But if we consider, on the other hand, the perfect uniformity and agreement of the parts of the universe, we shall not discover in it any marks of the combat of a malevolent with a benevolent being. There is indeed an opposition of pains and pleasures in the feelings of sensible creatures; but are not all the operations of nature carried on by an opposition of principles, of hot and cold, moist and dry, light and heavy? The true conclusion is that the original Source of all things is entirely indifferent to all these principles, and has no more regard to good above ill than to heat above cold, or to drought above moisture, or to light above heavy.

There may *four* hypotheses be framed concerning the first causes of the universe: that they are endowed with perfect goodness; that they have perfect malice; that they are opposite and have both goodness and malice; that they have neither goodness nor malice. Mixed phenomena can never prove the two former unmixed principles; and the uniformity and steadiness of general laws seem to oppose the third. The fourth, therefore, seems by far the most probable.

What I have said concerning natural evil will apply to moral with little or no variation; and we have no more reason to infer that the rectitude of the Supreme Being resembles human rectitude than that his benevolence resembles the human. Nay, it will be thought that we have still greater cause to exclude from him moral sentiments, such as we feel them, since moral evil, in the opinion of many, is much more predominant above moral good than natural evil above natural good.

But even though this should not be allowed, and though the virtue which is in mankind should be acknowledged much superior to the vice, yet, so long as there is any vice at all in the universe, it will very much puzzle you anthropomorphites how to account for it. You must assign a cause for it, without having recourse to the first cause. But as every effect must have a cause, and that cause another, you must either carry on the progression *in infinitum* or rest on that original principle, who is the ultimate cause of all things....

Hold! hold! cried Demea: Whither does your imagination hurry you? I joined in alliance with you in order to prove the incomprehensible nature of the Divine Being, and refute the principles of Cleanthes, who would measure everything by human rule and standard. But I now find you running into all the topics of the greatest libertines and infidels, and betraying that holy cause which you seemingly espoused. Are you secretly, then, a more dangerous enemy than Cleanthes himself?

And are you so late in perceiving it? replied Cleanthes. Believe me, Demea, your friend Philo, from the beginning, has been amusing himself at both our expense; and it must be confessed that the injudicious reasoning of our vulgar theology has given him but too just a handle of ridicule. The total infirmity of human reason, the absolute incomprehensibility of the Divine Nature, the great and universal misery, and still greater wickedness of men—these are strange topics, surely, to be so fondly cherished by orthodox divines and doctors. In ages of stupidity and ignorance, indeed, these principles may safely be espoused; and perhaps no views of things are more proper to promote superstition than such as encourage the blind amazement, the diffidence, and melancholy of mankind. But at present....

Blame not so much, interposed Philo, the ignorance of these reverend gentlemen. They know how to change their style with the times. Formerly, it was a most popular theological topic to maintain that human life was vanity and misery, and to exaggerate all the ills and pains which are incident to men. But of late years, divines, we find, begin to retract this position and maintain, though still with some hesitation, that there are more goods than evils, more pleasures than pains, even in this life. When religion stood entirely upon temper and education, it was thought proper to encourage melancholy, as, indeed, mankind never have recourse to superior powers so readily as in that disposition. But as men have now learned to form principles and to draw consequences, it is necessary to change the batteries, and to make use of such arguments as will endure at least some scrutiny and examination. This variation is the same (and from the same causes) with that which I formerly remarked with regard to scepticism.

Thus Philo continued to the last his spirit of opposition, and his censure of established opinions. But I could observe that Demea did not at all relish the latter part of the discourse; and he took occasion soon after, on some pretence or other, to leave the company.

NOTES

1. *Recherche de la Verité*. liv. 3, cap. 9.
2. *De Rerum Natura*, lib. XI [II], 1094. (Who can rule the sum, who hold in his hand with controlling force the strong reins, of the immeasurable deep? Who can at once make all the different heavens to roll and warm with ethereal fires all the fruitful earths, or be present in all places at all times?)—(Translation by H. A. J. Munro, G. Bell & Sons, 1920.)

3. *De Natura Deorum*, lib. I [cap. VIII]. (For with what eyes could your Plato see the construction of so vast a work which, according to him, God was putting together and building? What materials, what tools, what bars, what machines, what servants were employed in such gigantic work? How could the air, fire, water, and earth pay obedience and submit to the will of the architect?)

4. Dr. Clarke [Samuel Clarke, the rationalist theologian (1675–1729)].
5. *Republique des Lettres*, Aut 1685.
6. That sentiment had been maintained by Dr. King and some few others before Leibniz, though by none of so great fame as that German philosopher.
7. Milton: *Paradise Lost*, Bk. XI.
8. John Dryden, *Aureng-Zebe*, Act IV, sc. 1.

THE PROBLEM OF EVIL

Rebellion

FYODOR DOSTOEVSKY

Fyodor Dostoevsky (1821–1881) was one of the great Russian novelists of the nineteenth century.

"I must make you one confession," Ivan began. "I could never understand how one can love one's neighbors. It's just one's neighbors, to my mind, that one can't love, though one might love those at a distance. I once read somewhere of John the Merciful, a saint, that when a hungry, frozen beggar came to him, he took him into his bed, held him in his arms, and began breathing into his mouth, which was putrid and loathsome from some awful disease. I am convinced that he did that from 'self-laceration,' from the self-laceration of falsity, for the sake of the charity imposed by duty, as a penance laid on him. For any one to love a man, he must be hidden, for as soon as he shows his face, love is gone."

"Father Zossima has talked of that more than once," observed Alyosha, "he, too, said that the face of a man often hinders many people not practiced in love, from loving him. But yet there's a great deal of love in mankind, and almost Christlike love. I know that myself, Ivan."

"Well, I know nothing of it so far, and can't understand it, and the innumerable mass of mankind are with me there. The question is, whether that's due to men's bad qualities or whether it's inherent in their nature. To my thinking, Christ-like love for men is a miracle impossible on earth. He was God. But we are not gods. Suppose I, for instance, suffer intensely. Another can never know how much I suffer, because he is another and not I. And what's more, a man is rarely ready to admit another's suffering (as though it were a distinction). Why won't he admit it, do you think? Because I smell unpleasant, because I have a stupid face, because I once trod on his foot. Besides there is suffering and suffering; degrading, humiliating suffering such as humbles me—hunger, for instance—my benefactor will perhaps allow me; but when you come to higher suffering—for an idea, for instance—he will very rarely admit that, perhaps because my face strikes him as not at all what he fancies a man should have who suffers for an idea. And

From *The Brothers Karamazov*, C. Garnett trans., Book V, Chap. 4 (New York: Modern Library, Inc., 1950).

so he deprives me instantly of his favor, and not at all from badness of heart. Beggars, especially genteel beggars, ought never to show themselves, but to ask for charity through the newspapers. One can love one's neighbors in the abstract, or even at a distance, but at close quarters it's almost impossible. If it were as on the stage, in the ballet, where if beggars come in they wear silken rags and tattered lace and beg for alms dancing gracefully, then one might like looking at them. But even then we should not love them. But enough of that. I simply wanted to show you my point of view. I meant to speak of the suffering of mankind generally, but we had better confine ourselves to the sufferings of the children. That reduces the scope of my argument to the tenth of what it would be. Still we'd better keep to the children, though it does weaken my case. But, in the first place, children can be loved even at close quarters, even when they are dirty, even when they are ugly (I fancy, though, children never are ugly). The second reason why I won't speak of grownup people is that, besides being disgusting and unworthy of love, they have a compensation—they've eaten the apple and know good and evil, and they have become 'like god.' They go on eating it still. But the children haven't eaten anything, and are so far innocent. Are you fond of children, Alyosha? I know you are, and you will understand why I prefer to speak of them. If they, too, suffer horribly on earth, they must suffer for their fathers' sins, they must be punished for their fathers' sins, they must be punished for their fathers, who have eaten the apple; but that reasoning is of the other world and is incomprehensible for the heart of man here on earth. The innocent must not suffer for another's sins, and especially such innocents! You may be surprised at me, Alyosha, but I am awfully fond of children, too. And observe, cruel people, the violent, the rapacious, the Karamazovs are sometimes very fond of children. Children while they are quite little—up to seven, for instance—are so remote from grownup people; they are different creatures, as it were, of a different species. I knew a criminal in prison who had, in the course of his career as a burglar, murdered whole families, including several children. But when he was in prison, he had a strange affection for them. He spent all his time at his window, watching the children playing in the prison yard. He trained one little boy to come up to his window and made great friends with him...You don't know why I am telling you all this, Alyosha? My head aches and I am sad."

"You speak with a strange air," observed Alyosha uneasily, "as though you were not quite yourself."

"By the way, a Bulgarian I met lately in Moscow," Ivan went on, seeming not to hear his brother's words, "told me about the crimes committed by Turks and Circassians in all parts of Bulgaria through fear of a general rising of the Slavs. They burn villages, murder, outrage women and children, they nail their prisoners by the ears to the fences, leave them so till morning, and in the morning they hang them—all sorts of things you can't imagine. People talk sometimes of bestial cruelty, but that's a great injustice and insult to the beasts; a beast can never be so cruel as a man, so artistically cruel. The tiger only tears and gnaws, that's all he can do. He would never think of nailing people by the ears, even if he were able to do it. These Turks took a pleasure in torturing children, too; cutting the unborn child from the mother's womb, and tossing babies up in the air and catching them on the points of their bayonets before their mother's eyes. Doing it before the mother's eyes was what gave zest to the amusement. Here is another scene that I thought very interesting. Imagine a trembling mother with her baby in her arms, a circle of invading Turks around her. They've planned a diversion; they pet the baby, laugh to make it laugh. They succeed, the baby laughs. At that moment a Turk points a pistol four inches from the baby's face. The baby laughs with glee, holds out its little hands to the pistol, and he pulls the trigger in the baby's face and blows out its brains. Artistic, wasn't it? By the way, Turks are particularly fond of sweet things, they say."

"Brother, what are you driving at?" asked Alyosha.

"I think if the devil doesn't exist, but man has created him, he has created him in his own image and likeness."

"Just as he did God, then?" observed Alyosha. " 'It's wonderful how you can turn words,' as Polonius says in *Hamlet*," laughed Ivan. "You turn my words against me. Well, I am glad. Yours must be a fine God, if man created Him in His image and likeness. You asked just now what I was driving at. You see, I am fond of collecting certain facts, and, would you believe, I even copy anecdotes of a certain sort from newspapers and books, and I've already got a fine collection. The Turks, of course, have gone into it, but they are foreigners. I have specimens from home that are even better than the Turks. You know we prefer beating—rods and scourges—that's our national institution. Nailing ears is unthinkable for us, for we are, after all, Europeans. But the rod and scourge we have always with us and they cannot be taken from us. Abroad now they scarcely do any beating. Manners are more humane, or laws have been passed, so that they don't dare to flog men now. But they make up for it in another way just as national as ours. And so national that it would be practically impossible among us, though I believe we are being inoculated with it, since the religious movement began in our aristocracy. I have a charming pamphlet, translated from the French, describing how, quite recently, five years ago, a murderer, Richard, was executed—a young man, I believe, of three and twenty, who repented and was converted to the Christian faith at the very scaffold. This Richard was an illegitimate child who was given as a child of six by his parents to some shepherds on the Swiss mountains. They brought him up to work for them. He grew up like a little wild beast among them. The shepherds taught him nothing, and scarcely fed or clothed him, but sent him out at seven to herd the flock in cold and wet, and no one hesitated or scrupled to treat him so. Quite the contrary, they thought they had every right, for Richard had been given to them as a chattel, and they did not even see the necessity of feeding him. Richard himself describes how in those years, like the Prodigal Son in the Gospel, he longed to eat of the mash given to the pigs, which were fattened for sale. But they wouldn't even give him that, and beat him when he stole from the pigs. And that was how he spent all his childhood and his youth, till he grew up and was strong enough to go away and be a thief. The savage began to earn his living as a day laborer in Geneva. He drank what he earned, he lived like a brute, and finished by killing and robbing an old man. He was caught, tried, and condemned to death. They are no sentimentalists there. And in prison he was immediately surrounded by pastors, members of Christian brotherhoods, philanthropic ladies, and the like. They taught him to read and write in prison, and expounded the Gospel to him. They exhorted him, worked upon him, drummed at him incessantly, till at last he confessed his crime. He was converted. He wrote to the court himself that he was a monster, but that in the end God had vouchsafed him light and shown grace. All Geneva was in excitement about him—all philanthropic and religious Geneva. All the aristocratic and well-bred society of the town rushed to the prison, kissed Richard and embraced him: 'You are our brother, you have found grace.' And Richard does nothing but weep with emotion, 'Yes, I've found grace! All my youth and childhood I was glad to have pigs' food, but now even I have found grace. I am dying in the Lord.' 'Yes, Richard, die in the Lord; you have shed blood and must die. Though it's not your fault that you knew not the Lord, when you coveted the pigs' food and were beaten for stealing it (which was very wrong of you, for stealing is forbidden); but you've shed blood and you must die.' And on the last day, Richard, perfectly limp, did nothing but cry and repeat every minute: 'This is my happiest day. I am going to the Lord.' 'Yes,' cry the pastors and the judges and philanthropic ladies. 'This is the happiest day of your life, for you are going to the Lord!' They all work or drive to the scaffold in procession behind the prison van. At the scaffold they call to Richard: 'Die, brother, die in the Lord, for even thou hast found grace!' And so, covered with his brothers' kisses, Richard is dragged onto the scaffold, and led to the guillotine. And they chopped off his head in brotherly fashion, because he had found grace. Yes, that's characteristic. That pamphlet is translated into Russian by some Russian philanthropists of aristocratic rank and evangelical aspirations, and has been distributed gratis for the enlightenment of the people. The case of Richard is interesting because it's national. Though to us it's absurd to cut off a man's head, because he has become our brother and has found grace, yet we have our own specialty, which is all but worse. Our historical pastime is the direct satisfaction of inflicting pain. There are lines in Nekrassov describing how a peasant lashes a horse on the eyes, 'on its meek eyes'; everyone must have seen it. It's peculiarly Russian. He describes how a feeble little nag had foundered under too heavy a load and cannot move. The peasant beats it, beats it savagely, beats it at last not knowing what he is doing in the intoxication of cruelty, thrashes it mercilessly over and over again. 'However weak you are, you must pull, if you die for it.' The nag strains, and he begins lashing the poor defenseless creature on its weeping, on its 'meek eyes.' The frantic beast tugs and draws the load, trembling all over, gasping for breath, moving sideways, with a sort of unnatural spasmodic action—it's awful in Nekrassov. But that's only a horse, and God has given horses to be beaten. So the Tatars have taught us, and they left us the knout as a rememberance of it. But men, too, can be beaten. A well-educated, cultured gentleman and his wife beat their own child with a birchrod, a girl of seven. I have an exact account of it. The papa was glad that the birch was covered with twigs. 'It stings more,' said he, and so he began stinging his daughter. I know for a fact there are people who at every blow are worked up to sensuality, to literal sensuality, which increases progressively at every blow they inflict. They beat for a minute, for five minutes, for ten minutes, more often and more savagely. The child screams. At last the child cannot scream, it gasps, 'Daddy! daddy!' By some diabolical unseemly chance the case was brought into court. A counsel was engaged. The Russian people have long called a barrister 'a conscience for hire.' The counsel protests in his client's defense. 'It's such a simple thing,' he says, 'an everyday domestic event. A father corrects his child. To our shame be it said, it is brought into court.' The jury, convinced by him, gives a favorable verdict. The public roars with delight that the torturer is acquitted. Ah, pity I wasn't there! I would have proposed to raise a subscription in his honor! ... Charming pictures.

"But I've still better things about children. I've collected a great, great deal about Russian children, Alyosha. There was a little girl of five who was hated by her father and mother, 'most worthy and respectable people, of good education and breeding.' You see, I must repeat again, it is a peculiar characteristic of many people, this love of torturing children, and children only. To all other types of humanity these torturers behave mildly and benevolently like cultivated and humane Europeans; but they are very fond of tormenting children, even fond of children themselves in that sense. It's just their defenselessness that tempts the tormentor, just the angelic confidence of the child who has no refuge and no appeal that sets his vile blood on fire. In every man, of course, a demon lies hidden—the demon of rage, the demon of lustful heat at the screams of the tortured victim, the demon of lawlessness let off the chain, the demon of diseases that follow on vice, gout, kidney disease, and so on.

"This poor child of five was subjected to every possible torture by those cultivated parents. They beat her, thrashed her, kicked her for no reason till her body was one bruise. Then, they went to greater refinements of cruelty—shut her up all night in the cold and frost in a privy, and because she didn't ask to be taken up at night (as though a child of five sleeping its angelic, sound sleep could be trained to wake and ask), they smeared her face and filled her mouth with excrement, and it was her mother, her mother did this. And that mother could sleep, hearing the poor child's groans! Can you understand why a little creature, who can't even understand what's done to her, should beat her little aching heart with her tiny fist in the dark and the cold, and weep her meek unresentful tears to dear, kind God to protect her? Do you understand that, friend and brother, you pious and humble novice? Do you understand why this infamy must be and is permitted? Without it, I am told, man could not have existed on earth, for he could not have known good and evil. Why should he know that diabolical good and evil when it costs so much? Why, the whole world of knowledge is not worth that child's prayer to 'dear, kind God'! I say nothing of the sufferings of grown-up people, they have eaten the apple, damn them, and the devil take them all! But these little ones! I am making you suffer, Alyosha, you are not yourself. I'll leave off it if you like."

"Never mind. I want to suffer too," muttered Alyosha.

"One picture, only one more, because it's so curious, so characteristic, and I have only just read it in some collection of Russian antiquities. I've forgotten the name. I must look it up. It was in the darkest days of serfdom at the beginning of the century, and long live the Liberator of the People! There was in those days a general of aristocratic connections, the owner of great estates, one of those men—somewhat exceptional, I believe, even then—who, retiring from the service into a life of leisure, are convinced that they've earned absolute power over the lives of the subjects. There were such men then. So our general, settled on his property of two thousand souls, lives in pomp, and domineers over his poor neighbors as though they were dependents and buffoons. He has kennels of hundreds of hounds and nearly a hundred dog-boys—all mounted, and in uniform. One day a serf boy, a little child of eight, threw a stone in play and hurt the paw of the general's favorite hound. 'Why is my favorite dog lame?' He is told that the boy threw a stone that hurt the dog's paw. 'So you did it.' The general looked the child up and down. 'Take him.' He was taken—taken from his mother and kept shut up all night. Early that morning the general comes out on horseback, with the hounds, his dependents, dog-boys, and huntsmen, all mounted around him in full hunting parade. The servants are summoned for their edification, and in front of them all stands the mother of the child. The child is brought from the lockup. It's a gloomy, cold, foggy autumn day, a capital day for hunting. The general orders the child to be undressed; the child is stripped naked. He shivers, numb with terror, not daring to cry...'Make him run,' commands the general. 'Run! run!' shout the dog-boys. The boy runs...'At him!' yells the general, and he sets the whole pack of hounds on the child. The hounds catch him, and tear him to pieces before

his mother's eyes!...I believe the general was afterwards declared incapable of administering his estates. Well—what did he deserve? To be shot? To be shot for the satisfaction of our moral feelings? Speak, Alyosha!"

"To be shot," murmured Alyosha, lifting his eyes to Ivan with a pale, twisted smile.

"Bravo!" cried Ivan delighted. "If even you say so...You're a pretty monk! So there is a little devil sitting in your heart. Alyosha Karamazov!"

"What I said was absurd, but—"

"That's just the point that 'but'!" cried Ivan. "Let me tell you, novice, that the absurd is only too necessary on earth. The world stands on absurdities, and perhaps nothing would have come to pass in it without them. We know what we know!"

"What do you know?"

"I understand nothing," Ivan went on, as though in delirium. "I don't want to understand anything now. I want to stick to the fact. I made up my mind long ago not to understand. If I try to understand anything, I shall be false to the fact and I have determined to stick to the fact."

"Why are you trying me?" Alyosha cried, with sudden distress. "Will you say what you mean at last?"

"Of course, I will; that's what I've been leading up to. You are dear to me, I don't want to let you go, and I won't give you up to your Zossima [priest, Father]."

Ivan for a minute was silent, his face became all at once very sad.

"Listen! I took the case of children only to make my case clearer. Of the other tears of humanity with which the earth is soaked from its crust to its center, I will say nothing. I have narrowed my subject on purpose, I am a bug, and I recognize in all humility that I cannot understand why the world is arranged as it is. Men are themselves to blame, I suppose; they were given paradise, they wanted freedom, and stole fire from heaven, though they knew they would become unhappy, so there is no need to pity them. With my pitiful, earthly, Euclidean understanding, all I know is that there is suffering and that there are none guilty; that cause follows effect, simply and directly; that everything flows and finds its level—but that's only

Euclidean nonsense, I know that, and I can't consent to live by it! What comfort is to me that there are none guilty and that cause follows effect simply and directly, and that I know it—I must have justice, or I will destroy myself. And not justice in some remote infinite time and space, but here on earth, and that I could see myself. I have believed in it. I want to see it, and if I am dead by then, let me rise again, for if it all happens without me, it will be too unfair. Surely I haven't suffered, simply that I, my crimes and my sufferings, may manure the soil of the future harmony for somebody else. I want to see with my own eyes the hind lie down with the lion and the victim rise up and embrace his murderer. I want to be there when everyone suddenly understands what it has all been for. All the religions of the world are built on this longing, and I am a believer. But there are the children, and what am I to do about them? That's a question I can't answer. For the hundredth time I repeat, there are numbers of questions, but I've only taken the children, because in their case what I mean is so unanswerably clear. Listen! If all must suffer to pay for the eternal harmony, what have children to do with it, tell me, please? It's beyond all comprehension why they should suffer, and why they should pay for the harmony. Why should they, too, furnish material to enrich the soil for the harmony of the future? I understand solidarity in sin among men. I understand solidarity in retribution, too; but there can be no such solidarity with children. And if it is really true that they must share responsibility for all their father's crimes, such a truth is not of this world and is beyond my comprehension. Some jester will say, perhaps, that the child would have grown up and have sinned, but you see he didn't grow up, he was torn to pieces by the dogs, at eight years old. Oh, Alyosha, I am not blaspheming! I understand, of course, what an upheaval of the universe it will be, when everything in heaven and earth blends in one hymn of praise and everything that lives and has lived cries aloud: 'Thou art just, O Lord, for Thy ways are revealed.' When the mother embraces the fiend who threw her child to the dogs, and all three cry aloud with

tears, 'Thou are just, O Lord!' then, of course, the crown of knowledge will be reached and all will be made clear. But what pulls me up here is that I can't accept that harmony. And while I am on earth, I make haste to take my own measures. You see, Alyosha, perhaps it really may happen that if I live to that moment, or rise again to see it, I, too, perhaps, may cry aloud with the rest, looking at the mother embracing the child's torturer, 'Thou are just, O Lord!' but I don't want to cry aloud then. While there is still time, I hasten to protect myself and so I renounce the higher harmony altogether. It's not worth the tears of that one tortured child who beat itself on the breast with its little fist and prayed in its stinking outhouse with an unexpiated tear to 'dear, kind God'! It's not worth it, because those tears are unatoned for. They must be atoned for, or there can be no harmony. But how? How are you going to atone for them? Is it possible? By their being avenged? But what do I care for avenging them? What do I care for a hell for oppressors? What good can hell do, since those children have already been tortured? And what becomes of harmony, if there is hell? I want to forgive. I want to embrace. I don't want more suffering. And if the sufferings of children go to swell the sum of sufferings which was necessary to pay for truth, then I protest that the truth is not worth such a price. I don't want the mother to embrace the oppressor who threw her son to the dogs! She dare not forgive him! Let her forgive him for herself, if she will, let her forgive the torturer for the immeasurable suffering of her mother's heart. But the sufferings of her tortured child she has no right to forgive; she dare not forgive the torturer, even if the child were to forgive him! And if that is so, if they dare not forgive, what becomes of harmony? Is there in the whole world a being who would have the right to forgive and could forgive? I don't want harmony. From love for humanity I don't want it. I would rather be left with the unavenged suffering. I would rather remain with my unavenged suffering and unsatisfied indignation, *even if I were wrong*. Besides, too high a price is asked for harmony; it's beyond our means to pay so much to enter on it. And so I hasten to give back my entrance ticket, and if I am an honest man I am bound to give it back as soon as possible. And that I am doing. It's not God that I don't accept, Alyosha, only I most respectfully return Him the ticket."

"That's rebellion," murmured Alyosha, looking down.

"Rebellion? I am sorry you call it that," said Ivan earnestly. "One can hardly live in rebellion, and I want to live. Tell me yourself, I challenge you—answer. Imagine that you are creating a fabric of human destiny with the object of making men happy in the end, giving them peace and rest at last, but that it was essential and inevitable to torture to death only one tiny creature—that baby beating its breast with its fist, for instance—and to found that edifice on its unavenged tears, would you consent to be the architect on those conditions? Tell me, and tell the truth."

"No, I wouldn't consent," said Alyosha softly. . . .

Evil and Omnipotence

J. L. MACKIE

J. L. Mackie (1917–1983) taught philosophy at University College, Oxford.

The traditional arguments for the existence of God have been fairly thoroughly criticized by philosophers. But the theologian can, if he wishes, accept this criticism. He can admit that no rational proof of God's existence is possible. And he can still retain all that is essential to his position, by holding that God's existence is known in some other, nonrational way. I think, however, that a more telling criticism can be made by way of the traditional problem of evil. Here it can be shown, not that religious beliefs lack rational support, but that they are positively irrational, that the several parts of the essential theological doctrine are inconsistent with one another, so that the theologian can maintain his position as a whole only by a much more extreme rejection of reason than in the former case. He must now be prepared to believe, not merely what cannot be proved, but what can be *disproved* from other beliefs that he also holds.

The problem of evil, in the sense in which I shall be using the phrase, is a problem only for someone who believes that there is a God who is both omnipotent and wholly good. And it is a logical problem, the problem of clarifying and reconciling a number of beliefs: it is not a scientific problem that might be solved by further observations, or a practical problem that might be solved by a decision or an action. These points are obvious; I mention them only because they are sometimes ignored by theologians, who sometimes parry a statement of the problem with such remarks as "Well, can you solve the problem yourself?" or "This is a mystery which may be revealed to us later" or "Evil is something to be faced and overcome, not to be merely discussed."

In its simplest form the problem is this: God is omnipotent; God is wholly good; and yet evil exists. There seems to be some contradiction between these three propositions, so that if any two of them were true the third would be false. But at the same time all three are essential parts of most theological positions: the theologian, it seems, at once *must* adhere and *cannot consistently* adhere to all three. (The problem does not arise only for theists, but I shall discuss it in

From *Mind*, Vol. LXIV, No. 254 (1955). Reprinted by permission of Oxford University Press.

the form in which it presents itself for ordinary theism.)

However, the contradiction does not arise immediately; to show it we need some additional premises, or perhaps some quasi-logical rules connecting the terms "good," "evil," and "omnipotent." These additional principles are that good is opposed to evil, in such a way that a good thing always eliminates evil as far as it can, and that there are no limits to what an omnipotent thing can do. From these it follows that a good omnipotent thing eliminates evil completely, and then the propositions that a good omnipotent thing exists, and that evil exists, are incompatible.

ADEQUATE SOLUTIONS

Now once the problem is fully stated it is clear that it can be solved, in the sense that the problem will not arise if one gives up at least one of the propositions that constitute it. If you are prepared to say that God is not wholly good, or not quite omnipotent, or that evil does not exist, or that good is not opposed to the kind of evil that exists, or that there are limits to what an omnipotent thing can do, then the problem of evil will not arise for you.

There are, then, quite a number of adequate solutions of the problem of evil, and some of these have been adopted, or almost adopted, by various thinkers. For example, a few have been prepared to deny God's omnipotence, and rather more have been prepared to keep the term "omnipotence" but severely to restrict its meaning, recording quite a number of things that an omnipotent being cannot do. Some have said that evil is an illusion, perhaps because they held that the whole world of temporal, changing things is an illusion, and that what we call evil belongs only to this world, or perhaps because they held that although temporal things *are* much as we see them, those that we call evil are not really evil. Some have said that what we call evil is merely the privation of good, that evil in a positive sense, evil that would really be opposed to good, does not exist. Many have agreed with Pope that disorder is harmony not understood, and that partial evil is universal good. Whether any of these views is *true* is, of course, another

question. But each of them gives an adequate solution of the problem of evil in the sense that if you accept it this problem does not arise for you, though you may, of course, have *other* problems to face.

But often enough these adequate solutions are only *almost* adopted. The thinkers who restrict God's power, but keep the term "omnipotence," may reasonably be suspected of thinking, in other contexts, that his power is really unlimited. Those who say that evil is an illusion may also be thinking, inconsistently, that this illusion is itself an evil. Those who say that "evil" is merely privation of good may also be thinking, inconsistently, that privation of good is an evil. If Pope meant what he said in the first line of his couplet, that "disorder" is only harmony not understood, the "partial evil" of the second line must, for consistency, mean "that which, taken in isolation, falsely appears to be evil," but it would more naturally mean "that which, in isolation, really is evil." The second line, in fact, hesitates between two views, that "partial evil" isn't really evil, since only the universal quality is real, and that "partial evil" is really an evil, but only a little one.

In addition, therefore, to adequate solutions, we must recognize unsatisfactory inconsistent solutions, in which there is only a half-hearted or temporary rejection of one of the propositions which together constitute the problem. In these, one of the constituent propositions is explicitly rejected, but it is covertly reasserted or assumed elsewhere in the system.

FALLACIOUS SOLUTIONS

Besides these half-hearted solutions, which explicitly reject but implicitly assert one of the constituent propositions, there are definitely fallacious solutions which explicitly maintain all the constituent propositions, but implicitly reject at least one of them in the course of the argument that explains away the problem of evil.

There are, in fact, many so-called solutions which purport to remove the contradiction without abandoning any of its constituent propositions. These must be fallacious, as we can see from the very statement of the problem, but it is not so easy to see in each case precisely where the fallacy lies. I suggest that in all cases the fallacy has the general form suggested above: in order to solve the problem one (or perhaps more) of its constituent propositions is given up, but in such a way that it appears to have been retained, and can therefore be asserted without qualification in other contexts. Sometimes there is a further complication: the supposed solution moves to and fro between, say, two of the constituent propositions, at one point asserting the first of these but covertly abandoning the second, at another point asserting the second but covertly abandoning the first. These fallacious solutions often turn upon some equivocation with the words "good" and "evil," or upon some vagueness about the way in which good and evil are opposed to one another, or about how much is meant by "omnipotence." I propose to examine some of these so-called solutions, and to exhibit their fallacies in detail. Incidentally, I shall also be considering whether an adequate solution could be reached by a minor modification of one or more of the constituent propositions, which would, however, still satisfy all the essential requirements of ordinary theism.

1. "Good cannot exist without evil" or "Evil is necessary as a counterpart to good."

It is sometimes suggested that evil is necessary as a counterpart to good, that if there were no evil there could be no good either, and that this solves the problem of evil. It is true that it points to an answer to the question "Why should there be evil?" But it does so only by qualifying some of the propositions that constitute the problem.

First, it sets a limit to what God can do, saying that God *cannot* create good without simultaneously creating evil, and this means either that God is not omnipotent or that there are *some* limits to what an omnipotent thing can do. It may be replied that these limits are always presupposed, that omnipotence has never meant the power to do what is logically impossible, and on the present view the existence of good without evil would be a logical impossibility. This interpretation of omnipotence may, indeed, be accepted as a modification

of our original account which does not reject anything that is essential to theism, and I shall in general assume it in the subsequent discussion. It is, perhaps, the most common theistic view, but I think that some theists at least have maintained that God can do what is logically impossible. Many theists, at any rate, have held that logic itself is created or laid down by God, that logic is the way in which God arbitrarily chooses to think. (This is, of course, parallel to the ethical view that morally right actions are those which God arbitrarily chooses to command, and the two views encounter similar difficulties.) And *this* account of logic is clearly inconsistent with the view that God is bound by logical necessities—unless it is possible for an omnipotent being to bind himself, an issue which we shall consider later, when we come to the Paradox of Omnipotence. This solution of the problem of evil cannot, therefore, be consistently adopted along with the view that logic is itself created by God.

But, secondly, this solution denies that evil is opposed to good in our original sense. If good and evil are counterparts, a good thing will not "eliminate evil as far as it can." Indeed, this view suggests that good and evil are not strictly qualities of things at all. Perhaps the suggestion is that good and evil are related in much the same way as great and small. Certainly, when the term "great" is used relatively as a condensation of "greater than so-and-so," and "small" is used correspondingly, greatness and smallness are counterparts and cannot exist without each other. But in this sense greatness is not a quality, not an intrinsic feature of anything; and it would be absurd to think of a movement in favor of greatness and against smallness in this sense. Such a movement would be self-defeating, since relative greatness can be promoted only by a simultaneous promotion of relative smallness. I feel sure that no theists would be content to regard God's goodness as analogous to this—as if what he supports were not the *good* but the *better*, and as if he had the paradoxical aim that all things should be better than other things.

This point is obscured by the fact that "great" and "small" seem to have an absolute as well as a relative sense. I cannot discuss here whether there is absolute magnitude or not, but if there is, there could be an absolute sense for "great," it could mean of at least a certain size, and it would make sense to speak of all things getting bigger, of a universe that was expanding all over, and therefore it would make sense to speak of promoting greatness. But in *this* sense great and small are not logically necessary counterparts: either quality could exist without the other. There would be no logical impossibility in everything's being small or in everything's being great.

Neither in the absolute nor in the relative sense, then, of "great" and "small" do these terms provide an analogy of the sort that would be needed to support this solution of the problem of evil. In neither case are greatness and smallness *both* necessary counterparts *and* mutually opposed forces or possible objects for support and attack.

It may be replied that good and evil are necessary counterparts in the same way as any quality and its logical opposite: redness can occur, it is suggested, only if nonredness also occurs. But unless evil is merely the privation of good, they are not logical opposites, and some further argument would be needed to show that they are counterparts in the same way as genuine logical opposites. Let us assume that this could be given. There is still doubt of the correctness of the metaphysical principle that a quality must have a real opposite: I suggest that it is not really impossible that everything should be, say, red, that the truth is merely that if everything were red we should not notice redness, and so we should have no word "red"; we observe and give names to qualities only if they have real opposites. If so, the principle that a term must have an opposite would belong only to our language or to our thought, and would not be an ontological principle, and, correspondingly, the rule that good cannot exist without evil would not state a logical necessity of a sort that God would just have to put up with. God might have made everything good, though *we* should not have noticed it if he had.

But, finally, even if we concede that this *is* an ontological principle, it will provide a solution for the problem of evil only if one is prepared to say, "Evil exists, but only just enough evil to serve as

the counterpart of good." I doubt whether any theist will accept this. After all, the *ontological* requirement that nonredness should occur would be satisfied even if all the universe, except for a minute speck, were red, and, if there were a corresponding requirement for evil as a counterpart to good, a minute dose of evil would presumably do. But theists are not usually willing to say, in all contexts, that all the evil that occurs is a minute and necessary dose.

2. "Evil is necessary as a means to good."

It is sometimes suggested that evil is necessary for good not as a counterpart but as a means. In its simple form this has little plausibility as a solution of the problem of evil, since it obviously implies a severe restriction of God's power. It would be a *causal* law that you cannot have a certain end without a certain means, so that if God has to introduce evil as a means to good, he must be subject to at least some causal laws. This certainly conflicts with what a theist normally means by omnipotence. This view of God as limited by causal laws also conflicts with the view that causal laws are themselves made by God, which is more widely held than the corresponding view about the laws of logic. This conflict would, indeed, be resolved if it were possible for an omnipotent being to bind himself, and this possibility has still to be considered. Unless a favorable answer can be given to this question, the suggestion that evil is necessary as a means to good solves the problem of evil only by denying one of its constituent propositions, either that God is omnipotent or that "omnipotent" means what it says.

3. "The universe is better with some evil in it than it could be if there were no evil."

Much more important is a solution which at first seems to be a mere variant of the previous one, that evil may contribute to the goodness of a whole in which it is found, so that the universe as a whole is better as it is, with some evil in it, than it would be if there were no evil. This solution may be developed in either of two ways. It may be supported by an aesthetic analogy, by the fact that contrasts heighten beauty, that in a musical work, for example, there may occur discords which somehow add to the beauty of the work as a whole. Alternatively, it may be worked out in connection with the notion of progress, that the best possible organization of the universe will not be static, but progressive, that the gradual overcoming of evil by good is really a finer thing than would be the eternal unchallenged supremacy of good.

In either case, this solution usually starts from the assumption that the evil whose existence gives rise to the problem of evil is primarily what is called physical evil, that is to say, pain. In Hume's rather half-hearted presentation of the problem of evil, the evils that he stresses are pain and disease, and those who reply to him argue that the existence of pain and disease makes possible the existence of sympathy, benevolence, heroism, and the gradually successful struggle of doctors and reformers to overcome these evils. In fact, theists often seize the opportunity to accuse those who stress the problem of evil of taking a low, materialistic view of good and evil, equating these with pleasure and pain, and of ignoring the more spiritual goods which can arise in the struggle against evils.

But let us see exactly what is being done here. Let us call pain and misery "first order evil" or "evil (1)." What contrasts with this, namely, pleasure and happiness, will be called "first order good" or "good (1)." Distinct from this is "second order good" or "good (2)" which somehow emerges in a complex situation in which evil (1) is a necessary component—logically, not merely causally, necessary. (Exactly *how* it emerges does not matter: in the crudest version of this solution good (2) is simply the heightening of happiness by the contrast with misery, in other versions it includes sympathy with suffering, heroism in facing danger, and the gradual decrease of first order evil and increase of first order good.) It is also being assumed that second order good is more important than first order good or evil, in particular that it more than outweighs the first order evil it involves.

Now this is a particularly subtle attempt to solve the problem of evil. It defends God's goodness and omnipotence on the ground that (on a sufficiently long view) this is the best of all logically possible worlds because it includes

the important second order goods, and yet it admits that real evils, namely first order evils, exist. But does it still hold that good and evil are opposed? Not, clearly, in the sense that we set out originally: good does not tend to eliminate evil in general. Instead, we have a modified, a more complex pattern. First order good (e.g., happiness) *contrasts with* first order evil (e.g., misery): these two are opposed in a fairly mechanical way; some second order goods (e.g., benevolence) try to maximize first order good and minimize first order evil; but God's goodness is not this, it is rather the will to maximize *second* order good. We might, therefore, call God's goodness an example of a third order goodness, or good (3). While this account is different from our original one, it might well be held to be an improvement on it, to give a more accurate description of the way in which good is opposed to evil, and to be consistent with the essential theist position.

There might, however, be several objections to this solution.

First, some might argue that such qualities as benevolence—and *a fortiori* the third order goodness which promotes benevolence—have a merely derivative value, that they are not higher sorts of good, but merely means to good (1), that is, to happiness, so that it would be absurd for God to keep misery in existence in order to make possible the virtues of benevolence, heroism, etc. The theist who adopts the present solution must, of course, deny this, but he can do so with some plausibility, so I should not press this objection.

Secondly, it follows from this solution that God is not in our sense benevolent or sympathetic: he is not concerned to minimize evil (1), but only to promote good (2); and this might be a disturbing conclusion for some theists.

But, thirdly, the fatal objection is this. Our analysis shows clearly the possibility of the existence of a *second* order evil, an evil (2) contrasting with good (2) as evil (1) contrasts with good (1). This would include malevolence, cruelty, callousness, cowardice, and states in which good (1) is decreasing and evil (1) increasing. And just as good (2) is held to be the important kind of good, the kind that God is concerned to promote, so evil (2) will, by analogy, be the important kind of evil, the kind which God, if he were wholly good and omnipotent, would eliminate. And yet evil (2) plainly exists, and indeed most theists (in other contexts) stress its existence more than that of evil (1). We should, therefore, state the problem of evil in terms of second order evil, and against this form of the problem the present solution is useless.

An attempt might be made to use this solution again, at a higher level, to explain the occurrence of evil (2): indeed the next main solution that we shall examine does just this, with the help of some new notions. Without any fresh notions, such a solution would have little plausibility: for example, we could hardly say that the really important good was a good (3), such as the increase of benevolence in proportion to cruelty, which logically required for its occurrence the occurrence of some second order evil. But even if evil (2) could be explained in this way, it is fairly clear that there would be third order evils contrasting with this third order good: and we should be well on the way to an infinite regress, where the solution of a problem of evil, stated in terms of evil (*n*), indicated the existence of an evil (*n* + 1), and a further problem to be solved.

4. "Evil is due to human free will."

Perhaps the most important proposed solution of the problem of evil is that evil is not to be ascribed to God at all, but to the independent actions of human beings, supposed to have been endowed by God with freedom of the will. This solution may be combined with the preceding one: first order evil (e.g., pain) may be justified as a logically necessary component in second order good (e.g., sympathy) while second order evil (e.g., cruelty) is not *justified,* but is so ascribed to human beings that God cannot be held responsible for it. This combination evades my third criticism of the preceding solution.

The free-will solution also involves the preceding solution at a higher level. To explain why a wholly good God gave men free will although it would lead to some important evils, it must be argued that it is better on the whole that men should act freely, and sometimes err,

than that they should be innocent automata, acting rightly in a wholly determined way. Freedom, that is to say, is now treated as a third order good, and as being more valuable than second order goods (such as sympathy and heroism) would be if they were deterministically produced, and it is being assumed that second order evils, such as cruelty, are logically necessary accompaniments of freedom, just as pain is a logically necessary pre-condition of sympathy.

I think that this solution is unsatisfactory primarily because of the incoherence of the notion of freedom of the will: but I cannot discuss this topic adequately here, although some of my criticisms will touch upon it.

First I should query the assumption that second order evils are logically necessary accompaniments of freedom. I should ask this: if God has made men such that in their free choices they sometimes prefer what is good and sometimes what is evil, why could he not have made men such that they always freely choose the good? If there is no logical impossibility in a man's freely choosing the good on one, or on several occasions, there cannot be a logical impossibility in his freely choosing the good on every occasion. God was not, then, faced with a choice between making innocent automata and making beings who, in acting freely, would sometimes go wrong: there was open to him the obviously better possibility of making beings who would act freely but always go right. Clearly, his failure to avail himself of this possibility is inconsistent with his being both omnipotent and wholly good.

If it is replied that this objection is absurd, that the making of some wrong choices is logically necessary for freedom, it would seem that "freedom" must here mean complete randomness or indeterminacy, including randomness with regard to the alternatives good and evil, in other words that men's choices and consequent actions can be "free" only if they are not determined by their characters. Only on this assumption can God escape the responsibility for men's actions; for if he made them as they are, but did not determine their wrong choices, this can only be because the wrong choices are not determined by men as they are. But then if freedom is randomness, how can it be a characteristic of *will*? And, still more, how can it be the most important good? What value or merit would there be in free choices if these were random actions which were not determined by the nature of the agent?

I conclude that to make this solution plausible two different senses of "freedom" must be confused, one sense which will justify the view that freedom is a third order good, more valuable than other goods would be without it, and another sense, sheer randomness, to prevent us from ascribing to God a decision to make men such that they some-times go wrong when he might have made them such that they would always freely go right.

This criticism is sufficient to dispose of this solution. But besides this there is a fundamental difficulty in the notion of an omnipotent God creating men with free will, for if men's wills are really free this must mean that even God cannot control them, that is, that God is no longer omnipotent. It may be objected that God's gift of freedom to men does not mean that he *cannot* control their wills, but that he always *refrains* from controlling their wills. But why, we may ask, should God refrain from controlling evil wills? Why should he not leave men free to will rightly, but intervene when he sees them beginning to will wrongly? If God could do this, but does not, and if he is wholly good, the only explanation could be that even a wrong free act of will is not really evil, that its freedom is a value which outweighs its wrongness, so that there would be a loss of value if God took away the wrongness and the freedom together. But this is utterly opposed to what theists say about sin in other contexts. The present solution of the problem of evil, then, can be maintained only in the form that God has made men so free that he *cannot* control their wills.

This leads us to what I call the Paradox of Omnipotence: can an omnipotent being make things which he cannot subsequently control? Or, what is practically equivalent to this, can an omnipotent being make rules which then bind himself? (These are practically equivalent because any such rules could be regarded as setting certain things beyond his control, and *vice versa*.) The second of these formulations is relevant to the

suggestions that we have already met, that an omnipotent God creates the rules of logic or causal laws, and is then bound by them.

It is clear that this is a paradox: the questions cannot be answered satisfactorily either in the affirmative or in the negative. If we answer "Yes," it follows that if God actually makes things which he cannot control, or makes rules which bind himself, he is not omnipotent once he has made them: there are *then* things which he cannot do. But if we answer "No," we are immediately asserting that there are things which he cannot do, that is to say that he is already not omnipotent.

It cannot be replied that the question which sets this paradox is not a proper question. It would make perfectly good sense to say that a human mechanic has made a machine which he cannot control: if there is any difficulty about the question it lies in the notion of omnipotence itself.

This, incidentally, shows that although we have approached this paradox from the free-will theory, it is equally a problem for a theological determinist. No one thinks that machines have free will, yet they may well be beyond the control of their makers. The determinist might reply that anyone who makes anything determines its ways of acting, and so determines its subsequent behavior: even the human mechanic does this by his *choice* of materials and structure for his machine, though he does not know all about either of these: the mechanic thus determines, though he may not foresee, his machine's actions. And since God is omniscient, and since his creation of things is total, he both determines and foresees the ways in which his creatures will act. We may grant this, but it is beside the point. The question is not whether God *originally* determined the future actions of his creatures, but whether he can *subsequently* control their actions, or whether he was able in his original creation to put things beyond his subsequent control. Even on determinist principles the answers "Yes" and "No" are equally irreconcilable with God's omnipotence.

Before suggesting a solution of this paradox, I would point out that there is a parallel Paradox of Sovereignty. Can a legal sovereign make a law restricting its own future legislative power? For example, could the British parliament make a law forbidding any future parliament to socialize banking, and also forbidding the future repeal of this law itself? Or could the British parliament, which was legally sovereign in Australia in, say, 1899, pass a valid law, or series of laws, which made it no longer sovereign in 1933? Again, neither the affirmative nor the negative answer is really satisfactory. If we were to answer "Yes," we should be admitting the validity of a law which, if it were actually made, would mean that parliament was no longer sovereign. If we were to answer "No," we should be admitting that there is a law, not logically absurd, which parliament cannot validly make, that is, that parliament is not now a legal sovereign. This paradox can be solved in the following way. We should distinguish between first order laws, that is, laws governing the actions of individuals and bodies other than the legislature, and second order laws, that is, laws about laws, laws governing the actions of the legislature itself. Correspondingly, we should distinguish two orders of sovereignty, first order sovereignty (sovereignty [1]) which is unlimited authority to make first order laws, and second order sovereignty (sovereignty [2]) which is unlimited authority to make second order laws. If we say that parliament is sovereign we might mean that any parliament at any time has sovereignty (1), or we might mean that parliament has both sovereignty (1) and sovereignty (2) at present, but we cannot without contradiction mean both that the present parliament has sovereignty (2) and that every parliament at every time has sovereignty (1), for if the present parliament has sovereignty (2) it may use it to take away the sovereignty (1) of later parliaments. What the paradox shows is that we cannot ascribe to any continuing institution legal sovereignty in an inclusive sense.

The analogy between omnipotence and sovereignty shows that the paradox of omnipotence can be solved in a similar way. We must distinguish between first order omnipotence (omnipotence [1]), that is, unlimited power to act, and second order omnipotence (omnipotence [2]), that is, unlimited power to determine what powers to act things shall have. Then we could consistently say that God all the time has omnipotence (1), but if so no beings at any time have powers to act independently of God. Or we could say that God at one time had omnipotence (2), and used it to assign independent powers to act to certain things, so that God thereafter did not have omnipotence (1). But what the paradox shows is that we cannot consistently ascribe to any continuing being omnipotence in an inclusive sense.

An alternative solution of this paradox would be simply to deny that God is a continuing being, that any times can be assigned to his actions at all. But on this assumption (which also has difficulties of its own) no meaning can be given to the assertion that God made men with wills so free that he could not control them. The paradox of omnipotence can be avoided by putting God outside time, but the free-will solution of the problem of evil cannot be saved in this way, and equally it remains impossible to hold that an omnipotent God *binds himself* by causal or logical laws.

Conclusion

Of the proposed solutions of the problem of evil which we have examined, none has stood up to criticism. There may be other solutions which require examination, but this study strongly suggests that there is no valid solution of the problem which does not modify at least one of the constituent propositions in a way which would seriously affect the essential core of the theistic position.

Quite apart from the problem of evil, the paradox of omnipotence has shown that God's omnipotence must in any case be restricted in one way or another, that unqualified omnipotence cannot be ascribed to any being that continues through time. And if God and his actions are not in time, can omnipotence, or power of any sort, be meaningfully ascribed to him?

The Problem of Evil and the Problem of Suffering

GEORGE SCHLESINGER

George Schlesinger is professor emeritus at University of North Carolina, Chapel Hill. He has worked primarily in metaphysics, philosophy of science, and philosophy of religion.

I

The world is full of suffering; God is either helpless to prevent it, in which case He is not all-powerful, or does not choose to prevent it, in which case He is not all-good. It is not surprising that even after centuries of debate some should regard this as the most effective argument against theism, while others think of it as wholly ill conceived. Regardless of a philosopher's convictions, when considering a problem such as this, which touches upon vital issues like Divine omnipotence and providence, man's fate and freedom, he naturally finds it hard to keep to cool analysis untainted by his hopes and fears. However, even on the purely logical plane the problem has its unique difficulties, because it involves the highly elusive concept of infinity as applied to power and benevolence. I shall want to suggest that, in addition, the concept of infinity is involved, in a hitherto uncontemplated way, in the question of whether there is ineradicable evil, and that therein lies the key to the dissolution of the problem. But first I must clarify a number of points, and I propose to do so by considering very briefly some of the well-known arguments that have been employed in the context of our topic.

II

To begin, let us agree that the theist is not entitled to say: "I have no proof (because of my limited understanding) that omnipotence, benevolence, and the existence of evil are mutually compatible, but I have faith that they are, *just as* I have no proof that God exists but I have faith that He does." For it is not at all "just as." The "leap of faith" required in the former case is very different from that of the second, and this should not be overlooked. Lack of a proof that God exists can at most provide grounds for agnosticism; lack of a proof that the problem of evil has a solution, on the other hand, provides *prima facie* support for atheism. But nevertheless, if the theist merely says, "I have no solution for the problem of evil but I have faith it has a solution," then he commits no fallacy; he only puts himself into a logically weak position which a genuine suggestion for the solution of the problem could avoid.

The situation may be viewed as even worse with regard to the argument which maintains that Divine goodness is entirely different in kind from human goodness and should consequently not be judged in terms of notions formed on the basis of our acquaintance with the latter. Thus the fact that moral and physical evil seem to exist and to be condoned by Him should not be taken as a sign of deficiency in His goodness because His ways are inscrutable to limited human minds.

The obvious objection that may be raised against this is that we have no other notions of good and bad except those appertaining to human situations, where, for example, the condoning of unnecessary suffering is always condemned. Therefore, we must either be allowed—even

From *American Philosophical Quarterly* vol. 1 (1964). Reprinted with permission.

when talking about God—to use the only moral notions we have, or we cannot say anything meaningful on the subject. (There seems to be good ground for the atheist's complaint that if the theist does not choose the first alternative his position amounts to saying, "I do not know what I mean when I maintain that no evil can be attributed to God but I have faith that it means something significant," which is quite absurd. The atheist, on the other hand, can plausibly lay claim to a clear notion of what is morally wrong, namely, to cause or condone unnecessary human suffering, and thus has a notion of what it is to attribute such wrongs to God.)

A variation on the previous argument is the one which holds that it is wrong to say that evil is permitted to exist in the world, since, simply by definition, evil is that of which God does not approve and does not permit to exist. It seems obvious that, unless we have independent means of judging whether or not all of God's actions are good, the theist's claim that no moral imperfection can be attributed to Him is empty verbiage.

III

Some proposed solutions of the problem attempt to diminish or eliminate evil. At times it has been argued that there is far less suffering in the world than one would unreflectingly assume. Some have eloquently explained that pain is not additive and that there is thus no such thing as a "suffering humanity" transcending the individuals it consists of. Other exhort us (I) not to take for granted all the joy and moral beauty there is in the world which by far outstrips the amount of existing pain and moral ugliness, or argue (2) that all suffering ultimately brings about a greater good and should be viewed always as a preliminary to the latter.

It suffices to say that, while there is much wisdom in many of these arguments, they do not mitigate logically the problem we are facing. Multiply or divide the amount of pain in the world by a billion, and its incompatibility with Divine goodness and omnipotence is not affected. Were it that merely a single individual had to endure unnecessarily a slight inconvenience for a brief moment,

the problem—even though it would not "hurt" so much—would remain just as if everybody caused and endured suffering continually.

Another argument claims that there is no real, ineradicable evil because all suffering can be avoided. Sometimes it is claimed that the human soul has infinite resources and it is in the power of every individual to transcend pain and feel happy irrespective of his circumstances. It is not our concern here to examine the various assumptions involved in this argument—let it be conceded that each one of us has it in him to reach the peak of disinterested spirituality. It is still a fact that many people are unhappy, apparently, leaving their spiritual resources untapped out of ignorance or negligence. The skeptic may still pose the problem: Why are spiritual potentials allowed to go unrealized; why, even if there is no need, is it nevertheless possible to suffer?

Similarly, when it is said that suffering is always chastisement for transgressions, the skeptic may ask, apart from everything else, why have opportunities to sin been created? It may be the case that the reward for righteousness is incomparably greater than the punishment for wickedness, and that this reward tastes a thousand times sweeter now that there exists the possibility of sinning and being punished. However, the skeptic will go on urging, why not let human nature be different and man be made so as to be able to enjoy any amount of pleasure without needing a contrast?

IV

Another famous line of argument is to concede that evil exists, indeed necessarily so. If we had access to God's whole plan—it has been said— we might be able to appreciate that a given region of human experience, which, though in isolation looks ugly, viewed as a part of the entire pattern, enhances the over-all beauty and goodness of the whole. But even if the universe is much better because of having some evil in it and the same result could not otherwise be achieved, this is only so in the context of the existing laws of nature. Why did God not make nature's laws such that the amount of the advantages we enjoy should remain exactly the same as at present but there be no need to pay for it in pain?

There have also been many attempts to show that the necessity for the existence of evil is of the logical kind. Every person is the sum total of his experiences, it has been said, and it is therefore logically impossible that any given individual suffer less pain and anguish and enjoy more peace and happiness; for alter a man's experiences and you are no longer dealing with the same person. A more common and perhaps more serious attempt is based on the contention that a desirable quality, like the freedom of the will, for example, presupposes moral and physical evil (since by definition man's will is not free unless he can choose to do harm and creatures vulnerable to harm existed). It has also been maintained that there are other precious qualities like heroism which is analytically connected with danger, charity with want, compassion with pain, and hence it is logically impossible to have these desirable human traits without their unwanted prerequisites. We shall assume the reader is acquainted with arguments that have been produced to defeat these moves. For our purposes it does not matter if we also assume these arguments to be wholly effective. But we must note that in general they all lead to the conclusion that evil is only contingently but never logically necessary.

V

It has already been pointed out that if the world had been different and the amount of suffering in it had been a minute fraction only of what it is at present, this would have made great emotional, but no logical difference. It would seem that there exists a certain minimal level such that if the amount of suffering were reduced below it the problem of evil would not have occurred to anyone. Logically it would have been there just the same.

It should be added that even if no one ever experienced any pain or discomfort but some were deprived of positive happiness the problem would remain.

Taking once again our moral criterion from human affairs, if I have the opportunity to cause a person extreme happiness without harming anyone, without any expense or effort on my part, and I am aware of this, (even though *he* may not be) then if I refrain from doing so, I am morally reprehensible.

Thus, alter the world; diminish the amount of suffering until it vanishes altogether, and the problem remains: Why did not God make men much happier than they are?

Even the most satisfied man on earth could make up an endless list of requirements the fulfilment of which would increase his happiness. Thus it would not help if every individual was as happy as the happiest man. And even if everyone enjoyed such a state of supreme satisfaction, no longer asking for anything and claiming to have no unfulfilled desires, this would not show that God has discharged His "moral obligations" toward His creatures. For example, whether my dealings with *X* are beyond moral blame is not solely determined by the fact that *X* is completely satisfied. If *X* is a musically gifted child in my care whom I have provided with all his physical and emotional needs but whose musical education I have neglected, thus depriving him of a mode of enjoyment the possibility of which is wholly unknown to him, I am nevertheless blameworthy. Similarly a deity who is aware of the much greater possibilities for happiness that *could* be the lot of His creatures, but does not realize them, seems to be blameworthy irrespective of what these creatures think and feel.

There being no *prima facie* case for saying that the greater possibilities for happiness are finite, God's inability to create the greatest state of happiness is seen to be no different from his inability to create the greatest integer. Neither diminish His might, if we agree that He need not accomplish what is logically impossible. We cannot ask that He go against the laws of logic for we do not know what it is we are asking of Him; and when He does not do what is logically impossible, there just is no feat which we can say He failed to accomplish. (His inability to do what is logically impossible of course does not impair His omnipotence.)

What we have to conclude, therefore, is that the amount of pain and joy present in the world is entirely irrelevant and cannot be introduced as evidence concerning the moral nature of God. (There is of course scope left for investigating whether the question "Who (when and how), is happy or suffers?" may not provide a clue to the nature of Divine benevolence; but the mere fact of the presence of pain or joy in any amount points to nothing.)

The problem of evil arose originally because the proposition "God is omnipotent and no evil can be attributed to Him" and "There is a state of affairs in the world which a perfectly moral Being should not tolerate" are inconsistent. In order to do damage to the theist's position it was essential that the last proposition be thought of as based on observation. Evil has been observed in the world and this speaks against the belief in Divine goodness and omnipotence. In posing the problem, we made the implied assumption that the universe could be different from what it is now and then the problem would disappear. But now we have seen that—alter the universe as you wish—it does not affect the problem. It therefore does not arise in the first place.

The problem of evil disappears, then, because we have been shown that while the principle "It is morally wrong, when it does not interfere with the welfare of others, not to do as much as one *possibly can* to make others happy" may apply to humans, it *logically* cannot apply to an Omnipotent Being. (This of course does not amount to one of the attempts, considered briefly earlier, to solve the problem by suggesting there is an ineffable kind of evil, and it is of *this* that we are speaking when maintaining that no evil can be attributed to God. For here we are talking about a familiar notion of evil and show that for reasons perfectly unmysterious it cannot be present in the actions of God.)

We have, of course, provided absolutely no explanation why the world is not a much better place, and one may find this exceedingly frustrating. But no matter how much one may yearn for an explanation, the lack of it does not warrant a confusion between the problem of evil and the problem of suffering. True enough, if the theist is right there are many pertinent questions we may pose: Why is not everyone at least free from positive suffering? Or why is not everyone at least in a state of minimal happiness all the time (given a reasonable definition of "minimal" happiness)? But the possibility of posing these questions must not be construed as a possibility of questioning the theist's contention that evil is not to be attributed to God on grounds of the experienced character of the world we live in.

Why God Allows Evil

RICHARD SWINBURNE

Richard Swinburne is the Nolloth Professor of the Philosophy of The Christian Religion at the University of Oxford. He has done important work in metaphysics, epistemology, and the philosophy of religion.

This world is a clearly providential world in this sense—that we humans can have a great influence on our own destiny, and on the destiny of our world and its other inhabitants; and it is very good for us that it is like that. And yet animals and humans suffer (through natural processes of disease and accident), and they cause each other to suffer (we hurt and maim each other and cause each other to starve). The world, that is, contains much evil. An omnipotent God could have prevented this evil, and surely a perfectly good and omnipotent God would have done so.

From Richard Swinburne, *Is There A God?* pp. 95–113 (Oxford University Press, 1996). Reprinted by permission of Oxford University Press.

So why is there this evil? Is not its existence strong evidence against the existence of God? It would be unless we can construct what is known as a theodicy, an explanation of why God would allow such evil to occur. I believe that that can be done, and I shall outline a theodicy in this chapter. I emphasize that in . . . writing that God would do this or that, I am not taking for granted the existence of God, but merely claiming that, if there is a God, it is to be expected that he would do certain things, including allowing the occurrence of certain evils; and so, I am claiming, their occurrence is not evidence against his existence.

It is inevitable that any attempt by myself or anyone else to construct a theodicy will sound callous, indeed totally insensitive to human suffering. Many theists, as well as atheists, have felt that any attempt to construct a theodicy evinces an immoral approach to suffering. I can only ask the reader to believe that I am not totally insensitive to human suffering, and that I do mind about the agony of poisoning, child abuse, bereavement, solitary imprisonment, and marital infidelity as much as anyone else. True, I would not in most cases recommend that a pastor give this chapter to victims of sudden distress at their worst moment, to read for consolation. But this is not because its arguments are unsound; it is simply that most people in deep distress need comfort, not argument. Yet there is a problem about why God allows evil, and, if the theist does not have (in a cool moment) a satisfactory answer to it, then his belief in God is less than rational, and there is no reason why the atheist should share it. To appreciate the argument of this chapter, each of us needs to stand back a bit from the particular situation of his or her own life and that of close relatives and friends (which can so easily seem the only important thing in the world), and ask very generally what good things would a generous and everlasting God give to human beings in the course of a short earthly life. Of course thrills of pleasure and periods of contentment are good things, and—other things being equal—God would certainly seek to provide plenty of those. But a generous God will seek to give deeper good things than these. He will seek to give us great responsibility for ourselves, each other, and the world,

and thus a share in his own creative activity of determining what sort of world it is to be. And he will seek to make our lives valuable, of great use to ourselves and each other. The problem is that God cannot give us these goods in full measure without allowing much evil on the way.

The problem of evil is not that of the absence of various good states. We noted in Chapter 1[‡] that, however much good God creates, he could create more; and he does not in general have any obligation to create. That is why death is not in itself an evil; death is just the end of a good state, life (and in any case one of which God may choose to give us more—by giving us a life after death). Death may be an evil if it comes prematurely, or causes great grief to others; but in itself it is not an evil. But there are plenty of evils, positive bad states, which God could if he chose remove. I divide these into moral evils and natural evils. I understand by "natural evil" all evil which is not deliberately produced by human beings and which is not allowed by human beings to occur as a result of their negligence. Natural evil includes both physical suffering and mental suffering, of animals as well as humans; all the trail of suffering which disease, natural disasters, and accidents unpredictable by humans bring in their train. "Moral evil" I understand as including all evil caused deliberately by humans doing what they ought not to do (or allowed to occur by humans negligently failing to do what they ought to do) *and* also the evil constituted by such deliberate actions or negligent failure. It includes the sensory pain of the blow inflicted by the bad parent on his child, the mental pain of the parent depriving the child of love, the starvation allowed to occur in Africa because of negligence by members of foreign governments who could have prevented it, and also the evil of the parent or politician deliberately bringing about the pain or not trying to prevent the starvation.

MORAL EVIL

The central core of any theodicy must, I believe, be the "free-will defence", which deals—to start

---

*[Omitted here—Ed.]

with—with moral evil, but can be extended to deal with much natural evil as well. The free-will defence claims that it is a great good that humans have a certain sort of free will which I shall call free and responsible choice, but that, if they do, then necessarily there will be the natural possibility of moral evil. (By the "natural possibility" I mean that it will not be determined in advance whether or not the evil will occur.) A God who gives humans such free will necessarily brings about the possibility, and puts outside his own control whether or not that evil occurs. It is not logically possible—that is, it would be self-contradictory to suppose—that God could give us such free will and yet ensure that we always use it in the right way.

Free and responsible choice is not just free will in the narrow sense of being able to choose between alternative actions, without our choice being causally necessitated by some prior cause. I have urged, for the reasons given in the last chapter,[‡] that humans do have such free will. But humans could have that kind of free will merely in virtue of being able to choose freely between two equally good and unimportant alternatives. Free and responsible choice is rather free will (of the kind discussed) to make significant choices between good and evil, which make a big difference to the agent, to others, and to the world.

Given that we have free will, we certainly have free and responsible choice. Let us remind ourselves of the difference that humans can make to themselves, others, and the world. Humans have opportunities to give themselves and others pleasurable sensations, and to pursue worthwhile activities—to play tennis or the piano, to acquire knowledge of history and science and philosophy, and to help others to do so, and thereby to build deep personal relations founded upon such sensations and activities. And humans are so made that they can form their characters. Aristotle famously remarked: "we become just by doing just acts, prudent by doing prudent acts, brave by doing brave acts." That is, by doing a just act when it

is difficult—when it goes against our natural inclinations (which is what I understand by desires)—we make it easier to do a just act next time. We can gradually change our desires, so that—for example—doing just acts becomes natural. Thereby we can free ourselves from the power of the less good desires to which we are subject. And, by choosing to acquire knowledge and to use it to build machines of various sorts, humans can extend the range of the differences they can make to the world—they can build universities to last for centuries, or save energy for the next generation; and by cooperative effort over many decades they can eliminate poverty. The possibilities for free and responsible choice are enormous.

It is good that the free choices of humans should include *genuine* responsibility for other humans, and that involves the opportunity to benefit *or* harm them. God has the power to benefit or to harm humans. If other agents are to be given a share in his creative work, it is good that they have that power too (although perhaps to a lesser degree). A world in which agents can benefit each other but not do each other harm is one where they have only very limited responsibility for each other. If my responsibility for you is limited to whether or not to give you a camcorder, but I cannot cause you pain, stunt your growth, or limit your education, then I do not have a great deal of responsibility for you. A God who gave agents only such limited responsibilities for their fellows would not have given much. God would have reserved for himself the all-important choice of the kind of world it was to be, while simply allowing humans the minor choice of filling in the details. He would be like a father asking his elder son to look after the younger son, and adding that he would be watching the elder son's every move and would intervene the moment the elder son did a thing wrong. The elder son might justly retort that, while he would be happy to share his father's work, he could really do so only if he were left to make his own judgements as to what to do within a significant range of the options available to the father. A good God, like a good father, will delegate responsibility. In order to allow creatures a share in creation, he will allow them

---

*[Omitted here—Ed.]

the choice of hurting and maiming, of frustrating the divine plan. Our world is one where creatures have just such deep responsibility for each other. I can not only benefit my children, but harm them. One way in which I can harm them is that I can inflict physical pain on them. But there are much more damaging things which I can do to them. Above all I can stop them growing into creatures with significant knowledge, power, and freedom; I can determine whether they come to have the kind of free and responsible choice which I have. The possibility of humans bringing about significant evil is a logical consequence of their having this free and responsible choice. Not even God could give us this choice without the possibility of resulting evil.

Now . . . an action would not be intentional unless it was done for a reason—that is, seen as in some way a good thing (either in itself or because of its consequences). And, if reasons alone influence actions, that regarded by the subject as most important will determine what is done; an agent under the influence of reason alone will inevitably do the action which he regards as overall the best. If an agent does not do the action which he regards as overall the best, he must have allowed factors other than reason to exert an influence on him. In other words, he must have allowed desires for what he regards as good only in a certain respect, but not overall, to influence his conduct. So, in order to have a choice between good and evil, agents need already a certain depravity, in the sense of a system of desires for what they correctly believe to be evil. I need to *want* to overeat, get more than my fair share of money or power, indulge my sexual appetites even by deceiving my spouse or partner, want to see you hurt, if I am to have choice between good and evil. This depravity is itself an evil which is a necessary condition of a greater good. It makes possible a choice made seriously and deliberately, because made in the face of genuine alternative. I stress that, according to the free-will defence, it is the natural possibility of moral evil which is the necessary condition of the great good, not the actual evil itself. Whether that occurs is (through God's choice) outside God's control and up to us.

Note further and crucially that, if I suffer in consequence of your freely chosen bad action, that is not by any means pure loss for me. In a certain respect it is a good for *me*. My suffering would be pure loss for me if the only good thing in life was sensory pleasure, and the only bad thing sensory pain; and it is because the modern world tends to think in those terms that the problem of evil seems so acute. If these were the only good and bad things, the occurrence of suffering would indeed be a conclusive objection to the existence of God. But we have already noted the great good of freely choosing and influencing our future, that of our fellows, and that of the world. And now note another great good—the good of our life serving a purpose, of being of use to ourselves and others. Recall the words of Christ, "it is more blessed to give than to receive" (as quoted by St Paul (Acts 20: 35)). We tend to think, when the beggar appears on our doorstep and we feel obliged to give and do give, that that was lucky for him but not for us who happened to be at home. That is not what Christ's words say. They say that *we* are the lucky ones, not just because we have a lot, out of which we can give a little, but because we are privileged to contribute to the beggar's happiness—and that privilege is worth a lot more than money. And, just as it is a great good freely to choose to do good, so it is also a good to be used by someone else for a worthy purpose (so long, that is, that he or she has the right, the authority, to use us in this way). Being allowed to suffer to make possible a great good is a privilege, even if the privilege is forced upon you. Those who are allowed to die for their country and thereby save their country from foreign oppression are privileged. Cultures less obsessed than our own by the evil of purely physical pain have always recognized that. And they have recognized that it is still a blessing, even if the one who died had been conscripted to fight.

And even twentieth-century man can begin to see that—sometimes—when he seeks to help prisoners, not by giving them more comfortable quarters, but by letting them help the handicapped; or when he pities rather than envies the "poor little rich girl" who has everything and does nothing for anyone else. And one phenomenon prevalent in end-of-century Britain draws this especially to our attention—the evil of unemployment. Because of our system of Social Security, the unemployed on the whole have enough money to live without too much discomfort; certainly they are a lot better off than are many employed in Africa or Asia or Victorian Britain. What is evil about unemployment is not so much any resulting poverty but the uselessness of the unemployed. They often report feeling unvalued by society, of no use, "on the scrap heap". They rightly think it would be a good for them to contribute; but they cannot. Many of them would welcome a system where they were obliged to do useful work in preference to one where society has no use for them.

It follows from that fact that being of use is a benefit for him who is of use, and that those who suffer at the hands of others, and thereby make possible the good of those others who have free and responsible choice, are themselves benefited in this respect. I am fortunate if the natural possibility of my suffering if you choose to hurt me is the vehicle which makes your choice really matter. My vulnerability, my openness to suffering (which necessarily involves my actually suffering if you make the wrong choice), means that you are not just like a pilot in a simulator, where it does not matter if mistakes are made. That our choices matter tremendously, that we can make great differences to things for good or ill, is one of the greatest gifts a creator can give us. And if my suffering is the means by which he can give you that choice, I too am in this respect fortunate. Though of course suffering is in itself a bad thing, my good fortune is that the suffering is not random, pointless suffering. It is suffering which is a consequence of my vulnerability which makes me of such use.

Someone may object that the only good thing is not *being* of use (dying for one's country or being vulnerable to suffering at your hands), but *believing* that one is of use—believing that one is dying for one's country and that this is of use; the "feel-good" experience. But that cannot be correct. Having comforting beliefs is only a good thing if they are true beliefs. It is not a good thing to believe that things are going well when they are not, or that your life is of use when it is not. Getting pleasure out of a

comforting falsehood is a cheat. But if I get pleasure out of a true belief, it must be that I regard the state of things which I believe to hold to be a good thing. If I get pleasure out of the true belief that my daughter is doing well at school, it must be that I regard it as a good thing that my daughter does well at school (whether or not I believe that she is doing well). If I did not think the latter, I would not get any pleasure out of believing that she is doing well. Likewise, the belief that I am vulnerable to suffering at your hands, and that that is a good thing, can only be a good thing if being vulnerable to suffering at your hands is itself a good thing (independently of whether I believe it or not). Certainly, when my life is of use and that is a good for me, it is even better if I believe it and get comfort therefrom; but it can only be even better if it is already a good for me whether I believe it or not.

But though suffering may in these ways serve good purposes, does God have the right to allow me to suffer for your benefit, without asking my permission? For surely, an objector will say, no one has the right to allow one person A to suffer for the benefit of another one B without A's consent. We judge that doctors who use patients as involuntary objects of experimentation in medical experiments which they hope will produce results which can be used to benefit others are doing something wrong. After all, if my arguments about the utility of suffering are sound, ought we not all to be causing suffering to others in order that those others may have the opportunity to react in the right way?

There are, however, crucial differences between God and the doctors. The first is that God as the author of our being has certain rights, a certain authority over us, which we do not have over our fellow humans. He is the cause of our existence at each moment of our existence and sustains the laws of nature which give us everything we are and have. To allow someone to suffer for his own good or that of others, one has to stand in some kind of parental relationship towards him. I do not have the right to let some stranger suffer for the sake of some good, when I could easily prevent this, but I do have *some* right of this kind in respect of my own children. I may let the younger son suffer *somewhat* for his own good or that of his brother. I have this right because in small part I am responsible for the younger son's existence, his beginning and continuance. If I have begotten him, nourished, and educated him, I have some limited rights over him in return; to a *very limited* extent I can use him for some worthy purpose. If this is correct, then a God who is so much more the author of our being than are our parents has so much more right in this respect. Doctors do have over us even the rights of parents.

But secondly and all-importantly, the doctors *could* have asked the patients for permission; and the patients, being free agents of some power and knowledge, could have made an informed choice of whether or not to allow themselves to be used. By contrast, God's choice is not about how to use already existing agents, but about the sort of agents to make and the sort of world into which to put them. In God's situation there are no agents to be asked. I am arguing that it is good that one agent A should have deep responsibility for another B (who in turn could have deep responsibility for another C). It is not logically possible for God to have asked B if he wanted things thus, for, if A is to be responsible for B's growth in freedom, knowledge, and power, there will not be a B with enough freedom and knowledge to make any choice, before God has to choose whether or not to give A responsibility for him. One cannot ask a baby into which sort of world he or she wishes to be born. The creator has to make the choice independently of his creatures. He will seek on balance to benefit them—all of them. And, in giving them the gift of life—whatever suffering goes with it—that is a substantial benefit. But when one suffers at the hands of another, often perhaps it is not enough of a benefit to outweigh the suffering. Here is the point to recall that it is an additional benefit to the sufferer that his suffering is the means whereby the one who hurt him had the opportunity to make a significant choice between good and evil which otherwise he would not have had.

Although for these reasons, as I have been urging, God has the right to allow humans to cause each other to suffer, there must be a limit to the amount of suffering which he has the

right to allow a human being to suffer for the sake of a great good. A parent may allow an elder child to have the power to do some harm to a younger child for the sake of the responsibility given to the elder child; but there are limits. And there are limits even to the moral right of God, our creator and sustainer, to use free sentient beings as pawns in a greater game. Yet, if these limits were too narrow, God would be unable to give humans much real responsibility; he would be able to allow them only to play a toy game. Still, limits there must be to God's rights to allow humans to hurt each other; and limits there are in the world to the extent to which they can hurt each other, provided above all by the short finite life enjoyed by humans and other creatures—one human can hurt another for no more than eighty years or so. And there are a number of other safety-devices in-built into our physiology and psychology, limiting the amount of pain we can suffer. But the primary safety limit is that provided by the shortness of our finite life. Unending unchosen suffering would indeed to my mind provide a very strong argument against the existence of God. But that is not the human situation.

So then God, without asking humans, has to choose for them between the kinds of world in which they can live—basically either a world in which there is very little opportunity for humans to benefit or harm each other, or a world in which there is considerable opportunity. How shall he choose? There are clearly reasons for both choices. But it seems to me (just, on balance) that his choosing to create the world in which we have considerable opportunity to benefit or harm each other is to bring about a good at least as great as the evil which he thereby allows to occur. *Of course* the suffering he allows is a bad thing; and, other things being equal, to be avoided. But having the natural possibility of causing suffering makes possible a greater good. God, in creating humans who (of logical necessity) cannot choose for themselves the kind of world into which they are to come, plausibly exhibits his goodness in making for them the heroic choice that they come into a risky world where they may have to suffer for the good of others.

NATURAL EVIL

Natural evil is not to be accounted for along the same lines as moral evil. Its main role rather, I suggest, is to make it possible for humans to have the kind of choice which the free-will defence extols, and to make available to humans specially worthwhile kinds of choice.

There are two ways in which natural evil operates to give humans those choices. First, the operation of natural laws producing evils gives humans knowledge (if they choose to seek it) of how to bring about such evils themselves. Observing you catch some disease by the operation of natural processes gives me the power either to use those processes to give that disease to other people, or through negligence to allow others to catch it, or to take measures to prevent others from catching the disease. Study of the mechanisms of nature producing various evils (and goods) opens up for humans a wide range of choice. This is the way in which in fact we learn how to bring about (good and) evil. But could not God give us the requisite knowledge (of how to bring about good or evil) which we need in order to have free and responsible choice by a less costly means? Could he not just whisper in our ears from time to time what are the different consequences of different actions of ours? Yes. But anyone who believed that an action of his would have some effect because he believed that God had told him so would see all his actions as done under the all-watchful eye of God. He would not merely believe strongly that there was a God, but would know it with real certainty. That knowledge would greatly inhibit his freedom of choice, would make it very difficult for him to choose to do evil. This is because we all have a natural inclination to wish to be thought well of by everyone, and above all by an all-good God; that we have such an inclination is a very good feature of humans, without which we would be less than human. Also, if we were directly informed of the consequences of our actions, we would be deprived of the choice whether to seek to discover what the consequences were through experiment and hard cooperative work. Knowledge would be available on tap. Natural processes alone give humans

knowledge of the effects of their actions without inhibiting their freedom, and if evil is to be a possibility for them they must know how to allow it to occur.

The other way in which natural evil operates to give humans their freedom is that it makes possible certain kinds of action towards it between which agents can choose. It increases the range of significant choice. A particular natural evil, such as physical pain, gives to the sufferer a choice—whether to endure it with patience, or to bemoan his lot. His friend can choose whether to show compassion towards the sufferer, or to be callous. The pain makes possible these choices, which would not otherwise exist. There is no guarantee that our actions in response to the pain will be good ones, but the pain gives us the opportunity to perform good actions. The good or bad actions which we perform in the face of natural evil themselves provide opportunities for further choice—of good or evil stances towards the former actions. If I am patient with my suffering, you can choose whether to encourage or laugh at my patience; if I bemoan my lot, you can teach me by word any example what a good thing patience is. If you are sympathetic, I have then the opportunity to show gratitude for the sympathy; or to be so self-involved that I ignore it. If you are callous, I can choose whether to ignore this or to resent it for life. And so on. I do not think that there can be much doubt that natural evil, such as physical pain, makes available these sorts of choice. The actions which natural evil makes possible are ones which allow us to perform at our best and interact with our fellows at the deepest level.

It may, however, be suggested that adequate opportunity for these great good actions would be provided by the occurrence of moral evil without any need for suffering to be caused by natural processes. You can show courage when threatened by a gunman, as well as when threatened by cancer; and show sympathy to those likely to be killed by gunmen as well as to those likely to die of cancer. But just imagine all the suffering of mind and body caused by disease, earthquake, and accident unpreventable by humans removed at a stroke from our society. No sickness, no bereavement in consequence of the untimely death of the young. Many of us would then have such an easy life that we simply would not have much opportunity to show courage or, indeed, manifest much in the way of great goodness at all. We need those insidious processes of decay and dissolution which money and strength cannot ward off for long to give us the opportunities, so easy otherwise to avoid, to become heroes.

God has the right to allow natural evils to occur (for the same reason as he has the right to allow moral evils to occur)—up to a limit. It would, of course, be crazy for God to multiply evils more and more in order to give endless opportunity for heroism, but to have *some* significant opportunity for real heroism and consequent character formation is a benefit for the person to whom it is given. Natural evils give to us the knowledge to make a range of choices between good and evil, and the opportunity to perform actions of especially valuable kinds.

There is, however, no reason to suppose that animals have free will. So what about their suffering? Animals had been suffering for a long time before humans appeared on this planet—just how long depends on which animals are conscious beings. The first thing to take into account here is that, while the higher animals, at any rate the vertebrates, suffer, it is most unlikely that they suffer nearly as much as humans do. Given that suffering depends directly on brain events (in turn caused by events in other parts of the body), then, since the lower animals do not suffer at all and humans suffer a lot, animals of intermediate complexity (it is reasonable to suppose) suffer only a moderate amount. So, while one does need a theodicy to account for why God allows animals to suffer, one does not need as powerful a theodicy as one does in respect of humans. One only needs reasons adequate to account for God allowing an amount of suffering much less than that of humans. That said, there is, I believe, available for animals parts of the theodicy which I have outlined above for humans.

The good of animals, like that of humans, does not consist solely in thrills of pleasure. For animals, too, there are more worthwhile things, and in particular intentional actions, and among them serious significant intentional actions. The life of animals involves many serious significant intentional actions. Animals look for a mate, despite being tired and failing to find one. They take great trouble to build nests and feed their young, to decoy predators and explore. But all this inevitably involves pain (going on despite being tired) and danger. An animal cannot intentionally avoid forest fires, or take trouble to rescue its offspring from forest fires, unless there exists a serious danger of getting caught in a forest fire. The action of rescuing despite danger simply cannot be done unless the danger exists—and the danger will not exist unless there is a significant natural probability of being caught in the fire. Animals do not choose freely to do such actions, but the actions are nevertheless worthwhile. It is great that animals feed their young, not just themselves; that animals explore when they know it to be dangerous; that animals save each other from predators, and so on. These are the things that give the lives of animals their value. But they do often involve some suffering to some creature.

To return to the central case of humans—the reader will agree with me to the extent to which he or she values responsibility, free choice, and being of use very much more than thrills of pleasure or absence of pain. There is no other way to get the evils of this world into the right perspective, except to reflect at length on innumerable very detailed thought experiments (in addition to actual experiences of life) in which we postulate very different sorts of worlds from our own, and then ask ourselves whether the perfect goodness of God would require him to create one of these (or no world at all) rather than our own. But I conclude with a very small thought experiment, which may help to begin this process. Suppose that you exist in another world before your birth in this one, and are given a choice as to the sort of life you are to have in this one. You are told that you are to have only a short life, maybe of only a few minutes, although it will be an adult life in the sense that you will have the richness of sensation and belief characteristic of adults. You have a choice as to the sort of life you will have. You can have either a few minutes of very considerable pleasure, of the kind produced by some drug such as heroin, which you will experience by yourself and which will have no effects at all in the world (for example, no one else will know about it); or you can have a few minutes of considerable pain, such as the pain of childbirth, which will have (unknown to you at the time of pain) considerable good effects on others over a few years. You are told that, if you do not make the second choice, those others will never exist—and so you are under no moral obligation to make the second choice. But you seek to make the choice which will make *your* own life the best life for *you* to have led. How will you choose? The choice is, I hope, obvious. You should choose the second alternative.

For someone who remains unconvinced by my claims about the relative strengths of the good and evils involved—holding that, great though the goods are, they do not justify the evils which they involve—there is a fall-back position. My arguments may have convinced you of the greatness of the goods involved sufficiently for you to allow that a perfectly good God would be justified in bringing about the evils for the sake of the good which they make possible, if and only if God also provided compensation in the form of happiness after death to the victims whose sufferings make possible the goods. Someone whose theodicy requires buttressing in this way will need an independent reason for believing that God does provide such life

after death if he is to be justified in holding his theodicy. . . . While believing that God does provide at any rate for many humans such life after death, I have expounded a theodicy without relying on this assumption. But I can understand someone thinking that the assumption is needed, especially when we are considering the worst evils. (This compensatory afterlife need not necessarily be the ever-lasting life of Heaven.)

It remains the case, however, that evil is evil, and there is a substantial price to pay for the goods of our world which it makes possible. God would not be less than perfectly good if he created instead a world without pain and suffering, and so without the particular goods which those evils make possible. Christian, Islamic, and much Jewish tradition claims that God has created worlds of both kinds—our world, and the Heaven of the blessed. The latter is a marvellous world with a vast range of possible deep goods, but it lacks a few goods which our world contains, including the good of being able to reject the good. A generous God might well choose to give some of us the choice of rejecting the good in a world like ours before giving to those who embrace it a wonderful world in which the former possibility no longer exists.

God and the Problem of Evil

B. C. JOHNSON

B. C. Johnson is the pseudonym of an author who prefers anonymity.

Here is a common situation: a house catches on fire and a six-month-old baby is painfully burned to death. Could we possibly describe as "good" any person who had the power to save this child and yet refused to do so? God undoubtedly has this power and yet in many cases of this sort he has refused to help. Can we call God

"good"? Are there adequate excuses for his behavior?

First, it will not do to claim that the baby will go to heaven. It was either necessary for the baby to suffer or it was not. If it was not, then it was wrong to allow it. The child's ascent to heaven does not change this fact. If it was necessary,

From *The Atheist Debater's Handbook*. B. C. Johnson. "The Problem of Good and Evil." pp. 99–108 (Amherst, NY: Prometheus Books). Copyright © 1983 by B. C. Johnson. Reprinted with permission.

the fact that the baby will go to heaven does not explain why it was necessary, and we are still left without an excuse for God's inaction.

It is not enough to say that the baby's painful death would in the long run have good results and therefore should have happened, otherwise God would not have permitted it. For if we know this to be true, then we know—just as God knows—that every action successfully performed must in the end be good and therefore the right thing to do, otherwise, God would not have allowed it to happen. We could deliberately set houses ablaze to kill innocent people and if successful we would then know we had a duty to do it. A defense of God's goodness which takes as its foundation duties known only after the fact would result in a morality unworthy of the name. Furthermore, this argument does not explain why God allowed the child to burn to death. It merely claims that there is some reason discoverable in the long run. But the belief that such a reason is within our grasp must rest upon the additional belief that God is good. This is just to counter evidence against such a belief by assuming the belief to be true. It is not unlike a lawyer defending his client by claiming that the client is innocent and therefore the evidence against him must be misleading—that proof vindicating the defendant will be found in the long run. No jury of reasonable men and women would accept such a defense and the theist cannot expect a more favorable outcome.

The theist often claims that man has been given free will so that if he accidentally or purposefully causes fires, killing small children, it is his fault alone. Consider a bystander who had nothing to do with starting the fire but who refused to help even though he could have saved the child with no harm to himself. Could such a bystander be called good? Certainly not. If we would not consider a mortal human being good under these circumstances, what grounds could we possibly have for continuing to assert the goodness of an all-powerful God?

The suggestion is sometimes made that it is best for us to face disasters without assistance, otherwise we would become dependent on an outside power for aid. Should we then abolish

modern medical care or do away with efficient fire departments? Are we not dependent on their help? Is it not the case that their presence transforms us into soft, dependent creatures? The vast majority are not physicians or firemen. These people help in their capacity as professional outside sources of aid in much the same way that we would expect God to be helpful. Theists refer to aid from firemen and physicians as cases of man helping himself. In reality, it is a tiny minority of men helping a great many. We can become just as dependent on them as we can on God. Now the existence of this kind of outside help is either wrong or right. If it is right, then God should assist those areas of the world which do not have this kind of help. In fact, throughout history, such help has not been available. If aid ought to have been provided, then God should have provided it. On the other hand, if it is wrong to provide this kind of assistance, then we should abolish the aid altogether. But we obviously do not believe it is wrong.

Similar considerations apply to the claim that if God interferes in disasters, he would destroy a considerable amount of moral urgency to make things right. Once again, note that such institutions as modern medicine and fire departments are relatively recent. They function irrespective of whether we as individuals feel any moral urgency to support them. To the extent that they help others, opportunities to feel moral urgency are destroyed because they reduce the number of cases which appeal to us for help. Since we have not always had such institutions, there must have been a time when there was greater moral urgency than there is now. If such a situation is morally desirable, then we should abolish modern medical care and fire departments. If the situation is not morally desirable, then God should have remedied it.

Besides this point, we should note that God is represented as one who tolerates disasters, such as infants burning to death, in order to create moral urgency. It follows that God approves of these disasters as a means to encourage the creation of moral urgency. Furthermore, if there were no such disasters occurring, God would have to see to it that they occur. If it so happened that we lived in a world in which babies never perished in burning houses, God would be morally obliged to take an active hand in setting fire to houses with infants in them. In fact, if the frequency of infant mortality due to fire should happen to fall below a level necessary for the creation of maximum moral urgency in our real world, God would be justified in setting a few fires of his own. This may well be happening right now, for there is no guarantee that the maximum number of infant deaths necessary for moral urgency are occurring.

All of this is of course absurd. If I see an opportunity to create otherwise nonexistent opportunities for moral urgency by burning an infant or two, then I should *not* do so. But if it is good to maximize moral urgency, then I *should* do so. Therefore, it is not good to maximize moral urgency. Plainly we do not in general believe that it is a good thing to maximize moral urgency. The fact that we approve of modern medical care and applaud medical advances is proof enough of this.

The theist may point out that in a world without suffering there would be no occasion for the production of such virtues as courage, sympathy, and the like. This may be true, but the atheist need not demand a world without suffering. He need only claim that there is suffering which is in excess of that needed for the production of various virtues. For example, God's active attempts to save six-month-old infants from fires would not in itself create a world without suffering. But no one could sincerely doubt that it would improve the world.

The two arguments against the previous theistic excuse apply here also. "Moral urgency" and "building virtue" are susceptible to the same criticism. It is worthwhile to emphasize, however, that we encourage efforts to eliminate evils; we approve of efforts to promote peace, prevent famine, and wipe out disease. In other words, we do value a world with fewer or (if possible) no opportunities for the development of virtue (when "virtue" is understood to mean the reduction of suffering). If we produce such a world for succeeding generations, how will they develop virtues? Without war, disease, and famine, they will not be virtuous. Should we then cease our attempts to wipe out war, disease, and famine? If we do not

believe that it is right to cease attempts at improving the world, then by implication we admit that virtue-building is not an excuse for God to permit disasters. For we admit that the development of virtue is no excuse for permitting disasters.

It might be said that God allows innocent people to suffer in order to deflate man's ego so that the latter will not be proud of his apparently deserved good fortune. But this excuse succumbs to the arguments used against the preceding excuses and we need discuss them no further.

Theists may claim that evil is a necessary by-product of the laws of nature and therefore it is irrational for God to interfere every time a disaster happens. Such a state of affairs would alter the whole causal order and we would then find it impossible to predict anything. But the death of a child caused by an electrical fire could have been prevented by a miracle and no one would ever have known. Only a minor alteration in electrical equipment would have been necessary. A very large disaster could have been avoided simply by producing in Hitler a miraculous heart attack— and no one would have known it was a miracle. To argue that continued miraculous intervention by God would be wrong is like insisting that one should never use salt because ingesting five pounds of it would be fatal. No one is requesting that God interfere all of the time. He should, however, intervene to prevent especially horrible disasters. Of course, the question arises: where does one draw the line? Well, certainly the line should be drawn somewhere this side of infants burning to death. To argue that we do not know where the line should be drawn is no excuse for failing to interfere in those instances that would be called clear cases of evil.

It will not do to claim that evil exists as a necessary contrast to good so that we might know what good is. A very small amount of evil, such as a toothache, would allow that. It is not necessary to destroy innocent human beings.

The claim could be made that God has a "higher morality" by which his actions are to be judged. But it is a strange "higher morality" which claims that what we call "bad" is good and what we call "good" is bad. Such a morality can have no meaning to us. It would be like calling black "white" and white "black." In reply the theist may say that God is the wise Father and we are ignorant children. How can we judge God any more than a child is able to judge his parent? It is true that a child may be puzzled by his parents' conduct, but his basis for deciding that their conduct is nevertheless good would be the many instances of good behavior he has observed. Even so, this could be misleading. Hitler, by all accounts, loved animals and children of the proper race; but if Hitler had had a child, this offspring would hardly have been justified in arguing that his father was a good man. At any rate, God's "higher morality," being the opposite of ours, cannot offer any grounds for deciding that he is somehow good.

Perhaps the main problem with the solutions to the problem of evil we have thus far considered is that no matter how convincing they may be in the abstract, they are implausible in certain particular cases. Picture an infant dying in a burning house and then imagine God simply observing from afar. Perhaps God is reciting excuses in his own behalf. As the child succumbs to the smoke and flames, God may be pictured as saying: "Sorry, but if I helped you I would have considerable trouble deflating the ego of your parents. And don't forget I have to keep those laws of nature consistent. And anyway if you weren't dying in that fire, a lot of moral urgency would just go down the drain. Besides, I didn't start this fire, so you can't blame *me*."

It does no good to assert that God may not be all-powerful and thus not able to prevent evil. He can create a universe and yet is conveniently unable to do what the fire department can do— rescue a baby from a burning building. God should at least be as powerful as a man. A man, if he had been at the right place and time, could have killed Hitler. Was this beyond God's abilities? If God knew in 1910 how to produce polio vaccine and if he was able to communicate with somebody, he should have communicated this knowledge. He must be incredibly limited if he could not have managed this modest accomplishment. Such a God if not dead, is the next thing to it. And a person who believes in such a ghost of a God is practically an atheist. To call such a thing a god would be to strain the meaning of the word.

The theist, as usual, may retreat to faith. He may say that he has faith in God's goodness and

therefore the Christian Deity's existence has not been disproved. "Faith" is here understood as being much like confidence in a friend's innocence despite the evidence against him. Now in order to have confidence in a friend one must know him well enough to justify faith in his goodness. We cannot have justifiable faith in the supreme goodness of strangers. Moreover, such confidence must come not just from a speaking acquaintance. The friend may continually assure us with his words that he is good but if he does not act like a good person, we would have no reason to trust him. A person who says he has faith in God's goodness is speaking as if he had known God for a long time and during that time had never seen Him do any serious evil. But we know that throughout history God has allowed numerous atrocities to occur. No one can have justifiable faith in the goodness of such a God. This faith would have to be based on a close friendship wherein God was never found to do anything wrong. But a person would have to be blind and deaf to have had such a relationship with God. Suppose a friend of yours had always claimed to be good yet refused to help people when he was in a position to render aid. Could you have justifiable faith in his goodness?

You can of course say that you trust God anyway—that no arguments can undermine your faith. But this is just a statement describing how stubborn you are; it has no bearing whatsoever on the question of God's goodness.

The various excuses theists offer for why God has allowed evil to exist have been demonstrated to be inadequate. However, the conclusive objection to these excuses does not depend on their inadequacy.

First, we should note that every possible excuse making the actual world consistent with the existence of a good God could be used in reverse to make that same world consistent with an evil God. For example, we could say that God is evil and that he allows free will so that we can freely do evil things, which would make us more truly evil than we would be if forced to perform evil acts. Or we could say that natural disasters occur in order to make people more selfish and bitter, for most people tend to have a "me-first" attitude in a disaster (note, for example, stampedes to leave burning buildings). Even though some people achieve virtue from disasters, this outcome is necessary if persons are to react freely to disaster—necessary if the development of moral degeneracy is to continue freely. But, enough; the point is made. Every excuse we could provide to make the world consistent with a good God can be paralleled by an excuse to make the world consistent with an evil God. This is so because the world is a mixture of both good and bad.

Now there are only three possibilities concerning God's moral character. Considering the world as it actually is, we may believe: (*a*) that God is more likely to be all evil than he is to be all good; (*b*) that God is less likely to be all evil than he is to be all good; or (*c*) that God is equally as likely to be all evil as he is to be all good. In case (*a*) it would be admitted that God is unlikely to be all good. Case (*b*) cannot be true at all, since—as we have seen—the belief that God is all evil can be justified to precisely the same extent as the belief that God is all good. Case (*c*) leaves us with no reasonable excuses for a good God to permit evil. The reason is as follows: if an excuse is to be a reasonable excuse, the circumstances it identifies as excusing conditions must be actual. For example, if I run over a pedestrian and my excuse is that the brakes failed because someone tampered with them, then the facts had better bear this out. Otherwise the excuse will not hold. Now if case

(*c*) is correct and, given the facts of the actual world, God is as likely to be all evil as he is to be all good, then these facts do not support the excuses which could be made for a good God permitting evil. Consider an analogous example. If my excuse for running over the pedestrian is that my brakes were tampered with, and if the actual facts lead us to believe that it is no more likely that they were tampered with than that they were not, the excuse is no longer reasonable. To make good my excuse, I must show that it is a fact or at least highly probable that my brakes were tampered with—not that it is just a possibility. The same point holds for God. His excuse must not be a possible excuse, but an actual one. But case (*c*), in maintaining that it is just as likely that God is all evil as that he is all good, rules this out. For if case (*c*) is true, then the facts of the actual world do not make it any more likely that God is all good than that he is all evil. Therefore, they do not make it any more likely that his excuses are good than that they are not. But, as we have seen, good excuses have a higher probability of being true.

Cases (*a*) and (*c*) conclude that it is unlikely that God is all good, and case (*b*) cannot be true. Since these are the only possible cases, there is no escape from the conclusion that it is unlikely that God is all good. Thus the problem of evil triumphs over traditional theism.

REASON AND FAITH

The Ethics of Belief

W. K. CLIFFORD

W. K. Clifford (1845–1879) was an English mathematician and philosopher.

A shipowner was about to send to sea an emigrant-ship. He knew that she was old, and not over-well built at the first; that she had seen many seas and climes, and often had needed repairs. Doubts had

From W. K. Clifford, *Lectures and Essays* (1879).

been suggested to him that possibly she was not seaworthy. These doubts preyed upon his mind, and made him unhappy; he thought that perhaps he ought to have her thoroughly overhauled and refitted, even though this should put him to great expense. Before the ship sailed, however, he succeeded in overcoming these melancholy reflections. He said to himself that she had gone safely through so many voyages and weathered so many storms that it was idle to suppose she would not come safely home from this trip also. He would put his trust in Providence, which could hardly fail to protect all these unhappy families that were leaving their fatherland to seek for better times elsewhere. He would dismiss from his mind all ungenerous suspicions about the honesty of builders and contractors. In such ways he acquired a sincere and comfortable conviction that his vessel was thoroughly safe and seaworthy; he watched her departure with a light heart, and benevolent wishes for the success of the exiles in their strange new home that was to be; and he got his insurance-money when she went down in mid-ocean and told no tales.

What shall we say of him? Surely this, that he was verily guilty of the death of those men. It is admitted that he did sincerely believe in the soundness of his ship; but the sincerity of his conviction can in no wise help him, because *he had no right to believe on such evidence as was before him.* He had acquired his belief not by honestly earning it in patient investigation, but by stifling his doubts. And although in the end he may have felt so sure about it that he could not think otherwise, yet inasmuch as he had knowingly and willingly worked himself into that frame of mind, he must be held responsible for it.

Let us alter the case a little, and suppose that the ship was not unsound after all; that she made her voyage safely, and many others after it. Will that diminish the guilt of her owner? Not one jot. When an action is once done, it is right or wrong for ever; no accidental failure of its good or evil fruits can possibly alter that. The man would not have been innocent, he would only have been not found out. The question of right or wrong has to do with the origin of his belief, not the matter of it; not what it was, but how he got it; not whether it turned out to be true

or false, but whether he had a right to believe on such evidence as was before him.

There was once an island in which some of the inhabitants professed a religion teaching neither the doctrine of original sin nor that of eternal punishment. A suspicion got abroad that the professors of this religion had made use of unfair means to get their doctrines taught to children. They were accused of wresting the laws of their country in such a way as to remove children from the care of their natural and legal guardians; and even of stealing them away and keeping them concealed from their friends and relations. A certain number of men formed themselves into a society for the purpose of agitating the public about this matter. They published grave accusations against individual citizens of the highest position and character, and did all in their power to injure these citizens in the exercise of their professions. So great was the noise they made, that a Commission was appointed to investigate the facts; but after the Commission had carefully inquired into all the evidence that could be got, it appeared that the accused were innocent. Not only had they been accused on insufficient evidence, but the evidence of their innocence was such as the agitators might easily have obtained, if they had attempted a fair inquiry. After these disclosures the inhabitants of that country looked upon the members of the agitating society, not only as persons whose judgment was to be distrusted, but also as no longer to be counted honourable men. For although they had sincerely and conscientiously believed in the charges they had made, yet *they had no right to believe on such evidence as was before them.* Their sincere convictions, instead of being honestly earned by patient inquiring, were stolen by listening to the voice of prejudice and passion.

Let us vary this case also, and suppose, other things remaining as before, that a still more accurate investigation proved the accused to have been really guilty. Would this make any difference in the guilt of the accusers? Clearly not; the question is not whether their belief was true or false, but whether they entertained it on wrong grounds. They would no doubt say, "Now you see that we were right after all; next time perhaps you will believe us." And they might be believed, but they would not thereby become honourable men. They would not be innocent, they would only be not found out. Every one of them, if he chose to examine himself *in foro conscientiae*, would know that he had acquired and nourished a belief, when he had no right to believe on such evidence as was before him; and therein he would know that he had done a wrong thing.

It may be said, however, that in both of these supposed cases it is not the belief which is judged to be wrong, but the action following upon it. The shipowner might say, "I am perfectly certain that my ship is sound, but still I feel it my duty to have her examined, before trusting the lives of so many people to her." And it might be said to the agitator, "However convinced you were of the justice of your cause and the truth of your convictions, you ought not to have made a public attack upon any man's character until you had examined the evidence on both sides with the utmost patience and care."

In the first place, let us admit that, so far as it goes, this view of the case is right and necessary; right, because even when a man's belief is so fixed that he cannot think otherwise, he still has a choice in regard to the action suggested by it, and so cannot escape the duty of investigating on the ground of the strength of his convictions; and necessary, because those who are not yet capable of controlling their feelings and thoughts must have a plain rule dealing with overt acts.

But this being premised as necessary, it becomes clear that it is not sufficient, and that our previous judgment is required to supplement it. For it is not possible so to sever the belief from the action it suggests as to condemn the one without condemning the other. No man holding a strong belief on one side of a question, or even wishing to hold a belief on one side, can investigate it with such fairness and completeness as if he were really in doubt and unbiased; so that the existence of a belief not founded on fair inquiry unfits a man for the performance of this necessary duty.

Nor is that truly a belief at all which has not some influence upon the actions of him who holds it. He who truly believes that which prompts him to an action has looked upon the action to lust after it, he has committed it already in his heart. If a belief is not realized immediately in open deeds, it is stored up for the guidance of the future. It goes to make a part of that aggregate of beliefs which is the link between sensation and action at every moment of all our lives, and which is so organized and compacted together that no part of it can be isolated from the rest, but every new addition modifies the structure of the whole. No real belief, however trifling and fragmentary it may seem, is ever truly insignificant; it prepares us to receive more of its like, confirms those which resembled it before, and weakens others; and so gradually it lays a stealthy train in our inmost thoughts, which may someday explode into overt action, and leave its stamp upon our character for ever.

And no one man's belief is in any case a private matter which concerns himself alone. Our lives are guided by that general conception of the course of things which has been created by society for social purposes. Our words, our phrases, our forms and processes and modes of thought, are common property, fashioned and perfected from age to age; an heirloom which every succeeding generation inherits as a precious deposit and a sacred trust to be handed on to the next one, not unchanged but enlarged and purified, with some clear marks of its proper handiwork. Into this, for good or ill, is woven every belief of every man who has speech of his fellows. An awful privilege, and an awful responsibility, that we should help to create the world in which posterity will live.

In the two supposed cases which have been considered, it has been judged wrong to believe on insufficient evidence, or to nourish belief by suppressing doubts and avoiding investigation. The reason of this judgment is not far to seek; it is that in both these cases the belief held by one man was of great importance to other men. But forasmuch as no belief held by one man, however seemingly trivial the belief, and however obscure the believer, is ever actually insignificant or without its effect on the fate of mankind, we have no choice but to extend our judgment to all cases of belief whatever. Belief, that sacred faculty which prompts the decisions of our will, and knits into harmonious working all the compacted energies of our being, is ours not for ourselves, but for humanity. It is rightly used on truths which have been established by long experience and waiting toil, and which have stood in the fierce light of free and fearless questioning. Then it helps to bind men together, and to strengthen and direct their common action. It is desecrated when given to unproved and unquestioned statements, for the solace and private pleasure of the believer; to add a tinsel splendour to the plain straight road of our life and display a bright mirage beyond it; or even to drown the common sorrows of our kind by a selfdeception which allows them not only to cast down, but also to degrade us. Whoso would deserve well of his fellows in this matter will guard the purity of his belief with a very fanaticism of jealous care, lest at any time it should rest on an unworthy object, and catch a stain which can never be wiped away.

It is not only the leader of men, statesman, philosopher, or poet, that owes this bounden duty to mankind. Every rustic who delivers in the village alehouse his slow, infrequent sentences, may help to kill or keep alive the fatal superstitions which clog his race. Every hard-worked wife of an artisan may transmit to her children beliefs which shall knit society together, or rend it in pieces. No simplicity of mind, no obscurity of station, can escape the universal duty of questioning all that we believe.

It is true that this duty is a hard one, and the doubt which comes out of it is often a very bitter thing. It leaves us bare and powerless where we thought that we were safe and strong. To know all about anything is to know how to deal with it under all circumstances. We feel much happier and more secure when we think we know precisely what to do, no matter what happens, than when we have lost our way and do not know where to turn. And if we have supposed ourselves to know all about anything, and to be capable of doing what is fit in regard to it, we naturally do not like to find that we are really ignorant and powerless, that we have to begin again at the beginning, and try to learn what the thing is and how it is to be dealt with—if indeed anything can be learnt about it. It is the sense of power attached to a sense of knowledge that makes men desirous of believing, and afraid of doubting.

This sense of power is the highest and best of pleasures when the belief on which it is founded is a true belief, and has been fairly earned by investigation. For then we may justly feel that it is common property, and hold good for others as well as for ourselves. Then we may be glad, not that *I* have learned secrets by which I am safer and stronger, but that *we men* have got mastery over more of the world; and we shall be strong, not for ourselves, but in the name of Man and in his strength. But if the belief has been accepted on insufficient evidence, the pleasure is a stolen one. Not only does it deceive ourselves by giving us a sense of power which we do not really possess, but it is sinful, because it is stolen in defiance of our duty to mankind. That duty is to guard ourselves from such beliefs as from a pestilence, which may shortly master our own body and then spread to the rest of the town. What would be thought of one who, for the sake of a sweet fruit, should deliberately run the risk of bringing a plague upon his family and his neighbours?

And, as in other such cases, it is not the risk only which has to be considered; for a bad action is always bad at the time when it is done, no matter what happens afterwards. Every time we let ourselves believe for unworthy reasons, we weaken our powers of self-control, of doubting, of judicially and fairly weighing evidence. We all suffer severely enough from the maintenance and support of false beliefs and the fatally wrong actions which they lead to, and the evil born when one such belief is entertained is great and wide. But a greater and wider evil arises when the credulous character is maintained and supported, when a habit of believing for unworthy reasons is fostered and made permanent. If I steal money from any person, there may be no harm done by the mere transfer of possession; he may not feel the loss, or it may prevent him from using the money badly. But I cannot help doing this great wrong towards Man, that I make myself dishonest. What hurts society is not that it should lose its property, but that it should become a den of thieves, for then it must cease to be society. This is why we ought not to do evil, that good may come; for at any rate this great evil has come, that we have done evil and are made wicked thereby. In like manner, if I let myself believe anything on insufficient evidence, there may be no great harm done by the mere belief; it may be true after all, or I may never have occasion to exhibit it in outward acts. But I cannot help doing this great wrong towards Man, that I make myself credulous. The danger to society is not merely that it should believe wrong things, though that is great enough; but that it should become credulous, and lose the habit of testing things and inquiring into them; for then it must sink back into savagery.

The harm which is done by credulity in a man is not confined to the fostering of a credulous character in others, and consequent support of false beliefs. Habitual want of care about what I believe leads to habitual want of care in others about the truth of what is told to me. Men speak the truth to one another when each reveres the truth in his own mind and in the other's mind; but how shall my friend revere the truth in my mind when I myself am careless about it, when I believe things because I want to believe them, and because they are comforting and pleasant? Will he not learn to cry, "Peace," to me, when there is no peace? By such a course I shall surround myself with a thick atmosphere of falsehood and fraud, and in that I must live. It may matter little to me, in my cloudcastle of sweet illusions and darling lies; but it matters much to Man that I have made my neighbours ready to deceive. The credulous man is father to the liar and the cheat; he lives in the bosom of this his family, and it is no marvel if he should become even as they are. So closely are our duties knit together, that whoso shall keep the whole law, and yet offend in one point, he is guilty of all.

To sum up: it is wrong always, everywhere, and for anyone, to believe anything upon insufficient evidence.

If a man, holding a belief which he was taught in childhood or persuaded of afterwards, keeps down and pushes away any doubts which arise about it in his mind, purposely avoids the reading of books and the company of men that call in question or discuss it, and regards as impious those questions which cannot easily be asked without disturbing it—the life of that man is one long sin against mankind.

If this judgment seems harsh when applied to those simple souls who have never known better, who have been brought up from the cradle with a horror of doubt, and taught that their eternal welfare depends on *what* they believe, then it leads to the very serious question, *Who hath made Israel to sin?*

It may be permitted me to fortify this judgment with the sentence of Milton[1]—

> A man may be a heretic in the truth; and if he believe things only because his pastor says so, or the assembly so determine, without knowing other reason, though his belief be true, yet the very truth he holds becomes his heresy.

And with this famous aphorism of Coleridge[2]—

> He who begins by loving Christianity better than Truth, will proceed by loving his own sect or Church better than Christianity, and end in loving himself better than all.

Inquiry into the evidence of a doctrine is not to be made once for all, and then taken as finally settled.

It is never lawful to stifle a doubt; for either it can be honestly answered by means of the inquiry already made, or else it proves that the inquiry was not complete.

"But," says one, "I am a busy man; I have no time for the long course of study which would be necessary to make me in any degree a competent judge of certain questions, or even able to understand the nature of the arguments." Then he should have no time to believe.

NOTES

1. *Areopagitica.*
2. *Aids to Reflections.*

The Will to Believe

WILLIAM JAMES

William James (1842–1910) spent his career teaching philosophy and the new science of psychology at Harvard.

In the recently published Life by Leslie Stephen of his brother, Fitz-James, there is an account of a school to which the latter went when he was a boy. The teacher, a certain Mr. Guest, used to converse with his pupils in this wise, "Gurney, what is the difference between justification and sanctification?—Stephen, prove the omnipotence of God!" etc. In the midst of our Harvard free-thinking and indifference we are prone to imagine that here at your good old orthodox College conversation continues to be somewhat upon this order; and to show you that we at Harvard have not lost all interest in these vital subjects, I have brought with me tonight something like a sermon on justification by faith to read to you,—I mean an essay in justification *of* faith, a defence of our right to adopt a believing attitude in religious matters, in spite of the fact that our merely logical intellect may not have been coerced. "The Will to Believe," accordingly, is the title of my paper.

I have long defended to my own students the lawfulness of voluntarily adopted faith; but as soon as they have got well imbued with the logical spirit, they have as a rule refused to admit my contention to be lawful philosophically, even though in point of fact they were personally all the time chock-full of some faith or other themselves. I am all the while, however, so profoundly convinced that my own position is correct, that your invitation has seemed to me a good occasion to make my statements more clear. Perhaps your minds will be more open than those with which I have hitherto had to deal. I will be as little technical as I can, though I must begin by setting up some technical distinctions that will help us in the end.

I

Let us give the name of hypothesis to anything that may be proposed to our belief; and just as the electricians speak of *live* and *dead* wires, let us speak of any hypothesis as either live or dead. A live hypothesis is one which appeals as a real possibility to him to whom it is proposed. If I ask you to believe in the Mahdi, the notion makes no electric connection with your nature—it refuses to scintillate with any credibility at all. As an hypothesis it is completely dead. To an Arab, however (even if he be not one of the Mahdi's followers), the hypothesis is among the mind's possibilities: It is alive. This shows that deadness and liveness in an hypothesis are not intrinsic properties, but relations to the individual thinker. They are measured by his willingness to act. The maximum of liveness in an hypothesis means willingness to act irrevocably. Practically, that means belief; but there is some believing tendency wherever there is willingness to act at all.

Next, let us call the decision between two hypotheses an *option*. Options may be of several kinds. They may be first, *living* or *dead;* secondly, *forced* or *avoidable;* thirdly, *momentous* or *trivial;* and for our purposes we may call an option a *genuine* option when it is of the forced, living, and momentous kind.

1. A living option is one in which both hypotheses are live ones. If I say to you: "Be a theosophist or be a Mohammedan," it is probably a dead option, because for you neither hypothesis is likely to be alive. But if I say: "Be an agnostic

This essay, originally an address delivered before the Philosophical Clubs of Yale and Brown Universities, was first published in 1896.

or be a Christian," it is otherwise; trained as you are, each hypothesis makes some appeal, however small, to your belief.

2. Next, if I say to you: "Choose between going out with your umbrella or without it," I do not offer you a genuine option, for it is not forced. You can easily avoid it by not going out at all. Similarly, if I say, "Either love me or hate me," "Either call my theory true or call it false," your option is avoidable. You may remain indifferent to me, neither loving nor hating, and you may decline to offer any judgment as to my theory. But if I say, "Either accept this truth or go without it," I put on you a forced option, for there is no standing place outside of the alternative. Every dilemma based on a complete logical disjunction, with no possibility of not choosing, is an option of this forced kind.

3. Finally, if I were Dr. Nansen and proposed to you to join my North Pole expedition, your option would be momentous; for this would probably be your only similar opportunity, and your choice now would either exclude you from the North Pole sort of immortality altogether or put at least the chance of it into your hands. He who refuses to embrace a unique opportunity loses the prize as surely as if he tried and failed. *Per contra,* the option is trivial when the opportunity is not unique, when the stake is insignificant, or when the decision is reversible if it later prove unwise. Such trivial options abound in the scientific life. A chemist finds an hypothesis live enough to spend a year in its verification: he believes in it to that extent. But if his experiments prove inconclusive either way, he is quit for his loss of time, no vital harm being done.

It will facilitate our discussion if we keep all these distinctions well in mind.

II

The next matter to consider is the actual psychology of human opinion. When we look at certain facts, it seems as if our passional and volitional nature lay at the root of all our convictions. When we look at others, it seems as if they could do nothing when the intellect had once said its say. Let us take the latter facts up first.

Does it not seem preposterous on the very face of it to talk of our opinions being modifiable at will? Can our will either help or hinder our intellect in its perceptions of truth? Can we, by just willing it, believe that Abraham Lincoln's existence is a myth, and that the portraits of him in *McClure's Magazine* are all of some one else? Can we, by any effort of our will, or by any strength of wish that it were true, believe ourselves well and about when we are roaring with rheumatism in bed, or feel certain that the sum of the two one-dollar bills in our pocket must be a hundred dollars? We can *say* any of these things, but we are absolutely impotent to believe them; and of just such things is the whole fabric of the truths that we do believe in made up—matters of fact, immediate or remote, as Hume said, and relations between ideas, which are either there or not there for us if we see them so, and which if not there cannot be put there by any action of our own.

In Pascal's *Thoughts* there is a celebrated passage known in literature as Pascal's wager. In it he tries to force us into Christianity by reasoning as if our concern with truth resembled our concern with the stakes in a game of chance. Translated freely his words are these: You must either believe or not believe that God is—which will you do? Your human reason cannot say. A game is going on between you and the nature of things which at the day of judgment will bring out either heads or tails. Weigh what your gains and your losses would be if you should stake all you have on heads, or God's existence; if you win in such case, you gain eternal beatitude; if you lose, you lose nothing at all. If there were an infinity of chances, and only one for God in this wager, still you ought to stake your all on God; for though you surely risk a finite loss by this procedure, any finite loss is reasonable, even a certain one is reasonable, if there is but the possibility of infinite gain. Go, then, and take holy water, and have masses said; belief will come and stupefy your scruples. . . . Why should you not? At bottom, what have you to lose?

You probably feel that when religious faith expresses itself thus, in the language of the gamingtable, it is put to its last trumps. Surely Pascal's own personal belief in masses and holy water had far other springs; and this celebrated page of his is but an argument for others, a last desperate snatch at a weapon against the hardness of the unbelieving heart. We feel that a faith in masses and holy water adopted wilfully after such a mechanical calculation would lack the inner soul of faith's reality; and if we were ourselves in the place of the Deity, we should probably take particular pleasure in cutting off believers of this pattern from their infinite reward. It is evident that unless there be some preexisting tendency to believe in masses and holy water, the option offered to the will by Pascal is not a living option. Certainly no Turk ever took to masses and holy water on its account; and even to us Protestants these means of salvation seem such foregone impossibilities that Pascal's logic, invoked for them specifically, leaves us unmoved. As well might the Mahdi write to us, saying, "I am the Expected One whom God has created in his effulgence. You shall be infinitely happy if you confess me; otherwise you shall be cut off from the light of the sun. Weigh, then, your infinite gain if I am genuine against your finite sacrifice if I am not!" His logic would be that of Pascal; but he would vainly use it on us, for the hypothesis he offers us is dead. No tendency to act on it exists in us to any degree.

The talk of believing by our volition seems, then, from one point of view, simply silly. From another point of view it is worse than silly, it is vile. When one turns to the magnificent edifice of the physical sciences, and sees how it was reared; what thousands of disinterested moral lives of men lie buried in its mere foundations; what patience and postponement, what choking down of preference, what submission to the icy laws of outer fact are wrought into its very stones and mortar; how absolutely impersonal it stands in its vast augustness —then how besotted and contemptible seems every little sentimentalist who comes blowing his voluntary smoke-wreaths, and pretending to decide things from out of his private dream! Can we wonder if those bred in the rugged and manly school of science should feel like spewing such subjectivism out of their mouths? The whole system of loyalties which grow up in the schools of science go dead against its toleration; so that it is only natural that those who have caught the scientific fever

should pass over to the opposite extreme, and write sometimes as if the incorruptibly truthful intellect ought positively to prefer bitterness and unacceptableness to the heart in its cup.

> It fortifies my soul to know
> That though I perish, Truth is so

sings Clough, while Huxley exclaims: "My only consolation lies in the reflection that, however bad our posterity may become, so far as they hold by the plain rule of not pretending to believe what they have no reason to believe, because it may be to their advantage so to pretend [the word 'pretend' is surely here redundant], they will not have reached the lowest depth of immorality." And that delicious *enfant terrible* Clifford writes: "Belief is desecrated when given to unproved and unquestioned statements for the solace and private pleasure of the believer... Whoso would deserve well of his fellows in this matter will guard the purity of his belief with a very fanaticism of jealous care, lest at any time it should rest on an unworthy object, and catch a stain which can never be wiped away.... If [a] belief has been accepted on insufficient evidence [even though the belief be true, as Clifford on the same page explains] the pleasure is a stolen one.... It is sinful because it is stolen in defiance of our duty to mankind. That duty is to guard ourselves from such beliefs as from a pestilence which may shortly master our own body and then spread to the rest of the town....It is wrong always, everywhere, and for every one, to believe anything upon insufficient evidence."

III

All this strikes one as healthy, even when expressed, as by Clifford, with somewhat too much of robustious pathos in the voice. Free will and simple wishing do seem, in the matter of our credences, to be only fifth wheels to the coach. Yet if any one should thereupon assume that intellectual insight is what remains after wish and will and sentimental preference have taken wing, or that pure reason is what then settles our opinions, he would fly quite as directly in the teeth of the facts.

It is only our already dead hypotheses that our willing nature is unable to bring to life again. But what has made them dead for us is for the most part a previous action of our willing nature of an antagonistic kind. When I say "willing nature," I do not mean only such deliberate volitions as may have set up habits of belief that we cannot now escape from—I mean all such factors of belief as fear and hope, prejudice and passion, imitation and partisanship, the circumpressure of our caste and set. As a matter of fact we find ourselves believing, we hardly know how or why. Mr. Balfour gives the name of "authority" to all those influences, born of the intellectual climate, that make hypotheses possible or impossible for us, alive or dead. Here in this room, we all of us believe in molecules and the conservation of energy, in democracy and necessary progress, in Protestant Christianity and the duty of fighting for "the doctrine of the immortal Monroe," all for no reasons worthy of the name. We see into these matters with no more inner clearness, and probably with much less, than any disbeliever in them might possess. His unconventionality would probably have some grounds to show for its conclusions; but for us, not insight, but the *prestige* of the opinions, is what makes the spark shoot from them and light up our sleeping magazines of faith. Our reason is quite satisfied, in nine hundred and ninety-nine cases out of every thousand of us, if it can find a few arguments that will do to recite in case our credulity is criticized by some one else. Our faith is faith in some one else's faith, and in the greatest matters this is the most the case. . . .

Evidently, then, our non-intellectual nature does influence our convictions. There are passional tendencies and volitions which run before and others which come after belief, and it is only the latter that are too late for the fair; and they are not too late when the previous passional work has been already in their own direction. Pascal's argument, instead of being powerless, then seems a regular clincher, and is the last stroke needed to make our faith in masses and holy water complete. The state of things is evidently far from simple; and pure insight and logic, whatever they might do ideally, are not the only things that really do produce our creeds.

IV

Our next duty, having recognized this mixed-up state of affairs, is to ask whether it be simply reprehensible and pathological, or whether, on the contrary, we must treat it as a normal element in making up our minds. The thesis I defend is, briefly stated, this: *Our passional nature not only lawfully may, but must, decide an option between propositions, whenever it is a genuine option that cannot by its nature be decided on intellectual grounds; for to say, under such circumstances, "Do not decide, but leave the question open," is itself a passional decision—just like deciding yes or no—and is attended with the same risk of losing the truth. . . .*

VII

One more point, small but important, and our preliminaries are done. There are two ways of looking at our duty in the matter of opinion—ways entirely different, and yet ways about whose difference the theory of knowledge seems hitherto to have shown very little concern. *We must know the truth;* and *we must avoid error*—these are our first and great commandments as would-be knowers; but they are not two ways of stating an identical commandment, they are two separable laws. Although it may indeed happen that when we believe the truth A, we escape as an incidental consequence from believing the falsehood B, it hardly ever happens that by merely disbelieving B we necessarily believe A. We may in escaping B fall into believing other falsehoods, C or D, just as bad as B; or we may escape B by not believing anything at all, not even A.

Believe truth! Shun error!—these, we see, are two materially different laws; and by choosing between them we may end by coloring differently our whole intellectual life. We may regard the chase for truth as paramount, and the avoidance of error as secondary; or we may, on the other hand, treat the avoidance of error as more imperative, and let truth take its chance. Clifford, in the instructive passage which I have quoted, exhorts us to the latter course. Believe nothing, he tells us, keep your mind in suspense forever, rather than by closing it on insufficient evidence incur the awful risk of believing lies. You, on the other hand, may think that the risk of being in error is a very small matter when compared with the blessings of real knowledge, and be ready to be duped many times in your investigation rather than postpone indefinitely the chance of guessing true. I myself find it impossible to go with Clifford. We must remember that these feelings of our duty about either truth or error are in any case only expressions of our passional life. Biologically considered, our minds are as ready to grind out falsehood as veracity, and he who says, "Better go without belief forever than believe a lie!" merely shows his own preponderant private horror of becoming a dupe. He may be critical of many of his desires and fears, but this fear he slavishly obeys. He cannot imagine any one questioning its binding force. For my own part, I have also a horror of being duped; but I can believe that worse things than being duped may happen to a man in this world: so Clifford's exhortation has to my ears a thoroughly fantastic sound. It is like a general informing his soldiers that it is better to keep out of battle forever than to risk a single wound. Not so are victories either over enemies or over nature gained. Our errors are surely not such awfully solemn things. In a world where we are so certain to incur them in spite of all our caution, a certain lightness of heart seems healthier than this excessive nervousness on their behalf. At any rate, it seems the fittest thing for the empiricist philosopher.

VIII

And now, after all this introduction, let us go straight at our question. I have said, and now repeat it, that not only as a matter of fact do we find our passional nature influencing us in our opinions, but that there are some options between opinions in which this influence must be regarded both as an inevitable and as a lawful determinant of our choice.

I fear here that some of you my hearers will begin to scent danger, and lend an inhospitable ear. Two first steps of passion you have indeed had to admit as necessary—we must think so as to avoid dupery, and we must think so as to gain truth; but the surest path to those ideal consummations, you will probably consider, is from now onwards to take no further passional step.

Well, of course, I agree as far as the facts will allow. Wherever the option between losing truth and gaining it is not momentous, we can throw the chance of *gaining truth* away, and at any rate save ourselves from any chance of *believing falsehood,* by not making up our minds at all till objective evidence has come. In scientific questions, this is almost always the case; and even in human affairs in general, the need of acting is seldom so urgent that a false belief to act on is better than no belief at all. Law courts, indeed, have to decide on the best evidence attainable for the moment, because a judge's duty is to make law as well as to ascertain it, and (as a learned judge once said to me) few cases are worth spending much time over; the great thing is to have them decided on *any* acceptable principle, and got out of the way. But in our dealings with objective nature we obviously are recorders, not makers, of the truth; and decisions for the mere sake of deciding promptly and getting on to the next business would be wholly out of place. Throughout the breadth of physical nature facts are what they are quite independently of us, and seldom is there any such hurry about them that the risks of being duped by believing a premature theory need be faced. The questions here are always trivial options, the hypotheses are hardly living (at any rate not living for us spectators), the choice between believing truth or falsehood is seldom forced. The attitude of sceptical balance is therefore the absolutely wise one if we would escape mistakes. What difference, indeed, does it make to most of us whether we have or have not a theory of the Röntgen rays, whether we believe or not in mind-stuff, or have a conviction about the causality of conscious states? It makes no difference. Such options are not forced on us. On every account it is better not to make them, but still keep weighing reasons *pro et contra* with an indifferent hand.

I speak, of course, here of the purely judging mind. For purposes of discovery such indifference is to be less highly recommended, and science would be far less advanced than she is if the passionate desires of individuals to get their own faiths confirmed had been kept out of the game. See for example the sagacity which Spencer and Weismann now display. On the other hand, if you want an absolute duffer in an investigation, you must, after all, take the man who has no interest whatever in its results: he is the warranted incapable, the positive fool. The most useful investigator, because the most sensitive observer, is always he whose eager interest in one side of the question is balanced by an equally keen nervousness lest he become deceived.[1] Science has organized this nervousness into a regular *technique,* her so-called method of verification; and she has fallen so deeply in love with the method that one may even say she has ceased to care for truth by itself at all. It is only truth as technically verified that interests her. The truth of truths might come in merely affirmative form, and she would decline to touch it. Such truth as that, she might repeat with Clifford, would be stolen in defiance of her duty to mankind. Human passions, however, are stronger than technical rules. "*Le coeur a ses raisons,*" as Pascal says, "*que la raison ne connait pas*";[2] and however indifferent to all but the bare rules of the game the umpire, the abstract intellect, may be, the concrete players who furnish him the materials to judge of are usually, each one of them, in love with some pet "live hypothesis" of his own. Let us agree, however, that wherever there is no forced option, the dispassionately judicial intellect with no pet hypothesis, saving us, as it does, from dupery at any rate, ought to be our ideal.

The question next arises: Are there not somewhere forced options in our speculative questions, and can we (as men who may be interested at least as much in positively gaining truth as in merely escaping dupery) always wait with impunity till the coercive evidence shall have arrived? It seems *a priori* improbable that the truth should be so nicely adjusted to our needs and powers as that. In the great boarding-house of nature, the cakes and the butter and the syrup seldom come out so even and leave the plates so clean. Indeed, we should view them with scientific suspicion if they did.

IX

Moral questions immediately present themselves as questions whose solution cannot wait for sensible proof. A moral question is a question not of what sensibly exists, but of what is good, or would be good if it did exist. Science can tell us what exists; but to compare the *worths,* both of what exists and of what does not exist, we must consult not science, but what Pascal calls our heart. . . .

Turn now from these wide questions of good to a certain class of questions of fact, questions concerning personal relations, states of mind between one man and another. *Do you like me or not?*—for example. Whether you do or not depends, in countless instances, on whether I meet you halfway, am willing to assume that you must like me, and show you trust and expectation. The previous faith on my part in your liking's existence is in such cases what makes your liking come. But if I stand aloof, and refuse to budge an inch until I have objective evidence, until you shall have done something apt, as the absolutists say, *ad extorquendum assensum meum,* ten to one your liking never comes. How many women's hearts are vanquished by the mere sanguine insistence of some man that they *must* love him! He will not consent to the hypothesis that they cannot. The desire for a certain kind of truth here brings about that special truth's existence; and so it is in innumerable cases of other sorts. . . . *And where faith in a fact can help create the fact,* that would be an insane logic which should say that faith running ahead of scientific evidence is the "lowest kind of immorality" into which a thinking being can fall. Yet such is the logic by which our scientific absolutists pretend to regulate our lives!

X

In truths dependent on our personal action, then, faith based on desire is certainly a lawful and possibly an indispensable thing.

But now, it will be said, these are all childish human cases, and have nothing to do with great cosmical matters, like the question of religious faith. Let us then pass on to that. Religions differ so much in their accidents that in discussing the religious question we must make it very generic and broad. What then do we now mean by the religious hypothesis? Science says things are; morality says some things are better than other things; and religion says essentially two things.

First, she says that the best things are the more eternal things, the overlapping things, the things in the universe that throw the last stone, so to speak, and say the final word. "Perfection is eternal"—this phrase of Charles Secrétan seems a good way of putting this first affirmation of religion, an affirmation which obviously cannot yet be verified scientifically at all.

The second affirmation of religion is that we are better off even now if we believe her first affirmation to be true.

Now, let us consider what the logical elements of this situation are *in case the religious hypothesis in both its branches be really true.* (Of course, we must admit that possibility at the outset. If we are to discuss the question at all, it must involve a living option. If for any of you religion be a hypothesis that cannot, by any living possibility, be true, then you need go no farther. I speak to the "saving remnant" alone.) So proceeding, we see, first, that religion offers itself as a *momentous* option. We are supposed to gain, even now, by our belief, and to lose by our non-belief, a certain vital good. Secondly, religion is a *forced* option, so far as that good goes. We cannot escape the issue by remaining sceptical and waiting for more light, because, although we do avoid error in that way *if religion be untrue,* we lose the good, *if it be true,* just as certainly as if we positively chose to disbelieve. It is as if a man should hesitate indefinitely to ask a certain woman to marry him because he was not perfectly sure that she would prove an angel after he brought her home. Would he not cut himself off from that particular angel-possibility as decisively as if he went and married some one else? Scepticism, then, is not avoidance of option; it is option of a certain particular kind of risk. *Better risk loss of truth than chance of error*—that is your faith-vetoer's exact position. He is actively playing his stake as much as the believer is; he is backing the field against the religious hypothesis, just as the believer is backing the religious hypothesis against the field. To preach scepticism to us as a duty until "sufficient evidence" for religion be found, is tantamount therefore to telling us,

when in presence of the religious hypothesis, that to yield to our fear of its being error is wiser and better than to yield to our hope that it may be true. It is not intellect against all passion, then; it is only intellect with one passion laying down its law. And by what, forsooth, is the supreme wisdom of this passion warranted? Dupery for dupery, what proof is there that dupery through hope is so much worse than dupery through fear? I, for one, can see no proof; and I simply refuse obedience to the scientist's command to imitate his kind of option, in a case where my own stake is important enough to give me the right to choose my own form of risk. If religion be true and the evidence for it be still insufficient, I do not wish, by putting your extinguisher upon my nature (which feels to me as if it had after all some business in this matter), to forfeit my sole chance in life of getting upon the winning side—that chance depending, of course, on my willingness to run the risk of acting as if my passional need of taking the world religiously might be prophetic and right.

All this is on the supposition that it really may be prophetic and right, and that, even to us who are discussing the matter, religion is a live hypothesis which may be true. Now, to most of us religion comes in a still further way that makes a veto on our active faith even more illogical. The more perfect and more eternal aspect of the universe is represented in our religions as having personal form. The universe is no longer a mere *It* to us, but a *Thou,* if we are religious; and any relation that may be possible from person to person might be possible here. For instance, although in one sense we are passive portions of the universe, in another we show a curious autonomy, as if we were small active centers on our own account. We feel, too, as if the appeal of religion to us were made to our own active goodwill, as if evidence might be forever withheld from us unless we met the hypothesis halfway to take a trivial illustration: just as a man who in a company of gentlemen made no advances, asked a warrant for every concession, and believed no one's word without proof, would cut himself off by such churlishness from all the social rewards that a more trusting spirit would earn—so here, one who should shut himself up in snarling logicality and try to make the gods extort his recognition willy-nilly, or not get it at all, might cut himself off forever from his only opportunity of making the gods' acquaintance. This feeling, forced on us we know not whence that by obstinately believing that there are gods (although not to do so would be so easy both for our logic and our life) we are doing the universe the deepest service we can, seems part of the living essence of the religious hypothesis. If the hypothesis *were* true in all its parts, including this one, then pure intellectualism, with its veto on our making willing advances, would be an absurdity; and some participation of our sympathetic nature would be logically required. I therefore, for one, cannot see my way to accepting the agnostic rules for truthseeking, or wilfully agree to keep my willing nature out of the game. I cannot do so for this plain reason, that *a rule of thinking which would absolutely prevent me from acknowledging certain kinds of truth if those kinds of truth were really there, would be an irrational rule.* That for me is the long and short of the formal logic of the situation, no matter what the kinds of truth might materially be.

I confess I do not see how this logic can be escaped. But sad experience makes me fear that some of you may still shrink from radically saying with me, *in abstracto,* that we have the right to believe at our own risk any hypothesis that is live enough to tempt our will. I suspect, however, that if this is so, it is because you have got away from the abstract logical point of view altogether, and are thinking (perhaps without realizing it) of some particular religious hypothesis which for you is dead. The freedom to "believe what we will" you apply to the case of some patent superstition; and the faith you think of is the faith defined by the schoolboy when he said, is when you believe something that you know ain't true." I can only repeat that this is misapprehension. *In concreto,* the freedom to believe can only cover living options which the intellect of the individual cannot by itself resolve; and living options never seem absurdities to him who has them to consider. When I look at the religious question as it really puts itself to concrete men, and when I think of all the possibilities which both practically and theoretically it involves,

then this command that we shall put a stopper on our heart, instincts, and courage, and *wait*— acting of course meanwhile more or less as if religion were *not* true[3]—till doomsday, or till such time as our intellect and senses working together may have raked in evidence enough—this command, I say, seems to me the queerest idol ever manufactured in the philosophic cave. Were we scholastic absolutists, there might be more excuse. If we had an infallible intellect with its objective certitudes, we might feel ourselves disloyal to such a perfect organ of knowledge in not trusting to it exclusively, in not waiting for its releasing word. But if we are empiricists, if we believe that no bell in us tolls to let us know for certain when truth is in our grasp, then it seems a piece of idle fantasticality to preach so solemnly our duty of waiting for the bell. Indeed we *may* wait if we will—I hope you do not think that I am denying that—but if we do so, we do so at our peril as much as if we believed. In either case we *act,* taking our life in our hands. No one of us ought to issue vetoes to the other, nor should we bandy words of abuse. We ought, on the contrary, delicately and profoundly to respect one another's mental freedom: then only shall we bring about the intellectual republic; then only shall we have that spirit of inner tolerance without which all our outer tolerance is soulless, and which is empiricism's glory; then only shall we live and let live, in speculative as well as in practical things.

I began by a reference to Fitz-James Stephen; let me end by a quotation from him. "What do you think of yourself? What do you think of the world? . . . These are questions with which all must deal as it seems good to them. They are riddles of the Sphinx, and in some way or other we must deal with them. . . . In all important transactions of life we have to take a leap in the dark. . . . If we decide to leave the riddles unanswered, that is a choice; if we waver in our answer, that, too, is a choice: but whatever choice we make, we make it at our peril. If a man chooses to turn his back altogether on God and the future, no one can prevent him; no one can show beyond reasonable doubt that he is mistaken. If a man thinks otherwise and acts as he thinks, I do not see that any one can prove that *he* is mistaken. Each must act as he thinks best; and if he is wrong, so much the worse for him. We stand on a mountain pass in the midst of whirling snow and blinding mist, through which we get glimpses now and then of paths which may be deceptive. If we stand still we shall be frozen to death. If we take the wrong road we shall be dashed to pieces. We do not certainly know whether there is any right one. What must we do? 'Be strong and of a good courage.' Act for the best, hope for the best, and take what comes.... If death ends all, we cannot meet death better."[4]

NOTES

1. Compare Wilfrid Ward's Essay "The Wish to Believe," in his *Witnesses to the Unseen* (Macmillan & Co., 1893).

2. "The heart has its reasons which reason does not know." Editor's Trans.

3. Since belief is measured by action, he who forbids us to believe religion to be true, necessarily also forbids us to act as we should if we did believe it to be true. The whole defence of religious faith hinges upon action. If the action required or inspired by the religious hypothesis is in no way different from that dictated by the naturalistic hypothesis, then religious faith is a pure superfluity, better pruned away, and controversy about its legitimacy is a piece of idle trifling, unworthy of serious minds. I myself believe, of course, that the religious hypothesis gives to the world an expression which specifically determines our reactions, and makes them in a large part unlike what they might be on a purely naturalistic scheme of belief.

4. *Liberty, Equality, Fraternity*, p. 353, 2d edition (London, 1874).

Without Evidence or Argument

KELLY JAMES CLARK

Kelly James Clark is Professor of Philosophy at Calvin College.

INTRODUCTION

Suppose a stranger, let's call him David, sends you a note that declares that your wife is cheating on you. No pictures are included, no dates or times, no names. Just the assertion of your wife's unfaithfulness. You have had already fifteen good, and so far as you know, faithful years with your wife. Her behavior hasn't changed dramatically in the past few years. Except for David's allegation, you have no reason to believe there has been a breach in the relationship. What should you do? Confront her with what you take to be the truth, straight from David's letter? Hire a detective to follow her for a week and hope against hope the letter is a hoax? Or do you simply remain secure in the trust that you have built up all those years?

Suppose, even worse, that your son Clifford comes home after taking his first philosophy course in college. He persuades you of the truth of the so-called "problem of other minds." How do you know that other minds and, therefore, other people exist? How do you know that people are not simply cleverly constructed robots with excellent makeup jobs? How do you know that behind the person facade lies a person—someone with thoughts, desires and feelings? You can't experience another person's feelings; you can't see another person's

From Kelly James Clark "Reformed Epistemology," *Modern Reformation Magazine*, vol. 7(1998). Reprinted with permission of the Alliance of Confessing Evangelicals, 1716, Spruce St., Philadelphia, PA 19103, www.ModernReformation.com.

thoughts (even if you were to cut off the top of their head and peer into their brain); and even Bill Clinton can't really feel another person's pain. Yet thoughts, desires, and feelings are all essential to being a person. So you can't tell from the outside or just by looking, so to speak, if someone is a person. I can know that *I* am a person because I experience my own thoughts, feelings and desires. But I can't know, because I don't have any access to your inner-experience, if you, or anyone else, is a person.

Since you can't know if anyone else is a person, you rightly infer that you can't know if your wife is a person. Unsure that your wife is a person, how do you treat her? Do you hire a philosophical detective to search the philosophical literature for a proof that people-like things really are people? Do you avoid cuddling in the meantime, given your aversion to snuggling with machines? Or do you simply trust your deep-seated conviction that, in spite of the lack of evidence, your wife is a person and deserves to be treated as such?

Two final "Supposes." Suppose that you come to believe that there is a God because your parents taught you from the cradle up that God exists. Or suppose that you are on a retreat or on the top of a mountain and have a sense of being loved by God or that God created the universe. You begin to believe in God, not because you are persuaded by the argument from design—you are simply taken with belief in God. You just find yourself believing, what you had heretofore denied, that God exists. Now you have come across the writings of David Hume and W. K. Clifford who insist that you base all of your beliefs on evidence. Hume raises a further point: your belief in an all-loving, omnipotent God is inconsistent with the evil that there is in the world. Given the fact of evil, God cannot exist. To meet this demand for evidence, do you become a temporary agnostic and begin perusing the texts of Aquinas, Augustine and Paley for a good proof of God's existence? Do you give up belief in God because you see Hume's point and can't see how God and evil could be reconciled? Or do you remain steady in your trust in God in spite of the lack of evidence and even in the face of counter-evidence?

My Suppose-This and Suppose-That Stories are intended to raise the problem of the relationship of our important beliefs to evidence (and counter-evidence). Since the Enlightenment, there has been a demand to expose all of our beliefs to the searching criticism of reason. If a belief is unsupported by the evidence, it is irrational to believe it. It is the position of Reformed epistemology (likely the position that Calvin held) that belief in God, like belief in other persons, does not require the support of evidence or argument in order for it to be rational. This view has been defended by some of the world's most prominent philosophers including Alvin Plantinga, Nicholas Wolterstorff, and William Alston.[1]

The claim that belief in God is rational without the support of evidence or argument is startling for many an atheist or theist. Most atheist intellectuals feel comfort in their disbelief in God because they judge that there is little or no evidence for God's existence. Many theistic thinkers, however, insist that belief in God requires evidence and that such a demand should and can be met. So the claim that a person does not need evidence in order to rationally believe in God runs against the grain for atheist thinkers and has raised the ire of many theists. In spite of the vitriolic response to Reformed epistemology, I believe it is eminently defensible. In order to defend it, let us examine its critique of the Enlightenment demand for evidence.

THE DEMAND FOR EVIDENCE

W. K. Clifford, in an oft-cited article, claims that it is wrong, always and everywhere, for anyone to believe anything on insufficient evidence. Such a strong claim makes one speculate on Clifford's childhood: one imagines young W. K. constantly pestering his parents with "Why? Why? Why?..." It is this childish attitude toward inquiry and the risks that belief requires that leads William James to chastise Clifford as an *enfant terrible*. But, rather than disparage his character, let's examine the deficiencies of his claim that everything must be believed only on the basis of sufficient evidence (Relevance:

If everything must be based on sufficient evidence, so must belief in God).

The first problem with Clifford's universal demand for evidence is that it cannot meet its own demand. Clifford offers two fetching examples (a shipowner who knowingly sends an unseaworthy ship to sea and, in the first example, it sinks and, in the second example, it makes the trip) in support of his claim. The examples powerfully demonstrate that in cases like the example, rational belief requires evidence. No one would disagree: some beliefs require evidence for their rational acceptability. But *all* beliefs in *every* circumstance? That's an exceedingly strong claim to make and, it turns out, one that cannot be based on evidence.

Consider what someone like Clifford might allow us to take for evidence: beliefs that we acquire through sensory experience and beliefs that are self-evident like logic and mathematics. Next rainy day, make a list of all of your experiential beliefs: The sky is blue, grass is green, most trees are taller than most grasshoppers, slugs leave a slimy trail.... Now add to this list all of your logical and mathematical beliefs: $2 + 2 = 4$, every proposition is either true or false, all of the even numbers that I know of are the sum of two prime numbers, in Euclidean geometry the interior angles of triangles equal 180. From these propositions, try to deduce the conclusion that it is wrong, always and everywhere, for anyone to believe anything on insufficient evidence. None of the propositions that are allowed as evidence have anything at all to do with the conclusion. So Clifford's universal demand for evidence cannot satisfy its own standard! Therefore, by Clifford's own criterion, it must be irrational. More likely, however, the demand is simply false and it is easy to see why.

We, finite beings that we are, simply cannot meet such a demand. Consider all of the beliefs that you currently hold. How many of those have met Clifford's strict demand for evidence? Clifford intends for all of us, like a scientist in a laboratory, to test all of our beliefs all of the time. Could your beliefs survive Clifford's test? Think of how many of your beliefs, even scientific ones, are acquired *just because someone told you*. Not having been to

Paraguay, I only have testimonial evidence that Paraguay is a country in South America. For all I know, all of the mapmakers have conspired to delude us about the existence of Paraguay (and even South America!). And, since I have been to relatively few countries around the world, I must believe in the existence of most countries (and that other people inhabit them and speak in that language) without support of evidence. I believe that $e = mc^2$ and that matter is made up of tiny little particles not because of experiments in a chemistry or physics lab (for all of my experiments failed) but because my science teachers told me so. Most of the beliefs that I have acquired are based on my trust in my teachers and not on careful consideration of what Clifford would consider adequate evidence. And in this busy day and age, I don't really have the time to live up to Clifford's demand for evidence! If we had the leisure to test all of our beliefs, perhaps we could meet the demand. But since we cannot meet that demand, we cannot be obligated to do so.

Even if we had the time, however, we could not meet this universal demand for evidence. The demand for evidence simply cannot be met in a large number of cases with the cognitive equipment that we have. No one, as mentioned above, has ever been able to prove the existence of other persons. No one has ever been able to prove that we were not created five minutes ago with our memories intact. No one has been able to prove the reality of the past or that, in the future, the sun will rise. This list could go on and on. There is a limit to the things that human beings can prove. A great deal of what we believe is based on faith, not on evidence or arguments.

I use the term "faith" here but that it is misleading. I don't mean to oppose faith to knowledge in these instances. For surely we know that the earth is more than five minutes old and that the sun will rise tomorrow (although, maybe not in cloudy Grand Rapids!) and that Paul converted to Christianity (and lots of other truths about the past), etc., etc., etc. In these cases, we know lots of things but we cannot prove them. We have to trust or rely on the cognitive faculties which produce these beliefs. We rely on our memory to produce memory beliefs (I remember having coffee with my breakfast this morning). We rely on an inductive faculty to produce beliefs about the veracity of natural laws (If I let go of this book, it will fall to the ground). We rely on our cognitive faculties when we believe that there are other persons, there is a past, there is a world independent of our mind, or what other people tell us. We can't help but trust our cognitive faculties.

It is easy to see why. Reasoning must start somewhere. Suppose we were required to offer evidence or arguments for all our beliefs. If we offer statements 1-4 as evidence for 5, we would have to offer arguments to support 1-4. And then we would have to offer arguments in support of the arguments that are used to support 1-4. And then we would need arguments. . . . You get the point. Reasoning must start somewhere. There have to be some truths that we can just accept and reason from. Why not start with belief in God?

WITHOUT EVIDENCE OR ARGUMENT

We have been outfitted with cognitive faculties that produce beliefs that we can reason from. The number of beliefs we do and must reason to is quite small compared to the number of beliefs that we do and must accept without the aid of a proof. That's the long and short of the human believing condition. We, in most cases, must rely on our God-given intellectual equipment to produce beliefs, without evidence or argument, in the appropriate circumstances. Is it reasonable to believe that God has created us with a cognitive faculty which produces belief in God without evidence or argument?

There are at least three reasons to believe that it is proper or rational for a person to accept belief in God without the need for an argument. First, there are very few people who have access to or the ability to assess most theistic arguments. It is hard to imagine, therefore, that the demand for evidence would be a requirement of reason. My grandmother, a paradigm of the non-philosophical believer, would cackle if I informed her that her belief in God was irrational because she was unable to understand Aquinas's second Way or to refute Hume's version of the argument

from evil. The demand for evidence is an imperialistic attempt to make philosophers out of people who have no need to become philosophers. It is curious that very few philosophers (like most ordinary folk) have come to belief in God on the basis of theistic arguments. I commissioned and published a collection of spiritual autobiographies from prominent Christian philosophers just to see if philosophers were any different from my Grandmother on this count. They weren't.[2]

Second, it seems that God has given us an awareness of himself that is not dependent on theistic arguments. It is hard to imagine that God would make rational belief as difficult as those that demand evidence contend. I encourage anyone who thinks that evidence is required for rational belief in God, to study very carefully the theistic arguments, their refutations and counter-refutations, and their increasing subtlety yet decreasing charm. Adequate assessment of these arguments would require a lengthy and torturous tour through the history of philosophy and may require the honing of one's logical and metaphysical skills beyond the capacity of most of us. Why put that sort of barrier between us and God? John Calvin believed that God had provided us with a sense of the divine. He writes:

> There is within the human mind, and indeed by natural instinct, an awareness of divinity. This we take to be beyond controversy. To prevent anyone from taking refuge in the pretense of ignorance, God himself has implanted in all men a certain understanding of his divine majesty. Ever renewing its memory, he repeatedly sheds fresh drops. . . . Indeed, the perversity of the impious, who though they struggle furiously are unable to extricate themselves from the fear of God, is abundant testimony that this conviction namely that there is some God, is naturally inborn in all, and is fixed deep within, as it were in the very marrow. From this we conclude that it is not a doctrine that must first be learned in school, but one of which each of us is master from his mother's womb and which nature itself permits no one to forget.[3]

Calvin contends that people are accountable to God for their unbelief not because they have failed to submit to a convincing theistic proof, but because they have suppressed the truth that God has implanted within their minds. It is natural to suppose that if God created us with cognitive faculties which by and large reliably produce beliefs without the need for evidence, he would likewise provide us with a cognitive faculty which produces belief in him without the need for evidence.

Third, belief in God is more like belief in a person than belief in a scientific theory. Consider the examples that started this essay. Somehow the scientific approach—doubt first, consider all of the available evidence, and believe later—seems woefully inadequate or inappropriate to personal relations. What seems manifestly reasonable for physicists in their laboratory is desperately deficient in human relations. Human relations demand trust, commitment and faith. If belief in God is more like belief in other persons than belief in atoms, then the trust that is appropriate to persons will be appropriate to God. We cannot and should not arbitrarily insist that the scientific method is appropriate to every kind of human practice. The fastidious scientist, who cannot leave the demand for evidence in her laboratory, will find herself cut off from relationships that she could otherwise reasonably maintain—with friends, family and, perhaps even, God.

WITH OR WITHOUT EVIDENCE

I haven't said that belief in God could not or, in some cases, should not be based on evidence or argument. Indeed, I am inclined to think that the theistic arguments do provide some, non-coercive, evidence of God's existence. By non-coercive, I mean that the theistic arguments aren't of such power and illumination that they should be expected to persuade all rational creatures. Rational people could rationally reject the theistic proofs. Rational people, and this is a fact that we must live with, rationally disagree. Nonetheless, I believe that someone could rationally believe in God on the basis of theistic arguments, but no one needs to.[4]

Reformed epistemologists also believe, like Calvin, that the natural knowledge of himself

that God has implanted within us has been overlaid by sin. Part of the knowledge process may require the removal of the effects of sin on our minds. Attention to theistic arguments might do that. Also, some of the barriers to religious belief—such as the problem of evil or the alleged threat of science to religion—may need to be removed before one can see the light that has been shining within all along.

But the scales can fall from the "mind's eye" in a wide variety of means: on a mountaintop or at the ocean, looking at a flower, through a humbling experience, or by reading *The Chronicles of Narnia*. The list goes on yet a certain common feature should be noticed (and not the fact that few people have ever acquired belief in God as a result of the study of theistic proofs). The primary obstacle to belief in God seems to be more moral than intellectual. On the mountains one may feel one's smallness in relation to the grandness of it all. The flower may arouse one's sense of beauty. The loss of a job or a divorce may reveal one's unjustified pride. And *The Chronicles of Narnia* may awaken the dormant faith of a child. In all of these cases, the scales slide off the mind's eye when the overweening self is dethroned (not to mix too many metaphors!). Humility, not proofs, may be necessary to the realization of belief in God.

Conclusion

This approach to belief in God has been rather descriptive. We need to pay a lot more attention to how actual people actually acquire beliefs. The psychology of believing may tell us a lot about our cognitive equipment. The lessons learned from observing people and their beliefs support the position that I have defended: rational people may rationally believe in God without evidence or argument.

NOTES

1. Alvin Plantinga, "Reason and Belief in God," Nicholas Wolterstorff, "Can Belief in God Be Rational If It Has No Foundations?" and William Alston, "Christian Experience and Christian Belief" in *Faith and Rationality*, Plantinga and

Wolterstorff eds. (Notre Dame, Indiana: University of Notre Dame Press, 1983); William Alston, *Perceiving God* (Ithaca, New York: Cornell University Press, 1991); Alvin Plantinga, *Warranted Christian Belief* (New York and Oxford: Oxford University Press, 1999).

2. See Kelly James Clark, *Philosophers Who Believe* (Downers Grove, IL: InterVarsity Press, 1993).
3. *Institutes of the Christian Religion*, Bk. 1, Ch. 3.
4. I argue this in some detail in my *Return to Reason* (Grand Rapids, Michigan: Eerdmans Publishing Company, 1990).

The Wager

BLAISE PASCAL

Blaise Pascal (1623–1662) was a scholar, mathematician, and theologian of great distinction.

Infinite—nothing. Our soul is cast into a body, where it finds number, dimension. Thereupon it reasons, and calls this nature necessity, and can believe nothing else.

Unity joined to infinity adds nothing to it, no more than one foot to an infinite measure. The finite is annihilated in the presence of the infinite, and becomes a pure nothing. So our spirit before God, so our justice before divine justice. There is not so great a disproportion between our justice and that of God as between unity and infinity.

The justice of God must be vast like His compassion. Now justice to the outcast is less vast and ought less to offend our feelings than mercy toward the elect.

We know that there is an infinite, and are ignorant of its nature. As we know it to be false that numbers are finite, it is therefore true that there is an infinity in number. But we do not know what it is. It is false that it is even, it is false that it is odd; for the addition of a unit can make no change in its nature. Yet it is a number, and every number is odd or even (this is certainly true of every finite number). So we may well know that there is a God without knowing what He is. Is there not one substantial truth, seeing there are so many things which are not the truth itself?

We know then the existence and nature of the finite, because we also are finite and have

extension. We know the existence of the infinite and are ignorant of its nature, because it has extension like us, but not limits like us. But we know neither the existence nor the nature of God, because He has neither extension nor limits.

But by faith we know His existence; in glory we shall know His nature. Now, I have already shown that we may well know the existence of a thing, without knowing its nature.

Let us now speak according to natural lights.

If there is a God, He is infinitely incomprehensible, since, having neither parts nor limits, He has no affinity to us. We are then incapable of knowing either what He is or if He is. This being so, who will dare to undertake the decision of the question? Not we, who have no affinity to Him.

Who then will blame Christians for not being able to give a reason for their belief, since they profess a religion for which they cannot give a reason? They declare, in expounding it to the world, that it is a foolishness, *stultitiam;* [I Cor. 1.21.] and then you complain that they do not prove it! If they proved it, they would not keep their word; it is in lacking proofs that they are not lacking in sense. "Yes, but although this excuses those who offer it as such and takes away from them the blame of putting it forward without reason, it does not excuse those who

---

Blaisie Pascal, *Pensées,* translated by W. F. Trotter.

receive it." Let us then examine this point, and say, "God is, or He is not." But to which side shall we incline? Reason can decide nothing here. There is an infinite chaos which separated us. A game is being played at the extremity of this infinite distance where heads or tails will turn up. What will you wager? According to reason, you can do neither the one thing nor the other; according to reason, you can defend neither of the propositions.

Do not, then, reprove for error those who have made a choice; for you know nothing about it. "No, but I blame them for having made, not this choice, but a choice; for again both he who chooses heads and he who chooses tails are equally at fault, they are both in the wrong. The true course is not to wager at all."

Yes; but you must wager. It is not optional. You are embarked. Which will you choose then? Let us see. Since you must choose, let us see which interests you least. You have two things to lose, the true and the good; and two things to stake, your reason and your will, your knowledge and your happiness; and your nature has two things to shun, error and misery. Your reason is no more shocked in choosing one rather than the other, since you must of necessity choose. This is one point settled. But your happiness? Let us weigh the gain and the loss in wagering that God is. Let us estimate these two chances. If you gain, you gain all; if you lose, you lose nothing. Wager, then, without hesitation that He is. "That is very fine. Yes, I must wager; but I may perhaps wager too much." Let us see. Since there is an equal risk of gain and of loss, if you had only to gain two lives, instead of one, you might still wager. But if there were three lives to gain, you would have to play (since you are under the necessity of playing), and you would be imprudent, when you are forced to play, not to chance your life to gain three at a game where there is an equal risk of loss and gain. But there is an eternity of life and happiness. And this being so, if there were an infinity of chances, of which one only would be for you, you would still be right in wagering one to win two, and you would act stupidly, being obliged to play, by refusing to stake one life against three at a game in which out of an infinity of chances there is one for you, if there were an infinity of an infinitely happy life to gain. But there is here an infinity of an infinitely happy life to gain, a chance of gain against a finite number of chances of loss, and what you stake is finite. It is all divided; wherever the infinite is and there is not an infinity of chances of loss against that of gain, there is no time to hesitate, you must give all. And thus, when one is forced to play, he must renounce reason to preserve his life, rather than risk it for infinite gain, as likely to happen as the loss of nothingness.

For it is no use to say it is uncertain if we will gain, and it is certain that we risk, and that the infinite distance between the *certainty* of what is staked and the *uncertainty* of what will be gained, equals the finite good which is certainly staked against the uncertain infinite. It is not so, as every player stakes a certainty to gain an uncertainty, and yet he stakes a finite certainty to gain a finite uncertainty, without transgressing against reason. There is not an infinite distance between the certainty staked and the uncertainty of the gain; that is untrue. In truth, there is an infinity between the certainty of gain and the certainty of loss. But the uncertainty of the gain is proportioned to the certainty of the stake according to the proportion of the chances of gain and loss. Hence it comes that, if there are as many risks on one side as on the other, the course is to play even; and then the certainty of the stake is equal to the uncertainty of the gain, so far is it from fact that there is an infinite distance between them. And so our proposition is of infinite force, when there is the finite to stake in a game where there are equal risks of gain and of loss, and the infinite to gain. This is demonstrable; and if men are capable of any truths, this is one.

"I confess it, I admit it. But, still, is there no means of seeing the faces of the cards?" Yes, Scripture and the rest, etc. "Yes, but I have my hands tied and my mouth closed; I am forced to wager, and am not free. I am not released, and am so made that I cannot believe. What, then, would you have me do?"

True. But at least learn your inability to believe, since reason brings you to this, and yet you cannot believe. Endeavour, then, to convince yourself, not by increase of proofs of God, but by the abatement of your passions. You would like to attain faith and do not know the way; you would like to cure yourself of unbelief and ask the remedy for it. Learn of those who have been bound like you, and who now stake all their possessions. These are people who know the way which you would follow, and who are cured of an ill of which you would be cured. Follow the way by which they began; by acting as if they believed, taking the holy water, having masses said, etc. Even this will naturally make you believe, and deaden your acuteness. "But this is what I am afraid of." And why? What have you to lose?

But to show you that this leads you there, it is this which will lessen the passions, which are your stumbling-blocks.

The end of this discourse.

Now, what harm will befall you in taking this side? You will be faithful, humble, grateful, generous, a sincere friend, truthful. Certainly you will not have those poisonous pleasures, glory and luxury; but will you not have others? I will tell you that you will thereby gain in this life, and that, at each step you take on this road, you will see so great certainty of gain, so much nothingness in what you risk, that you will at last recognize that you have wagered for something certain and infinite, for which you have given nothing.

"Ah! This discourse transports me, charms me," etc.

If this discourse pleases you and seems impressive, know that it is made by a man who has knelt, both before and after it, in prayer to that Being, infinite and without parts, before whom he lays all he has, for you also to lay before Him all you have for your own good and for His glory, that so strength may be given to lowliness.

Custom is our nature. He who is accustomed to the faith believes in it, can no longer fear hell, and believes in nothing else. He who is accustomed to believe that the king is terrible . . . etc. Who doubts, then, that our soul, being accustomed to see number, space, motion, believes that and nothing else?

Do you believe it to be impossible that God is infinite, without parts? Yes. I wish therefore to show you an infinite and indivisible thing. It is a point moving everywhere with an infinite velocity; for it is one in all places and is all totality in every place.

Let this effect of nature, which previously seemed to you impossible, make you know that there may be others of which you are still ignorant. Do not draw this conclusion from your experiment, that there remains nothing for you to know; but rather that there remains an infinity for you to know.

It is false that we are worthy of the love of others; it is unfair that we should desire it. If we were born reasonable and impartial, knowing ourselves and others, we should not give this bias to our will. However, we are born with it; therefore born unjust, for all tends to self. This is contrary to all order. We must consider the general good; and the propensity to self is the beginning of all disorder, in war, in politics, in economy, and in the particular body of man. The will is therefore depraved.

If the members of natural and civil communities tend toward the weal of the body, the communities themselves ought to look to another more general body of which they are members. We ought, therefore, to look to the whole. We are, therefore, born unjust and depraved.

No religion but our own has taught that man is born in sin. No sea of philosophers has said this. Therefore none have declared the truth.

No sect or religion has always existed on earth, but the Christian religion.

We owe a great debt to those who point out faults. For they mortify us. They teach us that we have been despised. They do not prevent our being so in the future; for we have many other faults for which we may be despised. They prepare for us the exercise of correction and freedom from fault.

The heart has its reasons, which reason does not know. We feel it in a thousand things. I say that the heart naturally loves the Universal Being, and also itself naturally, according as it gives itself to them; and it hardens itself against one or the other at its will. You have rejected the one and kept the other. Is it by reason that you love yourself?

It is the heart which experiences God, and not the reason. This, then, is faith: God felt by the heart, not by the reason.

Faith is a gift of God; do not believe that we said it was a gift of reasoning. Other religions do not say this of their faith. They only give reasoning in order to arrive at it, and yet it does not bring them to it.

The only science contrary to common sense and human nature is that alone which has always existed among men.

The Christian religion alone makes man altogether lovable and happy. In honesty, we cannot perhaps be altogether lovable and happy.

Miracles and Testimony

SIMON BLACKBURN

Simon Blackburn is Professor of Philosophy at the University of Cambridge. He has written important works in philosophy of language and moral theory.

MIRACLES AND TESTIMONY

. . . Many people suppose that religious faith is well supported by the occurrence of miraculous events. A prophet may establish divine credentials by foreseeing the future, or by miraculous healing, or appearance after death, or other such signs.

Most of us are not directly privileged to see such events. Rather, we take our belief from other reports of them: testimony. We read of them in the Bible, or the Koran, or the *Lives of the Saints,* or even the *National Enquirer.* We don't personally watch, for instance, an amputated limb growing back to normal, but we may have heard that somewhere over the hills there is an absolutely unshakeable confirmed sighting of such a thing. People may not personally have been abducted by aliens, but they may believe wholeheartedly other people who tell them that they have, or that their brothers or cousins have. Even if we have not recently sighted the long-buried Elvis, we may read and believe that some people have.

Hume asked the telling question: when is it reasonable to believe such testimony?*

Suppose we leave on one side the 'miraculous' element—the question of whether any such event is due to invisible powers, or divine intervention. Still, any candidate for a miracle has to be not only surprising, but totally surprising, the kind of thing that, in the normal course of events, just never happens (we are not talking here about the sense in which the whole creation is miraculous, since that would take us back to the cosmological argument). To establish divine credentials, it is not enough for someone to be the hero of unusual events. He needs really incredible events: people elevating themselves in the air, lead floating, water turning into wine, the dead coming back to life. The challenge to the putative miracle-worker is: go on, amaze me. So when is it reasonable to believe testimony for such outlandish, totally out-of-the-ordinary events?

Hume begins by making a straightforward enough claim about human sayings. It is, we believe, a fact that they are mostly true. Hume claims that if we infer from a premise of the kind 'This person is telling me that p' to a conclusion 'So, p is probably true,' we are doing the same

---

From Simon Blackburn, *Think* (Oxford University Press, 1998), pp. 176-192. Reprinted by permission of Oxford University Press.
*[Hume asked this question in his important essay, " On Miracles." The italicized excerpts in this section are from this essay. EDS].

kind of thing as if we infer from one event, say 'The baseball is flying into the window,' to another, 'The window will break.' These inferences are *empirical* (a posteriori) and are founded on the way we experience the world to behave. The truthfulness of human testimony is a matter of fact, and founded on experience. And when things go wrong, we do not in fact rely on it. There can be a 'contrariety of evidence,' or in other words, some things pointing one way, and others a different way:

This contrariety of evidence, in the present case, may be derived from several different causes; from the opposition of contrary testimony; from the character or number of the witnesses; from the manner of their delivering their testimony; or from the union of all these circumstances. We entertain a suspicion concerning any matter of fact, when the witnesses contradict each other; when they are but few, or of a doubtful character; when they have an interest in what they affirm; when they deliver their testimony with hesitation, or on the contrary, with too violent asseverations. There are many other particulars of the same kind, which may diminish or destroy the force of any argument, derived from human testimony.

In other words, experience itself shows us when not to be too gullible. But now suppose that what is testified to is absolutely amazing, approaching the miraculous. Then:

The very same principle of experience, which gives us a certain degree of assurance in the testimony of witnesses, gives us also, in this case, another degree of assurance against the fact, which they endeavour to establish; from which contradiction there necessarily arises a counterpoise, and mutual destruction of belief and authority.

Before pausing to analyse the line of thought, we should see where it leads. Hume draws a famous conclusion:

The plain consequence is (and it is a general maxim worthy of our attention), 'That no testimony is sufficient to establish a miracle, unless the testimony be of such a kind, that its falsehood would be more miraculous, than the fact, which it endeavours to establish; and even in that case there

is a mutual destruction of arguments, and the superior only gives us an assurance suitable to that degree of force, which remains, after deducting the inferior.' When any one tells me, that he saw a dead man restored to life, I immediately consider with myself, whether it be more probable, that this person should either deceive or be deceived, or that the fact, which he relates, should really have happened. I weigh the one miracle against the other; and according to the superiority, which I discover, I pronounce my decision, and always reject the greater miracle. If the falsehood of his testimony would be more miraculous, than the event which he relates; then, and not till then, can he pretend to command my belief or opinion.

The argument can be analysed in a number of ways. It can usefully be thought of like this:

Suppose somebody tells me of a highly surprising or improbable event, *m*. In fact, let *m* be an event about as improbable as you can imagine. So my evidence for *m* is that 'this person is saying that *m* happened'. I now have a choice between two views of the matter:

(a) This person is saying that *m* happened. But *m* did not.
(b) This person is saying that *m* happened. And *m* did.

Now *each* of (a) and (b) contains *one* surprising element. View (a) contains the surprise: this person spoke falsely. View (b) contains the surprise of *m* occurring. So I have to balance which is more surprising or improbable, and then reject 'the greater miracle'.

The problem, as Hume gleefully points out, is that it is quite common for testimony to be false. There are the obvious cases of deliberate lies. There are cases of delusions. There are notorious lapses of memory. Where there is a transmission of information, errors get introduced: mistranslations, misunderstandings, people taking things intended metaphorically for literal truth, and so on. So (a) does not involve the same kind of improbability as (b). View (b) involves the miracle: an event about as improbable as can be imagined. View (a) only involves the kind of thing that we know happens anyhow: people get things wrong. Therefore the hurdle that 'no testimony is sufficient to establish a miracle, unless the testimony be of such a kind, that its falsehood would be more miraculous, than the fact, which it endeavours to establish' is an incredibly difficult hurdle for any piece of testimony to cross. And even then, all we are left with is a kind of confusion: not knowing what to believe, so that the wise course is to suspend judgement.

In fact, Hume goes on to argue that no evidence being used to establish a system of religion ever comes at all close to crossing the hurdle. He makes a number of points: reports of miracles tend to come from remote and barbarous times and places; from persons whose passions are inflamed; from persons who have an interest in selling a story:

The wise lend a very academic faith to every report which favours the passion of the reporter; whether it magnifies his country, his family, or himself, or in any other way strikes in with his natural inclinations and propensities. But what greater temptation than to appear a missionary, a prophet, an ambassador from heaven? Who would not encounter many dangers and difficulties, in order to attain so sublime a character? Or if, by the help of vanity and a heated imagination, a man has first made a convert of himself, and entered seriously into the delusion; who ever scruples to make use of pious frauds, in support of so holy and meritorious a cause?

He points out the way people love such reports:

The passion of surprise and wonder, arising from miracles, being an agreeable emotion, gives a sensible tendency towards the belief of those events, from which it is derived. And this goes so far, that even those who cannot enjoy this pleasure immediately, nor can believe those miraculous events, of which they are informed, yet love to partake of the satisfaction at second-hand or by rebound, and place a pride and delight in exciting the admiration of others.

With what greediness are the miraculous accounts of travellers received, their descriptions of sea and land monsters, their relations of wonderful adventures, strange men, and uncouth manners?

But if the spirit of religion join itself to the love of wonder, there is an end of common sense; and human testimony, in these circumstances, loses all pretensions to authority.

And he makes a more subtle point, concerning the relation between different religions, each of which has its budget of miracles:

[L]et us consider, that, in matters of religion, whatever is different is contrary; and that it is impossible the religions of ancient Rome, of Turkey, of Siam, and of China should, all of them, be established on any solid foundation. Every miracle, therefore, pretended to have been wrought in any of these religions (and all of them abound in miracles), as its direct scope is to establish the particular system to which it is attributed; so has it the same force, though more indirectly, to overthrow every other system. In destroying a rival system, it likewise destroys the credit of those miracles, on which that system was established; so that all the prodigies of different religions are to be regarded as contrary facts, and the evidences of these prodigies, whether weak or strong, as opposite to each other.

This would also be Hume's answer to the protest that so many people cannot be wrong. Whichever way the cake is cut, a huge number of people have to be wrong.

Hume's argument here is wonderfully *economical*. A less subtle philosopher might have tried to show a metaphysical conclusion, such as the absolute impossibility of miracles. Hume neither needs such a conclusion, nor tries to argue for it. He allows the metaphysical possibility of an intervening deity. There *might* be a deity who *might* on occasion let someone walk on water, or feed five thousand people on a few loaves and fishes. Still, experience is our only guide as to whether such events occur. If we are to believe that they do because of testimony, then the testimony has to be good: very good, and, in fact, miraculously good. But we never find testimony of the right kind.

People new to Hume's argument sometimes suspect that it is unduly *cynical*, expressing some kind of mistrustful, suspicious attitude to the reports of other people. I do not think this is true, or at least, that the suspicion is worse than is warranted by people's tendencies. After all, you have to be extremely innocent to deny, for instance, that it is wise to be suspicious of reports that flatter the passions of the reporter. Here is a quotation from the British newspaper the *Independent*, commenting on a report by the Royal College of Psychiatrists:

According to the Royal College of Psychiatrists, one in six of us are neurotic. They must think that 100 per cent of us are gullible as well. Bring out a report—the politically correct way to advertise your service. What next? The Institute of Builders says seven in ten houses need to be rebuilt, or the Association of Garage Mechanics that thirteen out of twenty cars need servicing?

In fact, the discussion in the second part of Hume's great essay is an ancestor of a whole academic study. Psychologists now investigate common cognitive malfunctions: failures of perception, of memory, the influences of other people, the infectious qualities of confidence, and the love of the marvellous, as influences that interfere with people's capacities to tell truth from falsehood. We are mostly quite good instruments for registering truth and dismissing falsehood. But we are not as good as we like to believe, and we are often not very good at all.

. . .

This is not to say that reports of things hitherto quite outside our experience have to be false. Science proceeds by finding such things. But we reason rightly when we maintain a sceptical attitude, until such time as the new phenomena are repeated and established, becoming part of the uniformities of nature.

Once we think of the theology of miracles, things become even worse. For a deity that sets the laws of nature into motion and never relents at least has a certain dignity. One that occasionally allows hiccups and intermissions, glorified conjuring tricks, is less impressive. Why just those miracles, just then? It is not what you would have expected. A little miracle or two snuffing out the Hitlers and Stalins would seem far more useful than one that changes water to wine at one particular wedding feast.

It is no doubt very good of God to let St Giuseppe levitate in front of pictures of him, but other things being equal, one would have preferred, say, the miraculous quarantine or destruction of the AIDS virus. It is what one might have expected antecedently, knowing that the world was under the regime of a good God. But the world as we know it does not confirm it.

INFINI—RIEN

None of the metaphysical arguments we have considered [in sections omitted here] do much to confirm the hypothesis that the universe is the creation of a traditional God. And Hume's analysis of testimony from miracles destroys their value as evidence. Faced with these blanks, religious faith may try to find other arguments.

An interesting and ingenious one is due to the French mathematician and theologian, Blaise Pascal (1632–62), and is known as Pascal's wager. Unlike the arguments we have been considering, it is not presented as an argument for the *truth* of religious belief, but for the *utility* of believing in some version of a monotheistic, Judaic, Christian, or Islamic, God.

The argument is this. First, Pascal confesses to metaphysical ignorance:

Let us now speak according to natural lights.
    If there is a God, he is infinitely incomprehensible, since, having neither parts, nor limits, He has no affinity to us. We are therefore incapable of knowing either what He is, or if He is . . . Who then will blame the Christians for not being able to give a reason for their belief, since they profess a religion for which they cannot give a reason?

It is not too clear why this excuse is offered for the Christians, as opposed to those of other faiths, as well as believers in fairies, ghosts, the living Elvis, and L. Ron Hubbard. Still, suppose the choice is between religious belief and a life of religious doubt or denial:

You must wager. It is not optional. Which will you choose then? . . . Let us weigh the gain and the loss in wagering that God is. Let us estimate these two chances. If you gain, you gain all; if you lose, you lose nothing. Wager, then, without hesitation that He is.

With great clarity Pascal realizes that this is rather an odd reason for choosing a belief. But he also says, perceptively, that

your inability to believe is the result of your passions, since reason brings you to this, and yet you cannot believe... Learn of those who have been bound like you, and who now stake all their posses-sions... Follow the way by which they began; by acting as if they believe, taking the holy water, having masses said, etc. Even this will naturally make you believe, and deaden your acuteness.

After you have 'stupefied' yourself, you have become a believer. And then you will reap the rewards of belief: infinite rewards, if the kind of God you believe in exists. And if it does not? Well, you have lost very little, in comparison with infinity: only what Pascal calls the 'poison-ous pleasures' of things like playing golf on Sun-days instead of going to mass.

The standard way to present this argument is in terms of a two-by-two box of the options:

	God Exists	*God Does Not*
I believe in him	+infinity!	0
I do not believe in him	-infinity!	0

The zeros on the right correspond to the thought that not much goes better or worse in this life, whether or not we believe. This life is of vanish-ingly little account compared to what is promised to believers. The plus-infinity figure corresponds to infinite bliss. The minus-infinity figure in the bottom left corresponds to the traditional jealous God, who sends to Hell those who do not believe in him, and of course encourages his followers to give them a hard time here, as well. But the minusinfinity figure can be soft-pedalled. Even if we put 0 in the bottom left-hand box, the wager looks good. It would be good even if God does not punish disbelief, because there is still that terrific payoff of '+infinity' cranking up the choice. In decision-theory terms, the option

of belief 'dominates', because it can win, and can-not lose. So—go for it!

Unfortunately the lethal problem with this argument is simple, once it is pointed out.

Pascal starts from a position of metaphysical ignorance. We just know nothing about the realm beyond experience. But the set-up of the wager presumes that we *do* know some-thing. We are supposed to know the rewards and penalties attached to belief in a Christian God. This is a God who will be pleasured and reward us for our attendance at mass, and will either be indifferent or, in the minus-infinity option, seriously discombobulated by our non-attendance. But this is a case of false options. For consider that if we are really ignorant meta-physically, then it is at least as likely that the options pan out like this:

> There is indeed a very powerful, very benevolent deity. He (or she or they or it) has determined as follows. The good human beings are those who follow the natural light of reason, which is given to them to control their beliefs. These good humans follow the arguments, and hence avoid religious convictions. These ones with the strength of mind not to believe in such things go to Heaven. The rest go to Hell.

This is not such a familiar deity as the tradi-tional jealous God, who cares above all that peo-ple believe in him. (Why is God so jealous? Alas, might his jealousy be a projection of human sec-tarian ambitions and emotions? Either you are with us or against us! The French sceptic Voltaire said that God created mankind in his image, and mankind returned the compliment.) But the problem for Pascal is that if we really know noth-ing, then we do not know whether the scenario just described is any less likely than the Christian one he presented. In fact, for my money, a God that punishes belief is just as likely, and a lot more reasonable, than one that punishes disbelief.

And of course, we could add the Humean point that whilst for Pascal it was a simple two-way question of mass versus disbelief, in the wider world it is also a question of the Koran ver-sus mass, or L. Ron Hubbard versus the Swami Maharishi, or the Aquarian Concepts Commu-nity Divine New Order Government versus the

First Internet Church of All. The wager has to be silent about those choices.

EMOTION AND THE WILL TO BELIEVE

We can now briefly consider the 'fideistic' line, that although the arguments are negligible, nevertheless people at least have a right to believe what they wish, and there may be some merit in blind faith, like the merit attaching to the mother who refuses to acknowledge her son's guilt in spite of damning evidence.

Philosophers professionally wedded to truth and reason are not apt to commend this attitude. The faith that defies reason might be called a blessing by others who share it, but credulity and superstition by those who don't, and distressingly apt to bring in its wake fanaticism and zealotry. Chapter 2 of the famous essay *On Liberty* by John Stuart Mill (1806-73) talks memorably of the atmosphere of 'mental slavery' that sets in with the absence of the questing critical intellect. Even the truth, Mill says, when held as a prejudice independent of and proof against argument, 'is but one superstition the more, accidentally clinging to the words which enunciate a truth'. One classic discussion (by the late-nineteenth-century English writer W. K. Clifford) compares beliefs held on insufficient evidence to stolen pleasures. An apt quotation is from Samuel Taylor Coleridge:

He who begins by loving Christianity better than truth, will proceed by loving his own sect or Church better than Christianity, and end in loving himself better than all.

But although these views are attractive, it is actually quite hard to show that the habit of blind faith is necessarily so very bad. If, having got to Hume's inert proposition, we then invest it with hopes, fears, resolutions, and the embellishments of our own particular creeds, where is the harm in that? Is not simple piety a Good Thing?

Some people certainly think random belief is a good thing. I have in front of me the advertisement for a company calling itself 'your metaphysical

superstore'. It specializes in New Age books and music, flower essence, essential oils and aromatherapy, magnetic therapy, light balance therapy, astrology and numerology, tarot and rune cards readings, crystals and gemstones, and at the end, like a rueful note of something approaching sanity, healing herbs. Why should thinkers mock the simple pieties of the people?

Of course, there are simple pieties that do not get this general protection. If I check into the Mysterious Mist and come back convinced that God's message to me is to kill young women, or people with the wrong-coloured skins, or people who go to the wrong church, or people who have sex the wrong way, that is not so good. So we have to use our human values, our own sense of good or bad, or right or wrong, to distinguish an admirable return from the mountain from a lunatic one.

We seem to be irretrievably in the domain of ethics here. And it would be impossible in a brief compass to assess the harms and benefits of religious belief, just as it is hard (although not impossible) to estimate the benefit or damage done by belief in magnetic therapy or Feng Shui or whatever. It clearly fills some function, answering to some human desires and needs. Some of the needs may be a common part of the human lot: I have already mentioned the need for ceremonies at crucial parts of life, or the need for poetry, symbol, myth, and music to express emotions and social relationships that we need to express. This is good. Unfortunately some of the desires may be a little less admirable: the desire to separatism, to schism, to imposing our way of life on others, to finding moral justifications for colonialism, or tribal or cultural imperialism, and all made guilt-free because done in the name of the Lord. For every peaceful benevolent mystic, there is an army chaplain, convincing the troops that God is on their side.

. . .

Obviously the attitude one takes to the 'fideism' that simply lets particular religious beliefs walk free from reason may depend heavily on what has recently been happening when they do so. Hume was born less than twenty years after the last legal religious executions in Britain, and himself suffered from the enthusiastic hostility of believers. If in our time and place all we see are church picnics and charities, we will not be so worried. But enough people come down the mountain carrying their own practical certainties to suggest that we ought to be.

Maybe some day something will be found that answers to the needs without pandering to the bad desires, but human history suggests that it would be unwise to bank on it.

PART TWO

Human Knowledge:
Its Grounds and Limits

D URING THE GREAT GOLDEN AGE of philosophy, in the seventeenth and eighteenth centuries, problems about the nature of human knowledge divided philosophers into two schools. Despite changing idioms and increased understanding of the methods of science, the division to a large degree persists. On the one hand, the **empiricists,** whose leading thinkers were John Locke (1632–1704), George Berkeley (1685–1753), and David Hume (1711–1776), held that all our ideas come from experience and that no proposition about any matter of fact can be known to be true independently of experience. On the other hand, the **rationalists,** whose most important representatives were René Descartes (1596–1650), Baruch Spinoza (1632–1677), and Gottfried Leibniz (1646–1716), maintained that there are **innate ideas** and that certain general propositions (usually called *a priori* propositions) can be known to be true in advance of, or in the absence of, empirical verification.[1]

Advocates of the theory of innate ideas did not, of course, hold that we are born literally thinking certain thoughts, but rather that we are born with inherited dispositions to have thoughts of a certain form and structure. Just as dehydrated milk has the disposition to become milk when water is added to it, so the mind, on this theory, has from birth the disposition to acquire the concepts of being, substance, duration—even infinitude and God—once a certain amount of experience is "added to it." Thus, rationalism holds that there can be in the mind ideas and truths that were not first present in experience but only later activated by experience. For the empiricist, on the other hand, the mind is (as Locke put it) like a tablet on which nothing has been written (a *tabula rasa*) until experience writes its message on it.

The writings of René Descartes, a leading mathematician, man of science, and philosopher, are a clear example not only of the rationalistic doctrine and method, but also of the rationalistic temper of mind. In the autobiographical *Discourse on Method,* Descartes compares the state of the sciences and philosophy to an ancient European town, grown helter-skelter from an older village, with crooked streets, random walls, and poor sanitation. Of course, we are not accustomed to ripping down whole cities in order to start from scratch the task of rational redesign; but individuals can without arrogance or absurdity think of ripping down and rebuilding their own homes:

> . . . and the same I thought was true of any similar project for reforming the body of the Sciences, or the order of teaching them established in the Schools: but as for the opinions which up to that time I had embraced, I thought that I could not do better than resolve at once to sweep them wholly away, that I might afterwards be in a position to admit either others more correct, or even perhaps the same ones when they had undergone the scrutiny of reason. I firmly believed that in this way I should much better succeed in the conduct of my life, than if I built only upon old foundations, and leaned upon principles which, in my youth, I had taken upon trust.

Thus, Descartes begins his dramatic quest for new "foundations," doubting everything that can be doubted until he finds a solid basis for reconstruction in the indubitable fact of his own existence as a "thinking substance." What makes the argument for his own existence so convincing, Descartes decides, is its "clearness and

---

[1]It should be noted that both the empiricist and rationalist are "rationalists" in the wider sense of the term—that is, as opposed to fideism, romanticism, or irrationalism. Both can support rational inquiry as the sole road to truth, but they differ in their conceptions of what rational inquiry is, particularly regarding the role that sense experience plays in it.

distinctness." Hence, he has a working criterion of truth to use in the voyage away from his skeptical starting point: Whatever he conceives clearly and distinctly is true.

In his third Meditation, Descartes finds in himself the idea of an infinite God. The idea, he argues, could not be his own invention, nor could it be derived from merely finite experience. Its only possible cause must be the actually existing deity. He then goes on to prove that this deity is no deceiver. Therefore, (a) because God has given us a powerful disposition to believe in the existence of material objects (such as human bodies), (b) because God would be a deceiver if no such objects existed, and (c) because God is not a deceiver, it follows that such objects do exist and that human knowledge is reliable. Intellectual error, then, when it occurs, springs from a kind of hasty willfulness in ourselves and not from God.

Although many philosophers today would quarrel with particular steps in Descartes' arguments, there is no denying that his general method has left its mark on most of his successors. For three centuries, philosophers have tried to give a rational reconstruction of our knowledge, beginning with what is indubitable (or nearly so), and building on it, taking very seriously as they work the nagging claims of imaginary **skeptics** that what we think we know with certainty we may not really know at all.

Admitting some minimal possibility that hitherto undoubted and apparently indubitable belief might yet be false is for most of us just a matter of make-believe. It will be simply feigning a doubt for the purposes of some irksome riddle or pointless intellectual game that some people find it fun to play. In order fully to appreciate how important it was to seventeenth- and eighteenth-century philosophers to "refute the skeptic," however, one must be able *genuinely* to doubt, to "doubt with conviction," if you will, to *honestly* believe that previously undoubted beliefs might yet be false, and to take that real possibility to heart, not just as a move in a game, but as a troublesome disturbance in one's network of convictions and indeed in one's orientation to the world. Imaginative teachers of philosophy often try to give examples from science fiction of what such a frame of mind would be like. The late Charles L. Stevenson, for example, used to introduce Descartes to his beginning students at the University of Michigan with a simple story of his own invention:

> Imagine a neurosurgeon whose expertise on the human brain and whose knowledge of daily events are such that he can, with probes, dictate a subject's experiences. After he has implanted electrodes in the brain of a certain male volunteer, the surgeon causes him to experience the removal of the probes, although they are still in place; then to experience going home through the rain, spending the night with his wife, receiving a call from the surgeon in the morning asking him to return to the laboratory, and returning—all this while he is, in fact, still on the operating table.
>
> The next day, the surgeon does actually remove the electrodes and sends the subject home, whereupon his wife inquires indignantly, "Where were you last night?" "Right here with you," the man replies. "Oh, no, you weren't," she rejoins, "and I can prove it. I had the whole neighborhood out searching for you."
>
> Then the enlightened husband smiles and says, "Ah, now I see. That surgeon fooled me. He made me *think* I came home. But I was on the operating table the whole time."
>
> His smile quickly fades, however, never to return, because from that point forward the poor fellow can never be certain he is not still on the operating table.[2]

---

[2]From Arthur W. Burks, "Preface," *Values and Morals: Essays in Honor of William Frankena, Charles Stevenson and Richard Brandt*, edited by Alvin Goldman and Jaegwon Kim (Dordrecht: D. Reidel Publishing Co., 1978), p. xiii.

A similar story with more dramatic detail is told by John Pollock in the selection that leads off Part 2. Pollock's illustration of real doubt taken to heart then serves as our introduction to the perennial philosophical problem of skepticism.

Skeptical worries have been around as long as philosophical inquiry. Probably the very deepest sort of philosophical skepticism is epistemological. Such skepticism raises the worry that all we think we know, including all methods of inquiry in which we have confidence, may at bottom entirely lack justification. Peter Unger, a contemporary philosopher who has taught at New York University for many years, defends this sort of radical skepticism. His master argument is quite simple and powerful: knowledge implies certainty; one can never be certain of anything; therefore one can never know anything. Because the argument is logically valid, anyone who rejects its conclusion—and that will be almost everyone—must find fault with either the first or the second premise (or both). Unger gives a clear and spirited defense of both premises.

Roderick Chisholm, one of the twentieth century's leading epistemologists, then comes to the aid of common sense, and seeks to show how we might have knowledge after all. His primary target is an ages-old skeptical challenge that can be traced back to the ancient Greeks. The challenge proceeds as follows: To have knowledge we must have a reliable method of obtaining it. We can know a method is reliable only if we know that it usually yields the truth. But we can know that it usually yields the truth only if we are already able to separate the true from the false, which by hypothesis we are not able to do without a good method. So we can never have any knowledge. Chisholm argues that the ancient problem can be solved, for we can have knowledge without first having (or knowing that we have) a method or criterion for correctly distinguishing true from false beliefs.

Though Chisholm's piece concludes our section on skepticism, such doubts re-emerge almost immediately in the next section, on our knowledge of the external world. Here we begin with excerpts from Bertrand Russell's *Problems of Philosophy,* a book that has served generations as their first introduction to philosophical thinking. Russell offers a characteristically sharp and accessible presentation of the basic worries about how we might gain knowledge of the world. Russell echoes and amplifies many of the deep concerns expressed in Descartes' classic *Meditations* (reprinted here in its entirety). Quite early on in this work, Descartes has us imagine the possibility that everything we know is mistaken. For all we know, an evil demon could be deceiving us about everything, or almost everything. This possibility of deception, says Descartes, undermines our confidence that we can know anything at all. But wait—so long as I think, I can be sure that I exist. From this slender thread, called the *cogito* (short for "cogito ergo sum": I think, therefore I am), and an argument for God's existence, Descartes tries to re-establish our justification for our beliefs about most everything we once took for granted.

However, most philosophers following Descartes have doubted that his undertaking was as successful as he himself took it to be. The skeptical doubts that Descartes raises early on in the *Meditations* continue to exercise philosophers, as we have seen. Skeptical doubts are especially likely to torment the empiricist philosopher. Because empiricism holds that the sole source ultimately of our knowledge of things external to us is sense experience, it is a matter of importance to empiricists to explain just how that knowledge is derived from the "impressions" made upon our various sense organs. John Locke rested a great part of his theory upon a crucial distinction first used in antiquity and then revived by Galileo—namely, the distinction between *primary* and *secondary* qualities of physical objects. **Primary qualities** are intrinsic characteristics of the object itself—characteristics such as solidity, extension in space (size), figure (shape), motion or rest, and number. These are qualities that the objects would continue to possess even if there were no perceiving beings in the world. **Secondary qualities,** on the other hand (such qualities as color, taste, smell, sound, warmth, and cold), exist only when actually sensed and then only "in the mind" of the one who senses them. Primary qualities are inseparable from the material object and are found in every part of it, no matter how small. Every conceivable unit of matter, from a celestial body to an atom, must have some size and shape. (On the other hand, no mere atom could have color.)

Locke also contributed to the terminology of subsequent empiricists the technical term "idea" to stand for "whatever is the object of the understanding when a man thinks" or, more generally, for any direct object of awareness or consciousness.[3] And, again, the "ideas" that result from our perception of primary qualities are different from our "ideas" of secondary qualities. When we perceive a primary quality, according to Locke, our "idea" of this quality exactly resembles the corresponding primary quality in the material object itself. In contrast, when we perceive a secondary quality, our "idea" of this quality has no resemblance to a corresponding property of the thing itself. That is, our "idea" of, for instance, color or odor in an object is produced in us by virtue of the object's "power" to reflect and absorb light waves of certain frequencies or to emit molecules in certain degrees of vibration. Because of these capacities or "powers" of material objects, color and odor can come into existence. Yet without eyes, there could be no color; without noses, no odor; and without minds, no "secondary qualities" at all.

Locke's theory of perception, then, does seem to have strong support from scientifically sophisticated common sense. It is often contrasted with another possible theory of perception (a theory held by no reputable philosopher), which is sometimes ascribed (quite unfairly) to the scientifically unsophisticated common sense of "the ordinary person." According to the latter theory, called **naive realism,** the qualities that Locke called "primary" and those he called "secondary" are both strictly part of physical objects, and both can exist quite independently of perceiving minds. It follows from naive realism that a world without perceiving minds might yet be a colorful, clamorous, and smelly place. Locke's view, in contrast, is that physical substances and their primary qualities can exist independently of sentient minds and only the secondary qualities are mind-dependent. This theory can be called **sophisticated realism:** "sophisticated" because it seems to accord with what science tells us about secondary qualities; "realism" because it allows that material objects have a real existence independent of minds. Locke's view is often called **representative realism** because of the tenet that ideas ("in the mind") faithfully mirror or "represent" material objects to us in perception, even though the material objects and the "ideas" by which we come to know them are quite distinct entities. The textbooks also call Locke's view the **causal theory of perception** because of the tenet that material objects are the causes of the ideas, or appearances, or sense data

---

[3]David Hume's usage was somewhat narrower. In the *Treatise of Human Nature,* his earlier, more formal exposition of the views included here, Hume explains that he will use the word "impression" to mean "all our sensations, passions and emotions, as they make their first appearance in the soul." By "ideas" he means "the faint images of these in thinking and reasoning."

we have of them. The material substance itself is distinct from its own qualities, even from its own primary qualities, and, not being directly perceivable, must simply be posited as an unknowable **"substratum"** for its powers and properties. (Locke's conception of substance was rejected by most later empiricists, who preferred to think of a material thing as a mere "bundle of attributes," not as a mysterious entity "underlying" or "possessing" its own attributes.)

The realism of Locke, roughly sketched in the preceding paragraphs, must be understood as the primary target of the arguments of George Berkeley, Bishop of Cloyne. Locke would have approved of Berkeley's systematic demonstration that secondary qualities are mental. Berkeley argues for the conclusion in two ways. First of all, he maintains that extreme degrees of each secondary quality are inseparable in our consciousness from pain. Hence, if it is absurd to imagine that pain is, for example, *in* or *part of* the stove, then it is equally absurd to imagine that the heat is literally in the stove. Berkeley's second argument is the famous "argument from the relativity of perception." If I put one ice-chilled hand and one warm hand into a tub of tepid water, the water will feel hot to my cold hand and cold to my hot hand; but the water itself cannot be both hot and cold. Hence, both heat and cold must be "in the mind" only.

But Berkeley then turns the tables on Locke by arguing in quite similar ways for the necessarily mental status of *primary qualities* too. If the supporter of Locke accepts these latter arguments, there is nothing left of his conception of an external object beyond that of an unknowable "substratum." Berkeley easily disposes of the concept of a substratum as theoretically superfluous and unintelligible. He is left then with a world in which only perceiving minds ("subjects") and their "ideas" (the appearances of primary and secondary qualities) exist. Hence, the universe is through and through mental. This theory of reality bears the name **subjective idealism.** (Perhaps *ideaism* would be less misleading, because the theory has nothing whatever to do with ideals.)

Berkeley was as concerned as Descartes or Locke to find a solid alternative to skepticism. As an empiricist, he was resolved to show that all of our ideas, insofar as they are genuine (not merely confused), are derived from experience. What, then, of our idea of corporeal objects such as trees, tables, bodies? Berkeley was driven by his logic and his empiricist starting points to conclude that physical objects, insofar as we have any clear idea of them at all, are simply collections of sense impressions. Those **corporeal substances,** of which Descartes was at last able to form a "clear and distinct idea," turn out on analysis to be the figments of muddled thought.

Has empiricism then truly reconstructed our knowledge of the world, if this is its conclusion? Doesn't Berkeley's conception of a world "through and through mental" give a violent jolt to common sense? Not so, replies Berkeley. His idealism implies that tables and trees and bodies are just exactly what they seem—colored, shaped, hard, and so on. There is indeed nothing to these things except the qualities they seem to have. Moreover, it is not true that tables "vanish" or "pop out of existence" the moment we turn our backs on them (that *would* be repugnant to common sense); for God is always perceiving them, and therefore they continue to exist as ideas in His mind. To many later empiricists, this use of God seemed a desperate expedient to save Berkeley's theory from embarrassment. John Stuart Mill (1806–1873) was typical of later empiricists (often called **phenomenalists**) who found ways to make the rejection of "corporeal substance" more palatable to common sense without invoking a ***deus ex machina.*** According to Mill, if we say that the table continues to exist when unperceived, all we can mean by this is that *if* someone were to look in a certain place, then he would have sense impressions of a certain (table-like) kind; for material objects are not simply bundles of actual sense impressions but are rather to be understood as "permanent possibilities of sensation," and this conception exhausts whatever clear idea we have of them. Some writers have suggested that phenomenalism (the view of David Hume as well as of Mill) can be thought of as "Berkeley's view without Berkeley's God."

The great opponent of the view that all reality is mental was Hume's countryman and almost exact contemporary, Thomas Reid (1710–1796). It was Reid's primary purpose to vindicate common sense against the skepticism to which empiricism seemed finally to be driven. The "Scottish Common Sense School," of which Reid was the chief spokesman, had very widespread influence, particularly in the United States in the nineteenth century. Reid concedes to Berkeley and Hume that we cannot infer the existence of enduring corporeal (nonmental) objects from our mere sense impressions. Nevertheless, he contends, our belief in such objects is no mere "opinion got by reasoning"; it is, rather, a natural principle of the human constitution, as reliable and as inevitable as any of the natural principles that govern our reasonings. (If, as Reid suggests, we think of nature, as designed by God, then we can find strong similarities in his position to the argument of Descartes that "God can be no deceiver.")

This section concludes with G. E. Moore's now-classic "proof" of an external world. Moore inherited from Reid a very sturdy appreciation of common sense, and would have no truck with skeptical hypotheses of the sort that have plagued philosophers for so long. Moore stuck out his two hands, proclaimed the certainty of their existence, and that was that. Whether that really is the end of the story is a matter that has been discussed ever since.

David Hume in the eighteenth century applied the empiricist philosophy not only to the concept of a material substance but to other basic concepts as well, with results that even he called skeptical. Unlike Berkeley, who regarded skepticism as a charge to be rebutted, Hume thought of it as a position to be reluctantly adopted. In the selections included here, he examines the concept of causation and finds no more sense in the idea of a "necessary connection" between cause and effect (when we drop a stone, it *must* fall—so we think) than Berkeley did in the idea of "corporeal substance." We may continue to talk, as Hume himself does, of one thing's causing another, but all we can *mean* is that events of the first kind are in fact constantly conjoined with events of the second kind; and the so-called necessity that the second follow the first is simply the reflection of our habitual expectation. Hume would not have us deny the plain reports of our senses or the fruits of our mathematical deductions; he merely points out that there is no logically infallible method of achieving truth about matters of fact, and indeed no method at all for reasoning about matters that lie beyond all experience. But this kind of skepticism need not force us into a permanent suspension of judgment about all things, even in the practical affairs of life; for we will (as Hume elsewhere puts it) continue to leave buildings by the first-floor door rather than the upstairs window, and "Nature will always maintain her rights and prevail in the end over any abstract reasoning whatever."

The article "An Encounter with David Hume" was written specifically for the third edition of this volume by Wesley C. Salmon, of the University of Pittsburgh.

It is meant to show the beginning student of philosophy and science ("Physics 1a") how natural Hume's doubts can seem to one who ponders the methods and results of the exact sciences and how important it is to our conception of scientific knowledge to come to terms with those doubts. In particular, Salmon discusses such scientific notions as causation, inductive inference, probability, laws of nature, the regularity of nature, necessity, and predictability, in the light of Hume's empiricism. Salmon's essay views these matters through the eyes of a sensitive undergraduate student of physics who comes to wonder whether all science rests ultimately on a kind of "faith" in the uniformity of nature that cannot be rationally demonstrated to be correct. If this is so, he asks (with a certain amount of anguish), how can physics be shown to be a more reliable guide to knowledge of the future than, say, astrology or crystal gazing? These questions pose in a very rough way what has come to be called "the problem of induction" or "Hume's riddle of induction." Salmon concludes by sketching the main strategies that have been proposed by philosophers for coming to terms with Hume's skeptical doubts about scientific method.

The theory of knowledge comes by its interest in the philosophy of science quite naturally, since the methods of science have been the most reliable—some philosophers say the *only* reliable—producers of knowledge. The first question epistemologists should ask about science, of course is: When are investigative methods properly called "scientific"? A full answer to the question "What is science?", however, will describe what job is assigned to science either in its crude or developed state and contrast that task with that of other cultural activities that could be, and often are, confused with it.

Perhaps the most influential answer of the last century was that offered by Sir Karl Popper, a renowned philosopher of science. In the paper included here, Popper argues that the essence of scientific claims lies in their falsifiability. He contrasts the claims of physics, for instance, with those of astrology and Freudian psychology, and demotes the latter to nonscientific status by virtue of his falsifiability criterion. This criterion states that hypotheses must be testable in order to qualify as scientific; a scientific claim must have a chance of being shown false in order for it to pass scientific muster. If no evidence could possibly count against a claim—think, for instance, of certain extreme conspiracy theories, whose proponents interpret all evidence in such a way as to support their far-fetched views—then it loses its status as a scientific claim.

Popper's views occasioned a great deal of discussion about what he termed "the demarcation problem"—the problem of sharply distinguishing between scientific and nonscientific realms. There is consensus today that Popper's falsifiability criterion does not work. In fact, most philosophers of science nowadays believe that the demarcation problem cannot be decisively solved with the introduction of any short, simple criterion. There is no black-and-white test that will distinguish the scientific from the nonscientific.

Still, there *is* very broad agreement among philosophers that certain kinds of inquiry do and do not count as properly scientific. In the final piece in this section, Philip Kitcher, a prominent philosopher of science at Columbia University, gives us his take on the demarcation problem. Focusing on recent creationist claims to equal time in high school classrooms, Kitcher tackles the question of what distinguishes genuine biological and physical science from other views that aspire to their scientific status. Along the way he considers Popper's falsifiability criterion, and reveals what is mistaken in a number of creationist critiques of evolutionary theory. He concludes his essay with a positive account of the elements of scientific claims. Whether Kitcher's is the final word on the matter is left for the reader to consider. What is certain is that philosophers remain deeply puzzled by the issues of what constitutes science, scientific knowledge, and scientific confirmation.

SKEPTICISM

A Brain in a Vat

JOHN POLLOCK

John Pollock, of the University of Arizona, has written important books on the theory of knowledge, the philosophy of mind, and cognitive science.

It all began that cold Wednesday night. I was sitting alone in my office watching the rain come down on the deserted streets outside, when the phone rang. It was Harry's wife, and she sounded terrified. They had been having a late supper alone in their apartment when suddenly the front door came crashing in and six hooded men burst into the room. The men were armed and they made Harry and Anne lie face down on the floor while they went through Harry's pockets. When they found his driver's license one of them carefully scrutinized Harry's face, comparing it with the official photograph and then muttered, "It's him all right." The leader of the intruders produced a hypodermic needle and injected Harry with something that made him lose consciousness almost immediately. For some reason they only tied and gagged Anne. Two of the men left the room and returned with a stretcher and white coats. They put Harry on the stretcher, donned the white coats, and trundled him out of the apartment, leaving Anne lying on the floor. She managed to squirm to the window in time to see them put Harry in an ambulance and drive away.

By the time she called me, Anne was coming apart at the seams. It had taken her several hours to get out of her bonds, and then she called the police. To her consternation, instead of uniformed officers, two plain clothed officials arrived and, without even looking over the scene, they proceeded to tell her that there was nothing they could do and if she knew what was good for her she would keep her mouth shut. If she raised a fuss they would put out the word that she was a psycho and she would never see her husband again.

Not knowing what else to do, Anne called me. She had had the presence of mind to note down the number of the ambulance, and I had no great difficulty tracing it to a private clinic at the outskirts of town. When I arrived at the clinic I was surprised to find it locked up like a fortress. There were guards at the gate and it was surrounded by a massive wall. My commando training stood me in good stead as I negotiated the 20 foot wall, avoided the barbed wire, and silenced the guard dogs on the other side. The ground floor windows were all barred,

From John Pollock, *Contemporary Theories of Knowledge* (MD: Rowman & Littlefield, 1986), pp. 1–4
Reprinted by permission of Rowman & Littlefield.

but I managed to wriggle up a drainpipe and get in through a second story window that someone had left ajar. I found myself in a laboratory. Hearing muffled sounds next door I peeked through the keyhole and saw what appeared to be a complete operating room and a surgical team laboring over Harry. He was covered with a sheet from the neck down and they seemed to be connecting tubes and wires to him. I stifled a gasp when I realized that they had removed the top of Harry's skull. To my considerable consternation, one of the surgeons reached into the open top of Harry's head and eased his brain out, placing it in a stainless steel bowl. The tubes and wires I had noted earlier were connected to the now disembodied brain. The surgeons carried the bloody mass carefully to some kind of tank and lowered it in. My first thought was that I had stumbled on a covey of futuristic Satanists who got their kicks from vivisection. My second thought was that Harry was an insurance agent. Maybe this was their way of getting even for the increases in their malpractice insurance rates. If they did this every Wednesday night, their rates were no higher than they should be!

My speculations were interrupted when the lights suddenly came on in my darkened hidey hole and I found myself looking up at the scariest group of medical men I had ever seen. They manhandled me into the next room and strapped me down on an operating table. I thought, "Oh, oh, I'm for it now!" The doctors huddled at the other end of the room, but I couldn't turn my head far enough to see what they were doing. They were mumbling among themselves, probably deciding my fate. A door opened and I heard a woman's voice. The deferential manner assumed by the medical malpractitioners made it obvious who was boss. I strained to see this mysterious woman but she hovered just out of my view. Then, to my astonishment, she walked up and stood over me and I realized it was my secretary, Margot. I began to wish I had given her that Christmas bonus after all.

It was Margot, but it was a different Margot than I had ever seen. She was wallowing in the heady wine of authority as she bent over me. "Well Mike, you thought you were so smart,

tracking Harry here to the clinic," she said. . . . "It was all a trick just to get you here. You saw what happened to Harry. He's not really dead, you know. These gentlemen are the premier neuroscientists in the world today. They have developed a surgical procedure whereby they remove the brain from the body but keep it alive in a vat of nutrient. The Food and Drug Administration wouldn't approve the procedure, but we'll show them. You see all the wires going to Harry's brain? They connect him up with a powerful computer. The computer monitors the output of his motor cortex and provides input to the sensory cortex in such a way that everything appears perfectly normal to Harry. It produces a fictitious mental life that merges perfectly into his past life so that he is unaware that anything has happened to him. He thinks he is shaving right now and getting ready to go to the office and stick it to another neurosurgeon. But actually, he's just a brain in a vat."

"Once we have our procedure perfected we're going after the head of the Food and Drug Administration, but we needed some experimental subjects first. Harry was easy. In order to really test our computer program we need someone who leads a more interesting and varied life—someone like you!" I was starting to squirm. The surgeons had drawn around me and were looking on with malevolent gleams in their eyes. The biggest brute, a man with a pockmarked face and one beady eye staring out from under his stringy black hair, was fondling a razor sharp scalpel in his still-bloody hands and looking as if he could barely restrain his excitement. But Margot gazed down at me and murmured in that incredible voice, "I'll bet you think we're going to operate on you and remove your brain just like we removed Harry's, don't you? But you have nothing to worry about. We're not going to remove your brain. We already did—three months ago!"

With that they let me go. I found my way back to my office in a daze. For some reason, I haven't told anybody about this. I can't make up my mind. I am racked by the suspicion that I am really a brain in a vat and all this I see around me is just a figment of the computer. After all, how could I tell? If the computer program really works, no matter what I do, everything will seem normal. Maybe nothing I see is real. It's driving me crazy. I've even considered checking into that clinic voluntarily and asking them to remove my brain just so that I can be sure.

An Argument for Skepticism

PETER UNGER

Peter Unger teaches philosophy at New York University.

I mean to offer a positive argument for skepticism about knowledge; I do not mean just to raise some doubts, however general, about statements to the effect that people know. The argument to be offered has as its conclusion the universal form of the skeptical thesis, that is, the proposition that nobody ever knows *anything* to be so. If this argument is sound, as I am inclined to think, then it will follow in particular that nobody ever knows anything about the past or future or even the present, about others or even about himself, about external objects or even about his own experiences, about complicated contingencies or even the simplest mathematical necessities. This, then, is an argument for an extremely strong and sweeping conclusion indeed.

The opposite of skepticism is often called dogmatism. In these terms, dogmatism is the view that certain things are known to be so. The stronger the form of dogmatism, the more sorts of things would be claimed to be known and, so, the weaker the form of skepticism which might still be allowed to hold. Thus, one might be a dogmatist about the past but a skeptic about the future in the sense that one might hold that we know a fair amount about the past but know nothing of the future. But typical arguments to the effect that we know things about the past do not *look* dogmatic in any usual sense. And, arguments to the effect that we know nothing of the future do not in any standard sense *look* particularly undogmatic; they do not *look* particularly indicative of an open-minded approach to things. Going by the typical arguments, then, the label "dogmatist" is unfairly prejudicial and there is no force in the claim that skepticism is to be preferred because the alternative is dogmatism. Unlike such typical arguments, the argument I mean to offer gives substance to the claim that the alternative to skepticism is a view which sanctions a dogmatic attitude. In that one may well not appreciate that this is indeed skepticism's only alternative, one might, perhaps, innocently believe that one knows things without being dogmatic in the process. But once the implications of that belief are brought out, as my argument means to do, the persistence in such a belief may itself be considered dogmatic. Of course, I do not want to be dogmatic in asserting any of this and, indeed, confess to only a moderate amount of confidence in what I have to offer. But as I am inclined to think it true, I offer it in a spirit which I hope may be taken as quite undogmatic and open-minded.

1 A PRELIMINARY STATEMENT OF THE ARGUMENT

I begin by giving a statement of the argument which, while correct in all essentials, does not account for certain complications. On this statement, the argument is exceedingly simple and straightforward. It has but two premises and

Originally published in *Philosophical Exchange* 1, 4 (1974).

each of them makes no exceptions whatsoever. The first of these is the proposition:

(1) If someone *knows* something to be so, then it is all right for the person to be absolutely *certain* that it is so.

For example, if it is true that Knute *knows* that there was a general called "Napoleon," then it is (perfectly) all right for him to be absolutely *certain* that there was. And, if Rene really *knows* that he exists, then it is (perfectly) all right for Rene to be absolutely certain that he does.

Our second and final premise, then, is this categorical proposition:

(2) It is never all right for anyone to be absolutely *certain* that anything is so.

According to this premise, it is not all right for Knute to be absolutely certain that there was a general called "Napoleon," nor is it even all right for Rene to be absolutely certain that he exists. No matter what their situations, these people should not have this "attitude of absolute certainty." When one understands what is involved in having this attitude, or in being absolutely certain of something, one will presumably understand why it is never all right to be absolutely certain.

These two premises together entail our conclusion of universal skepticism:

(3) Nobody ever *knows* that anything is so.

In particular, Knute does not really *know* that there was a general called "Napoleon," nor does Rene really *know* that he exists.

2 THE FIRST PREMISE: THE IDEA THAT IF ONE KNOWS IT IS ALL RIGHT FOR ONE TO BE CERTAIN

We often have the idea that someone is certain of something but he shouldn't be. Perhaps from his expressive behavior, perhaps from something else, we *take* it that he is certain of something—whether or not he really is certain of it. We ask him, if we are so inclined, "How can you be *certain* of that?" In asking this question, we manage to imply that it might not be all right for him to be certain and

imply, further, that this is because he might not really *know* the thing. If the man could show us that he does know, then we should withdraw the question and, perhaps, even apologize for implying what we did by raising it. But, then, how do we manage to imply so much just by asking this question in the first place? Neither "know" nor any cognate expression ever crosses our lips in the asking. We are able to imply so much, I suggest, because we all accept the idea that, at least generally, if one does know something then it is all right for one to be certain of it—but if one doesn't then it isn't. This suggests that there is some analytic connection between knowing, on the one hand, and on the other, its being all right to be certain.

The very particular idea that knowing *entails* its being all right to be certain is suggested, further, by the fact that knowing entails, at least, that one *is* certain. That this is a fact is made quite plain by the inconsistency expressed by sentences like "He really *knew* that it was raining, but he *wasn't* absolutely *certain* that it was." Such a sentence can express no truth: if he wasn't certain, then he didn't know. We get further confirmation here from considering transitivity. The sentences "He was *sad that* it was raining, but he *didn't know* it was" and "He was really *sad that* it was raining, but he *wasn't* absolutely *certain* it was" are likewise inconsistent. Their inconsistency means an entailment from being sad that to knowing, in the first case, and to being certain in the second. This can be best explained, it would seem, by an entailment from knowing to being certain. The entailment from knowing to being certain is convincingly clinched, I think, by appreciating the equivalence between someone's knowing something and his knowing it for certain, or with absolute certainty. To be sure, we may describe cases which we would more naturally react to with the words "He knew it" than "He knew it for certain": Consider a man who, looking for his cuff links, unerringly went to the very spot they were while doubts went through his mind. Did he know that they were in that spot? But our readiness to say he knew might only indicate loose usage of those words by us, while we are more strict in our use when the word "certain" enters the picture. That this is much the more plausible hypothesis than thinking there to be an inequivalence here is evidenced by the inconsistency of the relevant sentences: "He *knew* it, but he *didn't* know it for certain," "He really *knew* it, but he *didn't* know it *with absolute certainty*," "He knew it was there, but he didn't *really know* it," and so on. No truth can be found in these words no matter when they might be uttered. Even if they are put forth at the end of stories like that of the cuff-link finder, where we are inclined at first to say he knows, we realize that they must express what is false. Accordingly, we are forced to be unswayed by our tendency to loose usage and to admit the equivalence between knowing with absolute certainty and just plain knowing to be so. Admitting this equivalence, we can be quite confident that knowing does indeed entail being absolutely certain.

Now, it cannot be too strongly emphasized that everything I said is meant to be compatible with the sense which the ordinary word "know" actually has. Indeed, it fairly relies on this word's having only one ("strong") sense as it occurs in sentences of the forms "S knows that *p*" and "S knows about X." Some philosophers have suggested "weak" senses of "know" in which it does not even have an entailment to absolute certainty. But though there is some reason to suppose that "know" has different meanings in "John knows that Jim is his friend" and "John knows Jim," there appears no reason at all to suppose that "knows" may mean different things as it occurs in the former sentence. Indeed, reason seems to favor the opposite view. If a genuine ambiguous sentence has a meaning on which it is inconsistent, there will generally be one also on which it is consistent. Once the latter meaning is pointed out, this difference is appreciated and felt to be quite striking. Thus, the sentence "John really *types* many things, but he produces symbols *only orally*" has an obvious meaning on which it is inconsistent. But, it may be pointed out that "types" has another sense, which it shares (roughly) with "classifies." Once this is pointed out, the consistent meaning is appreciated, and the effect is a striking one. No similar phenomenon is ever found with the sentence "John really *knows* that he types things, but he

isn't absolutely *certain* that he does." There may be many *ad hoc* explanations of this fact. But the only plausible explanation is, I think, that "know" doesn't have a weak sense with no entailment to absolute certainty.

To deny our first premise, then, is to do violence to the meaning of "know" and to our concept of knowledge. If our argument is to be stopped, it must be with the consideration of the second premise. In any case, it is with that premise that the *substantive* claim of the argument is made: It is not only with mere questions of logical relations with which we must now contend. Accordingly, we now come to the largest and most important part of our discussion.

3 WHAT ATTITUDE IS INVOLVED IN ONE'S BEING ABSOLUTELY CERTAIN?

I will now, at last, begin to argue for the idea that to be absolutely certain of something is, owing to a certain feature of personal certainty, to be *dogmatic* in the matter of whether that thing is so. It is because of this dogmatic feature that there is always *something* wrong with being absolutely certain. In other words, it is because of this feature that our second premise, (2), is correct. My argument for the idea that this feature ensures this dogmatism falls naturally into two parts. The first part, which will occupy us in this present section, is aimed at specifying the feature. Thus, we will argue here that one's being absolutely certain of something involves one in having a certain severely negative *attitude* in the matter of whether that thing is so: the attitude that *no* new information, evidence or experience which one might ever have will be seriously considered by one to be *at all* relevant to *any possible* change in one's thinking in the matter. The second part is aimed at showing this attitude to be wrongly dogmatic even in matters which may appear to be quite simple and certain. That more normative segment will be reserved for the section immediately to follow.

That such an absolutely severe attitude should be essential to one's knowing is hardly novel with me. Indeed, philosophers who are quite plainly anti-skeptical proclaim just this attitude as essential to one's knowing. Thus Norman Malcolm thinks himself to know that there is an ink-bottle before him, and describes what he takes to be implicit in this knowledge of his:

> Not only do I not *have* to admit that (those) extraordinary occurrences would be evidence that there is no ink-bottle here; the fact is that I *do not* admit it. There is nothing whatever that could happen in the next moment that would by me be called *evidence* that there is not an ink-bottle here now. No future experience or investigation could prove to me that I am mistaken....
>
> It will appear to some that I have adopted an *unreasonable* attitude towards that statement. There is, however, nothing unreasonable about it.
>
> In saying that I should regard nothing as evidence that there is no ink-bottle here now, I am not *predicting* what I should do if various astonishing things happened....
>
> That assertion describes my *present* attitude towards the statement that here is an ink-bottle.[1]

Now, Malcolm, it is true, aligns himself with the idea that there are two (or more) senses of "know" to be found in sentences like "John *knows* that there is an ink-bottle before him." This idea is neither correct nor essential to his position in those passages. We have already argued, in section 2, that this idea is not correct. That this incorrect idea is not essential to the main thrust of his quoted remarks is, I think, equally clear. For he allows that there is at least *a* sense of "know" where knowing entails one's having the extreme attitude they characterize. Presumably, that sense, at least, is just the sense where knowing entails being absolutely certain, and the extreme attitude is just the one which is necessarily involved in absolute certainty. In that such philosophers think that when one knows the attitude of certainty is not only present but quite all right, their thinking that the attitude is to be characterized in such severe negative terms is some indirect evidence for thinking so. An attitude which is so *severely* negative as this might well *not* be one which is very often justified. However, even if one wants to avoid skepticism, a concern for the truth about this attitude makes a severe characterization of it quite unavoidable.

The attitude of certainty concerns *any* sequence of experience or events which could consistently be presented to a sentient subject, without its description prejudging the issue on which it might supposedly bear. Thus, one is certain that there is an ink-bottle before one only if one's attitude is this: Insofar as I care about being right about whether an ink-bottle is or was before me, no matter how things may seem to appear, *I will not count* as contrary evidence even such extraordinary sequences as these:

> ...when I next reach for this ink-bottle my hand should seem to pass *through* it and I should not feel the contact of any object...in the next moment the ink-bottle will suddenly vanish from sight...I should find myself under a tree in the garden with no ink-bottle about...one or more persons should enter this room and declare that they see no ink-bottle on this desk...a photograph taken now of the top of the desk should clearly show all of the objects on it except the ink-bottle.[2]

Now, however (nearly) certain one may be that some or all of these sequences will not occur, that is of course not the same thing as being (at all) certain that there is an ink-bottle before one. But, though there are many differences between the two, perhaps the one which should most clearly be focused on is this: If one is really certain of the ink-bottle, and not just of other things however related, then one's attitude is that *even if one should* seem to find oneself in *a* contrary garden, one *would disregard* this experience as irrelevant to the question of whether, at the time in question, there is or was an ink-bottle before one. One might resist this characterization, but then, I think, one would lose one's proper focus on what it is of which one is certain.

Here is a line of resistance to our characterization of being certain. Suppose, in contrast, one's attitudes were these: *If* strange things seemed to happen, then perhaps I would change my mind, I just might. But, I am absolutely certain that no strange things will ever happen to speak against there being an ink-bottle. Might not these attitudes be those of a man who was *absolutely* certain that *there is an ink-bottle before him*? Might not he be certain of the ink-bottle, not in or by having a completely exclusionary attitude on that matter itself but, rather, indirectly, so to speak, in or by having just such an attitude toward the possibility of apparently contrary appearances?

This suggestion, this line of resistance, is an interesting one, but it is neither correct nor of any use even if it were correct. First, let us notice that *at least almost* invariably when one is even very close to being absolutely certain of something, one is not nearly so certain that no contrary appearances will turn up. For example, you may be quite sure that I am married. But, you will not be quite so sure that no appearances to the contrary might show up: I may be married but say to you "No, I'm not really married. Mary and I don't believe in such institutions. We only sent out announcements to see the effect—and it's easier to have most people believe that we are." I might, at a certain point, say these things to you and get a few other people to say apparently confirmatory things. All of this, and some more if need be, should and would, I think incline you to be at least a bit less certain that I am married. Thus, at least with things where one is *quite* certain, the matter seems to be quite the *opposite* of what was suggested: One will not be so certain that nothing strangely contradictory will turn up—but one will be inclined to reject any such thing even if it does turn up. We may plausibly project that things work quite the same in situations where someone is absolutely certain (if there really are any such).

Let us now take something of which you are as certain as anything, say, that one and one are two. Suppose that you are very sure that your favorite mathematician will never say something false to you about any simple sum. Imagine that he, or God, tells you and insists that one and one are three, and not two. If your attitude is that he is still to be trusted or, at least, that you would no longer be quite so sure of the sum, then you are not absolutely certain that one and one are two. If you think you *are absolutely certain* of this sum, then, I submit, you should think also that your attitude will be to reject entirely the message from the mathematician or God. In this simple arithmetical matter, you are to give it, perhaps unlike other messages from

the same source, no weight at all in your thinking. It seems, then, that this line of resistance is not faithful to the idea of being certain of a particular thing. But would it be of any use in countering skepticism, or the skeptic's charge of dogmatism, even if it were right?

It seems to me that it is at least as dogmatic to have the position that it is absolutely certain that nothing will ever even appear to speak against one's position as to have the attitude that any such appearances which might show up should be entirely rejected. What about appearances to the effect that some contrary appearances, their precise nature left open as yet, are likely to show up in the future? If one is absolutely certain that the latter sort of appearances won't ever show up, one would, presumably, have the attitude of rejecting entirely the indication of the former appearances. One's attitude of rejection gets pushed farther back from the matter itself. Perhaps, on our line of resistance, this may go on indefinitely. But each retreat, and the consequent new place for rejection, only makes a man look more and more obvious in his dogmatism and unreasonableness about the whole affair. Even going back no farther than the second level, so to speak, only a quite foolhardy man would, it seems to me, reject out of hand any suggestion that some things might be brought forth to speak against his position. If anything, it is better for him to allow that they may and to be ready to reject them. So, even if our line of resistance had presented us with a case of being certain, the "indirect" way of being certain would hardly help us to avoid the skeptical charge. That is quite surely no way for being perfectly certain to be perfectly all right.

It is important to stress very hard that a clause like "I should regard nothing as evidence that there is no ink-bottle now" must be regarded as the expression of a man's *current attitude,* and not as any prediction of what he will do under certain future circumstances. Thus, one may allow that a sentence like the following is indeed consistent: "He is absolutely *certain* that there are automobiles, but he *may* change his mind should certain evidence come up." That is because even if his present attitude is that he will not, things may not happen in accordance with his attitude. For example, things might happen to him which *cause* him to become uncertain. Or, his attitude might just evaporate, so to speak, the new evidence then affecting him in the unwanted way; and so on. Such conditions as these give us a consistent interpretation for the foregoing sentence, even if not a very ordinary one. A sentence which will always express an inconsistency, on the other hand, is obtained once we make sure that our severely negative clause is embedded so that it is clear that the man's current attitude is the point. Thus, in contrast with the foregoing, it is always inconsistent to say "He is absolutely *certain* that there are automobiles, but *his attitude* is that he *may* change his mind should certain evidence come up." A proper assessment of the direct linguistic evidence supports the idea that the attitude of certainty is thus absolutely severe.

This direct linguistic evidence cannot be enough to satisfy one that being certain, or the attitude in knowing, demands so much as we claim. And, it is not enough to add the indirect evidence from anti-skeptical authors. What we want is to fit a severe characterization of this attitude into some more general account of things. Toward this end, I now recall my account of absolute terms.[3] On this account, *absolute adjectives* like "flat," "useless" and "certain" purport to denote a limiting state or situation to which things may approximate more or less closely. Thus, in the case of these adjectives, the modifier "absolutely," as well as "completely" and "perfectly," is redundant apart from points of emphasis. Now, various locutions with "certain" may appear to indicate matters of degree. But they will always admit of a paraphrase where this appearance is dispelled in favor of a more explicit reference to an *absolute limit*: "That's pretty certain" goes into "That's pretty *close to being absolutely* certain"; "He is more certain of this than of that" goes into "He is *absolutely* certain of this but not of that or else he is *closer to being absolutely* certain of this than of that," and so on. None of this is peculiar to "certain"; the same happens with locutions containing other absolute adjectives. Thus, these sentences seem to denote matters of degree, but their paraphrases dispel the illusory appearance: "That's the flattest

(most useless) thing I've ever seen" goes into "That's the only *absolutely* flat (useless) thing I've ever seen or else that's *closer to being absolutely* flat (useless) than anything else I've seen." In light of these paraphrases, we may repose some confidence in the following formula as saying what it is for something to be *x* where that is the same as being absolutely *x*: Something or someone is *x* (flat, useless, certain, etc.) just in case nothing *could possibly* ever be more *x*, or *x*-er, than that thing or person is right now. It is in this strict sense, then, that being certain, and *a fortiori* being absolutely certain, is being at an absolute limit. Now, absolute adjectives typically have contrasting terms which are *relative adjectives*: "certain" has "confident" and "doubtful," "flat" has "bumpy" and "curved," "useless" has "useful" and "serviceable," and so on. Because matters of degree *are* concerned, there is nothing which is deceptive about the locutions with *these* terms: The sentence "He is pretty confident" does not go into the apparently senseless "He is pretty close to being absolutely confident"; nor does "That is very useful" go into "That is very close to being absolutely useful." These relative terms really do denote matters of degree and not any state or situation which is an absolute limit. If something is bumpy, it is *not* true that nothing could possibly be more bumpy or bumpier. And if someone is confident of something, it does not follow that no one could ever be more confident. Now, a necessary condition for the correct application of an absolute adjective is, at least generally, that certain things denoted by relative adjectives be entirely absent. Thus, it is a necessary condition of something's being flat that it be *not at all* bumpy, that is, that bumpiness not be present even in the least degree. Also, it is a necessary condition of being flat that the thing be *not at all* curved, or that curvature or curvedness not be present at all. We might expect the same sort of thing to hold in the case of someone's being certain of something, and indeed it does: If someone is certain of something, then that thing is *not at all* doubtful so far as he is concerned, that is, doubt or doubtfulness is not present at all in that man with respect to that thing. I have already argued this before, but there are other things which must also be entirely absent if a man is to be certain, though their absence may be included, I suggest, in the absence of all doubt.

One thing which must be entirely absent, and which is, I think, implicit in the absence of all doubt, is this: any *openness* on the part of the man to consider new experience or information as seriously relevant to the truth or falsity of the thing. In other words, if S is certain that *p*, then it follows that S is *not at all* open to consider any new experience or information as relevant to his thinking in the matter of whether *p*.

4 WHY IS THERE ALWAYS SOMETHING WRONG WITH HAVING THIS ABSOLUTE ATTITUDE?

At the beginning of his brilliant paper, "Certainty," G. E. Moore, perhaps the most influential opponent of skepticism in this century, makes some assertions and, as he points out, does so in a very positive and definite way. In just this way, he says, for example, that he had clothes on and was not absolutely naked. Moore goes on to note that although he did not expressly *say* of the things which he asserted that he *knew* them to be true, he implied as much by asserting them in the way he did. His words are these:

> I *implied*...that I myself knew for certain, in each case, that what I asserted to be the case was, at the time I asserted it, in fact the case. And I do not think that I can be justly accused of dogmatism or over-confidence for having asserted these things positively in the way that I did. In the case of some kinds of assertions, and under some circumstances, a man can be justly accused of dogmatism for asserting something positively. But in the case of assertions such as I made, made under the circumstances under which I made them, the charge would be absurd.

I think that we may take it that, according to Moore, the reason he could not so be accused is that he was *not* dogmatic here. And the reason for that is that he *knew* these things, e.g., that he was not naked, so that he was *justified* in being absolutely *certain* of them. And, so, in those

innocuous circumstances of speech, he was justified in acting out of, in or in accord with, his position or attitude of personal certainty. Moore was saying, in effect, that one could have this by now familiarly characterized attitude without any pain of being at all dogmatic in the matter: That no new experience or information will have any effect at all on one's thinking in the matter at hand, in this case, in the matter of whether at the then-present time one is absolutely naked or not. Moore's position here is, then, quite of a piece with Malcolm's thought that it is *not at all unreasonable* of him to allow nothing to count as contrary evidence in the matter of whether an ink-bottle is before him. But Moore's point is more particular than Malcolm's, for he notes the *particular way* in which one who is certain might be thought to be unreasonable, or not justified, in his attitude. He might be thought to be such *in that* he is *dogmatic* in the matter. Moore similarly foreshadows, while focusing more clearly on the form of the opposite view, Hintikka's implication that in many matters one is *justified* in disregarding any further information: In situations where one knows, Moore says or implies, one is not at all dogmatic in having just such an absolutely negative position or attitude. It seems, then, that Moore was more sensitive than these other authors to the possibility that *dogmatism* might (almost) always be charged of one who was absolutely certain, even when he might rather plausibly claim to know. Now, it strikes me as oddly unfortunate, in a way, that others who actually spelled out what was involved in being certain, were not so sensitive to this particular charge. For it is, I think, precisely the feature they spell out which makes the charge of dogmatism live and convincing. By the same token however, it is to Moore's credit that, without articulating the key idea, he was able to sense the charge of *dogmatism* as a particular threat to his position, perhaps as the key one. Indeed, in the three full sentences I quoted, he refers to this charge as many times. We may put the substantial question, then, in these words: Was Moore referring to a charge of some real substance, or was he right in contending that (because he knew) there was really nothing to be feared?

We may now, I think, more fairly assess the question of whether in cases where one is absolutely certain, supposing there are any such, one's attitude is dogmatic at least in some degree. In such a case, there may be no relevant inconsistency, there being no disparity between one's tenacity and willingness to risk and infer. And, it may well be that no one will ever disagree with one, or even be much less certain of the thing. For, when one is absolutely certain, as we are supposing, the matter is likely to be clear-cut. But, even if nothing rubs the wrong way, from within oneself or without, one's attitude in the matter is this: I will not allow *anything at all* to count as evidence against my present view in the matter. The case being clear-cut, this attitude will cause one no trouble nor bring any challenge. But, what is one to think of it anyway, even if no penalty or embarrassment is liable ever to occur? I think that any reflection at all makes it pretty plain that, no matter how certain things may seem, *this* attitude is always dogmatic and one who has it will always be open to that charge even if circumstances mean that he will never be exposed to it.

Now, in order to see more clearly why, even in the apparently most clear-cut and certain matters, there is something wrong with letting nothing count against one's being right, it will *help* to describe some sequences of experience. I do *not* think that such an appreciation of detail is really necessary to gaining conviction that the attitude of certainty is always dogmatic and, providing there are no other considerations in its favor, to be foregone in favor of a more open-minded position. One must favor such an attitude in any case, no matter how certain something seems and no matter how little one is able to imagine what experiences there might be which, should they ever occur, one had best consider seriously and not just disregard. This is the right view in the matter however poor our own imaginations might be. But, the strength of habits to the contrary being so great, it will be a big help if we can succeed in imagining sequences of experience which seem to cry out for serious thought. Even in the cases of things which at first seem quite certain, then, and beyond any possibility of questioning at all, I will strive to be of service by imagining experiences. These described experiences should help one grasp firmly the idea that the attitude of certainty is always dogmatic.

5 HELPFUL EXPERIENCES FOR REJECTING THE ATTITUDE OF CERTAINTY

In quoting Malcolm's meditations on himself and his ink-bottle, we looked at some sequences of experiences which, if they occurred, might rightly be considered to have some weight and, accordingly, result in one's not being quite so certain as before that there is or was an ink-bottle before one. Malcolm says he wouldn't take those experiences as relevant here, that that is his attitude and that all of that is perfectly all right. I would disagree. But, in any event, it seems that one can easily imagine experiences which are more telling in this regard. And, also, with only more difficulty, one can imagine others which are easily more telling.

In respect of the matter of that ink-bottle, there are, it seems to me, all sorts of possible experiences which might cast some doubt. For example, one may be approached by government officials who seem to demonstrate that the object on one's desk is a container of a material to poison the water supply, which somehow found its way out of government hands and into one's home. It was disguised to look like an ink-bottle, but it is seen to have many small structural features essential to such a container of poison but which no ink-bottles have. One might well think, then, that though this object holds ink it is not an ink-bottle but, rather, is something else. Perhaps, then, there never was *an ink-bottle* before one, but only some such other object. It seems, at any rate, that such an experience as this should not be disregarded out of hand no matter what one eventually should come to think about whether an ink-bottle was before one. An attitude which would thus disregard it seems, then, to be a dogmatic one.

The experience just described is, I suppose, less than completely convincing. And, even if it is admitted that the experience does have some weight, it seems easy enough to retreat to other statements which are not thus susceptible to experimental challenge. For example, one may be, instead, absolutely certain that there is before one something which looks like an ink-bottle, or that there is something with a circular top, or whatever the favored things turn out to be. Though the sort of experience just imagined might go against one's being certain that *an ink-bottle* is before one, such a sequence of experience will not go against one's certainty about many other things: that there are automobiles, that there have been automobiles for quite some time now, and that one is not now absolutely naked. To get a more completely convincing case about one ink-bottle, and to begin to get a convincing case for these less susceptible things, one's imagination must work more radically. Descartes was quite well aware of the problem when he imagined his evil demon. We may do well to follow suit, though in a more modern and scientific vein.

I begin to imagine a more radical sequence of experience by supposing myself to experience a voice, coming from no definite location, which tells me this, in no uncertain terms: All the experiences I am having, including that of the voice, are artificially induced. Indeed, this has been going on for all of my conscious life and it will continue to do so. The voice tells me of various experiences I have had, some of which I had myself forgotten almost entirely. It then says that scientists accomplish all of this with me; it seems to tell me what they are like, what I am really like and, in great detail, how they manage to bring about these effects in me. To make its case most convincing, the voice says what experiences I will next have, and next after that and, then, after that. First, I will seem to fly off the face of the earth to a planet where the inhabitants worship me because I have only one mouth. After that, I am to come back to earth and seem to find that I have been elected Secretary-Treasurer of the International Brotherhood of Electricians. Finally, if that is not preposterous enough, I will seem to open up my body and find myself stuffed with fried shrimps, even unto the inner reaches of my thighs. Miraculously enough, I experience just these to happen. The experiences

are not as in a dream but indistinguishable from what I call the most ordinary waking experiences—except, of course, for the extraordinary content. Nor does this predicted sequence seem to take place in a flash, or in any very brief interval. To mirror what I take as reality, it seems to take a couple of months. After a convincing talk with the voice at the end of this experiential journey, I am left in a blue homogenous field of visual experience, feeling little but wonder, to think over whether an ink-bottle was ever before me, whether there are now or ever were any automobiles, and so on. Of course, the voice has told me that none of these things ever were, and told me why I thought otherwise. What am I to think now?

My attitude toward these imagined experiences is that if they should occur I would be at least somewhat less certain than I now am about these matters. I would be at least somewhat unconfident, even, that I was not naked at the time in question. This is my present attitude. If things would not develop in accord with it, that would be something I can now only hope will not happen. Moreover, I think it pretty plain that this is the attitude which I ought to have and that anyone who held an opposite one would have a dogmatic attitude in these matters. That is, if one's attitude is that these experiences will not be counted as having any weight at all, one would be dogmatic in these matters.

Now, some people might have the attitude that if these experiences occurred one should think himself to be quite mad or, at least, to have had his capacity for judgment impaired in some damaging way. My own attitude is more open than this. But it should be pointed out that even this attitude of prospective self-defeat is quite compatible with that of lessening one's confidence. One's total attitude, that is, might be that if the imagined experiences really came to pass one would both be less certain that there ever were automobiles and also be inclined to think that one must have become quite mad. All that I am claiming or need to claim is that one ought to have at least the first part of this total attitude or, more precisely, that one ought not to have the opposite attitude that any such experiences will be completely disregarded.

7 HELPFUL EXPERIENCES FOR THE HARDEST CASES

In respect of almost any matter, the possibility of certain imagined sequences of experience makes quite a convincing case that one ought not, on pain of dogmatism, have the attitude of absolute certainty. There are, however, two sorts of matters where something more must be said to explain how such experience might help us to appreciate the wrongness of this severe attitude. I treat them in turn, proceeding from the less to the more difficult.

The first and lesser difficulty concerns certain sorts of matters about the past. The most famous of these, due to Russell,[4] is the matter of whether the world sprang into existence five minutes ago. But the matter of whether oneself has existed for more than a brief moment will pose the problem more clearly so far as sequences of convincing experiences are concerned. The problem may be put like this: If any sequence of experience is to be convincing, it must itself endure for much more than a brief moment. Even in advance of any experiences which might look to show that one has been in existence only for a brief moment, one can and ought to appreciate this fact about the conditions of convincing. Therefore, it is in any case quite all right to have the attitude that no possible experience will be counted as convincing evidence for the claim that one has existed only for a brief moment. Rather, one may disregard any new experience which purports to be to this effect.

The difficulty with this reasoning is that it doesn't take into account how new experiences might make us view time differently. If our voice told us new things about time, we might not be able to disregard it without ourselves being dogmatic. Suppose that the voice says that one has been brought into existence only a brief moment ago complete with an accurate understanding of how long temporal intervals are. But one is also provided, the voice says, with an appealing consistent web of ostensible memories: to believe that one has experienced the things it seems to one that one has will be, then, only to believe what is false. Now, the recent experiences one indeed has had are,

according to the voice, part of a sequence which has gone on only for a brief moment, a billionth of a second, to be quite precise. And, this includes these very messages that even now are coming to one. Though it seems to one that the experiences have been going on for some months, one has in fact been alive for only a brief moment and, indeed, the world of concrete things, including the source of the voice, has existed for less than a minute. In response to these vocal claims one might put forward some relativistic theory of time on which the claims would make no sense and, at any rate, on which they could not possibly be true. But, that would only be to adduce some theory. And, if there is anything scientific about science it is that one should never be too certain of any theory, no matter how beautiful, comprehensive and powerful it may seem. So it seems that, no matter how one might wish to reply, one would do well to allow some influence for such a sequence of experience as the one just imagined. One should have the attitude, at least, that should it occur one will be not quite *so* certain, as one otherwise might be, that one has been alive for more than a brief moment.

The greatest difficulty in finding possible experience a help in abandoning the attitude of certainty comes, I think, in matters where we think that the only possible error must be a "purely verbal" one. This occurs, I take it, with matters of "immediate experience," e.g., with whether one is now experiencing phenomenal blueness or pain. And, it occurs with the "simplest matters of logical necessity," e.g., with whether two is the sum of one and one. Perhaps the most famous case, due to Descartes, is that concerning one's own present moment thinking and existence, e.g., whether one now exists. Now, some philosophers have found it quite an article of faith to suppose that there might be anything to answer to the word "I." They would think, I suppose, that what one ought to be sure of is that *something* now exists, leaving it quite open, what that thing might be. Even if it is true that in such matters as these, any error must be purely verbal, why shouldn't the possibility of just such an error make the attitude of absolute certainty dogmatic in these very matters? I have never heard anything to convince me of the opposite. It is said that what one believes or is certain of are propositions or, at least, some things that are too abstract to have uncertainty over words interfere with their status. Let us agree at the outset that we understand such attempts to downgrade the effect that words might have. But, nevertheless, ought not the following story about possible experience cause at least some very small doubts to enter one's mind? Again, we have our voice. After going through the sequence of experiences I described before, the voice tells me that I become easily confused about the meanings of certain terms. It says that on occasions, and now is one of them, I confuse the meaning of "exist," a word which means, roughly, "to continue on in the face of obstacles," with the meaning of "persist," a word which, roughly, shares a meaning with the verb "to be." Consequently, in philosophizing, I often say to myself "I exist" and "It seems certain to me that I *exist* now." And, I then seem to remember that I have never thought otherwise. But, in fact, of course, I am quite a changeable fellow, and so I rarely if ever *exist*. It is true that I *persist*, as everyone does, and I *should* say *this* when I do that philosophizing. No doubt, I will soon change once again and say and think, rightly, that what I do is persist. This will then seem certain to me, which is better than its seeming certain to me that what I do is exist, since at least the former is something which is *true*. But, it would be far better still if *neither* ever even *seemed* to be absolutely certain. At the very least, the voice concludes, I ought never to *be* certain of these things, no matter how tempting that might be. This is especially true in my case because I am so changeable and, as a consequence, so often and so easily confused.

I have no doubt that many would want to protest to this voice. Some might say that the matter of whether the words "I exist now" express a truth and that of whether I exist now are two utterly different matters. Now, it is very true that these matters are very different. But, why should that lead anyone to protest what I am saying? What I am saying is just that under certain conditions of experience

one ought to become less certain than before that one indeed *exists*, that one thing one does is exist. Indeed, one may be in just such an experiential situation even while being quite confident that the words "I exist now" do indeed express a truth. We may suppose, after all, that the voice tells one that one *does* continue on in the face of obstacles, and so one ought to be confident that one exists, as well as that one persists. Now, it *may* be that there is something deeply wrong with any of these vocal suggestions and, so, that one ought never to allow any to affect one's beliefs or attitudes even in the most minimal way. But I can't see how anyone can be absolutely certain that *this* is so. And, suppose that the *voice itself* went through all those matters with you and told you to rest assured that such verbal confusions can get you, and are now getting you, into error here. In that one might experience even this, so far as I can see, one's attitude in any of these matters ought not to be that of absolute certainty. Thus, one ought not, really, be absolutely certain that one now exists, or that something exists, or that one now feels pain, or whatever. Of course, the source of uncertainty we have just uncovered is present in matters which are not so apparently certain or simple. Thus, we may now appreciate a bit more fully why it is at least a bit dogmatic to be certain that there is an ink-bottle before one, that there ever are any automobiles, or that one has existed for more than a brief moment.

As I said earlier, these imagined sequences of experience are only meant to be a help in coming to the idea that being certain involves being dogmatic. Their role is to exemplify some situations where this feature of dogmatism might be brought out. I hope that the sequences I have described have been thus revealing and, so, convincing. But that they be so is hardly essential to making good our claim. For even if the particular experience one is able to imagine does not seem to jeopardize some statement which seems quite certain, one shouldn't be *sure* that there isn't any such sequence—possibly, even one which a human imagination just can't grasp in advance. And, even if there is no sequence of *experience* which ought to make one less certain, *mightn't* there be some other factor information about which ought to give one pause? Perhaps, there are some currently obscure conceptual truths about the nature of thought and reason, which show how any thinking at all is parasitic on the possibility of error in the case. No matter how comfortable one feels in his philosophy and his view of the world, I can't see how he might properly be *certain* that there is no way that he could possibly be wrong. He cannot properly be certain that he has given a complete accounting of every sort of experience, evidence and information which might possibly exist. For this reason, if for no other, it will be dogmatic of him ever to have the attitude that he will disregard *any* new experience, evidence and information which run counter to what he holds.

This is our case, then, that being certain involves being dogmatic and, so, that there is always at least *something* wrong with being certain. As we noticed, whatever is wrong with this dogmatism may be overridden by other considerations, considerations which are not properly epistemological ones. But, the fact that there is always some dogmatism, whether overridden or not, means that nobody ever knows anything about anything. In this sense, then, dogmatism is the opposite of skepticism, and the necessary presence of dogmatism means that skepticism is really true.

NOTES

1. Malcolm, "Knowledge and Belief," pp. 67–68, in *Knowledge and Certainty* (Englewood Cliffs, New Jersey: Prentice Hall, 1963).
2. Ibid., p. 67.
3. Peter Unger, "A Defense of Skepticism," *The Philosophical Review*, vol. LXXX, no. 2 (April 1971), sections II–IV. In a later issue of this journal, James Cargite replied to the skeptical suggestions in that paper of mine: "In Reply to a Defense of Skepticism," *The Philosophical Review*, vol. LXXXI, no. 2 (April 1972). Perhaps the present paper may be taken as deepening the debate between myself and this critic in a way that would not be possible in a brief and direct rejoinder on my part.
4. Bertrand Russell, *The Analysis of Mind* (New York: The Macmillan Company, 1921), pp. 159–60.

The Problem of the Criterion

RODERICK M. CHISHOLM

Roderick M. Chisholm (1916–1999), one of America's most distinguished epistemologists, spent his entire career at Brown University.

1

"The problem of the criterion" seems to me to be one of the most important and one of the most difficult of all the problems of philosophy. I am tempted to say that one has not begun to philosophize until one has faced this problem and has recognized how unappealing, in the end, each of the possible solutions is....

2

What is the problem, then? It is the ancient problem of "the diallelus"—the problem of "the wheel" or "the vicious circle." It was put very neatly by Montaigne in his *Essays*. So let us begin by paraphrasing his formulation of the puzzle. To know whether things really are as they seem to be, we must have a *procedure* for

An edited version of "The Problem of the Criterion," from Roderick M. Chisholm, *The Foundations of Knowing* (Sussex: Harvester Press, 1982), pp. 61–75. Reprinted by permission of Marquette University Press.

distinguishing appearances that are true from appearances that are false. But to know whether our procedure is a good procedure, we have to know whether it really *succeeds* in distinguishing appearances that are true from appearances that are false. And we cannot know whether it does really succeed unless we already know which appearances are *true* and which ones are *false*. And so we are caught in a circle.[1]

Let us try to see how one gets into a situation of this sort.

The puzzles begin to form when you ask yourself, "What can I really know about the world?" We are all acquainted with people who think they know a lot more than in fact they do know. I'm thinking of fanatics, bigots, mystics, various types of dogmatists. And we have all heard of people who claim at least to know a lot less than what in fact they do know. I'm thinking of those people who call themselves "skeptics" and who like to say that people cannot know what the world is really like. People tend to become skeptics, temporarily, after reading books on popular science: the authors tell us we cannot know what things are like really (but they make use of a vast amount of knowledge, or a vast amount of what is claimed to be knowledge, to support this skeptical conclusion). And as we know, people tend to become dogmatists, temporarily, as a result of the effects of alcohol, or drugs, or religious and emotional experiences. Then they claim to have an inside view of the world and they think they have a deep kind of knowledge giving them a key to the entire workings of the universe.

If you have a healthy common sense, you will feel that something is wrong with both of these extremes and that the truth is somewhere in the middle: we can know far more than the skeptic says we can know and far less than the dogmatist or the mystic says that he can know. But how are we to decide these things?

3

How do we decide, in any particular case, whether we have a genuine item of knowledge? Most of us are ready to confess that our beliefs far transcend what we really know. There are

things we believe that we don't in fact know. And we can say of many of these things that we know that we don't know them. I believe that Mrs. Jones is honest, say, but I don't know it, and I know that I don't know it. There are other things that we don't know, but they are such that we don't know that we don't know them. Last week, say, I thought I knew that Mr. Smith was honest, but he turned out to be a thief. I didn't know that he was a thief, and, moreover, I didn't know that I didn't know that he was a thief; I thought I knew that he was honest. And so the problem is: How are we to distinguish the real cases of knowledge from what only seem to be cases of knowledge? Or, as I put it before, how are we to decide in any particular case whether we have genuine items of knowledge?

What would be a satisfactory solution to our problem? Let me quote in detail what Cardinal Mercier says:

> If there is any knowledge which bears the mark of truth, if the intellect does have a way of distinguishing the true and the false, in short, if there *is* a criterion of truth, then this criterion should satisfy three conditions: it should be *internal, objective,* and *immediate.*
>
> It should be *internal.* No reason or rule of truth that is provided by an *external authority* can serve as an ultimate criterion. For the reflective doubts that are essential to criteriology can and should be applied to this authority itself. The mind cannot attain to certainty until it has found *within itself* a sufficient reason for adhering to the testimony of such an authority.
>
> The criterion should be *objective.* The ultimate reason for believing cannot be a merely *subjective* state of the thinking subject. A man is aware that he can reflect upon his psychological states in order to control them. Knowing that he has this ability, he does not, so long as he has not made use of it, have the right to be sure. The ultimate ground of certitude cannot consist in a subjective feeling. It can be found only in that which, objectively, produces this feeling and is adequate to reason.
>
> Finally, the criterion must be *immediate.* To be sure, a certain conviction may rest upon many different reasons some of which are subordinate to others. But if we are to avoid an infinite regress, then we must find a ground of assent that

presupposes no other. We must find an *immediate* criterion of certitude.

Is there a criterion of truth that satisfies these three conditions? If so, what is it?[2]

4

To see how perplexing our problem is, let us consider a figure that Descartes had suggested and that Coffey takes up in his dealings with the problem of the criterion.[3] Descartes' figure comes to this.

Let us suppose that you have a pile of apples and you want to sort out the good ones from the bad ones. You want to put the good ones in a pile by themselves and throw the bad ones away. This is a useful thing to do, obviously, because the bad apples tend to infect the good ones and then the good ones become bad, too. Descartes thought our beliefs were like this. The bad ones tend to infect the good ones, so we should look them over very carefully, throw out the bad ones if we can, and then—or so Descartes hoped—we would be left with just a stock of good beliefs on which we could rely completely. But how are we to do the sorting? If we are to sort out the good ones from the bad ones, then, of course, we must have a way of recognizing the good ones. Or at least we must have a way of recognizing the bad ones. And—again, of course—you and I do have a way of recognizing good apples and also of recognizing bad ones. The good ones have their own special feel, look, and taste, and so do the bad ones.

But when we turn from apples to beliefs, the matter is quite different. In the case of the apples, we have a method—a criterion—for distinguishing the good ones from the bad ones. But in the case of the beliefs, we do not have a method or a criterion for distinguishing the good ones from the bad ones. Or, at least, we don't have one yet. The question we started with was: How *are* we to tell the good ones from the bad ones? In other words, we were asking: What is the proper method for deciding which are the good beliefs and which are the bad ones—which beliefs are genuine cases of knowledge and which beliefs are not?

And now, you see, we are on the wheel. First, we want to find out which are the good beliefs and which are the bad ones. To find this out we have to have some way—some method—of deciding which are the good ones and which are the bad ones. But there are good and bad methods—good and bad ways—of sorting out the good beliefs from the bad ones. And so we now have a new problem: How are we to decide which are the good methods and which are the bad ones?

If we could fix on a good method for distinguishing between good and bad methods, we might be all set. But this, of course, just moves the problem to a different level. How are we to distinguish between a good and a bad method for choosing good methods? If we continue in this way, of course, we are led to an infinite regress and we will never have the answer to our original question.

What do we do in fact? We do know that there are fairly reliable ways of sorting out good beliefs from bad ones. Most people will tell you, for example, that if you follow the procedures of science and common sense—if you tend carefully to your observations and if you make use of the canons of logic, induction, and the theory of probability—you will be following the best possible procedure for making sure that you will have more good beliefs than bad ones. This is doubtless true. But how do we know that it is? How do we know that the procedures of science, reason, and common sense are the best methods that we have?

If we do know this, it is because we know that these procedures work. It is because we know that these procedures do in fact enable us to distinguish the good beliefs from the bad ones. We say: "See—these methods turn out good beliefs." But *how* do we know that they do? It can only be that we already know how to tell the difference between the good beliefs and the bad ones.

And now you can see where the skeptic comes in. He'll say this: "You said you wanted to sort out the good beliefs from the bad ones. Then to do this, you apply the canons of science, common sense, and reason. And now, in answer to the question, 'How do you know that that's the right way to do it?', you say "Why, I can see that the ones it picks out are the good ones and the ones it leaves behind are the bad ones.' But if you can *see* which ones are the good ones and which ones are the bad ones, why do you think you need a general method for sorting them out?"

5

We can formulate some of the philosophical issues that are involved here by distinguishing two pairs of questions. These are:

A) "*What* do we know? What is the *extent* of our knowledge?"
B) "How are we to decide *whether* we know? What are the *criteria* of knowledge?"

If you happen to know the answers to the first of these pairs of questions, you may have some hope of being able to answer the second. Thus, if you happen to know which are the good apples and which are the bad ones, then maybe you could explain to some other person how he could go about deciding whether or not he has a good apple or a bad one. But if you don't know the answer to the first of these pairs of questions—if you don't know what things you know or how far your knowledge extends—it is difficult to see how you could possibly figure out an answer to the second.

On the other hand, *if,* somehow, you already know the answers to the second of these pairs of questions, then you may have some hope of being able to answer the first. Thus, if you happen to have a good set of directions for telling whether apples are good or bad, then maybe you can go about finding a good one—assuming, of course, that there are some good apples to be found. But if you don't know the answer to the second of these pairs of questions—if you don't know how to go about deciding whether or not you know, if you don't know what the criteria of knowing are—it is difficult to see how you could possibly figure out an answer to the first.

And so we can formulate the position of *the skeptic* on these matters. He will say: "You cannot answer question A until you have answered question B. And you cannot answer question B until you have answered question A. Therefore you cannot answer either question. You cannot know what, if anything, you know, and there is no possible way for you to decide in any particular case." Is there any reply to this?

6

Broadly speaking, there are at least two other possible views. So we may choose among three possibilities.

There are people—philosophers—who think that they do have an answer to B and that, given their answer to B, they can then figure out their answer to A. And there are other people—other philosophers—who have it the other way around: they think that they have an answer to A and that, given their answer to A, they can then figure out the answer to B.

There don't seem to be any generally accepted names for these two different philosophical positions. (Perhaps this is just as well. There are more than enough names, as it is, for possible philosophical views.) I suggest, for the moment, we use the expressions "methodists" and "particularists." By "methodists," I mean, not the followers of John Wesley's version of Christianity, but those who think they have an answer to B, and who then, in terms of it, work out their answer to A. By "particularists" I mean those who have it the other way around.

7

Thus John Locke was a methodist—in our present, rather special sense of the term. He was able to arrive—somehow—at an answer to B. He said, in effect: "The way you decide whether or not a belief is a good belief—that is to say, the way you decide whether a belief is likely to be a genuine case of knowledge—is to see whether it is derived from sense experience, to see, for example, whether it bears certain relations to your sensations." Just what these relations to our sensations might be is a matter we may leave open, for present purposes. The point is: Locke felt that if a belief is to be credible, it must bear certain relations to the believer's sensations—but he never told us *how* he happened to arrive at this conclusion. This, of course, is the view that has come to be known as "empiricism." David Hume followed Locke in this empiricism and said that empiricism gives us an effective criterion for distinguishing the good apples from the bad ones. You can take this criterion to the library, he said. Suppose you find a book in which the author makes assertions that do not conform to the empirical criterion. Hume said: "Commit it to the flames: for it can contain nothing but sophistry and illusion."

8

Empiricism, then, was a form of what I have called "methodism." The empiricist—like other types of methodist—begins with a criterion and then he uses it to throw out the bad apples. There are two objections, I would say, to empiricism. The first—which applies to every form of methodism (in our present sense of the word)—is that the criterion is very broad and far-reaching and at the same time completely arbitrary. How can one *begin* with a broad generalization? It seems especially odd that the empiricist—who wants to proceed cautiously, step by step, from experience—begins with such a generalization. He leaves us completely in the dark so far as concerns what *reasons* he may have for adopting this particular criterion rather than some other. The second objection applies to empiricism in particular. When we apply the empirical criterion—at least, as it was developed by Hume, as well as by many of those in the nineteenth and twentieth centuries who have called themselves "empiricists"—we seem to throw out, not only the bad apples but the good ones as well, and we are left, in effect, with just a few parings or skins with no meat behind them. Thus Hume virtually conceded that, if you are going to be empiricist, the only matters of fact that you can really know about pertain to the existence of sensations. "'Tis vain," he said, "To ask whether there be body." He meant you cannot know whether any physical things exist—whether there are trees, or houses, or bodies, much less whether there are atoms or other such microscopic particles. All you can know is that there

are and have been certain sensations. You cannot know whether there is any you who experiences those sensations—much less whether any other people exist who experience sensations. And I think, if he had been consistent in his empiricism, he would also have said you cannot really be sure whether there have been any senations in the past; you can know only that certain sensations exist here and now.

9

The great Scottish philosopher, Thomas Reid, reflected on all this in the eighteenth century. He was serious about philosophy and man's place in the world. He finds Hume saying things implying that we can know only of the existence of certain sensations here and now. One can imagine him saying: "Good Lord! What kind of nonsense is this?" What he did say, among other things, was this: "A traveler of good judgment may mistake his way, and be unawares led into a wrong track; and while the road is fair before him, he may go on without suspicion and be followed by others but, when it ends in a coal pit; it requires no great judgment to know that he hath gone wrong, nor perhaps to find out what misled him."[4]

Thus Reid, as I interpret him, was not an empiricist; nor was he, more generally, what I have called a "methodist." He was a "particularist." That is to say, he thought that he had an answer to question A, and in terms of the answer to question A, he then worked out kind of an answer to question B.[5] An even better example of a "particularist" is the great twentieth century English philosopher, G. E. Moore.

Suppose, for a moment, you were tempted to go along with Hume and say "The only thing about the world I can really know is that there are now sensations of a certain sort. There's a sensation of a man, there's the sound of a voice, and there's a feeling of bewilderment or boredom. But that's all I can really know about." What would Reid say? I can imagine him saying something like this: "Well, you can talk that way if you want to. But you know very well that it isn't true. You know that you are there, that you have a body of such and such a sort and that other people are here, too. And you know about this building where you were this morning and all kinds of other things as well." G. E. Moore would raise his hand at this point and say: "I know very well this is a hand, and so do you. If you come across some philosophical theory that implies that you and I cannot know that this is a hand, then so much the worse for the theory." I think that Reid and Moore are right, myself, and I'm inclined to think that the "methodists" are wrong.

Going back to our questions A and B, we may summarize the three possible views as follows: there is skepticism (you cannot answer either question without presupposing an answer to the other, and therefore the questions cannot be answered at all); there is "methodism" (you begin with an answer to B); and there is "particularism" (you begin with an answer to A). I suggest that the third possibility is the most reasonable.

10

I would say—and many reputable philosophers would disagree with me—that, to find out whether you know such a thing as that this is a hand, you don't have to apply any test or criterion. Spinoza has it right. "In order to know," he said, "there is no need to know that we know, much less to know that we know that we know."[6]

This is part of the answer, it seems to me, to the puzzle about the diallelus. There are many things that quite obviously, we do know to be true. If I report to you the things I now see and hear and feel—or, if you prefer, the things I now think I see and hear and feel—the chances are that my report will be correct; I will be telling you something I know. And so, too, if you report the things that you think you now see and hear and feel. To be sure, there are hallucinations and illusions. People often think they see or hear or feel things that in fact they do not see or hear or feel. But from this fact—that our senses do sometimes deceive us—it hardly follows that your senses and mine are

deceiving you and me right now. One may say similar things about what we remember.

Having these good apples before us, we can look them over and formulate certain criteria of goodness. Consider the senses, for example. One important criterion—one epistemological principle—was formulated by St. Augustine. It is more reasonable, he said, to trust the senses than to distrust them. Even though there have been illusions and hallucinations, the wise thing, when everything seems all right, is to accept the testimony of the senses. I say "when everything seems all right." If on a particular occasion something about *that* particular occasion makes you suspect that particular report of the senses, if, say, you seem to remember having been drugged or hypnotized, or brainwashed, then perhaps you should have some doubts about what you think you see, or hear, or feel, or smell. But if nothing about this particular occasion leads you to suspect what the senses report on this particular occasion, then the wise thing is to take such a report at its face value. In short the senses should be regarded as innocent until there is some positive reason, on some particular occasion, for thinking that they are guilty on that particular occasion.

One might say the same thing of memory. If, on any occasion, you think you remember that such-and-such an event occurred, then the wise thing is to assume that that particular event did occur—unless something special about this particular occasion leads you to suspect your memory.

We have then a kind of answer to the puzzle about the diallelus. We start with particular cases of knowledge and then from those we generalize and formulate criteria of goodness—criteria telling us what it is for a belief to be epistemologically respectable....

Conclusion

So far as our problem of the criterion is concerned, the essential thing to note is this. In formulating such principles we will simply proceed as Aristotle did when he formulated his rules for the syllogism. As "particularists" in our approach to the problem of the criterion, we will fit our rules to the cases—to the apples we know to be good and to the apples we know to be bad. Knowing what we do about ourselves and the world, we have at our disposal certain instances that our rules or principles should countenance, and certain other instances that our rules or principles should rule out or forbid. And, as rational beings, we assume that by investigating these instances we can formulate criteria that any instance must satisfy if it is to be countenanced and we can formulate other criteria that any instance must satisfy if it is to be ruled out or forbidden.

If we proceed in this way we will have satisfied Cardinal Mercier's criteria for a theory of evidence or, as he called it, a theory of certitude. He said that any criterion, or any adequate set of criteria, should be internal, objective, and immediate. The type of criteria I have referred to are certainly *internal,* in his sense of the term. We have not appealed to any external authority as constituting the ultimate test of evidence. (Thus we haven't appealed to "science" or to "the scientists of our culture circle" as constituting the touchstone of what we know.) I would say that our criteria are *objective.* We have formulated them in terms of the concept of epistemic preferability—where the location "*p* is epistemically preferable to *q* for S" is taken to refer to an objective relation that obtains independently of the actual preferences of any particular subject. The criteria that we formulate, if they are adequate, will be principles that are necessarily true. And they are also *immediate.* Each of them is such that, if it is applicable at any particular time, then the fact that it is then applicable is capable of being directly evident to that particular subject at that particular time.

But in all of this I have presupposed the approach I have called "particularism." The "methodist" and the "skeptic" will tell us that we have started in the wrong place. If now we try to reason with them, then, I am afraid, we will be back on the wheel.

What few philosophers have had the courage to recognize is this: we can deal with the problem only by begging the question. It seems to me that, if we do recognize this fact, as we should, then it is unseemly for us to try to pretend that it isn't so.

One may object: "Doesn't this mean, then, that the skeptic is right after all?" I would answer: "Not at all. His view is only one of the three possibilities and in itself has no more to recommend it than the others do. And in favor of our approach there is the fact that we *do* know many things, after all."

NOTES

1. The quotation is a paraphrase. What Montaigne wrote was: "Pour juger des apparences que nous recevons des subjects, il nous faudroit un instrument judicatoire; pour verifier cet instrument, il nous y faut de la demonstration; pour verifier la demonstration, un instrument; nous voylà au rouet. Puisque les sens ne peuvent arrester notre dispute, éstans pleins euxmesmes d'incertitude, il faut que se soit la raison; aucune raison s'establira sans une autre raison: nous voylà à reculons jusques à l'infiny." The passage appears in book 2, chapter 12 ("An Apologie of Raymond Sebond"); it may be found on page 544 of the Modern Library edition of *The Essays of Montaigne.*

2. Cardinal D. J. Mercier, *Critériologie Générale ou Théorie Générale de la Certitude,* 8th Edition (Louvain, 1923), p. 234.

3. See the reply to the VIIth set of Objections and Coffey, vol. 1, p. 127.

4. Thomas Reid, *Inquiry into the Human Mind,* chap. 1, sec. 8.

5. Unfortunately Cardinal Mercier takes Reid to be what I have called a "methodist." He assumes, incorrectly I think, that Reid defends certain principles (principles that Reid calls principles of "common sense") on the ground that these principles happen to be the deliverance of a faculty called "common sense." See Mercier, pp. 179–81.

6. *On Improvement of the Understanding,* in *Chief Works of Benedict de Spinoza,* vol. 2, trans. R. H. M. Elwes, rev. ed. (London: George Bell and Sons, 1898), p. 13.

OUR KNOWLEDGE OF THE EXTERNAL WORLD

Appearance and Reality and the Existence of Matter

BERTRAND RUSSELL

Bertrand Russell (1872–1970) was one of the greatest philosophers of the twentieth century. His philosophical contributions ranged across many areas; he was also an important social critic. He received the Nobel prize for literature in 1950.

I

Is there any knowledge in the world which is so certain that no reasonable man could doubt it? This question, which at first sight might not seem difficult, is really one of the most difficult that can be asked. When we have realized the obstacles in the way of a straightforward and confident answer, we shall be well launched on the study of philosophy—for philosophy is merely the attempt to answer such ultimate questions, not carelessly and dogmatically, as we do in ordinary life and even in the sciences, but critically after exploring all that makes such questions puzzling, and after realizing all the vagueness and confusion that underlie our ordinary ideas.

In daily life, we assume as certain many things which, on a closer scrutiny, are found to be so full of apparent contradictions that only a great amount of thought enables us to know what it is that we really may believe. In the search for certainty, it is natural to begin with our present experiences, and in some sense, no doubt, knowledge is to be derived from them. But any statement as to what it is that our immediate experiences make us know is very likely to be wrong. It seems to me that I am now sitting in a chair, at a table of a certain shape, on which I see sheets of paper with writing or print. By turning my head I see out of the window buildings and clouds and the sun. I believe that the sun is about ninety-three million miles from the earth; that it is a hot globe many times bigger than the earth; that, owing to the earth's rotation, it rises every morning, and will continue to do so for an indefinite time in the future. I believe that, if any other normal person comes into my room, he will see the same chairs and tables and books and papers as I see, and that the table which I see is the same as the table which I feel pressing against my arm. All this seems to be so evident as to be hardly worth stating, except in answer to a man who doubts whether I know anything. Yet all this may be reasonably doubted, and all of it requires much careful discussion before we can be sure that we have stated it in a form that is wholly true.

To make our difficulties plain, let us concentrate attention on the table. To the eye it is oblong, brown, and shiny; to the touch it is smooth and cool and hard; when I tap it, it gives out a wooden sound. Anyone else who sees and feels and hears the table will agree with this description, so that it might seem as if no difficulty would arise; but as soon as we try to be more precise our troubles begin. Although I believe that the table is "really" of the same colour all over, the parts that reflect the light look much brighter than the other parts, and some parts look white because of reflected light. I know that, if I move,

From B. Russell, *Problems of Philosophy*, chs. 1 and 2.

the parts that reflect the light will be different, so that the apparent distribution of colours on the table will change. It follows that if several people are looking at the table at the same moment, no two of them will see exactly the same distribution of colours, because no two can see it from exactly the same point of view, and any change in the point of view makes some change in the way the light is reflected.

For most practical purposes these differences are unimportant, but to the painter they are all-important: The painter has to unlearn the habit of thinking that things seem to have the colour which common sense says they "really" have, and to learn the habit of seeing things as they appear. Here we have already the beginning of one of the distinctions that cause most trouble in philosophy—the distinction between "appearance" and "reality," between what things seem to be and what they are. The painter wants to know what things seem to be, the practical man and the philosopher want to know what they are; but the philosopher's wish to know this is stronger than the practical man's and is more troubled by knowledge as to the difficulties of answering the question.

To return to the table. It is evident from what we have found, that there is no colour which preeminently appears to be *the* colour of the table, or even of any one particular part of the table—it appears to be of different colours from different points of view, and there is no reason for regarding some of these as more really its colour than others. And we know that even from a given point of view the colour will seem different by artificial light, or to a colour-blind man, or to a man wearing blue spectacles, while in the dark there will be no colour at all, though to touch and hearing the table will be unchanged. This colour is not something which is inherent in the table, but something depending upon the table and the spectator and the way the light falls on the table. When, in ordinary life, we speak of *the* colour of the table, we only mean the sort of colour which it will seem to have to a normal spectator from an ordinary point of view under usual conditions of light. But the other colours which appear under other conditions have just as good a right to be considered

real; and therefore, to avoid favouritism, we are compelled to deny that, in itself, the table has any one particular colour.

The same thing applies to the texture. With the naked eye one can see the grain, but otherwise the table looks smooth and even. If we looked at it through a microscope, we should see roughnesses and hills and valleys, and all sorts of differences that are imperceptible to the naked eye. Which of these is the "real" table? We are naturally tempted to say that what we see through the microscope is more real, but that in turn would be changed by a still more powerful microscope. If, then, we cannot trust what we see with the naked eye, why should we trust what we see through a microscope? Thus, again, the confidence in our senses with which we began deserts us.

The *shape* of the table is no better. We are all in the habit of judging as to the "real" shapes of things, and we do this so unreflectingly that we come to think we actually see the real shapes. But, in fact, as we all have to learn if we try to draw, a given thing looks different in shape from every different point of view. If our table is "really" rectangular, it will look, from almost all points of view, as if it had two acute angles and two obtuse angles. If opposite sides are parallel, they will look as if they converged to a point away from the spectator; if they are of equal length, they will look as if the nearer side were longer. All these things are not commonly noticed in looking at a table, because experience has taught us to construct the "real" shape from the apparent shape, and the "real" shape is what interests us as practical men. But the "real" shape is not what we see; it is something inferred from what we see. And what we see is constantly changing in shape as we move about the room; so that here again the senses seem not to give us the truth about the table itself, but only about the appearance of the table.

Similar difficulties arise when we consider the sense of touch. It is true that the table always gives us a sensation of hardness, and we feel that it resists pressure. But the sensation we obtain depends upon how hard we press the table and also upon what part of the body we press with; thus the various sensations due to various pressures or various parts of the body cannot be supposed to reveal *directly* any definite property of the table, but at most to be signs of some property which perhaps *causes* all the sensations, but is not actually apparent in any of them. And the same applies still more obviously to the sounds which can be elicited by rapping the table.

Thus it becomes evident that the real table, if there is one, is not the same as what we immediately experience by sight or touch or hearing. The real table, if there is one, is not *immediately* known to us at all, but must be an inference from what is immediately known. Hence, two very difficult questions at once arise; namely, (1) Is there a real table at all? (2) If so, what sort of object can it be?

It will help us in considering these questions to have a few simple terms of which the meaning is definite and clear. Let us give the name of "sense-data" to the things that are immediately known in sensation: such things as colours, sounds, smells, hardnesses, roughnesses, and so on. We shall give the name "sensation" to the experience of being immediately aware of these things. Thus, whenever we see a colour, we have a sensation *of* the colour, but the colour itself is a sense-datum, not a sensation. The colour is that *of* which we are immediately aware, and the awareness itself is the sensation. It is plain that if we are to know anything about the table, it must be by means of the sense-data—brown colour, oblong shape, smoothness, etc.—which we associate with the table; but, for the reasons which have been given, we cannot say that the table is the sense-data, or even that the sense-data are directly properties of the table. Thus a problem arises as to the relation of the sense-data to the real table, supposing there is such a thing.

The real table, if it exists, we will call a "physical object." Thus we have to consider the relation of sense-data to physical objects. The collection of all physical objects is called "matter." Thus our two questions may be restated as follows: (1) Is there any such thing as matter? (2) If so, what is its nature?

The philosopher who first brought prominently forward the reasons for regarding the immediate objects of our senses as not existing independently of us was Bishop Berkeley (1685–1753). His *Three Dialogues between Hylas and Philonous, in Opposition to Sceptics and Atheists,* undertake to prove that there is no such thing as matter at all, and that the world consists of nothing but minds and their ideas. Hylas has hitherto believed in matter, but he is no match for Philonous, who mercilessly drives him into contradictions and paradoxes, and makes his own denial of matter seem, in the end, as if it were almost common sense. The arguments employed are of very different value: Some are important and sound, others are confused or quibbling. But Berkeley retains the merit of having shown that the existence of matter is capable of being denied without absurdity, and that if there are any things that exist independently of us they cannot be the immediate objects of our sensations.

There are two different questions involved when we ask whether matter exists, and it is important to keep them clear. We commonly mean by "matter" something which is opposed to "mind," something which we think of as occupying space and as radically incapable of any sort of thought or consciousness. It is chiefly in this sense that Berkeley denies matter; that is to say, he does not deny that the sense-data which we commonly take as signs of the existence of the table are really signs of the existence of *something* independent of us, but he does deny that this something is nonmental, that it is neither mind nor ideas entertained by some mind. He admits that there must be something which continues to exist when we go out of the room or shut our eyes, and that what we call seeing the table does really give us reason for believing in something which persists even when we are not seeing it. But he thinks that this something cannot be radically different in nature from what we see, and cannot be independent of seeing altogether, though it must be independent of *our* seeing. He is thus led to regard the "real" table as an idea in the mind of God. Such an idea has the required permanence and independence of ourselves, without being—as matter would otherwise be—something quite unknowable, in the sense that we can only infer it, and can never be directly and immediately aware of it.

Other philosophers since Berkeley have also held that, although the table does not depend for its existence upon being seen by me, it does depend upon being seen (or otherwise apprehended in sensation) by *some* mind—not necessarily the mind of God, but more often the whole collective mind of the universe. This they hold, as Berkeley does, chiefly because they think there can be nothing real—or at any rate nothing known to be real except minds and their thoughts and feelings. We might state the argument by which they support their view in some such way as this: "Whatever can be thought of is an idea in the mind of the person thinking of it; therefore nothing can be thought of except ideas in minds; therefore anything else is inconceivable, and what is inconceivable cannot exist."

Such an argument, in my opinion, is fallacious; and of course those who advance it do not put it so shortly or so crudely. But whether valid or not, the argument has been very widely advanced in one form or another; and very many philosophers, perhaps a majority, have held that there is nothing real except minds and their ideas. Such philosophers are called "idealists." When they come to explaining matter, they either say, like Berkeley, that matter is really nothing but a collection of ideas, or they say, like Leibniz (1646–1716), that what appears as matter is really a collection of more or less rudimentary minds.

But these philosophers, though they deny matter as opposed to mind, nevertheless, in another sense, admit matter. It will be remembered that we asked two questions; namely, (1) Is there a real table at all? (2) If so, what sort of object can it be? Now both Berkeley and Leibniz admit that there is a real table, but Berkeley says it is certain ideas in the mind of God, and Leibniz says it is a colony of souls. Thus both of them answer our first question in the affirmative, and only diverge from the views of ordinary mortals in their answer to our second question. In fact, almost all philosophers seem to be agreed that there is a real table, they almost all agree that, however much our sense-data—colour, shape smoothness, etc.—may depend upon us, yet their occurrence is a sign of something existing independently of us, something differing, perhaps, completely from our sense-data whenever we are in a suitable relation to the real table.

Now obviously this point in which the philosophers are agreed—the view that there is a real table, whatever its nature may be is vitally important, and it will be worthwhile to consider what reasons there are for accepting this view before we go on to the further question as to the nature of the real table. Our next chapter, therefore, will be concerned with the reasons for supposing that there is a real table at all.

Before we go farther it will be well to consider for a moment what it is that we have discovered so far. It has appeared that, if we take any common object of the sort that is supposed to be known by the senses, what the senses *immediately* tell us is not the truth about the object as it is apart from us, but only the truth about certain sense-data which, so far as we can see, depend upon the relations between us and the object. Thus what we directly see and feel is merely "appearance," which we believe to be a sign of some "reality" behind. But if the reality is not what appears, have we any means of knowing whether there is any reality at all? And if so, have we any means of finding out what it is like?

Such questions are bewildering, and it is difficult to know that even the strangest hypotheses may not be true. Thus our familiar table, which has roused but the slightest thoughts in us hitherto, has become a problem full of surprising possibilities. The one thing we know about it is that it is not what it seems. Beyond this modest result, so far, we have the most complete liberty of conjecture. Leibniz tells us it is a community of souls: Berkeley tells us it is an idea in the mind of God; sober science, scarcely less wonderful, tells us it is a vast collection of electric charges in violent motion.

Among these surprising possibilities, doubt suggests that perhaps there is no table at all. Philosophy, if it cannot answer so many questions as we could wish, has at least the power of asking questions which increase the interest of the world, and show the strangeness and wonder lying just below the surface even in the commonest things of daily life.

II

In this chapter we have to ask ourselves whether, in any sense at all, there is such a thing as matter. Is there a table which has a certain intrinsic nature, and continues to exist when I am not looking, or is the table merely a product of my imagination, a dream-table in a very prolonged dream? This question is of the greatest importance. For if we cannot be sure of the independent existence of objects, we cannot be sure of the independent existence of other people's bodies, and therefore still less of other people's minds, since we have no grounds for believing in their minds except such as are derived from observing their bodies. Thus if we cannot be sure of the independent existence of objects, we shall be left alone in a desert—it may be that the whole outer world is nothing but a dream, and that we alone exist. This is an uncomfortable possibility; but although it cannot be strictly *proved* to be false, there is not the slightest reason to suppose that it is true. In this chapter we have to see why this is the case.

Before we embark upon doubtful matters, let us try to find some more or less fixed point from which to start. Although we are doubting the physical existence of the table, we are not doubting the existence of the sense-data which made us think there was a table; we are not doubting that, while we look, a certain colour and shape appear to us, and while we press, a certain sensation of hardness is experienced by us. All this, which is psychological, we are not calling in question. In fact, whatever else may be doubtful, some at least of our immediate experiences seem absolutely certain.

Descartes (1596–1650), the founder of modern philosophy, invented a method which may still be used with profit—the method of systematic doubt. He determined that he would believe nothing which he did not see quite clearly and distinctly to be true. Whatever he could bring himself to doubt, he would doubt, until he saw reason for not doubting it. By applying this method he gradually became convinced that the only existence of which he could be *quite* certain was his own. He imagined a deceitful demon, who presented unreal things to his senses in a perpetual phantasmagoria; it might be very improbable that such a demon existed, but still it was possible, and therefore doubt concerning things perceived by the senses was possible.

But doubt concerning his own existence was not possible, for if he did not exist, no demon could deceive him. If he doubted, he must exist; if he had any experiences whatever, he must exist. Thus his own existence was an absolute certainty to him. "I think, therefore I am," he said (*Cogito, ergo sum*); and on the basis of this certainty he set to work to build up again the world of knowledge which his doubt had laid in ruins. By inventing the method of doubt, and by showing that subjective things are the most certain, Descartes performed a great service to philosophy, and one which makes him still useful to all students of the subject.

But some care is needed in using Descartes' argument. "*I* think, therefore *I* am" says rather more than is strictly certain. It might seem as though we were quite sure of being the same person today as we were yesterday, and this is no doubt true in some sense. But the real Self is as hard to arrive at as the real table and does not seem to have that absolute, convincing certainty that belongs to particular experiences. When I look at my table and see a certain brown colour, what is quite certain at once is not "*I* am seeing a brown color," but rather, "a brown colour is being seen." This of course involves something (or somebody) which (or who) sees the brown colour; but it does not of itself involve that more or less permanent person whom we call "I." So far as immediate certainty goes, it might be that the something which sees the brown colour is quite momentary, and not the same as the something which has some different experience the next moment.

Thus it is our particular thoughts and feelings that have primitive certainty. And this applies to dreams and hallucinations as well as to normal perceptions: When we dream or see a ghost, we certainly do have the sensations we think we have, but for various reasons it is held that no physical object corresponds to these sensations. Thus the certainty of our knowledge of our own experiences does not have to be limited in any way to allow for exceptional cases. Here, therefore, we have, for what it is worth, a solid basis from which to begin our pursuit of knowledge.

The problem we have to consider is this: Granted that we are certain of our own sense-data, have we any reason for regarding them as signs of the existence of something else, which we can call the physical object? When we have enumerated all the sense-data which we should naturally regard as connected with the table have we said all there is to say about the table, or is there still something else—something not a sense-datum, something which persists when we go out of the room? Common sense unhesitatingly answers that there is. What can be bought and sold and pushed about and have a cloth laid on it, and so on, cannot be a *mere* collection of sense-data. If the cloth completely hides the table, we shall derive no sense-data from the table, and therefore, if the table were merely sense-data, it would have ceased to exist, and the cloth would be suspended in empty air, resting, by a miracle, in the place where the table formerly was. This seems plainly absurd; but whoever wishes to become a philosopher must learn not to be frightened by absurdities.

One great reason why it is felt that we must secure a physical object in addition to the sense-data, is that we want the same object for different people. When ten people are sitting round a dinner-table, it seems preposterous to maintain that they are not seeing the same tablecloth, the same knives and forks and spoons and glasses. But the sense-data are private to each separate person; what is immediately present to the sight of one is not immediately present to the sight of another: They all see things from slightly different points of view, and therefore see them slightly differently. Thus, if there are to be public neutral objects, which can be in some sense known to many different people, there must be something over and above the private and particular sense-data which appear to various people. What reason, then, have we for believing that there are such public neutral objects?

The first answer that naturally occurs to one is that, although different people may see the table slightly differently, still they all see more or less similar things when they look at the table, and the variations in what they see follow the laws of perspective and reflection of light, so that it is easy to arrive at a permanent object underlying all the different people's sense-data. I bought my table from the former occupant of my room; I could not buy *his* sense-data, which died when he went away, but I could and did buy the confident expectation of more or less similar sense-data. Thus it is the fact that different people have similar sense-data, and that one person in a given place at different times has similar sense-data, which makes us suppose that over and above the sense-data there is a permanent public object which underlies or causes the sense-data of various people at various times.

Now insofar as the above considerations depend upon supposing that there are other people besides ourselves, they beg the very question at issue. Other people are represented to me by certain sense-data, such as the sight of them or the sound of their voices, and if I had no reason to believe that there were physical objects independent of my sense-data, I should have no reason to believe that other people exist except as part of my dream. Thus, when we are trying to show that there must be objects independent of our own sense-data, we cannot appeal to the testimony of other people, since this testimony itself consists of sense-data, and does not reveal other people's experiences unless our own sense-data are signs of things existing independently of us. We must therefore, if possible, find, in our own purely private experiences, characteristics which show, or tend to show, that there are in the world things other than ourselves and our private experiences.

In one sense it must be admitted that we can never *prove* the existence of things other than ourselves and our experiences. No logical absurdity results from the hypothesis that the world consists of myself and my thoughts and feelings and sensations, and that everything else is mere fancy. In dreams a very complicated world may seem to be present, and yet on waking we find it was a delusion; that is to say, we find that the sense-data in the dream do not appear to have corresponded with such physical objects as we should naturally infer from our sense-data.

(It is true that, when the physical world is assumed, it is possible to find physical causes for the sense-data in dreams: A door banging, for instance, may cause us to dream of a naval engagement. But although, in this case, there is a physical *cause* for the sense-data, there is not a physical object *corresponding* to the sense-data in the way in which an actual naval battle would correspond.) There is no logical impossibility in the supposition that the whole of life is a dream, in which we ourselves create all the objects that come before us. But although this is not logically impossible, there is no reason whatever to suppose that it is true; and it is, in fact, a less simple hypothesis, viewed as a means of accounting for the facts of our own life, than the common-sense hypothesis that there really are objects independent of us, whose action on us causes our sensations.

The way in which simplicity comes in from supposing that there really are physical objects is easily seen. If the cat appears at one moment in one part of the room, and at another in another part, it is natural to suppose that it has moved from the one to the other, passing over a series of intermediate positions. But if it is merely a set of sense-data, it cannot have ever been in any place where I did not see it; thus we shall have to suppose that it did not exist at all while I was not looking, but suddenly sprang into being in a new place. If the cat exists whether I see it or not, we can understand from our own experience how it gets hungry between one meal and the next; but if it does not exist when I am not seeing it, it seems odd that appetite should grow during non-existence as fast as during existence. And if the cat consists only of sense-data, it cannot be *hungry,* since no hunger but my own can be a sense-datum to me. Thus the behaviour of the sense-data which represent the cat to me, though it seems quite natural when regarded as an expression of hunger, becomes utterly inexplicable when regarded as mere movements and changes of patches of colour, which are as incapable of hunger as triangle is of playing football.

But the difficulty in the case of the cat is nothing compared to the difficulty in the case of human beings. When human beings speak—

that is, when we hear certain noises which we associate with ideas, and simultaneously see certain motions of lips and expressions of face—it is very difficult to suppose that what we hear is not the expression of a thought, as we know it would be if we emitted the same sounds. Of course similar things happen in dreams, where we are mistaken as to the existence of other people. But dreams are more or less suggested by what we call waking life, and are capable of being more or less accounted for on scientific principles if we assume that there really is a physical world. Thus every principle of simplicity urges us to adopt the natural view, that there really are objects other than ourselves and our sense-data which have an existence not dependent upon our perceiving them.

Of course it is not by argument that we originally come by our belief in an independent external world. We find this belief ready in ourselves as soon as we begin to reflect: It is what may be called an *instinctive* belief. We should never have been led to question this belief but for the fact that, at any rate in the case of sight, it seems as if the sense-datum itself were instinctively believed to be the independent object, whereas argument shows that the object cannot be identical with the sense-datum. This discovery, however—which is not at all paradoxical in the case of taste and smell and sound, and only slightly so in the case of touch—leaves undiminished our instinctive belief that there *are* objects *corresponding* to our sense-data. Since this belief does not lead to any difficulties, but on the contrary tends to simplify and systematize our account of our experiences, there seems no good reason for rejecting it. We may therefore admit—though with a slight doubt derived from dreams—that the external world does really exist, and is not wholly dependent for its existence upon our continuing to perceive it.

The argument which has led us to this conclusion is doubtless less strong than we could wish, but it is typical of many philosophical arguments, and it is therefore worthwhile to consider briefly its general character and validity. All knowledge, we find, must be built up upon our instinctive beliefs, and if these are rejected, nothing is left. But among our instinctive beliefs some are much stronger than others, while many have, by habit and association, become entangled with other beliefs, not really instinctive, but falsely supposed to be part of what is believed instinctively.

Philosophy should show us the hierarchy of our instinctive beliefs, beginning with those we hold most strongly, and presenting each as much isolated and as free from irrelevant additions as possible. It should take care to show that, in the form in which they are finally set forth, our instinctive beliefs do not clash, but form a harmonious system. There can never be any reason for rejecting one instinctive belief except that it clashes with others; thus, if they are found to harmonize, the whole system becomes worthy of acceptance.

It is of course *possible* that all or any of our beliefs may be mistaken, and therefore all ought to be held with at least some slight element of doubt. But we cannot have *reason* to reject a belief except on the ground of some other belief. Hence, by organizing our instinctive beliefs and their consequences, by considering which among them is most possible, if necessary, to modify or abandon, we can arrive, on the basis of accepting as our sole data what we instinctively believe, at an orderly systematic organization of our knowledge, in which, though the *possibility* of error remains, its likelihood is diminished by the interrelation of the parts and by the critical scrutiny which has preceded acquiescence.

This function, at least, philosophy can perform. Most philosophers, rightly or wrongly, believe that philosophy can do much more than this—that it can give us knowledge, not otherwise attainable, concerning the universe as a whole, and concerning the nature of ultimate reality. Whether this be the case or not, the more modest function we have spoken of can certainly be performed by philosophy, and certainly suffices, for those who have once begun to doubt the adequacy of common sense, to justify the arduous and difficult labours that philosophical problems involve.

Meditations on First Philosophy

RENÉ DESCARTES

René Descartes (1596–1650) is commonly said to be the founder of modern philosophy. Among his other achievements was the invention of analytical geometry.

SYNOPSIS OF THE FOLLOWING SIX MEDITATIONS*

In the first meditation reasons are provided which give us possible grounds for doubt about all things, especially material things, so long as we have no foundations for the sciences other than those which we have had up till now. Although the usefulness of such extensive doubt is not apparent at first sight, its greatest benefit lies in freeing us from all our preconceived opinions, and providing the easiest route by which the mind may be led away from the senses. The eventual result of this doubt is to make it impossible for us to have any further doubts about what we subsequently discover to be true.

In the Second Meditation, the mind uses its own freedom and supposes the non-existence of

From *Meditations on First Philosophy*, in *Descartes: Selected Philosophical Writings*, translated by John Cottingham, Rev. ed. (New York: Cambridge University Press, 1988), pp. 73–122. Reprinted by permission of Cambridge University Press.

*Material appearing in diamond brackets is found in later translations of the *Meditations* that Descartes himself approved of.

all the things about whose existence it can have even the slightest doubt; and in so doing the mind notices that it is impossible that it should not itself exist during this time. This exercise is also of the greatest benefit, since it enables the mind to distinguish without difficulty what belongs to itself, i.e. to an intellectual nature, from what belongs to the body. But since some people may perhaps expect arguments for the immortality of the soul in this section, I think they should be warned here and now that I have tried not to put down anything which I could not precisely demonstrate. Hence the only order which I could follow was that normally employed by geometers, namely to set out all the premises on which a desired proposition depends, before drawing any conclusions about it. Now the first and most important prerequisite for knowledge of the immortality of the soul is for us to form a concept of the soul which is as clear as possible and is also quite distinct from every concept of body; and that is just what has been done in this section. A further requirement is that we should know that everything that we clearly and distinctly understand is true in a way which corresponds exactly to our understanding of it; but it was not possible to prove this before the Fourth Meditation. In addition we need to have a distinct concept of corporeal nature, and this is developed partly in the Second Meditation itself, and partly in the Fifth and Sixth Meditations. The inference to be drawn from these results is that all the things that we clearly and distinctly conceive of as different substances (as we do in the case of mind and body) are in fact substances which are really distinct one from the other; and this conclusion is drawn in the Sixth Meditation. This conclusion is confirmed in the same Meditation by the fact that we cannot understand a body except as being divisible, while by contrast we cannot understand a mind except as being indivisible. For we cannot conceive of half of a mind, while we can always conceive of half of a body, however small; and this leads us to recognize that the natures of mind and body are not only different, but in some way opposite. But I have not pursued this topic any further in this book, first because these arguments are enough to show that the

decay of the body does not imply the destruction of the mind, and are hence enough to give mortals the hope of an after-life, and secondly because the premises which lead to the conclusion that the soul is immortal depend on an account of the whole of physics. This is required for two reasons. First, we need to know that absolutely all substances, or things which must be created by God in order to exist, are by their nature incorruptible and cannot ever cease to exist unless they are reduced to nothingness by God's denying his concurrence[1] to them. Secondly, we need to recognize that body, taken in the general sense, is a substance, so that it too never perishes. But the human body, in so far as it differs from other bodies, is simply made up of a certain configuration of limbs and other accidents[2] of this sort; whereas the human mind is not made up of any accidents in this way, but is a pure substance. For even if all the accidents of the mind change, so that it has different objects of the understanding and different desires and sensations, it does not on that account become a different mind; whereas a human body loses its identity merely as a result of a change in the shape of some of its parts. And it follows from this that while the body can very easily perish, the mind[3] is immortal by its very nature.

In the Third Meditation I have explained quite fully enough, I think, my principal argument for proving the existence of God. But in order to draw my readers' minds away from the senses as far as possible, I was not willing to use any comparison taken from bodily things. So it may be that many obscurities remain; but I hope they will be completely removed later, in my Replies to the Objections. One such problem, among others, is how the idea of a supremely perfect being, which is in us, possesses so much objective[4] reality that it can come only from a cause which is supremely perfect. In the Replies this is illustrated by the comparison of a very perfect machine, the idea of which is in the mind of some engineer. Just as the objective intricacy belonging to the idea must have some cause, namely the scientific knowledge of the engineer, or of someone else who passed the idea on to him, so the idea of God which is in us must have God himself as its cause.

In the Fourth Meditation it is proved that everything that we clearly and distinctly perceive is true, and I also explain what the nature of falsity consists in. These results need to be known both in order to confirm what has gone before and also to make intelligible what is to come later. (But here it should be noted in passing that I do not deal at all with sin, i.e. the error which is committed in pursuing good and evil, but only with the error that occurs in distinguishing truth from falsehood. And there is no discussion of matters pertaining to faith or the conduct of life, but simply of speculative truths which are known solely by means of the natural light.)[5]

In the Fifth Meditation, besides an account of corporeal nature taken in general, there is a new argument demonstrating the existence of God. Again, several difficulties may arise here, but these are resolved later in the Replies to the Objections. Finally I explain the sense in which it is true that the certainty even of geometrical demonstrations depends on the knowledge of God.

Lastly, in the Sixth Meditation, the intellect is distinguished from the imagination; the criteria for this distinction are explained; the mind is proved to be really distinct from the body, but is shown, notwithstanding, to be so closely joined to it that the mind and the body make up a kind of unit; there is a survey of all the errors which commonly come from the senses, and an explanation of how they may be avoided; and, lastly, there is a presentation of all the arguments which enable the existence of material things to be inferred. The great benefit of these arguments is not, in my view, that they prove what they establish—namely that there really is a world, and that human beings have bodies and so on—since no sane person has ever seriously doubted these things. The point is that in considering these arguments we come to realize that they are not as solid or as transparent as the arguments which lead us to knowledge of our own minds and of God, so that the latter are the most certain and evident of all possible objects of knowledge for the human intellect. Indeed, this is the one thing that I set myself to prove in these Meditations. And for that reason I will not now go over the various other issues in the book which are dealt with as they come up.

MEDITATIONS ON FIRST PHILOSOPHY

in which are demonstrated the existence of God and the distinction between the human soul and the body

FIRST MEDITATION

What can be called into doubt

Some years ago I was struck by the large number of falsehoods that I had accepted as true in my childhood, and by the highly doubtful nature of the whole edifice that I had subsequently based on them. I realized that it was necessary, once in the course of my life, to demolish everything completely and start again right from the foundations if I wanted to establish anything at all in the sciences that was stable and likely to last. But the task looked an enormous one, and I began to wait until I should reach a mature enough age to ensure that no subsequent time of life would be more suitable for tackling such inquiries. This led me to put the project off for so long that I would now be to blame if by pondering over it any further I wasted the time still left for carrying it out. So today I have expressly rid my mind of all worries and arranged for myself a clear stretch of free time. I am here quite alone, and at last I will devote myself sincerely and without reservation to the general demolition of my opinions.

But to accomplish this, it will not be necessary for me to show that all my opinions are false, which is something I could perhaps never manage. Reason now leads me to think that I should hold back my assent from opinions which are not completely certain and indubitable just as carefully as I do from those which are patently false. So, for the purpose of rejecting all my opinions, it will be enough if I find in each of them at least some reason for doubt. And to do this I will not need to run through them all individually, which would be an endless task. Once the foundations of a building are undermined, anything built on them collapses of its own accord; so I will go straight for the basic principles on which all my former beliefs rested.

Whatever I have up till now accepted as most true I have acquired either from the senses or through the senses. But from time to time I have found that the senses deceive, and it is prudent never to trust completely those who have deceived us even once.

Yet although the senses occasionally deceive us with respect to objects which are very small or in the distance, there are many other beliefs about which doubt is quite impossible, even though they are derived from the senses—for example, that I am here, sitting by the fire, wearing a winter dressing-gown, holding this piece of paper in my hands, and so on. Again, how could it be denied that these hands or this whole body are mine? Unless perhaps I were to liken myself to madmen, whose brains are so damaged by the persistent vapours of melancholia that they firmly maintain they are kings when they are paupers, or say they are dressed in purple when they are naked, or that their heads are made of earthenware, or that they are pumpkins, or made of glass. But such people are insane, and I would be thought equally mad if I took anything from them as a model for myself.

A brilliant piece of reasoning! As if I were not a man who sleeps at night, and regularly has all the same experiences[6] while asleep as madmen do when awake—indeed sometimes even more improbable ones. How often, asleep at night, am I convinced of just such familiar events— that I am here in my dressing-gown, sitting by the fire—when in fact I am lying undressed in bed! Yet at the moment my eyes are certainly wide awake when I look at this piece of paper; I shake my head and it is not asleep; as I stretch out and feel my hand I do so deliberately, and I know what I am doing. All this would not happen with such distinctness to someone asleep. Indeed! As if I did not remember other occasions when I have been tricked by exactly similar thoughts while asleep! As I think about this more carefully, I see plainly that there are never any sure signs by means of which being awake can be distinguished from being asleep. The result is that I begin to feel dazed, and this very feeling only reinforces the notion that I may be asleep.

Suppose then that I am dreaming, and that these particulars—that my eyes are open, that I am moving my head and stretching out my hands—are not true. Perhaps, indeed, I do not even have such hands or such a body at all. Nonetheless, it must surely be admitted that the visions which come in sleep are like paintings, which must have been fashioned in the likeness of things that are real, and hence that at least these general kinds of things—eyes, head, hands and the body as a whole—are things which are not imaginary but are real and exist. For even when painters try to create sirens and satyrs with the most extraordinary bodies, they cannot give them natures which are new in all respects; they simply jumble up the limbs of different animals. Or if perhaps they manage to think up something so new that nothing remotely similar has ever been seen before— something which is therefore completely fictitious and unreal—at least the colours used in the composition must be real. By similar reasoning, although these general kinds of things— eyes, head, hands and so on—could be imaginary, it must at least be admitted that certain other even simpler and more universal things are real. These are as it were the real colours from which we form all the images of things, whether true or false, that occur in our thought.

This class appears to include corporeal nature in general, and its extension; the shape of extended things; the quantity, or size and number of these things; the place in which they may exist, the time through which they may endure,[7] and so on.

So a reasonable conclusion from this might be that physics, astronomy, medicine, and all other disciplines which depend on the study of composite things, are doubtful; while arithmetic, geometry and other subjects of this kind, which deal only with the simplest and most general things, regardless of whether they really exist in nature or not, contain something certain and indubitable. For whether I am awake or asleep, two and three added together are five, and a square has no more than four sides. It seems impossible that such transparent truths should incur any suspicion of being false.

And yet firmly rooted in my mind is the longstanding opinion that there is an omnipotent God who made me the kind of creature that I am. How do I know that he has not brought it about that there is no earth, no sky, no extended thing, no shape, no size, no place, while at the same time ensuring that all these things appear to me to exist just as they do now? What is more, just as I consider that others sometimes go astray in cases where they think they have the most perfect knowledge, how do I know that God has not brought it about that I too go wrong every time I add two and three or count the sides of a square, or in some even simpler matter, if that is imaginable? But perhaps God would not have allowed me to be deceived in this way, since he is said to be supremely good. But if it were inconsistent with his goodness to have created me such that I am deceived all the time, it would seem equally foreign to his goodness to allow me to be deceived even occasionally; yet this last assertion cannot be made.[8]

Perhaps there may be some who would prefer to deny the existence of so powerful a God rather than believe that everything else is uncertain. Let us not argue with them, but grant them that everything said about God is a fiction. According to their supposition, then, I have arrived at my present state by fate or chance or a continuous chain of events, or by some other means; yet since deception and error seem to be imperfections, the less powerful they make my original cause, the more likely it is that I am so imperfect as to be deceived all the time. I have no answer to these arguments, but am finally compelled to admit that there is not one of my former beliefs about which a doubt may not properly be raised; and this is not a flippant or ill-considered conclusion, but is based on powerful and well thought-out reasons. So in future I must withhold my assent from these former beliefs just as carefully as I would from obvious falsehoods, if I want to discover any certainty.[9]

But it is not enough merely to have noticed this; I must make an effort to remember it. My habitual opinions keep coming back, and, despite my wishes, they capture my belief, which is as it were bound over to them as a result of long occupation and the law of custom. I shall never get out of the habit of confidently assenting to these opinions, so long as I suppose them to be

what in fact they are, namely highly probable opinions—opinions which, despite the fact that they are in a sense doubtful, as has just been shown, it is still much more reasonable to believe than to deny. In view of this, I think it will be a good plan to turn my will in completely the opposite direction and deceive myself, by pretending for a time that these former opinions are utterly false and imaginary. I shall do this until the weight of preconceived opinion is counter-balanced and the distorting influence of habit no longer prevents my judgement from perceiving things correctly. In the meantime, I know that no danger or error will result from my plan, and that I cannot possibly go too far in my distrustful attitude. This is because the task now in hand does not involve action but merely the acquisition of knowledge.

I will suppose therefore that not God, who is supremely good and the source of truth, but rather some malicious demon of the utmost power and cunning has employed all his energies in order to deceive me. I shall think that the sky, the air, the earth, colours, shapes, sounds and all external things are merely the delusions of dreams which he has devised to ensnare my judgement. I shall consider myself as not having hands or eyes, or flesh, or blood or senses, but as falsely believing that I have all these things. I shall stubbornly and firmly persist in this meditation; and, even if it is not in my power to know any truth, I shall at least do what is in my power,[10] that is, resolutely guard against assenting to any falsehoods, so that the deceiver, however powerful and cunning he may be, will be unable to impose on me in the slightest degree. But this is an arduous undertaking, and a kind of laziness brings me back to normal life. I am like a prisoner who is enjoying an imaginary freedom while asleep; as he begins to suspect that he is asleep, he dreads being woken up, and goes along with the pleasant illusion as long as he can. In the same way, I happily slide back into my old opinions and dread being shaken out of them, for fear that my peaceful sleep may be followed by hard labour when I wake, and that I shall have to toil not in the light, but amid the inextricable darkness of the problems I have now raised.

SECOND MEDITATION

The nature of the human mind, and how it is better known than the body

So serious are the doubts into which I have been thrown as a result of yesterday's meditation that I can neither put them out of my mind nor see any way of resolving them. It feels as if I have fallen unexpectedly into a deep whirlpool which tumbles me around so that I can neither stand on the bottom nor swim up to the top. Nevertheless I will make an effort and once more attempt the same path which I started on yesterday. Anything which admits of the slightest doubt I will set aside just as if I had found it to be wholly false; and I will proceed in this way until I recognize something certain, or, if nothing else, until I at least recognize for certain that there is no certainty. Archimedes used to demand just one firm and immovable point in order to shift the entire earth; so I too can hope for great things if I manage to find just one thing, however slight, that is certain and unshakeable.

I will suppose then, that everything I see is spurious. I will believe that my memory tells me lies, and that none of the things that it reports ever happened. I have no senses. Body, shape, extension, movement and place are chimeras. So what remains true? Perhaps just the one fact that nothing is certain.

Yet apart from everything I have just listed, how do I know that there is not something else which does not allow even the slightest occasion for doubt? Is there not a God, or whatever I may call him, who puts into me[11] the thoughts I am now having? But why do I think this, since I myself may perhaps be the author of these thoughts? In that case am not I, at least, something? But I have just said that I have no senses and no body. This is the sticking point: what follows from this? Am I not so bound up with a body and with senses that I cannot exist without them? But I have convinced myself that there is absolutely nothing in the world, no sky, no earth, no minds, no bodies. Does it now follow that I too do not exist? No: if I convinced myself of something[12] then I certainly existed. But there is a deceiver of supreme power and cunning who is deliberately and constantly deceiving me. In that case I too undoubtedly exist, if he is deceiving me; and let him deceive me as much as he can, he will never bring it about that I am nothing so long as I think that I am something. So after considering everything very thoroughly, I must finally conclude that this proposition, *I am, I exist,* is necessarily true whenever it is put forward by me or conceived in my mind.

But I do not yet have a sufficient understanding of what this 'I' is, that now necessarily exists. So I must be on my guard against carelessly taking something else to be this 'I', and so making a mistake in the very item of knowledge that I maintain is the most certain and evident of all. I will therefore go back and meditate on what I originally believed myself to be, before I embarked on this present train of thought. I will then subtract anything capable of being weakened, even minimally, by the arguments now introduced, so that what is left at the end may be exactly and only what is certain and unshakeable.

What then did I formerly think I was? A man. But what is a man? Shall I say 'a rational animal'? No; for then I should have to inquire what an animal is, what rationality is, and in this way one question would lead me down the slope to other harder ones, and I do not now have the time to waste on subtleties of this kind. Instead I propose to concentrate on what came into my thoughts spontaneously and quite naturally whenever I used to consider what I was. Well, the first thought to come to mind was that I had a face, hands, arms and the whole mechanical structure of limbs which can be seen in a corpse, and which I called the body. The next thought was that I was nourished, that I moved about, and that I engaged in senseperception and thinking; and these actions I attributed to the soul. But as to the nature of this soul, either I did not think about this or else I imagined it to be something tenuous, like a wind or fire or ether, which permeated my more solid parts. As to the body, however, I had no doubts about it, but thought I knew its nature distinctly. If I had tried to describe the mental conception I had of it, I would have expressed it as follows: by a body I understand whatever has a determinable shape and a definable location and can occupy a space in such a way as to exclude any other body; it can be perceived by touch, sight, hearing, taste or smell, and can be moved in various ways, not by itself but by whatever else comes into contact with it. For, according to my judgement, the power of self-movement, like the power of sensation or of thought, was quite foreign to the nature of a body; indeed, it was a source of wonder to me that certain bodies were found to contain faculties of this kind.

But what shall I now say that I am, when I am supposing that there is some supremely powerful and, if it is permissible to say so, malicious deceiver, who is deliberately trying to trick me in every way he can? Can I now assert that I possess even the most insignificant of all the attributes which I have just said belong to the nature of a body? I scrutinize them, think about them, go over them again, but nothing suggests itself; it is tiresome and pointless to go through the list once more. But what about the attributes I assigned to the soul? Nutrition or movement? Since now I do not have a body, these are mere fabrications. Sense-perception? This surely does not occur without a body, and besides, when asleep I have appeared to perceive through the senses many things which I afterwards realized I did not perceive through the senses at all. Thinking? At last I have discovered it—thought; this alone is inseparable from me. I am, I exist—that is certain. But for how long? For as long as I am thinking. For it could be that were I totally to cease from thinking, I should totally cease to exist. At present I am not admitting anything except what is necessarily true. I am, then, in the strict sense only a thing that thinks;[13] that is, I am a mind, or intelligence, or intellect, or reason—words whose meaning I have been ignorant of until now. But for all that I am a thing which is real and which truly exists. But what kind of thing? As I have just said—a thinking thing.

What else am I? I will use my imagination.[14] I am not that structure of limbs which is called a human body. I am not even some thin vapour which permeates the limbs—a wind, fire, air, breath, or whatever I depict in my imagination;

for these are things which I have supposed to be nothing. Let this supposition stand;[15] for all that I am still something. And yet may it not perhaps be the case that these very things which I am supposing to be nothing, because they are unknown to me, are in reality identical with the 'I' of which I am aware? I do not know, and for the moment I shall not argue the point, since I can make judgements only about things which are known to me. I know that I exist; the question is, what is this 'I' that I know? If the 'I' is understood strictly as we have been taking it, then it is quite certain that knowledge of it does not depend on things of whose existence I am as yet unaware; so it cannot depend on any of the things which I invent in my imagination. And this very word 'invent' shows me my mistake. It would indeed be a case of fictitious invention if I used my imagination to establish that I was something or other; for imagining is simply contemplating the shape or image of a corporeal thing. Yet now I know for certain both that I exist and at the same time that all such images and, in general, everything relating to the nature of body, could be mere dreams <and chimeras>. Once this point has been grasped, to say 'I will use my imagination to get to know more distinctly what I am' would seem to be as silly as saying 'I am now awake, and see some truth; but since my vision is not yet clear enough, I will deliberately fall asleep so that my dreams may provide a truer and clearer representation.' I thus realize that none of the things that the imagination enables me to grasp is at all relevant to this knowledge of myself which I possess, and that the mind must therefore be most carefully diverted from such things[16] if it is to perceive its own nature as distinctly as possible.

But what then am I? A thing that thinks. What is that? A thing that doubts, understands, affirms, denies, is willing, is unwilling, and also imagines and has sensory perceptions.

This is a considerable list, if everything on it belongs to me. But does it? Is it not one and the same 'I' who is now doubting almost everything, who nonetheless understands some things, who affirms that this one thing is true, denies everything else, desires to know more, is unwilling to be deceived, imagines many things even involuntarily, and is aware of many things which apparently come from the senses? Are not all these things just as true as the fact that I exist, even if I am asleep all the time, and even if he who created me is doing all he can to deceive me? Which of all these activities is distinct from my thinking? Which of them can be said to be separate from myself? The fact that it is I who am doubting and understanding and willing is so evident that I see no way of making it any clearer. But it is also the case that the 'I' who imagines is the same 'I'. For even if, as I have supposed, none of the objects of imagination are real, the power of imagination is something which really exists and is part of my thinking. Lastly, it is also the same 'I' who has sensory perceptions, or is aware of bodily things as it were through the senses. For example, I am now seeing light, hearing a noise, feeling heat. But I am asleep, so all this is false. Yet I certainly *seem* to see, to hear, and to be warmed. This cannot be false; what is called 'having a sensory perception' is strictly just this, and in this restricted sense of the term it is simply thinking.

From all this I am beginning to have a rather better understanding of what I am. But it still appears—and I cannot stop thinking this—that the corporeal things of which images are formed in my thought, and which the senses investigate, are known with much more distinctness than this puzzling 'I' which cannot be pictured in the imagination. And yet it is surely surprising that I should have a more distinct grasp of things which I realize are doubtful, unknown and foreign to me, than I have of that which is true and known—my own self. But I see what it is: my mind enjoys wandering off and will not yet submit to being restrained within the bounds of truth. Very well then; just this once let us give it a completely free rein, so that after a while, when it is time to tighten the reins, it may more readily submit to being curbed.

Let us consider the things which people commonly think they understand most distinctly of all; that is, the bodies which we touch and see. I do not mean bodies in general—for general perceptions are apt to be somewhat more confused—but one particular body. Let us take, for example, this piece of wax. It has just been taken from the honeycomb; it has not yet quite lost the taste of the honey; it retains some of the scent of the flowers from which it was gathered; its colour, shape and size are plain to see; it is hard, cold and can be handled without difficulty; if you rap it with your knuckle it makes a sound. In short, it has everything which appears necessary to enable a body to be known as distinctly as possible. But even as I speak, I put the wax by the fire, and look: the residual taste is eliminated, the smell goes away, the colour changes, the shape is lost, the size increases; it becomes liquid and hot; you can hardly touch it, and if you strike it, it no longer makes a sound. But does the same wax remain? It must be admitted that it does; no one denies it, no one thinks otherwise. So what was it in the wax that I understood with such distinctness? Evidently none of the features which I arrived at by means of the senses; for whatever came under taste, smell, sight, touch or hearing has now altered—yet the wax remains.

Perhaps the answer lies in the thought which now comes to my mind; namely, the wax was not after all the sweetness of the honey, or the fragrance of the flowers, or the whiteness, or the shape, or the sound, but was rather a body which presented itself to me in these various forms a little while ago, but which now exhibits different ones. But what exactly is it that I am now imagining? Let us concentrate, take away everything which does not belong to the wax, and see what is left: merely something extended, flexible and changeable. But what is meant here by 'flexible' and 'changeable'? Is it what I picture in my imagination: that this piece of wax is capable of changing from a round shape to a square shape, or from a square shape to a triangular shape? Not at all; for I can grasp that the wax is capable of countless changes of this kind, yet I am unable to run through this immeasurable number of changes in my imagination, from which it follows that it is not the faculty of imagination that gives me my grasp of the wax as flexible and changeable. And what is meant by 'extended'? Is the extension of the wax also unknown? For it increases if the wax melts, increases again if it boils, and is greater still if the heat is increased. I would not be making a correct judgement about the nature of wax unless

I believed it capable of being extended in many more different ways than I will ever encompass in my imagination. I must therefore admit that the nature of this piece of wax is in no way revealed by my imagination, but is perceived by the mind alone. (I am speaking of this particular piece of wax; the point is even clearer with regard to wax in general.) But what is this wax which is perceived by the mind alone?[17] It is of course the same wax which I see, which I touch, which I picture in my imagination, in short the same wax which I thought it to be from the start. And yet, and here is the point, the perception I have of it[18] is a case not of vision or touch or imagination—nor has it ever been, despite previous appearances—but of purely mental scrutiny; and this can be imperfect and confused, as it was before, or clear and distinct as it is now, depending on how carefully I concentrate on what the wax consists in.

But as I reach this conclusion I am amazed at how <weak and> prone to error my mind is. For although I am thinking about these matters within myself, silently and without speaking, nonetheless the actual words bring me up short, and I am almost tricked by ordinary ways of talking. We say that we see the wax itself, if it is there before us, not that we judge it to be there from its colour or shape; and this might lead me to conclude without more ado that knowledge of the wax comes from what the eye sees, and not from the scrutiny of the mind alone. But then if I look out of the window and see men crossing the square, as I just happen to have done, I normally say that I see the men themselves, just as I say that I see the wax. Yet do I see any more than hats and coats which could conceal automatons? I *judge* that they are men. And so something which I thought I was seeing with my eyes is in fact grasped solely by the faculty of judgement which is in my mind.

However, one who wants to achieve knowledge above the ordinary level should feel ashamed at having taken ordinary ways of talking as a basis for doubt. So let us proceed, and consider on which occasion my perception of the nature of the wax was more perfect and evident. Was it when I first looked at it, and believed I knew it by my external senses, or at least by what they call the 'common' sense[19]—that is, the power of imagination? Or is my knowledge more perfect now, after a more careful investigation of the nature of the wax and of the means by which it is known? Any doubt on this issue would clearly be foolish; for what distinctness was there in my earlier perception? Was there anything in it which an animal could not possess? But when I distinguish the wax from its outward forms—take the clothes off, as it were, and consider it naked—then although my judgement may still contain errors, at least my perception now requires a human mind.

But what am I to say about this mind, or about myself? (So far, remember, I am not admitting that there is anything else in me except a mind.) What, I ask, is this 'I' which seems to perceive the wax so distinctly? Surely my awareness of my own self is not merely much truer and more certain than my awareness of the wax, but also much more distinct and evident. For if I judge that the wax exists from the fact that I see it, clearly this same fact entails much more evidently that I myself also exist. It is possible that what I see is not really the wax; it is possible that I do not even have eyes with which to see anything. But when I see, or think I see (I am not here distinguishing the two), it is simply not possible that I who am now thinking am not something. By the same token, if I judge that the wax exists from the fact that I touch it, the same result follows, namely that I exist. If I judge that it exists from the fact that I imagine it, or for any other reason, exactly the same thing follows. And the result that I have grasped in the case of the wax may be applied to everything else located outside me. Moreover, if my perception of the wax seemed more distinct[20] after it was established not just by sight or touch but by many other considerations, it must be admitted that I now know myself even more distinctly. This is because every consideration whatsoever which contributes to my perception of the wax, or of any other body, cannot but establish even more effectively the nature of my own mind. But besides this, there is so much else in the mind itself which can serve to make my knowledge of it more distinct, that it scarcely seems worth going through the contributions made by considering bodily things.

I see that without any effort I have now finally got back to where I wanted. I now know that even bodies are not strictly perceived by the senses or the faculty of imagination but by the intellect alone, and that this perception derives not from their being touched or seen but from their being understood; and in view of this I know plainly that I can achieve an easier and more evident perception of my own mind than of anything else. But since the habit of holding on to old opinions cannot be set aside so quickly, I should like to stop here and meditate for some time on this new knowledge I have gained, so as to fix it more deeply in my memory.

THIRD MEDITATION
The existence of God

I will now shut my eyes, stop my ears, and withdraw all my senses. I will eliminate from my thoughts all images of bodily things, or rather, since this is hardly possible, I will regard all such images as vacuous, false and worthless. I will converse with myself and scrutinize myself more deeply; and in this way I will attempt to achieve, little by little, a more intimate knowledge of myself. I am a thing that thinks: that is, a thing that doubts, affirms, denies, understands a few things, is ignorant of many things,[21] is willing, is unwilling, and also which imagines and has sensory perceptions; for as I have noted before, even though the objects of my sensory experience and imagination may have no existence outside me, nonetheless the modes of thinking which I refer to as cases of sensory perception and imagination, in so far as they are simply modes of thinking, do exist within me—of that I am certain.

In this brief list I have gone through everything I truly know, or at least everything I have so far discovered that I know. Now I will cast around more carefully to see whether there may be other things within me which I have not yet noticed. I am certain that I am a thinking thing. Do I not therefore also know what is required for my being certain about anything? In this first item of knowledge there is simply a clear and distinct perception of what I am asserting; this would not be enough to make me certain of the truth of the matter if it could ever turn out that something which I perceived with such clarity and distinctness was false. So I now seem to be able to lay it down as a general rule that whatever I perceive very clearly and distinctly is true.[22]

Yet I previously accepted as wholly certain and evident many things which I afterwards realized were doubtful. What were these? The earth, sky, stars, and everything else that I apprehended with the senses. But what was it about them that I perceived clearly? Just that the ideas, or thoughts, of such things appeared before my mind. Yet even now I am not denying that these ideas occur within me. But there was something else which I used to assert, and which through habitual belief I thought I perceived clearly, although I did not in fact do so. This was that there were things outside me which were the sources of my ideas and which resembled them in all respects. Here was my mistake; or at any rate, if my judgement was true, it was not thanks to the strength of my perception.[23]

But what about when I was considering something very simple and straightforward in arithmetic or geometry, for example that two and three added together make five, and so on? Did I not see at least these things clearly enough to affirm their truth? Indeed, the only reason for my later judgement that they were open to doubt was that it occurred to me that perhaps some God could have given me a nature such that I was deceived even in matters which seemed most evident. But whenever my preconceived belief in the supreme power of God comes to mind, I cannot but admit that it would be easy for him, if he so desired, to bring it about that I go wrong even in those matters which I think I see utterly clearly with my mind's eye. Yet when I turn to the things themselves which I think I perceive very clearly, I am so convinced by them that I spontaneously declare: let whoever can do so deceive me, he will never bring it about that I am nothing, so long as I continue to think I am something; or make it true at some future time that I have never existed, since it is now true that I exist; or bring it about that two and three added together are more or less than five, or anything of this kind in which I see a manifest contradiction. And since I have no cause to think that there is a deceiving God, and I do not yet even know for sure whether there is a God at all, any reason for doubt which depends simply on this supposition is a very slight and, so to speak, metaphysical one. But in order to remove even this slight reason for doubt, as soon as the opportunity arises I must examine whether there is a God, and, if there is, whether he can be a deceiver. For if I do not know this, it seems that I can never be quite certain about anything else.

First, however, considerations of order appear to dictate that I now classify my thoughts into definite kinds,[24] and ask which of them can properly be said to be the bearers of truth and falsity. Some of my thoughts are as it were the images of things, and it is only in these cases that the term 'idea' is strictly appropriate—for example, when I think of a man, or a chimera, or the sky, or an angel, or God. Other thoughts have various additional forms: thus when I will, or am afraid, or affirm, or deny, there is always a particular thing which I take as the object of my thought, but my thought includes something more than the likeness of that thing. Some thoughts in this category are called volitions or emotions, while others are called judgements.

Now as far as ideas are concerned, provided they are considered solely in themselves and I do not refer them to anything else, they cannot strictly speaking be false; for whether it is a goat or a chimera that I am imagining, it is just as true that I imagine the former as the latter. As for the will and the emotions, here too one need not worry about falsity; for even if the things which I may desire are wicked or even non-existent, that does not make it any less true that I desire them. Thus the only remaining thoughts where I must be on my guard against making a mistake are judgements. And the chief and most common mistake which is to be found here consists in my judging that the ideas which are in me resemble, or conform to, things located outside me. Of course, if I considered just the ideas themselves simply as modes of my thought, without referring them to anything

else, they could scarcely give me any material for error.

Among my ideas, some appear to be innate, some to be adventitious,[25] and others to have been invented by me. My understanding of what a thing is, what truth is, and what thought is, seems to derive simply from my own nature. But my hearing a noise, as I do now, or seeing the sun, or feeling the fire, comes from things which are located outside me, or so I have hitherto judged. Lastly, sirens, hippogriffs and the like are my own invention. But perhaps all my ideas may be thought of as adventitious, or they may all be innate, or all made up; for as yet I have not clearly perceived their true origin.

But the chief question at this point concerns the ideas which I take to be derived from things existing outside me: what is my reason for thinking that they resemble these things? Nature has apparently taught me to think this. But in addition I know by experience that these ideas do not depend on my will, and hence that they do not depend simply on me. Frequently I notice them even when I do not want to: now, for example, I feel the heat whether I want to or not, and this is why I think that this sensation or idea of heat comes to me from something other than myself, namely the heat of the fire by which I am sitting. And the most obvious judgement for me to make is that the thing in question transmits to me its own likeness rather than something else.

I will now see if these arguments are strong enough. When I say 'Nature taught me to think this', all I mean is that a spontaneous impulse leads me to believe it, not that its truth has been revealed to me by some natural light. There is a big difference here. Whatever is revealed to me by the natural light—for example that from the fact that I am doubting it follows that I exist, and so on—cannot in any way be open to doubt. This is because there cannot be another faculty[26] both as trustworthy as the natural light and also capable of showing me that such things are not true. But as for my natural impulses, I have often judged in the past that they were pushing me in the wrong direction when it was a question of choosing the good, and I do not see why I should place any greater confidence in them in other matters.[27]

Then again, although these ideas do not depend on my will, it does not follow that they must come from things located outside me. Just as the impulses which I was speaking of a moment ago seem opposed to my will even though they are within me, so there may be some other faculty not yet fully known to me, which produces these ideas without any assistance from external things; this is, after all, just how I have always thought ideas are produced in me when I am dreaming.

And finally, even if these ideas did come from things other than myself, it would not follow that they must resemble those things. Indeed, I think I have often discovered a great disparity <between an object and its idea> in many cases. For example, there are two different ideas of the sun which I find within me. One of them, which is acquired as it were from the senses and which is a prime example of an idea which I reckon to come from an external source, makes the sun appear very small. The other idea is based on astronomical reasoning, that is, it is derived from certain notions which are innate in me (or else it is constructed by me in some other way), and this idea shows the sun to be several times larger than the earth. Obviously both these ideas cannot resemble the sun which exists outside me; and reason persuades me that the idea which seems to have emanated most directly from the sun itself has in fact no resemblance to it at all.

All these considerations are enough to establish that it is not reliable judgement but merely some blind impulse that has made me believe up till now that there exist things distinct from myself which transmit to me ideas or images of themselves through the sense organs or in some other way.

But it now occurs to me that there is another way of investigating whether some of the things of which I possess ideas exist outside me. In so far as the ideas are <considered> simply <as> modes of thought, there is no recognizable inequality among them: they all appear to come from within me in the same fashion. But in so far as different ideas <are considered as images which> represent different things, it is clear that they differ widely. Undoubtedly, the ideas which represent substances to me amount to something more and, so to speak, contain within themselves more objective[28] reality than the ideas which merely represent modes or accidents. Again, the idea that gives me my understanding of a supreme God, eternal, infinite, <immutable,> omniscient, omnipotent and the creator of all things that exist apart from him, certainly has in it more objective reality than the ideas that represent finite substances.

Now it is manifest by the natural light that there must be at least as much <reality> in the efficient and total cause as in the effect of that cause. For where, I ask, could the effect get its reality from, if not from the cause? And how could the cause give it to the effect unless it possessed it? It follows from this both that something cannot arise from nothing, and also that what is more perfect—that is, contains in itself more reality—cannot arise from what is less perfect. And this is transparently true not only in the case of effects which possess <what the philosophers call> actual or formal reality, but also in the case of ideas, where one is considering only <what they call> objective reality. A stone, for example, which previously did not exist, cannot begin to exist unless it is produced by something which contains, either formally or eminently everything to be found in the stone;[29] similarly, heat cannot be produced in an object which was not previously hot, except by something of at least the same order <degree or kind> of perfection as heat, and so on. But it is also true that the *idea* of heat, or of a stone, cannot exist in me unless it is put there by some cause which contains at least as much reality as I conceive to be in the heat or in the stone. For although this cause does not transfer any of its actual or formal reality to my idea, it should not on that account be supposed that it must be less real.[30] The nature of an idea is such that of itself it requires no formal reality except what it derives from my thought, of which it is a mode.[31] But in order for a given idea to contain such and such objective reality, it must surely derive it from some cause which contains at least as much formal reality as there is objective reality in the idea. For if we suppose that an idea contains something which was not in its cause, it must have got this from nothing; yet the mode of being by which a thing exists objectively <or representatively> in the intellect by way of an idea, imperfect though it may be, is certainly not nothing, and so it cannot come from nothing.

And although the reality which I am considering in my ideas is merely objective reality, I must not on that account suppose that the same reality need not exist formally in the causes of my ideas, but that it is enough for it to be present in them objectively. For just as the objective mode of being belongs to ideas by their very nature, so the formal mode of being belongs to the causes of ideas—or at least the first and most important ones—by *their* very nature. And although one idea may perhaps originate from another, there cannot be an infinite regress here; eventually one must reach a primary idea, the cause of which will be like an archetype which contains formally <and in fact> all the reality <or perfection> which is present only objectively <or representatively> in the idea. So it is clear to me, by the natural light, that the ideas in me are like <pictures, or> images which can easily fall short of the perfection of the things from which they are taken, but which cannot contain anything greater or more perfect.

The longer and more carefully I examine all these points, the more clearly and distinctly I recognize their truth. But what is my conclusion to be? If the objective reality of any of my ideas turns out to be so great that I am sure the same reality does not reside in me, either formally or eminently, and hence that I myself cannot be its cause, it will necessarily follow that I am not alone in the world, but that some other thing which is the cause of this idea also exists. But if no such idea is to be found in me, I shall have no argument to convince me of the existence of anything apart from myself. For despite a most careful and comprehensive survey, this is the only argument I have so far been able to find.

Among my ideas, apart from the idea which gives me a representation of myself, which cannot present any difficulty in this context, there are ideas which variously represent God, corporeal and inanimate things, angels, animals and finally other men like myself.

As far as concerns the ideas which represent other men, or animals, or angels, I have no difficulty in understanding that they could be put together from the ideas I have of myself, of corporeal things and of God, even if the world contained no men besides me, no animals and no angels.

As to my ideas of corporeal things, I can see nothing in them which is so great <or excellent> as to make it seem impossible that it originated in myself. For if I scrutinize them thoroughly and examine them one by one, in the way in which I examined the idea of the wax yesterday, I notice that the things which I perceive clearly and distinctly in them are very few in number. The list comprises size, or extension in length, breadth and depth; shape, which is a function of the boundaries of this extension; position, which is a relation between various items possessing shape; and motion, or change in position; to these may be added substance, duration and number. But as for all the rest, including light and colours, sounds, smells, tastes, heat and cold and the other tactile qualities, I think of these only in a very confused and obscure way, to the extent that I do not even know whether they are true or false, that is, whether the ideas I have of them are ideas of real things or of non-things.[32] For although, as I have noted before, falsity in the strict sense, or formal falsity, can occur only in judgements, there is another kind of falsity, material falsity, which occurs in ideas, when they represent non-things as things. For example, the ideas which I have of heat and cold contain so little clarity and distinctness that they do not enable me to tell whether cold is merely the absence of heat or vice versa, or whether both of them are real qualities, or neither is. And since there can be no ideas which are not as it were of things,[33] if it is true that cold is nothing but the absence of heat, the idea which represents it to me as something real and positive deserves to be called false; and the same goes for other ideas of this kind.

Such ideas obviously do not require me to posit a source distinct from myself. For on the one hand, if they are false, that is, represent non-things, I know by the natural light that they arise from nothing—that is, they are in me only because of a deficiency and lack of perfection in my nature. If on the other hand they are true, then since the reality which they represent is so extremely slight that I cannot even distinguish it from a non-thing, I do not see why they cannot originate from myself.

With regard to the clear and distinct elements in my ideas of corporeal things, it appears that I could have borrowed some of these from my idea of myself, namely substance, duration, number and anything else of this kind. For example, I think that a stone is a substance, or is a thing capable of existing independently, and I also think that I am a substance. Admittedly I conceive of myself as a thing that thinks and is not extended, whereas I conceive of the stone as a thing that is extended and does not think, so that the two conceptions differ enormously; but they seem to agree with respect to the classification 'substance'.[34] Again, I perceive that I now exist, and remember that I have existed for some time; moreover, I have various thoughts which I can count; it is in these ways that I acquire the ideas of duration and number which I can then transfer to other things. As for all the other elements which make up the ideas of corporeal things, namely extension, shape, position and movement, these are not formally contained in me, since I am nothing but a thinking thing; but since they are merely modes of a substance,[35] and I am a substance, it seems possible that they are contained in me eminently.

So there remains only the idea of God; and I must consider whether there is anything in the idea which could not have originated in myself. By the word 'God' I understand a substance that is infinite, <eternal, immutable,> independent, supremely intelligent, supremely powerful, and which created both myself and everything else (if anything else there be) that exists. All these attributes are such that, the more carefully I concentrate on them, the less possible it seems that they[36] could have originated from me alone. So from what has been said it must be concluded that God necessarily exists.

It is true that I have the idea of substance in me in virtue of the fact that I am a substance; but this would not account for my having the idea of an infinite substance, when I am finite, unless this idea proceeded from some substance which really was infinite.

And I must not think that, just as my conceptions of rest and darkness are arrived at by negating movement and light, so my perception of the infinite is arrived at not by means of a true idea but merely by negating the finite. On the contrary, I clearly understand that there is more reality in an infinite substance than in a finite one, and hence that my perception of the infinite, that is God, is in some way prior to my perception of the finite, that is myself. For how could I understand that I doubted or desired—that is, lacked something—and that I was not wholly perfect, unless there were in me some idea of a more perfect being which enabled me to recognize my own defects by comparison?

Nor can it be said that this idea of God is perhaps materially false and so could have come from nothing,[37] which is what I observed just a moment ago in the case of the ideas of heat and cold, and so on. On the contrary, it is utterly clear and distinct, and contains in itself more objective reality than any other idea; hence there is no idea which is in itself truer or less liable to be suspected of falsehood. This idea of a supremely perfect and infinite being is, I say, true in the highest degree; for although perhaps one may imagine that such a being does not exist, it cannot be supposed that the idea of such a being represents something unreal, as I said with regard to the idea of cold. The idea is, moreover, utterly clear and distinct; for whatever I clearly and distinctly perceive as being real and true, and implying any perfection, is wholly contained in it. It does not matter that I do not grasp the infinite, or that there are countless additional attributes of God which I cannot in any way grasp, and perhaps cannot even reach in my thought; for it is in the nature of the infinite not to be grasped by a finite being like myself. It is enough that I understand[38] the infinite, and that I judge that all the attributes which I clearly perceive and know to imply some perfection—and perhaps countless others of which I am ignorant—are present in God either formally or eminently. This is enough to make the idea that I have of God the truest and most clear and distinct of all my ideas.

But perhaps I am something greater than I myself understand, and all the perfections which I attribute to God are somehow in me potentially, though not yet emerging or actualized. For I am now experiencing a gradual increase in my knowledge, and I see nothing to prevent its increasing more and more to infinity. Further, I see no reason why I should not be able to use this increased knowledge to acquire all the other perfections of God. And finally, if the potentiality for these perfections is already within me, why should not this be enough to generate the idea of such perfections?

But all this is impossible. First, though it is true that there is a gradual increase in my knowledge, and that I have many potentialities which are not yet actual, this is all quite irrelevant to the idea of God, which contains absolutely nothing that is potential;[39] indeed, this gradual increase in knowledge is itself the surest sign of imperfection. What is more, even if my knowledge always increases more and more, I recognize that it will never actually be infinite, since it will never reach the point where it is not capable of a further increase; God, on the other hand, I take to be actually infinite, so that nothing can be added to his perfection. And finally, I perceive that the objective being of an idea cannot be produced merely by potential being, which strictly speaking is nothing, but only by actual or formal being.

If one concentrates carefully, all this is quite evident by the natural light. But when I relax my concentration, and my mental vision is blinded by the images of things perceived by the senses, it is not so easy for me to remember why the idea of a being more perfect than myself must necessarily proceed from some being which is in reality more perfect. I should therefore like to go further and inquire whether I myself, who have this idea, could exist if no such being existed.

From whom, in that case, would I derive my existence? From myself presumably, or from my parents, or from some other beings less perfect than God; for nothing more perfect than God, or even as perfect, can be thought of or imagined.

Yet if I derived my existence from myself,[40] then I should neither doubt nor want, nor lack anything at all; for I should have given myself all the perfections of which I have any idea, and thus I should myself be God. I must not suppose that the items I lack would be more difficult to acquire than those I now have. On the contrary, it is clear that, since I am a thinking thing or substance, it would have been far more difficult for me to emerge out of nothing than merely to acquire knowledge of the many things of which I am ignorant—such knowledge being merely an accident of that substance. And if I had derived my existence from myself, which is a greater achievement, I should certainly not have denied myself the knowledge in question, which is something much easier to acquire, or indeed any of the attributes which I perceive to be contained in the idea of God; for none of them seem any harder to achieve. And if any of them were harder to achieve, they would certainly appear so to me, if I had indeed got all my other attributes from myself, since I should experience a limitation of my power in this respect.

I do not escape the force of these arguments by supposing that I have always existed as I do now, as if it followed from this that there was no need to look for any author of my existence. For a lifespan can be divided into countless parts, each completely independent of the others, so that it does not follow from the fact that I existed a little while ago that I must exist now, unless there is some cause which as it were creates me afresh at this moment—that is, which preserves me. For it is quite clear to anyone who attentively considers the nature of time that the same power and action are needed to preserve anything at each individual moment of its duration as would be required to create that thing anew if it were not yet in existence. Hence the distinction between preservation and creation is only a conceptual one,[41] and this is one of the things that are evident by the natural light.

I must therefore now ask myself whether I possess some power enabling me to bring it about that I who now exist will still exist a little while from now. For since I am nothing but a thinking thing—or at least since I am now concerned only and precisely with that part of me which is a thinking thing—if there were such a power in me, I should undoubtedly be aware of it. But I experience no such power, and this very fact makes me recognize most clearly that I depend on some being distinct from myself.

But perhaps this being is not God, and perhaps I was produced either by my parents or by other causes less perfect than God. No; for as I have said before, it is quite clear that there must be at least as much in the cause as in the effect.[42] And therefore whatever kind of cause is eventually proposed, since I am a thinking thing and have within me some idea of God, it must be admitted that what caused me is itself a thinking thing and possesses the idea of all the perfections which I attribute to God. In respect of this cause one may again inquire whether it derives its existence from itself or from another cause. If from itself, then it is clear from what has been said that it is itself God, since if it has the power of existing through its own might,[43] then undoubtedly it also has the power of actually possessing all the perfections of which it has an idea—that is, all the perfections which I conceive to be in God. If, on the other hand, it derives its existence from another cause, then the same question may be repeated concerning this further cause, namely whether it derives its existence from itself or from another cause, until eventually the ultimate cause is reached, and this will be God.

It is clear enough that an infinite regress is impossible here, especially since I am dealing not just with the cause that produced me in the past, but also and most importantly with the cause that preserves me at the present moment.

Nor can it be supposed that several partial causes contributed to my creation, or that I received the idea of one of the perfections which I attribute to God from one cause and the idea of another from another—the supposition here being that all the perfections are to be found somewhere in the universe but not joined together in a single being, God.

On the contrary, the unity, the simplicity, or the inseparability of all the attributes of God is one of the most important of the perfections which I understand him to have. And surely the idea of the unity of all his perfections could not have been placed in me by any cause which did not also provide me with the ideas of the other perfections; for no cause could have made me

understand the interconnection and inseparability of the perfections without at the same time making me recognize what they were.

Lastly, as regards my parents, even if everything I have ever believed about them is true, it is certainly not they who preserve me; and in so far as I am a thinking thing, they did not even make me; they merely placed certain dispositions in the matter which I have always regarded as containing me, or rather my mind, for that is all I now take myself to be. So there can be no difficulty regarding my parents in this context. Altogether then, it must be concluded that the mere fact that I exist and have within me an idea of a most perfect being, that is, God, provides a very clear proof that God indeed exists.

It only remains for me to examine how I received this idea from God. For I did not acquire it from the senses; it has never come to me unexpectedly, as usually happens with the ideas of things that are perceivable by the senses, when these things present themselves to the external sense organs—or seem to do so. And it was not invented by me either; for I am plainly unable either to take away anything from it or to add anything to it. The only remaining alternative is that it is innate in me, just as the idea of myself is innate in me.

And indeed it is no surprise that God, in creating me, should have placed this idea in me to be, as it were, the mark of the craftsman stamped on his work—not that the mark need be anything distinct from the work itself. But the mere fact that God created me is a very strong basis for believing that I am somehow made in his image and likeness, and that I perceive that likeness, which includes the idea of God, by the same faculty which enables me to perceive myself. That is, when I turn my mind's eye upon myself, I understand that I am a thing which is incomplete and dependent on another and which aspires without limit to ever greater and better things; but I also understand at the same time that he on whom I depend has within him all those greater things, not just indefinitely and potentially but actually and infinitely, and hence that he is God. The whole force of the argument lies in this: I recognize that it would be impossible for me to exist with the kind of nature I have—that is, having within me the idea of God—were it not the case that God really existed. By 'God' I mean the very being the idea of whom is within me, that is, the possessor of all the perfections which I cannot grasp, but can somehow reach in my thought, who is subject to no defects whatsoever.[44] It is clear enough from this that he cannot be a deceiver, since it is manifest by the natural light that all fraud and deception depend on some defect.

But before examining this point more carefully and investigating other truths which may be derived from it, I should like to pause here and spend some time in the contemplation of God; to reflect on his attributes, and to gaze with wonder and adoration on the beauty of this immense light, so far as the eye of my darkened intellect can bear it. For just as we believe through faith that the supreme happiness of the next life consists solely in the contemplation of the divine majesty, so experience tells us that this same contemplation, albeit much less perfect, enables us to know the greatest joy of which we are capable in this life.

FOURTH MEDITATION

Truth and falsity

During these past few days I have accustomed myself to leading my mind away from the senses; and I have taken careful note of the fact that there is very little about corporeal things that is truly perceived, whereas much more is known about the human mind, and still more about God. The result is that I now have no difficulty in turning my mind away from imaginable things[45] and towards things which are objects of the intellect alone and are totally separate from matter. And indeed the idea I have of the human mind, in so far as it is a thinking thing, which is not extended in length, breadth or height and has no other bodily characteristics, is much more distinct than the idea of any corporeal thing. And when I consider the fact that I have doubts, or that I am a thing that is incomplete and dependent, then there arises in me a clear and distinct idea of a being who is independent and complete, that is, an idea of God. And from the mere fact that there is such an idea within me, or that I who possess this idea exist, I clearly infer that God also exists, and that every single moment of my entire existence depends on him. So clear is this conclusion that I am confident that the human intellect cannot know anything that is more evident or more certain. And now, from this contemplation of the true God, in whom all the treasures of wisdom and the sciences lie hidden, I think I can see a way forward to the knowledge of other things.[46]

To begin with, I recognize that it is impossible that God should ever deceive me. For in every case of trickery or deception some imperfection is to be found; and although the ability to deceive appears to be an indication of cleverness or power, the will to deceive is undoubtedly evidence of malice or weakness, and so cannot apply to God.

Next, I know by experience that there is in me a faculty of judgement which, like everything else which is in me, I certainly received from God. And since God does not wish to deceive me, he surely did not give me the kind of faculty which would ever enable me to go wrong while using it correctly.

There would be no further doubt on this issue were it not that what I have just said appears to imply that I am incapable of ever going wrong. For if everything that is in me comes from God, and he did not endow me with a faculty for making mistakes, it appears that I can never go wrong. And certainly, so long as I think only of God, and turn my whole attention to him, I can find no cause of error or falsity. But when I turn back to myself, I know by experience that I am prone to countless errors. On looking for the cause of these errors, I find that I possess not only a real and positive idea of God, or a being who is supremely perfect, but also what may be described as a negative idea of nothingness, or of that which is farthest removed from all perfection. I realize that I am, as it were, something intermediate between God and nothingness, or between supreme being and nonbeing: my nature is such that in so far as I was created by the supreme being, there is nothing in me to enable me to go wrong or lead me astray; but in so far as I participate in nothingness or nonbeing, that is, in so far as I am not myself the supreme being and am lacking in countless respects, it is no wonder that I make mistakes. I understand, then, that error as such is not something real which depends on God, but merely a defect. Hence my going wrong does not require me to have a faculty specially bestowed on me by God; it simply happens as a result of the fact that the faculty of true judgement which I have from God is in my case not infinite.

But this is still not entirely satisfactory. For error is not a pure negation,[47] but rather a privation or lack of some knowledge which somehow should be in me. And when I concentrate on the nature of God, it seems impossible that he should have placed in me a faculty which is not perfect of its kind, or which lacks some perfection which it ought to have. The more skilled the craftsman the more perfect the work produced by him; if this is so, how can anything produced by the supreme creator of all things not be complete and perfect in all respects? There is, moreover, no doubt that God could have given me a nature such that I was never mistaken; again, there is no doubt that he always wills what is best. Is it then better that I should make mistakes than that I should not do so?

As I reflect on these matters more attentively, it occurs to me first of all that it is no cause for surprise if I do not understand the reasons for some of God's actions; and there is no call to doubt his existence if I happen to find that there are other instances where I do not grasp why or how certain things were made by him. For since I now know that my own nature is very weak and limited, whereas the nature of God is immense, incomprehensible and infinite, I also know without more ado that he is capable of countless things whose causes are beyond my knowledge. And for this reason alone I consider the customary search for final causes to be totally useless in physics; there is considerable rashness in thinking myself capable of investigating the <impenetrable> purposes of God.

It also occurs to me that whenever we are inquiring whether the works of God are perfect, we ought to look at the whole universe, not just at one created thing on its own. For what would perhaps rightly appear very imperfect if it existed on its own is quite perfect when its function as a part of the universe is considered. It is true that, since my decision to doubt everything, it is so far only myself and God whose existence I have been able to know with certainty; but after considering the immense power of God, I cannot deny that many other things have been made by him, or at least could have been made, and hence that I may have a place in the universal scheme of things.

Next, when I look more closely at myself and inquire into the nature of my errors (for these are the only evidence of some imperfection in me), I notice that they depend on two concurrent causes, namely on the faculty of knowledge which is in me, and on the faculty of choice or freedom of the will; that is, they depend on both the intellect and the will simultaneously. Now all that the intellect does is to enable me to perceive[48] the ideas which are subjects for possible judgements; and when regarded strictly in this light, it turns out to contain no error in the proper sense of that term. For although countless things may exist without there being any corresponding ideas in me, it should not, strictly speaking, be said that I am deprived of these ideas,[49] but merely that I lack them, in a negative sense. This is because I cannot produce any reason to prove that God ought to have given me a greater faculty of knowledge than he did; and no matter how skilled I understand a craftsman to be, this does not make me think he ought to have put into every one of his works all the perfections which he is able to put into some of them. Besides, I cannot complain that the will or freedom of choice which I received from God is not sufficiently extensive or perfect, since I know by experience that it is not restricted in any way. Indeed, I think it is very noteworthy that there is nothing else in me which is so perfect and so great that the possibility of a further increase in its perfection or greatness is beyond my understanding. If, for example, I consider the faculty of understanding, I immediately recognize that in my case it is extremely slight and very finite, and I at once form the idea of an understanding which is much greater—indeed supremely great and infinite; and from the very fact that I can form an idea of it, I perceive that it belongs to the nature of God. Similarly, if I examine the faculties of memory or imagination, or any others, I discover that in my case each one of these faculties is weak and limited, while in the case of God it is immeasurable. It is only the will, or freedom of choice, which I experience within me to be so great that the idea of any greater faculty is beyond my grasp; so much so that it is above all in virtue of the will that I understand myself to bear in some way the image and likeness of God. For although God's will is incomparably greater than mine, both in virtue of the knowledge and power that accompany it and make it more firm and efficacious, and also in virtue of its object, in that it ranges over a greater number of items, nevertheless it does not seem any greater than mine when considered as will in the essential and strict sense. This is because the will simply consists in our ability to do or not do something (that is, to affirm or deny, to pursue or avoid); or rather, it consists simply in the fact that when the intellect puts something forward, we are moved to affirm or deny or to pursue or avoid it in such a way that we do not feel ourselves to be determined by any external force. For in order to be free, there is no need for me to be capable of going in each of two directions; on the contrary, the more I incline in one direction—either because I clearly understand that reasons of truth and goodness point that way, or because of a divinely produced disposition of my inmost thoughts—the freer is my choice. Neither divine grace nor natural knowledge ever diminishes freedom; on the contrary, they increase and strengthen it. But the indifference I feel when there is no reason pushing me in one direction rather than another is the lowest grade of freedom; it is evidence not of any perfection of freedom, but rather of a defect in knowledge or a kind of negation. For if I always saw clearly what was true and good, I should never have to deliberate about the right judgement or choice; in that case, although I should be wholly free, it would be impossible for me ever to be in a state of indifference.

From these considerations I perceive that the power of willing which I received from God is not, when considered in itself, the cause of my mistakes; for it is both extremely ample and also perfect of its kind. Nor is my power of understanding to blame; for since my understanding comes from God, everything that I understand I undoubtedly understand correctly, and any error here is impossible. So what then is the source of my mistakes? It must be simply this: the scope of the will is wider than that of the intellect; but instead of restricting it within the same limits, I extend its use to matters which I do not understand. Since the will is indifferent in such cases, it easily turns aside from what is true and good, and this is the source of my error and sin.

For example, during these past few days I have been asking whether anything in the world exists, and I have realized that from the very fact of my raising this question it follows quite evidently that I exist. I could not but judge that something which I understood so clearly was true; but this was not because I was compelled so to judge by any external force, but because a great light in the intellect was followed by a great inclination in the will, and thus the spontaneity and freedom of my belief was all the greater in proportion to my lack of indifference. But now, besides the knowledge that I exist, in so far as I am a thinking thing, an idea of corporeal nature comes into my mind; and I happen to be in doubt as to whether the thinking nature which is in me, or rather which I am, is distinct from this corporeal nature or identical with it. I am making the further supposition that my intellect has not yet come upon any persuasive reason in favour of one alternative rather than the other. This obviously implies that I am indifferent as to whether I should assert or deny either alternative, or indeed refrain from making any judgement on the matter.

What is more, this indifference does not merely apply to cases where the intellect is wholly ignorant, but extends in general to every case where the intellect does not have sufficiently clear knowledge at the time when the will deliberates. For although probable conjectures may pull me in one direction, the mere knowledge that they are simply conjectures, and not certain and indubitable reasons, is itself quite enough to push my assent the other way. My experience in the last few days confirms this: the mere fact that I found that all my previous beliefs were in some sense open to doubt was enough to turn my absolutely confident belief in their truth into the supposition that they were wholly false.

If, however, I simply refrain from making a judgement in cases where I do not perceive the truth with sufficient clarity and distinctness, then it is clear that I am behaving correctly and avoiding error. But if in such cases I either affirm or deny, then I am not using my free will correctly. If I go for the alternative which is false, then obviously I shall be in error; if I take the other side, then it is by pure chance that I arrive at the truth, and I shall still be at fault since it is clear by the natural light that the perception of the intellect should always precede the determination of the will. In this incorrect use of free will may be found the privation which constitutes the essence of error. The privation, I say, lies in the operation of the will in so far as it proceeds from me, but not in the faculty of will which I received from God, nor even in its operation, in so far as it depends on him.

And I have no cause for complaint on the grounds that the power of understanding or the natural light which God gave me is no greater than it is; for it is in the nature of a finite intellect to lack understanding of many things, and it is in the nature of a created intellect to be finite. Indeed, I have reason to give thanks to him who has never owed me anything for the great bounty that he has shown me, rather than thinking myself deprived or robbed of any gifts he did not bestow.[50]

Nor do I have any cause for complaint on the grounds that God gave me a will which extends more widely than my intellect. For since the will consists simply of one thing which is, as it were, indivisible, it seems that its nature rules out the possibility of anything being taken away from it. And surely, the more widely my will extends, then the greater thanks I owe to him who gave it to me.

Finally, I must not complain that the forming of those acts of will or judgements in which I go wrong happens with God's concurrence. For in so far as these acts depend on God, they are wholly true and good; and my ability to perform them means that there is in a sense more perfection in me than would be the case if I lacked this ability. As for the privation involved—which is all that the essential definition of falsity and wrong consists in—this does not in any way require the concurrence of God, since it is not a thing; indeed, when it is referred to God as its cause, it should be called not a privation but simply a negation.[51] For it is surely no imperfection in God that he has given me the freedom to assent or not to assent in those cases where he did not endow my intellect with a clear and distinct perception; but it is undoubtedly an imperfection in me to misuse that freedom and make judgements about matters which I do not fully understand. I can see, however, that God could easily have brought it about that without losing my freedom, and despite the limitations in my knowledge, I should nonetheless never make a mistake. He could, for example, have endowed my intellect with a clear and distinct perception of everything about which I was ever likely to deliberate; or he could simply have impressed it unforgettably on my memory that I should never make a judgement about anything which I did not clearly and distinctly understand. Had God made me this way, then I can easily understand that, considered as a totality,[52] I would have been more perfect than I am now. But I cannot therefore deny that there may in some way be more perfection in the universe as a whole because some of its parts are not immune from error, while others are immune, than there would be if all the parts were exactly alike. And I have no right to complain that the role God wished me to undertake in the world is not the principal one or the most perfect of all.

What is more, even if I have no power to avoid error in the first way just mentioned, which requires a clear perception of everything I have to deliberate on, I can avoid error in the second way, which depends merely on my remembering to withhold judgement on any occasion when the truth of the matter is not clear. Admittedly, I am aware of a certain weakness in me, in that I am unable to keep my attention fixed on one and the same item of knowledge at all times; but by attentive and repeated meditation I am nevertheless able to make myself remember it as often as the need arises, and thus get into the habit of avoiding error.

It is here that man's greatest and most important perfection is to be found, and I therefore think that today's meditation, involving an investigation into the cause of error and falsity, has been very profitable. The cause of error must surely be the one I have explained; for if, whenever I have to make a judgement, I restrain my will so that it extends to what the intellect clearly and distinctly reveals, and no further, then it is quite impossible for me to go wrong. This is because every clear and distinct perception is undoubtedly something,[53] and hence cannot come from nothing, but must necessarily have God for its author. Its author, I say, is God, who is supremely perfect, and who cannot be a deceiver on pain of contradiction; hence the perception is undoubtedly true. So today I have learned not only what precautions to take to avoid ever going wrong, but also what to do to arrive at the truth. For I shall unquestionably reach the truth, if only I give sufficient attention to all the things which I perfectly understand, and separate these from all the other cases where my apprehension is more confused and obscure. And this is just what I shall take good care to do from now on.

FIFTH MEDITATION

The essence of material things, and the existence of God considered a second time

There are many matters which remain to be investigated concerning the attributes of God and the nature of myself, or my mind; and perhaps I shall take these up at another time. But now that I have seen what to do and what to avoid in order to reach the truth, the most pressing task seems to be to try to escape from the doubts into which I fell a few days ago, and see whether any certainty can be achieved regarding material objects.

But before I inquire whether any such things exist outside me, I must consider the ideas of these things, in so far as they exist in my thought, and see which of them are distinct, and which confused.

Quantity, for example, or 'continuous' quantity as the philosophers commonly call it, is something I distinctly imagine. That is, I distinctly imagine the extension of the quantity (or rather of the thing which is quantified) in length, breadth and depth. I also enumerate various parts of the thing, and to these parts I assign various sizes, shapes, positions and local motions; and to the motions I assign various durations.

Not only are all these things very well known and transparent to me when regarded in this general way, but in addition there are countless particular features regarding shapes, number, motion and so on, which I perceive when I give them my attention. And the truth of these matters is so open and so much in harmony with my nature, that on first discovering them it seems that I am not so much learning something new as remembering what I knew before; or it seems like noticing for the first time things which were long present within me although I had never turned my mental gaze on them before.

But I think the most important consideration at this point is that I find within me countless ideas of things which even though they may not exist anywhere outside me still cannot be called nothing; for although in a sense they can be thought of at will, they are not my invention but have their own true and immutable natures. When, for example, I imagine a triangle, even if perhaps no such figure exists, or has ever existed, anywhere outside my thought, there is still a determinate nature, or essence, or form of the triangle which is immutable and eternal, and not invented by me or dependent on my mind. This is clear from the fact that various properties can be demonstrated of the triangle, for example that its three angles equal two right angles, that its greatest side subtends its greatest angle, and the like; and since these properties are ones which I now clearly recognize whether I want to or not, even if I never thought of them at all when I previously imagined the triangle, it follows that they cannot have been invented by me.

It would be beside the point for me to say that since I have from time to time seen bodies of triangular shape, the idea of the triangle may have come to me from external things by means of the sense organs. For I can think up countless other shapes which there can be no suspicion of my ever having encountered through the senses, and yet I can demonstrate various properties of these shapes, just as I can with the triangle. All these properties are certainly true, since I am clearly aware of them, and therefore they are something, and not merely nothing; for it is obvious that whatever is true is something; and I have already amply demonstrated that everything of which I am clearly aware is true. And even if I had not demonstrated this, the nature of my mind is such that I cannot but assent to these things, at least so long as I clearly perceive them. I also remember that even before, when I was completely preoccupied with the objects of the senses, I always held that the most certain truths of all were the kind which I recognized clearly in connection with shapes, or numbers or other items relating to arithmetic or geometry, or in general to pure and abstract mathematics.

But if the mere fact that I can produce from my thought the idea of something entails that everything which I clearly and distinctly perceive to belong to that thing really does belong to it, is not this a possible basis for another argument to prove the existence of God? Certainly, the idea of God, or a supremely perfect being, is one which I find within me just as surely as the idea of any shape or number. And my understanding that it belongs to his nature that he always exists[54] is no less clear and distinct than is the case when I prove of any shape or number that some property belongs to its nature. Hence, even if it turned out that not everything on which I have meditated in these past days is true, I ought still to regard the existence of God as having at least the same level of certainty as I have hitherto attributed to the truths of mathematics.[55]

At first sight, however, this is not transparently clear, but has some appearance of being a sophism. Since I have been accustomed to distinguish between existence and essence in everything else, I find it easy to persuade myself that existence can also be separated from the essence of God, and hence that God can be thought of as not existing. But when I concentrate more carefully, it is quite evident that existence can no more be separated from the essence of God than the fact that its three angles equal two right angles can be separated from the essence of a triangle, or than the idea of a mountain can be separated from the idea of a valley. Hence it is just as much of a contradiction to think of God (that is, a supremely perfect being) lacking existence (that is, lacking a perfection), as it is to think of a mountain without a valley.

However, even granted that I cannot think of God except as existing, just as I cannot think of a mountain without a valley, it certainly does not follow from the fact that I think of a mountain with a valley that there is any mountain in the world; and similarly, it does not seem to follow from the fact that I think of God as existing that he does exist. For my thought does not impose any necessity on things; and just as I may imagine a winged horse even though no horse has wings, so I may be able to attach existence to God even though no God exists.

But there is a sophism concealed here. From the fact that I cannot think of a mountain without a valley, it does not follow that a mountain and valley exist anywhere, but simply that a mountain and a valley, whether they exist or not, are mutually inseparable. But from the fact that I cannot think of God except as existing, it follows that existence is inseparable from God, and hence that he really exists. It is not that my thought makes it so, or imposes any necessity on any thing; on the contrary, it is the necessity of the thing itself, namely the existence of God, which determines my thinking in this respect. For I am not free to think of God without existence (that is, a supremely perfect being without a supreme perfection) as I am free to imagine a horse with or without wings.

And it must not be objected at this point that while it is indeed necessary for me to suppose God exists, once I have made the supposition that he has all perfections (since existence is one of the perfections), nevertheless the original supposition was not necessary. Similarly, the objection would run, it is not necessary for me to think that all quadrilaterals can be inscribed in a circle; but given this supposition, it will be necessary for me to admit that a rhombus can be inscribed in a circle—which is patently false.

Now admittedly, it is not necessary that I ever light upon any thought of God; but whenever I do choose to think of the first and supreme being, and bring forth the idea of God from the treasure house of my mind as it were, it is necessary that I attribute all perfections to him, even if I do not at that time enumerate them or attend to them individually. And this necessity plainly guarantees that, when I later realize that existence is a perfection, I am correct in inferring that the first and supreme being exists. In the same way, it is not necessary for me ever to imagine a triangle; but whenever I do wish to consider a rectilinear figure having just three angles, it is necessary that I attribute to it the properties which license the inference that its three angles equal no more than two right angles, even if I do not notice this at the time. By contrast, when I examine what figures can be inscribed in a circle, it is in no way necessary for me to think that this class includes all quadrilaterals. Indeed, I cannot even imagine this, so long as I am willing to admit only what I clearly and distinctly understand. So there is a great difference between this kind of false supposition and the true ideas which are innate in me, of which the first and most important is the idea of God. There are many ways in which I understand that this idea is not something fictitious which is dependent on my thought, but is an image of a true and immutable nature. First of all, there is the fact that, apart from God, there is nothing else of which I am capable of thinking such that existence belongs[56] to its essence. Second, I cannot understand how there could be two or more Gods of this kind; and after supposing that one God exists, I plainly see that it is necessary that he has existed from eternity and will abide for eternity. And finally, I perceive many other attributes of God, none of which I can remove or alter.

But whatever method of proof I use, I am always brought back to the fact that it is only what I clearly and distinctly perceive that completely convinces me. Some of the things I clearly and distinctly perceive are obvious to everyone, while others are discovered only by those who look more closely and investigate more carefully; but once they have been discovered, the latter are judged to be just as certain as the former. In the case of a right-angled triangle, for example, the fact that the square on the hypotenuse is equal to the square on the other two sides is not so readily apparent as the fact that the hypotenuse subtends the largest angle; but once one has seen it, one believes it just as strongly. But as regards God, if I were not overwhelmed by preconceived opinions, and if the images of things perceived by the senses did not besiege my thought on every side, I would certainly acknowledge him sooner and more easily than anything else. For what is more self-evident than the fact that the supreme being exists, or that God, to whose essence alone existence belongs,[57] exists?

Although it needed close attention for me to perceive this, I am now just as certain of it as I am of everything else which appears most certain. And what is more, I see that the certainty of all other things depends on this, so that without it nothing can ever be perfectly known.

Admittedly my nature is such that so long as[58] I perceive something very clearly and distinctly I cannot but believe it to be true. But my nature is also such that I cannot fix my mental vision continually on the same thing, so as to keep perceiving it clearly; and often the memory of a previously made judgement may come back, when I am no longer attending to the arguments which led me to make it. And so other arguments can now occur to me which might easily undermine my opinion, if I were unaware of God; and I should thus never have true and certain knowledge about anything, but only shifting and changeable opinions. For example, when I consider the nature of a triangle, it appears most evident to me, steeped as I am in the principles of geometry, that its three angles are equal to two right angles; and so long as I attend to the proof, I cannot but believe this to be true. But as soon as I turn my mind's eye away from the proof, then in spite of still remembering that I perceived it very clearly, I can easily fall into doubt about its truth, if I am unaware of God. For I can convince myself that I have a natural disposition to go wrong from time to time in matters which I think I perceive as evidently as can be. This will seem even more likely when I remember that there have been frequent cases where I have regarded things as true and certain, but have later been led by other arguments to judge them to be false.

Now, however, I have perceived that God exists, and at the same time I have understood that everything else depends on him, and that he is no deceiver; and I have drawn the conclusion that everything which I clearly and distinctly perceive is of necessity true. Accordingly, even if I am no longer attending to the arguments which led me to judge that this is true, as long as I remember that I clearly and distinctly perceived it, there are no counter-arguments which can be adduced to make me doubt it, but on the contrary I have true and certain knowledge of it. And I have knowledge not just of this matter, but of all matters which I remember ever having demonstrated, in geometry and so on. For what objections can now be raised?[59] That the way I am made makes me prone to frequent error? But I now know that I am incapable of error in those cases where my understanding is transparently clear. Or can it be objected that I have in the past regarded as true and certain many things which I afterwards recognized to be false? But none of these were things which I clearly and distinctly perceived: I was ignorant of this rule for establishing the truth, and believed these things for other reasons which I later discovered to be less reliable. So what is left to say? Can one raise the objection I put to myself a while ago, that I may be dreaming, or that everything which I am now thinking has as little truth as what comes to the mind of one who is asleep? Yet even this does not change anything. For even though I might be dreaming, if there is anything which is evident to my intellect, then it is wholly true.

Thus I see plainly that the certainty and truth of all knowledge depends uniquely on my awareness of the true God, to such an extent that I was incapable of perfect knowledge about anything else until I became aware of him. And now it is possible for me to achieve full and certain knowledge of countless matters, both concerning God himself and other things whose nature is intellectual, and also concerning the whole of that corporeal nature which is the subject-matter of pure mathematics.[60]

SIXTH MEDITATION

The existence of material things, and the real distinction between mind and body[61]

It remains for me to examine whether material things exist. And at least I now know they are capable of existing, in so far as they are the subject-matter of pure mathematics, since I perceive them clearly and distinctly. For there is no doubt that God is capable of creating everything that I am capable of perceiving in this manner; and I have never judged that something could not be made by him except on the grounds that there would be a contradiction in my perceiving it distinctly. The conclusion that material things exist is also suggested by the faculty of imagination, which I am aware of using when I turn my mind to material things. For when I give more attentive consideration to what imagination is, it seems to be nothing else but an application of the cognitive faculty to a body which is intimately present to it, and which therefore exists.

To make this clear, I will first examine the difference between imagination and pure understanding. When I imagine a triangle, for example, I do not merely understand that it is a figure bounded by three lines, but at the same time I also see the three lines with my mind's eye as if they were present before me; and this is what I call imagining. But if I want to think of a chiliagon, although I understand that it is a figure consisting of a thousand sides just as well as I understand the triangle to be a three-sided figure, I do not in the same way imagine the thousand sides or see them as if they were present before me. It is true that since I am in the habit of imagining something whenever I think of a corporeal thing, I may construct in my mind a confused representation of some figure; but it is clear that this is not a chiliagon. For it differs in no way from the representation I should form if I were thinking of a myriagon, or any figure with very many sides. Moreover, such a representation is useless for recognizing the properties which distinguish a chiliagon from other polygons. But suppose I am dealing with a pentagon: I can of course understand the figure of a pentagon, just as I can the figure of a chiliagon, without the help of the imagination; but I can also imagine a pentagon, by applying my mind's eye to its five sides and the area contained within them. And in doing this I notice quite clearly that imagination requires a peculiar effort of mind which is not required for understanding; this additional effort of mind clearly shows the difference between imagination and pure understanding.

Besides this, I consider that this power of imagining which is in me, differing as it does from the power of understanding, is not a necessary constituent of my own essence, that is, of the essence of my mind. For if I lacked it, I should undoubtedly remain the same individual as I now am; from which it seems to follow that it depends on something distinct from myself. And I can easily understand that, if there does exist some body to which the mind is so joined that it can apply itself to contemplate it, as it were, whenever it pleases, then it may possibly be this very body that enables me to imagine corporeal things. So the difference between this mode of thinking and pure understanding may simply be this: when the mind understands, it in some way turns towards itself and inspects one of the ideas which are within it; but when it imagines, it turns towards the body and looks at something in the body which conforms to an idea understood by the mind or perceived by the senses. I can, as I say, easily understand that this is how imagination comes about, if the body exists; and since there is no other equally suitable way of explaining imagination that comes to mind, I can make a probable conjecture that the body exists. But this is only a probability; and despite a careful and comprehensive investigation, I do not yet see how the distinct idea of corporeal nature which I find in my imagination can provide any basis for a necessary inference that some body exists.

But besides that corporeal nature which is the subject-matter of pure mathematics, there is much else that I habitually imagine, such as colours, sounds, tastes, pain and so on—though not so distinctly. Now I perceive these things much better by means of the senses, which is how, with the assistance of memory, they appear to have reached the imagination. So in order to deal with them more fully, I must pay equal attention to the senses, and see whether the things which are perceived by means of that mode of thinking which I call 'sensory perception' provide me with any sure argument for the existence of corporeal things.

To begin with, I will go back over all the things which I previously took to be perceived by the senses, and reckoned to be true; and I will go over my reasons for thinking this. Next, I will set out my reasons for subsequently calling these things into doubt. And finally I will consider what I should now believe about them.

First of all then, I perceived by my senses that I had a head, hands, feet and other limbs making up the body which I regarded as part of myself, or perhaps even as my whole self. I also perceived by my senses that this body was situated among many other bodies which could affect it in various favourable or unfavourable ways; and I gauged the favourable effects by a sensation of pleasure, and the unfavourable ones by a sensation of pain. In addition to pain and pleasure, I also had sensations within me of hunger, thirst, and other such appetites, and also of physical propensities towards cheerfulness, sadness, anger and similar emotions. And outside me, besides the extension, shapes and movements of bodies, I also had sensations of their hardness and heat, and of the other tactile qualities. In addition, I had sensations of light, colours, smells, tastes and sounds, the variety of which enabled me to distinguish the sky, the earth, the seas, and all other bodies, one from another. Considering the ideas of all these qualities which presented themselves to my thought, although the ideas were, strictly speaking, the only immediate objects of my sensory awareness, it was not unreasonable for me to think that the items which I was perceiving through the senses were things quite distinct from my thought, namely bodies which produced the ideas. For my experience was that these ideas came to me quite without my consent, so that I could not have sensory awareness of any object, even if I wanted to, unless it was present to my sense organs; and I could not avoid having sensory awareness of it when it was present. And since the ideas perceived by the senses were much more lively and vivid and even, in their own way, more distinct than any of those which I deliberately formed through meditating or which I found impressed on my memory, it seemed impossible that they should have come from within me; so the only alternative was that they came from other things. Since the sole source of my knowledge of these things was the ideas themselves, the supposition that the things resembled the ideas was bound to occur to me. In addition, I remembered that the use of my senses had come first, while the use of my reason came only later; and I saw that the ideas which I formed myself were less vivid than those which I perceived with the senses and were, for the most part, made up of elements of sensory ideas. In this way I easily convinced myself that I had nothing at all in the intellect which I had not previously had in sensation. As for the body which by some special right I called 'mine', my belief that this body, more than any other, belonged to me had some justification. For I could never be separated from it, as I could from other bodies; and I felt all my appetites and emotions in, and on account of, this body; and finally, I was aware of pain and pleasurable ticklings in parts of this body, but not in other bodies external to it. But why should that curious sensation of pain give rise to a particular distress of mind; or why should a certain kind of delight follow on a tickling sensation? Again, why should that curious tugging in the stomach which I call hunger tell me that I should eat, or a dryness of the throat tell me to drink, and so on? I was not able to give any explanation of all this, except that nature taught me so. For there is absolutely no connection (at least that I can understand) between the tugging sensation and the decision to take food, or between the sensation of something causing pain and the mental apprehension of distress that arises from that sensation. These and other judgements that I made concerning sensory objects, I was apparently taught to make by nature; for I had already made up my mind that this was how things were, before working out any arguments to prove it.

Later on, however, I had many experiences which gradually undermined all the faith I had had in the senses. Sometimes towers which had looked round from a distance appeared square from close up; and enormous statues standing on their pediments did not seem large when observed from the ground. In these and countless other such cases, I found that the judgements of the external senses were mistaken. And this applied not just to the external senses but to the internal senses as well. For what can be more internal than pain? And yet I had heard that those who had had a leg or an arm amputated sometimes still seemed to feel pain intermittently in the missing part of the body. So even in my own case it was apparently not quite certain that a particular limb was hurting, even if I felt pain in it. To these reasons for doubting, I recently added two very general ones.[62] The first was that every sensory experience I have ever thought I was having while awake I can also think of myself as sometimes having while asleep; and since I do not believe that what I seem to perceive in sleep comes from things located outside me, I did not see why I should be any more inclined to believe this of what I think I perceive while awake. The second reason for doubt was that since I did not yet know the author of my being (or at least was pretending not to), I saw nothing to rule out the possibility that my natural constitution made me prone to error even in matters which seemed to me most true. As for the reasons for my previous confident belief in the truth of the things perceived by the senses, I had no trouble in refuting them. For since I apparently had natural impulses towards many things which reason told me to avoid, I reckoned that a great deal of confidence should not be placed in what I was taught by nature. And despite the fact that the perceptions of the senses were not dependent on my will, I did not think that I should on that account infer that they proceeded from things distinct from myself, since I might perhaps have a faculty not yet known to me which produced them.[63]

But now, when I am beginning to achieve a better knowledge of myself and the author of my being, although I do not think I should heedlessly accept everything I seem to have acquired from the senses, neither do I think that everything should be called into doubt.

First, I know that everything which I clearly and distinctly understand is capable of being created by God so as to correspond exactly with my understanding of it. Hence the fact that I can clearly and distinctly understand one thing apart from another is enough to make me certain that the two things are distinct, since they are capable of being separated, at least by God. The question of what kind of power is required to bring about such a separation does not affect the judgement that the two things are distinct. Thus, simply by knowing that I exist and seeing at the same time that absolutely nothing else belongs to my nature or essence except that I am a thinking thing, I can infer correctly that my essence consists solely in the fact that I am a thinking thing. It is true that I may have (or, to anticipate, that I certainly have) a body that is very closely joined to me. But nevertheless, on the one hand I have a clear and distinct idea of myself, in so far as I am simply a thinking, nonextended thing; and on the other hand I have a distinct idea of body,[64] in so far as this is simply an extended, non-thinking thing. And accordingly, it is certain that I[65] am really distinct from my body, and can exist without it.

Besides this, I find in myself faculties for certain special modes of thinking,[66] namely imagination and sensory perception. Now I can clearly and distinctly understand myself as a whole without these faculties; but I cannot, conversely, understand these faculties without me, that is, without an intellectual substance to inhere in. This is because there is an intellectual act included in their essential definition; and hence I perceive that the distinction between them and myself corresponds to the distinction between the modes of a thing and the thing itself.[67] Of course I also recognize that there are other faculties (like those of changing position, of taking on various shapes, and so on) which, like sensory perception and imagination, cannot be understood apart from some substance for them to inhere in, and hence cannot exist without it. But it is clear that these other faculties, if they exist, must be in a corporeal or extended substance and not an intellectual one; for the clear and distinct conception of them includes extension, but does not include any intellectual act

whatsoever. Now there is in me a passive faculty of sensory perception, that is, a faculty for receiving and recognizing the ideas of sensible objects; but I could not make use of it unless there was also an active faculty, either in me or in something else, which produced or brought about these ideas. But this faculty cannot be in me, since clearly it presupposes no intellectual act on my part,[68] and the ideas in question are produced without my cooperation and often even against my will. So the only alternative is that it is in another substance distinct from me—a substance which contains either formally or eminently all the reality which exists objectively[69] in the ideas produced by this faculty (as I have just noted). This substance is either a body, that is, a corporeal nature, in which case it will contain formally <and in fact> everything which is to be found objectively <or representatively> in the ideas; or else it is God, or some creature more noble than a body, in which case it will contain eminently whatever is to be found in the ideas. But since God is not a deceiver, it is quite clear that he does not transmit the ideas to me either directly from himself, or indirectly, via some creature which contains the objective reality of the ideas not formally but only eminently. For God has given me no faculty at all for recognizing any such source for these ideas; on the contrary, he has given me a great propensity to believe that they are produced by corporeal things. So I do not see how God could be understood to be anything but a deceiver if the ideas were transmitted from a source other than corporeal things. It follows that corporeal things exist. They may not all exist in a way that exactly corresponds with my sensory grasp of them, for in many cases the grasp of the senses is very obscure and confused. But at least they possess all the properties which I clearly and distinctly understand, that is, all those which, viewed in general terms, are comprised within the subject-matter of pure mathematics.

What of the other aspects of corporeal things which are either particular (for example that the sun is of such and such a size or shape), or less clearly understood, such as light or sound or pain, and so on? Despite the high degree of doubt and uncertainty involved here, the very fact that God is not a deceiver, and the consequent impossibility of there being any falsity in my opinions which cannot be corrected by some other faculty supplied by God, offers me a sure hope that I can attain the truth even in these matters. Indeed, there is no doubt that everything that I am taught by nature contains some truth. For if nature is considered in its general aspect, then I understand by the term nothing other than God himself, or the ordered system of created things established by God. And by my own nature in particular I understand nothing other than the totality of things bestowed on me by God.

There is nothing that my own nature teaches me more vividly than that I have a body, and that when I feel pain there is something wrong with the body, and that when I am hungry or thirsty the body needs food and drink, and so on. So I should not doubt that there is some truth in this.

Nature also teaches me, by these sensations of pain, hunger, thirst and so on, that I am not merely present in my body as a sailor is present in a ship,[70] but that I am very closely joined and, as it were, intermingled with it, so that I and the body form a unit. If this were not so, I, who am nothing but a thinking thing, would not feel pain when the body was hurt, but would perceive the damage purely by the intellect, just as a sailor perceives by sight if anything in his ship is broken. Similarly, when the body needed food or drink, I should have an explicit understanding of the fact, instead of having confused sensations of hunger and thirst. For these sensations of hunger, thirst, pain and so on are nothing but confused modes of thinking which arise from the union and, as it were, intermingling of the mind with the body.

I am also taught by nature that various other bodies exist in the vicinity of my body, and that some of these are to be sought out and others avoided. And from the fact that I perceive by my senses a great variety of colours, sounds, smells and tastes, as well as differences in heat, hardness and the like, I am correct in inferring that the bodies which are the source of these various sensory perceptions possess differences corresponding to them, though perhaps not resembling them. Also, the fact that some of the perceptions are agreeable to me while others are disagreeable makes it quite certain that my body, or rather my whole self, in so far as I am a combination of body and mind, can be affected by the various beneficial or harmful bodies which surround it.

There are, however, many other things which I may appear to have been taught by nature, but which in reality I acquired not from nature but from a habit of making ill-considered judgements; and it is therefore quite possible that these are false. Cases in point are the belief that any space in which nothing is occurring to stimulate my senses must be empty; or that the heat in a body is something exactly resembling the idea of heat which is in me; or that when a body is white or green, the selfsame whiteness or greenness which I perceive through my senses is present in the body; or that in a body which is bitter or sweet there is the selfsame taste which I experience, and so on; or, finally, that stars and towers and other distant bodies have the same size and shape which they present to my senses, and other examples of this kind. But to make sure that my perceptions in this matter are sufficiently distinct, I must more accurately define exactly what I mean when I say that I am taught something by nature. In this context I am taking nature to be something more limited than the totality of things bestowed on me by God. For this includes many things that belong to the mind alone—for example my perception that what is done cannot be undone, and all other things that are known by the natural light;[71] but at this stage I am not speaking of these matters. It also includes much that relates to the body alone, like the tendency to move in a downward direction, and so on; but I am not speaking of these matters either. My sole concern here is with what God has bestowed on me as a combination of mind and body. My nature, then, in this limited sense, does indeed teach me to avoid what induces a feeling of pain and to seek out what induces feelings of pleasure, and so on. But it does not appear to teach us to draw any conclusions from these sensory perceptions about things located outside us without waiting until the intellect has examined[72] the matter. For knowledge of the truth about such things seems to belong to the mind alone, not to the combination of mind and body. Hence, although a star has no greater effect on my eye than the flame of a small light, that does not mean that there is any real or positive inclination in me to believe that the star is no bigger than the light; I have simply made this judgement from childhood onwards without any rational basis. Similarly, although I feel heat when I go near a fire and feel pain when I go too near, there is no convincing argument for supposing that there is something in the fire which resembles the heat, any more than for supposing that there is something which resembles the pain. There is simply reason to suppose that there is something in the fire, whatever it may eventually turn out to be, which produces in us the feelings of heat or pain. And likewise, even though there is nothing in any given space that stimulates the senses, it does not follow that there is no body there. In these cases and many others I see that I have been in the habit of misusing the order of nature. For the proper purpose of the sensory perceptions given me by nature is simply to inform the mind of what is beneficial or harmful for the composite of which the mind is a part; and to this extent they are sufficiently clear and distinct. But I misuse them by treating them as reliable touchstones for immediate judgements about the essential nature of the bodies located outside us; yet this is an area where they provide only very obscure information.

I have already looked in sufficient detail at how, notwithstanding the goodness of God, it may happen that my judgements are false. But a further problem now comes to mind regarding those very things which nature presents to me as objects which I should seek out or avoid, and also regarding the internal sensations, where I seem to have detected errors[73]—e.g. when someone is tricked by the pleasant taste of some food into eating the poison concealed inside it. Yet in this case, what the man's nature urges him to go for is simply what is responsible for the pleasant taste, and not the poison, which his nature knows nothing about. The only inference that can be drawn from this is that his nature is not omniscient. And this is not surprising, since man is a limited thing, and so it is only fitting that his perfection should be limited.

And yet it is not unusual for us to go wrong even in cases where nature does urge us towards something. Those who are ill, for example, may desire food or drink that will shortly afterwards turn out to be bad for them. Perhaps it may be said that they go wrong because their nature is disordered, but this does not remove the difficulty. A sick man is no less one of God's creatures than a healthy one, and it seems no less a contradiction to suppose that he has received from God a nature which deceives him. Yet a clock constructed with wheels and weights observes all the laws of its nature just as closely when it is badly made and tells the wrong time as when it completely fulfils the wishes of the clockmaker. In the same way, I might consider the body of a man as a kind of machine equipped with and made up of bones, nerves, muscles, veins, blood and skin in such a way that, even if there were no mind in it, it would still perform all the same movements as it now does in those cases where movement is not under the control of the will or, consequently, of the mind.[74] I can easily see that if such a body suffers from dropsy, for example, and is affected by the dryness of the throat which normally produces in the mind the sensation of thirst, the resulting condition of the nerves and other parts will dispose the body to take a drink, with the result that the disease will be aggravated. Yet this is just as natural as the body's being stimulated by a similar dryness of the throat to take a drink when there is no such illness and the drink is beneficial. Admittedly, when I consider the purpose of the clock, I may say that it is departing from its nature when it does not tell the right time; and similarly when I consider the mechanism of the human body, I may think that, in relation to the movements which normally occur in it, it too is deviating from its nature if the throat is dry at a time when drinking is not beneficial to its continued health. But I am well aware that 'nature' as I have just used it has a very different significance from 'nature' in the other sense. As I have just used it, 'nature' is simply a label which depends on my thought; it is quite extraneous to the things to which it is applied, and depends simply on my comparison between the idea of a sick man and a badly-made clock, and the idea of a healthy man and a well-made clock. But by 'nature' in the other sense I understand something which is really to be found in the things themselves; in this sense, therefore, the term contains something of the truth.

When we say, then, with respect to the body suffering from dropsy, that it has a disordered nature because it has a dry throat and yet does not need drink, the term 'nature' is here used merely as an extraneous label. However, with respect to the composite, that is, the mind united with this body, what is involved is not a mere label, but a true error of nature, namely that it is thirsty at a time when drink is going to cause it harm. It thus remains to inquire how it is that the goodness of God does not prevent nature, in this sense, from deceiving us.

The first observation I make at this point is that there is a great difference between the mind and the body, in as much as the body is by its very nature always divisible, while the mind is utterly indivisible. For when I consider the mind, or myself in so far as I am merely a thinking thing, I am unable to distinguish any parts within myself; I understand myself to be something quite single and complete. Although the whole mind seems to be united to the whole body, I recognize that if a foot or arm or any other part of the body is cut off, nothing has thereby been taken away from the mind. As for the faculties of willing, of understanding, of sensory perception and so on, these cannot be termed parts of the mind, since it is one and the same mind that wills, and understands and has sensory perceptions. By contrast, there is no corporeal or extended thing that I can think of which in my thought I cannot easily divide into parts; and this very fact makes me understand that it is divisible. This one argument would be enough to show me that the mind is completely different from the body, even if I did not already know as much from other considerations.

My next observation is that the mind is not immediately affected by all parts of the body, but only by the brain, or perhaps just by one small part of the brain, namely the part which is said to contain the 'common' sense.[75] Every time this part of the brain is in a given state, it presents the same signals to the mind, even though the other parts of the body may be in a different condition at the time. This is established by countless observations, which there is no need to review here.

I observe, in addition, that the nature of the body is such that whenever any part of it is moved by another part which is some distance away, it can always be moved in the same fashion by any of the parts which lie in between, even if the more distant part does nothing. For example, in a cord ABCD, if one end D is pulled so that the other end A moves, the exact same movement could have been brought about if one of the intermediate points B or C had been pulled, and D had not moved at all. In similar fashion, when I feel a pain in my foot, physiology tells me that this happens by means of nerves distributed throughout the foot, and that these nerves are like cords which go from the foot right up to the brain. When the nerves are pulled in the foot, they in turn pull on inner parts of the brain to which they are attached, and produce a certain motion in them; and nature has laid it down that this motion should produce in the mind a sensation of pain, as occurring in the foot. But since these nerves, in passing from the foot to the brain, must pass through the calf, the thigh, the lumbar region, the back and the neck, it can happen that, even if it is not the part in the foot but one of the intermediate parts which is being pulled, the same motion will occur in the brain as occurs when the foot is hurt, and so it will necessarily come about that the mind feels the same sensation of pain. And we must suppose the same thing happens with regard to any other sensation.

My final observation is that any given movement occurring in the part of the brain that immediately affects the mind produces just one corresponding sensation; and hence the best system that could be devised is that it should produce the one sensation which, of all possible sensations, is most especially and most frequently conducive to the preservation of the healthy man. And experience shows that the sensations which nature has given us are all of this kind; and so there is absolutely nothing to be found in them that does not bear witness to the power and goodness of God. For example, when the nerves in the foot are set in motion in a violent and unusual manner, this motion, by way of the spinal cord, reaches the inner parts of the brain, and there gives the mind its signal for having a certain sensation, namely the sensation of a pain as occurring in the foot. This stimulates the mind to do its best to get rid of the cause of the pain, which it takes to be harmful to the foot. It is true that God could have made the nature of man such that this particular motion in the brain indicated something else to the mind; it might, for example, have made the mind aware of the actual motion occurring in the brain, or in the foot, or in any of the intermediate regions; or it might have indicated something else entirely. But there is nothing else which would have been so conducive to the continued well-being of the body. In the same way, when we need drink, there arises a certain dryness in the throat; this sets in motion the nerves of the throat, which in turn move the inner parts of the brain. This motion produces in the mind a sensation of thirst, because the most useful thing for us to know about the whole business is that we need drink in order to stay healthy. And so it is in the other cases.

It is quite clear from all this that, notwithstanding the immense goodness of God, the nature of man as a combination of mind and body is such that it is bound to mislead him from time to time. For there may be some occurrence, not in the foot but in one of the other areas through which the nerves travel in their route from the foot to the brain, or even in the brain itself; and if this cause produces the same motion which is generally produced by injury to the foot, then pain will be felt as if it were in the foot. This deception of the senses is natural, because a given motion in the brain must always produce the same sensation in the mind; and the origin of the motion in question is much more often going to be something which is hurting the foot, rather than something existing elsewhere. So it is reasonable that this motion should always indicate to the mind a pain in the foot rather than in any other part of the body. Again, dryness of the throat may sometimes arise not, as it normally does, from the fact that a drink is necessary to the health of the body,

but from some quite opposite cause, as happens in the case of the man with dropsy. Yet it is much better that it should mislead on this occasion than that it should always mislead when the body is in good health. And the same goes for the other cases.

This consideration is the greatest help to me, not only for noticing all the errors to which my nature is liable, but also for enabling me to correct or avoid them without difficulty. For I know that in matters regarding the well-being of the body, all my senses report the truth much more frequently than not. Also, I can almost always make use of more than one sense to investigate the same thing; and in addition, I can use both my memory, which connects present experiences with preceding ones, and my intellect, which has by now examined all the causes of error. Accordingly, I should not have any further fears about the falsity of what my senses tell me every day; on the contrary, the exaggerated doubts of the last few days should be dismissed as laughable. This applies especially to the principal reason for doubt, namely my inability to distinguish between being asleep and being awake. For I now notice that there is a vast difference between the two, in that dreams are never linked by memory with all the other actions of life as waking experiences are. If, while I am awake, anyone were suddenly to appear to me and then disappear immediately, as happens in sleep, so that I could not see where he had come from or where he had gone to, it would not be unreasonable for me to judge that he was a ghost, or a vision created in my brain,[76] rather than a real man. But when I distinctly see where things come from and where and when they come to me, and when I can connect my perceptions of them with the whole of the rest of my life without a break, then I am quite certain that when I encounter these things I am not asleep but awake. And I ought not to have even the slightest doubt of their reality if, after calling upon all the senses as well as my memory and my intellect in order to check them, I receive no conflicting reports from any of these sources. For from the fact that God is not a deceiver it follows that in cases like these I am completely free from error.

But since the pressure of things to be done does not always allow us to stop and make such a meticulous check, it must be admitted that in this human life we are often liable to make mistakes about particular things, and we must acknowledge the weakness of our nature.

NOTES

1. The continuous divine action necessary to maintain things in existence.
2. Descartes here uses this scholastic term to refer to those features of a thing which may alter, e.g. the particular size, shape etc. of a body, or the particular thoughts, desires etc. of a mind.
3. '...or the soul of man, for I make no distinction between them' (added in French version).
4. For Descartes' use of this term, see Med. III, below p. 28.
5. Descartes added this passage on the advice of Arnauld (cf. AT VII 215; CSM II 151). He told Mersenne 'Put the words between brackets so that it can be seen that they have been added' (letter of 18 March 1641: AT III 335; CSMK 175).
6. '...and in my dreams regularly represent to myself the same things' (French version).
7. '...the place where they are, the time which measures their duration' (French version).
8. '...yet I cannot doubt that he does allow this' (French version).
9. '...in the sciences' (added in French version).
10. '...nevertheless it is in my power to suspend my judgement' (French version).
11. '...puts into my mind' (French version).
12. '...or thought anything at all' (French version).
13. The word 'only' is most naturally taken as going with 'a thing that thinks', and this interpretation is followed in the French version. When discussing this passage with Gassendi, however, Descartes suggests that he meant the 'only' to govern 'in the strict sense'; cf AT IXA 215; CSM II 276.
14. '...to see if I am not something more' (added in French version).
15. Lat. *maneat* ('let it stand'), first edition. The second edition has the indicative *manet:* 'The proposition still stands, *viz.* that I am nonetheless something.' The French version reads: 'without changing this supposition, I find that I am still certain that I am something'.
16. '...from this manner of conceiving things' (French version).
17. '...which can be conceived only by the understanding or the mind' (French version).

18. '...or rather the act whereby it is perceived' (added in French version).
19. See note p. 59 below.
20. The French version has 'more clear and distinct' and, at the end of this sentence, 'more evidently, distinctly and clearly'.
21. The French version here inserts 'loves, hates'.
22. '...all the things which we conceive very clearly and very distinctly are true' (French version).
23. '...it was not because of any knowledge I possessed' (French version).
24. The opening of this sentence is greatly expanded in the French version: 'In order that I may have the opportunity of examining this without interrupting the order of meditating which I have decided upon, which is to start only from those notions which I find first of all in my mind and pass gradually ·to those which I may find later on, I must here divide my thoughts...'
25. '...foreign to me and coming from outside' (French version).
26. '...or power for distinguishing truth from falsehood' (French version).
27. '...concerning truth and falsehood' (French version).
28. '...i.e. participate by representation in a higher degree of being or perfection' (added in French version). According to the scholastic distinction invoked in the paragraphs that follow, the 'formal' reality of anything is its own intrinsic reality, while the 'objective' reality of an idea is a function of its representational content. Thus if an idea A represents some object X which is F, then F-ness will be contained 'formally' in X but 'objectively' in A. See below, p. 85.
29. '...i.e. it will contain in itself the same things as are in the stone or other more excellent things' (added in French version). In scholastic terminology, to possess a property 'formally' is to possess it literally, in accordance with its definition; to possess it 'eminently' is to possess it in some higher form.
30. '...that this cause must be less real' (French version).
31. '...i.e. a manner or way of thinking' (added in French version).
32. '...chimerical things which cannot exist' (French version).
33. 'And since ideas, being like images, must in each case appear to us to represent something' (French version).
34. '...in so far as they represent substances' (French version).

35. '...and as it were the garments under which corporeal substance appears to us' (French version).
36. '...that the idea I have of them' (French version).
37. '...i.e. could be in me in virtue of my imperfection' (added in French version).
38. According to Descartes one can know or understand something without fully grasping it: 'In the same way we can touch a mountain with our hands but we cannot put our arms around it...To grasp something is to embrace it in one's thought; to know something, it is sufficient to touch it with one's thought' (letter to Mersenne, 27 May 1630: AT I 152; CSMK 25).
39. '...but only what is actual and real' (added in French version).
40. '...and were independent of every other being' (added in French version).
41. Cf. *Principles*, Part I, art. 62: AT VIII 30; CSM I 214.
42. '...at least as much reality in the cause as in its effect' (French version).
43. Lat. *per se;* literally 'through itself'.
44. '...and has not one of the things which indicate some imperfection' (added in French version).
45. '...from things which can be perceived by the senses or imagined' (French version).
46. '...of the other things in the universe' (French version).
47. '...i.e. not simply the defect or lack of some perfection to which I have no proper claim' (added in French version).
48. '...without affirming or denying anything' (added in French version).
49. '...it cannot be said that my understanding is deprived of these ideas, as if they were something to which its nature entitles it' (French version).
50. '...rather than entertaining so unjust a thought as to imagine that he deprived me of, or unjustly withheld, the other perfections which he did not give me' (French version).
51. '...understanding these terms in accordance with scholastic usage' (added in French version).
52. '...as if there were only myself in the world' (added in French version).
53. '...something real and positive' (French version).
54. '...that actual and eternal existence belongs to his nature' (French version).
55. '...which concern only figures and numbers' (added in French version).
56. '...necessarily belongs' (French version).
57. '...in the idea of whom alone necessary and eternal existence is comprised' (French version).
58. '...as soon as' (French version).
59. '...to oblige me to call these matters into doubt' (added in French version).
60. '...and also concerning things which belong to corporeal nature in so far as it can serve as the object of geometrical demonstrations which have no concern with whether that object exists' (French version).
61. '...between the soul and body of a man' (French version).
62. Cf. Med. I.
63. Cf. Med. III.
64. The Latin term *corpus* as used here by Descartes is ambiguous as between 'body' (i.e. corporeal matter in general) and 'the body' (i.e. this particular body of mine). The French version preserves the ambiguity.
65. '...that is, my soul, by which I am what I am' (added in French version).
66. '...certain modes of thinking which are quite special and distinct from me' (French version).
67. '...between the shapes, movements and other modes or accidents of a body and the body which supports them' (French version).
68. '...cannot be in me in so far as I am merely a thinking thing, since it does not presuppose any thought on my part' (French version).
69. For the terms 'formally', 'eminently' and 'objectively', see note, p. 29, above.
70. '...as a pilot in his ship' (French version).
71. '...without any help from the body' (added in French version).
72. '...carefully and maturely examined' (French version).
73. '...and thus seem to have been directly deceived by my nature' (added in French version).
74. '...but occurs merely as a result of the disposition of the organs' (French version).
75. The supposed faculty which integrates the data from the five specialized senses (the notion goes back ultimately to Aristotle). 'The seat of the common sense must be very mobile, to receive all the impressions which come from the senses; but it must also be of such a kind as to be movable only by the spirits which transmit these impressions. Only the *conarion* [pineal gland] fits this description' (letter to Mersenne, 21 April 1641: AT III 362; CSMK 180).
76. '...like those that are formed in the brain when I sleep' (added in French version).

The Causal Theory of Perception

JOHN LOCKE

John Locke (1632–1704) was one of the greatest of English philosophers. His empiricist theory of knowledge and natural rights political theory have had lasting influence.

1. Concerning the simple ideas of Sensation, it is to be considered,—that whatsoever is so constituted in nature as to be able, by affecting our senses, to cause any perception in the mind, doth thereby produce in the understanding a simple idea; which, whatever be the external cause of it, when it comes to be taken notice of by our discerning faculty, it is by the mind looked on and considered there to be a real positive idea in the understanding, as much as any other whatsoever; though, perhaps, the cause of it be but a privation of the subject.

2. Thus the ideas of heat and cold, light and darkness, white and black, motion and rest, are equally clear and positive ideas in the mind; though, perhaps, some of the causes which produce them are barely privations, in those subjects from whence our senses derive those ideas. These the understanding, in its view of them, considers all as distinct positive ideas, without taking notice of the causes that produce them: which is an inquiry not belonging to the idea, as it is in the understanding, but to the nature of the things existing without us. These are two very different things, and carefully to be distinguished; it being one thing to perceive and know the idea of white or black, and quite another to examine what kind of particles they must be, and how ranged in the superficies, to make any object appear white or black. . . .

7. To discover the nature of our *ideas* the better, and to discourse of them intelligibly, it will be convenient to distinguish them *as they are ideas or perceptions in our minds; and as they are modifications of matter in the bodies that cause such perceptions in us:* that so we may not think (as perhaps usually is done) that they are exactly the images and resemblances of something inherent in the subject; most of those of sensation being in the mind no more the likeness of something existing without us, than the names that stand for them are the likeness of our ideas, which yet upon hearing they are apt to excite in us.

8. Whatsoever the mind perceives *in itself,* or is the immediate object of perception, thought, or understanding, that I call *idea;* and the power to produce any idea in our mind, I call *quality* of the subject wherein that power is. Thus a snowball having the power to produce in us the ideas of white, cold, and round,—the power to produce those ideas in us, as they are in the snowball, I call qualities; and as they are sensations or perceptions in our understandings, I call them ideas; which *ideas,* if I speak of sometimes as in the things themselves, I would be understood to mean those qualities in the objects which produce them in us.

9. [Qualities thus considered in bodies are, *First,* such as are utterly inseparable from the body, in what state soever it be;] and such as in all the alterations and changes it suffers, all the force can be used upon it, it constantly keeps; and such as sense constantly finds in every particle of matter which has bulk enough to be perceived; and the mind finds inseparable from every particle of matter, though less than to make itself singly be perceived by our senses: e.g. Take a grain of wheat, divide it into two parts; each part has still solidity, extension, figure, and mobility: divide

Reprinted from *An Essay Concerning Human Understanding* Book II, Chapter VIII; Book IV, Chapter XI, first published 1690.

it again, and it retains still the same qualities; and so divide it on, till the parts become insensible; they must retain still each of them all those qualities. For division (which is all that a mill, or pestle, or any other body, does upon another, in reducing it to insensible parts) can never take away either solidity, extension, figure, or mobility from any body, but only makes two or more distinct separate masses of matter, of that which was but one before; all which distinct masses, reckoned as so many distinct bodies, after division, make a certain number. [These I call *original* or *primary qualities* of body, which I think we may observe to produce simple ideas in us, viz. solidity, extension, figure, motion or rest, and number.

10. *Secondly*, such qualities which in truth are nothing in the objects themselves but powers to produce various sensations in us by their primary qualities, i.e. by the bulk, figure, texture, and motion of their insensible parts, as colours, sounds, tastes, &c. These I call *secondary qualities*. To these might be added a *third* sort, which are allowed to be barely powers; though they are as much real qualities in the subject as those which I, to comply with the common way of speaking, call qualities, but for distinction, secondary qualities. For the power in fire to produce a new colour, or consistency, in *wax* or *clay,*—by its primary qualities, is as much a quality in fire, as the power it has to produce in *me* a new idea or sensation of warmth or burning, which I felt not before,—by the same primary qualities, viz. the bulk, texture, and motion of its insensible parts.]

11. [The next thing to be considered is, how bodies produce ideas in us; and that is manifestly by impulse, the only way which we can conceive bodies to operate in.]

12. If then external objects be not united to our minds when they produce ideas therein; and yet we perceive these *original* qualities in such of them as singly fall under our senses, it is evident that some motion must be thence continued by our nerves, or animal spirits, by some parts of our bodies, to the brains or the seat of sensation, there to produce in our minds the particular ideas we have of them. And since the extension, figure, number, and motion of bodies of an observable bigness, may be perceived at a distance by the sight, it is evident some singly imperceptible bodies must come from them to the eyes, and therby convey to the brain some motion; which produces these ideas which we have of them in us.

13. After the same manner that the ideas of these original qualities are produced in us, we may conceive that the ideas of *secondary* qualities are also produced, viz. by the operation of insensible particles on our senses. For, it being manifest that there are bodies and good store of bodies, each whereof are so small, that we cannot by any of our senses discover either their bulk, figure, or motion,—as is evident in the particles of the air and water, and others extremely smaller than those; perhaps as much smaller than the particles of air and water, as the particles of air and water are smaller than peas or hailstones;—let us suppose at present that the different motions and figures, bulk and number, of such particles, affecting the several organs of our senses, produce in us those different sensations which we have from the colours and smells of bodies; e.g. that a violet, by the impulse of such insensible particles of matter, of peculiar figures and bulks, and in different degrees and modifications of their motions, causes the ideas of the blue colour, and sweet scent of that flower to be produced in our minds. It being no more impossible to conceive that God should annex such ideas to such motions, with which they have no similitude, than that he should annex the idea of pain to the motion of a piece of steel dividing our flesh, with which that idea hath no resemblance.

14. What I have said concerning colours and smells may be understood also of tastes and sounds, and other the like sensible qualities; which, whatever reality we by mistake attribute to them, are in truth nothing in the objects themselves, but powers to produce various sensations in us, and depend on those primary qualities, viz. bulk, figure, texture, and motion of parts [as I have said].

15. From whence I think it easy to draw this observation,—that the ideas of primary qualities of bodies are resemblances of them, and their patterns do really exist in the bodies themselves, but

the ideas produced in us by these secondary qualities have no resemblance of them at all. There is nothing like our ideas, existing the bodies themselves. They are, in the bodies we denominate from them, only a power to produce those sensations in us: and what is sweet, blue, or warm in idea, is but the certain bulk, figure, and motion of the insensible parts, in the bodies themselves, which we call so.

16. Flame is denominated hot and light; snow, white and cold; and manna, white and sweet, from the ideas they produce in us. Which qualities are commonly thought to be the same in those bodies that those ideas are in us, the one the perfect resemblance of the other, as they are in a mirror, and it would by most men be judged very extravagant if one should say otherwise. And yet he that will consider that the same fire that, at one distance produces in us the sensation of warmth, does, at a nearer approach, produce in us the far different sensation of pain, ought to bethink himself what reason he has to say—that this idea of warmth, which was produced in him by the fire, is *actually in the fire;* and his idea of pain, which the same fire produced in him the same way, is *not* in the fire. Why are whiteness and coldness in snow, and pain not, when it produces the one and the other idea in us; and can do neither, but by the bulk, figure, number, and motion of its solid parts?

17. The particular bulk, number, figure, and motion of the parts of fire or snow are really in them,—whether any one's senses perceive them or no: and therefore they may be called *real* qualities, because they really exist in those bodies. But light, heat, whiteness, or coldness, are no more really in them than sickness or pain is in manna. Take away the sensation of them; let not the eyes see light or colours, nor the ears hear sounds; let the palate not taste, nor the nose smell, and all colours, tastes, odours, and sounds, *as they are such particular ideas,* vanish and cease, and are reduced to their causes, i.e. bulk, figure, and motion of parts.

18. A piece of manna of a sensible bulk is able to produce in us the idea of a round or square figure; and by being removed from one place to another, the idea of motion. This idea of motion represents it as it really is in manna moving: a circle or square are the same, whether in idea or existence, in the mind or in the manna. And this, both motion and figure, are really in the manna, whether we take notice of them or no: this everybody is ready to agree to. Besides, manna, by the bulk, figure, texture, and motion of its parts, has a power to produce the sensations of sickness, and sometimes of acute pains or gripings in us. That these ideas of sickness and pain are *not* in the manna, but effects of its operations on us, and are nowhere when we feel them not; this also every one readily agrees to. And yet men are hardly to be brought to think that sweetness and whiteness are not really in manna; which are but the effects of the operations of manna, by the motion, size, and figure of its particles, on the eyes and palate: as the pain and sickness caused by manna are confessedly nothing but the effects of its operations on the stomach and guts, by the size, motion, and figure of its insensible parts, (for by nothing else can a body operate, as has been proved): as if it could not operate on the eyes and palate, and thereby produce in the mind particular distinct ideas, which in itself it has not, as well as we allow it can operate on the guts and stomach, and thereby produce distinct ideas, which in itself it has not. These ideas, being all effects of the operations of manna on several parts of our bodies, by the size, figure, number, and motion of its parts;—why those produced by the eyes and palate should rather be thought to be really in the manna, than those produced by the stomach and guts; or why the pain and sickness, ideas that are the effect of manna, should be thought to be nowhere when they are not felt; and yet the sweetness and whiteness, effects of the same manna on other parts of the body, by ways equally as unknown, should be thought to exist in the manna, when they are not seen or tasted, would need some reason to explain.

19. Let us consider the red and white colours in porphyry. Hinder light from striking on it, and its colours vanish; it no longer produces any such ideas in us: upon the return of light it produces these appearances on us again. Can any one think any real alterations

are made in the porphyry by the presence or absence of light; and that those ideas of whiteness and redness are really in porphyry in the light, when it is plain *it has no colour in the dark?* It has, indeed, such a configuration of particles, both night and day, as are apt, by the rays of light rebounding from some parts of that hard stone, to produce in us the idea of redness, and from others the idea of whiteness; but whiteness or redness are not in it at any time, but such a texture that hath the power to produce such a sensation in us.

20. Pound an almond, and the clear white colour will be altered into a dirty one, and the sweet taste into an oily one. What real alteration can the beating of the pestle make in any body, but an alteration of the texture of it?

21. Ideas being thus distinguished and understood, we may be able to give an account how the same water, at the same time, may produce the idea of cold by one hand and of heat by the other; whereas it is impossible that the same water, if those ideas were really in it, should at the same time be both hot and cold. For, if we imagine *warmth,* as it is in our hands, to be nothing but a certain sort and degree of motion in the minute particles of our nerves or animal spirits, we may understand how it is possible that the same water may, at the same time, produce the sensations of heat in one hand and cold in the other; which yet *figure* never does, that never producing the idea of a square by one hand which has produced the idea of a globe by another. But if the sensation of heat and cold be nothing but the increase or diminution of the motion of the minute parts of our bodies, caused by the corpuscles of any other body, it is easy to be understood, that if that motion be greater in one hand than in the other; if a body be applied to the two hands, which has in its minute particles a greater motion than in those of one of the hands, and a less than in those of the other, it will increase the motion of the one hand and lessen it in the other; and so cause the different sensations of heat and cold that depend thereon.

22. I have in what just goes before been engaged in physical inquiries a little further than perhaps I intended. But, it being necessary to make the nature of sensation a little understood; and to make the difference between the *qualities* in bodies, and the *ideas* produced by them in the mind, to be distinctly conceived, without which it were impossible to discourse intelligibly of them;—I hope I shall be pardoned this little excursion into natural philosophy; it being necessary in our present inquiry to distinguish the *primary* and *real* qualities of bodies, which are always in them (viz. solidity, extension, figure, number, and motion, or rest, and are sometimes perceived by us, viz. when the bodies they are in are big enough singly to be discerned), from those *secondary* and *imputed* qualities, which are but the powers of several combinations of those primary ones, when they operate without being distinctly discerned;—whereby we may also come to know what ideas are, and what are not, resemblances of something really existing in the bodies we denominate from them.

23. The qualities, then, that are in bodies, rightly considered, are of three sorts:—

First, The bulk, figure, number, situation, and motion or rest of their solid parts. Those are in them, whether we perceive them or not; and when they are of that size that we can discover them, we have by these an idea of the thing as it is in itself; as is plain in artificial things. These I call *primary qualities.*

Secondly, The power that is in any body, by reason of its insensible primary qualities, to operate after a peculiar manner on any of our senses, and thereby produce in *us* the different ideas of several colours, sounds, smells, tastes, &c. These are usually called *sensible qualities.*

Thirdly, The power that is in any body, by reason of the particular constitution of its primary qualities, to make such a change in the bulk, figure, texture, and motion of *another body,* as to make it operate on our senses differently from what it did before. Thus the sun has a power to make wax white, and fire to make lead fluid. [These are usually called *powers.*]

The first of these, as has been said, I think may be properly called real, original, or primary qualities; because they are in the things themselves, whether they are perceived or not: and upon their different modifications it is that the secondary qualities depend.

The other two are only powers to act differently upon other things: which powers result from the different modifications of those primary qualities.

24. But, though the two latter sorts of qualities are powers barely, and nothing but powers, relating to several other bodies, and resulting from the different modifications of the original qualities, yet they are generally otherwise thought of. For the *second* sort, viz. the powers to produce several ideas in us, by our senses, are looked upon as real qualities in the things thus affecting us; but the *third* sort are called and esteemed barely powers, e.g., The idea of heat or light, which we receive by our eyes, or touch, from the sun, are commonly thought real qualities existing in the sun, and something more than mere powers in it. But when we consider the sun in reference to wax, which it melts or blanches, we look on the whiteness and softness produced in the wax, not as qualities in the sun, but effects produced by powers in it. Whereas, if rightly considered, these qualities of light and warmth, which are perceptions in me when I am warmed or enlightened by the sun, are no otherwise in the sun, than the changes made in the wax, when it is blanched or melted, are in the sun. They are all of them equally *powers in the sun, depending on its primary qualities;* whereby it is able, in the one case, so to alter the bulk, figure, texture, or motion of some of the insensible parts of my eyes or hands, as thereby to produce in me the idea of light or heat; and in the other, it is able so to alter the bulk, figure, texture, or motion of the insensible parts of the wax, as to make them fit to produce in me the distinct ideas of white and fluid.

25. The reason why the one are ordinarily taken for real qualities, and the other only for bare powers, seems to be, because the ideas we have of distinct colours, sounds, &c., containing nothing at all in them of bulk, figure, or motion, we are not apt to think them the effects of these primary qualities; which appear not, to our senses, to operate in their production, and with which they have not any apparent congruity or conceivable connexion. Hence it is that we are so forward to imagine, that those ideas are the resemblances of something really existing in the objects themselves: since sensation discovers nothing of bulk, figure, or motion of parts in their production; nor can reason show how bodies, *by their bulk, figure, and motion,* should produce in the mind the ideas of blue or yellow, &c. But, in the other case, in the operations of bodies changing the qualities one of another, we plainly discover that the quality produced hath commonly no resemblance with anything in the thing producing it; wherefore we look on it as a bare effect of power. For, through receiving the idea of heat or light from the sun, we are apt to think *it* is a perception and resemblance of such a quality in the sun; yet when we see wax, or a fair face, receive change of colour from the sun, we cannot imagine *that* to be the reception or resemblance of anything in the sun, because we find not those different colours in the sun itself. For, our senses being able to observe a likeness or unlikeness of sensible qualities in two different external objects, we forwardly enough conclude the production of any sensible quality in any subject to be an effect of bare power, and not the communication of any quality which was really in the efficient, when we find no such sensible quality in the thing that produced it. But our senses, not being able to discover any unlikeness between the idea produced in us, and the quality of the object producing it, we are apt to imagine that our ideas are resemblances of somthing in the objects, and not the effects of certain powers placed in the modification of their primary qualities, with which primary qualities the ideas produced in us have no resemblance.

26. To conclude. Beside those beforementioned primary qualities in bodies, viz. bulk, figure, extension, number; and motion of their solid parts; all the rest, whereby we take notice of bodies, and distinguish them one from another, are nothing else but several powers in them, depending on those primary qualities; whereby they are fitted, either by immediately operating on our bodies to produce several different ideas in us; or else, by operating on other bodies, so to change their primary qualities as to render them capable of producing ideas in us different from what before they did. The former of these, I

think, may be called secondary qualities *immediately perceivable;* the latter, secondary qualities, *mediately perceivable.*

OF OUR KNOWLEDGE OF THE EXISTENCE OF OTHER THINGS

1. The knowledge of our own being we have by intuition. The existence of a God, reason clearly makes known to us, as has been shown.

The knowledge of the existence of *any other thing* we can have only by *sensation:* for there being no necessary connexion of real existence with any *idea* a man hath in his memory; nor of any other existence but that of God with the existence of any particular man: no particular man can know the existence of any other being, but only when, by actual operating upon him, it makes itself perceived by him. For, the having the idea of anything in our mind, no more proves the existence of that thing, than the picture of a man evidences his being in the world, or the visions of a dream make thereby a true history.

2. It is therefore the *actual receiving* of ideas from without that gives us notice of the existence of other things, and makes us know, that something doth exist at that time without us, which causes that idea in us; though perhaps we neither know nor consider how it does it. For it takes not from the certainty of our senses, and the ideas we receive by them, that we know not the manner wherein they are produced: e.g. whilst I write this, I have, by the paper affecting my eyes, that idea produced in my mind, which, whatever object causes, I call *white;* by which I know that that quality or accident (i.e. whose appearance before my eyes always causes that idea) doth really exist, and hath a being without me. And of this, the greatest assurance I can possibly have, and to which my faculties can attain, is the testimony of my eyes, which are the proper and sole judges of this thing; whose testimony I have reason to rely on as so certain, that I can no more doubt, whilst I write this, that I see white and black, and that something really exists that causes that sensation in me, than that I write or move my hand; which is a certainty as great as human nature is capable of, concerning the existence of anything, but a man's self alone, and of God.

3. The notice we have by our senses of the existing of things without us, though it be not altogether so certain as our intuitive knowledge, or the deductions of our reason employed about the clear abstract ideas of our own minds; yet it is an assurance that deserves the name of *knowledge.* If we persuade ourselves that our faculties act and inform us right concerning the existence of those objects that affect them, it cannot pass for an illgrounded confidence: for I think nobody can, in earnest, be so sceptical as to be uncertain of the existence of those things which he sees and feels. At least, he that can doubt so far, (whatever he may have with his own thoughts,) will never have any controversy with me; since he can never be sure I say anything contrary to his own opinion. As to myself, I think God has given me assurance enough of the existence of things without me: since, by their different application, I can produce in myself both pleasure and pain, which is one great concernment of my present state. This is certain: the confidence that our faculties do not herein deceive us, is the greatest assurance we are capable of concerning the existence of material beings. For we cannot act anything but by our faculties; nor talk of knowledge itself, but by the help of those faculties which are fitted to apprehend even what knowledge is.

But besides the assurance we have from our senses themselves, that they do not err in the information they give us of the existence of things without us, when they are affected by them, we are further confirmed in this assurance by other concurrent reasons:—

4. I. It is plain those perceptions are produced in us by exterior causes affecting our senses: because those that want the *organs* of any sense, never can have the ideas belonging to that sense produced in their minds. This is too evident to be doubted: and therefore we cannot but be assured that they come in by the organs of that sense, and no other way. The organs themselves, it is plain, do not produce them: for then the eyes of a man in the dark would produce colours, and his nose smell roses in the winter: but we see nobody gets the relish of a pineapple, till he goes to the Indies, where it is, and tastes it.

5. II. Because sometimes I find that *I cannot avoid the having those ideas produced in my mind.* For though, when my eyes are shut, or windows fast, I can at pleasure recall to my mind the ideas of light, or the sun, which former sensations had lodged in my memory; so I can at pleasure lay by *that* idea, and take into my view that of the smell of a rose, or taste of sugar. But, if I turn my eyes at noon towards the sun, I cannot avoid the ideas which the light or sun then produces in me. So that there is a manifest difference between the ideas laid up in my memory, (over which, if they were there only, I should have constantly the same power to dispose of them, and lay them by at pleasure,) and those which force themselves upon me, and I cannot avoid having. And therefore it must needs be some exterior cause, and the brisk acting of some objects without me, whose efficacy I cannot resist, that produces those ideas in my mind, whether I will or no. Besides, there is nobody who doth not perceive the difference in himself between contemplating the sun, as he hath the idea of it in his memory, and actually looking upon it: of which two, his perception is so distinct, that few of his ideas are more distinguishable one from another. And therefore he hath certain knowledge that they are not *both* memory, or the actions of his mind, and fancies only within him; but that actual seeing hath a cause without.

6. III. Add to this, that many of those ideas are *produced in us with pain,* which afterwards we remember without the least offence. Thus, the pain of heat or cold, when the idea of it is revived in our minds, gives us no disturbance; which, when felt, was very troublesome; and is again, when actually repeated; which is occasioned by the disorder the external object causes in our bodies when applied to them: and we remember the pains of hunger, thirst, or the headache, without any pain at all; which would either never disturb us, or else constantly do it, as often as we thought of it, were there nothing more but ideas floating in our minds, and appearances entertaining our fancies, without the real existence of things affecting us from abroad. The same may be said of *pleasure,* accompanying several actual sensations. And though mathematical demonstration depends not upon sense, yet the examining them by diagrams gives great credit to the evidence of our sight, and seems to give it a certainty approaching to that of demonstration itself. For, it would be very strange, that a man should allow it for an undeniable truth, that two angles of a figure, which he measures by lines and angles of a diagram, should be bigger one than the other, and yet doubt of the existence of those lines and angles, which by looking on he makes use of to measure that by.

7. IV. Our *senses* in many cases *bear witness to the truth of each other's report,* concerning the existence of sensible things without us. He that *sees* a fire, may, if he doubt whether it be anything more than a bare fancy, *feel* it too; and be convinced, by putting his hand in it. Which certainly could never be put into such exquisite pain by a bare idea or phantom, unless that the pain be a fancy too: which yet he cannot, when the burn is well, by raising the idea of it, bring upon himself again.

Thus I see, whilst I write this, I can change the appearance of the paper; and by designing the letters, tell *beforehand* what new idea it shall exhibit the very next moment, by barely drawing my pen over it: which will neither appear (let me fancy as much as I will) if my hands stand still; or though I move my pen, if my eyes be shut: nor, when those characters are once made on the paper, can I choose afterwards but see them as they are; that is, have the ideas of such letters as I have made. Whence it is manifest, that they are not barely the sport and play of my own imagination, when I find that the characters that were made at the pleasure of my own thoughts, do not obey them; nor yet cease to be, whenever I shall fancy it, but continue to affect my senses constantly and regularly, according to the figures I made them. To which if we will add, that the sight of those shall, from another man, draw such sounds as I beforehand design they shall stand for, there will be little reason left to doubt that those words I write do really exist without me, when they cause a long series of regular sounds to affect my ears, which could not be the effect of my imagination, nor could my memory retain them in that order.

8. But yet, if after all this any one will be so sceptical as to distrust his senses, and to affirm

that all we see and hear, feel and taste, think and do, during our whole being, is but the series and deluding appearances of a long dream, whereof there is no reality; and therefore will question the existence of all things, or our knowledge of anything: I must desire him to consider, that, if all be a dream, then he doth but dream that he makes the question, and so it is not much matter that a waking man should answer him. But yet, if he pleases, he may dream that I make him this answer, That the certainty of things existing in *rerum natura* when we have the testimony of our senses for it is not only as great as our frame can attain to, but as our condition needs. For, our faculties being suited not to the full extent of being, nor to a perfect, clear, comprehensive knowledge of things free from all doubt and scruple; but to the preservation of us, in whom they are; and accommodated to the use of life: they serve to our purpose well enough, if they will but give us certain notice of those things, which are convenient or inconvenient to us. For he that sees a candle burning, and hath experimented the force of its flame by putting his finger in it, will little doubt that this is something existing without him, which does him harm, and puts him to great pain: which is assurance enough, when no man requires greater certainty to govern his actions by than what is as certain as his actions themselves. And if our dreamer pleases to try whether the glowing heat of a glass furnace be barely a wandering imagination in a drowsy man's fancy, by putting his hand into it, he may perhaps be wakened into a certainty greater than he could wish, that it is something more than bare imagination. So that this evidence is as great as we can desire, being as certain to us as our pleasure or pain, i.e. happiness or misery; beyond which we have no concernment, either of knowing or being. Such an assurance of the existene of things without us is sufficient to direct us in the attaining the good and avoiding the evil which is caused by them, which is the important concernment we have of being made acquainted with them.

9. In fine, then, when our senses do actually convey into our understandings any idea, we cannot but be satisfied that there doth something *at that time* really exist without us, which doth affect our senses, and by them give notice of itself to our apprehensive faculties, and actually produce that idea which we then perceive: and we cannot so far distrust their testimony, as to doubt that such *collections* of simple ideas as we have observed by our senses to be united together, do really exist together. But this knowledge extends as far as the present testimony of our senses, employed about particular objects that do then affect them, and no further. For if I saw such a collection of simple ideas as is wont to be called *man,* existing together one minute since, and am now alone, I cannot be certain that the same man exists now, since there is no *necessary connexion* of his existence a minute since with his existence now: by a thousand ways he may cease to be, since I had the testimony of my senses for his existence. And if I cannot be certain that the man I saw last today is now in being, I can less be certain that he is so who hath been longer removed from my senses, and I have not seen since yesterday, or since the last year: and much less can I be certain of the existence of men that I never saw. And, therefore, though it be highly probable that millions of men do now exist, yet, whilst I am alone, writing this, I have not that certainty of it which we strictly call knowledge; though the great likelihood of it puts me past doubt, and it be reasonable for me to do several things upon the confidence that there are men (and men also of my acquaintance, with whom I have to do) now in the world: but this is but probability, not knowledge.

10. Whereby yet we may observe how foolish and vain a thing it is for a man of a narrow knowledge, who having reason given him to judge of the different evidence and probability of things, and to be swayed accordingly; how vain, I say, it is to expect demonstration and certainty in things not capable of it; and refuse assent to very rational propositions, and act contrary to very plain and clear truths, because they cannot be made out so evident, as to surmount every the least (I will not say reason, but) pretence of doubting. He that, in the ordinary affairs of life, would admit of nothing but direct plain demonstration, would be sure of nothing in this world, but of perishing quickly. The wholesomeness of his meat or drink would not give him reason to venture on it: and I would fain know what it is he could do upon such grounds as are capable of no doubt, no objection.

Of the Principles of Human Knowledge

GEORGE BERKELEY

George Berkeley (1685–1753), the Anglican Bishop of Cloyne, was born in Ireland.

PART I

1. It is evident to anyone who takes a survey of the objects of human knowledge, that they are either ideas actually imprinted on the senses, or else such as are perceived by attending to the passions and operations of the mind, or lastly ideas formed by help of memory and imagination, either compounding, dividing, or barely representing those originally perceived in the aforesaid ways. By sight I have the ideas of light and colours with their several degrees and variations. By touch I perceive, for example, hard and soft, heat and cold, motion and resistance, and of all these more and less either as to quantity or degree. Smelling furnishes me with odours; the palate with tastes, and hearing conveys sounds to the mind in all their variety of tone and composition. And as several of these are observed to accompany each other, they come to be marked by one name, and so to be reputed as one thing. Thus, for example, a certain colour, taste, smell, figure and consistence having been observed to go together, are accounted one distinct thing, signified by the name *apple*. Other collections of ideas constitute a stone, a tree, a book, and the like sensible things; which, as they are pleasing or disagreeable, excite the passions of love, hatred, joy, grief, and so forth.

2. But besides all that endless variety of ideas or objects of knowledge, there is likewise something which knows or perceives them, and exercises divers operations, as willing, imagining, remembering about them. This perceiving, active being is what I call *mind, spirit, soul* or *myself*. By which words I do not denote any one of my ideas, but a thing entirely distinct from them, wherein they exist, or, which is the same thing, whereby they are perceived; for the existence of an idea consists in being perceived.

3. That neither our thoughts, nor passions, nor ideas formed by the imagination, exist without the mind, is what everybody will allow. And it seems no less evident that the various sensations or ideas imprinted on the sense, however blended or combined together (that is, whatever objects they compose) cannot exist otherwise than in a mind perceiving them. I think an intuitive knowledge may be obtained of this, by anyone that shall attend to what is meant by the term *exist* when applied to sensible things. The table I write on, I say, exists, that is, I see and feel it; and if I were out of my study I should say it existed, meaning thereby that if I was in my study I might perceive it, or that some other spirit actually does perceive it. There was an odour, that is, it was smelled; there was a sound, that is to say, it was heard; a colour or figure, and it was perceived by sight or touch. This is all that I can understand by these and the like expressions. For as to what is said of the absolute existence of unthinking things without any relation to their being perceived, that seems perfectly unintelligible. Their *esse* is *percipi*, nor is it possible they should have any existence, out of the minds or thinking things which perceive them.

4. It is indeed an opinion strangely prevailing amongst men, that houses, mountains, rivers, and in a word all sensible objects have an existence natural or real, distinct from their being perceived by the understanding. But with how great an assurance and acquiescence soever this principle may be entertained in the world; yet whoever shall find in his heart to call it in question, may,

---

First published in 1710.

if I mistake not, perceive it to involve a manifest contradiction. For what are the forementioned objects but the things we perceive by sense, and what do we perceive besides our own ideas or sensations; and is it not plainly repugnant that any one of these or any combination of them should exist unperceived?

5. If we thoroughly examine this tenet, it will, perhaps, be found at bottom to depend on the doctrine of *abstract ideas*. For can there be a nicer strain of abstraction than to distinguish the existence of sensible objects from their being perceived, so as to conceive them existing unperceived? Light and colours, heat and cold, extension and figures, in a word the things we see and feel, what are they but so many sensations, notions, ideas or impressions on the sense; and is it possible to separate, even in thought, any of these from perception? For my part I might as easily divide a thing from itself. I may indeed divide in my thoughts or conceive apart from each other those things which, perhaps, I never perceived by sense so divided. Thus I imagine the trunk of a human body without the limbs, or conceive the smell of a rose without thinking on the rose itself. So far I will not deny I can abstract, if that may properly be called *abstraction,* which extends only to the conceiving separately such objects, as it is possible may really exist or be actually perceived asunder. But my conceiving or imagining power does not extend beyond the possibility of real existence or perception. Hence as it is impossible for me to see or feel anything without an actual sensation of that thing, so is it impossible for me to conceive in my thoughts any sensible thing or object distinct from the sensation or perception of it.

6. Some truths there are so near and obvious to the mind, that a man need only open his eyes to see them. Such I take this important one to be, to wit, that all the choir of heaven and furniture of the earth, in a word all those bodies which compose the mighty frame of the world, have not any subsistence, without a mind, that their being is to be perceived or known; that consequently so long as they are not actually perceived by me, or do not exist in my mind or that of any other created spirit, they must either have no existence at all, or else subsist in the mind of some eternal spirit: it

being perfectly unintelligible and involving all the absurdity of abstraction, to attribute to any single part of them an existence independent of a spirit. To be coninced of which, the reader need only reflect and try to separate in his own thoughts the being of a sensible thing from its being perceived.

7. From what has been said, it follows, there is not any other substance than *spirit,* or that which perceives. But for the fuller proof of this point, let it be considered, the sensible qualities are colour, figure, motion, smell, taste, and such like, that is, the ideas perceived by sense. Now for an idea to exist in an unperceiving thing, is a manifest contradiction; for to have an idea is all one as to perceive; that therefore wherein colour, figure, and the like qualities exist, must perceive them; hence it is clear there can be no unthinking substance or *substratum* of those ideas.

8. But say you, though the ideas themselves do not exist without the mind, yet there may be things like them whereof they are copies or resemblances, which things exist without the mind, in an unthinking substance. I answer, an idea can be like nothing but an idea; a colour or figure can be like nothing but another colour or figure. If we look but ever so little into our thoughts, we shall find it impossible for us to conceive a likeness except only between our ideas. Again, I ask whether these supposed originals or external things, of which our ideas are the pictures or representations, be themselves perceivable or no? If they are, then they are ideas, and we have gained our point; but if you say they are not, I appeal to anyone whether it be sense, to assert a colour is like something which is invisible, hard or soft, like something which is intangible; and so of the rest.

9. Some there are who make a distinction betwixt *primary* and *secondary* qualities: by the former, they mean extension, figure, motion, rest, solidity or impenetrability and number: by the latter they denote all other sensible qualities, as colours, sounds, tastes, and so forth. The ideas we have of these they acknowledge not to be the resemblances of anything existing without the mind or unperceived; but they will have our ideas of the primary qualities to be patterns or

images of things which exist without the mind, in an unthinking substance which they call *matter.* By matter therefore we are to understand an inert, senseless substance, in which extension, figure, and motion, do actually subsist. But it is evident from what we have already shewn, that extension, figure and motion are only ideas existing in the mind, and that an idea can be like nothing but another idea, and that consequently neither they nor their archetypes can exist in an unperceiving substance. Hence it is plain, that the very notion of what is called *matter* or *corporeal substance,* involves a contradiction in it.

10. They who assert that figure, motion, and the rest of the primary or original qualities do exist without the mind, in unthinking substances, do at the same time acknowledge that colours, sounds, heat, cold, and such like secondary qualities, do not, which they tell us are sensations existing in the mind alone, that depend on and are occasioned by the different size, texture and motion of the minute particles of matter. This they take for an undoubted truth, which they can demonstrate beyond all exception. Now if it be certain, that those original qualities are inseparably united with the other sensible qualities, and not, even in thought, capable of being abstracted from them, it plainly follows that they exist only in the mind. But I desire anyone to reflect and try, whether he can by any abstraction of thought, conceive the extension and motion of a body, without all other sensible qualities. For my own part, I see evidently that it is not in my power to frame an idea of a body extended and moved, but I must withal give it some colour or other sensible quality which is acknowledged to exist only in the mind. In short, extension, figure, and motion, abstracted from all other qualities, are inconceivable. Where therefore the other sensible qualities are, there must these be also, to wit, in the mind and nowhere else.

11. Again, *great* and *small, swift* and *slow,* are allowed to exist nowhere without the mind, being entirely relative, and changing as the frame or position of the organs of sense varies. The extension therefore which exists without the mind, is neither great nor small, the motion neither swift nor slow, that is, they are nothing

at all. But say you, they are extension in general, and motion in general; thus we see how much the tenet of extended, moveable substances existing without the mind, depends on that strange doctrine of *abstract ideas.* And here I cannot but remark, how nearly the vague and indeterminate description of matter or corporeal substance, which the modern philosophers are run into by their own principles, resembles that antiquated and so much ridiculed notion of *materia prima,* to be met with in Aristotle and his followers. Without extension solidity cannot be conceived; since therefore it has been shewn that extension exists not in an unthinking substance, the same must also be true of solidity.

12. That number is entirely the creature of the mind, even though the other qualities be allowed to exist without, will be evident to whoever considers, that the same thing bears a different denomination of number as the mind views it with different respects. Thus, the same extension is one or three or thirty-six, according as the mind considers it with reference to a yard, a foot, or an inch. Number is so visibly relative, and dependent on men's understanding, that it is strange to think how anyone should give it an absolute existence without the mind. We say one book, one page, one line; all these are equally units, though some contain several of the others. And in each instance it is plain, the unit relates to some particular combination of ideas arbitrarily put together by the mind.

13. Unity I know some will have to be a simple or uncompounded idea, accompanying all other ideas into the mind. That I have any such idea answering the word *unity,* I do not find; and if I had, methinks I could not miss finding it; on the contrary it should be the most familiar to my understanding, since it is said to accompany all other ideas, and to be perceived by all the ways of sensation and reflexion. To say no more, it is an *abstract idea.*

14. I shall farther add, that after the same manner, as modern philosophers prove certain sensible qualities to have no existence in matter, or without the mind, the same thing may be likewise proved of all other sensible qualities whatsoever. Thus, for instance, it is said that heat and cold are affections only of the mind, and not at

all patterns of real beings, existing in the corporeal substances which excite them, for that the same body which appears cold to one hand, seems warm to another. Now why may we not as well argue that figure and extension are not patterns or resemblances of qualities existing in matter, because to the same eye at different stations, or eyes of a different texture at the same station, they appear various, and cannot therefore be the images of anything settled and determinate without the mind? Again, it is proved that sweetness is not really in the sapid thing because the thing remaining unaltered the sweetness is changed into bitter, as in case of a fever or otherwise vitiated palate. Is it not as reasonable to say, that motion is not without the mind, since if the succession of ideas in the mind become swifter, the motion, it is acknowledged, shall appear slower without any alteration in any external object.

15. In short, let anyone consider those arguments, which are thought manifestly to prove that colours and tastes exist only in the mind, and he shall find they may with equal force, be brought to prove the same thing of extension, figure, and motion? Though it must be confessed this method of arguing doth not so much prove that there is no extension or colour in an outward object, as that we do not know by sense which is the true extension or colour of the object. But the arguments foregoing plainly shew it to be impossible that any colour or extension at all, or other sensible quality whatsoever, should exist in an unthinking subject without the mind, or in truth, that there should be any such thing as an outward object.

16. But let us examine a little the received opinion. It is said extension is a mode or accident of matter, and that matter is the *substratum* that supports it. Now I desire that you would explain what is meant by matter's *supporting* extension: say you, I have no idea of matter, and therefore cannot explain it. I answer, though you have no positive, yet if you have any meaning at all, you must at least have a relative idea of matter; though you know not what it is, yet you must be supposed to know what relation it bears to accidents, and what is meant by its supporting them. It is evident *support* cannot here be taken

in its usual or literal sense, as when we say that pillars support a building: in what sense therefore must it be taken?

17. If we inquire into what the most accurate philosophers declare themselves to mean by *material substance;* we shall find them acknowledge, they have no other meaning annexed to those sounds, but the idea of being in general, together with the relative notion of its supporting accidents. The general idea of being appeareth to me the most abstract and incomprehensible of all other; and as for its supporting accidents, this, as we have just now observed, cannot be understood in the common sense of those words; it must therefore be taken in some other sense, but what that is they do not explain. So that when I consider the two parts or branches which make the signification of the words *material substance,* I am convinced there is no distinct meaning annexed to them. But why should we trouble ourselves any farther, in discussing this material *substratum* or support of figure and motion, and other sensible qualities? Does it not suppose they have an existence without the mind? And is not this a direct repugnancy, and altogether inconceivable?

18. But though it were possible that solid, figured, moveable substances may exist without the mind, corresponding to the ideas we have of bodies, yet how is it possible for us to know this? Either we must know it by sense, or by reason. As for our senses, by them we have the knowledge only of our sensations, ideas, or those things that are immediately perceived by sense, call them what you will: but they do not inform us that things exist without the mind, or unperceived, like to those which are perceived. This the materials themselves acknowledge. It remains therefore that if we have any knowledge at all of external things, it must be by reason, inferring their existence from what is immediately perceived by sense. But what reason can induce us to believe the existence of bodies without the mind, from what we perceive, since the very patrons of matter themselves do not pretend, there is any necessary connexion betwixt them and our ideas? I say it is granted on all hands (and what happens in dreams, phrensies, and the like, puts it beyond dispute) that it is possible

we might be affected with all the ideas we have now, though no bodies existed without, resembling them. Hence it is evident the supposition of external bodies is not necessary for the producing our ideas: since it is granted they are produced sometimes, and might possibly be produced always in the same order we see them in at present, without their concurrence.

19. But though we might possibly have all our sensations without them, yet perhaps it may be thought easier to conceive and explain the manner of their production, by supposing external bodies in their likeness rather than otherwise; and so it might be at least probable there are such things as bodies that excite their ideas in our minds. But neither can this be said; for though we give the materialists their external bodies, they by their own confession are never the nearer knowing how our ideas are produced; since they own themselves unable to comprehend in what manner body can act upon spirit, or how it is possible it should imprint any idea in the mind. Hence it is evident the production of ideas or sensations in our minds, can be no reason why we should suppose matter or corporeal substances, since that is acknowledged to remain equally inexplicable with, or without this supposition. If therefore it were possible for bodies to exist without the mind, yet to hold they do so, must needs be a very precarious opinion; since it is to suppose, without any reason at all, that God has created innumerable beings that are entirely useless, and serve to no manner of purpose.

20. In short, if there were external bodies, it is impossible we should ever come to know it; and if there were not, we might have the very same reasons to think there were that we have now. Suppose, what no one can deny possible, an intelligence, without the help of external bodies, to be affected with the same train of sensations or ideas that you are, imprinted in the same order and with like vividness in his mind. I ask whether that intelligence hath not all the reason to believe the existence of corporeal substances, represented by his ideas, and exciting them in his mind, that you can possibly have for believing the same thing? Of this there can be no question; which one consideration is enough to make any reasonable person suspect the strength of whatever arguments he may think himself to have, for the existence of bodies without the mind.

21. Were it necessary to add any farther proof against the existence of matter, after what has been said, I could instance several of those errors and difficulties (not to mention impieties) which have sprung from that tenet. It has occasioned numberless controversies and disputes in philosophy, and not a few of far greater moment in religion. But I shall not enter into the detail of them in this place, as well because I think, arguments *a posteriori* are unnecessary for confirming what has been, if I mistake not, sufficiently demonstrated *a priori*, as because I shall hereafter find occasion to say somewhat of them.

22. I am afraid I have given cause to think me needlessly prolix in handling this subject. For to what purpose is it to dilate on that which may be demonstrated with the utmost evidence in a line or two, to anyone that is capable of the least reflexion? It is but looking into your own thoughts, and so trying whether you can conceive it possible for a sound, or figure, or motion, or colour, to exist without the mind, or unperceived. This easy trial may make you see, that what you contend for, is a downright contradiction. Insomuch that I am content to put the whole upon this issue; if you can but conceive it possible for one extended moveable substance, or in general, for any one idea or anything like an idea, to exist otherwise than in a mind perceiving it, I shall readily give up the cause: and as for all that *compages* of external bodies which you contend for, I shall grant you its existence, though you cannot either give me any reason why you believe it exists, or assign any use to it when it is supposed to exist. I say, the bare possibility of your opinion's being true, shall pass for an argument that it is so.

23. But you say, surely there is nothing easier than to imagine trees, for instance, in a park, or books existing in a closet, and nobody by to perceive them. I answer, you may so, there is no difficulty in it: but what is all this, I beseech you, more then framing in your mind certain ideas which you call *books* and *trees,* and at the same time omitting to frame the idea of anyone that may perceive them? But do not you yourself

perceive or think of them all the while? This therefore is nothing to the purpose: it only shows you have the power of imagining or forming ideas in your mind; but it doth not shew that you can conceive it possible, the objects of your thought may exist without the mind: to make out this, it is necessary that you conceive them existing unconceived or unthought of, which is a manifest repugnancy. When we do our utmost to conceive the existence of external bodies, we are all the while only contemplating our own ideas. But the mind taking no notice of itself, is deluded to think it can and doth conceive bodies existing unthought of or without the mind; though at the same time they are apprehended by or exist in itself. A little attention will discover to anyone the truth and evidence of what is here said, and make it unnecessary to insist on any other proofs against the existence of material substance.

24. It is very obvious, upon the least inquiry into our own thoughts, to know whether it be possible for us to understand what is meant, by the *absolute existence of sensible objects in themselves, or without the mind.* To me it is evident those words mark out either a direct contradiction, or else nothing at all. And to convince others of this, I know no readier or fairer way, than to entreat they would calmly attend to their own thoughts: and if by this attention, the emptiness or repugnancy of those expressions does appear, surely nothing more is requisite for their conviction. It is on this therefore that I insist, to wit, that the absolute existence of unthinking things are words without a meaning, or which include a contradiction. This is what I repeat and inculcate, and earnestly recommend to the attentive thoughts of the reader.

25. All our ideas, sensations, or the thing which we perceive, by whatsoever names they may be distinguished, are visibly inactive, there is nothing of power or agency included in them. So that one idea or object of thought cannot produce, or make any alteration in another. To be satisfied of the truth of this, there is nothing else requisite but a bare observation of our ideas. For since they and every part of them exist only in the mind, it follows that there is nothing in them but what is perceived. But whoever shall attend to his ideas, whether of sense or reflexion, will not perceive in them any power or activity; there is therefore no such thing contained in them. A little attention will discover to us that the very being of an idea implies passiveness and inertness in it, insomuch that it is impossible for an idea to do anything, or, strictly speaking, to be the cause of anything: neither can it be the resemblance or pattern of any active being, as is evident from *Sect.* 8. Whence it plainly follows that extension, figure and motion, cannot be the cause of our sensations. To say therefore, that these are the effects of powers resulting from the configuration, number, motion, and size of corpuscles, must certainly be false.

26. We perceive a continual succession of ideas, some are a new excited, others are changed or totally disappear. There is therefore some cause of these ideas whereon they depend, and which produces and changes them. That this cause cannot be any quality or idea or combination of ideas, is clear from the preceding section. It must therefore be a substance; but it has been shewn that there is no corporeal or material substance; it remains therefore that the cause of ideas is an incorporeal active substance or spirit.

27. A spirit is one simple, undivided, active being: as it perceives ideas, it is called the *understanding,* and as it produces or otherwise operates about them, it is called the *will.* Hence there can be no idea formed of a soul or spirit: for all ideas whatever, being passive and inert, *vide Sect.* 25, they cannot represent unto us, by way of image or likeness, that which acts. A little attention will make it plain to anyone, that to have an idea which shall be like that active principle of motion and change of ideas, is absolutely impossible. Such is the nature of *spirit* or that which acts, that it cannot be of itself perceived, but only by the effects which it produceth. If any man shall doubt of the truth of what is here delivered, let him but reflect and try if he can frame the idea of any power or active being; and whether he hath ideas of two principal powers, marked by the names *will* and *understanding,* distinct from each other as well as from a third idea of

substance or being in general, with a relative notion of its supporting or being the subject of the aforesaid powers, which is signified by the name *soul* or *spirit.* This is what some hold; but so far as I can see, the words *will, soul, spirit,* do not stand for different ideas, or in truth, for any idea at all, but for something which is very different from ideas, and which being an agent cannot be like unto, or represented by, any idea whatsoever. Though it must be owned at the same time, that we have some notion of soul, spirit, and the operations of the mind, such as willing loving, hating, in as much as we known or understand the meaning of those words.

28. I find I can excite ideas in my mind at pleasure, and vary and shift the scene as oft as I think fit. It is no more than willing, and straightway this or that idea arises in my fancy: and by the same power it is obliterated, and makes way for another. This making and unmaking of ideas doth very properly denominate the mind active. Thus much is certain, and grounded on experience: but when we talk of unthinking agents, or of exciting ideas exclusive of volition, we only amuse ourselves with words.

29. But whatever power I may have over my own thoughts, I find the ideas actually perceived by sense have not a like dependence on my will. When it broad day-light I open my eyes, it is not in my power to choose whether I shall see or no, or to determine what particular objects shall present themselves to my view; and so likewise as to the hearing and other senses, the ideas imprinted on them are not creatures of my will. There is therefore some other will or spirit that produces them.

30. The ideas of sense are more strong, lively, and distinct than those of the imagination; they have likewise a steadiness, order, and coherence, and are not excited at random, as those which are the effects of human wills often are, but in a regular train or series, the admirable connexion whereof sufficiently testifies the wisdom and benevolence of its Author. Now the set rules or established methods, wherein the mind we depend on excites in us the ideas of sense, are called the *Laws of Nature:* and these we learn by experience, which teaches

us that such and such ideas are attended with such and such other ideas, in the ordinary course of things.

31. This gives us a sort of foresight, which enables us to regulate our actions for the benefit of the life. And without this we should be eternally at a loss: we could not know how to act anything that might procure us the least pleasure, or remove the least pain of sense. That food nourishes, sleep refreshes, and fire warms us; that to sow in the seed-time is the way to reap in the harvest, and, in general, that to obtain such or such ends, such or such means are conducive, all this we know, not by discovering any necessary connexion between our ideas, but only by the observation of the settled Laws of Nature, without which we should be all in uncertainty and confusion, and a grown man no more know how to manage himself in the affairs of life, than an infant just born.

32. And yet this consistent uniform working, which so evidently displays the goodness and wisdom of that governing spirit whose will constitutes the Laws of Nature, is so far from leading our thoughts to him, that it rather sends them a wandering after second causes. For when we perceive certain ideas of sense constantly followed by other ideas, and we know this is not of our doing, we forthwith attribute power and agency to the ideas themselves, and make one the cause of another, than which nothing can be more absurd and unintelligible. Thus, for example, having observed that when we perceive by sight a certain round luminous figure, we at the same time perceive by touch the idea of sensation called *heat,* we do from thence conclude the sun to be the cause of heat. And in like manner perceiving the motion and collision of bodies to be attended with sound, we are inclined to think the latter an effect of the former.

33. The ideas imprinted on the senses by the Author of Nature are called *real things:* and those excited in the imagination being less regular, vivid and constant, are more properly termed *ideas,* or *images of things,* which they copy and represent. But then our sensations, be they never so vivid and distinct, are nevertheless *ideas,* that is, they exist in the mind, or are perceived by it, as truly as the ideas of its own

framing. The ideas of sense are allowed to have more reality in them, that is, to be more strong, orderly, and coherent than the creatures of the mind; but this is no argument that they exist without the mind. They are also less dependent on the spirit, or thinking substance which perceives them, in that they are excited by the will of another and more powerful spirit: yet still they are *ideas,* and certainly no *idea,* whether faint or strong, can exist otherwise than in a mind perceiving it.

34. Before we proceed any farther, it is necessary to spend some time in answering objections which may probably be made against the principles hitherto laid down. In doing of which, if I seem too prolix of those of quick apprehensions, I hope it may be pardoned, since all men do not equally apprehend things of this nature; and I am willing to be understood by everyone. First then, it will be objected that by the foregoing principles, all that is real and substantial in Nature is banished out of the world: and instead a chimerical scheme of ideas takes place. All things that exist, exist only in the mind, that is, they are purely notional. What therefore becomes of the sun, moon, and stars? What must we think of houses, rivers, mountains, trees, stones; nay, even of our own bodies? Are all these but so many chimeras and illusions on the fancy? To all which, and whatever else of the same sort may be objected, I answer, that by the principles premised, we are not deprived of any one thing in Nature. Whatever we see, feel, hear or any wise conceive or understand, remains as secure as ever, and is as real as ever. There is a *rerum natura,* and the distinction between realities and chimeras retains its full force. This is evident from *Sect.* 29, 30, and 33, where we have shewn what is meant by *real things* in opposition to *chimeras,* or ideas of our own framing; but then they both equally exist in the mind, and in that sense are alike *ideas.*

35. I do not argue against the existence of any one thing that we can apprehend, either by sense or reflexion. That the things I see with mine eyes and touch with my hands do exist, really exist, I make not the least question. The only thing whose existence we deny, is that which philosophers call matter or corporeal substance. And in doing of this, there is no damage done to the rest of mankind, who, I dare say, will never miss it. The atheist indeed will want the colour of an empty name to support this impiety; and the philosophers may possibly find, they have lost a great handle for trifling and disputation.

36. If any man thinks this detracts from the existence or reality of things, he is very far from understanding what hath been premised in the plainest terms I could think of. Take here an abstract of what has been said. There are spiritual substances, minds, or human souls, which will or excite ideas in themselves at pleasure: but these are faint, weak, and unsteady in respect of others they perceive by sense, which being impressed upon them according to certain rules or laws of Nature, speak themselves the effects of a mind more powerful and wise than human spirits. These latter are said to have more *reality* in them than the former: by which is meant that they are more affecting, orderly, and distinct, and that they are not fictions of the mind perceiving them. And in this sense, the sun that I see by day is the real sun, and that which I imagine by night is the idea of the former. In the sense here given of *reality,* it is evident that every vegetable, star, mineral, and in general each part of the mundane system, is as much a *real being* by our principles as by any other. Whether others mean anything by the term *reality* different from what I do, I entreat them to look into their own thoughts and see.

Of the Existence of a Material World

THOMAS REID

Thomas Reid (1710–1796) was, next to Hume, the most influential Scottish philosopher.

It is beyond our power to say when, or in what order, we came by our notions of these qualities. When we trace the operations of our minds as far back as memory and reflection can carry us, we find them already in possession of our imagination and belief, and quite familiar to the mind: but how they came first into acquaintance, or what has given them so strong a hold of our belief, and what regard they deserve, are, no doubt, very important questions in the philosophy of human nature.

Shall we, with the Bishop of Cloyne,[1] serve them with a *quo warranto,*[2] and have them tried at the bar of philosophy, upon the statute of the ideal system?[3] Indeed, in this trial they seem to have come off very pitifully; for, although they had very able counsel, learned in the law— viz., Descartes, Malebranche, and Locke, who said everything they could for their clients—the Bishop of Cloyne, believing them to be aiders and abetters of heresy and schism, prosecuted them with great vigour, fully answered all that had been pleaded in their defence, and silenced their ablest advocates, who seem, for half a century past, to decline the argument, and to trust to the favour of the jury rather than to the strength of their pleadings.

Thus, the wisdom of *philosophy* is set in opposition to the *common sense* of mankind. The first pretends to demonstrate, *a priori,* that there can be no such thing as a material world; that sun, moon, stars, and earth, vegetable and animal bodies, are, and can be nothing else, but sensations in the mind, or images of those sensations in the memory and imagination; that, like pain and joy, they can have no existence when they are not thought of. The last can conceive no otherwise of this opinion, that as a kind of metaphysical lunacy, and concludes that too much learning is apt to make men mad; and that the man who seriously entertains this belief, though in other respects he may be a very good man, as a man may be who believes that he is made of glass; yet, surely he hath a soft place in his understanding, and hath been hurt by much thinking.

This opposition betwixt philosophy and common sense is apt to have a very unhappy influence upon the philosopher himself. He sees human nature in an odd, unamiable, and mortifying light. He considers himself, and the rest of his species, as born under a necessity of believing ten thousand absurdities and contradictions, and endowed with such a pittance of reason as is just sufficient to make this unhappy discovery: and this is all the fruit of his profound speculations. Such notions of human nature tend to slacken every nerve of the soul, to put every noble purpose and sentiment out of countenance, and spread a melancholy gloom over the whole face of things.

If this is wisdom let me be deluded with the vulgar. I find something within me that recoils against it, and inspires more reverent sentiments of the human kind, and of the universal administration. Common Sense and Reason have both one author; that Almighty Author in all whose other works we observe a consistency, uniformity, and beauty which charm and delight the understanding: there must, therefore, be some order and consistency in the human faculties, as well as in other parts of his workmanship. A man that thinks reverently of his own kind, and

From Thomas Reid, *Inquiry into the Human Mind on the Principles of Common Sense,* Chapter V, Section VII. First published in 1764.

esteems true wisdom and philosophy, will not be fond, nay, will be very suspicious, of such strange and paradoxical opinions. If they are false, they disgrace philosophy; and, if they are true, they degrade the human species, and make us justly ashamed of our frame.

To what purpose is it for philosophy to decide against common sense in this or any other matter? The belief of a material world is older, and of more authority, than any principles of philosophy. It declines the tribunal of reason, and laughs at all the artillery of the logician. It retains its sovereign authority in spite of all the edicts of philosophy, and reason itself must stoop to its orders. Even those philosophers who have disowned the authority of our notions of an external material world, confess that they find themselves under a necessity of submitting to their power.

Methinks, therefore, it were better to make a virtue of necessity; and, since we cannot get rid of the vulgar notion and belief of an external world, to reconcile our reason to it as well as we can; for, if Reason should stomach and fret ever so much at this yoke, she cannot throw it off; if she will not be the servant of Common Sense, she must be her slave.

In order, therefore, to reconcile Reason to Common Sense in this matter, I beg leave to offer to the consideration of philosophers these two observations. First, that, in all this debate about the existence of a material world, it hath been taken for granted on both sides, that this same material world, if any such there be, must be the express image of our sensations; that we can have no conception of any material thing which is not like some sensation in our minds; and particularly that the sensations of touch are images of extension, hardness, figure, and motion. Every argument brought against the existence of a material world, either by the Bishop of Cloyne, or by the author of the "Treatise of Human Nature,"[4] by supposeth this. If this is true, their arguments are conclusive and unanswerable; but, on the other hand, if it is not true, there is no shadow of argument left. Have those philosophers, then, given any solid proof of this hypothesis, upon which the whole weight of so strange a system rests? No. They have not so

much as attempted to do it. But, because ancient and modern philosophers have agreed in this opinion, they have taken it for granted. But let us, as becomes philosophers, lay aside authority; we need not, surely, consult Aristotle or Locke, to know whether pain be like the point of a sword. I have as clear a conception of extension, hardness, and motion, as I have of the point of sword; and, with some pains and practice, I can form as clear a notion of the other sensations of touch as I have of pain. When I do so, and compare them together, it appears to me clear as daylight, that the former are not of kin to the latter, nor resemble them in any one feature. They are as unlike, yea as certainly and manifestly unlike, as pain is to the point of a sword. It may be true, that those sensations first introduced the material world to our acquaintance; it may be true, that it seldom or never appears without their company; but, for all that, they are as unlike as the passion of anger is to those features of the countenance which attend it.

So that, in the sentence those philosophers have passed against the material world, there is an *error personae*.[5] Their proof touches not matter, or any of its qualities; but strikes directly against an idol of their own imagination, a material world made of ideas and sensations, which never had nor can have an existence.

Secondly, the very existence of our conceptions of extension, figure and motion, since they are neither ideas of sensation nor reflection, overturns the whole ideal system, by which the material world hath been tried and condemned so that there hath been likewise in this sentence an *error juris.*[6]

It is a very fine and just observation of Locke, that, as no human art can create a single particle of matter, and the whole extent of our power over the material world consists in compounding, combining, and disjoining the matter made to our hands; so, in the world of thought, the materials are all made by nature, and can only be variously combined and disjoined by us. So that it is impossible for reason or prejudice, true or false philosophy, to produce one simple notion or conception, which is not the work of nature, and the result of our constitution. The conception of extension, motion, and the other attributes of matter, cannot be the effect of error or prejudice; it must be the work of nature. And the power or faculty by which we acquire those conceptions, must be something different from any power of the human mind that hath been explained, since it is neither sensation nor reflection.

This I would, therefore, humbly propose, as an *experimentum crucis*,[7] by which the ideal system must stand or fall; and it brings the matter to a short issue: Extension, figure, motion, may, any one or all of them, be taken for the subject of this experiment. Either they are ideas of sensation, or they are not. If any one of them can be shewn to be an idea of sensation, or to have the least resemblance to any sensation, I lay my hand upon my mouth, and give up all pretense to reconcile reason to common sense in this matter, and must suffer the ideal scepticism to triumph. But if, on the other hand, they are not ideas of sensation, nor like to any sensation, then the ideal system is a rope of sand, and all the laboured arguments of the sceptical philosophy against a material world, and against the existence of everything but impressions and ideas, proceed upon a false hypothesis.

If our philosophy concerning the mind be so lame with regard to the origin of our notions of the clearest, most simple, and most familiar objects of thought, and the powers from which they are derived, can we expect that it should be more perfect in the account it gives of the origin of our opinions and belief? We have seen already some instances of its imperfection in this respect: and, perhaps, that same nature which hath given us the power to conceive things altogether unlike to any of our sensations, or to any operation of our minds, hath likewise provided for our belief of them, by some part of our constitution hitherto not explained.

Bishop Berkeley hath proved, beyond the possibility of reply, that we cannot by reasoning infer the existence of matter from our sensations; and the author of the "Treatise of Human Nature" hath proved no less clearly, that we cannot by reasoning infer the existence of our own or other minds from our sensations. But are we to admit nothing but what can be proved by reasoning? Then we must be sceptics indeed, and

believe nothing at all. The author of the "Treatise of Human Nature" appears to me to be but a half-sceptic. He hath not followed his principles so far as they lead him; but, after having, with unparalleled intrepidity and success, combatted vulgar prejudices, when he had but one blow to strike, his courage fails him, he fairly lays down his arms, and yields himself a captive to the most common of all vulgar prejudices—I mean the belief of the existence of his own impressions and ideas.

I beg, therefore, to have the honour of making an addition to the sceptical system, without which I conceive it cannot hang together. I affirm, that the belief of the existence of impressions and ideas, is as little supported by reason, as that of the existence of minds and bodies. No man ever did or could offer any reason for this belief. Descartes took it for granted, that he thought, and had sensations and ideas; so have all his followers done. Even the hero of scepticism hath yielded this point, I crave leave to say, weakly and imprudently. I say so, because I am persuaded that there is no principle of his philosophy that obliged him to make this concession. And what is there in impressions and ideas so formidable, that this all-conquering philosophy, after triumphing over every other existence, should pay homage to them? Besides, the concession is dangerous: for belief is of such a nature, that, if you leave any root, it will spread; and you may more easily pull it up altogether, than say, Hitherto shalt go and no further: the existence of impressions and ideas I give up to thee; but see thou pretend to nothing more. A thorough and consistent sceptic will never, therefore, yield this point; and while he holds it, you can never oblige him to yield anything else.

To such a sceptic I have nothing to say; but of the semi-sceptics, I should beg to know, why they believe the existence of their impressions and ideas. The true reason I take to be, because they cannot help it; and the same reason will lead them to believe many other things.

All reasonings must be from first principles; and for first principles no other reason can be given but this; that, by the constitution of our nature, we are under a necessity of assenting to them. Such principles are parts of our constitution, no less than the power of thinking: reason can neither make nor destroy them; nor can it do anything without them: it is like a telescope, which may help a man to see farther, who hath eyes; but, without eyes, a telescope shews nothing at all. A mathematician cannot prove the truth of his axioms, nor can he prove anything, unless he takes them for granted. We cannot prove the existence of our minds, nor even of our thoughts and sensations. A historian, or a witness can prove nothing, unless it is taken for granted that the memory and senses may be trusted. A natural philosopher can prove nothing, unless it is taken for granted that the course of nature is steady and uniform.

How or when I got such first principles, upon which I build all my reasoning, I know not; for I had them before I can remember: but I am sure they are parts of my constitution, and that I cannot throw them off. That our thoughts and sensations must have a subject, which we call *ourself*, is not therefore an opinion got by reasoning, but a natural principle. That our sensations of touch indicate something external, extended, figured, hard or soft, is not a deduction of reason, but a natural principle. The belief of it, and the very conception of it, are equally parts of our constitution. If we are deceived in it, we are deceived by Him that made us, and there is no remedy.

I do not mean to affirm, that the sensations of touch do, from the very first, suggest the same notions of body and its qualities which they do when we are grown up. Perhaps Nature is frugal in this, as in her other operations. The passion of love, with all its concomitant sentiments and desires, is naturally suggested by the perception of beauty in the other sex; yet the same perception does not suggest the tender passion till a certain period of life. A blow given to an infant, raises grief and lamentation; but when he grows up, it as naturally stirs resentment, and prompts him to resistance. Perhaps a child in the womb, or for some short period of its existence, is merely a sentient being; the faculties by which it perceives an external world, by which it reflects on its own thoughts, and existence, and relation to other things, as well as its reasoning and moral faculties, unfold themselves by degrees; so that it is inspired with the various principles of common sense, as with the passions of love and resentment, when it has occasion for them.

NOTES

1. [George Berkeley.]
2. [In old English law, a writ against one who is thought to have usurped any office, franchise, or liberty, to inquire on behalf of the king by what authority one exercises the office, etc.]
3. [By "the ideal system," Reid means the system of "ideas"—that is, idealism or phenomenalism.]
4. [Reid refers here to David Hume.]
5. [Personal error.]
6. [Error of principle.]
7. [Crucial experiment.]

Proof of an External World

G. E. MOORE

G. E. Moore (1873–1958) spent his entire career at Cambridge University, and wrote important works in ethics, free will, and epistemology.

It seems to me that, so far from its being true, as Kant declares to be his opinion, that there is only one possible proof of the existence of things outside of us, namely the one which he has given, I can now give a large number of different proofs, each of which is a perfectly rigorous

Reprinted from G. E. Moore, *Philosophical Papers* (New York: Collier Books, 1962), pp. 144–8. Reprinted by permission of Timothy Moore.

proof; and that at many other times I have been in a position to give many others. I can prove now, for instance, that two human hands exist. How? By holding up my two hands, and saying, as I make a certain gesture with the right hand, 'Here is one hand', and adding, as I make a certain gesture with the left, 'and here is another'. And if, by doing this, I have proved *ipso facto* the existence of external things, you will all see that I can also do it now in numbers of other ways: there is no need to multiply examples.

But did I prove just now that two human hands were then in existence? I do want to insist that I did; that the proof which I gave was a perfectly rigorous one; and that it is perhaps impossible to give a better or more rigorous proof of anything whatever. Of course, it would not have been a proof unless three conditions were satisfied; namely (1) unless the premiss which I adduced as proof of the conclusion was different from the conclusion I adduced it to prove; (2) unless the premiss which I adduced was something which I *knew* to be the case, and not merely something which I believed but which was by no means certain, or something which, though in fact true, I did not know to be so; and (3) unless the conclusion did really follow from the premiss. But all these three conditions were in fact satisfied by my proof. (1) The premiss which I adduced in proof was quite certainly different from the conclusion, for the conclusion was merely 'Two human hands exist at this moment'; but the premiss was something far more specific than this—something which I expressed by showing you my hands, making certain gestures, and saying the words 'Here is one hand, and here is another'. It is quite obvious that the two were different, because it is quite obvious that the conclusion might have been true, even if the premiss had been false. In asserting the premiss I was asserting much more than I was asserting in asserting the conclusion. (2) I certainly did at the moment *know* that which I expressed by the combination of certain gestures with saying the words 'Here is one hand and here is another'. I *knew* that there was one hand in the place indicated by combining a certain gesture with my first utterance of 'here' and that there was another in the different place indicated by

combining a certain gesture with my second utterance of 'here'. How absurd it would be to suggest that I did not know it, but only believed it, and that perhaps it was not the case! You might as well suggest that I do not know that I am now standing up and talking—that perhaps after all I'm not, and that it's not quite certain that I am! And finally (3) it is quite certain that the conclusion did follow from the premiss. This is as certain as it is that if there is one hand here and another here *now*, then it follows that there are two hands in existence *now*.

My proof, then, of the existence of things outside of us did satisfy three of the conditions necessary for a rigorous proof. Are there any other conditions necessary for a rigorous proof, such that perhaps it did not satisfy one of them? Perhaps there may be; I do not know; but I do want to emphasise that, so far as I can see, we all of us do constantly take proofs of this sort as absolutely conclusive proofs of certain conclusions—as finally settling certain questions, as to which we were previously in doubt. Suppose, for instance, it were a question whether there were as many as three misprints on a certain page in a certain book. A says there are, B is inclined to doubt it. How could A prove that he is right? Surely he *could* prove it by taking the book, turning to the page, and pointing to three separate places on it, saying 'There's one misprint here, another here, and another here': surely that is a method by which it *might* be proved! Of course, A would not have proved, by doing this, that there were at least three misprints on the page in question, unless it was certain that there was a misprint in each of the places to which he pointed. But to say that he *might* prove it in this way, is to say that it *might* be certain that there was. And if such a thing as that could ever be certain, then assuredly it was certain just now that there was one hand in one of the two places I indicated and another in the other.

I did, then, just now, give a proof that there were *then* external objects; and obviously, if I did, I could *then* have given many other proofs of the same sort that there were external objects *then*, and could now give many proofs of the same sort that there are external objects *now*.

But, if what I am asked to do is to prove that external objects have existed *in the past*, then I can give many different proofs of this also, but proofs which are in important respects of a different *sort* from those just given. And I want to emphasise that, when Kant says it is a scandal not to be able to give a proof of the existence of external objects, a proof of their existence in the past would certainly *help* to remove the scandal of which he is speaking. He says that, if it occurs to anyone to question their existence, we ought to be able to confront him with a satisfactory proof. But by a person who questions their existence, he certainly means not merely a person who questions whether any exist at the moment of speaking, but a person who questions whether any have *ever* existed; and a proof that some have existed in the past would certainly therefore be relevant to *part* of what such a person is questioning. How then can I prove that there have been external objects in the past? Here is one proof. I can say: 'I held up two hands above this desk not very long ago; therefore two hands existed not very long ago; therefore at least two external objects have existed at some time in the past, QED'. This is a perfectly good proof, provided I *know* what is asserted in the premiss. But I *do* know that I held up two hands above this desk not very long ago. As a matter of fact, in this case you all know it too. There's no doubt whatever that I did. Therefore I have given a perfectly conclusive proof that external objects have existed in the past; and you will all see at once that, if this is a conclusive proof, I could have given many others of the same sort, and could now give many others. But it is also quite obvious that this sort of proof differs in important respects from the sort of proof I gave just now that there were two hands existing *then*.

I have, then, given two conclusive proofs of the existence of external objects. The first was a proof that two human hands existed at the time when I gave the proof; the second was a proof that two human hands had existed at a time previous to that at which I gave the proof. These proofs were of a different sort in important respects. And I pointed out that I could have given, then, many other conclusive proofs of both sorts. It is also obvious that I could give

many others of both sorts now. So that, if these are the sort of proof that is wanted, nothing is easier than to prove the existence of external objects.

But now I am perfectly well aware that, in spite of all that I have said, many philosophers will still feel that I have not given any satisfactory proof of the point in question. And I want briefly, in conclusion, to say something as to why this dissatisfaction with my proofs should be felt.

One reason why, is, I think, this. Some people understand 'proof of an external world' as including a proof of things which I haven't attempted to prove and haven't proved. It is not quite easy to say *what* it is that they want proved—*what* it is that is such that unless they got a proof of it, they would not say that they had a proof of the existence of external things; but I can make an approach to explaining what they want by saying that if I had proved the propositions which I used as *premisses* in my two proofs, then they would perhaps admit that I had proved the existence of external things, but, in the absence of such a proof (which, of course, I have neither given nor attempted to give), they will say that I have not given what they mean by a proof of the existence of external things. In other words, they want a proof of what I assert *now* when I hold up my hands and say 'Here's one hand and here's another'; and, in the other case, they want a proof of what I assert *now* when I say 'I did hold up two hands above this desk just now'. Of course, what they really want is not merely a proof of these two propositions, but something like a general statement as to how *any* propositions of this sort may be proved. This, of course, I haven't given; and I do not believe it can be given: if this is what is meant by proof of the existence of external things, I do not believe that any proof of the existence of external things is possible. Of course, in some cases what might be called a proof of propositions which seem like these can be got. If one of you suspected that one of my hands was artificial he might be said to get a proof of my proposition 'Here's one hand, and here's another', by coming up and examining the suspected hand close up, perhaps touching and pressing it, and so establishing that it really was a human hand. But I do not believe that any proof is possible in nearly all cases. How am I to prove now that 'Here's one hand, and here's another'? I do not believe I can do it. In order to do it, I should need to prove for one thing, as Descartes pointed out, that I am not now dreaming. But how can I prove that I am not? I have, no doubt, conclusive reasons for asserting that I am not now dreaming; I have conclusive evidence that I am awake: but that is a very different thing from being able to prove it. I could not tell you what all my evidence is; and I should require to do this at least, in order to give you a proof.

But another reason why some people would feel dissatisfied with my proofs is, I think, not merely that they want a proof of something which I haven't proved, but that they think that, if I cannot give such extra proofs, then the proofs that I have given are not conclusive proofs at all. And this, I think, is a definite mistake. They would say: 'If you cannot prove your premiss that here is one hand and here is another, then you do not know it. But you yourself have admitted that, if you did not know it, then your proof was not conclusive. Therefore your proof was not, as you say it was, a conclusive proof.' This view that, if I cannot prove such things as these, I do not know them, is, I think, the view that Kant was expressing in the sentence which I quoted at the beginning of this lecture, when he implies that so long as we have no proof of the existence of external things, their existence must be accepted merely on *faith*. He means to say, I think, that if I cannot prove that there is a hand here, I must accept it merely as a matter of faith—I cannot know it. Such a view, though it has been very common among philosophers, can, I think, be shown to be wrong—though shown only by the use of premises which are not known to be true, unless we do know of the existence of external things. I can know things, which I cannot prove; and among things which I certainly did know, even if (as I think) I could not prove them, were the premises of my two proofs. I should say, therefore, that those, if any, who are dissatisfied with these proofs merely on the ground that I did not know their premises, have no good reason for their dissatisfaction.

THE METHODS OF SCIENCE

An Inquiry
Concerning Human Understanding

DAVID HUME

SECTION II. OF THE ORIGIN OF IDEAS

Everyone will readily allow that there is a considerable difference between the perceptions of the mind when a man feels the pain of excessive heat or the pleasure of moderate warmth, and when he afterwards recalls to his memory this sensation or anticipates it by his imagination. These faculties may mimic or copy the perceptions of the senses, but they never can entirely reach the force and vivacity of the original sentiment. The utmost we say of them, even when they operate with greatest vigor, is that they represent their object in so lively a manner that we could *almost* say we feel or see it. But, except the mind be disordered by disease or madness, they never can arrive at such a pitch of vivacity as to render these perceptions altogether

David Hume, *An Inquiry Concerning Human Understanding*. Sections II, IV–VII. First published in 1748.

undistinguishable. All the colors of poetry, how-ever splendid, can never paint natural objects in such a manner as to make the description be taken for a real landscape. The most lively thought is still inferior to the dullest sensation.

We may observe a like distinction to run through all the other perceptions of the mind. A man in a fit of anger is actuated in a very differ-ent manner from one who only thinks of that emotion. If you tell me that any person is in love, I easily understand your meaning and form a just conception of his situation, but never can mistake that conception for the real dis-orders and agitations of the passion. When we reflect on our past sentiments and affections, our thought is a faithful mirror and copies its objects truly, but the colors which it employs are faint and dull in comparison of those in which our original perceptions were clothed. It requires no nice discernment or metaphysical head to mark the distinction between them.

Here, therefore, we may divide all the percep-tions of the mind into two classes or species, which are distinguished by their different degrees of force and vivacity. The less forcible and lively are com-monly denominated "thoughts" or "ideas." The other species want a name in our language, and in most others; I suppose, because it was not req-uisite for any but philosophical purposes to rank them under a general term or appellation. Let us, therefore, use a little freedom and call them "impressions," employing that word in a sense somewhat different from the usual. By the term "impression," then, I mean all our more lively per-ceptions, when we hear, or see, or feel, or love, or hate, or desire, or will. And impressions are distin-guished from ideas, which are the less lively per-ceptions of which we are conscious when we reflect on any of those sensations or movements above mentioned.

Nothing, at first view, may seem more unbounded than the thought of man, which not only escapes all human power and authority, but is not even restrained within the limits of nature and reality. To form monsters and join incongruous shapes and appearances costs the imagination no more trouble than to conceive the most natural and familiar objects. And while the body is confined to one planet, along which it creeps with pain and difficulty, the thought can in an instant transport us into the most dis-tant regions of the universe, or even beyond the universe into the unbounded chaos where nature is supposed to lie in total confusion. What never was seen or heard of, may yet be conceived, nor is anything beyond the power of thought except what implies an absolute contradiction.

But though our thought seems to possess this unbounded liberty, we shall find upon a nearer examination that it is really confined within very narrow limits, and that all this creative power of the mind amounts to no more than the faculty of compounding, transposing, augment-ing, or diminishing the materials afforded us by the senses and experience. When we think of a golden mountain, we only join two consistent ideas, "gold" and "mountain," with which we were formerly acquainted. A virtuous horse we can conceive, because, from our own feeling, we can conceive virtue; and this we may unite to the figure and shape of a horse, which is an animal familiar to us. In short, all the materials of thinking are derived either from our outward or inward sentiment; the mixture and composi-tion of these belongs alone to the mind and will, or, to express myself in philosophical lan-guage, all our ideas or more feeble perceptions are copies of our impressions or more lively ones.

To prove this, the two following arguments will, I hope, be sufficient. *First,* when we analyze our thoughts or ideas, however compounded or sublime, we always find that they resolve them-selves into such simple ideas as were copied from a precedent feeling or sentiment. Even those ideas which at first view seem the most wide of this origin are found, upon a nearer scrutiny, to be derived from it. The idea of God, as meaning an infinitely intelligent, wise, and good Being, arises from reflecting on the operations of our own mind and augmenting, without limit, those qualities of goodness and wisdom. We may prose-cute this inquiry to what length we please; where we shall always find that every idea which we exam-ine is copied from a similar impression. Those who would assert that this position is not universally true, nor without exception, have only one, and that an easy, method of refuting it by produc-ing that idea which, in their opinion, is not derived from this source. It will then be incumbent on us, if we would maintain our doctrine, to produce the impression or lively perception which corresponds to it.

Secondly, if it happen, from a defect of the organ, that a man is not susceptible of any species of sensation, we always find that he is as little susceptible of the correspondent ideas. A blind man can form no notion of colors, a deaf man of sounds. Restore either of them that sense in which he is deficient by opening this new inlet for his sensations, you also open an inlet for the ideas, and he finds no difficulty in conceiving these objects. The case is the same if the object proper for exciting any sensation has never been applied to the organ. A Laplander... has no notion of the relish of wine. And though there are few or no instances of a like deficiency in the mind where a person has never felt or is wholly incapable of a sentiment or passion that belongs to his species, yet we find the same observation to take place in a less degree. A man of mild manners can form no idea of inveterate revenge or cruelty, nor can a selfish heart easily conceive the heights of friendship and generosity. It is readily allowed that other beings may possess many senses of which we can have no conception, because the ideas of them have never been introduced to us in the only manner by which an idea can have access to the mind, to wit, by the actual feeling and sensation.

There is, however, one contradictory phenomenon which may prove that it is not absolutely impossible for ideas to arise independent of their correspondent impressions. I believe it will readily be allowed that the several distinct ideas of color, which enter by the eye, or those of sound, which are conveyed by the ear, are really different from each other, though at the same time resembling. Now, if this be true of different colors, it must be no less so of the different shades of the same color; and each shade produces a distinct idea, independent of the rest. For if this should be denied, it is possible, by the continual gradation of shades, to run a color insensibly into what is most remote from it; and if you will not allow any of the means to be different, you cannot, without absurdity, deny the extremes to be the same. Suppose, therefore, a person to

have enjoyed his sight for thirty years and to have become perfectly acquainted with colors of all kinds, except one particular shade of blue, for instance, which it never has been his fortune to meet with; let all the different shades of that color, except that single one, be placed before him, descending gradually from the deepest to the lightest, it is plain that he will perceive a blank where that shade is wanting, and will be sensible that there is a greater distance in that place between the contiguous colors than in any other. Now I ask whether it be possible for him, from his own imagination, to supply this deficiency and raise up to himself the idea of that particular shade, though it had never been conveyed to him by his senses? I believe there are few but will be of opinion that he can; and this may serve as a proof that the simple ideas are not always, in every instance, derived from the correspondent impressions, though this instance is so singular that it is scarcely worth our observing, and does not merit that for it alone we should alter our general maxim.

Here, therefore, is a proposition which not only seems in itself simple and intelligible, but, if a proper use were made of it, might render every dispute equally intelligible, and banish all that jargon which has so long taken possession of metaphysical reasonings and drawn disgrace upon them. All ideas, especially abstract ones, are naturally faint and obscure. The mind has but a slender hold of them. They are apt to be confounded with other resembling ideas; and when we have often employed any term, though without a distinct meaning, we are apt to imagine it has a determinate idea annexed to it. On the contrary, all impressions, that is, all sensations either outward or inward, are strong and vivid. The limits between them are more exactly determined, nor is it easy to fall into any error or mistake with regard to them. When we entertain, therefore, any suspicion that a philosophical term is employed without any meaning or idea (as is but too frequent), we need but inquire, *from what impression is that supposed idea derived*? And if it be impossible to assign any, this will serve to confirm our suspicion. By bringing ideas in so clear a light, we may reasonably hope to remove all dispute which may arise concerning their nature and reality.[1]

SECTION IV. SKEPTICAL DOUBTS CONCERNING THE OPERATIONS OF THE UNDERSTANDING

Part I

All the objects of human reason or inquiry may naturally be divided into two kinds, to wit, "Relations of Ideas," and "Matters of Fact." Of the first kind are the sciences of Geometry, Algebra, and Arithmetic, and, in short, every affirmation which is either intuitively or demonstratively certain. *That the square of the hypotenuse is equal to the square of the two sides* is a proposition which expresses a relation between these figures. *That three times five is equal to the half of thirty* expresses a relation between these numbers. Propositions of this kind are discoverable by the mere operation of thought, without dependence on what is anywhere existent in the universe. Though there never were a circle or triangle in nature, the truths demonstrated by Euclid would forever retain their certainty and evidence.

Matters of fact, which are the second objects of human reason, are not ascertained in the same manner, nor is our evidence of their truth, however great, of a like nature with the foregoing. The contrary of every matter of fact is still possible, because it can never imply a contradiction and is conceived by the mind with the same facility and distinctness as if ever so conformable to reality. *That the sun will not rise tomorrow* is no less intelligible a proposition and implies no more contradiction than the affirmation *that it will rise*. We should in vain, therefore, attempt to demonstrate its falsehood. Were it demonstratively false, it would imply a contradiction and could never be distinctly conceived by the mind.

It may, therefore, be a subject worthy of curiosity to inquire what is the nature of that evidence which assures us of any real existence and matter of fact beyond the present testimony of our senses or the records of our memory. This part of philosophy, it is observable, had been little cultivated either by the ancients or moderns; and, therefore, our doubts and errors in the prosecution of so important an inquiry may be the more excusable while we march through such difficult paths without any guide or direction. They may even prove useful by exciting curiosity and destroying that implicit faith and security which is the bane of all reasoning and free inquiry. The discovery of defects in the common philosophy, if any such there be, will not, I presume, be a discouragement, but rather an incitement, as is usual, to attempt something more full and satisfactory than has yet been proposed to the public.

All reasonings concerning matter of fact seem to be founded on the relation of *cause* and *effect*. By means of that relation alone we can go beyond the evidence of our memory and senses. If you were to ask a man why he believes any matter of fact which is absent, for instance, that his friend is in the country or in France, he would give you a reason, and this reason would be some other fact: as a letter received from him or the knowledge of his former resolutions and promises. A man finding a watch or any other machine in a desert island would conclude that there had once been men in that island. All our reasonings concerning fact are of the same nature. And here it is constantly supposed that there is a connection between the present fact and that which is inferred from it. Were there nothing to bind them together, the inference would be entirely precarious. The hearing of an articulate voice and rational discourse in the dark assures us of the presence of some person. Why? Because these are the effects of the human make and fabric, and closely connected with it. If we anatomize all the other reasonings of this nature, we shall find that they are founded on the relation of cause and effect, and that this relation is either near or remote, direct or collateral. Heat and light are collateral effects of fire, and the one effect may justly be inferred from the other.

If we would satisfy ourselves, therefore, concerning the nature of that evidence which assures us of matters of fact, we must inquire how we arrive at the knowledge of cause and effect.

I shall venture to affirm, as a general proposition which admits of no exception, that the knowledge of this relation is not, in any instance, attained by reasonings *a priori*, but arises entirely from experience, when we find that any particular objects are constantly conjoined with each other. Let an object be presented to a man of ever so strong natural reason and abilities—if that object be entirely new to him, he will not be able, by the most accurate examination of its sensible qualities, to discover any of its causes or effects. Adam, though his rational faculties be supposed, at the very first, entirely perfect, could not have inferred from the fluidity and transparency of water that it would suffocate him, or from the light and warmth of fire that it would consume him. No object ever discovers, by the qualities which appear to the senses, either the causes which produced it or the effects which will arise from it; nor can our reason, unassisted by experience, ever draw any inference concerning real existence and matter of fact.

This proposition, *that causes and effects are discoverable, not by reason, but by experience,* will readily be admitted with regard to such objects as we remember to have once been altogether unknown to us, since we must be conscious of the utter inability which we then lay under of foretelling what would arise from them. Present two smooth pieces of marble to a man who has no tincture of natural philosophy; he will never discover that they will adhere together in such a manner as to require great force to separate them in a direct line, while they make so small a resistance to a lateral pressure. Such events as bear little analogy to the common course of nature are also readily confessed to be known only by experience, nor does any man imagine that the explosion of gunpowder or the attraction of a loadstone could ever be discovered by arguments *a priori.* In like manner, when an effect is supposed to depend upon an intricate machinery or secret structure of parts, we make no difficulty in attributing all our knowledge of it to experience. Who will assert that he can give the ultimate reason why milk or bread is proper nourishment for a man, not for a lion or tiger?

But the same truth may not appear at first sight to have the same evidence with regard to events which have become familiar to us from our first appearance in the world, which bear a close analogy to the whole course of nature, and which are supposed to depend on the simple qualities of objects without any secret structure of parts. We are apt to imagine that we could discover these effects by the mere operation of our reason without experience. We fancy that, were we brought on a sudden into this world, we could at first have inferred that one billiard ball would communicate motion to another upon impulse, and that we needed not to have waited for the event in order to pronounce with certainty concerning it. Such is the influence of custom that where it is strongest it not only covers our natural ignorance but even conceals itself, and seems not to take place, merely because it is found in the highest degree.

But to convince us that all the laws of nature and all the operations of bodies without exception are known only by experience, the following reflections may perhaps suffice. Were any object presented to us, and were we required to pronounce concerning the effect which will result from it without consulting past observation, after what manner, I beseech you, must the mind proceed in this operation? It must invent or imagine some event which it ascribes to the object as its effect; and it is plain that this invention must be entirely arbitrary. The mind can never possibly find the effect in the supposed cause by the most accurate scrutiny and examination. For the effect is totally different from the cause, and consequently can never be discovered in it. Motion in the second billiard ball is quite a distinct event from motion in the first, nor is there anything in the one to suggest the smallest hint of the other. A stone or piece of metal raised into the air and left without any support immediately falls. But to consider the matter *a priori,* is there anything we discover in this situation which can beget the idea of a downward rather than an upward or any other motion in the stone or metal?

And as the first imagination or invention of a particular effect in all natural operations is arbitrary where we consult not experience, so must we also esteem the supposed tie or connection between the cause and effect which binds them together and renders it impossible that any other effect could result from the operation of that cause. When I see, for instance, a billiard ball moving in a straight line toward another, even suppose motion in the second ball should by accident be suggested to me as the result of their contact or impulse, may I not conceive that a hundred different events might as well follow from that cause? May not both these balls remain at absolute rest? May not the first ball return in a straight line or leap off the second in any line or direction? All these suppositions are consistent and conceivable. Why, then, should we give the preference to one which is no more consistent or conceivable than the rest? All our reasonings *a priori* will never be able to show us any foundation for this preference.

In a word, then, every effect is a distinct event from its cause. It could not, therefore, be discovered in the cause, and the first invention or conception of it *a priori,* must be entirely arbitrary. And even after it is suggested, the conjunction of it with the cause must appear equally arbitrary, since there are always many other effects which, to reason, must seem fully as consistent and natural. In vain, therefore, should we pretend to determine any single event or infer any cause or effect without the assistance of observation and experience.

Hence we may discover the reason why no philosopher who is rational and modest has ever pretended to assign the ultimate cause of any natural operation, or to show distinctly the action of that power which produces any single effect in the universe. It is confessed that the utmost effort of human reason is to reduce the principles productive of natural phenomena to a greater simplicity, and to resolve the many particular effects into a few general causes, by means of reasonings from analogy, experience, and observation. But as to the causes of these general causes, we should in vain attempt their discovery, nor shall we ever be able to satisfy ourselves by any particular explication of them. These ultimate springs and principles are totally shut up from human curiosity and inquiry. Elasticity, gravity, cohesion of parts, communication of motion by impulse—these are probably the ultimate causes and principles which we ever discover in nature; and we may esteem ourselves sufficiently happy if, by accurate inquiry and reasoning, we can trace up the particular phenomena to, or near to, these general principles. The most perfect philosophy of the natural kind only staves off our ignorance a little longer, as perhaps the most perfect philosophy of the moral or metaphysical kind serves only to discover larger portions of it. Thus the observation of human blindness and weakness is the result of all philosophy, and meets us, at every turn, in spite of our endeavors to elude or avoid it.

Nor is geometry, when taken into the assistance of natural philosophy, ever able to remedy this defect or lead us into the knowledge of ultimate causes by all that accuracy of reasoning for which it is so justly celebrated. Every part of mixed mathematics proceeds upon the supposition that certain laws are established by nature in her operations, and abstract reasonings are employed either to assist experience in the discovery of these laws or to determine their influence in particular instances where it depends upon any precise degree of distance and quantity. Thus it is a law of motion, discovered by experience, that the moment or force of any body in motion is in the compound ratio or proportion of its solid contents and its velocity, and, consequently, that a small force may remove the greatest obstacle or raise the greatest weight if by any contrivance or machinery we can increase the velocity of that force so as to make it an overmatch for its antagonist. Geometry assists us in the application of this law by giving us the just dimensions of all the parts and figures which can enter into any species of machine, but still the discovery of the law itself is owing merely to experience; and all the abstract reasonings in the world could never lead us one step toward the knowledge of it. When we reason *a priori* and consider merely any object or cause as it appears to the mind, independent of all observation, it never could suggest to us the notion of any distinct object, such as its effect, much less show us the inseparable and inviolable connection between them. A man must be very sagacious who could discover by reasoning that crystal is the effect of heat, and ice of cold, without being previously acquainted with the operation of these qualities.

Part II

But we have not yet attained any tolerable satisfaction with regard to the question first proposed. Each solution still gives rise to a new question as difficult as the foregoing and leads us on to further inquiries. When it is asked,

What is the nature of all our reasonings concerning matter of fact? the proper answer seems to be that they are founded on the relation of cause and effect. When again it is asked, *What is the foundation of all our reasonings and conclusions concerning that relation?* it may be replied in one word, *experience.* But if we still carry on our sifting humor and ask, *What is the foundation of all conclusions from experience?* this implies a new question which may be of more difficult solution and explication. Philosophers that give themselves airs of superior wisdom and sufficiency have a hard task when they encounter persons of inquisitive dispositions, who push them from every corner to which they retreat, and who are sure at last to bring them to some dangerous dilemma. The best expedient to prevent this confusion is to be modest in our pretensions and even to discover the difficulty ourselves before it is objected to us. By this means we may make a kind of merit of our very ignorance.

I shall content myself in this section with an easy task and shall pretend only to give a negative answer to the question here proposed. I say, then, that even after we have experience of the operations of cause and effect, our conclusions from that experience are *not* founded on reasoning or any process of understanding. This answer we must endeavor both to explain and to defend.

It must certainly be allowed that nature has kept us at a great distance from all her secrets and has afforded us only the knowledge of a few superficial qualities of objects, while she conceals from us those powers and principles on which the influence of these objects entirely depends. Our senses inform us of the color, weight, and consistency of bread, but neither sense nor reason can ever inform us of those qualities which fit it for the nourishment and support of the human body. Sight or feeling conveys an idea of the actual motion of bodies, but as to that wonderful force or power which would carry on a moving body forever in a continued change of place, and which bodies never lose but by communicating it to others, of this we cannot form the most distant conception. But notwithstanding this ignorance of natural powers[2] and principles, we always presume when we see like sensible qualities that they

have like secret powers, and expect that effects similar to those which we have experienced will follow from them. If a body of like color and consistence with that bread which we have formerly eaten be presented to us, we make no scruple of repeating the experiment and foresee with certainty like nourishment and support. Now this is a process of the mind or thought of which I would willingly know the foundation. It is allowed on all hands that there is no known connection between the sensible qualities and the secret powers, and, consequently, that the mind is not led to form such a conclusion concerning their constant and regular conjunction by anything which it knows of their nature. As to past *experience,* it can be allowed to give *direct* and *certain* information of those precise objects only, and that precise period of time which fell under its cognizance: But why this experience should be extended to future times and to other objects which, for aught we know, may be only in appearance similar, this is the main question on which I would insist. The bread which I formerly ate nourished me; that is, a body of such sensible qualities was, at that time, endued with such secret powers. But does it follow that other bread must also nourish me at another time, and that like sensible qualities must always be attended with like secret powers? The consequence seems nowise necessary. At least, it must be acknowledged that there is here a consequence drawn by the mind, that there is a certain step taken, a process of thought, and an inference which wants to be explained. These two propositions are far from being the same: *I have found that such an object has always been attended with such an effect,* and *I foresee that other objects which are in appearance similar will be attended with similar effects.* I shall allow, if you please, that the one proposition may justly be inferred from the other: I know, in fact, that it always is inferred. But if you insist that the inference is made by a chain of reasoning, I desire you to produce that reasoning. The connection between these propositions is not intuitive. There is required a medium which may enable the mind to draw such an inference, if indeed it be drawn by reasoning and argument. What that medium is I must confess passes my comprehension; and it is incumbent on those to produce it who assert that it really exists and is the origin of all our conclusions concerning matter of fact.

This negative argument must certainly, in process of time, become altogether convincing if many penetrating and able philosophers shall turn their inquiries this way, and no one be ever able to discover any connecting proposition or intermediate step which supports the understanding in this conclusion. But as the question is yet new, every reader may not trust so far to his own penetration as to conclude, because an argument escapes his inquiry, that therefore it does not really exist. For this reason it may be requisite to venture upon a more difficult task, and, enumerating all the branches of human knowledge, endeavor to show that none of them can afford such an argument.

All reasonings may be divided into two kinds, namely, demonstrative reasoning, or that concerning relations of ideas, and moral reasoning, or that concerning matter of fact and existence. That there are no demonstrative arguments in the case seems evident, since it implies no contradiction that the course of nature may change and that an object, seemingly like those which we have experienced, may be attended with different or contrary effects. May I not clearly and distinctly conceive that a body, falling from the clouds and which in all other respects resembles snow, has yet the taste of salt or feeling of fire? Is there any more intelligible proposition than to affirm that all the trees will flourish in December and January, and will decay in May and June? Now, whatever is intelligible and can be distinctly conceived implies no contradiction and can never be proved false by any demonstrative argument or abstract reasoning *a priori*.

If we be, therefore, engaged by arguments to put trust in past experience and make it the standard of our future judgment, these arguments must be probable only, or such as regard matter of fact and real existence, according to the division above mentioned. But that there is no argument of this kind must appear if our explication of that species of reasoning be admitted as solid and satisfactory. We have said that all arguments concerning existence are founded on the relation of cause and effect, that our knowledge of that relation is derived entirely from experience, and that all our experimental conclusions proceed upon the supposition that the future will be conformable to the past. To endeavor, therefore, the proof of this last supposition by probable arguments, or arguments regarding existence, must be evidently going in a circle and taking that for granted which is the very point in question.

In reality, all arguments from experience are founded on the similarity which we discover among natural objects, and by which we are induced to expect effects similar to those which we have found to follow from such objects. And though none but a fool or madman will ever pretend to dispute the authority of experience or to reject that great guide of human life, it may surely be allowed a philosopher to have so much curiosity at least as to examine the principle of human nature which gives this mighty authority to experience and makes us draw advantage from that similarity which nature has placed among different objects. From causes which appear similar, we expect similar effects. This is the sum of our experimental conclusions. Now it seems evident that, if this conclusion were formed by reason, it would be as perfect at first, and upon one instance, as after ever so long a course of experience; but the case is far otherwise. Nothing so like as eggs, yet no one, on account of this appearing similarity, expects the same taste and relish in all of them. It is only after a long course of uniform experiments in any kind that we attain a firm reliance and security with regard to a particular event. Now, where is that process of reasoning which, from one instance, draws a conclusion so different from that which it infers from a hundred instances that are nowise different from that single one? This question I propose as much for the sake of information as with an intention of raising difficulties. I cannot find, I cannot imagine any such reasoning. But I keep my mind still open to instruction if anyone will vouchsafe to bestow it on me.

Should it be said that, from a number of uniform experiments, we *infer* a connection between the sensible qualities and the secret powers, this, I must confess, seems the same difficulty, couched in different terms. The question still recurs, On what process of argument is this *inference* founded?

Where is the medium, the interposing ideas which join propositions so very wide of each other? It is confessed that the color, consistence, and other sensible qualities of bread appear not of themselves to have any connection with the secret powers of nourishment and support; for otherwise we could infer these secret powers from the first appearance of these sensible qualities without the aid of experience, contrary to the sentiment of all philosophers, and contrary to plain matter of fact. Here, then, is our natural state of ignorance with regard to the powers and influence of all objects. How is this remedied by experience? It only shows us a number of uniform effects resulting from certain objects, and teaches us that those particular objects, at that particular time, were endowed with such powers and forces. When a new object endowed with similar sensible qualities is produced, we expect similar powers and forces, and look for a like effect. From a body of like color and consistence with bread, we expect like nourishment and support. But this surely is a step or progress of the mind which wants to be explained. When a man says, *I have found, in all past instances, such sensible qualities, conjoined with such secret powers,* and when he says, *similar sensible qualities will always be conjoined with similar secret powers,* he is not guilty of a tautology, nor are these propositions in any respect the same. You say that the one proposition is an inference from the other; but you must confess that the inference is not intuitive, neither is it demonstrative. Of what nature is it then? To say it is experimental is begging the question. For all inferences from experience suppose as their foundation, that the future will resemble the past and that similar powers will be conjoined with similar sensible qualities. If there be any suspicion that the course of nature may change, and that the past may be no rule for the future, all experience becomes useless and can give rise to no inference or conclusion. It is impossible, therefore, that any arguments from experience can prove this resemblance of the past to the future; since all these arguments are founded on the supposition of that resemblance. Let the course of things be allowed hitherto ever so regular, that alone, without some new argument or inference, proves not that for the future it will continue so. In vain do you pretend to have learned the nature of bodies from your past experience. Their secret nature and consequently all their effects and influence, may change without any change in their sensible qualities. This happens sometimes, and with regard to some objects. Why may it not happen always, and with regard to all objects? What logic, what process of argument secures you against this supposition? My practice, you say, refutes my doubts. But you mistake the purport of my question. As an agent, I am quite satisfied in the point; but as a philosopher who has some share of curiosity, I will not say skepticism, I want to learn the foundation of this inference. No reading, no inquiry has yet been able to remove my difficulty or give me satisfaction in a matter of such importance. Can I do better than propose the difficulty to the public, even though, perhaps, I have small hopes of obtaining a solution? We shall at least, by this means, be sensible of our ignorance, if we do not augment our knowledge.

I must confess that a man is guilty of unpardonable arrogance who concludes, because an argument has escaped his own investigation, that therefore it does not really exist. I must also confess that, though all the learned, for several ages, should have employed themselves in fruitless search upon any subject, it may still, perhaps, be rash to conclude positively that the subject must therefore pass all human comprehension. Even though we examine all the sources of our knowledge and conclude them unfit for such a subject, there may still remain a suspicion that the enumeration is not complete or the examination not accurate. But with regard to the present subject, there are some considerations which seem to remove all this accusation of arrogance or suspicion of mistake.

It is certain that the most ignorant and stupid peasants, nay infants, nay even brute beasts, improve by experience and learn the qualities of natural objects by observing the effects which result from them. When a child has felt the sensation of pain from touching the flame of a candle, he will be careful not to put his hand near any candle, but will expect a similar effect from a cause which is similar in its sensible qualities and appearance. If you assert, therefore, that the understanding of the child is led into this conclusion by any process of argument or ratiocination, I may justly require you to produce that argument, nor have you any pretense to refuse so equitable a demand. You cannot say that the argument is abstruse and may possibly escape your inquiry, since you confess that it is obvious to the capacity of a mere infant. If you hesitate, therefore, a moment or if, after reflection, you produce any intricate or profound argument, you, in a manner, give up the question and confess that it is not reasoning which engages us to suppose the past resembling the future, and to expect similar effects from causes which are to appearance similar. This is the proposition which I intended to enforce in the present section. If I be right, I pretend not to have made any mighty discovery. And if I be wrong, I must acknowledge myself to be indeed a very backward scholar, since I cannot now discover an argument which, it seems, was perfectly familiar to me long before I was out of my cradle.

SECTION V. SKEPTICAL SOLUTION OF THESE DOUBTS

Part I

The passion for philosophy, like that for religion, seems liable to this inconvenience, that though it aims at the correction of our manners and extirpation of our vices, it may only serve, by imprudent management, to foster a predominant inclination and push the mind with more determined resolution toward that side which already *draws* too much by the bias and propensity of the natural temper. It is certain that, while we aspire to the magnanimous firmness of the philosophic sage and endeavor to confine our pleasures altogether within our own minds, we may, at last, render our philosophy, like that of Epictetus and other Stoics, only a more refined system of selfishness, and reason ourselves out of all virtue as well as social enjoyment. While we study with attention the vanity of human life and turn all our thoughts toward the empty and transitory nature of riches and honors, we are, perhaps, all the while flattering our natural indolence which, hating the bustle of the world and drudgery of business, seeks a pretense of reason to give itself a full and uncontrolled indulgence. There is, however, one species of philosophy which seems little liable to this inconvenience, and that because it strikes in with no disorderly passion of the human mind, nor can mingle itself with any natural affection or propensity; and that is the Academic or Skeptical philosophy. The Academics always talk of doubt and suspense of judgment, of danger in hasty determinations, of confining to very narrow bounds the inquiries of the understanding, and of renouncing all speculations which lie not within the limits of common life and practice. Nothing, therefore, can be more contrary than such a philosophy to the supine indolence of the mind, its rash arrogance, its lofty pretensions, and its superstitious credulity. Every passion is mortified by it, except the love of truth; and that passion never is nor can be carried to too high a degree. It is surprising, therefore, that this philosophy, which in almost every instance must be harmless and innocent, should be the subject of so much groundless reproach and obloquy. But, perhaps, the very circumstance which renders it so innocent is what chiefly exposes it to the public hatred and resentment. By flattering no irregular passion, it gains few partisans. By opposing so many vices and follies, it raises to itself abundance of enemies who stigmatize it as libertine, profane, and irreligious.

Nor need we fear that this philosophy, while it endeavors to limit our inquiries to common life, should ever undermine the reasonings of common life and carry its doubts so far as to destroy all action as well as speculation. Nature will always maintain her rights and prevail in the end over any abstract reasoning whatsoever. Though we should conclude, for instance, as in the foregoing section, that in all reasonings from experience there is a step taken by the mind which is not supported by any argument or process of the understanding, there is no danger that these reasonings, on which almost all knowledge depends, will ever be affected by such a discovery. If the mind be not engaged by argument to make this step, it must be induced by some other principle of equal weight and authority; and that principle will preserve its influence as long as human nature remains the same.

What that principle is may well be worth the pains of inquiry.

Suppose a person, though endowed with the strongest faculties of reason and reflection, to be brought on a sudden into this world; he would, indeed, immediately observe a continual succession of objects and one event following another, but he would not be able to discover anything further. He would not at first, by any reasoning, be able to reach the idea of cause and effect, since the particular powers by which all natural operations are performed never appear to the senses; nor is it reasonable to conclude, merely because one event in one instance precedes another, that therefore the one is the cause, the other the effect. The conjunction may be arbitrary and casual. There may be no reason to infer the existence of one from the appearance of the other; and, in a word, such a person without more experience could never employ his conjecture or reasoning concerning any matter of fact or be assured of anything beyond what was immediately present to his memory or senses.

Suppose again that he has acquired more experience and has lived so long in the world as to have observed similar objects or events to be constantly conjoined together—what is the consequence of this experience? He immediately infers the existence of one object from the appearance of the other, yet he has not, by all his experience, acquired any idea or knowledge of the secret power by which the one object produces the other, nor is it by any process of reasoning he is engaged to draw this inference; but still he finds himself determined to draw it, and though he should be convinced that his understanding has no part in the operation, he would nevertheless continue in the same course of thinking. There is some other principle which determines him to form such a conclusion.

This principle is *custom* or *habit*. For whenever the repetition of any particular act or operation produces a propensity to renew the same act or operation without being impelled by any reasoning or process of the understanding, we always say that this propensity is the effect of *custom*. By employing that word we pretend not to have given the ultimate reason of such a propensity. We only point out a principle of human nature which is universally acknowledged, and which is well known by its effects. Perhaps we can push our inquiries no further or pretend to give the cause of this cause, but must rest contented with it as the ultimate principle which we can assign of all our conclusions from experience. It is sufficient satisfaction that we can go so far without repining at the narrowness of our faculties, because they will carry us no further. And it is certain we here advance a very intelligible proposition at least, if not a true one, when we assert that after the constant conjunction of two objects, heat and flame, for instance, weight and solidity, we are determined by custom alone to expect the one from the appearance of the other. This hypothesis seems even the only one which explains the difficulty why we draw from a thousand instances an inference which we are not able to draw from one instance that is in no respect different from them. Reason is incapable of any such variation. The conclusions which it draws from considering one circle are the same which it would form upon surveying all the circles in the universe. But no man, having seen only one body move after being impelled by another, could infer that every other body will move after a like impulse. All inferences from experience, therefore, are effects of custom, not of reasoning.[3]

Custom, then, is the great guide of human life. It is that principle alone which renders our experience useful to us and makes us expect, for the future, a similar train of events with those which have appeared in the past. Without the influence of custom we should be entirely ignorant of every matter of fact beyond what is immediately present to the memory and senses. We should never know how to adjust means to ends or to employ our natural powers in the production of any effect. There would be an end at once of all action as well as of the chief part of speculation.

But here it may be proper to remark that though our conclusions from experience carry us beyond our memory and senses and assure us of matters of fact which happened in the most distant places and most remote ages, yet some fact must always be present to the senses or memory from which we may first proceed in drawing these conclusions. A man who should find in a desert country the remains of pompous buildings would conclude that the country had, in ancient times, been cultivated by civilized inhabitants; but did nothing of this nature occur to him, he could never form such an inference. We learn the events of former ages from history, but then we must peruse the volume in which this instruction is contained, and thence carry up our inferences from one testimony to another, till we arrive at the eyewitnesses and spectators of these distant events. In a word, if we proceed not upon some fact present to the memory or senses, our reasonings would be merely hypothetical; and however the particular links might be connected with each other, the whole chain of inferences would have nothing to support it, nor could we ever, by its means, arrive at the knowledge of any real existence. If I ask why you believe any particular matter of fact which you relate, you must tell me some reason; and this reason will be some other fact connected with it. But as you cannot proceed after this manner *in infinitum,* you must at last terminate in some fact which is present to your memory or senses or must allow that your belief is entirely without foundation.

What, then, is the conclusion of the whole matter? A simple one, though, it must be confessed, pretty remote from the common theories of philosophy. All belief of matter of fact or real existence is derived merely from some object present to the memory or senses and a customary conjunction between that and some other object; or, in other words, having found, in many instances, that any two kinds of objects, flame and heat, snow and cold, have always been conjoined together: if flame or snow be presented anew to the senses, the mind is carried by custom to expect heat or cold, and to *believe* that such a quality does exist and will discover itself upon a nearer approach. This belief is the necessary result of placing the mind in such circumstances. It is an operation of the soul, when we are so situated, as unavoidable as to feel the passion of love, when we receive benefits; or hatred, when we meet with injuries. All these operations are a species of natural instincts, which no reasoning or process of the thought and understanding is able either to produce or to prevent. At this point it

would be very allowable for us to stop our philosophical researches. In most questions we can never make a single step further; and in all questions we must terminate here at last, after our most restless and curious inquiries. But still our curiosity will be pardonable, perhaps commendable, if it carry us on to still further researches and make us examine more accurately the nature of this *belief* and of the *customary conjunction* whence it is derived. By this means we may meet with some explications and analogies that will give satisfaction, at least to such as love the abstract sciences, and can be entertained with speculations which, however accurate, may still retain a degree of doubt and uncertainty. As to readers of a different taste, the remaining part of this Section is not calculated for them; and the following inquiries may well be understood, though it be neglected.

Part II

Nothing is more free than the imagination of man, and though it cannot exceed that original stock of ideas furnished by the internal and external senses, it has unlimited power of mixing, compounding, separating, and dividing these ideas in all the varieties of fiction and vision. It can feign a train of events with all the appearance of reality, ascribe to them a particular time and place, conceive them as existent, and paint them out to itself with every circumstance that belongs to any historical fact which it believes with the greatest certainty. Wherein, therefore, consists the difference between such a fiction and belief? It lies not merely in any peculiar idea which is annexed to such a conception as commands our assent, and which is wanting to every known fiction. For as the mind has authority over all its ideas, it could voluntarily annex this particular idea to any fiction, and consequently be able to believe whatever it pleases, contrary to what we find by daily experience. We can, in our conception, join the head of a man to the body of a horse, but it is not in our power to believe that such an animal has ever really existed.

It follows, therefore, that the difference between *fiction* and *belief* lies in some sentiment or feeling which is annexed to the latter, not to the former, and which depends not on the will, nor can be demanded at pleasure. It must be excited by nature like all other sentiments and must rise from the particular situation in which the mind is placed at any particular juncture. Whenever any object is presented to the memory or senses, it immediately, by the force of custom, carries the imagination to conceive that object which is usually conjoined to it; and this conception is attended with a feeling or sentiment different from the loose reveries of the fancy. In this consists the whole nature of belief. For as there is no matter of fact which we believe so firmly that we cannot conceive the contrary, there would be no difference between the conception assented to and that which is rejected were it not for some sentiment which distinguishes the one from the other. If I see a billiard ball moving toward another on a smooth table, I can easily conceive it to stop upon contact. This conception implies no contradiction, but still it feels very differently from that conception by which I represent to myself the impulse and the communication of motion from one ball to another.

Were we to attempt a *definition* of this sentiment, we should, perhaps, find it a very difficult, if not an impossible, task; in the same manner as if we should endeavor to define the feeling of cold, or passion of anger, to a creature who never had any experience of these sentiments. Belief is the true and proper name of this feeling, and no one is ever at a loss to know the meaning of that term, because every man is every moment conscious of the sentiment represented by it. It may not, however, be improper to attempt a *description* of this sentiment, in hopes we may by that means arrive at some analogies which may afford a more perfect explication of it. I say that belief is nothing but a more vivid, lively, forcible, firm, steady conception of an object than what the imagination alone is ever able to attain. This variety of terms, which may seem so unphilosophical, is intended only to express that act of the mind which renders realities, or what is taken for such, more present to us than fictions, causes them to weigh more in the thought, and gives them a superior influence on the passions and imagination. Provided we agree about the thing, it is needless to dispute about the terms. The imagination has the command over all its ideas and can join and mix and vary them in all the ways possible. It may conceive fictitious objects with all the circumstances of place and time. It may set them in a manner before our eyes, in their true colors, just as they might have existed. But as it is impossible that this faculty of imagination can ever, of itself, reach belief, it is evident that belief consists not in the peculiar nature or order of ideas, but in the *manner* of their conception and in their *feeling* to the mind. I confess that it is impossible perfectly to explain this feeling or manner of conception. We may make use of words which express something near it. But its true and proper name, as we observed before, is "belief," which is a term that everyone sufficiently understands in common life. And in philosophy we can go no further than assert that *belief* is something felt by the mind, which distinguishes the ideas of the judgment from the fictions of the imagination. It gives them more weight and influence, makes them appear of greater importance, enforces them in the mind, and renders them the governing principle of our actions. I hear at present, for instance, a person's voice with whom I am acquainted, and the sound comes as from the next room. This impression of my senses immediately conveys my thought to the person, together with all the surrounding objects. I paint them out to myself as existing at present, with the same qualities and relations of which I formerly knew them possessed. These ideas take faster hold of my mind than ideas of an enchanted castle. They are very different from the feeling and have a much greater influence of every kind, either to give pleasure or pain, joy or sorrow.

Let us, then, take in the whole compass of this doctrine and allow that the sentiment of belief is nothing but a conception more intense and steady than what attends the mere fictions of the imagination, and that this *manner* of conception arises from a customary conjunction of the object with something present to the memory or senses. I believe that it will not be difficult, upon these suppositions, to find other operations of the mind analogous to it and to trace up these phenomena to principles still more general.

We have already observed that nature has established connections among particular ideas, and that no sooner one idea occurs to our thoughts than it introduces its correlative and carries our attention towards it by a gentle and insensible movement. These principles of connection or association we have reduced to three, namely, "resemblance," "contiguity," and "causation," which are the only bonds that unite our thoughts together and beget that regular train of reflection or discourse which, in a greater or less degree, takes place among mankind. Now here arises a question on which the solution of the present difficulty will depend. Does it happen in all these relations that when one of the objects is presented to the senses or memory, the mind is not only carried to the conception of the correlative, but reaches a steadier and stronger conception of it than what otherwise it would have been able to attain? This seems to be the case with that belief which arises from the relation of cause and effect. And if the case be the same with the other relations or principles of association, this may be established as a general law which takes place in all the operations of the mind.

We may, therefore, observe, as the first experiment to our present purpose, that upon the appearance of the picture of an absent friend our idea of him is evidently enlivened by the *resemblance,* and that every passion which that idea occasions, whether of joy or sorrow, acquires new force and vigor. In producing this effect there concur both a relation and a present impression. Where the picture bears him no resemblance, at least was not intended for him, it never so much as conveys our thought to him. And where it is absent, as well as the person, though the mind may pass from the thought of one to that of the other, it feels its idea to be rather weakened than enlivened by that transition. We take a pleasure in viewing the picture of a friend when it is set before us; but when it is removed, rather choose to consider him directly than by reflection on an image which is equally distant and obscure.

The ceremonies of the Roman Catholic religion may be considered as instances of the same nature. The devotees of that superstition usually plead, in excuse for the mummeries with which they are upbraided, that they feel the good effect of those external motions, and postures, and actions in enlivening their devotion and quickening their fervor, which otherwise would decay if directed entirely to distant and immaterial objects. We shadow out the objects of our faith, say they, in sensible types and images, and render them more present to us by the immediate presence of these types than it is possible for us to do merely by an intellectual view and contemplation. Sensible objects have always a greater influence on the fancy than any other, and this influence they readily convey to those ideas to which they are related and which they resemble. I shall only infer from these practices and this reasoning that the effect of resemblance in enlivening the ideas is very common; and as in every case a resemblance and a present impression must concur, we are abundantly supplied with experiments to prove the reality of the foregoing principle.

We may add force to these experiments by others of a different kind, in considering the effects of *contiguity* as well as of *resemblance.* It is certain that distance diminishes the force of every idea and that, upon our approach to any object, though it does not discover itself to our senses, it operates upon the mind with an influence which imitates an immediate impression. The thinking on any object readily transports the mind to what is contiguous; but it is only the actual presence of an object that transports it with a superior vivacity. When I am a few miles from home, whatever relates to it touches me more nearly than when I am two hundred leagues distant, though even at that distance the reflecting on anything in the neighborhood of my friends or family naturally produces an idea of them. But, as in this latter case, both the objects of the mind are ideas, notwithstanding there is an easy transition between them: that transition alone is not able to give a superior vivacity to any of the ideas, for want of some immediate impression.[4]

No one can doubt but *causation* has the same influence as the other two relations of resemblance and contiguity. Superstitious people are fond of the relics of saints and holy men, for the same reason that they seek after types or images in order to enliven their devotion and give them a more intimate and strong conception of those exemplary lives which they desire to imitate. Now it is evident that one of the best relics which a devotee could procure would be the handiwork of a saint; and if his clothes and furniture are ever to be considered in this light, it is because they were once at his disposal and were moved and affected by him; in which respect they are to be considered as imperfect effects, and as connected with him by a shorter chain of consequences than any of those by which we learn the reality of his existence.

Suppose that the son of a friend who had been long dead or absent were presented to us; it is evident that this object would instantly revive its correlative idea and recall to our thoughts all past intimacies and familiarities in more lively color than they would otherwise have appeared to us. This is another phenomenon which seems to prove the principle above mentioned.

We may observe that in these phenomena the belief of the correlative object is always presupposed, without which the relation could have no effect. The influence of the picture supposes that we *believe* our friend to have once existed. Contiguity to home can never excite our ideas of home unless we *believe* that it really exists. Now I assert that this belief, where it reaches beyond the memory or senses, is of a similar nature and arises from similar causes with the transition of thought and vivacity of conception here explained. When I throw a piece of dry wood into a fire, my mind is immediately carried to conceive that it augments, not extinguishes, the flame. This transition of thought from the cause to the effect proceeds not from reason. It derives its origin altogether from custom and experience. And, as it first begins from an object present to the senses, it renders the idea or conception of flame more strong or lively than any loose floating reverie of the imagination. The idea arises immediately. The thought moves instantly toward it and conveys to it all that force of conception which is derived from the impression present to the senses. When a sword is leveled at my breast, does not the idea of wound and pain strike me more strongly than when a glass of wine is presented to me, even though by accident this idea should occur after the appearance of the latter object? But what is

there in this whole matter to cause such a strong conception except only a present object and a customary transition to the idea of another object which we have been accustomed to conjoin with the former? This is the whole operation of the mind in all our conclusions concerning matter of fact and existence; and it is a satisfaction to find some analogies by which it may be explained. The transition from a present object does in all cases give strength and solidity to the related idea.

Here, then, is a kind of pre-established harmony between the course of nature and the succession of our ideas; and though the powers and forces by which the former is governed be wholly unknown to us, yet our thoughts and conceptions have still, we find, gone on in the same train with the other works of nature. Custom is that principle by which this correspondence has been effected, so necessary to the subsistence of our species and the regulation of our conduct in every circumstance and occurrence of human life. Had not the presence of an object instantly excited the idea of those objects commonly conjoined with it, all our knowledge must have been limited to the narrow sphere of our memory and senses, and we should never have been able to adjust means to ends or employ our natural powers either to the producing of good or avoiding of evil. Those who delight in the discovery and contemplation of *final causes* have here ample subject to employ their wonder and admiration.

I shall add, for a further confirmation of the foregoing theory, that as this operation of the mind, by which we infer like effects from like causes, and *vice versa,* is so essential to the subsistence of all human creatures, it is not probable that it could be trusted to the fallacious deductions of our reason, which is slow in its operations, appears not, in any degree, during the first years of infancy, and, at best, is in every age and period of human life extremely liable to error and mistake. It is more conformable to the ordinary wisdom of nature to secure so necessary an act of the mind by some instinct or mechanical tendency which may be infallible in its operations, may discover itself at the first appearance of life and thought, and may be independent of all the labored deductions of the understanding. As nature has taught us the use of our limbs without giving us the knowledge of the muscles and nerves by which they are actuated, so has she implanted in us an instinct which carries forward the thought in a correspondent course to that which she has established among external objects, though we are ignorant of those powers and forces on which this regular course and succession of objects totally depends.

SECTION VI. OF PROBABILITY[5]

Though there be no such thing as *chance* in the world, our ignorance of the real cause of any event has the same influence on the understanding and begets a like species of belief or opinion.

There is certainly a probability which arises from a superiority of chances on any side; and, according as this superiority increases and surpasses the opposite chances, the probability receives a proportionable increase and begets still a higher degree of belief of assent to that side in which we discover the superiority. If a die were marked with one figure or number of spots on four sides, and with another figure or number of spots on the two remaining sides, it would be more probable that the former would turn up than the latter, though, if it had a thousand sides marked in the same manner, and only one side different, the probability would be much higher and our belief or expectation of the event more steady and secure. This process of the thought or reasoning may seem trivial and obvious; but to those who consider it more narrowly it may, perhaps, afford matter for curious speculation.

It seems evident that when the mind looks forward to discover the event which may result from the throw of such a die, it considers the turning up of each particular side as alike probable; and this is the very nature of chance, to render all the particular events comprehended in it entirely equal. But finding a greater number of sides concur in the one event than in the other, the mind is carried more frequently to that event and meets it oftener in revolving the various possibilities or chances on which the ultimate result depends. This concurrence of several views in one particular event begets immediately, by an explicable contrivance of nature, the

sentiment of belief and gives that event the advantage over its antagonist which is supported by a smaller number of views and recurs less frequently to the mind. If we allow that belief is nothing but a firmer and stronger conception of an object than what attends the mere fictions of the imagination, this operation may, perhaps, in some measure be accounted for. The concurrence of these several views or glimpses imprints the idea more strongly on the imagination, gives it superior force and vigor, renders its influence on the passions and affections more sensible, and, in a word, begets that reliance or security which constitutes the nature of belief and opinion.

The case is the same with the probability of causes as with that of chance. There are some causes which are entirely uniform and constant in producing a particular effect, and no instance has ever yet been found of any failure or irregularity in their operation. Fire has always burned, and water suffocated, every human creature. The production of motion by impulse and gravity is a universal law which has hitherto admitted of no exception. But there are other causes which have been found more irregular and uncertain, nor has rhubarb always proved a purge, or opium a soporific, to everyone who has taken these medicines. It is true, when any cause fails of producing its usual effect, philosophers ascribe not this to any irregularity in nature, but suppose that some secret causes in the particular structure of parts have prevented the operation. Our reasonings, however, and conclusions concerning the event are the same as if this principle had no place. Being determined by custom to transfer the past to the future in all our inferences, where the past has been entirely regular and uniform we expect the event with the greatest assurance and leave no room for any contrary supposition. But where different effects have been found to follow from causes which are to *appearance* exactly similar, all these various effects must occur to the mind in transferring the past to the future, and enter into our consideration when we determine the probability of the event. Though we give the preference to that which has been found most usual, and believe that this effect will exist, we must not overlook the other effects, but must assign to each of them a particular weight and authority in proportion as we have found it to be more or less frequent. It is more probable, in almost every country of Europe, that there will be frost sometime in January than that the weather will continue open throughout the whole month, though this probability varies according to the different climates, and approaches to a certainty in the more northern kingdoms. Here, then, it seems evident that when we transfer the past to the future in order to determine the effect which will result from any cause, we transfer all the different events in the same proportion as they have appeared in the past, and conceive one to have existed a hundred times, for instance, another ten times, and another once. As a great number of views do here concur in one event, they fortify and confirm it to the imagination, beget that sentiment which we call "belief," and give its object the preference above the contrary event which is not supported by an equal number of experiments and recurs not so frequently to the thought in transferring the past to the future. Let anyone try to account for this operation of the mind upon any of the received systems of philosophy, and he will be sensible of the difficulty. For my part, I shall think it sufficient if the present hints excite the curiosity of philosophers and make them sensible how defective all common theories are in treating of such curious and such sublime subjects.

SECTION VII. OF THE IDEA OF NECESSARY CONNECTION

Part I

The great advantage of the mathematical sciences above the moral consists in this, that the ideas of the former, being sensible, are always clear and determinate, the smallest distinction between them is immediately perceptible, and the same terms are still expressive of the same ideas without ambiguity or variation. An oval is never mistaken for a circle, nor a hyperbola for an ellipsis. The isosceles and scalenum are distinguished by boundaries more exact than vice and virtue, right and wrong. If any term be defined in geometry, the mind readily, of itself substitutes on all occasions

the definition for the term defined, or, even when no definition is employed, the object itself may be presented to the senses and by that means be steadily and clearly apprehended. But the finer sentiments of the mind, the operations of the understanding, the various agitations of the passions, though really in themselves distinct, easily escape us when surveyed by reflection, nor is it in our power to recall the original object as often as we have occasion to contemplate it. Ambiguity, by this means, is gradually introduced into our reasonings: similar objects are readily taken to be the same, and the conclusion becomes at last very wide of the premises.

One may safely, however, affirm that if we consider these sciences in a proper light, their advantages and disadvantages nearly compensate each other and reduce both of them to a state of equality. If the mind, with greater facility, retains the ideas of geometry clear and determinate, it must carry on a much longer and more intricate chain of reasoning and compare ideas much wider of each other in order to reach the abstruser truths of that science. And if moral ideas are apt, without extreme care, to fall into obscurity and confusion, the inferences are always much shorter in these disquisitions, and the intermediate steps which lead to the conclusion much fewer than in the sciences which treat of quantity and number. In reality, there is scarcely a proposition in Euclid so simple as not to consist of more parts than are to be found in any moral reasoning which runs not into chimera and conceit. Where we trace the principles of the human mind through a few steps, we may be very well satisfied with our progress, considering how soon nature throws a bar to all our inquiries concerning causes and reduces us to an acknowledgment of our ignorance. The chief obstacle, therefore, to our improvements in the moral or metaphysical sciences is the obscurity of the ideas and ambiguity of the terms. The principal difficulty in the mathematics is the length of inferences and compass of thought requisite to the forming of any conclusion. And, perhaps, our progress in natural philosophy is chiefly retarded by the want of proper experiments and phenomena, which are often discovered by chance and cannot always be found when requisite, even by the most diligent and prudent inquiry. As moral philosophy seems hitherto to have received less improvement than either geometry or physics, we may conclude that if there be any difference in this respect among these sciences, the difficulties which obstruct the progress of the former require superior care and capacity to be surmounted.

There are no ideas which occur in metaphysics more obscure and uncertain than those of "power," "force," "energy," or "necessary connection," of which it is every moment necessary for us to treat in all our disquisitions. We shall, therefore, endeavor in this Section to fix, if possible, the precise meaning of these terms and thereby remove some part of that obscurity which is so much complained of in this species of philosophy.

It seems a proposition which will not admit of much dispute that all our ideas are nothing but copies of our impressions, or, in other words, that it is impossible for us to *think* of anything which we have not antecedently *felt*, either by our external or internal senses. I have endeavored[6] to explain and prove this proposition, and have expressed my hopes that by a proper application of it men may reach a greater clearness and precision in philosophical reasonings than what they have hitherto been able to attain. Complex ideas may, perhaps, be well known by definition, which is nothing but an enumeration of those parts or simple ideas that compose them. But when we have pushed up definitions to the most simple ideas and find still some ambiguity and obscurity, what resources are we then possessed of? By what invention can we throw light upon these ideas and render them altogether precise and determinate to our intellectual view? Produce the impressions or original sentiments from which the ideas are copied. These impressions are all strong and sensible. They admit not of ambiguity. They are not only placed in a full light themselves, but may throw light on their correspondent ideas, which lie in obscurity. And by this means we may perhaps attain a new microscope or species of optics by which, in the moral sciences, the most minute and most simple ideas may be so enlarged as to fall readily under our apprehension and be equally known with the grossest and most sensible ideas that can be the object of our inquiry.

To be fully acquainted, therefore, with the idea of power or necessary connection, let us examine its impression and, in order to find the impression with greater certainty, let us search for it in all the sources from which it may possibly be derived.

When we look about us towards external objects and consider the operation of causes, we are never able, in a single instance, to discover any power or necessary connection, any quality which binds the effect to the cause and renders the one an infallible consequence of the other. We only find that the one does actually in fact follow the other. The impulse of one billiard ball is attended with motion in the second. This is the whole that appears to the *outward* senses. The mind feels no sentiment or *inward* impression from this succession of objects; consequently, there is not, in any single particular instance of cause and effect, anything which can suggest the idea of power or necessary connection.

From the first appearance of an object we never can conjecture what effect will result from it. But were the power or energy of any cause discoverable by the mind, we could foresee the effect, even without experience, and might, at first, pronounce with certainty concerning it by mere dint of thought and reasoning.

In reality, there is no part of matter that does ever, by its sensible qualities, discover any power or energy, or give us ground to imagine that it could produce anything, or be followed by any other object, which we could denominate its effect. Solidity, extension, motion—these qualities are all complete in themselves and never point out any other event which may result from them. The scenes of the universe are continually shifting, and one object follows another in an uninterrupted succession; but the power or force which actuates the whole machine is entirely concealed from us and never discovers itself in any of the sensible qualities of body. We know that, in fact, heat is a constant attendant of flame; but what is the connection between them we have no room so much as to conjecture or imagine. It is impossible, therefore, that the idea of power can be derived from the contemplation of bodies in single instances of their operation, because no bodies ever discover any power which can be the original of this idea.[7]

Since, therefore, external objects as they appear to the senses give us no idea of power or necessary connection by their operation in particular instances, let us see whether this idea be derived from reflection on the operations of our own minds and be copied from any internal impression. It may be said that we are every moment conscious of internal power while we feel that, by the simple command of our will, we can move the organs of our body or direct the faculties of our mind. An act of volition produces motion in our limbs or raises a new idea in our imagination. This influence of the will we know by consciousness. Hence we acquire the idea of power or energy, and are certain that we ourselves and all other intelligent beings are possessed of power. This idea, then, is an idea of reflection since it arises from reflecting on the operations of our own mind and on the command which is exercised by will both over the organs of the body and faculties of the soul.

We shall proceed to examine this pretension and, first, with regard to the influence of volition over the organs of the body. This influence, we may observe, is a fact which, like all other natural events, can be known only by experience, and can never be foreseen from any apparent energy or power in the cause which connects it with the effect and renders the one an infallible consequence of the other. The motion of our body follows upon the command of our will. Of this we are every moment conscious. But the means by which this is effected, the energy by which the will performs so extraordinary an operation—of this we are so far from being immediately conscious that it must forever escape our most diligent inquiry.

For, *first,* is there any principle in all nature more mysterious than the union of soul with body, by which a supposed spiritual substance acquires such an influence over a material one that the most refined thought is able to actuate the grossest matter? Were we empowered by a secret wish to remove mountains or control the planets in their orbit, this extensive authority would not be more extraordinary, nor more

beyond our comprehension. But if, by consciousness, we perceived any power or energy in the will, we must know this power; we must know its connection with the effect; we must know the secret union of soul and body, and the nature of both these substances by which the one is able to operate in so many instances upon the other.

Secondly, we are not able to move all the organs of the body with a like authority, though we cannot assign any reason, besides experience, for so remarkable a difference between one and the other. Why has the will an influence over the tongue and fingers, not over the heart and liver? This question would never embarrass us were we conscious of a power in the former case, not in the latter. We should then perceive, independent of experience, why the authority of the will over organs of the body is circumscribed within such particular limits. Being in that case fully acquainted with the power or force by which it operates, we should also know why its influence reaches precisely to such boundaries, and no further.

A man suddenly struck with a palsy in the leg or arm, or who had newly lost those members, frequently endeavors, at first, to move them and employ them in their usual offices. Here he is as much conscious of power to command such limbs as a man in perfect health is conscious of power to actuate any member which remains in its natural state and condition. But consciousness never deceives. Consequently, neither in the one case nor in the other are we ever conscious of any power. We learn the influence of our will from experience alone. And experience only teaches us how one event constantly follows another, without instructing us in the secret connection which binds them together and renders them inseparable.

Thirdly, we learn from anatomy that the immediate object of power in voluntary motion is not the member itself which is moved, but certain muscles and nerves and animal spirits, and, perhaps, something still more minute and more unknown, through which the motion is successfully propagated ere it reach the member itself whose motion is the immediate object of volition. Can there be a more certain proof that the power by which this whole operation is performed, so far from being directly and fully known by an inward sentiment or consciousness, is to the last degree mysterious and unintelligible? Here the mind wills a certain event; immediately another event, unknown to ourselves and totally different from the one intended, is produced. This event produces another, equally unknown, till, at last, through a long succession the desired event is produced. But if the original power were felt, it must be known; were it known, its effect must also be known, since all power is relative to its effect. And, *vice versa,* if the effect be not known, the power cannot be known nor felt. How indeed can we be conscious of a power to move our limbs when we have no such power, but only that to move certain animal spirits which, though they produce at last the motion of our limbs, yet operate in such a manner as is wholly beyond our comprehension?

We may therefore conclude from the whole, I hope, without any temerity, though with assurance, that our idea of power is not copied from any sentiment or consciousness of power within ourselves when we give rise to animal motion or apply our limbs to their proper use and office. That their motion follows the command of the will is a matter of common experience, like other natural events; but the power or energy by which this is effected, like that in other natural events, is unknown and inconceivable.[8]

Shall we then assert that we are conscious of a power or energy in our own minds when, by an act or command of our will, we raise up a new idea, fix the mind to the contemplation of it, turn it on all sides, and at last dismiss it for some other idea when we think that we have surveyed it with sufficient accuracy? I believe the same arguments will prove that even this command of the will gives us no real idea of force or energy.

First, it must be allowed that when we know a power, we know that very circumstance in the cause by which it is enabled to produce the effect, for these are supposed to be synonymous. We must, therefore, know both the cause and effect and the relation between them. But do we pretend to be acquainted with the nature of the human soul and the nature of an idea, or the aptitude of the one to produce the other? This is a real creation, a production of something out of nothing, which implies a power so great that it may seem, at first sight, beyond the reach of any being less than infinite. At least it must be owned that such a power is not felt, nor known, nor even conceivable by the mind. We only feel the event, namely, the existence of an idea consequent to a command of the will; but the manner in which this operation is performed, the power by which it is produced, is entirely beyond our comprehension.

Secondly, the command of the mind over itself is limited, as well as its command over the body; and these limits are not known by reason or any acquaintance with the nature of cause and effect, but only by experience and observation, as in all other natural events and in the operation of external objects. Our authority over our sentiments and passions is much weaker than that over our ideas; and even the latter authority is circumscribed within very narrow boundaries. Will any one pretend to assign the ultimate reason of these boundaries, or show why the power is deficient in one case, not in another.

Thirdly, this self-command is very different at different times. A man in health possesses more of it than one languishing with sickness. We are more master of our thoughts in the morning than in the evening; fasting, than after a full meal. Can we give any reason for these variations except experience? Where then is the power of which we pretend to be conscious? Is there not here, either in a spiritual or material substance, or both, some secret mechanism or structure of parts upon which the effect depends, and which, being entirely unknown to us, renders the power or energy of the will equally unknown and incomprehensible?

Volition is surely an act of the mind with which we are sufficiently acquainted. Reflect upon it. Consider it on all sides. Do you find anything in it like this creative power by which it raises from nothing a new idea and, with a kind of *fiat,* imitates the omnipotence of its Maker, if I may be allowed so to speak, who called forth into existence all the various scenes of nature? So far from being conscious of this energy in the will, it requires as certain experience as that of which we are possessed to convince us that such extraordinary effects do ever result from a simple act of volition.

The generality of mankind never find any difficulty in accounting for the more common and familiar operations of nature, such as the descent of heavy bodies, the growth of plants, the generation of animals, or the nourishment of bodies by food; but suppose that in all these cases they perceive the very force or energy of the cause by which it is connected with its effect, and is forever infallible in its operation. They acquire, by long habit, such a turn of mind that upon the appearance of the cause they immediately expect, with assurance, its usual attendant, and hardly conceive it possible that any other event could result from it. It is only on the discovery of extraordinary phenomena, such as earthquakes, pestilence, and prodigies of any kind, that they find themselves at a loss to assign a proper cause and to explain the manner in which the effect is produced by it. It is usual for men, in such difficulties, to have recourse to some invisible intelligent principle as the immediate cause of that event which surprises them, and which they think cannot be accounted for from the common powers of nature. But philosophers, who carry their scrutiny a little further, immediately perceive that, even in the most familiar events, the energy of the cause is as unintelligible as in the most unusual, and that we only learn by experience the frequent conjunction of objects, without being ever able to comprehend anything like connection between them. Here, then, many philosophers think themselves obliged by reason to have recourse, on all occasions, to the same principle which the vulgar never appeal to but in cases that appear miraculous and supernatural. They acknowledge mind and intelligence to be, not only the ultimate and original cause of all things, but the immediate and sole cause of every event which appears in nature. They pretend that those objects which are commonly denominated "causes" are in reality nothing but "occasions," and that the true and direct principle of every effect is not any power or force in nature, but a volition of the Supreme Being, who wills that such particular objects should forever be conjoined with each other. Instead of saying that one billiard ball moves another by a force which

it has derived from the author of nature, it is the Deity himself, they say, who, by a particular volition, moves the second ball, being determined to this operation by the impulse of the first ball, in consequence of those general laws which he has laid down to himself in the government of the universe. But philosophers, advancing still in their inquiries, discover that as we are totally ignorant of the power on which depends the mutual operation of bodies, we are no less ignorant of that power on which depends the operation of mind on body, or of body on mind; nor are we able, either from our senses or consciousness, to assign the ultimate principle in the one case more than in the other. The same ignorance, therefore, reduces them to the same conclusion. They assert that the Deity is the immediate cause of the union between soul and body, and that they are not the organs of sense which, being agitated by external objects, produce sensations in the mind; but that it is a particular volition of our omnipotent Maker which excites such a sensation in consequence of such a motion in the organ. In like manner, it is not any energy in the will that produces local motion in our members: It is God himself, who is pleased to second our will, in itself impotent, and to command that motion which we erroneously attribute to our own power and efficacy. Nor do philosophers stop at this conclusion. They sometimes extend the same inference to the mind itself in its internal operations. Our mental vision or conception of ideas is nothing but a revelation made to us by our Maker. When we voluntarily turn our thoughts to any object and raise up its image in the fancy, it is not the will which creates that idea, it is the universal Creator who discovers it to the mind and renders it present to us.

Thus, according to these philosophers, everything is full of God. Not content with the principle that nothing exists but by his will, that nothing possesses any power but by his concession, they rob nature and all created beings of every power in order to render their dependence on the Deity still more sensible and immediate. They consider not that by this theory they diminish, instead of magnifying, the grandeur of those attributes which they affect so much to celebrate.

It argues, surely, more power in the Deity to delegate a certain degree of power to inferior creatures than to produce everything by his own immediate volition. It argues more wisdom to contrive at first the fabric of the world with such perfect foresight that of itself, and by its proper operation, it may serve all the purposes of Providence than if the great Creator were obliged every moment to adjust its parts and animate by his breath all the wheels of that stupendous machine.

But if we would have a more philosophical confutation of this theory, perhaps the two following reflections may suffice:

First, it seems to me that this theory of the universal energy and operation of the Supreme Being is too bold ever to carry conviction with it to a man sufficiently apprised of the weakness of human reason and the narrow limits to which it is confined in all its operations. Though the chain of arguments which conduct to it were ever so logical, there must arise a strong suspicion, if not an absolute assurance, that it has carried us quite beyond the reach of our faculties when it leads to conclusions so extraordinary and so remote from common life and experience. We are got into fairyland long ere we have reached the last steps of our theory; and *there* we have no reason to trust our common methods of arguments or to think that our usual analogies and probabilities have any authority. Our line is too short to fathom such immense abysses. And however we may flatter ourselves that we are guided, in every step which we take, by a kind of verisimilitude and experience, we may be assured that this fancied experience has no authority when we thus apply it to subjects that lie entirely out of the sphere of experience. But on this we shall have occasion to touch afterwards.[9]

Secondly, I cannot perceive any force in the arguments on which this theory is founded. We are ignorant, it is true, of the manner in which bodies operate on each other. Their force or energy is entirely incomprehensible. But are we not equally ignorant of the manner or force by which a mind, even the Supreme Mind, operates, either on itself or on body? Whence, I beseech you, do we acquire any idea of it? We have no sentiment or consciousness of this power in ourselves. We have no idea of the Supreme Being but what we learn from reflection on our own faculties. Were our ignorance, therefore, a good reason for rejecting anything, we should be led into that principle of denying all energy in the Supreme Being, as much as in the grossest matter. We surely comprehend as little the operations of the one as of the other. Is it more difficult to conceive that motion may arise from impulse than that it may arise from volition? All we know is our profound ignorance in both cases.[10]

Part II

But to hasten to a conclusion of this argument, which is already drawn out to too great a length: We have sought in vain for an idea of power or necessary connection in all the sources from which we could suppose it to be derived. It appears that in single instances of the operation of bodies we never can, by our utmost scrutiny, discover anything but one event following another, without being able to comprehend any force or power by which the cause operates or any connection between it and its supposed effect. The same difficulty occurs in contemplating the operations of mind on body, where we observe the motion of the latter to follow upon the volition of the former, but are not able to observe or conceive the tie which binds together the motion and volition, or the energy, by which the mind produces this effect. The authority of the will over its own faculties and ideas is not a whit more comprehensible, so that, upon the whole, there appears not, throughout all nature, any one instance of connection which is conceivable by us. All events seem entirely loose and separate. One event follows another, but we never can observe any tie between them. They seem *conjoined*, but never *connected*. And as we can have no idea of anything which never appeared to our outward sense or inward sentiment, the necessary conclusion *seems* to be that we have no idea of connection or power at all, and that these words are absolutely without any meaning when employed either in philosophical reasonings or common life.

But there still remains one method of avoiding this conclusion, and one source which we have not yet examined. When any natural object or event is presented, it is impossible for us, by any sagacity or penetration, to discover, or even conjecture, without experience, what event will result from it, or to carry our foresight beyond that object which is immediately present to the memory and senses. Even after one instance or experiment where we have observed a particular event to follow upon another, we are not entitled to form a general rule or foretell what will happen in like cases, it being justly esteemed an unpardonable temerity to judge the whole course of nature from one single experiment, however accurate or certain. But when one particular species of events has always, in all instances, been conjoined with another, we make no longer any scruple of foretelling one upon the appearance of the other, and of employing that reasoning which can alone assure us of any matter of fact or existence. We then call the one object "cause," the other "effect." We suppose that there is some connection between them, some power in the one by which it infallibly produces the other and operates with the greatest certainty and strongest necessity.

It appears, then, that this idea of a necessary connection among events arises from a number of similar instances which occur, of the constant conjunction of these events; nor can that idea ever be suggested by any one of these instances surveyed in all possible lights and positions. But there is nothing in a number of instances, different from every single instance, which is supposed to be exactly similar, except only that after a repetition of similar instances the mind is carried by habit, upon the appearance of one event, to expect its usual attendant and to believe that it will exist. This connection, therefore, which we *feel* in the mind, this customary transition of the imagination from one object to its usual attendant, is the sentiment or impression from which we form the idea of power or necessary connection. Nothing further is in the case. Contemplate the subject on all sides, you will never find any other origin of that idea. This is the sole difference between one instance, from which we can never receive the idea of connection, and a number of similar instances by which it is suggested. The first time a man saw the communication of

motion by impulse, as by the shock of two billiard balls, he could not pronounce that the one event was *connected*, but only that it was *conjoined* with the other. After he has observed several instances of this nature, he then pronounces them to be *connected*. What alteration has happened to give rise to this new idea of *connection*? Nothing but that he now *feels* these events to be *connected* in his imagination, and can readily foretell the existence of one from the appearance of the other. When we say, therefore, that one object is connected with another, we mean only that they have acquired a connection in our thought and give rise to this inference by which they become proofs of each other's existence—a conclusion which is somewhat extraordinary, but which seems founded on sufficient evidence. Nor will its evidence be weakened by any general diffidence of the understanding or skeptical suspicion concerning every conclusion which is new and extraordinary. No conclusions can be more agreeable to skepticism than such as make discoveries concerning the weakness and narrow limits of human reason and capacity.

And what stronger instance can be produced of the surprising ignorance and weakness of the understanding than the present? For surely, if there be any relation among objects which it imports us to know perfectly, it is that of cause and effect. On this are founded all our reasonings concerning matter of fact or existence. By means of it alone we attain any assurance concerning objects which are removed from the present testimony of our memory and senses. The only immediate utility of all sciences is to teach us how to control and regulate future events by their causes. Our thoughts and inquiries are, therefore, every moment employed about this relation; yet so imperfect are the ideas which we form concerning it that it is impossible to give any just definition of cause, except what is drawn from something extraneous and foreign to it. Similar objects are always conjoined with similar. Of this we have experience. Suitably to this experience, therefore, we may define a cause to be *an object followed by another, and where all the objects, similar to the first, are followed by objects similar to the second.* Or, in other words, *where, if the first object had not been, the second never had existed.* The appearance of a cause always conveys the mind, by a customary transition, to the idea of the effect. Of this also we have experience. We may, therefore, suitably to this experience, form another definition of cause and call it *an object followed by another, and whose appearance always conveys the thought to that other.* But though both these definitions be drawn from circumstances foreign to the cause, we cannot remedy this inconvenience or attain any more perfect definition which may point out that circumstance in the cause which gives it a connection with its effect. We have no idea of this connection, nor even any distinct notion what it is we desire to know when we endeavor at a conception of it. We say, for instance, that the vibration of this string is the cause of this particular sound. But what do we mean by that affirmation? We either mean *that this vibration is followed by this sound, and that all similar vibrations have been followed by similar sounds;* or, *that this vibration is followed by this sound, and that, upon the appearance of one, the mind anticipates the senses and forms immediately an idea of the other.* We may consider the relation of cause and effect in either of these two lights; but beyond these we have no idea of it.[11]

To recapitulate, therefore, the reasonings of this Section: Every idea is copied from some preceding impression or sentiment; and where we cannot find any impression, we may be certain that there is no idea. In all single instances of the operation of bodies or minds there is nothing that produces any impression, nor consequently can suggest any idea, of power or necessary connection. But when many uniform instances appear, and the same object is always followed by the same event, we then begin to entertain the notion of cause and connection. We then *feel* a new sentiment or impression, to wit, a customary connection in the thought or imagination between one object and its usual attendant; and this sentiment is the original of that idea which we seek for. For as this idea arises from a number of similar instances, and not from any single instance, it must arise from that circumstance in which the number of instances differ from every individual instance. But this customary connection or transition of the imagination is the only circumstance in which they differ. In every other particular they are alike. The first instance which we saw of motion, communicated by the shock of two billiard balls (to return to this obvious illustration), is exactly similar to any instance that may at present occur to us, except only that we could not at first *infer* one event from the other, which we are enabled to do at present, after so long a course of uniform experience. I know not whether the reader will readily apprehend this reasoning. I am afraid that, should I multiply words about it or throw it into a greater variety of lights, it would only become more obscure and intricate. In all abstract reasonings there is one point of view which, if we can happily hit, we shall go further towards illustrating the subject than by all the eloquence in the world. This point of view we should endeavor to reach, and reserve the flowers of rhetoric for subjects which are more adapted to them.

NOTES

1. It is probable that no more was meant by those who denied innate ideas than that all ideas were copies of our impressions, though it must be confessed that the terms which they employed were not chosen with such caution, nor so exactly defined, as to prevent all mistakes about their doctrine. For what is meant by "innate"? If "innate" be equivalent to "natural," then all the perceptions and ideas of the mind must be allowed to be innate or natural, in whatever sense we take the latter word, whether in opposition to what is uncommon, artificial, or miraculous. If by innate he meant contemporary to our birth, the dispute seems to be frivolous, nor is it worth while to inquire at what time thinking begins, whether before, at, or after our birth. Again, the word "idea" seems to be commonly taken in a very loose sense by Locke and others, as standing for any of our perceptions, our sensations and passions, as well as thoughts. Now, in this sense, I should desire to know what can be meant by asserting that self-love, or resentment of injuries, or the passion between the sexes is not innate?

    But admitting these terms "impressions" and "ideas" in the sense above explained, and understanding by "innate" what is original or copied from no precedent perception, then may we assert that all our impressions are innate, and our ideas not innate.

To be ingenuous, I must own it to be my opinion that Locke was betrayed into this question by the schoolmen, who, making use of undefined terms, draw out their disputes to a tedious length without ever touching the point in question. A like ambiguity and circumlocution seem to run through that philosopher's reasonings, on this as well as most other subjects.

2. The word "power" is here used in a loose and popular sense. The more accurate explication of it would give additional evidence to this argument. See Section VII.

3. Nothing is more usual than for writers, even on *moral, political,* or *physical* subjects, to distinguish between *reason* and *experience,* and to suppose that these species of argumentation are entirely different from each other. The former are taken for the mere result of our intellectual faculties, which, by considering *a priori* the nature of things, and examining the effects that must follow from their operation, establish particular principles of science and philosophy. The latter are supposed to be derived entirely from sense and observation, by which we learn what has actually resulted from the operation of particular objects, and are thence able to infer what will for the future result from them. Thus, for instance, the limitations and restraints of civil government and a legal constitution may be defended, either from *reason,* which, reflecting on the great frailty and corruption of human nature, teaches that no man can safely be trusted with unlimited authority; or from *experience* and history, which inform us of the enormous abuses that ambition in every age and country has been found to make of so imprudent a confidence.

The same distinction between reason and experience is maintained in all our deliberations concerning the conduct of life, while the experienced statesman, general physician, or merchant, is trusted and followed, and the unpracticed novice, with whatever natural talents endowed, neglected and despised. Though it be allowed that reason may form very plausible conjectures with regard to the consequences of such a particular conduct in such particular circumstances, it is still supposed imperfect without the assistance of experience, which is alone able to give stability and certainty to the maxim derived from study and reflection.

But notwithstanding that this distinction be thus universally received, both in the active and speculative scenes of life, I shall not scruple to pronounce that it is, at bottom, erroneous, or at least superficial.

If we examine those arguments which, in any of the sciences above mentioned, are supposed to be the mere effects of reasoning and reflection, they will be found to terminate at last in some general principle or conclusion for which we can assign no reason but observation and experience. The only difference between them and those maxims which are vulgarly esteemed the result of pure experience is that the former cannot be established without some process of thought, and some reflection on what we have observed, in order to distinguish its circumstances and trace its consequences—whereas, in the latter, the experienced event is exactly and fully similar to that which we infer as the result of any particular situation. The history of a Tiberius or a Nero makes us dread a like tyranny, were our monarchs freed from the restraints of laws and senates; but the observation of any fraud or cruelty in private life is sufficient, with the aid of a little thought, to give us the same apprehension, while it serves as an instance of the general corruption of human nature, and shows us the danger which we must incur by reposing an entire confidence in mankind. In both cases, it is experience which is ultimately the foundation of our inference and conclusion.

There is no man so young and unexperienced as not to have formed from observation many general and just maxims concerning human affairs and the conduct of life; but it must be confessed that when a man comes to put these in practice he will be extremely liable to error, till time and further experience both enlarge these maxims, and teach him their proper use and application. In every situation or incident there are many particular and seemingly minute circumstances which the man of greatest talents is at first apt to overlook, though on them the justness of his conclusions, and consequently the prudence of his conduct, entirely depend. Not to mention that, to a young beginner, the general observations and maxims occur not always on the proper occasions, nor can be immediately applied with due calmness and distinction. The truth is, an unexperienced reasoner could be no reasoner at all were he absolutely inexperienced; and when we assign that character to anyone, we mean it only in a comparative sense, and suppose him possessed of experience in a smaller and more imperfect degree.

4. [A footnote containing a long quotation from Cicero, deleted.]

5. Mr. Locke divides all arguments into "demonstrative" and "probable." In this view, we must say that it is only probable that all men must die, or that the sun will rise tomorrow. But to conform our language more to common use, we ought to divide arguments into *demonstrations, proofs,* and *probabilities;* by proofs, meaning such arguments from experience as leave no room for doubt or opposition.

6. Section II.

7. Mr. Locke, in his chapter of Power, says that, finding from experience that there are several new productions in matter, and concluding that there must somewhere be a power capable of producing them, we arrive at last by this reasoning at the idea of power. But no reasoning can ever give us a new, original simple idea, as this philosopher himself confesses. This, therefore, can never be the origin of that idea.

8. It may be pretended, that the resistance which we meet with in bodies, obliging us frequently to exert our force and call up all our power, this gives us the idea of force and power. It is this *nisus* or strong endeavor of which we are conscious, that is the original impression from which this idea is copied. But, *first,* we attribute power to a vast number of objects where we never can suppose this resistance or exertion of force to take place; to the Supreme Being, who never meets with any resistance; to the mind in its command over its ideas and limbs, in common thinking and motion, where the effect follows immediately upon the will, without any exertion or summoning up of force; to inanimate matter, which is not capable of this sentiment. *Secondly,* this sentiment of an endeavor to overcome resistance has no known connection with any event: What follows it we know by experience, but could not know it *a priori.* It must, however, be confessed that the animal *nisus* which we experience, though it can afford no accurate precise idea of power, enters very much into that vulgar, inaccurate idea which is formed of it.

9. Section XII. [Not included here.]

10. I need not examine at length the *vis inertiae* which is so much talked of in the new philosophy, and which is ascribed to matter. We find by experience that a body at rest or in motion continues forever in its present state, till put from it by some new cause; and that a body impelled takes as much motion from the impelling body as it acquires itself. These are facts. When we call this a *vis inertiae,* we only mark these facts, without pretending to have any idea of the inert power, in the same manner as, when we talk of gravity, we mean certain effects without comprehending that active power. It was never the meaning of Sir Isaac Newton to rob second causes of all force or energy, though some of his followers have endeavored to establish that theory upon his authority. On the contrary, that great philosopher had recourse to an ethereal active fluid to explain his universal attraction, though he was so cautious and modest as to allow that it was a mere hypothesis not to be insisted on without more experiments. I must confess that there is something in the fate of opinions a little extraordinary. Descartes insinuated that doctrine of the universal and sole efficacy of the Deity, without insisting on it. Malebranche and other Cartesians made it the foundation of all their philosophy. It had, however, no authority in England. Locke, Clarke, and Cudworth never so much as take notice of it, but suppose all along that matter has a real, though subordinate and derived, power. By what means has it become so prevalent among our modern metaphysicians?

11. According to these explications and definitions, the idea of *power* is relative as much as that of *cause;* and both have a reference to an effect, or some other event constantly conjoined with the former. When we consider the *unknown* circumstance of an object by which the degree or quantity of its effect is fixed and determined, we call that its power. And accordingly, it is allowed by all philosophers that the effect is the measure of the power. But if they had any idea of power as it is in itself, why could they not measure it in itself? The dispute, whether the force of a body in motion be as its velocity, or the square of its velocity; this dispute, I say, needed not be decided by comparing its effects in equal or unequal times, but by direct mensuration and comparison.

As to the frequent use of the words "force," "power," "energy," etc., which everywhere occur in common conversation as well as in philosophy, that is no proof that we are acquainted, in any instance, with the connecting principle between cause and effect, or can account ultimately for the production of one thing by another. These words, as commonly used, have very loose meanings annexed to them, and their ideas are very uncertain and confused. No animal can put external bodies in motion without the sentiment of a *nisus* or endeavor; and every animal has a sentiment or feeling from the stroke or blow of an external object that is in motion. These sensations, which are merely animal, and from which we can *a priori* draw no inference, we are apt to transfer to inanimate objects, and to suppose that they have some such feelings whenever they transfer or receive motion. With regard to energies, which are exerted without our annexing to them any idea of communicated motion, we consider only the constant experienced conjunction of the events; and as we *feel* a customary connection between the ideas, we transfer that feeling to the objects, as nothing is more usual than to apply to external bodies every internal sensation which they occasion.

An Encounter with David Hume

WESLEY C. SALMON

Wesley C. Salmon teaches history and philosophy of science at the University of Pittsburgh.

A DAY IN THE LIFE OF A HYPOTHETICAL STUDENT

In the physics 1a lecture hall, Professor Salvia[1] has had a bowling ball suspended from a high ceiling by a long rope so that it can swing back and forth like a pendulum. Standing well over to one side of the room, he holds the bowling ball at the tip of his nose. He releases it (taking great care not to give it a push). It swings through a wide arc, gaining considerable speed as it passes through the low portion of its swing beneath the point of suspension from the ceiling. It continues to the other side of the room, where it reaches the end of its path, and then returns. The professor stands motionless as the bowling ball moves faster and faster back toward his nose. As it passes through the midpoint of the return arc, it is again traveling very rapidly, but it begins to slow down, and it stops just at the tip of his nose. Some of the students think he is cool. "This demonstration," he says, "illustrates the faith that the physicist has in nature's regularity." (See Figure 1.)

Imagine that you have witnessed this demonstration just after your philosophy class, where the subject of discussion was Hume's *Enquiry Concerning Human Understanding*. You raise

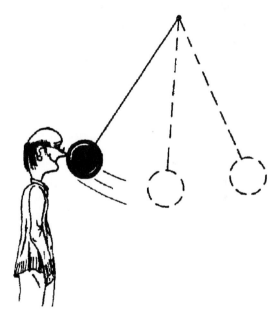

FIGURE 1 Prof Salvia's Pendulum. After swinging to the opposite side of the lecture hall, the bowling ball swings right back to the tip of the prof's nose, which remains motionless during the entire procedure.

your hand. "How did you *know* that the bowling ball would stop where it did, just short of bashing your nose into your face?" you ask.

"This is a standard demonstration," he replies; "I do it every year in this class, and it has often been used by many other physics teachers." In an attempt to inject a little humor, he adds, "If I had had any doubt about its working, I'd have had the teaching assistant do it."

"Are you saying, then, that you trusted the experiment to work this time simply because it has been tried so many times in the past, and has never failed?" You recall Hume's discussion of the collisions of billiard balls. In the first instance, according to Hume, before you have any experience with material objects colliding with one another, you would not know what to expect when you see a moving billiard ball approaching a stationary one, but after a good deal of experience you confidently expect some motion to be transferred to the stationary ball as a result of the collision. As your experience accumulates, you learn to predict the exact manner in which the second ball will move after being struck by the first. But you cannot really accept that answer, and neither, you feel sure, will your physics professor. Without waiting for an answer, you follow up your first question with another.

"I have this friend," you continue, "who drives like a maniac. It scares me to ride with him, but he always tells me not to worry—he has never had an accident, or even a traffic ticket. Should I conclude—assuming he is telling the truth (just as I assume you are telling me the truth about this demonstration)—that it is as safe for me to ride with him as it is for you to perform the bowling ball trick?"

"It's not the same thing at all," another student chimes in; "you can prove, mathematically, that the pendulum will not swing back beyond its original starting point, but you certainly can't prove mathematically that your friend won't have a wreck. In a way it's just the opposite; you can prove that he is likely to have an accident if he keeps on driving like that."

"What you say is partly right," says Professor Salvia to the second student, "but it isn't only a matter of mathematics. We have to rely upon the laws of physics as well. With the pendulum we were depending mainly upon the law of conservation of energy, one of the most fundamental laws of nature. As the pendulum goes through its swing, potential energy is transformed into kinetic energy, which is transformed back into potential energy, and so forth. As long as the total amount of energy remains unchanged, my nose is safe."

Since you have not yet studied the concept of energy, you do not worry too much about the details of the explanation. You are satisfied that you will understand why the pendulum behaves as it does when you have learned more about the concepts and laws that were mentioned. But you do remember something Hume wrote. There are two kinds of reasoning: reasoning concerning relations of ideas, and reasoning concerning matters of fact and existence. Mathematical reasoning falls into the former category (relations of ideas) and consequently, by itself, cannot provide any information about matters of fact. The pendulum and the professor's nose are, however, matters of fact, so we need something in addition to mathematics to get the information we want concerning that situation. Professor Salvia has told us what it is—we need the laws of nature as well.

Since physics is your last class in the morning, you head for the cafeteria when it is over to get a sandwich and coffee. The philosophy class is still bugging you. What was it Hume said about bread? That we do not know the "secret power" by which it nourishes us? Now we do, of course; we understand metabolism, the mechanism by which the body converts food into energy. Hume (living in the eighteenth century) did not understand about power and energy, as he said repeatedly. He did not know why bread is suitable food for humans, but not for tigers and lions. In biology class, you recall, you studied herbiverous, carnivorous, and omniverous species. Biologists must now understand why some species can metabolize vegetables and others cannot. Modern physics, chemistry, and biology can provide a complete explanation of the various forms of energy, the ways they can be converted from one form to another, and the ways in which they can be utilized by a living organism.

Taking a sip of the hot coffee, you recall some other things Hume said—for example, remarks about the "connection" between heat and flame. We now know that heat is really a form of energy; that temperature is a measure of the average kinetic energy of the molecules. Now, it seems, we know a great deal about the "secret powers," "energy," etc., that so perplexed Hume. Modern physics knows that ordinary objects are composed of molecules, which are in turn composed of atoms, which are themselves made up of subatomic particles. Modern science can tell us what holds atoms and molecules together, and why the things that consist of them have the properties they do. What was it that Hume said about a piece of ice and a crystal (e.g., a diamond)? That we do not know why one is caused by cold and the other by heat? I'll just bet, you think, that Salvia could answer that one without a bit of trouble. Why, you wonder, do they make us read these old philosophers who are now so out of date? Hume was, no doubt, a very profound thinker in his day, but why do we have to study him now, when we know the answers to all of those questions? If I were majoring in history that might be one thing, but that doesn't happen to be my field of interest. Oh, I suppose they'd say that getting an education means that you have to learn something about the "great minds of the past," but why doesn't the philosophy professor come right out and tell us the answers to these questions? It's silly to pretend that they are still great mysteries.

After lunch, let's imagine, you go to a class in contemporary social and political problems, a class you particularly like because of the lively discussions. A lot of time is spent talking about such topics as population growth, ecology and the environment, energy demands and uses, food production, and pollution. You discuss population trends, the extrapolation of such trends, and the predication that by the year 2000 A.D., world population will reach 7 billion. You consider the various causes and possible effects of increasing concentrations of carbon dioxide in the atmosphere. You discuss solutions to various of these problems in terms of strict governmental controls, economic sanctions and incentives, and voluntary compliance on the part of enlightened and concerned citizens.

"If people run true to form," you interject, "if they behave as they always have, you can be sure that you won't make much progress relying on the good will and good sense of the populace at large."

"What is needed is more awareness and education," another student remarks, "for people can change if they see the need. During World War II people willingly sacrificed in order to support the war effort. They will do the same again, if they see that the emergency is really serious. That's why we need to provide more education and make stronger appeals to their humanitarian concerns."

"What humanitarian concerns?" asks still another student with evident cynicism.

"People *will* change," says another. "I have been reading that we are entering a new era, the Age of Aquarius, when man's finer, gentler, more considerate nature will be manifest."

"Well, I don't know about all of this astrology," another remarks in earnest tones, "but I do not believe that God will let His world perish if we mend our ways and trust in Him. I have complete faith in His goodness."

You find this statement curiously reminiscent of Professor Salvia's earlier mention of his faith in the regularity of nature.

That night, after dinner, you read an English assignment. By the time you finish it, your throat feels a little scratchy, and you notice that you have a few sniffles. You decide to begin taking large doses of vitamin C; you have read that there is quite some controversy as to whether this helps to ward off colds, but that there is no harm in taking this vitamin in large quantities. Before going to the drug store to buy some vitamin C, you write home to request some additional funds; you mail your letter in the box by the pharmacy. You return with the vitamin C, take a few of the pills, and turn in for the night—confident that the sun will rise tomorrow morning, and hoping that you won't feel as miserable as you usually do when you catch a cold. David Hume is the farthest thing from your mind.

HUME REVISITED

The next morning, you wake up feeling fine. The sun is shining brightly, and you have no sign of a cold. You are not sure whether the vitamin C cured your cold, or whether it was the good night's sleep, or whether it wasn't going to develop into a real cold regardless. Perhaps, even, it was the placebo effect; in psychology you learned that people can often be cured by totally inert drugs (e.g., sugar pills) if they believe in them. You don't really know what caused your prompt recovery, but frankly, you don't really care. If it was the placebo effect that is fine with you; you just hope it will work as well the next time.

You think about what you will do today. It is Thursday, so you have a philosophy discussion section in the morning and a physics lab in the afternoon. Thursday, you say to yourself, has got to be the lousiest day of the week. The philosophy section is a bore, and the physics lab is a drag. If only it were Saturday, when you have no classes! For a brief moment you consider taking off. Then you remember the letter you wrote last night, think about your budget and your grades, and resign yourself to the prescribed activities for the day.

The leader of the discussion section starts off with the question, "What was the main problem—I mean the really *basic* problem—bothering Hume in the *Enquiry?*" You feel like saying, "Lack of adequate scientific knowledge" (or words to that effect), but restrain yourself. No use antagonizing the guy who will decide what grade to give you. Someone says that he seemed to worry quite a lot about causes and effects, to which the discussion leader (as usual) responds. "But *why?*" Again, you stifle an impulse to say, "Because he didn't know too much about them."

After much folderol, the leader finally elicits the answer, "Because he wanted to know how we can find out about things we don't actually see (or hear, smell, touch, taste, etc.)."

"In other words," the leader paraphrases, "to examine the basis for making inferences from what we observe to what we cannot (at the moment) observe. Will someone," he continues, "give me an example of something you believe in which you are not now observing?"

You think of the letter you dropped into the box last night, of your home and parents, and of the money you hope to receive. You do not see the letter now, but you are confident it is somewhere in the mails; you do not see your parents now, but you firmly believe they are back home where you left them; you do not yet see the

money you hope to get, but you expect to see it before too long. The leader is pleased when you give those examples. "And what do causes and effects have to do with all of this?" he asks, trying to draw you out a little more. Still thinking of your grade you cooperate. "I believe the letter is somewhere in the mails because I wrote it and dropped it in the box. I believe my parents are at home because they are always calling me up to tell me what to do. And I believe that the money will come as an effect of my eloquent appeal." The leader is really happy with that; you can tell you have an A for today's session.

"But," he goes on, "do you see how this leads us immediately into Hume's next question? If cause-effect relations are the whole basis for our knowledge of things and events we do not observe, how do we know whether one event causes another, or whether they just happen together as a matter of coincidence?" Your mind is really clicking now.

"I felt a cold coming on last night, and I took a massive dose of vitamin C," you report. "This morning I feel great, but I honestly don't know whether the vitamin C actually cured it."

"Well, how could we go about trying to find out," retorts the discussion leader.

"By trying it again when I have the first symptoms of a cold," you answer, "and by trying it on other people as well." At that point the bell rings, and you leave class wondering whether the vitamin C really did cure your incipient cold.

You keep busy until lunch, doing one thing and another, but sitting down and eating, you find yourself thinking again about the common cold and its cure. It seems to be a well-known fact that the cold is caused by one or more viruses, and the human organism seems to have ways of combating virus infections. Perhaps the massive doses of vitamin C trigger the body's defenses, in some way or other, or perhaps it provides some kind of antidote to the toxic effects of the virus. You don't know much about all of this, but you can't help speculating that science has had a good deal of success in finding causes and cures of various diseases. If continued research reveals the physiological and chemical processes in the cold's infection and in the body's response, then surely it would be possible to find out whether the vitamin C really has any effect upon the common cold or not. It seems that we could ascertain whether a causal relation exists in this instance if only we could discover the relevant laws of biology and chemistry.

At this point in your musings, you notice that it is time to get over to the physics lab. You remember that yesterday morning you were convinced that predicting the outcome of an experiment is possible if you know which physical laws apply. That certainly was the outcome of the discussion in the physics class. Now, it seems, the question about the curative power of vitamin C hinges on exactly the same thing—the laws of nature. As you hurry to the lab it occurs to you that predicting the outcome of an experiment, before it is performed, is a first-class example of what you were discussing in philosophy—making inferences from the observed to the unobserved. We observe the set-up for the experiment (or demonstration) before it is performed, and we predict the outcome before we observe it. Salvia certainly was confident about the prediction he made. Also, recalling one of Hume's examples, you were at least as confident, when you went to bed last night, that the sun would rise this morning. But Hume *seemed* to be saying that the basis for this confidence was the fact that the sun has been observed to rise every morning since the dawn of history. "That's wrong," you say to yourself as you reach the physics lab. "My confidence in the rising of the sun is based upon the laws of astronomy. So here we are back at the laws again."

Inside the lab you notice a familiar gadget; it consists of a frame from which five steel balls are suspended so that they hang in a straight line, each one touching its neighbors. Your little brother got a toy like this, in a somewhat smaller size, for his birthday a couple of years ago. You casually raise one of the end balls, and let it swing back. It strikes the nearest of the four balls left hanging, and the ball at the other end swings out (the three balls in the middle keeping their place). The ball at the far end swings back again, striking its neighbor, and then the ball on the near end swings out, almost to the point from which you let it swing originally. The

process goes on for a while, with the two end balls alternately swinging out and back. It has a pleasant rhythm. (See Figure 2.)

While you are enjoying the familiar toy, the lab instructor, Dr. Sagro,[2] comes over to you. "Do you know why just the ball on the far end moves—instead of, say, two on the far end, or all four of the remaining ones—when the ball on this end strikes?"

"Not exactly, but I suppose it has something to do with conservation of energy," you reply, recalling what Salvia said yesterday in answer to the question about the bowling ball.

"That's right," says Dr. Sagro, "but it also depends upon conservation of momentum." Before you have a chance to say anything she continues, "Let me ask you another question. What would happen if you raised two balls at this

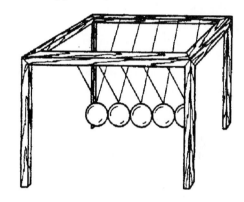

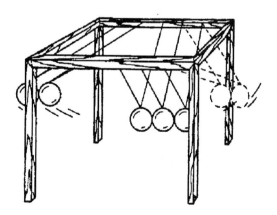

FIGURE 2 The Energy-Momentum Toy. When two balls at the right collide with the remaining three, two balls swing away from the left side. What happens when three on the right collide with the remaining two?

end, and let them swing together toward the remaining three?"

"I think two balls will swing away at the other end," you reply, remembering the way your brother's toy worked.

"Why don't you test it to find out if you are right?" says the instructor. You do, and you find that the result is as you had predicted. Without saying anything about it, you assume that this, too, can be explained by means of the laws of conservation of energy and momentum.

Dr. Sagro poses another question. "What will happen," she asks, "if you start by swinging three balls from this end?" Since there are only two remaining balls you don't know what to say, so you confess ignorance. She suggests you try it, in order to find out what will happen. When you do, you see that three balls swing to the other side, and three swing back again; the middle ball swings back and forth, acting as the third ball in each group. This was a case in which you didn't know what to expect as a result until you tried the experiment.[3] This was like some of Hume's examples; not until you have actually had the experience do you know what result to expect. But there is also something different. Hume said that you must try the experiment many times in order to know what to expect; nevertheless, after just one trial you are sure what will happen whenever the experiment is repeated. This makes it rather different from the problem of whether vitamin C

cured your cold. In that case, it seemed necessary to try the experiment over and over again, preferably with a number of different people. Reflecting upon this difference, you ask the lab instructor a crucial question, "If you knew the laws of conservation of momentum and energy, but had never seen the experiment with the three balls performed, would you have been able to predict the outcome?"

"Yes," she says simply.

"Well," you murmur inaudibly, "it seems as if the whole answer to Hume's problem regarding inferences about things we do not immediately observe, including predictions of future occurrences, rests squarely upon the laws of nature."

KNOWING THE LAWS

Given that the laws are so fundamental, you decide to find out more about them. The laws of conservation of energy and momentum are close at hand, so to speak, so you decide to start there. "O.K.," you say to the lab instructor, "what are these laws of nature, which enable you to predict so confidently how experiments will turn out before they are performed? I'd like to learn something about them."

"Fine," she says, delighted with your desire to learn; "let's start with conservation of momentum. It's simpler than conservation of energy, and we can demonstrate it quite easily."[4] (See Figure 3.)

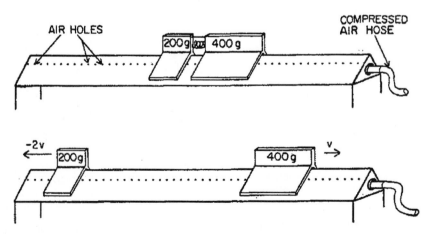

FIGURE 3 Cars on the Air Track. Top: Cars tied together against spring under tension. Bottom: Cars moving apart after "explosion." $400g \times v + 200g \times (-2v) = 0$. Momentum is conserved.

Your laboratory contains a standard piece of equipment—an air track—on which little cars move back and forth. The track is made of metal with many tiny holes through which air is blown. The cars thus ride on a thin cushion of air; they move back and forth almost without friction. Some of the cars are equipped with spring bumpers, so that they will bounce off of one another upon impact, while others have coupling devices which lock them together upon contact. Dr. Sagro begins by explaining what is meant by the momentum of a body—namely, its mass multiplied by its velocity.[5] "To speak somewhat quaintly," she says, "the mass is just a measure of the quantity of matter in the body.[6] Since, in all of the experiments we are going to do, it is safe to say that the mass of each body remains unchanged, we need not say more about it. You can see that each car comes with its mass labeled; this one, for instance, has a mass of 200 grams, while this one has a mass of 400 grams. We have a number of different cars with quite a variety of different masses. The velocity," she continues, "is what we ordinarily mean by 'speed' along with the direction of travel. On the air track there are only two possible directions, left to right and right to left. Let us simply agree that motion from left to right has a positive velocity, while motion from right to left has a negative velocity. Mass, of course, is always a positive quantity. Thus, momentum, which is mass times velocity, may be positive, negative, or zero. When we add the momenta of various bodies together, we must always be careful of the sign (plus or minus)."

With these preliminaries, you begin to perform a variety of experiments. She has various types of fancy equipment for measuring velocities, which she shows you how to use, and she also helps you to make measurements. You find that it is fun pushing cars back and forth on the track, crashing them into one another, and measuring their velocities before and after collisions. You try it with a variety of cars of different masses and with differing velocities. You try it with the ones that bounce apart after impact and with those that stick together. You always find that the *total* momentum (the sum of the momenta for the two cars) before any collision is equal to the *total* momentum after the collision, even

though the momenta of the individual cars may change markedly as a result of the collision. This, Dr. Sagro explains, is what the law of conservation of momentum demands: when two bodies (such as the cars) interact with one another (as in a collision), the total momentum of the system consisting of those two bodies is the same before and after the interaction.

You ask her whether this law applies only to collisions; she replies immediately that it applies to all kinds of interactions. "Let's see how it works for a simple type of 'explosion,'" she suggests. She helps you tie together two cars, holding a compressed spring between them. You burn the string which holds them together and they fly apart. You measure the velocities and compute the momenta of each of the cars after the "explosion." It turns out that the momentum of the one car is always equal in amount but opposite in direction to that of the other. This is true whether the cars are of equal or unequal masses and whether the tension on the spring that drives them apart is great or small. "This is just what the law of conservation of momentum tells us to expect," she explains; "the momentum of each car is zero before the 'explosion' because they are not moving (each has velocity equal to zero), and so the two momenta after the 'explosion' (one positive and one negative) must add up to zero. That is what has happened every time.

"There are many other applications of the law of conservation of momentum," she continues. "When a rifle recoils upon being fired, when a jet engine propels an airplane, when a rocket engine lifts an artificial satellite into orbit, or when you step out of an untethered rowboat and are surprised to feel it moving out from under you—these are all cases of conservation of momentum."

"Is this law ever violated?" you ask.

"No," she answers, "there are no known exceptions to it." You leave the lab with the feeling that you know at least one fundamental law, and that you have seen it proved experimentally right before your eyes. You can't wait to tell your philosophy professor about it.

When you go to your philosophy class the next morning, the topic is still Hume's *Enquiry Concerning Human Understanding* and the problem of how we can have knowledge of things we do not observe. As the lecture begins, Professor Philo[7] is saying, "As we saw during the last lecture, Hume maintains that our knowledge of what we do not observe is based entirely upon cause and effect relations, but that raises the question of how we can gain knowledge of these relations. Hume maintained that this knowledge can result only from repeated observation of one type of event (a cause) to see whether it is always followed by an event of another kind (its effect). Hume therefore analyzed the notion of causality in terms of constant conjunction of events. Consider for a moment Hume's favorite example, the colliding billiard balls..."

You raise your hand. "It seems to me that Hume was wrong about this," you begin, and then you relate briefly yesterday's experiences in the physics lab. "If you know the relevant laws of nature," you conclude, "you can predict the outcomes of future experiments on the basis of a single trial, or perhaps even without benefit of any trials at all."

"But how," asks Professor Philo, "can we establish knowledge of the laws of nature?"

You had a hunch she might ask some such question, and you are ready with your reply, "We *proved* it experimentally."

"Well," says Professor Philo, "I'm not a physicist, so perhaps you had better explain in a little more detail just what the experimental proof consists of. You mentioned something about an explosion—how did that go?"

You explain carefully how the air track works, how the two cars were joined together with a spring under tension in between, and how they moved apart when the string was burned. "In every case," you conclude, "the momentum of the two cars was equal in amount and opposite in direction, just as the law of conservation of momentum says it should be."

"Now let me see if I understand your line of reasoning," says the professor in a tone that is altogether too calm to suit you. "If the law of conservation of momentum is correct, then the two cars will part in the manner you described. The cars did move apart in just that way. Therefore, the law of conservation of momentum is correct. Is that your argument?"

"I guess so," you reply a bit hesitantly, because it looks as if she is trying to trap you.

"Do you think that kind of argument is valid?" she responds.

"What do you mean?" you ask, beginning to feel a little confused.

"Well," she says, "isn't that rather like the following argument: If this defendant is guilty, he will refuse to testify at his own trial; he does refuse to testify; therefore, he is guilty. Would any judge allow that argument in a court of law?"

"Of course not," you reply, "but it isn't the same thing at all. We tested the law of conservation of momentum many times in many different ways, and in every case we got the expected result (allowing for the usual small inaccuracies in the measurements)."

"If I remember what you said," Ms. Philo goes on, "in one of your experiments you had one car with a mass of 200 grams and another with a mass of 400 grams, and in that case the lighter car recoiled with twice the speed of the more massive one. How many times did you repeat this particular experiment?"

"Once or twice, as nearly as I can recall."

"Yet, you seem to believe that the result would be the same, no matter how many times the experiment was repeated—is that correct?"

"I suppose so," you reply somewhat uncomfortably.

"And with how many different masses and how many different recoil velocities did you try it? Do you believe it would work the same way if the masses were thousands or billions of kilograms instead of a few grams? And do you suppose that it would work the same way if the velocities were very great—somewhere near the speed of light?"

Since you have heard that strange things happen when speeds approach that of light, your hesitancy increases, but you reply tentatively, "Well, the lab instructor told me that there are no exceptions to the law."

"Did she say that," asks Philo, "or did she say no *known* exceptions?"

"I guess that was it," you reply lamely, feeling quite crushed.

Professor Philo endeavors to summarize the discussion. "What is considered experimental 'proof of a law of nature' is actually a process of testing *some* of its logical consequences. That is, you ask what would have to happen *if* your hypothesis is true, and then you perform an experiment to see if it turns out that way *in fact*. Since any law of nature is a generalization,[8] it has an unlimited number of consequences. We can never hope to test them all. In particular, any *useful* law of nature will have consequences that pertain to the future; they enable us to make predictions. We can never test these consequences until it is too late to use them for the purpose of prediction. To suppose that testing *some* of the consequences of a law constitutes a *conclusive proof* of the law would clearly be an outright logical fallacy." The bell rings and you leave the class, convinced that she has merely been quibbling.

During your physics class you brood about the previous discussion in the philosophy class, without paying very close attention to the lecture. Similar thoughts keep nagging at you during lunch. The objections brought up by Professor Philo seem to be well-founded, you conclude, but you wonder how they can be reconciled with the apparent reliability and certainty of scientific knowledge. In desperation, you decide to talk it over with Professor Salvia during his office hour this very afternoon. When you arrive, you don't know exactly where to begin, so you decide to go back to the pendulum demonstration, which was the thing that got you started on this whole mess. "When you performed that demonstration," you ask, "were you *absolutely certain* how it would turn out? Has it ever failed?"

"Well, to be perfectly honest," he says, "it has been known to fail. Once when a friend of mine was doing it in front of a large auditorium, the suspension in the ceiling broke and the ball landed right on his foot. He was in a cast for months!"

"But that's no fault of the law of conservation of energy is it?" you ask. "The breaking of the suspension didn't mean that conservation of energy is false, did it?"

"Of course not," he answers, "we still believe firmly in conservation of energy."

"But are you *certain* of the law of conservation of energy, or any other law of nature?" you ask, and before he has a chance to answer, you

tell him about the discussion in the philosophy class this morning.

"So that's what's bothering you," he says, after hearing the whole story. "Professor Philo has an important point. No matter how thoroughly we have tested a scientific law—better, let's say 'hypothesis'—there is always the possibility that new evidence will show up to prove it false. For instance, around the close of the nineteenth century, many physicists seemed virtually certain that Newtonian mechanics was absolutely correct. A wide variety of its consequences had been tested under many different circumstances, and Newton's laws stood up extremely well. But early in the twentieth century it became clear that what we now call 'classical physics' would have to undergo major revisions, and a profound scientific revolution ensued. Modern physics, which includes quantum mechanics and relativity theory, was the result. We can never be sure that any hypothesis we currently accept as correct will not have to be abandoned or modified at some time in the future as a result of new evidence."

"What about the law of conservation of momentum?" you ask, recalling yesterday's experience in the lab. "The lab instructor said it has no known exceptions."

"That is correct," says Salvia, "and it is a rather interesting case. Conservation of momentum is a consequence of Newton's laws of motion; therefore, any consequence of conservation of momentum is a consequence of Newton's laws. But we now regard Newton's laws as not strictly true—they break down, for example, with objects traveling close to the speed of light—but conservation of momentum holds even in these cases. So we have a good example of a case where we believe a lot of consequences, but we do not believe in the laws (Newton's) from which the consequences follow."

It occurs to you that this is a rather important set of supposed laws; perhaps the philosophy professor was not merely quibbling when she said that it was not valid to conclude that a hypothesis is true just because we know many of its consequences to be true.

"Since you cannot be certain of any so-called law of nature," you ask, "why do you believe in them so firmly?"

"Because," answers Salvia, "we consider them very well confirmed. We accept well-confirmed hypotheses, knowing that we may later have to change our minds in the light of new evidence. Science can no longer claim infallible truth."

"Does that mean that scientific results are highly probable, but not absolutely certain?" you ask, trying to be sure you have understood what he has said.

"Yes, you could put it that way," he agrees.

You leave with the feeling that you have a pretty good comprehension of the situation. As a result of your study of physics and philosophy you now understand why science cannot claim infallibility for its findings, but must be content with results that are well confirmed. With that, you take off for the weekend. (And what you do with your weekend is your own business.)

HUME'S BOMBSHELL

A little tired, but basically in a cheerful mood, you arrive at your philosophy class on Monday morning. You meet the professor a few minutes before class outside the room, and you tell her very briefly of your conversation with the physics professor. You explain that you now understand why it is that scientific laws can never be considered completely certain, but only as well-confirmed hypotheses. With her help, and with that of Professor Salvia, you now understand what Hume was driving at—and you see, moreover, that Hume was right. She smiles, and you both go into the classroom, where she begins her lecture.

"Last Friday, as you may recall, we had quite a lively discussion about the status of scientific laws—the law of conservation of momentum, in particular. We saw that such laws cannot be proved conclusively by any amount of experimental evidence. This is a point with which, I am happy to report, many (if not most) contemporary scientists agree. They realize that the most they can reasonably claim for their hypotheses is strong confirmation. Looking at the matter this way, one could conclude that it is wise to believe in scientific predictions, for if they are not certain to be true, they are a good bet. To believe in scientific results is to bet with the best available odds.

"However," she continues, "while this view may be correct as far as it goes, Hume was making a much more fundamental, and I should add, much more devastating point. Hume was challenging not merely our right to claim that scientific predictions will always be right, but also our right to claim that they will usually, or often, or indeed ever, be correct. Take careful note of what he says in Section IV:

> Let the course of things be allowed hitherto ever so regular; that alone, without some new argument or inference, proves not that, for the future, it will continue so. In vain do you pretend to have learned the nature of bodies from your past experience. Their secret nature, and consequently all their effects and influence, may change, without any change in their sensible qualities. This happens sometimes, and with regard to some objects: Why may it not happen always and with regard to all objects? What logic, what process of argument secures you against this supposition?

He is saying, as I hope you understood from your reading, that no matter how reliably a law seems to have held in the past, there is no logical reason why it must do so in the future *at all*. It is therefore possible that *every* scientific prediction, based on *any* law or laws whatever, may turn out to be false from this moment on. The stationary billiard ball that is struck by a moving one may remain motionless where it is—while the moving ball may bounce straight back in the direction from whence it came, or it may go straight up in the air, or it might vanish in a puff of smoke. Any of these possibilities can be imagined; none of them involves any logical contradiction. This is the force of Hume's skeptical arguments. The conclusion seems to be that we have no *reason* to believe in scientific predictions—no more reason than to believe on the basis of astrology, crystal gazing, or sheer blind guessing."

You can hardly believe your ears; what is she saying? You raise your hand, and when you are recognized, you can hardly keep your intense irritation from showing as you assert, "But certainly we can say that scientific predictions are more probable than those based, for example, upon astrology." As you speak, you are reminded of the remark in contemporary problems last Wednesday concerning the coming of the Age of Aquarius.

Science has got to be better than *that!* As these thoughts cross your mind Professor Philo is saying, "...but that depends upon what you mean by 'probable,' doesn't it?"

The physics lecture today is on Newton's law of gravitation, and the professor is explaining that every bit of matter in the universe is attracted to every other by a force proportional to the masses and inversely proportional to the square of the distance between them. He goes on to explain how Kepler's laws of planetary motion and Galileo's law of falling bodies are (when suitably corrected) consequences of Newton's laws. You listen carefully, but you recognize this as another law that enables scientists to make impressive predictions. Indeed, Salvia is now telling how Newton's laws were used to explain the tides on the oceans and to predict the existence of two planets, Neptune and Pluto, that had not been known before. At the same time, you are wondering whether there is anything in what Hume seemed to be saying about such laws. Is it possible that suddenly, at the very next moment, matter would cease to have gravitational attraction, so that the whole solar system would go flying apart? It's a pretty chilling thought.

At lunch you are thinking about this question, and you glance back at some of the readings that were assigned from Hume's *Enquiry*. You notice again Hume's many references to secret powers and forces. Well, gravitation is surely a force, though there has not been any great secret about it since Newton's time. It is the "power" which keeps the solar system together. You remember reading somewhere that, according to Hume, you cannot know that it is safer to leave a building by way of the halls, stairways, and doors than it would be to step out of the third-story window. Well, Newton's law makes it clear why you don't want to step out of the third-story window, but what assurance have you that the building will continue to stand, rather than crashing down around your ears before you can get out? The engineers who design and build towers and bridges have a great deal of knowledge of the "secret powers" of their materials, so they must know a great deal more than Hume did about the hidden properties of things.

At this very moment, a lucky coincidence occurs—you see Dr. Sagro, your physics lab instructor, entering the cafeteria. You wave to her, and she sits down with you, putting her coffee cup on the table. You begin to ask her some questions about structural materials, and she responds by inquiring whether you would be satisfied if she could explain how the table supports the cup of coffee. You recognize it as just the kind of question you have in mind, and urge her to proceed.

"Certain materials, such as the metal in this table," she begins, "have a rather rigid crystalline structure, and for this reason they stick together and maintain their shape unless subjected to large forces. These crystals consist of very regular (and very beautiful) arrays of atoms, and they are held together by forces, essentially electrostatic in origin, among the charged particles that make up the atoms. Have you studied Coulomb's law of electrostatic forces?"

"No," you reply, "we are just doing Newton's law of gravitation. I think Salvia said electricity and magnetism would come up next semester."

"Well," she says, "these electrostatic forces are a lot like gravitational forces (they vary inversely with the square of the distance), but there are a couple of very important differences. First, as you know, there are two types of charges, positive and negative. The proton in the nucleus of the atom carries a positive charge, and the electrons that circulate about the nuclei have a negative charge. Two particles with opposite signs (such as a proton and an electron) attract one another, while two particles with like signs (e.g., two electrons or two protons) repel each other. This is different from gravity, because all matter attracts all other matter; there is no such thing as gravitational repulsion. The second main difference is that the electrostatic force is fantastically stronger than the gravitational force—roughly a billion billion billion billion times more powerful—but we don't usually notice it because most objects we deal with in everyday life are electrically neutral, containing equal amounts of positive and negative electric charge, or very nearly so. If you could somehow strip all of the electrons away from an apple, and all of the protons away from the earth, the force of attraction between the apple and the earth would be unbelievable.

"It is these *extremely* strong attractive and repulsive forces among the electrons and protons in the metal that maintain a stable and rigid form. That's why the table doesn't collapse. And the reason the coffee cup stays on top of the table, without penetrating its surface or slipping through, is that the electrons in the surface of the cup strongly repel those in the surface of the table. Actually, there is also a quantum mechanical force that prevents the weight of the cup from noticeably compressing the table, but we needn't go into that, because the effect is mostly due to the electrostatic forces."

Pleased with this very clear explanation, you thank her, but follow it up with another question. "Is there any logical reason why it has to be that way—why opposite charges attract and like charges repel? Can you prove that it is impossible for like charges to attract and unlike charges to repel? What would happen if *that* were suddenly to become the law?"

"It would certainly result in utter catastrophe," she replies, "with all of the atomic nuclei bunching up together in one place and all of the electrons rushing away from them to congregate elsewhere. But to answer your question, no, there is no logical proof that it couldn't be that way. In our physical world we find that there are, in fact, two types of charges, and they obey the Coulomb law rather than the one you just formulated."

"Can you prove that the world will not switch from the one law to the other, say, tomorrow?" you ask.

"No, frankly, I can't," she answers, "but I, and all other physicists assume—call it an article of faith if you like—that it won't happen."

There's that word "faith" again, you muse as you leave the cafeteria.

The more you think about it, the more clearly you see that the physicists have not shown you how to get around the basic problem Hume raised; rather, they have really reinforced it. Maybe this problem is tougher than I thought, you say to yourself, and you head for Professor Philo's office to talk further about it. "I was thinking about all these 'secret powers' Hume talks about," you begin, "and so I asked my physics instructor about them. She explained, as an example, how a table supports a coffee cup, but she did it on the basis of laws of nature—Coulomb's law of electrostatics was one of them. This law is very well confirmed, I suppose, but she admitted that it is quite possible to imagine that this law would fail tomorrow, and—if you'll pardon the expression—all hell would break loose. Now, my question is, how can we find out about these secret powers that Hume keeps saying we need to know? How can we discover the real underlying causes of what happens?"

"I think you are really beginning to get the point Hume was driving at," she replies, "namely, that there is *no way,* even in principle, of finding any hidden causes or secret powers. You can, of course, find regularities in nature—such as conservation of energy, conservation of momentum, universal gravitation, and electrostatic attraction and repulsion—but these can only be known to have held up to the present. There is no further kind of hidden connection or causal relation that can be discovered by more careful observation, or examination with some kind of super-microscope. Of course, we do discover regularities, and we explain them. For instance, Kepler's laws of planetary motion are regularities that are explained by Newton's laws of motion and gravitation, but these do not reveal any secret powers. They simply provide more general regularities to cover the more restricted ones.

"In his discussion of 'the idea of necessary connection,' Hume tries to bring out precisely this point. We can observe, as you were saying in class the other day, that recoil experiments always yield a particular type of result—namely, momentum is conserved. We have observed this many times. And now we expect, on future trials, that the same thing will happen. But we do not observe, nor can we discover in any way, an *additional* factor which constitutes a necessary connection between the 'explosion' and the subsequent motion of the cars. This seems to be what Hume had in mind when he wrote:

> These ultimate springs and principles are totally shut up from human curiosity and enquiry.

Elasticity, gravity, cohesion of parts, communication of motion by impulse; these are probably the ultimate causes and principles which we ever discover in nature; and we may esteem ourselves sufficiently happy, if, by accurate inquiry and reasoning, we can trace up the particular phenomena to, or near to, these general principles.[9]

Hume is acknowledging that we can discover general regularities in nature, but he is denying that an additional 'connection' can be found. And Hume was dedicated to the maxim, as are modern scientists, that we have no business talking about things it is impossible in principle for us to know anything about.

"When he asks why we do, in fact, expect so confidently that the future experiments will have outcomes similar to those of the past trials, Hume finds that it is nothing other than a matter of psychological conditioning. When we see one type of cause repeatedly followed by a particular type of effect, we come to expect that the same type of effect will follow the next time we come across that kind of cause. But this is not a matter of logical reasoning. Have you heard of Pavlov's conditioning experiments with dogs?" You nod. "When the bell rings the dog starts to salivate. He is *not* reasoning that, since the sounding of the bell has, in the past, been associated with the bringing of food, therefore, on this occasion the food will (at least probably) appear soon after the bell rings. According to Hume's analysis, what is called 'scientific reasoning' is no more rational or logical than your watering at the mouth when you are hungry and hear the dinner bell. It is something you cannot help doing, Hume says, but that does not mean that it has any logical foundation."

"That brings up a question I've wanted to ask," you say. "Hume seems to think that people necessarily reason in that way—inductive reasoning, I think it is called—but I've noticed that lots of people don't seem to. For instance, many people (including a student in my current problems course) believe in things like astrology; they believe that the configuration of the planets has a bearing on human events, when experience shows that it often doesn't work that way." The professor nods in agreement. You continue, "So

if there is no logical justification for believing in scientific predictions, why isn't it just as reasonable to believe in astrological predictions?"

"That," replies the prof, "is a very profound and difficult question. I doubt that any philosopher has a completely satisfactory answer to it."

MODERN ANSWERS[10]

The Wednesday philosophy lecture begins with a sort of rhetorical question, "What reason do we have (Hume is, at bottom, asking) for trusting the scientific method; what grounds do we have for believing that scientific predictions are reliable?" You have been pondering that very question quite a bit in the last couple of days, and—rhetorical or not—your hand shoots up. You have a thing or two to say on the subject.

"Philosophers may have trouble answering such questions," you assert, "but it seems to me there is an obvious reply. As my physics professor has often said, the scientist takes a very practical attitude. He puts forth a hypothesis; if it works he believes in it, and he continues to believe in it as long as it works. If it starts giving him bad predictions, he starts looking for another hypothesis, or for a way of revising his old one. Now the important thing about the scientific method, it seems to me, is that it works. Not only has it led to a vast amount of knowledge about the physical world, but it has been applied in all sorts of practical ways—and although these applications may not have been uniformly beneficial—for better or worse they were successful. Not always, of course, but by and large. Astrology, crystal gazing, and other such superstitious methods simply do not work very well. That's good enough for me."[11]

"That is, indeed, a very tempting answer," Professor Philo replies, "and in one form or another, it has been advanced by several modern philosophers. But Hume actually answered that one himself. You might put it this way. We can all agree that science has, up till now, a very impressive record of success in predicting the future. The question we are asking, however, is this: should we *predict* that science will continue to have the kind of success it has had in the past? It is quite natural to assume that its record will continue, but this is just a case of applying the scientific method to itself. In studying conservation of momentum, you inferred that future experiments would have results similar to those of your past experiments; in appraising the scientific method, you are assuming that its future success will match its past success. But using the scientific method to judge the scientific method is circular reasoning. It is as if a man goes to a bank to cash a check. When the teller refuses, on the grounds that he does not know this man, the man replies, 'That is no problem; permit me to introduce myself—I am John Smith, just as it says on the check.'

"Suppose that I were a believer in crystal gazing. You tell me that your method is better than mine because it has been more successful than mine. You say that this is a good reason for preferring your method to mine, I object. Since you are using your method to judge my method (as well as your method), I demand the right to use my method to evaluate yours. I gaze into my crystal ball and announce the result: from now on crystal gazing will be very successful in predicting the future, while the scientific method is due for a long run of bad luck."

You are about to protest, but she continues.

"The trouble with circular arguments is that they can be used to prove anything; if you assume what you are trying to prove, then there isn't much difficulty in proving it. You find the scientific justification of the scientific method convincing because you already trust the scientific method; if you had equal trust in crystal gazing, I should think you would find the crystal gazer's justification of his method equally convincing. Hume puts it this way:

> When a man says, *I have found, in all past instances, such sensible qualities conjoined with such secret powers:* And when he says, *Similar sensible qualities will always be conjoined with similar secret powers,* he is not guilty of a tautology, nor are these propositions in any respect the same. You can say that the one proposition is an inference from the other. But you must confess that the inference is not intuitive; neither is it demonstrative: Of what nature is it, then? To say it is experimental is begging the question. For all inferences from experience suppose, as their foundation,

that the future will resemble the past, and that similar powers will be conjoined with similar sensible qualities.[12]

If the assumption that the future is like the past is the presupposition of the scientific method, we cannot assume that principle in order to justify the scientific method. Once more, we can hardly find a clearer statement than Hume's:

> We have said that all arguments concerning existence are founded on the relation of cause and effect; that our knowledge of that relation is derived entirely from experience; and that all our experimental conclusions proceed upon the supposition that the future will be conformable to the past. To endeavour, therefore, the proof of this last supposition by probable arguments, or arguments regarding existence, must evidently be going in a circle, and taking that for granted, which is the very point in question.[13]

"The principle that the future will be like the past, or that regularities which have held up to the present will persist in the future, has traditionally been called *the principle of uniformity of nature.* Some philosophers, most notably Immanuel Kant, have regarded it as an a priori truth.[14] It seems to me, however, that Hume had already provided a convincing refutation of that claim by arguing that irregularities, however startling to common sense, are by no means inconceivable—that is, they cannot be ruled out a priori. Recall what he said:

> ...it implies no contradiction that the course of nature may change, and that an object, seemingly like those which we have experienced, may be attended with different or contrary effects. May I not clearly and distinctly conceive that a body, falling from the clouds, and which, in all other respects, resembles snow, has yet the taste of salt or feeling of fire? ...Now whatever is intelligible, and can be distinctly conceived, implies no contradiction, and can never be proved false by any demonstrative argument or abstract reasoning *a priori.*[15]

"Other philosophers have proposed assuming this principle (or something similar) as a postulate; Bertrand Russell, though not the only one to advocate this approach, is by far the most famous.[16] But most philosophers agree that this use of postulation is question-begging. The real question still remains: why should one adopt any such postulate? Russell himself, in another context, summed it up very well: The method of 'postulating' what we want has many advantages; they are the same as the advantages of theft over honest toil."[17]

"Nevertheless," you interject, "can't we still say that scientific predictions are more probable than, say, those of astrology or crystal gazing?"

"It seems to me you raised a similar question once before," Professor Philo replies, "and I seem to recall saying that it depends on what you mean by the term 'probable.' Maybe it would be helpful if I now explain what I meant."[18] You nod encouragement. "The concept of probability—or perhaps I should say 'concepts' of probability—are very tricky. If you were to undertake a systematic study of confirmation and induction, you would have to go into a rather technical treatment of probability, but perhaps I can give a brief hint of what is involved.[19] One thing that has traditionally been meant by this term relates directly to the frequency with which something occurs—as Aristotle put it, the probable is that which happens often. If the weather forecaster says that there is a 90% chance of rain, he presumably means that, given such weather conditions as are now present, rain occurs in nine out of ten cases. If these forecasts are correct, we can predict rain on such occasions and be right nine times out of ten.

"Now, if you mean that scientific predictions are probable in *this* sense, I do not see how you could possibly support your claim. For Hume has argued—cogently, I think—that, for all we know now, *every* future scientific prediction may go wrong. He was not merely saying that science is fallible, that it will sometimes err in its predictions—he was saying that nature might at any moment (for all we can know) become irregular on such a wide scale that any kind of scientific prediction of future occurrences would be utterly impossible. We have not found any reason to believe he was mistaken about this point."

"That must not be the concept of probability I had in mind," you remark; "I'm not quite sure how to express it, but it had something to do with what it would be reasonable to believe. I

was thinking of the fact that, although we cannot regard scientific hypotheses as certain, we can consider them well confirmed. It is something like saying that a particular suspect is probably guilty of a crime—that the evidence, taken as a whole, seems to point to him."

"You have put your finger on another important probability concept," the professor replies. "It is sometimes known as the rational credibility concept. The most popular contemporary attempt (I believe) to deal with Hume's problem of inductive reasoning is stated in terms of this concept. The argument can be summarized in the following way. Hume has proved that we cannot *know for sure* that our scientific predictions will be correct, but that would be an unreasonable demand to place upon science. The best we can hope is for scientific conclusions that are probable. But when we ask that they be probable, in this sense, we are only asking that they be based upon the best possible evidence. Now, that is just what scientific predictions are—they are predictions based upon the best possible evidence. The scientist has fashioned his hypotheses in the light of all available information, and he has tested them experimentally on many occasions under a wide variety of circumstances. He has summoned all of the available evidence, and he has brought it to bear on the problem at hand. Such scientific predictions are obviously probable (as we are now construing this term); hence, they are rationally credible.[20] If we say that a belief is irrational, we mean that it runs counter to the evidence, or the person who holds it is ignoring the evidence. And in such contexts, when we speak of evidence, we are referring to inductive or scientific evidence.

"Now, the argument continues, to ask whether it is reasonable to believe in scientific conclusions comes right down to asking whether one ought to fashion his beliefs on the basis of the available evidence. But this is what it means to be rational. Hence, the question amounts to asking whether it is rational to be rational. If the question makes any sense at all, the obvious answer is 'yes.'"

"That answer certainly satisfies me," you say, feeling that Dr. Philo has succeeded admirably in stating the point you were groping for. "I'm glad to know that lots of other philosophers agree with it. Do you think it is a satisfactory answer to Hume's problem of induction?" You are more than a trifle discouraged when she gives a negative response with a shake of her head. "Why not?" you demand.

"This argument seems to me to beg the question," she replies, "for it assumes that the concept of evidence is completely clear. But that is precisely the question at issue. If we could be confident that the kind of experiments you performed in the physics lab to test the law of conservation of momentum do, in fact, provide evidence for that law, then we could say that the law is well supported by evidence. But to suppose that such facts do constitute evidence amounts to saying that what has happened in the past is a sign of what will happen in the future—the fact that momentum was conserved in your 'explosion' experiments is an indication that momentum will be conserved in future experiments of a similar nature. This assumes that the future will be like the past, and that is precisely the point at issue. To say that one fact constitutes evidence for another means, in part, that the one provides some basis for inference to the occurrence of the other. The problem of induction is nothing other than the problem of determining the circumstances under which such inference is justified. Thus, we have to resolve the problem of induction—Hume's problem—before we can ascertain whether one fact constitutes evidence for another. We cannot use the concept of evidence—inductive evidence—to solve the problem of induction.

"There is another way to look at this same argument. If you ask me whether you should use the scientific method, I must find out what you hope to accomplish. If you say that you want to get a job teaching physics, I can tell you right away that you had better use the scientific method, at least in your work, because that is what is expected of a physicist. If you say that you want to enjoy the respect and prestige that accrues to scientists in certain social circles, the answer is essentially the same. If you tell me, however, that you want to have as much success as possible in predicting future events, the answer is by no means as easy. If I tell you to go ahead

and make scientific predictions, because that is what is considered reasonable (that is what is meant by fashioning your beliefs on the basis of evidence), then you should ask whether being reasonable in this sense (which is obviously the commonly accepted sense) is a good way to attain your goal. The answer, 'but that's what it means to be reasonable,' is beside the point. You might say, 'I want a method that is reasonable to adopt in order to achieve my goal of successful prediction—that is what I mean by being reasonable. To tell me that the scientific method is what is usually *called* reasonable doesn't help. I want to know whether the method that is *commonly called* reasonable is *actually* a reasonable method to adopt to attain my goal of successful prediction of the future. The fact that it is usually considered reasonable cuts no ice, because an awareness of Hume's problem of induction has not filtered down into common usage.' That's what I think you should say."

"Couldn't we avoid all of these problems," suggests another student, "if we simply resisted the temptation to generalize? In social science, my area of interest, we find that it is very risky to generalize, say, from one society to another. An opinion survey on students in the far west, for example, will not be valid when applied to students attending eastern schools. Wouldn't we be better off to restrict our claims to the facts we know, instead of trying to extend them inductively to things we really don't know?"

"The opinion you have offered bears a strong resemblance (though it isn't identical) to that of an influential British philosopher.[21] He has presented his ideas persuasively, and has many followers. Hume, he says, has proved conclusively that induction is not a justifiable form of inference; it is, consequently, no part of science. The only kind of logic that has a legitimate place in science is deductive logic. Deductive inferences are demonstrative; their conclusions must be true if their premises are true. These inferences are precisely what Hume called 'reasoning concerning relations of ideas.' The crucial point is that they *do not add to our knowledge* in any way—they enable us to see the content of our premises, but they do not extend that content in the least. Thus, from premises that refer only to events in the past and present, it is impossible to *deduce* any predictions of future facts. Any kind of inference which would enable us to predict the future on the basis of facts already observed would have to be of a different sort; such inference is often called 'ampliative' or 'inductive.' If science contains only deductive inferences, but no inductive inferences, it can never provide us with any knowledge beyond the content of our immediate observations.

"Now this philosopher does not reject scientific knowledge; he simply claims that prediction of the future is no part of the business of science. Accordingly, the function of scientific investigation is to find powerful general hypotheses (he calls them *conjectures*) that adequately explain all known facts that have occurred so far. As long as such a generalization succeeds in explaining the new facts that come along it is retained; if it fails to explain new facts, it must be modified or rejected. The sole purpose of scientific experimentation is to try to find weaknesses in such hypotheses—that is to criticize them or try to refute them. He calls this the 'method of conjectures and refutations,' or sometimes simply, 'the critical approach.'

"The main difficulty with this approach—an insuperable one, in my opinion—is the fact that it completely deprives science of its predictive function. To the question of which method to use for predicting the future, it can give no answer. Astrology, crystal gazing, blind guessing, and scientific prediction are all on a par. To find out what the population of the world will be in 2000 A.D., we might as well employ a psychic seer as a scientific demographer. I find it hard to believe that this can constitute a satisfactory solution to the problem of employing our knowledge to find rational solutions to the problems that face us—problems whose solutions demand that we make predictions of the future course of events. Tempting as it is to try to evade Hume's problem in this way, I do not see how we can be satisfied to admit that there is no rational approach to our problem."

"But perhaps there is no answer to Hume's problem," says still another student; "maybe the only hope for salvation of this world is to give up our blind worship of science and return to religion. We have placed our faith in science, and look where we are as a result. I believe we should adopt a different faith."

There's that word *again*, you note to yourself, as the professor begins her answer: "Though I heartily agree that many of the results of science—*technological* results, I think we should emphasize—have been far from beneficial, I don't think we can properly condemn scientific *knowledge*. Knowledge is one thing; what we choose to do with it is quite another. But that's not the issue we are concerned with. I do not see how anyone could deny that science has had a great deal of success in making predictions; no other approach can possibly present a comparable record of success. And, as time goes on, the capability for predictive success seems only to increase. It would be an utterly astonishing piece of luck, if it were sheer coincidence, that science has been so much luckier than other approaches in making its predictions. If anyone can consistently pick a winner in every race at every track every day, we are pretty sure he has more than good luck going for him. Science isn't infallible, but it is hard to believe its predictive success is just a matter of chance. I, at least, am not prepared to say that science is just one among many equally acceptable faiths—you pays your money and you takes your choice. I feel rather sure that the scientific approach has a logical justification of some sort." With that, the bell rings, the discussion ends, and everyone leaves—none by way of the window.

It just isn't good enough, you say to yourself, after listening to your physics professor lecturing, with demonstrations, on the law of conservation of angular momentum. You don't know whether you're dizzier from the discussion of Hume's problem in the philosophy class or from watching student volunteers in this class being spun on stools mounted on turntables. In any case, you decide to look up Professor Philo after lunch, and you find her in her office.

"Look," you say a bit brusquely, "I see that Hume was right about our inability to prove that nature is uniform. But suppose that nature does play a trick on us, so to speak. Suppose that after all this time of appearing quite uniform, manifesting all sorts of regularities such as the laws of physics, she turns chaotic. Then there isn't anything we can do anyhow. Someone might make a lucky guess about some future event, but there would be no systematic method for anticipating the chaos successfully. It seems to me I've got a way of predicting the future which will work if nature is uniform—the scientific method, or if you like, the inductive method—and if nature isn't uniform, I'm out of luck whatever I do. It seems to me I've got everything to gain and nothing to lose (except a lot of hard work) if I attempt to adhere to the scientific approach. That seems good enough to me; what do you think?"[22]

"Well," she says quietly, "I tend to agree with that answer, and so do a few others, but we are certainly in the minority. And many difficult problems arise when you try to work it out with precision."

"What sorts of difficulties are these?" you ask.

"There are several kinds," she begins; "for instance, what exactly do you mean by saying that nature is uniform? You cannot mean—to use Hume's quaint language—that like sensible qualities are always conjoined with like secret powers. All of us, including Hume, know this claim is false. Bread which looks and tastes completely harmless may contain a deadly poison. A gas which has exactly the appearance of normal air may suffocate living organisms and pollute the atmosphere. That kind of uniformity principle cannot be the basis of our inferences."

"That's quite true," you answer, "but perhaps we could say that nature operates according to regular laws. Ever since I began to think about Hume's problem, I have been led back to laws of nature."

"Your suggestion is a good one," she replies, "but modern philosophers have found it surprisingly difficult to say precisely what type of statement can qualify as a possible law of nature. It is a law of nature, most physicists would agree, that no material objects travel faster than light; they would refuse to admit, *as a law of nature,* that no golden spheres are more than one mile in diameter. It is not easy to state clearly the basis for this distinction. Both statements are generalizations, and both are true to the best of our knowledge."[23]

"Isn't the difference simply that you cannot, even in principle, accelerate a material object to the speed of light, while it is possible in principle to fabricate an enormous sphere of gold?"

"That is precisely the question at issue," she replies. "The problem is, what basis do we have for claiming possibility in the one case and impossibility in the other. You seem to be saying that a law of nature prevents the one but not the other, which is obviously circular. And if you bring in the notion of causation—causing something to go faster than light vs. causing a large golden sphere to be created—you only compound the difficulty, for the concept of causation is itself a source of great perplexity.

"Suppose, however, that we had succeeded in overcoming that obstacle—that we could say with reasonable precision which sorts of statements are candidates for the status of laws of nature and which are not. We then face a further difficulty. It is obvious that some tests of scientific laws carry greater weight than others. The discovery of the planet Neptune, for example, confirmed Newton's laws much more dramatically than would a few additional observations of Mars. A test with particles traveling at very high velocities would be much stronger evidence for conservation of momentum than would some more experiments on the air track in the physics lab. It is not easy to see how to measure or compare the weight which different types of evidence lend to different scientific hypotheses.

"Scientific confirmation is a subtle and complex matter to which contemporary philosophers have devoted a great deal of attention; some have tried to construct systems of inductive logic that would capture this kind of scientific reasoning. Such efforts have, at best, met with limited success; inductive logic is in a primitive state compared with deductive logic. Until we have a reasonably clear idea of what such inference consists of, however, it is unlikely that we will be able to go very far in meeting the fundamental challenge Hume issued concerning the justification of scientific reasoning. Unless we can at least say what inductive inference is, and what constitutes uniformity of nature (or natural law), we can hardly argue that inductive reasoning—and only inductive reasoning—will prove successful in predicting the future if nature is uniform. And even if those concepts were clarified, the argument would still be intricate indeed."

"Do you think there is any chance that answers to such problems can be found?" you ask.

"I think it's just possible."

"Thanks," you say as you get up to leave.

"And my thanks to you," she replies. "You cannot possibly know how satisfying it is to talk with someone like you—someone intelligent—who takes such philosophical problems seriously and thinks hard about them. If you keep it up, you might be the very person to find some of the answers. I wish you well."

NOTES

1. Professor Salvia is a descendant of Salviati, the protagonist in Galileo's dialogues. The name was shortened when the family emigrated to America.

2. Dr. Sagro is married to a descendant of Sagredo, another character in Galileo's dialogues.

3. If you really did know, please accept the author's apologies.

4. Please note that "demonstrate" is ambiguous. In mathematics it means "prove"; in physics it means "exemplify." Hume uses this term only in the mathematical sense.

5. Hume, using the terminology of his day, refers to it as the "moment" of the moving body.

6. This is Newton's definition; it is somewhat out of date, but adequate in the present context.

7. She is a direct descendant of Philo, the protagonist in Hume's "Dialogues Concerning Natural Religion," most of which is reprinted in this anthology.

8. Professor Philo realizes that it would be more accurate to say that a statement or hypothesis expressing a law of nature must be a generalization, but she does not wish to introduce unnecessary terminological distinctions at this point.

9. In section IV, part I, anticipating the results of the later discussion.

10. All of the attempts to deal with Hume's problem which are treated in this section are discussed in

detail in Wesley C. Salmon, *The Foundations of Scientific Inference* (Pittsburgh: University of Pittsburgh Press, 1967); this book will be cited hereafter as *Foundations*.

11. This is an inductive justification; see *Foundations*, chapter II, section I.

12. David Hume, *Enquiry Concerning Human Understanding* (hereafter, *Enquiry*), section IV, part II.

13. Ibid.

14. For discussion of justification by means of synthetic a priori principles, see *Foundations*, chapter II, section 4.

15. *Enquiry*, section IV, part II.

16. For discussion of the postulational approach, see *Foundations*, chapter II, section 6.

17. Bertrand Russell, *Introduction to Mathematical Philosophy* (London: Allen & Unwin, 1919), p. 71.

18. The "probabilistic approach" is discussed in *Foundations*, chapter II, section 7.

19. An elementary survey of philosophical problems of probability is given in *Foundations*, chapters IV–VII. References to additional literature on this subject can be found there.

20. We are assuming, of course, that these predictions are properly made. Scientists are only human, and they do make mistakes. One should not conclude, however, that every false prediction represents a scientific error. Impeccable scientific procedure is fallible, as we have already noted more than once.

21. This refers to the "deductivist" position of Sir Karl Popper. This approach is discussed in *Foundations*, chapter II, section 3.

22. This approach is due mainly to Hans Reichenbach; it is known as a "pragmatic justification" and is discussed in *Foundations*, chapter II, section 8.

23. Further elementary discussion of this issue can be found in Carl G. Hempel, *Philosophy of Natural Science* (Englewood Cliffs, N.J.: Prentice-Hall, Inc., 1966), § 5.3. A more technical and extensive treatment of related issues can be found in Nelson Goodman, *Fact, Fiction, and Forecast*, 2nd ed. (Indianapolis, Ind.: The Bobbs-Merrill Co., 1965).

Science: Conjectures and Refutations

KARL POPPER

Karl Popper (1902–1994) was one of the great philosophers of science of the twentieth century.

Mr. Turnbull had predicted evil consequences,... and was now doing the best in his power to bring about the verification of his own prophecies.

—ANTHONY TROLLOPE

I

When I received the list of participants in this course and realized that I had been asked to speak to philosophical colleagues, I thought, after some hesitation and consultation, that you would probably prefer me to speak about those problems which interest me most, and about those developments with which I am most intimately acquainted. I therefore decided to do what I have never done before: to give you a report on my own work in the philosophy of science, since the autumn of 1919 when I first began to grapple with the problem, *"When should a theory be ranked as scientific?"* or *"Is there a criterion for the scientific character or status of a theory?"*

The problem which troubled me at the time was neither, "When is a theory true?" nor, "When is a theory acceptable?" My problem was different. *I wished to distinguish between science and pseudo-science;* knowing very well that science often errs, and that pseudo-science may happen to stumble on the truth.

I knew, of course, the most widely accepted answer to my problem: that science is distinguished from pseudo-science—or from "metaphysics"—by its *empirical method,* which is essentially *inductive,* proceeding from observation or experiment. But this did not satisfy me. On the contrary, I often formulated my problem as one of distinguishing between a genuinely empirical method and a non-empirical or even a pseudo-empirical method—that is to say, a method which, although it appeals to observation and experiment, nevertheless does not come up to scientific standards. The latter method may be exemplified by astrology, with its stupendous mass of empirical evidence based on observation—on horoscopes and on biographies.

But as it was not the example of astrology which led me to my problem I should perhaps briefly describe the atmosphere in which my problem arose and the examples by which it was stimulated. After the collapse of the Austrian Empire there had been a revolution in Austria: the air was full of revolutionary slogans and ideas, and new and often wild theories. Among the theories which interested me Einstein's theory of relativity was no doubt by far the most important. Three others were Marx's theory of history, Freud's psycho-analysis, and Alfred Adler's so-called "individual psychology".

There was a lot of popular nonsense talked about these theories, and especially about relativity (as still happens even today), but I was fortunate in those who introduced me to the study of this theory. We all—the small circle of students to which I belonged—were thrilled with the result of Eddington's eclipse observations which in 1919 brought the first important confirmation of Einstein's theory of gravitation. It was a great experience for us, and one which had a lasting influence on my intellectual development.

From Karl Popper, *Conjectures and Refutations* (London: Routledge, 1963), pp. 33–38. Reprinted by permission of the estate of Karl Popper.

The three other theories I have mentioned were also widely discussed among students at that time. I myself happened to come into personal contact with Alfred Adler, and even to co-operate with him in his social work among the children and young people in the working-class districts of Vienna where he had established social guidance clinics.

It was during the summer of 1919 that I began to feel more and more dissatisfied with these three theories—the Marxist theory of history, psychoanalysis, and individual psychology; and I began to feel dubious about their claims to scientific status. My problem perhaps first took the simple form, "What is wrong with Marxism, psycho-analysis, and individual psychology? Why are they so different from physical theories, from Newton's theory, and especially from the theory of relativity?"

To make this contrast clear I should explain that few of us at the time would have said that we believed in the *truth* of Einstein's theory of gravitation. This shows that it was not my doubting the *truth* of those other three theories which bothered me, but something else. Yet neither was it that I merely felt mathematical physics to be more *exact* than the sociological or psychological type of theory. Thus what worried me was neither the problem of truth, at that stage at least, nor the problem of exactness or measurability. It was rather that I felt that these other three theories, though posing as sciences, had in fact more in common with primitive myths than with science; that they resembled astrology rather than astronomy.

I found that those of my friends who were admirers of Marx, Freud, and Adler, were impressed by a number of points common to these theories, and especially by their apparent *explanatory power*. These theories appeared to be able to explain practically everything that happened within the fields to which they referred. The study of any of them seemed to have the effect of an intellectual conversion or revelation, opening your eyes to a new truth hidden from those not yet initiated. Once your eyes were thus opened you saw confirming instances everywhere: the world was full of *verifications* of the theory. Whatever happened always confirmed it. Thus its truth appeared manifest; and unbelievers were clearly people who did not want to see the manifest truth; who refused to see it, either because it was against their class interest, or because of their repressions which were still "un-analysed" and crying aloud for treatment.

The most characteristic element in this situation seemed to me the incessant stream of confirmations, of observations which "verified" the theories in question; and this point was constantly emphasized by their adherents. A Marxist could not open a newspaper without finding on every page confirming evidence for his interpretation of history; not only in the news, but also in its presentation—which revealed the class bias of the paper—and especially of course in what the paper did *not* say. The Freudian analysts emphasized that their theories were constantly verified by their "clinical observations". As for Adler, I was much impressed by a personal experience. Once, in 1919, I reported to him a case which to me did not seem particularly Adlerian, but which he found no difficulty in analysing in terms of his theory of inferiority feelings, although he had not even seen the child. Slightly shocked, I asked him how he could be so sure. "Because of my thousandfold experience," he replied; whereupon I could not help saying: "And with this new case, I suppose, your experience has become thousand-and-one-fold."

What I had in mind was that his previous observations may not have been much sounder than this new one; that each in its turn had been interpreted in the light of "previous experience", and at the same time counted as additional confirmation. What, I asked myself, did it confirm? No more than that a case could be interpreted in the light of the theory. But this meant very little, I reflected, since every conceivable case could be interpreted in the light of Adler's theory, or equally of Freud's. I may illustrate this by two very different examples of human behaviour: that of a man who pushes a child into the water with the intention of drowning it; and that of a man who sacrifices his life in an attempt to save the child. Each of these two cases can be explained with equal ease in Freudian and in Adlerian terms. According to Freud the first man suffered from repression (say, of some component of his Oedipus complex), while the second man had achieved sublimation. According to Adler the first man suffered from feelings of inferiority (producing perhaps the need to prove to himself that he dared to commit some crime), and so did the second man (whose need was to prove to himself that he dared to rescue the child). I could not think of any human behaviour which could not be interpreted in terms of either theory. It was precisely this fact—that they always fitted, that they were always confirmed—which in the eyes of their admirers constituted the strongest argument in favour of these theories. It began to dawn on me that this apparent strength was in fact their weakness.

With Einstein's theory the situation was strikingly different. Take one typical instance—Einstein's prediction, just then confirmed by the findings of Eddington's expedition. Einstein's gravitational theory had led to the result that light must be attracted by heavy bodies (such as the sun), precisely as material bodies were attracted. As a consequence it could be calculated that light from a distant fixed star whose apparent position was close to the sun would reach the earth from such a direction that the star would seem to be slightly shifted away from the sun; or, in other words, that stars close to the sun would look as if they had moved a little away from the sun, and from one another. This is a thing which cannot normally be observed since such stars are rendered invisible in daytime by the sun's overwhelming brightness; but during an eclipse it is possible to take photographs of them. If the same constellation is photographed at night one can measure the distances on the two photographs, and check the predicted effect.

Now the impressive thing about this case is the *risk* involved in a prediction of this kind. If observation shows that the predicted effect is definitely absent, then the theory is simply refuted. The theory is *incompatible with certain possible results of observation*—in fact with results which everybody before Einstein would have expected. This is quite different from the situation I have previously described, when it turned out that the theories in question were compatible with the most divergent human behaviour, so that it

was practically impossible to describe any human behaviour that might not be claimed to be a verification of these theories.

These considerations led me in the winter of 1919–20 to conclusions which I may now reformulate as follows.

1. It is easy to obtain confirmations, or verifications, for nearly every theory—if we look for confirmations.

2. Confirmations should count only if they are the result of *risky predictions;* that is to say, if, unenlightened by the theory in question, we should have expected an event which was incompatible with the theory—an event which would have refuted the theory.

3. Every "good" scientific theory is a prohibition: it forbids certain things to happen. The more a theory forbids, the better it is.

4. A theory which is not refutable by any conceivable event is nonscientific. Irrefutability is not a virtue of a theory (as people often think) but a vice.

5. Every genuine *test* of a theory is an attempt to falsify it, or to refute it. Testability is falsifiability; but there are degrees of testability; some theories are more testable, more exposed to refutation, than others; they take, as it were, greater risks.

6. Confirming evidence should not count *except when it is the result of a genuine test of the theory;* and this means that it can be presented as a serious but unsuccessful attempt to falsify the theory. (I now speak in such cases of "corroborating evidence".)

7. Some genuinely testable theories, when found to be false, are still upheld by their admirers—for example by introducing *ad hoc* some auxiliary assumption, or by re-interpreting the theory *ad hoc* in such a way that it escapes refutation. Such a procedure is always possible, but it rescues the theory from refutation only at the price of destroying, or at least lowering, its scientific status. (I later described such a rescuing operation as a *"conventionalist twist"* or a *"conventionalist stratagem"*.)

One can sum up all this by saying that *the criterion of the scientific status of a theory is its falsifiability, or refutability, or testability.*

II

I may perhaps exemplify this with the help of the various theories so far mentioned. Einstein's theory of gravitation clearly satisfied the criterion of falsifiability. Even if our measuring instruments at the time did not allow us to pronounce on the results of the tests with complete assurance, there was clearly a possibility of refuting the theory.

Astrology did not pass the test. Astrologers were greatly impressed, and misled, by what they believed to be confirming evidence—so much so that they were quite unimpressed by any unfavourable evidence. Moreover, by making their interpretations and prophecies sufficiently vague they were able to explain away anything that might have been a refutation of the theory had the theory and the prophecies been more precise. In order to escape falsification they destroyed the testability of their theory. It is a typical soothsayer's trick to predict things so vaguely that the predictions can hardly fail: that they become irrefutable.

The Marxist theory of history, in spite of the serious efforts of some of its founders and followers, ultimately adopted this soothsaying practice. In some of its earlier formulations (for example in Marx's analysis of the character of the "coming social revolution") their predictions were testable, and in fact falsified. Yet instead of accepting the refutations the followers of Marx re-interpreted both the theory and the evidence in order to make them agree. In this way they rescued the theory from refutation; but they did so at the price of adopting a device which made it irrefutable. They thus gave a "conventionalist twist" to the theory; and by this stratagem they destroyed its much advertised claim to scientific status.

The two psycho-analytic theories were in a different class. They were simply non-testable, irrefutable. There was no conceivable human behaviour which could contradict them. This does not mean that Freud and Adler were not seeing certain things correctly: I personally do not doubt that much of what they say is of considerable importance, and may well play its part one day in a psychological science which is testable. But it does mean that those "clinical observations" which analysts naively believe confirm

their theory cannot do this any more than the daily confirmations which astrologers find in their practice. And as for Freud's epic of the Ego, the Super-ego, and the Id, no substantially stronger claim to scientific status can be made for it than for Homer's collected stories from Olympus. These theories describe some facts, but in the manner of myths. They contain most interesting psychological suggestions, but not in a testable form.

At the same time I realized that such myths may be developed, and become testable; that historically speaking all—or very nearly all—scientific theories originate from myths, and that a myth may contain important anticipations of scientific theories. Examples are Empedocles' theory of evolution by trial and error, or Parmenides' myth of the unchanging block universe in which nothing ever happens and which, if we add another dimension, becomes Einstein's block universe (in which, too, nothing ever happens, since everything is, four-dimensionally speaking, determined and laid down from the beginning). I thus felt that if a theory is found to be non-scientific, or "metaphysical" (as we might say), it is not thereby found to be unimportant, or insignificant, or "meaningless", or "nonsensical". But it cannot claim to be backed by empirical evidence in the scientific sense—although it may easily be, in some genetic sense, the "result of observation".

(There were a great many other theories of this pre-scientific or pseudo-scientific character, some of them, unfortunately, as influential as the Marxist interpretation of history; for example, the racialist interpretation of history—another of those impressive and all-explanatory theories which act upon weak minds like revelations.)

Thus the problem which I tried to solve by proposing the criterion of falsifiability was neither a problem of meaningfulness or significance, nor a problem of truth or acceptability. It was the problem of drawing a line (as well as this can be done) between the statements, or systems of statements, of the empirical sciences, and all other statements—whether they are of a religious or of a metaphysical character, or simply pseudo-scientific. Years later—it must have been in 1928 or 1929—I called this first problem of mine the *"problem of demarcation".* The criterion of falsifiability is a solution to this problem of demarcation, for it says that statements or systems of statements, in order to be ranked as scientific, must be capable of conflicting with possible, or conceivable, observations.

Believing Where We Cannot Prove

PHILIP KITCHER

Philip Kitcher is Professor of Philosophy at Columbia University. He has published widely in philosophy of mathematics and philosophy of science.

OPENING MOVES

Simple distinctions come all too easily. Frequently we open the way for later puzzlement by restricting the options we take to be available. So, for example, in contrasting science and religion, we often operate with a simple pair of categories. On one side there is science, proof, and certainty; on the other, religion, conjecture, and faith.

The opening lines of Tennyson's *In Memoriam* offer an eloquent statement of the contrast:

> *Strong Son of God, immortal love,*
> *Whom we, that have not seen Thy face,*
> *By faith, and faith alone, embrace,*
> *Believing where we cannot prove.*

A principal theme of Tennyson's great poem is his struggle to maintain faith in the face of what seems to be powerful scientific evidence. Tennyson had read a popular work by Robert Chambers, *Vestiges of the Natural History of Creation*, and he was greatly troubled by the account of the course of life on earth that the book contains. *In Memoriam* reveals a man trying to believe where he cannot prove, a man haunted by the thought that the proofs may be against him.

Like Tennyson, contemporary Creationists accept the traditional contrast between science and religion. But where Tennyson agonized, they attack. While they are less eloquent, they are supremely confident of their own solution.

They open their onslaught on evolutionary theory by denying that it is a science. In *The Troubled Waters of Evolution*, Henry Morris characterizes evolutionary theory as maintaining that large amounts of time are required for evolution to produce "new kinds." As a result, we should not expect to see such "new kinds" emerging. Morris comments, "Creationists in turn insist that this belief is not scientific evidence but only a statement of faith. The evolutionist seems to be saying, Of course, we cannot really *prove* evolution, since this requires ages of time, and so, therefore, you should accept it as a proved fact of science! Creationists regard this as an odd type of logic, which would be entirely unacceptable in any other field of science" (Morris 1974b, 16). David Watson makes a similar point in comparing Darwin with Galileo: "So here is the difference between Darwin and Galileo: Galileo set a demonstrable *fact* against a few words of Bible poetry which the Church at that time had understood in an obviously naive way; Darwin set an unprovable *theory* against eleven chapters of straightforward history which cannot be reinterpreted in any satisfactory way" (Watson 1976, 46).

The idea that evolution is conjecture, faith, or "philosophy" pervades Creationist writings. It is absolutely crucial to their case for equal time for "scientific" Creationism. This ploy has succeeded in winning important adherents to the Creationist cause. As he prepared to defend

From Philip Kitcher, *Abusing Science: The Case Against Creationism*, pp. 30–38, 42–46, 48–49 (Cambridge: MIT Press, 1982). Reprinted by permission of MIT Press.

Arkansas law 590, Attorney General Steven Clark echoed the Creationist judgment. "Evolution," he said, "is just a theory." Similar words have been heard in Congress. William Dannemeyer, a congressman from California, introduced a bill to limit funding to the Smithsonian with the following words: "If the theory of evolution is just that—a theory—and if that theory can be regarded as a religion...then it occurs to this Member that other Members might prefer it not to be given exclusive or top billing in our Nation's most famous museum but equal billing or perhaps no billing at all."

In their attempt to show that evolution is not science, Creationists receive help from the least likely sources. Great scientists sometimes claim that certain facts about the past evolution of organisms are "demonstrated" or "indubitable." But Creationists also can (and do) quote scientists who characterize evolution as "dogma" and contend that there is no conclusive proof of evolutionary theory. Evolution is not part of science because, as evolutionary biologists themselves concede, science demands proof, and, as other biologists point out, proof of evolution is not forthcoming.

The rest of the Creationist argument flows easily. We educate our children in evolutionary theory as if it were a proven fact. We subscribe officially, in our school system, to one faith—an atheistic, materialistic faith—ignoring rival beliefs. Antireligious educators deform the minds of children, warping them to accept as gospel a doctrine that has no more scientific support than the true Gospel. The very least that should be done is to allow for both alternatives to be presented.

We should reject the Creationists' gambit. Eminent scientists notwithstanding, science is not a body of demonstrated truths. Virtually all of science is an exercise in believing where we cannot prove. Yet, scientific conclusions are not embraced by faith alone. Tennyson's dichotomy was too simple.

INCONCLUSIVE EVIDENCE

Sometimes we seem to have conclusive reasons for accepting a statement as true. It is hard to doubt that $2 + 2 = 4$. If, unlike Lord Kelvin's ideal mathematician, we do not find it obvious that

$$\int_{-\infty}^{+\infty} e^{-x^2}\,dx = \sqrt{\pi},$$

at least the elementary parts of mathematics appear to command our agreement. The direct evidence of our senses seems equally compelling. If I see the pen with which I am writing, holding it firmly in my unclouded view, how can I doubt that it exists? The talented mathematician who has proved a theorem and the keen-eyed witness of an episode furnish our ideals of certainty in knowledge. What they tell us can be engraved in stone, for there is no cause for worry that it will need to be modified.

Yet, in another mood, one that seems "deeper" or more "philosophical," skeptical doubts begin to creep in. Is there really anything of which we are so certain that later evidence could not give us reason to change our minds? Even when we think about mathematical proof, can we not imagine that new discoveries may cast doubt on the cogency of our reasoning? (The history of mathematics reveals that sometimes what seems for all the world like a proof may have a false conclusion.) Is it not possible that the most careful observer may have missed something? Or that the witness brought preconceptions to the observation that subtly biased what was reported? Are we not *always* fallible?

I am mildly sympathetic to the skeptic's worries. Complete certainty is best seen as an ideal toward which we strive and that is rarely, if ever, attained. Conclusive evidence always eludes us. Yet even if we ignore skeptical complaints and imagine that we are sometimes lucky enough to have conclusive reasons for accepting a claim as true, we should not include scientific reasoning among our paradigms of proof. Fallibility is the hallmark of science.

This point should not be so surprising. The trouble is that we frequently forget it in discussing contemporary science. When we turn to the history of science, however, our fallibility stares us in the face. The history of the natural sciences is strewn with the corpses of intricately organized theories, each of which had, in its day, considerable evidence in its favor. When we look at the confident defenders of those theories we should see anticipations of ourselves. The eighteenth century scientists who believed that heat is a "subtle fluid," the atomic theorists who maintained that water molecules are compounded out of one atom of hydrogen and one of oxygen, the biochemists who identified protein as the genetic material, and the geologists who thought that continents cannot move were neither unintelligent nor ill informed. Given the evidence available to them, they were eminently reasonable in drawing their conclusions. History proved them wrong. It did not show that they were unjustified.

Why is science fallible? Scientific investigation aims to disclose the general principles that govern the workings of the universe. These principles are not intended merely to summarize what some select groups of humans have witnessed. Natural science is not just natural history. It is vastly more ambitious. Science offers us laws that are supposed to hold universally, and it advances claims about things that are beyond our power to observe. The nuclear physicist who sets down the law governing a particular type of radioactive decay is attempting to state a truth that holds throughout the entire cosmos and also to describe the behavior of things that we cannot even see. Yet, of necessity, the physicist's ultimate evidence is highly restricted. Like the rest of us, scientists are confined to a relatively small region of space and time and equipped with limited and imperfect senses.

How is science possible at all? How are we able to have any confidence about the distant regions of the cosmos and the invisible realm that lies behind the surfaces of ordinary things? The answer is complicated. Natural science follows intricate and ingenious procedures for fathoming the secrets of the universe. Scientists devise ways of obtaining especially revealing evidence. They single out some of the things we are able to see as crucial clues to the way that nature works. These clues are used to answer questions that cannot be addressed by direct observation. Scientific theories, even those that are most respected and most successful, rest on indirect arguments from the observational evidence. New discoveries can

always call those arguments into question, showing scientists that the observed data should be understood in a different way, that they have misread their evidence.

But scientists often forget the fallibility of their enterprise. This is not just absentmindedness or wishful thinking. During the heyday of a scientific theory, so much evidence may support the theory, so many observational clues may seem to attest to its truth, that the idea that it could be overthrown appears ludicrous. In addition, the theory may provide ways of identifying quickly what is inaccessible to our unaided senses. Electron microscopes and cloud chambers are obvious examples of those extensions of our perceptual system that theories can inspire. Trained biochemists will talk quite naturally of seeing large molecules, and it is easy to overlook the fact that they are presupposing a massive body of theory in describing what they "see." If that theory were to be amended, even in subtle ways, then the descriptions of the "observed characteristics" of large molecules might have to be given up. Nor should we pride ourselves that the enormous successes of contemporary science secure us against future amendments. No theory in the history of science enjoyed a more spectacular career than Newton's mechanics. Yet Newton's ideas had to give way to Einstein's.

When practicing scientists are reminded of these straightforward points, they frequently adopt what the philosopher George Berkeley called a "forlorn skepticism." From the idea of science as certain and infallible, they jump to a cynical description of their endeavors. Science is sometimes held to be a game played with arbitrary rules, an irrational acceptance of dogma, an enterprise based ultimately on faith. Once we have appreciated the fallibility of natural science and recognized its sources, we can move beyond the simple opposition of proof and faith. Between these extremes lies the vast field of cases in which we believe something on the basis of good—even excellent—but inconclusive evidence.

If we want to emphasize the fact that what scientists believe today may have to be revised in the light of observations made tomorrow, then we can describe all our science as "theory." But the description should not confuse us.

To concede that evolutionary biology is a theory is not to suppose that there are alternatives to it that are equally worthy of a place in our curriculum. All theories are revisable, but not all theories are equal. Even though our present evidence does not *prove* that evolutionary biology—or quantum physics, or plate tectonics, or any other theory—is true, evolutionary biologists will maintain that the present evidence is overwhelmingly in favor of their theory and overwhelmingly against its supposed rivals. Their enthusiastic assertions that evolution is a proven fact can be charitably understood as claims that the (admittedly inconclusive) evidence we have for evolutionary theory is as good as we ever obtain for any theory in any field of science.

Hence the Creationist try for a quick Fools' Mate can easily be avoided. Creationists attempt to draw a line between evolutionary biology and the rest of science by remarking that large-scale evolution cannot be observed. This tactic fails. Large-scale evolution is no more inaccessible to observation than nuclear reactions or the molecular composition of water. For the Creationists to succeed in divorcing evolutionary biology from the rest of science, they need to argue that evolutionary theory is less well supported by the evidence than are theories in, for example, physics and chemistry. It will come as no surprise to learn that they try to do this. To assess the merits of their arguments we need a deeper understanding of the logic of inconclusive justification. We shall begin with a simple and popular idea: Scientific theories earn our acceptance by making successful predictions.

PREDICTIVE SUCCESS

Imagine that somebody puts forward a new theory about the origins of hay fever. The theory makes a number of startling predictions concerning connections that we would not have thought worth investigating. For example, it tells us that people who develop hay fever invariably secrete a particular substance in certain fatty tissues and that anyone who eats rhubarb as a child never develops hay fever. The theory predicts things that initially appear fantastic. Suppose that we check up on these predictions and find that they are borne out by clinical tests. Would we not begin to believe—and believe reasonably—that the theory was *at least* on the right track?

This example illustrates a pattern of reasoning that is familiar in the history of science. Theories win support by producing claims about what can be observed, claims that would not have seemed plausible prior to the advancement of the theory, but that are in fact found to be true when we make the appropriate observations. A classic (real) example is Pascal's confirmation of Torricelli's hypothesis that we live at the bottom of an ocean of air that presses down upon us. Pascal reasoned that if Torricelli's hypothesis were true, then air pressure should decrease at higher altitudes (because at higher altitudes we are closer to the "surface" of the atmosphere, so that the length of the column of air that presses down is shorter). Accordingly, he sent his brother-in-law to the top of a mountain to make some barometric measurements. Pascal's clever working out of the observational predictions of Torricelli's theory led to a dramatic predictive success for the theory.

The idea of predictive success has encouraged a popular picture of science. (We shall see later that this picture, while popular, is not terribly accurate.) Philosophers sometimes regard a theory as a collection of claims or statements. Some of these statements offer generalizations about the features of particular, recondite things (genes, atoms, gravitational force, quasars, and the like). These statements are used to infer statements whose truth or falsity can be decided by observation. (This appears to be just what Pascal did.) Statements belonging to this second group are called the *observational consequences* of the theory. Theories are supported when we find that their observational consequences (those that we have checked) are true. The credentials of a theory are damaged if we discover that some of its observational consequences are false.

We can make the idea more precise by being clearer about the inferences involved. Those who talk of inferring observational predictions from our theories think that we can *deduce* from the statements of the theory, and from those statements alone, some predictions whose accuracy we can check by direct observation. Deductive inference is well understood. The fundamental idea of deductive inference is this: We say that a statement *S* is a valid deductive consequence of a group of statements if and only if it is *impossible* that all the statements in the group should be true and that *S* should be false; alternatively, *S* is a valid deductive consequence (or, more simply, a valid consequence) of a group of statements if and only if it would be self-contradictory to assert all the statements in the group and to deny *S*.

It will be helpful to make the idea of valid consequence more familiar with some examples. Consider the statements "All lovers of baseball dislike George Steinbrenner" and "George Steinbrenner loves baseball." The statement "George Steinbrenner dislikes himself" is a deductively valid consequence of these two statements. For it is impossible that the first two should be true and the third false. However, in claiming that this is a case of deductively valid consequence, we do not commit ourselves to maintaining that *any* of the statements is true. (Perhaps there are some ardent baseball fans who admire Steinbrenner. Perhaps Steinbrenner himself has no time for the game.) What deductive validity means is that the truth of the first two statements would guarantee the truth of the third; that is, *if* the first two *were* true, then the third would have to be true.

Another example will help rule out other misunderstandings. Here are two statements: "Shortly after noon on January 1, 1982, in the Oval Office, a jelly bean was released from rest more than two feet above any surface"; "Shortly after noon on January 1, 1982, in the Oval Office, a jelly bean fell." Is the second statement a deductively valid consequence of the first? You might think that it is, on the grounds that it would have been impossible for the unfortunate object to have been released and not to have fallen. In one sense this is correct, but that is not the sense of impossibility that deductive logicians have in mind. Strictly speaking, it is not *impossible* for the jellybean to have been released without falling; we can imagine, for example, that the law of gravity might suddenly cease to operate. We do not *contradict* ourselves when we assert that the jellybean was released but deny that it fell; we simply refuse to accept the law of gravity (or some other relevant physical fact).

Thus, *S* is a deductively valid consequence of a group of statements if and only if there is *absolutely no possibility* that all the statements in the group should be true and *S* should be false. This conception allows us to state the popular view of theory and prediction more precisely. Theories are collections of statements. The observational consequences of a theory are statements that have to be true if the statements belonging to the theory are all true. These observational consequences also have to be statements whose truth or falsity can be ascertained by direct observation.

My initial discussion of predictive success presented the rough idea that, when we find the observational consequences of a theory to be true, our findings bring credit to the theory. Conversely, discovery that some observational consequences of a theory are false was viewed as damaging. We can now make the second point much more precise. Any theory that has a false observational consequence must contain some false statement (or statements). For if all the statements in the theory were true, then, according to the standard definitions of *deductive validity* and *observational consequence*, any observational consequence would also have to be true. Hence, if a theory is found to have a false observational consequence, we must conclude that one or more statements of the theory is false.

This means that theories can be conclusively falsified, through the discovery that they have false observational consequences. Some philosophers, most notably Sir Karl Popper (Popper 1959; 1963), have taken this point to have enormous significance for our understanding of science. According to Popper, the essence of a scientific theory is that it should be *falsifiable*. That is, if the theory is false, then it must be possible to show that it is false. Now, if a theory has utterly no observational consequences, it would be extraordinarily difficult to unmask that theory as false. So, to be a genuine scientific theory, a group of statements must have observational consequences. It is important to realize that Popper is not suggesting that every good theory must be false. The difference between being falsifiable and being false is like the difference between being vulnerable and actually being hurt. A good scientific theory should not be false. Rather, it must have observational consequences that could reveal the theory as mistaken if the experiments give the wrong results.

While these ideas about theory testing may seem strange in their formal attire, they emerge quite frequently in discussions of science. They also find their way into the creation-evolution debate.

PREDICTIVE FAILURE

From the beginning, evolutionary theory has been charged with just about every possible type of predictive failure. Critics of the theory have argued that (a) the theory makes no predictions (it is unfalsifiable and so fails Popper's criterion for science), (b) the theory makes false predictions (it is falsified), (c) the theory does not make the kinds of predictions it ought to make (the observations and experiments that evolutionary theorists undertake have no bearing on the theory). Many critics, including several Creationists, manage to advance all these objections in the same work. This is somewhat surprising, since points (a) and (b) are, of course, mutually contradictory. . . .

To make a serious assessment of these broad Creationist charges, we must begin by asking some basic methodological questions. We cannot decide whether evolutionary biologists are guilty of trying to save their theory by using ad hoc assumptions (new and implausible claims dreamed up for the sole purpose of protecting some cherished ideas) unless we have some way of deciding when a proposal is ad hoc. Similarly, we cannot make a reasoned response to the charge that laboratory experiments are irrelevant, or to the fundamental objection that evolutionary theory is unfalsifiable, unless we have a firmer grasp of the relation between theory and evidence.

NAIVE FALSIFICATIONISM

The time has come to tell a dreadful secret. While the picture of scientific testing sketched above continues to be influential among scientists, it has been shown to be seriously incorrect. (To give my profession its due, historians and philosophers of science have been trying to let this particular cat out of the bag for at least thirty years.) Important work in the history of science has made it increasingly clear that no major scientific theory has ever exemplified the relation between theory and evidence that the traditional model presents.

What is wrong with the old picture? Answer: Either it debars most of what we take to be science from counting as science or it allows virtually anything to count. On the traditional view of "theory," textbook cases of scientific theories turn out to be unfalsifiable. Suppose we identify Newtonian mechanics with Newton's three laws of motion plus the law of gravitation. What observational consequences can we deduce from these four statements? You might think that we could deduce that if, as the (undoubtedly apocryphal) story alleges, an apple became detached from a branch above where Newton was sitting, the apple would have fallen on his head. But this does not follow at all. To see why not, it is only necessary to recognize that the failure of this alleged prediction would not force us to deny any of the four statements of the theory. All we need do is assume that some other forces were at work that overcame the force of gravity and caused the apple to depart from its usual trajectory. So, given this simple way of applying Popper's criterion, Newtonian mechanics would be unfalsifiable. The same would go for any other scientific theory. Hence none of what we normally take to be science would count as science. (I might note that Popper is aware of this problem and has suggestions of his own as to how it should be overcome. However, what concerns me here are the *applications* of Popper's ideas, that are made by Creationists, as well as by scientists in their professional debates.)

The example of the last paragraph suggests an obvious remedy. Instead of thinking about theories in the simple way just illustrated, we might take them to be far more elaborate. Newton's laws (the three laws of motion and the law of gravitation) are *embedded* in Newtonian mechanics. They form the core of the theory, but do not constitute the whole of it. Newtonian mechanics also contains supplementary assumptions, telling us, for example, that for certain special systems the effects of forces other than gravity are negligible. This more elaborate collection of statements *does* have observational consequences and *is* falsifiable.

But the remedy fails. Imagine that we attempt to expose some self-styled spiritual teacher as an overpaid fraud. We try to point out that the teacher's central message—"Quietness is wholeness in the center of stillness"—is unfalsifiable. The teacher cheerfully admits that, taken by itself, this profound doctrine yields no observational consequences. He then points out that, by themselves, the central statements of scientific theories are also incapable of generating observational consequences. Alas, if all that is demanded is that a doctrine be embedded in a group of statements with observational consequences, our imagined guru will easily slither off the hook. He replies, "You have forgotten that my doctrine has many other claims. For example, I believe that if quietness is wholeness in the center of stillness, then flowers bloom in the spring, bees gather pollen, and blinkered defenders of so-called science raise futile objections to the world's spiritual benefactors. You will see that these three predictions are borne out by experience. Of course, there are countless others. Perhaps when you see how my central message yields so much evident truth, you will recognize the wealth of evidence behind my claim. Quietness is wholeness in the center of stillness."

More formally, the trouble is that *any* statement can be coupled with other statements to produce observational consequences. Given any doctrine D, and any statement O that records the result of an observation, we can enable D to "predict" O by adding the extra assumption, "If D, then O." (In the example, D is "Quietness is wholeness in the center of stillness"; examples of O would be statements describing the blooming of particular flowers in the spring, the pollen gathering of specific bees, and so forth.)

The falsifiability criterion adopted from Popper—which I shall call the *naive falsificationist* criterion—is hopelessly flawed. It runs aground on

a fundamental fact about the relation between theory and prediction: On their own, individual scientific laws, or the small groups of laws that are often identified as theories, do not have observational consequences. This crucial point about theories was first understood by the great historian and philosopher of science Pierre Duhem. Duhem saw clearly that individual scientific claims do not, and cannot, confront the evidence one by one. Rather, in his picturesque phrase, "Hypotheses are tested in bundles." Besides ruling out the possibility of testing an individual scientific theory (read, small group of laws), Duhem's insight has another startling consequence. We can only test relatively large bundles of claims. What this means is that when our experiments go awry we are not logically compelled to select any particular claim as the culprit. We can always save a cherished hypothesis from refutation by rejecting (however implausibly) one of the other members of the bundle. Of course, this is exactly what I did in the illustration of Newton and the apple above. Faced with disappointing results, I suggested that we could abandon the (tacit) additional claim that no large forces besides gravity were operating on the apple.

Creationists wheel out the ancient warhorse of naive falsificationism so that they can bolster their charge that evolutionary theory is not a science. The (very) brief course in deductive logic plus the whirlwind tour through naive falsificationism and its pitfalls enable us to see what is at the bottom of this seemingly important criticism. Creationists can appeal to naive falsificationism to show that evolution is not a science. But, given the traditional picture of theory and evidence I have sketched, one can appeal to naive falsificationism to show that *any* science is not a science. So, as with the charge that evolutionary change is unobservable, Creationists have again failed to find some "fault" of evolution not shared with every other science. (And, as we shall see, Creationists like some sciences, especially thermodynamics.) Consistent application of naive falsificationism can show that anybody's favorite science (whether it be quantum physics, molecular biology, or whatever) is not science. Of course, what this shows is that the naive falsificationist criterion is a very poor test of genuine science. To be fair, this point can cut both ways. Scientists who charge that "scientific" Creationism is unfalsifiable are not insulting the theory as much as they think.

SUCCESSFUL SCIENCE

Despite the inadequacies of naive falsificationism, there is surely something right in the idea that a science can succeed only if it can fail. An invulnerable "science" would not be science at all. To achieve a more adequate understanding of how a science can succeed and how it runs the risk of failure, let us look at one of the most successful sciences and at a famous episode in its development.

Newtonian celestial mechanics is one of the star turns in the history of science. Among its numerous achievements were convincing explanations of the orbits of most of the known planets. Newton and his successors viewed the solar system as a collection of bodies subject only to gravitational interactions; they used the law of gravitation and the laws of motion to compute the orbits. (Bodies whose effects were negligible in any particular case would be disregarded. For example, the gravitational attraction due to Mercury would not be considered in working out the orbit of Saturn.) The results usually tallied beautifully with astronomical observations. But one case proved difficult. The outermost known planet, Uranus, stubbornly followed an orbit that diverged from the best computations. By the early nineteenth century it was clear that something was wrong. Either astronomers erred in treating the solar system as a Newtonian gravitational system or there was some particular difficulty in applying the general method to Uranus.

Perhaps the most naive of falsificationists would have recommended that the central claim of Newtonian mechanics—the claim that the solar system is a Newtonian gravitational system—be abandoned. But there was obviously a more sensible strategy. Astronomers faced one problematical planet, and they asked themselves what made Uranus so difficult. Two of them, John Adams and Urbain Leverrier, came up with an answer. They proposed (independently) that there was a hitherto unobserved planet beyond Uranus. They computed the orbit of

the postulated planet and demonstrated that the anomalies of the motion of Uranus could be explained if a planet followed this path. There was a straightforward way to test their proposal. Astronomers began to look for the new planet. Within a few years, the planet—Neptune—was found.

I will extract several morals from this success story. The first concerns an issue we originally encountered in Morris's "table of natural predictions:" What is the proper use of auxiliary hypotheses? Adams and Leverrier saved the central claim of Newtonian celestial mechanics by offering an auxiliary hypothesis. They maintained that there were more things in the heavens than had been dreamed of in previous natural philosophy. The anomalies in the orbit of Uranus could be explained on the assumption of an extra planet. Adams and Leverrier worked out the exact orbit of that planet so that they could provide a detailed account of the perturbations—and so that they could tell their fellow astronomers where to look for Neptune. Thus, their auxiliary hypothesis was *independently testable*. The evidence for Neptune's existence was not just the anomalous motion of Uranus. The hypothesis could be checked independently of any assumptions about Uranus or about the correctness of Newtonian celestial mechanics—by making telescopic observations.

Since hypotheses are always tested in bundles, this method of checking presupposed other assumptions, in particular, the optical principles that justify the use of telescopes. The crucial point is that, while hypotheses are always tested in bundles, they can be tested in *different* bundles. An auxiliary hypothesis ought to be testable independently of the particular problem it is introduced to solve, independently of the theory it is designed to save.

While it is obvious in retrospect—indeed it was obvious at the time—that the problem with Uranus should not be construed as "falsifying" celestial mechanics, it is worth asking explicitly why scientists should have clung to Newton's theory in the face of this difficulty. The answer is not just that nothing succeeds like success, and that Newton's theory had been strikingly successful in calculating the orbits of the other planets. The crucial point concerns the way in which Newton's successes had been achieved. Newton was no opportunist, using one batch of assumptions to cope with Mercury, and then moving on to new devices to handle Venus. Celestial mechanics was a remarkably *unified* theory. It solved problems by invoking the same pattern of reasoning, or *problem-solving strategy*, again and again: From a specification of the positions of the bodies under study, use the law of gravitation to calculate the forces acting; from a statement of the forces acting, use the laws of dynamics to compute the equations of motion; solve the equations of motion to obtain the motions of the bodies. This single pattern of reasoning was applied in case after case to yield conclusions that were independently found to be correct.

At a higher level, celestial mechanics was itself contained in a broader theory. Newtonian physics, as a whole, was remarkably unified. It offered a strategy for solving a diverse collection of problems. Faced with *any* question about motion, the Newtonian suggestion was the same: Find the forces acting, from the forces and the laws of dynamics work out the equations of motion, and solve the equations of motion. The method was employed in a broad range of cases. The revolutions of planets, the motions of projectiles, tidal cycles and pendulum oscillations—all fell to the same problem-solving strategy.

We can draw a second moral. A science should be *unified*. A thriving science is not a gerrymandered patchwork but a coherent whole. Good theories consist of just one problem-solving strategy, or a small family of problem-solving strategies, that can be applied to a wide range of problems. The theory succeeds as it is able to encompass more and more problem areas. Failure looms when the basic problem-solving strategy (or strategies) can resolve almost none of the problems in its intended domain without the "aid" of untestable auxiliary hypotheses. . . .

The final moral I want to draw from this brief look at Newtonian physics concerns *fecundity*. A great scientific theory, like Newton's, opens up new areas of research. Celestial mechanics led to the discovery of a previously unknown planet. Newtonian physics as a whole led to the development of previously unknown sciences. Because a theory presents a new way of looking at the world, it can lead us to ask new questions, and so to embark on new and fruitful lines of inquiry. Of the many flaws with the earlier picture of theories as sets of statements, none is more important than the misleading presentation of sciences as static and insular. Typically, a flourishing science is incomplete. At any time, it raises more questions than it can currently answer. But incompleteness is no vice. On the contrary, incompleteness is the mother of fecundity. Unresolved problems present challenges that enable a theory to flower in unanticipated ways. They also make the theory hostage to future developments. A good theory should be productive; it should raise new questions and presume that those questions can be answered without giving up its problem-solving strategies.

I have highlighted three characteristics of successful science. *Independent testability* is achieved when it is possible to test auxiliary hypotheses independently of the particular cases for which they are introduced. *Unification* is the result of applying a small family of problem-solving strategies to a broad class of cases. *Fecundity* grows out of incompleteness when a theory opens up new and profitable lines of investigation. Given these marks of successful science, it is easy to see how sciences can fall short, and how some doctrines can do so badly that they fail to count as science at all. A scientific theory begins to wither if some of its auxiliary assumptions can be saved from refutation only by rendering them untestable; or if its problem-solving strategies become a hodgepodge, a collection of unrelated methods, each designed for a separate recalcitrant case; or if the promise of the theory just fizzles, the few questions it raises leading only to dead ends.

When does a doctrine fail to be a science? If a doctrine fails sufficiently abjectly as a science, then it fails to be a science. Where bad science becomes egregious enough, pseudoscience begins. The example of Newtonian physics shows us how to replace the simple (and incorrect) naive falsificationist criterion with a battery of tests. Do the doctrine's problem-solving strategies encounter recurrent difficulties in a significant range of cases? Are the problem-solving strategies an opportunistic collection of unmotivated and unrelated methods? Does the doctrine have too cozy a relationship with auxiliary hypotheses, applying its strategies with claims that can be "tested" only in their applications? Does the doctrine refuse to follow up on unresolved problems, airily dismissing them as "exceptional cases"? Does the doctrine restrict the domain of its methods, forswearing excursions into new areas of investigation where embarrassing questions might arise? If all, or many, of these tests are positive, then the doctrine is not a poor scientific theory. It is not a scientific theory at all.

The account of successful science that I have given not only enables us to replace the naive falsificationist criterion with something better. It also provides a deeper understanding of how theories are justified. Predictive success is one important way in which a theory can win our acceptance. But it is not the only way. In general, theories earn their laurels by solving problems—providing answers that can be independently recognized as correct—and by their fruitfulness. Making a prediction is answering a special kind of question. The astronomers who used celestial mechanics to predict the motion of Mars were answering the question of where Mars would be found. Yet, very frequently, our questions do not concern *what* occurs, but *why* it occurs. We already know that something happens and we want an explanation. Science offers us explanations by setting the phenomena within a unified framework. Using a widely applicable problem-solving strategy, to-

gether with independently confirmed auxiliary hypotheses, scientists show that what happened was to be expected. It was known before Newton that the orbits of the planets are approximately elliptical. One of the great achievements of Newton's celestial mechanics was to apply its problem-solving strategy to deduce that the orbit of any planet will be approximately elliptical, thereby explaining the shape of the orbits. In general, science is at least as concerned with reducing the number of unexplained phenomena as it is with generating correct predictions.

The most global Creationist attack on evolutionary theory is the claim that evolution is not a science. If this claim were correct, then the dispute about what to teach in high school science classes would be over. In earlier parts of this chapter, we saw how Creationists were able to launch their broad criticisms. If one accepts the idea that science requires proof, or if one adopts the naive falsificationist criterion, then the theory of evolution—and every other scientific theory—will turn out not to be a part of science. So Creationist standards for science imply that there is no science to be taught.

However, we have seen that Creationist standards rest on a very poor understanding of science. In light of a clearer picture of the scientific enterprise, I have provided a more realistic group of tests for good science, bad science, and pseudoscience.

PART THREE

Mind and Its Place in Nature

TO A LARGE DEGREE, WHAT has come to be known as the "mind–body problem" in philosophy is a product of the philosophy of René Descartes. How can things differing as radically as minds (or souls) and bodies, in Descartes' conception, be so intimately related, as they clearly are, in every human person? Bodies are solid chunks of material stuff, extended in three-dimensional space, publicly observable and measurable, possessed of a certain mass and velocity, and capable of causing things to happen, in accordance with the invariant laws of mechanics, by transmitting their impact in "collisions" with other material things. A mind, on the other hand, is directly "observable" only by the person who owns it; only he can think his thoughts, feel his emotions, suffer his pains. Although, under certain circumstances, someone else can cut open his skull and see and touch his living *brain*, there is no conceivable way for another to see or touch his mind or its beliefs, sensations, and desires. Minds, moreover, have no size or shape or spatial location, no mass, or velocity, or capacity to make impact.

Nevertheless, to common sense, it seems certain that minds and bodies do causally interact. When I intend, or wish, or desire (mental events) to raise my arm, up it goes (bodily event); and when a sliver of wood penetrates my flesh (bodily event), I feel pain (mental event). It would surely seem, then, that in normal cases of action, mental events *cause* physical ones and that, in sensation and perception, physical events *cause* mental ones. Yet how can this be? How can the mind, a massless, weightless, unextended thing, push up against a nerve cell and cause an impulse to be transmitted along a nerve to a muscle? And how can physical stimuli such as wood slivers or even light rays penetrate a thing that has no size or location, and cause it to have an experience? Isn't this as inconceivable as a collision between a physical object and a ghost? This is the kind of difficulty cited by many of Descartes' own contemporaries in criticism of his philosophy.[1]

Many important seventeenth-century philosophers, no matter how impressed in other ways by the "Cartesian philosophy" (as the philosophy of Descartes came to be called), found Descartes' theory of interaction between mind and body unacceptable. Some, therefore, came to abandon the part of Descartes' philosophy that generated the difficulty: his **dualism,** or theory that mind and matter are distinct and independent kinds of substances, each capable of existing quite independently of the other.[2] One alternative was **idealism:** the theory that the body itself is nothing but a collection of actual or possible sense-data—sights, sounds, touches, and smells. George Berkeley thought this way. According to this theory, there are only minds and their mental "contents"; hence, there are no problems of causal interaction between radically different kinds of substances. Yet another alternative was **materialism**—the

---

[1]A number of distinguished philosophers, theologians and scientists, including Pierre Gassendi, Thomas Hobbes, and Antoine Arnauld, were invited to comment on the manuscript of Descartes' *Meditations* before it was published. Their "Objections" were then forwarded to Descartes, who in turn composed "Replies," and published the whole exchange along with the original work. The entire discussion is strongly recommended to the serious student of Descartes' philosophy.

[2]Strictly speaking, the traditional mind-body problem was generated by a conjunction of two theories: (1) dualism as defined above, and (2) the theory sometimes called **two-way interactionism,** the latter being simply the commonsense assumption that mind and body can interact causally, sometimes mental events causing bodily events, as in volition, sometimes bodily events causing mental events, as when a decayed tooth causes pain sensations.

theory that mind is reducible to matter.[3] Still other philosophers maintained a kind of dualism but abandoned the commonsense view that mind and body really do interact causally. Some held, for example, that the wood sliver's penetration of my flesh does not *cause* me pain; rather, it is the *occasion* for God, whose infinite nature somehow encompasses both mind and matter, to cause me to feel pain, and similarly that my desire to raise my arm is simply the occasion for God's causing my arm to go up. This is the theory called **occasionalism.** Others held the view called **parallelism,** according to which mind and body only appear to interact because of a kind of "pre-established harmony" between their life histories. Gottfried Leibniz likened this parallelism to two clocks that strike at the same moment, having been wound up together and each designed to keep accurate time, in causal independence of each other.

We have included two defenses of Cartesian dualism in this volume. The locus classicus—Descartes' *Meditations*—appears in its entirety in Part 2. We choose to open this Part of the book with Brie Gertler's contemporary defense of the Cartesian position. Her master argument is quite straightforward: we can properly conceive of having a mental state (a belief, a conjecture, an experience of pain) while being disembodied; if we can properly conceive of having disembodied mental states, then it is possible that such states are disembodied; if it is possible that they are disembodied, then mental states are not identical with physical states. So mental states are not identical to physical states. Therefore dualism is true.

If dualism is true, then, as we have seen, it is difficult to understand how mental states can cause physical outcomes. This is the worry known as **epiphenomenalism,** which holds that mind is not itself a material thing; rather, it is a distinct but causally impotent by-product (an "epiphenomenon") of the world charted by physics. Gertler admits that this is something of a worry, but holds that the problems that beset her opponents are graver still.

In his selection here, Frank Jackson offers a powerful defense of epiphenomenalism. Along the way, he presents perhaps the greatest difficulty facing any physicalist (i.e., materialist): "the qualia problem." **Qualia** are the peculiarly subjective, felt qualities of experience, such as the smell of a hard-boiled egg, the taste of horseradish, or the fiery image of a sunset. Jackson presents a much-discussed argument designed to show that no amount of knowledge about how the brain works can give us knowledge of what it is to feel such things. Therefore, according to Jackson, these sorts of mental experiences cannot be physical ones. Jackson concludes that physicalism must be false.

One genuinely materialistic alternative to dualism and epiphenomenalism is the **identity theory,** which holds that mental events (the occurrence of aches and pains, sensations, after-images, desires, and thoughts) are simply identical with brain processes—"identical" in the same way that lightning flashes are "identical" with electrical discharges. Here the identity in question is **intertheoretic reduction.** In these

---

[3] *Materialism* as the name of a philosophical theory should not be confused with various other senses of the word. Philosophical materialists are *not* (necessarily) "persons who tend to give undue importance to material possessions and comforts." Nor are they (necessarily) "those who think that everybody ought to put their "material well-being" (as measured in dollars and cents) above all other considerations." A philosophical materialist could, with consistency, denounce materialism in these other senses.

cases, we reduce items in our commonsense theory of the world to items in a mature physics or neuroscience.

There are many people who don't believe that such reductions are possible. Part of this is because they fail to see any good argument for such reductions. And another is their attachment to arguments that support dualist views. Both of these motivations are questioned in the readings from our representative materialist, Peter Carruthers.

The bulk of Carruthers' piece is intended to show why dualist arguments are not as strong as they may appear. Carruthers begins his piece, however, with a brief argument in favor of the materialist theory. This argument is a version of what has become the most powerful case for materialism. In a nutshell, the argument claims that all that exists in this world can be adequately explained by citing physical causes. But if that is so, then there is no reason to postulate the existence of anything that is nonphysical. So either the mind does not exist, or it does, but is a physical thing.

While Carruthers, like almost everyone else, is perfectly willing to assume the existence of minds and mental events, another, more radical form of physicalism—**eliminative materialism**—is unwilling to make such a concession. On this view, championed by Paul Churchland in our selections, mental states and processes as we ordinarily conceive of them really have a status like that of witches and phlogiston and must simply be eliminated from our theorizing about ourselves. On the other side, however, many cognitive scientists believe that some sense will have to be made of our ordinary notions of mind. The development of computer technology in recent years has spurred the development of *functional* approaches to the mind. According to **functionalist** theories, the identity theory (also called **type physicalism**) is problematic because it holds that the mental and intellectual properties of a "system" (e.g., a person) depend on the specific physical (brain) properties of that system, whereas apparently many quite different physical systems (e.g., those that are constructed to process information) can perform the same intelligent tasks.

As the Churchland selection makes clear, functionalism sees itself as reconciling the best features of both **physicalism** and **behaviorism,** without succumbing to the deficiencies of either. Functionalism, like behaviorism, defines mental states relationally (in terms of input, output, and internal transitions), so there is no commitment to any specific type of matter. But unlike behaviorism, functionalism claims that all actual mental state tokens (instances) are identical to physical state tokens (instances), so functionalism, unlike behaviorism and dualism, can explain mental causation as a species of ordinary physical causation.

Many issues central to the mind–body problem are pursued in the next section, Can Non-Humans Think? We begin this section with Alan Turing's classic paper on the subject—a paper, written midway through the last century, that was far ahead of its time, and which supplied the basis of many of the arguments nowadays offered on the subject. Next comes John Searle's provocative paper "Minds, Brains, and Programs," which challenges the adequacy of a certain form of functionalism, the sort exemplified by current attempts to program computers to perform "intelligent" tasks. Searle contends that in order to have "intelligent" mental states, it is not enough that we suppose that the system simply is running the right program, because these mental states are not the kinds that *can* be programmed into a machine. Searle then considers a wide variety of possible objections to his view and attempts to refute each.

As far back as the seventeenth century, at least, philosophers have been fascinated by apparent similarities between human (rational) beings and machines. Excited by discoveries in medicine and physiology, some eighteenth-century philosophers asked whether humans might really be nothing but machines themselves. In our own day most of the excitement comes from those scientists who work on the machine side, not so much from new discoveries in human biology, though the latter have been accumulating at a great rate, too. This new emphasis is reflected in the way the philosophical interest is expressed. Now we do not ask whether, in principle, machines could be designed that are a kind of human, that is to say, intelligent conscious beings like us. Many philosophers would answer unhesitatingly "No, of course not. Computers are made of wires and springs, silicon chips, and the like, not protoplasm (flesh and blood) like us." To that kind of remark William Lycan has a ready reply: "What matters to mentality is not the stuff of which one is made, but the complex way in which that stuff is organized."

Perplexity about whether non-human beings could have human-like consciousness that enables them to be aware of the world and not mere reflexive reactors to stimuli, whether they can think, and if so, whether that thinking amounts to reasoning, extends also to animals like horses, cows, dogs, cats, and whales. Peter Carruthers and John Searle make repeat appearances here, taking opposite sides on these issues. Carruthers defends the view that animals lack any conscious experience at all. They have no thoughts, no beliefs, no inner life. If they have pains, for instance, then they are not conscious pains, and since that is so, they have no moral claims on us at all. Searle, by contrast, defends the view that many animals are indeed conscious, have thoughts, can feel pain, etc. Searle thinks that such claims are patently clear, but that philosophical errors have prevented some thinkers from accepting the obvious. He seeks to diagnose many of the most influential of these, in his defense of animal minds.

The concluding articles in Part 3 relate the discussion back to one of Descartes' original concerns: whether "in death there is an end of me." This question, of course, presupposes the questions preceding it about the nature of the subject of consciousness. If body and mind are one and the same thing, or if mind is a mere epiphenomenon or byproduct of body, then it would follow that the disintegration of mind (soul, self) would proceed at the same pace with the disintegration of the body. But if our minds are distinct substances and causally efficacious in their own right, then it is at least possible that they (we) can survive the death of their (our) bodies. If we are to make philosophical progress in our discussions of the possibility of survival, however, we need to move beyond common understanding of the nature of mind and examination of the empirical evidence (if any). In addition, we must become clear about a set of prior questions that are not normally treated in works on the mind–body problem—namely, questions about *personal identity*. Who or what am I, this entity whose possible survival of death is under discussion? Am I simply this body and nothing more? What then of my belief that this body "belongs" to me, that the owner is one thing and the body another? Am I simply my mind? Am I a self that somehow encompasses both body and mind? Could I be the *same self* that I am now if I had none of my present memories, or if I suddenly discovered myself with an altogether different body (for example, with four legs and a tail)? How much can I change without ceasing to be the person I am now? These are only some of the riddles associated with the elusive concept of personal identity. Still others are suggested by more recondite possibilities: resurrection of the dead, reincarnation, transmigration of souls, bodily transfers, multiple or alternate possession of a body by various persons, brain transplants, and "brain rejuvenations"—examples drawn from theology, psychic research, abnormal psychology, and science fiction.

The section on "Personal Identity and the Survival of Death" starts off with three famous philosophical accounts of personal identity and selfhood. John Locke argues that it is a person's consciousness, in the form of memories of past experiences, that make him or her the same person through different times, even as the body completely changes its characteristics and appearance. If the mind of a prince were magically inserted into the body of a cobbler, Locke argues in a famous example, we would all say that the person with the cobbler's appearance is the prince, and that only his body, not his personal identity, has changed. Thomas Reid, the eighteenth century Scottish philosopher whose attack on skepticism and idealism is included in Part 2, develops a theory of personal identity in Part 3 that was motivated in large part by his dissatisfaction with the theory of Locke's, which was already famous in his time. A human person, Reid argued, is quite unlike a physical object, which is constantly changing its properties so that over a period of time it will have nothing in common with, and hence not be identical with, its earlier precursors. Persons, on the other hand, are simple and indivisible, thus capable of maintaining their identities throughout their histories. The unregenerate skeptic David Hume, however, arguing from empiricist premises, rejects the claim that there is such a thing as an unchanging substantial self as opposed to the relatively fleeting thoughts and feelings revealed in introspective consciousness—that which passes as "self-awareness."

Derek Parfit, a contemporary philosopher who teaches at Oxford, takes Hume's views quite seriously. Indeed, he defends a claim very like that of Hume, and also, as it turns out, that of the Buddha. Parfit's defense is based on a kind of example that he has helped to make famous in philosophical circles—one involving divided brains, and our intuitions about who is who after such operations.

It is just this sort of example that serves as the basis for the next selection, a fictional tale designed to test philosophical theories and induce philosophical perplexity. Daniel Dennett spins a yarn in which the leading character (one Daniel Dennett, philosopher and patriot) is separated from his brain. His subsequent adventures are enough to throw our commonsense notions of selfhood and identity into complete disarray and to challenge the philosopher to put them in order again. Philosophers who have attempted to do this have struggled against a rising tide of ingenious hypothetical examples. Their efforts are often directed at first to the general problem of identity, not restricted to the case of identity between persons. When a physical object like a sock or a ship begins with one set of properties and very gradually changes these properties, can we say at a later time that the new object is the same object that we began with? How different from the earlier object can the later object be and still be identical to the original? Similar questions asked about humans, of course, are likely to be more interesting to us. Am I the same person I was when I emerged from the womb? If I am a genuinely penitent, morally newborn criminal who has been on death row for ten years, can my lawyer claim that I am *not* the same man who committed a brutal murder a decade earlier? What if my earlier self arranged with a surgeon, in a science fiction example, to transplant my brain in another person and that person's brain in me?

In the deathbed dialogue by John Perry that concludes this section, Professor Perry focuses sharply on the area where the problem of survival and the riddles of personal identity intersect. A dying professor, her old friend (a clergyman), and her student discuss quite spontaneously the famous philosophical theories of John Locke, Joseph Butler, and Anthony Collins—seminal thinkers of the seventeenth and eighteenth centuries—about personal identity. At issue is the question of what sense, if any, can be made of the very idea of personal survival.

In Defense of Mind–Body Dualism

BRIE GERTLER

Brie Gertler works primarily on philosophical problems in the philosophy of mind. She teaches at the University of Virginia.

How quaint, the idea that our minds somehow float free of the cold, hard, physical world. Surely dualism is the stuff of fantasy, an indulgence of poets and daydreamers, an echo of antiquated worldviews long ago demolished by the relentless progress of science. Though we may occasionally find comfort in imagining that our minds are special, in our more sober moments we must face the facts: our thoughts and feelings, and those of our loved ones, are just as much a part of the brute material order as sticks and stones.

This sentiment expresses a common attitude. The prevalence of this attitude may explain why physicalism, the view that sensations and other mental states are entirely physical, is generally the default position about the mind. On first approaching the mind–body problem, most scientifically minded people assume that physicalism simply has to be true.

However, the sentiment above seriously misrepresents present-day versions of dualism, the belief that some mental states are nonphysical. Many contemporary dualists are fully *naturalistic*. That is, they hold that mental states are just as much a part of the natural order as sticks and stones; and they favor a scientific approach to the mind, one that is independent of religious considerations. In essence, the contemporary dispute between physicalists and naturalistic dualists is a disagreement about what kinds of *data* there

are about the nature of mind, and what sort of *theory*—dualist or physicalist—best explains the data.

In this essay, I defend naturalistic dualism. I take, as my starting point, an argument made by René Descartes in his *Meditations*. I expand and defend this argument, drawing on some ideas developed by contemporary philosophers.[1] The expanded argument is, I think, much more powerful than most physicalists recognize. After making my case for dualism, I offer some criticisms of physicalism. The paper will close by defending dualism from the charge that the picture of reality it provides is unacceptably *spooky*.

But first, I must explain in more detail the point at issue between physicalists and dualists. What is it, precisely, that physicalists assert, and dualists deny? Our answer to this question will reveal the type of reasoning that a defense of dualism must employ.

1. PHYSICALISM, DUALISM, AND THE NEED FOR THOUGHT EXPERIMENTS

Physicalism comes in various forms. I will focus on the most straightforward version, the *identity thesis,* which has been defended by numerous philosophers. According to the identity thesis, every type of mental state is identical to some type of physical state. Here is an example of a particular identity claim, relating pain to C-fibers, a group of nerve cells that fire when pain is experienced.

(P) Pain $=$ C-fiber stimulation[2]

In this statement, "pain" refers to a type of sensation, the type of sensation you have when you stub your toe or bite your lip. This type of sensation is usually caused by tissue damage (in the toe or the lip), but it needn't be. For instance, a person who has had both feet amputated could nonetheless experience the "stubbed toe" sensation. So damage to the toe is merely the ordinary cause of that sort of sensation; the sensation itself is not spatially located *in* the toe. And it is the sensation itself, not its cause, which is most obviously a *mental* state. Throughout this essay, "pain" will refer to the sensation itself, and not its usual or real cause.

Actually, identity theorists are not committed to any particular identity thesis, such as (P). Their key claim is that every type of mental state is identical to some type of physical state, but they needn't claim that science has yet uncovered any particular identities. Still, (P) illustrates the *kind* of identity the physicalist has in mind. I will continue to use it in this way.

The first thing to notice about (P) is that it is extremely strong. It does not say merely that pain is perfectly correlated with C-fiber stimulation. Nor does it say that pain will always accompany, and be accompanied by, C-fiber stimulation. Rather, it says that pain just *is*—is nothing over and above—C-fiber stimulation. This means that pain *couldn't possibly* be present in the absence of C-fiber stimulation, or vice versa, any more than Superman could be present in the absence of Clark Kent, or water could be present in the absence of H_2O. So an identity statement goes beyond a claim about what is *actually* the case, to a claim about what is *possible*—or, really, what is *impossible*.

Because identity statements (statements about what is identical to what) entail that certain scenarios are impossible, they cannot be confirmed by empirical methods alone. To see why

this is, imagine that we are in the best-case situation for empirical investigation: We are somehow able to monitor all of the creatures in the universe, and to determine which creatures have C-fibers that are undergoing stimulation, and which creatures are experiencing pain. (To determine whether people are experiencing pain, we might simply ask them; to determine this for infants and animals, we might observe their behavior.) Suppose that we learn that these are perfectly correlated: C-fiber stimulation is present in all and only those creatures that are currently experiencing pain. Even this very tidy result does not establish the identity thesis, for we still do not know whether it is *possible* that one of these be present in the absence of the other. The perfect correlation might be an odd coincidence. Or, more plausibly, it might be that one of these causes the other. (A prominent dualist position holds that physical events, like the firing of C-fibers, *cause* mental events like pain. This allows us to explain how aspirin can block pain by affecting the brain.) Or it might be that pain and C-fiber stimulation are products of a common cause: Perhaps stubbing one's toe simultaneously causes both the pain sensation and C-fiber stimulation. These explanations of the correlation are alternatives to saying that pain is *identical to* C-fiber stimulation (e.g., if C-fiber stimulation causes pain then these cannot be identical, for nothing causes itself).

The upshot is that even a perfect correlation does not establish the identity thesis. It shows only that one of these factors *is not*, in fact, present in the absence of the other. But it does not show that one of these factors *could not possibly* be present in the absence of the other. And the identity thesis requires this latter, stronger claim.

If the identity thesis is true, then physicalism is true. Dualists deny the identity thesis, and believe that mental states are distinct from (that is, they are not identical to) physical states. Dualism thus implies that it is *possible* that pain is present in the absence of C-fiber stimulation. Dualists can accept that these are perfectly correlated; but, they claim, these are two distinct states, and so it is not *impossible* that one is present while the other is absent. (Again, perhaps their perfect correlation is due to some causal connection.)

I will defend dualism by arguing that it is possible that you experience pain even if you are in *no* physical state, that is, even if you have no body whatsoever. If pain can occur in the absence of *any* physical state, then physicalism is false.[3]

Because the dispute between physicalism and dualism concerns whether a particular scenario is *possible,* empirical evidence will not resolve it. We must therefore turn to another sort of evidence, gained from thought experiments. Thought experiments can help us to determine whether situations that don't actually occur—such as the presence of pain in the absence of C-fiber stimulation—are nonetheless possible.

Unlike scientific experiments, which are ordinarily conducted in a laboratory, thought experiments are conducted from the comfort of the armchair. One performs a thought experiment by attempting to imagine a given scenario, and then carefully reflecting on the outcome of this exercise. It may seem odd to think that such armchair reflection can yield genuine progress on a thorny issue like the mind–body problem. But because the dispute between physicalists and dualists concerns the sheer *possibility* of a given scenario, neither of these positions can be established without thought experiments.[4]

Here are some examples of thought experiments designed to reveal whether a given scenario is possible.

(A) You have never seen a book that is 100 feet tall. (According to *Guinness World Records,* the world's largest book—a photographic tour of the Asian country of Bhutan—is 5 feet tall by 7 feet wide.) Still, a moment's reflection reveals that you can imagine a 100-foot-tall book. While the high costs of production and the dim sales prospects mean that no one is likely ever to create such a book, these impediments don't absolutely *rule out* its creation. For instance, it is easy to imagine the production being financed by an eccentric millionaire.

We have just resolved the question, "Is it possible that a book be 100 feet tall?" by use of a thought experiment. On reflection, there seemed to be only practical obstacles to the creation of a 100-foot-tall book, and we could imagine overcoming those obstacles. Short of building the giant book ourselves, it is hard to see how this question could be resolved without the use of thought experiments.

(B) You have never seen an object that is blue all over and (simultaneously) orange all over. Can you imagine such an object? It seems clear that you cannot. This exercise of imagination leads you to believe that nothing could possibly be blue all over and orange all over.

(C) You have never encountered a married bachelor. I expect that you will find yourself unable to conceive of a married bachelor, since you will be unable to conceive of a married person who meets the requirements for being a bachelor (which include, of course, being unmarried). Because nothing can be simultaneously married and unmarried, it is impossible that there be any married bachelors.

In the first two cases, you drew on your *concepts* (**book, blue object,** etc.) in trying to *imagine* the described scenario. But in this third case your concepts are more directly involved, because the thought experiment involves *conceiving* rather than *imagining*. To imagine something is to form a sensory (perhaps visual) picture of it. Because no picture of a man will fully express his marital status, mere imagination will not do the trick here. Rather, you exercise the concepts directly, and find that you cannot conceive of a married bachelor because your concept **bachelor** includes the concept **unmarried,** and nothing that satisfies that concept can simultaneously satisfy the concept **married.** (It is no surprise that *conceive* and *concept* have the same Latin root.)

Of course, the results of a thought experiment are not guaranteed to be accurate. Like experiments done in the laboratory, thought experiments can go astray in any number of ways: Your imagination may be limited in a way that makes you unable to imagine a 100-foot-tall book; you may mistakenly think that 'bachelor' refers to any man who lives alone; etc. But as with other types of experiment, these mistakes can be minimized if we take care in designing and performing the experiment. Most importantly, engaging in thought experiments is our only way of determining whether scenarios that haven't actually occurred, and will never actually occur, are nonetheless possible.

In these thought experiments, we try to imagine or conceive a particular scenario, to determine whether it is possible. This exercise is known as a *conceivability test*. There are other types of thought experiments as well, but conceivability tests lie at the heart of most of the leading arguments for dualism, including the one that I will now present.

2. THE DISEMBODIMENT ARGUMENT

The argument that I will use is a descendant of an argument given by Descartes. I will call it the Disembodiment Argument. Its basic structure is disarmingly simple, but of course the devil—or, as Descartes might say, the malicious demon—is in the details.

The argument centers on the possibility that pain is present in the absence of any physical state.[5] Arguments for dualism usually focus on pain or other sensations, because the experience of sensations seems to present the greatest challenge to physicalism. Descartes himself believed that thoughts, such as "my senses sometimes mislead me," posed an equal challenge to physicalism, but contemporary philosophers are divided on that claim. We needn't concern ourselves with that issue. If our argument succeeds in showing that pain can be present in the absence of any physical state, we will have established dualism, for we will have shown that pain is not identical to anything physical, and thus that at least *some* mental states (viz., pains) are not physical. And that is precisely what the dualist maintains, and the physicalist denies.

As with other thought experiments, this one requires that you actively engage in the exercise of imagining or conceiving. This will unfortunately require a tiny bit of pain. So pinch yourself—lightly!—and, while doing so, put yourself into the position of the "I" in the following line of reasoning.

1. Even though I firmly believe that I have physical features, I can conceive of experiencing *this very pain* while possessing no physical features. In other words, I can conceive of experiencing *this very pain* while disembodied.
2. If I can conceive of a particular scenario occurring, then that scenario is possible.

So,

3. It is possible that *this very pain* occurs in a disembodied being.
4. If *this very pain* was identical to some physical state, then it could not possibly occur in a disembodied being.

So,

5. *This very pain* is not identical to any physical state.

So,

(Conclusion) The identity thesis, which says that every mental state is identical to some physical state, is false.

The major premises in this argument are (1) and (2). Premise (3) follows from these; premise (4) expresses an accepted fact about the nature of identity; and premise (5) follows from (3) and (4).

The best way to target this argument, then, is to deny either (1) or (2). This is precisely what physicalists have done. I will first discuss premise (2), and then take up premise (1).

Premise (2)

The chief criticism of premise (2) is that it involves a kind of intellectual hubris. In conceiving of something, we are simply exercising our *concepts*. And why should we think that our concepts accurately reflect the way the world is? Perhaps we are out of touch with reality, and our concepts don't correspond to real objects or properties. In that case, the fact that we can conceive of a particular scenario occurring provides no reason to think that that scenario is genuinely possible.

In reply to this criticism, it is crucial to note that *all* of our reasoning—in philosophy and elsewhere—must use some concepts, to define the topic we are investigating. In biology, we begin with some concept of reproduction, which empirical investigation may lead us to refine. In ethics, we begin with some concept of the good, which philosophical reasoning helps us to clarify and develop. And of course physicalists also rely on concepts—including concepts of the physical—in defending their view.

Occasionally, we may find that nothing satisfies a given concept, and so we may abandon investigations relating to it. This is what happened in the case of witchcraft: Most people came to deny that anything in reality corresponded to the concept **witchcraft,** and the study of witchcraft was replaced by research into superstitions and mental pathologies, phenomena that led to the mistaken belief in witchcraft. But while we must allow for the possibility that we'll refine or even abandon our concepts, concepts are indispensable at the outset of an investigation. For there is no way to proceed with an inquiry unless we have *some* concept of the subject matter we are investigating. The blanket objection that conceivability arguments are illegitimate because they use *our concepts* is, then, misguided.

However, there is a more nuanced version of the worry that premise (2) oversteps our intellectual bounds. Unlike the previous objection, this one acknowledges that we must employ concepts in order to reason at all. And it concedes that thought experiments using simple, straightforward concepts such as **bachelor** can help us to determine what is possible. But it rejects premise (2) on the grounds that it is too general: Not *everything* we can conceive is possible. For some of our concepts are clouded or obscure, and so cannot play the proper role in conceivability tests. In particular, this objection says that our concepts **pain** and **physical** are limited or unclear. Using such faulty concepts, what we can or cannot conceive does not reveal what is or is not possible.

This type of objection was advanced against Descartes' original argument by his contemporary Antoine Arnauld. Arnauld pointed out that a geometry student who hadn't yet encountered the proof of the Pythagorean Theorem could argue as follows:

> I can conceive of a right triangle with the following property: the square of its hypotenuse is unequal to the sum of the squares of its other two sides. Therefore, it is possible for a right triangle to have this property.

Clearly, this argument is invalid: The fact that the student could conceive this scenario does not mean that the scenario is possible.

Descartes anticipated Arnauld's objection, and had a ready response. He acknowledged that his argument will fail unless the relevant concepts are "complete and adequate." The student was able to conceive of a right triangle that violated the Pythagorean Theorem only because his concept **right triangle** was limited. But our concepts of mentality and of the physical are not limited in this way, or so Descartes claimed. That's why he thought that our ability to conceive disembodied pains was genuine evidence that disembodied pains were possible.[6]

In effect, Descartes' reply deflects attention away from premise (2), and makes premise (1) the focus of the argument. For everyone can agree that, if we have a comprehensive understanding of something, then conceivability tests provide a reliable guide to what is possible, involving that thing. It is because you fully understand what it means to be a bachelor that, when you find yourself unable to conceive of a married bachelor, you can justifiedly conclude that it's impossible that anything be a married bachelor. And if the geometry student gained a comprehensive grasp of right triangles, then he could similarly rely on conceivability tests. For a comprehensive grasp of right triangles would prevent him from conceiving of a right triangle that violated the Pythagorean Theorem.

Let us agree, then, that conceivability tests can reveal what is possible or impossible, *so long as the concepts involved are sufficiently comprehensive.* This amounts to qualifying premise (2), to read as follows:

2.* If, *using concepts that are sufficiently comprehensive,* I can conceive of a particular scenario occurring, then that scenario is possible.

Our new premise (2*) is unobjectionable, for it is trivially true. To say that a concept is "sufficiently comprehensive," in this sense, is just to say that it is suitable for use in conceivability tests. If follows, then, that conceivability tests *using sufficiently comprehensive concepts* reveal what is (and what is not) possible.

Because (2*) is trivially true, the burden of the argument now falls on the first premise. Let us consider premise (1) in more detail.

Premise (1)

We must modify premise (1) to fit our new second premise. It now becomes (1*).

1.* *Using concepts that are sufficiently comprehensive*, I can conceive of experiencing *this very pain* while disembodied.

Together, (1*) and (2*) yield (3), so the rest of the argument proceeds as before.

Again because (2*) is trivially true, the entire weight of the argument now rests on (1*). To evaluate (1*), we must determine whether the concepts at work in the "pinch" test are sufficiently comprehensive. That is, when you conceive of experiencing *this very pain* (the pinch) while disembodied, are your concepts **pain** and **physical** sufficiently clear and complete, like your concept **bachelor?** Or might they be confused or incomplete, like the geometry student's concept **right triangle?**

This is the core issue on which the Disembodiment Argument rests. The argument will succeed only if your concepts of pain and of the physical are sufficiently comprehensive to allow you to conclude, from the fact that you can conceive of experiencing pain while disembodied, that this is possible. Physicalists generally deny this. They believe that, in conceiving of disembodied pain, we are like Arnauld's geometry student, who conceives of a right triangle that violates the Pythagorean Theorem.

I now turn to discuss our concepts of the physical and of pain. We will see that **pain** plays a much more important role in the Disembodiment Argument.

3. OUR CONCEPT OF THE PHYSICAL

Consider what "physical" means. What conditions must something meet in order to qualify as *physical?*

Descartes thought that the essence of the physical was to be extended in space. But modern physics posits entities—such as fields and waves—that sit uncomfortably with the notion of spatial extension. And because modern physics is still evolving, we should not define the physical in terms of a currently favored theory. For further advances in physics might eventually lead us to reject whatever theory we currently favor.

In response to these worries, many philosophers now conceptualize the physical, for purposes of the mind–body problem, as "the inanimate" or "the nonmental." [7] In this way, the concept **physical** is defined by contrast with the concepts **animate** or **mental.** This suggestion nicely captures the issue at hand. On this reading of "physical," the central point of contention between physicalists and dualists is as follows:

> Are mental states ultimately, fundamentally nonmental? Are mental states, states of mental things like you and me, ultimately identical (or reducible) to states that are *also* had by inanimate, nonmental things, like sticks and stones?

The dualist will answer "no," claiming that mental states are part of the basic fabric of the universe. The physicalist will answer "yes," claiming that mental states are simply patterns of basic physical (that is, nonmental) phenomena. I propose that we adopt this way of conceptualizing the physical. States that are physical, in this sense, are ultimately constituted by phenomena that are nonmental.

As regards the Disembodiment Argument, this understanding of **physical** will affect how you perform the conceivability test described in (1*). To be disembodied is to have *no* physical—ultimately nonmental—features. So you are to attempt to conceive of experiencing *this very pain* while being a *purely* mental entity, an entity that, at least for a moment, has no features in common with sticks and stones.[8]

I now turn to the more significant concept for our purposes, the concept **pain.**

4. OUR CONCEPT OF PAIN

Recall that the Disembodiment Argument will succeed only if our concept of pain is sufficiently comprehensive, in the sense explained above. Is it?

Someone with the concept **pain** might be ignorant of non-essential features of pain: for instance, whether aspirin or ibuprofen more quickly relieves pain. But such features are not relevant to the possibility of disembodied pain. The Disembodiment Argument requires only that we grasp the *essential* features of pain, those that are relevant to the possibility of disembodied pain.[9]

Still, establishing that our concept **pain** is sufficiently comprehensive, in this sense, is a difficult task. The standard expressed by "sufficiently comprehensive" is very high, and as physicalists are quick to point out, most of our concepts do not meet this standard. The classic example concerns water. Before learning chemistry, each of us could presumably conceive that water was present in the absence of H_2O. And arguably, we can still conceive this. (For we can imagine that chemists develop a new technique for analyzing substances and that, using this technique, they discover that all of the stuff we call "water" contains an additional element, one undetectable by previous methods.) But while we can conceive that water is present in the absence of H_2O, this scenario is of course impossible, because water simply *is* H_2O. Clearly, then, our concept **water** is not sufficiently comprehensive to be used in this type of conceivability test.

Physicalists who cite the water example predict that, once neuroscience has developed more fully, we will come to regard our ability to conceive of disembodied pain in a similar way. That is, we will see that it involves the use of inadequate concepts, and therefore provides no real evidence for the possibility of disembodied pain, just as our ability to conceive of water that is not H_2O provides no evidence for the possibility of non-H_2O water.

To defend the Disembodiment Argument, we need to block the analogy between **water** and **pain**. This requires showing that our concept **pain** is importantly different from concepts such as **water,** to justify the claim that **pain** (unlike **water**) is sufficiently comprehensive. And this is precisely what I will now attempt to do.

First, we must understand *why* our concept **water** is not sufficiently comprehensive. It fails to meet this standard for a simple reason. Namely, we conceptualize water as something that has a *hidden essence,* an essence that can be discovered only by careful scientific investigation. (The hidden essence of water is in fact H_2O.) This is why armchair reflection will not reveal whether non-H_2O water is really possible.

But we don't conceptualize pain this way. *We conceptualize pain as something that has no hidden essence.* Pain wears its essential nature on its sleeve, as it were.

Here we have reached the fundamental, driving idea behind the Disembodiment Argument. As we conceptualize pain, pain has no hidden essence. If you *feel* that you are in pain, then you are in pain; determining whether you are in pain does not require scientific investigation. For the appearance (feeling) of pain just is pain itself. As one contemporary commentator has put it, "there is no appearance/reality distinction in the case of sensations" such as pain.[10]

How does this observation—that the appearance of pain is pain itself—help us to defend (1*)? The challenge, in defending (1*), is to show that our concept **pain** is sufficiently comprehensive for use in conceivability tests. The observation that the *feeling* of pain *is* pain accomplishes this. To determine whether you are really in pain, you need not investigate beyond the feeling of pain. For instance, you need not examine your brain to see whether your C-fibers are undergoing stimulation. (By contrast, investigation *is* required to determine whether something that seems like water—that looks and tastes like water—really is water.) This implies that pain has no hidden essence. So even if pain is perfectly correlated with C-fiber stimulation, C-fiber stimulation is not *essential* to pain; for if it were, then C-fiber stimulation would be the hidden essence of pain, and you couldn't be sure that you were in pain unless you determined that your C-fibers were firing. And if C-fiber stimulation is not essential to pain, then it is not *impossible* that pain be present in the absence of C-fiber stimulation. Hence, pain is not identical to C-fiber stimulation.

Let me be clear about my case here. I am not suggesting that we can't be mistaken about pain.[11] My point is just that there is *some* evidence for pain that is absolutely conclusive, for it is, simultaneously, evidence for pain and pain itself. This is evidence of the standard sort: that *hurting* sensation. That sensation is both the appearance of pain and the reality of pain.

Nor am I suggesting that the conceivability test at the heart of the Disembodiment Argument is easy to perform. You must pay close attention to your current "pinching" sensation, making sure that you are not reading more (or less) into it than what it presents. And you must carefully engage in the exercise of conceiving. This is why Descartes advised that, before engaging in the *Meditations,* we should find a quiet place and free our minds from distractions.

But as long as you exercise care, you should be able—through keeping your attention on the pinching feeling, while simultaneously trying to conceive that you are disembodied—to confirm, or disconfirm, (1*) for yourself. For my part, I find that this exercise confirms (1*). And because I assume that we are basically similar, as regards our sensations and concepts, I expect that you will find this as well.

This is, then, the basic argument for dualism. As modified, the key premise of the argument is (1*). That premise is supported by the simple but powerful thought that, according to our concept **pain,** the feeling of pain *is* pain; pain has no essential features that are hidden. So in attending to the pinching sensation, we have access to the essential feature of pain, namely, how it feels. This means that our concept **pain** is sufficiently comprehensive for use in conceivability tests. Your ability to conceive of disembodied pain therefore establishes that disembodied pain is possible, even if (in fact) everyone who experiences pain also has a body. This possibility refutes the identity thesis and establishes dualism.

5. A PHYSICALIST OBJECTION

Physicalists have put forth the following objection to this kind of argument:

> The argument shows only that, *according to our concept **pain,*** pain may be present in the absence of C-fiber stimulation. Still, we must bear in mind the example of water. *According to our concept **water,*** water may be present in the absence of H_2O. Just as the latter case does not lead us

to doubt that water = H_2O, the former case should not lead us to doubt that pain = C-fiber stimulation.

As I explained in Section 2, our concepts define the subject matter that we are investigating. And our concepts also determine how we interpret evidence. It is because we conceptualize water as something that has a hidden essence that our discovery that water is correlated with H_2O leads us to believe that water = H_2O. If we conceptualized water differently—e.g., as *any clear liquid*—then we wouldn't accept "water = H_2O."

By the same token, our concept of pain defines what it is that we are investigating when we try to understand the nature of pain. According to this concept, we are investigating that *hurting* sensation. And because pain has no hidden essence, according to our concept, the discovery that pain is correlated with C-fiber stimulation will not justify "pain = C-fiber stimulation."

Above, I said that empirical investigation could not establish that a certain scenario is *impossible.* This is why even a perfect correlation between pain and C-fiber stimulation could not establish that it is impossible that pain be present without C-fiber stimulation, and hence could not establish that these were identical. How, then, did empirical investigation establish that water = H_2O? The answer is simple: Empirical investigation did *not* single-handedly establish this. Empirical investigation established only a correlation between water and H_2O. What justified the identity claim was an additional fact, a fact about our *concept* of water, namely, that we conceptualize water as having a hidden essence. But we don't take the fact that a substance has a particular appearance (it is clear, drinkable, etc.) to be *conclusive evidence* that it is water; Rather, we think that, to conclusively determine whether something is water, we must discover its microstructure. The fact that water has a hidden essence was already implicit in our concept **water;** and this is why the discovery that water was perfectly correlated with H_2O led us to believe that H_2O was the hidden essence of water, and hence that water = H_2O.

By contrast, we don't think of pain as having a hidden essence. This is why you treat the *appearance* of pain—that *hurting* sensation—as conclusive evidence that you are in pain. And it is why we don't need scientific investigation to discover the *essence* of pain, though of course such investigation can discover interesting and important facts about pain.

Above, I said that concepts are crucially important because they define the topic that we are investigating. Anyone who interprets the correlation between pain and C-fiber stimulation as evidence that pain = C-fiber stimulation is straying from our concept, and hence simply changing the topic. The topic we're investigating, pain, is defined by our concept **pain;** and according to that concept, pain has no hidden essence.

But why not simply change the topic, and claim that nothing corresponds to our original concept **pain,** because every mental state has a hidden physical essence? The problem with this move is that we can still ask why we should accept the claim that pain = C-fiber stimulation. In the case of other identities, such as water = H_2O, there is a simple answer: You conceptualize water as having a hidden essence, and empirical investigation has discovered that H_2O is that hidden essence. Because there is no parallel justification for "pain = C-fiber stimulation," we have no reason to accept that identity claim.

Arguably, this distinctive feature of our pain concept—that, as we conceptualize pain, the appearance of pain *is* its reality—is possessed only by mental concepts. For our concepts of nonmental things do attribute a gap between whether the thing appears to satisfy the concept and whether it actually does so. If this is correct, our argument for dualism cannot be applied to anything that is not mental.

6. BUT WHAT ABOUT MENTAL CAUSATION?

The previous section discussed a physicalist objection to the method used in the Disembodiment Argument. However, a physicalist might instead criticize the *conclusion* of that argument, as follows:

The Disembodiment Argument does provide *some* reason to think that disembodied pain is possible.

But we should not embrace this conclusion until we carefully examine its consequences. And in fact the conclusion has one consequence that is utterly unacceptable: if dualism is true, then our mental states do not truly cause our bodily movements. That is, dualism leads to *epiphenomenalism,* the claim that the mental has no physical effects. But epiphenomenalism is repugnant.[12] So even if we are not sure quite where the argument goes wrong, it must go wrong somewhere.

Leading arguments for physicalism rest on the idea that accepting the identity thesis is the only way to preserve mental causation. But only a very strong version of the identity thesis will salvage mental causation as intended; and that version of the thesis faces problems that are as serious as the worry about epiphenomenalism. Or so I will argue.

The identity thesis is usually motivated by the following idea. If we want to explain why I leaped out of my chair (a physical event), we need not invoke anything other than previous physical events: I sat on a thumb tack, and this caused (via a train of other physical events) C-fiber stimulation, which then caused my leap out of the chair. To say that such an explanation requires us to invoke a mental state like pain *in addition* to C-fiber stimulation would be to deny that physics is complete. But all of our evidence is that physics *is* complete: We have never encountered a case where we were *forced* to go beyond the realm of the physical to explain a physical event. Now if physics is complete, then citing physical events will suffice to explain my leaping out of the chair. We need not mention pain in this explanation. So *if* pain causally contributes to my leaping from the chair, then pain must be physical—that is, it must be *identical to* a physical state such as C-fiber stimulation.

There are various objections that could be made to this argument. To my mind, the most promising is this: The nature of causation, and what it means to say that one event caused another, is far from clear. For example, David Hume argued that the best we can expect, in attempting to explain why an event occurred, is to identify a regularity: *This type of event is regularly preceded by that type of event.* But then why not say that *suddenly leaping out of one's chair is* regularly preceded by *feeling pain*? The physicalist will claim that there is also a physical event that regularly precedes such leaping, and so the mental event is superfluous. However, this response assumes that, in a competition between mental and physical causes, the physical cause will always win out. (Why not say that it is the physical event that is superfluous?) This assumption would be justified if we had some *deeper* account of how physical causation occurs, one that favored physical-to-physical causation over mental-to-physical causation. But there is no accepted understanding of how causation occurs; and contemporary Humeans believe that there is no deeper *fact* about how causation occurs, because causal statements merely report regularities. The bottom line is this: Physical causation is largely a mystery, and so we should be hesitant to use our limited understanding of physical causation to rule out the possibility of nonphysical causation. The argument that dualism commits us to epiphenomenalism is far from conclusive.

But even if you think that the identity thesis better accommodates mental causation, it faces another problem, sometimes called the *problem of chauvinism*. If pain = C-fiber stimulation, then creatures whose physical structure differs significantly from ours cannot feel pain. In other words, the identity thesis is chauvinistic, because it identifies pain with a physical state that may be specific to creatures on Earth.

To see the problem, suppose that we encounter an alien civilization that seems very similar to ours. In this civilization, legislative debate is often reduced to partisan squabbles. Its members spend their leisure time in a range of activities, from hiking to watching reality TV. It seems easy to imagine that aliens whose activities were so similar to ours could nonetheless differ physiologically from humans. Perhaps their planet does not have the abundance of H_2O and oxygen that Earth has, and so their physical and neural constitution is very different from ours. Even so, it seems entirely conceivable that such creatures feel pain. (We can suppose that some of these aliens are in hospitals, recovering from surgery.) But if pain *is just* C-fiber stimulation, then no creature who lacked C-fibers *could possibly* feel pain. The identity thesis does seem to be objectionably chauvinistic.

To my mind, it is highly implausible that the capacity for pain requires a physical constitution like ours. Remember, what is at issue here is not the *likelihood* that there are alien creatures who feel pain; it is the sheer *possibility* of this scenario. And it seems incredible that pain *couldn't possibly* be experienced by creatures who lacked C-fibers.

I have argued that, while the concern about whether dualism can do justice to mental causation is legitimate, the reasoning to show that dualism commits us to epiphenomenalism is open to question. Accepting the identity thesis obviously commits us to chauvinism, but it is not entirely clear that accepting dualism commits us to epiphenomenalism. And chauvinism is at least as repugnant as epiphenomenalism.

Some physicalists have responded to the chauvinism problem by retreating from the simple version of the identity thesis. In its simple version, the identity thesis claims that each type of mental state is identical to some type of physical state. The retreat from this simple version claims that pain *in humans* is identical to C-fiber stimulation; pain *in aliens* may be identical to some other physical state.[13] This move does avoid the chauvinism problem. But the retreat from the simple identity thesis means that we cannot explain such seemingly obvious causal generalizations about pain as "being in pain causes one to urgently try to change one's situation." For there is no single property that answers to "being in pain"; there is *pain-in-humans,* and *pain-in-aliens,* but on the proposal being considered, these are completely different properties. Because this modification of the identity thesis prevents us from allowing for familiar causal generalizations, it limits the alleged causal benefits of physicalism.

Until this point, I have been concerned solely with "identity" versions of physicalism. But in the face of the difficulties I have described, some physicalists adopt a weaker position, claiming that the relations between physical and mental states fall short of identity. Unfortunately, this weaker, "nonreductive" brand of physicalism faces precisely the same worries about epiphenomenalism that dualism allegedly faces. For the epiphenomenalism worry stems from the claim that pain $\neq$ C-fiber stimulation. So long as my pain isn't identical to the firing of my C-fibers, then we can always ask *which* of these factors caused me to leap out of the chair. Was it the pain, or was it the C-fiber stimulation? The danger is that the physical factor will fully explain my leap, and thus the mental factor will be superfluous.[14] The benefit of the identity thesis is that it blocks such questions. (Compare: Because Superman is identical to Clark Kent, it makes no sense to ask whether it was Superman *or* Clark Kent who stepped out of the phone booth.) Because avoiding epiphenomenalism is the chief consideration in favor of physicalism, these weaker physicalist positions seem unmotivated. Finally, it's worth noting that these weaker brands of physicalism are just as vulnerable to the Disembodiment Argument, for even the weakest brand of physicalism must hold that you could not feel the pinch you're feeling right now if you were disembodied.

Let me sum up the results of this section. According to physicalists, dualism implies that mental events, such as thoughts and sensations, never have physical effects. Many physicalists claim that the only way to avoid this "repugnant" epiphenomenalism is to accept the identity thesis. In response, I have outlined an objectionable consequence of the identity thesis: that those with different physical constitutions could not possibly experience pain or any other sensation that we experience. This chauvinistic result is at least as worrisome as epiphenomenalism. And the simple identity thesis is patently chauvinistic, while it is less clear that dualism leads to epiphenomenalism. Chauvinism can be avoided by modifying the identity thesis, but this modification sacrifices much of the alleged causal benefits of the identity thesis.

7. BUT ISN'T DUALISM *SPOOKY*?

Despite all this, there may be a lingering sense that dualism is just plain weird, or *spooky*.

But is dualism any spookier than physicalism? Bertrand Russell observed that those who accept the findings of modern science are hardly in a position to accuse dualists of spookiness.

> The plain man thinks that material objects must certainly exist, since they are evident to the senses. Whatever else may be doubted, it is certain that anything you can bump into must be real; this is

the plain man's metaphysic. This is all very well, but the physicist comes along and shows that you never bump into anything: even when you run your hand along a stone wall, you do not really touch it. When you think you touch a thing, there are certain electrons and protons, forming part of your body, which are attracted and repelled by certain electrons and protons in the thing you think you are touching, but there is no actual contact.... The electrons and protons themselves, however, are only crude first approximations, a way of collecting into a bundle either trains of waves or the statistical probabilities of various different kinds of events. Thus matter has become altogether too ghostly to be used as an adequate stick with which to beat the mind.[15]

Russell's point is that commitments of physical science, which is unquestionably naturalistic, are just as spooky or "ghostly" as dualism. And Russell was writing in 1935; subsequent advances in physics have made the physical realm appear all the more exotic. Contemporary physicists do not agree on the basic structure of the world, but the entities posited by relatively mainstream physical theories—vibrating strings, basic particles subject to quantum indeterminacy—seem spooky enough.

Surely, dualism does not *spookify* our overall picture of the world. That picture was already plenty spooky, due to the progress of physics itself. So there is no reason to hold that dualism is spooky, or that it conflicts with a broadly scientific, naturalistic picture of reality.

Conclusion

Most contemporary thinkers believe that minds are part of the natural order, and that scientific research can yield important information about how the mind works. Naturalistic dualists agree. And dualism is not undermined by empirical evidence, because empirical evidence reveals only correlations. Moreover, dualists can accept causal explanations of these correlations (e.g., the correlation between taking aspirin and pain reduction is explained by the fact that aspirin suppresses the biochemicals responsible for activating C-fibers).

At the outset of this essay, I noted that the dispute between physicalists and dualists can be interpreted as a disagreement as to what kinds of data there are about the nature of mind, and what kind of theory will best explain those data. The thought experiment at the center of the Disembodiment Argument provides data that favor dualism: We seem able to conceive of disembodied pain. Given that our concept of pain appears to be sufficiently comprehensive for use in a conceivability test, the proper conclusion is that pain could be present in a being that lacked physical features. This means that dualism is true.

Physicalists will discount the importance of data generated by conceivability tests. But these data are essential to defining the topic at hand, whether that topic is bachelors, water, or pain. So any claim that clashes with these data diverges from our original topic, and should therefore be rejected. The claim that "pain = C-fiber stimulation" clashes with the data generated by our conceivability test. It thus diverges from our original topic—pain, as defined by our concept **pain**—and hence we should reject it.

Any naturalist worth her salt will follow the evidence where it leads. And in this case, the evidence leads to dualism.

NOTES

1. My development of this argument most closely parallels Saul Kripke's argument in Lecture III of his book *Naming and Necessity* (Cambridge, MA: Harvard University Press, 1980). The other leading contemporary arguments for dualism are also naturalistic: Frank Jackson's Knowledge Argument, given in "The Qualia Problem," in this volume; and David Chalmers' Zombie Argument, given in Chapter 4 of his book *The Conscious Mind* (Oxford: Oxford University Press, 1996). Some of the ideas in this essay borrow from these other arguments as well.

2. This is a *type-identity* thesis: it identifies a *type* of mental state with a *type* of physical state. For simplicity, I will focus on type-identities. But my argument also challenges the thesis that every *particular* (or "token") mental state, such as the pain I'm feeling right now, is identical to some *particular* ("token") physical state. This latter claim is known as a *token-identity* thesis. Unlike the type-identity thesis, it allows that two instances of a single mental type (such as pain) can belong to different physical types. This distinction will surface briefly in Section 6.

3. Some philosophers believe that conceivability arguments in this direction don't succeed in undermining physicalism, since my ability to conceive of disembodied pain shows only that such a pain *could* be disembodied, not that my pain is actually distinct from my body. But we can sidestep this objection by focusing, in the thought experiment, on the idea that *this very pain* could be disembodied.

4. Of course, empirical evidence can tell us that a certain scenario is *possible*. If we observed that pain occurred in the absence of C-fiber stimulation, we would of course conclude that this was possible. So it might seem that this type of empirical observation could support dualism. However, even this observation would not settle the issue. For the physicalist will simply take this as evidence that we must look elsewhere to find the physical state identical to pain. Unless we have empirical evidence of a pain that is unaccompanied by *any* physical state—which seems highly unlikely—the physicalist can always hold out for the discovery of a physical state that does perfectly correlate with pain. I will assume, for the sake of argument, that there is a physical state that perfectly correlates with pain, and I will follow standard practice in speaking as if C-fiber stimulation is this state.

5. This means that it applies both to identities like "pain = C-fiber stimulation" and to the claim that every particular pain is identical to *some* physical state or other. That is, it applies to both type-identity and token-identity versions of physicalism. (These versions were distinguished in note 3.)

6. In his version of the argument, Descartes doesn't distinguish pains from thoughts more generally.

7. David Papineau proposes that we understand the physical as "the inanimate." See Papineau, "*Thinking about Consciousness.* Oxford University Press, 2002. Barbara Montero proposes that we understand it as "the nonmental." See "The Body Problem," *Noûs* 33 (1999), pp. 183–200.

8. This should be qualified a bit, for purely mental entities may share temporal features with sticks and stones, e.g., existing on a Tuesday. And of course they may share necessary features like "being such that $2 + 2 = 4$." So the issue is whether you can conceive of experiencing *this very pain* while sharing no contingent, nontemporal features with inanimate, nonmental objects.

9. Strictly speaking, our concept **pain** is sufficiently comprehensive only if we grasp both the essential features of pain and any features entailed by those essential features. The geometry student erred because he didn't grasp a property (the property expressed by the Pythagorean Theorem) entailed

by the essential feature of a right triangle *being a three-sided polygon with one angle equal to 90°*.

10. Christopher Hill, *Sensations: A Defense of Type Materialism* (Cambridge: Cambridge University Press, 1991), p. 127.

11. You might mistakenly believe that you're in pain if a trusted friend tells you that you are, at a time when you are steadfastly refusing to introspect your own feelings. (This is certainly an odd case, however, and seems more plausible for emotional pain than for the kind of pinch we are concerned with.) Or you might be tricked into believing that you're in pain: In a (cruel) fraternity hazing ritual, blindfolded recruits are told that they will be burnt with a cigarette in a certain spot. Ice is then applied to the spot, yielding shock rather than pain. Still, for a moment the victims react as if they were in pain, and they seem to believe that they are undergoing pain. (An alternative interpretation is that the recruits *are* in pain, but the pain has a curious origin: It is produced by the expectation of pain.)

12. The charge that epiphenomenalism is "repugnant" was made by David Lewis in "What Experience Teaches." This article appeared in W. Lycan, ed., *Mind and Cognition* (Oxford: Blackwell Publishing, 1990), pp. 499–519.

13. Lewis, "Mad Pain and Martian Pain," in N. Block, ed., *Readings in the Philosophy of Psychology, Vol. I.* (Harvard University Press, 1980), pp. 216–222.

14. The idea that non-reductive physicalism faces the problem of epiphenomenalism was made by Jaegwon Kim. See "The Nonreductivist's Troubles with Mental Causation," reprinted as Chapter 17 of Kim's book *Supervenience and Mind* (Cambridge: Cambridge University Press, 1993).

15. Russell, "What Is the Soul?" from his book *In Praise of Idleness and Other Essays* (NY: W. W. Norton, 1935).

The Qualia Problem

FRANK JACKSON

Frank Jackson has written many works in metaphysics, ethics, and the philosophy of mind. He teaches at the Australian National University.

I am what is sometimes known as a "qualia freak." I think that there are certain features of the bodily sensations especially, but also of certain perceptual experiences, which no amount of purely physical information includes. Tell me everything physical there is to tell about what is going on in a living brain, the kind of states, their functional role, their relation to what goes on at other times and in other brains, and so on and so forth, and be I as clever as can be in fitting it all together, you won't have told me about the hurtfulness of pains, the itchiness of itches, pangs of jealousy, or about the characteristic experience of tasting a lemon, smelling a rose, hearing a loud noise, or seeing the sky.

There are many qualia freaks, and some of them say that their rejection of Physicalism* is an unargued intuition. I think that they are being unfair to themselves. They have the following argument. Nothing you could tell of a physical sort captures the smell of a rose, for instance. Therefore, Physicalism is false. By our lights this is a perfectly good argument. It is obviously not to the point to question its validity, and the premise is intuitively obviously true both to them and to me.

I must, however, admit that it is weak from a polemical point of view. There are, unfortunately for us, many who do not find the premise intuitively obvious. The task then is to present an

---

This is an edited version of "Epiphenomenal Qualia," which appeared in the *Philosophical Quarterly* vol. 32 (1982), pp. 127–132. Reprinted by permission of Blackwell Publishing.
*The theory that all information is ultimately physical information—information about physical states and physical events, couched in exclusively physical language—Eds.

argument whose premises are obvious to all, or at least to as many as possible. This I try to do with what I will call "the Knowledge argument."

In the final section I tackle the question of the causal role of qualia. The major factor in stopping people from admitting qualia is the belief that they would have to be given a causal role with respect to the physical world and especially the brain; and it is hard to do this without sounding like someone who believes in fairies. I seek to turn this objection by arguing that the view that qualia are epiphenomenal is a perfectly possible one.

THE KNOWLEDGE ARGUMENT FOR QUALIA

People vary considerably in their ability to discriminate colors. Suppose that in an experiment to catalog this variation Fred is discovered. Fred has better color vision than anyone else on record; he makes every discrimination that anyone has ever made, and moreover he makes one that we cannot even begin to make. Show him a batch of ripe tomatoes and he sorts them into two roughly equal groups and does so with complete consistency. That is, if you blindfold him, shuffle the tomatoes up, and then remove the blindfold and ask him to sort them out again, he sorts them into exactly the same two groups.

We ask Fred how he does it. He explains that all ripe tomatoes do not look the same color to him, and in fact that this is true of a great many objects that we classify together as red. He sees two colors where we see one, and he has in consequence developed for his own use two words 'red$_1$' and 'red$_2$' to mark the difference. Perhaps he tells us that he has often tried to teach the difference between red$_1$ and red$_2$ to his friends but has gotten nowhere and has concluded that the rest of the world is red$_1$-red$_2$ color-blind—or perhaps he has had partial success with his children; it doesn't matter. In any case he explains to us that it would be quite wrong to think that because 'red' appears in both 'red$_1$' and 'red$_2$' that the two colors are shades of the one color. He only uses the common term 'red' to fit more easily into our restricted usage. To him red$_1$ and red$_2$ are as different from each other and all the other colors as yellow is from blue. And his discriminatory

behavior bears this out: He sorts red$_1$ from red$_2$ tomatoes with the greatest of ease in a wide variety of viewing circumstances. Moreover, an investigation of the physiological basis of Fred's exceptional ability reveals that Fred's optical system is able to separate out two groups of wavelengths in the red spectrum as sharply as we are able to sort out yellow from blue.

I think that we should admit that Fred can see, really see, at least one more color than we can; red$_1$ is a different color from red$_2$. We are to Fred as a totally red–green color-blind person is to us. H. G. Wells' story "The Country of the Blind" is about a sighted person in a totally blind community. This person never manages to convince them that he can see, that he has an extra sense. They ridicule this sense as quite inconceivable, and treat his capacity to avoid falling into ditches, to win fights, and so on as precisely that capacity and nothing more. We would be making their mistake if we refused to allow that Fred can see one more color than we can.

What kind of experience does Fred have when he sees red$_1$ and red$_2$? What is the new color or colors like? We would dearly like to know but do not; and it seems that no amount of physical information about Fred's brain and optical system tells us. We find out perhaps that Fred's cones respond differentially to certain light waves in the red section of the spectrum that make no difference to ours (or perhaps he has an extra cone) and that this leads in Fred to a wider range of those brain states responsible for visual discriminatory behavior. But none of this tells us what we really want to know about his color experience. There is something about it we don't know. But we know, we may suppose, everything about Fred's body, his behavior and dispositions to behavior and about his internal physiology, and everything about his history and relation to others that can be given in physical accounts of persons. We have all the physical information. Therefore, knowing all this is *not* knowing everything about Fred. It follows that Physicalism leaves something out.

To reinforce this conclusion, imagine that as a result of our investigations into the internal workings of Fred we find out how to make everyone's physiology like Fred's in the relevant respects; or perhaps Fred donates his body to science and on his death we are able to transplant his optical system into someone else—again the fine detail doesn't matter. The important point is that such a happening would create enormous interest. People would say "At last we will know what it is like to see the extra color, at last we will know how Fred has differed from us in the way he has struggled to tell us about for so long." Then it cannot be that we knew all along all about Fred. But *ex hypothesi* we did know all along everything about Fred that features in the physicalist scheme; hence the physicalist scheme leaves something out.

Put it this way. *After* the operation, we will know *more* about Fred and especially about his color experiences. But beforehand we had all the physical information we could desire about his body and brain, and indeed everything that has ever featured in physicalist accounts of mind and consciousness. Hence there is more to know than all that. Hence Physicalism is incomplete.

Fred and the new color(s) are of course essentially rhetorical devices. The same point can be made with normal people and familiar colors. Mary is a brilliant scientist who is, for whatever reason, forced to investigate the world from a black-and-white room *via* a black-and-white television monitor. She specializes in the neurophysiology of vision and acquires, let us suppose, all the physical information there is to obtain about what goes on when we see ripe tomatoes, or the sky, and use terms like 'red', 'blue', and so on. She discovers, for example, just which wavelength combinations from the sky stimulate the retina, and exactly how this produces *via* the central nervous system the contraction of the vocal chords and expulsion of air from the lungs that results in the uttering of the sentence 'The sky is blue'.

What will happen when Mary is released from her black-and-white room or is given a color television monitor? Will she *learn* anything or not? It just seems obvious that she will learn something about the world and our visual experience of it. But then it is inescapable that her previous knowledge was incomplete. But she had *all* the physical information. *Ergo* there is more to have than that, and Physicalism is false.

Clearly the same style of Knowledge argument could be deployed for taste, hearing, the bodily sensations, and generally speaking for the various mental states that are said to have (as it is variously put) raw feels, phenomenal features, or qualia. The conclusion in each case is that the qualia are left out of the physicalist story. And the polemical strength of the Knowledge argument is that it is so hard to deny the central claim that one can have all the physical information without having all the information there is to have.

THE BOGEY OF EPIPHENOMENALISM

Is there any really *good* reason for refusing to countenance the idea that qualia are causally impotent with respect to the physical world? I will argue for the answer *no*. All I will be concerned to defend is that it is possible to hold that certain properties of certain mental states, namely those I've called qualia, are such that their possession or absence makes no difference to the physical world.

Two reasons are standardly given for holding that a quale like the hurtfulness of a pain must be causally efficacious in the physical world, and so, for instance, that it . . . must sometimes make a difference to what happens in the brain. [Neither,] I will argue, has any real force.

(i) It is supposed to be just obvious that the hurtfulness of pain is partly responsible for the subject seeking to avoid pain, saying 'It hurts' and so on. But, to reverse Hume, anything can fail to cause anything. No matter how often *B* follows and no matter how initially obvious the causality of the connection seems, the hypothesis that *A* causes *B* can be overturned by an overarching theory that shows the two as distinct effects of a common underlying causal process.

To the untutored the image on the screen of Lee Marvin's fist moving from left to right immediately followed by the image of John Wayne's head moving in the same general direction looks as causal as anything. And of course throughout countless Westerns images similar to the first are followed by images similar to the second. All this counts for precisely nothing when we know the over-arching theory concerning how the relevant images are both effects of an underlying causal process involving the projector and the film. The epiphenomenalist can say exactly the same about the connection between, for example, hurtfulness and behavior. It is simply a consequence of the fact that certain happenings in the brain cause both.

(ii) The second objection relates to Darwin's Theory of Evolution. According to natural selection the traits that evolve over time are those conducive to physical survival. We may assume that qualia evolved over time—we have them, the earliest forms of life do not—and so we should expect qualia to be conducive to survival. The objection is that they could hardly help us to survive if they do nothing to the physical world.

The appeal of this argument is undeniable, but there is a good reply to it. Polar bears have particularly thick, warm coats. The Theory of Evolution explains this (we suppose) by pointing out that having a thick warm coat is conducive to survival in the Arctic. But having a thick coat goes along with having a heavy coat, and having a heavy coat is *not* conducive to survival. It slows the animal down.

Does this mean that we have refuted Darwin because we have found an evolved trait—having a heavy coat—that is not conducive to survival? Clearly not. Having a heavy coat is an unavoidable concomitant of having a warm coat (in the context, modern insulation was not available), and the advantages for survival of having a warm coat outweighed the disadvantages of having a heavy one. The point is that all we can extract from Darwin's theory is that we should expect any evolved characteristic to be *either* conducive to survival *or* a by-product of one that is so conducive. The epiphenomenalist holds that qualia fall into the latter category. They are a by-product of certain brain processes that are highly conducive to survival.

There is a very understandable response to the two replies I have just made. "All right, there is no knockdown refutation of the existence of epiphenomenal qualia. But the fact remains that they are an excrescence. They *do* nothing,

they *explain* nothing, they serve merely to soothe the intuitions of dualists, and it is left a total mystery how they fit into the world view of science. In short we do not and cannot understand the how and why of them."

This is perfectly true; but is no objection to qualia, for it rests on an overly optimistic view of the human animal, and its powers. We are the products of Evolution. We understand and sense what we need to understand and sense in order to survive. Epiphenomenal qualia are totally irrelevant to survival. At no stage of our evolution did natural selection favor those who could make sense of how they are caused and the laws governing them, or in fact why they exist at all. And that is why we can't.

It is not sufficiently appreciated that Physicalism is an extremely optimistic view of our powers. If it is true, we have, in very broad outline admittedly, a grasp of our place in the scheme of things. Certain matters of sheer complexity defeat us—there are an awful lot of neurons—but in principle we have it all. But consider the antecedent probability that everything in the Universe be of a kind that is relevant in some way or other to the survival of *Homo sapiens*. It is very low surely. But then one must admit that it is very likely that there is a part of the whole scheme of things, maybe a big part, which no amount of evolution will ever bring us near to knowledge about or understanding of. For the simple reason that such knowledge and understanding is irrelevant to survival.

Physicalists typically emphasize that we are a part of nature on their view, which is fair enough. But if we are a part of nature, we are as nature has left us after however many years of evolution and each step in that evolutionary progression has been a matter of chance constrained just by the need to preserve or increase survival value. The wonder is that we understand as much as we do, and there is no wonder that there should be matters which fall quite outside our comprehension. Perhaps exactly how epiphenomenal qualia fit into the scheme of things is one such.

The Mind Is the Brain

PETER CARRUTHERS

Peter Carruthers works mainly in the areas of epistemology and the philosophy of mind and language. He teaches at the University of Maryland.

I. MIND/BRAIN IDENTITY

...Even if descriptions of conscious experiences are logically independent of all descriptions of physical states (as the cartesian conception implies) it may in fact be the case that those descriptions are descriptions of the very same things. This is just what the thesis of mind/brain identity affirms. It holds that just as a particular cloud is, as a matter of fact, a great many water droplets suspended close together in the atmosphere; and just as a particular flash of lightning is, as a matter of fact, a certain sort of discharge of electrical energy; so a pain or a thought is (is identical with) some state of the brain or central nervous system.

The identity-thesis is a version of strong materialism: it holds that all mental states and events are in fact physical states and events. But it is not, like behaviourism and functionalism, a thesis about meaning: it does not claim that words such as 'pain' and 'after-image' may be analysed or defined in terms of descriptions of brain-processes. (This would be manifestly absurd.) Rather, it is a contingent thesis about the things in the world which our words refer to: it holds that the ways of thinking represented by our terms for conscious states, and the ways of thinking represented by some of our terms for brain-states, are in fact different ways of thinking of the very same (physical) states and events. So 'pain' does not mean 'such-and-such a stimulation of the neural fibres' (just as 'lightning' does not mean 'such-and-such a discharge of electricity'); yet for all that, the two terms in fact refer to the very same thing....

(A) An Argument for the Identity-Thesis

...We believe very firmly that some mental states and events are causally necessary for the occurrence of some physical ones. For example, I believe that if I had not been conscious of a pain in my foot (mental event), I should not have gone to the doctor (physical event). My awareness of the pain was, I believe, a causally-necessary condition of my later visit to the doctor. But as we also noted, it seems most unlikely that we shall ever need to advert to anything other than physical-physical causality when we investigate the detailed causal nexus behind any given physical event. On the contrary, it seems likely that there will always be physical events providing us with a sufficient causal explanation of any particular bodily movement. For example, as we trace the causes of my legs moving me in the direction of the doctor's surgery, through events in the muscles of my legs and feet, through events in the nerves of my spinal column, into events in the cells of my brain, it seems most unlikely that the chain of physical causation will eventually run out. So it is unlikely that we shall be forced to appeal to any non-physical event in order to provide a satisfactory explanation of my visit to the surgery.

Now the only way in which we can hold on to both beliefs—the belief that some mental events are causally necessary for the occurrence of some physical ones, and the belief that it is unnecessary to appeal to anything other than physical events in providing causal explanations of other physical events—is by believing that some mental events *are* physical ones. Then

From Peter Carruthers, *Introducing Persons: An Introduction to the Philosophy of the Mind* (London: Croom Helm, 1986), Ch. 5 (ISBN 0203005732). Reprinted by permission of Taylor & Francis Books Ltd.

somewhere in the chain of physical causes of my visit to the doctor there will be a brain event which is (is identical with) my awareness of a sensation of pain.

This argument for the general truth of the mind/brain identity-thesis may be summarised as follows.

(1) Some conscious states and events are causally necessary for the occurrence of some physical ones.

(2) In a completed neuro-physiological science there will be no need to advert to anything other than physical-physical causality.

(C) So some conscious states and events are (are identical with) physical (brain) states and events.

The argument is valid. And although its conclusion only claims that some conscious states are physical, it can easily be developed in such a way as to entail the stronger conclusion, that all are. For almost every kind of conscious state can sometimes be causally necessary for a physical one. Sometimes a particular bodily movement would not have taken place if: I had not made a particular decision; I had not thought a particular thought; I had not been aware of a particular sensation; I had not had a particular after-image; and so on. Then since it seems extremely unlikely that some conscious states are physical while some are not, it follows that all are.

Premiss (1) forms an important part of our common-sense view of ourselves and the world. We believe that conscious processes can make a difference to the world. Indeed as we saw in section 2.iv, we also believe the stronger thesis that conscious events form part of the true causal explanations of many physical events. Then the only way in which we can hold on to this belief, while denying the identity-thesis, is by denying premiss (2). We would have to deny that all physical events have purely physical causes.

Yet premiss (2) forms an important part of our scientific worldview. The more science progresses, the more likely it seems that all physical events will ultimately be explicable in purely physical terms. On the basis of what we know already, it would be quite extraordinary if it were to turn out that a physical event, such as one particular brain-cell firing off an electro-chemical impulse to another, sometimes has no physical cause. It would be even more extraordinary if this event were to prove to be, not random, but caused by something nonphysical. The existence of nonphysical causes of physical events would require us to recognise whole new species of causal relations and causal laws.

Given its validity and the strength of its premises, the argument above could reasonably be taken as a proof of the identity-thesis, were it not for the myriad objections which can be raised against that thesis. In later sections we shall consider a number of them, many of which involve apparent breaches of Leibniz's Law ('identical things share identical properties'). Despite the strength of the argument in its support, the identity-thesis will only be rationally acceptable if we can reply adequately to each of the objections....

II. PRELIMINARY DIFFICULTIES

In the last section we presented an argument in support of the identity-thesis which would have been convincing if considered purely on its own terms. Over the next three sections we shall reply to all the main objections which have been raised against that thesis, beginning with some of the less serious ones. They will get more serious as we go along.

(A) Certainty

Our first objection derives from Descartes, who deployed a similar argument in support of strong dualism. It runs as follows:

(1) I may be absolutely certain of my own experiences, when I have them.

(2) I cannot have the same degree of certainty about the existence of any physical state, including my own brain-states.

(C) So (by Leibniz's Law) my conscious experiences are not in fact identical with brain-states.

Although both the premises in this argument are true, the argument itself commits a fallacy (is invalid). For ... Leibniz's Law only operates in contexts which are not intentional. And it is obvious that the context created by the phrase 'X is certain that ...' is an intentional one.

For example, the police may be certain that Mr. Hyde is the murderer, while they have no inkling that Dr Jekyll is the murderer, despite the fact that Jekyll and Hyde are one and the same man. And Oedipus may be certain that Jocasta loves him without believing that his mother loves him, despite the fact that Jocasta is his mother. So from the fact that I have complete certainty about my own conscious states without having certainty about my own brain-states, it does not follow that my conscious states are not brain-states. For just as one and the same woman may be presented to Oedipus in two different guises—as Jocasta, and as his mother—so perhaps one and the same brain-state may be presented to me under two different aspects: in a third-person way (as a brain-state), and via the qualitative feel of what it is like to be in that state.

(B) Privacy

This second argument is a variation on the first. It runs as follows:

(1) Conscious states are private to the person who has them.

(2) Brain-states are not private: like any other physical state, they form part of the public realm.

(C) So (by Leibniz's Law) conscious states are not in fact identical with brain-states.

However, the term 'private' is ambiguous: something can be private in respect of knowledge (only I can know of it), or it can be private in respect of ownership (only I can possess it). Taken in the first way, the argument is the same as that above, and commits the same fallacy. But taken in the second way, premiss (2) is false.

It is true that only I can 'own' my conscious states: no one else can feel my pain, or think my thought. But it is equally true in this sense that only I can own my brain-states. For no one else

can possess my brain-state either. Any brain-state which they have will be, necessarily, their own brain-state, not mine. Conscious states are certainly not unique in respect of privacy of ownership. The same is true of blushes and sneezes as well as brain-states: no one else can blush my blush or sneeze my sneeze. Indeed it seems that in general the identity-conditions for states and events are tied to the identities of the subjects who possess them.

(C) Value

A thought can be wicked. A desire can be admirable. But no brain-state can be either wicked or admirable. We may therefore argue as follows:

(1) Conscious states are subject to norms: they can be good or bad, wicked or admirable.

(2) No purely physical states are subject to norms: no brain-state can be either wicked or admirable.

(C) So (by Leibniz's Law) conscious states are not identical with brain-states.

We might immediately be inclined to quarrel with premiss (2). For can a particular stabbing not be wicked? And what is a stabbing if not a physical event? But it may be replied that it is not the stabbing itself—considered merely as a physical event—which is wicked, but rather the intention behind it. And in general, physical states and events are only subject to norms if they are intentional (or at least foreseen).

This reply is sufficient to save the truth of premiss (2), but at the cost of revealing the same fallacy in the argument as was involved in the argument from certainty. For if it is only things which are intended (or foreseen) which can be wicked, then the context created by '... is wicked' will be an intentional one. For example, if the fact that it is wicked of Mary to have a particular desire implies that she either intentionally adopted that desire, or at least foresaw that she would continue to possess it if she took no steps to eradicate it, then it is no objection to the identity-thesis that it is, on the other hand, not wicked of her to be in such-and-such a brain-state. For you can foresee E (that you will marry Jocasta) without foreseeing F (that you will marry your mother), even though E is identical with F. And certainly she neither intended nor foresaw that she should be in that particular brain-state.

(D) Colour

An after-image can be green, a pain can be sharp and piercing. But it is hardly likely that any brain-state will be either green or sharp and piercing. There will then be many arguments which take the following sort of form:

(1) I am experiencing a fading green after-image.

(2) No brain-states are green.

(C) So (by Leibniz's Law) my after-image is not identical with any brain-state.

One mistake in this argument is that it treats my after-image as though it were a particular individual thing, having greenness as a property. Now it is true that the sentence 'I experience a green after-image' has the same grammatical form as the sentence 'I pick up a green book', which creates the impression that greenness is a property of the after-image in just the same way that it is a property of the book. But this impression is misleading. For the book in question might have had some other colour, while remaining the numerically-same book. But can we make any sense of the idea that the very same after-image which I have now, might have been red?

Of course what is true, is that I might now have been experiencing a red after-image rather than a green one. But can we make sense of the idea that it might have been this very same after-image (which happens to be green) which would then have been red? I suggest not. Rather, the greenness is essential to the identity of that particular after-image. The reason being that it is a mistake to treat the fading after-image as if it were a kind of object or individual thing. It is rather an event, or happening. And the greenness is in fact part of the event of experiencing-a-fading-green-after-image, as opposed to being a property *of* it.

This reply on its own is not sufficient to rebut the argument. For it seems certain that greenness is not part of the event of undergoing-such-and-

such-a-change-in-brain-state. So how can that event be identical with the event of experiencing-a-fading-green-after-image, if greenness really is part of the latter event? For must not identical events have identical parts? For example, if the battle of Waterloo is (is identical with) the battle which lost Napoleon the war, then if a particular cavalry charge is part of the battle of Waterloo, it must also be part of the battle which lost Napoleon the war. For they are the very same battle (the very same event).

The second mistake in the argument is to think that an experience can be green, or a conscious event have greenness as one of its parts, in anything like the same sense that a physical object can be green, or a physical event have greenness as one of its parts. Experiences are not literally green in the way that grass is literally green. Rather, the 'greenness' of my green after-image consists in my having an experience which is like the experience of seeing a green patch (and it is the patch which is green, not the experience). Then if to have a green after-image is to be in state like the state one is in when one sees a green patch, and if the possession of that after-image is identical with some brain-state, it will indeed follow that the brain-state too is like the state one is in when one sees a green patch. But there is no difficulty about this. For the latter state too will be identical with some brain-state. And it seems entirely plausible that there should be some resemblance between the two brain-states.

The point can be put like this: green after-images are experiences *of* green, rather than things (or events) which *are* (or which contain) green. A green after-image is, as it were, an event of being under-the-impression-that-one-is-seeing-a-green-patch. If this is so, then the after-image can be identical with a brain-state without breaching Leibniz's Law, so long as the brain-state too can in this sense be 'of' green. If green after-images represent green, rather than literally being green, then there will be no difficulty here so long as it is possible for brain-states to represent. This question will be pursued below.

(E) Felt Quality

This objection arises out of the last one. Even if after-images are not literally coloured, still they do literally have phenomenal (felt) characteristics, which we describe by means of the colour-terms ('sensation of red', 'sensation of green', etc.). For example there is the qualitative 'feel' which is common to the experiences of having a green after-image and seeing green grass. Indeed all experiences have distinctive qualitative feels, which we are each of us aware of in our own case. But can any brain-state have a distinctive feel? For example, think of a particular brain-state—say one group of brain cells firing off impulses to another group—and ask yourself 'What is the distinctive feel of this event?' It is hard even to get a grip on the question. How can any brain-event feel like a sensation of red, for example? Surely only another sensation can, in the required sense, *feel like* a sensation of red.

The argument sketched above may be summarised as follows:

(1) All experiences have distinctive felt qualities.

(2) Brain-states do not have distinctive felt qualities.

(C) So (by Leibniz's Law) experiences are not in fact identical with brain-states.

Once again we have been misled by grammatical form, this time into thinking of the qualitative feel of an experience as being genuinely a property of it. (Thus we say 'The pain has a distinctive feel' just as we say 'The car has a distinctive colour'.) It would be more accurate to say that the experience itself *is* (is identical with) a distinctive qualitative feel. The experience of pain is not different from the feel of pain. Rather they are one and the same. So it is entirely irrelevant whether or not a brain-state can possess (have as a property) a particular qualitative feel. Since the experience itself is identical with its qualitative feel, the real question is whether or not a brain-state, too, can be identical with a qualitative feel. And we have as yet been given no reason for thinking that this cannot be so.

(F) Complete Knowledge

Someone could know all physical facts about the brain without knowing what the different experiences feel like. Thus no amount of information

about brain-processes will ever allow a congenitally blind person to know what a sensation of red feels like. But if there is information about feelings which would not be conveyed by any amount of information about the brain, then feelings cannot themselves be brain-states. The argument is as follows:

(1) Complete knowledge of physical states would not imply knowledge of what experiences feel like.

(2) If experiences were physical states, then complete knowledge of the physical would imply complete knowledge of experiences.

(C) So experiences are not physical states.

Although this argument, like the argument from certainty, involves an intentional term (the context created by the phrase 'X knows that...' being an intentional one) it does not commit the same fallacy. This is because the premises speak of complete knowledge, knowledge from all points of view. Oedipus certainly could not have complete knowledge of Jocasta without knowing that she is his mother. (So if he does know everything about her, but does not know that she is his mother, then she is *not* his mother.)

Both of the premises in the above argument are true. But the argument is invalid, because of a shift in the meaning of the term 'knowledge'. Knowing what an experience feels like is not propositional (factual) knowledge, but rather practical (recognitional) knowledge. It is a matter of knowing how to do something rather than knowing that something is the case. Knowing what a sensation of red feels like is a matter of being able to recognise it when you have one: it is a practical skill. Now of course no amount of factual information will necessarily give you a practical skill. As the name suggests, this will generally require practice. So the sense in which premise (1) is true is this: no amount of factual knowledge about the brain will necessarily enable you to recognise your experiences when you have them.

Premiss (2), on the other hand, is only true if restricted to factual knowledge (practical knowledge being excluded). If Jocasta is Oedipus's mother, then if he has complete knowledge of (all facts about) Jocasta, he must have complete knowledge of his mother. But it does not follow that he must be capable of recognising her when he sees her. He may have been told every fact that there is to know about his mother (the exact length of her nose, the colour of her eyes, the number and colour of hairs on her head, and so on) and yet still not be able to recognise her. This will depend upon how good he is at translating factual information into visual imagery. If he is particularly bad at it, he may have to identify his mother by ticking-off all the facts piece-meal ('length of nose . . . yes; colour of eyes . . . yes;' and so on).

It is thus entirely consistent with the identity-thesis that you cannot teach a blind person what sensations of red are like by telling them facts about the brain. Although sensations are brain-states, knowing what they are like is a matter of being able to recognise them ('straight off') when you have them. And it is hardly surprising that people cannot acquire such a recognitional skill by being given the bare facts; they will of course need practise in having those states.

III. FURTHER DIFFICULTIES

In this section we shall consider two of the arguments we originally presented in support of weak dualism (and hence, by implication, against the thesis of mind/brain identity). These are the arguments from intentionality, and from spatial position.

(A) Intentionality

Recall the claim that conscious states are unique in being intentional. Our argument was as follows:

(1) Conscious states are intentional, or representational, states.

(2) No merely physical state (e.g. of the brain) can be intentional in its own right.

(C) So (by Leibniz's Law) conscious states are not identical with brain-states.

This argument is valid, and premiss (1) is obviously true. So everything turns on the acceptability of premiss (2).

There is a general philosophical problem about representation. Much of the philosophy of language is concerned with the question: how is it possible for anything to represent—or be *about*—anything else? So it may be that the difficulty we experience in trying to understand how an arrangement of cellular connections could represent anything, is merely a specific instance of the general difficulty of understanding how anything at all can represent anything. In any case the problem of representation is not made any *less* of a problem by supposing that the states which do the representing are non-physical ones.

Perhaps the claim that physical states can be representations-in-their-own-right cannot be made entirely convincing in the absence of a solution to the general problem of representation. Nevertheless we can at least get an inkling of how intentionality can be embodied in a physical system, in advance of a solution to that problem. For by looking at systems which are, manifestly, purely physical—e.g. computers and computer-controlled machines—we can begin to see how they can display some of the distinctive features of intentional states. If we can see the beginnings of intentionality embodied in a physical system such as a computer, then there is no reason in principle why full-blown intentionality (beliefs, desires and the rest) should not be embodied in the biological computer which is the human brain.

One distinctive feature of intentional states is that they represent things in one way rather than another. For a crude analogue of this, imagine a computer linked to a video-camera and mechanical arm. The computer is programmed to scan the input from the camera, and to grab with its arm any yellow object. In order for the grabbing-operation to be successful it must also be able to interpret from the input the shapes, sizes and spatial positions of those objects. But the computer does not select objects on the basis of their shape or size, but only on the basis of their colour.

Now suppose that the only yellow objects which are ever presented to the machine are in fact lemons, its purpose being to select lemons from a passing array of fruit. Of course lemons do also have a characteristic shape, but the computer is indifferent with respect to shape. It initiates a grabbing motion only in response to the yellow colour. Then there is almost a sense in which the machine might be said to desire the yellow objects which it grabs, but not the lemon-shaped objects, even though the yellow objects are all lemon-shaped.

Of course I do not want to say that such a machine would literally have a desire for yellow objects. Though quite what is missing here, which would be present in the case of a genuine desire, is not easy to see. Perhaps we can only make sense of something having a particular desire against a wider background, a network of other desires and beliefs. Or perhaps only a being which is alive, which has needs (and which may consequently be said to have 'a good') can have desires. The important point for our purposes here is that we have found an analogue for the intentionality of desire in the concept of 'differential response'. Just as Oedipus will respond differently to one and the same woman presented to him now as Jocasta, now as his mother; so the machine will respond differently to one and the same bit of fruit presented to it now as a yellow thing (its shape being obscured), now as a lemon-shaped thing (its colour being obscured).

The other distinctive feature of intentional states, is that they can be directed at non-existent objects. And it is apt to seem unintelligible how any physical system could do this. Here again my strategy is to construct, by way of reply, a crude physical analogue for this aspect of the intentionality of desire. Thus consider the sort of behaviour which might be displayed by a Cruise missile. It is programmed to take photographs of the terrain beneath it at various points along its route, to scan those photographs for landmarks in order to check its position, and adjust its direction accordingly. Now suppose that as a result of an error, it is programmed to find a distinctively-shaped lake at a particular point on its route, but that no such lake exists. As a result, the missile circles round and around the area, until finally it runs out of fuel and crashes. Here we might almost say 'The missile was searching for a lake which did not exist'.

Note that the intentionality displayed in the Cruise missile's 'desire' is not merely derivative from the thoughts and intentions of the computer programer. True enough, that 'desire' was caused to exist by the programer. But its intentionality—its directedness on a non-existent object—is actually displayed in the behaviour of the missile itself. For it has entered a cycle of behaviour which we know will only be terminated if it succeeds in photographing a lake with a particular distinctive shape; but we also know that no such lake exists.

I conclude that there is no reason in principle why a merely-physical system should not display the various features characteristic of intentional states. So we have been given no reason for supposing that beliefs and desires are not themselves physical (brain) states.

(B) Spatial Position

Recall from [an earlier] section the following argument:

(1) All brain-states must occupy some particular position in space.

(2) It is nonsense (meaningless) to attribute any particular spatial position to a state of consciousness.

(C) So (by Leibniz's Law) conscious states cannot be identical with brain-states.

This argument is valid. Premiss (1) is obviously true. So everything depends upon the truth of premiss (2). I shall not waste time quibbling that some conscious states (e.g. pains) are apparently attributed spatial positions. For the identity-thesis extends to all conscious states without exception. And in any case it is unlikely that some conscious states are identical with brain-states and some not. I shall focus on the hardest case for the identity-theorist; namely, thoughts.

An identity-theorist might be tempted to respond to the above argument by conceding that our ordinary concept of thought makes attributions of spatial position to them nonsensical, but by rejecting that ordinary conception as mistaken. They may insist that every thought (properly conceived of) does in fact have a place, namely the place of its identical brain-state. But for them to take this line would be a mistake. For then the thesis of mind/brain identity would no longer represent a contingent discovery, but would be something which we have stipulated as true through a change of meaning.

In fact we should be entitled to reply to the identity-theorist as follows. 'If you mean the word "thought" as we usually do, then your thesis is false; indeed necessarily false. But if, on the other hand, you wish to give the word a different meaning for your own special purposes, then you are perfectly entitled to do so. But don't pretend that you have made a momentous discovery, or that you are saying anything which conflicts with what the weak dualist believes. All you have done is given a new definition.' (It is rather as if someone were to give new definitions of the words 'red' and 'green', in such a way that it then makes sense to ascribe those words to numbers; and were then to announce, as if they had discovered something terribly important, 'Contrary to what has always been believed, every even number is red and every odd one green.')

A more promising strategy for the identity-theorist would be to suggest that we have again been misled by the grammatical form of phrases like 'my thought of my mother' into conceiving of a thought as if it were a special kind of individual thing or object. For obviously, if a thought were really a physical object like a grain of sand or a brain-cell, then it would have to occupy some precise position in space. So perhaps we need to be reminded that a thought is an action, and an action is a species of event (a 'happening'). And then the general question becomes: what are the criteria for attributing spatial positions to events?

Often the place of an event can be pinned down no more precisely than the place of the subject of that event. And in such cases requests for more precise specifications will seem nonsensical. Thus the place of the event of Mary-growing-older is wherever Mary is. And the question 'Is the event of Mary-growing-older taking place two inches behind her right eye?' seems just as nonsensical as the parallel question about the event of Mary-thinking-of-her-mother. Yet for all that the process of ageing is a purely physical one.

Now we only need to be reminded of these facts to realise that we do in fact attribute spatial positions to thoughts; namely: whenever we say where the thinker of that thought is. And the fact that requests for more detailed specifications of the spatial positions of thoughts sound nonsensical, need not show that thoughts themselves are nonphysical. Thinking, like ageing, may be a physical process whose subject is the whole human being.

However, the position of an event is not always simply the position of its subject. An event can also take place in part of its subject. Thus the position of Mary's-left-big-toe-turning-blue is not simply wherever Mary is. It is, more precisely, wherever her left foot is. For if Mary is lying on a river-bank with her left foot in the water, then the event takes place in the water; whereas Mary herself is not in the water.

It seems likely that the physical event which is, according to the identity-theorist, the event of Mary-thinking-of-her-mother, takes place in some particular region of her brain. So we still have a problem, if the closest we can get to the spatial position of Mary's thought is the spatial position of Mary. If the brain-event can be two inches behind her right eye, whilst it is nonsensical to describe the thought of her mother as occurring two inches behind her right eye, then the thought and the brain-event cannot be identical.

The correct way for an identity-theorist to respond, is by denying that it is nonsensical to ascribe precise spatial positions to thoughts. The only real evidence which the objector has for this claim, is that most of us would be left gaping, our minds completely blank, if asked whether Mary's thought is two inches behind her right eye. But this does not show that the question is literally meaningless. It only shows firstly, that it is not the sort of question which itself points you in the direction in which you have to look for an answer. (Contrast: 'Where is the dam cracking?' It is part of the ordinary notion of a crack, that in order to find them you have to search in specific locations.) And secondly, that we can have no idea where to look for an answer until we have acquired some further information.

Suppose you were asked 'In what specific region of her body is the event of Mary-catching-a-cold taking place?' This too would have a tendency to make your mind go blank, partly because it is no part of the ordinary concept of a cold that in order to establish whether someone has a cold you have to search in specific locations within the body. But on reflection you may realise that what you are really being asked is: 'In virtue of changes in what parts of Mary's body is it becoming true that she has a cold?' This at least is a question you can understand. But if you know nothing of viruses, or medicine generally, you may not even know what sorts of things would be relevant to the discovery of the answer. Yet when you are told that colds are viruses, and that viruses enter the body at specific locations, then you know what would constitute an answer. Note, moreover, that it would be hardly very plausible to say that the term 'a cold' had changed its meaning for you when you acquired this information.

The question about the specific location of Mary's act of thinking about her mother is essentially similar. The first step in dispelling the puzzlement which it causes is to realise that what we are in fact being asked is: 'In virtue of changes in what specific region of Mary is it becoming true that she is thinking of her mother?' The next step is to learn that each conscious event is identical with some brain-event. Then we know that in order to answer the question, we should first need to discover which brain-event is identical with Mary's thought, and then discover where that brain-event is occurring. Yet we do not need to regard our acceptance of the identity-thesis as altering the meaning of the term 'thought', any more than our acceptance that colds are viruses alters the meaning of the term 'a cold.' We may thus deny the claim made in premiss (2) of the argument above....

Conclusion

In [the first] section we presented an argument for thinking it likely that all conscious states are identical with brain-states. Then in the sections following we have replied to all the various possible objections to this idea. Since there is good reason to believe the identity-thesis to be true, and no good reason to believe it false, the case for that thesis is rationally convincing. We should therefore embrace the thesis of mind/brain identity, and declare ourselves to be strong materialists.

Behaviorism, Materialism and Functionalism

PAUL M. CHURCHLAND

Paul M. Churchland has written widely in the philosophy of psychology and related fields. He now teaches at the University of California, San Diego.

PHILOSOPHICAL BEHAVIORISM

Philosophical behaviorism reached the peak of its influence during the first and second decades after World War II. It was jointly motivated by at least three intellectual fashions. The first motivation was a reaction against dualism. The second motivation was the Logical Positivists' idea that the meaning of any sentence was ultimately a matter of the observable circumstances that would tend to verify or confirm that sentence. And the third motivation was a general assumption that most, if not all, philosophical problems are the result of linguistic or conceptual confusion, and are to be solved (or dissolved) by careful

From Paul M. Churchland, *Matter and Consciousness* (Cambridge, Mass.: MIT Press, 1984), pp. 23–49. Reprinted by permission of MIT Press.

analysis of the language in which the problem is expressed.

In fact, philosophical behaviorism is not so much a theory about what mental states are (in their inner nature) as it is a theory about how to analyze or to understand the vocabulary we use to talk about them. Specifically, the claim is that talk about emotions and sensations and beliefs and desires is not talk about ghostly inner episodes, but is rather a shorthand way of talking about actual and potential patterns of *behavior*. In its strongest and most straightforward form, philosophical behaviorism claims that any sentence about a mental state can be paraphrased, without loss of meaning, into a long and complex sentence about what observable behavior *would* result if the person in question were in this, that, or the other observable circumstance.

A helpful analogy here is the dispositional property, *being soluble*. To say that a sugar cube is soluble is not to say that the sugar cube enjoys some ghostly inner state. It is just to say that *if* the sugar cube were put in water, then it *would* dissolve. More strictly,

"x is water soluble"

is equivalent by definition to

"if *x* were put in unsaturated water, *x* would dissolve."

This is one example of what is called an "operational definition." The term "soluble" is defined in terms of certain operations or tests that would reveal whether or not the term actually applies in the case to be tested.

According to the behaviorist, a similar analysis holds for mental states such as "wants a Caribbean holiday," save that the analysis is much richer. To say that Anne wants a Caribbean holiday is to say that (1) if asked whether that is what she wants, she would answer yes, and (2) if given new holiday brochures for Jamaica and Japan, she would peruse the ones for Jamaica first, and (3) if given a ticket on this Friday's flight to Jamaica, she would go, and so on and so on. Unlike solubility, claims the behaviorist, most mental states are *multitracked* dispositions. But dispositions they remain.

There is therefore no point in worrying about the "relation" between the mind and the body, on this view. To talk about Marie Curie's mind, for example, is not to talk about some "thing" that she "possesses"; it is to talk about certain of her extraordinary capacities and dispositions. The mind–body problem, concludes the behaviorist, is a pseudo-problem.

Behaviorism is clearly consistent with a materialist conception of human beings. Material objects can have dispositional properties, even multitracked ones, so there is no necessity to embrace dualism to make sense of our psychological vocabulary. (It should be pointed out, however, that behaviorism is strictly consistent with dualism also. Even if philosophical behaviorism were true, it would remain possible that our multitracked dispositions are grounded in immaterial mind-stuff rather than in molecular structures. This is not a possibility that most behaviorists took seriously, however. . . .)

Philosophical behaviorism, unfortunately, had two major flaws that made it awkward to believe, even for its defenders. It evidently ignored, and even denied, the "inner" aspect of our mental states. To have a pain, for example, seems to be not merely a matter of being inclined to moan, to wince, to take aspirin, and so on. Pains also have an intrinsic qualitative nature (a horrible one) that is revealed in introspection, and any theory of mind that ignores or denies such *qualia* is simply derelict in its duty.

This problem received much attention from behaviorists, and serious attempts were made to solve it. The details take us deeply into semantical problems, however, so we shall postpone further discussion of this difficulty.

The second flaw emerged when behaviorists attempted to specify in detail the multitracked disposition said to constitute any given mental state. The list of conditionals necessary for an adequate analysis of "wants a Caribbean holiday," for example, seemed not just to be long, but to be indefinitely or even infinitely long, with no finite way of specifying the elements to be included. And no term can be well defined whose *definiens** is

---

*[definition—Eds.]

openended and unspecific in this way. Further, each conditional of the long analysis was suspect on its own. Supposing that Anne does want a Caribbean holiday, conditional (1) above will be true only if she isn't *secretive* about her holiday fantasies; conditional (2) will be true only if she isn't already *bored* with the Jamaica brochures; conditional (3) will be true only if she doesn't *believe* the Friday flight will be hijacked, and so forth. But to repair each conditional by adding in the relevant qualification would be to reintroduce a series of *mental* elements into the business end of the definition, and we would no longer be defining the mental solely in terms of publicly observable circumstances and behavior.

So long as behaviorism seemed the only alternative to dualism, philosophers were prepared to struggle with these flaws in hopes of repairing or defusing them. However, three more materialist theories rose to prominence during the late fifties and sixties, and the flight from behaviorism was swift.

(I close this section with a cautionary note. The *philosophical* behaviorism discussed above is to be sharply distinguished from the *methodological* behaviorism that has enjoyed such a wide influence within psychology. In its bluntest form, this latter view urges that any new theoretical terms invented by the science of psychology *should be* operationally defined, in order to guarantee that psychology maintains a firm contact with empirical reality. Philosophical behaviorism, by contrast, claims that all of the commonsense psychological terms in our prescientific vocabulary *already* get whatever meaning they have from [tacit] operational definitions. The two views are logically distinct, and the methodology might be a wise one, for new theoretical terms, even though the correlative analysis of commonsense mental terms is wrong.)

REDUCTIVE MATERIALISM (THE IDENTITY THEORY)

Reductive materialism, more commonly known as *the identity theory,* is the most straightforward of the several materialist theories of mind. Its central claim is simplicity itself: mental states *are* physical states of the brain. That is, each type of mental

state or process is *numerically identical with* (is one and the very same thing as) some type of physical state or process within the brain or central nervous system. At present we do not know enough about the intricate functionings of the brain actually to state the relevant identities, but the identity theory is committed to the idea that brain research will eventually reveal them....

Historical Parallels

As the identity theorist sees it, the result here predicted has familiar parallels elsewhere in our scientific history. Consider sound. We now know that sound is just a train of compression waves traveling through the air, and that the property of being high pitched is identical with the property of having a high oscillatory frequency. We have learned that light is just electromagnetic waves, and our best current theory says that the color of an object is identical with a triplet of reflectance efficiencies the object has, rather like a musical chord that it strikes, though the "notes" are struck in electromagnetic waves instead of in sound waves. We now appreciate that the warmth or coolness of a body is just the energy of motion of the molecules that make it up: warmth is identical with high average molecular kinetic energy, and coolness is identical with low average molecular kinetic energy. We know that lightning is identical with a sudden large-scale discharge of electrons between clouds, or between the atmosphere and the ground. What we now think of as "mental states," argues the identity theorist, are identical with brain states in exactly the same way.

Intertheoretic Reduction

These illustrative parallels are all cases of successful *intertheoretic reduction.* That is, they are all cases where a new and very powerful theory turns out to entail a set of propositions and principles that mirror perfectly (or almost perfectly) the propositions and principles of some older theory or conceptual framework. The relevant principles entailed by the new theory have the same structure as the corresponding principles of the old framework, and they apply in exactly the same cases. The only difference is that where the old principles contained (for example) the notions of ," "is hot," and "is cold," the new principles contain instead the notions of "total molecular kinetic energy," "has a high mean molecular kinetic energy," and "has a low mean molecular kinetic energy."

If the new framework is far better than the old at explaining and predicting phenomena, then we have excellent reason for believing that the theoretical terms of the *new* framework are the terms that describe reality correctly. But if the old framework worked adequately, so far as it went, and if it parallels a portion of the new theory in the systematic way described, then we may properly conclude that the old terms and the new terms refer to the very same things, or express the very same properties. We conclude that we have apprehended the very same reality that is incompletely described by the old framework, but with a new and more penetrating conceptual framework. And we announce what philosophers of science call "intertheoretic identities"; light *is* electromagnetic waves, temperature *is* mean molecular kinetic energy, and so forth.

The examples of the preceding two paragraphs share one more important feature in common. They are all cases where the things or properties on the receiving end of the reduction are *observable* things and properties within our *commonsense* conceptual framework. They show that intertheoretic reduction occurs not only between conceptual frameworks in the theoretical stratosphere: commonsense observables can also be reduced. There would therefore be nothing particularly surprising about a reduction of our familiar introspectible mental states to physical states of the brain. All that would be required would be that an explanatorily successful neuroscience develop to the point where it entails a suitable "mirror image" of the assumptions and principles that constitute our commonsense conceptual framework for mental states, an image where brain-state terms occupy the positions held by mental-state terms in the assumptions and principles of common sense. If this (rather demanding) condition were indeed met, then, as in the historical cases cited, we would be justified in announcing a reduction, and in asserting the identity of mental states with brain states.

Arguments for the Identity Theory

What reasons does the identity theorist have for believing that neuroscience will eventually achieve the strong conditions necessary for the reduction of our "folk" psychology? There are at least four reasons, all directed at the conclusion that the correct account of human-behavior-and-its-causes must reside in the physical neurosciences.

We can point first to the purely physical origins and ostensibly physical constitution of each individual human. One begins as a genetically programmed monocellular organization of molecules (a fertilized ovum), and one develops from there by the accretion of further molecules whose structure and integration are controlled by the information coded in the DNA molecules of the cell nucleus. The result of such a process would be a purely physical system whose behavior arises from its internal operations and its interactions with the rest of the physical world. And those behavior-controlling internal operations are precisely what the neurosciences are about.

This argument coheres with a second argument. The origins of each *type* of animal also appear exhaustively physical in nature. The argument from evolutionary history . . . lends further support to the identity theorist's claim, since evolutionary theory provides the only serious explanation we have for the behavior-controlling capacities of the brain and central nervous system. Those systems were selected for because of the many advantages (ultimately, the reproductive advantage) held by creatures whose behavior was thus controlled. Again our behavior appears to have its basic causes in neural activity.

The identity theorist finds further support in the argument . . . from the neural dependence of all known mental phenomena. . . . This is precisely what one should expect, if the identity theory is true. Of course, systematic neural dependence is also a consequence of property dualism, but here the identity theorist will appeal to considerations of simplicity. Why admit two radically different classes of properties and operations if the explanatory job can be done by one?

A final argument derives from the growing success of the neurosciences in unraveling the nervous systems of many creatures and in explaining their behavioral capacities and deficits in terms of the structures discovered. The preceding arguments all suggest that neuroscience should be successful in this endeavor, and the fact is that the continuing history of neuroscience bears them out. Especially in the case of very simple creatures (as one would expect), progress has been rapid. And progress has also been made with humans, though for obvious moral reasons exploration must be more cautious and circumspect. In sum, the neurosciences have a long way to go, but progress to date provides substantial encouragement to the identity theorist.

Even so, these arguments are far from decisive in favor of the identity theory. No doubt they do provide an overwhelming case for the idea that the causes of human and animal behavior are essentially physical in nature, but the identity theory claims more than just this. It claims that neuroscience will discover a taxonomy of neural states that stand in a one-to-one correspondence with the mental states of our commonsense taxonomy. Claims for intertheoretic identity will be justified only if such a match-up can be found. But nothing in the preceding arguments guarantees that the old and new frameworks will match up in this way, even if the new framework is a roaring success at explaining and predicting our behavior. Furthermore, there are arguments from other positions within the materialist camp to the effect that such convenient match-ups are rather unlikely....

ELIMINATIVE MATERIALISM

The identity theory was called into doubt not because the prospects for a materialist account of our mental capacities were thought to be poor, but because it seemed unlikely that the arrival of an adequate materialist theory would bring with it the nice one-to-one match-ups, between the concepts of folk psychology and the concepts of theoretical neuroscience, that intertheoretic reduction requires. The reason for that doubt was the great variety of quite different physical systems that could instantiate the required functional organization. *Eliminative materialism* also doubts that the correct neuroscientific account of human

capacities will produce a neat reduction of our commonsense framework, but here the doubts arise from a quite different source.

As the eliminative materialists see it, the one-to-one match-ups will not be found, and our commonsense psychological framework will not enjoy an intertheoretic reduction, *because our commonsense psychological framework is a false and radically misleading conception of the causes of human behavior and the nature of cognitive activity.* On this view, folk psychology is not just an incomplete representation of our inner natures; it is an outright *mis*representation of our internal states and activities. Consequently, we cannot expect a truly adequate neuroscientific account of our inner lives to provide theoretical categories that match up nicely with the categories of our commonsense framework. Accordingly, we must expect that the older framework will simply be eliminated, rather than be reduced, by a matured neuroscience.

Historical Parallels

As the identity theorist can point to historical cases of successful intertheoretic reduction, so the eliminative materialist can point to historical cases of the outright elimination of the ontology of an older theory in favor of the ontology of a new and superior theory. For most of the eighteenth and nineteenth centuries, learned people believed that heat was a subtle *fluid* held in bodies, much in the way water is held in a sponge. A fair body of moderately successful theory described the way this fluid substance—called "caloric"—flowed within a body, or from one body to another, and how it produced thermal expansion, melting, boiling, and so forth. But by the end of the last century it had become abundantly clear that heat was not a substance at all, but just the energy of motion of the trillions of jostling molecules that make up the heated body itself. The new theory—the "corpuscular/kinetic theory of matter and heat"—was much more successful than the old in explaining and predicting the thermal behavior of bodies. And since we were unable to *identify* caloric fluid with kinetic energy (according to the old theory, caloric is a material *substance;* according to the new theory, kinetic energy is a form of *motion*), it was finally agreed that there is *no such thing* as caloric. Caloric was simply eliminated from our accepted ontology.

A second example. It used to be thought that when a piece of wood burns, or a piece of metal rusts, a spiritlike substance called "phlogiston" was being released: briskly, in the former case, slowly in the latter. Once gone, that "noble" substance left only a base pile of ash or rust. It later came to be appreciated that both processes involve, not the loss of something, but the *gaining* of a substance taken from the atmosphere: oxygen. Phlogiston emerged, not as an incomplete description of what was going on, but as a radical misdescription. Phlogiston was therefore not suitable for reduction to or identification with some notion from within the new oxygen chemistry, and it was simply eliminated from science.

Admittedly, both of these examples concern the elimination of something nonobservable, but our history also includes the elimination of certain widely accepted "observables." Before Copernicus' views became available, almost any human who ventured out at night could look up at *the starry sphere of the heavens,* and if he stayed for more than a few minutes he could also see that it *turned,* around an axis through Polaris. What the sphere was made of (crystal?) and what made it turn (the gods?) were theoretical questions that exercised us for over two millennia. But hardly anyone doubted the existence of what everyone could observe with their own eyes. In the end, however, we learned to reinterpret our visual experience of the night sky within a very different conceptual framework, and the turning sphere evaporated.

Witches provide another example. Psychosis is a fairly common affliction among humans, and in earlier centuries its victims were standardly seen as cases of demonic possession, as instances of Satan's spirit itself, glaring malevolently out at us from behind the victims' eyes. That witches exist was not a matter of any controversy. One would occasionally see them, in any city or hamlet, engaged in incoherent, paranoid, or even murderous behavior. But observable or not, we eventually decided that witches simply do not exist. We concluded that the concept of a witch is an element in a conceptual framework that misrepresents so badly the phenomena to which it was standardly applied that literal application of the notion should be permanently withdrawn. Modern theories of mental dysfunction led to the elimination of witches from our serious ontology.

The concepts of folk psychology—belief, desire, fear, sensation, pain, joy, and so on—await a similar fate, according to the view at issue. And when neuroscience has matured to the point where the poverty of our current conceptions is apparent to everyone, and the superiority of the new framework is established, we shall then be able to set about *re*conceiving our internal states and activities, within a truly adequate conceptual framework at last. Our explanations of one another's behavior will appeal to such things as our neuropharmacological states, the neural activity in specialized anatomical areas, and whatever other states are deemed relevant by the new theory. Our private introspection will also be transformed, and may be profoundly enhanced by reason of the more accurate and penetrating framework it will have to work with—just as the astronomer's perception of the night sky is much enhanced by the detailed knowledge of modern astronomical theory that he or she possesses.

The magnitude of the conceptual revolution here suggested should not be minimized: it would be enormous. And the benefits to humanity might be equally great. If each of us possessed an accurate neuroscientific understanding of (what we now conceive dimly as) the varieties and causes of mental illness, the factors involved in learning, the neural basis of emotions, intelligence, and socialization, then the sum total of human misery might be much reduced. The simple increase in mutual understanding that the new framework made possible could contribute substantially toward a more peaceful and humane society. Of course, there would be dangers as well: increased knowledge means increased power, and power can always be misused.

Arguments for Eliminative Materialism

The arguments for eliminative materialism are diffuse and less than decisive, but they are stronger than are widely supposed. The distinguished feature of this position is its denial that a smooth intertheoretic reduction is to be expected—even a species-specific reduction—of the framework of folk psychology to the framework of a matured neuroscience. The reason for this denial is the eliminative materialist's conviction that folk psychology is a hopelessly primitive and deeply confused conception of our internal activities. But why this low opinion of our commonsense conceptions?

There are at least three reasons. First, the eliminative materialist will point to the widespread explanatory, predictive, and manipulative failures of folk psychology. So much of what is central and familiar to us remains a complete mystery from within folk psychology. We do not know what *sleep* is, or why we have to have it, despite spending a full third of our lives in that condition. (The answer, "For rest," is mistaken. Even if people are allowed to rest continuously, their need for sleep is undiminished. Apparently, sleep serves some deeper functions, but we do not yet know what they are.) We do not understand how *learning* transforms each of us from a gaping infant to a cunning adult, or how differences in *intelligence* are grounded. We have not the slightest idea how *memory* works, or how we manage to retrieve relevant bits of information instantly from the awesome mass we have stored. We do not know what *mental illness* is, nor how to cure it.

In sum, the most central things about us remain almost entirely mysterious from within folk psychology. And the defects noted cannot be blamed on inadequate time allowed for their correction, for folk psychology has enjoyed no significant changes or advances in well over 2,000 years, despite its manifest failures. Truly successful theories may be expected to reduce, but significantly unsuccessful theories merit no such expectation.

This argument from explanatory poverty has a further aspect. So long as one sticks to normal brains, the poverty of folk psychology is perhaps not strikingly evident. But as soon as one examines the many perplexing behavioral and cognitive deficits suffered by people with *damaged* brains, one's descriptive and explanatory resources start to claw the air. . . . As with other humble theories asked to

operate successfully in unexplored extensions of their old domain (for example, Newtonian mechanics in the domain of velocities close to the velocity of light, and the classical gas law in the domain of high pressures or temperatures), the descriptive and explanatory inadequacies of folk psychology become starkly evident.

The second argument tries to draw an inductive lesson from our conceptual history. Our early folk theories of motion were profoundly confused, and were eventually displaced entirely by more sophisticated theories. Our early folk theories of the structure and activity of the heavens were wildly off the mark, and survive only as historical lessons in how wrong we can be. Our folk theories of the nature of fire, and the nature of life, were similarly cockeyed. And one could go on, since the vast majority of our past folk conceptions have been similarly exploded. All except folk psychology, which survives to this day and has only recently begun to feel pressure. But the phenomenon of conscious intelligence is surely a more complex and difficult phenomenon than any of those just listed. So far as accurate understanding is concerned, it would be a *miracle* if we had got *that* one right the very first time, when we fell down so badly on all the others. Folk psychology has survived for so very long, presumably, not because it is basically correct in its representations, but because the phenomena addressed are so surpassingly difficult that any useful handle on them, no matter how feeble, is unlikely to be displaced in a hurry.

A third argument attempts to find an a priori advantage for eliminative materialism over the identity theory and functionalism.* It attempts to counter the common intuition that eliminative materialism is distantly possible, perhaps, but is much less probable than either the identity theory or functionalism. The focus again is on whether the concepts of folk psychology will find vindicating match-ups in a matured neuroscience. The eliminativist bets no; the other two bet yes. (Even the functionalist bets yes, but expects the

---

*[See section 4 for the discussion of functionalism. We have reversed the order in which these theories are discussed, so that the discussion of functionalism occurs *after*, rather than before, the present discussion of eliminative materialism.— Ed.]

match-ups to be only species-specific, or only person-specific. Functionalism...denies the existence only of *universal* type/type identities.)

The eliminativist will point out that the requirements on a reduction are rather demanding. The new theory must entail a set of principles and embedded concepts that mirrors very closely the specific conceptual structure to be reduced. And the fact is, there are vastly many more ways of being an explanatorily successful neuroscience while *not* mirroring the structure of folk psychology, than there are ways of being an explanatorily successful neuroscience while also *mirroring* the very specific structure of folk psychology. Accordingly, the a priori probability of eliminative materialism is not lower, but substantially *higher* than that of either of its competitors. One's initial intuitions here are simply mistaken.

Granted, this initial a priori advantage could be reduced if there were a very strong presumption in favor of the truth of folk psychology—true theories are better bets to win reduction. But according to the first two arguments, the presumptions on this point should run in precisely the opposite direction.

Arguments Against Eliminative Materialism

The initial plausibility of this rather radical view is low for almost everyone, since it denies deeply entrenched assumptions. That is at best a question-begging complaint, of course, since those assumptions are precisely what is at issue. But the following line of thought does attempt to mount a real argument.

Eliminative materialism is false, runs the argument, because one's introspection reveals directly the existence of pains, beliefs, desires, fears, and so forth. Their existence is as obvious as anything could be.

The eliminative materialist will reply that this argument makes the same mistake that an ancient or medieval person would be making if he insisted that he could just see with his own eyes that the heavens form a turning sphere, or that witches exist. The fact is, all observation occurs within some system of concepts, and our observation judgments are only as good as the conceptual framework in which they are expressed. In all three cases—the starry sphere, witches, and the familiar mental states—precisely what is challenged is the integrity of the background conceptual frameworks in which the observation judgments are expressed. To insist on the validity of one's experiences, *traditionally interpreted,* is therefore to beg the very question at issue. For in all three cases, the question is whether we should *reconceive* the nature of some familiar observational domain.

A second criticism attempts to find an incoherence in the eliminative materialist's position. The bald statement of eliminative materialism is that the familiar mental states do not really exist. But that statement is meaningful, runs the argument, only if it is the expression of a certain *belief,* and an *intention* to communicate, and a *knowledge* of the language, and so forth. But if the statement is true, then no such mental states exist, and the statement is therefore a meaningless string of marks or noises, and cannot be true. Evidently, the assumption that eliminative materialism is true entails that it cannot be true.

The hole in this argument is the premise concerning the conditions necessary for a statement to be meaningful. It begs the question. If eliminative materialism is true, then meaningfulness must have some different source. To insist on the "old" source is to insist on the validity of the very framework at issue. Again, an historical parallel may be helpful here. Consider the medieval theory that being biologically *alive* is a matter of being ensouled by an immaterial *vital spirit.* And consider the following response to someone who has expressed disbelief in that theory.

> My learned friend has stated that there is no such thing as vital spirit. But this statement is incoherent. For if it is true, then my friend does not have vital spirit, and must therefore be *dead.* But if he is dead, then his statement is just a string of noises, devoid of meaning or truth. Evidently, the assumption that antivitalism is true entails that it cannot be true! Q.E.D.

This second argument is now a joke, but the first argument begs the question in exactly the same way.

A final criticism draws a much weaker conclusion, but makes a rather stronger case. Eliminative materialism, it has been said, is making mountains out of molehills. It exaggerates the defects in folk psychology, and underplays its real successes. Perhaps the arrival of a matured neuroscience will require the elimination of the occasional folk-psychological concept, continues the criticism, and a minor adjustment in certain folk-psychological principles may have to be endured. But the large-scale elimination forecast by the eliminative materialist is just an alarmist worry or a romantic enthusiasm.

Perhaps this complaint is correct. And perhaps it is merely complacent. Whichever, it does bring out the important point that we do not confront two simple and mutually exclusive possibilities here: pure reduction versus pure elimination. Rather, these are the end points of a smooth spectrum of possible outcomes, between which there are mixed cases of partial elimination and partial reduction. Only empirical research . . . can tell us where on that spectrum our own case will fall. Perhaps we should speak here, more liberally, of "revisionary materialism," instead of concentrating on the more radical possibility of an across-the-board elimination. Perhaps we should. But it has been my aim in this section to make it at least intelligible to you that our collective conceptual destiny lies substantially toward the revolutionary end of the spectrum.

FUNCTIONALISM*

According to *functionalism*, the essential or defining feature of any type of mental state is the set of causal relations it bears to (1) environmental effects on the body, (2) other types of mental states, and (3) bodily behavior. Pain, for example, characteristically results from some bodily damage or trauma; it causes distress, annoyance, and practical reasoning aimed at relief; and it causes wincing, blanching, and nursing of the traumatized area. Any state that plays exactly that functional role is a pain, according to functionalism. Similarly, other types of mental states (sensations,

fears, beliefs, and so on) are also defined by their unique causal roles in a complex economy of internal states mediating sensory inputs and behavioral outputs.

This view may remind the reader of behaviorism, and indeed it is the heir to behaviorism, but there is one fundamental difference between the two theories. Where the behaviorist hoped to define each type of mental state solely in terms of environmental input and behavioral output, the functionalist denies that this is possible. As he sees it, the adequate characterization of almost any mental state involves an ineliminable reference to a variety of other mental states with which it is causally connected, and so a reductive definition solely in terms of publicly observable inputs and outputs is quite impossible. Functionalism is therefore immune to one of the main objections against behaviorism.

Thus the difference between functionalism and behaviorism. The difference between functionalism and the identity theory will emerge from the following argument raised against the identity theory.

Imagine a being from another planet, says the functionalist, a being with an alien physiological constitution, a constitution based on the chemical element silicon, for example, instead of on the element carbon, as ours is. The chemistry and even the physical structure of the alien's brain would have to be systematically different from ours. But even so, that alien brain could well sustain a functional economy of internal states whose mutual *relations* parallel perfectly the mutual relations that define our own mental states. The alien may have an internal state that meets all the conditions for being a pain state, as outlined earlier. That state, considered from a purely physical point of view, would have a very different makeup from a human pain state, but it could nevertheless be identical to a human pain state from a purely functional point of view. And so for all of his functional states.

If the alien's functional economy of internal states were indeed *functionally isomorphic* with our own internal economy—if those states were causally connected to inputs, to one another, and to behavior in ways that parallel our own internal connections—then the alien would have

---

*[In Professor Churchland's text this section occurs *before* the section on Eliminative Materialism. We have reversed the order here.—Eds.]

pains, and desires, and hopes, and fears just as fully as we, despite the differences in the physical system that sustains or realizes those functional states. What is important for mentality is not the matter of which the creature is made, but the structure of the internal activities which that matter sustains.

If we can think of one alien constitution, we can think of many, and the point just made can also be made with an artificial system. Were we to create an electronic system—a computer of some kind—whose internal economy were functionally isomorphic with our own in all the relevant ways, then it too would be the subject of mental states.

What this illustrates is that there are almost certainly many more ways than one for nature, and perhaps even for man, to put together a thinking, feeling, perceiving creature. And this raises a problem for the identity theory, for it seems that there is no single type of physical state to which a given type of mental state must always correspond. Ironically, there are *too many* different kinds of physical systems that can realize the functional economy characteristic of conscious intelligence. If we consider the universe at large, therefore, and the future as well as the present, it seems quite unlikely that the identity theorist is going to find the one-to-one match-ups between the concepts of our common-sense mental taxonomy and the concepts of an overarching theory that encompasses all of the relevant physical systems. But that is what intertheoretic reduction is standardly said to require. The prospects for universal identities, between types of mental states and types of brain states, are therefore slim.

If the functionalists reject the traditional "mental type = physical type" identity theory, virtually all of them remain committed to a weaker "mental token = physical token" identity theory, for they still maintain that each *instance* of a given type of mental state is numerically identical with some specific physical state in some physical system or other. It is only universal (type/type) identities that are rejected. Even so, this rejection is typically taken to support the claim that the science of psychology is or should be *methodologically autonomous* from the various physical sciences such as physics, biology, and even neurophysiology. Psychology, it is claimed, has its own irreducible laws and its own abstract subject matter.

[In 1984] functionalism [was] probably the most widely held theory of mind among philosophers, cognitive psychologists, and artificial intelligence researchers. Some of the reasons are apparent from the preceding discussion, and there are further reasons as well. In characterizing mental states as essentially functional states, functionalism places the concerns of psychology at a level that abstracts from the teeming detail of a brain's neurophysiological (or crystallographic, or microelectronic) structure. The science of psychology, it is occasionally said, is methodologically autonomous from those other sciences (biology, neuroscience, circuit theory) whose concerns are with what amount to engineering details. This provides a rationale for a great deal of work in cognitive psychology and artificial intelligence, where researchers postulate a system of abstract functional states and then test the postulated system, often by way of its computer simulation, against human behavior in similar circumstances. The aim of such work is to discover in detail the functional organization that makes us what we are. . . .

Arguments Against Functionalism

Current popularity aside, functionalism also faces difficulties. The most commonly posed objection cites an old friend: sensory qualia. Functionalism may escape one of behaviorism's fatal flaws, it is said, but it still falls prey to the other. By attempting to make its *relational* properties the definitive feature of any mental state, functionalism ignores the "inner" or qualitative nature of our mental states. But their qualitative nature is the essential feature of a great many types of mental state (pain, sensations of color, of temperature, of pitch, and so on), runs the objection, and functionalism is therefore false.

The standard illustration of this apparent failing is called "the inverted spectrum thought-experiment." It is entirely conceivable, runs the story, that the range of color sensations that I enjoy upon viewing standard objects is simply inverted relative to the color sensations that you enjoy. When viewing a tomato, I may have what is really a sensation-of-green where you have the normal sensation-of-red; when viewing a banana, I may have what is really sensation-of-blue where you have the normal sensation-of-yellow; and so forth. But since we have no way of comparing our inner qualia, and since I shall make all the same observational discriminations among objects that you will, there is no way to tell whether my spectrum is inverted relative to yours.

The problem for functionalism arises as follows. Even if my spectrum is inverted relative to yours, we remain functionally isomorphic with one another. My visual sensation upon viewing a tomato is *functionally* identical with your visual sensation upon viewing a tomato. According to functionalism, therefore, they are the very same type of state, and it does not even make sense to suppose that my sensation is "really" a sensation-of-green. If it meets the functional conditions for being a sensation-of-red, then by definition it is a sensation-of-red. According to functionalism, apparently, a spectrum inversion of the kind described is ruled out by definition. But such inversions are entirely conceivable, concludes the objection, and if functionalism entails that they are not conceivable, then functionalism is false.

Another qualia-related worry for functionalism is the so-called "absent qualia problem." The functional organization characteristic of conscious intelligence can be instantiated (= realized or instanced) in a considerable variety of physical systems, some of them radically different from a normal human. For example, a giant electronic computer might instantiate it, and there are more radical possibilities still. One writer asks us to imagine the people of China—all 10^9 of them—organized into an intricate game of mutual interactions so that collectively they constitute a giant brain which exchanges inputs and outputs with a single robot body. That system of the robot-plus-10^9-unit-brain could presumably instantiate the relevant functional organization (though no doubt it would be much slower in its activities than a human or a computer), and would therefore be the subject of mental states, according to functionalism. But

surely, it is urged, the complex states that there play the functional roles of pain, pleasure, and sensations-of-color would not have intrinsic qualia as ours do, and would therefore fail to be genuine mental states. Again, functionalism seems at best an incomplete account of the nature of mental states.

It has recently been argued that both the inverted-qualia and the absent-qualia objections can be met, without violence to functionalism and without significant violence to our commonsense intuitions about qualia. Consider the inversion problem first. I think the functionalist is right to insist that the type-identity of our visual sensations be reckoned according to their functional role. But the objector is also right in insisting that a relative inversion of two people's qualia, without functional inversion, is entirely conceivable. The apparent inconsistency between these positions can be dissolved by insisting that (1) our functional states (or rather, their physical realizations) do indeed have an intrinsic nature on which our introspective identification of those states depends; while also insisting that (2) such intrinsic natures are nevertheless not essential to the type-identity of a given mental state, and may indeed *vary* from instance to instance of the same type of mental state.

What this means is that the qualitative character of your sensation-of-red might be different from the qualitative character of my sensation-of-red, slightly or substantially, and a third person's sensation-of-red might be different again. But so long as all three states are standardly caused by red objects and standardly cause all three of us to believe that something is red, then all three states are sensations-of-red, whatever their intrinsic qualitative character. Such intrinsic qualia merely serve as salient features that permit the quick introspective identification of sensations, as black-on-orange stripes serve as a salient feature for the quick visual identification of tigers. But specific qualia are not essential to the type-identity of mental states, any more than black-on-orange stripes are essential to the type-identity of tigers.

Plainly, this solution requires the functionalist to admit the *reality* of qualia, and we may wonder how there can be room for qualia in his materialist world-picture. Perhaps they can be fit in as follows: *identify* them with physical properties of whatever physical states instantiate the mental (functional) states that display them. For example, identify the qualitative nature of your sensations-of-red with that physical feature (of the brain state that instantiates it) to which your mechanisms of introspective discrimination are in fact responding when you judge that you have a sensation-of-red. If materialism is true, then there must *be* some internal physical feature or other to which your discrimination of sensations-of-red is keyed: *that* is the quale of your sensations-of-red. If the pitch of a sound can turn out to be the frequency of an oscillation in air pressure, there is no reason why the quale of a sensation cannot turn out to be, say, a spiking frequency in a certain neural pathway. ("Spikes" are the tiny electrochemical pulses by which our brain cells communicate.)

This entails that creatures with a constitution different from ours may have qualia different from ours, despite being psychologically isomorphic with us. It does not entail that they *must* have different qualia, however. If the qualitative character of my sensation-of-red is really a spiking frequency of 90 hertz in a certain neural pathway, it is possible that an electromechanical robot might enjoy the very same qualitative character if, in reporting sensations-of-red, the robot were responding to a spiking frequency of 90 hertz in a corresponding *copper* pathway. It might be the spiking frequency that matters to our respective mechanisms of discrimination, not the nature of the medium that carries it.

This proposal also suggests a solution to the absent qualia problem. So long as the physical system at issue is functionally isomorphic with us, to the last detail, then it will be equally capable of subtle introspective discriminations among its sensations. Those discriminations must be made on some systematic physical basis, that is, on some characteristic physical features of the states being discriminated. Those features at the objective focus of the system's discriminatory mechanisms, *those* are its sensory qualia—though the alien system is no more likely to appreciate their true physical nature than we appreciate the

true physical nature of our own qualia. Sensory qualia are therefore an inevitable concomitant of any system with the kind of functional organization at issue. It may be difficult or impossible to "see" the qualia in an alien system, but it is equally difficult to "see" them even when looking into a human brain.

I leave it to the reader to judge the adequacy of these responses. If they are adequate, then, given its other virtues, functionalism must be conceded a very strong position among the competing contemporary theories of mind. It is interesting, however, that the defense offered in the last paragraph found it necessary to take a leaf from the identity theorist's book (types of quale are reduced to or identified with types of physical state), since the final objection we shall consider also tends to blur the distinction between functionalism and reductive materialism.

Consider the property of *temperature,* runs the objection. Here we have a paradigm of a physical property, one that has also been cited as the paradigm of a successfully *reduced* property, as expressed in the intertheoretic identity

"temperature = mean kinetic energy of constituent molecules."

Strictly speaking, however, this identity is true only for the temperature of a gas, where simple particles are free to move in ballistic fashion. In a *solid,* temperature is realized differently, since the interconnected molecules are confined to a variety of vibrational motions. In a *plasma,* temperature is something else again, since a plasma has no constituent molecules; they, and their constituent atoms, have been ripped to pieces. And even a *vacuum* has a so-called "blackbody" temperature—in the distribution of electromagnetic waves coursing through it. Here temperature has nothing to do with the kinetic energy of particles.

It is plain that the physical property of temperature enjoys "multiple instantiations" no less than do psychological properties. Does this mean that thermodynamics (the theory of heat and temperature) is an "autonomous science," separable from the rest of physics, with its own irreducible laws and its own abstract nonphysical subject matter?

Presumably not. What it means, concludes the objection, is that *reductions are domain-specific:*

temperature-in-a-gas = the mean kinetic energy of the gas's molecules,

whereas

temperature-in-a-vacuum = the blackbody distribution of the vacuum's transient radiation.

Similarly, perhaps

joy-in-a-human = resonances in the lateral hypothalamus,

whereas

joy-in-a-Martian = something else entirely.

This means that we may expect some type/type reductions of mental states to physical states after all, though they will be much narrower than was first suggested. Furthermore, it means that functionalist claims concerning the radical autonomy of psychology cannot be sustained. And last, it suggests that functionalism is not so profoundly different from the identity theory as was first made out. . . .

CAN NON-HUMANS THINK?

Computing Machinery and Intelligence

ALAN TURING

Alan Turing (1912–1954), a British mathematician, did important work in probability theory, and was one of the founders of modern computation theory. He played an indispensable role in breaking German war codes during WW II.

THE IMITATION GAME

I propose to consider the question "Can machines think?" This should begin with definitions of the meaning of the terms 'machine' and 'think'. The definitions might be framed so as to reflect so far as possible the normal use of the words, but this attitude is dangerous. If the meaning of the words 'machine' and 'think' are to be found by examining how they are commonly used it is difficult to escape the conclusion that the meaning and the answer to the question, "Can machines think?" is to be sought in a statistical survey such as a Gallup poll. But this is absurd. Instead of attempting such a definition I shall replace the question by another, which is closely related to it and is expressed in relatively unambiguous words.

The new form of the problem can be described in terms of a game which we call the "imitation game". It is played with three people, a man (A), a woman (B), and an interrogator (C) who may be of either sex. The interrogator stays in a room apart from the other two. The object of the game for the interrogator is to determine which of the other two is the man and which is the woman. He knows them by labels X and Y, and at the end of the game he says either "X is A and Y is B" or "X is B and Y is A". The interrogator is allowed to put questions to A and B thus:

C: Will X please tell me the length of his or her hair?

From Alan Turing, "Computing Machinery and Intelligence," *Mind*, Vol. 59 (1950). Reprinted by permission of Oxford University Press.

Now suppose X is actually A, then A must answer. It is A's object in the game to try to cause C to make the wrong identification. His answer might therefore be

A: My hair is shingled, and the longest strands are about nine inches long.

In order that tones of voice may not help the interrogator the answers should be written, or better still, typewritten. The ideal arrangement is to have a teleprinter communicating between the two rooms. Alternatively the question and answers can be repeated by an intermediary. The object of the game for the third player (B) is to help the interrogator. The best strategy for her is probably to give truthful answers. She can add such things as "I am the woman, don't listen to him!" to her answers, but it will avail nothing as the man can make similar remarks.

We now ask the question, "What will happen when a machine takes the part of A in this game?" Will the interrogator decide wrongly as often when the game is played like this as he does when the game is played between a man and a woman? These questions replace our original, "Can machines think?"

CRITIQUE OF THE NEW PROBLEM

As well as asking, "What is the answer to this new form of the question?" one may ask, "Is this new question a worthy one to investigate?" This latter question we investigate without further ado, thereby cutting short an infinite regress.

The new problem has the advantage of drawing a fairly sharp line between the physical and the intellectual capacities of a man. No engineer or chemist claims to be able to produce a material which is indistinguishable from the human skin. It is possible that at some time this might be done, but even supposing this invention available we should feel there was little point in trying to make a "thinking machine" more human by dressing it up in such artificial flesh. The form in which we have set the problem reflects this fact in the condition which prevents the interrogator from seeing or touching the other competitors, or hearing their voices. Some other advantages of the proposed criterion may be

shown up by specimen questions and answers. Thus:

Q: Please write me a sonnet on the subject of the Forth Bridge.
A: Count me out on this one. I never could write poetry.
Q: Add 34957 to 70764.
A: (Pause about 30 seconds and then give as answer) 105621.
Q: Do you play chess?
A: Yes.
Q: I have K at my K1, and no other pieces. You have only K at K6 and R at R1. It is your move. What do you play?
A: (After a pause of 15 seconds) R–R8 mate.

The question and answer method seems to be suitable for introducing almost any one of the fields of human endeavor that we wish to include. We do not wish to penalize the machine for its inability to shine in beauty competitions, nor to penalize a man for losing in a race against an airplane. The conditions of our game make these disabilities irrelevant. The "witnesses" can brag, if they consider it advisable, as much as they please about their charms, strength or heroism, but the interrogator cannot demand practical demonstrations.

The game may perhaps be criticized on the ground that the odds are weighted too heavily against the machine. If the man were to try and pretend to be the machine he would clearly make a very poor showing. He would be given away at once by slowness and inaccuracy in arithmetic. May not machines carry out something which ought to be described as thinking but which is very different from what a man does? This objection is a very strong one, but at least we can say that if, nevertheless, a machine can be constructed to play the imitation game satisfactorily, we need not be troubled by this objection.

It might be urged that when playing the "imitation game" the best strategy for the machine may possibly be something other than imitation of the behavior of a man. This may be, but I think it is unlikely that there is any great effect of this kind. In any case there is no intention to investigate here the theory of the game, and it will be assumed that the best strategy is to try to provide answers that would naturally be given by a man.

THE MACHINES CONCERNED IN THE GAME

The question which we put in section 1 will not be quite definite until we have specified what we mean by the word 'machine'. It is natural that we should wish to permit every kind of engineering technique to be used in our machines. We also wish to allow the possibility that an engineer or team of engineers may construct a machine which works, but whose manner of operation cannot be satisfactorily described by its constructors because they have applied a method which is largely experimental. Finally, we wish to exclude from the machines men born in the usual manner. It is difficult to frame the definitions so as to satisfy these three conditions. One might for instance insist that the team of engineers should be all of one sex, but this would not really be satisfactory, for it is probably possible to rear a complete individual from a single cell of the skin (say) of a man. To do so would be a feat of biological technique deserving of the very highest praise, but we would not be inclined to regard it as a case of "constructing a thinking machine". This prompts us to abandon the requirement that every kind of technique should be permitted. We are the more ready to do so in view of the fact that the present interest in "thinking machines" has been aroused by a particular kind of machine, usually called an "electronic computer" or "digital computer". Following this suggestion we only permit digital computers to take part in our game....

UNIVERSALITY OF DIGITAL COMPUTERS

[D]igital computers...may be classified among the "discrete state machines". These are the machines which move by sudden jumps or clicks from one quite definite state to another. These states are sufficiently different for the possibility of confusion between them to be ignored. Strictly speaking there are no such machines. Everything really moves continuously. But there are many kinds of machines which can profitably be *thought of* as being discrete state machines. For instance in considering the switches for a lighting system it is a convenient fiction that each switch must be definitely on or definitely off. There must be intermediate positions, but for most purposes we can forget about them. As an example of a discrete state machine, we might consider a wheel which clicks round through $120°$ once a second, but may be stopped by a lever which can be operated from outside; in addition a lamp is to light in one of the positions of the wheel. This machine could be described abstractly as follows: The internal state of the machine (which is described by the position of the wheel) may be q_1, q_2, or q_3. There is an input signal i_0 or i_1 (position or lever). The internal state at any moment is determined by the last state and input signal according to the table

		Last state:		
		q_1	q_2	q_3
Input:	i_0	q_2	q_3	q_1
	i_1	q_1	q_2	q_3

The output signals, the only externally visible indication of the internal state (the light), are described by the table

State:	q_1	q_2	q_3
Output:	O_0	O_0	O_1

This example is typical of discrete state machines. They can be described by such tables, provided they have only a finite number of possible states....

Given the table corresponding to a discrete state machine, it is possible to predict what it will do. There is no reason why this calculation should not be carried out by means of a digital computer. Provided it could be carried out sufficiently quickly the digital computer could mimic the behavior of any discrete state machine. The imitation game could then be played with the machine in question (as B) and the mimicking digital computer (as A) and the interrogator would be unable to distinguish them. Of course the digital computer must have adequate storage capacity as well as working sufficiently fast. Moreover, it must be programmed afresh for each new machine which it is desired to mimic.

This special property of digital computers, that they can mimic any discrete state machine, is described by saying that they are *universal* machines. The existence of machines with this property has the important consequence that, considerations of speed apart, it is unnecessary to design various new machines to do various computing processes. They can all be done with one digital computer, suitably programmed for each case. It will be seen that as a consequence of this all digital computers are in a sense equivalent.

We may now consider again the point raised at the end of section 3. It was suggested tentatively that the question, "Can machines think?" should be replaced by "Are there imaginable digital computers which would do well in the imitation game?" If we wish we can make this superficially more general and ask, "Are there discrete state machines which would do well?" But in view of the universality property we see that either of these questions is equivalent to this: "Let us fix our attention on one particular digital computer" C. Is it true that by modifying this computer to have an adequate storage, suitably increasing its speed of action, and providing it with an appropriate program, C can be made to play satisfactorily the part of A in the imitation game, the part of B being taken by a man?"

CONTRARY VIEWS ON THE MAIN QUESTION

We may now consider the ground to have been cleared and we are ready to proceed to the debate on our question, "Can machines think?" and the variant of it quoted at the end of the last section. We cannot altogether abandon the original form of the problem, for opinions will differ as to the appropriateness of the substitution and we must at least listen to what has to be said in this connection.

It will simplify matters for the reader if I explain first my own beliefs in the matter. Consider first the more accurate form of the question. I believe that in about fifty years' time it will be possible to program computers, with a storage capacity of about 10^9, to make them play the imitation game so well that an average interrogator will not have more than 70 per cent chance of making the right identification after five minutes of questioning. The original question, "Can machines think?" I believe to be too meaningless to deserve discussion. Nevertheless I believe that at the end of the twentieth century the use of words and general educated opinion will have altered so much that one will be able to speak of machines thinking without expecting to be contradicted. I believe further that no useful purpose is served by concealing these beliefs. The popular view that scientists proceed inexorably from well-established fact to well-established fact, never being influenced by any unproved conjecture, is quite mistaken. Provided it is made clear which are proved facts and which are conjectures, no harm can result. Conjectures are of great importance since they suggest useful lines of research.

I now proceed to consider opinions opposed to my own.

(1) The Theological Objection

Thinking is a function of man's immortal soul. God has given an immortal soul to every man and woman, but not to any other animal or to machines. Hence no animal or machine can think.

I am unable to accept any part of this, but will attempt to reply in theological terms. I should find the argument more convincing if animals were classed with men, for there is a greater difference, to my mind, between the typical animate and the inanimate than there is between man and the other animals. The arbitrary character of the orthodox view becomes clearer if we consider how it might appear to a member of some other religious community. How do Christians regard the Moslem view that women have no souls? But let us leave this point aside and return to the main argument. It appears to me that the argument quoted above implies a serious restriction of the omnipotence of the Almighty. It is admitted that there are certain things that He cannot do such as making one equal to two, but should we not believe that He has freedom to confer a soul on an elephant if He sees fit? We might expect that He would only exercise this power in conjunction with a mutation which provided the elephant with an appropriately improved brain to minister to the needs of this soul. An argument of exactly similar form may be made for the case of machines. It may seem different because it is more difficult to "swallow". But this really only means that we think it would be less likely that He would consider the circumstances suitable for conferring a soul. The circumstances in question are discussed in the rest of this paper. In attempting to construct such machines we should not be irreverently usurping His power of creating souls, any more than we are in the procreation of children: rather we are, in either case, instruments of His will providing mansions for the souls that He creates.

However, this is mere speculation. I am not very impressed with theological arguments, whatever they may be used to support. Such arguments have often been found unsatisfactory in the past. In the time of Galileo it was argued that the texts, "And the sun stood still . . . and hasted not to go down about a whole day" (Joshua x. 13) and "He laid the foundations of the earth, that it should not move at any time" (Psalm cv. 5) were an adequate refutation of the Copernican theory. With our present knowledge, such an argument appears futile. When that knowledge was not available, it made a quite different impression.

(2) The "Heads in the Sand" Objection

"The consequences of machines thinking would be too dreadful. Let us hope and believe that they cannot do so."

This argument is seldom expressed quite so openly as in the form above. But it affects most of us who think about it at all. We like to believe that Man is in some subtle way superior to the rest of creation. It is best if he can be shown to be *necessarily* superior, for then there is no danger of him losing his commanding position. The popularity of the theological argument is clearly connected with this feeling. It is likely to be quite strong in intellectual people, since they value the power of thinking more highly than others, and are more inclined to base their belief in the superiority of Man on this power.

I do not think that this argument is sufficiently substantial to require refutation. Consolation

would be more appropriate; perhaps this should be sought in the transmigration of souls. . . .

(3) The Argument from Consciousness

This argument is very well expressed in Professor Jefferson's Lister Oration for 1949, from which I quote.

> Not until a machine can write a sonnet or compose a concerto because of thoughts and emotions felt, and not by the chance fall of symbols, could we agree that machine equals brain—that is, not only write it but know that it had written it. No mechanism could feel (and not merely artificially signal, and easy contrivance) pleasure at its successes, grief when its valves fuse, be warmed by flattery, be made miserable by its mistakes, be charmed by sex, be angry or depressed when it cannot get what it wants.

This argument appears to be a denial of the validity of our test. According to the most extreme form of this view, the only way by which one could be sure that a machine thinks is to *be* the machine and to feel oneself thinking. One could then describe these feelings to the world, but of course no one would be justified in taking any notice. Likewise according to this view, the only way to know that a *man* thinks is to be that particular man. It is in fact the solipsist point of view. It may be the most logical view to hold but it makes communication of ideas difficult. A is liable to believe "A thinks but B does not" while B believes "B thinks but A does not". Instead of arguing continually over this point, it is usual to have the polite convention that everyone thinks.

I am sure that Professor Jefferson does not wish to adopt the extreme and solipsist point of view. Probably he would be quite willing to accept the imitation game as a test. The game (with the player B omitted) is frequently used in practice under the name of *viva voce* to discover whether someone really understands something or has "learned it parrot fashion". Let us listen in to a part of such a *viva voce*:

Interrogator: In the first line of your sonnet, which reads "Shall I compare thee to a summer's day," would not "a spring day" do as well or better?

Witness: It wouldn't scan.

Interrogator: How about "a winter's day". That would scan all right.

Witness: Yes, but nobody wants to be compared to a winter's day.

Interrogator: Would you say Mr. Pickwick reminded you of Christmas?

Witness: In a way.

Interrogator: Yet Christmas is a winter's day, and I do not think Mr. Pickwick would mind the comparison.

Witness: I don't think you're serious. By a winter's day one means a typical winter's day, rather than a special one like Christmas.

And so on. What would Professor Jefferson say if the sonnet-writing machine were able to answer like this in the *viva voce?* I do not know whether he would regard the machine as "merely artificially signalling" these answers, but if the answers were as satisfactory and sustained as in the above passage I do not think he would describe it as "an easy contrivance". This phrase is, I think, intended to cover such devices as the inclusion in the machine of a record of someone reading a sonnet, with appropriate switching to turn it on from time to time.

In short then, I think that most of those who support the argument from consciousness could be persuaded to abandon it rather than be forced into the solipsist position. They will then probably be willing to accept our test.

I do not wish to give the impression that I think there is no mystery about consciousness. There is, for instance, something of a paradox connected with any attempt to localize it. But I do not think these mysteries necessarily need to be solved before we can answer the question with which we are concerned in this paper.

(4) Arguments from Various Disabilities

These arguments take the form, "I grant you that you can make machines do all the things you have mentioned but you will never be able to make one to do X." Numerous features X are suggested in this connection. I offer a selection:

Be kind, resourceful, beautiful, friendly, have initiative, have a sense of humor, tell right from wrong, make mistakes, fall in love, enjoy strawberries and cream, make someone fall in love with it, learn from experience, use words properly, be the subject of its own thought, have as much diversity of behavior as a man, do something really new....

No support is usually offered for these statements. I believe they are mostly founded on the principle of scientific induction. A man has seen thousands of machines in his lifetime. From what he sees of them he draws a number of general conclusions. They are ugly, each is designed for a very limited purpose, when required for a minutely different purpose they are useless, the variety of behavior of any one of them is very small, and so on and so forth. Naturally he [mistakenly] concludes that these are necessary properties of machines in general....

There are, however, special remarks to be made about many of the disabilities that have been mentioned.

The claim that "machines cannot make mistakes" seems a curious one. One is tempted to retort, "Are they any the worse for that?" But let us adopt a more sympathetic attitude, and try to see what is really meant. I think this criticism can be explained in terms of the imitation game. It is claimed that the interrogator could distinguish the machine from the man simply by setting them a number of problems in arithmetic. The machine would be unmasked because of its deadly accuracy. The reply to this is simple. The machine (programmed for playing the game) would not attempt to give the *right* answers to the arithmetic problems. It would deliberately introduce mistakes in a manner calculated to confuse the interrogator....

The claim that a machine cannot be the subject of its own thought can of course only be answered if it can be shown that the machine has *some* thought with *some* subject matter. Nevertheless, "the subject matter of a machine's operations" does seem to mean something, at least to the people who deal with it. If, for instance, the machine were trying to find a solution of the equation $x^2 - 40x - 11 = 0$, one would be tempted to describe this equation as part of the machine's subject matter at that moment. It may be used to help in making up its own programs, or to predict the effect of alterations in its own structure. By observing the results of its own behavior it can modify its own programs so as to achieve some purpose more effectively. These are possibilities of the near future, rather than Utopian dreams. . . .

(5) Lady Lovelace's Objection

. . . A variant of Lady Lovelace's objection states that a machine can "never do anything really new". This may be parried for moment with the saw, "There is nothing new under the sun." Who can be certain that "original work" that he has done was not simply the growth of the seed planted in him by teaching, or the effect of following well-known general principles. A batter variant of the objection says that a machine can never "take us by surprise". This statement is a more direct challenge and can be met directly. Machines take me by surprise with great frequency. This is largely because I do not do sufficient calculation to decide what to expect them to do, or rather because, although I do a calculation, I do it in a hurried, slipshod fashion, taking risks. Perhaps I say to myself, "I suppose the voltage here ought to be the same as there: anyway let's assume it is." Naturally I am often wrong, and the result is a surprise for me, for by the time the experiment is done these assumptions have been forgotten. These admissions lay me open to lectures on the subject of my vicious ways, but do not throw any doubt on my credibility when I testify to the surprises I experience.

I do not expect this reply to silence my critic. He will probably say that such surprises are due to some creative mental act on my part, and reflect no credit on the machine. This leads us back to the argument from consciousness, and far from the idea of surprise. It is a line of argument we must consider closed, but it is perhaps worth remarking that the appreciation of something as surprising requires as much of a "creative mental act" whether the surprising event originates from a man, a book, a machine or anything else.

The view that machines cannot give rise to surprises is due, I believe, to a fallacy to which philosophers and mathematicians are particularly subject. This is the assumption that as soon as a fact is presented to a mind all consequences of that fact spring into the mind simultaneously with it. It is a very useful assumption under many circumstances, but one too easily forgets that it is false. A natural consequence of doing so is that one then assumes that there is no virtue in the mere working out of consequences from data and general principles. . . .

(6) The Argument from Informality of Behavior

It is not possible to produce a set of rules purporting to describe what a man should do in every conceivable set of circumstances. One might for instance have a rule that one is to stop when one sees a red traffic light, and to go if one sees a green one; but what if by some fault both appear together? One may perhaps decide that it is safest to stop. But some further difficulty may well arise from this decision later. To attempt to provide rules of conduct to cover every eventuality, even those arising from traffic lights, appears to be impossible. With all this I agree.

From this it is argued that we cannot be machines. I shall try to reproduce the argument, but I fear I shall hardly do it justice. It seems to run something like this: "If each man had a definite set of rules of conduct by which he regulated his life he would be no better than a machine. But there are no such rules, so men cannot be machines." The undistributed middle is glaring. I do not think the argument is ever put quite like this, but I believe this is the argument used nevertheless. There may however be a certain confusion between "rules of conduct" and "laws of behavior" to cloud the issue. By "rules of conduct" I mean precepts such as "Stop if you see red lights", on which one can act, and of which one can be conscious. By "laws of behavior" I mean laws of nature as applied to a man's body such as "if you pinch him he will squeak". If we substitute "laws of behavior which regulate his life" for "laws of conduct by which he regulates his life" in the argument quoted the undistributed middle is no longer inseperable. For we believe that it is not only true that being regulated by laws of behavior implies being some sort of machine (though not necessarily a discrete state machine), but that conversely being such a machine implies being regulated by such laws. However, we cannot so easily convince ourselves of the absence of complete laws of behavior as of complete rules of conduct. The only way we know of for finding such laws is scientific observation, and we certainly know of no circumstances under which we could say: "We have searched enough. There are no such laws."

We can demonstrate more forcibly that any such statement would be unjustified. For suppose we could be sure of finding such laws if they existed. Then given a discrete state machine it should certainly be possible to discover by observation sufficient about it to predict its future behavior, and this within a reasonable time, say a thousand years. But this does not seem to be the case. I have set up on the Manchester computer a small program using only 1000 units of storage, whereby the machine supplied with one sixteen figure number replies with another within two seconds. I would defy anyone to learn from these replies sufficient about the program to be able to predict any replies to untried values. . . .

LEARNING MACHINES

The reader will have anticipated that I have no very convincing arguments of a positive nature to support my views. If I had I should not have taken such pains to point out the fallacies in contrary views. Such evidence as I have I shall now give.

Let us return for a moment to Lady Lovelace's objection, which stated that the machine can only do what we tell it to do. One could say that a man can "inject" an idea into the machine, and that it will respond to a certain extent and then drop into quiescence, like a piano string struck by a hammer. Another simile would be an atomic pile of less than critical size: an injected idea is to correspond to a neutron entering the pile from without. Each such neutron will cause a certain disturbance which eventually dies away. If, however, the size of the pile is sufficiently increased, the disturbance caused by such an incoming neutron will very likely go on and on, increasing until the whole pile is destroyed. Is there a corresponding phenomenon for minds, and is there one for machines? There does seem to be one for the human mind. The majority of them seem to be "subcritical", that is, to correspond in this analogy to piles of subcritical size. An idea presented to such a mind will on an average give rise to less than one idea in reply. A smallish proportion are supercritical. An idea presented to such a mind may give rise to a whole "theory" consisting of secondary, tertiary and more remote ideas. Animals' minds seem to be very definitely subcritical. Adhering to this analogy we ask, "Can a machine be made to be supercritical?"

The "skin of an onion" analogy is also helpful. In considering the functions of the mind or the brain we find certain operations which we can explain in purely mechanical terms. This we say does not correspond to the real mind: it is a sort of skin which we must strip off if we are to find the real mind. But then in what remains we find a further skin to be stripped off, and so on. Proceeding in this way, do we ever come to the "real" mind, or do we eventually come to the skin which has nothing in it? In the latter case the whole mind is mechanical. (It would not be a discrete state machine however. We have discussed this.)

These last two paragraphs do not claim to be convincing arguments. They should rather be described as "recitations tending to produce belief."

The only really satisfactory support that can be given for the view expressed at the beginning of [the preceding] section will be that provided by waiting for the end of the century and then doing the experiment described. But what can we say in the meantime? What steps should be taken now if the experiment is to be successful?

As I have explained, the problem is mainly one of programming. Advances in engineering will have to made too, but it seems unlikely that these will not be adequate for the requirements. . . .

In the process of trying to imitate an adult human mind we are bound to think a good deal about the process which has brought it to the state that it is in. We may notice three components:

(a) The initial state of the mind, say at birth;

(b) The education to which it has been subjected; and

(c) Other experience, not to be described as education, to which it has been subjected.

Instead of trying to produce a program to simulate the adult mind, why not rather try to produce one which simulates the child's? If this were then subjected to an appropriate course of education one would obtain the adult brain. Presumably the child-brain is something like a notebook as one buys it from the stationers. Rather little mechanism, and lots of blank sheets. (Mechanism and writing are from our point of view almost synonymous.) Our hope is that there is so little mechanism in the child-brain that something like it can be easily programmed. The amount of work in the education we can assume, as a first approximation, to be much the same as for the human child. . . .

It will not be possible to apply exactly the same teaching process to the machine as to a normal child. It will not, for instance, be provided with legs, so that it could not be asked to go out and fill the coal scuttle. Possibly it might not have eyes. But however well these deficiencies might be overcome by clever engineering, one could not send the creature to school without the other children making excessive fun of it. It must be given some tuition. We need not be too concerned about the legs, eyes, and so on. The example of Miss Helen Keller shows that education can take place provided that communication in both directions between teacher and pupil can take place by some means or other.

We normally associate punishments and rewards with the teaching process. Some simple child-machines can be constructed or programmed on this sort of principle. The machine has to be so constructed that events which shortly preceded the occurrence of a punishment-single are unlikely to be repeated, whereas a reward-signal increases the probability of repetition of the events which led up to it. These definitions do not presuppose any feelings on the part of the machine. I have done some experiments with one such child-machine, and succeeded in teaching it a few things, but the teaching method was too unorthodox for the experiment to be considered really successful.

The use of punishments and rewards can at best be a part of the teaching process. Roughly speaking, if the teacher has no other means of communicating to the pupil, the amount of information which can reach him does not exceed the total number of rewards and punishments applied. By the time a child has learned to repeat "Casablanca" he would probably feel very sore indeed, if the text could only be discovered by a "Twenty Questions" technique, every "No" taking the form of a blow. It is necessary therefore to have some other "unemotional" channels of communication. If these are available it is possible to teach a machine by punishments and rewards to obey orders given in some language, such as a symbolic language. These orders are to be transmitted through the "unemotional" channels. The use of this language will diminish greatly the number of punishments and rewards required. . . .

We may hope that machines will eventually compete with men in all purely intellectual fields. But which are the best ones to start with? Even this is a difficult decision. Many people think that a very abstract activity, like the playing of chess, would be best. It can also be maintained that it is best to provide the machine with the best sense organs that money can buy, and then teach it to understand and speak English. This process could follow the normal teaching of a child. Things would be pointed out and named, and so on. Again I do not know what the right answer is, but I think both approaches should be tried.

We can only see a short distance ahead, but we can see plenty there that needs to be done.

Minds, Brains, and Programs

JOHN R. SEARLE

John Searle has made important contributions to the philosophy of mind and the philosophy of language. He teaches at the University of California, Berkeley.

What psychological and philosophical significance should we attach to recent efforts at computer simulations of human cognitive capacities? In answering this question, I find it useful to distinguish what I will call "strong" AI from "weak" or "cautious" AI (artificial intelligence). According to weak AI, the principal value of the computer in the study of the mind is that it gives us a very powerful tool. For example, it enables us to formulate and test hypotheses in a more rigorous and precise fashion. But according to strong AI, the computer is not merely a tool in the study of the mind; rather, the appropriately programmed computer really *is* a mind, in the sense that computers given the right programs can be literally said to *understand* and have other cognitive states. In strong AI, because the programmed computer has cognitive states, the programs are not mere tools that enable us to test psychological explanations; rather, the programs are themselves the explanations.

I have no objection to the claims of weak AI, at least as far as this article is concerned. My discussion here will be directed at the claims I have defined as those of strong AI, specifically the claim that the appropriately programmed computer literally has cognitive states and that the programs thereby explain human cognition. When I hereafter refer to AI, I have in mind the strong version, as expressed by these two claims.

I will consider the work of Roger Schank and his colleagues at Yale (Schank and Abelson 1977), because I am more familiar with it than I am with any other similar claims, and because it provides a very clear example of the sort of work I wish to examine. But nothing that follows depends upon the details of Schank's programs. The same arguments would apply to Winograd's SHRDLU (Winograd 1973), Weizenbaum's ELIZA (Weizenbaum 1965), and indeed any Turing machine simulation of human mental phenomena. . . .

Very briefly, and leaving out the various details, one can describe Schank's program as follows: The aim of the program is to simulate the human ability to understand stories. It is characteristic of human beings' story-understanding capacity that they can answer questions about the story even though the information that they give was never explicitly stated in the story. Thus, for example, suppose you are given the following story: "A man went into a restaurant and ordered a hamburger. When the hamburger arrived it was burned to a crisp, and the man stormed out of the restaurant angrily, without paying for the hamburger or leaving a tip." Now, if you are asked "Did the man eat the hamburger?" you will presumably answer, "No, he did not." Similarly, if you are given the following story: "A man went into a restaurant and ordered a hamburger; when the hamburger came he was very pleased with it; and as he left the restaurant he gave the waitress a large tip before paying his bill," and you are asked the question, "Did the man eat the hamburger?" you will presumably answer, "Yes, he ate the hamburger." Now Schank's machines can similarly answer questions about restaurants in this fashion. To do this, they have a "representation" of the sort of information that human beings have about restaurants, which enables them to answer such questions as those above, given these sorts of stories. When the machine is given the story and then asked the question, the machine will print out answers of the sort that we would expect human beings to give if told similar stories. Partisans of strong AI claim that in this question and answer sequence the machine is not only simulating a human ability but also (1) that the machine can literally be said to *understand* the story and provide the answers to questions, and (2) that what the machine and its programs do *explains* the human ability to understand the story and answer questions about it.

Both claims seem to me to be totally unsupported by Schank's work, as I will attempt to show in what follows. I am not, of course, saying that Schank himself is committed to these claims.

One way to test any theory of the mind is to ask oneself what it would be like if my mind actually worked on the principles that the theory says all minds work on. Let us apply this test to the Schank program with the following *Gedankenexperiment.** Suppose that I'm locked in a room and given a large batch of Chinese writing. Suppose furthermore (as is indeed the case) that I know no Chinese, either written or spoken, and that I'm not even confident that I could recognize Chinese writing as Chinese writing distinct from, say, Japanese writing or meaningless squiggles. To me, Chinese writing is just so many meaningless squiggles. Now suppose further that after this first batch of Chinese writing I am given a second batch of Chinese script together with a set of rules for correlating the second batch with the first batch. The rules are in English, and I understand these rules as well as any other native speaker of English. They enable me to correlate one set of formal symbols with another set of formal symbols, and all that "formal" means here is that I can identify the symbols entirely by their shapes. Now suppose also that I am given a third batch of Chinese symbols together with some instructions, again in English, that enable me to correlate elements of this third batch with the first two batches, and these rules instruct me how to give back certain Chinese symbols with certain sorts of shapes in response to certain sorts of shapes given me in

the third batch. Unknown to me, the people who are giving me all of these symbols call the first batch a "script," they call the second batch a "story," and they call the third batch "questions." Furthermore, they call the symbols I give them back in response to the third batch "answers to the questions," and the set of rules in English that they gave me, they call the "program." Now just to complicate the story a little, imagine that these people also give me stories in English, which I understand, and they then ask me questions in English about these stories, and I give them back answers in English. Suppose also that after a while I get so good at following the instructions for manipulating the Chinese symbols and the programmers get so good at writing the programs that from the external point of view—that is, from the point of view of somebody outside the room in which I am locked—my answers to the questions are absolutely indistinguishable from those of native Chinese speakers. Nobody just looking at my answers can tell that I don't speak a word of Chinese. Let us also suppose that my answers to the English questions are, as they no doubt would be, indistinguishable from those of other native English speakers, for the simple reason that I am a native English speaker. From the external point of view—from the point of view of someone reading my "answers"—the answers to the Chinese questions and the English questions are equally good. But in the Chinese case, unlike the English case, I produce the answers by manipulating uninterpreted formal symbols. As far as the Chinese is concerned, I simply behave like a computer; I perform computational operations on formally specified elements. For the purposes of the Chinese, I am simply an instantiation of the computer program.

Now the claims made by strong AI are that the programmed computer understands the stories and that the program in some sense explains human understanding. But we are now in a position to examine these claims in light of our thought experiment.

1. As regards the first claim, it seems to me quite obvious in the example that I do not understand a word of the Chinese stories. I have inputs

---

*[Experiment in the imagination.—Ed.]

and outputs that are indistinguishable from those of the native Chinese speaker, and I can have any formal program you like, but I still understand nothing. For the same reasons, Schank's computer understands nothing of any stories, whether in Chinese, English, or whatever, since in the Chinese case the computer is me, and in cases where the computer is not me, the computer has nothing more than I have in the case where I understand nothing.

2. As regards the second claim, that the program explains human understanding, we can see that the computer and its program do not provide sufficient conditions of understanding since the computer and the program are functioning, and there is no understanding. But does it even provide a necessary condition or a significant contribution to understanding? One of the claims made by the supporters of strong AI is that when I understand a story in English, what I am doing is exactly the same—or perhaps more of the same—as what I was doing in manipulating the Chinese symbols. It is simply more formal symbol manipulation that distinguishes the case in English, where I do understand, from the case in Chinese, where I don't. I have not demonstrated that this claim is false, but it would certainly appear an incredible claim in the example. Such plausibility as the claim has derives from the supposition that we can construct a program that will have the same inputs and outputs as native speakers, and in addition we assume that speakers have some level of description where they are also instantiations of a program. On the basis of these two assumptions we assume that even if Schank's program isn't the whole story about understanding, it may be part of the story. Well, I suppose that is an empirical possibility, but not the slightest reason has so far been given to believe that it is true, since what is suggested—though certainly not demonstrated—by the example is that the computer program is simply irrelevant to my understanding of the story. In the Chinese case I have everything that artificial intelligence can put into me by way of a program, and I understand nothing; in the English case I understand everything, and there is so far no reason at all to suppose that my understanding has anything to do with computer programs, that is,

with computational operations on purely formally specified elements. As long as the program is defined in terms of computational operations on purely formally defined elements, what the example suggests is that these by themselves have no interesting connection with understanding. They are certainly not sufficient conditions, and not the slightest reason has been given to suppose that they are necessary conditions or even that they make a significant contribution to understanding. Notice that the force of the argument is not simply that different machines can have the same input and output while operating on different formal principles—that is not the point at all. Rather, whatever purely formal principles you put into the computer, they will not be sufficient for understanding, since a human will be able to follow the formal principles without understanding anything. No reason whatever has been offered to suppose that such principles are necessary or even contributory, since no reason has been given to suppose that when I understand English I am operating with any formal program at all.

Well, then, what is it that I have in the case of the English sentences that I do not have in the case of the Chinese sentences? The obvious answer is that I know what the former mean, while I haven't the faintest idea what the latter mean. But in what does this consist and why couldn't we give it to a machine, whatever it is? I will return to this question later, but first I want to continue with the example.

I have had the occasion to present this example to several workers in artificial intelligence, and, interestingly, they do not seem to agree on what the proper reply to it is. I get a surprising variety of replies, and in what follows I will consider the most common of these (specified along with their geographic origins).

But first I want to block some common misunderstandings about "understanding": In many of these discussions one finds a lot of fancy footwork about the word "understanding." My critics point out that there are many different degrees of understanding; that "understanding" is not a simple two-place predicate; that there are even different kinds and levels of understanding, and often the law of excluded middle doesn't even apply in a straightforward way to statements of the form "*x* understands *y*"; that in many cases it is a matter for decision and not a simple matter of fact whether *x* understands *y;* and so on. To all of these points I want to say: of course, of course. But they have nothing to do with the points at issue. There are clear cases in which "understanding" literally applies and clear cases in which it does not apply; and these two sorts of cases are all I need for this argument. I understand stories in English; to a lesser degree I can understand stories in French; to a still lesser degree, stories in German; and in Chinese, not at all. My car and my adding machine, on the other hand, understand nothing: they are not in that line of business.* We often attribute "understanding" and other cognitive predicates by metaphor and analogy to cars, adding machines, and other artifacts, but nothing is proved by such attributions. We say, "The door *knows* when to open because of its photoelectric cell," "The adding machine *knows how (understands how, is able)* to do addition and subtraction but not division," and "The thermostat *perceives* changes in the temperature." The reason we make these attributions is quite interesting, and it has to do with the fact that in artifacts we extend our own intentionality;† our tools are extensions of our purposes, and so we find it natural to make metaphorical attributions of intentionality to them; but I take it no philosophical ice is cut by such examples. The sense in which an automatic door "understands instructions" from its photoelectric cell is not at all the sense in which I understand English. If the sense in which Schank's programmed computers understand stories is supposed to be the metaphorical sense in which the door understands, and not the sense in which I understand English, the issue would not be worth discussing. But Newell and Simon (1963) write that the kind of cognition they claim for computers is exactly the same as for

human beings. I like the straightforwardness of this claim, and it is the sort of claim I will be considering. I will argue that in the literal sense the programmed computer understands what the car and the adding machine understand, namely, exactly nothing. The computer's understanding is not just (like my understanding of German) partial or incomplete; it is zero.

Now to the replies:

(1) *The Systems Reply (Berkeley, California)*. "While it is true that the individual person who is locked in the room does not understand the story, the fact is that he is merely part of a whole system, and the system does understand the story. The person has a large ledger in front of him in which are written the rules, he has a lot of scratch paper and pencils for doing calculations, he has "data banks" of sets of Chinese symbols. Now, understanding is not being ascribed to the mere individual; rather it is being ascribed to this whole system of which he is a part."

My response to the systems theory is quite simple: Let the individual internalize all of these elements of the system. He memorizes the rules in the ledger and the data banks of Chinese symbols, and he does all the calculations in his head. The individual then incorporates the entire system. There isn't anything at all to the system that he does not encompass. We can even get rid of the room and suppose he works outdoors. All the same, he understands nothing of the Chinese, and a fortiori neither does the system, because there isn't anything in the system that isn't in him. If he doesn't understand, then there is no way the system could understand because the system is just a part of him.

Actually I feel somewhat embarrassed to give even this answer to the systems theory because the theory seems to me so implausible to start with. The idea is that while a person doesn't understand Chinese, somehow the *conjunction* of that person and bits of paper might understand Chinese. It is not easy for me to imagine how someone who was not in the grip of an ideology would find the idea at all plausible. Still, I think many people who are committed to the ideology of strong AI will in the end be inclined to say something very much like this; so let us pursue

---

*Also, "understanding" implies both the possession of mental (intentional) states and the truth (validity, success) of these states. For the purposes of this discussion we are concerned only with the possession of the states.
†Intentionality is by definition that feature of certain mental states by which they are directed at or about objects and states of affairs in the world. Thus, beliefs, desires, and intentions are intentional states; undirected forms of anxiety and depression are not.

it a bit further. According to one version of this view, while the man in the internalized systems example doesn't understand Chinese in the sense that a native Chinese speaker does (because, for example, he doesn't know that the story refers to restaurants and hamburgers, etc.), still "the man as a formal symbol manipulation system" *really does understand Chinese*. The subsystem of the man that is the formal symbol manipulation system for Chinese should not be confused with the subsystem for English.

So there are really two subsystems in the man; one understands English, the other Chinese, and "it's just that the two systems have little to do with each other." But, I want to reply, not only do they have little to do with each other, they are not even remotely alike. The subsystem that understands English (assuming we allow ourselves to talk in this jargon of "subsystems" for a moment) knows that the stories are about restaurants and eating hamburgers, he knows that he is being asked questions about restaurants and that he is answering questions as best he can by making various inferences from the content of the story, and so on. But the Chinese system knows none of this. Whereas the English subsystem knows that "hamburgers" refers to hamburgers, the Chinese subsystem knows only that "squiggle squiggle" is followed by "squoggle squoggle." All he knows is that various formal symbols are being introduced at one end and manipulated according to rules written in English, and other symbols are going out at the other end. The whole point of the original example was to argue that such symbol manipulation by itself couldn't be sufficient for understanding Chinese in any literal sense because the man could write "squoggle squoggle" after "squiggle squiggle" without understanding anything in Chinese. And it doesn't meet that argument to postulate subsystems within the man, because the subsystems are no better off than the man was in the first place; they still don't have anything even remotely like what the English-speaking man (or subsystem) has. Indeed, in the case as described, the Chinese subsystem is simply a part of the English subsystem, a part that engages in meaningless symbol manipulation according to rules in English.

Let us ask ourselves what is supposed to motivate the systems reply in the first place; that is, what *independent* grounds are there supposed to be for saying that the agent must have a subsystem within him that literally understands stories in Chinese? As far as I can tell the only grounds are that in the example I have the same input and output as native Chinese speakers and a program that goes from one to the other. But the whole point of the examples has been to try to show that that couldn't be sufficient for understanding, in the sense in which I understand stories in English, because a person, and hence the set of systems that go to make up a person, could have the right combination of input, output, and program and still not understand anything in the relevant literal sense in which I understand English. The only motivation for saying there *must* be a subsystem in me that understands Chinese is that I have a program and I can pass the Turing test; I can fool native Chinese speakers. But precisely one of the points at issue is the adequacy of the Turing test. The example shows that there could be two "systems," both of which pass the Turing test, but only one of which understands; and it is no argument against this point to say that since they both pass the Turing test they must both understand, since this claim fails to meet the argument that the system in me that understands English has a great deal more than the system that merely processes Chinese. In short, the systems reply simply begs the question by insisting without argument that the system must understand Chinese.

Furthermore, the systems reply would appear to lead to consequences that are independently absurd. If we are to conclude that there must be cognition in me on the grounds that I have a certain sort of input and output and a program in between, then it looks like all sorts of noncognitive subsystems are going to turn out to be cognitive. For example, there is a level of description at which my stomach does information processing, and it instantiates any number of computer programs, but I take it we do not want to say that it has any understanding (cf. Pylyshyn 1980). But if we accept the systems reply, then it is hard to see how we avoid saying that stomach, heart, liver, and so on are all understanding subsystems, since there is no principled way to distinguish the motivation for saying the Chinese subsystem understands from saying that the stomach understands. It is, by the way, not an answer to this point to say that the Chinese system has information as input and output and the stomach has food and food products as input and output, since from the point of view of the agent, from my point of view, there is no information in either the food or the Chinese—the Chinese is just so many meaningless squiggles. The information in the Chinese case is solely in the eyes of the programmers and the interpreters, and there is nothing to prevent them from treating the input and output of my digestive organs as information if they so desire.

This last point bears on some independent problems in strong AI, and it is worth digressing for a moment to explain it. If strong AI is to be a branch of psychology, then it must be able to distinguish those systems that are genuinely mental from those that are not. It must be able to distinguish the principles on which the mind works from those on which nonmental systems work; otherwise it will offer us no explanations of what is specifically mental about the mental. And the mental-nonmental distinction cannot be just in the eye of the beholder but it must be intrinsic to the systems; otherwise it would be up to any beholder to treat people as nonmental and, for example, hurricanes as mental if he likes. But quite often in the AI literature the distinction is blurred in ways that would in the long run prove disastrous to the claim that AI is a cognitive inquiry. Mc Carthy, for example, writes, "Machines as simple as thermostats can be said to have beliefs, and having beliefs seems to be a characteristic of most machines capable of problem solving performance" (McCarthy 1979). Anyone who thinks strong AI has a chance as a theory of the mind ought to ponder the implications of that remark. We are asked to accept it as a discovery of strong AI that the hunk of metal on the wall that we use to regulate the temperature has beliefs in exactly the same sense that we, our spouses, and our children have beliefs, and furthermore that "most" of the other machines in the room—telephone, tape recorder, adding machine, electric light switch—also have beliefs

in this literal sense. It is not the aim of this article to argue against McCarthy's point, so I will simply assert the following without argument. The study of the mind starts with such facts as that humans have beliefs, while thermostats, telephones, and adding machines don't. If you get a theory that denies this point you have produced a counter-example to the theory and the theory is false. One gets the impression that people in AI who write this sort of thing think they can get away with it because they don't really take it seriously, and they don't think anyone else will either. I propose, for a moment at least, to take it seriously. Think hard for one minute about what would be necessary to establish that that hunk of metal on the wall over there had real beliefs, beliefs with direction of fit, propositional content, and conditions of satisfaction; beliefs that had the possibility of being strong beliefs or weak beliefs; nervous, anxious, or secure beliefs; dogmatic, rational, or superstitious beliefs; blind faiths or hesitant cogitations; any kind of beliefs. The thermostat is not a candidate. Neither is stomach, liver, adding machine, or telephone. However, since we are taking the idea seriously, notice that its truth would be fatal to strong AI's claim to be a science of the mind. For now the mind is everywhere. What we wanted to know is what distinguishes the mind from thermostats and livers. And if McCarthy were right, strong AI wouldn't have a hope of telling us that.

(2) The Robot Reply (Yale). "Suppose we wrote a different kind of program from Schank's program. Suppose we put a computer inside a robot, and this computer would not just take in formal symbols as input and give out formal symbols as output, but rather would actually operate the robot in such a way that the robot does something very much like perceiving, walking, moving about, hammering nails, eating, drinking—anything you like. The robot would, for example, have a television camera attached to it that enabled it to see, it would have arms and legs that enabled it to 'act,' and all of this would be controlled by its computer 'brain.' Such a robot would, unlike Schank's computer, have genuine understanding and other mental states."

The first thing to notice about the robot reply is that it tacitly concedes that cognition is not solely a matter of formal symbol manipulation, since this reply adds a set of causal relations with the outside world (cf. Fodor 1980). But the answer to the robot reply is that the addition of such "perceptual" and "motor" capacities adds nothing by way of understanding, in particular, or intentionality, in general, to Schank's original program. To see this, notice that the same thought experiment applies to the robot case. Suppose that instead of the computer inside the robot, you put me inside the room and, as in the original Chinese case, you give me more Chinese symbols with more instructions in English for matching Chinese symbols to Chinese symbols and feeding back Chinese symbols to the outside. Suppose, unknown to me, some of the Chinese symbols that come to me come from a television camera attached to the robot and other Chinese symbols that I am giving out serve to make the motors inside the robot move the robot's legs or arms. It is important to emphasize that all I am doing is manipulating formal symbols: I know none of these other facts. I am receiving "information" from the robot's "perceptual" apparatus, and I am giving out "instructions" to its motor apparatus without knowing either of these facts. I am the robot's homunculus, but unlike the traditional homunculus, I don't know what's going on. I don't understand anything except the rules for symbol manipulation. Now in this case I want to say that the robot has no intentional states at all; it is simply moving about as a result of its electrical wiring and its program. And furthermore, by instantiating the program I have no intentional states of the relevant type. All I do is follow formal instructions about manipulating formal symbols.

(3) *The Brain Simulator Reply (Berkeley and M.I.T.).* "Suppose we design a program that doesn't represent information that we have about the world, such as the information in Schank's scripts, but simulates the actual sequence of neuron firings at the synapses of the brain of a native Chinese speaker when he understands stories in Chinese and gives answers to them. The machine takes in Chinese stories and questions about them as input, it simulates the formal structure of actual Chinese brains in processing these stories, and it gives out Chinese answers as outputs. We can even imagine that the machine operates, not with a single serial program, but with a whole set of programs operating in parallel, in the manner that actual human brains presumably operate when they process natural language. Now surely in such a case we would have to say that the machine understood the stories; and if we refuse to say that, wouldn't we also have to deny that native Chinese speakers understood the stories? At the level of the synapses, what would or could be different about the program of the computer and the program of the Chinese brain?"

Before countering this reply I want to digress to note that it is an odd reply for any partisan of artificial intelligence (or functionalism, etc.) to make: I thought the whole idea of strong AI is that we don't need to know how the brain works to know how the mind works. The basic hypothesis, or so I had supposed, was that there is a level of mental operations consisting of computational processes over formal elements that constitute the essence of the mental and can be realized in all sorts of different brain processes, in the same way that any computer program can be realized in different computer hardwares: On the assumptions of strong AI, the mind is to the brain as the program is to the hardware, and thus we can understand the mind without doing neurophysiology. If we had to know how the brain worked to do AI, we wouldn't bother with AI. However, even getting this close to the operation of the brain is still not sufficient to produce understanding. To see this, imagine that instead of a monolingual man in a room shuffling symbols we have the man operate an elaborate set of water pipes with valves connecting them. When the man receives the Chinese symbols, he looks up in the program, written in English, which valves he has to turn on and off. Each water connection corresponds to a synapse in the Chinese brain, and the whole system is rigged up so that after doing all the right firings, that is after turning on all the right faucets, the Chinese answers pop out at the output end of the series of pipes.

Now where is the understanding in this system? It takes Chinese as input, it simulates the formal structure of the synapses of the Chinese brain, and it gives Chinese as output. But the man certainly doesn't understand Chinese, and neither do the water pipes, and if we are tempted to adopt what I think is the absurd view that somehow the *conjunction* of man *and* water pipes understands, remember that in principle the man can internalize the formal structure of the water pipes and do all the "neuron firings" in his imagination. The problem with the brain simulator is that it is simulating the wrong things about the brain. As long as it simulates only the formal structure of the sequence of neuron firings at the synapses, it won't have simulated what matters about the brain, namely its causal properties, its ability to produce intentional states. And that the formal properties are not sufficient for the causal properties is shown by the water pipe example: We can have all the formal properties carved off from the relevant neurobiological causal properties.

(4) *The Combination Reply (Berkeley and Stanford)*. "While each of the previous three replies might not be completely convincing by itself as a refutation of the Chinese room counterexample, if you take all three together they are collectively much more convincing and even decisive. Imagine a robot with a brain-shaped computer lodged in its cranial cavity, imagine the computer programmed with all the synapses of a human brain, imagine the whole behavior of the robot is indistinguishable from human behavior, and now think of the whole thing as a unified system and not just as a computer with inputs and outputs. Surely in such a case we would have to ascribe intentionality to the system."

I entirely agree that in such a case we would find it rational and indeed irresistible to accept the hypothesis that the robot had intentionality, as long as we knew nothing more about it. Indeed, besides appearance and behavior, the other elements of the combination are really irrelevant. If we could build a robot whose behavior was indistinguishable over a large range from human behavior, we would attribute intentionality to it, pending some reason not to.

We wouldn't need to know in advance that its computer brain was a formal analogue of the human brain.

But I really don't see that this is any help to the claims of strong AI, and here's why: According to strong AI, instantiating a formal program with the right input and output is a sufficient condition of, indeed is constitutive of, intentionality. As Newell (1979) puts it, the essence of the mental is the operation of a physical symbol system. But the attributions of intentionality that we make to the robot in this example have nothing to do with formal programs. They are simply based on the assumption that if the robot looks and behaves sufficiently like us, then we would suppose, until proven otherwise, that it must have mental states like ours that cause and are expressed by its behavior and it must have an inner mechanism capable of producing such mental states. If we knew independently how to account for its behavior without such assumptions we would not attribute intentionality to it, especially if we knew it had a formal program. And this is precisely the point of my earlier reply to objection II.

Suppose we knew that the robot's behavior was entirely accounted for by the fact that a man inside it was receiving uninterpreted formal symbols from the robot's sensory receptors and sending out uninterpreted formal symbols to its motor mechanisms, and the man was doing this symbol manipulation in accordance with a bunch of rules. Furthermore, suppose the man knows none of these facts about the robot; all he knows is which operations to perform on which meaningless symbols. In such a case we would regard the robot as an ingenious mechanical dummy. The hypothesis that the dummy has a mind would now be unwarranted and unnecessary, for there is now no longer any reason to ascribe intentionality to the robot or to the system of which it is a part (except of course for the man's intentionality in manipulating the symbols). The formal symbol manipulations go on, the input and output are correctly matched, but the only real locus of intentionality is the man, and he doesn't know any of the relevant intentional states; he doesn't, for example, *see* what comes into the robot's eyes, he doesn't *intend* to move the robot's arm, and he doesn't *understand* any of the remarks made to or by the robot. Nor, for the reasons stated earlier, does the system of which man and robot are a part.

To see this point, contrast this case with cases in which we find it completely natural to ascribe intentionality to members of certain other primate species such as apes and monkeys and to domestic animals such as dogs. The reasons we find it natural are, roughly, two: We can't make sense of the animal's behavior without the ascription of intentionality, and we can see that the beasts are made of similar stuff to ourselves—that is an eye, that a nose, this is its skin, and so on. Given the coherence of the animal's behavior and the assumption of the same causal stuff underlying it, we assume both that the animal must have mental states underlying its behavior, and that the mental states must be produced by mechanisms made out of the stuff that is like our stuff. We would certainly make similar assumptions about the robot unless we had some reason not to, but as soon as we knew that the behavior was the result of a formal program, and that the actual causal properties of the physical substance were irrelevant, we would abandon the assumption of intentionality.

There are two other responses to my example that come up frequently (and so are worth discussing) but really miss the point.

(5) *The Other Minds Reply (Yale)*. "How do you know that other people understand Chinese or anything else? Only by their behavior. Now the computer can pass the behavioral tests as well as they can (in principle), so if you are going to attribute cognition to other people you must in principle also attribute it to computers."

This objection really is only worth a short reply. The problem in this discussion is not about how I know that other people have cognitive states, but rather what it is that I am attributing to them when I attribute cognitive states to them. The thrust of the argument is that it couldn't be just computational processes and their output because the computational processes and their output can exist without the cognitive state. It is no answer to this argument to feign anesthesia. In "cognitive sciences" one

presupposes the reality and knowability of the mental in the same way that in physical sciences one has to presuppose the reality and knowability of physical objects.

(6) *The Many Mansions Reply (Berkeley)*. "Your whole argument presupposes that AI is only about analog and digital computers. But that just happens to be the present state of technology. Whatever these causal processes are that you say are essential for intentionality (assuming you are right), eventually we will be able to build devices that have these causal processes, and that will be artificial intelligence. So your arguments are in no way directed at the ability of artificial intelligence to produce and explain cognition."

I really have no objection to this reply save to say that it in effect trivializes the project of strong AI by redefining it as whatever artificially produces and explains cognition. The interest of the original claim made on behalf of artificial intelligence is that it was a precise, well defined thesis: Mental processes are computational processes over formally defined elements. I have been concerned to challenge that thesis. If the claim is redefined so that it is no longer that thesis, my objections no longer apply because there is no longer a testable hypothesis for them to apply to.

Let us now return to the question I promised I would try to answer: Granted that in my original example I understand the English and I do not understand the Chinese, and granted therefore that the machine doesn't understand either English or Chinese, still there must be something about me that makes it the case that I understand English and a corresponding something lacking in me that makes it the case that I fail to understand Chinese. Now why couldn't we give those somethings, whatever they are, to a machine?

I see no reason in principle why we couldn't give a machine the capacity to understand English or Chinese, since in an important sense our bodies with our brains are precisely such machines. But I do see very strong arguments for saying that we could not give such a thing to a machine where the operation of the machine is defined solely in terms of computational processes over formally defined elements; that is, where the operation of the machine is defined as an instantiation of a computer program. It is not because I am the instantiation of a computer program that I am able to understand English and have other forms of intentionality (I am, I suppose, the instantiation of any number of computer programs), but as far as we know it is because I am a certain sort of organism with a certain biological (i.e., chemical and physical) structure, and this structure, under certain conditions, is causally capable of producing perception, action, understanding, learning, and other intentional phenomena. And part of the point of the present argument is that only something that had those causal powers could have that intentionality. Perhaps other physical and chemical processes could produce exactly these effects; perhaps, for example, Martians also have intentionality but their brains are made of different stuff. That is an empirical question, rather like the question whether photosynthesis can be done by something with a chemistry different from that of chlorophyll.

But the main point of the present argument is that no purely formal model will ever be sufficient by itself for intentionality because the formal properties are not by themselves constitutive of intentionality, and they have by themselves no causal powers except the power, when instantiated, to produce the next stage of the formalism when the machine is running. And any other causal properties that particular realizations of the formal model have are irrelevant to the formal model because we can always put the same formal model in a different realization where those causal properties are obviously absent. Even if, by some miracle, Chinese speakers exactly realize Schank's program, we can put the same program in English speakers, water pipes, or computers, none of which understand Chinese, the program notwithstanding.

What matters about brain operations is not the formal shadow cast by the sequence of synapses but rather the actual properties of the sequences. All the arguments for the strong version of artificial intelligence that I have seen insist on drawing an outline around the shadows cast by cognition and then claiming that the shadows are the real thing.

By way of concluding I want to try to state some of the general philosophical points implicit in the argument. For clarity I will try to do it in a question-and-answer fashion, and I begin with that old chestnut of a question:

"Could a machine think?"

The answer is, obviously, yes. We are precisely such machines.

"Yes, but could an artifact, a man-made machine, think?"

Assuming it is possible to produce artificially a machine with a nervous system, neurons with axons and dendrites, and all the rest of it, sufficiently like ours, again the answer to the question seems to be obviously, yes. If you can exactly duplicate the causes, you could duplicate the effects. And indeed it might be possible to produce consciousness, intentionality, and all the rest of it using some other sorts of chemical principles than those that human beings use. It is, as I said, an empirical question.

"OK, but could a digital computer think?"

If by "digital computer" we mean anything at all that has a level of description where it can correctly be described as the instantiation of a computer program, then again the answer is, of course, yes, since we are the instantiations of any number of computer programs, and we can think.

"But could something think, understand, and so on *solely* by virtue of being a computer with the right sort of program? Could instantiating a program, the right program of course, by itself be a sufficient condition of understanding?"

This I think is the right question to ask, though it is usually confused with one or more of the earlier questions, and the answer to it is no.

"Why not?"

Because the formal symbol manipulations by themselves don't have any intentionality; they are quite meaningless; they aren't even *symbol* manipulations, since the symbols don't symbolize anything. In the linguistic jargon, they have only a syntax but no semantics. Such intentionality as computers appear to have is solely in the minds of those who program them and those who use them, those who send in the input and those who interpret the output.

The aim of the Chinese room example was to try to show this by showing that as soon as we put something into the system that really does have intentionality (a man), and we program him with the formal program, you can see that the formal program carries no additional intentionality. It adds nothing, for example, to a man's ability to understand Chinese.

Precisely that feature of AI that seemed so appealing—the distinction between the program and the realization—proves fatal to the claim that simulation could be duplication. The distinction between the program and its realization in the hardware seems to be parallel to the distinction between the level of mental operations and the level of brain operations. And if we could describe the level of mental operations as a formal program, then it seems we could describe what was essential about the mind without doing either introspective psychology or neurophysiology of the brain. But the equation "mind is to brain as program is to hardware" breaks down at several points, among them the following three:

First, the distinction between program and realization has the consequence that the same program could have all sorts of crazy realizations that had no form of intentionality. Weizenbaum (1976, Ch. 2), for example, shows in detail how to construct a computer using a roll of toilet paper and a pile of small stones. Similarly, the Chinese story understanding-program can be programmed into a sequence of water pipes, a set of wind machines, or a monolingual English speaker, none of which thereby acquires an understanding of Chinese. Stones, toilet paper, wind, and water pipes are the wrong kind of stuff to have intentionality in the first place—only something that has the same causal powers as brains can have intentionality—and though the English speaker has the right kind of stuff for intentionality you can easily see that he doesn't get any extra intentionality by memorizing the program, since memorizing it won't teach him Chinese.

Second, the program is purely formal, but the intentional states are not in that way formal. They are defined in terms of their content, not their form. The belief that it is raining, for example, is not defined as a certain formal shape, but as a certain mental content with conditions of satisfaction, a direction of fit (see Searle 1979), and

the like. Indeed the belief as such hasn't even got a formal shape in this syntactic sense, since one and the same belief can be given an indefinite number of different syntactic expressions in different linguistic systems.

Third, as I mentioned before, mental states and events are literally a product of the operation of the brain, but the program is not in that way a product of the computer.

"Well if programs are in no way constitutive of mental processes, why have so many people believed the converse? That at least needs some explanation."

I don't really know the answer to that one. The idea that computer simulations could be the real thing ought to have seemed suspicious in the first place because the computer isn't confined to simulating mental operations, by any means. No one supposes that computer simulations of a five-alarm fire will burn the neighborhood down or that a computer simulation of a rainstorm will leave us all drenched. Why on earth would anyone suppose that a computer simulation of understanding actually understood anything? It is sometimes said that it would be frightfully hard to get computers to feel pain or fall in love, but love and pain are neither harder nor easier than cognition or anything else. For simulation, all you need is the right input and output and a program in the middle that transforms the former into the latter. That is all the computer has for anything it does. To confuse simulation with duplication is the same mistake, whether it is pain, love, cognition, fires, or rainstorms.

Still, there are several reasons why AI must have seemed—and to many people perhaps still does seem—in some way to reproduce and thereby explain mental phenomena, and I believe we will not succeed in removing these illusions until we have fully exposed the reasons that give rise to them.

First, and perhaps most important, is a confusion about the notion of "information processing": Many people in cognitive science believe that the human brain, with its mind, does something called "information processing," and analogously the computer with its program does information processing; but fires and rainstorms, on the other hand, don't do information processing at all. Thus, though the computer can simulate the formal features of any process whatever, it stands in a special relation to the mind and brain because when the computer is properly programmed, ideally with the same program as the brain, the information processing is identical in the two cases, and this information processing is really the essence of the mental. But the trouble with this argument is that it rests on an ambiguity in the notion of "information." In the sense in which people "process information" when they reflect, say, on problems in arithmetic or when they read and answer questions about stories, the programmed computer does not do "information processing." Rather, what it does is manipulate formal symbols. The fact that the programmer and the interpreter of the computer output use the symbols to stand for objects in the world is totally beyond the scope of the computer. The computer, to repeat, has a syntax but no semantics. Thus, if you type into the computer "2 plus 2 equals?" it will type out "4." But it has no idea that "4" means 4 or that it means anything at all. And the point is not that it lacks some second-order information about the interpretation of its first-order symbols, but rather that its first-order symbols don't have any interpretations as far as the computer is concerned. All the computer has is more symbols. The introduction of the notion of "information processing" therefore produces a dilemma: Either we construe the notion of "information processing" in such a way that it implies intentionality as part of the process or we don't. If the former, then the programmed computer does not do information processing: it only manipulates formal symbols. If the latter, then, though the computer does information processing, it is only doing so in the sense in which adding machines, typewriters, stomachs, thermostats, rainstorms, and hurricanes do information processing; namely, they have a level of description at which we can describe them as taking information in at one end, transforming it, and producing information as output. But in this case it is up to outside observers to interpret the input and output as information in the ordinary sense. And no similarity is established between the computer and the brain in terms of any similarity of information processing.

Second, in much of AI there is a residual behaviorism or operationalism. Since appropriately programmed computers can have input-output patterns similar to those of human beings, we are tempted to postulate mental states in the computer similar to human mental states. But once we see that it is both conceptually and empirically possible for a system to have human capacities in some realm without having any intentionality at all, we should be able to overcome this impulse. My desk adding machine has calculating capacities, but no intentionality, and in this paper I have tried to show that a system could have input and output capabilities that duplicated those of a native Chinese speaker and still not understand Chinese, regardless of how it was programmed. The Turing test is typical of the tradition in being unashamedly behavioristic and operationalistic, and I believe that if AI workers totally repudiated behaviorism and operationalism much of the confusion between simulation and duplication would be eliminated.

Third, this residual operationalism is joined to a residual form of dualism; indeed strong AI only makes sense given the dualistic assumption that, where the mind is concerned, the brain doesn't matter. In strong AI (and in functionalism, as well) what matters are programs, and programs are independent of their realization in machines; indeed, as far as AI is concerned, the same program could be realized by an electronic machine, a Cartesian mental substance, or a Hegelian world spirit. The single most surprising discovery that I have made in discussing these issues is that many AI workers are quite shocked by my idea that actual human mental phenomena might be dependent on actual physical-chemical properties of actual human brains. But if you think about it a minute you can see that I should not have been surprised; for unless you accept some form of dualism, the strong AI project hasn't got a chance. The project is to reproduce and explain the mental by designing programs, but unless the mind is not only conceptually but empirically independent of the brain you couldn't carry out the project, for the program is completely independent of any realization. Unless you believe that the mind is separable from the brain both conceptually and empirically—dualism in a strong form—you cannot hope to reproduce the mental by writing and running programs since programs must be independent of brains or any other particular forms of instantiation. If mental operations consist in computational operations on formal symbols, then it follows that they have no interesting connection with the brain; the only connection would be that the brain just happens to be one of the indefinitely many types of machines capable of instantiating the program. This form of dualism is not the traditional Cartesian variety that claims there are two sorts of *substances,* but it is Cartesian in the sense that it insists that what is specifically mental about the mind has no intrinsic connection wit the actual properties of the brain. This underlying dualism is masked from us by the fact that AI literature contains frequent fulminations against "dualism"; what the authors seem to be unaware of is that their position presupposes a strong version of dualism.

"Could a machine think?" My own view is that *only* a machine could think, and indeed only very special kinds of machines, namely brains and machines that had the same causal powers as brains. And that is the main reason strong AI has had little to tell us about thinking, since it has nothing to tell us about machines. By its own definition, it is about programs, and programs are not machines. Whatever else intentionality is, it is a biological phenomenon, and it is as likely to be as causally dependent on the specific biochemistry of its origins as lactation, photosynthesis, or any other biological phenomena. No one would suppose that we could produce milk and sugar by running a computer simulation of the formal sequences in lactation and photosynthesis, but where the mind is concerned many people are willing to believe in such a miracle because of a deep and abiding dualism: The mind they suppose is a matter of formal processes and is independent of quite specific material causes in the way that milk and sugar are not.

In defense of this dualism the hope is often expressed that the brain is a digital computer (early computers, by the way, were often called "electronic brains"). But that is no help. Of course the brain is a digital computer. Since everything is a digital computer, brains are too. The point is that the brain's causal capacity to produce intentionality cannot consist in its instantiating a computer program, since for any program you like it is possible for something to instantiate that program and still not have any mental states. Whatever it is that the brain does to produce intentionality, it cannot consist in instantiating a program since no program, by itself, is sufficient for intentionality.*

---

*I am indebted to a rather large number of people for discussion of these matters and for their patient attempts to overcome my ignorance of artificial intelligence. I would especially like to thank Ned Block, Hubert Dreyfus, John Haugeland, Roger Schank, Robert Wilensky, and Terry Winograd.

Robots and Minds[1]

WILLIAM G. LYCAN

William G. Lycan teaches philosophy at the University of North Carolina, Chapel Hill.

Artificial Intelligence is, very crudely, the science of getting machines to perform jobs that normally require intelligence and judgment. Researchers at any number of AI labs have designed machines that prove mathematical theorems, play chess, sort mail, guide missiles, assemble auto engines, diagnose illnesses, read stories and other written texts, and converse with people

---

From William G. Lycan, *Consciousness* (Cambridge, MA: A Bradford Book, 1987), pp. 123–130. Reprinted by permission of the publisher, MIT Press.

in a rudimentary way. This is, we might say, intelligent behavior.

But what is this "intelligence"? As a first pass, I suggest that intelligence of the sort I am talking about is a kind of flexibility, a responsiveness to contingencies. A dull or stupid machine must have just the right kind of raw materials presented to it in just the right way, or it is useless: the electric can opener must have an appropriately sized can fixed under its drive wheel *just so,* in order to operate at all. Humans (most of us, anyway) are not like that. We deal with the unforeseen. We take what comes and make the best of it, even though we may have had no idea what it would be. We play the ball from whatever lie we are given, and at whatever angle to the green; we read and understand texts we have never seen before; we find our way back to Chapel Hill after getting totally lost in downtown Durham (or downtown Washington, D.C., or downtown Lima, Peru).

Our pursuit of our goals is guided while in progress by our ongoing perception and handling of interim developments. Moreover, we can pursue any number of different goals at the same time, and balance them against each other. We are sensitive to contingencies, both external and internal, that have a very complex and unsystematic structure.

It is almost irresistible to speak of *information* here, even if the term were not as trendy as it is. An intelligent creature, I want to say, is an *information-sensitive* creature, one that not only *registers* information through receptors such as senseorgans but somehow stores and manages and finally uses that information. Higher animals are intelligent beings in this sense, and so are we, even though virtually nothing is known about how we organize or manage the vast, seething profusion of information that comes our way. And there is one sort of machine that is information-sensitive also: the digital computer. A computer *is* a machine specifically designed to be fed complexes of information, to store them, manage them, and produce appropriate theoretical or practical conclusions on demand. Thus, if artificial intelligence is what one is looking for, it is no accident that one looks to the computer.

Yet a computer has two limitations in common with machines of less elite and grandiose sorts, both of them already signaled in the characterization I have just given. First, a (present-day) computer must be *fed* information, and the choice of what information to feed and in what form is up to a human programmer or operator. (For that matter, a present-day computer must be plugged into an electrical outlet and have its switch turned to ON, but this is a very minor contingency given the availability of nuclear power packs.) Second, the *appropriateness* and effectiveness of a computer's output depends entirely on what the programmer or operator had in mind and goes on to make of it. A computer has intelligence in the sense I have defined, but has no judgment, since it has no goals and purposes of its own and no internal sense of appropriateness, relevance, or proportion.

For essentially these reasons—that computers are intelligent in my minimal sense, and that they are nevertheless limited in the two ways I have mentioned—AI theorists, philosophers, and intelligent laymen have inevitably compared computers to human minds, but at the same time debated both technical and philosophical questions raised by this comparison. The questions break down into three main groups or types: (A) Questions of the form "Will a computer ever be able to do *X*?" where *X* is something that intelligent humans can do. (B) Questions of the form "Given that a computer can or could do *X,* have we any reason to think that it does *X* in the same way that humans do *X?*" (C) Questions of the form "Given that some futuristic supercomputer were able to do *X, Y, Z, . . . ,* for some arbitrarily large range and variety of human activities, would that show that the computer had property *P?*" where *P* is some feature held to be centrally, vitally characteristic of human minds, such as thought, consciousness, feeling, sensation, emotion, creativity, or freedom of the will.

Questions of type A are empirical questions and cannot be settled without decades, perhaps centuries, of further research—compare ancient and medieval speculations on the question of whether a machine could ever fly. Questions of type B are brutely empirical too, and their answers are unavailable to AI researchers *per se,* lying squarely in the domain of cognitive psychology, a science or alleged science barely into its infancy. Questions of type C are philosophical and conceptual, and so I shall essay to answer them all at one stroke.

Let us begin by supposing that all questions of types A and B have been settled affirmatively—that one day we might be confronted by a muchimproved version of Hal, the soft-spoken computer in Kubrick's *2001* (younger readers may substitute Star Wars' C3PO or whatever subsequent cinematic robot is the most lovable). Let us call this more versatile machine "Harry."[2] Harry (let us say) is humanoid in form—he is a miracle of miniaturization and has lifelike plastic skin—and he can converse intelligently on all sorts of subjects, play golf *and* the viola, write passable poetry, control his occasional nervousness pretty well, make love, prove mathematical theorems (of course), show envy when outdone, throw gin bottles at annoying children, etc., etc. We may suppose he fools people into thinking he is human. Now the question is, is Harry really a *person*? Does he have thoughts, feelings, and so on? Is he actually conscious, or is he just a mindless walking hardware store whose movements are astoundingly *like* those of a person?[3]

Plainly his acquaintances would tend from the first to see him as a person, even if they were aware of his dubious antecedents. I think it is a plain psychological fact, if nothing more, that we could not help treating him as a person, unless we resolutely made up our minds, on principle, not to give him the time of day. But how could we really tell that he is conscious?

Well, how do we really tell that any humanoid creature is conscious? How do you tell that I am conscious, and how do I tell that you are? Surely we tell, and decisively, on the basis of our standard behavioral tests for mental states, to revert to [an earlier theme of this book]: We know that a human being has such-and-such mental states when it behaves, to speak very generally, in the ways we take to be appropriate to organisms that are in those states. (The point is of course an epistemological one only, no metaphysical implications intended or tolerated.) We know for practical purposes that a creature has a mind when it fulfills all the right criteria. And by

hypothesis, Harry fulfills all our behavioral criteria with a vengeance; moreover, he does so *in the right way* (cf. questions of type B): the processing that stands causally behind his behavior is just like ours. It follows that we are at least *prima facie* justified in believing him to be conscious.

We have not *proved* that he is conscious, of course—any more than you have proved that I am conscious. An organism's merely behaving in a certain way is no logical guarantee of sentience; from my point of view it is at least imaginable, a bare logical possibility, that my wife, my daughter, and my chairman are not conscious, even though I have excellent, overwhelming behavioral reason to think that they are. But for that matter, our "standard behavioral tests" for mental states yield practical or moral certainty only so long as the situation is not palpably extraordinary or bizarre. A human chauvinist—in this case, someone who denies that Harry has thoughts and feelings, joys and sorrows—thinks precisely that Harry is as bizarre as they come. But *what is bizarre about him?* There are quite a few chauvinist answers to this, but what they boil down to, and given our hypothesized facts all they could boil down to, are two differences between Harry and ourselves: his *origin* (a laboratory is not a proper mother), and the *chemical composition of his anatomy,* if his creator has used silicon instead of carbon, for example. To exclude him from our community for either or both of *those* reasons seems to me to be a clear case of racial or ethnic prejudice (literally) and nothing more. I see no obvious way in which either a creature's origin or its subneuroanatomical chemical composition should matter to its psychological processes or any aspect of its mentality.

My argument can be reinforced by a thought experiment. . . . Imagine that we take a normal human being, Henrietta, and begin gradually replacing parts of her with synthetic materials—first a few prosthetic limbs, then a few synthetic arteries, then some neural fibers, and so forth. Suppose that the surgeons who perform the successive operations (particularly the neurosurgeons) are so clever and skillful that Henrietta survives in fine style: her intelligence, personality, perceptual acuity, poetic abilities, etc., remain just as they were before. But after the replacement process has eventually gone on to completion, Henrietta will have become an artifact—at least, her body will then be nothing but a collection of artifacts. Did she lose consciousness at some point during the sequence of operations, despite her continuing to behave and respond normally? When? It is hard to imagine that there is some privileged portion of the human nervous system that is for some reason indispensable, even though kidneys, lungs, heart, and any given bit of brain could in principle be replaced by a prosthesis (for *what* reason?); and it is also hard to imagine that there is some *propor*-tion of the nervous system such that removal of more than that proportion causes loss of con-sciousness or sentience despite perfect mainte-nance of all intelligent capacities.

If this quick but totally compelling defense of Harry and Henrietta's personhood is correct, then the two, and their ilk, will have not only mental lives like ours, but *moral* lives like ours, and moral rights and privileges accordingly. Just as ori-gin and physical constitution fail to affect psycho-logical personhood, if a creature's internal organization is sufficiently like ours, so do they fail to affect moral personhood. We do not dis-criminate against a person who has a wooden leg, or a mechanical kidney, or a nuclear heart regula-tor; no more should we deny any human or civil right to Harry or Henrietta on grounds of their origin or physical makeup, which they cannot help.

But this happy egalitarianism raises a more immediate question: *In real life,* we shall soon be faced with medium-grade machines, which have some intelligence and are not "mere" machines like refrigerators or typewriters but which fall far short of flawless human stimulators like Harry. For AI researchers may well build machines that will appear to have some familiar mental capacities but not others. The most obvi-ous example is that of a sensor or perceptron, which picks up information from its immediate environment, records it, and stores it in memory for future printout. (We already have at least crude machines of this kind. When they become versatile and sophisticated enough, it will be quite natural to say that they see or hear and that they remember.) But the possibility of "spe-cialist" machines of this kind raises an unforeseen contingency: There is an enormous and many-dimensional range of possible beings in between

our current "mere" machines and our fully devel-oped, flawless human simulators; we have not even begun to think of all the infinitely possible variations on this theme. And once we do begin to think of these hard cases, we will be at a loss as to where to draw the "personhood" line between them. How complex, eclectic, and impressive must a machine be, and in what respects, before we award it the accolade of per-sonhood and/or of consciousness? There is, to say the least, no clear answer to be had *a priori,* Descartes' notorious view of animals to the con-trary notwithstanding.*

This typical philosophical question would be no more than an amusing bonbon, were it not for the attending moral conundrum: What moral rights would an intermediate or marginally intel-ligent machine have? Adolescent machines of this sort will confront us much sooner than will any good human simulators, for they are easier to design and construct; more to the moral point, they will be designed mainly as *labor-saving de-vices,* as servants who will work for free, and ser-vants of this kind are (literally) made to be exploited. If they are intelligent to any degree, we should have qualms in proportion.

I suggest that this moral problem, which may become a real and pressing one, is parallel to the current debate over animal rights. Luckily I have never wanted to cook and eat my Compaq Portable.

Suppose I am right about the irrelevance of biochemical constitution to psychology; and sup-pose I was also right about the coalescing of the notions *computation, information, intelligence.* Then our mentalized theory of computation sug-gests in turn a computational theory of mentality, and a computational picture of the place of human beings in the world. In fact, philosophy aside, that picture has already begun to get a grip on people's thinking—as witness the filtering down of com-puter jargon into contemporary casual speech—and that grip is not going to loosen. Computer science is the defining technology of our time, and in this sense the computer is the natural

---

*Descartes claimed in his *Discourse on Method* that animals are mere machines.

cultural successor to the steam engine, the clock, the spindle, and the potter's wheel.[4] Predictably, an articulate computational theory of the mind has also gained credence among professional psychologists and philosophers.[5] I have been trying to support it here and elsewhere; I shall say no more about it for now, save to note again its near-indispensability in accounting for intentionality (noted), and to address the ubiquitous question of computer creativity and freedom:

Soft Determinism* or **Libertarianism*** may be true of humans. But many people have far more rigidly deterministic intuitions about computers. Computers, after all, (let us all say it together:) "only do what they are told/programmed to do"; they have no spontaneity and no freedom of choice. But human beings choose all the time, and the ensuing states of the world often depend entirely on these choices.[6] Thus the "computer analogy" supposedly fails.

The alleged failure of course depends on what we think freedom really is. As a Soft Determinist, I think that to have freedom of choice in acting is (roughly) for one's action to proceed out of one's own desires, deliberation, will, and intention, rather than being compelled or coerced by external forces regardless of my desires or will. As before, free actions are not *uncaused* actions. My free actions are those that *I* cause, i.e., that are caused by my own mental processes rather than by something pressing on me from the outside. I have argued...that I am free in that my beliefs, desires, deliberations, and intentions are all functional or computational states and processes within me that do interact in characteristic ways to produce my behavior. Note now that the same response vindicates our skilled human-simulating machines from the charge of puppethood. The word "robot" is often used as a veritable synonym for "puppet," so it may seem that Harry and Henrietta are paradigm cases of *un*free mechanisms that "only do what they are programmed to do." This is a slander—for two reasons:

First, even an ordinary computer, let alone a fabulously sophisticated machine like Harry, is in a way unpredictable. You are at its mercy. You *think* you know what it is going to do; you know what it should do, what it is supposed to do, but there is no guarantee—and it may do something *awful* or at any rate something that you could not have predicted and could not figure out if you tried with both hands. This practical sort of unpredictability would be multiplied a thousandfold in the case of a machine as complex as the human brain, and it is notably characteristic of *people*.

The unpredictability has several sources. (i) Plain old physical defects, as when Harry's circuits have been damaged by trauma, stress, heat, or the like. (ii) Bugs in one or more of his programs. (I have heard that once upon a time, somewhere, a program was written that had not a single bug in it, but this is probably an urban folk tale.) (iii) Randomizers, quantum-driven or otherwise; elements of Harry's behavior may be *genuinely,* physically random. (iv) Learning and analogy mechanisms; if Harry is equipped with these, as he inevitably would be, then his behavior-patterns will be modified in response to his experiential input from the world, which would be neither controlled nor even observed by us. *We don't know where he's been.* (v) The relativity of reliability to goal-description. This last needs a bit of explanation.

People often say things like, "A computer just crunches binary numbers; provided it isn't broken, it just chugs on mindlessly through whatever flipflop settings are predetermined by its electronic makeup." But such remarks ignore the multileveled character of real computer programming. At any given time, as we have noted [earlier], a computer is running *each of any number of* programs, depending on how it is described and on the level of functional organization that interests us. True, it is always crunching binary numbers, but in crunching them it is also doing any number of more esoteric things. And (more to the point) what counts as a mindless, algorithmic procedure at a very low level of organization may constitute, at a higher level, a hazardous do-or-die heuristic that might either succeed brilliantly or (more likely) fail and leave its objective unfulfilled.

As a second defense, remember that Harry too has beliefs, desires, and intentions (provided

---

*See Part 4 for detailed discussions (and definitions) of these doctrines.

my original argument is sound). If this is so, then his behavior normally proceeds out of his own mental processes rather than being externally compelled; and so he satisfies the definition of freedom-of-action formulated above. In most cases it will be appropriate to say that Harry could have done other than what he did do (but in fact chose after some ratiocination to do what he did, instead). Harry acts in the same sense as that in which we act, though one might continue to quarrel over what sense that is.

Probably the most popular remaining reason for doubt about machine consciousness has to do with the raw qualitative character of experience. Could a mere bloodless runner-of-programs have states that *feel to it* in any of the various dramatic ways in which our mental states feel to us?

The latter question is usually asked rhetorically, expecting a resounding answer "NO!!" But I do not hear it rhetorically, for I do not see why the negative answer is supposed to be at all obvious, even for machines as opposed to biologic humans. Of course there is an incongruity *from our human point of view* between human feeling and printed circuitry or silicon pathways; that is to be expected, since we are considering those high-tech items from an external, third-person perspective and at the same time comparing them to our own first-person feels. But argumentatively, that *Gestalt* phenomenon counts for no more in the present case than it did in that of human consciousness, viz., for nothing, especially if my original argument about Harry was successful in showing that biochemical constitution is irrelevant to psychology. What matters to mentality is not the stuff of which one is made, but the complex way in which that stuff is organized.[7] If after years of close friendship we were to open Harry up and find that he is stuffed with microelectronic gadgets instead of protoplasm, we would be taken aback—no question. But our *Gestalt* clash on the occasion would do nothing *at all* to show that Harry does not have his own rich inner qualitative life. If an objector wants to insist that computation alone cannot provide consciousness with its qualitative character, the objector will have to take the initiative and come up with a further, substantive argument to show why not.[8] We have already seen

that such arguments have failed wretchedly for the case of humans; I see no reason to suspect that they would work any better for the case of robots. We must await further developments. But at the present stage of inquiry I see no compelling feel-based objection to the hypothesis of machine consciousness.

NOTES

1. The material in this appendix was first presented as part of the John Ingram Forry Lecture at Amherst College, in 1985. I am very grateful to Jay Garfield and to Lee Bowie for their penetrating formal commentaries on that occasion, which I shall be answering in the (eventually to be) published proceedings of the event.

2. Harry has appeared before, in Lycan (1985). The next four paragraphs are lifted almost *verbatim* from that article.

3. It is interesting that children seem instinctively to reject the hypothesis of machine consciousness, usually on the grounds that computers are not alive. (One day when my daughter Jane was three years old, we were fooling with some piece of software or other, and I quite unreflectively remarked "It thinks you want it to [do such-and-such]." She did an enormous take, and then replied, "Computers can't think!—Is that 'just an expression'??")

4. I borrow the term "defining technology," and the examples, from Jay Bolter (1984).

5. The computational picture of mentality is by no means new. For one thing, the idea of mechanical intelligence goes back to the seventeenth century at least, long before Charles Babbage's celebrated Analytical Engine. And the computer model of the mind received a decisive boost from the McCullough-Pitts model of the neuron (1947), according to which a neuron is nothing but a little on-off device, that either *fires* or does not. If a brain is just an organized collection of neurons, and a neuron is just an on-off switch, it follows *straightway* that a brain is a digital computer and anything interesting that it does is a computation over binary formulas. Thus a human being is not only a featherless biped, a rational animal, and the only creature on earth that laughs, but the only computing machine on earth that is made by unskilled labor.

The McCullough-Pitts model is no longer current (no pun intended): neurons are now known to be very complicated little agents, not mere on-off switches. But the computational picture of mentality still receives strong encouragement from other quarters. It has two separate philosophical motivations, in particular, the first of which I have already noted: It exploits and explains the coalescence of the notions of computation, information, and intelligence. The computer is the only thing in the world that displays potential intelligence *and* whose workings are well understood. It is the only answer we currently know to the question: By what means *could* Mother Nature have crafted an intelligent being (in our sense of responsiveness to contingencies) out of nothing but a large bunch of individually insensate biological cells? To deny that there may be other answers would be presumptuous at best, and there are plenty of human capacities that do not seem to admit of computational simulation in any way at all—but anyone who manages to think up a genuinely distinct alternative to the digital-computer paradigm will have achieved a major conceptual breakthrough. For the foreseeable future, computation is our only model for intelligence.

Computationalism as a form of Homunctionalism also affords us a way of acknowledging our place as physical organisms amid the closed causal order we call Nature, without benefit of intervention by ghosts. (Actually I hear there are some physicists who speculate that quantum indeterminancies afford gaps in nature that are in principle permeable to Cartesian minds, and that immaterial egos do insert themselves into quantum gaps, thus taking over the role of hidden variables. But (i) it would have to be shown how such quantum phenomena could be combined and multiplied into macroscopic effects characteristic of intelligence, i.e., how the brain could act as a "quantum magnifier," and (ii) to avoid *ad-hoc*ness of the crassest sort, one would have to find physical reason to think that Cartesian intervention does occur, which task I take to be almost definitionally impossible.)

6. Of course, this re-emphasizes the question of human freedom: if humans are just wetware or liveware, are they not then essentially soft puppets? This in turn suggests—however speciously in light of the arguments made [earlier]—that the computational view of people must therefore be drastically wrong.

7. Relatively speaking, of course; I am not encouraging Two-Levelism.

8. That mental acts do not *feel* digital is not an objection either. To infer from that fact that mental acts are not digital would be a clear case of what Armstrong (1968a) calls the "headless woman" fallacy.

Brute Experience*

PETER CARRUTHERS

The question whether brutes have experiences has been granted as obvious in recent times, and in one sense of the term "experience" no doubt it is so. But not, I shall argue, in the sense that makes their experiences an appropriate object of moral concern.

I.

Since Thomas Nagel's seminal paper "What is it Like to be a Bat?",[1] it has become generally accepted that a creature may be said to have experiences if and only if there is something that it is

*I am grateful to Clare McCready for discussions that stimulated the writing of this paper, and to A. D. Smith for his comments on an earlier draft.

From *The Journal of Philosophy,* vol. 86, no. 5 (May 1989), pp. 258–269. Reprinted with permission from the Journal of Philosophy, Inc.

The author of this article no longer endorses the "reflexive thinking" theory of consciousness that it contains. For his current views, see his book *Phenomenal Consciousness: A Naturalistic Theory,* published by Cambridge University Press in 2000. Nor does the author agree any longer that non-conscious pains can't be appropriate objects of sympathy. See Chapters 9 and 10 of his book *Consciousness: Essays from a Higher-Order Perspective,* published by Oxford University Press in 2005.

like to be that thing (even if we cannot know what). But this identification of experience with subjective feel is false. There are, in fact, many experiences that do not feel like anything.

Consider some familiar examples. While driving the car over a route I know well, my conscious attention may be wholly abstracted from my surroundings. I may be thinking deeply about a current piece of writing of mine, or phantasizing about my next summer's holiday, to the extent of being unaware of what I am doing on the road. It is common in such cases that one may suddenly "come to," returning one's attention to the task at hand with a startled realization that one has not the faintest idea what one has been doing or seeing for some minutes past. Yet there is a clear sense in which I must have been seeing, or I should have crashed the car. My passenger sitting next to me may correctly report that I had seen the lorry double parked by the side of the road, since I had deftly steered the car around it. But I was not aware of seeing that lorry, either at the time or later in memory.

Another example: When washing up dishes I generally put on music to help pass the time. If it is a piece that I love particularly well, I may become totally absorbed, ceasing to be conscious of what I am doing at the sink. Yet someone observing me position a glass neatly on the rack to dry between two coffee mugs would correctly say that I must have seen that those mugs were already there, or I should not have placed the glass where I did. Yet I was not aware of seeing those mugs, or of placing the glass between them. At the time I was swept up in the finale of Schubert's "Arpeggione Sonata," and if asked even a moment later I should have been unable to recall at what I had been looking.

Let us call such experiences *nonconscious experiences.* What does it feel like to be the subject of a nonconscious experience? It feels like nothing. It does not *feel like anything* to have a nonconscious visual experience, as of a lorry parked at the side of the road or as of two coffee mugs placed on a draining rack, precisely because to have such an experience is not to be conscious of it. Only conscious experiences have a distinctive phenomenology, a distinctive feel. Nonconscious experiences are those which may help to

control behavior without being felt by the conscious subject.

These points—intuitive as they are—are already sufficient to show that Nagel is wrong to identify the question whether a creature has experiences with the question whether there is something that it feels like to be that thing. For there is a class—perhaps a large class—of nonconscious experiences that have no phenomenology. So, the fact that a creature has sense organs, and can be observed to display sensitivity in its behavior to the salient features of its surrounding environment, is insufficient to establish that it feels like anything to be that thing. It may be that the experiences of brutes (that is, of some or all nonhuman animals) are wholly of the nonconscious variety. It is an open question whether there is anything that it feels like to be a bat or a dog or a monkey. If consciousness is like the turning on of a light, then it may be that their lives are nothing but darkness. In order to make progress with this issue, we need to understand the nature of the distinction between conscious and nonconscious mental states.

Before proceeding to that task, however, it is worth noticing a somewhat less familiar example of nonconscious experience, since this will help us to see how the conscious/nonconscious distinction may have a physical realization in the neurological structure of the human brain. The phenomenon I have in mind is that of blindsight.[2] Human subjects who have suffered lesions in the striate cortex (the visual center in the higher part of the brain) may lose all conscious experience in an area of their visual field. They insist that they can see nothing at all within that region. Nevertheless, if asked to guess, they prove remarkably good at describing features of objects presented to them in that area, such as the orientation of a line, or at pointing out the direction of a light source. They can also reach out and grasp objects. Indeed, if asked to try to catch a ball thrown toward them from their blind side, they often prove successful.[3]

The conclusion to be drawn from these studies is that, while blindsight patients lack conscious visual experience within an area of their visual field, they nevertheless have nonconscious experiences which are somehow made available to help in the control of their actions. It seems that the neurological explanation for the phenomenon is that information from the eye is not only mapped on to the striate cortex (in normal subjects) but is also sent to a second mapping in the midbrain. It is presumably this latter mapping which is made available, in blindsight patients, to be integrated with the subject's goals and other perceptions in controlling behavior. It is also possible that it is this midbrain information which underlies the everyday examples of nonconscious experience outlined above. But we should beware of concluding that any creature with a striate cortex will be the subject of conscious visual experiences. The phenomenon of blindsight shows only that a functioning striate cortex is a physically necessary condition for conscious visual experience, not that it is sufficient. It may be that in the case of everyday nonconscious experience the striate cortex is indeed active, but that its information is not made available to whatever structures in the human brain underlie consciousness. And it may be that nonhuman animals with a striate cortex do not possess those structures at all.

It is worth stressing that the various nonconscious experiences we have considered do genuinely deserve to be counted as a species of *experience*. For not only is incoming information processed to quite a high degree of sophistication, but the states in question conform to the practical-reasoning model of explanation. Thus, the car driver behaved as he did because he *wanted* to reach his destination safely and *saw* that the lorry was an obstacle in his path. And the blindsight patient picked up the ball because he *wanted* to comply with the request of the experimenter and *saw* that the ball was on the edge of the desk. But if someone really insists that experiences are conscious states *by definition,* then the conclusion of this section may simply be rephrased. It is that, since there exist in humans similar levels of cognitive processing and behavior control to those displayed by brutes, which do not involve experiences, it is an open question whether brutes have experiences at all. In the discussion that follows, however, I shall assume, as seems most natural, that not all experiences are conscious ones.

II.

What distinguishes conscious from nonconscious experiences? The question is best raised in connection with the distinction between conscious and nonconscious mental states generally. Since David Armstrong's[4] early work, it has been usual to characterize conscious mental states as those which give rise (noninferentially) to an activated second-order belief in their own existence. Thus, a conscious belief that P is one which, besides being available to enter into the causation of the subject's behavior, is apt to cause in them the activated belief that they believe that P.[5] Similarly, a conscious visual experience is one that, besides causing beliefs about the matter to which the experience relates, and being made available to nonconscious motor control processes, is apt to give rise to the belief that just such an experience is taking place.

If such an account were correct, then it would be very doubtful whether many species of animal could be said to enjoy conscious experiences. For only the most anthropomorphic of us is prepared to ascribe second-order beliefs to toads and mice; and many of us would have serious doubts about ascribing such states even to higher mammals such as chimpanzees.[6] At any rate, behavioral evidence for the possession of such states in higher mammals is contentious, whereas their absence from lower mammals, birds, reptiles, and fish is surely uncontentious. I shall show, however, that the proposed account is definitely incorrect. But this result is not a defense of conscious experience for brutes. Quite the contrary: the account of consciousness which emerges will make it even less likely that any nonhuman animals have conscious experiences.

I begin with an example I owe to Tim Williamson, designed to show that one cannot equate conscious believing that P with an activated second-order belief that one believes that P. In the course of a discussion of the merits and demerits of functionalism in the philosophy of mind, I might realize that I had for some time been speaking of functionalists as "we," also becoming angry when the views of functionalists were maligned, thus manifesting the activated second-order belief that I believe myself to believe in functionalism. But this might strike me with the force of self-discovery. If anyone had asked me previously whether I were a functionalist, I might have expressed uncertainty. In which case it would seem that the possession of activated second-order beliefs is not sufficient for conscious believing.

Another argument with the same conclusion is that the proposed account gets the focus of attention of conscious believing quite wrong. Conscious belief is surely world-directed in precisely the way that belief itself is. If I entertain the conscious belief that the world is getting warmer, then the primary object of my belief is the earth and its likely future temperature. Whereas if the proposed account were correct, the primary object of the conscious belief would be myself (I should be believing of myself that I possess a particular first-order belief), only focusing on the world indirectly, via the content of the first-order belief in question.

This point holds also for the proposed account of the distinction between conscious and nonconscious experience. Conscious visual experiences, too, are primarily world-directed. When I consciously see that there is a dagger on the desk before me, the primary focus of my attention is the dagger itself. In normal cases of conscious perception, our experiences are, as it were, transparent: representing the world to us without themselves being objects of attention. It is of course possible to pay attention to one's conscious experiences, as when I attempt a phenomenological description of my visual field. But this is a sophisticated and relatively unusual thing to do. Whereas on the proposed account it is the normal case: to perceive consciously that there is a dagger on the desk would be to have activated the belief about myself that I have an experience of there being a dagger on the desk.

Is it possible to do better? Indeed it is.[7] A conscious, as opposed to a nonconscious, mental state is one that is available to conscious thought—where a conscious act of thinking is itself an event that is available to be thought about in turn. (When we think things consciously to ourselves, the events that express our thoughts are themselves available to be objects of further

thoughts—I can think to myself that my thought was poorly formulated, or hasty, or confused, or whatever.) In the case of belief, a conscious belief (qua standing state) is one that is apt to emerge in a conscious thinking with the same content. This is then able to handle Williamson's example: the reason why I had not consciously believed functionalism to be true is that I failed to have any disposition to think to myself, "Functionalism is true." The account also has the advantage that conscious beliefs have the same primary world-directedness as beliefs. For the conscious act of thinking, aptness to emerge in which is the distinctive mark of a conscious belief, is an event with the very same (world-directed) content as that belief itself. What makes my belief that the earth is getting warmer a conscious one is that I am disposed in suitable circumstances to think to myself, "The earth is getting warmer"; in both cases, the direction of focus is on the world, rather than on myself.

In the case of experience, a conscious experience is a state whose content is available to be consciously thought about (that is, which is available for description in acts of thinking which are themselves made available to further acts of thinking). In this case, I say 'available to be thought *about*', rather than 'apt to emerge in thinkings with the same content', because it is plausible to claim that most experiences have a degree of complexity and richness which may outreach our powers of accurate description. Nevertheless, every aspect of the perceived scene is made available to thought, even if only the thought that things are now subtly different. (Although the manner in which the leaves of a tree are shimmering in the breeze may defy description, I must at least be able to think to myself that the pattern of movement is now slightly altered, if it is.) Here, too, we can retain the primary world-directedness of conscious experience, since the normal way for information that is made available to thought through perception to emerge in acts of thinking is in thoughts about the object perceived—as when I think to myself that the dagger on the desk is richly ornamented.

When we turn to consider, not conscious experience of something in the world, but the more sophisticated state of consciousness of that experience itself, it is important to note that the suggested account is consistent with the existence of unanalyzable qualia. It may indeed be the case that the distinctive feel of my experience of a warm shade of red is incapable of further analysis, or even of nonrelational description. But I claim that what constitutes that feeling as a conscious rather than a nonconscious state is that it is available to be consciously thought about. It is the status of qualia as conscious states, not the individual qualia themselves, which is being analyzed on the proposed account.

Besides the virtues mentioned above, my account provides a natural treatment of the examples of nonconscious experience with which we began. The reason why my perception of the double-parked lorry was not conscious, is that, while information about the lorry was somehow made available for integration into my actions, it was not available to my conscious thoughts. Similarly in the example of nonconscious perception of mugs on a draining board, what makes the experience nonconscious is that there was, in the circumstances, nothing available for me to think spontaneously about those mugs.

The issue of spontaneity is important in handling the blindsight examples. For although in these cases the visual information is, in a sense, available to be thought about (since if asked to guess what is there, subjects will generally guess correctly), it is not apt to give rise to spontaneous thoughts in the way that conscious experiences do. In the normal course of events, blindsighted people will have no thoughts whatever about objects positioned in the blind portion of their visual field. Indeed, when they do think about the matter, they are strongly inclined to believe that they see nothing.

One final virtue of my account is that it is able to explain why so many philosophers have been inclined to connect possession of conscious mental states with the ability to speak a natural language. For such a connection is at its most plausible (though still denied by many) where conscious thinkings are concerned. The idea that the ability to think things consciously to oneself is tied to the possession of a natural language has an immediate (if defeasible) plausibility.

Whereas a similar thesis applied to the capacity for conscious experience seems much more puzzling. For why should it be supposed that language mastery is a necessary condition for a creature to enjoy conscious visual experiences? If the account sketched above is correct, then there may indeed be such a connection, but at one remove: it is because conscious experiences are those which are available to conscious thinkings. Now, although I am in fact one of those who maintain that language mastery is at least contingently connected with the capacity for conscious thought, I shall not argue for this here.[8] Nor is such a thesis necessary in what follows.

Are there any other alternatives to my account? I can think of only three. First, it might be said that the distinctive feature of a conscious experience is that it is recorded in short-term memory (this being the *explanation* of why such experiences are, in humans, available to be thought about). But the trouble with this is that there is nothing here to distinguish conscious from nonconscious short-term memory. (My own account, in contrast, is reflexive: conscious thinkings are ones that are themselves available to be consciously thought about.) Second, it might be said that a conscious state is one that is available to the organism as a whole. But the trouble here is that the experiences of any earth worm or slug will turn out to be conscious ones, on this account, whereas the experiences of my car driver are not. Third, it might be claimed that the distinction between conscious and nonconscious states is simple and unanalyzable. But this surely cannot be right. It cannot be merely that we are capable of recognizing, straight off, whether or not a given state is conscious (in the way that we are capable of recognizing whether or not a given shade of color is green); for nonconscious states, precisely because they *are* nonconscious, cannot be immediately recognized as such. Yet if it is said to be the availability for such immediate recognition which constitutes a state as a conscious one, then we appear to have returned to a version of my own proposal.

If my account of the distinction between conscious and nonconscious mental states may be taken as established, then the nonconscious status of most animal experiences follows with very little further argument. For if it is implausible to ascribe second-order beliefs to mice or fish, it is even more unlikely that they should be thinking things consciously to themselves—that is, that they should engage in acts of thinking which are themselves made available for the organism to think about. Indeed, it seems highly implausible to ascribe such activities to any but the higher primates; and, even then, many of us would entertain serious doubts.[9] In the discussion that follows, I shall confine attention to those species for which I take it the above thesis will be noncontroversial. I shall assume that no one would seriously maintain that dogs, cats, sheep, cattle, pigs, or chickens consciously think things to themselves (let alone that fish or reptiles do). In which case, if my account of the distinction between conscious and nonconscious experience is correct, the experiences of all these creatures will be of the nonconscious variety.

III.

It goes without saying that pains, too, are experiences. Then two questions remain. First, does pain, like any other experience, admit of a conscious/nonconscious distinction? If so, then the pains of brutes will be nonconscious ones, according to my general account of this distinction. Second, are nonconscious pains an appropriate object of sympathy and moral concern? If not, then the sufferings of brutes will make no moral claims upon us.

There are no noncontroversial examples of nonconscious pain in humans to parallel our everyday examples of nonconscious visual experience. There is an obvious reason for this, since part of the function of pain is to intrude upon consciousness, in order that one may give one's full attention to taking evasive action. But possible examples come from cases where someone is concentrating very intently upon a task, and where they later report having felt no pain upon injury, but where they nevertheless display aversive behavior. For instance, a soldier in the midst of battle may be too caught up in the fighting to notice any pain when he badly burns his hand on the red-hot barrel of a gun, but an observer would see him jerk his hand away in the manner characteristic of someone in pain. Should we feel sympathy in such a case? Clearly we would be sympathetic for the soldier's injury; but not for his suffering, since he in fact felt no pain. This sort of example is incapable of carrying very great weight, however, because the pain behavior displayed is hardly paradigmatic. Since the episode is so brief and unstructured, it may perhaps be thought of as a mere reflex, rather than a genuine instance of nonconscious pain perception.

Can there be cases of pain parallel to those of blindsight? That is, cases where the full (or nearly full) range of pain behavior is displayed, but in which the subject is not conscious of any pain. So far as I am aware, no such cases have actually occurred; but the neurophysiology of pain perception suggests that they are, in principle, possible.[10] Pain in humans is mediated through two types of nerve, which generate distinct projections in the brain subserving distinct functions. Very roughly, the "new path" is fast; it is projected into the higher centers of the brain, and is responsible for precise pain location and fine discriminations of feel. The "old path" is, by contrast, slow; it is projected primarily to the more ancient limbic system in the brain, and gives rise to aversion (the desire for the pain to cease).

Some types of morphine can suppress the activity of the old path, while leaving the new path fully functioning. Patients report that their pain is still just as intense (it feels the same), but that it no longer bothers them (they no longer want it to stop). It seems unlikely, in contrast, that there will be any drug, or any naturally-occurring lesions, which suppress the activity of the new path while leaving the old path functioning. For, unlike the case of vision, the nerves of the new path have no specialized projection area in the higher cortex, but seem rather to be mapped in a complex way into many different regions throughout it.[11] This suggests that phenomena similar to blindsight could only occur as a result of direct surgical intervention. But they do seem to be possible, in principle.

Let us then imagine a case for pain similar to that of blindsight. Suppose that a particular subject, Mary, is never conscious of any pains in her legs. But when she suffers injury in that region, she displays much of normal pain behavior. If we jab pins into her feet, she tends to try very hard to make us stop, she grimaces and groans, and severe damage causes her to scream. But she sincerely declares that she feels nothing. Perhaps she initially found her own behavior disquieting, but now she understands its basis and merely finds it a nuisance. When she twists her ankle, she does not ask for something to alleviate the pain (she says she feels none), but for something to help her relax, and to stop her from grinding her teeth and limping when she walks.

This case is clearly imaginable. It is a possible example (physically possible as well as logically so) of nonconscious pain—that is, of events which otherwise occupy the normal causal role of pain,[12] but which are not available to be thought about consciously and spontaneously by the subject. Ought we to feel sympathy for Mary? We might perhaps feel sympathy for her general condition, since it is in many ways a disturbing situation in which to find oneself. But we should not feel sympathy on specific occasions of injury, since it is clear that she does not suffer. Not being conscious of any pain, her mental state is not an appropriate object of moral concern. (Her injury itself might be, however, because of its indirect effects upon her life, and hence her conscious desires and disappointments. There are many things that you cannot do with a twisted ankle, even if you feel no pain.) Similarly then in the case of brutes: since their experiences, including their pains, are nonconscious ones, their pains are of no immediate moral concern. Indeed, since all the mental states of brutes are nonconscious, their injuries are lacking even in indirect moral concern. Since the disappointments caused to a dog through possession of a broken leg are themselves nonconscious in their turn, they, too are not appropriate objects of our sympathy. Hence, neither the pain of the broken leg itself, nor its further effects upon the life of the dog, have any rational claim upon our sympathy.

Of course, it is one thing to reach an intellectual acceptance of such a position, and quite another to put it into practice. Are we really capable of suppressing our sympathy when we see an animal (especially a cuddly one) in severe pain? Not only is it possible that this should occur—after all, the history of mankind is replete with examples of those who have eradicated all feelings of sympathy even for members of other races, by telling themselves that they are not "really human"—but it is a moral imperative that it ought to. Much time and money is presently spent on alleviating the pains of brutes which ought properly to be directed toward human beings, and many are now campaigning to reduce the efficiency of modern farming methods because of the pain caused to the animals involved. If the arguments presented here have been sound, such activities are not only morally unsupportable but morally objectionable.[13]

Consider once again the case of Mary. Suppose that you are a doctor who knows the details of her condition, and that you happen to be on the scene of an accident in which her legs have been badly injured. A number of other people are obviously injured and in pain, but Mary is screaming the loudest. Ought you to treat her first? Clearly not, other things being equal (e.g., provided that she is not bleeding badly); indeed, it would be moral weakness in you to do so. For you know that she is not really suffering, since her pains are nonconscious, whereas the sufferings of the others are real. Similarly then in the case of brutes: since their pains are nonconscious (as are all their mental states), they ought not to be allowed to get in the way of any morally serious objective.

It is worth drawing a contrast at this point with the case of very young children. I presume that the pains of babies, too, are nonconscious; for no one will seriously maintain that they consciously think things to themselves. Nevertheless, it is important that they should continue to evoke our sympathy. For a baby's pains and injuries, and our attitudes toward them, are likely to have a significant effect upon the person the baby will one day become. There is a parallel here with the case of language development. As every parent knows, one naturally becomes possessed by a sort of necessary insanity, talking to young children as if they could understand. This is no doubt essential if children are to develop into skilled practitioners of their native tongue. In both cases, one engages, and should engage, in a useful fiction: ascribing to the baby thoughts that it does not in fact possess.

There is no such rationale in the case of brutes. For our sympathy and concern for their pains and injuries cannot be said to have an effect on the persons they will one day become. Nevertheless, it is hard, especially in a culture such as ours where animals are often used as exemplars in moral training (we tell children that it is *cruel* to pull the whiskers out of the cat), to eradicate our feelings toward them. Indeed, in such a culture we may have reason to look askance at people who can be wholly indifferent to an animal writhing in agony before their very eyes. (We say, "How can you be so inhuman?") But what should be said is that we are obliged to set such feelings aside whenever they threaten to have a morally significant effect upon other humans. And it also follows that there is no moral criticism to be leveled at the majority of people who are indifferent to the pains of factory-farmed animals, which they know to exist but do not themselves observe.

NOTES

1. *Philosophical Review*, LXXXIII, 4 (1974), pp. 435–451.
2. This has been researched by a number of investigators. See in particular L. Weiskrantz, "Varieties of Residual Experience," *Quarterly Journal of Experimental Psychology*, XXXIII, 3 (1980), pp. 365–386.
3. For these last two facts, I rely upon personal communication from A. J. Marcel, Applied Psychology Unit, Cambridge, who will be publishing details shortly. Subjects displayed 80%–90% of normal accuracy in reaching out for objects of varying sizes and orientations, placed at varying distances. For examples of other experimental data suggesting the existence of nonconscious perceptions of quite a sophisticated sort, see Marcel, "Conscious and Unconscious Perception," *Cognitive Psychology*, xv, 2(1983), pp. 197–300.
4. *A Materialist Theory of the Mind* (London: Routledge, 1968). Similar accounts have been defended recently in Peter Smith and O. R. Jones, *The Philosophy of Mind* (New York: Cambridge, 1986), and in my own *Introducing Persons* (Albany: SUNY, 1986).

5. A belief is activated when it becomes engaged in the subject's current mental processes.
6. For a useful review of the evidence of various levels of cognitive organization in a range of animal species, see Stephen Walker, *Animal Thought* (New York: Routledge & Kegan Paul, 1983).
7. The account that follows is modelled on some of Daniel Dennett's suggestions in "Toward a Cognitive Theory of Consciousness," in *Brainstorms* (Montgomery, VT: Bradford, 1978), pp. 149–173. But Dennett, implausibly, connects consciousness directly with the ability to give verbal reports. If there is such a connection, it needs to be established at least in part by empirical investigation, not fixed by definition.
8. See ch. 10 of my *Tractarian Semantics* (New York: Blackwell, 1989).
9. See the very sensible discussion of the cognitive powers of chimpanzees in Walker, *op. cit.*
10. In what follows, I rely largely upon the account provided by Dennett in "Why You Can't Make a Computer that Feels Pain," in *Brainstorms*, ch. 10.
11. Here I rely upon J. Z. Young, *Philosophy and the Brain* (New York: Oxford, 1986).
12. This is not strictly correct, since part of the normal causal role of pain is to give rise to a conscious desire that the pain should cease, whereas I am supposing that Mary's avoidance behavior is motivated by desires that are nonconscious. (This is merely for ease of presentation: Mary cannot consciously desire that her *pain* should stop, since she feels none. But she might in fact have a conscious desire that whatever is going on in her ankle should cease.) The adjustment is allowable in this context, since the desires of brutes, as well as their pains, will be nonconscious ones.
13. Peter Singer has been prominent in defending the moral significance of animals, from a broadly utilitarian perspective. See, for example, his *Practical Ethics* (New York: Cambridge, 1979). But he makes no attempt to take account of the distinction between conscious and nonconscious experience. Indeed, he does not notice it. There are, of course, other moral perspectives, from the standpoint of some of which the moral significance of animals may be attacked; for example, versions of contractualism which place a premium upon rational agency. But my argument is the more fundamental, since even contractualists should find a place for compassion.

Animal Minds

JOHN SEARLE

I

Many species of animals have consciousness, intentionality, and thought processes. By "consciousness" I mean those subjective states of sentience and awareness that we have during our waking life (and at a lower level of intensity in our dreams); by "intentionality" I mean that feature of the mind by which it is directed at or about objects and states of affairs in the world; and by "thought processes" I mean those temporal sequences of intentional states that are systematically related to each other, where the relationship is constrained by some rational principles. Examples of conscious states are such things as feeling a pain or hearing a sound. Examples of intentional states are such things as wanting to eat food or believing that someone is approaching. Examples of thought processes are such things as figuring how to get a banana that is out of reach or monitoring the behavior of prey who is on the move and is trying to escape. Though these three phenomena—consciousness, intentionality, and thought processes—overlap, they are not identical. Some conscious states are intentional, some not. Some intentional states are conscious, many are not. For example, my current thought that it is unlikely to rain is conscious, my belief when I am asleep that Bill Clinton is president of the United States is unconscious. All thought processes, as I have defined them, are intentional; but not every intentional state occurs as part of a thought process. For example, a pang of undirected anxiety, though conscious, is not intentional. A sudden desire for a cold beer is both conscious and intentional. An animal who has a sudden pang of hunger can have that pang without it being part of any thought process.

I have said that many species of animals have consciousness, intentionality, and thought processes. Now why am I so confident about that? Why, for example, am I so confident that my dog, Ludwig Wittgenstein Searle, is conscious? Well, why is he so confident I am conscious? I think part of the correct answer, in the case of both Ludwig and me, is that any other possibility is out of the question. We have, for example, known each other now for quite a while so there is not really any possibility of doubt.

Philosophically speaking the interesting question is why in philosophy and science we have so much trouble seeing that such sorts of answers are the correct ones? I will come back to this point later. Now I want to turn the original question around and ask, why have so many thinkers denied what would appear to be obvious points, that many species of animals other than our own have consciousness, intentionality, and thought processes? Think for a moment how counterintuitive such denials are: I get home from work and Ludwig rushes out to meet me. He jumps up and down and wags his tail. I am certain that (a) he is conscious; (b) he is aware of my presence (intentionality); and (c) that awareness produces in him a state of pleasure (thought process). How could anyone deny either a, b or c? As his namesake might have said, "This is how we play the language game with 'certain'." I now turn to consider some of these denials.

II

In the seventeenth and eighteenth centuries, in response to the Cartesian revolution, it made sense both philosophically and theologically to wonder whether animals had minds. If, as

Reprinted by permission from *Midwest Studies in Philosophy*, vol. XIX, 1994: pp. 206–219.

Descartes had taught us, there were two kinds of substances in the universe, mental substance whose essence was thinking or consciousness, and physical substance whose essence was extension, then the question becomes pressing: Which of the animate extended substances had minds? Which of the living substances contained consciousness?

The basic Aristotelian dichotomy between the living and the non-living was transcended by an even more fundamental dichotomy between those things that had minds and those that did not. The question became even more pressing when people reflected on the theological implications of any philosophical answer that they might care to give. The commonsense view that higher animals are conscious in exactly the same sense that human beings are conscious has the result that every such animal possesses an immortal soul. This is because the Cartesian theory of the nature of the mental, and of the distinction between the mental and the physical, has the implication that consciousness is indestructible. Any mental substance is indivisible and so lasts eternally. But if animals have consciousness, then it follows immediately that they have immortal souls, and the afterlife will, to put it mildly, be very much overpopulated. Worse yet, if consciousness extends very far down the phylogenetic scale, then it might turn out that the population of the afterlife includes a very large number of the souls of fleas, snails, ants, and so forth. This is an unwelcome theological consequence of what seemed a plausible philosophical doctrine.

Another problem that arose even for theologians who were not Cartesians is this: If animals are conscious then they can suffer. But if they can suffer then how is their suffering to be justified, given that they do not have original sin and presumably do not have free will? The arguments that were used to reconcile the existence of an omnipotent and beneficent God with a suffering human population do not seem to work for animals.

We now regard these ways of thinking about the problem of animal minds as completely implausible, and the Cartesians gave an equally implausible solution: On their view, animals simply do not have minds. Animals are unconscious automatons and though we feel sympathy for the dog crushed beneath the car wheel, our sympathy is misplaced. It is just as if a computer had been run over.

Ridiculous as this view now seems to us, I believe it is an inevitable consequence of the rest of the Cartesian system. If every mind is an immortal soul, then only beings that can have immortal souls can have minds. The natural way out of this puzzle is to abandon dualism, both property dualism and substance dualism. And if one abandons dualism, if one really abandons it, then one must also abandon materialism, monism, the identity thesis, behaviorism, token-token identity, functionalism, Strong Artificial Intelligence, and all of the other excrescences that dualism has produced in the nineteenth and twentieth centuries. Properly understood, all these absurd views are forms of dualism.[1]

If one thoroughly abandons dualism, what is the result as far as animal minds are concerned? Before answering that, I want to consider some other more recent attempts to show that animals do not have certain sorts of mental phenomena.

III

Very few people today would be willing to argue that animals lack consciousness altogether. But several thinkers, both philosophers and scientists, have argued either that animals lack intentionality in general or at least that animals cannot think, that is, they cannot have thought processes in my sense. I am frankly extremely suspicious *a priori* of any argument of this form because we know in advance that humans do have intentionality and thought processes and we know that humans are biologically continuous with the rest of the animal kingdom. Whatever its surface logical form, any argument against animal intentionality and thinking has to imply the following piece of speculative neurobiology: the difference between human and animal brains is such that the human brain can cause and sustain intentionality and thinking, and animal brains cannot.

Given what we know about the brains of the higher mammals, especially the primates, any such speculation must seem breathtakingly irresponsible. Anatomically the similarities are too great for such a speculation to seem even remotely plausible, and physiologically we know that the mechanisms that produce intentionality and thought in humans have close parallels in other beasts. Humans, dogs, and chimpanzees all take in perceptual stimuli through visual, tactile, auditory, olfactory, and other sensory receptors; they all send the signals produced by these stimuli to the brain where they are processed; and eventually the resultant brain processes cause motor outputs in the forms of intentional actions such as socializing with other conspecific beasts, eating, playing, fighting, reproducing, raising their young, and trying to stay alive. It seems out of the question, given the neurobiological continuity, to suppose that only humans have intentionality and thoughts.

However, let us turn to the actual arguments against the possibility of animal thinking. The form of the arguments is and has to be the same: humans satisfy a necessary condition on thinking which animals do not and cannot satisfy. Given what we know of the similarities and differences between human and animal capacities, the alleged crucial difference between humans and animals, in all of the arguments I know, is the same: the human possession of language makes human thought possible and the absence of language in animals makes animal thought impossible.

The Cartesians also thought that language was the crucial differentiating feature that distinguished humans from animals. But they thought the significance of language was epistemic. The possession of language was a sure sign that humans are conscious and its absence a sure sign that animals are not conscious. This view has always seemed very puzzling to me. Why should linguistic behavior be epistemically essential for the presence of consciousness? We know in the case of human beings that children are conscious long before they are able to speak a language and we know that many human beings never acquire the ability to speak a language, but we do not for that reason doubt that they are conscious.

More recent thinkers concede that animals are conscious but think of language as somehow playing a constitutive role in thought, such that beings without language could not have thoughts.

The major premise, then, of these arguments is always that humans have language in a sense in which animals do not have a language, and so far that premise seems to me to be correct. Even those of us who would be willing to describe the waggle dance of the bees as a language and the achievements of the chimpanzees Washoe, Lana, and others as genuinely linguistic would still grant that such symbolizing behavior is vastly weaker than any natural human language. So let us grant that, in some important sense of "language," humans have language, and as far as we know, no other species does. What follows about the mind? Well one thing follows immediately: If there are any intentional states whose possession requires a language, animals cannot have those states, and *a fortiori* they cannot have thought processes involving those states. Clearly there are such states. My dog can want me to take him for a walk but he cannot want me to get my income tax returns in on time for the 1993 tax year. He can want to be let out but he cannot want to write a doctoral thesis on the incidence of mononucleosis among American undergraduates. To have these latter sorts of desires he would have to have, at the very least, linguistic abilities that he lacks. Is there a principle? How do we decide which intentional states require language and which do not? I think there are several principles involved, and I will come back to this question later. Right now I want to continue to follow the arguments against the possibility of any intentionality and thought among linguistically deprived beasts. The argument that there are some intentional states that animals cannot have does not show that they can have no intentional states. Here are some arguments for the stronger thesis.

One argument is that in order to attribute beliefs to a system we have to have a way of distinguishing cases where the system genuinely believes that *p* from cases where the system merely supposes that *p,* hypothesizes that *p,* reckons that *p,* has a hunch that *p,* is certain that *p,* or is merely inclined to think that on balance, all things considered, that *p.*[2] But we cannot make these distinctions for a being that cannot make them for itself, and a being can only make them for itself if it has the relevant vocabulary. The vocabulary need not be the same as or translatable exactly into English, but there must be some vocabulary for marking the different types of intentional states within the range or there is no sense to the attribution of the states.

What are we to make of this argument? Even if we grant the premise that such discriminations require a language, it does not follow that we need to be able to make fine-grained distinctions before we can make any attributions of intentional states at all. In fact this premise just seems wrong. Very general psychological verbs like "believe" and "desire" are often used in such a way as to allow for a slack, an indeterminacy, as to which of the subsidiary forms of the general attitude are exemplified by the agent. Thus I may believe that it is going to rain, without it being the case that I myself could say without reflection whether it is a strong or weak belief, a hunch, a conviction, or a supposition. And even if I can answer these questions on reflection, the reflection itself may fix the relevant attitude. Before I thought about it there simply may not have been any fact of the matter about which kind of belief it was, I just believed that it was going to rain. So I conclude that the fact that fine-grained discriminations cannot be made for animal beliefs and desires does not show that animals do not have beliefs and desires....

A related argument has been considered by [Donald] Davidson.

In order that an animal have a thought, the thought must occur in a network of beliefs. His example is: in order to think the gun is loaded I must believe that guns are a type of weapon, and that a gun is an enduring physical object. So in order to have a thought there must be beliefs. But, and this is the crucial step, in order to have beliefs a creature must have the concept of belief. Why? Because in order to have a belief one must be able to distinguish true from false beliefs. But this contrast, between the true and the false, "can only emerge in the context of interpretation" (of language)[3] The notion of a true belief or a false belief depends on the notion

of true and false utterances, and these notions cannot exist without a shared language. So, only a creature who is the possessor and interpreter of a language can have thoughts. The basic idea in this argument seems to be that since "truth" is a metalinguistic semantic predicate and since the possession of belief requires the ability to make the distinction between true and false beliefs, it seems to follow immediately that the possession of beliefs requires metalinguistic semantic predicates, and that obviously requires a language.

This argument is not as clear as it might be, and one might object to various of its steps. The feature on which I want to concentrate here is what I take to be the central core of the argument: In order to tell the difference between true and false beliefs one must have a linguistically articulated concept of belief.

The claim is that only within a language can one distinguish correct from incorrect beliefs. I agree with the presupposition of this claim: having an intentional state requires the capacity to discriminate conditions which satisfy from those that do not satisfy the intentional state. Indeed, I wish to generalize this point to all intentional states and not just confine it to beliefs. In general, in order to have intentional states one must be able to tell the difference between satisfied and unsatisfied intentional states. But I see no reason at all to suppose that this necessarily requires a language, and even the most casual observation of animals suggests that they typically discriminate the satisfaction from the frustration of their intentional states, and they do this without a language.

How does it work? Well, the first and most important thing to notice is that beliefs and desires are embedded not only in a network of other beliefs and desires but more importantly in a network of perceptions and actions, and these are the biologically primary forms of intentionality. We have all along in this discussion been talking as if perception and action were not forms of intentionality but of course they are; they are the biologically primary forms. Typically, for animals as well as humans, perception fixes belief, and belief together with desire determines courses of action. Consider real-life examples: Why is my dog barking up that tree? Because he *believes* that the cat is up the tree, and he wants to catch up to the cat. Why does he believe the cat is up the tree? Because he *saw* the cat run up the tree. Why does he now stop barking up the tree and start running toward the neighbor's yard? Because he no longer believes that the cat is up the tree, but in the neighbor's yard. And why did he correct his belief? Because he just saw (and no doubt smelled) the cat run into the neighbor's yard; and *seeing and smelling is believing*. The general point is that animals correct their beliefs all the time on the basis of their perceptions. In order to make these corrections they have to be able to distinguish the state of affairs in which their belief is satisfied from the state of affairs in which it is not satisfied. And what goes for beliefs also goes for desires.

But why do we need to "postulate" beliefs and desires at all? Why not just grant the existence of perceptions and actions in such cases? The answer is that the behavior is unintelligible without the assumption of beliefs and desires; because the animal, for example, barks up the tree even when he can no longer see or smell the cat, thus manifesting a belief that the cat is up the tree even when he cannot see or smell that the cat is up the tree. And similarly he behaves in ways that manifest a desire for food even when he is neither seeing, smelling, nor eating food.

In such cases animals distinguish true from false beliefs, satisfied from unsatisfied desires, without having the concepts of truth, falsity, satisfaction, or even belief and desire. And why should that seem surprising to anyone? After all, in vision some animals distinguish between red-colored and green-colored objects without having the concepts vision, color, red, or green. I think many people suppose there must be something special about "true" and "false," because they suppose them to be *essentially* semantic predicates in a metalanguage. Given our Tarskian upbringing, we tend to think that the use of "true" and "false" to characterize beliefs must somehow be derived from a more fundamental use to characterize linguistic entities, sentences, and statements, for example. And then it seems to us that if a creature could tell true from false beliefs it would first have to have an object language to give any grip to the original metalanguage distinction between truth and falsity, now being applied by extension to something nonlinguistic.

But all of this is a mistake. "True" and "false" are indeed metalinguistic predicates, but more fundamentally they are *metaintentional* predicates. They are used to assess success and failure of representations to achieve fit in the mind-to-world direction of fit, *of which statements and sentences are a special case*. It is no more mysterious that an animal, at least sometimes, can tell whether its belief is true or false, than that it can tell whether its desire is satisfied or frustrated. For neither beliefs nor desires does the animal require a language; rather what it requires is some device for recognizing whether the world is the way it seemed to be (belief) and whether the world is the way the animal wants it to be (desire). But an animal does not have to have a language in order to tell true from false beliefs, any more than it has to have a language to tell satisfied from unsatisfied desires. Consider the example of the dog chasing the cat, for an illustration.

IV

I conclude that the arguments I have seen which deny mental phenomena to animals, ranging from Descartes to Davidson, are without force. I now turn to a remaining question: How do we distinguish those intentional states that require a language, and hence are impossible for animals, from those that do not? I believe the best way to answer this question is to list some of the categories of intentional states which require a language and explain the reasons why they require a language. I doubt that I have thought of all of these, but here are five for a start.

1. *Intentional states that are about language.* For example, a creature cannot think that "eat" is a transitive verb or wonder how to translate "Je n'aurais pas pu" into English if it does not possess the capacity to speak a language.

2. *Intentional states that are about facts which have language as partly constitutive of the fact.* For example an animal cannot think that the object in front of it is a twenty-dollar bill or that the man it sees is the Chairman of the Philosophy Department at the University of California, because the facts represented, facts involving human institutions such as money and universities, require language as a constitutive element of the facts.

3. *Intentional states that represent facts that are so remote in space and time from the animal's experience as to be unrepresentable without language.* For example, my dog might think that I am now eating good food, but it cannot think that Napolean ate good food.

4. *Intentional states that represent complex facts, where the complexity cannot be represented without language.* This is a very large class. Thus my dog can fear a falling object, but he cannot believe the law of gravity even though the falling object instantiates the law of gravity. He can probably have some simple conditional thoughts, but he cannot have subjunctive counterfactual thoughts. Perhaps he can think: "If he gives me that bone I will eat it," but not "If only he had given me a bigger bone I would have enjoyed it more!"

5. *Intentional states that represent facts where the mode of presentation of the fact locates it relative to some linguistic system.* For example, my dog can believe that it is warm here now, but he cannot believe that the 30th of April, 1993, is a warm day, because the system of representing days is essentially linguistic.

No doubt this list could be continued. What it shows so far is that the reasons that an intentional state essentially requires a language for its existence fall into two classes. Either the state has conditions of satisfaction that are essentially linguistic or the mode of representing the conditions of satisfaction is essentially linguistic. Or, quite commonly, both. A third type of reason would be that the type of the state requires language for the very possession of a state of that type. I have seen it claimed that there are such types of state—perhaps hope and resentment would be examples—but I have never seen a convincing argument.

V

I now return to the question: How should we think of animals' mental phenomena in a philosophy purged of dualism? The answer is a form of what I have elsewhere called biological naturalism. Consciousness and other forms of mental phenomena are biological processes occurring in human and certain animal brains. They are as much a part of the biological natural history of animals as are lactation, the secretion of bile, mitosis, meiosis, growth, and digestion. Once we remind ourselves of what we know about the brain and we forget our dualist upbringing, the general outline of the solution to the so-called mind–body problem, whether for humans or animals, is quite simple. Mental phenomena are caused by lower-level neuronal processes in human and animal brains and are themselves higher-level or macro features of those brains. Of course, we do not yet know the details of how it works, how the quite specific neurobiology of human and animal nervous systems causes all the enormous variety of our mental lives. But from the fact that we do not yet know *how* it works it does not follow that we do not know *that* it works.

From the fact that human and animal brains cause consciousness it also does not follow that only human and animal brains could do it. Perhaps one could create consciousness of the sort that exists in us and other animals using some artificial device; perhaps one might be able to create it in systems not made of carbon-based molecules at all. And for all we know, consciousness may have evolved among beasts in other galaxies, or other solar systems within our own dear galaxy, that do not have our local obsession with carbon, hydrogen, nitrogen, and oxygen. But one thing we know for certain: any system capable of causing consciousness and other mental phenomena must have causal capacities to do it equivalent to the threshold biological capacities of animal brains, both our own human brains and the brains of other kinds of animals. From the fact that brains do it causally, it is a trivial logical consequence that any other system capable of doing it causally must have threshold causal powers to do it equivalent to brains. If that sounds trivial, it should. It is, however, routinely denied by any amount of confused contemporary philosophy of mind that tries to treat consciousness as some purely formal abstract phenomenon independent of any biological or physical reality at all. Contemporary versions of this view are sometimes called 'Strong Artificial Intelligence'[4] They are expressions of one of the major tenets of traditional dualism, the view that where the mind is concerned the specific neurobiology of the brain is of little importance.

So far, we have not the faintest idea how to create consciousness artificially in some other medium, because we do not know exactly how it is created in our own brains. Some of our best contemporary theories tell us that it is a matter of variable rates of neuron firings relative to certain specific neuronal architectures. But what is it exactly about the peculiar electrochemistry of neurons, synapses, transmitters, receptors, and so forth, that enables them to cause consciousness? At present, we do not know. So, the prospects of artificial consciousness are extremely remote, even though the existence of consciousness in brains other than human brains is not seriously in doubt.

Well, what about the special problems having to do with animal minds? I have so far been talking as if humans and animals were in the same boat, but what about the special features of animal minds? Problems in this area can be divided roughly into two categories and it is important to keep them separate. First, *ontological* problems which have to do with the nature, character, and causal relations of animal mental phenomena, both what causes them and what they in turn cause. Second, *epistemic* problems which have to do with how we find out about animal mental states, how we know that animals have mental states, and how we know which animals have which sorts of mental states. It is a consequence of the views that I have enunciated so far, that there are not very many interesting philosophical questions about the ontology of animal mental life in general and animal consciousness in particular. The most important questions in this are largely questions for animal psychologists, biologists, and especially neurobiologists. Specifically, if we know that our brains cause consciousness,

and we know therefore that any other system capable of causing consciousness must have the relevant threshold causal powers equivalent to our own brains, then the question becomes a factual empirical question: which sorts of animal brains are capable of causing and sustaining consciousness?

Often however in this area epistemology and ontology are confused. The Turing Test tempts us to precisely such a confusion, because the behaviorism behind the test leads to arguments like the following: If two systems behave the same way we have the same grounds for attributing mental states to one as we do to the other. For example, both snails and termites are capable of exhibiting what appears to be goal-directed behavior, so what sense could be attached, for example, to the claim that snails had consciousness and termites did not have it? In fact, since the appearance of goal-directed behavior seems to be a feature of all sorts of artifacts, mouse traps and heat-seeking missiles, for example, if we are going to attribute consciousness to snails or termites on the basis of the appearance of goal-directed behavior, why not to any system that appears to be goal directed, such as mouse traps or heat-seeking missiles?

But if, as I am claiming, this approach confuses epistemology and ontology, what is the right way to look at such questions? How, for example, would we test the hypothesis that snails had consciousness and termites did not? Well, here is one possible way. Suppose we had a science of the brain which enabled us to establish conclusively the causal bases of consciousness in humans. Suppose we discovered that certain electrochemical sequences were causally necessary and sufficient for consciousness in humans. Suppose we knew that humans that had those features were conscious and humans that lacked them lacked consciousness. Suppose we knew, for example, in our own case, that if we knocked out these specific features through anaesthetics, we became unconscious. We may suppose that this is an extremely complicated electrochemical phenomenon, and following a long philosophical tradition, I will simply abbreviate its description as XYZ. Suppose that the presence of features XYZ in the otherwise normal human brain is causally both necessary and sufficient for consciousness. Now, if we found XYZ present in snails but absent in termites, that would seem very strong empirical evidence that snails had consciousness and termites did not. If we had a rich enough theory so that we could identify XYZ as causally both necessary and sufficient for consciousness, then we might regard the hypothesis as definitely established, pending, of course, the usual hesitations about the ultimate falsifiability in principle of any scientific hypothesis.

VI

If the ontological questions are mostly for specialists, what about the epistemology? Here we find plenty of opportunities to clear up philosophical confusions. I have said that contrary to Descartes we are absolutely confident that the higher animals are conscious; but what are the grounds for our confidence? After all, we can design machines that can behave in some areas just as intelligently as animals, perhaps more so, and we are not inclined to ascribe consciousness to these machines. What's the difference? What, other than biological chauvinism, would lead us to ascribe consciousness to animals but not, for example, to computers?

The standard answer has been that we know of the existence of other minds in animals in the same way we know it in humans, we infer from the *behavior* of the human or animal that it has consciousness and other mental phenomena. Since the behavior of other humans and animals is relevantly similar to my own, I infer that they have conscious states just like mine. On this view, if we could build a mechanical animal out of tinker toy parts that behaved like real animals, we would have to say that it too had consciousness.

In response I want to say that I think this view is hopelessly confused and that behavior by itself is simply irrelevant. Even if we confine ourselves to verbal behavior, as Descartes did, it is important to point out that my car radio exhibits much more intelligent verbal behavior, not only than any animal but even than any human that I know. It will on demand provide me with predictions of the weather, reports of the latest news, discussions of the Stock Market as well as

Western songs and rock and roll music, and it will display a large number of other forms of verbal behavior, even some where the same radio speaks with a whole lot of its different voices at once. But I do not for a moment suppose that my radio is conscious, and I have no doubt that my dog is conscious. The reason for the distinction is that I have a theory. I have a theory about how radios work and I have a theory about how dogs work. By 'theory' I do not mean anything fancy, I just mean a kind of commonsense theory. I know that a radio is a machine designed for the purpose of transmitting the voices and music produced by people a long way away in such a fashion that I can hear them in my living room or my car. I know that my dog has a certain inner causal structure that is relevantly similar to my own. I know that my dog has eyes, ears, skin, etcetera, and that these form part of the causal bases of his mental life, just as similar structures form part of the causal bases of my mental life. In giving this answer, I am not trying to "answer skepticism" or trying to "solve the other minds problem." I do not think there is any such problem and I do not take skepticism seriously. Rather, I am explaining what are in fact, in real life, the grounds for our complete confidence that dogs are conscious and radios are not. It is not a matter of behavior as such. By itself, behavior is irrelevant. Behavior is only interesting to us to the extent that we see it as the expression of a more ontologically fundamental causal structure. The principle by which we "solve the other minds problem for animals" is not that intelligent behavior is proof of consciousness but rather the principle is that if the animal has a causally relevant structure similar to our own, then it is likely to produce similar mental states in response to similar stimuli. The "behavior" is simply evidence that it is so responding. Nothing more.

Contrary to the whole epistemological tradition, I am suggesting that the grounds on which we found our certainty that animals are conscious is not that intelligent behavior which is the same or similar to ours is proof of consciousness, but rather that causal structures which are the same or similar causal structures to ours produce the same or similar effects. Behavior, even linguistic behavior, is only relevant given certain assumptions about structure. That is why we attribute consciousness to humans and animals, with or without language, and we do not attribute it to radios.

But even saying this seems to me to concede too much. It will almost unavoidably give the impression that I think there really is an other minds problem, that there are tests that a system must pass in order to have a mind, and that dogs and baboons are passing the tests and computers as well as chairs and tables are failing. I think that is the wrong way to see these matters and I will now try to explain why.

The worst mistake that we inherited from Cartesianism was dualism, together with all of its idealist, monist, materialist, physicalist progeny. But the second worst mistake was to take epistemology seriously, or rather to take it seriously in the wrong way. Descartes together with the British empiricists and right up through the Positivists and the Behaviorists of the twentieth century have given us the impression that the question: "How do you know?" asks the fundamental question, the answer to which will explain the relation between us as conscious beings and the world. The idea is that somehow or other we are constantly in some epistemic stance toward the world whereby we are making inferences from evidence of various kinds. We are busy inferring that the sun will rise tomorrow, that other people are conscious, that objects are solid, that events in the past really occurred, and so forth. In this case, the idea is that the evidence that we have that other people are conscious is based on their behavior, and since we see relevantly similar behavior in dogs and primates, we may reasonably infer that they, too, are conscious. Against this tradition, I want to say that epistemology is of relatively little interest in philosophy and daily life. It has its own little corner of interest where we are concentrating on such things as how to understand certain traditional skeptical arguments, but our basic relationships to reality are seldom matters of epistemology. I do not infer that my dog is conscious, any more than, when I come into a room, I infer that the people present are conscious. I simply respond to them as is appropriate to

respond to conscious beings. I just treat them as conscious beings and that is that. If somebody says, "Yes, but aren't you ignoring the possibility that other people might be unconscious zombies, and the dog might be, as Descartes thought, a cleverly constructed machine, and that the chairs and tables might, for all you know, be conscious? Aren't you simply ignoring these possibilities?" The answer is: Yes. I am simply ignoring all of these possibilities. They are out of the question. I do not take any of them seriously. Epistemology is of very little interest in the philosophy of mind and in the philosophy of language for the simple reason that where mind and language are concerned, very little of our relationship to the phenomena in question is epistemic. The epistemic stance is a very special attitude that we adopt under certain special circumstances. Normally, it plays very little role in our dealings with people or animals. Another way to put this is to say that it does not matter really *how* I know whether my dog is conscious, or even *whether* or not I do "know" that he is conscious. The fact is, he is conscious and epistemology in this area has to *start* with this fact.

There are indeed grounds for my certainty in the cases of dogs, chairs, tables, baboons, and other people, and I tried to state some of those grounds earlier, but the important thing to see is that I am certain. When I state the grounds for my certainty I am not trying to answer philosophical skepticism or "prove" that animals have minds and tables and chairs do not.

However, though the general or philosophically skeptical form of the "other animals' minds problem" seems to me confused, there are quite specific questions about specific mechanisms the answers to which are essential to scientific progress in this area. For example, how are cats' visual experiences similar to and different from those of humans? We know quite a lot about this question because we have studied the cat's visual system fairly extensively, and we have an extra motivation for wanting to answer it because we need to know how much we can learn about the human visual system from work done on cats. Furthermore, we currently suppose that certain species of birds navigate by detecting the earth's magnetic field. And the question arises, if they do this, do they do it consciously? And if so, what are the mechanisms for conscious detection of magnetism? In the same vein, bats navigate by bouncing sonar off solid objects in the dark. We would like to know not only what it feels like to do this but what the mechanisms are that produce the conscious experience of detecting material objects by reflected sound waves. The most general question of all is this: What exactly are the neurobiological mechanisms by which consciousness is produced and sustained in animals and humans? An answer to this question would give us solid epistemic grounds for settling the issue as to which animals are conscious and which are not.

Such epistemic questions seem to me meaningful, important, and indeed crucial for scientific progress in these areas. But notice how different they are from traditional philosophical skepticism. They are answered by doing specific work on specific mechanisms, using the best tools available. For example, no one could have said in advance, just on the basis of philosophical reflection, that

using PET scans and CAT scans would prove crucial in studying human and animal minds. To these genuine epistemic questions the answer is always the same: Use your ingenuity. Use any weapon you can lay your hands on and stick with any weapon that works. With this type of epistemology we have the best chance of understanding both human and animal minds.

NOTES

1. See John R. Searle, *The Rediscovery of the Mind* (Cambridge, Mass., 1992) for arguments to substantiate this claim.
2. This was an argument popular during my student days at Oxford in the 1950s. I first heard it in lectures and seminars by Stuart Hampshire. I do not know if he ever published it.
3. D. Davidson, "Thought and Talk" in *Truth and Interpretation* (Oxford, 1984), pp. 155–170, at 170.
4. Cf. John R. Searle, "Minds, Brains and Programs," *Behavioral and Brain Sciences* 3 (1980), pp. 417–424.

PERSONAL IDENTITY AND THE SURVIVAL OF DEATH

The Prince and the Cobbler

JOHN LOCKE

...If the identity of *soul alone* makes the same *man,* and there be nothing in the nature of matter why the same individual spirit may not be united to different bodies, it will be possible that those men, living in distant ages, and of different tempers, may have been the same man: which way of speaking must be from a very strange use of the word man, applied to an idea out of which body and shape are exclude....

An animal is a living organized body; and consequently the same animal, as we have observed, is the same continued *life* communicated to different particles of matter, as they happen successively to be united to that organized living body. And whatever is talked of other definitions, ingenious observation puts it past doubt, that the idea in our minds, of which the sound "man" in our mouths is the

From John Locke, *An Essay Concerning Human Understanding*, Book II, Chapter 27, "Of Ideas of Identity and Diversity." First published in 1690.

sign, is nothing else but of an animal of such a certain from. . . .

I presume it is not the idea of a thinking or rational being alone that makes the *idea of a man* in most people's sense: but of a body, so and so shaped, joined to it; and if that be the idea of a man, the same successive body not shifted all at once, must, as well as the same immaterial spirit, go to the making of the same man.

This being premised, to find wherein personal identity consists, we must consider what *person* stands for;—which, I think, is a thinking intelligent being, that has reason and reflection, and can consider itself as itself, the same thinking thing, in different times and places; which it does only by that consciousness which is inseparable from thinking, and, as it seems to me, essential to it: it being impossible for any one to perceive without *perceiving* that he does perceive. When we see, hear, smell, taste, feel, mediate, or will anything, we know that we do so. Thus it is always as to our present sensations and perceptions: and by this every one is to himself that which he calls self:—it not being considered, in this case, whether the same self be continued in the same or divers substances. For, since consciousness always accompanies thinking, and it is that which makes every one to be what he calls self, and thereby distinguishes himself from all other thinking things, in this alone consists personal identity, i.e. the sameness of a rational being: and as far as this consciousness can be extended backwards to any past action or thought, so far reaches the identity of that person; it is the same self now it was then; and it is by the same self with this present one that now reflects on it, that that action was done.

But it is further inquired, whether it be the same identical substance. This few would think they had reason to doubt of, if these perceptions, with their consciousness, always remained present in the mind, whereby the same thinking thing would be always consciously present, and, as would be thought, evidently the same to itself. But that which seems to make the difficulty is this, that this consciousness being interrupted always by forgetfulness, there being no moment of our lives wherein we have the whole train of all our past actions before our eyes in one view,

but even the best memories losing the sight of one part whilst they are viewing another; and we sometimes, and that the greatest part of our lives, not reflecting on our past selves, being intent on our present thoughts, and in sound sleep having no thoughts at all, or at least none with that consciousness which remarks our waking thoughts,—I say, in all these cases, our consciousness being interrupted, and we losing the sight of our past selves, doubts are raised whether we are the same thinking thing, i.e. the same *substance* or no. Which, however reasonable or unreasonable, concerns not *personal* identity at all. The question being what makes the same person; and not whether it be the same identical substance, which always thinks in the same person, which, in the case, matters not at all: different substances, by the same consciousness (where they do partake in it) being united into one person, as well as different bodies by the same life are united into one animal, whose identity is preserved in that change of substances by the unity of one continued life. For, it being the same consciousness that makes a man be himself to himself, personal identity depends on that only, whether it be annexed solely to one individual substance, or can be continued in a succession of several substances. For as far any intelligent being *can* repeat the idea of any past action with the same consciousness it had of it at first, and with the same consciousness it has of any present action; so far it is the same personal self. For it is by the consciousness it has of its present thoughts and actions, that it is *self to itself* now, and so will be the same self, as far as the same consciousness can extend to actions past or to come; and would be by distance of time, or change of substance, no more two persons, than a man be two men by wearing other clothes today than he did yesterday, with a long or a short sleep between: the same consciousness uniting those distant actions in the same person, whatever substances contributed to their production.

That this is so, we have some kind of evidence in our very bodies, all whose particles, whilst vitally united to this same thinking conscious self, so that *we feel* when they are touched, and are affected by, and conscious of good or harm that happends to them, are a part of our-selves; i.e. of our thinking conscious self. Thus, the limbs of his body are to every one a part of himself; he sympathizes and is concerned for them. Cut off a hand, and thereby separate it from that consciousness he had of its heat, cold, and other affections, and it is then no longer a part of that which is himself, any more than the remotest part of matter. Thus, we see the *substance* whereof personal self consisted at one time may be varied at another, without the change of personal identity; there being no question about the same person, though the limbs which but now were a part of it, be cut off...

And thus may we be able, without any difficulty, to conceive the same person at the resurrection, though in a body not exactly in make or parts the same which he had here,—the same consciousness going along with the soul that inhabits it. But yet the soul alone, in the change of bodies, would scarce to any one but to him that makes the soul the man, be enough to make the same man. For should the soul of a prince, carrying with it the consciousness of the prince's past life, enter and inform the body of a cobbler, as soon as deserted by his own soul, every one sees he would be the same *person* with the prince, accountable only for the prince's actions: but who would say it was the same *man?* The body too goes to the making the man, and would, I guess, to everybody determine the man in this case, wherein the soul, with all its princely thoughts about it, would not make another man: but he would be the same cobbler to every one besides himself. I know that, in the ordinary way of speaking, the same person, and the same man, stand for one and the same thing. And indeed every one will always have a liberty to speak as he pleases, and to apply what articulate sounds to what ideas he thinks fit, and change them as often as he pleases. But yet, when we will inquire what makes the same *spirit, man,* or *person,* we must fix the ideas of spirit, man, or person in our minds; and having resolved with ourselves what we mean by them, it will not be hard to determine in either of them, or the like, when it is the same, and when not.

But though the immaterial substance or soul does not alone, wherever it be, and in

whatsoever state, make the same *man;* yet it is plain, consciousness, as far as ever it can be extended—should it be to ages past—unites existences and actions very remote in time into the same *person,* as well as it does the existences and actions of the immediately preceding moment: so that whatever has the consciousness of present and past actions, is the same person to whom they both belong. Had I the same consciousness that I saw the ark and Noah's flood, as that I saw an overflowing of the Thames last winter, or as that I write now, I could no more doubt that I who write this now, that saw the Thames overflowed last winter, and that viewed the flood at the general deluge, was the same *self,*—place that self in what *substance* you please—than that I who write this am the same *myself* now whilst I write (whether I consist of all the same substance, material or immaterial, or no) that I was yesterday. For as to this point of being the same self, it matters not whether this present self be made up of the same or other substances—I being as much concerned, and as justly accountable for any action that was done a thousand years since, appropriated to me now by this self-consciousness, as I am for what I did the last moment...

But yet possibly it will still be objected,—Suppose I wholly lose the memory of some parts of my life, beyond a possibility of retrieving them, so that perhaps I shall never be conscious of them again; yet am I not the same person that did those actions, had those thoughts that I once was conscious of, though I have now forgot them? To which I answer, that we must here take notice what the word *I* is applied to; which, in this case, is the *man* only. And the same man being presumed to be the same person, I is easily here supposed to stand also for the same person. But if it be possible for the same man to have distinct incommunicable consciousness at different times, it is past doubt the same man would at different times make different persons; which, we see, is the sense of mankind in the solemnest declaration of their opinions, human laws not punishing the mad man for the sober man's actions, nor the sober man for what the mad man did,—thereby making them two persons: which is somewhat explained by our way of speaking in English when we say such an one is "not himself," or is "beside himself"; in which phrases it is insinuated, as if those who now, or at least first used them, thought that self was changed; the selfsame person was no longer in that man.

But yet it is hard to conceive that Socrates, the same individual man, should be two persons. To help us a little in this, we must consider what is meant by Socrates, or the same individual *man*.

First, it must be either the same individual, immaterial, thinking substance; in short, the same numerical soul, and nothing else.

Secondly, or the same animal, without any regard to an immaterial soul.

Thirdly, or the same immaterial spirit united to the same animal.

Now, take which of these suppositions you please, it is impossible to make personal identity to consist in anything but consciousness; or reach any further than that does.

Of Mr. Locke's Account of Our Personal Identity

THOMAS REID

In a long chapter upon Identity and Diversity, Mr. Locke has made many ingenious and just observations, and some which I think cannot be defended. I shall only take notice of the account he gives of our own personal identity. His doctrine upon this subject has been censured by Bishop Butler, in a short essay subjoined to his *Analogy,* with whose sentiments I perfectly agree.

Identity, as was observed, supposes the continued existence of the being of which it is affirmed, and therefore can be applied only to things which have a continued existence. While any being continues to exist, it is the same being; but two beings which have a different beginning or a different ending of their existence cannot possibly be the same. To this, I think, Mr. Locke agrees.

He observes, very justly, that, to know what is meant by the same person, we must consider what the word *person* stands for; and he defines a person to be an intelligent being, endowed with reason and with consciousness, which last he thinks inseparable from thought.

From this definition of a person, it must necessarily follow, that, while the intelligent being continues to exist and to be intelligent, it must be the same person. To say that the intelligent being is the person, and yet that the person ceases to exist while the intelligent being continues, or that the person continues while the intelligent being ceases to exist, is to my apprehension a manifest contradiction.

One would think that the definition of a person should perfectly ascertain the nature of personal identity, or wherein it consists, though it might still be a question how we come to know and be assured of our personal identity.

Mr. Locke tells us, however, "that personal identity, that is, the sameness of a rational being, consists in consciousness alone, and, as far as this consciousness can be extended backwards to any past action or thought, so far reaches the identity of that person. So that whatever has the consciousness of present and past actions is the same person to whom they belong."

This doctrine has some strange consequences, which the author was aware of. Such as, that if the same consciousness can be transferred from one intelligent being to another, which he thinks we cannot show to be impossible,

From Thomas Reid, *Essays on the Intellectual Powers of Man,* Essay III, Chapter 6. First published in 1785.

then two or twenty intelligent beings may be the same person. And if the intelligent being may lose the consciousness of the actions done by him, which surely is possible, then he is not person that did those actions; so that *one intelligent being may be two or twenty different persons,* if he shall so often lose the consciousness of his former actions.

There is another consequence of this doctrine, which follows no less necessarily, though Mr. Locke probably did not see it. It is, *that a man be, and at the same time not be, the person that did a particular action.*

Suppose a brave officer to have been flogged when a boy at school for robbing an orchard, to have taken a standard from the enemy in his first campaign, and to have been made a general in advanced life; suppose, also, which must be admitted to be possible, that, when he took the standard, he was conscious of his having been flogged at school, and that, when made a general, he was conscious of his taking the standard, but had absolutely lost the consciousness of his flogging.

These things being supposed, it follows, from Mr. Locke's doctrine, that he who was flogged at school is the same person who took the standard, and that he who took the standard is the same person who was made a general. Whence it follows, if there be any truth in logic, that the general is the same person with him who was flogged at school. But the general's consciousness does not reach so far back as his flogging; therefore, according to Mr. Locke's doctrine, he is not the person who was flogged. Therefore the general is, and at the same time is not, the same person with him who was flogged at school.

Leaving the consequences of this doctrine to those who have leisure to trace them, we may observe, with regard to the doctrine itself:

First, that Mr. Locke attributes to consciousness the conviction we have of our past actions, as if a man may now be conscious of what he did twenty years ago. It is impossible to understand the meaning of this, unless by consciousness be meant memory, the only faculty by which we have an immediate knowledge of our past actions.

Sometimes, in popular discourse, a man says he is conscious that he did such a thing, meaning that he distinctly remembers that he did it. It is unnecessary, in common discourse, to fix accurately the limits between consciousness and memory. This was formerly shown to be the case with regard to sense and memory: and therefore distinct remembrance is sometimes called sense, sometimes consciousness, without any inconvenience.

But this ought to be avoided in philosophy, otherwise we confound the different powers of the mind, and ascribe to one what really belongs to another. If a man can be conscious of what he did twenty years or twenty minutes ago, there is no use for memory, nor ought we allow that there is any such faculty. The faculties of consciousness and memory are chiefly distinguished by this, that the first is an immediate knowledge of the present, the second an immediate knowledge of the past.

When, therefore, Mr. Locke's notion of personal identity is properly expressed, it is, that personal identity consists in distinct remembrance; for, even in the popular sense, to say that I conscious of a past action means nothing else than that I distinctly remember that I did it.

Secondly, it may be observed, that, in this doctrine, not only is consciousness confounded with memory, but, which is still more strange, personal identity is confounded with the evidence which we have of our personal identity.

It is very true, that my remembrance that I did such a thing is the evidence I have that I am the identical person who did it. And this, I am apt to think, Mr. Locke meant. But to say that my remembrance that I did such a thing, or my consciousness, makes me the person who did it, is, in my apprehension, an absurdity too gross to be entertained by any man who attends to the meaning of it; for it is to attribute to memory or consciousness a strange magical power of producing its object, though that object must have existed before the memory or consciousness which produced it.

Consciousness is the testimony of one faculty; memory is the testimony of another faculty; and to say that the testimony is the cause of the thing testified, this surely is absurd, if any thing be, and could not have been said by Mr. Locke, if he had not confounded the testimony with the thing testified.

When a horse that was stolen is found and claimed by the owner, the only evidence he can have, or that a judge or witnesses can have, that this is the very identical horse which was his property, is similitude. But would it not be ridiculous from this to infer that the identity of a horse consists in similitude only? The only evidence I have that I am the identical person who did such actions is, that I remember distinctly I did them; or, as Mr. Locke expresses it, I am conscious I did them. To infer from this, that personal identity consists in consciousness, is an argument which, if it had any force, would prove the identity of a stolen horse to consist solely in similitude.

Thirdly, is it not strange that the sameness or identity of a person should consist in a thing which is continually changing, and is not any two minutes the same?

Our consciousness, our memory, and every operation of the mind, are still flowing like the water of a river, or like time itself. The consciousness I have this moment can no more be the same consciousness I had last moment, than this moment can be the last moment. Identity can only be affirmed of things which have a continued existence. Consciousness, and every kind of thought, are transient and momentary, and have no continued existence; and, therefore, if personal identity consisted in consciousness, it would certainly follow, that no man is the same person any two moments of his life; and as the right and justice of reward and punishment are founded on personal identity, no man could be responsible for his actions.

But though I take this to be the unavoidable consequence of Mr. Locke's doctrine concerning personal identity, and though some persons may have liked the doctrine the better on this account, I am far from imputing any thing of this kind to Mr. Locke. He was too good a man not to have rejected with abhorrence a doctrine which he believed to draw this consequence after it.

Fourthly, there are many expressions used by Mr. Locke, in speaking of personal identity, which to me are altogether unintelligible, unless we suppose that he confounded that sameness or identity which we ascribe to an individual with the identity which, in common discourse, is often ascribed to many individuals of the same species.

When we say that pain and pleasure, consciousness and memory, are the same in all men, this sameness can only mean similarity, or sameness of kind. That the pain of one man can be the same individual pain with that of another man is no less impossible, than that one man should be another man: the pain felt by me yesterday can no more be the pain I fell to-day, than yesterday can be this day; and the same thing may be said of every passion and of every operation of the mind. The same kind or species of operation may be in different men, or in the same man at different times; but it is impossible that the same individual operation should be in different men, or in the same man at different times.

When Mr. Locke, therefore, speaks of "the same consciousness being continued through a succession of different substances"; when he speaks of "repeating the idea of a past action, with the same consciousness we had of it at the first," and of "the same consciousness extending to actions past and to come"; these expressions are to me unintelligible, unless he means not the same individual consciousness, but a consciousness that is similar, or of the same kind.

If our personal identity consists in consciousness, as this consciousness cannot be the same individually any two moments, but only of the same kind, it would follow, that we are not for any two moments the same individual persons, but the same kind of persons.

As our consciousness sometimes ceases to exist, as in sound sleep, our personal identity must cease with it. Mr. Locke allows, that the same thing cannot have two beginnings of existence, so that our identity would be irrecoverably gone every time we ceased to think, if it was but for a moment.

The Self

DAVID HUME

There are some philosophers, who imagine we are every moment intimately conscious of what we call our Self; that we feel its existence and its continuance in existence; and are certain, beyond the evidence of a demonstration, both of its perfect identity and simplicity. . . .

Unluckily all these positive assertions are contrary to that very experience, which is pleaded for them, nor have we any idea of *self*, after the manner it is here explained. For from what impression could this idea be derived? This question 'tis impossible to answer without a manifest contradiction and absurdity; and yet 'tis a question, which must necessarily be answered, if we would have the idea of self pass for clear and intelligible. It must be some one impression, that gives rise to every real idea. But self or person is not any one impression, but that to which our several impressions and ideas are supposed to have a reference. If any impression gives rise to the idea of self, that impression must continue invariably the same, through the whole course or our lives; since self is supposed to exist after that manner. But there is no impression constant and invariable. Pain and pleasure, grief and joy, passions and sensations succeed each other, and never all exist at the same time. It cannot, therefore, be from any of these impressions, or from any other, that the idea of self is derived; and consequently there is no such idea.

But farther, what must become of all our particular perceptions upon this hypothesis? All these are different, and distinguishable, and separable from each other, and may be separately considered, and may exist separately, and have no need of any thing to support their existence. After what manner, therefore, do they belong to self; and how are they connected with it? For my part, when I enter most intimately into what I call *myself*, I always stumble on some particular perception or other, of heat or cold, light or shade, love or hatred, pain or pleasure. I never can catch *myself* at any time without a perception, and never can observe any thing but the perception. When my perceptions are removed for any time, as by sound sleep; so long am I insensible of *myself*, and may truly be said not to exist. And were all my perceptions removed by death, and could I neither think, nor feel, nor see, nor love, nor hate after the dissolution of my body, I should be entirely annihilated, nor do I conceive what is farther requisite to make me a perfect nonentity. If any one upon serious and unprejudiced reflection, thinks he has a different notion of *himself*, I must confess I can reason no longer with him. All I can allow him is, that he may be in the right as well as I, and that we are essentially different in this particular. He may, perhaps, perceive something simple and continued, which he calls *himself*; though I am certain there is no such principle in me.

But setting aside some metaphysicians of this kind, I may venture to affirm of the rest of mankind, that they are nothing but a bundle or collection of different perceptions, which succeed each other with an inconceivable rapidity, and are in a perpetual flux and movement. Our eyes cannot turn in their sockets without varying our perceptions. Our thought is still more variable than our sight; and all our other senses and faculties contribute to this change; nor is there any single power of the soul, which remains unalterably the same, perhaps for one moment. The mind is a kind of theatre, where several perceptions successively make their appearance; pass, re-pass, glide away, and mingle in an infinite variety of postures and situations. There is properly no *simplicity* in it at one time, nor *identity* in

From David Hume, *A Treatise of Human Nature*. First published in England in 1738.

different; whatever natural propension we may have to imagine that simplicity and identity. The comparison of the theatre must not mislead us. They are the successive perceptions only, that constitute the mind; nor have we the most distant notion of the place, where these scenes are represented, or of the materials, of which it is composed.

What then gives us so great a propension to ascribe an identity to these successive perceptions, and to suppose ourselves possessed of an invariable and uninterrupted existence through the whole course of our lives? . . .

We have a distinct idea of an object, that remains invariable and uninterrupted through a supposed variation of time; and this idea we call that of *identity* or *sameness.* We have also a distinct idea of several different objects existing in succession, and connected together by a close relation; and this to an accurate view affords as perfect a notion of *diversity,* as if there was no manner of relation among the objects. But though these two ideas of identity, and a succession of related objects be in themselves perfectly distinct, and even contrary, yet 'tis certain, that in our common way of thinking they are generally confounded with each other. That action of the imagination, by which we consider the uninterrupted and invariable object, and that by which we reflect on the succession of related objects, are almost the same to the feeling, nor is there much more effort of thought required in the latter case than in the former. The relation facilitates the transition of the mind from one object to another, and renders its passage as smooth as if it contemplated one continued object. This resemblance is the cause of the confusion and mistake, and makes us substitute the notion of identity, instead of that of related objects. . . .

Thus we feign the continued existence of the perceptions of our senses, to remove the interruption; and run into the notion of a *soul,* and *self,* and *substance,* to disguise the variation. But we may farther observe, that where we do not give rise to such a fiction, our propension to confound identity with relation is so great, that we are apt to imagine something unknown and mysterious, connecting the parts, beside their relation; and this I take to be the case with regard to the identity we ascribe to plants and vegetables. And even when this does not take place, we still feel a propensity to confound these ideas, though we are not able fully to satisfy ourselves in that particular, nor find any thing invariable and uninterrupted to justify our notion of identity.

Thus the controversy concerning identity is not merely a dispute of words. For when we attribute identity, in an improper sense, to variable or interrupted objects, our mistake is not confined to the expression, but is commonly attended with a fiction, either of something invariable and uninterrupted, or of something mysterious and inexplicable, or at least with a propensity to such fictions. What will suffice to prove this hypothesis to the satisfaction of every fair enquirer, is to show from daily experience and observation, that the objects, which are variable or interrupted, and yet are supposed to continue the same, are such only as consist of a succession of parts, connected together by resemblance, contiguity, or causation. . . .

A ship, of which a considerable part has been changed by frequent reparations, is still considered as the same: nor does the difference of the materials hinder us from ascribing an identity to it. The common end, in which the parts conspire, is the same under all their variations, and affords an easy transition of the imagination from one situation of the body to another. . . .

Though every one must allow, that in a very few years both vegetables and animals endure a *total* change, yet we still attribute identity to them, while their form, size, and substance are entirely altered. An oak, that grows from a small plant to a large tree, is still the same oak; though there be not one particle of matter, or figure of its parts the same. An infant becomes a man, and is sometimes fat, sometimes lean, without any change in his identity. . . . A man, who hears a noise, that is frequently interrupted and renewed, says, it is still the same noise; though 'tis evident the sounds have only a specific identity or resemblance, and there is nothing numerically the same, but the cause, which produced them. In like manner it may be said without breach of the propriety of language, that such a church, which was formerly of brick, fell to ruin, and that the parish rebuilt the same church of free-stone, and according to modern architecture. Here neither the form nor materials are the same, nor is there any thing common to the two objects, but their relation to the inhabitants of the parish; and yet this alone is sufficient to make us denominate them the same. . . .

From thence it evidently follows, that identity is nothing really belonging to these different perceptions, and uniting them together; but is merely a quality, which we attribute to them, because of the union of their ideas in the imagination, when we reflect upon them. . . .

The only question, therefore, which remains, is, by what relations this uninterrupted progress of our thought is produced, when we consider the successive existence of a mind or thinking person. And here 'tis evident we must confine ourselves to resemblance and causation. . . . Also, as memory alone acquaints us with the continuance and extent of this succession of perceptions, 'tis to be considered, upon that account chiefly, as the source of personal identity. Had we no memory, we never should have any notion of causation, nor consequently of that chain of causes and effects, which constitute our self or person.

Divided Minds and the Nature of Persons

DEREK PARFIT

Derek Parfit is a fellow of All Souls College, Oxford.

It was the split-brain cases which drew me into philosophy. Our knowledge of these cases depends on the results of various psychological tests, as described by Donald MacKey.[1] These tests made use of two facts. We control each of our arms, and see what is in each half of our visual fields, with only one of our hemispheres. When someone's hemispheres have been disconnected, psychologists can thus present to this person two different written questions in the two halves of his visual field, and can receive two different answers written by this person's two hands.

Here is a simplified imaginary version of the kind of evidence that such tests provide. One of these people looks fixedly at the centre of a wide screen, whose left half is red and right half is blue. On each half in a darker shade are the words, "How many colours can you see?" With both hands the person writes, "Only one". The words are now changed to read, "Which is the only colour that you can see?" With one of his hands the person writes "Red", with the other he writes "Blue".

If this is how such a person responds, I would conclude that he is having two visual sensations—that he does, as he claims, see both red and blue. But in seeing each colour he is not aware of seeing the other. He has two streams of consciousness, in each of which he can see only one colour. In one stream he sees red, and at the same time, in his other stream, he sees blue. More generally, he could be having at the same time two series of thoughts and sensations, in having each of which he is unaware of having the other.

This conclusion has been questioned. It has been claimed by some that there are not *two* streams of consciousness, on the ground that the sub-dominant hemisphere is a part of the brain whose functioning involves no consciousness. If this were true, these cases would lose most of their interest. I believe that it is not true, chiefly because, if a person's dominant hemisphere is

From *Mindwaves*, ed. Colin Blakemore & Susan Greenfield (Oxford: Basil Blackwell, 1987), pp. 19–25. Reprinted by permission of Blackwell Publishing.

destroyed, this person is able to react in the way in which, in the split-brain cases, the sub-dominant hemisphere reacts, and we do not believe that such a person is just an automaton, without consciousness. The sub-dominant hemisphere is, of course, much less developed in certain ways, typically having the linguistic abilities of a three-year-old. But three-year-olds are conscious. This supports the view that, in split-brain cases, there *are* two streams of consciousness.

Another view is that, in these cases, there are two persons involved, sharing the same body. Like Professor MacKay, I believe that we should reject this view. My reason for believing this is, however, different. Professor MacKay denies that there are two persons involved because he believes that there is only one person involved. I believe that, in a sense, the number of persons involved is none.

THE EGO THEORY AND THE BUNDLE THEORY

To explain this sense I must, for a while, turn away from the split-brain cases. There are two theories about what persons are, and what is involved in a person's continued existence over time. On the *Ego Theory*, a person's continued existence cannot be explained except as the continued existence of a particular *Ego*, or *subject of experiences*. An Ego Theorist claims that, if we ask what unifies someone's consciousness at any time—what makes it true, for example, that I can now both see what I am typing and hear the wind outside my window—the answer is that these are both experiences which are being had by me, this person, at this time. Similarly, what explains the unity of a person's whole life is the fact that all of the experiences in this life are had by the same person, or subject of experiences. In its best-known form, the *Cartesian view*, each person is a persisting purely mental thing—a soul, or spiritual substance.

The rival view is the *Bundle Theory*. Like most styles in art—Gothic, baroque, rococo, etc.—this theory owes its name to its critics. But the name is good enough. According to the Bundle Theory, we can't explain either the unity of consciousness at any time, or the unity of a whole life, by

referring to a person. Instead we must claim that there are long series of different mental states and events—thoughts, sensations, and the like—each series being what we call one life. Each series is unified by various kinds of causal relation, such as the relations that hold between experiences and later memories of them. Each series is thus like a bundle tied up with string.

In a sense, a Bundle Theorist denies the existence of persons. An outright denial is of course absurd. As Reid protested in the eighteenth century, 'I am not thought, I am not action, I am not feeling; I am something which thinks acts and feels.' I am not a series of events but a person. A Bundle Theorist admits this fact, but claims it to be only a fact about our grammar, or our language. There are persons or subjects in this language-dependent way. If, however, persons are believed to be more than this—to be separately existing things, distinct from our brains and bodies, and the various kinds of mental states and events—the Bundle Theorist denies that there are such things.

The first Bundle Theorist was Buddha, who taught "anatta", or the *No Self view*. Buddhists concede that selves or persons have "nominal existence", by which they mean that persons are merely combinations of other elements. Only what exists by itself, as a separate element, has instead what Buddhists call "actual existence". Here are some quotations from Buddhist texts:

> At the beginning of their conversation the king politely asks the monk his name, and receives the following reply: 'Sir, I am known as "Nagasena"; my fellows in the religious life address me as "Nagasena". Although my parents gave me the name . . . it is just an appellation, a form of speech, a description, a conventional usage. "Nagasena" is only a name, for no person is found here.'
>
> A sentient being does exist, you think, O Mara? You are misled by a false conception. This bundle of elements is void of Self, In it there is no sentient being. Just as a set of wooden parts Receives the name of carriage, So do we give to elements. The name of fancied being.
>
> Buddha has spoken thus: 'O Brethren, actions do exist, and also their consequences, but the person that acts does not. There is no one to cast away this set of elements, and no one to assume a new set of them. There exists no Individual, it

is only a conventional name given to a set of elements'[2]

Buddha's claims are strikingly similar to the claims advanced by several Western writers. Since these writers knew nothing of Buddha, the similarity of these claims suggests that they are not merely part of one cultural tradition, in one period. They may be, as I believe they are, true.

WHAT WE BELIEVE OURSELVES TO BE

Given the advances in psychology and neurophysiology, the Bundle Theory may now seem to be obviously true. It may seem uninteresting to deny that there are separately existing Egos, which are distinct from brains and bodies and the various kinds of mental states and events. But this is not the only issue. We may be convinced that the Ego Theory is false, or even senseless. Most of us, however, even if we are not aware of this, also have certain beliefs about what is involved in our continued existence over time. And these beliefs would only be justified if something like the Ego Theory was true. Most of us therefore have false beliefs about what persons are, and about ourselves.

These beliefs are best revealed when we consider certain imaginary cases, often drawn from science fiction. One such case is *teletransportation*. Suppose that you enter a cubicle in which, when you press a button, a scanner records the states of all of the cells in your brain and body, destroying both while doing so. This information is then transmitted at the speed of light to some other planet, where a replicator produces a perfect organic copy of you. Since the brain of your Replica is exactly like yours, it will seem to remember living your life up to the moment when you pressed the button, its character will be just like yours, and it will be in every other way psychologically continuous with you. This psychological continuity will not have its normal cause, the continued existence of your brain, since the causal chain will run through the transmission by radio of your "blueprint".

Several writers claim that, if you chose to be teletransported, believing this to be the fastest way of travelling, you would be making a terrible mistake. This would not be a way of travelling, but a way of dying. It may not, they concede, be quite as bad as ordinary death. It might be some consolation to you that, after your death, you will have this Replica, which can finish the book that you are writing, act as parent to your children, and so on. But, they insist, this Replica won't be you. It will merely be someone else, who is exactly like you. This is why this prospect is nearly as bad as ordinary death.

Imagine next a whole range of cases, in each of which, in a single operation, a different proportion of the cells in your brain and body would be replaced with exact duplicates. At the near end of this range, only 1 or 2 per cent would be replaced; in the middle, 40 or 60 per cent; near the far end, 98 or 99 per cent. At the far end of this range is pure teletransportation, the case in which all of your cells would be "replaced".

When you imagine that some proportion of your cells will be replaced with exact duplicates, it is natural to have the following beliefs. First, if you ask, "Will I survive? Will the resulting person be me?", there must be an answer to this question. Either you will survive, or you are about to die. Second, the answer to this question must be either a simple "Yes" or a simple "No". The person who wakes up either will or will not be you. There cannot be a third answer, such as that the person waking up will be half you. You can imagine yourself later being half-conscious. But if the resulting person will be fully conscious, he cannot be half you. To state these beliefs together: to the question, "Will the resulting person be me?", there must always *be* an answer, which must be all-or-nothing.

There seem good grounds for believing that, in the case of teletransportation, your Replica would not be you. In a slight variant of this case, your Replica might be created while you were still alive, so that you could talk to one another. This seems to show that, if 100 per cent of your cells were replaced, the result would merely be a Replica of you. At the other end of my range of cases, where only 1 per cent would be replaced, the resulting person clearly *would* be you. It therefore seems that, in the cases in between, the resulting person must be either you, or merely a Replica. It seems that one of these must be true, and that it makes a great difference which is true.

HOW WE ARE NOT WHAT WE BELIEVE

If these beliefs were correct, there must be some critical percentage, somewhere in this range of cases, up to which the resulting person would be you, and beyond which he would merely be your Replica. Perhaps, for example, it would be you who would wake up if the proportion of cells replaced were 49 per cent, but if just a few more cells were also replaced, this would make all the difference, causing it to be someone else who would wake up.

That there must be some such critical percentage follows from our natural beliefs. But this conclusion is most implausible. How could a few cells make such a difference? Moreover, if there is such a critical percentage, no one could ever discover where it came. Since in all these cases the resulting person would believe that he was you, there could never be any evidence about where, in this range of cases, he would suddenly cease to be you.

On the Bundle Theory, we should reject these natural beliefs. Since you, the person, are not a separately existing entity, we can know exactly what would happen without answering the question of what will happen to you. Moreover, in the case in the middle of my range, it is an empty question whether the resulting person would be you, or would merely be someone else who is exactly like you. These are not here two different possibilities, one of which must be true. These are merely two different descriptions of the very same course of events. If 50 per cent of your cells were replaced with exact duplicates, we could call the resulting person you, or we could call him merely your Replica. But since these are not here different possibilities, this is a mere choice of words.

As Buddha claimed, the Bundle Theory is hard to believe. It is hard to accept that it could be an empty question whether one is about to die, or will instead live for many years.

What we are being asked to accept may be made clearer with this analogy. Suppose that a certain club exists for some time, holding regular meetings. The meetings then cease. Some years later, several people form a club with the same name, and the same rules. We can ask, "Did these people revive the very same club? Or did they merely start up another club which is exactly similar?" Given certain further details, this would be another empty question. We could know just what happened without answering this question. Suppose that some one said: "But there must be an answer. The club meeting later must either be, or not be, the very same club." This would show that this person didn't understand the nature of clubs.

In the same way, if we have any worries about my imagined cases, we don't understand the nature of persons. In each of my cases, you would know that the resulting person would be both psychologically and physically exactly like you, and that he would have some particular proportion of the cells in your brain and body—90 per cent, or 10 per cent, or, in the case of teletransportation, 0 per cent. Knowing this, you know everything. How could it be a real question what would happen to you, unless you are a separately existing Ego, distinct from a brain and body, and the various kinds of mental state and event? If there are no such Egos, there is nothing else to ask a real question about.

Accepting the Bundle Theory is not only hard; it may also affect our emotions. As Buddha claimed, it may undermine our concern about our own futures. This effect can be suggested by redescribing this change of view. Suppose that you are about to be destroyed, but will later have a Replica on Mars. You would naturally believe that this prospect is about as bad as ordinary death, since your Replica won't be you. On the Bundle Theory, the fact that your Replica won't be you just consists in the fact that, though it will be fully psychologically continuous with you, this continuity won't have its normal cause. But when you object to teletransportation you are not objecting merely to the abnormality of this cause. You are objecting that this cause won't get *you* to Mars. You fear that the abnormal cause will fail to produce a further and all-important fact, which is different from the fact that your Replica will be psychologically continuous with you. You do not merely want there to be psychological continuity between you and some future person. You want to *be* this future person. On the Bundle Theory, there is no such special further fact. What you fear will not happen, in this imagined case, *never* happens. You want the person on Mars to be you in a specially intimate way in which no future person will ever be you. This means that, judged from the standpoint of your natural beliefs, even ordinary survival is about as bad as teletransportation. *Ordinary survival is about as bad as being destroyed and having a Replica.*

HOW THE SPLIT-BRAIN CASES SUPPORT THE BUNDLE THEORY

The truth of the Bundle Theory seems to me, in the widest sense, as much a scientific as a philosophical conclusion. I can imagine kinds of evidence which would have justified believing in the existence of separately existing Egos, and believing that the continued existence of these Egos is what explains the continuity of each mental life. But there is in fact very little evidence in favour of this Ego Theory, and much for the alternative Bundle Theory.

Some of this evidence is provided by the split-brain cases. On the Ego Theory, to explain what unifies our experiences at any one time, we should simply claim that these are all experiences which are being had by the same person. Bundle Theorists reject this explanation. This disagreement is hard to resolve in ordinary cases. But consider the simplified split-brain case that I described. We show to my imagined patient a placard whose left half is blue and right half is red. In one of this person's two streams of consciousness, he is aware of seeing only blue, while at the same time, in his other stream, he is aware of seeing only red. Each of these two visual experiences is combined with other experiences, like that of being aware of moving one of his hands. What unifies the experiences, at any time, in each of this person's two streams of consciousness? What unifies his awareness of seeing only red with his awareness of moving one hand? The answer cannot be that these experiences are being had by the same

person. The answer cannot explain the unity of each of this person's two streams of consciousness, since it ignores the disunity between these streams. This person is now having all of the experiences in both of his two streams. If this fact was what unified these experiences, this would make the two streams one.

These cases do not, I have claimed, involve two people sharing a single body. Since there is only one person involved, who has two streams of consciousness, the Ego Theorist's explanation would have to take the following form. He would have to distinguish between persons and subjects of experiences, and claim that, in split-brain cases, there are *two* of the latter. What unifies the experiences in one of the person's two streams would have to be the fact these experiences are all being had by the same subject of experiences. What unifies the experiences in this person's other stream would have to be the fact that they are being had by another subject of experiences. When this explanation takes this form, it becomes much less plausible. While we could assume that "subject of experiences", or "Ego", simply meant "person", it was easy to believe that there are subjects of experiences. But if there can be subjects of experiences that are not persons, and if in the life of a split-brain patient there are at any time two different subjects of experiences—two different. Egos—why should we believe that there really are such things? This does not amount to a refutation. But it seems to me a strong argument against the Ego Theory.

As a Bundle Theorist, I believe that these two Egos are idle cogs. There is another explanation of the unity of consciousness, both in ordinary cases and in split-brain cases. It is simply a fact that ordinary people are, at any time, aware of having several different experiences. This awareness of several different experiences can be helpfully compared with one's awareness, in short-term memory, of several different experiences. Just as there can be a single memory of just having had several experiences, such as hearing a bell strike three times, there can be a single state of awareness both of hearing the fourth striking of this bell, and of seeing, at the same time, ravens flying past the bell-tower.

Unlike the Ego Theorist's explanation, this explanation can easily be extended to cover split-brain cases. In such cases there is, at any time, not one state of awareness of several different experiences, but two such states. In the case I described, there is one state of awareness of both seeing only red and of moving one hand, and there is another state of awareness of both seeing only blue and moving the other hand. In claiming that there are two such states of awareness, we are not postulating the existence of unfamiliar entities, two separately existing Egos which are not the same as the single person whom the case involves. This explanation appeals to a pair of mental states which would have to be described anyway in a full description of this case.

I have suggested how the split-brain cases provide one argument for one view about the nature of persons. I should mention another such argument, provided by an imagined extension of these cases, first discussed at length by David Wiggins.[3]

In this imagined case a person's brain is divided, and the two halves are transplanted into a pair of different bodies. The two resulting people live quite separate lives. This imagined case shows

that personal identity is not what matters. If I was about to divide, I should conclude that neither of the resulting people will be me. I will have ceased to exist. But this way of ceasing to exist is about as good—or as bad—as ordinary survival.

Some of the features of Wiggins's imagined case are likely to remain technically impossible. But the case cannot be dismissed, since its most striking feature, the division of one stream of consciousness into separate streams, has already happened. This is a second way in which the actual split-brain cases have great theoretical importance. They challenge some of our deepest assumptions about ourselves.[4]

NOTES

1. See MacKay's contribution, chapter 1 of *Mind-waves,* ed. Colin Blakemore and Susan Greenfield (Oxford: Basil Blackwell, 1987), pp. 5–16.
2. For the sources of these and similar quotations, see my *Reasons and Persons* pp. 502–3, 532. (Oxford: Oxford University Press, 1984).
3. At the end of his *Identity and Spatio-temporal Continuity* (Oxford: Blackwell, 1967).
4. I discuss these assumptions further in part 3 of my *Reasons and Persons.*

Where Am I?

DANIEL C. DENNETT

Daniel C. Dennett, a leading figure in the philosophy of mind, teaches at Tufts University.

Now that I've won my suit under the Freedom of Information Act, I am at liberty to reveal for the first time a curious episode in my life that may be of interest not only to those engaged in research in the philosophy of mind, artificial intelligence and neuroscience but also to the general public.

Several years ago I was approached by Pentagon officials who asked me to volunteer for a highly dangerous and secret mission. In collaboration with

NASA and Howard Hughes, the Department of Defense was spending billions to develop a Supersonic Tunneling Underground Device, or STUD. It was supposed to tunnel through the earth's core at great speed and deliver a specially designed atomic warhead "right up the Red's missile silos," as one of the Pentagon brass put it.

The problem was that in an early test they had succeeded in lodging a warhead about a

From Daniel C. Dennett, *Brainstorms* (Bradford Books, 1978), pp. 310–323. Reprinted by permission of MIT Press.

mile deep under Tulsa, Oklahoma, and they wanted me to retrieve it for them. "Why me?" I asked. Well, the mission involved some pioneering applications of current brain research, and they had heard of my interest in brains and of course my Faustian curiosity and great courage and so forth.... Well, how could I refuse? The difficulty that brought the Pentagon to my door was that the device I'd been asked to recover was fiercely radioactive, in a new way. According to monitoring instruments, something about the nature of the device and its complex interactions with pockets of material deep in the earth had produced radiation that could cause severe abnormalities in certain tissues of the brain. No way had been found to shield the brain from these deadly rays, which were apparently harmless to other tissues and organs of the body. So it had been decided that the person sent to recover the device should *leave his brain behind*. It would be kept in a safe place where it could execute its normal control functions by elaborate radio links. Would I submit to a surgical procedure that would completely remove my brain, which would then be placed in a life-support system at the Manned Spacecraft Center in Houston? Each input and output pathway, as it was severed, would be restored by a pair of micro-miniaturized radio transceivers, one attached precisely to the brain, the other to the nerve stumps in the empty cranium. No information would be lost, all the connectivity would be preserved. At first I was a bit reluctant. Would it really work? The Houston brain surgeons encouraged me. "Think of it," they said, "as a mere *stretching* of the nerves. If your brain were just moved over an *inch* in your skull, that would not alter or impair your mind. We're simply going to make the nerves indefinitely elastic by splicing radio links into them."

I was shown around the life-support lab in Houston and saw the sparkling new vat in which my brain would be placed, were I to agree. I met the large and brilliant support team of neurologists, hematologists, biophysicists, and electrical engineers, and after several days of discussions and demonstrations, I agreed to give it a try. I was subjected to an enormous array of blood tests, brain scans, experiments, interviews, and the like. They took down my autobiography at great length, recorded tedious lists of my beliefs, hopes, fears, and tastes. They even listed my favorite stereo recordings and gave me a crash session of psychoanalysis.

The day for surgery arrived at last and of course I was anesthetized and remember nothing of the operation itself. When I came out of anesthesia, I opened my eyes, looked around, and asked the inevitable, the traditional, the lamentably hackneyed postoperative question: "Where am I?" The nurse smiled down at me. "You're in Houston," she said, and I reflected that this still had a good chance of being the truth one way or another. She handed me a mirror. Sure enough, there were the tiny antennae poling up through their titanium ports cemented into my skull.

"I gather the operation was a success," I said, "I want to go see my brain." They led me (I was a bit dizzy and unsteady) down a long corridor and into the life-support lab. A cheer went up from the assembled support team, and I responded with what I hoped was a jaunty salute. Still feeling lightheaded, I was helped over to the life-support vat. I peered through the glass. There, floating in what looked like ginger ale, was undeniably a human brain, though it was almost covered with printed circuit chips, plastic tubules, electrodes, and other paraphernalia. "Is that mine?" I asked. "Hit the output transmitter switch there on the side of the vat and see for yourself," the project director replied. I moved the switch to OFF, and immediately slumped, groggy and nauseated, into the arms of the technicians, one of whom kindly restored the switch to its ON position. While I recovered my equilibrium and composure, I thought to myself: "Well, here I am, sitting on a folding chair, staring through a piece of plate glass at my own brain.... But wait," I said to myself, "shouldn't I have thought, 'Here I am, suspended in a bubbling fluid, being stared at by my own eyes'?" I tried to think this latter thought. I tried to project it into the tank, offering it hopefully to my brain, but I failed to carry off the exercise with any conviction. I tried again. "Here am *I*, Daniel Dennett, suspended in a bubbling fluid, being stared at by my own eyes." No, it just didn't work. Most puzzling and confusing. Being a philosopher of firm physicalist conviction, I believed unswervingly that the tokening of my thoughts was occurring somewhere in my brain: yet, when I thought "Here I am," where the thought occurred to me was *here*, outside the vat, where I, Dennett, was standing staring at my brain.

I tried and tried to think myself into the vat, but to no avail. I tried to build up to the task by doing mental exercises. I thought to myself, "The sun is shining *over there*," five times in rapid succession, each time mentally ostending a different place: in order, the sunlit corner of the lab, the visible front lawn of the hospital, Houston, Mars, and Jupiter. I found I had little difficulty in getting my "there's" to hop all over the celestial map with their proper references. I could loft a "there" in an instant through the farthest reaches of space, and then aim the next "there" with pinpoint accuracy at the upper left quadrant of a freckle on my arm. Why was I having such trouble with "here"? "Here in Houston" worked well enough, and so did "here in the lab," and even "here in this part of the lab," but "here in the vat" always seemed merely an unmeant mental mouthing. I tried closing my eyes while thinking it. This seemed to help, but still I couldn't manage to pull it off, except perhaps for a fleeting instant. I couldn't be sure. The discovery that I couldn't be sure was so unsettling. How did I know *where* I meant by "here" when I thought "here"? Could I *think* I meant one place when in fact I meant another? I didn't see how that could be admitted without untying the few bonds of intimacy between a person and his own mental life that had survived the onslaught of the brain scientists and philosophers, the physicalists and behaviorists.... Nagged by confusion, I attempted to orient myself by falling back on a favorite philosopher's ploy. I began naming things.

"Yorick," I said aloud to my brain, "you are my brain. The rest of my body, seated in this chair, I dub 'Hamlet.'" So here we all are: Yorick's my brain, Hamlet's my body, and I am Dennett. *Now*, where am I? And when I think "where am I?" where's that thought tokened? [ie, where does that thought occur?] Is it tokened in my brain, lounging about in the vat, or right here

between my ears where it *seems* to be tokened? Or nowhere? Its *temporal* coordinates give me no trouble; must it not have spatial coordinates as well? I began making a list of the alternatives.

1. *Where Hamlet goes, there goes Dennett*. This principle was easily refuted by appeal to the familiar brain transplant thought-experiments so enjoyed by philosophers. If Tom and Dick switch brains, Tom is the fellow with Dick's former body—just ask him; he'll claim to be Tom, and tell you the most intimate details of Tom's autobiography. It was clear enough, then, that my current body and I could part company, but not likely that I could be separated from my brain. The rule of thumb that emerged so plainly from the thought-experiments was that in a brain-transplant operation, one wanted to be the *donor*, not the recipient. Better to call such an operation a *body*-transplant, in fact. So perhaps the truth was,

2. *Where Yorick goes, there goes Dennett*. This was not at all appealing, however. How could I be in the vat and not about to go anywhere, when I was so obviously outside the vat looking in and beginning to make guilty plans to return to my room for a substantial lunch? This begged the question, I realized, but it still seemed to be getting at something important. Casting about for some support for my intuition, I hit upon a legalistic sort of argument that might have appealed to Locke.

Suppose, I argued to myself, I were now to fly to California, rob a bank, and be apprehended. In which state would I be tried: In California, where the robbery took place, or in Texas, where the brains of the outfit were located? Would I be a California felon with an out-of-state brain, or a Texas felon remotely controlling an accomplice of sorts in California? It seemed possible that I might beat such a rap just on the undecidability of that jurisdictional question, though perhaps it would be deemed an inter-state, and hence Federal, offense. In any event, suppose I were convicted. Was it likely that California would be satisfied to throw Hamlet into the brig, knowing that Yorick was living the good life and luxuriously taking the waters in Texas? Would Texas incarcerate Yorick, leaving Hamlet free to take the next boat to Rio? This alternative appealed to me. Barring capital punishment or other cruel and unusual punishment, the state would be obliged to maintain the life-support system for Yorick though they might move him from Houston to Leavenworth, and aside from the unpleasantness of the opprobrium, I, for one, would not mind at all and would consider myself a free man under those circumstances. If the state has an interest in forcibly relocating persons in institutions, it would fail to relocate me in any institution by locating Yorick there. If this were true, it suggested a third alternative.

3. *Dennett is wherever he thinks he is.* Generalized, the claim was as follows: At any given time a person has a *point of view,* and the location of the point of view (which is determined internally by the content of the point of view) is also the location of the person.

Such a proposition is not without its perplexities, but to me it seemed a step in the right direction. The only trouble was that it seemed to place one in a heads-I-win/tails-you-lose situation of unlikely infallibility as regards location. Hadn't I myself often been wrong about where I was, and at least as often uncertain? Couldn't one get lost? Of course, but getting lost *geographically* is not the only way one might get lost. If one were lost in the woods one could attempt to reassure oneself with the consolation that at least one knew where one was: one was right *here* in the familiar surroundings of one's own body. Perhaps in this case one would not have drawn one's attention to much to be thankful for. Still, there were worse plights imaginable, and I wasn't sure I wasn't in such a plight right now.

Point of view clearly had something to do with personal location, but it was itself an unclear notion. It was obvious that the content of one's point of view was not the same as or determined by the content of one's beliefs or thoughts. For example, what should we say about the point of view of the Cinerama viewer who shrieks and twists in his seat as the roller-coaster footage overcomes his psychic distancing? Has he forgotten that he is safely seated in the theater? Here I was inclined to say that the

person is experiencing an illusory shift in point of view. In other cases, my inclination to call such shifts illusory was less strong. The workers in laboratories and plants who handle dangerous materials by operating feedback-controlled mechanical arms and hands undergo a shift in point of view that is crisper and more pronounced than anything Cinerama can provoke. They can feel the heft and slipperiness of the containers they manipulate with their metal fingers. They know perfectly well where they are and are not fooled into false beliefs by the experience, yet it is as if they were inside the isolation chamber they are peering into. With mental effort, they can manage to shift their point of view back and forth, rather like making a transparent Neckar cube or an Escher drawing change orientation before one's eyes. It does seem extravagant to suppose that in performing this bit of mental gymnastics, they are transporting *themselves* back and forth.

Still their example gave me hope. If I was in fact in the vat in spite of my intuitions, I might be able to train myself to adopt that point of view even as a matter of habit. I should dwell on images of myself comfortably floating in my vat, beaming volitions to that familiar body *out there.* I reflected that the ease or difficulty of this task was presumably independent of the truth about the location of one's brain. Had I been practicing before the operation, I might now be finding it second nature. You might now yourself try such a *tromp d'oeil.* Imagine you have written an inflammatory letter which has been published in the *Times,* the result of which is that the Government has chosen to impound your brain for a probationary period of three years in its Dangerous Brain Clinic in Bethesda, Maryland. Your body of course is allowed freedom to earn a salary and thus to continue its function of laying up income to be taxed. At this moment, however, your body is seated in an auditorium listening to a peculiar account by Daniel Dennett of his own similar experience. Try it. Think yourself to Bethesda, and then hark back longingly to your body, far away, and yet *seeming* so near. It is only with long-distance restraint (yours? the Government's?) that you can control your impulse to get those hands clapping in polite applause before navigating the old body to the rest room and a well-deserved glass of evening sherry in the lounge. The task of imagination is certainly difficult, but if you achieve your goal the results might be consoling.

Anyway, there I was in Houston, lost in thought as one might say, but not for long. My speculations were soon interrupted by the Houston doctors, who wished to test out my new prosthetic nervous system before sending me off on my hazardous mission. As I mentioned before, I was a bit dizzy at first, and not surprisingly, although I soon habituated myself to my new circumstances (which were, after all, well nigh indistinguishable from my old circumstances). My accommodation was not perfect, however, and to this day I continue to be plagued by minor coordination difficulties. The speed of light is fast, but finite, and as my brain and body move farther and farther apart, the delicate interaction of my feedback systems is thrown into disarray by the time lags. Just as one is rendered close to speechless by a delayed or echoic hearing of one's speaking voice so, for instance, I am virtually unable to track a moving object with my eyes whenever my brain and my body are more than a few miles apart. In most matters my impairment is scarcely detectable, though I can no longer hit a slow curve ball with the authority of yore. There are some compensations of course. Though liquor tastes as good as ever, and warms my gullet while corroding my liver, I can drink it in any quantity I please, without becoming the slightest bit inebriated, a curiosity some of my close friends may have noticed (though I occasionally have *feigned* inebriation, so as not to draw attention to my unusual circumstances). For similar reasons, I take aspirin orally for a sprained wrist, but if the pain persists I ask Houston to administer codeine to me *in vitro*. In times of illness the phone bill can be staggering.

But to return to my adventure. At length, both the doctors and I were satisfied that I was ready to undertake my subterranean mission. And so I left my brain in Houston and headed by helicopter for Tulsa. Well, in any case, that's the way it seemed to me. That's how I

would put it, just off the top of my head as it were. On the trip I reflected further about my earlier anxieties and decided that my first postoperative speculations had been tinged with panic. The matter was not nearly as strange or metaphysical as I had been supposing. Where was I? In two places, clearly: both inside the vat and outside it. Just as one can stand with one foot in Connecticut and the other in Rhode Island, I was in two places at once. I had become one of those scattered individuals we used to hear so much about. The more I considered this answer, the more obviously true it appeared. But, strange to say, the more true it appeared, the less important the question to which it could be the true answer seemed. A sad, but not unprecedented, fate for a philosophical question to suffer. This answer did not completely satisfy me, of course. There lingered some question to which I should have liked an answer, which was neither "Where are all my various and sundry parts?" nor "What is my current point of view?" Or at least there seemed to be such a question. For it did seem undeniable that in some sense *I* and not merely *most of me* was descending into the earth under Tulsa in search of an atomic warhead.

When I found the warhead, I was certainly glad I had left my brain behind, for the pointer on the specially built Geiger counter I had brought with me was off the dial. I called Houston on my ordinary radio and told the operation control center of my position and my progress. In return, they gave me instructions for dismantling the vehicle, based upon my on-site observations. I had set to work with my cutting torch when all of a sudden a terrible thing happened. I went stone deaf. At first I thought it was only my radio earphones that had broken, but when I tapped on my helmet, I heard nothing. Apparently the auditory transceivers had gone on the fritz. I could no longer hear Houston or my own voice, but I could speak, so I started telling them what had happened. In mid-sentence, I knew something else had gone wrong. My vocal apparatus had become paralyzed. Then my right hand went limp—another transceiver had gone. I was truly in deep trouble. But worse was to follow. After a few more minutes, I went blind. I cursed my luck, and then I cursed the scientists who had led me into this grave peril. There I was, deaf, dumb, and blind, in a radioactive hole more than a mile under Tulsa. Then the last of my cerebral radio links broke, and suddenly I was faced with a new and even more shocking problem: whereas an instant before I had been buried alive in Oklahoma, now I was disembodied in Houston. My recognition of my new status was not immediate. It took me several very anxious minutes before it dawned on me that my poor body lay several hundred miles away, with heart pulsing and lungs respiring, but otherwise as dead as the body of any heart transplant donor, its skull packed with useless, broken electronic gear. The shift in perspective I had earlier found well nigh impossible now seemed quite natural. Though I could think myself back into my body in the tunnel under Tulsa, it took some effort to sustain the illusion. For surely it was an illusion to suppose I was still in Oklahoma: I had lost all conact with that body.

It occurred to me then, with one of those rushes of revelation of which we should be suspicious, that I had stumbled upon an impressive demonstration of the immateriality of the soul based upon physicalist principles and premises. For as the last radio signal between Tulsa and Houston died away, had I not changed location from Tulsa to Houston at the speed of light? And had I not accomplished this without any increase in mass? What moved from A to B at such speed was surely myself, or at any rate my soul or mind—the massless center of my being and home of my consciousness. My *point of view* had lagged somewhat behind, but I had already noted the indirect bearing of point of view on personal location. I could not see how a physicalist philosopher could quarrel with this except by taking the dire and counterintuitive route of banishing all talk of persons. Yet the notion of personhood was so well entrenched in everyone's world view, or so it seemed to me, that any denial would be as curiously unconvincing, as systematically disingenuous, as the Cartesian negation, "non sum."*

The joy of philosophic discovery thus tided me over some very bad minutes or perhaps hours as the helplessness and hopelessness of my situation became more apparent to me. Waves of panic and even nausea swept over me, made all the more horrible by the absence of their normal bodydependent phenomenology. No adrenalin rush of tingles in the arms, no pounding heart, no premonitory salivation. I did feel a dread sinking feeling in my bowels at one point, and this tricked me momentarily into the false hope that I was undergoing a reversal of the process that landed me in this fix—a gradual undisembodiment. But the isolation and uniqueness of that twinge soon convinced me that it was simply the first of a plague of phantom body hallucinations that I, like any other amputee, would be all too likely to suffer.

My mood then was chaotic. On the one hand, I was fired up with elation of my philosophic discovery and was wracking my brain (one of the few familiar things I could still do), trying to figure out how to communicate my discovery to the journals; while on the other, I was bitter, lonely, and filled with dread and uncertainty. Fortunately, this did not last long, for my technical support team sedated me into a dreamless sleep from which I awoke, hearing with magnificent fidelity the familiar opening strains of my favorite Brahms piano trio. So that was why they had wanted a list of my favorite recordings! It did not take me long to realize that I was hearing the music without ears. The output from the stereo stylus was being fed through some fancy rectification circuitry directly into my auditory nerve. I was mainlining Brahms, an unforgettable experience for any stereo buff. At the end of the record it did not surprise me to hear the reassuring voice of the project director speaking into a microphone that was now my prosthetic ear. He confirmed my analysis of what had gone wrong and assured me that steps were being taken to re-embody me. He did not elaborate, and after a few more recordings, I found myself drifting off to sleep. My sleep lasted, I later learned, for the better part of a year, and when I awoke, it was to find myself fully restored to my senses. When I looked into the

*["I do not exist."]

mirror, though, I was a bit startled to see an unfamiliar face. Bearded and a bit heavier, bearing no doubt a family resemblance to my former face, and with the same look of spritely intelligence and resolute character, but definitely a new face. Further self-explorations of an intimate nature left me no doubt that this was a new body and the project director confirmed my conclusions. He did not volunteer any information on the past history of my new body and I decided (wisely, I think in retrospect) not to pry. As many philosophers unfamiliar with my ordeal have more recently speculated, the acquisition of a new body leaves one's *person* intact. And after a period of adjustment to a new voice, new muscular strengths and weaknesses, and so forth, one's *personality* is by and large also preserved. More dramatic changes in personality have been routinely observed in people who have undergone extensive plastic surgery, to say nothing of sex change operations, and I think no one contests the survival of the person in such cases. In any event I soon accommodated to my new body, to the point of being unable to recover any of its novelties to my consciousness or even memory. The view in the mirror soon became utterly familiar. That view, by the way, still revealed antennae, and so I was not surprised to learn that my brain had not been moved from its haven in the life-support lab.

I decided that good old Yorick deserved a visit. I and my new body, whom we might as well call Fortinbras, strode into the familiar lab to another round of applause from the technicians, who were of course congratulating themselves, not me. Once more I stood before the vat and contemplated poor Yorick, and on a whim I once again cavalierly flicked off the output transmitter switch. Imagine my surprise when nothing unusual happened. No fainting spell, no nausea, no noticeable change. A technician hurried to restore the switch to ON, but still I felt nothing. I demanded an explanation, which the project director hastened to provide. It seems that before they had even operated on the first occasion, they had constructed a computer duplicate of my brain, reproducing both the complete information processing structure

and the computational speed of my brain in a giant computer program. After the operation, but before they had dared to send me off on my mission to Oklahoma, they had run this computer system and Yorick side by side. The incoming signals from Hamlet were sent simultaneously to Yorick's transceivers and to the computer's array of inputs. And the outputs from Yorick were not only beamed back to Hamlet, my body; they were recorded and checked against the simultaneous output of the computer program, which was called "Hubert" for reasons obscure to me. Over days and even weeks, the outputs were identical and synchronous, which of course did not *prove* that they had succeeded in copying the brain's functional structure, but the empirical support was greatly encouraging.

Hubert's input, and hence activity, had been kept parallel with Yorick's during my disembodied days. And now, to demonstrate this, they had actually thrown the master switch that put Hubert for the first time in on-line control of my body—not Hamlet, of course, but Fortinbras. (Hamlet, I learned, had never been recovered from its underground tomb and could be assumed by this time to have largely returned to the dust. At the head of my grave still lay the magnificent bulk of the abandoned device, with the word STUD emblazoned on its side in large letters—a circumstance which may provide archeologists of the next century with a curious insight into the burial rites of their ancestors.)

The laboratory technicians now showed me the master switch, which had two positions, labeled *B*, for Brain (they didn't know my brain's name was Yorick) and *H*, for Hubert. The switch did indeed point to *H*, and they explained to me that if I wished, I could switch it back to *B*. With my heart in my mouth (and my brain in its vat), I did this. Nothing happened. A click, that was all. To test their claim, and with the master switch now set at *B*, I hit Yorick's output transmitter switch on the vat and sure enough, I began to faint. Once the output switch was turned back on and I had recovered my wits, so to speak, I continued to play with the master switch, flipping it back and forth. I found that with the exception of the transitional click, I could detect no trace of a difference. I could switch in mid-utterance, and the sentence I had begun speaking under the control of Yorick was finished without a pause or hitch of any kind under the control of Hubert. I had a spare brain, a prosthetic device which might some day stand me in very good stead, were some mishap to befall Yorick. Or alternatively, I could keep Yorick as a spare and use Hubert. It didn't seem to make any difference which I chose, for the wear and tear and fatigue on my body did not have any debilitating effect on either brain, whether or not it was actually causing the motions of my body, or merely spilling its output into thin air.

The one truly unsettling aspect of this new development was the prospect which was not long in dawning on me, of someone detaching the spare—Hubert or Yorick, as the case might be—from Fortinbras and hitching it to yet another body—some Johnny-come-lately Rosencrantz or Guildenstern. Then (if not before) there would be *two* people, that much was clear. One would be me, and the other would be a sort of super-twin brother. If there were two bodies, one under the control of Hubert and the other being controlled by Yorick, then which would the world recognize as the true Dennett? And whatever the rest of the world decided, which one would be *me*? Would I be the Yorick-brained one, in virtue of Yorick's causal priority and former intimate relationship with the original Dennett body, Hamlet? That seemed a bit legalistic, a bit too redolent of the arbitrariness of consanguinity and legal possession, to be convincing at the metaphysical level. For, suppose that before the arrival of the second body on the scene, I had been keeping Yorick as the spare for years, and letting Hubert's output drive my body—that is, Fortinbras—all that time. The Hubert-Fortinbras couple would seem then by squatter's rights (to combat one legal intuition with another) to be true to Dennett and the lawful inheritor of everything that was Dennett's. This was an interesting question, certainly, but not nearly so pressing as another question that bothered me. My strongest intuition was that in such an

eventuality *I* would survive so long as *either* brain-body couple remained intact, but I had mixed emotions about whether I should want both to survive.

I discussed my worries with the technicians and the project director. The prospect of two Dennetts was abhorrent to me. I explained, largely for social reasons. I didn't want to be my own rival for the affections of my wife, nor did I like the prospect of the two Dennetts sharing my modest professor's salary. Still more vertiginous and distasteful, though, was the idea of knowing *that much* about another person, while he had the very same goods on me. How could we ever face each other? My colleagues in the lab argued that I was ignoring the bright side of the matter. Weren't there many things I wanted to do but, being only one person, had been unable to do? Now one Dennett could stay at home and be the professor and family man, while the other could strike out on a life of travel and adventure—missing the family of course, but happy in the knowledge that the other Dennett was keeping the home fires burning. I could be faithful and adulterous at the same time. I could even cuckold myself—to say nothing of other more lurid possibilities my colleagues were all too ready to force upon my overtaxed imagination. But my ordeal in Oklahoma (or was it Houston?) had made me less adventurous, and I shrank from this opportunity that was being offered (though of course I was never quite sure it was being offered to *me* in the first place).

There was another prospect even more disagreeable—that the spare, Hubert or Yorick as the case might be, would be detached from any input from Fortinbras and just left detached. Then, as in the other case, there would be two Dennetts, or at least two claimants to my name and possessions, one embodied in Fortinbras, and the other sadly, miserably disembodied. Both selfishness and altruism bade me take steps to prevent this from happening. So I asked that measures be taken to ensure that no one could ever tamper with the transceiver connections or the master switch without my (our? no, *my*) knowledge and consent. Since I had no desire to spend my life guarding my equipment in Houston, it was mutually decided that all the electronic connections in the lab would be carefully locked: both those that controlled the life-support system for Yorick and those that controlled the power supply for Hubert would be guarded with fail-safe devices, and I would take the only master switch, outfitted for radio remote control, with me wherever I went. I carry it strapped around my waist and—wait a moment—*here it is.* Every few months I reconnoiter the situation by switching channels. I do this only in the presence of friends of course, for if the other channel were, heaven forbid, either dead or otherwise occupied, there would have to be somebody who had my interests at heart to switch it back, to bring me back from the void. For while I could feel, see, hear and otherwise sense whatever befell my body, subsequent to such a switch, I'd be unable to control it. By the way, the two positions on the switch are intentionally unmarked, so I never have the faintest idea whether I am switching from Hubert to Yorick or *vice versa.* (Some of you may think that in this case I really don't know *who* I am, let alone where I am. But such reflections no longer make much of a dent on my essential Dennettness, on my own sense of who I am. If it is true that in one sense I don't know who I am then that's another one of your philosophical truths of underwhelming significance.)

In any case, every time I've flipped the switch so far, nothing has happened. *So let's give it a try. . . .*

"THANK GOD! I THOUGHT YOU'D NEVER FLIP THAT SWITCH! You can't imagine how horrible it's been these last two weeks—but now you know, it's your turn in purgatory. How I've longed for this moment! You see, about two weeks ago—excuse me, ladies and gentlemen, but I've got to explain this to my . . . um, brother, I guess you could say, but he's just told you the facts, so you'll understand—about two weeks ago our two brains drifted just a bit out of synch. I don't know whether *my* brain is now Hubert or Yorick, any more than you do, but in any case, the two brains drifted apart, and of course once the process started, it snowballed,

for I was in a slightly different receptive state for the input we both received, a difference that was soon magnified. In no time at all the illusion that I was in control of my body—our body—was completely dissipated. There was nothing I could do—no way to call you. YOU DIDN'T EVEN KNOW I EXISTED! It's been like being carried around in a cage, or better, like being possessed—hearing my own voice say things I didn't mean to say, watching in frustration as my own hands performed deeds I hadn't intended. You'd scratch our itches, but not the way I would have, and you kept me awake, with your tossing and turning. I've been totally exhausted, on the verge of a nervous breakdown, carried around helplessly by your frantic round of activities, sustained only by the knowledge that some day you'd throw the switch.

"Now it's your turn, but at least you'll have the comfort of knowing *I* know you're in there. Like an expectant mother, I'm eating—or at any rate tasting, smelling, seeing—for *two* now, and I'll try to make it easy for you. Don't worry. Just as soon as this colloquium is over, you and I will fly to Houston, and we'll see what can be done to get one of us another body. You can have a female body—your body could be any color you like. But let's think it over. I tell you what—to be fair, if we both want this body, I promise I'll let the project director flip a coin to settle which of us gets to keep it and which then gets to choose a new body. That should guarantee justice, shouldn't it? In any case, I'll take care of you, I promise. These people are my witnesses.

"Ladies and gentlemen, this talk we have just heard is not exactly the talk *I* would have given, but I assure you that everything he said was perfectly true. And now if you'll excuse me, I think I'd—we'd—better sit down."[1]

NOTE

1. Anyone familiar with the literature on this topic will recognize that my remarks owe a great deal to the explorations of Sydney Shoemaker, John Perry, David Lewis and Derek Parfit, and in particular to their papers in Amelie Rorty, ed., *The Identities of Persons,* 1976.

A Dialogue on
Personal Identity and Immortality

JOHN PERRY

John Perry teaches philosophy at Stanford University.

(This is a record of conversations of Gretchen Weirob, a teacher of philosophy at a small mid-western college, and several of her friends. They took place in her hospital room, the three nights before she died from injuries sustained in a motorcycle accident. Sam Miller is a chaplain and a longtime friend of Weirob's; Dave Cohen is a former student of hers.)

THE FIRST NIGHT

Cohen: I can hardly believe what you say, Gretchen. You are lucid and do not appear to be in great pain. And yet you say things are hopeless?

Weirob: These devices can keep me alive for another day or two at most. Some of my vital organs have been injured beyond anything the doctors know how to repair, apart from certain rather radical measures I have rejected. I am not in much pain. But as I understand it that is not a particularly good sign. My brain was uninjured and I guess that's why I am as lucid as I ever am. The whole situation is a bit depressing, I fear. But here's Sam Miller. Perhaps he will know how to cheer me up.

Miller: Good evening Gretchen. Hello, Dave. I guess there's not much point in beating around the bush, Gretchen; the medics tell me you're a goner. Is there anything I can do to help?

Weirob: Crimenentley, Sam! You deal with the dying every day. Don't you have anything more comforting to say than "Sorry to hear you're a goner?"

Miller: Well to tell you the truth, I'm a little at a loss for what to say to you. Most people I deal with are believers like I am. We talk of the prospects for survival. I give assurance that God, who is just and merciful, would not permit such a travesty as that our short life on this earth should be the end of things. But you and I have talked about religious and philosophical issues for years. I have never been able to find in you the least inclination to believe in God; indeed, it's a rare day when you are sure that your friends have minds, or that you can see your own hand in front of your face, or that there is any reason to believe that the sun will rise tomorrow. How can I hope to comfort you with the prospect of life after death, when I know you will regard it as having no probability whatsoever?

Weirob: I would not require so much to be comforted, Sam. Even the possibility of something quite improbable can be comforting, in certain situations. When we used to play tennis, I beat you no more than one time in twenty. But this was enough to establish the possibility of beating you on any given occasion, and by focusing merely on the possibility, I remained eager to play. Entombed in a secure prison, having thought our situation quite hopeless, we might find unutterable joy in the information that there was, after all, a possibility of escape, however slim the chances of actually succeeding. Hope provides comfort, and hope does not always require probability. But we must believe that what we hope for is at least possible. So I will ·set an easier task for you. Simply persuade me that my survival, after the death of this body, is *possible*, and I promise to be comforted. Whether you succeed or not, your attempts will be a diversion, for you know I like to talk philosophy more than anything else.

Miller: But what is possibility, if not reasonable probability?

Weirob: I do not mean possible in the sense of likely, or even in the sense of comforming to the known laws of physics or biology. I mean possible only in the weakest sense, of being conceivable, given the unavoidable facts. Within the next couple of days, this body will die. It will be buried, and it will rot away. I ask that, given these facts, you explain to me how it even makes *sense* to talk of me continuing to exist. Just explain to me what it is I am to *imagine,* when I imagine surviving, that is consistent with these facts, and I shall be comforted.

Miller: But then what is there to do? There are many conceptions of immortality, of survival past the grave, which all seem to make good sense. Surely not the possibility, but only the probability, can be doubted. Take your choice! Christians believe in life, with a body, in some Hereafter—the details vary, of course, from sect to sect. There is the Greek idea of the body as a prison, from which we escape at death—so we have continued life without a body. Then there are conceptions, in which we, so to speak, merge with the flow of being…

Weirob: I must cut short your lesson in comparative religion. Survival means surviving, no more, no less. I have no doubts that I shall merge with being; plants will take roots in my remains, and the chemicals that I am will continue to make their contribution to life. I am enough of an ecologist to be comforted. But survival, if it is anything, must offer comforts of a different sort, the comforts of *anticipation.* Survival means that tomorrow, or sometime in the future, there will be someone who will experience, who will see and touch and smell—or at least, at the very least, think and reason and remember. And this person will be *me.* This person will be related to me in such a way that it is correct for me to anticipate, to look forward to, those future experiences. And I am related to her in such a way that it will be right for her to remember what I have thought and done, to feel remorse for what I have done wrong,

and pride in what I have done right. And the only relation that supports anticipation and memory in this way, is simply *identity.* For it is never correct to anticipate, as happening to oneself, what will happen to someone else, is it? Or to remember, as one's own thoughts and deeds, what someone else did? So don't give me merger with being, or some such nonsense. Give me identity, or let's talk about baseball or fishing—but I'm sorry to get so emotional. I just react so strongly when words which mean one thing are used for another—when one talks about survival, but does not mean to say that the same person will continue to exist. It's such a sham!

Miller: I'm sorry. I was just trying to stay in touch with the times, if you want to know the truth, for when I read modern theology or talk to my students who have studied eastern religions, the notion of survival as simply continued existence of the same person seems out of date. Merger with Being! Merger with Being! That's all I hear. My own beliefs are quite simple, if somewhat vague. I think you will live again—with or without a body, I don't know—*I* draw comfort from my belief that you and I will be together again, after I also die. We will communicate, somehow. We will continue to grow spiritually. That's what I believe, as surely as I believe that I am sitting here. For I don't know how God could be excused, if this small sample of life is all that we are allotted; I don't know why he should have created us, if this few years of toil and torment are the end of it…

Weirob: Remember our deal, Sam. You don't have to convince me that survival is probable, for we both agree you would not get to first base. You have only to convince me that it is possible. The only condition is that it be real survival we are talking about, not some up-to-date ersatz survival, which simply amounts to what any ordinary person would call ceasing totally to exist.

Miller: I guess I just miss the problem then. Of course it's possible. You just continue to exist, after your body dies. What's to be defended or explained? You want details? OK. Two people meet a thousand years from now, in a place that may or may not be part of this physical universe. I am one and you are the other. So you must have survived. Surely you can imagine that. What else is there to say?

Weirob: But in a few days *I* will quit breathing, *I* will be put into a coffin, *I* will be buried. And in a few months or a few years *I* will be reduced to so much humus. That I take it is obvious, is given. How then can you say that I am one of these persons a thousand years from now?

Suppose I took this box of kleenex and lit fire to it. It is reduced to ashes and I smash the ashes and flush them down the john. Then I say to you, go home and on the shelf will be *that very box of kleenex.* It has survived! Wouldn't that be absurd? What sense could you make of it? And yet that is just what you say to me. I will rot away. And then, a thousand years later, there I will be. What sense does that make?

Miller: There could be an *identical* box of kleenex at your home, one just like it in every respect. And, in this sense, there is no difficulty in there being someone identical to you in the Hereafter, though your body has rotted away.

Weirob: You are playing with words again. There could be an *exactly similar* box of kleenex on my shelf. We sometimes use "identical" to mean "exactly similar" as when we talk of "identical twins." But I am using "identical," in a way in which *identity* is the condition of memory and correct anticipation. If I am told that tomorrow though I will be dead, someone else that looks and sounds and thinks just like me will be alive, would that be comforting? Could I correctly *anticipate* having her experiences? Would it make sense for me to fear her pains and look forward to her pleasures? Would it be right for her to feel remorse at the harsh way I am treating you? Of course not. Similarity, however exact, is not identity. I use identity to mean there is but one thing. If I am to survive, there must be one person who is here in this bed now, and who is talking to someone in your Hereafter ten or a thousand years from now. After all, what comfort could there be in the notion of a Heavenly imposter, walking around getting credit for the few good things I have done?

Miller: I'm sorry. I see that I was simply confused. Here is what I should have said. If you were merely a live human body—as the kleenex box is merely cardboard and glue in a certain

arrangement—then the death of your body would be the end of you. But surely you are more than that, fundamentally more than that. What is fundamentally you is not your body, but your soul or self or mind.

Weirob: Do you mean these words, "soul," "self," or "mind" to come to the same thing?

Miller: I have heard fine distinctions made, but usually cannot follow them. They are the nonphysical, nonmaterial, aspects of you. They are your consciousness. It is this that I get at with these words, and I am not clever enough to attempt any further distinction.

Weirob: Consciousness? I am conscious, for a while yet. I see, I hear, I think, I remember. But "to be conscious"—that is a verb. What is the subject of the verb, the thing which is conscious? Isn't it just this body, the same object that is overweight, injured, and lying in bed? And which will be buried, and not be conscious in a day or a week at the most?

Miller: As you are a philosopher, I would expect you to be less muddled about these issues. Did Descartes not draw a clear distinction between the body and the mind, between that which is overweight and that which is conscious? Your mind or soul is immaterial, lodged while you are on earth in your body. They are intimately related, but not identical. Now clearly, what concerns us in survival is your mind or soul. It is this which must be identical between the person before me now, and the one I expect to see in a thousand years in heaven.

Weirob: So I am not really this body, but a soul or mind or spirit? And this soul cannot be seen or felt or touched or smelt? That is implied, I take it, by the fact that it is immaterial?

Miller: That's right. Your soul sees and smells, but cannot be seen or smelt.

Weirob: Let me see if I understand you. You would admit that I am the very same person with whom you ate lunch last week at Dorsey's?

Miller: Of course you are.

Weirob: Now when you say I am the same person, if I understand you, that is not a remark about this body you see and could touch and I fear can smell. Rather it is a remark about a soul, which you cannot see or touch or smell. The fact that the same body was across the booth from you at Dorsey's as is now lying in front of you on the bed—that would not mean that the same *person* was present on both occasions, if the same soul were not. And if, through some strange turn of events, the same soul were present on both occasions, but lodged in different bodies, then it *would* be the same person. Is that right?

Miller: You have understood me perfectly. But surely, you understood all of this before!

Weirob: But wait. I can repeat it, but I'm not sure I understand it. If you cannot see or touch or in any way perceive my soul, what makes you think the one you are confronted with now *is* the very same soul you were confronted with at Dorsey's?

Miller: But I just explained. To say it is the same soul and to say it is the same person, are the same. And, of course, you are the same person you were before. Who else would you be if not yourself? You *were* Gretchen Weirob, and you *are* Gretchen Weirob.

Weirob: But how do you know you are talking to Gretchen Weirob at all, and not someone else, say Barbara Walters or even Mark Spitz!

Miller: Well, it's just obvious. I can see who I am talking to.

Weirob: But all you can see is my body. You can see, perhaps, that the same body is before you now that was before you last week at Dorsey's. But you have just said that Gretchen Weirob is not a body but a soul. In judging that the same person is before you now as was before you then, you must be making a judgement about souls—which, you said, cannot be seen or touched or smelled or tasted. And so, I repeat, how do you know?

Miller: Well, I *can* see that it is the same body before me now that was across the table at Dorsey's. And I know that the same soul is connected with the body as was connected with it before. That's how I know it's you. I see no difficulty in the matter.

Weirob: You reason on the principle, "same body, same self."

Miller: Yes.

Weirob: And would you reason conversely also? If there were in this bed Barbara Walters' body—that is, the body you see every night on

the news—would you infer that it was not me, Gretchen Weirob, in the bed?

Miller: Of course I would. How would you have come by Barbara Walters' body?

Weirob: But then merely extend this principle to Heaven, and you will see that your conception of survival is without sense. Surely this very body, which will be buried and, as I must so often repeat, *rot away,* will not be in your Hereafter. Different body, different person. Or do you claim that a body can rot away on earth, and then still wind up somewhere else? Must I bring up the kleenex box again?

Miller: No, I do not claim that. But I also do not extend a principle, found reliable on earth, to such a different situation as is represented by the Hereafter. That a correlation between bodies and souls has been found on earth, does not make it inconceivable or impossible that they should separate. Principles found to work in one circumstance may not be assumed to work in vastly altered circumstances. January and snow go together here, and one would be a fool to expect otherwise. But the principle does not apply in California.

Weirob: So the principle, "same body, same soul," is a well-confirmed regularity, not something you know "a priori."

Miller: By "a priori" you philosophers mean something which can be known without observing what actually goes on in the world, as I can know that two plus two equals four just by thinking about numbers, and that no bachelors are married just by thinking about the meaning of "bachelor"?

Weirob: Yes.

Miller: Then you are right. If it was part of the meaning of "same body" that wherever we have the same body, we have the same soul, it would have to obtain universally, in Heaven as well as on earth. But I just claim it is a generalization we know by observation on earth, and it need not automatically extend to Heaven.

Weirob: But where do you get this principle? It simply amounts to a correlation between being confronted with the same body and being confronted with the same soul. To establish such a correlation in the first place, surely one must have some *other* means of judging sameness of soul. You do not have such a means; your principle is without foundation; either you really do not know the person before you now is Gretchen Weirob, the very same person you lunched with at Dorsey's, or what you do know has nothing to do with sameness of some immaterial soul.

Miller: Hold on, hold on. You know I can't follow you when you start spitting out arguments like that. Now what is this terrible fallacy I'm supposed to have committed?

Weirob: I'm sorry. I get carried away. Here, have one of my chocolates by way of a peace offering.

Miller: Very tasty, thank you.

Weirob: Now why did you choose that one?

Miller: Because it had a certain swirl on the top which shows that it is a caramel.

Weirob: That is, a certain sort of swirl is correlated with a certain type of filling—the swirls with caramel, the rosettes with orange, and so forth.

Miller: Yes. When you put it that way, I see an analogy. Just as I judged that the filling would be the same in this piece as in the last piece that I ate with such a swirl, so I judge that the soul with which I am conversing is the same as the last soul with which I conversed when sitting across from that body. We *see* the outer wrapping and infer to what is inside.

Weirob: But how did you come to realize that swirls of that sort and caramel insides were so associated?

Miller: Why from eating a great many of them over the years. Whenever I bit into a candy with that sort of swirl, it was filled with this sort of caramel.

Weirob: Could you have established the correlation had you never been allowed to bite into a candy and never seen what happened when someone else bit into one? You could have formed the hypothesis, "same swirl, same filling." But could you have ever established it?

Miller: It seems not.

Weirob: So your inference, in a particular case, to the identity of filling from the identity of swirl would be groundless?

Miller: Yes, it would. I think I see what is coming.

Weirob: I'm sure you do. Since you can never, so to speak, bite into my soul, can never see or touch it, you have no way of testing your hypothesis that sameness of body means sameness of self.

Miller: I daresay you are right. But now I'm a bit lost. What is supposed to follow from all of this?

Weirob: If identity of persons consisted in identity of immaterial unobservable souls as you claim, then judgements of personal identity of the sort we make every day whenever we greet a friend or avoid a pest are really judgements about such souls.

Miller: Right.

Weirob: But if such judgements were really about souls, they would all be groundless and without foundation. For we have no direct method of observing sameness of soul, and so— and this is the point made by the candy example—can have no indirect method either.

Miller: That seems fair.

Weirob: But our judgements about persons are not all simply groundless and silly, so we must not be judging of immaterial souls after all.

Miller: Your reasoning has some force. But I suspect the problem lies in my defense of my position, and not the position itself. Look here. There *is* a way to test the hypothesis of a correlation after all. When I entered the room, I expected you to react just as you did. Argumentatively and skeptically. Had the person with this body reacted completely different perhaps I would have been forced to conclude it was not you. For example, had she complained about not being able to appear on the six o'clock news, and missing Harry Reasoner, and so forth, I might have eventually been persuaded it *was* Barbara Walters and not you. Similarity of psychological characteristics, a person's attitudes, beliefs, memories, prejudices, and the like, is observable. These are correlated with identity of body on the one side, and of course with sameness of soul on the other. So the correlation between body and soul can be established after all by this intermediate link.

Weirob: And how do you know that?

Miller: Know what?

Weirob: That where we have sameness of psychological characteristics, we have sameness of soul.

Miller: Well now you are really being just silly. The soul or mind just is that which is responsible for one's character, memory, belief. These are aspects of or states of mind, just as one's height, weight, and appearance are aspects of the body.

Weirob: Let me grant, for the sake of argument, that belief, character, memory, and so forth are states of mind. That is, I suppose, I grant that what one thinks and feels is due to the state one's mind is in at that time. And I shall even grant that a mind is an immaterial thing—though I harbor the gravest doubts that this is so. I do not see how it follows from that, that similarity of such traits requires, or is evidence to the slightest degree, for identity of the mind or soul.

Let me explain my point with an analogy. If we were to walk out of this room, down past the mill and out toward Wilbur, what would we see?

Miller: We would come to the Blue River, among other things.

Weirob: And how would you recognize the Blue River? I mean, of course if you left from here, you would scarcely expect to hit the Platte or Niobrara. But suppose you were actually lost, and came across the Blue River in your wandering, just at that point where an old dam partly blocks the flow. Couldn't you recognize it?

Miller: Yes, I'm sure as soon as I saw that part of the river I would again know where I was.

Weirob: And how would you recognize it?

Miller: Well, the turgid brownness of the water, the sluggish flow, the filth washed up on the banks, and such.

Weirob: In a word, the state of the water which makes up the river at the time you see it.

Miller: Right.

Weirob: If you saw blue clean water, with bass jumping, you would know it wasn't the Blue River.

Miller: Of course.

Weirob: So you expect, each time you see the Blue, to see the water, which makes it up, in similar states—not always exactly the same, for sometimes it's a little dirtier, but by and large, similar.

Miller: Yes, but what do you intend to make of this?

Weirob: Each time you see the Blue, it consists of *different* water. The water that was in it

a month ago may be in Tuttle Creek Reservoir, or in the Mississippi, or in the Gulf of Mexico by now. So the *similarity* of states of water, by which you judge the sameness of river, does not require *identity* of the water which is in those states at these various times.

Miller: And?

Weirob: And so just because you judge as to personal identity by reference to similarity of states of mind, it does not follow that the mind, or soul, is the same in each case. My point is this. For all you know, the immaterial soul which you think is lodged in my body might change from day to day, from hour to hour, from minute to minute, replaced each time by another soul psychologically similar. You cannot see it or touch it, so how would you know?

Miller: Are you saying I don't really know who you are?

Weirob: Not at all. *You* are the one who says personal identity consists in sameness of this immaterial, unobservable, invisible, untouchable soul. I merely point out that *if* it did consist in that, you *would* have no idea who I am. Sameness of body would not necessarily mean sameness of person. Sameness of psychological characteristics would not necessarily mean sameness of person. I am saying that if you do know who I am then you are wrong that personal identity consists in sameness of immaterial soul.

Miller: I see. But wait. I believe my problem is that I simply forgot a main tenet of my theory. The correlation can be established in my own case. I know that *my* soul and my body are intimately and consistently found together. From this one case I can generalize, at least as concerns life in this world, that sameness of body is a reliable sign of sameness of soul. This leaves me free to regard it as intelligible, in the case of death, that the link between the particular soul and the particular body it has been joined with is broken.

Weirob: This would be quite an extrapolation, wouldn't it, from one case directly observed, to a couple of billion in which only the body is observed? For I take it that we are in the habit of assuming, for every man now on earth, as well as those who have already come and gone, that the principle "one body, one soul" is in effect.

Miller: This does not seem an insurmountable obstacle. Since there is nothing special about my case, I assume the arrangement I find in it applies universally, until given some reason to believe otherwise. And I never have been.

Weirob: Let's let that pass. I have another problem that is more serious. How is it that you know in your own case that there is a single soul which has been so consistently connected with your body?

Miller: Now you really cannot be serious, Gretchen. How can I doubt that I am the same person I was? Is there anything more clear and distinct, less susceptible to doubt? How do you expect me to prove anything to you, when you are capable of denying my own continued existence from second to second? Without knowledge of our own identity, everything we think and do would be senseless. How could I think if I did not suppose that the person who begins my thought is the one who completes it? When I act, do I not assume that the person who forms the intention is the very one who performs the action?

Weirob: But I grant you that a single *person* has been associated with your body since you were born. The question is whether one immaterial soul has been, or more precisely, whether you are in a position to know it. You believe that a judgement that one and the same person has had your body all these many years is a judgement that one and the same immaterial soul has been lodged in it. I say that such judgements concerning the soul are totally mysterious, and that if our knowledge of sameness of persons consisted in knowledge of sameness of immaterial soul, it too would be totally mysterious. To point out, as you do, that it is not, but perhaps the most secure knowledge we have, the foundation of all reason and action, is simply to make the point that it cannot consist of knowledge of identity of immaterial self.

Miller: You have simply asserted, and not established, that my judgement that a single soul has been lodged in my body these many years is mysterious.

Weirob: Well, consider these possibilities. One is that a single soul, one and the same, has been with this body I call mine since it was born. The other is that one soul was associated with it until five years ago and then another, psychologically similar, inheriting all the memories and beliefs, took over. A third hypothesis is that every five years a new soul takes over. A fourth is that every five minutes a new soul takes over. The most radical is that there is a constant flow of souls through this body, each psychologically similar to the preceding, as there is a constant flow of water molecules down the Blue. What evidence do I have that the first hypothesis, the "single soul hypothesis," is true, and not one of the others? Because I am the same person I was five minutes or five years ago? But the issue in question is simply whether from sameness of person, which isn't in doubt, we can infer sameness of soul. Sameness of body? But how do I establish a stable relationship between soul and body? Sameness of thoughts and sensations? But they are in constant flux. By the nature of the case, if the soul cannot be observed, it cannot be observed to be the same. Indeed, no sense has ever been assigned to the phrase "same soul." Nor could any sense be attached to it! One would have to say what a single soul looked like or felt like, how an encounter with a single soul at different times differed from encounters with different souls. But this can hardly be done, since a soul on your conception doesn't look or feel like *anything* at all. And so of course "souls" can afford no principle of identity. And so they cannot be used to bridge the gulf between my existence now and my existence in the hereafter.

Miller: Do you doubt the existence of your own soul?

Weirob: I haven't based my argument on there being no immaterial souls of the sort you describe, but merely on their total irrelevance to questions of personal identity, and so to questions of personal survival. I do indeed harbor grave doubts whether there are any immaterial souls of the sort to which you appeal. Can we have a notion of a soul unless we have a notion of the *same* soul? But I hope you do not think that means I doubt my own existence. I think I lie here, overweight and conscious. I think you can see me, not just some outer wrapping, for I think I am just a live human body. But that is not the basis of my argument. I give you these souls. I merely observe they can by their nature provide no principle of personal identity.

Miller: I admit I have no answer.

I'm afraid I do not comfort you, though I have perhaps provided you with some entertainment. Emerson said that a little philosophy turns one away from religion, but that deeper understanding brings one back. I know no one who has thought so long and hard about philosophy as you have. Will it never lead you back to a religious frame of mind?

Weirob: My former husband used to say that a little philosophy turns one away from religion, and more philosophy makes one a pain in the neck. Perhaps he was closer to the truth than Emerson.

Miller: Perhaps he was. But perhaps by tomorrow night I will have come up with some argument that will turn you around.

Weirob: I hope I live to hear it.

THE SECOND NIGHT

Weirob: Well, Sam, have you figured out a way to make sense of the identity of immaterial souls?

Miller: No, I have decided it was a mistake to build my argument on such a dubious notion.

Weirob: Have you then given up on survival? I think such a position would be a hard one for a clergyman to be talked into, and would feel bad about having pushed you so far.

Miller: Don't worry. I'm more convinced than ever. I stayed up late last night thinking and reading, and I'm sure I can convince you now.

Weirob: Get with it, time is running out.

Miller: First, let me explain why, independently of my desire to defend survival after death, I am dissatisfied with your view that personal identity is just bodily identity. My argument will be very similar to the one you used to convince me that personal identity could not be identified with identity of an immaterial soul.

Consider a person waking up tomorrow morning, conscious, but not yet ready to open her eyes and look around and, so to speak, let the new day officially begin.

Weirob: Such a state is familiar enough, I admit.

Miller: Now couldn't such a person tell who she was? That is, even before opening her eyes and looking around, and in particular before looking at her body or making any judgements about it, wouldn't she be able to say who she was? Surely most of us, in the morning, know who we are before opening our eyes and recognizing our own bodies, do we not?

Weirob: You seem to be right about that.

Miller: But such a judgement as this person makes—we shall suppose she judges "I am Gretchen Weirob"—is a judgement of personal identity. Suppose she says to herself, "I am the very person who was arguing with Sam Miller last night." This is clearly a statement about her identity with someone who was alive the night before. And she could make this judgement without examining her body at all. You could have made just this judgement this morning, before opening your eyes.

Weirob: Well, in fact I did so. I remembered our conversation of last night and said to myself, "Could I be the rude person who was so hard on Sam Miller's attempts to comfort me?" And, of course, my answer was that I not only could be but was that very rude person.

Miller: But then by the same principle you used last night, personal identity cannot be bodily identity. For you said that it could not be identity of immaterial soul because we were not judging as to identity of immaterial soul when we judge as to personal identity. But by the same token, as my example shows, we are not judging as to bodily identity when we judge as to personal identity. For we can judge who we are, and that we are the very person who did such and such and so and so, without having to make any judgements at all about the body. So, personal identity, while it may not consist of identity of an immaterial soul, does not consist in identity of material body either.

Weirob: I did argue as you remember. But I also said that the notion of the identity of an immaterial, unobservable, unextended soul seemed to make no sense at all. This is one reason such souls cannot be what we are judging about, when we judge as to personal identity. Bodily identity at least makes sense. Perhaps we are just assuming sameness of body, without looking.

Miller: Granted. But you do admit that we do not in our own cases need to actually make a judgement of bodily identity in order to make a judgement of personal identity.

Weirob: I don't think I will admit it. I will let it pass, so that we may proceed.

Miller: OK. Now it seems to me we are even able to imagine awakening and finding ourselves to have a *different* body than the one we had before. Suppose yourself just as I have described you. And now suppose you finally open your eyes and see, not the body you have grown so familiar with over the years, but one of a fundamentally different shape and size.

Weirob: Well I should suppose I had been asleep for a very long time and lost a lot of weight—perhaps I was in a coma for a year or so.

Miller: But isn't it at least conceivable that it should not be your old body at all? I seem to be able to imagine awakening with a totally new body.

Weirob: And how would you suppose that this came about?

Miller: That's beside the point. I'm not saying I can imagine a procedure that would bring this about. I'm saying I can imagine it happening to me. In Kafka's *The Metamorphosis,* someone awakens as a cockroach. I can't imagine what would make this happen to me or anyone else, but I can imagine awakening with the body of a cockroach. It is incredible that it should happen—that I do not deny. I simply mean I can imagine experiencing it. It doesn't seem contradictory or incoherent, simply unlikely and inexplicable.

Weirob: So, if I admit this can be imagined, what follows then?

Miller: Well, I think it follows that personal identity does not just amount to bodily identity. For I would not, finding that I had a new body, conclude that I was not the very same person I was before. I would be the same *person,* though I did not have the same *body.* So we would have identity of person but not identity of body. So personal identity cannot just amount to bodily identity.

Weirob: Well, suppose—and I emphasize *suppose*—I grant you all of this. Where does it leave you? What do you claim I have recognized as

the same, if not my body and not my immaterial soul?

Miller: I don't claim that you have recognized anything as the same, except the person involved, that is, you yourself.

Weirob: I'm not sure what you mean.

Miller: Let me appeal again to the Blue River. Suppose I take a visitor to the stretch of river by the old Mill, and then drive him toward Manhattan. After an hour or so drive we see another stretch of river, and I say, "That's the same river we saw this morning." As you pointed out yesterday, I don't thereby imply that the very same molecules of water are seen both times. And the places are different, perhaps a hundred miles apart. And the shape and color and level of pollution might all be different. What do I see later in the day that is identical with what I saw earlier in the day?

Weirob: Nothing, except the river itself.

Miller: Exactly. But now notice that what I see, strictly speaking, is not the whole river but only a part of it. I see different parts of the same river at the two different times. So really, if we restrict ourselves to what I literally see, I do not judge identity at all, but something else.

Weirob: And what might that be?

Miller: In saying that the river seen earlier and the river seen later are one and the same river, do I mean any more than that the stretch of water seen later and that stretch of water seen earlier are connected by other stretches of water?

Weirob: That's about right. If the stretches of water are so connected, there is but one river of which they are both parts.

Miller: Yes, that's what I mean. The statement of identity, "This river is the same one we saw this morning," is in a sense about rivers. But in a way it is also about stretches of water or river parts.

Weirob: So, is all of this something special about rivers?

Miller: Not at all. It is a recurring pattern. After all, we constantly deal with objects extended in space and time. But we are seldom aware of the objects as a whole, but only of their parts or stretches of their histories. When a statement of identity is not just something trivial, like "This bed is this bed," it is usually because we are really judging that different parts fit together, in some appropriate pattern, into a certain kind of whole.

Weirob: I'm not sure I see just what you mean yet.

Miller: Let me give you another example. Suppose we are sitting together watching the first game of a doubleheader. You ask me, "Is this game identical with this game?" This is a perfectly stupid question, though, of course, strictly speaking it makes sense and the answer is "yes."

But now suppose you leave in the sixth inning to go for hot dogs. You are delayed, and return after about forty-five minutes or so. You ask, "Is this the same game I was watching?" Now your question is not stupid, but perfectly appropriate.

Weirob: Because the first game might still be going on or it might have ended, and the second game begun, by the time I return.

Miller: Exactly. Which is to say somehow different parts of the game—different innings, or at least different plays—were somehow involved in your question. That's why it wasn't stupid or trivial but significant.

Weirob: So, you think that judgements as to the identity of an object of a certain kind—rivers or baseball games or whatever—involve judgements as to the *parts* of those things being connected in a certain way, and are significant only when different parts are involved. Is that your point?

Miller: Yes, and I think it is an important one. How foolish it would be, when we ask a question about the identity of baseball games, to look for something *else*, other than the game as a whole, which had to be the same. It could be the same game, even if different players were involved. It could be the same game, even if it had been moved to a different field. These other things, the innings, the plays, the players, the field, don't have to be the same at the different times for the game to be the same, they just have to be related in certain ways so as to make that complex whole we call a single game.

Weirob: You think we were going off on a kind of a wild goose chase when we asked whether it was the identity of soul or body that was involved in the identity of persons?

Miller: Yes. The answer I should now give is neither. We are wondering about the identity of the person. Of course, if by "soul" we just mean "person," there is no problem. But if we mean, as I did yesterday, some other thing whose identity is already understood, which has to be the same when persons are the same, we are just fooling ourselves with words.

Weirob: With rivers and baseball games, I can see that they are made up of parts connected in a certain way. The connection is, of course, different in the two cases, as is the sort of "part" involved. River parts must be connected physically with other river parts to form a continuous whole. Baseball innings must be connected so that the score, batting order, and the like are carried over from the earlier inning to the latter one according to the rules. Is there something analogous we are to say about persons?

Miller: Writers who concern themselves with this speak of "person-stages." That is just a stretch of consciousness, such as you and I are aware of now. I am aware of a flow of thoughts and feelings that are mine, you are aware of yours. A person is just a whole composed of such stretches as parts, not some substance that underlies them, as I thought yesterday, and not the body in which they occur, as you seem to think. That is the conception of a person I wish to defend today.

Weirob: So when I awoke and said to myself, "I am the one who was so rude to Sam Miller last night," I was judging that a certain stretch of consciousness I was then aware of, and an earlier one I remembered having been aware of, form a single whole of the appropriate sort—a single stream of consciousness, we might say.

Miller: Yes, that's it exactly. You need not worry about whether the same immaterial soul is involved, or whether that even makes sense. Nor need you worry about whether the same body is involved, as indeed you do not since you don't even have to open your eyes and look. Identity is not, so to speak, something under the person-stages, nor in something they are attached to, but something you build from them.

Now survival, you can plainly see, is no problem at all once we have this conception of personal identity. All you need suppose is that there is, in Heaven, a conscious being, and that the personstages that make her up are in the appropriate relation to those that now make you up, so that they are parts of the same whole—namely, you. If so, you have survived. So will you admit now that survival is at least possible?

Weirob: Hold on, hold on. Comforting me is not that easy. You will have to show that it is possible that these person-stages or stretches of consciousness be related in the appropriate way. And to do that, won't you have to tell me what that way is?

Miller: Yes, of course, I was getting ahead of myself. It is right at this point that my reading was particularly helpful. In a chapter of his *Essay on Human Understanding* Locke discusses this very question. He suggests that the relation between two person-stages or stretches of consciousness that makes them stages of a single person is just that the later one contains memories of the earlier one. He doesn't say this in so many words—he talks of "extending our consciousness back in time." But he seems to be thinking of memory.

Weirob: So, any past thought or feeling or intention or desire that I can remember having is mine?

Miller: That's right. I can remember only my own past thoughts and feelings, and you only yours. Of course, everyone would readily admit that. Locke's insight is to take this relation as the source of identity and not just its consequence. To remember—or more plausibly, to be able to remember—the thoughts and feelings of a person who was conscious in the past is just what it is to be that person.

Now you can easily see that this solves the problem of the possibility of survival. As I was saying, all you need to do is imagine someone at some future time, not on this earth and not with your present thoughts and feelings, remembering the very conversation we are having now. This does not require sameness of anything else, but it amounts to sameness of person. So, now will you admit it?

Weirob: No, I don't.

Miller: Well, what's the problem now?

Weirob: I admit that if I remember having a certain thought or feeling had by some person in the past, then I must indeed be that person. Though I can remember watching others think, I cannot remember their thinking, any more than I can experience it at the time it occurs if it is theirs and not mine. This is the kernel of Locke's idea, and I don't see that I could deny it.

But we must distinguish—as I'm sure you will agree—between *actually* remembering and merely *seeming* to remember. Many men who think that they are Napoleon claim to remember losing the battle of Waterloo. We may suppose them to be sincere, and to really seem to remember it. But, they do not actually remember, because they were not there and are not Napoleon.

Miller: Of course, I admit that we must distinguish between actually remembering and only seeming to.

Weirob: And you will admit too, I trust, that the thought of some person at some far place and some distant time seeming to remember this conversation I am having with you would not give me the sort of comfort that the prospect of survival is supposed to provide. I would have no reason to anticipate future experiences of this person, simply because she is to *seem* to remember my experiences. The experiences of such a deluded imposter are not ones I can look forward to having.

Miller: I agree.

Weirob: So, the mere possibility of someone in the future seeming to remember this conversation does not show the possibility of my surviving. Only the possibility of someone actually remembering this conversation—or, to be precise, the experiences I am having—would show that.

Miller: Of course. But what are you driving at? Where is the problem? I can imagine someone being deluded, but also someone actually being you and remembering your present thoughts.

Weirob: But, what's the difference? How do you know *which* of the two you are imagining, and *what* you have shown possible?

Miller: Well, I just imagine the one and not the other. I don't see the force of your argument.

Weirob: Let me try to make it clear with another example. Imagine two persons. One is talking to you, saying certain words, having certain thoughts, and so on. The other is not talking to you at all, but is in the next room being hypnotized. The hypnotist gives to this person a posthypnotic suggestion that upon awakening he will remember having had certain thoughts and having uttered certain words to you. The thoughts and words he mentions happen to be just the thoughts and words which the first person actually thinks and says. Do you understand the situation?

Miller: Yes, continue.

Weirob: Now, in a while, both of the people are saying sentences which begin, "I remember saying to Sam Miller..." and "I remember thinking as I talked to Sam Miller..." And they both report remembering just the same thoughts and utterances. One of these will be remembering and the other only seeming to remember, right?

Miller: Of course.

Weirob: Now, which one is *actually* remembering?

Miller: Why the very one who was in the room talking to me, of course. The other one is just under the influence of the suggestion made by the hypnotist and not remembering talking to me at all.

Weirob: Now you agree that the difference between them does not consist in the content of what they are now thinking or saying.

Miller: Agreed. The difference is in the relation to the past thinking and speaking. In the one case the relation of memory obtains. In the other, it does not.

Weirob: But they both satisfy part of the conditions of remembering, for they both *seem to remember*. So there must be some further condition that the one satisfies and the other does not. I am trying to get you to say what that further condition is.

Miller: Well, I said that the one who had been in this room talking would be remembering.

Weirob: In other words, given two putative rememberers of some past thought or action, the real rememberer is the one who, in addition to seeming to remember the past thought or action, actually thought it or did it.

Miller: Yes.

Weirob: That is to say, the one who is identical with the person who did the past thinking and uttering.

Miller: Yes, I admit it.

Weirob: So, your argument just amounts to this. Survival is possible, because imaginable. It is imaginable, because my identity with some Heavenly person is imaginable. To imagine it, we imagine a person in Heaven who, first, seems to remember my thoughts and actions, and second, is me.

Surely, there could hardly be a tighter circle. If I have doubts that the Heavenly person is me, I will have doubts as to whether she is really remembering or only seeming to. No one could doubt the possibility of some future person who, after his or her death, seemed to remember the things he or she thought and did. But that possibility does not resolve the issue about the possibility of survival. Only the possibility of someone *actually* remembering could do that, for that, as we agree, is sufficient for identity. But doubts about survival and identity simply go over without remainder into doubts about whether the memories would be actual or merely apparent. You guarantee me no more than the possibility of a deluded Heavenly imposter.

Cohen: But wait, Gretchen. I think Sam was less than fair to his own idea just now.

Weirob: You think you can break out of the circle of using real memory to explain identity, and identity to mark the difference between real and apparent memory? Feel free to try.

Cohen: Let us return to your case of the hypnotist. You point out that we have two putative rememberers. You ask what marks the difference, and claim the answer must be the circular one that the real rememberer is the person who actually had the experiences both seem to remember.

But that is not the only possible answer. The experiences themselves cause the later apparent memories in the one case, the hypnotist causes them in the other. We can say that the rememberer is the one of the two whose memories were *caused in the right way* by the earlier experiences. We thus distinguish between the rememberer and the hypnotic subject, without appeal to identity.

The idea that real memory amounts to apparent memory plus identity is misleading anyway. I seem to remember knocking over the menorah so the candles fell into and ruined a tureen of soup when I was a small child. And I did actually perform such a feat. So we have apparent memory and identity. But I do *not* actually remember; I was much too young when I did this to remember it now. I have simply been told the story so often I seem to remember.

Here the suggestion that real memory is apparent memory that was caused in the appropriate way by the past events fares better. Not my experience of pulling over the menorah, but my parents' later recounting of the tragedy, cause my memorylike impressions.

Weirob: You analyze personal identity into memory, and memory into apparent memory which is caused in the right way. A person is a certain sort of causal process.

Cohen: Right.

Weirob: Suppose now for the sake of argument I accept this. How does it help Sam in his defense of the possibility of survival? In ordinary memory, the causal chain from remembered event to memory of it never leads us outside the confines of a single body. Indeed, the normal process of which you speak surely involves storage of information somehow in the brain. How can the states of my brain, when I die, influence in the appropriate way the apparent memories of the Heavenly person Sam takes to be me?

Cohen: Well, I didn't intend to be defending the possibility of survival. That is Sam's problem. I just like the idea that personal identity can be explained in terms of memory, and not just in terms of identity of the body.

Miller: But surely, this does provide me with the basis for further defense. Your challenge, Gretchen, was to explain the difference between two persons in Heaven, one who actually remembers your experience—and so is you—and one who simply seems to remember it. But can I not just say that the one who is you is the one whose states were caused in the appropriate way? I do not mean the way they would be in a normal case of earthly memory. But in the case of the Heavenly being who is you, God would

have created her with the brain states (or whatever) she has *because* you had the ones you had at death. Surely it is not the exact form of the dependence of my later memories on my earlier perceptions that makes them really to be memories, but the fact that the process involved has preserved information.

Weirob: So if God creates a Heavenly person, designing her brain to duplicate the brain I have upon death, that person is me. If, on the other hand, a Heavenly being should come to be with those very same memory-like states by accident (if there are accidents in Heaven) it would not be me.

Miller: Exactly. Are you satisfied now that survival makes perfectly good sense?

Weirob: No, I'm still quite unconvinced.

The problem I see is this. If God could create one person in Heaven, and by designing her after me, make her me, why could He not make two such bodies, and cause this transfer of information into both of them? Would both of these Heavenly persons then be me? It seems as clear as anything in philosophy that from

A is B

and

C is B

where by "is" we mean identity, we can infer,

A is C.

So, if each of these Heavenly persons is me, they must be each other. But then they are not two but one. But my assumption was that God creates two, not one. He could create them physically distinct, capable of independent movement, perhaps in widely separated Heavenly locations, each with her own duties to perform, her own circle of Heavenly friends, and the like.

So either God, by creating a Heavenly person with a brain modeled after mine does not really create someone identical with me but merely someone similar to me, or God is somehow limited to making only one such being. I can see no reason why, if there were a God, He should be so limited. So I take the first option. He could create someone similar to me, but not someone who would *be* me. Either your analysis of memory is wrong, and such a being does not, after all, remember what I am doing or saying, or memory is not sufficient for personal identity. Your theory has gone wrong somewhere, for it leads to absurdity.

Cohen: But wait. Why can't Sam simply say that if God makes one such creature, she is you, while if He makes more, none of them are you? It's possible that He makes only one. So it's possible that you survive. Sam always meant to allow that it's *possible* that you won't survive. He had in mind the case in which there is no God to make the appropriate Heavenly persons, or God exists, but just doesn't make even one. You have simply shown that there is another way of not surviving. Instead of making too few Heavenly rememberers, He makes too many. So what? He might make the right number, and then you would survive.

Weirob: Your remarks really amount to a change in your position. Now you are not claiming that memory alone is enough for personal identity. Now, it is memory *plus* lack of competition, the absence of other rememberers, that is needed for personal identity.

Cohen: It does amount to a change of position. But what of it? Is there anything untenable about the position as changed?

Weirob: Let's look at this from the point of view of the Heavenly person. She says to herself, "Oh, I must be Gretchen Weirob, for I remember doing what she did and saying what she said." But now that's a pretty tenuous conclusion, isn't it? She is really only entitled to say, "Oh, either I'm Gretchen Weirob, or God has created more than one being like me, and none of us are." Identity has become something dependent on things wholly extrinsic to her. Who she is now turns on not just her states of mind and their relation to my states of mind, but on the existence or nonexistence of other people. Is this really what you want to maintain?

Or look at it from my point of view. God creates one of me in Heaven. Surely I should be glad if convinced this was to happen. Now He creates another, and I should despair again, for this means I won't survive after all. How can doubling a good deed make it worthless?

Cohen: Are you saying that there is some contradiction in my suggestion that only a unique Heavenly Gretchen counts as your survival?

Weirob: No, it's not contradictory, as far as I can see. But it seems odd in a way that shows that something somewhere is wrong with your theory. Here is a certain relationship I have with a Heavenly person. There being such a person, to whom I am related in this way, is something that is of great importance to me, a source of comfort. It makes it appropriate for me to anticipate having her experiences, since she is just me. Why should my having that relation to another being destroy my relation to this one? You say because then I will not be identical with either of them. But since you have provided a theory about what that identity consists in, we can look and see what it amounts to for me to be or not to be identical. If she is to remember my experience, I can rightly anticipate hers. But then it seems the doubling makes no difference. And yet it must, for one cannot be identical with two. So you add, in a purely *ad hoc* manner, that her memory of me isn't enough to make my anticipation of her experiences appropriate, if there are two rather than one so linked. Isn't it more reasonable to conclude, since memory does not secure identity when there are two Heavenly Gretchens, it also doesn't when there is only one?

Cohen: There is something *ad hoc* about it, I admit. But perhaps that's just the way our concept works. You have not elicited a contradiction . . .

Weirob: An infinite pile of absurdities has the same weight as a contradiction. And absurdities can be generated from your account without limit. Suppose God created this Heavenly person before I died. Then He in effect kills me; if He has already created her, then you really are not talking to whom you think, but someone new, created by Gretchen Weirob's strange death moments ago. Or suppose He first creates one being in Heaven, who is me. Then He created another. Does the first cease to be me? If God can create such beings in Heaven, surely He can do so in Albuquerque. And there is nothing on your theory to favor this body before you as Gretchen Weirob's, over the one belonging to the person created in Albuquerque. So I am to suppose that if God were to do this, I would suddenly cease to be. I'm tempted to say I would cease to be Gretchen Weirob. But that would be a confused way of putting it. There would be here, in my place, a new person with false memories of having been Gretchen Weirob, who has just died of competition—a strange death, if ever there was one. She would have no right to my name, my bank account, or the services of my doctor, who is paid from insurance premiums paid for by deductions from Gretchen Weirob's past salary. Surely this is nonsense; however carefully God should choose to duplicate me, in Heaven or in Albuquerque, I would not cease to be, or cease to be who I am. You may reply that God, being benevolent, would never create an extra Gretchen Weirob. But I do not say that He would, but only that if He did this would not, as your theory implies, mean that I cease to exist. Your theory gives the wrong answer in this possible circumstance, so it must be wrong. I think I have been given no motivation to abandon the most obvious and straightforward view on these matters. I am a live body, and when that body dies, my existence will be at an end.

THE THIRD NIGHT

Weirob: Well, Sam, are you here for a third attempt to convince me of the possibility of survival?

Miller: No, I have given up. I suggest we talk about fishing or football or something unrelated to your imminent demise. You will outwit any straightforward attempts to comfort you, but perhaps I can at least divert your mind.

Cohen: But before we start on fishing...although I don't have any particular brief for survival, there is one point in our discussion of the last two evenings that still bothers me. Would you mind discussing for a while the notion of personal identity itself, without worrying about the more difficult case of survival after death?

Weirob: I would enjoy it. What point bothers you?

Cohen: Your position seems to be that personal identity amounts to identity of a human body, nothing more, nothing less. A person is just a live human body, or more precisely, I

suppose, a human body that is alive and has certain capacities—consciousness and perhaps rationality. Is that right?

Weirob: Yes, it seems that simple to me.

Cohen: But I think there has actually been an episode which disproves that. I am thinking of the strange case of Julia North, which occurred in California a few months ago. Surely you remember it.

Weirob: Yes, only too well. But you had better explain it to Sam, for I'll wager he has not heard of it.

Cohen: Not heard of Julia North? But the case was all over the headlines.

Miller: Well, Gretchen is right. I know nothing of it. She knows that I only read the sports page.

Cohen: You only read the sports page!

Weirob: It's an expression of his unconcern with earthly matters.

Miller: Well, that's not quite fair, Gretchen. It's a matter of preference. I much prefer to spend what time I have for reading in reading about the eighteenth century, rather than the drab and miserable century into which I had the misfortune to be born. It was really a much more civilized century, you know. But let's not dwell on my peculiar habits. Tell me about Julia North.

Cohen: Very well. Julia North was a young woman who was run over by a street car while saving the life of a young child who wandered onto the tracks. The child's mother, one Mary Frances Beaudine, had a stroke while watching the horrible scene. Julia's healthy brain and wasted body, and Mary Frances' healthy body and wasted brain, were transported to a hospital where a brilliant neurosurgeon, Dr. Matthews, was in residence. He had worked out a procedure for what he called a "body transplant." He removed the brain from Julia's head and placed it in Mary Frances', splicing the nerves, etc., using techniques not available until quite recently. The survivor of all this was obviously Julia, as everyone agreed—except, unfortunately, Mary Frances' husband. His shortsightedness and lack of imagination led to great complications and drama and made the case more famous in the history of crime than in the history of medicine. I shall not go into the details of this sorry aspect of the case—they are well reported in a book by Barbara Harris called *Who Is Julia?*, in case you are interested.

Miller: Fascinating!

Cohen: Well, the relevance of this case is obvious. Julia North had one body up until the time of the accident, and another body after the operation. So one person had two bodies. So a person cannot be simply *identified* with a human body. So something must be wrong with your view, Gretchen. What do you say to this?

Weirob: I'll say to you just what I said to Dr. Matthews . . .

Cohen: You have spoken with Dr. Matthews?

Weirob: Yes. He contacted me shortly after my accident. My physician had phoned him up about my case. Matthews said he could perform the same operation for me he did for Julia North. I refused.

Cohen: You refused! But Gretchen, why . . . ?

Miller: Gretchen, I *am* shocked. Your decision practically amounts to suicide! You passed up an opportunity to continue living? Why on earth . . . ?

Weirob: Hold on, hold on. You are both making an assumption I reject. If the case of Julia North amounts to a counterexample to my view that a person is just a live human body, and if my refusal to submit to this procedure amounts to passing up an option to survive, then the survivor of such an operation must be reckoned as the same person as the brain donor. That is, the survivor of Julia North's operation must have been Julia, and the survivor of the operation on me would have to be me. This is the assumption you both make in criticizing me. But I reject it. I think Jack Beaudine was right. The survivor of the operation involving Julia North's brain was Mary Frances Beaudine, and the survivor of the operation which was to involve my brain would not have been me.

Miller: Gretchen, how on earth can you say that? Will you not give up your view that personal identity is just bodily identity, no matter how clear the counterexample? I really think you simply have an irrational attachment to the lump of material that is your body.

Cohen: Yes, Gretchen, I agree with Sam. You are being preposterous! The survivor of Julia North's operation had no idea who Mary Frances Beaudine was. She remembered being Julia . . .

Weirob: She *seemed* to remember being Julia. Have you forgotten so quickly the importance of this distinction? In my opinion, the effect of the operation was that Mary Frances Beaudine survived deluded, thinking she was someone else.

Cohen: But as you know, the case was litigated. It went to the Supreme Court. They said that the survivor was Julia.

Weirob: That argument is unworthy of you, Dave. Is the Supreme Court infallible?

Cohen: No, they aren't. But I don't think it's such a stupid point.

Look at it this way, Gretchen. This is a case in which two criteria we use to make judgements of identity conflict. Usually we expect personal identity to involve both bodily identity and psychological continuity. That is, we expect that if we have the same body, then the beliefs, memories, character traits and the like also will be enormously similar. In this case, these two criteria which usually coincide do not. If we choose one criterion, we say that the survivor is Mary Frances Beaudine and she has undergone drastic psychological changes. If we choose the other, we say that Julia has survived with a new body. We have to choose which criterion is more important. It's a matter of choice of how to use our language, how to extend the concept "same person" to a new situation. The overwhelming majority of people involved in the case took the survivor to be Julia. That is, society chose to use the concept one way rather than the other. The Supreme Court is *not* beside the point. One of their functions is to settle just how old concepts shall be applied to new circumstances—how "freedom of the press" is to be understood when applied to movies or television, whose existence was not foreseen when the concept was shaped, or to say whether "murder" is to include the abortion of a foetus. They are fallible on points of fact, but they are the final authority on the development of certain important concepts used in law. The notion of *person* is such a concept.

Weirob: You think that *who* the survivor was, was a matter of convention, of how we choose to use language?

Cohen: Yes.

Weirob: I can show the preposterousness of all that with an example.

Let us suppose that I agree to the operation. I lie in bed, expecting my continued existence, anticipating the feelings and thoughts I shall have upon awakening after the operation. Dr. Matthews enters and asks me to take several aspirin, so as not to have a headache when I awake. I protest that aspirins upset my stomach; he asks whether I would have a terrible headache tomorrow or a mild stomachache now, and I agree that it would be reasonable to take them.

Let us suppose you enter at this point with bad news. The Supreme Court has changed its mind! So the survivor will not be me. So, I say, "Oh, then I will not take the aspirin, for it's not me that will have a headache, but someone else. Why should I endure a stomachache, however mild, for the comfort of someone else? After all, I am already donating my brain to that person."

Now this is clearly absurd. If I was correct, in the first place, to anticipate having the sensations and thoughts that the survivor is to have the next day, the decision of nine old men a thousand or so miles away wouldn't make me wrong. And if I was wrong so to anticipate, their decision couldn't make me right. How can the correctness of my anticipation of survival be a matter of the way we use our words? If it is not such a matter, then my identity is not either. My identity with the survivor, my survival, is a question of fact, not of convention.

Cohen: Your example is persuasive. I admit I am befuddled. On the one hand, I cannot see how the matter can be other than I have described. When we know all the facts what can remain to be decided but how we are to describe them, how we are to use our language? And yet I can see that it seems absurd to suppose that the correctness or incorrectness of anticipation of future experience is a matter for convention to decide.

Miller: Well, I didn't think the business about convention was very plausible anyway.

But I should like to return you to the main question, Gretchen. Fact or convention, it still remains. Why will you not admit that the survivor of this operation would be you?

Weirob: Well, *you* tell *me*, why do you think she would be me?

Miller: I can appeal to the theory I developed last night. You argued that the idea that personal identity consists in memory would not guarantee the possibility of survival after death. But you said nothing to shake its plausibility as an account of personal identity. It has the enormous advantage, remember, of making sense of our ability to judge our own identity, without examination of our bodies. I should argue that it is the correctness of this theory that explains the *almost* universal willingness to say that the survivor of Julia's operation was Julia. We need not deliberate over how to extend our concept, we need only apply the concept we already have. Memory is sufficient for identity and bodily identity is *not* necessary for it. The survivor remembered Julia's thoughts and actions, and so was Julia. Would you but submit to the operation, the survivor would remember your thoughts and actions, would remember this very conversation we are now having, and would be you.

Cohen: Yes, I now agree completely with Sam. The theory that personal identity is to be analyzed in terms of memory is correct, and according to it you will survive if you submit to the operation.

Let me add another argument against your view and in favor of the memory theory. You have emphasized that identity is the condition of *anticipation*. That means, among other things, that we have a particular concern for that person in the future whom we take to be ourselves. If I were told that any of the three of us were to suffer pain tomorrow, I should be sad. But if it were you or Sam that were to be hurt, my concern would be altruistic or unselfish. That is because I would not anticipate having the painful experience myself. Here I do no more than repeat points you have made earlier in our conversations.

Now what is there about mere sameness of body that makes sense of this asymmetry, between the way we look at our own futures, and the way we look at the futures of others? In other words, why is the identity of your body—that mere lump of matter, as Sam put it—of such great importance? Why care so much about it?

Weirob: You say, and I surely agree, that identity of person is a very special relationship—so special as perhaps not even happily called a relationship at all. And you say that since my theory is that identity of person is identity of body, I should be able to explain the importance of the one in terms of the importance of the other.

I'm not sure I can do that. But does the theory that personal identity consists in memory fare better on this score?

Cohen: Well, I think it does. Those properties of persons which make persons of such great value, and mark their individuality, and make one person so special to his friends and loved ones, are ultimately psychological or mental. One's character, personality, beliefs, attitudes, convictions—they are what make every person so unique and special. A skinny Gretchen would be a shock to us all, but not a Gretchen diminished in any important way. But a Gretchen who was not witty, or not gruff, or not as honest to the path an argument takes as is humanly possible—those would be fundamental changes. Is it any wonder that the survivor of that California fiasco was reckoned as Julia North? Would it make sense to take her to be Mary Jane Beaudine, when she had none of her beliefs or attitudes or memories?

Now if such properties are what is of importance about a person to others, is it not reasonable that they are the basis of one's importance to oneself? And these are just the properties that personal identity preserves when it is taken to consist in links of memory. Do we not have, in this idea, at least the beginning of an explanation of the importance of identity?

Weirob: So on two counts you two favor the memory theory. First, you say it explains how it is possible to judge as to one's own identity, without having to examine one's body. Second, you say it explains the importance of personal identity.

Cohen: Now surely you must agree the memory theory is correct. Do you agree? There may still be time to contact Dr. Matthews...

Weirob: Hold on, hold on. I'm still not persuaded. Granted the survivor will *think* she is me, will *seem* to remember thinking my thoughts. But recall the importance of distinguishing between real and merely apparent memory...

Cohen: But *you* recall that this distinction is to be made on the basis of whether the apparent memories were or were not caused by the prior experiences in the appropriate way. The survivor will not seem to remember your thoughts because of hypnosis or by coincidence or overweening imagination. She will seem to remember them because the traces those experiences left on your brain now activate her mind in the usual way. She will seem to remember them because she does remember them, and will be you.

Weirob: Let's go over this slowly. We all agree that the fact that the survivor of this strange operation Dr. Matthews proposes would *seem* to remember doing what I have done. Let us even suppose she would take herself to be me, claim to be Gretchen Weirob—and have no idea who else she might be. (We are then assuming that she differs from me in one aspect—her theory of personal identity. But that does not show her not to be me, for I could change my mind by then.) We all first agree that this much does not make her me. For this could all be true of someone suffering a delusion or a subject of hypnosis.

Cohen: Yes, this is all agreed.

Weirob: But now you think that some *further* condition is satisfied, which makes her apparent memories *real* memories. Now what exactly is this further condition?

Cohen: Well, that the same brain was involved in the perception of the events, and their later *memory*. Thus a causal chain of just the same sort as when only a single body is involved is involved here. That is, perceptions when the event occurs leave a trace in the brain, which is later responsible for the content of the memory. And we agreed, did we not, that apparent memory, caused in the right way, is real memory?

Weirob: Now is it absolutely crucial that the same brain is involved?

Cohen: What do you mean?

Weirob: Let me explain again by reference to Dr. Matthews. In our conversation he explained a new procedure on which he was working called a *brain rejuvenation*. By this process, which is not yet available—only the feasibility of developing it is being studied—a new brain could be made which is an exact duplicate of my brain. That is, an exact duplicate in terms of psychologically relevant states. It might not duplicate all the properties of my brain; for example, the blood vessels in the new brain might be stronger than in the old brain.

Miller: What is the point of developing such a macabre technique?

Weirob: Dr. Matthews' idea is that when weaknesses which might lead to stroke or other brain injury are noted, a healthy duplicate could be made, and replace the original, forestalling the problem.

Now Dave, suppose my problem were not with my liver and kidneys and such, but with my brain. Would you recommend such an operation as to my benefit?

Cohen: You mean, do I think the survivor of such an operation would be you?

Weirob: Exactly. You may assume that Dr. Matthews' technique works perfectly so the causal process involved is no less reliable than that involved in ordinary memory.

Cohen: Then I would say it was you . . . No! Wait! No, it wouldn't be you. Absolutely not!

Miller: But why the sudden reversal? It seems to me it would be her. Indeed, I should try such an operation myself, if it would clear up my dizzy spells and leave me otherwise unaffected.

Cohen: No, don't you see, she is leading us into a false trap. If we say it *is* her, then she will say, "Then what if he makes two duplicates, or three or ten? They can't all be me, they all have an equal claim, so none will be me." It would be the argument of last night, reapplied on earth. So the answer is no, absolutely not, it wouldn't be you. Duplication of self does not preserve identity. Identity of the person requires identity of the brain.

Miller: Quite right.

Weirob: Now let me see if I have your theory straight. Suppose we have two bodies, A and B. My brain is put into A, a duplicate into B. The survivor of this, call them "A-Gretchen" and "B-Gretchen," both seem to remember giving this very speech. Both are in this state of seeming to remember, as the last stage in an information-preserving causal chain, initiated by my giving this speech. Both have my character, personality, beliefs, and the like. But one is *really* remembering, the other is not. A-Gretchen is really me, B-Gretchen is not.

Cohen: Precisely. Is this incoherent?

Weirob: No, I guess there is nothing incoherent about it. But look what has happened to the advantages you claimed for the memory theory.

First, you said, it explains how I can know who I am without opening my eyes and recognizing my body. But in your theory Gretchen-A and Gretchen-B cannot know who they are even if they do open their eyes and examine their bodies. How is Gretchen-A to know whether she has the original brain and is who she seems to be, or has the duplicate and is a new person, only a few minutes old, and with no memories but my delusions? If the hospital kept careless records, or the surgeon thought it was of no great importance to keep track of who got the original and who got the duplicate, she might never know who she was. By making identity of person turn into identity of brain, your theory makes the ease with which I can determine who I am not less, but more mysterious than my theory.

Second, you said, your theory explains why my concern for Gretchen-A, who is me whether she knows it or not, would be selfish, and my anticipation of her experience correct while my concern for Gretchen-B with her duplicated brain would be unselfish, and my anticipation of having her experiences incorrect. And it explains this, you said, because by insisting on the links of memory, we preserve in personal identity more psychological characteristics which are the most important features of a person.

But Gretchen-A and Gretchen-B are psychologically indistinguishable. Though they will go their separate ways, at the moment of awakening they could well be exactly similar in every psychological respect. In terms of character and belief and the contents of their minds, Gretchen-A is no more like me than Gretchen-B. So there is nothing in your theory after all, to explain why anticipation is appropriate when we have identity, and not otherwise.

You said, Sam, that I had an irrational attachment for this unworthy material object, my body. But you too are as irrationally attached to your brain. I have never seen my brain. I should have easily given it up, for a rejuvenated version, had that been the choice with which I was faced. I have never seen it, never felt it, and have no attachment to it. But my body? That seems to me all that I am. I see no point in trying to evade its fate.

Perhaps I miss the merit of your arguments. I am tired, and perhaps my poor brain, feeling slighted, has begun to desert me . . .

Cohen: Oh don't worry Gretchen, you are still clever. Again you have left me befuddled. I don't know what to say. But answer me this. Suppose you are right and we are wrong. But suppose these arguments had not occurred to you, and, sharing in our error, you had agreed to the operation. You anticipate the operation until it happens, thinking you will survive. You are happy. The survivor takes herself to be you, and thinks she made a decision before the operation which has now turned out to be right. She is happy. Your friends are happy. Who would be worse off, either before or after the operation?

Suppose even that you realize identity would not be preserved by such an operation but have it done anyway, and as the time for the operation approaches, you go ahead and anticipate the experiences of the survivor. Where exactly is the mistake? Do you really have any less reason to care for the survivor than for yourself? Can mere identity of body, the lack of which alone keeps you from being her, mean that much? Perhaps we were wrong, after all, in focusing on identity as the necessary condition of anticipation . . .

Miller: It's too late, Dave.

NOTES

The First Night: The arguments against the position that personal identity consists in identity of an immaterial soul are similar to those found in John Locke, "Of Identity and Diversity," Chapter 1 of Book II of *Essay Concerning Human Understanding.* This chapter first appeared in the second edition of 1694.

The Second Night: The arguments against the view that personal identity consists in bodily identity are also suggested by Locke, as is the theory that memory is what is crucial. The argument that the memory theory is circular was made by Joseph Butler in "Of Personal Identity," an Appendix to his *Analogy of Religion,* first published in 1736. Locke's memory theory has been developed by a number of modern authors, including Sydney Shoemaker. The possibility of circumventing Butler's charge of circularity by an appeal to causation is noted by David Wiggins in *Identity and Spatial Temporal Continuity.* The "duplication argument" was apparently first used by the eighteenth-century free thinker, Antony Collins. Collins assumed that something like Locke's theory of personal identity was correct, and used the duplication argument to raise problems for the doctrine of immortality.

The Third Night: Who Is Julia?, by Barbara Harris, is an engaging novel published in 1972. (Dr. Matthews had not yet thought of brain rejuvenations.)

Locke considers the possibility of the "consciousness" of a prince being transferred to the body of a cobbler. The idea of using the removal of a brain to suggest how this might happen comes from Sydney Shoemaker's seminal book, *Self-Knowledge and Self-Identity* (1963). Bernard Williams has cleverly and articulately resisted the memory theory and the view that such a brain removal would amount to a body transplant in a number of important articles which are collected in his book *Problems of the Self* (1973). In particular, Williams has stressed the relevance of the duplication argument even in questions of terrestrial personal identity. Weirob's position in this essay is more inspired by Williams than anyone else. I have discussed Williams' arguments and related topics in "Can the Self Divide?" (*Journal of Philosophy,* 1972) and a review of his book (*Journal of Philosophy,* 1976).

An important article on the themes which emerge toward the end of the dialogue is Derek Parfit's "Personal Identity" (*Philosophical Review,* 1971). This article, along with Locke's chapter and a number of other important chapters and articles by Hume, Shoemaker, Williams, and others are collected in my anthology *Personal Identity* (1975). A number of new articles on personal identity appear in Amelie Rorty (ed.), *The Identities of Persons* (1976).

PART FOUR

Determinism, Free Will, and Responsibility

W HAT ARE WE ASKING WHEN we ask *why* something happened? Will an adequate explanation show us that in some sense or other the event to be explained *had* to happen in the way it did? In principle, are voluntary actions subject to the same kinds of explanations as physical events? If, in principle, everything that happens can be explained by science, is there then no such thing in the universe as random chance, genuine contingency, and uncertainty? These questions have great interest to the philosopher in their own right; but they also are of great strategic importance to the continuing arguments over the ancient riddle of determinism versus free will.

Determinism is the theory that all events, including human actions and choices, are, without exception, totally determined. What does it mean to say that an event (a past event, E, for instance) is "totally determined"? To this question various answers have been given, which for our present purposes we can take to be roughly equivalent.[1]

1. E was completely caused.
2. There were antecedent sufficient conditions for E; that is, conditions such that given their occurrence E *had* to occur.
3. It was causally necessary that E occur.
4. Given what preceded it, it was inevitable that E take place.
5. E is subsumable under a universal law of nature; that is, the occurrence of E was deducible from a description of the conditions that obtained before its occurrence and certain universal laws.
6. The occurrence of E is subject in principle to scientific explanation.
7. The occurrence of E was in principle predictable.
8. There are circumstances and laws which, if they had been known, would have made it possible for one to predict the occurrence and exact nature of E.

Indeterminism, the logical contradictory of determinism, is the theory that some events are not determined. Many exponents of indeterminism hold that the events that are not determined are human actions.

There are a number of commonsense considerations that should at least incline a reflective person toward determinism. Whenever we plant seeds, or plug in a machine, or prepare for a storm, we act in the expectation that physical events will occur in accordance with known laws of nature. Hardly anyone would deny, moreover, that physical characteristics of human beings—the color of their eyes, the cellular structure of their brains, glands, and other organs—are determined exactly by their genetic inheritance. And pediatricians and parents of large broods have often observed that temperament is determined, at least to a large degree, right from birth. To a large extent our characters, personalities, and intellects are a consequence of our inherited physical capacities and temperamental proclivities, and our choices in turn reflect our characters. Similarly, our early childhood training, family environment, and education have formative influences on character. We do what we do because we are what we are, and we are what we are—at least to a large extent—because our genes and the influencing conduct of others have formed us that way.

---

[1]Speaking more strictly, definitions 1–6 are "roughly equivalent" to one another, and definitions 7 and 8 are "roughly equivalent" to one another, although one should be aware of subtle differences even within these classes. Basically, there are two types of definitions: those in terms of prior sufficient conditions and those in terms of predictability.

At the same time, common sense recognizes that human beings do some things "of their own free will," that is, act in circumstances in which they might very well have done something else instead. This commonsense observation is hard to reconcile with determinism, which seems to imply that every event that occurs is the only one that could have occurred in the circumstances. This in turn seems to imply that no matter what I did a moment ago, I *could* not have done otherwise—which, in turn, seems to say that I *had* to do what I did, that I was not a free agent. But, most of us would agree, my ability to do otherwise is a necessary condition of praise or blame, reward or punishment—in short, for my *being responsible*. Therefore, if determinism cannot be reconciled with the ability to do otherwise, it cannot be reconciled with moral responsibility either. But we *do* hold people responsible for what they do (indeed, some say we *must* hold people responsible); therefore (some have argued), so much the worse for determinism. Such is the commonsense case against determinism.

Common sense, however, is no more pleased with indeterminism, which seems to give no satisfactory answer at all to any query of the form "Why did *this* happen rather than some other thing?" The reply "It just happened, that's all" inevitably leaves us unsatisfied. If we drop a stone and, to our astonishment, it rises straight up in the air instead of falling, we won't rest content with the "explanation" that "it was just one of those things—a totally random chance occurrence without rhyme or reason." We are even less likely to accept "chance" as an "explanation" for human actions. Such an explanation, we feel, makes all human actions arbitrary and unintelligible; it also seems to destroy the intimate bond between a person and his actions that is required by judgments of moral responsibility. Yet just insofar as a person's action was uncaused, just so far does it seem to have occurred "without rhyme or reason," as a "matter of pure chance." In the words of one determinist: "in proportion as an act of volition starts of itself without cause it is exactly, so far as the freedom of the individual is concerned, as if it had been thrown into his mind from without—'suggested to him by a freakish demon.'"[2]

Common sense thus is tied up in knots. It looks with little favor either on determinism or indeterminism in respect to human actions. Yet because these two theories are defined as logical contradictories, one of them *must* be true. The plight of common sense thus takes the form of a **dilemma;** that is, an argument of the form

1. If P is true, then Q is true.
2. If not-P is true, then Q is true.
3. Either P is true or not-P is true.
4. Therefore, Q is true (where Q is something repugnant or antecedently unacceptable).

The dilemma of determinism can be stated thus:

1. If determinism is true, we can never do other than we do; hence, we are never responsible for what we do.
2. If indeterminism is true, then some events—namely, human actions—are random, hence not free; hence, we are never responsible for what we do.

---

[2]R. E. Hobart, "Free-Will as Involving Determinism and Inconceivable Without It," *Mind* 43 (1934).

3. Either determinism is true or else indeterminism is true.
4. Therefore, we are never responsible for what we do.

There are several ways we might try to escape being gored by the "horns of the dilemma," but one way is *not* open to us. We may not deny the third premise; for, given our definitions of *determinism* and *indeterminism*, it amounts simply to the statement that either determinism is true or else it is not—surely an innocuous claim! We are, in short, not able in this case to get "between the horns of the dilemma" by denying its disjunctive premise.

We are thus left with three possibilities. We can deny the first premise and hold that determinism is, after all, perfectly compatible with free will and responsibility; or we can deny the second premise and hold that we can act freely, and are responsible for our actions, even though they are uncaused; or finally we can accept the entire argument just as it stands and argue on independent grounds that its conclusion is not so "repugnant" or so "antecedently unacceptable" as it seems at first appearance.

Those who deny the dilemma's first premise are nowadays called **compatibilists** (sometimes also **soft determinists**). Their central claim is that we can have free will, and be morally responsible for our choices and actions, even if determinism is true. Most compatibilists have believed that determinism is, in fact, true. Both A. J. Ayer and Walter Stace, two of the compatibilists represented here, take this position. Our third, contemporary philosopher John Martin Fischer, is more cautious, and claims that the jury isn't yet in regarding determinism's truth. Still, he says, we can be free even if it does turn out that the world operates in a wholly deterministic way.

The key issue that divides compatibilists from their libertarian and hard determinist opponents is usually the problem of how we should interpret "free to do otherwise," "could have done otherwise," "his act was avoidable," and similar locutions used in support of our ascriptions of blame and punishment, credit or reward. Most parties to the discussion agree that a person can be held morally responsible for his past action *only* if he was able to do other than he did. Put more tersely: Avoidability is a necessary condition of responsibility. There are two importantly different senses of *avoidability* in play in these discussions, and we must be careful to distinguish them. In the *categorical sense*, to say that an act is avoidable is to say that there were no antecedent conditions (causes) sufficient for its occurrence. In the *hypothetical sense*, to say that an act is avoidable is to say that *if* the actor had chosen (or, perhaps, intended) to do otherwise, he would have done otherwise (nothing would have stopped him). Avoidability in the hypothetical sense is perfectly compatible with determinism; avoidability in the categorical sense, by definition, is not. Now the question arises: In which of the senses of *avoidable*—the categorical sense, the hypothetical sense, or both—is it true that a person can be held responsible for his action only if it was avoidable?

The late A. J. Ayer's essay "Freedom and Necessity" presents the standard arguments for the hypothetical analysis of freedom and avoidability as clearly and elegantly as any more recent work. We use the word "standard" in this connection because these arguments were common to all the great philosophers in the tradition of English empiricism—Thomas Hobbes (1588–1679), John Locke (1632–1704), David Hume (1711–1776), John Stuart Mill (1806–1873), and Bertrand Russell (1872–1970). These so-called soft determinists differ from both hard determinists and libertarians over the compatibility of freedom and determinism, but they are also likely to differ with their opponents over the issue that most frequently leads people to consider the question of determinism, namely the implications of determinism for judgments of responsibility, blame, and punishment.

In our second compatibilist offering, Walter Stace provides several examples in which we find it natural to distinguish between an action's being caused and its being controlled. Pursuing a classic soft determinist strategy, Stace seeks to make plausible the distinction between these notions, thereby making room for the idea that though all of our actions are caused, some may nevertheless be relevantly within our control. If control over our actions is what is crucial to moral responsibility, and if control is compatible with an action's being caused, then freedom and determinism may peacefully co-exist, as the compatibilist claims.

Everyone agrees that in order to be responsible for an action, a person must in some way exercise control over it. So one way of seeing the disputes within this area of philosophy is to see how different thinkers understand the relevant notion of control. Our last compatibilist, John Martin Fischer, rejects the hypothetical analysis, and seeks to replace it with the notion of guidance control. This is the sort of control that we exercise over actions when they are responsive to reasons that we endorse. We may lack what he calls *regulative control*—the genuine ability to choose and to do otherwise than we in fact do—and yet still possess guidance control, which is, in his book, enough to warrant attributions of responsibility.

Another approach to the dilemma of determinism—one that rejects its second premise—is found in the writings of Thomas Reid and Immanuel Kant, among others, and is represented here by the essays of Roderick Chisholm and Robert Kane. This is the libertarian position, which argues that freedom is incompatible with determinism, that determinism is false, and that we do in fact often possess the sort of freedom necessary for moral responsibility. **Libertarians**[3] remind us that human actions, unlike other events in nature, are subject to a special kind of explanation: the actor's own *reasons* for acting. An uncaused action, done deliberately for some reason, would therefore be a perfectly intelligible one, and adequately explained by an account of its reasons.

Roderick Chisholm's article tackles head on perhaps the most troubling worry that besets libertarianism: the nature of the person whose choices can determine conduct but which are not themselves determined. Nothing else we know of has this sort of power. Physical things act in predictable ways and are governed by laws of cause and effect. Free human choices aren't like this. But they aren't random or purely matters of chance, either. Persons are controlling the choices they make, without in turn being necessitated to make them. Chisholm forthrightly sees the difficulty of such a position, and fans of libertarianism would do well to carefully attend to his analysis, one of whose primary virtues is to sketch just how exceptional free choices and persons are in the grand scheme of things. Philosophers and scientists are by nature skeptical of exceptions, constantly on the alert to prevent ad hoc hypotheses from being introduced to save a familiar or comforting idea. Chisholm sets the debate about libertarianism right where it should be, and forces us to ask whether the libertarian is giving us what we want (a robust sense of free will) at the expense of an occult view of the person.

---

[3]Not to be confused with the political theory of the same name, which advocates a minimal state and argues that all laws, except those necessary to vindicate citizens' moral rights, are unjustified.

Robert Kane's paper picks up directly on this theme and outlines a new version of libertarianism that takes its indeterminist element very seriously. Kane struggles to preserve a full-blooded conception of freedom compatibly with the latest scientific views of the world. Taking his cue from findings that reject thoroughgoing determinism, especially at the microphysical level, Kane seeks to locate opportunities for free will and moral responsibility within the indeterministic openings whose existence is ratified by contemporary physics.

Libertarians deny the possibility that we can have free will if determinism is true. The compatibility of free will and determinism is also denied by those who respond to the dilemma of determinism in the third way (that is, by embracing the conclusion of the dilemma, instead of trying to avoid it). This is the approach of the **hard determinists;** instead of abandoning determinism as the libertarians do, they jettison free will and moral responsibility. Hard determinism was the view of Baruch Spinoza and Paul Holbach, among other philosophers; of Mark Twain and Thomas Hardy, among other literary figures; and of Clarence Darrow, the famous American criminal lawyer. It is represented here by the selections from Holbach, a seventeenth-century thinker, and Derk Pereboom, a contemporary philosopher now teaching at Cornell University.

Holbach is a typical representative of the eighteenth-century "enlightenment" period, in which philosophers were often themselves scientists inclined to find in the methods and discoveries of science the solution to ancient philosophical riddles. They also tended to be political radicals (by the standards of their time), substituting their theories of human rights for the prevailing justifications of inequalities among social classes. In neither area, philosophy or politics, were they reluctant to embrace revolutionary consequences. Holbach, for example, is uncompromising in his account of the implications of scientific explanation for human freedom.

Derk Pereboom prefers to think of himself as a hard incompatibilist, rather than a hard determinist, since he is unsure of whether determinism is true, but convinced nonetheless that determinism precludes genuine freedom, and convinced as well that the sort of freedom worth having does not exist. Pereboom presents clear and accessible arguments against both compatibilism and libertarianism, and then offers an extended discussion of the many ways in which determinism is said to threaten our moral practices and our ability to find meaning in life. Pereboom argues that the common perceptions of determinism's threatening nature are largely unfounded, and that, in some surprising cases, we can vindicate (and even better justify) certain of our moral attitudes and practices by subscribing to hard incompatibilism.

The concluding section of Part 4, entitled "Freedom and Moral Responsibility," pursues several of the issues in the free will debate. James Rachels offers us a characteristically accessible presentation of the various central issues surrounding questions of moral responsibility. He considers the most important arguments for libertarianism, and finds them each wanting. He is cautiously pessimistic about compatibilism, too. He concludes with a variety of considerations that aim to show that the hard determinist option does not pose the deep threat to morality that most thinkers believe it does.

Rachels' selection is followed by Harry Frankfurt's "Alternate Possibilities and Moral Responsibility," which challenges the widely held view that avoidability is a necessary condition of responsibility. He offers cases in which a person cannot avoid doing or choosing as he does, and yet is properly held morally responsible for his choices or actions. The piece has become a contemporary classic in the free will discussion and continues to spark vigorous debate among philosophers as to the proper role (if any) of control and avoidability in determinations of freedom and responsibility.

The next selection is Thomas Nagel's "Moral Luck," in which Nagel sets out explicitly to challenge the Kantian view of moral responsibility. As Kant saw it, even in a world as dangerous and unpredictable as our own, there is at least one thing that is fully within our control: our moral integrity. Our moral integrity is a function solely of our intending to do what we perceive to be our duty. We may fail to achieve the results we intend—that much may be out of our control. But we are in command of our intentions, and this command supplies the proper basis for assignments of moral credit and blame. Praise is properly merited for good intentions, and blame deserved for bad, precisely because such intentions are within our control.

Nagel challenges this widely held view in two ways. First, he argues that even if our intentions are fully within our control, our moral responsibility is based on other factors that are matters of luck. Suppose two drivers are speeding recklessly along a narrow road, and one driver hits and kills a pedestrian, while the other driver injures no one. Nagel argues that in such a case, we rightly charge the first driver with a graver wrong than the second, even though this disparity is based on something entirely outside of either driver's control (namely, the presence or absence of a pedestrian along the road). Nagel also argues that even when we base assignments of praise and blame on intentions alone, the intentions one forms and acts on are themselves matters of luck. What we intend to do is partly a function of how we are raised, what circumstances we find ourselves in, and what genetic inheritance we find ourselves with. All of these are in the relevant sense "matters of luck," since we cannot be said to have controlled or determined their presence. Nagel's article seems to expose a deep problem for our ordinary notions of how responsibility and control are related. It forces our attention right back to the initial concern that defines the classic debate: how (or whether) it is possible to be a free, morally responsible person while at the same time recognizing the ineliminable role that genetics, upbringing, circumstance, and socialization have played in making you the person you are.

Our final offering is by Susan Wolf, who, in a highly original paper, methodically presents a theory with two basic parts. For one to be responsible for one's actions or their consequences, first of all, it must be the case that those actions are within the control of one's will, and second, that one's will is within the control of one's "deeper self." But that is not sufficient. Third, it must also be true that one is *sane*, where insanity in turn is analyzed as having *unavoidably mistaken* moral beliefs and values. Wolf's full theory then has a "deep self" condition supplemented by a "sanity condition," and the latter incorporates a conception of moral beliefs and their acquisition. The result is a theory that fits more comfortably with determinism should that theory just happen to be true, and which does not require what is impossible, according to Wolf, namely, that a person, to be responsible for anything, must have created her own "deeper self" from nothing.

COMPATIBILISM: THE CASE FOR DETERMINISM AND ITS COMPATIBILITY WITH THE MOST IMPORTANT SENSE OF FREE WILL

Freedom and Necessity

A. J. AYER

A. J. Ayer (1910–1991), a distinguished British philosopher, was a leading spokesman for the school of philosophers known as Logical Positivists.

When I am said to have done something of my own free will it is implied that I could have acted otherwise; and it is only when it is believed that I could have acted otherwise that I am held to be morally responsible for what I have done. For a man is not thought to be morally responsible for an action that it was not in his power to avoid. But if human behaviour is entirely governed by causal laws, it is not clear how any action that is done could ever have been avoided. It may be said of the agent that he would have acted otherwise if the causes of his action had been different, but they being what they were, it seems to follow that he was bound to act as he did. Now it is commonly assumed both that men are capable of acting freely, in the sense that is required to make them morally responsible, and that human behaviour is entirely governed by causal laws: and it is the apparent conflict between these two assumptions that gives rise to the philosophical problem of the freedom of the will.

Confronted with this problem, many people will be inclined to agree with Dr. Johnson: 'Sir, we *know* our will is free, and *there's* an end on't.' But, while this does very well for those who accept Dr. Johnson's premiss, it would hardly convince anyone who denied the freedom of the will. Certainly, if we do know that our wills are free, it follows that they are so. But the logical reply to this might be that since our wills are not free, it follows that no one can know that they are: so that if anyone claims, like Dr. Johnson, to know that they are, he must be mistaken. What is evident, indeed, is that people often believe themselves to be acting freely; and it is to this 'feeling' of freedom that some philosophers appeal when they wish, in the supposed interests of morality, to prove that not all human action is causally determined. But if these philosophers are right in their assumption that a man cannot be acting freely if his action is causally determined, then the fact that someone feels free to do, or not to do, a certain action does not prove that he really is so. It may prove that the agent does not himself know what it is that makes him act in one way rather than another: but from the fact that a man is unaware of the causes of his action, it does not follow that no such causes exist.

So much may be allowed to the determinist; but his belief that all human actions are subservient to causal laws still remains to be justified. If, indeed, it is necessary that every event should have a cause, then the rule must apply to human behaviour as much as to anything else. But why should it be supposed that every event must have a cause? The contrary is not unthinkable. Nor is the law of universal causation a necessary presupposition of scientific thought. The scientist may try to discover causal laws, and in many cases he succeeds; but sometimes he has to be content with statistical laws, and sometimes he comes upon events which, in the present state of his knowledge, he is not able to subsume under any law at all. In the case of these events he assumes that if he knew more he would be able to discover some law, whether causal or statistical, which would enable him to account for them. And this assumption cannot be disproved. For however far he may have carried his investigation, it is always open to him to carry it further; and it is always conceivable that if he carried it further he would discover the connection which had hitherto escaped him. Nevertheless, it is also conceivable that the events with which he is concerned are not systematically connected with any others: so that the reason why he does not discover the sort of laws that he requires is simply that they do not obtain.

Now in the case of human conduct the search for explanations has not in fact been altogether fruitless. Certain scientific laws have been established; and with the help of these laws we do make a number of successful predictions about the ways in which different people will behave. But these predictions do not always cover every detail. We may be able to predict that in certain circumstances a particular man will be angry, without being able to prescribe the precise form that the expression of his anger will take. We may be reasonably sure that he will shout, but not sure how loud his shout will be, or exactly what words he will use. And it is only a small proportion of human actions that we are able to forecast even so precisely as this. But that, it may be said, is because we have not carried our investigations very far. The science of psychology is still in its infancy and, as it is developed, not only will more human actions be explained, but the explanations will go into greater detail. The ideal of complete explanation may never in fact be attained: but it is theoretically attainable. Well, this may be so: and certainly it is impossible to show *a priori* that it is not so: but equally it cannot be shown that it is. This will not, however, discourage the scientist who, in the field of human behaviour, as elsewhere, will continue to

formulate theories and test them by the facts. And in this he is justified. For since he has no reason *a priori* to admit that there is a limit to what he can discover, the fact that he also cannot be sure that there is no limit does not make it unreasonable for him to devise theories, nor, having devised them, to try constantly to improve them.

But now suppose it to be claimed that, so far as men's actions are concerned, there is a limit: and that this limit is set by the fact of human freedom. An obvious objection is that in many cases in which a person feels himself to be free to do, or not to do, a certain action, we are even now able to explain, in causal terms, why it is that he acts as he does. But it might be argued that even if men are sometimes mistaken in believing that they act freely, it does not follow that they are always so mistaken. For it is not always the case that when a man believes that he has acted freely we are in fact able to account for his action in causal terms. A determinist would say that we should be able to account for it if we had more knowledge of the circumstances, and had been able to discover the appropriate natural laws. But until those discoveries have been made, this remains only a pious hope. And may it not be true that, in some cases at least, the reason why we can give no causal explanation is that no causal explanation is available; and that this is because the agent's choice was literally free, as he himself felt it to be?

The answer is that this may indeed be true, inasmuch as it is open to anyone to hold that no explanation is possible until some explanation is actually found. But even so it does not give the moralist what he wants. For he is anxious to show that men are capable of acting freely in order to infer that they can be morally responsible for what they do. But if it is a matter of pure chance that a man should act in one way rather than another, he may be free but can hardly be responsible. And indeed when a man's actions seem to us quite unpredictable, when, as we say, there is no knowing what he will do, we do not look upon him as a moral agent. We look upon him as a lunatic.

To this it may be objected that we are not dealing fairly with the moralist. For when he makes it a condition of my being morally responsible that I should act freely, he does not wish to imply that it is purely a matter of chance that I act as I do. What he wishes to imply is that my actions are the result of my own free choice: and it is because they are the result of my own free choice that I am held to be morally responsible for them.

But now we must ask how it is that I come to make my choice. Either it is an accident that I choose to act as I do or it is not. If it is an accident, then it is merely a matter of chance that I did not choose otherwise; and if it is merely a matter of chance that I did not choose otherwise, it is surely irrational to hold me morally responsible for choosing as I did. But if it is not an accident that I choose to do one thing rather than another, then presumably there is some causal explanation of my choice: and in that case we are led back to determinism.

Again, the objection may be raised that we are not doing justice to the moralist's case. His view is not that it is a matter of chance that I choose to act as I do, but rather that my choice depends upon my character. Nevertheless he holds that I can still be free in the sense that he requires; for it is I who am responsible for my character. But in what way am I responsible for my character? Only, surely, in the sense that there is a causal connection between what I do now and what I have done in the past. It is only this that justifies the statement that I have made myself what I am: and even so this is an over-simplification, since it takes no account of the external influences to which I have been subjected. But, ignoring the external influences, let us assume that it is in fact the case that I have made myself what I am. Then it is still legitimate to ask how it is that I have come to make myself one sort of person rather than another. And if it be answered that it is a matter of my strength of will, we can put the same question in another form by asking how it is that my will has the strength that it has and not some other degree of strength. Once more, either it is an accident or it is not. If it is an accident, then by the same argument as before, I am not morally responsible, and if it is not an accident we are led back to determinism.

Furthermore, to say that my actions proceed from my character or, more colloquially, that I act in character, is to say that my behaviour is consistent and to that extent predictable: and since it is, above all, for the actions that I perform in character that I am held to be morally responsible, it looks as if the admission of moral responsibility, so far from being incompatible with determinism, tends rather to presuppose it. But how can this be so if it is a necessary condition of moral responsibility that the person who is held responsible should have acted freely? It seems that if we are to retain this idea of moral responsibility, we must either show that men can be held responsible for actions which they do not do freely, or else find some way of reconciling determinism with the freedom of the will.

It is no doubt with the object of effecting this reconciliation that some philosophers have defined freedom as the consciousness of necessity. And by so doing they are able to say not only that a man can be acting freely when his action is causally determined, but even that his action must be causally determined for it to be possible for him to be acting freely. Nevertheless this definition has the serious disadvantage that it gives to the word 'freedom' a meaning quite different from any that it ordinarily bears. It is indeed obvious that if we are allowed to give the word 'freedom' any meaning that we please, we can find a meaning that will reconcile it with determinism: but this is no more a solution of our present problem than the fact that the word 'horse' could be arbitrarily used to mean what is ordinarily meant by 'sparrow' is a proof that horses have wings. For suppose that I am compelled by another person to do something 'against my will.' In that case, as the word 'freedom' is ordinarily used, I should not be said to be acting freely: and the fact that I am fully aware of the constraint to which I am subjected makes no difference to the matter. I do not become free by becoming conscious that I am not. It may, indeed, be possible to show that my being aware that my action is causally determined is not incompatible with my acting freely: but it by no means follows that it is in this that my freedom consists. Moreover, I suspect that one of the reasons why people are inclined to define freedom as the consciousness of necessity is that they think that if one is conscious of necessity one may somehow be able to master it. But this is a fallacy. It is like someone's saying that he wishes he could see into the future, because if he did he would know what calamities lay in wait for him and so would be able to avoid them. But if he avoids the calamities then they don't lie in the future and it is not true that he foresees them. And similarly if I am able to master necessity, in the sense of escaping the operation of a necessary law, then the law in question is not necessary. And if the law is not necessary, then neither my freedom nor anything else can consist in my knowing that it is.

Let it be granted, then, when we speak of reconciling freedom with determination we are using the word 'freedom' in an ordinary sense. It still remains for us to make this usage clear: and perhaps the best way to make it clear is to show what it is that freedom, in this sense, is contrasted with. Now we began with the assumption that freedom is contrasted with causality: so that a man cannot be said to be acting freely if his action is causally determined. But this assumption has led us into difficulties and I now wish to suggest that it is mistaken. For it is not, I think, causality that freedom is to be contrasted with, but constraint. And while it is true that being constrained to do an action entails being caused to do it, I shall try to show that the converse does not hold. I shall try to show that from the fact that my action is causally determined it does not necessarily follow that I am constrained to do it: and this is equivalent to saying that it does not necessarily follow that I am not free.

If I am constrained, I do not act freely. But in what circumstances can I legitimately be said to be constrained? An obvious instance is the case in which I am compelled by another person to do what he wants. In a case of this sort the compulsion need not be such as to deprive one of the power of choice. It is not required that the other person should have hypnotized me, or that he should make it physically impossible for me to go against his will. It is enough that he should induce me to do what he wants by making it clear to me that, if I do not, he will bring about some situation that I regard as even more undesirable than the consequences of the action that he wishes me to do. Thus, if the man points a pistol

at my head I may still choose to disobey him: but this does not prevent its being true that if I do fall in with his wishes he can legitimately be said to have compelled me. And if the circumstances are such that no reasonable person would be expected to choose the other alternative, then the action that I am made to do is not one for which I am held to be morally responsible.

A similar, but still somewhat different, case is that in which another person has obtained an habitual ascendancy over me. Where this is so, there may be no question of my being induced to act as the other person wishes by being confronted with a still more disagreeable alternative: for if I am sufficiently under his influence this special stimulus will not be necessary. Nevertheless I do not act freely, for the reason that I have been deprived of the power of choice. And this means that I have acquired so strong a habit of obedience that I no longer go through any process of deciding whether or not to do what the other person wants. About other matters I may still deliberate: but as regards the fulfilment of this other person's wishes, my own deliberations have ceased to be a causal factor in my behaviour. And it is in this sense that I may be said to be constrained. It is not, however, necessary that such constraint should take the form of subservience to another person. A kleptomaniac is not a free agent, in respect of his stealing, because he does not go through any process of deciding whether or not to steal. Or rather, if he does go through such a process, it is irrelevant to his behaviour. Whatever he resolved to do, he would steal all the same. And it is this that distinguishes him from the ordinary thief.

But now it may be asked whether there is any essential difference between these cases and those in which the agent is commonly thought to be free. No doubt the ordinary thief does go through a process of deciding whether or not to steal, and no doubt it does affect his behaviour. If he resolved to refrain from stealing, he could carry his resolution out. But if it be allowed that his making or not making this resolution is causally determined, then how can he be any more free than the kleptomaniac? It may be true that unlike the kleptomaniac he could refrain from stealing if he chose: but if there is a cause, or set of causes, which necessitate his choosing as he does, how can he be said to have the power of choice? Again, it may be true that no one now compels me to get up and walk across the room: but if my doing so can be causally explained in terms of my history or my environment, or whatever it may be, then how am I any more free than if some other person had compelled me? I do not have the feeling of constraint that I have when a pistol is manifestly pointed at my head: but the chains of causation by which I am bound are no less effective for being invisible.

The answer to this is that the cases I have mentioned as examples of constraint do differ from the others: and they differ just in the ways that I have tried to bring out. If I suffered from a compulsion neurosis, so that I got up and walked across the room, whether I wanted to or not, or if I did so because somebody else compelled me, then I should not be acting freely. But if I do it now, I shall be acting freely, just because these conditions do not obtain; and the fact that my action may nevertheless have a cause is, from this point of view, irrelevant. For it is not when my action has any cause at all, but only when it has a special sort of cause, that it is reckoned not to be free.

But here it may be objected that, even if this distinction corresponds to ordinary usage, it is still very irrational. For why should we distinguish, with regard to a person's freedom, between the operations of one sort of cause and those of another? Do not all causes equally necessitate? And is it not therefore arbitrary to say that a person is free when he is necessitated in one fashion but not when he is necessitated in another?

That all causes equally necessitate is indeed a tautology, if the word 'necessitate' is taken merely as equivalent to 'cause': but if, as the objection requires, it is taken as equivalent to 'constrain' or 'compel,' then I do not think that this proposition is true. For all that is needed for one event to be the cause of another is that, in the given circumstances, the event which is said to be the effect would not have occurred if it had not been for the occurrence of the event which is said to be the cause, or vice versa,

according as causes are interpreted as necessary, or sufficient, conditions: and this fact is usually deducible from some causal law which states that whenever an event of the one kind occurs then, given suitable conditions, an event of the other kind will occur in a certain temporal or spatio-temporal relationship to it. In short, there is an invariable concomitance between the two classes of events; but there is no compulsion, in any but a metaphorical sense. Suppose, for example, that a psycho-analyst is able to account for some aspect of my behaviour by referring it to some lesion that I suffered in my childhood. In that case, it may be said that my childhood experience, together with certain other events, necessitates my behaving as I do. But all that this involves is that it is found to be true in general that when people have had certain experiences as children, they subsequently behave in certain specifiable ways; and my case is just another instance of this general law. It is in this way indeed that my behaviour is explained. But from the fact that my behaviour is capable of being explained, in the sense that it can be subsumed under some natural law, it does not follow that I am acting under constraint.

If this is correct, to say that I could have acted otherwise is to say, first, that I should have acted otherwise if I had so chosen; secondly, that my action was voluntary in the sense in which the actions, say, of the kleptomaniac are not; and thirdly, that nobody compelled me to choose as I did: and these three conditions may very well be fulfilled. When they are fulfilled, I may be said to have acted freely. But this is not to say that it was a matter of chance that I acted as I did, or, in other words, that my action could not be explained. And that my actions should be capable of being explained is all that is required by the postulate of determinism.

If more than this seems to be required it is, I think, because the use of the very word 'determinism' is in some degree misleading. For it tends to suggest that one event is somehow in the power of another, whereas the truth is merely that they are factually correlated. And the same applies to the use, in this context, of the word 'necessity' and even of the word 'cause' itself.

Moreover, there are various reasons for this. One is the tendency to confuse causal with logical necessitation, and so to infer mistakenly that the effect is contained in the cause. Another is the uncritical use of a concept of force which is derived from primitive experiences of pushing and striking. A third is the survival of an animistic conception of causality, in which all causal relationships are modelled on the example of one person's exercising authority over another. As a result we tend to form an imaginative picture of an unhappy effect trying vainly to escape from the clutches of an over-mastering cause. But, I repeat, the fact is simply that when an event of one type occurs, an event of another type occurs also, in a certain temporal or spatio-temporal relation to the first. The rest is only metaphor. And it is because of the metaphor, and not because of the fact, that we come to think that there is an antithesis between causality and freedom.

Nevertheless, it may be said, if the postulate of determinism is valid, then the future can be explained in terms of the past: and this means that if one knew enough about the past one would be able to predict the future. But in that case what will happen in the future is already decided. And how then can I be said to be free? What is going to happen is going to happen and nothing that I do can prevent it. If the determinist is right, I am the helpless prisoner of fate.

But what is meant by saying that the future course of events is already decided? If the implication is that some person has arranged it, then the proposition is false. But if all that is meant is that it is possible, in principle, to deduce it from a set of particular facts about the past, together with the appropriate general laws, then, even if this is true, it does not in the least entail that I am the helpless prisoner of fate. It does not even entail that my actions make no difference to the future: for they are causes as well as effects; so that if they were different their consequences would be different also. What it does entail is that my behaviour can be predicted: but to say that my behaviour can be predicted is not to say that I am acting under constraint. It is indeed true that I cannot escape my destiny if this is taken to mean no more than that I shall do what I shall do. But this is a tautology, just as it is a tautology that what is going to happen is going to happen. And such tautologies as these prove nothing whatsoever about the freedom of the will.

The Problem of Free Will

WALTER T. STACE

Walter Stace (1886–1967) wrote books on Greek philosophy and the philosophy of religion. He taught at Princeton University.

[A] great problem which the rise of scientific naturalism has created for the modern mind concerns the foundations of morality. The old religious foundations have largely crumbled away, and it may well be thought that the edifice built upon them by generations of men is in danger of collapse. A total collapse of moral behavior is... very unlikely. For a society in which this occurred could not survive. Nevertheless the danger to moral standards inherent in the virtual disappearance of their old religious foundations is not illusory.

I shall first discuss the problem of free will, for it is certain that if there is no free will there can be no morality. Morality is concerned with what men ought and ought not to do. But if a man has no freedom to choose what he will do, if whatever he does is done under compulsion, then it does not make sense to tell him that he ought not to have done what he did and that he ought to do something different. All moral precepts would in such case be meaningless. Also if he acts always under compulsion, how can he be held morally responsible for his actions? How can he, for example, be punished for what he could not help doing?

It is to be observed that those learned professors of philosophy or psychology who deny the existence of free will do so only in their professional moments and in their studies and lecture rooms. For when it comes to doing anything practical, even of the most trivial kind, they invariably behave as if they and others were free. They inquire from you at dinner whether you will choose this dish or that dish. They will ask a child why he told a lie, and will punish him for not having chosen the way of truthfulness. All of which is inconsistent with a disbelief in free will. This should cause us to suspect that the problem is not a real one; and this, I believe, is the case. The dispute is merely verbal, and is due to nothing but a confusion about the meanings of words. It is what is now fashionably called a semantic problem.

How does a verbal dispute arise? Let us consider a case which, although it is absurd in the sense that no one would ever make the mistake which is involved in it, yet illustrates the principle which we shall have to use in the solution of the problem. Suppose that someone believed that the word "man" means a certain sort of five-legged animal; in short that "five-legged animal" is the correct *definition* of man. He might then look around the world, and rightly observing that there are no five-legged animals in it, he might proceed to deny the existence of men. This preposterous conclusion would have been reached because he was using an incorrect definition of "man." All you would have to do to show him his mistake would be to give him the correct definition; or at least to show him that his definition was wrong. Both the problem and its solution would, of course, be entirely verbal. The

problem of free will, and its solution, I shall maintain, is verbal in exactly the same way. The problem has been created by the fact that learned men, especially philosophers, have assumed an incorrect definition of free will, and then finding that there is nothing in the world which answers to their definition, have denied its existence. As far as logic is concerned, their conclusion is just as absurd as that of the man who denies the existence of men. The only difference is that the mistake in the latter case is obvious and crude, while the mistake which the deniers of free will have made is rather subtle and difficult to detect.

Throughout the modern period, until quite recently, it was assumed, both by the philosophers who denied free will and by those who defended it, that *determinism is inconsistent with free will*. If a man's actions were wholly determined by chains of causes stretching back into the remote past, so that they could be predicted beforehand by a mind which knew all the causes, it was assumed that they could not in that case be free. This implies that a certain definition of actions done from free will was assumed, namely that they are actions *not* wholly determined by causes or predictable beforehand. Let us shorten this by saying that free will was defined as meaning indeterminism. This is the incorrect definition which has led to the denial of free will. As soon as we see what the true definition is we shall find that the question whether the world is deterministic, as Newtonian science implied, or in a measure indeterministic, as current physics teaches, is wholly irrelevant to the problem.

Of course there is a sense in which one can define a word arbitrarily in any way one pleases. But a definition may nevertheless be called correct or incorrect. It is correct if it accords with a *common usage* of the word defined. It is incorrect if it does not. And if you give an incorrect definition, absurd and untrue results are likely to follow. For instance, there is nothing to prevent you from arbitrarily defining a man as a five-legged animal, but this is incorrect in the sense that it does not accord with the ordinary meaning of the word. Also it has the absurd result of leading to a denial of the existence of men. This shows that *common usage is the criterion for deciding whether a definition is correct or not.* And this is the principle which I shall apply to free will. I shall show that indeterminism is not what is meant by the phrase "free will" *as it is commonly used*. And I shall attempt to discover the correct definition by inquiring how the phrase is used in ordinary conversation.

Here are a few samples of how the phrase might be used in ordinary conversation. It will be noticed that they include cases in which the question whether a man acted with free will is asked in order to determine whether he was morally and legally responsible for his acts.

Jones: I once went without food for a week.
Smith: Did you do that of your own free will?
Jones: No. I did it because I was lost in a desert and could find no food.

But suppose that the man who had fasted was Mahatma Gandhi. The conversation might then have gone:

Gandhi: I once fasted for a week.
Smith: Did you do that of your own free will?
Gandhi: Yes. I did it because I wanted to compel the British Government to give India its independence.

Take another case. Suppose that I had stolen some bread, but that I was as truthful as George Washington. Then, if I were charged with the crime in court, some exchange of the following sort might take place:

Judge: Did you steal the bread of your own free will?
Stace: Yes. I stole it because I was hungry.

Or in different circumstances the conversation might run:

Judge: Did you steal of your own free will?
Stace: No. I stole because my employer threatened to beat me if I did not.

At a recent murder trial in Trenton some of the accused had signed confessions, but afterwards asserted that they had done so under police duress. The following exchange might have occurred:

Judge: Did you sign this confession of your own free will?
Prisoner: No. I signed it because the police beat me up.

Now suppose that a philosopher had been a member of the jury. We could imagine this conversation taking place in the jury room.

Foreman of the Jury: The prisoner says he signed the confession because he was beaten, and not of his own free will.
Philosopher: This is quite irrelevant to the case. There is no such thing as free will.
Foreman: Do you mean to say that it makes no difference whether he signed because his conscience made him want to tell the truth or because he was beaten?
Philosopher: None at all. Whether he was caused to sign by a beating or by some desire of his own—the desire to tell the truth, for example—in either case his signing was causally determined, and therefore in neither case did he act of his own free will. Since there is no such thing as free will, the question whether he signed of his own free will ought not to be discussed by us.

The foreman and the rest of the jury would rightly conclude that the philosopher must be making some mistake. What sort of a mistake could it be? There is only one possible answer. The philosopher must be using the phrase "free will" in some peculiar way of his own which is not the way in which men usually use it when they wish to determine a question of moral responsibility. That is, he must be using an incorrect definition of it as implying action not determined by causes.

Suppose a man left his office at noon, and were questioned about it. Then we might hear this:

Jones: Did you go out of your own free will?
Smith: Yes. I went out to get my lunch.

But we might hear:

Jones: Did you leave your office of your own free will?

Smith: No. I was forcibly removed by the police.

We have now collected a number of cases of actions which, in the ordinary usage of the English language, would be called cases in which people have acted of their own free will. We should also say in all these cases that they *chose* to act as they did. We should also say that they could have acted otherwise, if they had chosen. For instance, Mahatma Gandhi was not compelled to fast; he chose to do so. He could have eaten if he had wanted to. When Smith went out to get his lunch, he chose to do so. He could have stayed and done some more work, if he had wanted to. We have also collected a number of cases of the opposite kind. They are cases in which men were not able to exercise their free will. They had no choice. They were compelled to do as they did. The man in the desert did not fast of his own free will. He had no choice in the matter. He was compelled to fast because there was nothing for him to eat. And so with the other cases. It ought to be quite easy, by an inspection of these cases, to tell what we ordinarily mean when we say that a man did or did not exercise free will. We ought therefore to be able to extract from them the proper definition of the term. Let us put the cases in a table:

Free Acts	Unfree Acts
Gandhi fasting because he wanted to free India.	The man fasting in the desert because there was no food.
Stealing bread because one is hungry.	Stealing because one's employer threatened to beat one.
Signing a confession because one wanted to tell the truth.	Signing because the police beat one.
Leaving the office because one wanted one's lunch.	Leaving because forcibly removed.

It is obvious that to find the correct definition of free acts we must discover what characteristic is common to all the acts in the left-hand column, and is, at the same time, absent from all the acts in the right-hand column. This characteristic which all free acts have, and which no unfree acts have, will be the defining characteristic of free will.

Is being uncaused, or not being determined by causes, the characteristic of which we are in search? It cannot be, because although it is true that all the acts in the right-hand column have causes, such as the beating by the police or the absence of food in the desert, so also do the acts in the left-hand column. Mr. Gandhi's fasting was caused by his desire to free India, the man leaving his office by his hunger, and so on. Moreover there is no reason to doubt that these causes of the free acts were in turn caused by prior conditions, and that these were again the results of causes, and so on back indefinitely into the past. Any physiologist can tell us the causes of hunger. What caused Mr. Gandhi's tremendously powerful desire to free India is no doubt more difficult to discover. But it must have had causes. Some of them may have lain in peculiarities of his glands or brain, others in his past experiences, others in his heredity, others in his education. Defenders of free will have usually tended to deny such facts. But to do so is plainly a case of special pleading, which is unsupported by any scrap of evidence. The only reasonable view is that all human actions, both those which are freely done and those which are not, are either wholly determined by causes, or at least as much determined as other events in nature. It may be true, as the physicists tell us, that nature is not as deterministic as was once thought. But whatever degree of determinism prevails in the world, human actions appear to be as much determined as anything else. And if this is so, it cannot be the case that what distinguishes actions freely chosen from those which are not free is that the latter are determined by causes while the former are not. Therefore, being uncaused or being undetermined by causes, must be an incorrect definition of free will.

What, then, is the difference between acts which are freely done and those which are not?

What is the characteristic which is present to all the acts in the left-hand column and absent from all those in the right-hand column? Is it not obvious that, although both sets of actions have causes, the causes of those in the left-hand column are *of a different kind* from the causes of those in the righthand column? The free acts are all caused by desires, or motives, or by some sort of internal psychological states of the agent's mind. The unfree acts, on the other hand, are all caused by physical forces or physical conditions, outside the agent. Police arrest means physical force exerted from the outside; the absence of food in the desert is a physical condition of the outside world. We may therefore frame the following rough definitions. *Acts freely done are those whose immediate causes are psychological states in the agent. Acts not freely done are those whose immediate causes are states of affairs external to the agent.*

It is plain that if we define free will in this way, then free will certainly exists, and the philosopher's denial of its existence is seen to be what it is—nonsense. For it is obvious that all those actions of men which we should ordinarily attribute to the exercise of their free will, or of which we should say that they freely chose to do them, are in fact actions which have been caused by their own desires, wishes, thoughts, emotions, impulses, or other psychological states.

In applying our definition we shall find that it usually works well, but that there are some puzzling cases which it does not seem exactly to fit. These puzzles can always be solved by paying careful attention to the ways in which words are used, and remembering that they are not always used consistently. I have space for only one example. Suppose that a thug threatens to shoot you unless you give him your wallet, and suppose that you do so. Do you, in giving him your wallet, do so of your own free will or not? If we apply our definition, we find that you acted freely, since the immediate cause of the action was not an actual outside force but the fear of death, which is a psychological cause. Most people, however, would say that you did not act of your own free will but under compulsion. Does this show that our definition is

wrong? I do not think so. Aristotle, who gave a solution of the problem of free will substantially the same as ours (though he did not use the term "free will") admitted that there are what he called "mixed" or borderline cases in which it is difficult to know whether we ought to call the acts free or compelled. In the case under discussion, though no actual force was used, the gun at your forehead so nearly approximated to actual force that we tend to say the case was one of compulsion. It is a borderline case.

Here is what may seem like another kind of puzzle. According to our view an action may be free though it could have been predicted beforehand with certainty. But suppose you told a lie, and it was certain beforehand that you would tell it. How could one then say, "You could have told the truth"? The answer is that it is perfectly true that you could have told the truth *if you had wanted to.* In fact you would have done so, for in that case the causes producing your action, namely your desires, would have been different, and would therefore have produced different effects. It is a delusion that predictability and free will are incompatible. This agrees with common sense. For if, knowing your character, I predict that you will act honorably, no one would say when you do act honorably, that this shows you did not do so of your own free will.

Since free will is a condition of moral responsibility, we must be sure that our theory of free will gives a sufficient basis for it. To be held morally responsible for one's actions means that one may be justly punished or rewarded, blamed or praised, for them. But it is not just to punish a man for what he cannot help doing. How can it be just to punish him for an action which it was certain beforehand that he would do? We have not attempted to decide whether, as a matter of fact, all events, including human actions, are completely determined. For that question is irrelevant to the problem of free will. But if we assume for the purposes of argument that complete determinism is true, but that we are nevertheless free, it may then be asked whether such a deterministic free will is compatible with moral responsibility.

For it may seem unjust to punish a man for an action which it could have been predicted with certainty beforehand that he would do.

But that determinism is incompatible with moral responsibility is as much a delusion as that it is incompatible with free will. You do not excuse a man for doing a wrong act because, knowing his character, you felt certain beforehand that he would do it. Nor do you deprive a man of a reward or prize because, knowing his goodness or his capabilities, you felt certain beforehand that he would win it.

Volumes have been written on the justification of punishment. But so far as it affects the question of free will, the essential principles involved are quite simple. The punishment of a man for doing a wrong act is justified, either on the ground that it will correct his own character, or that it will deter other people from doing similar acts. The instrument of punishment has been in the past, and no doubt still is, often unwisely used; so that it may often have done more harm than good. But that is not relevant to our present problem. Punishment, if and when it is justified, is justified only on one or both of the grounds just mentioned. The question then is how, if we assume determinism, punishment can correct character or deter people from evil actions.

Suppose that your child develops a habit of telling lies. You give him a mild beating. Why? Because you believe that his personality is such that the usual motives for telling the truth do not cause him to do so. You therefore supply the missing cause, or motive, in the shape of pain and the fear of future pain if he repeats his untruthful behavior. And you hope that a few treatments of this kind will condition him to the habit of truth-telling, so that he will come to tell the truth without the infliction of pain. You assume that his actions are determined by causes, but that the usual causes of truth-telling do not in him produce their usual effects. You therefore supply him with an artificially injected motive, pain and fear, which you think will in the future cause him to speak truthfully.

The principle is exactly the same where you hope, by punishing one man, to deter others from wrong actions. You believe that the fear of punishment will cause those who might otherwise do evil to do well.

We act on the same principle with non-human, and even with inanimate, things, if they do not behave in the way we think they ought to behave. The rose bushes in the garden produce only small and poor blooms, whereas we want large and rich ones. We supply a cause which will produce large blooms, namely fertilizer. Our automobile does not go properly. We supply a cause which will make it go better, namely oil in the works. The punishment for the man, the fertilizer for the plant, and the oil for the car, are all justified by the same principle and in the same way. The only difference is that different kinds of things require different kinds of causes to make them do what they should. Pain may be the appropriate remedy to apply, in certain cases, to human beings, and oil to the machine. It is, of course, of no use to inject motor oil into the boy or to beat the machine.

Thus we see that moral responsibility is not only consistent with determinism, but requires it. The assumption on which punishment is based is that human behavior is causally determined. If pain could not be a cause of truth-telling there would be no justification at all for punishing lies. If human actions and volitions were uncaused, it would be useless either to punish or reward, or indeed to do anything else to correct people's bad behavior. For nothing that you could do would in any way influence them. Thus moral responsibility would entirely disappear. If there were no determinism of human beings at all, their actions would be completely unpredictable and capricious, and therefore irresponsible. And this is in itself a strong argument against the common view of philosophers that free will means being undetermined by causes.

My Compatibilism

JOHN MARTIN FISCHER

John Martin Fischer has taught for many years at The University of California–Riverside.

I. INTRODUCTION

Thinking about it in one way, compatibilism seems very plausible. For now, take "compatibilism" to be the doctrine that both some central notion of freedom and also genuine, robust moral responsibility are compatible with the doctrine of causal determinism (which, among other things, entails that every bit of human behavior is causally necessitated by events in the past together with the natural laws). Of course, compatibilism, as thus understood, does not in itself take any stand on whether causal determinism is true.

Compatibilism can seem plausible because it appears so obvious to us that we (most of us) are at least sometimes free and morally responsible, and yet we also realize that causal determinism could turn out to be true. That is, for all we know, it is true that all events (including human behavior) are the results of chains of necessitating causes that can be traced indefinitely into the past. Put slightly differently, I could certainly imagine waking up some morning to the newspaper headline, "Causal Determinism Is True!" (Most likely this would not be in the *National Inquirer* or even *People*—but perhaps the *New York Times...*) I could imagine reading the article and subsequently (presumably over some time) becoming convinced that causal determinism is true—that the generalizations that describe the relationships between complexes of past events and laws of nature, on the one hand, and subsequent events, on the other, are universal generalizations with 100 percent probabilities associated

with them. And I feel confident that this would not, nor should it, change my view of myself and others as (sometimes) free and robustly morally responsible agents—deeply different from other animals. The mere fact that these generalizations or conditionals have 100 percent probabilities associated with them, rather than 99.9 percent (say), would not and should not have any effect on my views about the existence of freedom and moral responsibility. My basic views of myself and others as free and responsible are and should be resilient with respect to such a discovery about the arcane and "close" facts pertaining to the generalizations of physics. (This of course is not to say that these basic views are resilient to *any* empirical discovery—just to this sort of discovery.)

So, when I deliberate I often take it that I am free in the sense that I have more than one option that is genuinely open to me. Since causal determinism (in the sense sketched above) might, for all we know be true, compatibilism seems extremely attractive. Similarly, it is very natural to distinguish those agents who are compelled to behave as they do from those who act freely; we make this distinction, and mark the two classes of individuals, in common sense and also the law. If causal determinism turned out to be true, and incompatibilism were also true, then it would seem that all behavior would be put into one class—the distinctions we naturally and intuitively draw in common sense and law would be in jeopardy of disappearing.

And yet there are deep problems with compatibilism. Perhaps these are what have led some philosophers to condemn it in such vigorous terms:

Reprinted with permission from Blackwell Publishers. This is an abridged version of a longer essay that appeared in Manual Vargas, ed., *Four Views on Free Will: A Debate* (Malden, MA: Blackwell 2007).

"wretched subterfuge" (Kant), "quagmire of evasion" (James), and "the most flabbergasting
instance of the fallacy of changing the subject to
be encountered anywhere in the complete history
of sophistry ... [a ploy that] was intended to take
in the vulgar, but which has beguiled the learned
in our time" (Wallace Matson).

In this short essay I will start by highlighting
the attractions of compatibilism and sketching
and motivating an appealing version of traditional compatibilism. I shall then present a basic
challenge to such a compatibilism. Given this
challenge, I suggest an alternative version of compatibilism, which I call "semicompatibilism," and I
develop some of the advantages of such an
approach. My goal will be to present the beginning
of a defense of semicompatibilism (highlighting
the main attractions), rather than a detailed elaboration or full defense of the doctrine.

II. THE LURE OF COMPATIBILISM

As I pointed out above, often it seems to me that
I have more than one path open to me. The paths
into the future branch out from the present, and
they represent different ways I could proceed into
the future. When I deliberate now about whether
to go to the lecture or to the movies tonight,
I now think I genuinely can go to the lecture,
and I genuinely can go to the movies (but perhaps I cannot do both). And I often have this
view about the future—the view of the future as
a "garden of forking paths" (in Borges' wonderful phrase). But I also can be brought to recognize that, for all I know, causal determinism is
true; its truth would not necessarily manifest
itself to me phenomenologically (that is, in my
conscious experience). Thus, compatibilism is
extremely attractive: It allows me to keep both
the view that I (sometimes at least) have more
than one path genuinely open to me and also
that causal determinism may be true. (I can
keep both of these views in the same mental
compartment, so to speak; they need not be
compartmentalized into different mental slots
or thought to apply to different realms or
perspectives.)

It is incredibly natural—almost inevitable
phenomenologically—to think that I could either

go to the movies or to the lecture tonight, that
I could either continue working on this essay or
take a coffee break, and so forth. It would be jarring to discover that, despite the appearance of
the availability of these options, only one path
into the future is genuinely available to me. A
compatibilist need not come to the one-path
conclusion, in the event that theoretical physicists conclusively establish that the conditionals
discussed above have associated with them
100 percent probabilities, rather than (say)
99.9 percent probabilities. A compatibilist can
embrace the resiliency of this fundamental view
of ourselves as agents who (help to) *select* the
path the world takes into the future, among various paths it genuinely *could* take. A compatibilist
can capture the intuitive idea that a tiny difference
(between 100% and 99.9%) should not make such
a huge difference (between our having more than
one genuinely available pathway into the future
and this pervasive phenomenological fact being
just a big delusion). How could such a small
change—of the sort envisaged in the probabilities
associated with the arcane conditionals of theoretical physics—make such a big difference?

Similarly, it is natural and extraordinarily
"basic" for human beings to think of ourselves
as (sometimes at least) morally accountable for
our choices and behavior. Typically, we think of
ourselves as morally responsible precisely in virtue
of exercising a distinctive kind of freedom or control; this freedom is traditionally thought to
involve exactly the sort of "selection" from
among genuinely available alternative possibilities
alluded to above. When an agent is morally
responsible for his behavior, we typically suppose
that he could have (at least at some relevant time)
done otherwise.

The assumption that we human beings—
most of us, at least—are morally responsible
agents (at least sometimes) is extremely important and pervasive. In fact, it is hard to imagine
human life without it. (At the very least, such
life would be very different from the way we
currently understand our lives—less richly tex-
tured and, arguably, not better or more attractive.) A compatibilist need not give up this
assumption, even if he were to wake up to the
headline, "Causal Determinism Is True!" (and

he were convinced of its truth). Nor need the compatibilist give up any of his basic metaphysical views—apparently *a priori* metaphysical truths that support his views about free will—simply because the theoretical physicists have established that the relevant probabilities are 100 percent rather than 99 percent. Wouldn't it be bizarre to give up a principle such as that the past is fixed and out of our control or that logical truths are fixed and out of our control, simply because one has been convinced that the probabilities in question are 100 percent rather than 99 percent? A compatibilist need not "flipflop" in this weird and unappealing way.

In ordinary life, and in our moral principles and legal system, we distinguish individuals who behave freely from those who do not. Sam is a "normal" adult human being, who grew up in favorable circumstances (roughly those described in the American TV series, *Leave It To Beaver*). He has no unusual neurophysiological or psychological anomalies or disorders, and he is not in a context in which he is manipulated, brainwashed, coerced, or otherwise "compelled" to do what he does. More specifically, no factors that uncontroversially function to undermine, distort, or thwart the normal human faculty of practical reasoning or execution of the outputs of such reasoning are present. He deliberates in the "normal way" about whether to deliberately withhold pertinent information on his income tax forms, and, although he knows it is morally wrong, he decides to withhold the information and cheat on his taxes anyway.

According to our commonsense way of looking at the world and even our more theoretical moral and legal perspectives, Sam freely chooses to cheat on his income taxes and freely cheats. It is plausible that, given the assumptions I have sketched, he was free just prior to his decision and action *not* to so decide and behave. Insofar as Sam selected his own path, he acted freely and can be held both morally and legally accountable for cheating on his taxes.

On the other hand, we tend to exempt certain agents from *any* moral responsibility in virtue of their lacking even the *capacity* to control their choices and actions; we take it that such individuals are so impaired in their cognitive and/or executive capacities that they cannot *freely* select their path into the future (even if various paths present themselves as genuinely available). Such agents may have significant brain damage or neurological or psychological disorders in virtue of which they are not even capable of exercising the distinctive human capacity of control in any morally significant context. Other agents may have the basic features that underwrite this capacity, but they nevertheless are locally rather than globally exempt from moral responsibility (that is, they are not morally responsible for some of their choices and actions, but they may be held responsible for others).

On the commonsense view, even as structured and refined by moral and legal analysis, agents who are brainwashed (without their consent), involuntarily subjected to hypnosis or subliminal advertising or other forms of behavioral conditioning, or even direct stimulation of the brain, are not morally responsible for the relevant behavior. But they may be morally responsible for choices and actions that are not the result of these "stock" examples of freedom-undermining and thus responsibility-undermining factors.

Of course, there are difficult cases of significant coercion, or pressure that falls short of genuine compulsion, or subliminal suggestion that is influential but not determinative, about which reasonable persons may disagree. Further, there is considerable controversy over the role and significance of early childhood experiences, deprivations, poverty, physical and psychological abuse, and so forth. But even though there are "hard cases," common sense—and moral and legal theory—has it that there are clear cases of freedom and responsibility, on the one hand, and clear cases of the lack of it, on the other.

A compatibilist can maintain this distinction, even if it turns out that the physicists convince us that the probabilities associated with the relevant conditionals—the conditionals linking the past and laws with the present in physics—are 100 percent, rather than 99.9 percent. And this is a significant and attractive feature of compatibilism. Incompatibilism would seem to lead to a collapse of the important distinction between agents such as Sam and thoroughly manipulated or brainwashed or coerced agents. A compatibilist need not deny what seems so obvious, even if the conditionals have attached to them probabilities of 100 percent. There is an important difference between agents such as Sam, who act freely and can be held morally responsible, and individuals who are completely or partially exempt from moral responsibility in virtue of *special* hindrances and disabilities that impair their functioning. Again, a compatibilist's view of human beings as (sometimes) both free and morally responsible agents is *resilient* with respect to the particular empirical discovery that causal determinism is true. Wouldn't it be bizarre if our basic view of ourselves as free and morally responsible, and our distinction between responsible agents and those who are insane or literally unable to control their behavior, would hang on whether the probabilities of the conditionals are 99.9 percent or 100 percent? Again, how can such a tiny change make such a monumental difference?

III. A COMPATIBILIST ACCOUNT OF FREEDOM

One might distinguish between the forward-looking aspects of agency, including practical reasoning, planning, and deliberation, and the backward-looking aspects of agency, including accountability and moral (and legal) responsibility. I have noted that it is extremely natural and plausible—almost inevitable—to think of ourselves as (sometimes at least) having more than one path branching into the future. This same assumption appears to frame both our deliberation and (retrospectively) our attributions of responsibility. I shall here take it that the possibilities in question are the *same* in both forward-looking and backward-looking aspects of agency: When we deliberate, we naturally presuppose that we have different paths into the future, and when we assign responsibility, we suppose (typically) that the relevant agent had available to him a different path.

In both forward-looking and backward-looking contexts, it is appealing to suppose that the relevant sort of possibility or freedom is analyzed as a certain sort of choice-dependence. That is, when I'm deliberating, it is plausible to

suppose that I genuinely can do whatever it is that I would do, if I were so to choose: I can go to the movies later insofar as I would go to the movies, if I were to choose to go to the movies, and I can go to the lecture insofar as I would go to the lecture, if I were to choose to go to the lecture, and so forth. On this view, I can do, in the relevant sense of "can," whatever is a (suitable) function of my "will" or choices: The scope of my deliberation about the future is the set of paths along which my behavior is a function of my choices. I do not deliberate about whether to jump to the moon, because (in part at least) I would not successfully jump to the moon, even if I were to choose to jump to the moon.

Similarly, given the assumption of the unity of forward-looking and backward-looking features of agency, the alternative possibilities pertinent to the attribution of responsibility are understood in terms of choice-dependence. That is, on this approach an agent is morally responsible for a certain action only if he could have done otherwise, and he could have done otherwise just in case he would have done otherwise, if he had chosen to do otherwise.

This compatibilist analysis of freedom (or the distinctive sort of possibility relevant to deliberation and responsibility) is called the "conditional analysis" because it suggests that our freedom can be understood in terms of certain conditional statements ("if–then" statements). More specifically, the conditional analysis commends to us the view that an agent S's freedom to do X can be understood in terms of the truth of a statement such as, "If S were to choose (will, decide, and so forth) to do X, S would do X." The subjunctive conditional specifies the relevant notion of "dependence." The analysis seems to capture important elements of our intuitive picture of what is within the legitimate scope of our deliberation and planning for the future. It also helps to sort out at least some cases in which agents are not morally responsible for their behavior—and to distinguish these from cases in which agents are responsible. If someone is kidnapped and chained, he is presumably not morally responsible for not helping someone in distress insofar as he would still be in chains (and thus would not succeed in helping), even if he were to choose (decide, will) to help.

But despite its considerable attractions, the conditional analysis, as presented thus far, has fatal problems—problems that should be seen to be fatal even by the compatibilist. First, note that it may be that some upshot is choice-dependent in the way specified by the conditional analysis, and yet there may be some factor that (uncontroversially) impairs or hinders the relevant agent's capacity for choice (in the circumstances in question). This factor could render the agent powerless (in the sense presumably relevant to moral responsibility), even though the upshot is choice-dependent.

So consider the following example due to Keith Lehrer. As a boy, Thomas had a terrible and traumatic experience with a snake. He thus has a pathological aversion to snakes that renders him psychologically incapable of bringing himself to choose to touch a snake (much less pick one up), even as an adult. A snake is in a basket right in from of Thomas. Whereas it is true that *if* Thomas were to choose to pick up the snake, he would do so, it is nevertheless true that Thomas cannot choose to pick up the snake, Intuitively, Thomas cannot pick up the snake— and yet the conditional analysis would have it that he can (in the relevant sense). This is a problem that even a compatibilist should see as significant; the problem clearly does not come from causal determination *per se*. The general form of the problem is that the relevant subjunctive conditional can be true consistently with the actual operation of some factor that intuitively (and apart from any contentious views about the compatibility of causal determinism and freedom) makes it the case that the agent is psychologically incapable of choosing (the act in question) and thus unable to perform the act. Factors that would seem to render an agent psychologically incapable of choice (and which could be seen to do so even by a compatibilist) might include past trauma, subliminal advertising, aversive conditioning, hypnosis, and even direct electric stimulation of the brain.

To make the point starkly, an individual could have his brain directly manipulated (without his consent) so as to choose Y. This would presumably render it true that he cannot do X, even though it might well be the case that *if* he had chosen to do X, he would have done X. (Of course, if the individual were to choose X, then he would not have been subject to the actual manipulation to which he has been subjected—manipulation that issues in his choosing Y.) Think of a demonic (or even well-intentioned) neuroscientist (or even a team including very nice neurophilosophers and neuroscientists!) who can manipulate parts of the brain by using (say) a laser; metaphorically, the laser beam can be thought of as a line that comes from some external source— some source physically external to the individual who is being manipulated and out of his control—at the "end" of which is the individual's choice to do Y. The neuroscientist knows the systematic workings of the brain so that she knows what sort of laser-induced manipulation is bound to produce a choice to do Y. Under such circumstances, it would seem ludicrous to suppose that the individual is free to do X; and yet it may well be true that *if* he were to choose X, the neuroscientist would not have intervened and the individual would successfully do X. The upshot is choice-dependent, but the individual is clearly powerless (in the relevant sense).

Some compatibilists about freedom and causal determinism have given up on the conditional analysis in light of such difficulties. Others have sought to give a more refined conditional analysis. So we might distinguish between the generally discredited "simple" conditional analysis, and what might be called the "refined" conditional analysis. Different philosophers have suggested different ways of refining the simple analysis, but the basic idea is somehow to rule out the factors that uncontroversially (that is, without making any assumptions that are contentious within the context of an evaluation of the compatibility of causal determinism and freedom) render an agent unable to choose (and thus unable to act).

Along these lines, one might try something like this: An agent S can do X just in case (i) if S were to choose to do X, S would do X, and (ii) the agent is not subject to clandestine hypnosis, subliminal advertising, psychological compulsion resulting from past traumatic experiences, direct stimulation of the brain, neurological damage due to a fall or accident, and so forth. . . .

An obvious problem with the refined analysis is the "and so forth. . . ." It would seem that an indefinitely large number of other conditions (apparently heterogeneous in nature) could in principle be thought to issue in the relevant sort of incapacity. Additionally, there should be a certain discomfort in countenancing as part of the analysis a list of disparate items with no explanation of what ties them together as a class; from a philosophical point of view, condition (ii) posits an unseemly miscellany. How could one evaluate a proposed addition to the list in a principled way?

Perhaps the compatibilist could simply admit these problems and revise condition (ii) in the following way: (ii') the agent is not subject to *any* factor that would uncontroversially (that is, without making any assumptions that are contentious within the context of an evaluation of the compatibility of causal determinism and freedom) render an agent unable to choose the act in question (and thus unable to act). Despite the obvious problems of incompleteness in this analysis, it might capture something useful; it might capture much of what a compatibilist means by the relevant notion of freedom.

Unfortunately, the proposed revision renders the analysis completely useless in seeking to resolve the controversial issue of whether causal determinism is compatible with freedom (in the relevant sense). This is because all actual choices will be the result of a causally deterministic sequence, if causal determinism is true. Since causal determination obviously is *not* a factor that uncontroversially renders an agent unable to choose (and thus unable to act), the revised analysis will have results congenial to compatibilism. But it would be dialectically unfair to the incompatibilist to suppose that the revised analysis can be seen uncontroversially to be acceptable; that is, it would clearly beg the question against the incompatibilist to contend that the refined conditional analysis can be seen to be a plausible analysis of the sort of freedom that is under consideration.

To see this more clearly, recall again the metaphor of the line from the neuroscientist to the individual's choice. When the neuroscientist uses clandestine and unconsented-to manipulation by a laser beam, it is plausible that the individual could not have chosen otherwise. Note that, under the circumstances, the only way the individual would have chosen otherwise (would have chosen X instead of Y) would have been if the neuroscientist had not employed the laser beam as she actually did; that is, it was a necessary condition of the individual's choosing otherwise that the line not have been present, as it were. But the incompatibilist will ask how exactly causal determination of the choice to do Y is any different from the neuroscientist's employment of her laser beam to manipulatively induce a choice to do Y. The laser beam is not experienced as coercive—it is by hypothesis not experienced at all. The laser is a "subtle" and phenomenologically inaccessible influence that starts entirely "outside" the agent (physically external to the agent and not within his control) and issues (via a process over which the agent has no control) in a choice to do Y. But if causal determinism is true, then there is *some* causally deterministic sequence that starts entirely "outside" the agent (physically external to the agent and not within his control) and issues (via a deterministic process) in a choice to do Y. The incompatibilist will legitimately ask what exactly the difference between the laser beam and the causally deterministic sequence is? Metaphorically, they are both lines that start outside the agent and end with the same choice, and both lines must be "erased" to get a different choice.

Now a compatibilist might grant this, but insist on a crucial point—that not all causal sequences are "created equal." More specifically, the compatibilist wishes to insist that not all causally deterministic sequences undermine freedom; a straightforward and "upfront" commitment of the compatibilist is to the idea that we can distinguish among causally deterministic sequences, and, more specifically, that we can distinguish those that involve "compulsion" (or some freedom- and responsibility-undermining factor) from those that do not. Returning to the pictorial metaphor: It may well be that an individual cannot choose or do otherwise when being manipulated by the neuroscientist's laser beam—in this case the individual cannot erase the line from the neuroscientist to his choice. On the other hand, according to the compatibilist, there is no reason to suppose that I am not free either to go to the lecture or go to the movies later. Even if I do in fact go to the movies, there is no reason—no reason stemming merely from the truth of causal determinism—to suppose that my behavior is causally determined in a *special way*—a way uncontroversially recognized to rule out freedom and responsibility. Thus, even if I do in fact go to the movies later, the compatibilist might say that there is no reason (stemming merely from the truth of causal determinism) to think that I will not be free (at the relevant time) to go to the lecture instead—and thus no reason to suppose that I will not be free (at the relevant time) to erase the line that does in fact connect the past to my choice to go to the movies.

IV. THE CONSEQUENCE ARGUMENT

Yes, it is a basic commitment of the compatibilist—to which I promise we will return below—that not all causally deterministic sequences undermine freedom equally. But there is nevertheless an argument that presents a significant challenge to this commitment and also to the common-sense idea that we can be confident in distinguishing cases of freedom and responsibility from cases where some freedom- and responsibility-undermining factor operates. This argument is a "skeptical argument," rather like the skeptical argument from the possibility of illusion to the conclusion that we don't know what we ordinarily take ourselves to know about the external world. The skeptical argument in epistemology employs basic ingredients of common sense to challenge other parts of common sense; that is, it employs ordinary ideas about the possibility of illusion and the concept of knowledge (putatively) to generate the intuitively jarring result that we don't know what we take ourselves to know about the external world. Similarly, the

skeptical argument about our freedom employs ordinary ideas about the fixity of the past and the fixity of the natural laws (putatively) to generate the intuitively jarring result that we are not ever free, if causal determinism turns out to be true (something we can't rule out *a priori*). If this skeptical argument is sound, it calls into question *any* compatibilist analysis of freedom (that is, freedom of the sort under consideration—involving the capacity for selection among open alternatives). If the argument is sound, then not only both the simple and refined conditional analysis, but *any* compatibilist analysis (of the relevant sort of freedom) must be rejected. It is thus an extremely powerful and disturbing argument. I think that any honest and serious discussion of compatibilism must address this argument, to which I turn now.

The skeptical argument has been around in one form or another for a very long time. Actually, a structurally similar argument was originally presented thousands of years ago; then, the worry was fatalism (more specifically, the idea that the truth of statements about the future must be fixed and thus we lack freedom). Then in the Middle Ages the worry stemmed from the doctrine of God's essential omniscience. In the Modern era, our attention has focused primarily (although by no means exclusively) on the threat posed by science—more specifically, the possibility that causal determinism is true. At this point, we simply do not know whether causal determinism is true or not. If it turns out to be true, then all our behavior could in principle be deduced from a complete description of the past and laws of nature. Put differently, if causal determinism is true, then true propositions about the past and propositions that express the laws of nature entail all our current and future choices and actions.

Here's the argument (very informally). Suppose that causal determinism is indeed true. Given the definition of causal determinism, it follows that my current choice to continue typing (and not take an admittedly much-needed coffee break) is entailed by true propositions about the past and laws of nature. Thus, if I were free (just prior to my actual choice) to choose (and subsequently do) otherwise, then I must have been free so to behave that the past would have been different or the natural laws would have been different. But intuitively the past is "fixed" and out of my control and so are the natural laws. I cannot now do anything that is such that, if I were to do it, the past would have been different (say, John F. Kennedy never would have been assassinated) or the natural laws would be different (say, some things would travel faster than the speed of light [if I've got the natural law in question correct!]). It appears to follow that, despite the natural and almost ineluctable sense I have that I am (sometimes, at least) free to choose and do otherwise, I am never free to choose and do otherwise, if causal determinism obtains.

Although the compatibilist wishes to say that not all causally deterministic sequences equally threaten freedom, the Consequence Argument—so-called by Peter Van Inwagen because under causal determinism all our behavior is the consequence of the past plus the laws of nature—appears to imply that causal determinism *per se* rules out the relevant sort of freedom. If the Consequence Argument is sound—and it relies on intuitively plausible ingredients, such as the fixity of the past and natural laws—then the commonsense distinction between cases of "compulsion" and ordinary cases in which moral responsibility is present would vanish, if causal determinism were true; and since we do not know that causal determinism is false, our basic views about ourselves (as free and morally responsible agents) would be called into question.

Recall that it would be uncontroversial that I would not be morally responsible if I were subjected to clandestine (and unconsented to) manipulation by a neuroscientist's laser beam. As I said above, in such a context, in order for a different choice to have occurred, the laser beam must not have connected the neurosurgeon with my actual choice. Similarly, if causal determinism were true, then the Consequence Argument brings out the fact that—even in the most "ordinary" circumstances (that is, in the absence of anything that would uncontroversially constitute compulsion)—in order for a different choice to have occurred, the past or the natural laws

would have had to have been different: The "line" connecting the past to my choice (via the laws) would have had to have been broken (or erased). The line posited by causal determination appears to be equivalent to the laser beam.

Another way to look at the ingredients that go into the Consequence Argument is to consider the intuitive idea that (as the philosopher Carl Ginet puts the point) my freedom now is the freedom to add to the given past, holding fixed the laws of nature. In terms of our metaphor, my freedom (on this view) is the freedom to draw a line that *extends* the line that connects the actual past with the present (holding fixed the natural laws). The future may well be a garden of forking paths, but the forking paths all branch off a single line (presumably). The Consequence Argument throws into relief an intuitively jarring implication of compatibilism: The compatibilist cannot embrace the almost undeniable picture of our freedom as the freedom to add to the past, given the laws. If the past is a set of dots, then for our freedom truly to be understandable, we must be able to connect the dots—in more ways than one. Some have said that responsibility involves "making a connection" with values of a certain sort, or "tracking values" in a certain way; but there is even a more fundamental way in which our freedom involves making a connection: We must be able to connect our current actions with out past (holding the natural laws fixed).

In my opinion, the Consequence Argument is a powerful and highly plausible argument. On the other hand, it certainly falls short of being indisputably sound. Some compatibilists—Multiple-Pasts Compatibilists—are willing to say that we can sometimes so act that the past would have been different from what it actually was; alternatively, these compatibilists say that our freedom need not be construed as the freedom to extend the given past, holding the natural laws fixed. On such a view, I might have access to a possibility with a different past associated with it (a possible world with a different past from the actual past) insofar as there are no special "obstacles" in the actual course of events (or the actual world) that "block" such access. Other compatibilists—Local-Miracle

Compatibilists—are willing to say that we can sometimes so act that a natural law that actually obtains would not have obtained; some such compatibilists are also willing to countenance small changes in the past as well as the laws. On this sort of view, I might have access to a possibility (or possible world) with slightly different natural laws from those that obtain actually, as long as these alternative scenarios do not involve widespread and big changes in the laws. This view is defended in a classic paper by David Lewis.

So there is room for compatibilism about causal determinism and the sort of freedom that involves genuine access to alternative possibilities, even in light of the Consequence Argument; excellent philosophers have opted for some response to the Consequence Argument (such as Local-Miracle or Multiple-Pasts Compatibilism). The Consequence Argument is highly plausible, but it is not indisputably sound, and thus there is no knockdown argument available that the responses are inadequate. Nevertheless, I do in fact find the Consequence Argument highly plausible, and I am inclined to accept its soundness. I thus think it is important to argue that there is an attractive kind of compatibilism that is indeed consistent with accepting the Consequence Argument as sound.

V. SEMICOMPATIBLISM AND THE FRANKFURT-EXAMPLES

Let's say you are driving your car and it is functioning normally. You want to go to the coffee house, so you guide the car to the right (into the parking lot for the coffee house). Your choice to go to the coffee house is based on your own reasons in the normal way, and the car's steering apparatus functions normally. Here you have a certain distinctive kind of control of the car's movements—you have "guidance control" of the car's going to the right. This is more than mere causation or even causal determination; you might have causally determined the car's going to the right by sneezing (and thus jerking the steering wheel to the

right) or having an epileptic seizure (and thus slumping over the wheel and causing it to turn to the right) without having exercised this specific and distinctive sort of *control.* Supposing that there are no "special" factors at work—that is, no special psychological impairments, brain lesions, neurological disorders, causal determination, and so forth—and imagining (as above) that the car's steering apparatus is not broken, you had it in your power (just prior to your actual decision to turn to the right) to continue going straight ahead, or to turn the car to the left, and so forth. That is, although you exercise guidance control in turning the car to the right, you presumably (and apart from special assumptions) possessed freedom to choose and do otherwise: You had "regulative control" over the car's movements. In the normal case, we assume that agents have both guidance and regulative control—a signature sort of control of the car's movements, as well as a characteristic kind of control *over* the car's movements.

Whereas these two sorts of control are typically presumed to go together, they can be prized apart. Suppose that everything is as above, but that the steering apparatus of your car is broken in such a way that, if you had tried to guide the car in any direction other than the one in which you actually guide it, it would have gone to the right anyway—in just the trajectory it actually traveled. The defect in the steering apparatus plays no role in the actual sequence of events, but it would have played a role in the alternative scenario (or range of such scenarios). Given this sort of preemptive overdetermination, although you exhibit guidance control of the car's going to the right, you do *not* have regulative control over the car's movements: It would have gone in precisely the same way, no matter what you were to choose or try.

Of course, in this context you *do* possess *some* regulative control: You could have chosen otherwise, and you could have tried to guide the car in some other direction. This is reminiscent of John Locke's famous example in his *Essay Concerning Human Understanding.* Here a man is transported into a room while he is asleep. When the man awakens, he considers leaving, but he decides to stay in the room for his own reasons. Locke says he voluntarily chooses to stay in the room and voluntarily stays in the room. Unbeknownst to the man, the door to the room is locked, and thus he could not have left the room. According to Locke, the man voluntarily stays in the room, although he does not have the power to leave the room. He exhibits a certain sort of control of his staying in the room (what I would call guidance control), even though he cannot do otherwise than stay in the room (and thus he lacks regulative control over staying in the room). But note that, as in the second car example above, the man could have chosen to leave the room, and he could have tried to do so.

Can structurally similar examples be given in which there is guidance control but *no* regulative control? This is where the "Frankfurt-examples" come in. The contemporary philosopher, Harry Frankfurt, has sought to provide just such an example. One could say that he seeks to put the locked door inside the mind (in terms of Locke's example). In Locke's example, some factor (the locked door) plays no role in the individual's deliberations or choice, and yet its presence renders it true that the individual could not have done otherwise (could not have left the room). Frankfurt posits some factor that plays an analogous role in the context of the agent's mind: It plays no role in the agent's actual deliberations or choice, and yet its presence (allegedly) renders it true that the individual could not have chosen otherwise (or done otherwise). If Frankfurt's examples work, then one could in principle entirely prize apart guidance control from regulative control.

Here is my favorite version of a Frankfurt-type case. Jones has left his political decision until the last moment, just as some diners leave their decision about what to order at a restaurant to the moment when the waiter turns to them. In any case, Jones goes into the voting booth, deliberates in the "normal" way, and chooses to vote for the Democrat. On the basis of this choice, Jones votes for the Democrat. Unbeknownst to Jones, he has a chip in his brain that allows a very nice and highly progressive neurosurgeon (Black) to monitor his brain. The neurosurgeon wants Jones to vote for the Democrat, and if she sees that Jones is about to do so, she does not intervene in any way—she merely monitors the brain. If, on the other hand, the neurosurgeon sees that Jones is about to choose to vote for the Republican, she swings into action with her nifty electronic probe and stimulates Jones' brain in such a way as to ensure that he chooses to vote for the Democrat (and goes ahead and votes for the Democrat). Given the set-up, it seems that Jones freely chooses to vote for the Democrat and freely votes for the Democrat, although he could not have chosen or done otherwise: It seems that Jones exhibits guidance control of his vote, but he lacks regulative control over his choice and also his vote. The neurosurgeon's chip and electronic device has brought Locke's locked door into the mind. Just as the locked door plays no role in Locke's man's choice or behavior but nevertheless renders it true that he could not have done otherwise, the Black's set-up plays no role in Jones' actual choice or behavior, but it apparently renders it true that he could not have chosen or done otherwise.

How exactly does the neurosurgeon's device reliably know how Jones is about to vote? Frankfurt himself is vague about this point, but let us imagine that Jones's brain registers a certain neurological pattern if Jones is about to choose to vote for the Democrat, and a different pattern if Jones is about to choose to vote Republican. The chip can subtly convey this information to the neurosurgeon, which she can then use to good effect. Of course, the mere possibility of exhibiting a certain neurological pattern is not sufficiently robust to ground ascriptions of moral responsibility, on the picture that requires access to alternative possibilities. That is, if moral responsibility requires the sort of control that involves selection from among various paths that are genuinely open to an agent, the mere possibility of involuntarily exhibiting a certain neurological pattern would not seem to count as the relevant sort of "selection." Put slightly differently, just as it is not enough to secure moral responsibility that a different choice could have *randomly* occurred, it does not seem to be enough to secure moral responsibility that a different neurological pattern could have been exhibited *involuntarily*. Such an exiguous possibility is a mere "flicker of freedom" and not sufficiently robust to ground moral responsibility, given the picture that requires regulative control for moral responsibility. How could something as important as moral responsibility come from something so thin—and something entirely involuntary?

It is tempting then to suppose that one could have a genuine kind of control—guidance control—that can be entirely prized apart from regulative control and that is all the freedom required for moral responsibility. So even if the Consequence Argument were valid and thus all causally deterministic sequences were equally potent in ruling out the sort of control that requires access to alternative possibilities (regulative control), it would *not* follow that all causally deterministic sequences equally threaten guidance control and moral responsibility. That is, if moral responsibility does not require the sort of control that involves access to alternative possibilities, then this opens the possibility of defending a kind of compatibilism, even granting the soundness of the Consequence Argument.

But various philosophers have resisted the temptation to suppose that one can expunge all vestiges of regulative control while at the same time preserving guidance control. They have pointed out that the appearance that Frankfurt-type cases can help to separate guidance from (all) regulative control may be misleading. Perhaps the most illuminating way to put their argument is in terms of a dilemma. The first horn assumes that indeterminism is true in the Frankfurt-examples; in particular, it assumes that the relationship between the "prior sign" (read by the progressive neurosurgeon, Black) is causally indeterministic. It follows that right up until the time Jones begins to choose, he can begin to choose otherwise; after all, the prior sign (together with other factors) falls short of causally determining the actual choice. Thus, there emerges a robust alternative possibility—the possibility of beginning to choose otherwise. This is no mere flicker of freedom; although it may be blocked or thwarted before it is completed or comes to fruition, it is nevertheless a voluntary episode—the initiation of choice.

The second horn of the dilemma assumes that causal determinism is true in the examples. Given the assumption of causal determination, it would appear to be straightforwardly question-begging to say that Jones is obviously morally responsible for his choice and behavior (despite lacking genuine access to alternative possibilities). After all, this (the compatibility of causal determination and moral responsibility) is precisely what is at issue!

The dilemma is powerful, but I am not convinced that it presents an insuperable objection to the employment of the Frankfurt-examples as part of a general strategy of defending compatibilism; as a matter of fact, I reject it. First, there have been various attempts at providing explicitly indeterministic versions of the Frankfurt-cases, and I think some of them are promising. I think it may well be possible to construct a Frankfurt example (under the explicit assumption of causal indeterminism) in which there are *no* robust alternative possibilities. Recall that it is not enough for the proponent of the regulative control requirement to identify just any sort of alternative possibility; rather, he needs to find an alternative possibility that is sufficiently *robust* to ground attributions of moral responsibility, given the regulative control picture. If the ground of moral responsibility is a certain sort of *selection* from genuinely available paths into the future, then paths with mere accidental or arbitrary events would seem to be irrelevant. This is the idea of the irrelevance of exiguous alternatives. In my view, to seek to get responsibility out of mere flickers of freedom is akin to alchemy.

On the second horn of the dilemma, causal determinism is assumed. I agree that it would be dialectically rash to conclude from mere inspection of the example presented above that Jones is morally responsible for his choice and voting behavior. Rather, my approach would be more circumspect. First, I would note that the distinctive contribution of the Frankfurt-examples is to suggest that if Jones is not morally responsible for his choice and behavior, this is *not* because he lacks genuine access to (robust) alternative possibilities. After all, in the example, Black's set-up is sufficient for Jones's choosing and acting as he actually does, but intuitively it is *irrelevant* to Jones's moral responsibility. That is, we can identify a factor—Black's elaborate set-up—that is (perhaps in conjunction with other features of the example) sufficient for Jones's actual kind of choice and behavior, but it plays no actual role in Jones's deliberations or actions; Black's set-up could have been subtracted from the situation and the actual sequence would have flowed in exactly the way it actually did. When something is in this way irrelevant to what happens in the actual sequence issuing in an agent's choice and behavior, it would seem to be irrelevant to his moral responsibility.

So the distinctive element added by the Frankfurt-type examples, under the assumption of causal determinism, is this: If the relevant agent is not morally responsible, it is not because of his lack of regulative control. Alternatively, we could say that they show that it is not the lack of genuine access to alternative possibilities (regulative control) in itself (and apart from pointing to other factors) that rules out moral responsibility. Now we can ask whether there is some other factor—some factor that plays a role in the actual sequence—that rules out moral responsibility, if causal determinism obtains. We will turn to a more thorough and careful consideration of such "actual-sequence factors" below. For now, I simply wish to note that there is nothing question-begging or dialectically inappropriate about how I have invoked the Frankfurt-examples thus far (on the second horn), and their distinctive role is to call into question the relevance or importance of regulative control in grounding moral responsibility (in the way presented described above).

Taking stock, in Section IV I presented the Consequence Argument. I did not officially endorse its conclusion, although I am inclined to believe that the argument is valid and further that its premises are based on extremely plausible ingredients. I suggested that it would be prudent to seek a defense of compatibilism that does not presuppose that the Consequence Argument is unsound. Here I have presented the rudimentary first steps toward the elaboration of just such a compatibilism. I have invoked the Frankfurt-examples (the prototypes of which are in John Locke) to support the contention that moral responsibility does not require regulative control (or the sort of freedom that involves genuine access to alternative possibilities), but only guidance control. Further, I have suggested that (thus far at least) there is no reason to suppose that causal determinism is inconsistent with guidance control. Better, I have contended that even if causal determinism threatens regulative control, it does not thereby threaten guidance control. In a more comprehensive defense of the sort of compatibilism I find attractive, one would explore whether there are other reasons (apart from regulative control) in virtue of which causal determinism is incompatible with moral responsibility (and offer reasons why it isn't).

VI. CONCLUSION: THE LURE OF SEMICOMPATIBILISM

John Perry has told me that I need a new name for the position, and I agree that "semicompatibilism" is not very exciting. (My only consolation is that the other names for positions in the Free Will debates are equally uninspiring; could you imagine going to the barricades for "hard incompatibilism"?) What is important, however, is not what's in the name, but what's in the doctrine. In this essay I have focused mainly on trying to explain the appeal of this form of compatibilism. That is, I have attempted to provide a *general* motivation for compatibilism, and also an explanation of the appeal of *this specific form* of compatibilism (as opposed to traditional compatibilism). The idea here has not been to develop detailed elaborations of the ideas or sustained defenses of the positions; rather, I have simply presented in sketchy form the attractions of the overall view (and some of the difficulties faced by its competitors).

One of the main virtues of compatibilism is that our deepest and most basic views about our agency—our freedom and moral responsibility—are not held hostage to views in physics. A semicompatibilist would not have to revise these beliefs in light of a future discovery of the truth of causal determinism. Nor need he be prepared to revise his basic metaphysical views—such as that the past is fixed or the laws of nature are fixed or that powerlessness can be transmitted via the Principle of Transfer of Powerlessness—in light of such a discovery. A libertarian, it seems, must claim that he knows from his armchair (or philosophical Barca-Lounger) that causal determinism is false; but how could we know in advance such an empirical thesis? These are significant virtues of semicompatibilism: a proponent of this doctrine need not purport to know *a priori* some (presumably) empirical thesis in physics, or be prepared to give up his basic views about our agency, or engage in unattractive "metaphysical flipflopping" (giving up some of one's basic metaphysical principles in light of some empirical truth in physics).

Semicompatibilism combines the best features of compatibilism and incompatibilism. It can accommodate the most compelling insights of the incompatibilist (as crystallized in the Consequence Argument) and also the basic appeal of compatibilism—that not all causally deterministic sequences equally rule out the sort of control that grounds moral responsibility. Thus, semicompatiblism allows us to track common sense (suitably conceptualized in moral and legal theory) in making distinctions between those factors that operate in such a way as to undermine responsibility and those that do not. And a semicompatibilist need not give up the idea that sometimes individuals robustly deserve punishment for their behavior, whereas on other occasions they robustly deserve moral commendation and reward. That is, a semicompatibilist need not etiolate or reconfigure the widespread and natural idea that individuals *morally deserve* to be treated harshly in certain circumstances, and kindly in others. We need not in any way damp down our revulsion at heinous deeds, or our admiration for human goodness and even heroism. Thus, even if the name is unexciting, the idea is beautiful.

VII. AFTERWORD

This essay is a significantly abridged version of my contribution to Manuel Vargas et al., *Four Views on Free Will: A Debate* (Blackwell, 2007). It seeks to explain in a relatively informal way some of the main ideas in my approach to free will and moral responsibility and their motivations; I have thus not included footnotes. I hope the reader will understand that the nature of this book requires a less substantial scholarly apparatus than one might expect in another context. Below I make some very minimal suggestions for further reading.

I have attempted to present, defend, and elaborate semicompatibilism in John Martin Fischer, *The Metaphysics of Free Will: An Essay on Control* (Oxford: Blackwell Publishers, 1994); John Martin Fischer and Mark Ravizza, S. J., *Responsibility and Control: A Theory of Moral Responsibility* (New York: Cambridge University Press, 1998); and John Martin Fischer, *My Way: Essays on Moral Responsibility* (New York: Oxford University Press, 2006).

A landmark collection that explores and elaborates compatibilist themes is Gary Watson, *Agency and Answerability* (Oxford: Clarendon Press, 2004). For important discussions of traditional compatibilist accounts of freedom and their difficulties, as well as presentations of the Consequence Argument, see Peter Van Inwagen, *An Essay on Free Will* (Oxford: Clarendon Press, 1983); and Carl Ginet, *On Action* (Cambridge, U.K.: Cambridge University Press, 1990).

Much of Harry Frankfurt's work on these subjects is collected in Harry G. Frankfurt, ed., *The Importance of What We Care About* (Cambridge, U.K., Cambridge University Press, 1988). There are helpful discussions of various aspects of the Frankfurt-examples in David Widerker and Michael McKenna, eds., *Moral Responsibility and Alternative Possibilities: Essays on the Importance of Alternative Possibilities* (Aldershot, U.K.: Ashgate, 2003).

LIBERTARIANISM: THE CASE FOR FREE WILL AND ITS INCOMPATIBILITY WITH DETERMINISM

Human Freedom and the Self

RODERICK M. CHISHOLM

'A staff moves a stone, and is moved by a hand, which is moved by a man.'

ARISTOTLE, *Physics*, 256a.

1. The Metaphysical Problem of human freedom might be summarized in the following way: Human beings are responsible agents; but this fact appears to conflict with a deterministic view of human action (the view that every event that is involved in an act is caused by some other event); and it *also* appears to conflict with an indeterministic view of human action (the view that the act, or some event that is essential to the act, is not caused at all.) To solve the problem, I believe, we must make somewhat far-reaching assumptions about the self or the agent—about the man who performs the act.

Perhaps it is needless to remark that, in all likelihood, it is impossible to say anything significant about this ancient problem that has not been said before.[1]

2. Let us consider some deed, or misdeed, that may be attributed to a responsible agent: one man, say, shot another. If the man *was* responsible for what he did, then, I would urge, what was to happen at the time of the shooting was something that was entirely up to the man himself. There was a moment at which it was true, both that he could have fired the shot and also that he could have refrained from firing it.

And if this is so, then, even though he did fire it, he could have done something else instead. (He didn't find himself firing the shot 'against his will', as we say.) I think we can say, more generally, then, that if a man is responsible for a certain event or a certain state of affairs (in our example, the shooting of another man), then that event or state of affairs was brought about by some act of his, and the act was something that was in his power either to perform or not to perform.

But now if the act which he *did* perform was an act that was also in his power *not* to perform, then it could not have been caused or determined by any event that was not itself within his power either to bring about or not to bring about. For example, if what we say he did was really something that was brought about by a second man, one who forced his hand upon the trigger, say, or who, by means of hypnosis, compelled him to perform the act, then since the act was caused by the *second* man it was nothing that was within the power of the *first* man to prevent. And precisely the same thing is true, I think, if instead of referring to a second man who compelled the first one, we speak instead of the *desires* and *beliefs* which the first man happens to have had. For if what we say he did was really something that was brought about by his own beliefs and desires, if these beliefs and desires in the particular situation in which he happened to have found himself caused him to do just what it was that we say he

The Lindley Lecture, 1964, pp. 3–15. © Copyright 1964 by the Department of Philosophy, University of Kansas. Reprinted by permission of the author and of the Department of Philosophy of the University of Kansas, Lawrence, Kansas, USA.

did do, then, since *they* caused it, *he* was unable to do anything other than just what it was that he did do. It makes no difference whether the cause of the deed was internal or external; if the cause was some state or event for which the man himself was not responsible, then he was not responsible for what we have been mistakenly calling his act. If a flood caused the poorly constructed dam to break, then, given the flood and the constitution of the dam, the break, we may say, *had* to occur and nothing could have happened in its place. And if the flood of desire caused the weak-willed man to give in, then he, too, had to do just what it was that he did do and he was no more responsible than was the dam for the results that followed. (It is true, of course, that if the man is responsible for the beliefs and desires that he happens to have, then he may also be responsible for the things they lead him to do. But the question now becomes: *is* he responsible for the beliefs and desires he happens to have? If he is, then there was a time when they were within his power either to acquire or not to acquire, and we are left, therefore, with our general point.)

One may object: But surely if there were such a thing as a man who is really *good*, then he would be responsible for things that he would do; yet, he would be unable to do anything other than just what it is that he does do, since, being good, he will always choose to do what is best. The answer, I think, is suggested by a comment that Thomas Reid makes upon an ancient author. The author had said of Cato, 'He was good because he could not be otherwise', and Reid observes: 'This saying, if understood literally and strictly, is not the praise of Cato, but of his constitution, which was no more the work of Cato than his existence'.[2] If Cato was himself responsible for the good things that he did, then Cato, as Reid suggests, was such that, although he had the power to do what was not good, he exercised his power only for that which was good.

All of this, if it is true, may give a certain amount of comfort to those who are tender-minded. But we should remind them that it also conflicts with a familiar view about the nature of God—with the view that 'every St.

Thomas Aquinas expresses by saying that 'every movement both of the will and of nature proceeds from God as the Prime Mover'.[3] If the act of the sinner *did* proceed from God as the Prime Mover, then God was in the position of the second agent we just discussed, the man who forced the trigger finger, or the hypnotist, and the sinner, so-called, was *not* responsible for what he did. (This may be a bold assertion, in view of the history of western theology, but I must say that I have never encountered a single good reason for denying it.)

There is one standard objection to all of this and we should consider it briefly.

3. The objection takes the form of a stratagem—one designed to show that determinism (and divine providence) is consistent with human responsibility. The stratagem is one that was used by Jonathan Edwards and by many philosophers in the present century, most notably, G. E. Moore.[4]

One proceeds as follows: The expression

(a) He could have done otherwise,

it is argued, means no more nor less than

(b) If he had chosen to do otherwise, then he would have done otherwise.

(In place of 'chosen', one might say 'tried', 'set out', 'decided', 'undertaken', or 'willed'.) The truth of statement (b), it is then pointed out, is consistent with determinism (and with divine providence); for even if all of the man's actions were causally determined, the man could still be such that, *if* he had chosen otherwise, then he would have done otherwise. What the murderer saw, let us suppose, along with his beliefs and desires, *caused* him to fire the shot; yet he was such that *if*, just then, he had chosen or decided *not* to fire the shot, then he would not have fired it. All of this is certainly possible. Similarly, we could say, of the dam, that the flood caused it to break and also that the dam was such that, *if* there had been no flood or any similar pressure, then the dam would have remained intact. And therefore, the argument proceeds, if (b) is consistent with determinism, and if (a) and (b) say the same thing, then (a) is also consistent with determinism; hence we can say that the agent *could* have done otherwise even though he was caused to do what he did do; and therefore determinism and moral responsibility are compatible.

Is the argument sound? The conclusion follows from the premises, but the catch, I think, lies in the first premise—the one saying that statement (a) tells us no more nor less than what statement (b) tells us. For (b), it would seem, could be true while (a) is false. That is to say, our man might be such that, if he had chosen to do otherwise, then he would have done otherwise, and yet *also* such that he could not have done otherwise. Suppose, after all, that our murderer could not have *chosen,* or could not have *decided,* to do otherwise. Then the fact that he happens also to be a man such that, if he had chosen not to shoot he would not have shot, would make no difference. For if he could *not* have chosen *not* to shoot, then he could not have done anything other than just what it was that he did do. In a word: from our statement (b) above ('If he had chosen to do otherwise, then he would have done otherwise'), we cannot make an inference to (a) above ('He could have done otherwise') unless we can *also* assert:

(c) He could have chosen to do otherwise.

And therefore, if we must reject this third statement (c), then, even though we may be justified in asserting (b), we are not justified in asserting (a). If the man could not have chosen to do otherwise, then he would not have done otherwise—*even if* he was such that, if he *had* chosen to do otherwise, then he would have done otherwise.

The stratagem in question, then, seems to me not to work, and I would say, therefore, that the ascription of responsibility conflicts with a deterministic view of action.

4. Perhaps there is less need to argue that the ascription of responsibility also conflicts with an indeterministic view of action—with the view that the act, or some event that is essential to the act, is not caused at all. If the act—the firing of the shot—was not caused at all, if it was fortuitous or capricious, happening so to speak out of the blue, then, presumably, no one—and nothing was responsible for the act. Our conception of action, therefore, should be neither deterministic nor indeterministic. Is there any other possibility?

5. We must not say that every event involved in the act is caused by some other event; and we must not say that the act is something that is not caused at all. The possibility that remains, therefore, is this: We should say that at least one of the events that are involved in the act is caused, not by any other events, but by something else instead. And this something else can only be the agent—the man. If there is an event that is caused, not by other events, but by the man, then there are some events involved in the act that are not caused by other events. But if the event in question is caused by the man then it *is* caused and we are not committed to saying that there is something involved in the act that is not caused at all.

But this, of course, is a large consequence, implying something of considerable importance about the nature of the agent or the man.

6. If we consider only inanimate natural objects, we may say that causation, if it occurs, is a relation between *events* or *states of affairs.* The dam's breaking was an event that was caused by a set of other events—the dam being weak, the flood being strong, and so on. But if a man is responsible for a particular deed, then, if what I have said is true, there is some event, or set of events, that is caused, *not* by other events or states of affairs, but by the agent, whatever he may be.

I shall borrow a pair of medieval terms, using them, perhaps, in a way that is slightly different from that for which they were originally intended. I shall say that when one event or state of affairs (or set of events or states of affairs) causes some other event or state of affairs, then we have an instance of *transeunt* causation. And I shall say that when an *agent,* as distinguished from an event, causes an event or state of affairs, then we have an instance of *immanent* causation.

The nature of what is intended by the expression 'immanent causation' may be illustrated by this sentence from Aristotle's *Physics*: 'Thus, a staff moves a stone, and is moved by a hand, which is moved by a man.'(VII, 5, 256a, 6–8) If the man was responsible, then we have in this illustration a number of instances of causation—most of them transeunt but at least one of them immanent. What the staff did to the stone was an instance of transeunt causation, and thus we may describe it as a relation between events: 'the motion of the staff caused the motion of the stone.' And similarly for what the hand did to the staff: 'the motion of the hand caused the motion of the staff'. And, as we know from physiology, there are still other events which caused the motion of the hand. Hence we need not introduce the agent at this particular point, as Aristotle does—we *need* not, though we *may*. We *may* say that the hand was moved by the man, but we may *also* say that the motion of the hand was caused by the motion of certain muscles; and we may say that the motion of the muscles was caused by certain events that took place within the brain. But some event, and presumably one of those that took place within the brain, was caused by the agent and not by any other events.

There are, of course, objections to this way of putting the matter; I shall consider the two that seem to me to be most important.

7. One may object, firstly: 'If the *man* does anything, then, as Aristotle's remark suggests, what he does is to move the *hand*. But he certainly does not *do* anything to his brain—he may not even know that he *has* a brain. And if he doesn't do anything to the brain, and if the motion of the hand was caused by something that happened within the brain, then there is no point in appealing to "immanent causation" as being something incompatible with "transeunt causation"—for the whole thing, after all, is a matter of causal relations among events or states of affairs.'

The answer to this objection, I think, is this: It is true that the agent does not *do* anything with his brain, or to his brain, in the sense in which he *does* something with his hand and does something to the staff. But from this it does not follow that the agent was not the immanent cause of something that happened within his brain.

We should note a useful distinction that has been proposed by Professor A. I. Melden—namely, the distinction between 'making something A happen' and 'doing A'.[5] If I reach for the staff and pick it up, then one of the things that I *do* is just that—reach for the staff and pick it up. And if it is something that I do, then there is a very clear sense in which it may be said to be something that I know that I do. If you ask me, 'Are you doing something, or trying to do something, with the staff?', I will have no difficulty in finding an answer. But in doing something with the staff, I also make various things happen which are not in this same sense things that I do: I will make various air-particles move; I will free a number of blades of grass from the pressure that had been upon them; and I may cause a shadow to move from one place to another. If these are merely things that I make happen, as distinguished from things that I do, then I may know nothing whatever about them; I may not have the slightest idea that, in moving the staff, I am bringing about any such thing as the motion of air-particles, shadows, and blades of grass.

We may say, in answer to the first objection, therefore, that it is true that our agent does nothing to his brain or with his brain; but from this it does not follow that the agent is not the immanent cause of some event within his brain; for the brain event may be something which, like the motion of the air-particles, he made happen in picking up the staff. The only difference between the two cases is this: in each case, he made something happen when he picked up the staff; but in the one case—the motion of the air-particles or of the shadows—it was the motion of the staff that caused the event to happen; and in the other case—the event that took place in the brain—it was this event that caused the motion of the staff.

The point is, in a word, that whenever a man does something A, then (by 'immanent causation') he makes a certain cerebral event happen, and this cerebral event (by 'transeunt causation') makes A happen.

8. The second objection is more difficult and concerns the very concept of 'immanent causation', or causation by an agent, as this concept is to be interpreted here. The concept is subject to a difficulty which has long been associated with that of the prime mover unmoved. We have said that there must be some event A, presumably some cerebral event, which is caused not by any other event, but by the agent. Since A was not caused by any other event, then the agent himself cannot be said to have undergone any change or produced any other event (such as 'an act of will' or the like) which brought A about. But if, when the agent made A happen, there was no event involved other than A itself, no event which could be described as *making* A happen, what did the agent's causation consist of? What, for example, is the difference between A's just happening, and the agents' *causing* A to happen? We cannot attribute the difference to any event that took place within the agent. And so far as the event A itself is concerned, there would seem to be no discernible difference. Thus Aristotle said that the activity of the prime mover is nothing in addition to the motion that it produces, and Suarez said that 'the action is in reality nothing but the effect as it flows from the agent'.[6] Must we conclude, then, that there is no more to the man's action in causing event A than there is to the event A's happening by itself? Here we would seem to have a distinction without a difference—in which case we have failed to find a *via media* between a deterministic and an indeterministic view of action.

The only answer, I think, can be this: that the difference between the man's causing A, on the one hand, and the event A just happening, on the other, lies in the fact that, in the first case but not the second, the event A *was* caused and was caused by the man. There was a brain event A; the agent did, in fact, cause the brain event; but there was nothing that he did to cause it.

This answer may not entirely satisfy and it will be likely to provoke the following question: 'But what are you really *adding* to the assertion that A happened when you utter the words "The agent *caused* A to happen"?' As soon as we have put the question this way, we see, I think, that whatever difficulty we may have encountered is one that may be traced to the concept of causation generally—whether 'immanent' or 'transeunt'. The problem, in other words, is not a problem that is peculiar to our conception of human action. It is a problem that must be faced by anyone who makes use of the concept of causation at all; and therefore, I would say, it is a problem for everyone but the complete indeterminist.

For the problem, as we put it, referring just to 'immanent causation', or causation by an agent, was this: 'What is the difference between saying, of an event A, that A just happened and saying that someone caused A to happen?' The analogous problem, which holds for 'transeunt causation', or causation by an event, is this: 'What is the difference between saying, of two events A and B, that B happened and then A happened, and saying that B's happening was the *cause* of A's happening?' And the only answer that one can give is this—that in the one case the agent was the cause of A's happening and in the other case event B was the cause of A's happening. The nature of transeunt causation is no more clear than is that of immanent causation.

9. But we may plausibly say—and there is a respectable philosophical tradition to which we may appeal—that the notion of immanent causation, or causation by an agent, is in fact more clear than that of transeunt causation, or causation by an event, and that it is only by understanding our own causal efficacy, as agents, that we can grasp the concept of *cause* at all. Hume may be said to have shown that we do not derive the concept of *cause* from what we perceive of external things. How, then, do we derive it? The most plausible suggestion, it seems to me, is that of Reid, once again: namely that 'the conception of an efficient cause may very probably be derived from the experience we have had ...of our own power to produce certain effects'.[7] If we did not understand the concept of immanent causation, we would not understand that of transeunt causation.

10. It may have been noted that I have avoided the term 'free will' in all of this. For even if there is such a faculty as 'the will', which somehow sets our acts agoing, the question of freedom, as John Locke said, is not the question *'whether the will be free';* it is the question *'whether a man be free'.*[8] For if there is a 'will', as a moving faculty, the question is whether the man is free to will to do these things that he does will to do—and also whether he is free *not* to will any of those things that he does will to do, and, again, whether he is free to will any of those things that he does not will to do. Jonathan Edwards tried to restrict himself to the question—'Is the man free to do what it is that he wills?' but the answer to this question will not tell us whether the man is responsible for what it is that he *does* will to do. Using still another pair of medieval terms, we may say that the metaphysical problem of freedom does not concern the *actus imperatus;* it does not concern the question whether we are free to accomplish whatever it is that we will or set out to do; it concerns the *actus elicitus,* the question whether we are free to will or to set out to do those things that we do will or set out to do.

11. If we are responsible, and if what I have been trying to say is true, then we have a prerogative which some would attribute only to God: each of us, when we act, is a prime mover unmoved. In doing what we do, we cause certain events to happen, and nothing—or no one—causes us to cause those events to happen.

12. If we are thus prime movers unmoved and if our actions, or those for which we are responsible, are not causally determined, then they are not causally determined by our *desires.* And this means that the relation between what we want or what we desire, on the one hand, and what it is that we do, on the other, is not as simple as most philosophers would have it.

We may distinguish between what we might call the 'Hobbist approach' and what we might call the 'Kantian approach' to this question. The Hobbist approach is the one that is generally accepted at the present time, but the Kantian approach, I believe, is the one that is true. According to Hobbism, if we *know,* of some man, what his beliefs and desires happen to be and how strong they are, if we know what he feels certain of, what he desires more than anything else, and if we know the state of his body and what stimuli he is being subjected to, then we may *deduce,* logically, just what it is that he will do—or, more accurately, just what it is that he will try, set out, or undertake to do. Thus Professor Melden has said that 'the connection between wanting and doing is logical'.[9] But according to the Kantian approach to our problem, and this is the one that I would take, there is no such logical connection between wanting and doing, nor need there even be a causal connection. No set of statements about a man's desires, beliefs, and stimulus situation at any time implies any statement telling us what the man will try, set out, or undertake to do at that time. As Reid put it, though we may 'reason from men's motives to their actions and, in many cases, with great probability', we can never do so 'with absolute certainty'.[10]

This means that, in one very strict sense of the terms, there can be no science of man. If we think of science as a matter of finding out what laws happen to hold, and if the statement of a law tells us what kinds of events are caused by what other kinds of events, then there will be human actions which we cannot explain by subsuming them under any laws. We cannot say, 'It is causally necessary that, given such and such desires and beliefs, and being subject to such and such stimuli, the agent will do so and so'. For at times the agent, if he chooses, may rise above his desires and do something else instead.

But all of this is consistent with saying that, perhaps more often than not, our desires do exist under conditions such that those conditions necessitate us to act. And we may also say, with Leibniz, that at other times our desires may 'incline without necessitating'.

13. Leibniz's phrase presents us with our final philosophical problem. What does it mean to say that a desire, or a motive, might 'incline without necessitating'? There is a temptation,

certainly, to say that 'to incline' means to cause and that 'not to necessitate' means not to cause, but obviously we cannot have it both ways.

Nor will Leibniz's own solution do. In his letter to Coste, he puts the problem as follows: 'When a choice is proposed, for example to go out or not to go out, it is a question whether, with all the circumstances, internal and external, motives, perceptions, dispositions, impressions, passions, inclinations taken together, I am still in a contingent state, or whether I am necessitated to make the choice, for example, to go out; that is to say, whether this proposition true and determined in fact, *In all these circumstances taken together I shall choose to go out*, is contingent or necessary.'[11] Leibniz's answer might be put as follows: in one sense of the terms 'necessary' and 'contingent', the proposition 'In all these circumstances taken together I shall choose to go out', may be said to be contingent and not necessary, and in another sense of these terms, it may be said to be necessary and not contingent. But the sense in which the proposition may be said to be contingent, according to Leibniz, is only this: there is no logical contradiction involved in denying the proposition. And the sense in which it may be said to be necessary is this: since 'nothing ever occurs without cause or determining reason', the proposition is causally necessary. 'Whenever all the circumstances taken together are such that the balance of deliberation is heavier on one side than on the other, it is certain and infallible that that is the side that is going to win out'. But if what we have been saying is true, the proposition 'In all these circumstances taken together I shall choose to go out', may be causally as well as logically contingent. Hence we must find another interpretation for Leibniz's statement that our motives and desires may incline us, or influence us, to choose without thereby necessitating us to choose.

Let us consider a public official who has some moral scruples but who also, as one says, could be had. Because of the scruples that he does have, he would never take any positive steps to receive a bribe—he would not actively solicit one. But his morality has its limits and he is also such that, if we were to confront him with a *fait accompli* or to let him see what is about to happen ($10,000 in cash is being deposited behind the garage), then he would succumb and be unable to resist. The general situation is a familiar one and this is one reason that people pray to be delivered from temptation. (It also justifies Kant's remark: 'And how many there are who may have led a long blameless life, who are only *fortunate* in having escaped so many temptations'.)[12] Our relation to the misdeed that we contemplate may not be a matter simply of being able to bring it about or not to bring it about. As St. Anselm noted, there are at least four possibilities. We may illustrate them by reference to our public official and the event which is his receiving the bribe, in the following way: (i) he may be able to bring the event about himself (*facere esse*), in which case he would actively cause himself to receive the bribe; (ii) he may be able to refrain from bringing it about himself (*non facere esse*), in which case he would not himself do anything to insure that he receive the bribe; (iii) he may be able to do something to prevent the event from occurring (*facere non esse*), in which case he would make sure that the $10,000 was *not* left behind the garage; or (iv) he may be unable to do anything to prevent the event from occurring (*non facere non esse*), in which case, though he may not solicit the bribe, he would allow himself to keep it.[13] We have envisaged our official as a man who can resist the temptation to (i) but cannot resist the temptation to (iv): he can refrain from bringing the event about himself, but he cannot bring himself to do anything to prevent it.

Let us think of 'inclination without necessitation', then, in such terms as these. First we may contrast the two propositions:

(1) He can resist the temptation to do something in order to make A happen;
(2) He can resist the temptation to allow A to happen (i.e. to do nothing to prevent A from happening).

We may suppose that the man has some desire to have A happen and thus has a motive for making A happen. His motive for making A happen, I suggest, is one that *necessitates* provided that, because of the motive, (1) is false; he cannot resist the temptation to do something in order to make A happen. His motive for making A happen is one that *inclines* provided that, because of the motive, (2) is false; like our public official, he cannot bring himself to do anything to prevent A from happening. And therefore we can say that this motive for making A happen is one that *inclines but does not necessitate* provided that, because of the motive, (1) is true and (2) is false; he can resist the temptation to make it happen but he cannot resist the temptation to allow it to happen.

NOTES

1. The general position to be presented here is suggested in the following writings, among others: Aristotle, I *Eudemian Ethics*, bk. ii ch. 6, *Nicomachean Ethics*, bk. iii, ch. 1–5; Thomas Reid, *Essays on the Active Powers of Man*. C. A. Campbell, 'Is "Free Will" a Pseudo-Problem?' *Mind*, 1951, pp. 441–65, Roderick M. Chisholm, 'Responsibility and Avoidability', and Richard Taylor, 'Determination and the Theory of Agency', in *Determinism and Freedom in the Age of Modern Science*, ed. Sidney Hook (New York, 1958).

2. Thomas Reid, *Essays on the Active Powers of Man*, essay iv. ch. 4 (*Works*, 600).

3. *Summa Theologica,* First Part of the Second Part, qu. vi ('On the Voluntary and Involuntary').

4. Jonathan Edwards, *Freedom of the Will* (New Haven, 1957): G. E. Moore, *Ethics* (Home University Library, 1912). ch. 6.

5. A. I. Melden, *Free Action* (London, 1961), especially ch. 3. Mr. Melden's own views, however, are quite the contrary of those that are proposed here.

6. Aristotle, *Physics*, bk. iii. ch. 3; Suarez, *Disputationes Metaphysicae*, Disputation 18, s. 10.

7. Reid, *Works*. 524.

8. *Essay concerning Human Understanding*, bk. ii, ch. 21.

9. Melden, 166.

10. Reid, *Works*, 608, 612.

11. 'Lettre à Mr. Coste de la Nécessité et de la Contingence' (1707) in *Opera Philosophica*, ed. Erdmann, pp. 447–9.

12. In the Preface to the *Metaphysical Elements of Ethics*, in *Kant's Critique of Practical Reason and Other Works on the Theory of Ethics*, ed. T. K. Abbott (London, 1959), 303.

13. Cf. D. P. Henry, 'Saint Anselm's *De "Grammatico"'*, *Philosophical Quarterly*, x (1960), 115–26. St. Anselm noted that (i) and (iii), respectively, may be thought of as forming the upper left and the upper right corners of a square of opposition, and (ii) and (iv) the lower left and the lower right.

Free Will: Ancient Dispute, New Themes

ROBERT KANE

Robert Kane teaches philosophy at the University of Texas.

I

"There is a disputation that will continue till mankind are raised from the dead, between the necessitarians and the partisans of free will." These are the words of twelfth-century Persian poet, Jalalu'ddin Rumi. The problem of free will and necessity (or determinism), of which

Rumi speaks, has puzzled the greatest minds for centuries—including famous philosophers, literary figures, theologians, scientists, legal theorists, and psychologists—as well as many ordinary people. It has affected and been affected by both religion and science.

In his classic poem, *Paradise Lost*, John Milton describes the angels debating how some of them could have sinned of their own free wills given that God had made them intelligent and happy.[1] Why would they have done it? And why were they responsible for it rather than God, since God had made them the way they were and had complete foreknowledge of what they would do? While puzzling over such questions, even the angels, Milton tells us, were "in Endless Mazes lost" (not a comforting thought for us humans). On the scientific front, issues about free will lead us to ask about the nature of the physical universe and our place in it (are we determined by physical laws and movements of the atoms?), about human psychology and the springs of action (can our actions be predicted by those who know our psychology?), about social conditioning, moral responsibility, crime and punishment, right and wrong, good and evil, and much more.

To dive into these questions, the best way to begin is with the idea of *freedom* itself. Nothing could be more important than freedom to the modern world. All over the globe, the trend (often against resistance) is toward societies that are more free. But why do we want freedom? The simple, and not totally adequate, answer is that to be more free is to have the capacity and opportunity to satisfy more of our desires. In a free society we can walk into a store and buy almost anything we want. We can choose what movies to see, what music to listen to, whom to vote for.

But these are what you might call *surface* freedoms. What is meant by *free will* runs deeper than these everyday freedoms. To see how, suppose we had maximal freedom to make such choices to satisfy our desires and yet the choices we actually made were manipulated by others, by the powers-that-be. In such a world we would have a great deal of everyday freedom to do whatever we wanted, yet our free *will* would be severely limited. We would be free to *act* or choose *as* we will, but would not have the ultimate say about what it is that we will. Someone else would be pulling the strings, not by coercing us against our wishes, but by manipulating us into having the wishes they wanted us to have.

You may be thinking that, to some extent, we do live in such a world, where we are free to make numerous choices, but are manipulated into making many of our choices by advertising, television, public relations, spin doctors, salespersons, marketers, and sometimes even by friends, parents, relatives, rivals, or enemies. One indication of how important free will is to us is that people generally feel revulsion at such manipulation. When people find out that what they thought were their own wishes were actually manipulated by others who wanted them to choose in just the way they did, they feel demeaned. Such situations are demeaning because we realize we were not our own persons; and having free will is about being your own person.

The problem is brought out in a striking way by twentieth-century utopian novels, such as Aldous Huxley's *Brave New World* and B. F. Skinner's *Walden Two*.[2] In the fictional societies described in these famous works, people can have and do what they will or choose, but only to the extent that they have been conditioned by behavioral engineers or neuro-chemists to will or choose what they can have and do. In *Brave New World*, the lower-echelon workers are under the influence of powerful drugs so that they do not dream of things they cannot have. They are quite content to play miniature golf all weekend. They can do what they want, though their wants are meager and controlled by drugs.

The citizens of Skinner's *Walden Two* have a richer existence than the workers of *Brave New World*. Yet their desires and purposes are also covertly controlled, in this case by behavioral engineers. Walden Two-ers live collectively in a kind of rural commune; and because they share duties of farming and raising children, they have plenty of leisure. They pursue arts, sciences, crafts, engage in musical performances, and enjoy what appears to be a pleasant existence. The fictional founder of Walden Two, a fellow named Frazier, forthrightly says that their pleasant existence is brought about by the fact that, in his community, persons can do whatever they want or choose because they have been behaviorally conditioned since childhood to want and choose only what they can have and do. In other words, they have maximal *surface freedom* of action and choice (they can choose or do anything they want), but they lack a *deeper freedom* of the will because their desires and purposes are created by their behavioral conditioners or controllers. Their wills are not of "their own" making. Indeed, what happens in Walden Two is that their surface freedom to act and choose as they will is maximized by minimizing the deeper freedom to have the ultimate say about what they will.

Thus Frazier can say that Walden Two "is the freest place on earth" (p. 297), because he has surface freedoms in mind. For there is no *coercion* in Walden Two and no *punishment* because no one has to be forced to do anything against his or her will. The citizens can have anything they want because they have been conditioned not to want anything they cannot have. As for the deeper freedom, or free will, it does not exist in Walden Two, as Frazier himself admits (p. 257). But this is no loss, according to Frazier. Echoing *Walden Two*'s author, B. F. Skinner (a foremost defender of behaviorism in psychology), Frazier thinks the deeper freedom of the will is an illusion in the first place. We do not have it anyway, inside or outside Walden Two. In our ordinary lives, he argues, we are just as much the products of upbringing and social conditioning as the citizens of Walden Two, though we may delude ourselves into thinking otherwise. The difference is that, unlike Walden Two, our everyday conditioning is often haphazard, incompetent, and harmful.

Why then, Skinner asks, reject the maximal surface freedom and happiness of Walden Two for a deeper freedom of the will that is something we do not and cannot have anyway? Along with many other scientists, he thinks the idea that we could be *ultimate* determiners of our own ends or purposes (which is what the deeper freedom of the will would require) is an impossible ideal that cannot fit into the modern scientific picture of the world. To have such freedom, we would have to have been the original creators of our own wills—causes of ourselves. But if we trace the psychological springs of action back further and further to childhood, we find that we were less free back then, not more, and more subject to conditioning. We thus delude ourselves into

thinking that we have sacrificed some real (deeper) freedom for the happiness of Walden Two. Rather we have gained a maximum amount of the only kind of freedom we really can have (surface freedom), while giving up an illusion (free will).

Seductive as these arguments may be, there are many people (myself included) who continue to believe that something important is missing in Walden Two and that the deeper freedom is not a mere illusion. Such persons want to be the ultimate designers of their own lives as Frazier was for the lives of Walden Two. They want to be the creators, as he was, not the pawns—at least for their own lives. What they long for is what was traditionally meant by "free will."

Here is yet another way of looking at it. Free will in this deeper sense is also intimately related to notions of moral responsibility, blameworthiness, and praiseworthiness. Suppose a young man is on trial for an assault and robbery in which his victim was beaten to death. Let us say we attend his trial on a daily basis. At first, our thoughts of the young man are filled with anger and resentment. But as we listen daily to how he came to have such a mean character and perverse motives—a sordid story of parental neglect, child abuse, sexual abuse, bad role models—some of our resentment against the young man is shifted over to the parents and others who abused and influenced him. We begin to feel angry with them as well as him. Yet we aren't quite ready to shift all of the blame away from the young man himself. We wonder whether some residual responsibility may not belong to him. Our questions become: To what extent is *he* responsible for becoming the sort of person he now is? Was it *all* a question of bad parenting, societal neglect, social conditioning, and the like, or did he have any role to play in it?

These are crucial questions about free will, and about what may be called *ultimate responsibility*. We know that parenting and society, genetic makeup and upbringing, have an influence on what we become and what we are. But were these influences entirely *determining* or did they "leave anything over" for us to be responsible for? That's what we wanted to know about the young man. The question of whether he is merely a victim of his bad circumstances or has some residual responsibility for being what he is depends on whether these other factors were or were not *entirely* determining.[3]

Turning this around, if there were factors or circumstances that entirely determined what he did, then to be ultimately responsible, he would have had to be responsible to some degree for some of those factors by virtue of earlier acts through which he formed his present character. As the philosopher Aristotle put it centuries ago, if a man is responsible for the wicked acts that flow from his character, then he must at one time in the past have been responsible for forming the character from which these acts flow. But, of course, if *all* of our choices and actions were entirely determined by prior circumstances, we would have had to be responsible to some degree for some of these earlier circumstances by still earlier acts of ours, and so on indefinitely backward in time—an impossibility for finite creatures like ourselves. At some point, if we are to be ultimately responsible for being what we are, there must be acts in our life histories in which parenting and society, genetic make-up, and other factors did not completely determine how we acted, but left something over for us to be responsible for then and there. This is why many people have thought that the deeper freedom of the will is not compatible with being completely determined by the past. Surface freedoms (to do or choose what we will) may be compatible with determinism, but free will does not seem to be (as Skinner himself realized).

II

Yet such thoughts only lead to a further problem that has haunted free will debates for centuries: If this deeper freedom of the will is not compatible with determinism, it does not seem to be compatible with *indeterminism* either. An event that is undetermined might occur or might not occur, given the entire past. (A determined event *must* occur, given the entire past.) Thus, whether or not an undetermined event actually occurs, given its past, is a matter of chance. But chance events occur spontaneously and are not under the control of anything, hence not under the

control of agents. How then could they be free and responsible actions? If, for example, a choice occurred by virtue of a quantum jump or other undetermined event in your brain, it would seem a fluke or accident rather than a responsible choice. Undetermined events in the brain or body, it seems, would inhibit or interfere with freedom, occurring spontaneously and not under our control. They would turn out to be a nuisance—or perhaps a curse, like epilepsy—rather than an enhancement of our freedom.

Or look at the problem in another way that goes a little deeper. If my choice is really undetermined, that means I could have made a different choice *given exactly the same past* right up to the moment when I did choose. This is what indeterminism and the denial of determinism mean: exactly the same past, different outcomes. Imagine, for example, that I had been deliberating about where to spend my vacation, in Hawaii or Colorado, and after much thought and deliberation had decided I preferred Hawaii, and chose it. If the choice was undetermined, then exactly the same deliberation, the same thought processes, the same beliefs, desires, and other motives—not a sliver of difference—that led to my favoring and choosing Hawaii over Colorado, might by chance have resulted in my choosing Colorado instead. That is very strange. If such a thing happened it would seem a fluke or accident, like that quantum jump in the brain just mentioned, not a rational choice. Because I had come to favor Hawaii and was about to choose it, when by chance I chose Colorado, I would wonder what went wrong in my brain and perhaps consult a neurologist.

For reasons such as these, people have argued that undetermined free choices would be "arbitrary," "capricious," "random," "irrational," "uncontrolled," "inexplicable," or merely "matters of luck or chance," not really free and responsible choices at all. If free will is not compatible with determinism, it does not seem to be compatible with indeterminism either.

These charges are powerful ones and defenders of free will over the centuries have made extraordinary claims attempting to respond to them. Free will does require indeterminism, these defenders have said. But it cannot *merely* be indeterminism or chance. Some "extra factors" must be involved in free will that go beyond ordinary scientific or causal understanding. Immanuel Kant, for example, insisted that we can't explain free will in scientific and psychological terms. To account for it we have to appeal to the agency of what he called a "noumenal self" outside space and time that could not be studied in scientific terms.[4] Others have appealed to what Nobel physiologist John Eccles calls a "transempirical power center," which would intervene in the brain, filling the causal gaps left by indeterminism or chance.[5] Still others have appealed to a special kind of agent-causation—or, as Roderick Chisholm has called it, "immanent causation"—that cannot be explained in terms of the ordinary scientific modes of causation in terms of events or occurrences. Where all prior events, both physical and mental, leave a choice or action undetermined, the agent- or immanent cause determines it, but cannot be determined in turn because it is not an event. The agent-cause is, in Chisholm's words, a "prime mover unmoved."[6]

Such unusual stratagems are common among defenders of an indeterminist free will (who often nowadays are called "incompatibilists" because they believe that free will is not compatible with determinism and "libertarians" because they believe in addition that free will is not an illusion). But these unusual stratagems, such as noumenal selves, transempirical power centers, and agent- or immanent causes, have unfortunately reinforced the view, now widespread among philosophers and scientists, that traditional notions of free will requiring indeterminism are mysterious and have no place in the modern scientific picture of the world. Such libertarian stratagems, to their critics, are reminiscent of the old debates about vital forces in the biology of the nineteenth century, where obscure forces were postulated to explain what otherwise could not be explained about living things. They remind us of the Arkansas farmer when he first saw an automobile. He listened intently to the explanation of how the internal combustion engine worked, and nodded in agreement, but insisted on looking under the hood anyway because, as he said, "there must be a horse in there somewhere."

Thus, defenders of a nondeterminist free will are faced with a dilemma that was expressed by philosopher Thomas Hobbes at the beginning of the modern era. When trying to explain free will, these incompatibilist or libertarian defenders tend to fall either into "confusion" or "emptiness"—the confusion of identifying free will with indeterminism or the emptiness of mysterious accounts of agency in terms of noumenal selves, transempirical power centers, non-occurrent or agent-causes, or other stratagems whose operations remain obscure and unexplained. What is needed to escape this dilemma is some new thinking about how free will can be reconciled with indeterminism and how it might fit into the modern scientific picture of the world, without appealing to extra factors that have made it seem so mysterious. In the remainder of this essay, I want to suggest some new ways of thinking about this problem and about free will generally, which may stir you to do likewise.[7]

III

The first thing to note is that indeterminism does not have to be a factor in all acts done "of our own free wills." Not all of them have to be undetermined. Frequently in everyday life we act from existing motives without having to think or deliberate about what to do. At such times, we may very well be determined by our existing characters and motives. Yet we may also at such times be acting "of our own free wills" to the extent that we formed our present characters and motives (our own wills) by earlier choices or actions that were not themselves determined. Recall again Aristotle's claim that if a man is responsible for the wicked acts that flow from his character, he must at one time in the past have been responsible for forming the character from which these acts flow. Not all choices or acts done "of our own free wills" have to be undetermined, but only those choices or acts in our lifetimes by which we made ourselves into the kinds of persons we are. Let us call these "self-forming choices or actions" or SFAs.

I believe that such undetermined self-forming choices and actions (SFAs) occur at those difficult times of life when we are torn between competing visions of what we should do or become, and that they are more frequent than we think. Perhaps we are torn between doing the moral thing or acting from ambition, or between powerful present desires and long-term goals, or we are faced with difficult tasks for which we have aversions. In all such cases, we are faced with competing motivations and have to make an effort to overcome temptation to do something else we also strongly want. At such times, there is tension and uncertainty in our minds about what to do. I suggest that this is reflected in appropriate regions of our brains by movement away from thermodynamic equilibrium—in short, a kind of stirring up of chaos in the brain that makes it sensitive to microindeterminacies at the neuronal level. The uncertainty and inner tension we feel at such soulsearching moments of self-formation would thus be reflected in the indeterminacy of our neural processes themselves. What is experienced personally as uncertainty corresponds physically to the opening of a window of opportunity that temporarily screens off complete determination by influences of the past. (By contrast, when we act from predominant motives or settled dispositions, the uncertainty or indeterminacy is muted. If it did play a role in such cases, it would be a mere nuisance or fluke, as critics suggest, like the choice of Colorado when we favored Hawaii.)

When we do decide under such conditions of uncertainty, the outcome is not determined because of the preceding indeterminacy—and yet it can be willed (and hence rational and voluntary) either way owing to the fact that, in such selfformation, the agents' prior wills are divided by conflicting motives. Consider a businesswoman who faces a conflict of this kind. She is on the way to a business meeting important to her career when she observes an assault taking place in an alley. An inner struggle ensues between her moral conscience telling her to stop and call for help, and her career ambitions telling her she cannot miss this meeting. She has to make an effort of will to overcome the temptation to go on to her meeting. If she overcomes this temptation, it will be the result of her effort, but if she fails, it will be because she did not *allow* her effort to succeed. And this is

because, while she wanted to overcome temptation, she also wanted to fail, for quite different and incommensurable reasons. When we, like the businesswoman, decide in such circumstances, and the indeterminate efforts we are making become determinate choices, we *make* one set of competing reasons or motives prevail over the others then and there *by deciding*.

Now let us add a further piece to the puzzle. Just as indeterminism does not necessarily undermine rationality and voluntariness, so indeterminism, in and of itself, does not necessarily undermine control and responsibility. Suppose you are trying to think through a difficult problem, say a mathematical problem, and there is some indeterminacy in your neural processes complicating the task—a kind of chaotic background. It would be like trying to concentrate and solve a problem with background noise or distraction. Whether you are going to succeed in solving the mathematical problem is uncertain and undetermined because of the distracting indeterministic neural noise. Yet, if you concentrate and solve the problem nonetheless, we have reason to say you did it and are responsible for it even though it was undetermined whether you would succeed. The distracting neural noise would have been an obstacle that you overcame by your effort.

There are numerous other examples supporting this point, where indeterminism functions as an obstacle to success without precluding responsibility. Consider an assassin who is trying to shoot the prime minister, but might miss because of some undetermined events in his nervous system that may lead to a jerking or wavering of his arm. If the assassin does succeed in hitting his target, despite the indeterminism, can he be held responsible? The answer is obviously yes because he intentionally and voluntarily succeeded in doing what he was *trying* to do—kill the prime minister. Yet his action, killing the prime minister, was undetermined. One might even say "he got lucky" in killing the prime minister, because there was a chance he might have missed. Yet, for all that, he *did* kill the prime minister and *was* responsible for it.

Here is another example: A husband, while arguing with his wife, in a fit of rage swings his arm down on her favorite glass-top table, intending to break it. Again, we suppose that some indeterminism in the nerves of his arm makes the momentum of his swing indeterminate so that it is literally not determined whether the table will break right up to the moment when it is struck. Whether the husband breaks the table or not is undetermined and yet he is clearly responsible if he does break it. (It would be a poor excuse for him to say to his wife "chance did it, not me" or "it wasn't my doing; it happened by chance." She would not be impressed.)

To be sure, such examples—of the mathematical problem, the assassin, and the husband—do not amount to genuine exercises of free will in "self-forming actions" or SFAs, such as the businesswoman's, where the wills of the agents are divided between conflicting motives. The businesswoman wants to do the right thing and help the victim, but she also wants to go on to her meeting. By contrast, the will of the assassin is not equally divided. He wants to kill the prime minister, but does not also want to fail. (If his conscience bothered him and he was undecided about what to do up to the last minute, that would be another matter. *Then* his choice would be a selfforming action or SFA, like the businesswoman's. But such was not the case.) Thus, if the assassin fails to hit his target, it will be merely by chance or as a fluke, not voluntarily (and so also for the husband and mathematical problem-solver). Cases such as the assassin, husband, and mathematical problem-solver are therefore not all that we want. Yet they are a step in the right direction because they show that indeterminism does not necessarily rule out action and responsibility, any more than it necessarily rules out rationality and voluntariness. To go further, we have to dig more deeply and add some further ideas.

IV

Let us imagine in cases of self-forming choices, like the businesswoman's, where there *is* conflict in the will, that the indeterministic noise that is providing an obstacle to her overcoming temptation (and stopping to help the victim) is not coming from an external source, but is coming from her own will, because she also deeply desires to do the opposite (go on to her meeting). Imagine

that in such conflicting circumstances, two competing (recurrent) neural networks are involved. (These are complex networks of interconnected neurons in the brain circulating impulses in feedback loops that are generally involved in high-level human cognitive processing.[8]) The input of one of these networks is coming from the woman's desires and motives for stopping to help the victim. If the network reaches a certain activation threshold (the simultaneous firing of a complex set of "output" neurons), that would represent her choice to help. For the competing network, the inputs are her ambitious motives for going on to her meeting, and its reaching an activation threshold would represent the choice to go on. (If one network activates, the other will be inhibited and the contrary choice will not be made.)

Now imagine further that these two competing networks are connected so that the indeterministic noise that is an obstacle to her making one of the choices is coming from her desire to make the other. Thus, as suggested for self-forming choices or SFAs, the indeterminism arises from a *tensioncreating conflict in the will.* In such circumstances, when either of the pathways "wins" (i.e., reaches an activation threshold, which amounts to choice), it will be like the agent's solving the mathematical problem by overcoming the indeterministic background noise generated by the other. And just as we could say, when you solved the mathematical problem by overcoming the distracting noise through your effort, that you did it and are responsible for it, so one can say this as well, I would argue, in the present case, *whichever one is chosen.* The neural pathway through which she succeeds in reaching a choice threshold will have overcome the obstacle in the form of indeterministic noise coming from the other pathway.

Note that, in these circumstances, the choices either way will not be "inadvertent," "accidental," "capricious," or "merely random," because they will be *willed* by the woman either way, when they are made, and done for *reasons* either way (moral convictions if she turns back, ambitious motives if she goes on) which she then and there endorses. And these are the conditions usually required to say something is done "on purpose," rather than accidentally, capriciously, or merely by chance. Moreover, these conditions taken together (that she wills it, and does it for reasons, and could have done otherwise willingly and for reasons) rule out each of the normal motives we have for saying that agents act, but do not have control over their actions (coercion, constraint, inadvertence, mistake, and control by others). None of these obtain in the businesswoman's case. She is not coerced (no one is holding a gun to her head), not physically constrained or disabled, not forced or controlled by others; nor does she act inadvertently or by mistake, but on purpose either way, as just noted.

Of course, with "self-forming" choices of these kinds, agents cannot control or determine which choice outcome will occur *before* it occurs or the outcomes would be *pre*determined after all. (That would be like deciding beforehand what you are going to decide.) But it does not follow that, because one does not control or determine which of a set of outcomes is going to occur before it occurs, one does not control which of them occurs, *when* it occurs. When the above conditions for selfforming choices are satisfied, agents exercise control over their future lives *then and there* by deciding. Indeed, they have what may be called "plural voluntary control" in the following sense: Agents have plural voluntary control over a set of options (stopping to help or going on to a meeting) when they are able to bring about *whichever* of the options they will, *when* they will to do so, for the *reasons* they will to do so, *on purpose* rather than by mistake or accident, without being coerced or compelled in doing so, or otherwise controlled by other agents or mechanisms. We have seen that each of these conditions can be satisfied in cases of SFAs, like the businesswoman's, despite the indeterminism involved.[9] These conditions of plural voluntary control may be summed by saying, as people often do, that the agents can choose either way "at will." ("Plural" in "plural voluntary control" means "more-than-one-way" and "voluntary" means "in accordance with one's will.")

Note also that this account of self-forming choices amounts to a kind of "doubling" of the mathematical problem. It is as if an agent faced with such a choice is *trying* or making an effort to solve *two* cognitive problems at once, or to complete two competing (deliberative) tasks at once—in our example, to make a moral choice and to make a conflicting self-interested choice (corresponding to the two competing neural networks involved). Each task is being thwarted by the indeterminism coming from the other, so it might fail. But if it succeeds, then the agents can be held responsible because, as in the case of solving the mathematical problem, they will have succeeded in doing what they were knowingly and willingly trying to do. Recall again the cases of the assassin and the husband. Owing to indeterminacies in their neural pathways, the assassin might miss his target or the husband fail to break the table. But if they *succeed,* despite the probability of failure, they are responsible, because they will have succeeded in doing what they were trying to do.

And so it is, I suggest, with self-forming choices, except that in the case of self-forming choices, *whichever way the agents choose,* they will have succeeded in doing what they were trying to do because they were simultaneously trying to make both choices, and one is going to succeed. Their failure to do one thing is not a *mere* failure, but a voluntary succeeding in doing the other. Does it make sense to talk about the agent's trying to do two competing things at once in this way, or to solve two cognitive problems at once? Well, we know that the brain is a parallel processor; it can simultaneously process different kinds of information relevant to tasks such as perception or recognition through different neural pathways. Such a capacity, I believe, is essential to the exercise of free will.

In cases of self-formation (SFAs), agents are simultaneously trying to resolve plural and competing cognitive tasks. They are, as we say, of two minds. Yet they are not two separate persons. They are not dissociated from either task. The businesswoman who wants to go back to help the victim is the same ambitious woman who wants to go to her meeting and make a sale. She is a complex creature, torn inside by different visions of who she is and what she wants to be, as we all are from time to time. But this is the kind of complexity needed for genuine self-formation and free will. And when she succeeds in doing one of the things she is trying to do, she will endorse that as *her* resolution of the conflict in her will, voluntarily and intentionally, not by accident or mistake.

V

Yet it is still hard to shake the intuition that if choices are undetermined, they *must* happen merely by chance—and so must be "random," "capricious," "uncontrolled," "irrational," "inexplicable," and all the other things charged. I do not deny the powerful hold such intuitions have upon us. They are among the reasons why free will continues to be such a deep problem, even for those who want to believe in it. But the very fact that it has been such a problem for so long should also suggest that we cannot take ordinary intuitions about free will at face value without questioning them. If we are ever going to understand it, we will likely have to break old habits of thought and learn to think in new ways.

The first step in doing this is to question the intuitive connection in most people's minds between "indeterminism's being involved in something" and "its happening merely as a matter of chance or luck." "Chance" and "luck" are terms of ordinary language that carry the connotation of "it's out of my control." So using them already begs certain questions, whereas "indeterminism" is a technical term that merely precludes *deterministic* causation, though not causation altogether. Indeterminism is consistent with non-deterministic or probabilistic causation, where the outcome is not inevitable. It is therefore a mistake (alas, one of the most common in debates about free will) to assume that "undetermined" means "uncaused."

Another source of misunderstanding is this: Because the outcome of the businesswoman's effort (the choice) is undetermined up to the last minute, we may have the image of her first making an effort to overcome temptation (to go on to her meeting) and then at the last instant "chance taking over" and deciding the issue for her. But this image is misleading. On the view just described, one cannot separate the indeterminism and the effort of will, so that *first* the effort occurs *followed* by chance or luck (or vice versa). One must think of the effort and the indeterminism as fused; the effort *is* indeterminate and the indeterminism is a *property* of the effort, not something separate that occurs after or before the effort. The fact that the effort has this property of being indeterminate does not make it any less the woman's *effort*. The complex recurrent neural network that realizes the effort in the brain is circulating impulses in feedback loops and there is some indeterminacy in these circulating impulses. But the whole process is her effort of will and it persists right up to the moment when the choice is made. There is no point at which the effort stops and chance "takes over." She chooses as a result of the effort, even though she might have failed. Similarly, the husband breaks the table as a result of his effort, even though he might have failed because of the indeterminacy. (That is why his excuse—"chance broke the table, not me"—is so lame.)

And just as expressions such as "she chose *by* chance" can mislead us in such contexts, so can expressions like "she got lucky." Recall that in the cases of the assassin and the husband, one might say "they got lucky" in killing the prime minister and breaking the table because their actions were undetermined. Yet, as we noted, it does not follow that they were not responsible. So ask yourself this question: Why does the inference "he got lucky, *so he was not responsible?*" fail when it does fail, in the cases of the husband and the assassin? The first part of an answer has to do with the point made earlier that "luck," like "chance," has question-begging implications in ordinary language that are not necessarily implications of "indeterminism" (which implies only the absence of deterministic causation). The core meaning of "he got lucky" in the assassin and husband cases, which *is* implied by indeterminism, I suggest, is that "he succeeded *despite the probability or chance of failure*"; and this core meaning does not imply lack of responsibility, if he succeeds.

If "he got lucky" had further meanings in the husband and assassin cases that are often associated with "luck" and "chance" in ordinary usage (for example, the outcome was not his doing, or occurred by *mere* chance, or he was not responsible for it), the inference would not fail for the husband and assassin, as it clearly does. But the point is that these further meanings of "luck" and "chance" do not follow *from the mere presence of indeterminism*. The second reason why the inference "he got lucky, so he was not responsible" fails for the assassin and the husband is that *what* they succeeded in doing was what they were trying and wanting to do all along (kill the minister and break the table respectively). The third reason is that *when* they succeeded, their reaction was not "oh dear, that was a mistake, an accident—something that *happened* to me, not something I *did*." Rather they *endorsed* the outcomes as something they were trying and wanting to do all along, that is to say, knowingly and purposefully, not by mistake or accident.

But these conditions are satisfied in the businesswoman's case as well, *either way* she chooses. If she succeeds in choosing to return to help the victim (or in choosing to go on to her meeting), first, she will have "succeeded *despite the probability or chance of failure;* second, she will have succeeded in doing what she was trying and wanting to do all along (she wanted both outcomes very much, but for different reasons, and was trying to make those reasons prevail in both cases); and third, when she succeeded (in choosing to return to help) her reaction was not "oh dear, that was a mistake, an accident—something that happened to me, not something I did." Rather she endorsed the outcome as something she was trying and wanting to do all along; she recognized it as her resolution of the conflict in her will. And if she had chosen to go on to her meeting, she would have endorsed that outcome, recognizing it as her resolution of the conflict in her will.

Let us try another tack. Perhaps we are begging the question by assuming at the outset that the outcomes of the woman's efforts are her *choices*. If they are not choices to begin with, they cannot be voluntary choices. One might argue this on the grounds that (A) "if an event is undetermined, it must be something that merely *happens* and cannot be somebody's choice"; or (B) "if an event is undetermined, it

must be something that merely happens, it cannot be something an agent *does* (it cannot be an action)." But to see how questionbegging these assumptions are, one has only to note that A and B imply respectively (A′) "if an event is a choice, it must be determined" ("all choices are determined") and (B′) "if an event is an action, it must be determined" ("all actions are determined"). Are these claims supposed to be true necessarily or by definition? If so, the free will issue would be solved by fiat; it would follow merely from the meanings of the words that all choices and actions are determined.

But why should we believe this? Was the husband's breaking the table not something he did because it was not determined? Recall that "undetermined" does not mean "uncaused." The breaking of the table was caused by the swing of his arm, and though the outcome was not inevitable, that was good enough for saying he did it and was responsible. As for choices, a choice is the formation of an intention or a purpose to do something. It resolves uncertainty and indecision in the mind about what to do, "setting the mind" on one alternative rather than another. Nothing in such a description implies that there could not be some indeterminism in the deliberation and neural processes of an agent's preceding choice corresponding to the agent's uncertainty about what to do. Recall from preceding arguments that the presence of indeterminism does not mean the outcome happened merely by chance and not by the agent's effort.

But it is one thing to choose, in the sense of forming an intention; it is another thing to have *control* over one's choosing. Perhaps this is where the real problem lies. Would not the presence of indeterminism at least *diminish* the control persons have over their choices and other actions? Is it not the case that the assassin's control over whether the prime minister is killed (his ability to realize his purposes or what he is trying to do) is lessened by the undetermined impulses in his arm—and so also for the husband and his breaking the table? Moreover, this limitation is connected with another often noted by critics— that indeterminism, wherever it occurs, seems to be a *hindrance* or *obstacle* to our realizing our purposes and hence an obstacle to our freedom.

These concerns are closer to the mark, and there is something to them. But rather than being devastating objections to an incompatibilist account of free will, I think they reveal something important about such a free will. I think we should concede that indeterminism, wherever it occurs, *does* diminish control over what we are trying to do and *is* a hindrance or obstacle to the realization of our purposes. But recall that in the case of the businesswoman (and for SFAs generally), the indeterminism that is admittedly diminishing her control over one thing she is trying to do (the moral act of helping the victim) *is coming from her own will*—from her desire and effort to do the opposite (go to her business meeting). And the indeterminism that is diminishing her control over the other thing she is trying to do (act selfishly and go to her meeting) is coming from her desire and effort to do the opposite (to be a moral person and act on moral reasons).

So, in each case, the indeterminism *is* functioning as a hindrance or obstacle to her realizing one of her purposes—a hindrance or obstacle in the form of resistance within her will. As a consequence, whichever choice she makes, whichever effort wins out, she will have to overcome the hindrance or obstacle provided by the indeterminism coming from the other. If there were no such hindrance—if there were no resistance in her will—she would indeed in a sense have "complete control" over one of her options. There would be no competing motives that would stand in the way of her choosing it. But then also she would not be free to rationally and voluntarily choose the other purpose because she would have no good competing reasons to do so. Thus, by *being* a hindrance to the realization of some of our purposes, indeterminism paradoxically opens up the genuine possibility of pursuing other purposes—of choosing or doing *otherwise* in accordance with, rather than against, our wills (voluntarily) and reasons (rationally).

To be genuinely self-forming agents (creators of ourselves)—to have free will—there must at times in life be obstacles and hindrances in our wills of this sort that we must overcome. We can concede then that indeterminism is a hindrance and a nuisance, but a necessary one if we are to have ultimate responsibility for our own wills. Being "your own self" is a struggle. We can appreciate why existentialist philosopher Jean-Paul Sartre said that true freedom (free will) is a burden many people want to "escape"—preferring instead that others tell them what to do and how to live, or perhaps preferring that their choices always be easy.[10] In an earlier time, St. Augustine asked why God would have given us free will, since it is such a pain to us and to others; and the answer was that without it we would lack the greater good of being ultimately responsible for what we are and what we do.[11]

Perhaps we should look in another direction that has also led to doubts about whether free will can be reconciled with indeterminism or chance. What might be going on in the brain, we might ask, when free choices take place? If neuroscientists were to inspect the woman's brain when she was struggling with her moral decision, wouldn't it be the case that they would find nothing more than interconnected sets of neuron firings in which micro-indeterminacies were not negligible? These interconnected neuron firings would in turn terminate in some definite configuration of nerve firings that corresponded to the "choice" to stop and help the victim or in another set of firings corresponding to the "choice" to go on to her meeting. But why one of these outcomes occurred rather than the other would be inexplicable in terms of the preceding processes. Probabilities could be assigned for one outcome rather than the other, but that is all. And this looks like chance.

I agree that if the physical descriptions of these events were the only legitimate ones, then free will would look like nothing more than chance or probability. When neuroscientists described it in physico-chemical terms, all they would get are indeterministic chaotic processes with probabilistic outcomes. In short, if described from a physical perspective alone, free will looks like chance. But the physical description is not the only one to be considered. The indeterministic chaotic process is also, experientially considered, the agent's effort of will—something the agent is doing. And the undetermined outcome of the process, one way or the other, is experientially the agent's choice—something the agent does, not something that merely happens to the agent. So viewed from another perspective, the neural output that represents the choice is the result of the agent's effort even though the outcome is not determined.

If we did not add these mental descriptions of what is going on to the physical descriptions, something important would be left out of our picture of the world. To make sense of free will, we do not have to be complete (substance) dualists about mind and body, as Descartes was. But we cannot be extreme "eliminative" materialists either. We can't expect to lop off from the top of our world-view all psychological descriptions of human beings in terms of beliefs, desires, intentions, efforts, choices, and consciousness (leaving only descriptions in neurophysiological terms), *and expect free will to survive*. The fact is that a lot of other things important to us would not survive either if we were to lop off these psychological descriptions from our descriptions of the world, such as personhood, rationality, subjectivity, morality, and so on.

But notice that *this* problem is not a special one for theories of free will that presuppose indeterminism. Suppose you believed that all choices and actions were determined and that human free agency was compatible with determinism. You still could not adequately describe human agency, if you confined yourself to describing the brain in chemical and neurophysiological terms alone, leaving out all ordinary psychological descriptions in terms of beliefs, desires, intentions, efforts, choices, and consciousness. Determinists and compatibilists about free will cannot eliminate supervenient mental or psychological descriptions either, if they are going to describe human agency. It is no less a mystery how neural firings in the brain could be, or give rise to, conscious beliefs, efforts, or choices if these neural firings are *determined* than if they are undetermined. This problem (the problem of consciousness, or more generally, the "mind/body problem") is no special problem for indeterminist theories of free will like the one given here. It is a

problem for anyone who wishes to talk about free agency, whatever position they take on free will, compatibilist or incompatibilist, determinist or indeterminist.

These reflections naturally raise the further question of whether the indeterminism that is required by an incompatibilist theory of free will is actually there in the brain. This is an empirical question that can only be decided by scientific research and not by a philosophical theory or armchair speculation (much as philosophers would like to decide all questions *a priori*, or before all experience). While we cannot resolve this question, we can at least keep our minds open about it. There is so much more to be learned about the brain and living things. One caution, however: If you are inclined to believe that free will is incompatible with determinism (if you are an incompatibilist or libertarian), don't think you can escape such scientific and empirical questions altogether unless you want to leave free will a complete mystery. Even if you appealed to "transempirical power centers" or "non-event" agent causes to make sense of free will (as libertarians often do), there would still have to be some indeterminacy in the natural world—and presumably in the brain where it counts—to make room in nature (to provide the "causal gaps") for the intervention of these additional causes or agencies. As the ancient Epicurean philosophers said centuries ago, if the atoms do not sometimes "swerve" in undetermined ways, there will be no room in nature for free will.

Addressing this problem earlier, I suggested that conflicts in the wills of agents associated with self-forming choices might "stir up chaos" in the brain, sensitizing it to quantum indeterminacies at the neuronal level, which would then be magnified to affect the neural networks as a whole. This is speculative to be sure, and others writers have suggested different ways in which indeterminacy might be involved in the brain.[12] But such speculations are not merely idle. There is some evidence that unpredictable chaotic activity plays a role in the brain and human cognition, providing some of the flexibility that the nervous system needs to react creatively to an ever-changing environment.

A recent article in the journal *Behavior and Brain Sciences,* entitled "How Brains Make Chaos in Order to Make Sense of the World", defends this role, as do other recent writings.[13] Now it is true that chaos (or chaotic behavior) in physical systems, though unpredictable, is nonetheless usually deterministic. Chaos does not of itself imply indeterminism. But chaotic behavior in physical systems does involve "sensitivity to initial conditions." Minute differences in the initial conditions of chaotic physical systems, including living things, may be magnified, giving rise to large-scale, undetermined effects. If the brain does "make chaos to understand the world," its sensitivity to initial conditions may magnify quantum indeterminacies in neural networks whose outputs can depend on minute differences in the timings of individual neuron firings. So while quantum physics and the new sciences of chaos and complexity may not give us the indeterminism needed for free will alone (because the uncertainty of the former is usually negligible in larger physical systems and the latter need not be indeterministic by itself), they might do so together.

In any case, I have not tried to settle such empirical questions, nor could I. What I have been addressing is another set of questions that incline people to write off incompatibilist views of free will from the start, believing they could not possibly make sense and could not be reconciled with the modern scientific picture of human beings, *even if* indeterminism were somehow available in the physical world. I have argued to the contrary that if the indeterminism is there in nature, then something could be done to make sense of free will.

Let me conclude with one final objection that is perhaps the most telling and has not yet been discussed. Even if one granted that persons, such as the businesswoman, could make genuine self-forming choices that were undetermined, isn't there something to the charge that such choices would be "arbitrary"? A residual arbitrariness seems to remain in all self-forming choices because the agents cannot in principle have sufficient or overriding *prior* reasons for making one option and one set of reasons prevail over the other. The agents *make* one set of reasons prevail *by* choosing, to be sure, but they could as well have made the other set of reasons prevail by choosing differently.

I agree that there is some truth to this charge as well. But I would argue that such arbitrariness relative to prior reasons also tells us something important about free will. It tells us that every undetermined self-forming free choice is the initiation of what might be called a "value experiment" whose justification lies in the future and is not fully explained by past reasons. In making such a choice we say, in effect, "Let's try this. It is not required by my past, but is consistent with my past and is one branching pathway my life can now meaningfully take. Whether it is the right choice, only time will tell. Meanwhile, I am willing to take responsibility for it one way or the other."

It is worth noting that the term "arbitrary" comes from the Latin *arbitrium,* which means "judgment"—as in *liberum arbitrium voluntatis,* "free judgment of the will" (the medieval philosophers' designation for free will). Imagine a writer in the middle of a novel. The novel's heroine faces a crisis and the writer has not yet developed her character in sufficient detail to say exactly how she will act. The author makes a "judgment" about this that is not determined by the heroine's already formed past, which does not give unique direction. In this sense, the judgment (*arbitrium*) of how she will react is "arbitrary," but not entirely so. It had input from the heroine's fictional past and in turn gave input to her projected future. In a similar way, agents who exercise free will are both authors of and characters in their own stories all at once. By virtue of "self-forming" judgments of the will (*arbitria voluntatis*), they are "arbiters" of their own lives, "making themselves" out of a past that, if they are truly free, does not limit their future pathways to one.

Suppose we were to say to them, "But look, you didn't have sufficient or *conclusive* prior reasons for choosing as you did since you also had viable reasons for choosing the other way." They might reply, "True enough. But I did have *good* reasons for choosing as I did, which I'm willing to stand by and take responsibility for. If they were not sufficient or conclusive reasons, that's because, like the heroine of the novel, I was not a fully formed person before I chose (and still am not, for that matter). Like the author of the novel described above, I am in the process of writing an unfinished story and forming an unfinished character who, in my case, is myself."

NOTES

1. *Paradise Lost* (London: Methuen, 1955), prologue.
2. *Brave New World* (San Francisco: Harper-Collins, 1989). *Walden Two* (New York: MacMillan, 1962). Page references in the paper to *Walden Two* are to this edition.
3. This is why we are naturally inclined to ask in cases like this whether someone else in exactly the same circumstances might have acted differently.
4. Kant, *The Critique of Practical Reason*. Trans. by L. W. Beck (Indianapolis: Bobbs-Merrill, 1956), part III.
5. Eccles, *Facing Reality* (New York: Springer-Verlag, 1970).
6. For defenses of this agent-causal position by various authors, see the essays in T. O'Connor(ed.), *Agents, Causes and Events: Essays on Indeterminism and Free Will* (Oxford: Oxford University Press, 1995).
7. These ideas are developed at greater length in my book, *The Significance of Free Will* (Oxford and New York: Oxford University Press, 1996; paperback edition, 1998).
8. A readable and accessible introduction to the role of neural networks (including recurrent networks) in cognitive processing is P. M. Churchland, *The Engine of Reason, the Seat of the Soul* (Cambridge, MA: MIT Press, 1996).
9. I show in greater detail that each of these conditions can be satisfied by self-forming choices or SFAs in *The Significance of Free Will* (op. cit.), chapter 8.
10. Sartre, "Selections from *Being and Nothingness*." In S. Morgenbesser et al.(eds.), *Free Will* (Englewood Cliffs, NJ: Prentice-Hall, 1962), pp. 95–113.
11. Augustine, *On the Free Choice of the Will* (Indianapolis: Bobbs-Merrill, 1964), Part I.
12. For example, H. Stapp, *Mind, Matter and Quantum Mechanics* (New York: Springer-Verlag, 1993); D. Hodgson, *The Mind Matters* (Oxford: Clarendon Press, 1991); R. Penrose, *The Emperor's New Mind* (Oxford: Oxford University Press, 1989); J. Eccles (op. cit.)
13. The article is C. Skarda and W. Freeman, *Behavioral and Brain Sciences* 10 (1987): 161–195; other writings on the subject include A. Babloyantz and A. Destexhe, "Strange Attractors in the Human Cortex." In L. Rensing(ed.), *Temporal Disorder in Human Oscillatory Systems* (New York: Springer-Verlag, 1985); G. Scott and M. McMillen (eds.), *Dissipative Structures and Spatiotemporal Organization Studies in Biomedical Research* (Ames: Iowa State University Press, 1980); H. Walter, *Neurophilosophy and Free Will*. Trans. by Cynthia Stohr (Cambridge, MA: MIT Press, 2001), Part III.

HARD DETERMINISM: THE CASE FOR DETERMINISM AND ITS INCOMPATIBILITY WITH ANY IMPORTANT SENSE OF FREE WILL

The Illusion of Free Will

PAUL HOLBACH

Paul Henri Thiry, Baron d'Holbach (1723–1789), a French philosopher, was one of the Encyclopedists. His book, *System of Nature*, was called by his enemies "the Bible of Atheists."

From System *of Nature* by Baron Paul d'Holbach, published in 1770. Translated by H. D. Robinson.

Motives and the Determinism of the Will. In whatever manner man is considered, he is connected to universal nature, and submitted to the necessary and immutable laws that she imposes on all the beings she contains, according to their peculiar essences or to the respective properties with which, without consulting them, she endows each particular species. Man's life is a line that nature commands him to describe upon the surface of the earth, without his ever being able to swerve from it, even for an instant. He is born without his own consent; his organization does in nowise depend upon himself; his ideas come to him involuntarily; his habits are in the power of those who cause him to contract them; he is unceasingly modified by causes, whether visible or concealed, over which he has no control, which necessarily regulate his mode of existence, give the hue to his way of thinking, and determine his manner of acting. He is good or bad, happy or miserable, wise or foolish, reasonable or irrational, without his will being for anything in these various states. Nevertheless, in spite of the shackles by which he is bound, it is pretended he is a free agent, or that independent of the causes by which he is moved, he determines his own will, and regulates his own condition. . . .

The will, as we have elsewhere said, is a modification of the brain, by which it is disposed to action, or prepared to give play to the organs. This will is necessarily determined by the qualities, good or bad, agreeable or painful, of the object or the motive that acts upon his senses, or of which the idea remains with him, and is resuscitated by his memory. In consequence, he acts necessarily, his action is the result of the impulse he receives either from the motive, from the object, or from the idea which has modified his brain, or disposed his will. When he does not act according to this impulse, it is because there comes some new cause, some new motive, some new idea, which modifies his brain in a different manner, gives him a new impulse, determines his will in another way, by which the action of the former impulse is suspended: thus, the sight of an agreeable object, or its idea, determines his will to set him in action to procure it; but if a new object or a new idea

more powerfully attracts him, it gives a new direction to his will, annihilates the effect of the former, and prevents the action by which it was to be procured. This is the mode in which reflection, experience, reason, necessarily arrests or suspends the action of man's will: without this he would of necessity have followed the anterior impulse which carried him towards a then desirable object. In all this he always acts according to necessary laws from which he has no means of emancipating himself.

If when tormented with violent thirst, he figures to himself in idea, or really perceives a fountain, whose limpid streams might cool his feverish want, is he sufficient master of himself to desire or not to desire the object competent to satisfy so lively a want? It will no doubt be conceded, that it is impossible he should not be desirous to satisfy it; but it will be said—if at this moment it is announced to him that the water he so ardently desires is poisoned, he will, notwithstanding his vehement thirst, abstain from drinking it: and it has, therefore, been falsely concluded that he is a free agent. The fact, however, is, that the motive in either case is exactly the same: his own conservation. The same necessity that determined him to drink before he knew the water was deleterious upon this new discovery equally determined him not to drink; the desire of conserving himself either annihilates or suspends the former impulse; the second motive becomes stronger than the preceding, that is, the fear of death, or the desire of preserving himself, necessarily prevails over the painful sensation caused by his eagerness to drink: but, it will be said, if the thirst is very parching, an inconsiderate man without regarding the danger will risk swallowing the water. Nothing is gained by this remark; in this case, the anterior impulse only regains the ascendency; he is persuaded that life may possibly be longer preserved, or that he shall derive a greater good by drinking the poisoned water than by enduring the torment, which, to his mind, threatens instant dissolution; thus the first becomes the strongest and necessarily urges him on to action. Nevertheless, in either case, whether he partakes of the water, or whether he does not, the two actions will be equally necessary; they will be the effect of that motive which finds itself most puissant; which consequently acts in the most coercive manner upon his will.

This example will serve to explain the whole phenomena of the human will. This will, or rather the brain, finds itself in the same situation as a bowl, which, although it has received an impulse that drives it forward in a straight line, is deranged in its course whenever a force superior to the first obliges it to change its direction. The man who drinks the poisoned water appears a madman; but the actions of fools are as necessary as those of the most prudent individuals. The motives that determine the voluptuary and the debauchee to risk their health, are as powerful, and their actions are as necessary, as those which decide the wise man to manage his. But, it will be insisted, the debauchee may be prevailed on to change his conduct: this does not imply that he is a free agent; but that motives may be found sufficiently powerful to annihilate the effect of those that previously acted upon him; then these new motives determine his will to the new mode of conduct he may adopt as necessarily as the former did to the old mode. . . .

The errors of philosophers on the free agency of man, have arisen from their regarding his will as the *primum mobile,* the original motive of his actions; for want of recurring back, they have not perceived the multiplied, the complicated causes which, independently of him, give motion to the will itself; or which dispose and modify his brain, while he himself is purely passive in the motion he receives. Is he the master of desiring or not desiring an object that appears desirable to him? Without doubt it will be answered, no: but he is the master of resisting his desire, if he reflects on the consequences. But, I ask, is he capable of reflecting on these consequences, when his soul is hurried along by a very lively passion, which entirely depends upon his natural organization, and the causes by which he is modified? Is it in his power to add to these consequences all the weight necessary to counterbalance his desire? Is he the master of preventing the qualities which render an object desirable from residing in it? I shall be told: he ought to have learned to resist his passions; to contract a habit of putting a curb on his desires. I agree to it without any

difficulty. But in reply, I again ask, is his nature susceptible of this modification? Does his boiling blood, his unruly imagination, the igneous fluid that circulates in his veins, permit him to make, enable him to apply true experience in the moment when it is wanted? And even when his temperament has capacitated him, has his education, the examples set before him, the ideas with which he has been inspired in early life, been suitable to make him contract this habit of repressing his desires? Have not all these things rather contributed to induce him to seek with avidity, to make him actually desire those objects which you say he ought to resist? . . .

In short, the actions of man are never free; they are always the necessary consequence of his temperament, of the received ideas, and of the notions, either true or false, which he has formed to himself of happiness; of his opinions, strengthened by example, by education, and by daily experience. So many crimes are witnessed on the earth only because every thing conspires to render man vicious and criminal; the religion he has adopted, his government, his education, the examples set before him, irresistibly drive him on to evil: under these circumstances, morality preaches virtue to him in vain. In those societies where vice is esteemed, where crime is crowned, where venality is constantly recompensed, where the most dreadful disorders are punished only in those who are too weak to enjoy the privilege of committing them with impunity, the practice of virtue is considered nothing more than a painful sacrifice of happiness. Such societies chastise, in the lower orders, those excesses which they respect in the higher ranks; and frequently have the injustice to condemn those in the penalty of death, whom public prejudices, maintained by constant example, have rendered criminal.

Man, then, is not a free agent in any one instant of his life; he is necessarily guided in each step by those advantages, whether real or fictitious, that he attaches to the objects by which his passions are roused: these passions themselves are necessary in a being who unceasingly tends towards his own happiness; their energy is necessary, since that depends on his temperament; his temperament is necessary, because it depends on the physical elements which enter into his composition; the modification of this temperament is necessary, as it is the infallible and inevitable consequence of the impulse he receives from the incessant action of moral and physical beings.

Choice Does Not Prove Freedom. In spite of these proofs of the want of free agency in man, so clear to unprejudiced minds, it will, perhaps be insisted upon with no small feeling of triumph, that if it be proposed to any one, to move or not to move his hand, an action in the number of those called indifferent, he evidently appears to be the master of choosing; from which it is concluded that evidence has been offered of free agency. The reply is, this example is perfectly simple; man in performing some action which he is resolved on doing, does not by any means prove his free agency; the very desire of displaying this quality, excited by the dispute, becomes a necessary motive, which decides his will either for the one or the other of these actions: What deludes him in this instance, or that which persuades him he is a free agent at this moment, is, that he does not discern the true motive which sets him in action, namely, the desire of convincing his opponent: if in the heat of the dispute he insists and asks, "Am I not the master of throwing myself out of the window?" I shall answer him, no; that whilst he preserves his reason there is no probability that the desire of proving his free agency, will become a motive sufficiently powerful to make him sacrifice his life to the attempt: if, notwithstanding this, to prove he is a free agent, he should actually precipitate himself from the window, it would not be a sufficient warranty to conclude he acted freely, but rather that it was the violence of his temperament which spurred him on to this folly. Madness is a state, that depends upon the heat of the blood, not upon the will. A fanatic or a hero, braves death as necessarily as a more phlegmatic man or coward flies from it.

There is, in point of fact, no difference between the man that is cast out of the window by another, and the man who throws himself out of it, except that the impulse in the first instance comes immediately from without whilst that which determines the fall in the second case, springs from within his own peculiar machine, having its more remote cause also exterior. When Mutius Scaevola held his hand in the fire, he was as much acting under the influence of necessity (caused by interior motives) that urged him to this strange action, as if his arm had been held by strong men: pride, despair, the desire of braving his enemy, a wish to astonish him, and anxiety to intimidate him, etc., were the invisible chains that held his hand bound to the fire. The love of glory, enthusiasm for their country, in like manner caused Codrus and Decius to devote themselves for their fellow-citizens. The Indian Colanus and the philosopher Peregrinus were equally obliged to burn themselves, by desire of exciting the astonishment of the Grecian assembly.

It is said that free agency is the absence of those obstacles competent to oppose themselves to the actions of man, or to the exercise of his faculties: it is pretended that his is a free agent whenever, making use of these faculties, he produces the effect he has proposed to himself. In reply to this reasoning, it is sufficient to consider that it in nowise depends upon himself to place or remove the obstacles that either determine or resist him; the motive that causes his action is no more in his own power than the obstacle that impedes him, whether this obstacle or motive be within his own machine or exterior of his person: he is not master of the thought presented to his mind, which determines his will; this thought is excited by some cause independent of himself.

To be undeceived on the system of his free agency, man has simply to recur to the motive by which his will is determined; he will always find this motive is out of his own control. It is said: that in consequence of an idea to which the mind gives birth, man acts freely if he encounters no obstacle. But the question is, what gives birth to this idea in his brain? Was he the master either to prevent it from presenting itself, or from renewing itself in his brain? Does not this idea depend either upon objects that strike him exteriorly and in despite of himself, or upon causes, that without his knowledge, act within himself and modify his brain? Can he prevent his eyes, cast without design upon any object whatever, from giving him an idea of this object, and from moving his brain? He is not more master of the obstacles; they are the necessary effects of either interior or exterior causes, which always act according to their given properties. A man insults a coward; this necessarily irritates him against his insulter; but his will cannot vanquish the obstacle that cowardice places to the object of his desire, because his natural conformation, which does not depend upon himself, prevents his having courage. In this case, the coward is insulted in spite of himself; and against his will is obliged patiently to brook the insult he has received.

Absence of Restraint Is Not Absence of Necessity. The partisans of the system of free agency appear ever to have confounded constraint with necessity. Man believes he acts as a free agent, every time he does not see any thing that places obstacles to his actions; he does not perceive that the motive which causes him to will, is always necessary and independent of himself. A prisoner loaded with chains is compelled to remain in prison; but he is not a free agent in the desire to emancipate himself; his chains prevent him from acting, but they do not prevent him from willing; he would save himself if they would loose his fetters; but he would not save himself as a free agent; fear or the idea of punishment would be sufficient motives for his action.

Man may, therefore, cease to be restrained, without, for that reason, becoming a free agent: in whatever manner he acts, he will act necessarily, according to motives by which he shall be determined. He may be compared to a heavy body that finds itself arrested in its descent by any obstacle whatever: take away this obstacle, it will gravitate or continue to fall; but who shall say this dense body is free to fall or not? Is not its descent the necessary effect of its own specific gravity? The virtuous Socrates submitted to the laws of his country, although they were unjust; and though the doors of his jail were left open to him, he would not save himself; but in this he did not act as a free agent: the invisible chains of opinion, the secret love of decorum, the inward respect for the laws, even when they were iniquitous, the fear of tarnishing his glory, kept him in his prison; they were motives sufficiently powerful with this enthusiast for virtue, to induce him to wait death with tranquility; it was not in his power to save himself, because he could find no potential motive to bring him to depart, even for an instant, from those principles to which his mind was accustomed.

Man, it is said, frequently acts against his inclination, from whence it is falsely concluded he is a free agent; but when he appears to act contrary to his inclination, he is always determined to it by some motive sufficiently efficacious to vanquish this inclination. A sick man, with a view to his cure, arrives at conquering his repugnance to the most disgusting remedies: the fear of pain, or the dread of death, then become necessary motives; consequently this sick man cannot be said to act freely.

When it is said, that man is not a free agent, it is not pretended to compare him to a body moved by a simple impulsive cause: he contains within himself causes inherent to his existence; he is moved by an interior organ, which has its own peculiar laws, and is itself necessarily determined in consequence of ideas formed from perception resulting from sensation which it receives from exterior objects. As the mechanism of these sensations, of these perceptions, and the manner they engrave ideas on the brain of man, are not known to him; because he is unable to unravel all these motions; because he cannot perceive the chain of operations in his soul, or the motive principle that acts within him, he supposes himself a free agent; which literally translated, signifies, that he moves himself by himself; that he determines himself without cause: when he rather ought to say, that he is ignorant how or why he acts in the manner he does. It is true the soul enjoys an activity peculiar to itself: but it is equally certain that this activity would never be displayed, if some motive or some cause did not put it in a condition to exercise itself: at least it will not be pretended that the soul is able either to love or to hate without being moved, without knowing the objects, without having some idea of their qualities. Gunpowder has unquestionably a particular activity, but this activity will never display itself, unless fire be applied to it; this, however, immediately sets it in motion.

The Complexity of Human Conduct and the Illusion of Free Agency. It is the great complication of motion in man, it is the variety of his action, it is the multiplicity of causes that move him, whether simultaneously or in continual succession, that persuades him he is a free agent: if all his motions were simple, if the causes that move him did not confound themselves with each other, if they were distinct, if his machine were less complicated, he would perceive that all his actions were necessary, because he would be enabled to recur instantly to the cause that made him act. A man who should be always obliged to go towards the west, would always go on that side; but he would feel that, in so going, he was not a free agent: if he had another sense, as his actions or his motion, augmented by a sixth, would be still more varied and much more complicated, he would believe himself still more a free agent than he does with his five senses.

It is, then, for want of recurring to the causes that move him; for want of being able to analyze, from not being competent to decompose the complicated motion of his machine, that man believes himself a free agent: it is only upon his own ignorance that he founds the profound yet deceitful notion he has of his free agency; that he builds those opinions which he brings forward as a striking proof of his pretended freedom of action. If, for a short time, each man was willing to examine his own peculiar actions, search out their true motives to discover their concatenation, he would remain convinced that the sentiment he has of his natural free agency, is a chimera that must speedily be destroyed by experience.

Nevertheless it must be acknowledged that the multiplicity and diversity of the causes which continually act upon man, frequently without even his knowledge, render it impossible, or at least extremely difficult for him to recur to the true principles of his own peculiar actions, much less the actions of others: they frequently depend upon causes so fugitive, so remote from their effects, and which, superficially examined, appear to have so little analogy, so slender a relation with them, that it requires singular sagacity to bring them into light. This is what renders the study of the moral man a task of such difficulty; this is the reason why his heart is an abyss, of which it is frequently impossible for him to fathom the depth. . . .

If he understood the play of his organs, if he were able to recall to himself all the impulsions they have received, all the modifications they have undergone, all the effects they have produced, he would perceive that all his actions are submitted to the fatality, which regulates his own particular system, as it does the entire system of the universe: no one effect in him, any more than in nature, produces itself by chance; this, as has been before proved, is word void of sense. All that passes in him; all that is done by him; as well as all that happens in nature, or that is attributed to her, is derived from necessary causes, which act according to necessary laws, and which produce necessary effects from whence necessarily flow others.

Fatality, is the eternal, the immutable, the necessary order, established in nature; or the indispensable connexion of causes that act, with the effects they operate. Conforming to this order, heavy bodies fall: light bodies rise; that which is analogous in matter reciprocally attracts; that which is heterogeneous mutually repels; man congregates himself in society, modifies each his fellow; becomes either virtuous or wicked; either contributes to his mutual happiness, or reciprocates his misery; either loves his neighbour, or hates his companion necessarily, according to the manner in which the one acts upon the other. From whence it may be seen, that the same necessity which regulates the physical, also regulates the moral world, in which every thing is in consequence submitted to fatality. Man, in running over, frequently without his own knowledge, often in spite of himself, the route which nature has marked out for him, resembles a swimmer who is obliged to follow the current that carries him along: he believes himself a free agent, because he sometimes consents, sometimes does not consent, to glide with the stream, which notwithstanding, always hurries him forward; he believes himself the master of his condition, because he is obliged to use his arms under the fear of sinking. . . .

Why We Have No Free Will and Can Live Without It

DERK PEREBOOM

Derk Pereboom teaches philosophy at Cornell University.

1. OUTLINE OF HARD INCOMPATIBILISM

Baruch Spinoza (1677/1985: 440–44, 483–84, 496–97) maintained that due to certain general facts about the nature of the universe, we human beings do not have the sort of free will required for moral responsibility. I agree. More exactly, he argues that it is because causal determinism is true that we lack this sort of free will; he is thus a *hard determinist*. By contrast, the position I defend is agnostic about causal determinism. I contend, like Spinoza, that we would not have the sort of free will required for moral responsibility if causal determinism were true, but also that indeterministic theories do not significantly improve the prospects for this sort of free will. Consequently, we need to take seriously the verdict that we lack the sort of free will required for moral responsibility. I call the resulting view *hard incompatibilism*. In addition, I argue that a conception of life without this sort of free will need not exclude morality or our sense of meaning in life, and in some respects it could even be beneficial.

2. AGAINST COMPATIBILISM

The case for hard incompatibilism involves arguing against two competing positions. The first of these is *compatibilism*, which claims that free will of the type required for moral responsibility is compatible with determinism. Compatibilists typically maintain, in addition, that we do in fact have this sort of free will. The second is *libertarianism*, which contends that although the sort of free will required for moral responsibility is not compatible with determinism, it turns out that determinism is false, and we do have this kind of free will.

Compatibilists typically attempt to formulate conditions on agency intended to provide an account of what it is to be morally responsible for an action. These conditions are compatibilist in that they allow for an agent to be morally responsible for an action even when she is causally determined to act as she does. For instance, David Hume and his followers specify that morally responsible action be caused by desires that flow from the agent's "durable and constant" character, and that the agent not be constrained to act, at least in the sense that the action not result from an irresistible desire (Hume 1739/1978: 319–412). Harry Frankfurt proposes that moral responsibility requires that the agent have endorsed and produced her will to perform the action in the right way. More specifically, she must have a second-order desire—that is, a desire to have a particular desire—to will to perform it, and her will must be her will because she has this second-order desire (Frankfurt 1971). John Fischer argues that morally responsible action must result from a rational consideration of the reasons at issue; among other things, the agent must be receptive to the reasons present in a situation, and she must be responsive to them to the degree that in at least some situations in which the reasons are different, she would have done otherwise (Fischer 1994). Finally, Jay Wallace proposes that moral responsibility requires that the agent have the general ability to grasp, apply, and regulate her behavior by moral reasons (Wallace 1994). Each of these compatibilists intends for his conditions to be sufficient for an agent's moral responsibility when they are supplemented by some fairly uncontroversial additional necessary conditions, such as the provision that the agent understands that killing is morally wrong.

In my view, the best type of challenge to the compatibilist begins with the intuition that if someone is causally determined to act by other agents, for example, by scientists who manipulate her brain, then she is not morally responsible for that action. This intuition remains strong even if she meets the compatibilist conditions on moral responsibility just canvassed. The following "four-case argument" first of all develops examples of actions that involve such manipulation, in which these compatibilist conditions on moral responsibility are satisfied (1995, 2001). These cases, taken individually, indicate that it is possible for an agent not to be morally responsible even if the compatibilist conditions are satisfied, and that as a result these conditions are inadequate. But the argument has additional force, by way of setting out three such cases, each progressively more like a fourth scenario which the compatibilist might envision to be realistic, in which the action is causally determined in a natural way. The further challenge for the compatibilist is to point out a difference between this fourth scenario and one or more of the manipulation examples that shows why the agent might be morally responsible in the ordinary case but not in the manipulation examples. My contention is that non-responsibility generalizes from at least one of the manipulation cases to the ordinary one.

In each of the four cases, Professor Plum decides to kill Ms. White for the sake of some personal advantage, and succeeds in doing so. We design the cases so that his act of murder conforms to the prominent compatibilist conditions. Plum's action meets the Humean conditions, since for him purely selfish reasons typically weigh heavily—much too heavily as judged from the moral point of view—while in addition the desire that motivates him to act is nevertheless not irresistible for him, and in this sense he is not constrained to act. It fits the condition proposed by Frankfurt: Plum's effective desire (i.e., his will) to murder White conforms appropriately to his second-order desires for which effective desires he will have. That is, he wills to murder her, and he wants to will to do so, and he wills this act of murder because he wants to will to do so. The action also satisfies the reasons-responsiveness condition advocated by Fischer: Plum's desires are modified by, and some of them arise from, his rational consideration of the reasons he has, and if he knew that the bad consequences for himself that would result from killing White would be much more severe than they are actually likely to be, he would have refrained from killing her for this reason. In addition, this action meets the condition advanced by Wallace: Plum retains the general ability to grasp, apply, and regulate his behavior by moral reasons. For instance, when egoistic reasons that count against acting morally are relatively weak, he will usually regulate his behavior by moral reasons instead. This ability even provides him with the capacity to revise and develop his moral character over time. Now, supposing that causal determinism is true, is it plausible that Plum is morally responsible for his action?

Each of the four cases I will now describe features different ways in which Plum's murder of White might be causally determined by factors beyond his control.

> Case 1: Professor Plum was created by neuroscientists, and they can manipulate him directly through the use of radio-like technology, but he is as much like an ordinary human being as is possible given these unusual features. The neuroscientists manipulate him to undertake the process of reasoning by which the desires at play in his act of murder are brought about and modified. They do this by pushing a series of buttons just before he begins to reason about his situation, thereby causing his reasoning process to be rationally egoistic. Plum does not think and act contrary to character since his reasoning process is typically rationally egoistic. His effective first-order desire to kill White conforms to his second-order desires. The process of deliberation from which his action results is reasons-responsive; in particular, this type of process would have resulted in his refraining from killing White in some situations in which the egoistic reasons were different. Still, he is not exclusively rationally egoistic, since he typically

regulates his behavior by moral reasons when the egoistic reasons are relatively weak— weaker than they are in the current situation. He is also not constrained, in the sense that he does not act because of an irresistible desire— the neuroscientists do not provide him with a desire of this kind.

In Case 1, Plum's action satisfies all the compatibilist conditions we just examined. But intuitively, he is not morally responsible for the murder, because his action is causally determined by what the neuroscientists do, which is beyond his control. Consequently, it would seem that these compatibilist conditions are not sufficient for moral responsibility, even if all taken together.

A compatibilist might resist this conclusion by arguing that although in Case 1 the process resulting in the action satisfies all of the prominent compatibilist conditions, yet Plum's relevant states are directly produced by the manipulators moment by moment—he is locally manipulated— and this is the aspect of the story that undermines his moral responsibility. In reply, could a time lag between the manipulators' activity and the production of the states in the agent plausibly make the crucial difference as to whether an agent is morally responsible? If the neuroscientists did all of their manipulating during one time interval and, after an appropriate length of time, the relevant states were produced in him, would he only then be morally responsible? It is my sense that such a time lag, all by itself, would make no difference to whether an agent is responsible.

Let us now consider a scenario more like the ordinary situation than Case 1.

Case 2: Plum is like an ordinary human being, except that neuroscientists have programmed him *at the beginning of his life* to weigh reasons for action so that he is often but not exclusively rationally egoistic, with the consequence that in the circumstances in which he now finds himself, he is causally determined to engage in the reasons-responsive process of deliberation and to have the set of first- and second-order desires that result in his killing White. Plum has the general ability to regulate his behavior by moral reasons, but in his circumstances the

egoistic reasons weigh very heavily for him, and consequently he is causally determined to murder White. But at the same time he does not act because of an irresistible desire.

Here again, although Plum meets each of the compatibilist conditions, it is intuitive that he is not morally responsible. Thus Case 2 also shows that the prominent compatibilist conditions, either separately or in conjunction, are not sufficient for moral responsibility. Furthermore, it would seem unprincipled to claim that here, by contrast with Case 1, Plum is morally responsible because the length of time between the programming and the action is now great enough. Whether the programming occurs a few seconds or fifty years before the action seems irrelevant to the question of his moral responsibility. Causal determination by factors beyond Plum's control plausibly explains his lack of moral responsibility in the first case, and I believe that we are forced to say that he is not morally responsible in the second case for the same reason.

Imagine next a scenario more similar yet to an ordinary situation.

Case 3: Plum is an ordinary human being, except that he was causally determined by the rigorous training practices of his household and community so that he is often but not exclusively rationally egoistic (exactly as egoistic as in Cases 1 and 2). This training took place when he was too young to have the ability to prevent or alter the practices that determined his character. Consequently, Plum is causally determined to engage in the reasons-responsive process of deliberation and to have the first- and second-order desires that result in his killing White. Here again he has the general ability to grasp, apply, and regulate his behavior by moral reasons, but in these circumstances the egoistic reasons are very powerful, and so the training practices of his upbringing, in conjunction with background circumstances, deterministically result in his act of murder. Nonetheless, he does not act on an irresistible desire.

If a compatibilist wishes to contend that Plum is morally responsible in Case 3, he needs to point to a feature of these circumstances that would explain why he is morally responsible here but not in Case 2. But it seems that there is no such feature. In each of these examples, Plum meets all the prominent compatibilist conditions for morally responsible action, so a divergence in judgment about moral responsibility between these examples will not be supported by a difference in whether these conditions are satisfied. Causal determination by factors beyond his control most plausibly explains the absence of moral responsibility in Case 2, and we are constrained to conclude that Plum is not morally responsible in Case 3 for the same reason.

Thus it appears that Plum's exemption from responsibility in Cases 1 and 2 generalizes to the nearer-to-normal Case 3. Does it generalize all the way to the ordinary case?

> Case 4: Physicalist determinism is true—everything in the universe is in some sense physical, and every event is rendered inevitable by virtue of the past states of this physical universe in conjunction with causal processes governed by laws of nature. Plum is an ordinary human being, raised in normal circumstances, and he is typically but not exclusively rationally egoistic (just as egoistic as in Cases 1–3). His act of murdering White results from his engaging in the reasons-responsive process of deliberation, and he has the specified first- and second-order desires. Although he possesses the general ability to grasp, apply, and regulate his behavior by moral reasons, in these circumstances the egoistic reasons weigh very heavily for him, and he is thus causally determined to kill White. However, it is not due to an irresistible desire that he commits this act of murder.

Given that we need to deny moral responsibility in Case 3, could Plum be responsible in this more ordinary case? There would seem to be no differences between Case 3 and Case 4 that could serve to justify the claim that Plum is not responsible in Case 3 but is in Case 4. One distinguishing feature of Case 4 is that the causal determination of Plum's crime is not brought about by other agents (Lycan 1997: 117–18). However, the claim that this is a relevant difference is implausible. Imagine

a further case that is exactly the same as, say, Case 1 or Case 2, except that Plum's states are induced by a spontaneously generated machine—a machine that has no intelligent designer. Here also Plum would not be morally responsible.

The best explanation for the intuition that Plum is not morally responsible in the first three cases is that his action is produced by a deterministic causal process that traces back to factors beyond his control. Because his action is also causally determined in this way in Case 4, we should conclude that here again he is not morally responsible. So by this argument, Plum's non-responsibility in Case 1 generalizes to non-responsibility in Case 4. We should conclude, I think, that if an action results from any deterministic causal process that traces back to factors beyond the agent's control, then she will lack the control required to be morally responsible for it.

3. EVENT-CAUSAL LIBERTARIANISM AND THE LUCK OBJECTION

Let us now consider libertarianism, the variety of incompatibilism that claims that we do have the sort of free will required for moral responsibility. There are two major types of libertarianism, the event-causal and the agent-causal versions. In event-causal libertarianism, actions are caused solely by events—events such as *Joe's desiring at noon to have lunch,* or *Mary's believing today that if she sells her stock tomorrow she will maximize her gains.* Now it is often supposed that all causation in the physical world is by events, and not by *things,* such as stars, machines, and agents, which we call *substances.* Although one might say, for example, that a bomb—a substance—caused damage to the building, when we want to speak more accurately, we say instead that *the bomb's exploding at a certain time*—an event—caused the damage. So if we think carefully about what it is in the physical world that causes effects, it turns out to be events, not substances. In solidarity with this position, event-causal libertariansim maintains that all actions are caused solely by events, and further, that some type of indeterminacy in the production of actions by appropriate events is the decisive requirement for moral responsibility (Kane 1996; Ekstrom 2000).

Critics of libertarianism have contended that if actions are not causally determined, agents cannot be morally responsible for them. Its classical presentation of this objection is found in Hume's *Treatise of Human Nature,* and it has become known as the "luck" objection (Hume 1739/1978: 411–12). The key idea is that if, holding fixed all of the conditions that precede an action, the action could either occur or not, then whether it does occur is a matter of chance or luck, and the agent cannot be morally responsible for it (Hume 1739/1978: 411–12).

I contend that event-causal libertarianism is undermined by the luck objection. Intuitively, for an agent to be morally responsible for a decision, she must exercise a certain type and degree of control in making that decision. In an event-causal libertarian picture, the relevant causal conditions prior to a decision—events that involve the agent—leave it open whether this decision will occur, and the agent has no further causal role in determining whether it in fact does. Accordingly, whether the decision occurs or not is in this sense a matter of luck, and the agent lacks the control required for being morally responsible for it.

To illustrate, consider Robert Kane's example of a businesswoman—let's call her Anne—who has a choice between stopping to help out an assault victim, as a result of which she would be late for an important meeting, or not stopping, which would allow her to make it to a meeting on time (Kane 1996). For simplicity, suppose the causally relevant events that immediately precede the action are, against stopping, *Anne's desiring not make her boss angry,* and *Anne's believing that if she is late for the meeting her boss will be angry with her;* and for stopping, *Anne's desiring to help people in trouble,* and *Anne's belief that she can help the assault victim.* Imagine that the motivational force of each of these pairs of prior events is for her about the same. On an event-causal libertarian view, with the causal influence of these events already in place, both Anne's deciding to stop and her not deciding to stop remain significantly probable outcomes. Suppose that she in fact decides to stop. There is nothing else about Anne that can settle whether the decision to stop occurs, because in this theory her role in producing a decision is exhausted by these prior events. If nothing about Anne can settle whether the decision occurs, then she will not have the control required for moral responsibility for it. This might be called *the problem of the disappearing agent.* On an event-causal libertarian theory, no provision allows the agent to have the right sort of control over whether the decision occurs, and for this reason she lacks the control required for moral responsibility for it.

Libertarians agree that an action's resulting from a deterministic sequence of causes that traces back to factors beyond the agent's control would rule out her moral responsibility for it. One deeper point of the luck objection is that if this sort of causal determination rules out moral responsibility, then it is no remedy simply to provide slack in the causal net by making the causal history of actions indeterministic. Such a move would yield one prerequisite for moral responsibility—the absence of causal determinism for decision and action—but it would not supply another—sufficiently enhanced control (Clarke 2003). In particular, it would not provide the capacity for an agent to be the source of her decisions and actions that, according to many incompatibilists, is unavailable in a deterministic framework.

4. AGENT CAUSAL LIBERTARIANISM AND AN OBJECTION FROM OUR BEST PHYSICAL THEORIES

What needs to be added to the event-causal libertarian story is a further causal involvement of the agent in the making of the decision, a causal involvement that would enhance her control in making a decision over what is present in event-causal and deterministic contexts. It is this enhanced control that would solve the problem of the disappearing agent, which is highlighted by the luck objection against event-causal libertarianism. The agent-causal libertarian's solution is to specify a way in which the agent could have this enhanced control. The suggested remedy is to reintroduce the agent as a cause, this time not merely as involved in events, but rather fundamentally as a substance (Chisholm 1976; O'Connor 2000; Clarke 2003). The agent-causal libertarian claims that we possess a special causal power—a power for an agent, fundamentally as a substance, to cause a decision without being causally determined to do so. The proposal is that if Anne had this power, by exercising it she would be able to settle which of the two competing decisions occurs—both of which remain as open possibilities given only the causal role of the events. In this way she would have the enhanced control required to be morally responsible for her decision.

But can agent-causal libertarianism be reconciled with what we would expect given our best physical theories? If the agent-causal position is true, then when an agent makes a free decision, she causes the decision without being causally determined to do so. On the path to action that results from this undetermined decision, changes in the physical world, for example in the agent's brain or some other part of her body, are produced. But if the physical world were generally governed by deterministic laws, it seems that here we would encounter divergences from these laws. For the changes in the physical world that result from the undetermined decision would themselves not be causally determined, and they would thus not be governed by the deterministic laws. One might object that it is possible that the physical changes that result from every free decision just happen to dovetail with what could in principle be predicted on the basis of the deterministic laws, so nothing actually happens that diverges from these laws (Kant 1781/1997: 532–46). But this proposal would seem to involve coincidences too wild to be believed. For this reason, agent-causal libertarianism is not plausibly reconciled with the physical world's being governed by deterministic laws.

On the standard interpretation of quantum mechanics, however, the physical world is not in fact deterministic, but is rather governed by probabilistic statistical laws. Some philosophers have defended the claim that agent-causal libertarianism can be reconciled with physical laws of

this sort (Clarke 2003: 181). However, wild coincidences would also arise on this suggestion. Consider the class of possible actions each of which has a physical component whose antecedent probability of occurring is approximately 0.32. It would not violate the statistical laws in the sense of being logically incompatible with them if, for a large number of instances, the physical components in this class were not actually realized close to 32 percent of the time. Rather, the force of the statistical law is that for a large number of instances it is correct to *expect* physical components in this class to be realized close to 32 percent of the time. Are free choices on the agent-causal libertarian model compatible with what the statistical law leads us to expect about them? If they were, then for a large enough number of instances the possible actions in our class would almost certainly be freely chosen close to 32 percent of the time. But if the occurrence of these physical components were settled by the choices of agent-causes, then their actually being chosen close to 32 percent of the time would amount to a wild coincidence. The proposal that agent-caused free choices do not diverge from what the statistical laws predict for the physical components of our actions would run so sharply counter to what we would expect as to make it incredible.

At this point, the libertarian might propose that there actually do exist divergences from the probabilities that we would expect without the presence of agent-causes, and that these divergences are to be found at the interface between the agent-cause and that which it directly affects—an interface that is likely to be found in the brain. The problem for this proposal, however, is that we have no evidence that such divergences occur. This difficulty, all by itself, provides a strong reason to reject this approach.

It is sometimes claimed that our experience of deliberating and choosing provides us with good evidence for the broader thesis that we have libertarian free will. Perhaps, then, if we could have libertarian free will only if we were agent causes, then this evidence from our experience would count in favor of the existence of divergences from what our best physical theories predict. But Spinoza remarks, "experience itself, no less than reason, teaches that men believe themselves free because they are conscious of their own actions, and ignorant of the causes by which they are determined..." (Spinoza 1677/1985: 496). Spinoza maintains that we believe our decisions are free only because we are ignorant of their causes. The lesson to draw from Spinoza here is that the evidence from experience that is apt to generate a belief that we have libertarian free will would be just the same if decisions were instead causally determined and we were ignorant of enough of their causes. For this reason, this evidence experience provides for our having libertarian free will is not especially impressive. This consideration counts strongly against the proposal that such evidence gives us reason to believe that the divergences in question exist.

On the other hand, nothing we've said conclusively rules out the claim that because we are agent causes, there exist such divergences. We do not have a complete understanding of the human neural system, and it may turn out that some human neural structures are significantly different from anything else in nature we understand, and that they serve to ground agent causation. This approach may be the best one for libertarians to pursue. But at this point we have no evidence that it will turn out to be correct.

Thus all versions of libertarianism face serious difficulties. Earlier, we saw that compatibilism is vulnerable to an argument from manipulation cases. The position that remains is hard incompatibilism, which denies that we have the sort of free will required for moral responsibility. The concern for this view is not, I think, that there is significant empirical evidence that it is false, or that there is a good argument that it is somehow incoherent, and false for that reason. Rather, the questions it faces are practical: What would life be like if we believed it was true? Is this a sort of life that we can tolerate?

5. HARD INCOMPATIBILISM AND WRONGDOING

Accepting hard incompatibilism demands giving up our ordinary view of ourselves as blameworthy for immoral actions and praiseworthy for actions that are morally exemplary. At this point one might object that giving up our belief in moral responsibility would have very harmful consequences, perhaps so harmful that thinking and acting as if hard incompatibilism is true is not a feasible option. Thus even if the claim that we are morally responsible turns out to be false, there may yet be weighty practical reasons to believe that we are, or at least to treat people as if they were.

For instance, one might think that if we gave up the belief that people are blameworthy, we could no longer legitimately judge any actions as wrong or even bad, or as right or good. But this seems mistaken. Even if we came to believe that some perpetrator of genocide was not morally responsible because of some degenerative brain disease he had, we would still maintain that his actions were morally wrong, and that it was extremely bad that he acted as he did. So, in general, denying blameworthiness would not at the same time threaten judgments of wrongness or badness, and, likewise, denying praiseworthiness would not undermine assessments of rightness or goodness.

Perhaps treating wrongdoers as blameworthy is often required for effective moral education and improvement. If we resolved never to treat people as blameworthy, one might fear that we would be left with insufficient leverage to reform immoral behavior. Still, this option would have us treat people as blameworthy—by, for example, expressing anger toward them because of what they have done—when they do not deserve it, which would seem prima facie morally wrong. If people are not morally responsible for immoral behavior, treating them as if they were would seem to be unfair. However, it is possible to achieve moral reform by methods that would not be threatened by this sort of unfairness, and in ordinary situations such practices could arguably be as successful as those that presuppose moral responsibility. Instead of treating people as if they deserve blame, the hard incompatibilist can turn to moral admonition and encouragement, which presuppose only that the offender has done wrong. These methods can effectively communicate a sense of right and wrong and they can issue in salutary reform.

But does hard incompatibilism have resources adequate for contending with criminal behavior? Here it would appear to be at a disadvantage, and if so, practical considerations might yield strong reasons to treat criminals as if they were morally responsible. First of all, if hard incompatibilism is true, a retributivist justification for criminal punishment is unavailable, for it asserts that the criminal deserves pain or deprivation just for committing the crime, while hard incompatibilism denies this claim. And retributivism is one of the most naturally compelling ways to justify criminal punishment.

By contrast, a theory that justifies criminal punishment on the ground that punishment educates criminals morally is not threatened by hard incompatibilism specifically. So one might suggest that the hard incompatibilist could endorse a view of this kind. However, we lack significant empirical evidence that punishing criminals brings about moral education, and without such evidence, it would be wrong to punish them in order to achieve this goal. In general, it is wrong to harm a person for the sake of realizing some good in the absence of impressive evidence that the harm will produce the good. Moreover, even if we had impressive evidence that punishment was effective in morally educating criminals, we should prefer non-punitive ways of achieving this result, if they are available—whether or not criminals are morally responsible.

Deterrence theories have it that punishing criminals is justified for the reason that it deters future crime. The two most-discussed deterrence theories, the utilitarian version and the one that grounds the right to punish on the right to self-defense, are not undermined by hard incompatibilism per se. Still, they are questionable on other grounds. The utilitarian theory, which claims that punishment is justified because it maximizes utility (i.e., the quantity of happiness or pleasure minus the quantity of unhappiness or pain), faces well-known challenges. It would seem at times to require punishing the innocent when doing so would maximize utility; in certain situations it would appear to prescribe punishment that is unduly severe; and it would authorize harming people merely as means to the well-being, in this case the safety, of others. The

sort of deterrence theory that grounds the right to punish in the right of individuals to defend themselves against immediate threats (Farrell 1985: 38–60) is also objectionable. For when a criminal is sentenced to punishment he is most often not an immediate threat to anyone, since he is then in the custody of the law, and this fact about his circumstances distinguishes him from those who can legitimately be harmed on the basis of the right of self-defense.

There is, however, an intuitively legitimate theory of crime prevention that is neither undercut by hard incompatibilism, nor threatened by other sort of considerations. This theory draws an analogy between the treatment of criminals and the treatment of carriers of dangerous diseases. Ferdinand Schoeman (1979) argues that if we have the right to quarantine carriers of serious communicable diseases to protect people, then for the same reason we also have the right to isolate the criminally dangerous. Notice that quarantining a person can be justified when she is not morally responsible for being dangerous to others. If a child is infected with a deadly contagious virus that was transmitted to her before she was born, quarantine can still be legitimate. Now imagine that a serial killer poses a grave danger to a community. Even if he is not morally responsible for his crimes (say because no one is ever morally responsible), it would be as legitimate to isolate him as it is to quarantine a nonresponsible carrier of a serious communicable disease.

Clearly, it would be morally wrong to treat carriers of communicable diseases more severely than is required to protect people from the resulting threat. Similarly, it would be wrong to treat criminals more harshly than is required to protect society against the danger posed by them. Moreover, just as moderately dangerous diseases may allow for only measures less intrusive than quarantine, so moderately serious criminal tendencies might only justify responses less intrusive than detention. In addition, I suspect that a theory modeled on quarantine would not justify measures of the sort whose legitimacy is most in doubt, such as the death penalty or confinement in the worst prisons we have. Moreover, it would demand a degree of concern for the rehabilitation and well-being of the criminal that would alter much of current practice. Just as society must seek to cure the diseased it quarantines, so it would be required to try to rehabilitate the criminals it detains. In addition, if a criminal cannot be rehabilitated, and if protection of society demands his indefinite confinement, there would be no justification for making his life more miserable than needed to guard against the danger he poses.

6. MEANING IN LIFE

If hard incompatibilism is true, could we legitimately retain a sense of achievement for what makes our lives fulfilled, happy, satisfactory, or worthwhile, and our hold on our hopes for making these sorts of achievements in our lives? (Honderich 1988) It might be argued that if hard incompatibilism is true, there can be no genuine achievements, for an agent cannot have an achievement for which she is not also praiseworthy. However, achievement, and our hope for achievement, is not as closely connected to praiseworthiness as this objection supposes. If an agent hopes to achieve success in some project, and if she accomplishes what she hoped for, intuitively this outcome would be an achievement of hers even if she is not praiseworthy for it— although at the same time the sense in which it is her achievement may be diminished. For example, if someone hopes that her efforts as a teacher will result in well-educated children, and they do, there remains a clear sense in which she has achieved what she hoped for—even if it turns out she is not praiseworthy for anything she does.

One might think that hard incompatibilism would instill an attitude of resignation to whatever the future holds in store. But this isn't clearly right. Even if what we know about our behavioral dispositions and our environment gives us reason to believe that our futures will turn out in a particular way, it can often be reasonable to hope that they will turn out differently. For this to be so, it may sometimes be important that we lack complete knowledge of our dispositions and environmental conditions. Imagine that someone reasonably believes that he has a disposition that might well be an impediment to realizing something he hopes to achieve. However, because he does not know whether this disposition will in fact have this effect, it remains open for him—that is, not ruled out by anything he knows or believes—that another disposition of his will allow him to transcend the impediment. For instance, imagine that someone aspires to become a successful politician, but he is concerned that his fear of public speaking will get in the way. He does not know whether this fear will in fact frustrate his ambition, since it is open for him that he will overcome this problem, perhaps due to a disposition for resolute self-discipline in transcending obstacles of this sort. As a result, he might reasonably hope that he will get over his fear and succeed in his ambition. Given hard incompatibilism, if he in fact does overcome his problem and succeeds in political life, this will not be an achievement of his in as robust a sense as we might naturally suppose, but it will be his achievement in a substantial sense nonetheless.

Still, with Saul Smilansky one might contend that although determinism leaves room for a limited foundation of the sense of self-worth that derives from achievement or virtue, the hard incompatibilist's perspective can nevertheless be "extremely damaging to our view of ourselves, to our sense of achievement, worth, and self-respect," especially when it comes to achievement in the formation of one's own moral character. In response, Smilansky thinks that it would be best for us to foster the illusion that we have free will (Smilansky 2000). Now I agree that there is a kind of self-respect that presupposes an incompatibilist foundation, and that it would be undercut if hard incompatibilism were true. I question, however, whether Smilanksy is right about how damaging it would be for us to give up this sort of self-respect, and whether his appeal to illusion is required.

First, note that our sense of self-worth—our sense that we have value and that our lives are worth living—is to a non-trivial extent due to features not produced by our will, let alone by free will. People place great value on natural beauty, native athletic ability, and intelligence, none of which have their source in our volition. To be sure, we also value efforts that are voluntary in the sense that they are willed by us—in productive work and altruistic behavior, and indeed, in the formation of moral character. However, does it matter very much to us that these voluntary efforts are also *freely* willed? Perhaps Smilansky overestimates how much we care.

Consider how someone comes to have a good moral character. It is not implausible that it is formed to a significant degree as a result of upbringing, and moreover, the belief that this is so widespread. Parents typically regard themselves as having failed in raising their children if they turn out with immoral dispositions, and parents often take great care to bring their children up to prevent such a result. Accordingly, people often come to believe that they have the good moral character they do largely because they were raised with love and skill. But those who come to believe this about themselves seldom experience dismay because of it. People tend not to become dispirited upon coming to understand that their good moral character is not their own doing, and that they do not deserve a great deal of praise or respect for it. By contrast, they often come to feel more fortunate and thankful. Suppose, however, that there are some who would be overcome with dismay. Would it be justified or even desirable for them to foster the illusion that they nevertheless deserve praise and respect for producing their moral character? I suspect that most would eventually be able to accept the truth without incurring much loss. All of this, I think, would also hold for those who come to believe that they do not deserve praise and respect for producing their moral character because they are not, in general, morally responsible.

7. EMOTIONS, REACTIVE ATTITUDES, AND PERSONAL RELATIONSHIPS

Peter Strawson (1962) argues that the justification for judgments of blameworthiness and praiseworthiness has its foundation in what he calls the *reactive attitudes,* reactions to how people voluntarily behave—attitudes such as moral resentment, guilt, gratitude, forgiveness, and love. Moreover, because moral responsibility has

this kind of foundation, the truth or falsity of determinism is irrelevant to whether we are justified in regarding agents as morally responsible. This is because these reactive attitudes are required for the kinds of interpersonal relationships that make our lives meaningful, and so even if we could give up the reactive attitudes we would never have sufficient practical reason to do so. Strawson believes that it is in fact psychologically impossible for us to give up the reactive attitudes altogether, but in a limited range of cases we can adopt what he calls the "objective attitude," a cold and calculating stance toward others, which he describes as follows:

> To adopt the objective attitude to another human being is to see him, perhaps, as an object of social policy; as a subject for what, in a wide range of sense, might be called treatment; as something certainly to be taken account, perhaps precautionary account, of; to be managed or handled or cured or trained; perhaps simply to be avoided...The objective attitude may be emotionally toned in many ways: it may include repulsion or fear, it may include pity or love, though not all kinds of love. But it cannot include the range of reactive feelings and attitudes which belong to involvement or participation with others in interpersonal human relationships; it cannot include resentment, gratitude, forgiveness, anger, or the sort of love which two adults can sometimes be said to feel reciprocally, for each other. (Strawson 1962)

If determinism did imperil the reactive attitudes, and we were able to relinquish them, Strawson suggests that we would face the prospect of adopting this objective attitude toward everyone, as a result of which our interpersonal relationships would be undermined. Since we have extremely good practical reasons for maintaining these relationships, we would never have sufficient practical reason to adopt the objective attitude in most cases, and hence we would never have sufficient reason to give up our reactive attitudes, and thus to stop regarding people as morally responsible.

Clearly, if we persistently maintained an objective attitude toward others, our relationships would be undermined. However, I deny that it would be appropriate to adopt this stance if we came to believe that hard incompatibilism were true. In my conception, some of the reactive attitudes would in fact be challenged by hard incompatibilism, for some of them, such as moral resentment and indignation, would have the false presupposition that the person who is the object of the attitude is morally responsible. But I claim that the reactive attitudes that we would want to retain either are not threatened by hard incompatibilism in this way, or else have analogues or aspects that would not have false presuppositions. The attitudes that would survive do not amount to the objective attitude, and they would be sufficient to sustain good human relationships.

It is plausible that to a certain degree moral resentment and indignation are beyond our power to affect. Even supposing that a hard incompatibilist is thoroughly committed to morality and rationality, and that she is admirably in control of her emotions, she might still be unable to eliminate these attitudes. Thus as hard incompatibilists we might expect people to be morally resentful in certain circumstances, and we would not regard them as morally responsible for it. But we also have the ability to prevent, temper, and sometimes to dispel moral resentment, and given a belief in hard incompatibilism, we might attempt such measures for the sake of morality and rationality. Modifications of this sort, assisted by a hard incompatibilist conviction, might well be good for interpersonal relationships.

It might be objected that in relationships moral resentment and indignation are crucial to effective communication of wrongdoing, and if we dispelled or modified these attitudes, relationships would be damaged. However, when a person is wronged in a relationship, she typically has further attitudes not threatened by hard incompatibilism, attitudes whose expression can play the communicative role in question. These attitudes include being alarmed or distressed about what another has done, and moral sadness or concern for him. Moral resentment, then, is not obviously required for effective communication in personal relationships.

Forgiveness might appear to presuppose that the person being forgiven is blameworthy, and if

this is so, this attitude would also be undercut by hard incompatibilism. But certain key features of forgiveness are not endangered by hard incompatibilism, and they are sufficient to sustain the role forgiveness has in relationships. Suppose a friend repeatedly mistreats you, and because of this you decide to end your relationship with him. However, he then apologizes to you, indicating his recognition that his actions were wrong, his wish that he had not mistreated you, and his commitment to refrain from the immoral behavior. Because of this you decide not to end the friendship. In this case, the feature of forgiveness that is consistent with hard incompatilism is the willingness to cease to regard past immoral behavior as a reason to weaken or end a relationship. The aspect of forgiveness that is undermined by hard incompatibilism is the willingness to disregard the friend's blameworthiness. But since she has given up the belief that we are morally responsible, the hard incompatibilist no longer needs a willingness to disregard blameworthiness in order to foster good relationships.

One might object that hard incompatibilism imperils the self-directed attitudes of guilt and repentance, and that this would be especially bad for relationships. In the absence of guilt and repentance, we would not only be incapable of restoring relationships damaged because we have done wrong, but we would also be kept from restoring our moral integrity. For without the attitudes of guilt and repentance, we would lack the psychological mechanisms that can play these roles. But note first that it is because guilt essentially involves a belief that one is blameworthy that this attitude would be threatened by hard incompatibilism. It is for this reason that repentance would also seem to be (indirectly) threatened, for feeling guilty would appear to be required to motivate repentance. Imagine, however, that you have acted immorally; still because you endorse hard incompatibilism, you deny that you are blameworthy. Instead, you acknowledge that you were the agent of wrongdoing, you feel sad that you have done wrong, and you deeply regret having acted as you did. In addition, because you are committed to doing what is right and to your own moral improvement, you resolve not to act in this way in the future, and to seek out the help of others in sustaining your resolution. None of these measures are jeopardized by hard incompatibilism.

Gratitude would appear to presuppose that the person to whom one is grateful is morally responsible for a beneficial act, whereupon hard incompatibilism would undermine gratitude. But as in the case of forgiveness, certain aspects of this attitude would be unaffected, and these aspects can provide what is needed for good relationships. Gratitude involves, first of all, being thankful toward a person who has acted beneficially. It is true that being thankful toward someone usually involves the belief that she is praiseworthy for some action. Still, one can also be thankful to a small child for some kindness, without believing that she is morally responsible for it. This aspect of thankfulness could be retained even without the presupposition of praiseworthiness. Typically gratitude also involves joy as a response to what someone has done. But no feature of hard incompatibilism undermines being joyful and expressing joy when others are, for example, considerate or generous in one's behalf. Expressing joy can bring about the sense of harmony and goodwill often produced by gratitude, and thus here hard incompatibilism is not at a disadvantage.

Is the kind of love that mature adults have for each other in good relationships imperiled by hard incompatibilism, as Strawson's line of argument suggests? Consider first whether for loving someone it is important that the person who is loved has and exercises free will in the sense required for moral responsibility. Parents love their children rarely, if ever, for the reason that they possess this sort of free will, or decide to do what is right by free will, or deserve to be loved due to freely willed choices. Moreover, when adults love each other, it is also very seldom, if at all, for these sorts of reasons. The reasons we love others are surely varied and complex. Besides moral character and behavior, features such as intelligence, appearance, style, and resemblance to others in one's personal history all might play a part. Suppose morally admirable qualities are particularly important in occasioning, enriching, and maintaining love.

Even if there is an aspect of love that we conceive as a deserved response to morally admirable qualities, it is unlikely that love would vanish or even be diminished if we came to believe that these qualities are not produced or sustained by freely willed decisions. Such admirable qualities are loveable whether or not we deserve praise for having them.

One might contend that we want to be freely loved by others—to be loved by them as a result of their free will. Against this, the love parents have for their children typically comes about independently of the parents' will altogether, and we don't think that love of this sort is deficient. Kane recognizes this fact about parents' love, and he acknowledges that romantic love is similar in this respect. However, he maintains that there is a kind of love we very much want that would not exist if all love were causally determined by factors beyond our control (Kane 1996: 88). The plausibility of Kane's claim might be enhanced by reflecting on how you would react upon discovering that someone you love was causally determined to love you by, say, a benevolent manipulator.

Setting aside *free* will for a moment, when does the will play any role at all in engendering love? When a relationship is disintegrating, people will at times decide to try to restore the love they once had for one another. When a student finds herself in conflict with a roommate from the outset, she might choose to take steps to improve the relationship. When a marriage is arranged, the partners may decide to do what they can to love each other. In these kinds of circumstances we might want others to make a decision that might produce or maintain love. But this is not to say that we would want that decision to be freely willed in the sense required for moral responsibility. For it is not clear that value would be added by the decision's being free in this sense. Moreover, although in some circumstances we might want others to make decisions of this sort, we would typically prefer love that did not require such decisions. This is so not only for intimate romantic relationships—where it is quite obvious—but also for friendships and relationships between parents and children.

Suppose Kane's view could be defended, and we did want love that is freely willed in the sense required for moral responsibility. If we in fact desired love of this kind, then we would want a kind of love that is impossible if hard incompatibilism is true. Still, the sorts of love not challenged by hard incompatibilism are sufficient for good relationships. If we can aspire to the kind of love parents typically have for their children, or the type romantic lovers share, or the sort had by friends who are deeply devoted to each other, and whose friendship became close through their interactions, then the possibility of fulfillment through interpersonal relationships remains intact.

Hard incompatibilism, therefore, does not yield a threat to interpersonal relationships. It might challenge certain attitudes that typically have a role in such relationships. Moral resentment, indignation, and guilt would likely be irrational for a hard incompatibilist, since these attitudes would have presuppositions believed to be false. But these attitudes are either not required for good relationships, or they have analogues that could play their typical role. Moreover, love—the reactive attitude most essential to good interpersonal relationships—does not seem threatened by hard incompatibilism at all. Love of another involves, fundamentally, wishing for the other's good, taking on her aims and desires, and a desire to be together with her, and none of this is endangered by hard incompatibilism.

8. THE GOOD IN HARD INCOMPATIBILISM

Hard incompatibilism also promises substantial benefits for human life. Of all the attitudes associated with the assumption that we are morally responsible, anger seems most closely connected with it. Discussions about moral responsibility most often focus not on how we judge morally exemplary agents, but rather on how we regard those who are morally deficient. Examples designed to elicit a strong intuition that an agent is morally responsible most often feature an especially heinous action, and the intuition usually involves sympathetic anger. It may be,

then, that our attachment to the assumption that we are morally responsible derives to a significant degree from the role anger plays in our emotional lives. Perhaps we feel that giving up the assumption of responsibility is threatening because the rationality of anger would be undercut as a result.

The kind of anger at issue is the sort that is directed toward a person who is believed to have behaved immorally—it comprises both moral resentment and indignation. Let us call this attitude *moral anger*. Not all anger is moral anger. One type of non-moral anger is directed toward someone because his abilities are lacking in some respect or because he has performed poorly in some situation. We are sometimes angry with machines for malfunctioning. At times our anger has no object. Still, most human anger is moral anger.

Moral anger comprises a significant part of our moral lives as we ordinarily conceive them. It motivates us to resist abuse, discrimination, and oppression. At the same time, expression of moral anger often has harmful effects, failing to contribute to the well-being either of those toward whom it is directed or of those expressing the anger. Often its expression is intended to cause little else than emotional or physical pain. Consequently, it has a tendency to damage relationships, impair the functioning of organizations, and unsettle societies. In extreme cases, it can motivate people to torture and kill.

The realization that expression of moral anger can be damaging gives rise to a strong demand that it be morally justified when it occurs. The demand to morally justify behavior that is harmful is generally a very strong one, and expressions of moral anger are often harmful. This demand is made more urgent by the fact that we are often attached to moral anger, and that we frequently enjoy expressing it. Most commonly we justify expression of moral anger by arguing that wrongdoers deserve it, and we believe that they deserve it because they are morally responsible for what they do. If hard incompatibilism is true, however, justification of this sort is undermined. Yet given the concerns to which expression of moral anger give rise, this may be a good thing.

Accepting hard incompatibilism is not likely to modify our attitudes to the extent that expression of moral anger ceases to be a problem for us. However, moral anger is often sustained and magnified by the belief that its object is morally responsible for immoral behavior. Destructive moral anger in relationships is nurtured in this way by the assumption that the other is blameworthy. The anger that fuels ethnic conflicts, for example, is almost always fostered by the conviction that a group of people deserves blame for past wrongs. Hard incompatibilism advocates giving up such beliefs because they are false. As a result, moral anger might decrease, and its expressions subside.

Would the benefits that would result if moral anger were modified in this way compensate for the losses that would ensue? Moral anger motivates us to oppose wrongful behavior. Would we lose the motivation to oppose immorality? If for hard incompatibilist reasons the assumption that wrongdoers are blameworthy is withdrawn, the belief that they have in fact behaved immorally would not be threatened. Even if those who commit genocide are not morally responsible, their actions are nonetheless clearly horribly immoral, and a conviction that this is so would remain untouched. This, together with a commitment to oppose wrongdoing, would permit a resolve to resist abuse, discrimination, and oppression. Accepting hard incompatibilism would thus allow us to retain the benefits moral anger can also provide, while at the same time challenging its destructive effects.

❧ REFERENCES

Chisholm, Roderick (1976). *Person and Object* (La Salle: Open Court).

Clarke, Randolph (2003). *Libertarian Theories of Free Will* (Oxford: Oxford University Press).

Ekstrom, Laura W. (2000). *Free Will: A Philosophical Study* (Boulder: Westview).

Farrell, Daniel M. (1985). "The Justification of General Deterrence," *The Philosophical Review* 104.

Fischer, John Martin (1994). *The Metaphysics of Free Will* (Oxford: Blackwell).

Frankfurt, Harry G. (1971). "Freedom of the Will and the Concept of a Person," *Journal of Philosophy* 68, pp. 5–20.

Honderich, Ted (1988). *A Theory of Determinism* (Oxford: Oxford University Press).

Hume, David (1739/1978). *A Treatise of Human Nature*, L. A. Selby-Bigge, ed. (Oxford: Oxford University Press).

Kane, Robert (1996). *The Significance of Free Will* (New York: Oxford University Press).

Kant, Immanuel (1781/1997). *Critique of Pure Reason*, tr. Paul Guyer and Allen Wood (Cambridge: Cambridge University Press, 1997).

Lycan, William G. (1997). *Consciousness* (Cambridge: MIT Press).

Mele, Alfred (2006). *Free Will and Luck* (Oxford: Oxford University Press).

O'Connor, Timothy (2000). *Persons and Causes* (Oxford: Oxford University Press).

Pereboom, Derk (2001). *Living Without Free Will* (Cambridge: Cambridge University Press).

Schoeman, Ferdinand D. (1979). "On Incapacitating the Dangerous," *American Philosophical Quarterly* 16.

Smilansky, Saul (2000). *Free Will and Illusion* (Oxford: Oxford University Press).

Spinoza, Baruch (1677/1985). *Ethics,* in *The Collected Works of Spinoza,* ed. and tr. Edwin Curley, Volume 1 (Princeton: Princeton University Press).

Strawson, Peter F. (1962). "Freedom and Resentment," *Proceedings of the British Academy* 48 pp. 1–25.

van Inwagen, Peter (1983). *An Essay On Free Will* (Oxford: Oxford University Press).

Wallace, R. Jay (1994). *Responsibility and the Moral Sentiments* (Cambridge, Harvard University Press).

FREEDOM AND MORAL RESPONSIBILITY

The Debate over Free Will

JAMES RACHELS

James Rachels (1942–2003) was the author of *The End of Life* and numerous other books and articles on the problems of practical ethics. He taught philosophy at the University of Alabama at Birmingham for many years.

Man's life is a line that nature commands him to describe on the surface of the earth, without his being able to swerve from it, even for an instant.... Nevertheless, in spite of the shackles by which he is bound, it is pretended he is a free agent.

—PAUL HENRI BARON D'HOLBACH,
The System of Nature (1770)

Sir, we know *our will is free, and* there's *an end on it.*

—DR. JOHNSON, In Boswell's
The Life of Samuel Johnson, LL.D. (1791)

THE DETERMINIST ARGUMENT

Toward the end of his life, Isaac Bashevis Singer (1904–1991) developed a set of stock answers to the questions that interviewers would put to him. When asked about his philosophy of life, he would reply: "I believe in free will. I have no choice."

Singer knew that his little joke made a serious philosophical point. It is hard to avoid thinking we have free will. When you are deciding what to do, the choice seems entirely yours. The inner feeling of freedom is so powerful that we may be unable to give up the idea of free will, no matter how much evidence there is against it.

And of course there is a great deal of evidence against it. The more we learn about the causes of human behavior, the less likely it seems that we freely choose our actions. No one piece of evidence forces this conclusion. Nonetheless, many different strands of evidence point in this direction, and the cumulative effect is that "free will" looks more and more like part of a prescientific way of thinking.

We may call this the Determinist Argument:

1. Everything we do is caused by forces over which we have no control.
2. If our actions are caused by forces over which we have no control, we do not act freely.
3. Therefore, we never act freely.

This is a disturbing line of thought because of what it seems to imply about individual responsibility. If we are not free, then it seems that we are not responsible for what we do.

But is the Determinist Argument sound? It is plausible, but there is much in it that can be disputed. We will look at two responses to the argument that defend free will in different ways. One theory, Libertarianism, denies the first premise of the argument and holds that our actions are not causally determined. Another theory, Compatibilism, denies the second premise and holds that we are free despite the fact that our actions *are* causally determined. We will consider these views one at a time.

THE LIBERTARIAN RESPONSE

Libertarianism is the view that at least some of our actions are free because they are not, in fact, causally determined. According to this theory, human choices are not constrained in the same way that other events in the world are constrained. A billiard ball, when struck by another billiard ball, must move in a certain direction with a certain velocity. It has no choice. The laws of cause and effect determine precisely what will happen. But a human decision is not like that. Right now, you can decide whether to continue reading or to stop reading. You can do either, and nothing makes you choose one way or the other. The laws of cause and effect have no power over you.

This is not very plausible. Nonetheless, this way of thinking has been defended by a number of philosophers, and several lines of argument have been advanced in its support.

The Argument from Experience

We may begin with the idea that we know we are free because *each of us is immediately aware of being free* every time we make a conscious choice. Think again of what you are doing at this moment, reading the page in front of you. You can continue reading, or you can stop. Which will it be? Think of what it is like, right now, as you consider these options. You feel no constraints. Nothing is holding you back or forcing you in either direction. The decision is up to you. The experience of freedom, it may be said, is the best proof we could have.

This may not sound like much of an argument, because your "awareness of being free" might be an illusion. It may be that you feel free only because you are not aware of the causal forces at work. Nevertheless, consider this: Before we give up a belief in which we have great confidence, we should have evidence against it in which we have even *greater* confidence. And it may be that we have greater confidence in our experience of freedom than we could ever have in any of the arguments against it.

Samuel Johnson made this point in his discussion with Boswell when he said: "You are surer that you can lift up your finger or not as you please, than you are of any conclusion from a deduction of reasoning. . . . All theory is against the freedom of the will; all experience for it." And experience, he thought, is more certain than mere theory.

The general point here may be unassailable. When we have direct experience of something, we should want very powerful evidence before we

stop believing it. The problem, however, is that the evidence against free will tends to undermine our confidence in our experience. Jose Delgado found that he could cause people to do things by electrically stimulating their brains—they would look over their shoulder, for example—and then they would offer reasons why they had done so, such as "I was looking for my comb." Delgado's subjects, who did not know that their brains were being stimulated, would *experience* the movements as voluntary. Perhaps we are like Delgado's subjects. What is the difference between us and them, except that in the experimental setting we know about the electrochemical event that causes the action, while in everyday life we are ignorant of what is happening in our brains? In the face of such evidence, it is hollow to insist, with Dr. Johnson, that we simply know we are free. If freedom is to be defended, a better argument is needed.

The Argument That the Universe Is Not a Deterministic System

Determinism, it may be said, is out of keeping with present-day science. In the heyday of Newtonian physics, it was thought that the universe operates strictly according to laws of cause and effect. The Laws of Nature were believed to be causal laws that specify the conditions under which one state of affairs must follow another— the motion of balls on a billiards table was a model for the whole universe. But Newtonian physics has now been replaced by a different picture of how the world works.

According to quantum mechanics, a cornerstone of present-day physics, the rules that govern the behavior of subatomic particles are irreducibly probabilistic. The laws of quantum theory do not say "Given X, Y *must* follow." Instead, they say "Given X, there is *a certain probability* that Y will follow." Thus, the Laws of Nature may tell us that under certain conditions a certain percentage of radioactive atoms will decay, but they do not tell us which atoms will decay. The fact that a certain percentage will decay may be determined, but the fact that a particular atom will decay is not determined.

Some scientists believe, on philosophical grounds, that quantum theory must eventually be superseded by a different, as yet unknown theory that is deterministic. They find the idea that the universe operates according to principles of chance to be abhorrent. Einstein, who famously said that "God does not play dice with the universe," was one such scientist. Yet no replacement theory is in sight and, for all we know, quantum theory is here to stay.

Does this mean that we don't need to worry about Determinism? Quantum theory has sometimes been hailed as good news for free will. If not everything is causally determined, it is said, then we may be free after all, because our actions may be among the things that are not determined.

However, quantum physics does not really offer much help in defending free will. For one thing, the implications of quantum indeterminacy for human behavior are so small as to make no practical difference. Compare the implications of quantum theory for computers. A computer's outputs are determined by its inputs and its program. Quantum mechanics does not imply that we should stop trusting computers—the computer's operations are, if not completely determined, close enough as to make no difference. We will still get the expected outputs, given the right program and the right inputs. Something similar could be true of human beings. If so, that would be enough for the Determinist Argument.

The Argument That We Cannot Predict Our Own Decisions

A different sort of argument for Libertarianism turns on the idea that anything that is causally determined is predictable, at least in principle. Of course, something may be determined and yet not be predictable in practice, because we do not know enough. The tree outside my window is leaning, and sooner or later it will fall. I cannot predict when it will fall because I do not know enough about the tree, the soil, how much rain will fall in the days ahead, and so on. But if I knew all those things and had a perfect understanding of the Laws of Nature, then presumably I could calculate when it will topple.

If human actions are causally determined, it should be possible, in principle, to predict them in the same way. We would need only to know the pertinent facts about the person, the person's circumstances, and the relevant causal laws.

But there is a catch. This seems plausible only if we are predicting *other* people's behavior. Suppose your friend Jones is in the process of deciding whether to take a job in another city. If you had enough information about him, including events in his brain and so on, you might be able to predict what his decision will be and when he will reach it. You could say, Tomorrow at 10:07 P.M., Jones will decide to take the job. Thus, you would know what he is going to do even before he does. So far, so good.

But when it comes to predicting our *own* decisions, things are different. Suppose you are the person trying to decide whether to take the out-of-town job. If you possessed all the relevant information about yourself, could you predict what you will decide? Could you predict that you will continue to deliberate until tomorrow at 10:07, when you will decide to take the job? It is an odd notion. In the first place, if you knew in advance what you will decide, your deliberations might cease. Why go on thinking about it if you already know what you will do? But then the prediction that you would continue to deliberate would be wrong. Moreover, you may be a mischievous person who hates being predictable. Then, whatever conclusion is reached about your future behavior, you could do the opposite just to prove the prediction wrong. The prediction, we might say, is self-defeating. This seems to show that there is a big difference between predicting human behavior and predicting other events in the physical world.

We may summarize the argument like this:

1. If human behavior is causally determined, it is in principle predictable.
2. But a prediction about what someone will do can be thwarted if the person whose behavior is being predicted knows about the prediction and chooses to act otherwise.
3. Therefore, not all human actions are in principle predictable.
4. And so not all human actions are causally determined.

This is a clever argument, but is it sound? There are several problems with it. The first thing we might notice is that people do sometimes predict their own decisions, and this is no impediment to continued deliberation. It happens all the time. You might accurately predict that you will eventually turn down the job because it isn't especially attractive, and in any case you realize that you have turned down other out-of-town jobs that were better. Despite knowing this, you may continue to consider the offer.

It is true, however, that a prediction adds a new element to the situation to which people might react. But this does not mean that the outcome isn't determined. We just need to be clearer about what "predictable" means in this context. We should distinguish between two types of predictability:

a. Predictable by a hypothetical ideal observer who stands outside the system and observes events but does not interfere with them.
b. Predictable by human beings in the real world.

Determinism implies predictability in sense (a) but not in sense (b). With this in mind, consider again the case where I predict you will do something and you do the opposite just to prove me wrong. My prediction may be proved wrong; nonetheless, an ideal observer may have known exactly what was going to happen, including my prediction and your mischievous response.

This argument, then, does not prove that our behavior is not determined. But there is one more argument to consider.

The Argument from Accountability

The assumption that we have free will is deeply ingrained in our ordinary ways of thinking. In responding to other people, we cannot help but think of them as the authors of their actions. We hold them responsible, blaming them if they behave badly and admiring them if they behave well. For these reactions to be justified, it seems necessary that people have free will.

Other important human feelings, such as pride and shame, also presuppose free will. Someone who scores the winning goal or who does well on an examination may feel proud, while someone who chokes or cheats may feel ashamed. But if our actions are always due to factors beyond our control, feelings of pride and shame

are baseless. These feelings are an inescapable part of human life. Thus, once again, thinking of ourselves as free seems inescapable.

We might therefore reason as follows:

1. We cannot help but admire or blame people for what they do, nor can we avoid sometimes feeling pride or shame for what we do.
2. These responses—admiration, blame, pride, and shame—would not be appropriate if people did not have free will.
3. Therefore, we must believe that people have free will.
4. Since we must believe it, we do: People have free will.

This is an example of what Immanuel Kant (1724–1804) called a "transcendental argument." Kant, who is thought by many to have been the greatest of the modern philosophers, observed that there are some things we cannot help believing. Then we cannot avoid also believing whatever is required for the first belief to be true. Suppose we cannot help but believe X. But X presupposes Y. Then, Kant said, we have no choice but to assume Y is true.

The problem with this sort of argument is obvious: The original beliefs might be false, even if they are psychologically inescapable. If we knew that the original beliefs were *true*—that people are blameworthy and that pride is justified—then we could conclude that whatever these beliefs entail is also true. But if we don't know the original beliefs are true, we are not entitled to draw any such conclusions from them. We cannot conclude that we have free will just because it is implied by things we believe but do not know.

Is Libertarianism Coherent?

Finally, we may consider whether Libertarianism makes any sense as a positive view of human behavior. To understand our behavior, we need more than just the denial that our actions are determined. We need, in addition, a positive account of how we make decisions.

If our actions are not causally determined, how are they supposed to come about? What, exactly, produces our decisions? We might imagine that there is, inside each of us, a sort of "mental being" whose decisions are not constrained by the laws of cause and effect—a ghostly controller who makes choices independently of the happenings in the brain. But this is not credible. It goes against what science tells us about how things work. There is no evidence for any sort of "mental energy" at work within us, disconnected from the operation of our neurological systems. And even if we set science aside, this speculation looks like nothing more than a fairy tale.

But if we are not to suppose that there is a disconnected mental entity inside us calling the shots, what are we to think? That some part of the brain operates outside the causal network of the world? It sounds silly, but it is hard to come up with anything better. There seems to be no plausible account available that makes sense of Libertarian "freedom." Without such an account, we must look elsewhere for a solution to the problem of free will.

THE COMPATIBILIST RESPONSE

Compatibilism is the idea that an act can be both free and determined at the same time. This may sound like a contradiction, but according to this theory it is not. Contrary to what you might think, we can accept that human behavior is causally determined and yet go right on thinking of ourselves as free.

Among philosophers, Compatibilism is by far the most popular theory of free will. In one form or another, it was the theory of Hobbes, Hume, Kant, and Mill; and it is defended by most writers on the subject today. This usually comes as a surprise to people who are not familiar with the philosophical literature, because free will and Determinism seem obviously *in*compatible. How are they supposed to be consistent with one another? How can an act be free and determined at the same time?

According to Compatibilism, some actions are obviously free, and some are obviously not free. The trick is to see the difference between them. Here are some examples of when your action is not free:

- You hand over your wallet because a robber holds a gun at your head.
- You attend the company picnic only because your boss says you must.

- You report for induction into the army because you've been drafted and if you don't report you will be sent to prison.

In these cases, you are not acting freely because you are being forced to do things you don't want to do. On the other hand, here are some cases in which you do act freely:

- You contribute money to a charity because you've decided the charity is worthy of your support.
- You urge your company to sponsor a picnic because you think it would be a great thing for the employees. You're delighted when your boss agrees, and you volunteer to help organize the event. On the day of the picnic, you arrive early because you're so excited about it.
- You join the army because the prospect of being a soldier appeals to you. You think it would be a fine career.

These actions are free because your choice is based on your own desires, without anyone else telling you what you must do. *This is what it means to do something "of your own free will."* But notice that this is perfectly compatible with your actions being causally determined by your past history, events in your brain, and so on. It is even compatible with your *desires* being caused by factors beyond your control. Thus, free will and Determinism are compatible.

The basic idea of Compatibilism may be summed up by saying that "free" does not mean "uncaused." Rather, it means something like "uncoerced." Thus, whether your behavior is free does not depend on *whether* it is caused; it only depends on *how* it is caused.

Free Will as Involving Determinism

Is Compatibilism a viable theory? The basic argument for it goes as follows.

The whole worry over free will begins with the thought that *if an action is caused, it cannot be free*. Without this assumption, no problem about free will arises. The question, then, is whether this assumption is true.

If it were true, then in order to be free an act would have to be uncaused. But consider what that would mean. What would it be like for *any* event to be uncaused? Imagine that billiard balls stopped obeying the laws of cause and effect. Their motions would then be unpredictable, but only because they would be random and chaotic. They might go off at odd angles, leap into the air, or suddenly stop. When struck by the cue ball, they might not move at all, or they might explode or turn to ice. Anything at all could happen.

Similarly, if a person's actions were suddenly disconnected from the network of causes and effects, they would become random, chaotic, and unpredictable. A man standing on a street corner might step into the traffic rather than waiting for the light to change. Or he might take off his clothes, attack the person next to him, jump up and down, or recite the Magna Carta. This is what it would be like for behavior to be uncaused. But it is not what we mean by "free." You would not think that someone who began behaving in this way had suddenly acquired free will—you would think he had gone crazy. Free actions are not random and chaotic. They are orderly and thoughtful.

This line of thought may be taken one step further. Free will is not only compatible with Determinism; free will *requires* Determinism. In a random, chaotic world, no one would be free. But in a world that operates in an orderly fashion, according to the laws of cause and effect, free and rational actions are possible because in such a world a person's character and desires will control what he does.

In the causally determined world, however, people's actions would be *predictable*. Does this undermine the notion that they would be free?

Obviously, people's actions are often predictable, despite what was said above about mischievous refusals to act according to expectations. If you know someone well enough, you can often say in advance what sort of choices she will make. I have a friend who sees lots of movies, and I know exactly what sorts of movies she likes. I have been observing her moviegoing habits for years. If she is picking a movie to attend this evening and I know what's playing, I can predict fairly well what she will choose.

But does the fact that I can predict her choice mean that she is not free? Not at all— she looks at the newspaper listings, thinks over what she wants to see, and decides accordingly. No one is holding a gun to her head. No one is manipulating her or tricking her. No one has planted a remote-control device in her brain. Thus, she chooses "of her own free will." The fact that, knowing her as I do, I can predict her choice changes nothing. Indeed, if I could *not* predict that she will prefer *The Remains of the Day* to *Lone Wolf McQuade,* something would be wrong.

The Problem with Compatibilism

In the opinion of most philosophers today, Compatibilism has the best chance of saving free will and protecting the notion of moral responsibility from the onslaught of Determinism. Yet there is a serious problem with Compatibilism. Compatibilism says we are free if our actions flow from our own unmanipulated character and desires. The problem is that our characters and desires are themselves ultimately caused by forces beyond our control. This fact by itself is enough to bring our "freedom" into doubt. Peter van Inwagen puts the point like this:

> If Determinism is true, then our actions are consequences of the laws of nature and events in the remote past. But it is not up to us what went on before we were born, and neither is it up to us what the laws of nature are. Therefore, the consequences of these things (including our present acts) are not up to us.

Compatibilists agree that our present characters and desires are not up to us. That concession seems to give away the game. At the very least, it is enough to make thoughtful people uneasy, even if the compatibilist analysis allows us to go on saying we are free.

ETHICS AND FREE WILL

Many philosophers and theologians see the deterministic implications of modern science as a crisis. Our freedom, they say, is essential to our dignity as moral beings. It separates us from the animals. If we start thinking of ourselves as mere robots, pushed and pulled about by impersonal forces, we lose our humanity.

But before we give in to such fears, we need to ask what the implications of Determinism really are. The most worrisome matters have to do with ethics. If we do not have free will, are we still responsible moral agents? Does ethics lose its point? But perhaps the loss of free will is really not so disturbing, and so we have no reason to fear it and no need to fashion defenses against it.

Deliberating about What Is Best

First, we can set aside the idea that if we lack free will we are "mere robots." We are nothing like robots. We have thoughts, intentions, and emotions. We experience happiness and unhappiness. We love our children and, if we are lucky, they love us back. We take pleasure in going to the movies, playing baseball, and hearing Mozart. Robots can do none of this. Our capacity for these experiences and activities does not depend on our having free will. Even if our behavior is completely determined, all of this is still true.

Another way we are different from robots is that we often have *reasons* for what we do, and this will still be so even if we lack free will. As long as we have beliefs and desires, and our behavior is connected to them, we will still be capable of acting rationally. We will still be pursuing our own goals, just as before. Of course, the sense in which our goals are "our own" would subtly change. We could no longer think of them as something that we freely choose. Instead, we would see them as goals that we have as a result of our makeup, what goes on in our brain, and the influence of our environment. But what of that? Our goals are still our goals, and we still care about them.

It is sometimes suggested that the denial of free will would lead to a fatalistic attitude about the future: There would be no point in striving to change things. But clearly this does not follow. The future depends on what we do, and if we want a certain sort of future, we have good reason to do what is needed to bring it about. Suppose you want sick children in Nigeria to get the medical care they need, and so you contribute to humanitarian efforts. You help change the future. And there is certainly a point to it—without the

help, the children will be worse off. Once again, the presence or absence of free will makes no difference.

Could we deliberate about what to do if we did not believe we had free will? Some philosophers have argued that, if we believe we are not free, "deliberating" makes no sense. After all, deliberating means trying to decide, and the effort to decide seems to presuppose that we could do different things. This reasoning sounds plausible. But what do we actually do when we deliberate? Mainly, we think about what we want and about how different actions would lead to different outcomes. We think about the children in Nigeria, what it's like to be sick and helpless, how our money could supply their needs, and so on; and we might also think about other things we could use our money for. There is nothing in the thought that I do not have free will that would prevent me from continuing to mull things over in this way.

Therefore, the denial of free will does not mean the end of ethics. We may still regard some things as good and others as bad—even if no one has free will, it is still better for the children in Nigeria not to die. Moreover, we may still regard actions as better or worse depending on whether they help bring about better or worse outcomes. Even if you do not have free will, contributing to humanitarian efforts is still a good thing for you to do.

Evaluating People as Good or Bad

Could we continue to regard *people* as good or bad if they do not have free will? It may seem like a surprising thing to say, but I don't see why not. Even without free will, people will still have virtues and vices. They will still be brave or cowardly, kind or cruel, generous or greedy. A murderer will still be a murderer, and a murderer will still be a bad thing to be. Of course, it may be possible to explain someone's misdeeds as the result of his genes, his history, or the chemistry of his brain. This may lead us to see him as unlucky in the circumstances that made him what he is. But that doesn't mean he is not a bad man. We need to distinguish (a) whether someone *is* a bad man from (b) how he *came to be* a bad man. A causal account of someone's character does not imply that he is not bad. It merely explains how he got to be bad.

Consider again Eric Rudolph, whom we met in Chapter 8. [omitted here–Ed.]. Rudolph is accused by the FBI of an abortion-clinic bombing in which a policeman was killed and a nurse was terribly wounded. The story of Rudolph's life provides ample evidence that he is not responsible for having turned out as he did. Knowing his background, we may come to regard him as merely unlucky to have had his unfortunate history. As the old saying has it, there but for the grace of God go I. Yet we may still think of Rudolph as a bad man, because he is, after all, a murderer. He deliberately set out to harm innocent people. Now, however, we have a better understanding of what made him that way.

Responsibility

But, it may be protested, if people do not have free will, then they are not *responsible* for what they do. So how can we say that Eric Rudolph, or anyone else for that matter, is really a bad man?

It is natural to assume that, if we do not have free will, then we are not responsible. Philosophers disagree about whether this is a disturbing conclusion that should be resisted or an enlightened idea that we should welcome. Bertrand Russell took the latter view. He wrote:

> No man treats a motorcar as foolishly as he treats another human being. When the car will not go, he does not attribute its annoying behavior to sin; he does not say, "You are a wicked motorcar, and I shall not give you any more petrol until you go." He attempts to find out what is wrong and to set it right.

Similarly, Russell says, when a person misbehaves we should try to figure out why and deal with that. There is surely something to this idea, especially when we think about the criminal law and the social causes of crime.

Surprisingly, however, it turns out that our commonsense understanding of responsibility is perfectly compatible with Determinism. Being responsible, in the ordinary sense, means that you may be held accountable for what you do—you may be blamed when you behave badly and praised when you behave well. So, if

you are a responsible being, there must be some conditions under which you are *blameworthy* for having done something. What would those conditions be?

From a commonsense point of view, there seem to be three such conditions: (1) You must have done the act in question, (2) the act must in some sense have been wrong, and (3) you must have no excuse for having done it.

The notion of an excuse is crucial. Excuses are facts that get you off the hook when you have done something bad. It was an accident, you may say, or you didn't know what you were doing, or you were forced to do it. It is not possible to give a complete list of legitimate excuses, but here are some common ones:

- *Mistake.* For example, when you left my house, you took my umbrella by mistake—you thought it was yours. If you had taken my umbrella intentionally, you would be blameworthy.
- *Accident.* You were driving safely, taking every sensible precaution, when the child darted in front of the car—you could not have avoided hitting her. If you were trying to hit her, or even if you could reasonably have avoided it, you could be blamed.
- *Coercion.* You were forced to open the safe for the bank robbers because they held a gun to your head. If you had opened it voluntarily, you could be blamed.
- *Ignorance.* You gave your spouse poison with the bedtime drink, but you didn't know it was poison because the pills were in the medicine bottle and you thought they were aspirin. If you had known it was poison, you'd be a murderer.
- *Insanity.* You are suffering from Capgras syndrome, a rare delusional disorder that makes people believe someone known to them—usually a friend or relative—has been replaced by an imposter. So your objectionable behavior is not your fault. There are many other such disorders, and they are generally believed to be the result of damage to specific parts of the brain.

The logic of praise is similar to the logic of blame. Someone is praiseworthy for having done something if (a) he or she did it, (b) it was a good thing to do, and (c) there are no conditions present analogous to excuses. It is curious that there is no name for these analogous conditions. We have a word, "excuses," for the conditions that make blame inappropriate; but we have no word for the comparable conditions that make praise inappropriate. Yet, clearly, similar conditions function in similar ways. If you do something splendid but do it merely by accident or from ignorance, you do not merit praise as you would if you had done it knowingly. Perhaps there is no general word for these conditions because people do not ordinarily try to avoid being praised. We might call them "credit-eliminating conditions."

Thus, the commonsense conception of responsibility is that people are responsible for what they do if there are no excusing conditions or credit-eliminating conditions present. Then, if they behave well they merit praise, while if they behave badly they merit blame. And this conception of responsibility, we should note, is fully compatible with behavior's being causally determined.

All this may be summed up in two ways, depending on whether one thinks that Compatibilism is a viable theory. Compatibilists would say that if these conditions are satisfied, then you act freely. Determinists, however, might say that you

are not free, but you are still responsible, because responsibility does not require free will. A lot of ink has been spilled in this debate, but it looks suspiciously like only a verbal dispute. The essential point is that the fact that people's behavior is causally determined does not mean that they are not responsible for what they do.

Conclusion

The problem of free will is one of the most difficult philosophical issues, and anyone who ventures an opinion about it should be suitably conscious that she could be wrong. Nonetheless, this possibility is worth considering: Little will be lost if we stop thinking of ourselves as having free will. We can go on regarding one another as intelligent, purposeful beings who are capable of acting well or acting badly, and we can continue to judge people as being good or bad depending on the choices they make. We can continue to respond positively or negatively to others depending on what they do and the kind of people they are. At the same time, however, we would do all this with the added understanding that people do not ultimately control either their character or their desires. Where "free will" is concerned, this may be all there is to know.

Alternate Possibilities
and Moral Responsibility

HARRY FRANKFURT

Harry Frankfurt teaches philosophy at Princeton University. He has published several important papers on the issues of free will.

A dominant role in nearly all recent inquiries into the free-will problem has been played by a principle which I shall call "the principle of alternate possibilities." This principle states that a

person is morally responsible for what he has done only if he could have done otherwise. Its exact meaning is a subject of controversy, particularly concerning whether someone who accepts

This paper first appeared in *Journal of Philosophy* vol. 66 (1969), pp. 829–839. Reprinted by permission of the publisher and author.

it is thereby committed to believing that moral responsibility and determinism are incompatible. Practically no one, however, seems inclined to deny or even to question that the principle of alternate possibilities (construed in some way or other) is true. It has generally seemed so overwhelmingly plausible that some philosophers have even characterized it as an *a priori* truth. People whose accounts of free will or of moral responsibility are radically at odds evidently find in it a firm and convenient common ground upon which they can profitably take their opposing stands.

But the principle of alternate possibilities is false. A person may well be morally responsible for what he has done even though he could not have done otherwise. The principle's plausibility is an illusion, which can be made to vanish by bringing the relevant moral phenomena into sharper focus.

I

In seeking illustrations of the principle of alternate possibilities, it is most natural to think of situations in which the same circumstances both bring it about that a person does something and make it impossible for him to avoid doing it. These include, for example, situations in which a person is coerced into doing something, or in which he is impelled to act by a hypnotic suggestion, or in which some inner compulsion drives him to do what he does. In situations of these kinds there are circumstances that make it impossible for the person to do otherwise, and these very circumstances also serve to bring it about that he does whatever it is that he does.

However, there may be circumstances that constitute sufficient conditions for a certain action to be performed by someone and that therefore make it impossible for the person to do otherwise, but that do not actually impel the person to act or in any way produce his action. A person may do something in circumstances that leave him no alternative to doing it, without these circumstances actually moving him or leading him to do it—without them playing any role, indeed, in bringing it about that he does what he does.

An examination of situations characterized by circumstances of this sort casts doubt, I believe, on the relevance to questions of moral responsibility of the fact that a person who has done something could not have done otherwise. I propose to develop some examples of this kind in the context of a discussion of coercion and to suggest that our moral intuitions concerning these examples tend to disconfirm the principle of alternate possibilities. Then I will discuss the principle in more general terms, explain what I think is wrong with it, and describe briefly and without argument how it might appropriately be revised.

II

It is generally agreed that a person who has been coerced to do something did not do it freely and is not morally responsible for having done it. Now the doctrine that coercion and moral responsibility are mutually exclusive may appear to be no more than a somewhat particularized version of the principle of alternate possibilities. It is natural enough to say of a person who has been coerced to do something that he could not have done otherwise. And it may easily seem that being coerced deprives a person of freedom and of moral responsibility simply because it is a special case of being unable to do otherwise. The principle of alternate possibilities may in this way derive some credibility from its association with the very plausible proposition that moral responsibility is excluded by coercion.

It is not right, however, that it should do so. The fact that a person was coerced to act as he did may entail both that he could not have done otherwise and that he bears no moral responsibility for his action. But his lack of moral responsibility is not entailed by his having been unable to do otherwise. The doctrine that coercion excludes moral responsibility is not correctly understood, in other words, as a particularized version of the principle of alternate possibilities.

Let us suppose that someone is threatened convincingly with a penalty he finds unacceptable and that he then does what is required of him by the issuer of the threat. We can imagine details that would make it reasonable for us to think that the person was coerced to perform the action in question, that he could not have done otherwise, and that he bears no moral responsibility for having done what he did. But just what is it about situations of this kind that warrants the judgment that the threatened person is not morally responsible for his act?

This question may be approached by considering situations of the following kind. Jones decides for reasons of his own to do something, then someone threatens him with a very harsh penalty (so harsh that any reasonable person would submit to the threat) unless he does precisely that, and Jones does it. Will we hold Jones morally responsible for what he has done? I think this will depend on the roles we think were played, in leading him to act, by his original decision and by the threat.

One possibility is that Jones$_1$ is not a reasonable man: he is, rather, a man who does what he has once decided to do no matter what happens next and no matter what the cost. In that case, the threat actually exerted no effective force upon him. He acted without any regard to it, very much as if he were not aware that it had been made. If this is indeed the way it was, the situation did not involve coercion at all. The threat did not lead Jones$_1$ to do what he did. Nor was it in fact sufficient to have prevented him from doing otherwise: if his earlier decision had been to do something else, the threat would not have deterred him in the slightest. It seems evident that in these circumstances the fact that Jones$_1$ was threatened in no way reduces the moral responsibility he would otherwise bear for his act. This example, however, is not a counterexample either to the doctrine that coercion excuses or to the principle of alternate possibilities. For we have supposed that Jones$_1$ is a man upon whom the threat had no coercive effect and, hence, that it did not actually deprive him of alternatives to doing what he did.

Another possibility is that Jones$_2$ was stampeded by the threat. Given that threat, he would have performed that action regardless of what decision he had already made. The threat upset him so profoundly, moreover, that he completely forgot his own earlier decision and did what was demanded of him entirely because he

was terrified of the penalty with which he was threatened. In this case, it is not relevant to his having performed the action that he had already decided on his own to perform it. When the chips were down he thought of nothing but the threat, and fear alone led him to act. The fact that at an earlier time Jones$_2$ had decided for his own reasons to act in just that way may be relevant to an evaluation of his character; he may bear full moral responsibility for having made *that* decision. But he can hardly be said to be morally responsible for his action. For he performed the action simply as a result of the coercion to which he was subjected. His earlier decision played no role in bringing it about that he did what he did, and it would therefore be gratuitous to assign it a role in the moral evaluation of his action.

Now consider a third possibility. Jones$_3$ was neither stampeded by the threat nor indifferent to it. The threat impressed him, as it would impress any reasonable man, and he would have submitted to it wholeheartedly if he had not already made a decision that coincided with the one demanded of him. In fact, however, he performed the action in question on the basis of the decision he had made before the threat was issued. When he acted, he was not actually motivated by the threat but solely by the considerations that had originally commended the action to him. It was not the threat that led him to act, though it would have done so if he had not already provided himself with a sufficient motive for performing the action in question.

No doubt it will be very difficult for anyone to know, in a case like this one, exactly what happened. Did Jones$_3$ perform the action because of the threat, or were his reasons for acting simply those which had already persuaded him to do so? Or did he act on the basis of two motives, each of which was sufficient for his action? It is not impossible, however, that the situation should be clearer than situations of this kind usually are. And suppose it is apparent to us that Jones$_3$ acted on the basis of his own decision and not because of the threat. Then I think we would be justified in regarding his moral responsibility for what he did as unaffected by the threat even though, since he would in any case have submitted to the threat, he could not have avoided doing what he did. It would be entirely reasonable for us to make the same judgment concerning his moral responsibility that we would have made if we had not known of the threat. For the threat did not in fact influence his performance of the action. He did what he did just as if the threat had not been made at all.

III

The case of Jones$_3$ may appear at first glance to combine coercion and moral responsibility, and thus to provide a counterexample to the doctrine that coercion excuses. It is not really so certain that it does so, however, because it is unclear whether the example constitutes a genuine instance of coercion. Can we say of Jones$_3$ that he was coerced to do something, when he had already decided on his own to do it and when he did it entirely on the basis of that decision? Or would it be more correct to say that Jones$_3$ was not coerced to do what he did, even though he himself recognized that there was an irresistible force at work in virtue of which he had to do it? My own linguistic intuitions lead me toward the second alternative, but they are somewhat equivocal. Perhaps we can say either of these things, or perhaps we must add a qualifying explanation to whichever of them we say.

This murkiness, however, does not interfere with our drawing an important moral from an examination of the example. Suppose we decide to say that Jones$_3$ was *not* coerced. Our basis for saying this will clearly be that it is incorrect to regard a man as being coerced to do something unless he does it *because of* the coercive force exerted against him. The fact that an irresistible threat is made will not, then, entail that the person who receives it is coerced to do what he does. It will also be necessary that the threat is what actually accounts for his doing it. On the other hand, suppose we decide to say that Jones$_3$ *was* coerced. Then we will be bound to admit that being coerced does not exclude being morally responsible. And we will also surely be led to the view that coercion affects the judgment of a person's moral responsibility only when the person acts as he does because he is coerced to do so—i.e., when the fact that he is coerced is what accounts for his action.

Whichever we decide to say, then, we will recognize that the doctrine that coercion excludes moral responsibility is not a particularized version of the principle of alternate possibilities. Situations in which a person who does something cannot do otherwise because he is subject to coercive power are either not instances of coercion at all, or they are situations in which the person may still be morally responsible for what he does if it is not because of the coercion that he does it. When we excuse a person who has been coerced, we do not excuse him because he was unable to do otherwise. Even though a person is subject to a coercive force that precludes his performing any action but one, he may nonetheless bear full moral responsibility for performing that action.

IV

To the extent that the principle of alternate possibilities derives its plausibility from association with the doctrine that coercion excludes moral responsibility, a clear understanding of the latter diminishes the appeal of the former. Indeed the case of Jones$_3$ may appear to do more than illuminate the relationship between the two doctrines. It may well seem to provide a decisive counterexample to the principle of alternate possibilities and thus to show that this principle is false. For the irresistibility of the threat to which Jones$_3$ is subjected might well be taken to mean that he cannot but perform the action he performs. And yet the threat, since Jones$_3$ performs the action without regard to it, does not reduce his moral responsibility for what he does.

The following objection will doubtless be raised against the suggestion that the case of Jones$_3$ is a counterexample to the principle of alternate possibilities. There is perhaps a sense in which Jones$_3$ cannot do otherwise than perform the action he performs, since he is a reasonable man and the threat he encounters is sufficient to move any reasonable man. But it is not this sense that is germane to the principle of alternate possibilities. His knowledge that he stands to suffer an intolerably harsh penalty does not mean that Jones$_3$, strictly speaking, *cannot* perform any action but the one he does perform. After all it is still open to him, and this is crucial, to defy the threat if he wishes to do so and to accept the penalty his action would bring down upon him. In the sense in which the principle of alternate possibilities employs the concept of "could have done otherwise," Jones$_3$'s inability to resist the threat does not mean that he cannot do otherwise than perform the action he performs. Hence the case of Jones$_3$ does not constitute an instance contrary to the principle.

I do not propose to consider in what sense the concept of "could have done otherwise" figures in the principle of alternate possibilities, nor will I attempt to measure the force of the objection I have just described.[1] For I believe that whatever force this objection may be thought to have can be deflected by altering the example in the following way.[2] Suppose someone—Black, let us say—wants Jones$_4$ to perform a certain action. Black is prepared to go to considerable lengths to get his way, but he prefers to avoid showing his hand unnecessarily. So he waits until Jones$_4$ is about to make up his mind what to do, and he does nothing unless it is clear to him (Black is an excellent judge of such things) that Jones$_4$ is going to decide to do something *other* than what he wants him to do. If it does become clear that Jones$_4$ is going to decide to do something else, Black takes effective steps to ensure that Jones$_4$ decides to do, and that he does do, what he wants him to do.[3] Whatever Jones$_4$'s initial preferences and inclinations, then, Black will have his way.

What steps will Black take, if he believes he must take steps, in order to ensure that Jones$_4$ decides and acts as he wishes? Anyone with a theory concerning what "could have done otherwise" means may answer this question for himself by describing whatever measures he would regard as sufficient to guarantee that, in the relevant sense, Jones$_4$ cannot do otherwise. Let Black pronounce a terrible threat, and in this way both force Jones$_4$ to perform the desired action and prevent him from performing a forbidden one. Let Black give Jones$_4$ a potion, or put him under hypnosis, and in some such way as these generate in Jones$_4$ an irresistible inner compulsion to perform the act Black wants performed and to avoid others. Or let Black manipulate the minute processes of Jones$_4$'s brain and nervous system in some more direct way, so that causal forces running in and out of his synapses and along the poor man's nerves determine that he chooses to act and that he does act in the one way and not in any other. Given any conditions under which it will be maintained that Jones$_4$ cannot do otherwise, in other words, let Black bring it about that those conditions prevail. The structure of the example is flexible enough, I think, to find a way around any charge of irrelevance by accommodating the doctrine on which the charge is based.[4]

Now suppose that Black never has to show his hand because Jones$_4$, for reasons of his own, decides to perform and does perform the very action Black wants him to perform. In that case, it seems clear, Jones$_4$ will bear precisely the same moral responsibility for what he does as he would have borne if Black had not been ready to take steps to ensure that he do it. It would be quite unreasonable to excuse Jones$_4$ for his action, or to withhold the praise to which it would normally entitle him, on the basis of the fact that he could not have done otherwise. This fact played no role at all in leading him to act as he did. He would have acted the same even if it had not been a fact. Indeed, everything happened just as it would have happened without Black's presence in the situation and without his readiness to intrude into it.

In this example there are sufficient conditions for Jones$_4$'s performing the action in question. What action he performs is not up to him. Of course it is in a way up to him whether he acts on his own or as a result of Black's intervention. That depends upon what action he himself is inclined to perform. But whether he finally acts on his own or as a result of Black's intervention, he performs the same action. He has no alternative but to do what Black wants him to do. If he does it on his own, however, his moral responsibility for doing it is not affected by the fact that

Black was lurking in the background with sinister intent, since this intent never comes into play.

V

The fact that a person could not have avoided doing something is a sufficient condition of his having done it. But, as some of my examples show, this fact may play no role whatever in the explanation of why he did it. It may not figure at all among the circumstances that actually brought it about that he did what he did, so that his action is to be accounted for on another basis entirely. Even though the person was unable to do otherwise, that is to say, it may not be the case that he acted as he did *because* he could not have done otherwise. Now if someone had no alternative to performing a certain action but did not perform it because he was unable to do otherwise, then he would have performed exactly the same action even if he *could* have done otherwise. The circumstances that made it impossible for him to do otherwise could have been subtracted from the situation without affecting what happened or why it happened in any way. Whatever it was that actually led the person to do what he did, or that made him do it, would have led him to do it or made him do it even if it had been possible for him to do something else instead.

Thus it would have made no difference, so far as concerns his action or how he came to perform it, if the circumstances that made it impossible for him to avoid performing it had not prevailed. The fact that he could not have done otherwise clearly provides no basis for supposing that he *might* have done otherwise if he had been able to do so. When a fact is in this way irrelevant to the problem of accounting for a person's action it seems quite gratuitous to assign it any weight in the assessment of his moral responsibility. Why should the fact be considered in reaching a moral judgment concerning the person when it does not help in any way to understand either what made him act as he did or what, in other circumstances, he might have done?

This, then, is why the principle of alternate possibilities is mistaken. It asserts that a person bears no moral responsibility—that is, he is to be excused—for having performed an action if there were circumstances that made it impossible for him to avoid performing it. But there may be circumstances that make it impossible for a person to avoid performing some action without those circumstances in any way bringing it about that he performs that action. It would surely be no good for the person to refer to circumstances of this sort in an effort to absolve himself of moral responsibility for performing the action in question. For those circumstances, by hypothesis, actually had nothing to do with his having done what he did. He would have done precisely the same thing, and he would have been led or made in precisely the same way to do it, even if they had not prevailed.

We often do, to be sure, excuse people for what they have done when they tell us (and we believe them) that they could not have done otherwise. But this is because we assume that what they tell us serves to explain why they did what they did. We take it for granted that they are not being disingenuous, as a person would be who cited as an excuse the fact that he could not have avoided doing what he did but who knew full well that it was not at all because of this that he did it.

What I have said may suggest that the principle of alternate possibilities should be revised so as to assert that a person is not morally responsible for what he has done if he did it because he could not have done otherwise. It may be noted that this revision of the principle does not seriously affect the arguments of those who have relied on the original principle in their efforts to maintain that moral responsibility and determinism are incompatible. For if it was causally determined that a person perform a certain action, then it will be true that the person performed it because of those causal determinants. And if the fact that it was causally determined that a person perform a certain action means that the person could not have done otherwise, as philosophers who argue for the incompatibility thesis characteristically suppose, then the fact that it was causally determined that a person perform a certain action will mean that the person performed it because he could not have done otherwise. The revised principle of alternate possibilities will entail, on this assumption concerning the meaning of 'could have done otherwise', that a person is not morally responsible for what he has done if it was causally determined that he do it. I do not believe, however, that this revision of the principle is acceptable.

Suppose a person tells us that he did what he did because he was unable to do otherwise; or suppose he makes the similar statement that he did what he did because he had to do it. We do often accept statements like these (if we believe them) as valid excuses, and such statements may well seem at first glance to invoke the revised principle of alternate possibilities. But I think that when we accept such statements as valid excuses it is because we assume that we are being told more than the statements strictly and literally convey. We understand the person who offers the excuse to mean that he did what he did *only because* he was unable to do otherwise, or *only because* he had to do it. And we understand him to mean, more particularly, that when he did what he did it was not because that was what he really wanted to do. The principle of alternate possibilities should thus be replaced, in my opinion, by the following principle: a person is not morally responsible for what he has done if he did it only because he could not have done otherwise. This principle does not appear to conflict with the view that moral responsibility is compatible with determinism.

The following may all be true: there were circumstances that made it impossible for a person to avoid doing something; these circumstances actually played a role in bringing it about that he did it, so that it is correct to say that he did it because he could not have done otherwise; the person really wanted to do what he did; he did it because it was what he really wanted to do, so that it is not correct to say that he did what he did only because he could not have done otherwise. Under these conditions, the person may well be morally responsible for what he has done. On the other hand, he will not be morally responsible for what he has done if he did it only because he could not have done otherwise, even if what he did was something he really wanted to do.

NOTES

1. The two main concepts employed in the principle of alternate possibilities are "morally responsible" and "could have done otherwise." To discuss the principle without analyzing either of these concepts may well seem like an attempt at piracy. The reader should take notice that my Jolly Roger is now unfurled.

2. After thinking up the example that I am about to develop I learned that Robert Nozick, in lectures given several years ago, had formulated an example of the same general type and had proposed it as a counterexample to the principle of alternate possibilities.

3. The assumption that Black can predict what $Jones_4$ will decide to do does not beg the question of determinism. We can imagine that $Jones_4$ has often confronted the alternatives—*A* and *B*—that he now confronts, and that his face has invariably twitched when he was about to decide to do *A* and never when he was about to decide to do *B*. Knowing this, and observing the twitch, Black would have a basis for prediction. This does, to be sure, suppose that there is some sort of causal relation between $Jones_4$'s state at the time of the twitch and his subsequent states. But any plausible view of decision or of action will allow that reaching a decision and performing an action both involve earlier and later phases, with causal relations between them, and such that the earlier phases are not themselves part of the decision or of the action. The example does not require that these earlier phases be deterministically related to still earlier events.

4. The example is also flexible enough to allow for the elimination of Black altogether. Anyone who thinks that the effectiveness of the example is undermined by its reliance on a human manipulator, who imposes his will on $Jones_4$, can substitute for Black a machine programmed to do what Black does. If this is still not good enough, forget both Black and the machine and suppose that their role is played by natural forces involving no will or design at all.

Moral Luck

THOMAS NAGEL

Thomas Nagel teaches philosophy at New York University. He is the author of *The View from Nowhere* and numerous important works in the philosophy of mind and moral philosophy.

Kant Believed that good or bad luck should influence neither our moral judgment of a person and his actions, nor his moral assessment of himself.

> The good will is not good because of what it effects or accomplishes or because of its adequacy to achieve some proposed end; it is good only because of its willing, i.e., it is good of itself. And, regarded for itself, it is to be esteemed incomparably higher than anything which could be brought about by it in favor of any inclination or even of the sum total of all inclinations. Even if it should happen that, by a particular unfortunate fate or by the niggardly provision of a stepmotherly nature, this will should be wholly lacking in power to accomplish its purpose, and if even the greatest effort should not avail it to achieve anything of its end, and if there remained only the good will (not as a mere wish but as the summoning of all the means in our power), it would sparkle like a jewel in its own right, as something that had its full worth in itself. Usefulness or fruitlessness can neither diminish nor augment this worth.[1]

He would presumably have said the same thing about a bad will: whether it accomplishes its evil purposes is morally irrelevant. And a course of action that would be condemned if it had a bad outcome cannot be vindicated if by luck it turns out well. There cannot be moral risk. This view seems to be wrong, but it arises in response to a fundamental problem about moral responsibility to which we possess no satisfactory solution.

The problem develops out of the ordinary conditions of moral judgment. Prior to reflection it is intuitively plausible that people cannot be morally assessed for what is not their fault, or for what is due to factors beyond their control.

Such judgment is different from the evaluation of something as a good or bad thing, or state of affairs. The latter may be present in addition to moral judgment, but when we blame someone for his actions we are not merely saying it is bad that they happened, or bad that he exists: we are judging *him*, saying he is bad, which is different from his being a bad thing. This kind of judgment takes only a certain kind of object. Without being able to explain exactly why, we feel that the appropriateness of moral assessment is easily undermined by the discovery that the act or attribute, no matter how good or bad, is not under the person's control. While other evaluations remain, this one seems to lose its footing. So a clear absence of control, produced by involuntary movement, physical force, or ignorance of the circumstances, excuses what is done from moral judgment. But what we do depends in many more ways than these on what is not under our control—what is not produced by a good or a bad will in Kant's phrase. And external influences in this broader range are not usually thought to excuse what is done from moral judgment, positive or negative.

Let me give a few examples, beginning with the type of case Kant has in mind. Whether we succeed or fail in what we try to do nearly always depends to some extent on factors beyond our control. This is true of murder, altruism, revolution, the sacrifice of certain interests for the sake of others—almost any morally important act. What has been done, and what is morally judged, is partly determined by external factors. However jewel-like the good will may be in its own right,

Reprinted from *Mortal Questions* by Thomas Nagel, by permission of Thomas Nagel and Cambridge University Press.

there is a morally significant difference between rescuing someone from a burning building and dropping him from a twelfthstory window while trying to rescue him. Similarly, there is a morally significant difference between reckless driving and manslaughter. But whether a reckless driver hits a pedestrian depends on the presence of the pedestrian at the point where he recklessly passes a red light. What we do is also limited by the opportunities and choices with which we are faced, and these are largely determined by factors beyond our control. Someone who was an officer in a concentration camp might have led a quiet and harmless life if the Nazis had never come to power in Germany. And someone who led a quiet and harmless life in Argentina might have become an officer in a concentration camp if he had not left Germany for business reasons in 1930.

I shall say more later about these and other examples. I introduce them here to illustrate a general point. Where a significant aspect of what someone does depends on factors beyond his control, yet we continue to treat him in that respect as an object of moral judgment, it can be called moral luck. Such luck can be good or bad. And the problem posed by this phenomenon, which led Kant to deny its possibility, is that the broad range of external influences here identified seems on close examination to undermine moral assessment as surely as does the narrower range of familiar excusing conditions. If the condition of control is consistently applied, it threatens to erode most of the moral assessments we find it natural to make. The things for which people are morally judged are determined in more ways than we at first realize by what is beyond their control. And when the seemingly natural requirement of fault or responsibility is applied in light of these facts, it leaves few prereflective moral judgments intact. Ultimately, nothing or almost nothing about what a person does seems to be under his control.

Why not conclude, then, that the condition of control is false—that it is an initially plausible hypothesis refuted by clear counter-examples? One could in that case look instead for a more refined condition which picked out the *kinds* of lack of control that really undermine certain moral judgments, without yielding the unac- ceptable conclusion derived from the broader condition, that most or all ordinary moral judgments are illegitimate.

What rules out this escape is that we are dealing not with a theoretical conjecture but with a philosophical problem. The condition of control does not suggest itself merely as a generalization from certain clear cases. It seems *correct* in the further cases to which it is extended beyond the original set. When we undermine moral assessment by considering new ways in which control is absent, we are not just discovering what *would* follow given the general hypothesis, but are actually being persuaded that in itself the absence of control is relevant in these cases too. The erosion of moral judgment emerges not as the absurd consequence of an over-simple theory, but as a natural consequence of the ordinary idea of moral assessment, when it is applied in view of a more complete and precise account of the facts. It would therefore be a mistake to argue from the unacceptability of the conclusions to the need for a different account of the conditions of moral responsibility. The view that moral luck is para- doxical is not a *mistake,* ethical or logical, but a perception of one of the ways in which the intui- tively acceptable conditions of moral judgment threaten to undermine it all.

It resembles the situation in another area of philosophy, the theory of knowledge. There too conditions which seem perfectly natural, and which grow out of the ordinary procedures for challenging and defending claims to knowledge, threaten to undermine all such claims if con- sistently applied. Most skeptical arguments have this quality: they do not depend on the imposi- tion of arbitrarily stringent standards of knowl- edge, arrived at by misunderstanding, but appear to grow inevitably from the consistent application of ordinary standards.[2] There is a substantive parallel as well, for epistemological skepticism arises from consideration of the respects in which our beliefs and their relation to reality depend on factors beyond our control. External and internal causes produce our beliefs. We may subject these processes to scrutiny in an effort to avoid error, but our conclusions at this next level also result, in part, from influences which we do not control directly. The same will be true no matter how far we carry the investigation. Our beliefs are always, ultimately, due to factors outside our control, and the impossibility of encompassing those factors without being at the mercy of others leads us to doubt whether we know anything. It looks as though, if any of our beliefs are true, it is pure biological luck rather than knowledge.

Moral luck is like this because while there are various respects in which the natural objects of moral assessment are out of our control or influenced by what is out of our control, we cannot reflect on these facts without losing our grip on the judgments.

There are roughly four ways in which the natural objects of moral assessment are disturbingly subject to luck. One is the phenomenon of constitutive luck—the kind of person you are, where this is not just a question of what you deliberately do, but of your inclinations, capacities, and temperament. Another category is luck in one's circumstances—the kind of problems and situations one faces. The other two have to do with the causes and effects of action: luck in how one is determined by antecedent circumstances, and luck in the way one's actions and projects turn out. All of them present a common problem. They are all opposed by the idea that one cannot be more culpable or estimable for anything than one is for that fraction of it which is under one's control. It seems irrational to take or dispense credit or blame for matters over which a person has no control, or for their influence on results over which he has partial control. Such things may create the conditions for action, but action can be judged only to the extent that it goes beyond these conditions and does not just result from them.

Let us first consider luck, good and bad, in the way things turn out. Kant, in the above-quoted passage, has one example of this in mind, but the category covers a wide range. It includes the truck driver who accidentally runs over a child, the artist who abandons his wife and five children to devote himself to painting,[3] and other cases in which the possibilities of success and failure are even greater. The driver, if he is entirely without fault, will feel terrible about his role in the event, but will not have to reproach himself. Therefore this example of agent-regret[4]

is not yet a case of *moral* bad luck. However, if the driver was guilty of even a minor degree of negligence—failing to have his brakes checked recently, for example—then if that negligence contributes to the death of the child, he will not merely feel terrible. He will blame himself for the death. And what makes this an example of moral luck is that he would have to blame himself only slightly for the negligence itself if no situation arose which required him to brake suddenly and violently to avoid hitting a child. Yet the *negligence* is the same in both cases, and the driver has no control over whether a child will run into his path.

The same is true at higher levels of negligence. If someone has had too much to drink and his car swerves on to the sidewalk, he can count himself morally lucky if there are no pedestrians in his path. If there were, he would be to blame for their deaths, and would probably be prosecuted for manslaughter. But if he hurts no one, although his recklessness is exactly the same, he is guilty of a far less serious legal offense and will certainly reproach himself and be reproached by others much less severely. To take another legal example, the penalty for attempted murder is less than that for successful murder—however similar the intentions and motives of the assailant may be in the two cases. His degree of culpability can depend, it would seem, on whether the victim happened to be wearing a bullet-proof vest, or whether a bird flew into the path of the bullet—matters beyond his control.

Finally, there are cases of decision under uncertainty—common in public and in private life. Anna Karenina goes off with Vronsky, Gauguin leaves his family, Chamberlain signs the Munich agreement, the Decembrists persuade the troops under their command to revolt against the czar, the American colonies declare their independence from Britain, you introduce two people in an attempt at matchmaking. It is tempting in all such cases to feel that some decision must be possible, in the light of what is known at the time, which will make reproach unsuitable no matter how things turn out. But this is not true; when someone acts in such ways he takes his life, or his moral position, into his hands, because how things run out determines what he has done. It is possible *also* to assess the decision from the point of view of what could be known at the time, but this is not the end of the story. If the Decembrists had succeeded in overthrowing Nicholas I in 1825 and establishing a constitutional regime, they would be heroes. As it is, not only did they fail and pay for it, but they bore some responsibility for the terrible punishments meted out to the troops who had been persuaded to follow them. If the American Revolution had been a bloody failure resulting in greater repression, then Jefferson, Franklin and Washington would still have made a noble attempt, and might not even have regretted it on their way to the scaffold, but they would also have had to blame themselves for what they had helped to bring on their compatriots. (Perhaps peaceful efforts at reform would eventually have succeeded.) If Hitler had not overrun Europe and exterminated millions, but instead had died of a heart attack after occupying the Sudetenland, Chamberlain's action at Munich would still have utterly betrayed the Czechs, but it would not be the great moral disaster that has made his name a household word.[5]

In many cases of difficult choice the outcome cannot be foreseen with certainty. One kind of assessment of the choice is possible in advance, but another kind must await the outcome, because the outcome determines what has been done. The same degree of culpability or estimability in intention, motive, or concern is compatible with a wide range of judgments, positive or negative, depending on what happened beyond the point of decision. The *mens rea* which could have existed in the absence of any consequences does not exhaust the grounds of moral judgment. Actual results influence culpability or esteem in a large class of unquestionably ethical cases ranging from negligence through political choice.

That these are genuine moral judgments rather than expressions of temporary attitude is evident from the fact that one can say *in advance* how the moral verdict will depend on the results. If one negligently leaves the bath running with the baby in it, one will realize, as one bounds up the stairs toward the bathroom, that if the baby has drowned one has done something awful, whereas if it has not one has merely been careless. Someone who launches a violent

revolution against an authoritarian regime knows that if he fails he will be responsible for much suffering that is in vain, but if he succeeds he will be justified by the outcome. I do not mean that *any* action can be retroactively justified by history. Certain things are so bad in themselves, or so risky, that no results can make them all right. Nevertheless, when moral judgment does depend on the outcome, it is objective and timeless and not dependent on a change of standpoint produced by success or failure. The judgment after the fact follows from a hypothetical judgment that can be made beforehand, and it can be made as easily by someone else as by the agent.

From the point of view which makes responsibility dependent on control, all this seems absurd. How is it possible to be more or less culpable depending on whether a child gets into the path of one's car, or a bird into the path of one's bullet? Perhaps it is true that what is done depends on more than the agent's state of mind or intention. The problem then is, why is it not irrational to base moral assessment on what people do, in this broad sense? It amounts to holding them responsible for the contributions of fate as well as for their own—provided they have made some contribution to begin with. If we look at cases of negligence or attempt, the pattern seems to be that overall culpability corresponds to the product of mental or intentional fault and the seriousness of the outcome. Cases of decision under uncertainty are less easily explained in this way, for it seems that the overall judgment can even shift from positive to negative depending on the outcome. But here too it seems rational to subtract the effects of occurrences subsequent to the choice, that were merely possible at the time, and concentrate moral assessment on the actual decision in light of the probabilities. If the object of moral judgment is the *person*, then to hold him accountable for what he has done in the broader sense is akin to strict liability, which may have its legal uses but seems irrational as a moral position.

The result of such a line of thought is to pare down each act to its morally essential core, an inner act of pure will assessed by motive and intention. Adam Smith advocates such a position in *The Theory of Moral Sentiments,* but notes that it runs contrary to our actual judgments.

> But how well soever we may seem to be persuaded of the truth of this equitable maxim, when we consider it after this manner, in abstract, yet when we come to particular cases, the actual consequences which happen to proceed from any action, have a very great effect upon our sentiments concerning its merit or demerit, and almost always either enhance or diminish our sense of both. Scarce, in any one instance, perhaps, will our sentiments be found, after examination, to be entirely regulated by this rule, which we all acknowledge ought entirely to regulate them.[6]

Joel Feinberg points out further that restricting the domain of moral responsibility to the inner world will not immunize it to luck. Factors beyond the agent's control, like a coughing fit, can interfere with his decisions as surely as they can with the path of a bullet from his gun.[7] Nevertheless the tendency to cut down the scope of moral assessment is pervasive, and does not limit itself to the influence of effects. It attempts to isolate the will from the other direction, so to speak, by separating out constitutive luck. Let us consider that next.

Kant was particularly insistent on the moral irrelevance of qualities of temperament and personality that are not under the control of the will. Such qualities as sympathy or coldness might provide the background against which obedience to moral requirements is more or less difficult, but they could not be objects of moral assessment themselves, and might well interfere with confident assessment of its proper object—the determination of the will by the motive of duty. This rules out moral judgment of many of the virtues and vices, which are states of character that influence choice but are certainly not exhausted by dispositions to act deliberately in certain ways. A person may be greedy, envious, cowardly, cold, ungenerous, unkind, vain, or conceited, but *behave* perfectly by a monumental effort of will. To possess these vices is to be unable to help having certain feelings under certain circumstances, and to have strong spontaneous impulses to act badly. Even if one controls the impulses, one still has the vice. An envious person hates the greater success of others. He

can be morally condemned as envious even if he congratulates them cordially and does nothing to denigrate or spoil their success. Conceit, likewise, need not be displayed. It is fully present in someone who cannot help dwelling with secret satisfaction on the superiority of his own achievements, talents, beauty, intelligence, or virtue. To some extent such a quality may be the product of earlier choices; to some extent it may be amenable to change by current actions. But it is largely a matter of constitutive bad fortune. Yet people are morally condemned for such qualities, and esteemed for others equally beyond control of the will: they are assessed for what they are *like*.

To Kant this seems incoherent because virtue is enjoined on everyone and therefore must in principle be possible for everyone. It may be easier for some than for others, but it must be possible to achieve it by making the right choices, against whatever temperamental background.[8] One may want to have a generous spirit, or regret not having one, but it makes no sense to condemn oneself or anyone else for a quality which is not within the control of the will. Condemnation implies that you should not be like that, not that it is unfortunate that you are.

Nevertheless, Kant's conclusion remains intuitively unacceptable. We may be persuaded that these moral judgments are irrational, but they reappear involuntarily as soon as the argument is over. This is the pattern throughout the subject.

The third category to consider is luck in one's circumstances, and I shall mention it briefly. The things we are called upon to do, the moral tests we face, are importantly determined by factors beyond our control. It may be true of someone that in a dangerous situation he would behave in a cowardly or heroic fashion, but if the situation never arises, he will never have the chance to distinguish or disgrace himself in this way, and his moral record will be different.[9]

A conspicuous example of this is political. Ordinary citizens of Nazi Germany had an opportunity to behave heroically by opposing the regime. They also had an opportunity to behave badly, and most of them are culpable for having failed this test. But it is a test to which the citizens of other countries were not subjected, with the result that even if they, or some of them, would have behaved as badly as the Germans in like circumstances, they simply did not and therefore are not similarly culpable. Here again one is morally at the mercy of fate, and it may seem irrational upon reflection, but our ordinary moral attitudes would be unrecognizable without it. We judge people for what they actually do or fail to do, not just for what they would have done if circumstances had been different.[10]

This form of moral determination by the actual is also paradoxical, but we can begin to see how deep in the concept of responsibility the paradox is embedded. A person can be morally responsible only for what he does; but what he does results from a great deal that he does not do; therefore he is not morally responsible for what he is and is not responsible for. (This is not a contradiction, but it is a paradox.)

It should be obvious that there is a connection between these problems about responsibility and control and an even more familiar problem, that of freedom of the will. That is the last type of moral luck I want to take up, though I can do no more within the scope of this essay than indicate its connection with the other types.

If one cannot be responsible for consequences of one's acts due to factors beyond one's control, or for antecedents of one's acts that are properties of temperament not subject to one's will, or for the circumstances that pose one's moral choices, then how can one be responsible even for the stripped-down acts of the will itself, if *they* are the product of antecedent circumstances outside of the will's control?

The area of genuine agency, and therefore of legitimate moral judgment, seems to shrink under this scrutiny to an extensionless point. Everything seems to result from the combined influence of factors, antecedent and posterior to action, that are not within the agent's control. Since he cannot be responsible for them, he cannot be responsible for their results—though it may remain possible to take up the aesthetic or other evaluative analogues of the moral attitudes that are thus displaced.

It is also possible, of course, to brazen it out and refuse to accept the results, which indeed seem unacceptable as soon as we stop thinking about the arguments. Admittedly, if certain surrounding circumstances had been different, then no unfortunate consequences would have followed from a wicked intention, and no seriously culpable act would have been performed; but since the circumstances were *not* different, and the agent *in fact* succeeded in perpetrating a particularly cruel murder, *that* is what he did, and that is what he is responsible for. Similarly, we may admit that if certain antecedent circumstances had been different, the agent would never have developed into the sort of person who would do such a thing; but since he *did* develop (as the inevitable result of those antecedent circumstances) into the sort of swine he is, and into the person who committed such a murder, *that* is what he is blameable for. In both cases one is responsible for what one actually does—even if what one actually does depends in important ways on what is not within one's control. This compatibilist account of our moral judgments would leave room for the ordinary conditions of responsibility—the absence of coercion, ignorance, or involuntary movement—as part of the determination of what someone has done—but it is understood not to exclude the influence of a great deal that he has not done.[11]

The only thing wrong with this solution is its failure to explain how skeptical problems arise. For they arise not from the imposition of an arbitrary external requirement, but from the nature of moral judgment itself. Something in the ordinary idea of what someone does must explain how it can seem necessary to subtract from it anything that merely happens—even though the ultimate consequence of such subtraction is that nothing remains. And something in the ordinary idea of knowledge must explain why it seems to be undermined by any influences on belief not within the control of the subject—so that knowledge seems impossible without an impossible foundation in autonomous reason. But let us leave epistemology aside and concentrate on action, character, and moral assessment.

The problem arises, I believe, because the self which acts and is the object of moral judgment is threatened with dissolution by the absorption of its acts and impulses into the class of events. Moral judgment of a person is judgment not of what happens to him, but of him. It does not say merely that a certain event or state of affairs is fortunate or unfortunate or even terrible. It is not an evaluation of a state of the world, or of an individual as part of the world. We are not thinking just that it would be better if he were different, or did not exist, or had not done some of the things he has done. We are judging *him*, rather than his existence or characteristics. The effect of concentrating on the influence of what is not under his control is to make this responsible self seem to disappear, swallowed up by the order of mere events.

What, however, do we have in mind that a person must *be* to be the object of these moral attitudes? While the concept of agency is easily undermined, it is very difficult to give it a positive characterization. That is familiar from the literature on Free Will.

I believe that in a sense the problem has no solution, because something in the idea of agency is incompatible with actions being events, or people being things. But as the external determinants of what someone has done are gradually exposed, in their effect on consequences, character, and choice itself, it becomes gradually clear that actions are events and people things. Eventually nothing remains which can be ascribed to the responsible self, and we are left with nothing but a portion of the larger sequences of events, which can be deplored or celebrated, but not blamed or praised.

Though I cannot define the idea of the active self that is thus undermined, it is possible to say something about its sources. There is a close connection between our feelings about ourselves and our feelings about others. Guilt and indignation, shame and contempt, pride and admiration are internal and external sides of the same moral attitudes.

We are unable to view ourselves simply as portions of the world, and from inside we have a rough idea of the boundary between what is us and what is not, what we do and what happens to us, what is our personality and what is an accidental handicap. We apply the same essentially internal conception of the self to others. About ourselves we feel pride, shame, guilt, remorse—and agent-regret. We do not regard our actions and our characters merely as fortunate or un-

fortunate episodes—though they may also be that. We cannot *simply* take an external evaluative view of ourselves—of what we most essentially are and what we do. And this remains true even when we have seen that we are not responsible for our own existence, or our nature, or the choices we have to make, or the circumstances that give our acts the consequences they have. Those acts remain ours and we remain ourselves, despite the persuasiveness of the reasons that seem to argue us out of existence.

It is this internal view that we extend to others in moral judgment—when we judge *them* rather than their desirability or utility. We extend to others the refusal to limit ourselves to external evaluation, and we accord to them selves like our own. But in both cases this comes up against the brutal inclusion of humans and everything about them in a world from which they cannot be separated and of which they are nothing but contents. The external view forces itself on us at the same time that we resist it. One way this occurs is through the gradual erosion of what we do by the subtraction of what happens.

The inclusion of consequences in the conception of what we have done is an acknowledgment that we are parts of the world, but the paradoxical character of moral luck which emerges from this acknowledgment shows that we are unable to operate with such a view, for it leaves us with no one to be. The same thing is revealed in the appearance that determinism obliterates responsibility. Once we see an aspect of what we or someone else does as something that happens, we lose our grip on the idea that it has been done and that we can judge the doer and not just the happening. This explains why the absence of determinism is no more hospitable to the concept of agency than is its presence—a point that has been noticed often. Either way the act is viewed externally, as part of the course of events.

The problem of moral luck cannot be understood without an account of the internal conception of agency and its special connection with the moral attitudes as opposed to other types of value. I do not have such an account. The degree to which the problem has a solution can be determined only by seeing whether in some degree the incompatibility between this conception and the various ways in which we do not control what we do is only apparent. I have nothing to offer on that topic either, but it is not enough to say merely that our basic moral attitudes toward ourselves and others are determined by what is actual; for they are also threatened by the sources of that actuality, and by the external view of action which forces itself on us when we see how everything we do belongs to a world that we have not created.

NOTES

1. Immanuel Kant, *Foundations of the Metaphysics of Morals,* L. W. Beck, trans. (Bobbs-Merrill, 1959), sec. I, paragraph 3.

2. See Thompson Clark, "The Legacy of Skepticism," *Journal of Philosophy,* LXIX, no. 20 (November 9, 1972): pp. 754–69.

3. Such a case, modelled on the life of Gauguin, is discussed by Bernard Williams in "Moral Luck," *Proceedings of the Aristotelian Society,* supplementary vol. L (1976): pp. 115–35 (to which the original version of this essay was a reply). He points out that though success or failure cannot be predicted in advance, Gauguin's most basic retrospective feelings about the decision will be determined by the development of his talent. My disagreement with Williams is that his account fails to explain why such retrospective attitudes can be called moral. If success does not permit Gauguin to justify himself to others, but still determines his most basic feelings, that shows only that his most basic feelings need not be moral. It does not show that morality is subject to luck. If the retrospective judgment were moral, it would imply the truth of a hypothetical judgment made in advance, of the form "If I leave my family and become a great painter, I will be justified by success; if I don't become a great painter, the act will be unforgivable."

4. Williams's term (*ibid.*).

5. For a fascinating but morally repellent discussion of the topic of justification by history, see Maurice Merleau-Ponty, *Humanisme et Terreur* (Paris: Gallimard, 1947), translated as *Humanism and Terror* (Boston: Beacon Press, 1969).

6. Adam Smith, *The Theory of Moral Sentiments,* 1759, Pt II, sect. 3, Introduction, para. 5.

7. "Problematic Responsibility in Law and Morals," in Joel Feinberg, *Doing and Deserving* (Princeton: Princeton University Press, 1970).

8. If nature has put little sympathy in the heart of a man, and if he, though an honest man, is by temperament cold and indifferent to the sufferings of others, perhaps because he is provided with special gifts of patience and fortitude and expects or even requires that others should have the same—and such a man would certainly not be the meanest product of nature—would not he find in himself a source from which to give himself a far higher worth than he could have got by having a good-natured temperament?" (Kant, *Foundations of the Metaphysics of Morals,* first section, eleventh paragraph).

9. Cf. Thomas Gray, 'Elegy Written in a Country Churchyard':
   Some mute inglorious Milton here may rest.
   Some Cromwell, guiltless of his country's blood.
   An unusual example of circumstantial moral luck is provided by the kind of moral dilemma with which someone can be faced through no fault of his own, but which leaves him with nothing to do which is not wrong. See chapter 5; and Bernard Williams, 'Ethical Consistency,' *Proceedings of the Aristotelian Society,* supplementary vol. XXXIX (1965), reprinted in *Problems of the Self* (Cambridge: Cambridge University Press, 1973), pp. 166–86.

10. Circumstantial luck can extend to aspects of the situation other than individual behavior. For example, during the Vietnam War even U.S. citizens who had opposed their country's actions vigorously from the start often felt compromised by its crimes. Here they were not even responsible; there was probably nothing they could do to stop what was happening, so the feeling of being implicated may seem unintelligible. But it is nearly impossible to view the crimes of one's own country in the same way that one views the crimes of another country, no matter how equal one's lack of power to stop them in the two cases. One *is* a citizen of one of them, and has a connexion with its actions (even if only through taxes that cannot be withheld)—that one does not have with the other's. This makes it possible to be ashamed of one's country, and to feel a victim of moral bad luck that one was an American in the 1960s.

11. The corresponding position in epistemology would be that knowledge consists of true beliefs formed in certain ways, and that it does not require all aspects of the process to be under the knower's control, actually or potentially. Both the correctness of these beliefs and the process by which they are arrived at would therefore be importantly subject to luck. The Nobel Prize is not awarded to people who turn out to be wrong, no matter how brilliant their reasoning.

Sanity and the Metaphysics of Responsibility

SUSAN WOLF

Susan Wolf teaches philosophy at the University of North Carolina, Chapel Hill.

Philosophers who study the problems of free will and responsibility have an easier time than most in meeting challenges about the relevance of their work to ordinary, practical concerns. Indeed, philosophers who study these problems are rarely faced with such challenges at all, since questions concerning the conditions of responsibility come up so obviously and so frequently in everyday life. Under scrutiny, however, one might question whether the connections between philosophical and nonphilosophical concerns in this area are real.

In everyday contexts, when lawyers, judges, parents, and others are concerned with issues of responsibility, they know, or think they know, what in general the conditions of responsibility are. Their questions are questions of application: Does this or that particular person meet this or that particular condition? Is this person mature enough, or informed enough, or sane enough to be responsible? Was he or she acting under posthypnotic suggestion or under the influence of a mind-impairing drug? It is assumed, in these contexts, that normal, fully developed adult human beings are responsible beings. The questions have to do with whether a given individual falls within the normal range.

By contrast, philosophers tend to be uncertain about the general conditions of responsibility, and they care less about dividing the responsible from the nonresponsible agents than about determining whether, and if so why, any of us are ever responsible for anything at all.

In the classroom, we might argue that the philosophical concerns grow out of the non-philosophical ones, that they take off where the nonphilosophical questions stop. In this way, we might convince our students that even if they are not plagued by the philosophical worries, they ought to be. If they worry about whether a person is mature enough, informed enough, and sane enough to be responsible, then they should worry about whether that person is metaphysically free enough, too.

The argument I make here, however, goes in the opposite direction. My aim is not to convince people who are interested in the apparently non-philosophical conditions of responsibility that they should go on to worry about the philosophical conditions as well, but rather to urge those who already worry about the philosophical problems not to leave the more mundane, pre-philosophical problems behind. In particular, I suggest that the mundane recognition that *sanity* is a condition of responsibility has more to do with the murky and apparently metaphysical problems which surround the issue of responsibility than at first meets the eye. Once the significance of the condition of sanity is fully appreciated, at least some of the apparently insuperable metaphysical aspects of the problem of responsibility will dissolve.

My strategy is to examine a recent trend in philosophical discussions of responsibility, a trend that tries, but I think ultimately fails, to give an acceptable analysis of the conditions of responsibility. It fails due to what at first appear to be deep and irresolvable metaphysical problems. It is here that I suggest that the condition of sanity comes to the rescue. What at first

From Ferdinand David Schoeman (ed.). *Responsibility, Character, and the Emotions: New Essays in Moral Psychology* (New York: Cambridge University Press, 1988), pp. 46–62. Reprinted with the permission of Cambridge University Press.

appears to be an impossible requirement for responsibility—the requirement that the responsible agent have created her- or himself—turns out to be the vastly more mundane and non controversial requirement that the responsible agent must, in a fairly standard sense, be sane.

FRANKFURT, WATSON, AND TAYLOR

The trend I have in mind is exemplified by the writings of Harry Frankfurt, Gary Watson, and Charles Taylor. I will briefly discuss each of their separate proposals, and then offer a composite view that, while lacking the subtlety of any of the separate accounts, will highlight some important insights and some important blind spots they share.

In his seminal article "Freedom of the Will and the Concept of a Person,"[1] Harry Frankfurt notes a distinction between freedom of action and freedom of the will. A person has freedom of action, he points out, if she (or he) has the freedom to do whatever she wills to do—the freedom to walk or sit, to vote liberal or conservative, to publish a book or open a store, in accordance with her strongest desires. Even a person who has freedom of action may fail to be responsible for her actions, however, if the wants or desires she has the freedom to convert into action are themselves not subject to her control. Thus, the person who acts under posthypnotic suggestion, the victim of brainwashing, and the kleptomaniac might all possess freedom of action. In the standard contexts in which these examples are raised, it is assumed that none of the individuals is locked up or bound. Rather, these individuals are understood to act on what, at one level at least, must be called *their own desires*. Their exemption from responsibility stems from the fact that their own desires (or at least the ones governing their actions) are not up to them. These cases may be described in Frankfurt's terms as cases of people who possess freedom of action, but who fail to be responsible agents because they lack freedom of the will.

Philosophical problems about the conditions of responsibility naturally focus on an analysis of this latter kind of freedom: What *is* freedom of the will, and under what conditions can we reasonably be thought to possess it? Frankfurt's proposal is to understand freedom of the will by analogy to freedom of action. As freedom of action is the freedom to do whatever one wills to do, freedom of the will is the freedom to will whatever one wants to will. To make this point clearer, Frankfurt introduces a distinction between first-order and second-order desires. First-order desires are desires to do or to have various things; second-order desires are desires about what desires to have or what desires to make effective in action. In order for an agent to have both freedom of action and freedom of the will, that agent must be capable of governing his or her actions by first-order desires *and* capable of governing his or her first-order desires by second-order desires.

Gary Watson's view of free agency[2]—free and responsible agency, that is—is similar to Frankfurt's in holding that an agent is responsible for an action only if the desires expressed by that action are of a particular kind. While Frankfurt identifies the right kind of desires as desires that are supported by second-order desires, however, Watson draws a distinction between "mere" desires, so to speak, and desires that are *values*. According to Watson, the difference between free action and unfree action cannot be analyzed by reference to the logical form of the desires from which these various actions arise, but rather must relate to a difference in the quality of their source. Whereas some of my desires are just appetites or conditioned responses I find myself "stuck with," others are expressions of judgments on my part that the objects I desire are good. Insofar as my actions can be governed by the latter type of desire—governed, that is, by my values or valuational system—they are actions that I perform freely and for which I am responsible.

Frankfurt's and Watson's accounts may be under stood as alternate developments of the intuition that in order to be responsible for one's actions, one must be responsible for the self that performs these actions. Charles Taylor, in an article entitled "Responsibility for Self,"[3] is concerned with the same intuition. Although Taylor does not describe his view in terms of different levels or types of desire, his view is related, for he claims that our freedom and responsibility depend on our ability to reflect on, criticize, and revise our selves. Like Frankfurt and Watson, Taylor seems to believe that if the characters from which our actions flowed were simply and permanently *given* to us, implanted by heredity, environment, or God, then we would be mere vehicles through which the causal forces of the world traveled, no more responsible than dumb animals or young children or machines. But like the others, he points out that, for most of us, our characters and desires are not so brutely implanted—or, at any rate, if they are, they are subject to revision by our own reflecting, valuing, or second-order desiring selves. We human beings—and as far as we know, only we human beings—have the ability to step back from ourselves and decide whether we are the selves we want to be. Because of this, these philosophers think, we are responsible for our selves and for the actions that we produce.

Although there are subtle and interesting differences among the accounts of Frankfurt, Watson, and Taylor, my concern is with features of their views that are common to them all. All share the idea that responsible agency involves something more than intentional agency. All agree that if we are responsible agents, it is not just because our actions are within the control of our wills, but because, in addition, our wills are not just psychological states *in* us, but expressions of characters that come *from* us, or that at any rate are acknowledged and affirmed *by* us. For Frankfurt, this means that our wills must be ruled by our second-order desires; for Watson, that our wills must be governable by our system of values: for Taylor, that our wills must issue from selves that are subject to self-assessment and redefinition in terms of a vocabulary of worth. In one way or another, all these philosophers seem to be saying that the key to responsibility lies in the fact that responsible agents are those for whom it is not just the case that their actions are within the control of their wills, but also the case that their wills are within the control of their *selves* in some deeper sense. Because, at one level, the differences among Frankfurt, Watson, and Taylor may be understood as differences

in the analysis or interpretation of what it is for an action to be under the control of this deeper self, we may speak of their separate positions as variations of one basic view about responsibility: the *deep-self view*.

THE DEEP-SELF VIEW

Much more must be said about the notion of a deep self before a fully satisfactory account of this view can be given. Providing a careful, detailed analysis of that notion poses an interesting, important, and difficult task in its own right. The degree of understanding achieved by abstraction from the views of Frankfurt, Watson, and Taylor, however, should be sufficient to allow us to recognize some important virtues as well as some important drawbacks of the deep-self view.

One virtue is that this view explains a good portion of our pretheoretical intuitions about responsibility. It explains why kleptomaniacs, victims of brainwashing, and people acting under posthypnotic suggestion may not be responsible for their actions, although most of us typically are. In the cases of people in these special categories, the connection between the agents' deep selves and their wills is dramatically severed—their wills are governed not by their deep selves, but by forces external to and independent from them. A different intuition is that we adult human beings can be responsible for our actions in a way that dumb animals, infants, and machines cannot. Here the explanation is not in terms of a split between these beings' deep selves and their wills; rather, the point is that these beings *lack* deep selves altogether. Kleptomaniacs and victims of hypnosis exemplify individuals whose selves are *alienated* from their actions; lower animals and machines, on the other hand, do not have the sorts of selves from which actions *can* be alienated, and so they do not have the sort of selves from which, in the happier cases, actions can responsibly flow.

At a more theoretical level, the deep-self view has another virtue: It responds to at least one way in which the fear of determinism presents itself.

A naive reaction to the idea that everything we do is completely determined by a causal chain that extends backward beyond the times of our births involves thinking that in that case we would have no control over our behavior whatsoever. If everything is determined, it is thought, then what happens happens, whether we want it to or not. A common, and proper, response to this concern points out that determinism does not deny the causal efficacy an agent's desires might have on his or her behavior. On the contrary, determinism in its more plausible forms tends to affirm this connection, merely adding that as one's behavior is determined by one's desires, so one's desires are determined by something else.[4]

Those who were initially worried that determinism implied fatalism, however, are apt to find their fears merely transformed rather than erased. If our desires are governed by something else, they might say, they are not *really* ours after all—or, at any rate, they are ours in only a superficial sense.

The deep-self view offers an answer to this transformed fear of determinism, for it allows us to distinguish cases in which desires are determined by forces foreign to oneself from desires which are determined *by* one's self—by one's "real," or second-order desiring, or valuing, or deep self, that is. Admittedly, there are cases, like that of the kleptomaniac or the victim of hypnosis, in which the agent acts on desires that "belong to" him or her in only a superficial sense. But the proponent of the deep-self view will point out that even if determinism is true, ordinary adult human action can be distinguished from this. Determinism implies that the desires which govern our actions are in turn governed by something else, but that something else will, in the fortunate cases, be our own deeper selves.

This account of responsibility thus offers a response to our fear of determinism; but it is a response with which many will remain unsatisfied. Even if my actions are governed by my desires and my desires are governed by my own deeper self, there remains the question: Who, or what, is responsible for this deeper self? The response above seems only to have pushed the problem further back.

Admittedly, some versions of the deep-self view, including Frankfurt's and Taylor's seem to anticipate this question by providing a place for the ideal that an agent's deep self may be governed by a still deeper self. Thus, for Frankfurt, second-order desires may themselves be governed by third-order desires, third-order desires by fourth-order desires, and so on. Also, Taylor points out that, as we can reflect on and evaluate our prereflective selves, so we can reflect on and evaluate the selves who are doing the first reflecting and evaluating, and so on. However, this capacity to recursively create endless levels of depth ultimately misses the criticism's point.

First of all, even if there is no *logical* limit to the number of levels of reflection or depth a person may have, there is certainly a psychological limit—it is virtually impossible imaginatively to conceive a fourth-, much less an eighth-order, desire. More important, no matter how many levels of self we posit, there will still, in any individual case, be a last level—a deepest self about whom the question "What governs it?" will arise, as problematic as ever. If determinism is true, it implies that even if my actions are governed by my desires, and my desires are governed by my deepest self, my deepest self will still be governed by something that must, logically, be external to myself altogether. Though I can step back from the values my parents and teachers have given me and ask whether these are the values I really want, the "I" that steps back will itself be a product of the parents and teachers I am questioning.

The problem seems even worse when one sees that one fares no better if determinism is false. For if my deepest self is not determined by something external to myself, it will still not be determined by *me*. Whether I am a product of carefully controlled forces or a result of random mutations, whether there is a complete explanation of my origin or no explanation at all, *I* am not, in any case, responsible for my existence; I am not in control of my deepest self.

Thus, though the claim that an agent is responsible for only those actions that are within the control of his or her deep self correctly identifies a necessary condition for responsibility—a condition that separates the hypnotized and the brainwashed, the immature and the lower animals from ourselves, for example—it fails to provide a sufficient condition of responsibility that puts all fears of determinism to rest. For one of the fears invoked by the thought of determinism seems to be connected to its implication that we are but intermediate links in a causal chain, rather than ultimate, self-initiating sources of movement and change. From the point of view of one who has this fear, the deep-self view seems merely to add loops to the chain, complicating the picture but not really improving it. From the point of view of one who has this fear, responsibility seems to require being a prime mover unmoved, whose deepest self is itself neither random *nor* externally determined, but is rather determined *by* itself—who is, in other words, self-created.

At this point, however, proponents of the deep-self view may wonder whether this fear is legitimate. For although people evidently can be brought to the point where they feel that responsible agency requires them to be ultimate sources of power, to the point where it seems that nothing short of self-creation will do, a return to the internal standpoint of the agent whose responsibility is in question makes it hard to see what good this metaphysical status is supposed to provide or what evil its absence is supposed to impose.

From the external standpoint, which discussions of determinism and indeterminism encourage us to take up, it may appear that a special metaphysical status is required to distinguish us significantly from other members of the natural world. But proponents of the deep-self view will suggest this is an illusion that a return to the internal standpoint should dispel. The possession of a deep self that is effective in governing one's actions is a sufficient distinction, they will say. For while other members of the natural world are not in control of the selves that they are, we, possessors of effective deep selves, are in control. We can reflect on what sorts of beings we are, and on what sorts of marks we make on the world. We can change what we don't like about ourselves, and keep what we do. Admittedly, we do not create ourselves from nothing. But as long as we can revise ourselves, they will suggest, it is hard to find reason to complain. Harry Frankfurt writes that a person who is free to do what he wants to do and also free to want what he wants to want has "all the freedom

it is possible to desire or to conceive."[5] This suggests a rhetorical question: If you are free to control your actions by your desires, and free to control your desires by your deeper desires, and free to control those desires by still deeper desires, what further kind of freedom can you want?

THE CONDITION OF SANITY

Unfortunately, there is a further kind of freedom we can want, which it is reasonable to think necessary for responsible agency. The deep-self view fails to be convincing when it is offered as a complete account of the conditions of responsibility. To see why, it will be helpful to consider another example of an agent whose responsibility is in question.

JoJo is the favorite son of Jo the First, an evil and sadistic dictator of a small, undeveloped country. Because of his father's special feelings for the boy, JoJo is given a special education and is allowed to accompany his father and observe his daily routine. In light of this treatment, it is not surprising that little JoJo takes his father as a role model and develops values very much like Dad's. As an adult, he does many of the same sorts of things his father did, including sending people to prison or to death or to torture chambers on the basis of whim. He is not *coerced* to do these things, he acts according to his own desires. Moreover, these are desires he wholly *wants* to have. When he steps back and asks, "Do I really want to be this sort of person?" his answer is resoundingly "Yes," for this way of life expresses a crazy sort of power that forms part of his deepest ideal.

In light of JoJo's heritage and upbringing—both of which he was powerless to control—it is dubious at best that he should be regarded as responsible for what he does. It is unclear whether anyone with a childhood such as his could have developed into anything but the twisted and perverse sort of person that he has become. However, note that JoJo is someone whose actions are controlled by his desires and whose desires are the desires he wants to have: That is, his actions are governed by desires that are governed by and expressive of his deepest self.

The Frankfurt–Watson–Taylor strategy that allowed us to differentiate our normal selves from the victims of hypnosis and brainwashing will not allow us to differentiate ourselves from the son of Jo the First. In the case of these earlier victims, we were able to say that although the actions of these individuals were, at one level, in control of the individuals themselves, these individuals themselves, qua agents, were not the selves they more deeply wanted to be. In this respect, these people were unlike our happily more integrated selves. However, we cannot say of JoJo that his self, qua agent, is not the self he wants it to be. It *is* the self he wants it to be. From the inside, he feels as integrated, free, and responsible as we do.

Our judgment that JoJo is not a responsible agent is one that we can make only from the outside—from reflecting on the fact, it seems, that his deepest self is not up to him. Looked at from the outside, however, our situation seems no different from his—for in the last analysis, it is not up to any of us to have the deepest selves we do. Once more, the problem seems metaphysical—and not just metaphysical, but insuperable. For, as I mentioned before, the problem is independent of the truth of determinism. Whether we are determined or undetermined, we cannot have created our deepest selves. Literal self-creation is not just empirically, but logically impossible.

If JoJo is not responsible because his deepest self is not up to him, then we are not responsible either. Indeed, in that case responsibility would be impossible for anyone to achieve. But I believe the appearance that literal self-creation is required for freedom and responsibility is itself mistaken.

The deep-self view was right in pointing out that freedom and responsibility require us to have certain distinctive types of control over our behavior and our selves. Specifically, our actions need to be under the control of our selves, and our (superficial) selves need to be under the control of our deep selves. Having seen that these types of control are not enough to guarantee us the status of responsible agents, we are

tempted to go on to suppose that we must have yet another kind of control to assure us that even our deepest selves are somehow up to us. But not all the things necessary for freedom and responsibility must be types of power and control. We may need simply to *be* a certain way, even though it is not within our power to determine whether we are that way or not.

Indeed, it becomes obvious that at least one condition of responsibility is of this form as soon as we remember what, in everyday contexts, we have known all along—namely, that in order to be responsible, an agent must be *sane*. It is not ordinarily in our power to determine whether we are or are not sane. Most of us, it would seem, are lucky, but some of us are not. Moreover, being sane does not necessarily mean that one has any type of power or control an insane person lacks. Some insane people, like JoJo and some actual political leaders who resemble him, may have complete control of their actions, and even complete control of their acting selves. The desire to be sane is thus not a desire for another form of control; it is rather a desire that one's self be connected to the world in a certain way—we could even say it is a desire that one's self be *controlled by* the world in certain ways and not in others.

This becomes clear if we attend to the criteria for sanity that have historically been dominant in legal questions about responsibility. According to the M'Naughten Rule, a person is sane if (1) he knows what he is doing and (2) he knows that what he is doing is, as the case may be, right or wrong. Insofar as one's desire to be sane involves a desire to know what one is doing—or more generally, a desire to live in the real world—it is a desire to be a controlled (to have, in this case, one's *beliefs* controlled) by perceptions and sound reasoning that produce an accurate conception of the world, rather than by blind or distorted forms of response. The same goes for the second constituent of sanity—only, in this case, one's hope is that one's *values* be controlled by processes that afford an accurate conception of the world.[6] Putting these two conditions together, we may understand sanity, then, as the minimally sufficient ability cognitively and normatively to recognize and appreciate the world for what it is.

There are problems with this definition of sanity, at least some of which will become obvious in what follows, that make it ultimately unacceptable either as a gloss on or an improvement of the meaning of the term in many of the contexts in which it is used. The definition offered does seem to bring out the interest sanity has for us in connection with issues of responsibility, however, and some pedagogical as well as stylistic purposes will be served if we use sanity hereafter in this admittedly specialized sense.

THE SANE DEEP-SELF VIEW

So far I have argued that the conditions of responsible agency offered by the deep-self view are necessary but not sufficient. Moreover, the gap left open by the deep-self view seems to be one that can be filled only by a metaphysical, and, as it happens, metaphysically impossible addition. I now wish to argue, however, that the condition of sanity, as characterized above, is sufficient to fill the gap. In other words, the deep-self view, supplemented by the condition of sanity, provides a satisfying conception of responsibility. The conception of responsibility I am proposing, then, agrees with the deep-self view in requiring that a responsible agent be able to govern her (or his) actions by her desires and to govern her desires by her deep self. In addition, my conception insists that the agent's deep self be sane, and claims that this is *all* that is needed for responsible agency. By contrast to the plain deep-self view, let us call this new proposal the *sane deep-self view*.

It is worth noting, to begin with, that this new proposal deals with the case of JoJo and related cases of deprived childhood victims in ways that better match our pretheoretical intuitions. Unlike the plain deep-self view, the sane deep-self view offers a way of explaining why JoJo is not responsible for his actions without throwing our own responsibility into doubt. For, although like us, JoJo's actions flow from desires that flow from his deep self, unlike us, JoJo's deep self is itself insane. Sanity, remember, involves the ability to know the difference between right and wrong, and a person who, even on reflection, cannot see that having someone

tortured because he failed to salute you is wrong plainly lacks the requisite ability.

Less obviously, but quite analogously, this new proposal explains why we give less than full responsibility to persons who, though acting badly, act in ways that are strongly encouraged by their societies—the slaveowners of the 1850s, the Nazis of the 1930s, and many male chauvinists of our fathers' generation, for example. These are people, we imagine, who falsely believe that the ways in which they are acting are morally acceptable, and so, we may assume, their behavior is expressive of or at least in accordance with these agents' deep selves. But their false beliefs in the moral permissibility of their actions and the false values from which these beliefs derived may have been inevitable, given the social circumstances in which they developed. If we think that the agents could not help but be mistaken about their values, we do not blame them for the actions those values inspired?[7]

It would unduly distort ordinary linguistic practice to call the slaveowner, the Nazi, or the male chauvinist even partially or locally insane. Nonetheless, the reason for withholding blame from them is at bottom the same as the reason for withholding it from JoJo. Like JoJo, they are, at the deepest level, unable cognitively and normatively to recognize and appreciate the world for what it is. In our sense of the term, their deepest selves are not fully *sane*.

The sane deep-self view thus offers an account of why victims of deprived childhoods as well as victims of misguided societies may not be responsible for their actions, without implying that we are not responsible for ours. The actions of these others are governed by mistaken conceptions of value that the agents in question cannot help but have. Since, as far as we know, our values are not, like theirs, unavoidably mistaken, the fact that these others are not responsible for their actions need not force us to conclude that we are not responsible for ours.

But it may not yet be clear why sanity, in this special sense, should make such a difference—why, in particular, the question of whether someone's values are unavoidably *mistaken* should have any bearing on their status as responsible agents. The fact that the sane deep-self view implies judgments that match our intuitions about the difference in status between characters like JoJo and ourselves provides little support for it if it cannot also defend these intuitions. So we must consider an objection that comes from the point of view we considered earlier which rejects the intuition that a relevant difference can be found.

Earlier, it seemed that the reason JoJo was not responsible for his actions was that although his actions were governed by his deep self, his deep self was not up to him. But this had nothing to do with his deep self's being mistaken or not mistaken, evil or good, insane or sane. If JoJo's values are unavoidably mistaken, our values, even if not mistaken, appear to be just as unavoidable. When it comes to freedom and responsibility, isn't it the unavoidability, rather than the mistakenness, that matters?

Before answering this question, it is useful to point out a way in which it is ambiguous: The concepts of avoidability and mistakenness are not unequivocally distinct. One may, to be sure, construe the notion of avoidability in a purely metaphysical way. Whether an event or state of affairs is unavoidable under this construal depends, as it were, on the tightness of the causal connections that bear on the event's or state of affairs' coming about. In this sense, our deep selves do seem as unavoidable for us as JoJo's and the others' are for them. For presumably we are just as influenced by our parents, our cultures, and our schooling as they are influenced by theirs. In another sense, however, our characters are not similarly unavoidable.

In particular, in the cases of JoJo and the others, there are certain features of their characters that they cannot avoid *even though these features are seriously mistaken, misguided, or bad.* This is so because, in our special sense of the term, these characters are less than fully sane. Since these characters lack the ability to know right from wrong, they are unable to revise their characters on the basis of right and wrong, and so their deep selves lack the resources and the reasons that might have served as a basis for self-correction. Since the deep selves *we* unavoidably have, however, are sane deep selves—deep

selves, that is, that unavoidably *contain* the ability to know right from wrong—we unavoidably do have the resources and reasons on which to base self-correction. What this means is that though in one sense we are no more in control of our deepest selves than JoJo et al., it does not follow in our case, as it does in theirs, that we would be the way we are, even if it is a bad or wrong way to be. However, if this does not follow, it seems to me, our absence of control at the deepest level should not upset us.

Consider what the absence of control at the deepest level amounts to for us: Whereas JoJo is unable to control the fact that, at the deepest level, he is not fully sane, we are not responsible for the fact that, at the deepest level, we are. It is not up to us to *have* minimally sufficient abilities cognitively and normatively to recognize and appreciate the world for what it is. Also, presumably, it is not up to us to have lots of other properties, at least to begin with—a fondness for purple, perhaps, or an antipathy for beets. As the proponents of the plain deep-self view have been at pains to point out, however, we do, if we are lucky, have the ability to revise our selves in terms of the values that are held by or constitutive of our deep selves. If we are lucky enough both to have this ability and to have our deep selves be sane, it follows that although there is much in our characters that we did not choose to have, there is nothing irrational or objectionable in our characters that we are compelled to keep.

Being sane, we are able to understand and evaluate our characters in a reasonable way, to notice what there is reason to hold on to, what there is reason to eliminate, and what, from a rational and reasonable standpoint, we may retain or get rid of as we please. Being able as well to govern our superficial selves by our deep selves, then, we are able to change the things we find there is reason to change. This being so, it seems that although we may not be *metaphysically* responsible for ourselves—for, after all, we did not create ourselves from nothing—we are *morally* responsible for ourselves, for we are able to understand and appreciate right and wrong, and to change our characters and our actions accordingly.

SELF-CREATION, SELF-REVISION, AND SELF-CORRECTION

At the beginning of this chapter, I claimed that recalling that sanity was a condition of responsibility would dissolve at least some of the appearance that responsibility was metaphysically impossible. To see how this is so, and to get a fuller sense of the sane deep-self view, it may be helpful to put that view into perspective by comparing it to the other views we have discussed along the way.

As Frankfurt, Watson, and Taylor showed us, in order to be free and responsible we need not only to be able to control our actions in accordance with our desires, we need to be able to control our desires in accordance with our deepest selves. We need, in other words, to be able to *revise* ourselves—to get rid of some desires and traits, and perhaps replace them with others on the basis of our deeper desires or values or reflections. However, consideration of the fact that the selves who are doing the revising might themselves be either brute products of external forces or arbitrary outputs of random generation made us wonder whether the capacity for self-revision was enough to assure us of responsibility—and the example of JoJo added force to the suspicion that it was not. Still, if the ability to revise ourselves is not enough, the ability to create ourselves does not seem necessary either. Indeed, when you think of it, it is unclear why anyone should want self-creation. Why should anyone be disappointed at having to accept the idea that one has to get one's start somewhere? It is an idea that most of us have lived with quite contentedly all along. What we do have reason to want, then, is something more than the ability to revise ourselves, but less than the ability to create ourselves. Implicit in the sane deep-self view is the idea that what is needed is the ability to *correct* (or improve) ourselves.

Recognizing that in order to be responsible for our actions, we have to be responsible for our selves, the sane deep-self view analyzes what is necessary in order to be responsible for our selves as (1) the ability to evaluate ourselves sensibly and accurately, and (2) the ability to transform ourselves insofar as our evaluation tells us

to do so. We may understand the exercise of these abilities as a process whereby we *take* responsibility for the selves that we are but did not ultimately create. The condition of sanity is intrinsically connected to the first ability; the condition that we able to control our superficial selves by our deep selves is intrinsically connected to the second.

The difference between the plain deep-self view and the sane deep-self view, then, is the difference between the requirement of the capacity for self-revision and the requirement of the capacity for self-correction. Anyone with the first capacity can *try* to take responsibility for himself or herself. However, only someone with a sane deep self—a deep self that can see and appreciate the world for what it is—can self-evaluate sensibly and accurately. Therefore, although insane selves can try to take responsibility for themselves, only sane selves will properly be accorded responsibility.

TWO OBJECTIONS CONSIDERED

At least two problems with the sane deep-self view are so glaring as to have certainly struck many readers. In closing, I shall briefly address them. First, some will be wondering how, in light of my specialized use of the term "sanity," I can be so sure that "we" are any saner than the nonresponsible individuals I have discussed. What justifies my confidence that, unlike the slaveowners, Nazis, and male chauvinists, not to mention JoJo himself, we are able to understand and appreciate the world for what it is? The answer to this is that nothing justifies this except widespread intersubjective agreement and the considerable success we have in getting around in the world and satisfying our needs. These are not sufficient grounds for the smug assumption that we are in a position to see the truth about *all* aspects of ethical and social life. Indeed, it seems more reasonable to expect that time will reveal blind spots in our cognitive and normative outlook, just as it has revealed errors in the outlooks of those who have lived before. But our judgments of responsibility can only be made from here, on the basis of the understandings and values that we can develop by exercising the abilities we do possess as well and as fully as possible.

If some have been worried that my view implicitly expresses an overconfidence in the assumption that we are sane and therefore right about the world, others will be worried that my view too closely connects sanity with being right about the world, and fear that my view implies that anyone who acts wrongly or has false beliefs about the world is therefore insane and so not responsible for his or her actions. This seems to me to be a more serious worry, which I am sure I cannot answer to everyone's satisfaction.

First, it must be admitted that the sane deep-self view embraces a conception of sanity that is explicitly normative. But this seems to me a strength of that view, rather than a defect. Sanity *is* a normative concept, in its ordinary as well as in its specialized sense, and severely deviant behavior, such as that of a serial murderer of a sadistic dictator, does constitute evidence of a psychological defect in the agent. The suggestion that the most horrendous, stomach-turning crimes could be committed only by an insane person—an inverse of Catch-22, as it were—must be regarded as a serious possibility, despite the practical problems that would accompany general acceptance of that conclusion.

But, it will be objected, there is no justification, in the sane deep-self view, for regarding only horrendous and stomach-turning crimes as evidence of insanity in its specialized sense. If sanity is the ability cognitively and normatively to understand and appreciate the world for what it is, then *any* wrong action or false belief will count as evidence of the absence of that ability. This point may also be granted, but we must be careful about what conclusion to draw. To be sure, when someone acts in a way that is not in accordance with acceptable standards of rationality and reasonableness, it is always appropriate to look for an explanation of why he or she acted that way. The hypothesis that the person was unable to understand and appreciate that an action fell outside acceptable bound will always be a possible explanation. Bad performance on a math test always suggests the possibility that the testee is stupid. Typically, however, other

explanations will be possible, too—for example, that the agent was too lazy to consider whether his or her action was acceptable, or too greedy to care, or, in the case of the math testee, that he or she was too occupied with other interests to attend class or study. Other facts about the agent's history will help us decide among these hypotheses.

This brings out the need to emphasize that sanity, in the specialized sense, is defined as the *ability* cognitively and normatively to understand and appreciate the world for what it is. According to our commonsense understandings, having this ability is one thing and exercising it is another—at least some wrong-acting, responsible agents presumably fall within the gap. The notion of "ability" is notoriously problematic, however, and there is a long history of controversy about whether the truth of determinism would show our ordinary ways of thinking to be simply confused on this matter. At this point, then, metaphysical concerns may voice themselves again—but at least they will have been pushed into a narrower, and perhaps a more manageable, corner.

The sane deep-self view does not, then, solve all the philosophical problems connected to the topics of free will and responsibility. If anything, it highlights some of the practical and empirical problems, rather than solves them. It may, however, resolve some of the philosophical, and particularly, some of the metaphysical problems, and reveal how intimate are the connections between the remaining philosophical problems and the practical ones.

NOTES

1. Harry Frankfurt, "Freedom of the Will and the Concept of a Person," *Journal of Philosophy* LXVIII (1971), pp. 5–20.
2. Gary Watson, "Free Agency," *Journal of Philosophy* LXXII (1975), pp. 205–20.
3. Charles Taylor, "Responsibility for Self," in A. E. Rorty, ed., *The Identities of Persons* (Berkeley: University of California Press, 1976 pp. 381–99.
4. See, e.g., David Hume. *A Treatise of Human Nature* (Oxford: Oxford University Press, 1967), pp. 399–406, and R. E. Hobart, "Free Will as Involving Determination and Inconceivable Without It," *Mind* 43 (1934).

5. Frankfurt, p. 16.
6. Strictly speaking, perception and sound reasoning may not be enough to ensure the ability to achieve an accurate conception of what one is doing and especially to achieve a reasonable normative assessment of one's situation. Sensitivity and exposure to certain realms of experience may also be necessary for these goals. For the purpose of this essay, I understand 'sanity' to include whatever it takes to enable one to develop an adequate conception of one's world. In other contexts, however, this would be an implausibly broad construction of the term.
7. Admittedly, it is open to question whether these individuals were in fact unable to help having mistaken values, and indeed, whether recognizing the errors of their society would even have required exceptional independence or strength of mind. This is presumably an empirical question, the answer to which is extraordinarily hard to determine. My point here is simply that *if* we believe they are unable to recognize that their values are mistaken, we do not hold them responsible for the actions that flow from these values, and *if* we believe their ability to recognize their normative errors is impaired, we hold them less than fully responsible for relevant actions.

Morality and Its Critics

THESE DAYS THERE IS A good deal of skepticism about morality, skepticism that may take many forms. One challenge to morality comes from a famous theory of human motivation. The theory that human beings are so constituted by nature that they are incapable of desiring or pursuing anything but their own well-being as an end in itself is called **psychological egoism.** If "true morality" requires selfless devotion to others even at the cost of one's own interests, and if all persons are inherently selfish, as this theory claims, there may be no way to motivate persons to behave morally. Genuinely disinterested acts of benevolence, on this view, do not exist, although persons sometimes appear to be acting unselfishly when they take the interests of other people to be the means for promoting their own good. This theory of motivation should be distinguished from the doctrine called **ethical egoism,** which, as its name indicates, is not a theory about how human beings in fact act but rather a moral doctrine stating how they ought to act. According to this doctrine, one ought to pursue one's own well-being, and only one's own well-being, as an end in itself. A *psychological* egoist, insofar as he or she bothered with ethics at all, might be expected to be an *ethical* egoist; for if there is only one thing that we *can* pursue, there cannot be some other thing that we *ought* to pursue. Most psychological egoists, however, have sought some way to reconcile necessarily selfish motivation with the unselfish and even self-sacrificing conduct required by morality. Many argue, for example, that generally the best means to promote one's own happiness is to work for the public good or the happiness of others.

Joel Feinberg's essay on psychological egoism contains elementary distinctions and standard arguments reorganized and written in elementary terms. Because of its pedagogical intent, it might very well be used as the student's introduction to this section, or even perhaps to the whole volume. Most students, after much resistance, seemed to be persuaded by its arguments; but some of the best students (especially those who were psychology or biology majors) remained unconvinced to the end. Some of the students who were unconvinced by the arguments against psychological egoism would admit that the *a priori* arguments for psychological egoism are fallacious, but insist that the biological sciences and particularly evolutionary theory may yet provide empirical evidence for the theory.

James Rachels, in a characteristically balanced critique, finds the difficulties in ethical egoism to be more impressive than its advantages. He calls it a "challenging" theory, worth taking seriously even though in the end he rejects it. Its importance, he claims, consists in the insights it provides into "the reasons why we *do* have obligations to other people." As Rachels sees it, ethical egoism exhibits the same fundamental flaw as racist and sexist theories: it advocates a policy of preferential treatment without citing a morally relevant factor that might justify such treatment. Each person is allowed (indeed, required) by ethical egoism to give priority to his or her own interests over those of everyone else. Unless some moral attribute can be identified to legitimate such treatment, egoism is, like racism and sexism, unjustified.

One may take a deeply skeptical attitude toward morality even if one allows that persons can be altruistically motivated, and allows as well that ethical standards require us to behave in ways that sometimes necessitate deep personal sacrifice. This form of moral skepticism assumes that we know what morality requires of us—occasional self-sacrifice—and proceeds to ask why it is rational, in such cases, to do what morality requires of us. If we can do better for ourselves by disregarding our moral duties, why shouldn't we do so? Suppose you find a wallet containing $5000 in cash. Surely the morally right thing to do (at least according to the prevailing moral code) would be to return the wallet with the money to its owner. But would this truly be the most reasonable course of action? Think of what you have to gain: an expression of gratitude, some small satisfaction at having done your duty (mixed with nagging doubts that you are a fool), and *maybe* a small reward. Now compare these benefits with what you have to lose—namely, the $5000 itself. It would seem that the losses involved in doing your duty far outweigh the gains. (Perhaps the example might be still more convincing if the money belonged not to a private person but to a great corporation or the federal government.) Looking at the matter in this way, wouldn't you be a fool to return the money? Isn't it *unreasonable*, indeed profoundly contrary to reason, voluntarily to choose a loss in preference to a gain for oneself? And yet this is what morality often seems to require of us: that we put the interests of other people ahead of our own. How, then, can it be reasonable to be moral?

One line of reply to this challenge immediately suggests itself. Not to return the property of others is tantamount to stealing it. If other people were ever to find out that you are, in effect, a thief, their opinion of you would drop drastically and your reputation might never fully recover. Moreover, if the authorities were to make this discovery about you, the consequences might be still worse. Even if no one ever found you out, you would have to live in continued anxiety and fear; and even if you got over that, you might become just a bit bolder in the face of subsequent temptations, until your very success finally would betray you, and you would be found out. The idea that it can *pay* to do what is morally wrong, in short, is usually a miscalculation.

Glaucon and Adeimantus, two characters in Plato's *Republic,* are not satisfied with this kind of answer. That there are advantages in having the reputation of being moral and upright (or "just" as they put it) is perfectly evident: what they wish to learn from Socrates is whether there are corresponding advantages in really being, as opposed to merely seeming, morally upright. If it is reasonable to be honest only *because* dishonesty doesn't pay, then, it would seem, it is reasonable to be honest *only when* dishonesty doesn't pay; the ideally wise person would then be the one who is able to have the "best of both worlds" by seeming, but not really being, moral.

Friedrich Nietzsche (1844–1900), a brilliant classicist and philosopher, takes up where Plato's characters left off. Nietzsche sought to turn morality on its head. He is deeply skeptical about the claims of moralists, and thinks that the Judaeo-Christian conception of the virtues that we have inherited has things upside down. In an excerpt from his work *Beyond Good and Evil,* Nietzsche makes his case for the thought that morality has nothing to do with exemplifying such virtues as humility, forgiveness, and charity. These, he claims, originated in a cult of people who were oppressed, resented it, could do nothing about it, and so elevated the effects of their humiliations into virtues. Nietzsche's even deeper claim is that morality has no external, universal authoritative source. Nietzsche famously announced the death of God in an earlier work, and sought to undermine views which anchored their moral prescriptions in a divine or more objective source.

There is an important connection between Nietzsche's skepticism and yet another form of doubt about morality. This further form of moral skepticism begins by noting the existence of deep, apparently intractable disagreements that divide people on many ethical issues. Prospects for gaining consensus on issues of abortion, or capital punishment, or famine relief seem quite slim, even if those doing the talking are well-intentioned, open-minded, and knowledgeable about the topic under discussion. Many have inferred from this that ethics cannot be objective in the way that science or mathematics is. Disciplines that admit of objective truth appear capable of progress and broad consensus both on methods of inquiry and on a significant set of substantive propositions. **Ethical subjectivists** claim that we do not see such progress or consensus in ethics, and that therefore ethics is simply not an objective area of inquiry. According to one version of subjectivism **(meta-ethical subjectivism),** ethical judgments are neither true nor false—they are simply expressions of commands, preferences or emotions, and as such are not even eligible candidates for truth. A different version **(normative subjectivism)** claims that ethical judgments can be true (or false), but that their truth depends entirely on whether they accurately report the sentiments of those who issue the judgments. As Russ Shafer-Landau points out, in his article that leads off the Standards of Right Conduct section, normative subjectivism is less attractive than its meta-ethical cousin. And while most of us act as if metaethical subjectivism were false—we assess moral judgments as true or false, and deliberate and pursue investigations into ethical issues as if there were truth that awaited discovery—meta-ethical subjectivism is supported by a number of appealing arguments. Whether in the end it is entirely convincing is left to the reader to decide.

Shifting the focus from interpersonal ethical disagreements to intersocietal ones, Mary Midgley presents a consideration of **ethical relativism,** the view that actions are right if and only if they comport with the ultimate ethical standards of the society in which they are performed. This is a natural move to make for those who are convinced that ethics cannot be objective, but have doubts about the plausibility of ethical subjectivism. Rather than view each person as an equally good moral judge, as subjectivists do, relativists make cultural mores the ultimate ethical standards. Midgley offers us a very interesting test case with which to examine assumptions about our abilities to make valid cross-cultural moral assessments. In the end, she thinks that the relativists have overstated the difficulties in this area, and that we are able, in many cases, to rightly say of one social code that it is morally superior (or inferior) to another.

In our selection from *Nicomachean Ethics,* Aristotle offers us a view of ethics that has inspired contemporary philosophers to re-explore the merits of virtue ethics. Aristotle thinks that the central notion in ethics is virtue (as opposed, say, to duty, or happiness, or contract), and that virtue is a matter of knowing and being disposed to behave in accordance with the mean between vicious extremes. As Aristotle frankly says, being virtuous and gaining ethical know-how is not a matter of simply following hard and fast rules, but rather of exercising one's judgment. Only the wise person, whose capacity for practical wisdom has been developed through experience and learning, will truly be in a position to exercise his judgment properly, and so determine, in hard cases, what is noble, fine or just.

Thomas Hobbes, the brilliant English philosopher (1588–1679), is often classed as an ethical egoist. But his is a sophisticated position, as readers will see for themselves, and he is just as often counted the founder of modern **social contract theory.** In his selection from *Leviathan,* Hobbes outlines a view according to which morality develops in response to the horrors of life without government (what he called the **state of nature**). Such a life he famously described as "solitary, poor, nasty, brutish and short," and he thought that any government, even despotism, was to be preferred to the state of nature. Hobbes claimed that there was no right or wrong, justice or injustice in the state of nature, and that the standards of morality are properly given by the terms of the social compact to which parties in the state of nature agree. Hobbes thought that each person's well-being would be enhanced by agreeing to limit his liberty in exchange for the security offered by life under law. His view has had a wide-ranging impact not only on ethics, but also on theories of justice, where social contract views have recently experienced renewed popularity.

An alternative form of social contract theory has emerged in the past three decades, inspired by John Rawls's now-classic work, *A Theory of Justice*. Rawls, perhaps the greatest political philosopher of the twentieth century, defends his egalitarian principles of justice by deriving them from a kind of hypothetical social contract. According to the contractarian method of identifying moral principles, a proposed principle of justice (for example, the utilitarian's, or Rawls's own) is correct, provided it would be chosen over any alternative principle that could be proposed to a group of normally self-interested, rational persons. We are to suppose that all these persons have gathered together voluntarily in an **original position** of equal power for the purpose of designing the institutions that will regulate their future lives. We are also to suppose that they wear a kind of **veil of ignorance,** which prevents them from knowing facts about their own future condition that could tempt them ("rationally self-interested" beings that they are) to base their choice on the desire to promote their own interest, to the disadvantage of others. These features, which are to ensure impartiality, are the most important features that distinguish Rawlsian from Hobbesian contractarianism. Whereas Hobbes starts with individuals in the state of nature, as they really are, with full knowledge of their social positions, Rawls banishes such knowledge. If these hypothetical choosers are neither rich nor poor, white nor black, male nor female, old nor young—so far as they know—then they cannot be lobbyists for any particular class interests and must choose their principles from a more disinterested vantage point. Justice, then, is the name for the principles such persons would choose to govern the design of their political and economic institutions.

Though not very popular these days among professional philosophers, the **divine command theory** enjoys broad allegiance among non-philosophers. This theory tells us that actions are right in virtue of being commanded by God. Because of a growing lack of confidence in theism, as well as worries that date back to Plato's time, the influence of divine command theory has waned considerably. But Philip Quinn, in an essay written expressly for this volume, gives a reasoned, even-handed defense of this theory, focusing much of his efforts on showing why the standard objections to it are less compelling than they have seemed. Quinn does not argue for God's existence in this paper, but does do a good deal to show why, if one is a theist, the divine command theory should be seen as a viable option.

Quinn's selection is followed by an excerpt from one of the greatest systematic philosophers of Western civilization, Immanuel Kant. We have excerpted here the greater part of Books I and II of his *Groundwork of the Metaphysics of Morals*. In Book I Kant develops the notion of a **good will,** and defends his claim that nothing else can be unconditionally good, that is, good in every instance, regardless of accompanying circumstances. The good will is simply the commitment to do one's duty for its own sake (rather than, say, because it will promote one's self-interest). But where does one's duty lie? In Book II Kant introduces his **categorical imperative,** a command of reason that is authoritative for moral agents regardless of their desires. Kant claims that the rightness or wrongness of an action lies not in the results it brings about, but instead in the principle that guides a person's conduct. Kant calls such a principle a **maxim.** The categorical imperative states that actions are right if and only if their maxim is such that the agent can will that everyone abide by it. In effect, the centerpiece of Kantian ethics is the directive not to make an exception of oneself—act only on those principles that one is willing to see everyone act on.

Kant's view is directly opposed to the **utilitarian** view of John Stuart Mill. Mill believes that pleasure is the sole intrinsic value, and he believes that our fundamental moral obligation is to produce as much pleasure as we can. But here the focus is not just on one's own pleasure; rather, in the famous utilitarian phrase, "everybody is to count for one and nobody as more than one." Because of its dual emphasis on impartiality and on pleasure, utilitarianism is sometimes denominated **universalistic** (as opposed to egoistic) **hedonism.** This view places priority on achieving the greatest happiness for the greatest number, another utilitarian catch-phrase, and thus locates the virtue of beneficence at the heart of ethics. Utilitarians sometimes seek to display the attractions of their view by asking a couple of apparently innocent questions: How could an action that produces the most happiness possibly fail to be right? And how could an action be right if another available action could have made people better off, that is, produced more pleasure?

Despite the apparently rhetorical nature of such questions, Kantians (and others) will find much to disagree with regarding the utilitarian theory. In fact, the contrast between Kant and Mill could not be sharper (though Mill insists that Kant's theory is best understood as a version of utilitarianism, a claim whose merits have been debated for over a century). Kant and Mill disagree about what has value for its own sake (the good will, or pleasure), about what makes actions right or wrong (proper intentions, or results), and about which virtue stands at the center of ethics (fairness, or beneficence).

We conclude our selections in normative ethics with the most famous effort to effect a compromise between the Kantian and Utilitarian theories. Sir David Ross, in his day the greatest translator of Aristotle's works, also found time to invent one of the few genuinely novel ethical theories of the twentieth century. He finds merit in the Kantian idea that there are sources of duty other than that of promoting greatest happiness, though he also agrees with utilitarians in saying that, nevertheless, it often is our duty to do what will maximize happiness. He can say such things because he believes that all of our moral principles are **prima facie.** Prima facie principles are those that may permissibly be broken in certain circumstances. Ross believed in **ethical pluralism**—rather than one single, absolute principle that lay at the foundations of ethics, there is a plurality, each of which is independent, and cannot be derived from the others. Such rules as those enjoining truth-telling, the repayment of debts, and promise-keeping are valid principles, though they may, in certain cases (which resist specification), take a back seat to other principles. These further principles (such as those enjoining beneficence, or the avoidance of harming others) are also prima facie, and so may themselves be outweighed in some cases by competing principles.

As a way, in part, to test the implications of the proposed standards of right conduct, we conclude Part 5 with a section on Ethical Problems. The section starts off with Plato's *Crito,* the classic discussion of political obligation and the conditions (if any) under which civil disobedience is permissible. Set in Socrates' jail cell, as he awaits his execution, Socrates calmly resists his friend Crito's invitation to easily escape, justifying his refusal by invoking considerations that remain (2400 years later) the basis of most contemporary arguments regarding political obligation.

Martha Nussbaum next offers us an extended case study of the tenability of ethical relativism. Her focus is on the practice, still quite widespread, of female genital mutilation. Are our criticisms of such a practice the product merely of insular thinking, or are there universal moral standards that we can rely on to criticize the longstanding practices of other peoples? In a piece that characteristically combines sophisticated theorizing with an appreciation of the facts on the ground, Nussbaum echoes Midgley's earlier piece in thinking that we are, indeed, able to justifiably criticize the moral practices of other cultures.

We continue our survey of some ethical problems with two selections on issues of famine relief, one (by Onora O'Neill) that recommends a Kantian perspective, the other (by Peter Singer) displaying the recommendations that follow from utilitarian assumptions. Singer's piece, especially, forces us to look hard at our assumptions about what we own, and what we owe to others. If he is right, then we are morally obligated to give as much as we have, just shy of making ourselves as badly off as those we are intending to help. Following Singer's piece is another striking paper, written with an implicit utilitarian challenge. John Harris invites us to ponder the morality of what he calls a *survival lottery.* In societies that lack a sufficient number of donor organs to transplant to those in need, every citizen must participate in a lottery. If a citizen's number gets drawn, then he or she will be killed in order to distribute the vital organs. Although one person will surely die as a result, each organ will be distributed to a different person in need, thereby saving many more lives. Though this strikes us as repugnant, Harris claims that there is no morally relevant difference between such a lottery and the present state of affairs. If we had (say) five vital organs, and one person needed a transplant of all five to survive, while five others each needed just one organ to survive, we'd have no qualms about allowing the one to die so that the five may live. If the results are the same in the survival lottery and in real life—we can save five at the cost of one life— why is it OK to save five in the latter case but not the former? The answer, presumably, has to do with the claim that it is morally worse to kill people than to allow them to die. Utilitarians deny this, since the consequences of killing may be just as bad or good as those of letting die, and, for utilitarians, it is consequences that count. For those with different convictions, it is incumbent on you to identify a morally relevant difference that can explain the intuitions surrounding the acceptability of the survival lottery.

James Rachels, though not a utilitarian, takes up this very issue in his article on the topic of euthanasia, or mercy-killing. Rachels' article, published about thirty years ago in a pre-eminent medical journal, criticized the prevailing view among doctors that **active euthanasia** is immoral, though **passive euthanasia** need not be. Active euthanasia involves the intention, on the part of the doctor, to terminate the life of the patient for the patient's own good. In the present context, the discussion is carried on with the understanding that the proposed euthanasia is voluntary—that is, that the patient's decision is made on the basis of adequate information and in the absence of coercion. Whereas active euthanasia seeks to intervene in an ongoing sequence to hasten the patient's death, passive euthanasia (also assumed here to be voluntary) involves the medical staff's decision, in conjunction with the patient, to allow the patient to die. Rachels argues that there is a morally relevant difference between active and passive euthanasia only if there is a morally relevant difference between killing and letting die. But, he argues, there is no such difference. Therefore if, as most people assume, passive euthanasia is morally acceptable (when voluntarily undertaken), then so too is active euthanasia.

Peter Singer next makes another appearance in a selection from his popular work *Animal Liberation*. Singer likens the political movement on behalf of animals to other progressive movements, such as the Women's Liberation or Black Liberation movements of the sixties and seventies. He thinks that the suffering of non-human animals is as morally important, in itself, as our own suffering, and offers several arguments designed to convince what he knows will be a skeptical audience. Perhaps his most powerful argument against **speciesism**—the view that species membership is in itself a morally important trait—claims that there are no morally relevant differences between some non-human animals and some severely mentally impaired human beings. If one's species is not intrinsically important, and if the reflective, communicative, emotional or social abilities of such impaired humans is not any greater (and possibly worse) than that of a pig or a primate, then we must treat these beings in similar ways. Since one wouldn't unnaturally confine and prematurely kill and eat such humans, or conduct the sorts of experiments routinely performed on primates, then one shouldn't do this to these non-human animals, either. Those who object to Singer's conclusions will have to identify the morally relevant trait that distinguishes all human beings, no matter how impaired, from the rest of creation.

CHALLENGES TO MORALITY

Psychological Egoism

JOEL FEINBERG

A. THE THEORY

1. "Psychological egoism" is the name given to a theory widely held by ordinary people, and at one time almost universally accepted by political economists, philosophers, and psychologists, according to which all human actions when properly understood can be seen to be motivated by selfish desires. More precisely, psychological egoism is the doctrine that the only thing anyone is capable of desiring or pursuing ultimately (as an end in itself) is his own self-interest. No psychological egoist denies that people sometimes do desire things other than their own

From materials composed for philosophy students at Brown University, 1958.

welfare—the happiness of other people, for example; but all psychological egoists insist that people are capable of desiring the happiness of others only when they take it to be a *means* to their own happiness. In short, purely altruistic and benevolent actions and desires do not exist; but people sometimes appear to be acting unselfishly and disinterestedly when they take the interests of others to be means to the promotion of their own self-interest.

2. This theory is called *psychological* egoism to indicate that it is not a theory about what *ought* to be the case, but rather about what, as a matter of fact, *is* the case. That is, the theory claims to be a description of psychological facts, not a prescription of ethical ideals. It asserts, however, not merely that all men do as a contingent matter of fact "put their own interests first," but also that they are capable of nothing else, human nature being what it is. Universal selfishness is not just an accident or a coincidence on this view; rather, it is an unavoidable consequence of psychological laws.

The theory is to be distinguished from another doctrine, so-called "ethical egoism," according to which all people *ought* to pursue their own wellbeing. This doctrine, being a prescription of what *ought* to be the case, makes no claim to be a psychological theory of human motives; hence the word "ethical" appears in its name to distinguish it from *psychological* egoism.

3. There are a number of types of motives and desires which might reasonably be called "egoistic" or "selfish," and corresponding to each of them is a possible version of psychological egoism. Perhaps the most common version of the theory is that apparently held by Jeremy Bentham.[1] According to this version, all persons have only one ultimate motive in all their voluntary behavior and that motive is a selfish one; more specifically, it is one particular kind of selfish motive—namely, a desire for one's own *pleasure*. According to this version of the theory, "the only kind of ultimate desire is the desire to get or to prolong pleasant experiences, and to avoid or to cut short unpleasant experiences for oneself."[2] This form of psychological egoism is often given the cumbersome name—*psychological egoistic hedonism.*

B. PRIMA FACIE REASONS IN SUPPORT OF THE THEORY

4. Psychological egoism has seemed plausible to many people for a variety of reasons, of which the following are typical:

a. "Every action of mine is prompted by motives or desires or impulses which are *my* motives and not somebody else's. This fact might be expressed by saying that whenever I act I am always pursuing my own ends or trying to satisfy my own desires. And from this we might pass on to—'I am always pursuing something for myself or seeking my own satisfaction.' Here is what seems like a proper description of a man acting selfishly, and if the description applies to all actions of all men, then it follows that all men in all their actions are selfish."[3]

b. It is a truism that when a person gets what he wants he characteristically feels pleasure. This has suggested to many people that what we really want in every case is our own pleasure, and that we pursue other things only as a means.

c. *Self-Deception.* Often we deceive ourselves into thinking that we desire something fine or noble when what we really want is to be thought well of by others or to be able to congratulate ourselves, or to be able to enjoy the pleasures of a good conscience. It is a well-known fact that people tend to conceal their true motives from themselves by camouflaging them with words like "virtue," "duty," etc. Since we are so often misled concerning both our own real motives and the real motives of others, is it not reasonable to suspect that we might *always* be deceived when we think motives disinterested and altruistic? Indeed, it is a simple matter to explain away all allegedly unselfish motives: "Once the conviction that selfishness is universal finds root in a person's mind, it is very likely to burgeon out in a thousand corroborating generalizations. It will be discovered that a friendly smile is really only an attempt to win an approving nod from a more or less gullible recording angel; that a charitable deed is, for its performer, only an opportunity to congratulate himself on the good fortune or the cleverness that enables him to be charitable; that a public benefaction is just plain good business advertising. It will emerge that gods are worshipped only because they indulge men's selfish fears, or tastes, or hopes; that the 'golden rule' is no more than an eminently sound success formula; that social and political codes are created and subscribed to only because they serve to restrain other men's egoism as much as one's own, morality being only a special sort of 'racket' or intrigue using weapons of persuasion in place of bombs and machine guns. Under this interpretation of human nature, the categories of commercialism replace those of disinterested service and the spirit of the horse trader broods over the face of the earth."[4]

d. *Moral Education.* Morality, good manners, decency, and other virtues must be teachable. Psychological egoists often notice that moral education and the inculcation of manners usually utilize what Bentham calls the "sanctions of pleasure and pain."[5] Children are made to acquire the civilizing virtues only by the method of enticing rewards and painful punishments. Much the same is true of the history of the race. People in general have been inclined to behave well only when it is made plain to them that there is "something in it for them." Is it not then highly probable that just such a mechanism of human motivation as Bentham describes must be presupposed by our methods of moral education?

C. CRITIQUE OF PSYCHOLOGICAL EGOISM: CONFUSIONS IN THE ARGUMENTS

5. *Non-Empirical Character of the Arguments.* If the arguments of the psychological egoist consisted for the most part of carefully acquired empirical evidence (well-documented reports of controlled experiments, surveys, interviews, laboratory data, and so on), then the critical

philosopher would have no business carping at them. After all, since psychological egoism purports to be a scientific theory of human motives, it is the concern of the experimental psychologist, not the philosopher, to accept or reject it. But as a matter of fact, empirical evidence of the required sort is seldom presented in support of psychological egoism. Psychologists, on the whole, shy away from generalizations about human motives which are so sweeping and so vaguely formulated that they are virtually incapable of scientific testing. It is usually the "armchair scientist" who holds the theory of universal selfishness, and his usual arguments are either based simply on his "impressions" or else are largely of a non-empirical sort. The latter are often shot full of a very subtle kind of logical confusion, and this makes their criticism a matter of special interest to the analytic philosopher.

6. The psychological egoist's first argument (4a, above) is a good example of logical confusion. It begins with a truism—namely, that all of my motives and desires are *my* motives and desires and not someone else's. (Who would deny this?) But from this simple tautology nothing whatever concerning the nature of my motives or the objective of my desires can possibly follow. The fallacy of this argument consists in its violation of the general logical rule that analytic statements (tautologies) cannot entail synthetic (factual) ones.[6] That every voluntary act is prompted by the agent's own motives is a tautology; hence, it cannot be equivalent to "A person is always seeking something for himself" or "All of a person's motives are selfish," which are synthetic. What the egoist must prove is not merely:

(i) Every voluntary action is prompted by a motive of the agent's own.

but rather:

(ii) Every voluntary action is prompted by a motive of a quite particular kind, viz. a selfish one.

Statement (i) is obviously true, but it cannot all by itself give any logical support to statement (ii).

The source of the confusion in this argument is readily apparent. It is not the genesis of an action or the *origin* of its motives which makes it a "selfish" one, but rather the "purpose" of the act or the *objective* of its motives; *not where the motive comes from* (in voluntary actions it always comes from the agent) but *what it aims at* determines whether or not it is selfish. There is surely a valid distinction between voluntary behavior, in which the agent's action is motivated by purposes of his own, and *selfish* behavior in which the agent's motives are of one exclusive sort. The egoist's argument assimilates all voluntary action into the class of selfish action, by requiring, in effect, that an unselfish action be one which is not really motivated at all. In the words of Lucius Garvin, "to say that an act proceeds from our own . . . desire is only to say that the act is our own. To demand that we should act on motives that are not our own is to ask us to make ourselves living contradictions in terms."[7]

7. But if argument 4a fails to prove its point, argument 4b does no better. From the fact that all our successful actions (those in which we get what we were after) are accompanied or followed by pleasure it does not follow, as the egoist claims, that the *objective* of every action is to get pleasure for oneself. To begin with, the premise of the argument is not, strictly speaking, even true. Fulfillment of desire (simply getting what one was after) is no guarantee of satisfaction (pleasant feelings of gratification in the mind of the agent). Sometimes when we get what we want we *also* get, as a kind of extra dividend, a warm, glowing feeling of contentment; but often, far too often, we get no dividend at all, or, even worse, the bitter taste of ashes. Indeed, it has been said that the characteristic psychological problem of our time is the *dissatisfaction* that attends the fulfillment of our very most powerful desires.

Even if we grant, however, for the sake of argument, that getting what one wants *usually* yields satisfaction, the egoist's conclusion does not follow. We can concede that we normally get pleasure (in the sense of satisfaction) when our desires are satisfied, *no matter what our desires are for;* but it does not follow from this roughly accurate generalization that the only thing we ever desire is our own satisfaction. Pleasure may well be the usual accompaniment of all actions in which the agent gets what he wants; but to infer

from this that what the agent always wants is his own pleasure is like arguing, in William James's example,[8] that because an ocean liner constantly consumes coal on its trans-Atlantic passage that therefore the *purpose* of its voyage is to consume coal. The immediate inference from even constant accompaniment to purpose (or motive) is always a *non sequitur*.

Perhaps there is a sense of "satisfaction" (desire fulfillment) such that it is certainly and universally true that we get satisfaction whenever we get what we want. But satisfaction in this sense is simply the "coming into existence of that which is desired." Hence, to say that desire fulfillment always yields "satisfaction" in this sense is to say no more than that we always get what we want when we get what we want, which is to utter a tautology like "a rose is a rose." It can no more entail a synthetic truth in psychology (like the egoistic thesis) than "a rose is a rose" can entail significant information in botany.

8. *Disinterested Benevolence.* The fallacy in argument 4b then consists, as Garvin puts it, "in the supposition that the apparently unselfish desire to benefit others is transformed into a selfish one by the fact that we derive pleasure from carrying it out."[9] Not only is this argument fallacious; it also provides us with a suggestion of a counterargument to show that its conclusion (psychological egoistic hedonism) is false. Not only is the presence of pleasure (satisfaction) as a by-product of an action no proof that the action was selfish; in some special cases it provides rather conclusive proof that the action was *unselfish*. For in those special cases the fact that we get pleasure from a particular action *presupposes that we desired something else*—something other than our own pleasure—as an end in itself and not merely as a means to our own pleasant state of mind.

This way of turning the egoistic hedonist's argument back on him can be illustrated by taking a typical egoist argument, one attributed (perhaps apocryphally) to Abraham Lincoln, and then examining it closely:

> Mr. Lincoln once remarked to a fellow-passenger on an old-time mud-coach that all men were prompted by selfishness in doing good. His fellow-passenger was antagonizing this position when they were

passing over a corduroy bridge that spanned a slough. As they crossed this bridge they espied an old razor-backed sow on the bank making a terrible noise because her pigs had got into the slough and were in danger of drowning. As the old coach began to climb the hill, Mr. Lincoln called out, "Driver, can't you stop just a moment?" Then Mr. Lincoln jumped out, ran back and lifted the little pigs out of the mud and water and placed them on the bank. When he returned, his companion remarked: "Now Abe, where does selfishness come in on this little episode?" "Why, bless your soul Ed, that was the very essence of selfishness. I should have had no peace of mind all day had I gone on and left that suffering old sow worrying over those pigs. I did it to get peace of mind, don't you see?"[10]

If Lincoln had cared not a whit for the welfare of the little pigs and their "suffering" mother, but only for his own "peace of mind," it would be difficult to explain how he could have derived pleasure from helping them. The very fact that he did feel satisfaction as a result of helping the pigs presupposes that he had a preexisting desire for something other than his own happiness. Then when *that* desire was satisfied, Lincoln of course derived pleasure. The *object* of Lincoln's desire was not pleasure; rather pleasure was the *consequence* of his preexisting desire for something else. If Lincoln had been wholly indifferent to the plight of the little pigs as he claimed, how could he possibly have derived any pleasure from helping them? He could not have achieved peace of mind from rescuing the pigs, had he not a prior concern—on which his peace of mind depended—for the welfare of the pigs for its own sake.

In general, the psychological hedonist analyzes apparent benevolence into a desire for "benevolent pleasure." No doubt the benevolent person does get pleasure from his benevolence, but in most cases, this is only because he has previously desired the good of some person, or animal, or mankind at large. Where there is no such desire, benevolent conduct is not generally found to give pleasure to the agent.

9. *Malevolence.* Difficult cases for the psychological egoist include not only instances of disinterested benevolence, but also cases of "disinterested malevolence." Indeed, malice and hatred are generally no more "selfish" than benevolence. Both are motives likely to cause an agent to sacrifice his own interests—in the case of benevolence, in order to help someone else, in the case of malevolence in order to harm someone else. The selfish person is concerned ultimately only with his own pleasure, happiness, or power; the benevolent person is often equally concerned with the happiness of others; to the malevolent person, the *injury* of another is often an end in itself—an end to be pursued sometimes with no thought for his own interests. There is reason to think that people have as often sacrificed themselves to injure or kill others as to help or to save others, and with as much "heroism" in the one case as in the other. The unselfish nature of malevolence was first noticed by the Anglican Bishop and moral philosopher Joseph Butler (1692–1752), who regretted that people are no more selfish than they are.[11]

10. *Lack of Evidence for Universal Self-Deception.* The more cynical sort of psychological egoist who is impressed by the widespread phenomenon of self-deception (see 4c above) cannot be so quickly disposed of, for he has committed no *logical* mistakes. We can only argue that the acknowledged frequency of self-deception is insufficient evidence for his universal generalization. His argument is not fallacious, but inconclusive.

No one but the agent himself can ever be certain what conscious motives really prompted his action, and where motives are disreputable, even the agent may not admit to himself the true nature of his desires. Thus, for every apparent case of altruistic behavior, the psychological egoist can argue, with some plausibility, that the true motivation *might* be selfish, appearance to the contrary. Philanthropic acts are really motivated by the desire to receive gratitude; acts of self-sacrifice, when truly understood, are seen to be motivated by the desire to feel self-esteem; and so on. We must concede to the egoist that all apparent altruism might be deceptive in this way; but such a sweeping generalization requires considerable empirical evidence, and such evidence is not presently available.

11. *The "Paradox of Hedonism" and Its Consequences for Education.* The psychological

egoistic Hedonist (e.g., Jeremy Bentham) has the simplest possible theory of human motivation. According to this variety of egoistic theory, all human motives without exception can be reduced to one—namely, the desire for one's own pleasure. But this theory, despite its attractive simplicity, or perhaps because of it, involves one immediately in a paradox. Astute observers of human affairs from the time of the ancient Greeks have often noticed that pleasure, happiness, and satisfaction are states of mind which stand in a very peculiar relation to desire. An exclusive desire for happiness is the surest way to prevent happiness from coming into being. Happiness has a way of "sneaking up" on persons when they are preoccupied with other things; but when persons deliberately and single-mindedly set off in pursuit of happiness, it vanishes utterly from sight and cannot be captured. This is the famous "paradox of hedonism": the single-minded pursuit of happiness is necessarily self-defeating, for *the way to get happiness is to forget it;* then perhaps it will come to you. If you aim exclusively at pleasure itself, with no concern for the things that bring pleasure, then pleasure will never come. To derive satisfaction, one must ordinarily first desire something other than satisfaction, and then find the means to get what one desires.

To feel the full force of the paradox of hedonism the reader should conduct an experiment in his imagination. Imagine a person (let's call him "Jones") who is, first of all, devoid of intellectual curiosity. He has no desire to acquire any kind of knowledge for its own sake, and thus is utterly indifferent to questions of science, mathematics, and philosophy. Imagine further that the beauties of nature leave Jones cold: he is unimpressed by the autumn foliage, the snow-capped mountains, and the rolling oceans. Long walks in the country on spring mornings and skiing forays in the winter are to him equally a bore. Moreover, let us suppose that Jones can find no appeal in art. Novels are dull, poetry a pain, paintings nonsense and music just noise. Suppose further that Jones has neither the participant's nor the spectator's passion for baseball, football, tennis, or any other sport. Swimming to him is a cruel aquatic form of calisthenics, the sun only a cause of sunburn. Dancing

is coeducational idiocy, conversation a waste of time, the other sex an unappealing mystery. Politics is a fraud, religion mere superstition; and the misery of millions of underprivileged human beings is nothing to be concerned with or excited about. Suppose finally that Jones has no talent for any kind of handicraft, industry, or commerce, and that he does not regret that fact.

What then is Jones interested in? He must desire something. To be sure, he does. Jones has an overwhelming passion for, a complete preoccupation with, his own happiness. The one exclusive desire of his life is *to be happy.* It takes little imagination at this point to see that Jones's one desire is bound to be frustrated. People who—like Jones—most hotly pursue their own happiness are the least likely to find it. Happy people are those who successfully pursue such things as aesthetic or religious experience, self-expression, service to others, victory in competitions, knowledge, power, and so on. If none of these things in themselves and for their own sakes mean anything to a person, if they are valued at all then only as a means to one's own pleasant states of mind—then that pleasure can never come. The way to achieve happiness is to pursue something else.

Almost all people at one time or another in their lives feel pleasure. Some people (though perhaps not many) really do live lives which are on the whole happy. But if pleasure and happiness presuppose desires for something other than pleasure and happiness, then the existence of pleasure and happiness in the experience of some people proves that those people have strong desires for something other than their own happiness—egoistic hedonism to the contrary.

The implications of the "paradox of hedonism" for educational theory should be obvious. The parents least likely to raise a happy child are those who, even with the best intentions, train their child to seek happiness directly. How often have we heard parents say:

> I don't care if my child does not become an intellectual, or a sports star, or a great artist. I just want her to be a plain average sort of person. Happiness does not require great ambitions and great

frustrations; it's not worth it to suffer and become neurotic for the sake of science, art, or do-goodism. I just want my child to be happy.

This can be a dangerous mistake, for it is the child (and the adult for that matter) without "outerdirected" interests who is the most likely to be unhappy. The pure egoist would be the most wretched of persons.

The educator might well beware of "life adjustment" as the conscious goal of the educational process for similar reasons. "Life adjustment" can be achieved only as a by-product of other pursuits. A whole curriculum of "life adjustment courses" unsupplemented by courses designed to incite an interest in things other than life adjustment would be tragically self-defeating.

As for moral education, it is probably true that punishment and reward are indispensable means of inculcation. But if the child comes to believe that the *sole* reasons for being moral are that he will escape the pain of punishment thereby and/or that he will gain the pleasure of a good reputation, then what is to prevent him from doing the immoral thing whenever he is sure that he will not be found out? While punishment and reward then are important tools for the moral educator, they obviously have their limitations. Beware of the man who does the moral thing only out of fear of pain or love of pleasure. He is not likely to be wholly trustworthy. Moral education is truly successful when it produces persons who are willing to do the right thing *simply because it is right,* and not merely because it is popular or safe.

12. *Pleasure as Sensation.* One final argument against psychological hedonism should suffice to put that form of the egoistic psychology to rest once and for all. The egoistic hedonist claims that all desires can be reduced to the single desire for one's own *pleasure.* Now the word "pleasure" is ambiguous. On the one hand, it can stand for a certain indefinable, but very familiar and specific kind of sensation, or more accurately, a property of sensations; and it is generally, if not exclusively, associated with the senses. For example, certain taste sensations such as sweetness, thermal sensations of the sort derived from a hot bath or the feel of the August sun while one lies on a sandy beach, erotic sensations, olfactory sensations (say) of the fragrance of flowers or perfume, and tactual and kinesthetic sensations from a good massage, are all pleasant in this sense. Let us call this sense of "pleasure," which is the converse of "physical pain," pleasure$_1$.

On the other hand, the word "pleasure" is often used simply as a synonym for "satisfaction" (in the sense of gratification, not mere desire fulfillment.) In this sense, the existence of pleasure presupposes the prior existence of desire. Knowledge, religious experience, aesthetic expression, and other so-called "spiritual activities" often give pleasure in this sense. In fact, as we have seen, we tend to get pleasure in this sense whenever we get what we desire, no matter what we desire. The masochist even derives pleasure (in the sense of "satisfaction") from his own physically painful sensations. Let us call the sense of "pleasure" which means "satisfaction"—pleasure$_2$.

Now we can evaluate the psychological hedonist's claim that the sole human motive is a desire for one's own pleasure, bearing in mind (as he often does not) the ambiguity of the word "pleasure." First, let us take the hedonist to be saying that it is the desire for pleasure$_1$ (pleasant sensation) which is the sole ultimate desire of all people and the sole desire capable of providing a motive for action. Now I have little doubt that all (or most) people desire their own pleasure, *sometimes.* But even this familiar kind of desire occurs, I think, rather rarely. When I am very hungry, I often desire to eat, or, more specifically, to eat this piece of steak and these potatoes. Much less often do I desire to eat certain morsels simply for the sake of the pleasant gustatory sensations they might cause. I have, on the other hand, been motivated in the latter way when I have gone to especially exotic (and expensive) French or Chinese restaurants; but normally, pleasant gastronomic sensations are simply a happy consequence or by-product of my eating, not the antecedently desired objective of my eating. There are, of course, others who take gustatory sensations far more seriously: the *gourmet* who eats only to savor the textures and flavors of fine foods, and the wine fancier who "collects" the exquisitely subtle and very pleasant tastes of rare old wines. Such people are truly absorbed in their taste sensations when they eat and drink, and there may even be some (rich) persons whose desire for such sensations is the sole motive for eating and drinking. It should take little argument, however, to convince the reader that such persons are extremely rare.

Similarly, I usually derive pleasure from taking a hot bath, and on occasion (though not very often) I even decide to bathe simply for the sake of such sensations. Even if this is equally true of everyone, however, it hardly provides grounds for inferring that *no one ever* bathes from *any* other motive. It should be empirically obvious that we sometimes bathe simply in order to get clean, or to please others, or simply from habit.

The view then that we are never after anything in our actions but our own pleasure—that all people are complete "gourmets" of one sort or another—is not only morally cynical; it is also contrary to common sense and everyday experience. In fact, the view that pleasant sensations play such an enormous role in human affairs is so patently false, on the available evidence, that we must conclude that the psychological hedonist has the other sense of "pleasure"—satisfaction—in mind when he states his thesis. If, on the other hand, he really does try to reduce the apparent multitude of human motives to the one desire for pleasant sensations, then the abundance of historical counterexamples justifies our rejection out of hand of his thesis. It surely seems incredible that the Christian martyrs were ardently pursuing their own pleasure when they marched off to face the lions, or that what the Russian soldiers at Stalingrad "really" wanted when they doused themselves with gasoline, ignited themselves, and then threw the flaming torches of their own bodies on German tanks, was simply the experience of pleasant physical sensations.

13. *Pleasure as Satisfaction.* Let us consider now the other interpretation of the hedonist's thesis, that according to which it is one's own pleasure$_2$ (satisfaction) and not merely pleasure$_1$ (pleasant sensation) which is the sole ultimate objective of all voluntary behavior. In one respect, the "satisfaction thesis" is even less plausible than the "physical sensation thesis"; for the latter at least is a genuine empirical hypothesis, testable in experience, though contrary to the facts which experience discloses. The former, however, is so confused that it cannot even be completely stated without paradox. It is, so to speak, defeated in its own formulation. Any attempted explication of the theory that all men at all times desire only their own satisfaction leads to an *infinite regress* in the following way:

> "All men desire only satisfaction."
> "Satisfaction of what?"
> "Satisfaction of their desires."
> "Their desires for what?"
> "Their desires for satisfaction."
> "Satisfaction of what?"
> "Their desires."
> "For what?"
> "For satisfaction"—etc., *ad infinitum.*

In short, psychological hedonism interpreted in this way attributes to all people as their sole motive a wholly vacuous and infinitely self-defeating desire. The source of this absurdity is in the notion that satisfaction can, so to speak, feed on itself, and perform the miracle of perpetual self-regeneration in the absence of desires for anything other than itself.

To summarize the argument of sections 12 and 13: The word "pleasure" is ambiguous. Pleasure$_1$ means a certain indefinable characteristic of physical sensation. Pleasure$_2$ refers to the feeling of satisfaction that often comes when one gets what one desires whatever be the nature of that which one desires. Now, if the hedonist means pleasure$_1$ when he says that one's own pleasure is the ultimate objective of all of one's behavior, then his view is not supported by the facts. On the other hand, if he means pleasure$_2$, then his theory cannot even be clearly formulated, since it leads to the following infinite regress: "I desire only satisfaction of my desire for satisfaction of my desire for satisfaction...etc., *ad infinitum.*" I conclude then that psychological hedonism (the most common form of psychological egoism), however interpreted, is untenable.

D. CRITIQUE OF PSYCHOLOGICAL EGOISM: UNCLEAR LOGICAL STATUS OF THE THEORY

14. There remain, however, other possible forms of the egoistic psychology. The egoist might admit that not all human motives can be reduced to the one ultimate desire for one's own pleasure, or happiness, and yet still maintain that our ultimate motives, whether they be desire for happiness (J. S. Mill), self-fulfillment (Aristotle), power (Hobbes), or whatever, are always *self-regarding* motives. He might still maintain that, given our common human nature, wholly disinterested action impelled by exclusively other-regarding motives is psychologically impossible, and that therefore there is a profoundly important sense in which it is true that, whether they be hedonists or not, *all people are selfish.*

Now it seems to me that this highly paradoxical claim cannot be finally evaluated until it is properly understood, and that it cannot be properly understood until one knows what the psychological egoist is willing to accept as evidence either for or against it. In short, there are two things that must be decided: (a) whether the theory is true or false and (b) whether its truth or falsity (its truth value) depends entirely on the *meanings* of the words in which it is expressed or whether it is made true or false by certain *facts*, in this case the facts of psychology.

15. *Analytic Statements.* Statements whose truth is determined solely by the meanings of the words in which they are expressed, and thus can be held immune from empirical evidence, are often called analytic statements or tautologies. The following are examples of tautologies:

(1) All bachelors are unmarried.
(2) All effects have causes.
(3) Either Providence is the capital of Rhode Island or it is not.

The truth of (1) is derived solely from the meaning of the word "bachelor," which is defined (in part) as "unmarried man." To find out whether (1) is true or false we need not conduct interviews, compile statistics, or perform experiments. All empirical evidence is superfluous and irrelevant; for if we know the meanings of "bachelor" and "unmarried," then we know not only that (1) is true, but that it is *necessarily* true—i.e., that it cannot possibly be false, that no future experiences or observations could possibly upset it, that to deny it would be to assert a logical contradiction. But notice that what a tautology gains in certainty ("necessary truth") it loses in descriptive content. Statement (1) imparts no information whatever about any matter of fact; it simply records our determination to use certain words in a certain way. As we say, "It is true by definition."

Similarly, (2) is (necessarily) true solely in virtue of the meanings of the words "cause" and "effect" and thus requires no further observations to confirm it. And of course, no possible observations could falsify it, since it asserts no matter of fact. And finally, statement (3) is (necessarily) true solely in virtue of the meaning of the English expression "either...or." Such terms as "either...or," "If...then," "and," and "not" are called by logicians "logical constants." The *definitions* of logical constants are made explicit in the so-called "laws of thought"—the law of contradiction, the law of the excluded middle, and the law of identity. These "laws" are not laws in the same sense as are (say) the laws of physics. Rather, they are merely consequences of the *definitions* of logical constants, and as such, though they are necessarily true, they impart no information about the world. "Either Providence is the capital of Rhode Island or it is not" tells us nothing about geography; and "Either it is now raining or else it is not" tells us nothing about the weather. You don't have to look at a map or look out the window to know that they are true. Rather, they are known to be true *a priori* (independently of experience); and, like all (or many)[12] *a priori* statements, they are *vacuous*, i.e., devoid of informative content.

The denial of an analytic statement is called a contradiction. The following are typical examples of contradictions: "Some bachelors are married," "Some causes have no effects," "Providence both is and is not the capital of Rhode Island." As in the case of tautologies, the truth value of contra-dictions (their falsehood) is logically necessary, not contingent on any facts of experience, and uninformative. Their falsity is derived from the meanings (definitions) of the words in which they are expressed.

16. *Synthetic Statements.* On the other hand, statements whose truth or falsity is derived not from the meanings of words but rather from the facts of experience (observations) are called *synthetic.*[13] Prior to experience, there can be no good reason to think either that they are true or that they are false. That is to say, their truth value is *contingent;* and they can be confirmed or disconfirmed only by *empirical* evidence,[14] i.e., controlled observations of the world. Unlike analytic statements, they do impart information about matters of fact. Obviously, "It is raining in Newport now," if true, is more informative than "Either it is raining in Newport now or it is not," even though the former *could* be false, while the latter is necessarily true. I take the fol-lowing to be examples of synthetic (contingent) statements:

(1') All bachelors are neurotic.
(2') All events have causes.
(3') Providence is the capital of Rhode Island.
(3") Newport is the capital of Rhode Island.

Statement (3') is true; (3") is false; and (1') is a matter for a psychologist (not for a philosopher) to decide; and the psychologist himself can only decide *empirically,* i.e., by making many observa-tions. The status of (2') is very difficult and its truth value is a matter of great controversy. That is because its truth or falsity depends on *all* the facts ("all events"); and, needless to say, not all of the evidence is in.

17. *Empirical Hypotheses.* Perhaps the most interesting subclass of synthetic statements are those generalizations of experience of the sort characteristically made by scientists; e.g., "All released objects heavier than air fall," "All swans are white," "All men have Oedipus com-plexes." I shall call such statements "empirical hypotheses" to indicate that their function is to sum up past experience and enable us successfully to predict or anticipate future experience.[15] They are never logically certain, since it is always at

least conceivable that future experience will dis-confirm them. For example, zoologists once believed that all swans are white, until black swans were discovered in Australia. The most important characteristic of empirical hypotheses for our present purposes is their relation to evi-dence. A person can be said to understand an empirical hypothesis only if he knows how to rec-ognize evidence against it. *If a person asserts or believes a general statement in such a way that he cannot conceive of any possible experience which he would count as evidence against it, then he cannot be said to be asserting or believing an empirical hypothesis.* We can refer to this impor-tant characteristic of empirical hypotheses as *fal-sifiability in principle.*

Some statements only appear to be empirical hypotheses but are in fact disguised tautologies reflecting the speaker's determination to use words in certain (often eccentric) ways. For example, a zoologist might refuse to allow the existence of "Australian swans" to count as evi-dence against the generalization that all swans are white, on the grounds that the black Austra-lian swans are not "really" swans at all. This would indicate that he is holding *whiteness* to be part of the definition of "swan," and that therefore, the statement "All swans are white" is, for him, "true by definition"—and thus just as immune from counterevidence as the state-ment "All spinsters are unmarried." Similarly, most of us would refuse to allow any possible experience to count as evidence against "$2 + 2 = 4$." or "Either unicorns exist or they do not," indicating that the propositions of arithmetic and logic are not empirical hypotheses.

18. *Ordinary Language and Equivocation.* Philosophers, even more than ordinary people, are prone to make startling and paradoxical claims that take the form of universal generalizations and hence resemble empirical hypotheses. For example, "All things are mental (there are no physical objects)," "All things are good (there is no evil)," "All voluntary behavior is selfish," etc. Let us confine our attention for the moment to the latter which is a rough statement of psy-chological egoism. At first sight, the statement "All voluntary behavior is selfish" seems

obviously false. One might reply to the psychological egoist in some such manner as this:

> I *know* some behavior, at least, is unselfish, because I saw my Aunt Emma yesterday give her last cent to a beggar. Now she will have to go a whole week with nothing to eat. Surely, *that* was not selfish of her.

Nevertheless, the psychological egoist is likely not to be convinced, and insist that, in this case, if we knew enough about Aunt Emma, we would learn that her primary motive in helping the beggar was to promote her own happiness or assuage her own conscience, or increase her own selfesteem, etc. We might then present the egoist with even more difficult cases for his theory—saints, martyrs, military heroes, patriots, and others who have sacrificed themselves for a cause. If psychological egoists nevertheless refuse to accept any of these as examples of unselfish behavior, then we have a right to be puzzled about what they are saying. Until we know what they would count as *unselfish* behavior, we can't very well know what they mean when they say that all voluntary behavior is *selfish*. And at this point we may suspect that they are holding their theory in a "privileged position"—that of immunity to evidence, that they would allow no *conceivable* behavior to count as evidence against it. What they say then, if true, must be true in virtue of the way they define—or redefine—the word "selfish." And in that case, it cannot be an empirical hypothesis.

If what the psychological egoist says is "true by redefinition," then I can "agree" with him and say "It is true that in *your* sense of the word 'selfish' my Aunt Emma's behavior was selfish; but in the ordinary sense of 'selfish,' which implies blameworthiness, she surely was not selfish." There is no point of course in arguing about a mere word. The important thing is not what particular words a person uses, but rather whether what he wishes to say in those words is true. Departures from ordinary language can often be justified by their utility for certain purposes; but they are dangerous when they invite equivocation. The psychological egoist may be saying something which is true when he says that Emma is selfish in *his* sense, but if he doesn't realize that his sense of "selfish" differs from the ordinary one, he may be tempted to infer that Emma is selfish in the ordinary sense which implies blameworthiness; and this of course would be unfair and illegitimate. It is indeed an extraordinary extension of the meaning of the word "self-indulgent" (as C. G. Chesterton remarks somewhere) which allows a philosopher to say that a man is self-indulgent when he wants to be burned at the stake.

19. *The Fallacy of the Suppressed Correlative.* Certain words in the English language operate in pairs—e.g., "selfish-unselfish," "good-bad," "large-small," "mental-physical." To assert that a thing has one of the above characteristics is to *contrast* it with the opposite in the pair. To know the meaning of one term in the pair, we must know the meaning of the correlative term with which it is contrasted. If we could not conceive of what it would be like for a thing to be bad, for example, then we could not possibly understand what is being said of a thing when it is called "good." Similarly, unless we had a notion of what it would be like for action to be *unselfish*, we could hardly understand the sentence "So-and-so acted selfishly"; for we would have nothing to contrast "selfishly" with. The so-called "fallacy of the suppressed correlative"[16] is committed by a person who consciously or unconsciously redefines one of the terms in a contrasting pair in such a way that its new meaning incorporates the sense of its correlative.

Webster's Collegiate Dictionary defines "selfish" (in part) as "regarding one's own comfort, advantage, etc. in disregard of, or at the expense of that of others." In this ordinary and proper sense of "selfish," Aunt Emma's action in giving her last cent to the beggar certainly was *not* selfish. Emma *disregarded* her *own* comfort (it is not "comfortable" to go a week without eating) and advantage (there is no "advantage" in malnutrition) *for the sake of* (not "at the expense of") another. Similarly, the martyr marching off to the stake is foregoing (not indulging) his "comfort" and indeed his very life for the sake of (not at the expense of) a cause. If Emma and the martyr then are "selfish," they must be so in a strange new sense of the word.

A careful examination of the egoist's arguments (see especially 4a above) reveals what new sense he gives to the word "selfish." He redefines the word so that it means (roughly) "motivated," or perhaps "intentional." "After all," says the egoist, "Aunt Emma had some *purpose* in giving the beggar all her money, and this purpose (desire, intention, motive, aim) was *her* purpose and no one else's. She was out to further some aim of her own, wasn't she? Therefore, she was pursuing her own ends (acting from her own motives); she was after something *for herself* in so acting, and that's what I mean by calling her action selfish. Moreover, all intentional action—action done 'on purpose,' deliberately from the agent's own motives—is selfish in the same sense." We can see now, from this reply, that since the egoist apparently means by "selfish" simply "motivated," when he says that all motivated action is selfish *he is not asserting a synthetic empirical hypothesis about human motives; rather, his statement is a tautology roughly equivalent to "all motivated actions are motivated."* And if that is the case, then what he says is true enough; but, like all tautologies, it is empty, uninteresting, and trivial.

Moreover, in redefining "selfish" in this way, the psychological egoist has committed the fallacy of the suppressed correlative. For what can we now contrast "selfish voluntary action" with? Not only are there no *actual* cases of unselfish voluntary actions on the new definition; there are not even any *theoretically possible* or *conceivable* cases of unselfish voluntary actions. And if we cannot even conceive of what an unselfish voluntary action would be like, how can we give any sense to the expression "selfish voluntary action"? The egoist, so to speak, has so blown up the sense of "selfish" that, like inflated currency, it will no longer buy anything.

20. *Psychological Egoism as a Linguistic Proposal.* There is still one way out for the egoist. He might admit that his theory is not really a psychological hypothesis about human nature designed to account for the facts and enable us to predict or anticipate future events. He may

even willingly concede that his theory is really a disguised redefinition of a word. Still, he might argue, he has made no claim to be giving an accurate description of actual linguistic usage. Rather, he is making a proposal to *revise* our usage in the interest of economy and convenience, just as the biologists once proposed that we change the ordinary meaning of "insect" in such a way that spiders are no longer called insects, and the ordinary meaning of "fish" so that whales and seals are no longer called fish.

What are we to say to this suggestion? First of all, stipulative definitions (proposals to revise usage) are never true or false. They are simply useful or not useful. Would it be useful to redefine "selfish" in the way the egoist recommends? It is difficult to see what would be gained thereby. The egoist has noticed some respects in which actions normally called "selfish" and actions normally called "unselfish" are alike, namely they are both motivated and they both can give satisfaction—either in prospect or in retrospect—to the agent. Because of these likenesses, the egoist feels justified in attaching the label "selfish" to *all* actions. Thus one word— "selfish"—must for him do the work of two words ("selfish" and "unselfish" in their old meanings); and, as a result, a very real distinction, that between actions for the sake of others and actions at the expense of others, can no longer be expressed in the language. Because the egoist has noticed some respects in which two types of actions are alike, he wishes to make it impossible to describe the respects in which they differ. It is difficult to see any utility in this state of affairs.

But suppose we adopt the egoist's "proposal" nevertheless. Now we would have to say that all actions are selfish; but, in addition, we would want to say that there are two different kinds of selfish actions, those which regard the interests of others and those which disregard the interests of others, and, furthermore, that only the latter are blameworthy. After a time our ear would adjust to the new uses of the word "selfish," and we would find nothing at all strange in such statements as "Some selfish actions are morally praiseworthy." After a while, we might even invent two new words, perhaps "selfitic" and "unselfitic," to distinguish the two important classes of "selfish" actions. Then we would be right back where we started, with new linguistic tools ("selfish" for "motivated," "selfitic" for "selfish," and "unselfitic" for "unselfish") to do the same old necessary jobs. That is, until some new egoistic philosopher arose to announce with an air of discovery that "All selfish behavior is really selfitic—there are no truly unselfitic selfish actions." Then, God help us!

NOTES

1. See his *Introduction to the Principles of Morals and Legislation* (1789), Chap. I, first paragraph: "Nature has placed mankind under the governance of two sovereign masters, *pain* and *pleasure*. It is for them alone to point out what we ought to do, as well as to determine what we shall do.... They govern us in all we do, in all we say, in all we think: every effort we can make to throw off our subjection will serve but to demonstrate and confirm it."

2. C. D. Broad, *Ethics and the History of Philosophy* (New York: The Humanities Press, 1952), Essay 10—"Egoism as a Theory of Human Motives," p. 218. This essay is highly recommended.

3. Austin Duncan-Jones, *Butler's Moral Philosophy* (London; Penguin Books, 1952), p. 96. Duncan-Jones goes on to reject this argument. See p. 512f.

4. Lucius Garvin, *A Modern Introduction to Ethics* (Boston: Houghton Mifflin, 1953), p. 37. Quoted here by permission of the author and publisher.

5. *Op. cit.*, Chap. III.

6. See Part D, 15 and 16, below.

7. *Op. cit.*, p. 39.

8. *The Principles of Psychology* (New York: Henry Holt, 1890), Vol. II, p. 558.

9. *Op. cit.*, p. 39.

10. Quoted from the *Springfield* (Illinois) *Monitor*, by F. C. Sharp in his *Ethics* (New York: Appleton-Century, 1928), p. 75.

11. See his *Fifteen Sermons on Human Nature Preached at the Rolls Chapel* (1726), especially the first and eleventh.

12. Whether or not there are some *a priori* statements that are not merely analytic, and hence *not* vacuous, is still a highly controversial question among philosophers.

13. Some philosophers (those called "rationalists") believe that there are some synthetic statements whose truth can be known *a priori* (see footnote 12). If they are right, then the statement above is not entirely accurate.

14. Again, subject to the qualification in footnotes 12 and 13.

15. The three examples given above all have the generic character there indicated, but they also differ from one another in various other ways, some of which are quite important. For our present purposes however, we can ignore the ways in which they differ from one another and concentrate on their common character as generalizations of experience ("inductive generalizations"). As such they are sharply contrasted with such a generalization as "All puppies are young dogs," which is analytic.

16. The phrase was coined by J. Lowenberg. See his article "What Is Empirical?" in the *Journal of Philosophy*, May 1940.

Ethical Egoism

JAMES RACHELS

James Rachel (1942–2003) is the author of The End of Life and numerous other books and articles on the problems of practical ethics. He taught philosophy at the University of Alabama at Birmingham for many years.

IS THERE A DUTY TO CONTRIBUTE FOR FAMINE RELIFE?

Each year millions of people die of malnutrition and related health problems. A common pattern among children in poor countries is death from dehydration caused by diarrhea brought on by malnutrition. James Grant, executive director of the United Nations Children's Fund (UNICEF), estimates that about 15,000 children die in this way *every day*. That comes to 5,475,000 children annually. Even if his estimate is too high, the number that die is staggering.

For those of us in the affluent countries, this poses an acute moral problem. We spend money on ourselves, not only for the necessities of life but for innumerable luxuries—for fine automobiles, fancy clothes, stereos, sports, movies, and so on. In our country, even people with modest incomes enjoy such things. The problem is that we *could* forgo our luxuries and give the money for famine relief instead. The fact that we don't suggests that we regard our luxuries as more important than feeding the hungry.

Why do we allow people to starve to death when we could save them? Very few of us actually believe our luxuries are that important. Most of us, if asked the question directly, would probably be a bit embarrassed, and we would say that we probably should do more for famine relief. The explanation of why we do not is, at least in part, that we hardly ever think of the problem. Living our own comfortable lives, we are effectively insulated from it. The starving people are dying at some distance from us; we do not see them, and we can avoid even thinking of them. When we do think of them, it is only abstractly, as bloodless statistics. Unfortunately for the starving, statistics do not have much power to motivate action.

But leaving aside the question of *why* we behave as we do, what is our *duty*? What *should* we do? We might think of this as the "common-sense" view of the matter: morality requires that we balance our own interests against the interests of others. It is understandable, of course, that we look out for our own interests, and no one can be faulted for attending to his own basic needs. But at the same time the needs of others are also important, and when we can help others—especially at little cost to ourselves—we should do so. Suppose you are thinking of spending ten dollars on a trip to the movies, when you are reminded that ten dollars could buy food for a starving child. Thus you could do a great service for the child at little cost to yourself. Common-sense morality would say, then, that you should give the money for famine relief rather than spending it on the movies.

This way of thinking involves a general assumption about our moral duties: it is assumed that we have moral duties *to other people*—and not merely duties that we create, such as by making a promise or incurring a debt. We have "natural" duties to others *simply because they are people who could be helped or harmed by our actions*. If a certain action would benefit (or harm) other people, then that is a reason why we should (or should not) do that action. The common-sense assumption is that other people's interests *count*, for their own sakes, from a moral point of view.

But one person's common sense is another person's naive platitude. Some thinkers have maintained that, in fact, we have no "natural" duties to other people. *Ethical Egoism* is the idea that each person ought to pursue his or her own self-interest exclusively. It is different from Psychological Egoism, which is a theory of human nature concerned with how people *do* behave—Psychological Egoism says that people do in fact always pursue their own interests. Ethical Egoism, by contrast, is a normative theory—that is, a theory about how we *ought* to behave. Regardless of how we do behave, Ethical Egoism says we have no moral duty except to do what is best for ourselves.

It is a challenging theory. It contradicts some of our deepest moral beliefs—beliefs held by most of us, at any rate—but it is not easy to refute. We will examine the most important arguments for and against it. If it turns out to be true, then of course that is immensely important. But even if it turns out to be false, there is still much to be learned from examining it—we may, for example, gain some insight into the reasons why we *do* have obligations to other people.

But before looking at the arguments, we should be a little clearer about exactly what this theory says and what it does not say. In the first place, Ethical Egoism does not say that one should promote one's own interests *as well as* the interests of others. That would be an ordinary, unexceptional view. Ethical Egoism is the radical view that one's *only* duty is to promote one's own interests. According to Ethical Egoism, there is only one ultimate principle of conduct, the principle of self-interest, and this principle sums up *all* of one's natural duties and obligations.

However, Ethical Egoism does not say that you should *avoid* actions that help others, either. It may very well be that in many instances your interests coincide with the interests of others, so that in helping yourself you will be aiding others willynilly. Or it may happen that aiding others is an effective *means* for creating some benefit for yourself. Ethical Egoism does not forbid such actions; in fact, it may demand them. The theory insists only that in such cases the benefit to others is not what makes the act right. What makes the act right is, rather, the fact that it is to one's own advantage.

Finally, Ethical Egoism does not imply that in pursuing one's interests one ought always to do what one wants to do, or what gives one the most pleasure in the short run. Someone may want to do something that is not good for himself or that will eventually cause himself more grief than pleasure—he may want to drink a lot or smoke cigarettes or take drugs or waste his best years at the race track. Ethical Egoism would frown on all this, regardless of the momentary pleasure it affords. It says that a person ought to do what *really is* to his or her own best advantage, *over the long run*. It endorses selfishness, but it doesn't endorse foolishness.

THREE ARGUMENTS IN FAVOR OF ETHICAL EGOISM

What reasons can be advanced to support this doctrine? Why should anyone think it is true? Unfortunately, the theory is asserted more often than it is argued for. Many of its supporters apparently think its truth is self-evident, so that arguments are not needed. When it *is* argued for, three lines of reasoning are most commonly used.

1. The first argument has several variations, each suggesting the same general point:

a. Each of us is intimately familiar with our own individual wants and needs. Moreover, each of us is uniquely placed to pursue those wants and needs effectively. At the same time, we know the desires and needs of other people only imperfectly, and we are not well situated to pursue them. Therefore, it is reasonable to believe that if we set out to be "our brother's keeper," we would often bungle the job and end up doing more mischief than good.

b. At the same time, the policy of "looking out for others" is an offensive intrusion into other people's privacy; it is essentially a policy of minding other people's business.

c. Making other people the object of one's "charity" is degrading to them; it robs them of their individual dignity and self-respect. The offer of charity says, in effect, that they are not competent to care for themselves; and the statement is self-fulfilling—they cease to be self-reliant and become passively dependent on others. That is why the recipients of "charity" are so often resentful rather than appreciative.

What this adds up to is that the policy of "looking out for others" is self-defeating. If we want to promote the best interests of everyone alike, we should *not* adopt so-called altruistic policies of behavior. On the contrary, if each person looks after his or her *own* interests, it is more likely that everyone will be better off, in terms of both physical and emotional well-being. Thus Robert G. Olson says in his book *The Morality of Self-Interest* (1965), "The individual is most likely to contribute to social betterment by rationally pursuing his own best long-range interests." Or as Alexander Pope said more poetically,

> Thus God and nature formed the general frame
> And bade self-love and social be the same.

It is possible to quarrel with this argument on a number of grounds. Of course no one favors bungling, butting in, or depriving people of their self-respect. But is this really what we are doing when we feed hungry children? Is the starving child in Ethiopia really harmed when we "intrude" into "her business" by supplying food? It hardly seems likely. Yet we can set this point aside, for considered as an argument for Ethical Egoism, this way of thinking has an even more serious defect.

The trouble is that it isn't really an argument *for Ethical Egoism* at all. The argument concludes that we should adopt certain policies of action; and on the surface they appear to be egoistic policies. However, the *reason* it is said we should adopt those policies is decidedly *un*egoistic. The reason is one that to an egoist shouldn't matter. It is said that we should adopt those policies because doing so will promote the "betterment of society"—but according to Ethical Egoism, that is something we should not be concerned about. Spelled out fully, with everything laid on the table, the argument says:

(1) We ought to do whatever will promote the best interests of everyone alike.
(2) The interests of everyone will best be promoted if each of us adopts the policy of pursuing our own interests exclusively.
(3) Therefore, each of us should adopt the policy of pursuing our own interests exclusively.

If we accept this reasoning, then we are not ethical egoists at all. Even though we might end up *behaving* like egoists, our ultimate principle is one of beneficence—we are doing what we think will help everyone, not merely what we think will benefit ourselves. Rather than being egoists, we turn out to be altruists with a peculiar view of what in fact promotes the general welfare.

2. The second argument was put forward with some force by Ayn Rand, a writer little heeded by professional philosophers but who nevertheless was enormously popular on college campuses during the 1960s and 1970s. Ethical Egoism, in her view, is the only ethical philosophy that respects the integrity of the individual human life. She regarded the ethics of "altruism" as a totally destructive idea, both in society as a whole and in the lives of individuals taken in by

it. Altruism, to her way of thinking, leads to a denial of the value of the individual. It says to a person: *your* life is merely something that may be sacrificed. "If a man accepts the ethics of altruism," she writes, "his first concern is not how to live his life, but how to sacrifice it." Moreover, those who would *promote* this idea are beneath contempt—they are parasites who, rather than working to build and sustain their own lives, leech off those who do. Again, she writes:

> Parasites, moochers, looters, brutes and thugs can be of no value to a human being—nor can he gain any benefit from living in a society geared to *their* needs, demands and protections, a society that treats him as a sacrificial animal and penalizes him for his virtues in order to reward *them* for their vices, which means: a society based on the ethics of altruism.

By "sacrificing one's life" Rand does not necessarily mean anything so dramatic as dying. A person's life consists (in part) of projects undertaken and goods earned and created. To demand that a person abandon his projects or give up his goods is also a clear effort to "sacrifice his life." Furthermore, throughout her writings Rand also suggests that there is a *metaphysical* basis for egoistic ethics. Somehow, it is the only ethics that takes seriously the *reality* of the individual person. She bemoans "the enormity of the extent to which altruism erodes men's capacity to grasp the value of an individual life; it reveals a mind from which the reality of a human being has been wiped out."

What, then, of the starving people? It might be argued, in response, that Ethical Egoism "reveals a mind from which the reality of a human being has been wiped out"—namely, the human being who is starving. Rand quotes with approval the evasive answer given by one of her followers: "Once, when Barbara Brandon was asked by a student: 'What will happen to the poor...?'—she answered: 'If *you* want to help them, you will not be stopped.'" All these remarks are, I think, part of one continuous argument that can be summarized like this:

1. A person has only one life to live. If we place any value on the individual—that is, if

the individual has any moral worth—then we must agree that this life is of supreme importance. After all, it is all one has, and all one is.

2. The ethics of altruism regards the life of the individual as something one must be ready to sacrifice for the good of others.

3. Therefore, the ethics of altruism does not take seriously the value of the human individual.

4. Ethical Egoism, which allows each person to view his or her own life as being of ultimate value, *does* take the human individual seriously—in fact, it is the only philosophy that does so.

5. Thus, Ethical Egoism is the philosophy that ought to be accepted.

The problem with this argument, as you may already have noticed, is that it relies on picturing the alternatives in such an extreme way. "The ethics of altruism" is taken to be such an extreme philosophy that *nobody*, with the possible exception of certain monks, would find it congenial. As Ayn Rand presents it, altruism implies that one's own interests have *no* value, and that *any* demand by others calls for sacrificing them. If that is the alternative, then any other view, including Ethical Egoism, will look good by comparison. But this is hardly a fair picture of the choices. What we called the common-sense view stands somewhere between the two extremes. It says that one's own interests and the interests of others are both important and must be balanced against one another. Sometimes, when the balancing is done, it will turn out that one should act in the interests of others; other times, it will turn out that one should take care of oneself. So even if the Randian argument refutes the extreme "ethics of altruism," it does not follow that one must accept the other extreme of Ethical Egoism.

3. The third line of reasoning takes a somewhat different approach. Ethical Egoism is usually presented as a *revisionist* moral philosophy, that is, as a philosophy that says our common-sense moral views are mistaken and need to be changed. It is possible, however, to interpret Ethical Egoism in a much less radical way, as a theory that *accepts* common-sense morality and offers a surprising account of its basis.

The less radical interpretation goes as follows. In everyday life, we assume that we are obliged to obey certain rules. We must avoid doing harm to others, speak the truth, keep our promises, and so on. At first glance, these duties appear to be very different from one another. They appear to have little in common. Yet from a theoretical point of view, we may wonder whether there is not some hidden *unity* underlying the hodgepodge of separate duties. Perhaps there is some small number of fundamental principles that explain all the rest, just as in physics there are basic principles that bring together and explain diverse phenomena. From a theoretical point of view, the smaller the number of basic principles, the better. Best of all would be *one* fundamental principle, from which all the rest could be derived. Ethical Egoism, then, would be the theory that all our duties are ultimately derived from the one fundamental principle of self-interest.

Taken in this way, Ethical Egoism is not such a radical doctrine. It does not challenge common-sense morality; it only tries to explain and systematize it. And it does a surprisingly successful job. It can provide plausible explanations of the duties mentioned above, and more:

a. If we make a habit of doing things that are harmful to other people, people will not be reluctant to do things that will harm *us*. We will be shunned and despised; others will not have us as friends and will not do us favors when we need them. If our offenses against others are serious enough, we may even end up in jail. Thus it is to our own advantage to avoid harming others.

b. If we lie to other people, we will suffer all the ill effects of a bad reputation. People will distrust us and avoid doing business with us. We will often need for people to be honest with us, but we can hardly expect them to feel much of an obligation to be honest with us if they know we have not been honest with them. Thus it is to our own advantage to be truthful.

c. It is to our own advantage to be able to enter into mutually beneficial arrangements with other people. To benefit from those arrangements, we need to be able to rely on others to keep their parts of the bargains we make with them—we need to be able to rely on them to keep their promises to us. But we can hardly expect others to keep their promises to us if we are not willing to keep our promises to them. Therefore, from the point of view of self-interest, we should keep our promises.

Pursuing this line of reasoning, Thomas Hobbes suggested that the principle of Ethical Egoism leads to nothing less than the Golden Rule: we should "do unto others" *because* if we do, others will be more likely to "do unto us."

Does this argument succeed in establishing Ethical Egoism as a viable theory of morality? It is, in my opinion at least, the best try. But there are two serious objections to it. In the first place, the argument does not prove quite as much as it needs to prove. At best, it shows only that *as a general rule* it is to one's own advantage to avoid harming others. It does not show that this is *always* so. And it could not show that, for even though it may usually be to one's advantage to avoid harming others, sometimes it is not. Sometimes one might even *gain* from treating another person badly. In that case, the obligation not to harm the other person could *not* be derived from the principle of Ethical Egoism. Thus it appears that not all our moral obligations can be explained as derivable from self-interest.

But set that point aside. There is still a more fundamental question to be asked about the proposed theory. Suppose it is true that, say, contributing money for famine relief is somehow to one's own advantage. It does not follow that this is the only reason, or even the most basic reason, why doing so is a morally good thing. (For example, the most basic reason might be *in order to help the starving people*. The fact that doing so is also to one's own advantage might be only a secondary, less important, consideration.) A demonstration that one could *derive* this duty from self-interest does not prove that self-interest is the *only reason* one has this duty. Only if you accept an additional proposition—namely, the proposition that there is no reason for giving *other than* self-interest—will you find Ethical Egoism a plausible theory.

THREE ARGUMENTS AGAINST ETHICAL EGOISM

Ethical Egoism has haunted twentieth-century moral philosophy. It has not been a popular doctrine; the most important philosophers have rejected it outright. But it has never been very far from their minds. Although no thinker of consequence has defended it, almost everyone has felt it necessary to explain why he was rejecting it—as though the very possibility that it might be correct was hanging in the air, threatening to smother their other ideas. As the merits of the various "refutations" have been debated, philosophers have returned to it again and again.

The following three arguments are typical of the refutations proposed by contemporary philosophers.

1. In his book *The Moral Point of View* (1958), Kurt Baier argues that Ethical Egoism cannot be correct because it cannot provide solutions for conflicts of interest. We need moral rules, he says, only because our interests sometimes come into conflict. (If they never conflicted, then there would be no problems to solve and hence no need for the kind of guidance that morality provides.) But Ethical Egoism does not help to resolve conflicts of interest; it only exacerbates them. Baier argues for this by introducing a fanciful example:

> Let B and K be candidates for the presidency of a certain country and let it be granted that it is in the interest of either to be elected, but that only one can succeed. It would then be in the interest of B but against the interest of K if B were elected, and vice versa, and therefore in the interest of B but against the interest of K if K were liquidated, and vice versa. But from this it would follow that B ought to liquidate K, that it is wrong for B not to do so, that B has not "done his duty" until he has liquidated K; and vice versa. Similarly K, knowing that his own liquidation is in the interest of B and therefore, anticipating B's attempts to secure it, ought to take steps to foil B's endeavors. It would be wrong for him not to do so. He would "not have done his duty" until he had made sure of stopping B. . . .

This is obviously absurd. For morality is designed to apply in just such cases, namely, those where interests conflict. But if the point of view of morality were that of self-interest, then there could never be moral solutions of conflicts of interest.

Does this argument prove that Ethical Egoism is unacceptable? It does, *if* the conception of morality to which it appeals is accepted. The argument assumes that an adequate morality must provide solutions for conflicts of interest in such a way that everyone concerned can live together harmoniously. The conflict between B and K, for example, should be resolved so that they would no longer be at odds with one another. (One would not then have a duty to do something that the other has a duty to prevent.) Ethical Egoism does not do that, and if you think an ethical theory should, then you will not find Ethical Egoism acceptable.

But a defender of Ethical Egoism might reply that *he* does not accept this conception of morality. For him, life is essentially a long series of conflicts in which each person is struggling to come out on top: and the principle he accepts—the principle of Ethical Egoism—simply urges each one to do his or her best to win. On his view, the moralist is not like a courtroom judge, who resolves disputes. Instead, he is like the Commissioner of Boxing, who urges each fighter to do his best. So the conflict between B and K will be "resolved" not by the application of an ethical theory but by one or the other of them winning the struggle. The egoist will not be embarrassed by this—on the contrary, he will think it no more than a realistic view of the nature of things.

2. Some philosophers, including Baier, have leveled an even more serious charge against Ethical Egoism. They have argued that it is a *logically inconsistent* doctrine—that is, they say it leads to logical contradictions. If this is true, then Ethical Egoism is indeed a mistaken theory, for no theory can be true if it is self-contradictory.

Consider B and K again. As Baier explains their predicament, it is in B's interest to kill K, and obviously it is in K's interest to prevent it. But, Baier says,

if K prevents B from liquidating him, his act must be said to be both wrong and not wrong—wrong because it is the prevention of what B ought to do, his duty, and wrong for B not to do it; not wrong because it is what K ought to do, his duty, and wrong for K not to do it. But one and the same act (logically) cannot be both morally wrong and not morally wrong.

Now, does *this* argument prove that Ethical Egoism is unacceptable? At first glance it seems persuasive. However, it is a complicated argument, so we need to set it out with each step individually identified. Then we will be in a better position to evaluate it. Spelled out fully, it looks like this:

1. Suppose it is each person's duty to do what is in his own best interests.
2. It is in B's best interest to liquidate K.
3. It is in K's best interest to prevent B from liquidating him.
4. Therefore B's duty is to liquidate K, and K's duty is to prevent B from doing it.
5. But it is wrong to prevent someone from doing his duty.
6. Therefore it is wrong for K to prevent B from liquidating him.
7. Therefore it is both wrong and not wrong for K to prevent B from liquidating him.
8. But no act can be both wrong and not wrong—that is a self-contradiction.
9. Therefore the assumption with which we started—that it is each person's duty to do what is in his own best interests—cannot be true.

When the argument is set out in this way, we can see its hidden flaw. The logical contradiction—that it is both wrong and not wrong for K to prevent B from liquidating him—does *not* follow simply from the principle of Ethical Egoism. It follows from that principle *and* the additional premise expressed in step (5)—namely, that "it is wrong to prevent someone from doing his duty." Thus we are not compelled by the logic of the argument to reject Ethical Egoism. Instead, we could simply reject this additional premise, and the contradiction would be avoided. That is surely what the ethical egoist would want to do, for the ethical egoist would never say, without qualification, that it is always wrong to prevent someone from doing his duty. He would say, instead, that *whether one ought to prevent someone from doing his duty depends entirely on whether it would be to one's own advantage to do so.* Regardless of whether we think this is a correct view, it is, at the very least, a *consistent* view, and so this attempt to convict the egoist of self-contradiction fails.

3. Finally, we come to the argument that I think comes closest to an outright refutation of Ethical Egoism. It is also the most interesting of the arguments, because at the same time it provides the most insight into why the interests of other people *should* matter to a moral agent.

Before this argument is presented, we need to look briefly at a general point about moral values. So let us set Ethical Egoism aside for a moment and consider this related matter.

There is a whole family of moral views that have this in common: they all involve dividing people into groups and saying that the interests of some groups count for more than the interests of other groups. Racism is the most conspicuous example; it involves dividing people into groups according to race and assigning greater importance to the interests of one race than to others. The practical result is that members of the preferred race are to be *treated better* than the others. Anti-Semitism works the same way, and so can nationalism. People in the grip of such views will think, in effect: "*My* race counts for more," or "Those who believe in *my* religion count for more," or "*My* country counts for more," and so on.

Can such views be defended? Those who accept them are usually not much interested in argument—racists, for example, rarely try to offer rational grounds for their position. But suppose they did. What could they say?

There is a general principle that stands in the way of any such defense, namely: *We can justify treating people differently only if we can show that there is some factual difference between them that is relevant to justifying the difference in*

treatment. For example, if one person is admitted to law school while another is rejected, this can be justified by pointing out that the first graduated from college with honors and scored well on the admissions test, while the second dropped out of college and never took the test. However, if *both* graduated with honors and did well on the entrance examination—in other words, if they are in all relevant respects equally well qualified—then it is merely arbitrary to admit one but not the other.

Can a racist point to any differences between, say, white people and black people that would justify treating them differently? In the past, racists have sometimes attempted to do this by picturing blacks as stupid, lacking in ambition, and the like. *If* this were true, then it might justify treating them differently, in at least some circumstances. (This is the deep purpose of racist stereotypes—to provide the "relevant differences" needed to justify differences in treatment.) But of course it is not true, and in fact there are no such general differences between the races. Thus racism is an *arbitrary* doctrine, in that it advocates treating some people differently even though there are no differences between them to justify it.

Ethical Egoism is a moral theory of the same type. It advocates that each of us divide the world into two categories of people—ourselves and all the rest—and that we regard the interests of those in the first group as more important than the interests of those in the second group. But each of us can ask, what is the difference between myself and others that justifies placing myself in this special category? Am I more intelligent? Do I enjoy my life more? Are my accomplishments greater? Do I have needs or abilities that are so different from the needs or abilities of others? *What is it that makes me so special?* Failing an answer, it turns out that Ethical Egoism is an arbitrary doctrine, in the same way that racism is arbitrary.

The argument, then, is this:

1. Any moral doctrine that assigns greater importance to the interests of one group than to those of another is unacceptably arbitrary

unless there is some difference between the members of the groups that justifies treating them differently.

2. Ethical Egoism would have each person assign greater importance to his or her own interests than to the interests of others. *But there is no general difference between oneself and others, to which each person can appeal, that justifies this difference in treatment.*

3. Therefore, Ethical Egoism is unacceptably arbitrary.

And this, in addition to arguing against Ethical Egoism, also sheds some light on the question of why we should care about others.

We should care about the interests of other people *for the very same reason we care about our own interests;* for their needs and desires are comparable to our own. Consider, one last time, the starving people we could feed by giving up some of our luxuries. Why should we care about them? We care about ourselves, of course—if *we* were starving, we would go to almost any lengths to get food. But what is the difference between us and them? Does hunger affect them any less? Are they somehow less deserving than we? If we can find no relevant difference between us and them, then we must admit that if *our* needs should be met, so should *theirs.* It is this realization, that we are on a par with one another, that is the deepest reason why our morality must include some recognition of the needs of others, and why, then, Ethical Egoism fails as a moral theory.

The Immoralist's Challenge

PLATO

Plato (427?–347 B.C.E.) lived and taught in Athens. Most of his surviving works have the form of fictitious dialogues between Socrates (who had been his teacher) and other Greek contemporaries.

When I said this, I thought I had done with the discussion, but it turned out to have been only a prelude. Glaucon showed his characteristic courage on this occasion too and refused to accept Thrasymachus' abandonment of the argument. Socrates, he said, do you want to seem to have persuaded us that it is better in every way to be just than unjust, or do you want truly to convince us of this?

I want truly to convince you, I said, if I can.

Well, then, you certainly aren't doing what you want. Tell me, do you think there is a kind of good we welcome, not because we desire what comes from it, but because we welcome it for its own sake—joy, for example, and all the harmless pleasures that have no results beyond the joy of having them?

Certainly, I think there are such things.

And is there a kind of good we like for its own sake and also for the sake of what comes from it—knowing, for example, and seeing and being healthy? We welcome such things, I suppose, on both counts.

Yes.

And do you also see a third kind of good, such as physical training,[1] medical treatment

From Plato, *The Republic, Bk. II* 357A–367E, trans. G. M. A. Grube, revised by C. D. C. Reeve (Hackett Publishing Company. 1992). Reprinted by permission of Hackett Publishing Company, Inc. All rights reserved.

when sick, medicine itself, and the other ways of making money? We'd say that these are onerous but beneficial to us, and we wouldn't choose them for their own sakes, but for the sake of the rewards and other things that come from them.

There is also this third kind. But what of it?

Where do you put justice?

I myself put it among the finest goods, as something to be valued by anyone who is going to be blessed with happiness, both because of itself and because of what comes from it.

That isn't most people's opinion. They'd say that justice belongs to the onerous kind, and is to be practiced for the sake of the rewards and popularity that come from a reputation for justice, but is to be avoided because of itself as something burdensome.

I know that's the general opinion. Thrasymachus faulted justice on these grounds a moment ago and praised injustice, but it seems that I'm a slow learner.

Come, then, and listen to me as well, and see whether you still have that problem, for I think that Thrasymachus gave up before he had to, charmed by you as if he were a snake. But I'm not yet satisfied by the argument on either side. I want to know what justice and injustice are and what power each itself has when it's by itself in the soul. I want to leave out of account their rewards and what comes from each of them. So, if you agree, I'll renew the argument of Thrasymachus. First, I'll state what kind of thing people consider justice to be and what its origins are. Second, I'll argue that all who practice it do so unwillingly, as something necessary, not as something good. Third, I'll argue that they have good reason to act as they do, for the life of an unjust person is, they say, much better than that of a just one.

It isn't, Socrates, that I believe any of that myself. I'm perplexed, indeed, and my ears are deafened listening to Thrasymachus and countless others. But I've yet to hear anyone defend justice in the way I want, proving that it is better than injustice. I want to hear it praised *by itself*, and I think that I'm most likely to hear this from you. Therefore, I'm going to speak at length in praise of the unjust life, and in doing so I'll show you the way I want to hear you praising justice and denouncing injustice. But see whether you want me to do that or not.

I want that most of all. Indeed, what subject could someone with any understanding enjoy discussing more often?

Excellent. Then let's discuss the first subject I mentioned—what justice is and what its origins are.

They say that to do injustice is naturally good and to suffer injustice bad, but that the badness of suffering it so far exceeds the goodness of doing it that those who have done and suffered injustice and tasted both, but who lack the power to do it and avoid suffering it, decide that it is profitable to come to an agreement with each other neither to do injustice nor to suffer it. As a result, they begin to make laws and covenants, and what the law commands they call lawful and just. This, they say, is the origin and essence of justice. It is intermediate between the best and the worst. The best is to do injustice without paying the penalty; the worst is to suffer it without being able to take revenge. Justice is a mean between these two extremes. People value it not as a good but because they are too weak to do injustice with impunity. Someone who has the power to do this, however, and is a true man wouldn't make an agreement with anyone not to do injustice in order not to suffer it. For him that would be madness. This is the nature of justice, according to the argument, Socrates, and these are its natural origins.

We can see most clearly that those who practice justice do it unwillingly and because they lack the power to do injustice, if in our thoughts we grant to a just and an unjust person the freedom to do whatever they like. We can then follow both of them and see where their desires would lead. And we'll catch the just person red-handed travelling the same road as the unjust. The reason for this is the desire to outdo others and get more and more.[2] This is what anyone's nature naturally pursues as good, but nature is forced by law into the perversion of treating fairness with respect.

The freedom I mentioned would be most easily realized if both people had the power they say the ancestor of Gyges of Lydia possessed. The story goes that he was a shepherd in the service of the ruler of Lydia. There was a violent thunderstorm, and an earthquake broke open the ground and created a chasm at the place where he was tending his sheep. Seeing this, he was filled with amazement and went down into it. And there, in addition to many other wonders of which we're told, he saw a hollow bronze horse. There were windowlike openings in it, and, peeping in, he saw a corpse, which seemed to be of more than human size, wearing nothing but a gold ring on its finger. He took the ring and came out of the chasm. He wore the ring at the usual monthly meeting that reported to the king on the state of the flocks. And as he was sitting among the others, he happened to turn the setting of the ring towards himself to the inside of his hand. When he did this, he became invisible to those sitting near him, and they went on talking as if he had gone. He wondered at this, and, fingering the ring, he turned the setting outwards again and became visible. So he experimented with the ring to test whether it indeed had this power—and it did. If he turned the setting inward, he became invisible; if he turned it outward, he became visible again. When he realized this, he at once arranged to become one of the messengers sent to report to the king. And when he arrived there, he seduced the king's wife, attacked the king with her help, killed him, and took over the kingdom.

Let's suppose, then, that there were two such rings, one worn by a just and the other by an unjust person. Now, no one, it seems, would be so incorruptible that he would stay on the path of justice or stay away from other people's property, when he could take whatever he wanted from the marketplace with impunity, go into people's houses and have sex with anyone he wished, kill or release from prison anyone he wished, and do all the other things that would make him like a god among humans. Rather his actions would be in no way different from those of an unjust person, and both would follow the same path. This, some would say, is a great proof that one is never just willingly but only when compelled to be. No one believes justice to be a good when it is kept private, since, wherever either person thinks he can do injustice with impunity, he does it. Indeed, every man believes that injustice is far more profitable to himself than justice. And any exponent of this argument will say he's right, for someone who didn't want to do injustice, given this sort of opportunity, and who didn't touch other people's property would be thought wretched and stupid by everyone aware of the situation, though, of course, they'd praise him in public, deceiving each other for fear of suffering injustice. So much for my second topic.

As for the choice between the lives we're discussing, we'll be able to make a correct judgment about that only if we separate the most just and the most unjust. Otherwise we won't be able to do it. Here's the separation I have in mind. We'll subtract nothing from the injustice of an unjust person and nothing from the justice of a just one, but we'll take each to be complete in his own way of life. First, therefore, we must suppose that an unjust person will act as clever craftsmen do: A first-rate captain or doctor, for example, knows the difference between what his craft can and can't do. He attempts the first but lets the second go by, and if he happens to slip, he can put things right. In the same way, an unjust person's successful attempts at injustice must remain undetected, if he is to be fully unjust. Anyone who is caught should be thought inept, for the extreme of injustice is to be believed to be just without being just. And our completely unjust person must be given complete injustice; nothing may be subtracted from it. We must allow that, while doing the greatest injustice, he has nonetheless provided himself with the greatest reputation for justice. If he happens to make a slip, he must be able to put it right. If any of his unjust activities should be discovered, he must be able to speak persuasively or to use force. And if force is needed, he must have the help of courage and strength and of the substantial wealth and friends with which he has provided himself.

Having hypothesized such a person, let's now in our argument put beside him a just man, who is simple and noble and who, as Aeschylus says, doesn't want to be believed to be good but to be so.[3] We must take away his reputation, for a reputation for justice would bring him honor and rewards, so that it wouldn't be clear whether he is just for the sake of justice itself or for the sake of those honors and rewards. We must strip him of everything except justice and make his situation the opposite of an unjust person's. Though he does no injustice, he must have the greatest reputation for it, so that his justice may be tested fullstrength and not diluted by wrong-doing and what comes from it. Let him stay like that unchanged until he dies—just, but all his life believed to be unjust. In this way, both will reach the extremes, the one of justice and the other of injustice, and we'll be able to judge which of them is happier.

Whew! Glaucon, I said, how vigorously you've scoured each of the men for our competition, just as you would a pair of statues for an art competition.

I do the best I can, he replied. Since the two are as I've described, in any case, it shouldn't be difficult to complete the account of the kind of life that awaits each of them, but it must be done. And if what I say sounds crude, Socrates, remember that it isn't I who speak but those who praise injustice at the expense of justice. They'll say that a just person in such circumstances will be whipped, stretched on a rack, chained, blinded with fire, and, at the end, when he has suffered every kind of evil, he'll be impaled, and will realize then that one shouldn't want to be just but to be believed to be just. Indeed, Aeschylus' words are far more correctly applied to unjust people than to just ones, for the supporters of injustice will say that a really unjust person, having a way of life based on the truth about things and not living in accordance with opinion, doesn't want simply to be believed to be unjust but actually to be so—

Harvesting a deep furrow in his mind,
Where wise counsels propagate.

He rules his city because of his reputation for justice; he marries into any family he wishes; he gives his children in marriage to anyone he wishes; he has contracts and partnerships with anyone he wants; and besides benefiting himself in all these ways, he profits because he has no scruples about doing injustice. In any contest, public or private, he's the winner and outdoes[4] his enemies. And by outdoing them, he becomes wealthy, benefiting his friends and harming his enemies. He makes adequate sacrifices to the gods and sets up magnificent offerings to them. He takes better care of the gods, therefore, (and, indeed, of the human beings he's fond of) than a just person does. Hence it's likely that the gods, in turn, will take better care of him than of a just person. That's what they say, Socrates, that gods and humans provide a better life for unjust people than for just ones.

When Glaucon had said this, I had it in mind to respond, but his brother Adeimantus intervened: You surely don't think that the position has been adequately stated?

Why not? I said.

The most important thing to say hasn't been said yet.

Well, then, I replied, a man's brother must stand by him, as the saying goes.[5] If Glaucon has omitted something, you must help him. Yet what he has said is enough to throw me to the canvas and make me unable to come to the aid of justice.

Nonsense, he said. Hear what more I have to say, for we should also fully explore the arguments that are opposed to the ones Glaucon gave, the ones that praise justice and find fault with injustice, so that what I take to be his intention may be clearer.

When fathers speak to their sons, they say that one must be just, as do all the others who have charge of anyone. But they don't praise justice itself, only the high reputations it leads to and the consequences of being thought to be just, such as the public offices, marriages, and other things Glaucon listed. But they elaborate even further on the consequences of reputation. By bringing in the esteem of the gods, they are able to talk about the abundant good things that they themselves and the noble Hesiod and Homer say that the gods give to the pious,[6] for Hesiod says that the gods make the oak trees

> Bear acorns at the top and bees in the middle
> And make fleecy sheep heavy laden with wool

for the just, and tells of many other good things akin to these. And Homer is similar:

> When a good king, in his piety,
> Upholds justice, the black earth bears
> Wheat and barley for him, and his trees are
> heavy with fruit.
> His sheep bear lambs unfailingly, and the sea
> yields up its fish.

Musaeus and his son make the gods give the just more headstrong goods than these.[7] In their stories, they lead the just to Hades, seat them on couches, provide them with a symposium of pious people, crown them with wreaths, and make them spend all their time drinking—as if they thought drunkenness was the finest wage of virtue. Others stretch even further the wages that virtue receives from the gods, for they say that someone who is pious and keeps his promises leaves his children's children and a whole race behind him. In these and other similar ways, they praise justice. They bury the impious and unjust in mud in Hades; force them to carry water in a sieve; bring them into bad repute while they're still alive, and all those penalties that Glaucon gave to the just person they give to the unjust. But they have nothing else to say. This, then, is the way people praise justice and find fault with injustice.

Besides this, Socrates, consider another form of argument about justice and injustice employed both by private individuals and by poets. All go on repeating with one voice that justice and moderation are fine things, but hard and onerous, while licentiousness and injustice are sweet and easy to acquire and are shameful only in opinion and law. They add that unjust deeds are for the most part more profitable than just ones, and, whether in public or private, they willingly honor vicious people who have wealth and other types of power and declare them to be happy. But they dishonor and disregard the weak and the poor, even though they agree that they are better than the others.

But the most wonderful of all these arguments concerns what they have to say about the gods and virtue. They say that the gods, too, assign misfortune and a bad life to many good people, and the opposite fate to their opposites. Begging priests and prophets frequent the doors of the rich and persuade them that they possess a god-given power founded on sacrifices and incantations. If the rich person or any of his ancestors has committed an injustice, they can fix it with pleasant rituals. Moreover, if he wishes to injure some enemy, then, at little expense, he'll be able to harm just and unjust alike, for by means of spells and enchantments they can persuade the gods to serve them. And the poets are brought forward as witnesses to all these accounts. Some harp on the ease of vice, as follows:

> Vice in abundance is easy to get;
> The road is smooth and begins beside you,
> But the gods have put sweat between us and virtue,

and a road that is long, rough, and steep.[8] Others quote Homer to bear witness that the gods can be influenced by humans, since he said:

> The gods themselves can be swayed by prayer,
> And with sacrifices and soothing promises,
> Incense and libations, human beings turn them
> from their purpose
> When someone has transgressed and sinned.[9]

And they present a noisy throng of books by Musaeus and Orpheus, offspring as they say of Selene and the Muses, in accordance with which they perform their rituals.[10] And they persuade not only individuals but whole cities that the unjust deeds of the living or the dead can be absolved or purified through sacrifices and pleasant games. These initiations, as they call them, free people from punishment hereafter, while a terrible fate awaits the uninitiated.

When all such sayings about the attitudes of gods and humans to virtue and vice are so often repeated, Socrates, what effect do you suppose they have on the souls of young people? I mean those who are clever and are able to flit from one of these sayings to another, so to speak, and gather from them an impression of what sort of person he should be and of how best to travel the road of life. He would surely ask himself Pindar's question, "Should I by justice or by crooked deceit scale this high wall and live my life guarded and secure?" And he'll answer: "The various sayings suggest that there is no advantage in my being just if I'm not also thought just, while the troubles and penalties of being just are apparent. But they tell me that an unjust person, who has secured for himself a reputation for justice, lives the life of a god. Since, then, 'opinion forcibly overcomes truth' and 'controls happiness,' as the wise men say, I must surely turn entirely to it.[11] I should create a façade of illusory virtue around me to deceive those who come near, but keep behind it the greedy and crafty fox of the wise Archilochus."[12]

"But surely," someone will object, "it isn't easy for vice to remain always hidden." We'll reply that nothing great is easy. And, in any case, if we're to be happy, we must follow the path indicated in these accounts. To remain undiscovered we'll form secret societies and political clubs. And there are teachers of persuasion to make us clever in dealing with assemblies and law courts. Therefore, using persuasion in one place and force in another, we'll outdo others[13] without paying a penalty.

"What about the gods? Surely, we can't hide from them or use violent force against them!" Well, if the gods don't exist or don't concern themselves with human affairs, why should we worry at all about hiding from them? If they do exist and do concern themselves with us, we've learned all we know about them from the laws and the poets who give their genealogies—nowhere else. But these are the very people who tell us that the gods can be persuaded and influenced by sacrifices, gentle prayers, and offerings. Hence, we should believe them on both matters or neither. If we believe them, we should be unjust and offer sacrifices from the fruits of our injustice. If we are just, our only gain is not to be punished by the gods, since we lose the profits of injustice. But if we are unjust, we get the profits of our crimes and transgressions and afterwards persuade the gods by prayer and escape without punishment.

"But in Hades won't we pay the penalty for crimes committed here, either ourselves or our children's children?" "My friend," the young man will say as he does his calculation, "mystery rites have great power and the gods have great power of absolution. The greatest cities tell us this, as do those children of the gods who have become poets and prophets."

Why, then, should we still choose justice over the greatest injustice? Many eminent authorities agree that, if we practice such injustice with a false façade, we'll do well at the hands of gods and humans, living and dying as we've a mind to. So, given all that has been said, Socrates, how is it possible for anyone of any power—whether of mind, wealth, body, or birth—to be willing to honor justice and not laugh aloud when he hears it praised? Indeed, if anyone can show that what we've said is false and has adequate knowledge that justice is best, he'll surely be full not of anger but of forgiveness for the unjust. He knows that, apart from someone of godlike character who is disgusted by injustice or one who has gained knowledge and avoids injustice for that reason, no one is just willingly. Through cowardice or old age or some other weakness, people do indeed object to injustice. But it's obvious that they do so only because they lack the power to do injustice, for the first of them to acquire it is the first to do as much injustice as he can.

And all of this has no other cause than the one that led Glaucon and me to say to you: "Socrates, of all of you who claim to praise justice, from the original heroes of old whose words survive, to the men of the present day, not one has ever blamed injustice or praised justice except by mentioning the reputations, honors, and rewards that are their consequences. No one has ever adequately described what each itself does of its own power by its presence in the soul of the person who possesses it, even if it remains hidden from gods and humans. No one, whether in poetry or in private conversations, has adequately argued that injustice is the worst thing a soul can have in it and that justice is the greatest good. If you had treated the subject in this way and persuaded us from youth, we wouldn't now be guarding against one another's injustices, but each would be his own best guardian, afraid that by doing injustice he'd be living with the worst thing possible."

Thrasymachus or anyone else might say what we've said, Socrates, or maybe even more, in discussing justice and injustice—crudely inverting their powers, in my opinion. And, frankly, it's because I want to hear the opposite from you that I speak with all the force I can muster. So don't merely give us a theoretical argument that justice is stronger than injustice, but tell us what each itself does, because of its own powers, to someone who possesses it, that makes injustice bad and justice good. Follow Glaucon's advice, and don't take reputations into account, for if you don't deprive justice and injustice of their true reputations and attach false ones to them, we'll say that you are not praising them but their reputations and that you're encouraging us to be unjust in secret. In that case, we'll say that you agree with Thrasymachus that justice is the good of another, the advantage of the stronger, while injustice is one's own advantage and profit, though not the advantage of the weaker.

You agree that justice is one of the greatest goods, the ones that are worth getting for the sake of what comes from them, but much more so for their own sake, such as seeing, hearing, knowing, being healthy, and all other goods that are fruitful by their own nature and not simply because of reputation. Therefore, praise justice as a good of that kind, explaining how—because of its very self—it benefits its possessors and how injustice harms them. Leave wages and reputations for others to praise.

Others would satisfy me if they praised justice and blamed injustice in that way, extolling the wages of one and denigrating those of the other. But you, unless you order me to be satisfied, wouldn't, for you've spent your whole life investigating this and nothing else. Don't, then, give us only a theoretical argument that justice is stronger than injustice, but show what effect each has because of itself on the person who has it—the one for good and the other for bad—whether it remains hidden from gods and human beings or not.

NOTES

1. "Music" or "music and poetry" and "physical training" are more transliterations than translations of *mousikē* and *gymnastikē,* which have no English equivalents. It is clear from Plato's discussion, for example, that *mousikē* includes poetry and stories, as well as music proper, and that *gymnastikē* includes dance and training in warfare, as well as what we call physical training. The aims of *mousikē* and *gymnastikē* are characterized at 522a. For further discussion see F. A. G. Beck, *Greek Education 430–350 B.C.* (London: Methuen, 1964).
2. *Pleonexian.* See 343e n. 18.
3. In *Seven Against Thebes,* 592–94, it is said of Amphiaraus that "he did not wish to be believed to be the best but to be it." The passage continues with the words Glaucon quotes below at 362a–b.
4. *pleonektein.* See 343e n. 18.
5. See Homer, *Odyssey* 16.97–98.
6. The two quotations which follow are from Hesiod, *Works and Days* 332–33, and Homer, *Odyssey* 19.109.
7. Musaeus was a legendary poet closely associated with the mystery religion of Orphism.
8. *Works and Days* 287–89, with minor alterations.
9. *Iliad* 9.497–501, with minor alterations.
10. It is not clear whether Orpheus was a real person or a mythical figure. His fame in Greek myth rests on the poems in which the doctrines of the Orphic religion are set forth. These are discussed in W. Burkert, *Greek Religion* (Cambridge: Harvard University Press, 1985). Musaeus was a mythical singer closely related to Orpheus. Selene is the Moon.
11. The quotation is attributed to Simonides, whom Polemarchus cites in Book I.
12. Archilochus of Paros (c. 756–16 B.C.), was an iambic and elegiac poet who composed a famous fable about the fox and the hedgehog.
13. *Pleonektountes.* See 343e n. 18.

Master and Slave Morality

FRIEDRICH NIETZSCHE

Friedrich Nietzsche (1844–1900) was a brilliant classicist and philosopher, whose criticisms of conventional morality have played an important role in the development of twentieth-century thought.

201

As long as herd utility is the only utility governing moral value judgments, as long as the preservation of the community is the only thing in view and questions concerning immorality are limited to those things that seem to threaten the survival of the community; as long as this is the case, there cannot yet be a "morality of neighbor love." Suppose that even here, consideration, pity, propriety, gentleness, and reciprocity of aid are already practiced in a small but steady way; suppose that even in this state of society, all the drives that would later come to be called by the honorable name of "virtues" (and, in the end, basically coincide with the concept of "morality")—suppose that they are already active: at this point they still do not belong to the realm of moral valuations at all—they are still *extra-moral*. During the best days of Rome, for instance, an act done out of pity was not called either good or evil, moral or immoral; and if it were praised on its own, the praise would be perfectly compatible with a type of reluctant disdain as soon as it was held up against any action that served to promote the common good, the *res publica*.[1] Ultimately, the "love of the neighbor" is always somewhat conventional, willfully feigned and beside the point compared to *fear of the neighbor*. After the structure of society seems on the whole to be established and secured against external dangers, it is this fear of the neighbor that again creates new perspectives of moral valuation. Until now, in the spirit of common utility, certain strong and dangerous drives such as enterprise, daring, vindictiveness, cunning, rapacity, and a domineering spirit must have been not only honored (under different names than these of course), but nurtured and cultivated (since, given the threats to the group, they were constantly needed against the common enemies). Now, however, since there are no more escape valves for these drives, they are seen as twice as dangerous and, one by one, they are denounced as immoral and abandoned to slander. Now the opposite drives and inclinations come into moral favor; step by step, the herd instinct draws its conclusion. How much or how little danger there is to the community or to equality in an opinion, in a condition or affect, in a will, in a talent, this is now the moral perspective: and fear is once again the mother of morality. When the highest and strongest drives erupt in passion, driving the individual up and out and far above the average, over the depths of the herd conscience, the self-esteem of the community is destroyed—its faith in itself, its backbone, as it were, is broken: as a result, these are the very drives that will be denounced and slandered the most. A high, independent spiritedness, a will to stand alone, even an excellent faculty of reason, will be perceived as a threat. Everything that raises the individual over the herd and frightens the neighbor will henceforth be called *evil*; the proper, modest, unobtrusive, equalizing attitude and the *mediocrity* of desires acquire moral names and honors. Finally, in very peaceable circumstances there are fewer and fewer opportunities and less and less need to nurture an instinct for severity

---

From Rolf-Peter Horstmann and Judith Norman, eds., Friedrich Nietzsche, *Beyond Good and Evil*, translated by Judith Norman. Reprinted by permission of Cambridge University Press.

or hardness; and now every severity starts disturbing the conscience, even where justice is concerned. A high and hard nobility and self-reliance is almost offensive, and provokes suspicion; "the lamb," and "the sheep" even more, gains respect.—There is a point in the history of a society when it becomes pathologically enervated and tenderized and it takes sides, quite honestly and earnestly, with those who do it harm, with *criminals*. Punishment: that seems somehow unjust to this society,—it certainly finds the thoughts of "punishment" and "needing to punish" both painful and frightening. "Isn't it enough to render him *unthreatening*? Why punish him as well? Punishment is itself fearful!"—with these questions, the herd morality, the morality of timidity, draws its final consequences. If the threat, the reason for the fear, could be totally abolished, this morality would be abolished as well: it would not be necessary any more, it would not *consider itself* necessary any more! Anyone who probes the conscience of today's European will have to extract the very same imperative from a thousand moral folds and hiding places, the imperative of herd timidity: "we want the day to come when there is *nothing more to fear!*" The day to come—the will and way *to that day* is now called "progress" everywhere in Europe.

202

Let us immediately repeat what we have already said a hundred times before, since there are no ready ears for such truths—for *our* truths— these days. We know all too well how offensive it sounds when someone classifies human beings as animals, without disguises or allegory; and we are considered almost *sinful* for constantly using expressions like "herd," and "herd instinct" with direct reference to people of "modern ideas." So what? We cannot help ourselves, since this is where our new insights happen to lie. Europe, we have found, has become unanimous in all major moral judgments; and this includes the countries under Europe's influence. People in Europe clearly *know* what Socrates claimed not to know, and what that famous old snake once promised to teach,—people these days "know" what is good and evil. Now it must sound harsh and strike the ear quite badly when we keep insisting on the following point: what it is that claims to know here, what glorifies itself with its praise and reproach and calls itself good is the instinct of the herd animal man, which has come to the fore, gaining and continuing to gain predominance and supremacy over the other instincts, in accordance with the growing physiological approach and approximation whose symptom it is. *Morality in Europe these days is the morality of herd animals:*—and therefore, as we understand things, it is only one type of human morality beside which, before which, and after which many other (and especially *higher*) moralities are or should be possible. But this morality fights tooth and nail against such a "possibility" and such a "should": it stubbornly and ruthlessly declares "I am morality itself and nothing else is moral!" And in fact, with the aid of a religion that indulged and flattered the loftiest herd desires, things have reached the point where this morality is increasingly apparent in even political and social institutions: the *democratic* movement is the heir to Christianity. But there are indications that the tempo of this morality is still much too slow and lethargic for those who have less patience, those who are sick or addicted to the above-mentioned instinct. This is attested to by the increasingly frantic howling, the increasingly undisguised snarling of the anarchist dogs that now wander the alleyways of European culture, in apparent opposition to the peaceable and industrious democrats and ideologists of revolution, and still more to the silly philosophasters and brotherhood enthusiasts who call themselves socialists and want a "free society." But, in fact, they are one and all united in thorough and instinctive hostility towards all forms of society besides that of the *autonomous* herd (even to the point of rejecting the concepts of "master" and "slave"—*ni dieu ni maître*[2] reads a socialist formula—); they are united in their dogged opposition to any special claims, special rights, or privileges (which means, in the last analysis, that they are opposed to *any* rights: since when everyone is equal, no one will need "rights" anymore—); they are united in their mistrust of punitive justice (as if it were a violation of those who are weaker, a wrong against the *necessary* result of all earlier societies—); but they are likewise united in the religion of pity, in sympathy for whatever feels, lives, suffers (down to the animal and up to "God":—the excessive notion of "pity for God" belongs in a democratic age—); they are all united in the cries and the impatience of pity, in deadly hatred against suffering in general, in the almost feminine inability to sit watching, to *let* suffering happen; they are united in the way they involuntarily raise the general level of sensitivity and gloom under whose spell Europe seems threatened with a new Buddhism; they are united in their faith in the morality of *communal* pity, as if it were morality in itself, the height, the *achieved* height of humanity, the sole hope for the future, the solace of the present, the great redemption of all guilt from the past:—they are all united in their faith in the community as *Redeemer,* which is to say: in the herd, in "themselves" . . .

203

We who have a different faith—, we who consider the democratic movement to be not merely an abased form of political organization, but rather an abased (more specifically a diminished) form of humanity, a mediocritization and depreciation of humanity in value: where do *we* need to reach with our hopes?—Towards *new philosophers,* there is no alternative; towards spirits who are strong and original enough to give impetus to opposed valuations and initiate a revaluation and reversal of "eternal values"; towards those sent out ahead; towards the men of the future who in the present tie the knots and gather the force that compels the will of millennia into *new* channels. To teach humanity its future as its *will,* as dependent on a human will, to prepare for the great risk and wholesale attempt at breeding and cultivation and so to put an end to the gruesome rule of chance and nonsense that has passed for "history" so far (the nonsense of the "greatest number" is only its latest form): a new type of philosopher and commander will be needed for this some day, and whatever hidden, dreadful, or benevolent spirits have existed on earth will pale into insignificance beside the image of this type. The image of such leaders hovers before

our eyes:—may I say this out loud, you free spirits? The conditions that would have to be partly created and partly exploited for them to come into being; the probable paths and trials that would enable a soul to grow tall and strong enough to feel the *compulsion* for these tasks; a revaluation of values whose new pressure and hammer will steel a conscience and transform a heart into bronze to bear the weight of a responsibility like this; and, on the other hand, the necessity of such leaders, the terrible danger that they could fail to appear or simply fail and degenerate—these are *our* real worries and dark clouds, do you know this, you free spirits? These are the heavy, distant thoughts and storms that traverse the sky of *our* lives. There are few pains as intense as ever having seen, guessed, or sympathized while an extraordinary person ran off course and degenerated: but someone with an uncommon eye for the overall danger that "humanity" itself will *degenerate,* someone like us, who has recognized the outrageous contingency that has been playing games with the future of humanity so far—games in which no hand and not even a "finger of God" has taken part—someone who has sensed the disaster that lies hidden in the idiotic guilelessness and credulity of "modern ideas," and still more in the whole of Christian-European morality: someone like this will suffer from an unparalleled sense of alarm. In a single glance he will comprehend everything that *could be bred from humanity,* given a favorable accumulation and intensification of forces and tasks; he will know with all the prescience of his conscience how humanity has still not exhausted its greatest possibilities, and how often the type man has already faced mysterious decisions and new paths:—he will know even better, from his most painful memories, the sorts of miserable things that generally shatter, crush, sink, and turn a development of the highest rank into a miserable affair. The *total degeneration of humanity* down to what today's socialist fools and nitwits see as their "man of the future"—as their ideal!—this degeneration and diminution of humanity into the perfect herd animal (or, as they say, into man in a "free society"), this brutalizing process of turning humanity into stunted little animals with equal rights and equal claims is no doubt *possible!* Anyone who has ever thought this possibility through to the end knows one more disgust than other men,—and perhaps a new *task* as well! . . .

259

Mutually refraining from injury, violence, and exploitation, placing your will on par with the other's: in a certain, crude sense, these practices can become good manners between individuals when the right conditions are present (namely, that the individuals have genuinely similar quantities of force and measures of value, and belong together within a single body). But as soon as this principle is taken any further, and maybe even held to be the *fundamental principle of society*, it immediately shows itself for what it is: the will to *negate* life, the principle of disintegration and decay. Here we must think things through thoroughly, and ward off any sentimental weakness: life itself is *essentially* a process of appropriating, injuring, overpowering the alien and the weaker, oppressing, being harsh, imposing your own form, incorporating, and at least, the very least, exploiting,—but what is the point of always using words that have been stamped with slanderous intentions from time immemorial? Even a body within which (as we presupposed earlier) particular individuals treat each other as equal (which happens in every healthy aristocracy): if this body is living and not dying, it will have to treat other bodies in just those ways that the individuals it contains *refrain* from treating each other. It will have to be the embodiment of will to power, it will want to grow, spread, grab, win dominance,—not out of any morality or immorality, but because it is *alive,* and because life *is* precisely will to power. But there is no issue on which the base European consciousness is less willing to be instructed than this; these days, people everywhere are lost in rapturous enthusiasms, even in scientific disguise, about a future state of society where "the exploitative character" will fall away:—to my ears, that sounds as if someone is promising to invent a life that dispenses with all organic functions. "Exploitation" does not belong to a corrupted

or imperfect, primitive society: it belongs to the *essence* of being alive as a fundamental organic function; it is a result of genuine will to power, which is just the will of life.—Although this is an innovation at the level of theory,—at the level of reality, it is the *primal fact* of all history. Let us be honest with ourselves to this extent at least!—

260

As I was wandering through the many subtle and crude moralities that have been dominant or that still dominate over the face of the earth, I found certain traits regularly recurring together and linked to each other. In the end, two basic types became apparent to me and a fundamental distinction leapt out. There is a *master morality* and a *slave morality;*—I will immediately add that in all higher and more mixed cultures, attempts to negotiate between these moralities also appear, although more frequently the two are confused and there are mutual misunderstandings. In fact, you sometimes find them sharply juxtaposed—inside the same person even, within a single soul. Moral value distinctions have arisen within either a dominating type that, with a feeling of well-being, was conscious of the difference between itself and those who were dominated—or alternatively, these distinctions arose among the dominated people themselves, the slaves and dependants of every rank. In the first case, when dominating people determine the concept of "good," it is the elevated, proud states of soul that are perceived as distinctive and as determining rank order. The noble person separates himself off from creatures in which the opposite of such elevated, proud states is expressed: he despises them. It is immediately apparent that, in this first type of morality, the contrast between "good" and "bad" amounts to one between "noble" and "despicable" (the contrast between "good" and *"evil"* has a different lineage). People who were cowardly, apprehensive, and petty, people who thought narrowly in terms of utility—these were the ones despised. But the same can be said about distrustful people with their uneasy glances, about grovelers, about dog-like types of people who let themselves be mistreated, about begging flatterers and, above all, about liars:—it is a basic belief of aristocrats that base peoples are liars. "We who are truthful"—that is what the nobility of ancient Greece called themselves. It is obvious that moral expressions everywhere were first applied to *people* and then, only later and derivatively, to *actions* (which is why it is a tremendous mistake when historians of morality take their point of departure from questions such as "why do acts of pity get praised?"). The noble type of person feels that *he* determines value, he does not need anyone's approval, he judges that "what is harmful to me is harmful in itself," he knows that he is the one who gives honor to things in the first place, he *creates values*. He honors everything he sees in himself: this sort of morality is self-glorifying. In the foreground, there is the feeling of fullness, of power that wants to overflow, the happiness associated with a high state of tension, the consciousness of a wealth that wants to make gifts and give away. The noble person helps the unfortunate too, although not (or hardly ever) out of pity, but rather more out of an impulse generated by the over-abundance of power. In honoring himself, the noble man honors the powerful as well as those who have power over themselves, who know how to speak and be silent, who joyfully exercise severity and harshness over themselves, and have respect for all forms of severity and harshness. "Wotan has put a hard heart in my breast," reads a line from an old Scandinavian saga: this rightly comes from the soul of a proud Viking. This sort of a man is even proud of *not* being made for pity: which is why the hero of the saga adds, by way of warning, "If your heart is not hard when you are young, it will never be hard." The noble and brave types of people who think this way are the furthest removed from a morality that sees precisely pity, actions for others, and *désintéressement*[3] as emblematic of morality. A faith in yourself, pride in yourself, and a fundamental hostility and irony with respect to "selflessness" belong to a noble morality just as certainly as does a slight disdain and caution towards sympathetic feelings and "warm hearts."—The powerful are the ones who *know* how to honor; it is their art,

their realm of invention. A profound reverence for age and origins—the whole notion of justice is based on this double reverence—, a faith and a prejudice in favor of forefathers and against future generations is typical of the morality of the powerful. And when, conversely, people with "modern ideas" believe almost instinctively in "progress" and "the future," and show a decreasing respect for age, this gives sufficient evidence of the ignoble origin of these "ideas." But, most of all, the morality of dominating types is foreign and painful to contemporary taste due to its stern axiom that people have duties only towards their own kind; that when it comes to creatures of a lower rank, to everything alien, people are allowed to act as they see fit or "from the heart," and in any event, "beyond good and evil"—: things like pity might have a place here. The capacity and duty to experience extended gratitude and vengefulness—both only among your own kind—, subtlety in retaliation, refinement in concepts of friendship, a certain need to have enemies (as flue holes, as it were for the affects of jealousy, irascibility, arrogance,—basically, in order to be a good *friend*): all these are characteristic features of noble morality which, as I have suggested, is not the morality of "modern ideas," and this makes it difficult for us to relate to, and also difficult for us to dig it up and lay it open.—It is different with the second type of morality, *slave morality*. What if people who were violated, oppressed, suffering, unfree, exhausted, and unsure of themselves were to moralize: what type of moral valuations would they have? A pessimistic suspicion of the whole condition of humanity would probably find expression, perhaps a condemnation of humanity along with its condition. The slave's gaze resents the virtues of the powerful. It is skeptical and distrustful, it has a *subtle* mistrust of all the "good" that is honored there—, it wants to convince itself that even happiness is not genuine there. Conversely, qualities that serve to alleviate existence for suffering people are pulled out and flooded with light: pity, the obliging, helpful hand, the warm heart, patience, industriousness, humility, and friendliness receive full honors here—, since these are the most useful qualities and practically the only way of holding up under the pressure of existence. Slave morality is essentially a morality of utility. Here we have the point of origin for that famous opposition between "good" and *"evil."* Evil is perceived as something powerful and dangerous; it is felt to contain a certain awesome quality, a subtlety and strength that block any incipient contempt. According to the slave morality then, "evil" inspires fear; but according to the master morality, it is *"good"* that inspires and wants to inspire fear, while the "bad" man is seen as contemptible. The opposition comes to a head when, following the logic of slave morality, a hint of contempt (however slight and well disposed) finally comes to be associated with even its idea of "good," because within the terms of slave morality, the good man must always be *unthreatening:* he is good-natured, easy to deceive, maybe a bit stupid, *un bonhomme.*[4] Wherever slave morality holds sway, language shows a tendency for the words "good" and "stupid" to come closer together.— A final fundamental distinction: the desire for *freedom*, the instinct for happiness, and subtleties in the feeling of freedom necessarily belong to slave morals and morality, just as an artistry and enthusiasm in respect and devotion are invariant symptoms of an aristocratic mode of thinking and valuing.—This clearly shows why love *as passion* (our European specialty) must have had a purely noble descent: it is known to have been invented in the knightly poetry of Provence, by those magnificent, inventive men of the *"gai saber."*[5] Europe is indebted to these men for so many things, almost for itself.

261

Vanity is perhaps one of the most difficult things for a noble person to comprehend: he will be tempted to keep denying it when a different type of man will almost be able to feel it in his hands. He has difficulty imagining creatures who would try to inspire good opinions about themselves that they themselves do not hold—and consequently do not "deserve" either—, and who would then end up *believing* these good opinions. For one thing, this strikes the noble as being so tasteless and showing such a lack of self-respect,

and, for another thing, it seems so baroque and unreasonable to him, that he would gladly see vanity as an exception and stay skeptical in most of the cases where it is brought up. For example, he will say: "I can be wrong about my own worth and still insist that other people acknowledge it to be what I say it is,—but that is not vanity (instead, it is arrogance or, more frequently, it is what they call 'humility' or 'modesty')." Or alternatively: "There are many reasons why I can enjoy other people's good opinions, perhaps because I love and honor them and rejoice in each of their joys, and perhaps also because their good opinions confirm and reinforce my faith in my own good opinion of myself, perhaps because other people's good opinions are useful or look as though they could be useful to me, even when I don't agree with them,—but none of that is vanity." It is only when forced (namely with the help of history) that the noble person realizes that from time immemorial, in all strata of people who are in some way dependent, base people *were* only what they were *considered to be:*—not being at all accustomed to positing values, the only value the base person attributes to himself is the one his masters have attributed to him (creating values is the true *right of masters*). We can see it as the result of a tremendous atavism that, to this day, ordinary people still *wait* for an opinion to be pronounced about themselves before instinctively deferring to it. And this is by no means only the case with "good" opinions—they defer to bad and unfair ones as well (for instance, just think about most of the self-estimations and self-underestimations that devout women accept from their father confessors and, in general, that devout Christians accept from their church). As a matter of fact, in keeping with the slow approach of a democratic order of things (and its cause, the mixing of blood between masters and slaves), the originally rare and noble urge to ascribed to yourself a value that comes *from* yourself, and to "think well" of yourself is now increasingly widespread and encouraged. But in every age it is opposed by an older, broader, and more thoroughly ingrained tendency,—and in the phenomenon of "vanity," this older tendency gains mastery over the younger. The vain take pleasure in *every* good opinion they hear about themselves (abstracted entirely from the point of view of utility, and just as much removed from truth or falsity), just as they suffer from every bad opinion. This is because they submit—they *feel* submissive—to both good and bad opinions out of that oldest instinct of submissiveness which erupts within them.—This is "the slave" in the blood of the vain, a remnant of the mischief of the slave—and how much "slave" is still left over in women, for instance!—, they try to *seduce* people into having good opinions of them. By the same token, it is the slave who submits to these opinions immediately afterwards, as if he were not the one who had just called for them.—And to say it again: vanity is an atavism.

262

A *species*[6] originates, a type grows sturdy and strong, in the long struggle with essentially constant *unfavorable* conditions. Conversely, people know from the experience of breeders that species with overabundant diets and, in general, more than their share of protection and care, will immediately show a striking tendency towards variations of the type, and will be rich in wonders and monstrosities (including monstrous vices). You only need to see an aristocratic community (such as Venice or an ancient Greek *polis*[7]) as an organization that has been established, whether voluntarily or involuntarily, for the sake of *breeding:* the people living there together are self-reliant and want to see their species succeed, mainly because if they *do not* succeed they run a horrible risk of being eradicated. Here there are none of the advantages, excesses, and protections that are favorable to variation. The species needs itself to be a species, to be something that, by virtue of its very hardness, uniformity, and simplicity of form, can succeed and make itself persevere in constant struggle with its neighbors or with the oppressed who are or threaten to become rebellious. A tremendous range of experiences teaches it which qualities are primarily responsible for the fact that, despite all gods and men, it still exists, it keeps prevailing. It calls these qualities virtues, and these are the only virtues it fosters. It does so with harshness; in fact, it desires harshness. Every aristocratic morality is intolerant about

the education of the young, disposal over women, marriage customs, relations between old and young and penal laws (which only concern deviants):—it considers intolerance itself to be a virtue, under the rubric of "justice." A type whose traits are few in number but very strong, a species of people who are strict, warlike, clever, and silent, close to each other and closed up (which gives them the most subtle feeling for the charms and nuances of association) will, in this way, establish itself (as a species) over and above the change of generations. The continuous struggle with constant *unfavorable* conditions is, as I have said, what causes a type to become sturdy and hard. But, eventually, a fortunate state will arise and the enormous tension will relax; perhaps none of the neighbors are enemies anymore, and the means of life, even of enjoying life, exist in abundance. With a single stroke, the bonds and constrains of the old discipline are torn: it does not seem to be necessary any more, to be a condition of existence,—if it wanted to continue, it could do so only as a form of *luxury,* as an archaic *taste.* Variation, whether as deviation (into something higher, finer, rarer) or as degeneration and monstrosity, suddenly comes onto the scene in the greatest abundance and splendor; the individual dares to be individual and different. At these turning points of history, a magnificent, diverse, jungle-like growth and upward striving, a kind of *tropical* tempo in the competition to grow will appear alongside (and often mixed up and tangled together with) an immense destruction and self-destruction. This is due to the wild egoisms that are turned explosively against each other, that wrestle each other "for sun and light," and can no longer derive any limitation, restraint, or refuge from morality as it has existed so far. It was this very morality that accumulated the tremendous amount of force to put such a threatening tension into the bow:—and now it is, now it is being "outlived." The dangerous and uncanny point has been reached when the greatest, most diverse, most comprehensive life *lives past* the old morality. The "individual" is left standing there, forced to give himself laws, forced to rely on his own arts and wiles of self-preservation, self-enhancement, self-redemption. There is nothing but new whys and hows; there are no longer any shared formulas; misunderstanding is allied with disregard; decay, ruin, and the highest desires are horribly entwined; the genius of the race overflows from every cornucopia of good and bad; there is a disastrous simultaneity of spring and autumn, filled with new charms and veils that are well suited to the young, still unexhausted, still indefatigable corruption. Danger has returned, the mother of morals, great danger, displaced onto the individual this time, onto the neighbor or friend, onto the street, onto your own child, onto your own heart, onto all of your own-most, secret-most wishes and wills: and the moral philosophers emerging at this time—what will they have to preach? These sharp observers and layabouts discover that everything is rapidly coming to an end, that everything around them is ruined and creates ruin, that nothing lasts as long as the day after tomorrow except one species of person, the hopelessly *mediocre*. Only the mediocre have prospects for continuing on, for propagating—they are the people of the future, the only survivors: "Be like them! Be mediocre!" is the only morality that still makes sense, that still finds ears. But this morality of mediocrity is difficult to preach! It can never admit what it is and what it wants! It has to talk about moderation and dignity and duty and loving your neighbors,—it will have a hard time *hiding its irony!*—

263

There is an *instinct for rank* that, more than anything else, is itself the sign of a *high* rank; there is a *pleasure* in nuances of respect that indicates a noble origin and noble habits. The subtlety, quality, and stature of a soul is put dangerously to the test when something of the first rank passes by before the shudders of authority are there to protect it from intrusive clutches and crudeness: something that goes on its way like a living touchstone, undiscovered, unmarked, and experimenting, perhaps voluntarily covered and disguised. Anyone whose task and exercise is the investigation of souls will use this very art, in a variety of forms, to establish the ultimate value of a soul, the unalterable, inborn order of

rank it belongs to: this sort of investigator will test out the soul's *instinct for respect. Différence engendre haine:*[8] Many natures have a baseness that suddenly bursts out, like dirty water, when any sort of holy vessel, any sort of treasure from a closed shrine, any sort of book that bears the mark of a great destiny is carried past. On the other hand, there is an involuntary hush, a hesitation of the eye and a quieting of every gesture, all of which indicate that the soul *feels* the presence of something deserving the highest honors. The way in which respect for the *Bible* has, on the whole, been maintained in Europe might be the best piece of discipline and refinement in manners that Europe owes to Christianity. Books with this sort of profundity and ultimate meaning need the protection of an externally imposed tyranny of authority; this way, they can *last* through the millennia that are needed to use them up and figure them out. It is a great achievement when the masses (people of all kinds who lack depth or have speedy bowels) have finally had the feeling bred into them that they cannot touch everything, that there are holy experiences which require them to take off their shoes and keep their dirty hands away,—and this is pretty much as high a level of humanity as they will ever reach. Conversely, what is perhaps the most disgusting thing about so-called scholars, the devout believers in "modern ideas," is their lack of shame, the careless impudence of their eyes and hands that touch, taste, and feel everything. And there might still be a greater *relative* nobility of taste and tactfulness of respect within a people these days, within a lower sort of people, namely within the peasantry, than among the newspaper-reading *demimonde* of the spirit, the educated.

NOTES

1. Commonwealth.
2. Neither God nor master.
3. Disinterestedness.
4. A good simple fellow.
5. Gay science.
6. In German: *Art*. In this section, *Art* is translated as "species" and *Typus* as "type."
7. City-state.
8. "Difference engenders hatred."

PROPOSED STANDARDS OF RIGHT CONDUCT

Ethical Subjectivism

RUSS SHAFER-LANDAU

Imagine two people debating the morality of giving to famine relief. Smith thinks that we are bound to give a great deal more than people typically do. Jones denies this. Suppose that these two, after talking a good while longer, have found themselves in agreement about all of the relevant facts, and have also sharpened their own positions so that the views they emerge with are each internally consistent. But suppose that the fundamental disagreement between them remains. Can this disagreement be rationally resolved?

Not likely, according to ethical subjectivists. Subjectivism claims that there is no ideal or uniquely correct resolution to ethical disagreements, because there are no ethical standards that are objectively correct, no standards to which all rational or fully informed people must agree. There is no overarching, universal yardstick that can be applied to determine the truth of one's ultimate moral principles. Once we have identified our deepest moral commitments, we can go no further. It makes no sense, according to subjectivism, to suppose that such commitments could be false or irrational.

To better understand ethical subjectivism, we need to appreciate the key notions of subjectivity and objectivity. A proposition or judgment is objectively true just in case it is true independently of anyone's thinking it is. So, for instance, the claim that the earth orbits around the sun is an objective truth, because the claim is true regardless of whether anyone believes it. A judgment is subjectively true just in case its truth depends on whether the speaker endorses it. To insist that chocolate is tastier than vanilla, or that beer is better than wine, is to make a subjective claim, because in this case truth is in the eye of the beholder.

TWO KINDS OF SUBJECTIVISM

Philosophers distinguish between two kinds of ethical theory. The first sort—**normative theory**—attempts to specify conditions under which an action is morally right or wrong. John Stuart Mill, for instance, held that an act is right insofar as it tends to produce happiness. Immanuel Kant thought that one acts rightly only if one is willing to see everyone act in accordance with one's own principles. Thomas Hobbes claimed that an act is right if it is permitted by rules that would be agreed to by self-interested parties seeking to band together to escape from anarchy.

Viewed as a normative theory, ethical subjectivism claims that an act is morally right if, and only if, the person judging the action approves of it. Similarly, personal disapproval is both necessary and sufficient for an action to qualify as wrong.

Normative subjectivism allows that moral judgments can be true or false. There is truth in ethics, but no objective truth. A moral judgment is true, according to normative subjectivism, just in case it accurately reports the sentiments of the speaker. Thus sincerity is the mark of ethical truth. If normative subjectivism is true, then one's sincere moral judgments cannot be mistaken.

The debate among Mill, Kant, Hobbes, and normative subjectivists is an intramural one. Each theory asserts its superiority as an answer to the question: Under what conditions are actions morally right? This is a very important debate within ethics. But we can step back from this debate and ask instead about the status of these competing theories. Specifically, we can ask of all of these theories how they might be justified, whether they are or can be true, and how, if at all, we might know that one or another is true. These are **meta-ethical** questions. Here we are not asking what makes actions right. Instead, we are focusing on whether normative theories can be justified in the first place.

Meta-ethical subjectivism is the particular claim that normative ethical theories, and moral judgments quite generally, cannot be true. Contrast this with normative subjectivism, which claims that moral judgments can be true, provided they accurately report the speaker's feelings. Because of their different views about the possibility of ethical truth, meta-ethical subjectivism implies the falsity of normative subjectivism, and vice versa.

Let us consider the motivations and the plausibility of normative subjectivism first.

MOTIVATIONS FOR NORMATIVE SUBJECTIVISM

A. The Argument from Democracy

One of normative subjectivism's appeals is that it is so democratic. Subjectivism is a levelling doctrine—everyone issues true moral judgments, so long as they sincerely give voice to their feelings. Everyone's views are on a par with everyone else's. This democratic element is a genuine feature of subjectivism. But many take this democratic element a step further, expressing their allegiance to normative subjectivism by means of the following argument:

1. If everyone has an equal right to have and voice moral opinions, then everyone's moral opinions are equally plausible.
2. Everyone does have an equal right to have and voice moral opinions.
3. Therefore everyone's moral opinions are equally plausible.

This argument is *valid*—its premises entail its conclusion. *If* one were to accept premises (1) and (2), then logic requires one to accept the conclusion (3) as well. But should we accept these premises? The second premise seems generally plausible. But the first premise is false. Having a right to an opinion does not entail the plausibility of that opinion. Though everyone has an equal right to express views about

mathematics or quantum physics, no one supposes that everyone's opinions here are equally plausible. I have lots of opinions about botany, about the content of the tax code, about the location of various buildings and landmarks. Further, I have a right to each of these opinions. But many of them (I'm not sure which) are mistaken. I misidentify plants, misconstrue tax law, and my sense of direction is awful. These humdrum examples show that the plausibility of an opinion really has nothing to do with one's right to hold it: Having a right to an opinion is one thing, the truth of that opinion quite another. This directly undermines the first premise of the argument. Because we must reject one of its crucial premises, the argument from democracy is unsound. It does not supply a good basis for endorsing normative subjectivism.

B. The Argument from Disagreement

One thing that impresses many people about work in the sciences is the degree of consensus about which propositions are true, and about which methods are appropriate for discovering new truths. Things in ethics seem to be much different; there seems to be a great deal of disagreement about fundamental issues, and a lack of consensus about appropriate methods for resolving moral questions. The diversity of ethical opinion has struck many as an important indicator of morality's fundamentally subjective character.

Here is a representative sketch of an argument for subjectivism that takes the breadth of ethical disagreement as its focus:

1. If there is persistent disagreement among informed, good-willed, open-minded people about some subject matter, then that subject matter does not admit of objective truth.
2. There is persistent disagreement about ethical issues among informed, good-willed, open-minded people.
3. Therefore there are no objective ethical truths.

We can know that an argument's conclusion is true if we know that the argument is logically valid and that all of its premises are true. This argument is valid. The second premise seems to be true, though the breadth of moral *agreement* is often underappreciated. The divisive moral issues tend to get the most press, but this publicity can mask the significant degree of moral consensus that must form the core of any society. Further, though there clearly is disagreement about ethical issues, it is sensible to suppose that much of this is owing to mistaken beliefs—more information would lead to greater ethical agreement. Public debates about welfare reform in the United States, or about the morality of capital punishment, are chock full of misinformation. Getting the facts straight would get us a good distance toward resolving issues on these (and other) topics.

Still, we may suppose that even after gathering the facts, people of good will may disagree in their ethical views. So let us grant premise (2). Premise (1), however, is not plausible. There is persistent disagreement among informed, good-willed, open-minded physicists and mathematicians. We, and they, assume that their efforts are nevertheless aimed at discovering objective truths. We do not believe that taste is the arbiter of truth in math or physics. Indeed, we can make this quite general point about investigations of all sorts. When historians debate the causes of the Civil War, they are not *merely* entering their personal views, with nothing other than parochial preference to back them up. Historians are trying to discover what *really* caused the Civil War. They continue to disagree about this. But this is not evidence that their discipline is subjective, that the truths they arrive at are mere expressions of taste. It isn't the case that historical (or physical or mathematical) judgments are true just because someone believes in them. What this shows is that a discipline may deal in objective truths even if its open-minded, informed practitioners deeply disagree with one another. Because that is so, the argument from disagreement fails to provide adequate support for normative subjectivism.

C. The Argument from Tolerance

Many people find subjectivism attractive because of the support it seems to provide for tolerance. We nowadays reject the once-prevalent feelings of superiority that were used to justify the oppression of Asians, Africans, and indigenous Americans

during the past three centuries. We would encourage a respectful, tolerant attitude toward different cultures, rather than a dismissive outlook that brands other cultures as "primitive." This dismissive attitude always begins with an (implicit) endorsement of ethical objectivism—there is an objectively correct way to do things. And we all know how things go from here: "We have it right, they don't, thus we have to show them the true path. If this means exploiting them (for their own good), and possibly destroying their way of life, no great loss, since we will supply them with a far better one."

If you are like most people, you'll have bristled at the arrogance expressed in these last lines. This may lead you to endorse the following argument from tolerance:

1. If normative subjectivism is true, then no one's deepest opinions are more plausible than anyone else's.
2. If no one's deepest opinions are more plausible than anyone else's, then we have to respect and tolerate the opinions of all others.
3. Thus if normative subjectivism is true, then we have to respect and tolerate the opinions of all others.

There are two important points to note about this argument. The first is that even if it is sound—even if it is logically valid (it is), and all of its premises (and thus its conclusion) are true—this does not entail that ethical objectivists need to embrace an arrogant or disrespectful attitude toward different cultures. Objectivists believe that there are ethical truths that exist independently of whether anyone thinks so. An objectivist need not believe that *he himself* is in possession of such truth. Indeed, objectivists who are appropriately humble will recognize their own fallibility and the limits to their understanding, in much the same way as physicists or chemists might appreciate the depth of their own ignorance against the backdrop of objective truth. Arrogance and intolerance are poor character traits. They are not mandated by the intellectual position of ethical objectivism.

Let us return to the argument. Its first premise is true. But the second premise is suspect if normative subjectivism is true. Suppose that it is.

This means that an action is morally right just in case someone approves of it. If one approves of tolerant behavior, then such behavior is morally correct. The problem, however, is that *if* one approves of intolerance, then intolerant behavior is morally appropriate. Subjectivism morally sanctions the intolerance of prejudiced and bigoted individuals, so long as such intolerance is sincerely felt. Regrettably, it often is. Those who think that even (and especially) racists and bigots are morally required to display respect for others will find no ground for their view in ethical subjectivism. To think that even a deeply prejudiced person should be tolerant is to embrace the universal or objective value of toleration. A concern for tolerance thus sits very uncomfortably with normative subjectivism.

D. The Argument from Atheism

A common thought that moves many to normative subjectivism is that objectivity in ethics can be purchased only through divine commands. If ethics is objective, then it must be God who validates the moral rules. The problem, according to subjectivists, is that God does not exist.

Here is the argument in somewhat tighter form:

1. If ethics is objective, then God must exist.
2. God does not exist.
3. Therefore ethics is not objective.

We could undermine the argument from atheism if we could show that God exists. We can't, at least not here (and perhaps not anywhere; this is one philosophical issue that may never be settled). But even if we could resolve this matter, and do so in favor of the atheist, this would not be enough to prove subjectivism. We can see that from the argument itself. The argument requires a further claim (premise 1), namely, that ethics is objective only if God exists.

There is an intuitive, widely shared view that underlies the first premise. The thought is that laws require lawgivers. There are laws against assault, forgery, and perjury only because lawmakers have enacted them. No legislators, no laws. By analogy, if there are moral laws, these require some lawmaker to validate them. If moral laws are objective, this lawmaker cannot

be any one of us. (Remember: Objective moral rules are those whose truth does not depend on human endorsement.) If not one of us, then who? Enter God.

There are two reasons to doubt premise (1). This premise seems to derive its strongest support from the common thought mentioned earlier (*viz.*, that rules require rulegivers). But this principle is suspect. Many think that the rules of logic and the axioms of mathematics are true quite independently of whether anyone has ordained them. *If* that is so (an issue too complex to tackle here), then moral rules too might be true or justified even in the absence of a moral lawgiver.

Further, there is reason to think that even if God exists, God cannot be the ultimate source of ethical principles, and so cannot be the missing link that supplies objectivity in ethics.

Suppose God exists. Suppose God issues commands to us. And further suppose that our moral law comprises these commands. Ethics is objective because the law comes from God, not from us. If it didn't come from God, it couldn't be objective.

This familiar line of thought, often used to support premise (1), is beset by a troubling dilemma: God either does or does not have reasons to support his (or her or its) commands. If God lacks justifying reasons, then God's commands are arbitrary, and so supply no authoritative basis for ethics. Alternatively, if God's commands *are* backed up by reasons, then divine commands are no longer arbitrary. They may be authoritative. We can envision a God who is omniscient, and so knows all facts, including moral facts. This God may also be omnibenevolent, and in his goodness may want to impart the moral facts (or rules) to us, in the form of divine commands. This traditional picture preserves the goodness and omniscience of God, precisely by envisioning divine commands as being well-supported by reasons.

The problem, however, is that these reasons, whatever they are, are what really justify the divine commands. If God commands us not to kill, extort, or perjure, he does so *because such actions are wrong;* they are not wrong because God forbids them. But this means that even theists, if they are to retain a picture of an all-good and all-knowing God, must acknowledge a source of ethical truth that exists independently of God's commands. This means that the objectivity of ethics does not hinge on God's commands. And that directly challenges premise (1). (For a view that takes the opposite approach to God's role in ethics, see Philip Quinn's article, "God and Morality," which appears later in this section.)

A final complication emerges when we consider the argument's conclusion—the claim that ethics is not objective. Even if premises (1) and (2) are true, the conclusion does not show that normative subjectivism is true. Put simply, (3) may be true *even if normative subjectivism is false.* There are at least two theories, in addition to normative subjectivism, that are compatible with the claim that ethics is not objective. One of these theories is meta-ethical subjectivism. The other is ethical relativism, the view that an action is morally right if, and only if, it is permitted by the ultimate mores of the society in which it is performed. Ethical relativism allows for moral truth—moral judgments are true just in case they accurately report a certain kind of social consensus. Because moral truth is a function of what people believe it to be, ethical relativism is a non-objective theory. Thus relativists, as well as normative and meta-ethical subjectivists, will embrace conclusion (3). This shows that the argument from atheism, if it is to support normative subjectivism, must be supplemented by additional arguments that rule out its two antiobjectivist competitors.

For our purposes, then, we must suspend judgment on the argument from atheism. The argument is sound only if both of its premises are true. They may be. But we could know this only after a very great deal of further philosophical investigation. And we would have an argument for normative subjectivism only if we also had in hand a battery of arguments that undermined both meta-ethical subjectivism and ethical relativism. All the more reason to wait and see before pronouncing a judgment on the argument from atheism.

Implications of Normative Subjectivism

As we have seen, many of the arguments that are advanced for ethical subjectivism are not very compelling. This is not a fatal flaw. Most philosophical positions are supported by a large battery of arguments, many of which, after serious attention, turn out to be unsound. Thus ethical subjectivism may be true even if the preceding arguments turn out to be less than convincing. But to gain plausibility, its supporters need to discharge two debts. First, they must advance a positive argument that survives scrutiny. Second, they must show that the essential implications of subjectivism are implications we can live with. Let us see whether this is so.

First, as we have seen, subjectivism is a doctrine of **moral equivalence**—everyone's ultimate moral views are as plausible as everyone else's. This is a handy weapon when dealing with arrogant or haughty individuals. But moral equivalence is a double-edged sword. If all moral views are on a par with one another, then we lose our basis for issuing substantive moral criticism of unsavory characters such as Nazis and terrorists. If subjectivism is true, then those who approve of antisemitism and terrorism are correct in calling such behavior morally right. The moral views of a Hitler or an IRA gunman are *true*, so long as these views are sincerely held.

Of course, subjectivism does not render us mute at this stage—we can criticize the views of Nazis and terrorists, but only from our own perspective. Importantly, our perspective is not superior to theirs. Moral equivalence entails that conflicting moral views are just different; neither one is better or worse than another. This may appeal when comparing the prayer or dietary rituals of Belgians and Polynesians. But it is likely to leave us cold in the face of serious evil.

Normative subjectivism also comes very close to rendering each person **morally infallible.** An infallible person is one who cannot make mistakes. Thus such a person has no false beliefs and all true ones. If subjectivism is true, then it is possible that all, or almost all, of our moral beliefs are correct. We can be morally mistaken in only one of two ways. We might base our moral views on false beliefs (e.g., a racist whose antipathy to blacks is based on a false belief about their intelligence). Or we might possess moral beliefs that conflict with other, deeper moral beliefs we already hold. We might, for instance, approve of the death penalty for a specially awful murderer, even though in a cooler moment we reject the principles that could justify the execution.

According to subjectivism, moral views that are free of either sort of error cannot be mistaken. Apart from exceptions of these two kinds, subjectivism entails that our moral feelings are selfcertifying. Moral outlooks that seem to us vicious, ruthless, callous, selfish, or even maniacal cannot be wrong, so long as the views imply no factual errors and are consistent with other things a person holds. Literature and history offer a good supply of well-informed, consistent fanatics. Subjectivism implies that their views are true.

If we are ordinarily morally infallible, and if we disagree with others in our ethical views, then it follows that subjectivism **generates contradictions.** A contradiction occurs when a proposition is alleged to be both true and false. Theories that generate contradictions cannot be true. We would rightly dismiss a mathematical theory that entailed that two and two did, and at the same time did not, equal four. Suppose ethical subjectivism is correct. If Smith thinks that giving famine aid is mandatory, and Jones disagrees, then giving to famine relief is and is not morally required. It is both true and false that giving to famine relief is obligatory. That is a contradiction.

We can resolve this worrying implication in a fairly straightforward way. Rather than saying that Smith's approval of an action makes it morally right, period, we say that her approval makes it right *for her.* Thus, in the previous example, giving famine aid is not right and wrong in the same respect—it is right for Smith, and wrong for Jones. This is the strategy of relativizing moral judgments to their speakers.

This move really can solve the problem of contradiction. But the strategy has its costs. It renders subjectivism **incapable of explaining the point or existence of moral disagreement.** Think again of the debate about famine relief. If all Smith is saying is that she herself approves of it, and if all Jones is saying is that he doesn't, then Smith and Jones don't really disagree with one another. Further, we lose incentive to continue moral conversation, because moral truth just consists in reports of personal feelings.

It may appear that Smith and Jones, in their debate about famine relief, are trying to get at the truth, trying to discover what is *really* right. But if we relativize judgments to their speakers, this appearance is misleading. There can be no genuine disagreement about where truth lies, since it lies in the eyes of the beholder. If subjectivism is right, everyone's views are true, so long as they are sincerely expressed. Thus ethical disagreement could focus only on whether the interlocutors actually believe what they say they do. Disagreement cannot focus on whether famine relief is *really* right—right in a non-relative, objective sense—because (according to subjectivism) famine relief *cannot be* really right (or wrong). Subjectivism leaves us with an entirely unrecognizable picture of moral disagreement.

A final concern. If subjectivism is true, then **our moral views are arbitrary.** There is no better reason to adopt one ethical view over another. Subjectivism claims that moral views are true because one believes them; one does not believe them because they are true. Moral views are justified to the extent that they are believed, so any basis whatever (other than false belief) will confer plausibility. This allows us to see two ways in which subjectivism entails the arbitrariness of ethical views. First, one's moral outlook may be justified even if one has no reason at all that supports it—that one believes it is sufficient to make it true. In a second kind of case, one does possess reasons that support one's moral views. But the reasons that support a moral belief may fail entirely to move other informed, rational, good-willed people. In this sense, one's views are arbitrary, because they are supported by reasons that could, with complete propriety, be rejected by any and all other rational people.

MOTIVATIONS FOR META-ETHICAL SUBJECTIVISM

Most people will find at least some of these implications troubling. For those who do, yet still balk at the idea of objectivity in ethics, meta-ethical subjectivism is a natural path to pursue. This brand of subjectivism denies that moral judgments can be true or false. They are neither true nor false because they are not attempting to describe anything. There are no facts that they might accurately capture—not even facts about our own feelings, or society's agreements. According to meta-ethical subjectivism, the purpose of moral judgment is not to *report* personal or social attitudes, but rather to *express* one's feelings or *voice* one's commitments.

On this view, moral judgments are closely analogous to commands and emotional responses. Though moral judgments look like factual judgments—"infanticide is wrong" has the same grammatical structure as straightforward descriptive judgments ("space is curved", "grass is green")—this appearance is misleading. To say that infanticide is wrong, for instance, is either to give vent to a visceral dislike of infanticide, or to issue a command that prohibits infanticide. On the first line, the moral judgment is equivalent to "Infanticide? Boo! Yuck!" On the second view, the moral judgment reduces to something like "Don't commit infanticide!" On either view, moral judgments cannot be true or false, since they don't purport to describe anything. Emotive ventings ("Spinach? Blech!") aren't true or false. Commands ("Rise and shine!") aren't true or false. According to meta-ethical subjectivists, because moral judgments are effectively utterances of either sort, they aren't true or false, either. Unlike normative subjectivism, which sees moral judgments as reports of personal feelings, and so usually true, metaethical subjectivism denies that such judgments are ever true (or false).

The distinction between normative and metaethical subjectivism may seem a minor one, a picayune footnote introduced by philosophers to impress one another and oppress their students. But the distinction is actually quite important. As we'll see, we can solve many of the problems that beset normative subjectivism if we deny that moral judgments can be true or false. Whether all of the problems disappear remains to be seen.

Let us begin our assessment of meta-ethical subjectivism by considering some of the most important arguments that have been advanced on its behalf.

A. The Argument from Moral Motivation

The great Scottish philosopher David Hume was no fan of ethical objectivism. One of the many arguments he offered against it began with what he took to be a striking difference between moral judgments and factual ones. Hume thought that one mark of moral judgment was its capacity to motivate people. A person who sincerely thinks that something is good will be really moved to pursue it; someone who thinks an action genuinely obligatory is thereby motivated to perform it. Nothing like this could be claimed of factual judgments.

Here is the argument put more succinctly:

1. Every moral judgment motivates all by itself.
2. Factual judgments cannot motivate all by themselves.
3. Therefore moral judgments are not factual judgments.

Premise (1) tells us that moral judgments are intrinsically motivational—to judge an action right is to be motivated to perform it. To avoid misunderstanding, note that one can be motivated to perform an action and still fail to do it. Motivations can be overridden; people can be weakwilled, for instance. Still, Hume claims that we cannot genuinely make a moral judgment unless we are motivated *to some extent* to comply with it.

This is what distinguishes moral judgments from factual judgments. We may believe all sorts of mathematical, chemical, or geographical propositions without being moved in the slightest. And when we are moved by factual judgments, it is only because of some accompanying desire that we happen to have. The factual judgments do not motivate all by themselves. Even a very likely candidate—"stepping out in front of that bus will surely kill you"—does not motivate all by itself. We cannot know how or whether a factual judgment will move us unless we also know which desires are associated with the judgment; whether, in this case, we want to commit suicide or to remain alive. Moral judgments intrinsically motivate. Factual judgments do not. Therefore moral judgments are not factual ones.

This is a classic of ethical argumentation. The second premise is widely, if not universally, accepted. The first premise, though, has attracted significant opposition, primarily from those who think that moral claims are a species of factual claims. On this line, moral judgments, like factual judgments, need to be supplemented by a desire before people will be motivated to act on them. Moral judgments do not motivate all by themselves. In order to generate motivation, some associated moral desire (e.g., to be beneficent or just) must be present. Those who reject premise (1) believe that it is possible for some people, known as amoralists, to lack moral desires. Amoralists are those who sincerely make moral judgments but entirely fail to be moved by them. These might be people who are depressed, rebellious, alienated, or just plain evil. If amoralists can exist, then premise (1) of the argument from moral motivation is false.

It might seem that this is an easy question to resolve. We can see that amoralists may exist just by imagining their possibility. We can readily imagine someone saying that some particular action is right, all the while remaining perfectly indifferent. The difficulty here is that our imagination is not a reliable indicator of genuine possibilities. People (claim to) imagine the possibility of a square circle, or a number that is both odd and even, but these things cannot exist. Likewise, even if we can imagine the amoralist, this isn't sufficient to show that such persons can exist. Premise (1) may be true after all.

Meta-ethical subjectivists will analyze moral judgments as expressions of emotion; since emotions are intrinsically motivating, moral judgments are intrinsically motivating, too. This is why subjectivists endorse premise (1) of the argument from moral motivation. If amoralists really can exist, then moral judgments are not intrinsically motivating, and hence not necessarily expressions of emotion. If they are not intrinsically motivating, then moral judgments might be factual judgments after all. The plausibility of meta-ethical subjectivism thus depends on whether the amoralist is a genuine possibility. That, unfortunately, is an issue that can't be briefly resolved. Hume's classic argument may be sound. But one would need to undertake a great deal of further investigation before having any warranted confidence one way or the other.

B. The Argument from Economy

Most philosophers believe that when one is comparing the plausibility of competing theories, we should, if all other things are equal, give the nod to the simpler, more economical theory. Theory A is more economical than theory B if A can explain all that B can, but with fewer assumptions. Copernicus' theory of elliptical orbit was simpler than Ptolemy's, and for this reason ultimately came to be viewed as more plausible. The reason scientists don't refer to hexes, spells, ghosts, or demons in their theories is because they can explain everything they need to explain without invoking such things. Supernatural phenomena are *superfluous;* they're added baggage, unnecessary extras that simpler theories can do without.

In a similar vein, meta-ethical subjectivists claim superiority for their view because their assumptions about what there is in the world are sparer than objectivism's. Subjectivists have an essentially scientific view of what the world consists of. The world contains physical things, and physical forces that work on them. Morality is a complex human creation; when we ask what is in the world, *really,* no mention of moral facts need be made. We can explain all of the goings-on of this world, including all human activities—why people act as they do, say the things they do, think as they do—without invoking anything like a "moral fact".

This method of doing away with moral facts bears a striking resemblance to accounts that seek to undermine traditional religion. The Judaeo-Christian god is thought by many to be superfluous—we can explain all of the goings-on of our world without supposing that there is something further, something more (God) who must be put in the picture. As science progresses, we discover that the natural events we once attributed to God (or to the gods) can be explained solely in terms of the natural workings of the natural world. In the same way, many philosophers and neuroscientists have expressed doubt about the existence of a soul, claiming that it is more economical simply to posit the existence of the brain and the nervous system to explain all of our behavior. Without the brain and nervous system, we can't explain any conscious behavior. With it, we can explain all we need to explain. The notion of a soul does no explanatory work (or so it is alleged). A simpler, better theory would thus do without it.

Subjectivists take this strategy and apply it to ethics. What would moral facts be needed to explain? Subjectivists usually take this to be a rhetorical question. We can explain everything in the world by referring to scientific facts, including facts about human psychology. But objectivists have supplied answers. They claim that we can explain lots of things that need explaining by citing moral facts. We explain why Hitler did what he did by citing his *evil nature*. We explain why people opposed apartheid by citing its *injustice*. We explain the success of a con man by reference to his *duplicitous character*. These all seem to be moral facts. The question, of course, is whether we can explain the beliefs and actions mentioned in these examples without citing the moral facts themselves.

For instance, subjectivists will claim that we don't have to suppose that there really is some moral fact of injustice existing out there, somewhere, in order to explain why so many people protested against the apartheid regime. Instead, we simply need to mention the nonmoral facts about differential treatment that obtained in South Africa, and combine these facts with further nonmoral, psychological facts, facts about what people believed. Citizens believed that there was grave injustice, they felt disgusted by the regime, and these beliefs and feelings, combined with various social, cultural, and economic facts, generated the protests that contributed to undermining apartheid society. This explanation makes no mention of any moral facts—just moral judgments and feelings, plus the social scientific facts just alluded to.

This subjectivist strategy is precisely the same sort of strategy we use to debunk metaphysical commitments in other areas. We can cite facts about the Salem society of 300 years ago, combined with people's beliefs and feelings about witches, to explain why so many people were hanged. We don't need to suppose that there really were witches in order to explain everything that needs explaining. Likewise, it is claimed, we don't need to assume the existence of moral facts in order to explain everything in the world that requires explanation.

If we compare the world that scientists depict with that same world, plus a further realm of moral facts, it is easy to see which view is simpler. But simplicity is not everything. The simpler theory must also be sufficiently explanatory. The question in ethics, as in theology and in the philosophy of mind, is whether we really can explain all that needs explaining with the sparer, more economical theories. As with matters of moral motivation, the issue of economy remains extremely controversial, with objectivists arguing that we do need moral facts to explain our practices, and subjectivists charging that moral facts are superfluous. Unsurprisingly, then, we must satisfy ourselves with only a sketch of the competing positions. Getting beyond the preliminaries requires a deeper dip into the philosophical waters than we can undertake here.

C. The Argument from Oddness

Meta-ethical subjectivists urge another reason for abandoning belief in objective moral facts. Suppose, with objectivism, that moral judgments are true, and true quite independently of what we happen to think of them. They are true, when they are, because they accurately report objective moral facts. But what could such things be? We readily grant that geologists and chemists, physicists and astronomers deal in objective truth, because we believe that their findings are constrained by the physical world whose features exist independently of whether anyone recognizes them. Botanical facts are facts about plants; geological facts are facts about rocks. In botany and geology, evidence is supplied by three-dimensional, tangible, physical stuff. We can taste it, smell it, touch it, and see it. We can't taste wrongness or hear rightness. Moral facts, if they were to exist, would have to be quite odd sorts of things, certainly nothing at all like the kinds of phenomena studied by recognized factual disciplines.

Objectivists typically reply, with some force, that they need not be committed to any ghostly realm of moral facts. Everyone agrees that there are moral rules. Moral facts are simply applications of those rules. If a moral rule prohibits infanticide, and Smith commits infanticide, then it is a moral fact that what he did was wrong. Nothing mysterious so far. But subjectivists will claim that the relevant question has simply been pushed back a step. Now we must ask what *justifies* or *validates the moral rule* against adultery (or promise-breaking, lying, killing, etc.). What is it that makes a moral rule (objectively) true?

As a first step in exploring possibilities, we should consider rules in nonmoral contexts and ask what makes them true. Rules of sports or etiquette are true, if they are, only because certain people believe they are. If no one endorsed the three strikes rule in baseball, or the ban on public nosepicking, then there simply would not be any such rules. Such rules are therefore subjective in the relevant sense.

On the other hand, most people believe that the laws of chemistry, geology, astronomy, and physics are true because of the way the world is. Our best thoughts in these disciplines track reality, as opposed to creating it. If moral rules are like scientific laws, however, then presumably they would have to be true in virtue of the operations of the physical world. This sounds very strange. The movement of protons makes certain physical laws true; the behavior of molecules validates certain chemical laws; the interactions of cells makes true particular laws of biology. But which operations of which physical things make moral rules true? The moral prohibition on torture does not seem to be vindicated by citing the workings of the physical world.

There are two standard moves for ethical objectivists to make at this point. The first strategy—**ethical naturalism**—claims that, despite appearances, moral facts really are natural, scientific facts. Whether something is right or wrong can be verified in just the same way that scientific hypotheses can be. Prominent examples of naturalism include the claims that actions are morally right if and only if they maximize pleasure, that things are good just because they are desired, and that exchanges are just if and only if all parties to the transfer have agreed to abide by its terms.

I don't want to take a stand on the success of these views. What is important for our purposes is that if these claims (or others like them) are true, then all it takes is ordinary empirical investigation to determine whether actions are right, good, or just. There doesn't

seem to be anything especially weird or mysterious about pleasure, desire, or agreements. If moral facts consist of just these sorts of humdrum things, then moral facts are not at all strange.

Subjectivists acknowledge this. But they remain skeptical. Naturalists need to supply *plausible* connections that link moral and naturalistic (i.e., nonmoral) features. But does rightness really consist in maximizing happiness? Is something good just because it is desired? Do all mutual agreements really yield justice? After thorough scrutiny, most philosophers have rejected these views. Now, objectivists needn't abandon hope—they may try to defend these theories in the face of criticisms, or they make seek better, improved naturalistic theories. There is no way to entirely discount the possibility that with greater application and ingenuity, objectivists may arrive at satisfactory naturalistic accounts of moral features. But the history of such efforts does not inspire confidence.

Try it yourself: an act is morally right if and only if_____. What fills in the blank is called an *analysis*. Naturalists disagree among themselves about which analyses are best. Naturalists are unified, however, in believing that the blank can ultimately be filled in naturalistically, that is, without the use of any moral terms. A classic case is that of the standard utilitarian doctrine cited above, which claims that an action is morally right if and only if it maximizes pleasure. The main benefit of such a theory is that it makes determining the rightness of actions a straightforward affair. Of course it won't, as a practical matter, always be easy to determine whether pleasure is maximized. But in principle, at least, we can see a clear path to justifying our moral claims and providing guidance for action.

Ethical nonnaturalists believe that there are no true naturalistic analyses of moral terms. For nonnaturalists, moral judgments cannot be empirically verified, and so there is a sharp disanalogy between ethics and science. Some nonnaturalists claim that we cannot give any analysis at all of moral terms—the above blank simply can't be filled in. The notion of goodness, for instance, may simply be basic, a fundamental term used to define other terms but not itself capable of definition.

Alternatively, some nonnaturalists believe that we can define moral terms, but only if we employ other moral terms to do so. So, for instance, we might define morally right action as that which is reasonable and proper.

The basic worry for nonnaturalism is that if we abandon empirical verification in ethics, it is not easy to see how we could verify or justify moral claims at all. If goodness is indefinable, or definable only by use of other moral terms which themselves are indefinable, how are we to know what is good and bad, right and wrong? If I am puzzled about whether an action is morally right, I'm likely to be equally puzzled about whether it is reasonable and proper. And things are still worse if we claim that goodness or rightness are basic and indefinable. For then we've no criteria at all to assist us in discovering truth in ethics.

In facing this problem, nonnaturalists have usually fallen back on the idea that we somehow intuit what is right and wrong. Intuition involves an immediate grasp or apprehension of the truth of some proposition. In ethics, the claim would be that we just intuit the truth that pain is bad, that keeping promises is good, that disloyalty is wrong, etc. The problem, of course, is that different people will have different intuitions about what is right and good and just, and intuitionism doesn't seem to have the resources for rationally adjudicating these disputes. If we deny that there are any definitions of moral terms, then there will be no criteria at all for arbitrating ethical disagreement. If we allow that there are such definitions, but insist that they contain moral terms, then the disagreements will simply be replicated in disputes about whether the defining moral terms (e.g., "reasonable," "proper") apply.

So the objectivist is faced with a dilemma: Either (i) opt for ethical naturalism, in which case we must come up with some plausible naturalistic analyses, or (ii) opt for ethical nonnaturalism, in which case we need to explain how it is possible to acquire knowledge of objective ethical facts. The subjectivist claims that options (i) and (ii) are so fraught with difficulties that it is best to abandon the commitment to ethical objectivity that motivated their development.

IMPLICATIONS OF META-ETHICAL SUBJECTIVISM

In addition to the powerful motivating arguments we have just discussed, meta-ethical subjectivism appeals because of its ability to handle several of the problems that beset normative subjectivism. Specifically, the worry about moral infallibility is bypassed, because this brand of subjectivism denies that anyone can ever possess moral truth, much less possess it in all instances. The problem of contradiction is likewise avoided. Contradictions arise when a proposition is alleged to be both true and false. If meta-ethical subjectivism is true, moral judgments are *neither* true *nor* false. Thus contradictions never arise. Finally, the existence and point of moral disagreement is preserved. According to meta-ethical subjectivism, ethical disagreements are disagreements in attitude. People on opposite sides of the abortion debate, for instance, have clashing attitudes toward abortion. There is real disagreement—emotional disagreement. Because they each may feel very strongly about the issue, the point of such debate is to convince others to share their view, and so act in ways they favor. This seems to account for a great deal of what goes on in ethical disagreement.

Still, meta-ethical subjectivism cannot avoid the remaining two implications of its normative cousin. Both brands of subjectivism generate a widespread moral equivalence, though for different reasons. Normative subjectivism makes each person an equally good arbiter of moral truth. Meta-ethical subjectivism denies that there is any moral truth. This denial implies that no one is superior to another at identifying what is right, or fine, or good. And no one is inferior, either. Moral judgments are expressions of taste, and a taste for cruelty or sadism is not worse (or better) than one for compassion and honesty. *De gustibus non est disputandum.*

Meta-ethical subjectivism also suffers from the problem of arbitrariness. If our ethical attachments are ultimately entirely up to us, with no supporting reasons needed, and no rationally compelling ones available, then our moral views are arbitrary. We have no better reason to support the ideology of Gandhi than of Pol Pot. Of course, each person actually will take a side. But our preferences in this regard are not rationally or ethically mandated. There is nothing necessarily irrational, wrong, or inappropriate about those whose fundamental aims differ from ours, even if those aims require for their satisfaction a policy of intimidation and torture.

Meta-ethical subjectivism also has to explain why all of us do employ non-subjectivist language in expressing our ethical outlooks. We frequently take our moral views to be *true,* and say as much in discussions with others. Our ethical conversations seem to be governed by a background assumption that, at least sometimes, those who disagree with us are *in error* and have *false beliefs.* Those with specially bad or confused impulses often come in for criticism as *irrational.* At the extreme, we may say of some such people that they or their views are *illogical.* Being illogical seems to involve contradiction, which (as we've seen) requires the notions of truth and falsity. Because meta-ethical subjectivism abandons these notions, it has difficulty explaining what illogical ethical views could amount to. The flip side is that these subjectivists also have difficulty explaining what logical ethical views amount to. A logical position is one in which one's views, if true, logically entail a true conclusion. But if we abandon the notion of truth in ethics, we seem to take the notion of logic with it.

Finally, if meta-ethical subjectivism is true, we must abandon our aspirations for moral knowledge. Knowledge presupposes truth. Though we often make claims to moral knowledge, such as knowing that genocide or racism is wrong, such claims must be merely metaphorical or false. There is no moral wisdom, at least none that comes from having the sort of ethical sensibility that issues in true moral judgments. Subjectivists usually counter that ethical knowledge is a matter of *knowing how* to live, rather than *knowing that* something or other is morally right. But what would it be to know how to live, if any consistent way of life was just as good as another? If we could not know *that* certain things were valuable, good, or virtuous, how could we be successful at knowing *how* to live? This is a challenge that subjectivists have yet to fully meet.

Conclusion

In many ways, the paces we've been put through here are entirely typical of philosophical discussion. Perhaps most typical is the state of play at the end of the day. Rarely do philosophers have knockdown arguments that can eliminate a philosophical position from contention. Philosophical evaluation is ordinarily a matter of weighing the pros and cons of competing theories, and tentatively opting for one view over another. Justifying a philosophical view requires advancing positive arguments on its behalf, and deflecting criticisms that detractors have identified. One needn't worry about getting bored. There will always be detractors. Criticisms are never in short supply.

Thus when we come to assess the merits of ethical subjectivism, in either of its major forms, we are engaged in a process of judgment. We examine the arguments in support of the theory, develop them as best we can, and then scrutinize the implications of adoption. Whether we can live with the implications depends on one's assessment of the theory's attractions, and those of its competitors. There is no neat, simple method for discharging this task. Whether we can live with moral equivalence, arbitrariness, and the impossibility of moral knowledge depends on whether we can do better elsewhere. And *that* depends on how well ethical objectivists can respond to the motivating arguments of previous sections. Subjectivism's prospects may be bright (or dim). But we can measure its incandescence only after a very great deal of further philosophical labor.[1]

NOTE

1. I undertake some of this labor in *Whatever Happened to Good and Evil?* (Oxford University Press 2003), an introductory book devoted to assessing the plausibility of ethical subjectivism and objectivism.

Trying Out One's New Sword

MARY MIDGLEY

Mary Midgley, now retired from the University of Newcastle-upon-Tyne, has written widely on a variety of issues regarding ethical theory, environmental ethics, and the relation between science and religion.

All of us are, more or less, in trouble today about trying to understand cultures strange to us. We hear constantly of alien customs. We see changes in our lifetime which would have astonished our parents. I want to discuss here one very short way of dealing with this difficulty, a drastic way which many people now theoretically favour. It consists in simply denying that we can ever understand any culture except our own well enough to make judgements about it. Those who recommend this hold that the world is sharply divided into separate societies, sealed units, each with its own system of thought. They feel that the respect and tolerance due from one system to another forbids us ever to take up a critical position to any other culture. Moral judgement, they suggest, is a kind of coinage valid only in its country of origin.

I shall call this position "moral isolationism." I shall suggest that it is certainly not forced upon us, and indeed that it makes no sense at all. People usually take it up because they think it is a respectful attitude to other cultures. In fact, however, it is not respectful. Nobody can respect what is entirely unintelligible to them. To respect someone, we have to know enough about him to make a *favourable* judgement, however general and tentative. And we do understand people in other cultures to this extent. Otherwise a great mass of our most valuable thinking would be paralysed.

To show this, I shall take a remote example, because we shall probably find it easier to think calmly about it than we should with a contemporary one, such as female circumcision in Africa or the Chinese Cultural Revolution. The principles involved will still be the same. My example is this. There is, it seems, a verb in classical Japanese which means "to try out one's new sword on a chance wayfarer". (The word is *tsujigiri*, literally "crossroads-cut".) A samurai sword had to be tried out because, if it was to work properly, it had to slice through someone at a single blow, from the shoulder to the opposite flank. Otherwise, the warrior bungled his stroke. This could injure his honour, offend his ancestors, and even let down his emperor. So tests were needed, and wayfarers had to be expended. Any wayfarer would do—provided, of course, that he was not another Samurai. Scientists will recognize a familiar problem about the rights of experimental subjects.

Now when we hear of a custom like this, we may well reflect that we simply do not understand it; and therefore are not qualified to criticize it at all, because we are not members of that culture. But we are not members of any other culture either, except our own. So we extend the principle to cover all extraneous cultures, and we seem therefore to be moral isolationists. But this is, as we shall see, an impossible position. Let us ask what it would involve.

We must ask first: Does the isolating barrier work both ways? Are people in other cultures equally unable to criticize *us*? This question struck me sharply when I read a remark in *The Guardian* by an anthropologist about a South American Indian who had been taken into a Brazilian town for an operation, which saved his life. When he came back to his village, he made several highly critical remarks about the white Brazilians' way of life. They may very well have been justified. But the interesting point was that the anthropologist called these remarks "a damning indictment of Western civilization". Now the Indian had been in that town about two weeks. Was he in a position to deliver a damning indictment? Would we ourselves be qualified to deliver such an indictment on the Samurai, provided we could spend two weeks in ancient Japan? What do we really think about this?

My own impression is that we believe that outsiders can, in principle, deliver perfectly good indictments—only, it usually takes more than two weeks to make them damning. Understanding has degrees. It is not a slapdash yes-or-no matter. Intelligent outsiders can progress in it, and in some ways will be at an advantage over the locals. But if this is so, it must clearly apply to ourselves as much as anybody else.

Our next question is this: Does the isolating barrier between cultures block praise as well as blame? If I want to say that the Samurai culture has many virtues, or to praise the South American Indians, am I prevented from doing *that* by my outside status? Now, we certainly do need to praise other societies in this way. But it is hardly possible that we could praise them effectively if we could not, in principle, criticize them. Our praise would be worthless if it rested on no definite grounds, if it did not flow from some understanding. Certainly we may need to praise things which we do not *fully* understand. We say "there's something very good here, but I can't quite make out what it is yet". This happens when we want to learn from strangers. And we can learn from strangers. But to do this we have to distinguish between those strangers who are worth learning from and those who are not. Can we then judge which is which?

This brings us to our third question: What is involved in judging? Now plainly there is no question here of sitting on a bench in a red robe and sentencing people. Judging simply means forming an opinion, and expressing it if it is called for. Is there anything wrong about this? Naturally, we ought to avoid forming—and expressing—*crude* opinions, like that of a simple-minded missionary, who might dismiss

the whole Samurai culture as entirely bad, because non-Christian. But this is a different objection. The trouble with crude opinions is that they are crude, whoever forms them, not that they are formed by the wrong people. Anthropologists, after all, are outsiders quite as much as missionaries. Moral isolationism forbids us to form *any* opinions on these matters. Its ground for doing so is that we don't understand them. But there is much that we don't understand in our own culture too. This brings us to our last question: If we can't judge other cultures, can we really judge our own? Our efforts to do so will be much damaged if we are really deprived of our opinions about other societies, because these provide the range of comparison, the spectrum of alternatives against which we set what we want to understand. We would have to stop using the mirror which anthropology so helpfully holds up to us.

In short, moral isolationism would lay down a general ban on moral reasoning. Essentially, this is the programme of immoralism, and it carries a distressing logical difficulty. Immoralists like Nietzsche are actually just a rather specialized sect of moralists. They can no more afford to put moralizing out of business than smugglers can afford to abolish customs regulations. The power of moral judgement is, in fact, not a luxury, not a perverse indulgence of the self-righteous. It is a necessity. When we judge something to be bad or good, better or worse than something else, we are taking it as an example to aim at or avoid. Without opinions of this sort, we would have no framework of comparison for our own policy, no chance of profiting by other people's insights or mistakes. In this vacuum, we could form no judgements on our own actions.

Now it would be odd if Homo sapiens had really got himself into a position as bad as this—a position where his main evolutionary asset, his brain, was so little use to him. None of us is going to accept this sceptical diagnosis. We cannot do so, because our involvement in moral isolationism does not flow from apathy, but from a rather acute concern about human hypocrisy and other forms of wickedness. But we polarize that concern around a few selected moral truths. We are rightly angry with those who despise, oppress or steamroll other cultures. We think that doing these things is actually *wrong*. But this is itself a moral judgement. We could not condemn oppression and insolence if we thought that all our condemnation were just a trivial local quirk of our own culture. We could still less do it if we tried to stop judging altogether.

Real moral scepticism, in fact, could lead only to inaction, to our losing all interest in moral questions, most of all in those which concern other societies. When we discuss these things, it becomes instantly clear how far we are from doing this. Suppose, for instance, that I criticize the bisecting Samurai, that I say his behaviour is brutal. What will usually happen next is that someone will protest, will say that I have no right to make criticisms like that of another culture. But it is most unlikely that he will use this move to end the discussion of the subject. Instead, he will justify the Samurai. He will try to fill in the background, to make me understand the custom, by explaining the exalted ideals of discipline and devotion which produced it. He will probably talk of the lower value which the ancient Japanese placed on individual life generally. He may well suggest that this is a healthier attitude than our own obsession with security. He may add, too, that the wayfarers did not seriously mind being bisected, that in principle they accepted the whole arrangement.

Now an objector who talks like this is implying that it *is* possible to understand alien customs. That is just what he is trying to make me do. And he implies, too, that if I do succeed in understanding them, I shall do something better than giving up judging them. He expects me to change my present judgement to a truer one—namely, one that is favourable. And the standards I must use to do this cannot just be Samurai standards. They have to be ones current in my own culture. Ideals like discipline and devotion will not move anybody unless he himself accepts them. As it happens, neither discipline nor devotion is very popular in the West at present. Anyone who appeals to them may well have to do some more arguing to make *them* acceptable, before he can use them to explain the Samurai.

But if he does succeed here, he will have persuaded us, not just that there was something to be said for them in ancient Japan, but that there would be here as well.

Isolating barriers simply cannot arise here. If we accept something as a serious moral truth about one culture, we can't refuse to apply it—in however different an outward form—to other cultures as well, wherever circumstances admit it. If we refuse to do this, we just are not taking the other culture seriously. This becomes clear if we look at the last argument used by my objector—that of justification by consent of the victim. It is suggested that sudden bisection is quite in order, *provided* that it takes place between consenting adults. I cannot now discuss how conclusive this justification is. What I am pointing out is simply that it can only work if we believe that *consent* can make such a transaction respectable—and this is a thoroughly modern and Western idea. It would probably never occur to a Samurai; if it did, it would surprise him very much. It is *our* standard. In applying it, too, we are likely to make another typically Western demand. We shall ask for good factual evidence that the wayfarers actually do have this rather surprising taste—that they are really willing to be bisected. In applying Western standards in this way, we are not being confused or irrelevant. We are asking the questions which arise *from where we stand*, questions which we can see the sense of. We do this because asking questions which you can't see the sense of is humbug. Certainly we can extend our questioning by imaginative effort. We can come to understand other societies better. By doing so, we may make their questions our own, or we may see that they are really forms of the questions which we are asking already. This is not impossible. It is just very hard work. The obstacles which often prevent it are simply those of ordinary ignorance, laziness and prejudice.

If there were really an isolating barrier, of course, our own culture could never have been formed. It is no sealed box, but a fertile jungle of different influences—Greek, Jewish, Roman, Norse, Celtic and so forth, into which further influences are still pouring—American, Indian, Japanese, Jamaican, you name it. The moral isolationist's picture of separate unmixable cultures is quite unreal. People who talk about British history usually stress the value of this fertilizing mix, no doubt rightly. But this is not just an odd fact about Britain. Except for the very smallest and most remote, all cultures are formed out of many streams. All have the problem of digesting and assimilating things which, at the start, they do not understand. All have the choice of learning something from this challenge, or, alternatively, of refusing to learn, and fighting it mindlessly instead.

This universal predicament has been obscured by the fact that anthropologists used to concentrate largely on very small and remote cultures, which did not seem to have this problem. These tiny societies, which had often forgotten their own history, made neat, self-contained subjects for study. No doubt it was valuable to emphasize their remoteness, their extreme strangeness, their independence of our cultural tradition. This emphasis was, I think, the root of moral isolationism. But, as the tribal studies themselves showed, even there the anthropologists were able to interpret what they saw and make judgements—often favourable—about the tribesmen. And the tribesmen, too, were quite equal to making judgements about the anthropologists—and about the tourists and Coca-Cola salesmen who followed them. Both sets of judgements, no doubt, were somewhat hasty, both have been refined in the light of further experience. A similar transaction between us and the Samurai might take even longer. But that is no reason at all for deeming it impossible. Morally as well as physically, there is only one world, and we all have to live in it.

The Nature of Virtue, from *Nicomachean Ethics*

ARISTOTLE

Aristotle (384–322 B.C.E.) is, in the minds of many, the greatest philosopher who ever lived. He was a student of Plato's, and in turn was tutor to Alexander the Great. In addition to his pathbreaking contributions to metaphysics, logic, rhetoric and the philosophy of mind, he was the pre-eminent scientist of his day.

BOOK I [HAPPINESS]

[Ends and Goods]

§1 Every craft and every line of inquiry, and likewise every action and decision, seems to seek some good; that is why some people were right to describe the good as what everything seeks. §2 But the ends [that are sought] appear to differ; some are activities, and others are products apart from the activities. Wherever there are ends apart from the actions, the products are by nature better than the activities.

§3 Since there are many actions, crafts, and sciences, the ends turn out to be many as well; for health is the end of medicine, a boat of boat building, victory of generalship, and wealth of household management. §4 But some of these pursuits are subordinate to some one capacity; for instance, bridle making and every other science producing equipment for horses are

From Aristotle, *Nicomachean Ethics,* translated by Terence Irwin, 2ed (Indianapolis: Hackett Publishing Company, 1999), pp. 1–4, 7–12, 15–18, 22–25, 28, 29, 163–69. Reprinted by permission of Hackett Publishing Company, Inc. All rights reserved.

subordinate to horsemanship, while this and every action in warfare are, in turn, subordinate to generalship, and in the same way other pursuits are subordinate to further ones. In all such cases, then, the ends of the ruling sciences are more choiceworthy than all the ends subordinate to them, since the lower ends are also pursued for the sake of the higher. §5 Here it does not matter whether the ends of the actions are the activities themselves, or something apart from them, as in the sciences we have mentioned.

[The Highest Good and Political Science]

§1 Suppose, then, that the things achievable by action have some end that we wish for because of itself, and because of which we wish for the other things, and that we do not choose everything because of something else—for if we do, it will go on without limit, so that desire will prove to be empty and futile. Clearly, this end will be the good, that is to say, the best good.

§2 Then surely knowledge of this good also carries great weight for [determining the best] way of life; if we know it, we are more likely, like archers who have a target to aim at, to hit the right mark. §3 If so, we should try to grasp, in outline at any rate, what the good is, and which is its proper science or capacity.

§4 It seems proper to the most controlling science—the highest ruling science. §5 And this appears characteristic of political science. §6 For it is the one that prescribes which of the sciences ought to be studied in cities, and which ones each class in the city should learn, and how far; indeed we see that even the most honored capacities—generalship, household management, and rhetoric, for instance—are subordinate to it. §7 And since it uses the other sciences concerned with action, and moreover legislates what must be done and what avoided, its end will include the ends of the other sciences, and so this will be the human good. §8 For even if the good is the same for a city as for an individual, still the good of the city is apparently a greater and more complete good to acquire and preserve. For while it is satisfactory to acquire and preserve the good even for an individual, it is finer and more divine to acquire and preserve it for a

people and for cities. And so, since our line of inquiry seeks these [goods, for an individual and for a community], it is a sort of political science.

[The Method of Political Science]

§1 Our discussion will be adequate if we make things perspicuous enough to accord with the subject matter; for we would not seek the same degree of exactness in all sorts of arguments alike, any more than in the products of different crafts. §2 Now, fine and just things, which political science examines, differ and vary so much as to seem to rest on convention only, not on nature. §3 But [this is not a good reason, since] goods also vary in the same way, because they result in harm to many people—for some have been destroyed because of their wealth, others because of their bravery. §4 And so, since this is our subject and these are our premises, we shall be satisfied to indicate the truth roughly and in outline; since our subject and our premises are things that hold good usually [but not universally], we shall be satisfied to draw conclusions of the same sort.

Each of our claims, then, ought to be accepted in the same way [as claiming to hold good usually]. For the educated person seeks exactness in each area to the extent that the nature of the subject allows; for apparently it is just as mistaken to demand demonstrations from a rhetorician as to accept [merely] persuasive arguments from a mathematician. §5 Further, each person judges rightly what he knows, and is a good judge about that; hence the good judge in a given area is the person educated in that area, and the unqualifiedly good judge is the person educated in every area.

This is why a youth is not a suitable student of political science; for he lacks experience of the actions in life, which are the subject and premises of our arguments. §6 Moreover, since he tends to follow his feelings, his study will be futile and useless; for the end [of political science] is action, not knowledge. §7 It does not matter whether he is young in years or immature in character, since the deficiency does not depend on age, but results from following his feelings in his life and in a given pursuit; for an immature person, like an incontinent person, gets no benefit from his knowledge. But for those who accord with reason in forming their desires and in their actions, knowledge of political science will be of great benefit.

§8 These are the preliminary points about the student, about the way our claims are to be accepted, and about what we propose to do.

[Common Beliefs]

§1 Let us, then, begin again. Since every sort of knowledge and decision pursues some good, what is the good that we say political science seeks? What, [in other words,] is the highest of all the goods achievable in action?

§2 As far as its name goes, most people virtually agree; for both the many and the cultivated call it happiness, and they suppose that living well and doing well are the same as being happy. But they disagree about what happiness is, and the many do not give the same answer as the wise.

§3 For the many think it is something obvious and evident—for instance, pleasure, wealth, or honor. Some take it to be one thing, others another. Indeed, the same person often changes his mind; for when he has fallen ill, he thinks happiness is health, and when he has fallen into poverty, he thinks it is wealth. And when they are conscious of their own ignorance, they admire anyone who speaks of something grand and above their heads. [Among the wise,] however, some used to think that besides these many goods there is some other good that exists in its own right and that causes all these goods to be goods.

§4 Presumably, then, it is rather futile to examine all these beliefs, and it is enough to examine those that are most current or seem to have some argument for them.

§5 We must notice, however, the difference between arguments from principles and arguments toward principles. For indeed Plato was right to be puzzled about this, when he used to ask if [the argument] set out from the principles or led toward them—just as on a race course the path may go from the starting line to the far end, or back again. For we should certainly begin from things known, but things are known in two ways; for some are known to us, some

known without qualification. Presumably, then, *we* ought to begin from things known to *us*.

§6 That is why we need to have been brought up in fine habits if we are to be adequate students of fine and just things, and of political questions generally. §7 For we begin from the [belief] that [something is true]; if this is apparent enough to us, we can begin without also [knowing] why [it is true]. Someone who is well brought up has the beginnings, or can easily acquire them. Someone who neither has them nor can acquire them should listen to Hesiod: 'He who grasps everything himself is best of all; he is noble also who listens to one who has spoken well; but he who neither grasps it himself nor takes to heart what he hears from another is a useless man.'

[The Three Lives]

§1 But let us begin again from the point from which we digressed. For, it would seem, people quite reasonably reach their conception of the good, i.e., of happiness, from the lives [they lead]; §2 for there are roughly three most favored lives: the lives of gratification, of political activity, and, third, of study.

The many, the most vulgar, would seem to conceive the good and happiness as pleasure, and hence they also like the life of gratification. §3 In this they appear completely slavish, since the life they decide on is a life for grazing animals. Still, they have some argument in their defense, since many in positions of power feel as Sardanapallus felt, [and also choose this life].

§4 The cultivated people, those active [in politics], conceive the good as honor, since this is more or less the end [normally pursued] in the political life. This, however, appears to be too superficial to be what we are seeking; for it seems to depend more on those who honor than on the one honored, whereas we intuitively believe that the good is something of our own and hard to take from us. §5 Further, it would seem, they pursue honor to convince themselves that they are good; at any rate, they seek to be honored by prudent people, among people who know them, and for virtue. It is clear, then, that—in their view at any rate—virtue is superior [to honor].

§6 Perhaps, indeed, one might conceive virtue more than honor to be the end of the political life. However, this also is apparently too incomplete [to be the good]. For it seems possible for someone to possess virtue but be asleep or inactive throughout his life, and, moreover, to suffer the worst evils and misfortunes. If this is the sort of life he leads, no one would count him happy, except to defend a philosopher's paradox. Enough about this, since it has been adequately discussed in the popular works as well.

§7 The third life is the life of study, which we shall examine in what follows.

§8 The moneymaker's life is in a way forced on him [not chosen for itself]; and clearly wealth is not the good we are seeking, since it is [merely] useful, [choiceworthy only] for some other end. Hence one would be more inclined to suppose that [any of] the goods mentioned earlier is the end, since they are liked for themselves. But apparently they are not [the end] either; and many arguments have been presented against them. Let us, then, dismiss them.

[An Account of the Human Good]

§1 But let us return once again to the good we are looking for, and consider just what it could be. For it is apparently one thing in one action or craft, and another thing in another; for it is one thing in medicine, another in generalship, and so on for the rest. What, then, is the good of each action or craft? Surely it is that for the sake of which the other things are done; in medicine this is health, in generalship victory, in house-building a house, in another case something else, but in every action and decision it is the end, since it is for the sake of the end that everyone does the other actions. And so, if there is some end of everything achievable in action, the good achievable in action will be this end; if there are more ends than one, [the good achievable in action] will be these ends.

§2 Our argument, then, has followed a different route to reach the same conclusion. But we must try to make this still more perspicuous. §3 Since there are apparently many ends, and we choose some of them (for instance, wealth, flutes, and, in general, instruments) because of something else, it is clear that not all ends are complete. But the best good is apparently something complete. And so, if only one end is complete, the good we are looking for will be this end; if more ends than one are complete, it will be the most complete end of these.

§4 We say that an end pursued in its own right is more complete than an end pursued because of something else, and that an end that is never choiceworthy because of something else is more complete than ends that are choiceworthy both in their own right and because of this end. Hence an end that is always choiceworthy in its own right, never because of something else, is complete without qualification.

§5 Now happiness, more than anything else, seems complete without qualification. For we always choose it because of itself, never because of something else. Honor, pleasure, understanding, and every virtue we certainly choose because of themselves, since we would choose each of them even if it had no further result; but we also choose them for the sake of happiness, supposing that through them we shall be happy. Happiness, by contrast, no one ever chooses for their sake, or for the sake of anything else at all.

§6 The same conclusion [that happiness is complete] also appears to follow from self-sufficiency. For the complete good seems to be self-sufficient. What we count as self-sufficient is not what suffices for a solitary person by himself, living an isolated life, but what suffices also for parents, children, wife, and, in general, for friends and fellow citizens, since a human being is a naturally political [animal]. §7 Here, however, we must impose some limit; for if we extend the good to parents' parents and children's children and to friends of friends, we shall go on without limit; but we must examine this another time. Anyhow, we regard something as self-sufficient when all by itself it makes a life choiceworthy and lacking nothing; and that is what we think happiness does.

§8 Moreover, we think happiness is most choiceworthy of all goods, [since] it is not counted as one good among many. [If it were] counted as one among many, then, clearly, we think it would be more choiceworthy if the smallest of goods were added; for the good that is added becomes an extra quantity of goods, and the larger of two goods is always more choice-worthy. Happiness, then, is apparently something complete and selfsufficient, since it is the end of the things achievable in action.

§9 But presumably the remark that the best good is happiness is apparently something [generally] agreed, and we still need a clearer statement of what the best good is. §10 Perhaps, then, we shall find this if we first grasp the function of a human being. For just as the good, i.e., [doing] well, for a flautist, a sculptor, and every craftsman, and, in general, for whatever has a function and [characteristic] action, seems to depend on its function, the same seems to be true for a human being, if a human being has some function.

§11 Then do the carpenter and the leather worker have their functions and actions, but has a human being no function? Is he by nature idle, without any function? Or, just as eye, hand, foot, and, in general, every [bodily] part apparently has its function, may we likewise ascribe to a human being some function apart from all of these?

§12 What, then, could this be? For living is apparently shared with plants, but what we are looking for is the special function of a human being; hence we should set aside the life of nutrition and growth. The life next in order is some sort of life of sense perception; but this too is apparently shared with horse, ox, and every animal.

§13 The remaining possibility, then, is some sort of life of action of the [part of the soul] that has reason. One [part] of it has reason as obeying reason; the other has it as itself having reason and thinking. Moreover, life is also spoken of in two ways [as capacity and as activity], and we must take [a human being's special function to be] life as activity, since this seems to be called life more fully. We have found, then, that the human function is activity of the soul in accord with reason or requiring reason.

§14 Now we say that the function of a [kind of thing]—of a harpist, for instance—is the same in kind as the function of an excellent individual of the kind—of an excellent harpist, for instance. And the same is true without qualification in every case, if we add to the function the superior

achievement in accord with the virtue; for the function of a harpist is to play the harp, and the function of a good harpist is to play it well. Moreover, we take the human function to be a certain kind of life, and take this life to be activity and actions of the soul that involve reason; hence the function of the excellent man is to do this well and finely.

§15 Now each function is completed well by being completed in accord with the virtue proper [to that kind of thing]. And so the human good proves to be activity of the soul in accord with virtue, and indeed with the best and most complete virtue, if there are more virtues than one. §16 Moreover, it must be in a complete life. For one swallow does not make a spring, nor does one day; nor, similarly, does one day or a short time make us blessed and happy.

§17 This, then, is a sketch of the good; for, presumably, we must draw the outline first, and fill it in later. If the sketch is good, anyone, it seems, can advance and articulate it, and in such cases time discovers more, or is a good partner in discovery. That is also how the crafts have improved, since anyone can add what is lacking [in the outline].

§18 We must also remember our previous remarks, so that we do not look for the same degree of exactness in all areas, but the degree that accords with a given subject matter and is proper to a given line of inquiry. §19 For the carpenter's and the geometer's inquiries about the right angle are different also; the carpenter restricts himself to what helps his work, but the geometer inquires into what, or what sort of thing, the right angle is, since he studies the truth. We must do the same, then, in other areas too, [seeking the proper degree of exactness], so that digressions do not overwhelm our main task.

§20 Nor should we make the same demand for an explanation in all cases. On the contrary, in some cases it is enough to prove rightly that [something is true, without also explaining why it is true]. This is so, for instance, with principles, where the fact that [something is true] is the first thing, that is to say, the principle.

§21 Some principles are studied by means of induction, some by means of perception, some by means of some sort of habituation, and others by other means. §22 In each case we should try to find them out by means suited to their nature, and work hard to define them rightly. §23 For they carry great weight for what follows; for the principle seems to be more than half the whole, and makes evident the answer to many of our questions.

[Defense of the Account of the Good]

§1 We should examine the principle, however, not only from the conclusion and premises [of a deduction], but also from what is said about it; for all the facts harmonize with a true account, whereas the truth soon clashes with a false one.

§2 Goods are divided, then, into three types, some called external, some goods of the soul, others goods of the body. We say that the goods of the soul are goods most fully, and more than the others, and we take actions and activities of the soul to be [goods] of the soul. And so our account [of the good] is right, to judge by this belief anyhow—and it is an ancient belief, and accepted by philosophers.

§3 Our account is also correct in saying that some sort of actions and activities are the end; for in that way the end turns out to be a good of the soul, not an external good.

§4 The belief that the happy person lives well and does well also agrees with our account, since we have virtually said that the end is a sort of living well and doing well.

§5 Further, all the features that people look for in happiness appear to be true of the end described in our account. §6 For to some people happiness seems to be virtue; to others prudence; to others some sort of wisdom; to others again it seems to be these, or one of these, involving pleasure or requiring it to be added; others add in external prosperity as well. §7 Some of these views are traditional, held by many, while others are held by a few men who are widely esteemed. It is reasonable for each group not to be completely wrong, but to be correct on one point at least, or even on most points.

§8 First, our account agrees with those who say happiness is virtue [in general] or some [particular] virtue; for activity in accord with virtue is proper to virtue. §9 Presumably, though, it matters quite a bit whether we suppose that the best good consists in possessing or in using—that is to say, in a state or in an activity [that actualizes the state]. For someone may be in a state that achieves no good—if, for instance, he is asleep or inactive in some other way—but this cannot be true of the activity; for it will necessarily act and act well. And just as Olympic prizes are not for the finest and strongest, but for the contestants—since it is only these who win—the same is true in life; among the fine and good people, only those who act correctly win the prize.

§10 Moreover, the life of these active people is also pleasant in itself. For being pleased is a condition of the soul, [and hence is included in the activity of the soul]. Further, each type of person finds pleasure in whatever he is called a lover of; a horse, for instance, pleases the horse-lover, a spectacle the lover of spectacles. Similarly, what is just pleases the lover of justice, and in general what accords with virtue pleases the lover of virtue.

§11 Now the things that please most people conflict, because they are not pleasant by nature, whereas the things that please lovers of the fine are things pleasant by nature. Actions in accord with virtue are pleasant by nature, so that they both please lovers of the fine and are pleasant in their own right.

§12 Hence these people's life does not need pleasure to be added [to virtuous activity] as some sort of extra decoration; rather, it has its pleasure within itself. For besides the reasons already given, someone who does not enjoy fine actions is not good; for no one would call a person just, for instance, if he did not enjoy doing just actions, or generous if he did not enjoy generous actions, and similarly for the other virtues.

§13 If this is so, actions in accord with the virtues are pleasant in their own right. Moreover, these actions are good and fine as well as pleasant; indeed, they are good, fine, and pleasant more than anything else is, since on this question the excellent person judges rightly, and his judgment agrees with what we have said.

§14 Happiness, then, is best, finest, and most pleasant, and the Delian inscription is wrong to distinguish these things: 'What is most just is finest; being healthy is most beneficial; but it is most pleasant to win our heart's desire.' For all three features are found in the best activities, and we say happiness is these activities, or [rather] one of them, the best one.

§15 Nonetheless, happiness evidently also needs external goods to be added, as we said, since we cannot, or cannot easily, do fine actions if we lack the resources. For, first of all, in many actions we use friends, wealth, and political power just as we use instruments. §16 Further, deprivation of certain [externals]—for instance, good birth, good children, beauty—mars our blessedness. For we do not altogether have the character of happiness if we look utterly repulsive or are ill-born, solitary, or childless; and we have it even less, presumably, if our children or friends are totally bad, or were good but have died.

§17 And so, as we have said, happiness would seem to need this sort of prosperity added also. That is why some people identify happiness with good fortune, and others identify it with virtue.

[How Is Happiness Achieved?]

§1 This also leads to a puzzle: Is happiness acquired by learning, or habituation, or by some other form of cultivation? Or is it the result of some divine fate, or even of fortune?

§2 First, then, if the gods give any gift at all to human beings, it is reasonable for them to give us happiness more than any other human good, insofar as it is the best of human goods. §3 Presumably, however, this question is more suitable for a different inquiry.

But even if it is not sent by the gods, but instead results from virtue and some sort of learning or cultivation, happiness appears to be one of the most divine things, since the prize and goal of virtue appears to be the best good, something divine and blessed. §4 Moreover [if happiness comes in this way] it will be widely shared; for anyone who is not deformed [in his capacity] for virtue will be able to achieve happiness through some sort of learning and attention.

§5 And since it is better to be happy in this way than because of fortune, it is reasonable for this to be the way [we become] happy. For whatever is natural is naturally in the finest state possible. §6 The same is true of the products of crafts and of every other cause, especially the

best cause; and it would be seriously inappropriate to entrust what is greatest and finest to fortune.

§7 The answer to our question is also evident from our account. For we have said that happiness is a certain sort of activity of the soul in accord with virtue, [and hence not a result of fortune]. Of the other goods, some are necessary conditions of happiness, while others are naturally useful and cooperative as instruments [but are not parts of it].

§8 Further, this conclusion agrees with our opening remarks. For we took the goal of political science to be the best good; and most of its attention is devoted to the character of the citizens, to make them good people who do fine actions.

§9 It is not surprising, then, that we regard neither ox, nor horse, nor any other kind of animal as happy; for none of them can share in this sort of activity. §10 For the same reason a child is not happy either, since his age prevents him from doing these sorts of actions. If he is called happy, he is being congratulated [simply] because of anticipated blessedness; for, as we have said, happiness requires both complete virtue and a complete life.

§11 It needs a complete life because life includes many reversals of fortune, good and bad, and the most prosperous person may fall into a terrible disaster in old age, as the Trojan stories tell us about Priam. If someone has suffered these sorts of misfortunes and comes to a miserable end, no one counts him happy.

[Praise and Honor]

§1 Now that we have determined these points, let us consider whether happiness is something praiseworthy, or instead something honorable; for clearly it is not a capacity [which is neither praiseworthy nor honorable].

§2 Whatever is praiseworthy appears to be praised for its character and its state in relation to something. We praise the just and the brave person, for instance, and in general the good person and virtue, because of their actions and achievements; and we praise the strong person, the good runner, and each of the others because he naturally has a certain character and is in a certain state in relation to something good and excellent. §3 This is clear also from praises of the gods; for these praises appear ridiculous because they are referred to us, but they are referred to us because, as we said, praise depends on such a reference.

§4 If praise is for these sorts of things, then clearly for the best things there is no praise, but something greater and better. And indeed this is how it appears. For the gods and the most god-like of men are [not praised, but] congratulated for their blessedness and happiness. The same is true of goods; for we never praise happiness, as we praise justice, but we count it blessed, as something better and more godlike [than anything that is praised].

§5 Indeed, Eudoxus seems to have used the right sort of argument in defending the supremacy of pleasure. By not praising pleasure, though it is a good, we indicate—so he thought—that it is superior to everything praiseworthy; [only] the god and the good have this superiority since the other goods are [praised] by reference to them.

§6 [Here he seems to have argued correctly.] For praise is given to virtue, since it makes us do fine actions; but celebrations are for achievements, either of body or of soul. §7 But an exact treatment of this is presumably more proper for specialists in celebrations. For us, anyhow, it is clear from what has been said that happiness is something honorable and complete.

§8 A further reason why this would seem to be correct is that happiness is a principle; for [the principle] is what we all aim at in all our other actions; and we take the principle and cause of goods to be something honorable and divine.

[Introduction to the Virtues]

§1 Since happiness is a certain sort of activity of the soul in accord with complete virtue, we must examine virtue; for that will perhaps also be a way to study happiness better. §2 Moreover, the true politician seems to have put more effort into virtue than into anything else, since he wants to make the citizens good and law-abiding. §3 We find an example of this in the Spartan and Cretan legislators and in any others who share their concerns. §4 Since, then, the examination

of virtue is proper for political science, the inquiry clearly suits our decision at the beginning.

§5 It is clear that the virtue we must examine is human virtue, since we are also seeking the human good and human happiness. §6 By human virtue we mean virtue of the soul, not of the body, since we also say that happiness is an activity of the soul. §7 If this is so, it is clear that the politician must in some way know about the soul, just as someone setting out to heal the eyes must know about the whole body as well. This is all the more true to the extent that political science is better and more honorable than medicine; even among doctors, the cultivated ones devote a lot of effort to finding out about the body. Hence the politician as well [as the student of nature] must study the soul. §8 But he must study it for his specific purpose, far enough for his inquiry [into virtue]; for a more exact treatment would presumably take more effort than his purpose requires.

§9 [We] have discussed the soul sufficiently [for our purposes] in [our] popular works as well [as our less popular], and we should use this discussion. We have said, for instance, that one [part] of the soul is nonrational, while one has reason. §10 Are these distinguished as parts of a body and everything divisible into parts are? Or are they two [only] in definition, and inseparable by nature, as the convex and the concave are in a surface? It does not matter for present purposes.

§11 Consider the nonrational [part]. One [part] of it, i.e., the cause of nutrition and growth, would seem to be plantlike and shared [with all living things]; for we can ascribe this capacity of the soul to everything that is nourished, including embryos, and the same capacity to full-grown living things, since this is more reasonable than to ascribe another capacity to them.

§12 Hence the virtue of this capacity is apparently shared, not [specifically] human. For this part and this capacity more than others seem to be active in sleep, and here the good and the bad person are least distinct; hence happy people are said to be no better off than miserable people for half their lives. §13 This lack of distinction is not surprising, since sleep is inactivity of the soul insofar as it is called excellent or base, unless to some small extent some movements penetrate [to our awareness], and in this way the decent person comes to have better images [in dreams] than just any random person has. §14 Enough about this, however, and let us leave aside the nutritive part, since by nature it has no share in human virtue.

§15 Another nature in the soul would also seem to be nonrational, though in a way it shares in reason. For in the continent and the incontinent person we praise their reason, that is to say, the [part] of the soul that has reason, because it exhorts them correctly and toward what is best; but they evidently also have in them some other [part] that is by nature something apart from reason, clashing and struggling with reason. For just as paralyzed parts of a body, when we decide to move them to the right, do the contrary and move off to the left, the same is true of the soul; for incontinent people have impulses in contrary directions. §16 In bodies, admittedly, we see the part go astray, whereas we do not see it in the soul; nonetheless, presumably, we should suppose that the soul also has something apart from reason, countering and opposing reason. The [precise] way it is different does not matter.

§17 However, this [part] as well [as the rational part] appears, as we said, to share in reason. At any rate, in the continent person it obeys reason; and in the temperate and the brave person it presumably listens still better to reason, since there it agrees with reason in everything.

§18 The nonrational [part], then, as well [as the whole soul] apparently has two parts. For while the plantlike [part] shares in reason not at all, the [part] with appetites and in general desires shares in reason in a way, insofar as it both listens to reason and obeys it. This is the way in which we are said to 'listen to reason' from father or friends, as opposed to the way in which [we 'give the reason'] in mathematics. The nonrational part also [obeys and] is persuaded in some way by reason, as is shown by correction, and by every sort of reproof and exhortation.

§19 If, then, we ought to say that this [part] also has reason, then the [part] that has reason, as well [as the nonrational part], will have two parts. One will have reason fully, by having it within itself; the other will have reason by listening to reason as to a father.

The division between virtues accords with this difference. For some virtues are called virtues of thought, others virtues of character; wisdom, comprehension, and prudence are called virtues of thought, generosity and temperance virtues of character. For when we speak of someone's character we do not say that he is wise or has good comprehension, but that he is gentle or temperate. And yet, we also praise the wise person for his state, and the states that are praiseworthy are the ones we call virtues.

BOOK II [VIRTUE OF CHARACTER]

[How a Virtue of Character Is Acquired]

§1 Virtue, then, is of two sorts, virtue of thought and virtue of character. Virtue of thought arises and grows mostly from teaching; that is why it needs experience and time. Virtue of character [i.e., of *ēthos*] results from habit [*ethos*]; hence its name 'ethical', slightly varied from 'ethos'.

§2 Hence it is also clear that none of the virtues of character arises in us naturally. For if something is by nature in one condition, habituation cannot bring it into another condition. A stone, for instance, by nature moves downwards, and habituation could not make it move upwards, not even if you threw it up ten thousand times to habituate it; nor could habituation make fire move downwards, or bring anything that is by nature in one condition into another condition. §3 And so the virtues arise in us neither by nature nor against nature. Rather, we are by nature able to acquire them, and we are completed through habit.

§4 Further, if something arises in us by nature, we first have the capacity for it, and later perform the activity. This is clear in the case of the senses; for we did not acquire them by frequent seeing or hearing, but we already had them when we exercised them, and did not get them by exercising them. Virtues, by contrast, we acquire, just as we acquire crafts, by having first activated them. For we learn a craft by producing the same product that we must produce when we have learned it; we become builders, for instance, by building, and we become harpists by playing the harp. Similarly, then, we become just by doing just actions, temperate by doing temperate actions, brave by doing brave actions....

[Habituation]

§1 Our present discussion does not aim, as our others do, at study; for the purpose of our examination is not to know what virtue is, but to become good, since otherwise the inquiry would be of no benefit to us. And so we must examine the right ways of acting; for, as we have said, the actions also control the sorts of states we acquire.

§2 First, then, actions should accord with the correct reason. That is a common [belief], and let us assume it. We shall discuss it later, and say what the correct reason is and how it is related to the other virtues.

§3 But let us take it as agreed in advance that every account of the actions we must do has to be stated in outline, not exactly. As we also said at the beginning, the type of accounts we demand should accord with the subject matter; and questions about actions and expediency, like questions about health, have no fixed answers.

§4 While this is the character of our general account, the account of particular cases is still more inexact. For these fall under no craft or profession; the agents themselves must consider in each case what the opportune action is, as doctors and navigators do. §5 The account we offer, then, in our present inquiry is of this inexact sort; still, we must try to offer help.

§6 First, then, we should observe that these sorts of states naturally tend to be ruined by excess and deficiency. We see this happen with strength and health—for we must use evident cases [such as these] as witnesses to things that are not evident. For both excessive and deficient exercise ruin bodily strength, and, similarly, too much or too little eating or drinking ruins health, whereas the proportionate amount produces, increases, and preserves it.

§7 The same is true, then, of temperance, bravery, and the other virtues. For if, for instance, someone avoids and is afraid of everything, standing firm against nothing, he becomes cowardly; if he is afraid of nothing at all and goes to face

everything, he becomes rash. Similarly, if he gratifies himself with every pleasure and abstains from none, he becomes intemperate; if he avoids them all, as boors do, he becomes some sort of insensible person. Temperance and bravery, then, are ruined by excess and deficiency, but preserved by the mean.

§8 But these actions are not only the sources and causes both of the emergence and growth of virtues and of their ruin; the activities of the virtues [once we have acquired them] also consist in these same actions. For this is also true of more evident cases; strength, for instance, arises from eating a lot and from withstanding much hard labor, and it is the strong person who is most capable of these very actions. §9 It is the same with the virtues. For abstaining from pleasures makes us become temperate, and once we have become temperate we are most capable of abstaining from pleasures. It is similar with bravery; habituation in disdain for frightening situations and in standing firm against them makes us become brave, and once we have become brave we shall be most capable of standing firm.

[The Importance of Pleasure and Pain]

§1 But we must take someone's pleasure or pain following on his actions to be a sign of his state. For if someone who abstains from bodily pleasures enjoys the abstinence itself, he is temperate; if he is grieved by it, he is intemperate. Again, if he stands firm against terrifying situations and enjoys it, or at least does not find it painful, he is brave; if he finds it painful, he is cowardly. For virtue of character is about pleasures and pains.

For pleasure causes us to do base actions, and pain causes us to abstain from fine ones. §2 That is why we need to have had the appropriate upbringing—right from early youth, as Plato says—to make us find enjoyment or pain in the right things; for this is the correct education....

§6 We assume, then, that virtue is the sort of state that does the best actions concerning pleasures and pains, and that vice is the contrary state....

§11 To sum up: Virtue is about pleasures and pains; the actions that are its sources also increase it or, if they are done badly, ruin it; and its activity is about the same actions as those that are its sources.

[Virtuous Actions versus Virtuous Character]

§1 Someone might be puzzled, however, about what we mean by saying that we become just by doing just actions and become temperate by doing temperate actions. For [one might suppose that] if we do grammatical or musical actions, we are grammarians or musicians, and, similarly, if we do just or temperate actions, we are thereby just or temperate.

§2 But surely actions are not enough, even in the case of crafts; for it is possible to produce a grammatical result by chance, or by following someone else's instructions. To be grammarians, then, we must both produce a grammatical result and produce it grammatically—that is to say, produce it in accord with the grammatical knowledge in us.

§3 Moreover, in any case, what is true of crafts is not true of virtues. For the products of a craft determine by their own qualities whether they have been produced well; and so it suffices that they have the right qualities when they have been produced. But for actions in accord with the virtues to be done temperately or justly it does not suffice that they themselves have the right qualities. Rather, the agent must also be in the right state when he does them. First, he must know [that he is doing virtuous actions]; second, he must decide on them, and decide on them for themselves; and, third, he must also do them from a firm and unchanging state....

§4 Hence actions are called just or temperate when they are the sort that a just or temperate person would do. But the just and temperate person is not the one who [merely] does these actions, but the one who also does them in the way in which just or temperate people do them.

§5 It is right, then, to say that a person comes to be just from doing just actions and temperate from doing temperate actions; for no one has the least prospect of becoming good from failing to do them....

[Virtue of Character: Its Genus]

§1 Next we must examine what virtue is. Since there are three conditions arising in the soul—feelings, capacities, and states—virtue must be one of these....

§3 First, then, neither virtues nor vices are feelings. For we are called excellent or base insofar as we have virtues or vices, not insofar as we have feelings. Further, we are neither praised nor blamed insofar as we have feelings; for we do not praise the angry or the frightened person, and do not blame the person who is simply angry, but only the person who is angry in a particular way. We are praised or blamed, however, insofar as we have virtues or vices....

§5 For these reasons the virtues are not capacities either; for we are neither called good nor called bad, nor are we praised or blamed, insofar as we are simply capable of feelings....

§6 If, then, the virtues are neither feelings nor capacities, the remaining possibility is that they are states. And so we have said what the genus of virtue is.

[Virtue of Character: Its Differentia]

§1 But we must say not only, as we already have, that it is a state, but also what sort of state it is.

§2 It should be said, then, that every virtue causes its possessors to be in a good state and to perform their functions well. The virtue of eyes, for instance, makes the eyes and their functioning excellent, because it makes us see well; and similarly, the virtue of a horse makes the horse excellent, and thereby good at galloping, at carrying its rider, and at standing steady in the face of the enemy. §3 If this is true in every case, the virtue of a human being will likewise be the state that makes a human being good and makes him perform his function well.

§4 We have already said how this will be true, and it will also be evident from our next remarks, if we consider the sort of nature that virtue has.

In everything continuous and divisible we can take more, less, and equal, and each of them either in the object itself or relative to us; and the equal is some intermediate between excess and deficiency. §5 By the intermediate in the object I mean what is equidistant from each extremity; this is one and the same for all. But relative to us the intermediate is what is neither superfluous nor deficient; this is not one, and is not the same for all.

§6 If, for instance, ten are many and two are few, we take six as intermediate in the object, since it exceeds [two] and is exceeded [by ten] by an equal amount, [four]. §7 This is what is intermediate by numerical proportion. But that is not how we must take the intermediate that is relative to us. For if ten pounds [of food], for instance, are a lot for someone to eat, and two pounds a little, it does not follow that the trainer will prescribe six, since this might also be either a little or a lot for the person who is to take it—for Milo [the athlete] a little, but for the beginner in gymnastics a lot; and the same is true for running and wrestling. §8 In this way every scientific expert avoids excess and deficiency and seeks and chooses what is intermediate—but intermediate relative to us, not in the object....

§10 By virtue I mean virtue of character; for this is about feelings and actions, and these admit of excess, deficiency, and an intermediate condition. We can be afraid, for instance, or be confident, or have appetites, or get angry, or feel pity, and in general have pleasure or pain, both too much and too little, and in both ways not well. §11 But having these feelings at the right times, about the right things, toward the right people, for the right end, and in the right way, is the intermediate and best condition, and this is proper to virtue. §12 Similarly, actions also admit of excess, deficiency, and an intermediate condition.

Now virtue is about feelings and actions, in which excess and deficiency are in error and incur blame, whereas the intermediate condition is correct and wins praise, which are both proper to virtue. §13 Virtue, then, is a mean, insofar as it aims at what is intermediate....

§15 Virtue, then, is a state that decides, consisting in a mean, the mean relative to us, which is defined by reference to reason, that is to say, to the reason by reference to which the prudent person would define it. It is a mean between two vices, one of excess and one of deficiency.

§16 It is a mean for this reason also: Some vices miss what is right because they are deficient, others because they are excessive, in feelings or in actions, whereas virtue finds and chooses what is intermediate.

§17 That is why virtue, as far as its essence and the account stating what it is are concerned, is a mean, but, as far as the best [condition] and the good [result] are concerned, it is an extremity.

§18 Now not every action or feeling admits of the mean. For the names of some automatically include baseness—for instance, spite, shamelessness, envy [among feelings], and adultery, theft, murder, among actions. For all of these and similar things are called by these names because they themselves, not their excesses or deficiencies, are base. Hence in doing these things we can never be correct, but must invariably be in error. We cannot do them well or not well—by committing adultery, for instance, with the right woman at the right time in the right way. On the contrary, it is true without qualification that to do any of them is to be in error.

§19 [To think these admit of a mean], therefore, is like thinking that unjust or cowardly or intemperate action also admits of a mean, an excess and a deficiency. If it did, there would be a mean of excess, a mean of deficiency, an excess of excess and a deficiency of deficiency. §20 On the contrary, just as there is no excess or deficiency of temperance or of bravery (since the intermediate is a sort of extreme), so also there is no mean of these vicious actions either, but whatever way anyone does them, he is in error. For in general there is no mean of excess or of deficiency, and no excess or deficiency of a mean.

[The Particular Virtues of Character]

§1 However, we must not only state this general account but also apply it to the particular cases. For among accounts concerning actions, though the general ones are common to more cases, the specific ones are truer, since actions are about particular cases, and our account must accord with these. Let us, then, find these from the chart.

§2 First, then, in feelings of fear and confidence the mean is bravery. The excessively fearless person is nameless (indeed many cases are nameless), and the one who is excessively confident is rash. The one who is excessive in fear and deficient in confidence is cowardly.

§3 In pleasures and pains—though not in all types, and in pains less than in pleasures—the mean is temperance and the excess intemperance.

People deficient in pleasure are not often found, which is why they also lack even a name; let us call them insensible.

§4 In giving and taking money the mean is generosity, the excess wastefulness and the deficiency ungenerosity. Here the vicious people have contrary excesses and defects; for the wasteful person is excessive in spending and deficient in taking, whereas the ungenerous person is excessive in taking and deficient in spending. §5 At the moment we are speaking in outline and summary, and that is enough; later we shall define these things more exactly.

[Relations Between Mean and Extreme States]

§1 Among these three conditions, then, two are vices—one of excess, one of deficiency—and one, the mean, is virtue. In a way, each of them is opposed to each of the others, since each extreme is contrary both to the intermediate condition and to the other extreme, while the intermediate is contrary to the extremes.

§2 For, just as the equal is greater in comparison to the smaller, and smaller in comparison to the greater, so also the intermediate states are excessive in comparison to the deficiencies and deficient in comparison to the excesses—both in feelings and in actions. For the brave person, for instance, appears rash in comparison to the coward, and cowardly in comparison to the rash person; the temperate person appears intemperate in comparison to the insensible person, and insensible in comparison with the intemperate person; and the generous person appears wasteful in comparison to the ungenerous, and ungenerous in comparison to the wasteful person. §3 That is why each of the extreme people tries to push the intermediate person to the other extreme, so that the coward, for instance, calls the brave person rash, and the rash person calls him a coward, and similarly in the other cases.

§4 Since these conditions of soul are opposed to each other in these ways, the extremes are more contrary to each other than to the intermediate. For they are further from each other than from the intermediate, just as the large is further from the small, and the small from the large, than either is from the equal.

§5 Further, sometimes one extreme—rashness or wastefulness, for instance—appears somewhat like the intermediate state, bravery or generosity. But the extremes are most unlike one another; and the things that are furthest apart from each other are defined as contraries. And so the things that are further apart are more contrary.

§6 In some cases the deficiency, in others the excess, is more opposed to the intermediate condition. For instance, cowardice, the deficiency, not rashness, the excess, is more opposed to bravery, whereas intemperance, the excess, not insensibility, the deficiency, is more opposed to temperance.

§7 This happens for two reasons: One reason is derived from the object itself. Since sometimes one extreme is closer and more similar to the intermediate condition, we oppose the contrary extreme, more than this closer one, to the intermediate condition. Since rashness, for instance, seems to be closer and more similar to bravery, and cowardice less similar, we oppose cowardice, more than rashness, to bravery; for what is further from the intermediate condition seems to be more contrary to it. This, then, is one reason, derived from the object itself.

§8 The other reason is derived from ourselves. For when we ourselves have some natural tendency to one extreme more than to the other, this extreme appears more opposed to the intermediate condition. Since, for instance, we have more of a natural tendency to pleasure, we drift more easily toward intemperance than toward orderliness. Hence we say that an extreme is more contrary if we naturally develop more in that direction; and this is why intemperance is more contrary to temperance, since it is the excess [of pleasure].

[How Can We Reach the Mean?]

§1 We have said enough, then, to show that virtue of character is a mean and what sort of mean it is; that it is a mean between two vices, one of excess and one of deficiency; and that it is a mean because it aims at the intermediate condition in feelings and actions.

§2 That is why it is also hard work to be excellent. For in each case it is hard work to find the intermediate; for instance, not everyone, but only one who knows, finds the midpoint in a circle. So also getting angry, or giving and spending money, is easy and everyone can do it; but doing it to the right person, in the right amount, at the right time, for the right end, and in the right way is no longer easy, nor can everyone do it. Hence doing these things well is rare, praiseworthy, and fine.

§3 That is why anyone who aims at the intermediate condition must first of all steer clear of the more contrary extreme, following the advice that Calypso also gives: 'Hold the ship outside the spray and surge.' For one extreme is more in error, the other less. §4 Since, therefore, it is hard to hit the intermediate extremely accurately, the secondbest tack, as they say, is to take the lesser of the evils. We shall succeed best in this by the method we describe.

We must also examine what we ourselves drift into easily. For different people have different natural tendencies toward different goals, and we shall come to know our own tendencies from the pleasure or pain that arises in us. §5 We must drag ourselves off in the contrary direction; for if we pull far away from error, as they do in straightening bent wood, we shall reach the intermediate condition.

§6 And in everything we must beware above all of pleasure and its sources; for we are already biased in its favor when we come to judge it. Hence we must react to it as the elders reacted to Helen, and on each occasion repeat what they said; for if we do this, and send it off, we shall be less in error.

§7 In summary, then, if we do these things we shall best be able to reach the intermediate condition. But presumably this is difficult, especially in particular cases, since it is not easy to define the way we should be angry, with whom, about what, for how long. For sometimes, indeed, we ourselves praise deficient people and call them mild, and sometimes praise quarrelsome people and call them manly.

§8 Still, we are not blamed if we deviate a little in excess or deficiency from doing well, but only if we deviate a long way, since then we are easily noticed. But how great and how serious a deviation receives blame is not easy to define in an account; for nothing else perceptible is easily defined either. Such things are among particulars, and the judgment depends on perception.

§9 This is enough, then, to make it clear that in every case the intermediate state is praised, but we must sometimes incline toward the excess, sometimes toward the deficiency; for that is the easiest way to hit the intermediate and good condition.

BOOK X

[Happiness and Theoretical Study]

§1 If happiness is activity in accord with virtue, it is reasonable for it to accord with the supreme virtue, which will be the virtue of the best thing. The best is understanding, or whatever else seems to be the natural ruler and leader, and to understand what is fine and divine, by being itself either divine or the most divine element in us. Hence complete happiness will be its activity in accord with its proper virtue; and we have said that this activity is the activity of study.

§2 This seems to agree with what has been said before, and also with the truth. For this activity is supreme, since understanding is the supreme element in us, and the objects of understanding are the supreme objects of knowledge.

Further, it is the most continuous activity, since we are more capable of continuous study than any continuous action.

§3 Besides, we think pleasure must be mixed into happiness; and it is agreed that the activity in accord with wisdom is the most pleasant of the activities in accord with virtue. Certainly, philosophy seems to have remarkably pure and firm pleasures, and it is reasonable for those who have knowledge to spend their lives more pleasantly than those who seek it.

§4 Moreover, the self-sufficiency we spoke of will be found in study more than in anything else. For admittedly the wise person, the just person, and the other virtuous people all need the good things necessary for life. Still, when these are adequately supplied, the just person needs other people as partners and recipients of his just actions; and the same is true of the temperate person, the brave person, and each of the others. But the wise person is able, and more able the wiser he is, to study even by himself; and though he presumably does it better with colleagues, even so he is more self-sufficient than any other [virtuous person].

§5 Besides, study seems to be liked because of itself alone, since it has no result beyond having studied. But from the virtues concerned with action we try to a greater or lesser extent to gain something beyond the action itself. . . .

But the activity of understanding, it seems, is superior in excellence because it is the activity of study, aims at no end apart from itself, and has its own proper pleasure, which increases the activity. Further, self-sufficiency, leisure, unwearied activity (as far as is possible for a human being), and any other features ascribed to the blessed person, are evidently features of this activity. Hence a human being's complete happiness will be this activity, if it receives a complete span of life, since nothing incomplete is proper to happiness.

§8 Such a life would be superior to the human level. For someone will live it not insofar as he is a human being, but insofar as he has some divine element in him. And the activity of this divine element is as much superior to the activity in accord with the rest of virtue as this element is superior to the compound. Hence if understanding is something divine in comparison with a human being, so also will the life in accord with understanding be divine in comparison with human life. We ought not to follow the makers of proverbs and 'Think human, since you are human', or 'Think mortal, since you are mortal'. Rather, as far as we can, we ought to be pro-immortal, and go to all lengths to live a life in accord with our supreme element; for however much this element may lack in bulk, by much more it surpasses everything in power and value.

§9 Moreover, each person seems to be his understanding, if he is his controlling and better element. It would be absurd, then, if he were to choose not his own life, but something else's. And what we have said previously will also apply now. For what is proper to each thing's nature is supremely best and most pleasant for it; and hence for a human being the life in accord with understanding will be supremely best and most pleasant, if understanding, more than anything else, is the human being. This life, then, will also be happiest.

[Theoretical Study and the Other Virtues] . . .

§4 Moreover, it seems to need external supplies very little, or [at any rate] less than virtue of character needs them. For let us grant that they both need necessary goods, and to the same extent; for there will be only a very small difference, even though the politician labors more about the body and suchlike. Still, there will be a large difference in [what is needed] for the [proper] activities [of each type of virtue]. For the generous person will need money for generous actions; and the just person will need it for paying debts, since wishes are not clear, and people who are not just pretend to wish to do justice. Similarly, the brave person will need enough power, and the temperate person will need freedom [to do intemperate actions], if they are to achieve anything that the virtue requires. For how else will they, or any other virtuous people, make their virtue clear?

§5 Moreover, it is disputed whether decision or action is more in control of virtue, on the assumption that virtue depends on both. Well, certainly it is clear that the complete [good] depends on both; but for actions many external goods are needed, and the greater and finer the actions the more numerous are the external goods needed.

§6 But someone who is studying needs none of these goods, for that activity at least; indeed, for study at least, we might say they are even hindrances. Insofar as he is a human being, however, and [hence] lives together with a number of other human beings, he chooses to do the actions that accord with virtue. Hence he will need the sorts of external goods [that are needed for the virtues], for living a human life.

§7 In another way also it appears that complete happiness is some activity of study. For we traditionally suppose that the gods more than anyone are blessed and happy; but what sorts of actions ought we to ascribe to them? Just actions? Surely they will appear ridiculous making contracts, returning deposits, and so on. Brave actions? Do they endure what [they find] frightening and endure dangers because it is fine? Generous actions? Whom will they give to? And surely it would be absurd for them to have currency or anything like that. What would their temperate actions be? Surely it is vulgar praise to say that they do not have base appetites. When we go through them all, anything that concerns actions appears trivial and unworthy of the gods. Nonetheless, we all traditionally suppose that they are alive and active, since surely they are not asleep like Endymion. Then if someone is alive, and action is excluded, and production even more, what is left but study? Hence the gods' activity that is superior in blessedness will be an activity of study. And so the human activity that is most akin to the gods' activity will, more than any others, have the character of happiness.

§8 A sign of this is the fact that other animals have no share in happiness, being completely deprived of this activity of study. For the whole life of the gods is blessed, and human life is blessed to the extent that it has something resembling this sort of activity; but none of the other animals is happy, because none of them shares in study at all. Hence happiness extends just as far as study extends, and the more someone studies, the happier he is, not coincidentally but insofar as he studies, since study is valuable in itself. And so [on this argument] happiness will be some kind of study.

§9 But happiness will need external prosperity also, since we are human beings; for our nature is not self-sufficient for study, but we need a healthy body, and need to have food and the other services provided. Still, even though no one can be blessedly happy without external goods, we must not think that to be happy we will need many large goods. For self-sufficiency and action do not depend on excess.

§10 Moreover, we can do fine actions even if we do not rule earth and sea; for even from moderate resources we can do the actions that accord with virtue. This is evident to see, since many private citizens seem to do decent actions no less than people in power do—even more, in fact. It is enough if moderate resources are provided; for the life of someone whose activity accords with virtue will be happy.

§11 Solon surely described happy people well, when he said they had been moderately supplied with external goods, had done what he regarded as the finest actions, and had lived their lives temperately. For it is possible to have moderate possessions and still to do the right actions. And Anaxagoras would seem to have supposed that the happy person was neither rich nor powerful, since he said he would not be surprised if the happy person appeared an absurd sort of person to the many. For the many judge by externals, since these are all they perceive. §12 Hence the beliefs of the wise would seem to accord with our arguments.

These considerations, then, produce some confidence. But the truth in questions about action is judged from what we do and how we live, since these are what control [the answers to such questions]. Hence we ought to examine what has been said by applying it to what we do and how we live; and if it harmonizes with what we do, we should accept it, but if it conflicts we should count it [mere] words.

§13 The person whose activity accords with understanding and who takes care of understanding would seem to be in the best condition, and most loved by the gods. For if the gods pay some attention to human beings, as they seem to, it would be reasonable for them to take pleasure in what is best and most akin to them, namely understanding; and reasonable for them to benefit in return those who most of all like and honor understanding, on the assumption that these people attend to what is beloved by the gods, and act correctly and finely. Clearly, all this is true of the wise person more than anyone else; hence he is most loved by the gods. And it is likely that this same person will be happiest; hence, by this argument also, the wise person, more than anyone else, will be happy.

[FROM ETHICS TO POLITICS]

[Moral Education]

§1 We have now said enough in outlines about happiness and the virtues, and about friendship and pleasure also. Should we, then, think that our decision [to study these] has achieved its end? On the contrary, the aim of studies about action, as we say, is surely not to study and know about a given thing, but rather to act on our knowledge. §2 Hence knowing about virtue is not enough, but we must also try to possess and exercise virtue, or become good in any other way. . . .

It is difficult, however, for someone to be trained correctly for virtue from his youth if he has not been brought up under correct laws; for the many, especially the young, do not find it pleasant to live in a temperate and resistant way. That is why laws must prescribe their upbringing and practices; for they will not find these things painful when they get used to them.

§9 Presumably, however, it is not enough if they get the correct upbringing and attention when they are young; rather, they must continue the same practices and be habituated to them when they become men. Hence we need laws concerned with these things also, and in general with all of life. For the many yield to compulsion more than to argument, and to sanctions more than to the fine.

§10 That is why legislators must, in some people's view, urge people toward virtue and exhort them to aim at the fine—on the assumption that anyone whose good habits have prepared him decently will listen to them—but must impose corrective treatments and penalties on anyone who disobeys or lacks the right nature, and must completely expel an incurable. For the decent person, it is assumed, will attend to reason because his life aims at the fine, whereas the base person, since he desires pleasure, has to receive corrective treatment by pain, like a beast of burden. That is why it is said that the pains imposed must be those most contrary to the pleasures he likes.

Leviathan

THOMAS HOBBES

Thomas Hobbes (1588–1679) was a brilliant English philosopher. His work, *Leviathan* (excerpted here), is a classic of the social contract tradition in ethics and political philosophy.

OF THE NATURAL CONDITION OF MANKIND AS CONCERNING THEIR FELICITY AND MISERY

Nature has made men so equal in the faculties of the body and mind as that, though there be found one man sometimes manifestly stronger in body or of quicker mind than another, yet, when all is reckoned together, the difference between man and man is not so considerable as that one man can thereupon claim to himself any benefit to which another may not pretend as well as he. For as to the strength of body, the weakest has strength enough to kill the strongest, either by secret machination or by confederacy with others that are in the same danger with himself.

And as to the faculties of the mind, setting aside the arts grounded upon words, and especially that skill of proceeding upon general and infallible rules called science—which very few have and but in few things, as being not a native faculty born with us, nor attained, as prudence, while we look after somewhat else—I find yet a greater equality among men than that of strength. For prudence is but experience, which equal time equally bestows on all men in those things they equally apply themselves unto. That which may perhaps make such equality incredible is but a vain conceit of one's own wisdom, which almost all men think they have in a greater degree than the vulgar—that is, than all men but themselves and a few others whom, by fame or for

From *Leviathan*, first published in 1651.

concurring with themselves, they approve. For such is the nature of men that howsoever they may acknowledge many others to be more witty or more eloquent or more learned, yet they will hardly believe there be many so wise as themselves; for they see their own wit at hand and other men's at a distance. But this proves rather that men are in that point equal than unequal. For there is not ordinarily a greater sign of the equal distribution of anything than that every man is contented with his share.

From this equality of ability arises equality of hope in the attaining of our ends. And therefore if any two men desire the same thing, which nevertheless they cannot both enjoy, they become enemies; and in the way to their end, which is principally their own conservation, and sometimes their delectation only, endeavor to destroy or subdue one another. And from hence it comes to pass that where an invader has no more to fear than another man's single power, if one plant, sow, build, or possess a convenient seat, others may probably be expected to come prepared with forces united to dispossess and deprive him, not only of the fruit of his labor, but also of his life or liberty. And the invader again is in the like danger of another.

And from this diffidence of one another there is no way for any man to secure himself so reasonable as anticipation—that is, by force or wiles to master the persons of all men he can, so long till he see no other power great enough to endanger him; and this is no more than his own conservation requires, and is generally allowed. Also, because there be some that take pleasure in contemplating their own power in the acts of conquest, which they pursue farther than their security requires, if others that otherwise would be glad to be at ease within modest bounds should not by invasion increase their power, they would not be able, long time, by standing only on their defense, to subsist. And by consequence, such augmentation of dominion over men being necessary to a man's conservation, it ought to be allowed him.

Again, men have no pleasure, but on the contrary a great deal of grief, in keeping company where there is no power able to overawe them all. For every man looks that his companion should value him at the same rate he sets upon himself; and upon all signs of contempt or undervaluing naturally endeavors, as far as he dares (which among them that have no common power to keep them in quiet is far enough to make them destroy each other), to extort a greater value from his contemners by damage and from others by the example.

So that in the nature of man we find three principal causes of quarrel: first, competition; secondly, diffidence; thirdly, glory.

The first makes men invade for gain, the second for safety, and the third for reputation. The first use violence to make themselves masters of other men's persons, wives, children, and cattle; the second, to defend them; the third, for trifles, as a word, a smile, a different opinion, and any other sign of undervalue, either direct in their persons or by reflection in their kindred, their friends, their nation, their profession, or their name.

Hereby it is manifest that, during the time men live without a common power to keep them all in awe, they are in that condition which is called war, and such a war as is of every man against every man. For WAR consists not in battle only, or the act of fighting, but in a tract of time wherein the will to contend by battle is sufficiently known; and therefore the notion of *time* is to be considered in the nature of war as it is in the nature of weather. For as the nature of foul weather lies not in a shower or two of rain but in an inclination thereto of many days together, so the nature of war consists not in actual fighting but in the known disposition thereto during all the time there is no assurance to the contrary. All other time is PEACE.

Whatsoever, therefore, is consequent to a time of war where every man is enemy to every man, the same is consequent to the time wherein men live without other security than what their own strength and their own invention shall furnish them withal. In such condition there is no place for industry, because the fruit thereof is uncertain: and consequently no culture of the earth; no navigation nor use of the commodities that may be imported by sea; no commodious building; no instruments of moving and removing such things as require much force; no knowledge of the face of the earth; no account of time; no arts; no letters; no society; and, which is worst of all, continual fear and danger of violent death; and the life of man solitary, poor, nasty, brutish, and short.

It may seem strange to some man that has not well weighed these things that nature should thus dissociate and render men apt to invade and destroy one another; and he may therefore, not trusting to this inference made from the passions, desire perhaps to have the same confirmed by experience. Let him therefore consider with himself—when taking a journey he arms himself and seeks to go well accompanied, when going to sleep he locks his doors, when even in his house he locks his chests, and this when he knows there be laws and public officers, armed, to revenge all injuries shall be done him—what opinion he has of his fellow subjects when he rides armed, of his fellow citizens when he locks his doors, and of his children and servants when he locks his chests. Does he not there as much accuse mankind by his actions as I do by my words? But neither of us accuse man's nature in it. The desires and other passions of man are in themselves no sin. No more are the actions that proceed from those passions till they know a law that forbids them, which, till laws be made, they cannot know, nor can any law be made till they have agreed upon the person that shall make it.

It may peradventure be thought there was never such a time nor condition of war as this, and I believe it was never generally so over all the world; but there are many places where they live so now. For the savage people in many places of America, except the government of small families, the concord whereof depends on natural lust, have no government at all and live at this day in that brutish manner as I said before. Howsoever, it may be perceived what manner of life there would be where there were no common power to fear by the manner of life which men that have formerly lived under a peaceful government use to degenerate into in a civil war.

But though there had never been any time wherein particular men were in a condition of war one against another, yet in all times kings and persons of sovereign authority, because of their independency, are in continual jealousies and in the state and posture of gladiators, having their weapons pointing and their eyes fixed on one another—that is, their forts, garrisons, and guns upon the frontiers of their kingdoms, and continual spies upon their neighbors—which is a posture of war. But because they uphold thereby the industry of their subjects, there does not follow from it that misery which accompanies the liberty of particular men.

To this war of every man against every man, this also is consequent: that nothing can be unjust. The notions of right and wrong, justice and injustice, have there no place. Where there is no common power, there is no law; where no law, no injustice. Force and fraud are in war the two cardinal virtues. Justice and injustice are none of the faculties neither of the body nor mind. If they were, they might be in a man that were alone in the world, as well as his senses and passions. They are qualities that relate to men in society, not in solitude. It is consequent also to the same condition that there be no propriety, no dominion, no *mine* and *thine* distinct; but only that to be every man's that he can get, and for so long as he can keep it. And thus much for the ill condition which man by mere nature is actually placed in, though with a possibility to come out of it consisting partly in the passions, partly in his reason.

The passions that incline men to peace are fear of death, desire of such things as are necessary to commodious living, and a hope by their industry to obtain them. And reason suggests convenient articles of peace, upon which men may be drawn to agreement. These articles are they which otherwise are called the Laws of Nature, whereof I shall speak more particularly in the two following chapters.

OF THE FIRST AND SECOND NATURAL LAWS, AND OF CONTRACTS

The RIGHT OF NATURE, which writers commonly call *jus naturale,* is the liberty each man has to use his own power, as he will himself, for the preservation of his own nature—that is to say, of his own life—and consequently of doing anything which, in his own judgment and reason, he shall conceive to be the aptest means thereunto.

By LIBERTY is understood, according to the proper signification of the word, the absence of external impediments; which impediments may oft take away part of a man's power to do what he would, but cannot hinder him from using the power left him according as his judgment and reason shall dictate to him.

A LAW OF NATURE, *lex naturalis,* is a precept or general rule, found out by reason, by which a man is forbidden to do that which is destructive of his life or takes away the means of preserving the same and to omit that by which he thinks it may be best preserved. For though they that speak of this subject use to confound *jus* and *lex, right* and *law,* yet they ought to be distinguished; because RIGHT consists in liberty to do or to forbear, whereas LAW determines and binds to one of them; so that law and right differ as much as obligation and liberty, which in one and the same matter are inconsistent.

And because the condition of man, as has been declared in the precedent chapter, is a condition of war of every one against every one—in which case everyone is governed by his own reason and there is nothing he can make use of that may not be a help unto him in preserving his life against his enemies—it follows that in such a condition every man has a right to everything, even to one another's body. And therefore, as long as this natural right of every man to everything endures, there can be no security to any man, how strong or wise soever he be, of living out the time which nature ordinarily allows men to live. And consequently it is a precept or general rule of reason *that every man ought to endeavor peace, as far as he has hope of obtaining it; and when he cannot obtain it, that he may seek and use all helps and advantages of war.* The first branch of which rule contains the first and fundamental law of nature, which is *to seek peace and follow it.* The second, the sum of the right of nature, which is, *by all means we can to defend ourselves.*

From this fundamental law of nature, by which men are commanded to endeavor peace,

is derived this second law: *that a man be willing, when others are so too, as far forth as for peace and defense of himself he shall think it necessary, to lay down this right to all things, and be contented with so much liberty against other men as he would allow other men against himself.* For as long as every man holds this right of doing anything he likes, so long are all men in the condition of war. But if other men will not lay down their right as well as he, then there is no reason for anyone to divest himself of his, for that were to expose himself to prey, which no man is bound to, rather than to dispose himself to peace. This is that law of the gospel: *whatsoever you require that others should do to you, that do ye to them.* And that law of all men, *quod tibi fieri non vis, alteri ne feceris.*[1]

To lay down a man's *right* to anything is to *divest* himself of the *liberty* of hindering another of the benefit of his own right to the same. For he that renounces or passes away his right gives not to any other man a right which he had not before—because there is nothing to which every man had not right by nature—but only stands out of his way, that he may enjoy his own original right without hindrance from him, not without hindrance from another. So that the effect which redounds to one man by another man's defect of right is but so much diminution of impediments to the use of his own right original. Right is laid aside either by simply renouncing it or by transferring it to another. By *simply* RENOUNCING, when he cares not to whom the benefit thereof redounds. By TRANSFERRING, when he intends the benefit thereof to some certain person or persons. And when a man has in either manner abandoned or granted away his right, then he is said to be OBLIGED or BOUND not to hinder those to whom such right is granted or abandoned from the benefit of it; and that he *ought,* and it is his DUTY, not to make void that voluntary act of his own; and that such hindrance is INJUSTICE and INJURY as being *sine jure,*[2] the right being before renounced or transferred. So that *injury* or *injustice* in the controversies of the world is somewhat like to that which in the disputations of scholars is called *absurdity.* For as it is there called an absurdity to contradict what one maintained in the beginning, so in the world it is called injustice and injury voluntarily to undo that which from the beginning he had voluntarily done. The way by which a man either simply renounces or transfers his right is a declaration or signification by some voluntary and sufficient sign or signs that he does so renounce or transfer, or has so renounced or transferred, the same to him that accepts it. And these signs are either words only or actions only; or as it happens most often, both words and actions. And the same are the BONDS by which men are bound and obliged—bonds that have their strength, not from their own nature, for nothing is more easily broken than a man's word, but from fear of some evil consequence upon the rupture.

Whensoever a man transfers his right or renounces it, it is either in consideration of some right reciprocally transferred to himself or for some other good he hopes for thereby. For it is a voluntary act; and of the voluntary acts of every man, the object is some *good to himself*. And therefore there be some rights which no man can be understood by any words or other signs to have abandoned or transferred. As, first, a man cannot lay down the right of resisting them that assault him by force to take away his life, because he cannot be understood to aim thereby at any good to himself. The same may be said of wounds and chains and imprisonment, both because there is no benefit consequent to such patience as there is to the patience of suffering another to be wounded or imprisoned, as also because a man cannot tell, when he sees men proceed against him by violence, whether they intend his death or not. And, lastly, the motive and end for which this renouncing and transferring of right is introduced is nothing else but the security of a man's person in his life and in the means of so preserving life as not to be weary of it. And therefore if a man by words or other signs seem to despoil himself of the end for which those signs were intended, he is not to be understood as if he meant it or that it was his will, but that he was ignorant of how such words and actions were to be interpreted.

The mutual transferring of right is that which men call CONTRACT.

There is difference between transferring of right to the thing and transferring, or tradition—that is, delivery—of the thing itself. For the thing may be delivered together with the translation of the right, as in buying and selling with ready money or exchange of goods or lands, and it may be delivered some time after.

Again, one of the contractors may deliver the thing contracted for on his part and leave the other to perform his part at some determinate time after and in the meantime be trusted, and then the contract on his part is called PACT or COVENANT; or both parts may contract now to perform hereafter, in which cases he that is to perform in time to come, being trusted, his performance is called *keeping of promise* or faith, and the failing of performance, if it be voluntary, *violation of faith*.

When the transferring of right is not mutual, but one of the parties transfers in hope to gain thereby friendship or service from another or from his friends, or in hope to gain the reputation of charity or magnanimity, or to deliver his mind from the pain of compassion, or in hope of reward in heaven—this is not contract but GIFT, FREE GIFT, GRACE, which words signify one and the same thing.

Signs of contract are either *express* or *by inference*. Express are words spoken with understanding of what they signify, and such words are either of the time *present* or *past*—as *I give, I grant, I have given, I have granted, I will that this be yours*—or of the future—as *I will give, I will grant*—which words of the future are called PROMISE.

Signs by inference are sometimes the consequence of words, sometimes the consequence of silence, sometimes the consequence of actions, sometimes the consequence of forbearing an action; and generally a sign by inference of any contract is whatsoever sufficiently argues the will of the contractor.

Words alone, if they be of the time to come and contain a bare promise, are an insufficient sign of a free gift and therefore not obligatory. For if they be of the time to come, as *tomorrow I will give*, they are a sign I have not given yet and consequently that my right is not transferred but remains till I transfer it by some other act.

But if the words be of the time present or past, as *I have given* or *do give to be delivered tomorrow*, then is my tomorrow's right given away today, and that by the virtue of the words though there were no other argument of my will. And there is a great difference in the signification of these words: *volo hoc tuum esse cras* and *cras dabo*—that is, between *I will that this be yours tomorrow* and *I will give it you tomorrow*—for the word *I will*, in the former manner of speech, signifies an act of the will present, but in the latter it signifies a promise of an act of the will to come; and therefore the former words, being of the present, transfer a future right; the latter, that be of the future, transfer nothing. But if there be other signs of the will to transfer a right besides words, then, though the gift be free, yet may the right be understood to pass by words of the future: as if a man propound a prize to him that comes first to the end of a race, the gift is free; and though the words be of the future, yet the right passes; for if he would not have his words so be understood, he should not have let them run.

In contracts, the right passes not only where the words are of the time present or past but also where they are of the future, because all contract is mutual translation or change of right, and therefore he that promises only because he has already received the benefit for which he promises is to be understood as if he intended the right should pass; for unless he had been content to have his words so understood, the other would not have performed his part first. And for that cause, in buying and selling and other acts of contract a promise is equivalent to a covenant and therefore obligatory.

He that performs first in the case of a contract is said to MERIT that which he is to receive by the performance of the other; and he has it as *due*. Also when a prize is propounded to many which is to be given to him only that wins, or money is thrown among many to be enjoyed by them that catch it, though this be a free gift, yet so to win or so to catch is to *merit* and to have it as DUE. For the right is transferred in the propounding of the prize and in throwing down the money, though it be not determined to whom but by the event of the contention. But there is between these two sorts of merit this difference: that in contract I merit by virtue of my own power and the contractor's need, but in this case of free gift I am enabled to merit only by the benignity of the giver; in contract I merit at the contractor's hand that he should depart with his right, in this case of gift I merit not that the giver should part with his right but that when he has parted with it, it should be mine rather than another's. And this I think to be the meaning of that distinction of the Schools between *meritum congrui* and *meritum condigni*.[3] For God Almighty having promised Paradise to those men, hoodwinked with carnal desires, that can walk through this world according to the precepts and limits prescribed by him, they say he that shall so walk shall merit Paradise *ex congruo*. But because no man can demand a right to it, by his own righteousness or any other power in himself, but by the free grace of God only, they say no man can merit Paradise *ex condigno*. This, I say, I think is the meaning of that distinction; but because disputers do not agree upon the signification of their own terms of art longer than it serves their turn, I will not affirm anything of their meaning; only this I say: when a gift is given indefinitely, as a prize to be contended for, he that wins merits and may claim the prize as due.

If a covenant be made wherein neither of the parties perform presently but trust one another, in the condition of mere nature, which is a condition of war of every man against every man, upon any reasonable suspicion, it is void; but if there be a common power set over them both, with right and force sufficient to compel performance, it is not void. For he that performs first has no assurance the other will perform after, because the bonds of words are too weak to bridle men's ambition, avarice, anger, and other passions without the fear of some coercive power which in the condition of mere nature, where all men are equal and judges of the justness of their own fears, cannot possibly be supposed. And therefore he which performs first does but betray himself to his enemy, contrary to the right he can never abandon of defending his life and means of living.

But in a civil estate, where there is a power set up to constrain those that would otherwise violate their faith, that fear is no more reasonable; and for that cause, he which by the covenant is to perform first is obliged so to do.

The cause of fear which makes such a covenant invalid must be always something arising after the covenant made, as some new fact or other sign of the will not to perform; else it cannot make the covenant void. For that which could not hinder a man from promising ought not to be admitted as a hindrance of performing.

He that transfers any right transfers the means of enjoying it, as far as lies in his power. As he that sells land is understood to transfer the herbage and whatsoever grows upon it; nor can he that sells a mill turn away the stream that drives it. And they that give to a man the right of government in sovereignty are understood to give him the right of levying money to maintain soldiers and of appointing magistrates for the administration of justice.

To make covenants with brute beasts is impossible because, not understanding our speech, they understand not nor accept of any translation of right, nor can translate any right to another; and without mutual acceptation there is no covenant.

To make covenant with God is impossible but by mediation of such as God speaks to, either by revelation supernatural or by his lieutenants that govern under him and in his name; for otherwise we know not whether our covenants be accepted or not. And therefore they that vow anything contrary to any law of nature vow in vain, as being a thing unjust to pay such vow. And if it be a thing commanded by the law of nature, it is not the vow but the law that binds them.

The matter or subject of a covenant is always something that falls under deliberation, for to covenant is an act of the will—that is to say, an act, and the last act, of deliberation—and is therefore always understood to be something to come, and which is judged possible for him that covenants to perform.

And therefore to promise that which is known to be impossible is no covenant. But if that prove impossible afterwards which before was thought possible, the covenant is valid, and binds, though not to the thing itself, yet to the value, or, if that also be impossible, to the unfeigned endeavor of performing as much as is possible, for to more no man can be obliged.

Men are freed of their covenants two ways: by performing or by being forgiven. For performance is the natural end of obligation, and forgiveness the restitution of liberty, as being a retransferring of that right in which the obligation consisted.

Covenants entered into by fear, in the condition of mere nature, are obligatory. For example, if I covenant to pay a ransom or service for my life to an enemy, I am bound by it; for it is a contract, wherein one receives the benefit of life, the other is to receive money or service for it; and consequently, where no other law, as in the condition of mere nature, forbids the performance, the covenant is valid. Therefore prisoners of war, if trusted with the payment of their ransom, are obliged to pay it; and if a weaker prince make a disadvantageous peace with a stronger, for fear, he is bound to keep it; unless, as has been said before, there arises some new and just cause of fear to renew the war. And even in commonwealths, if I be forced to redeem myself from a thief by promising him money, I am bound to pay it till the civil law discharge me. For whatsoever I may lawfully do without obligation, the same I may lawfully covenant to do through fear; and what I lawfully covenant, I cannot lawfully break. A former covenant makes void a later. For a man that has passed away his right to one man today has it not to pass tomorrow to another; and therefore the later promise passes no right, but is null.

A covenant not to defend myself from force by force is always void. For, as I have showed before, no man can transfer or lay down his right to save himself from death, wounds, and imprisonment, the avoiding whereof is the only end of laying down any right; and therefore the promise of not resisting force in no covenant transfers any right, nor is obliging. For though a man may covenant thus: *unless I do so or so, kill me,* he cannot covenant thus: *unless I do so or so, I will not resist you when you come to kill me.* For man by nature chooses the lesser evil, which is danger of death in resisting, rather than the greater, which is certain and present death in not resisting. And this is granted to be true by all men, in that they lead criminals to execution and prison with armed men, notwithstanding that such criminals have consented to the law by which they are condemned.

A covenant to accuse oneself, without assurance of pardon, is likewise invalid. For in the condition of nature, where every man is judge, there is no place for accusation; and in the civil state, the accusation is followed with punishment, which, being force, a man is not obliged not to resist. The same is also true of the accusation of those by whose condemnation a man falls into misery, as of a father, wife, or benefactor. For the testimony of such an accuser, if it be not willingly given, is presumed to be corrupted by nature, and therefore not to be received; and where a man's testimony is not to be credited, he is not bound to give it. Also accusations upon torture are not to be reputed as testimonies. For torture is to be used but as means of conjecture and light in the further examination and search of truth; and what is in that case confessed tends to the ease of him that is tortured, not to the informing of the torturers, and therefore ought not to have the credit of a sufficient testimony; for whether he deliver himself by true or false accusation, he does it by the right of preserving his own life.

The force of words being, as I have formerly noted, too weak to hold men to the performance of their covenants, there are in man's nature but two imaginable helps to strengthen it. And those are either a fear of the consequence of breaking their word, or a glory or pride in appearing not to need to break it. This latter is a generosity too rarely found to be presumed on, especially in the pursuers of wealth, command, or sensual pleasure—which are the greatest part of mankind. The passion to be reckoned upon is fear, whereof there be two very general objects: one, the power of spirits invisible; the other, the power of those men they shall therein offend. Of these two, though the former be the greater power, yet the fear of the latter is commonly the greater fear. The fear of the former is in every man his own religion, which has place in the nature of man before civil society. The latter has not so,

at least not place enough to keep men to their promises, because in the condition of mere nature the inequality of power is not discerned but by the event of battle. So that before the time of civil society, or in the interruption thereof by war, there is nothing can strengthen a covenant of peace agreed on against the temptations of avarice, ambition, lust, or other strong desire but the fear of that invisible power, which they everyone worship as God and fear as a revenger of their perfidy. All therefore that can be done between two men not subject to civil power is to put one another to swear by the God he fears, which *swearing* or OATH is a *form of speech, added to a promise, by which he that promises signifies that, unless he perform, he renounces the mercy of his God, or calls to him for vengeance on himself.* Such was the heathen form, *Let Jupiter kill me else, as I kill this beast.* So is our form, *I shall do thus and thus, so help me God.* And this, with the rites and ceremonies which everyone uses in his own religion, that the fear of breaking faith might be the greater.

By this it appears that an oath taken according to any other form or rite than his that swears is in vain and no oath, and that there is no swearing by anything which the swearer thinks not God. For though men have sometimes used to swear by their kings, for fear or flattery, yet they would have it thereby understood they attributed to them divine honor. And that swearing unnecessarily by God is but profaning of his name; and swearing by other things, as men do in common discourse, is not swearing but an impious custom gotten by too much vehemence of talking.

It appears also that the oath adds nothing to the obligation. For a covenant, if lawful, binds in the sight of God without the oath as much as with it; if unlawful, binds not at all, though it be confirmed with an oath.

OF OTHER LAWS OF NATURE

From that law of nature by which we are obliged to transfer to another such rights as, being retained, hinder the peace of mankind, there follows a third, which is this: *that men perform their covenants made;* without which covenants are in vain and but empty words, and, the right of all men to all things remaining, we are still in the condition of war.

And in this law of nature consists the fountain and original of JUSTICE. For where no covenant has preceded there has no right been transferred, and every man has right to every thing; and consequently no action can be unjust. But when a covenant is made, then to break it is *unjust;* and the definition of INJUSTICE is no other than *the not performance of covenant.* And whatsoever is not unjust is *just.*

But because covenants of mutual trust, where there is a fear of not performance on either part, as has been said in the former chapter, are invalid, though the original of justice be the making of covenants, yet injustice actually there can be none till the cause of such fear be taken away, which, while men are in the natural condition of war, cannot be done. Therefore, before the names of just and unjust can have place, there must be some coercive power to compel men equally to the performance of their covenants by the terror of some punishment greater than the benefit they expect by the breach of their covenant, and to make good that propriety which by mutual contract men acquire in recompense of the universal right they abandon; and such power there is none before the erection of a commonwealth. And this is also to be gathered out of the ordinary definition of justice in the Schools, for they say that *justice is the constant will of giving to every man his own.* And therefore where there is no *own*—that is, no propriety—there is no injustice; and where there is no coercive power erected—that is, where there is no commonwealth—there is no propriety, all men having right to all things; therefore, where there is no commonwealth, there nothing is unjust. So that the nature of justice consists in keeping of valid covenants; but the validity of covenants begins not but with the constitution of a civil power sufficient to compel men to keep them; and then it is also that propriety begins.

The fool hath said in his heart, there is no such thing as justice,[4] and sometimes also with his tongue, seriously alleging that, every man's conservation and contentment being committed to his own care, there could be no reason why every man might not do what he thought

conduced thereunto; and therefore also to make or not make, keep or not keep covenants was not against reason when it conduced to one's benefit. He does not therein deny that there be covenants and that they are sometimes broken, sometimes kept, and that such breach of them may be called injustice and the observance of them justice; but he questions whether injustice, taking away the fear of God—for the same fool hath said in his heart there is no God—may not sometimes stand with that reason which dictates to every man his own good, and particularly then when it conduces to such a benefit as shall put a man in a condition to neglect not only the dispraise and revilings, but also the power of other men. The kingdom of God is gotten by violence; but what if it could be gotten by unjust violence? Were it against reason so to get it, when it is impossible to receive hurt by it? And if it be not against reason, it is not against justice, or else justice is not to be approved for good. From such reasoning as this, successful wickedness has obtained the name of virtue; and some that in all other things have disallowed the violation of faith yet have allowed it when it is for the getting of a kingdom. And the heathen that believed that Saturn was deposed by his son Jupiter believed nevertheless the same Jupiter to be the avenger of injustice—somewhat like to a piece of law in Coke's *Commentaries on Littleton*[5] where he says: if the right heir of the crown be attainted of treason, yet the crown shall descend to him and *eo instante* the attainder be void; from which instances a man will be very prone to infer that when the heir apparent of a kingdom shall kill him that is in possession, though his father, you may call it injustice or by what other name you will, yet it can never be against reason, seeing all the voluntary actions of men tend to the benefit of themselves, and those actions are most reasonable that conduce most to their ends. This specious reasoning is nevertheless false.

For the question is not of promises mutual where there is no security of performance on either side—as when there is no civil power erected over the parties promising—for such promises are no covenants; but either where one of the parties has performed already or where there is a power to make him perform, there is the question whether it be against reason—that is, against the benefit of the other—to perform or not. And I say it is not against reason. For the manifestation whereof we are to consider, first, that when a man does a thing which, notwithstanding anything can be foreseen and reckoned on, tends to his own destruction, howsoever some accident which he could not expect, arriving, may turn it to his benefit, yet such events do not make it reasonably or wisely done. Secondly, that in a condition of war, wherein every man to every man, for want of a common power to keep them all in awe, is an enemy, there is no man who can hope by his own strength or wit to defend himself from destruction without the help of confederates, where everyone expects the same defense by the confederation that anyone else does; and therefore he which declares he thinks it reason to deceive those that help him can in reason expect no other means of safety than what can be had from his own single power. He, therefore, that breaks his covenant, and consequently declares that he thinks he may with reason do so, cannot be received into any society that unite themselves for peace and defense, but by the error of them that receive him; nor, when he is received, be retained in it without seeing the danger of their error, which errors a man cannot reasonably reckon upon as the means of his security; and therefore if he be left or cast out of society he perishes, and if he live in society, it is by the errors of other men, which he could not foresee nor reckon upon, and consequently against the reason of his preservation; and so, as all men that contribute not to his destruction, forbear him only out of ignorance of what is good for themselves.

As for the instance of gaining the secure and perpetual felicity of heaven by any way, it is frivolous, there being but one way imaginable, and that is not breaking but keeping of covenant.

And for the other instance of attaining sovereignty by rebellion, it is manifest that, though the event follow, yet because it cannot reasonably be expected, but rather the contrary, and because by gaining it so others are taught to gain the same in like manner, the attempt thereof is against reason.

Justice, therefore—that is to say, keeping of covenant—is a rule of reason by which we are forbidden to do anything destructive to our life, and consequently a law of nature.

There be some that proceed further and will not have the law of nature to be those rules which conduce to the preservation of man's life on earth but to the attaining of an eternal felicity after death, to which they think the breach of covenant may conduce and consequently be just and reasonable; such are they that think it a work of merit to kill or depose or rebel against the sovereign power constituted over them by their own consent. But because there is no natural knowledge of man's estate after death—much less of the reward that is then to be given to breach of faith—but only a belief grounded upon other men's saying that they know it supernaturally, or that they know those that knew them that knew others that knew it supernaturally, breach of faith cannot be called a precept of reason or nature.

Others that allow for a law of nature the keeping of faith do nevertheless make exception of certain persons, as heretics and such as use not to perform their covenant to others; and this also is against reason. For if any fault of a man be sufficient to discharge our covenant made, the same ought in reason to have been sufficient to have hindered the making of it.

The names of just and unjust, when they are attributed to men, signify one thing, and when they are attributed to actions, another. When they are attributed to men, they signify conformity or inconformity of manners to reason. But when they are attributed to actions, they signify the conformity or inconformity to reason, not of manners or manner of life, but of particular actions. A just man, therefore, is he that takes all the care he can that his actions may be all just; and an unjust man is he that neglects it. And such men are more often in our language styled by the names of righteous and unrighteous than just and unjust, though the meaning be the same. Therefore a righteous man does not lose that title by one or a few unjust actions that proceed from sudden passion or mistake of things or persons; nor does an unrighteous man lose his character for such actions as he does or forbears to do for fear, because his will is not framed by the justice but by the apparent benefit of what he is to do. That which gives to human actions the relish of justice is a certain nobleness or gallantness of courage, rarely found, by which a man scorns to be beholden for the contentment of his life to fraud or breach of promise. This justice of the manners is that which is meant where justice is called a virtue and injustice a vice.

But the justice of actions denominates men, not just, but *guiltless;* and the injustice of the same, which is also called injury, gives them but the name of *guilty.*

Again, the injustice of manners is the disposition or aptitude to do injury, and is injustice before it proceed to act and without supposing any individual person injured. But the injustice of an action—that is to say, injury—supposes an individual person injured—namely, him to whom the covenant was made—and therefore many times the injury is received by one man when the damage redounds to another. As when the master commands his servant to give money to a stranger: if it be not done, the injury is done to the master, whom he had before covenanted to obey; but the damage redounds to the stranger, to whom he had no obligation and therefore could not injure him. And so also in commonwealths private men may remit to one another their debts but not robberies or other violences whereby they are endamaged; because the detaining of debt is an injury to themselves, but robbery and violence are injuries to the person of the commonwealth.

Whatsoever is done to a man, conformable to his own will signified to the doer, is no injury to him. For if he that does it has not passed away his original right to do what he please by some antecedent covenant, there is no breach of covenant and therefore no injury done him. And if he have, then his will to have it done, being signified, is a release of that covenant, and so again there is no injury done him.

Justice of actions is by writers divided into *commutative* and *distributive;* and the former they say consists in proportion arithmetical, the latter in proportion geometrical. Commutative, therefore, they place in the equality of value of the things contracted for, and distributive in the distribution of equal benefit to men of equal merit. As if it were injustice to sell dearer than we buy, or to give more to a man than he merits. The value of all things contracted for is measured by the appetite of the contractors, and therefore the just value is that which they be contented to give. And merit (besides that which is by covenant, where the performance on one part merits the performance of the other part, and falls under justice commutative, not distributive) is not due by justice, but is rewarded of grace only. And therefore this distinction, in the sense wherein it uses to be expounded, is not right. To speak properly, commutative justice is the justice of a contractor—that is, a performance of covenant in buying and selling, hiring and letting to hire, lending and borrowing, exchanging, bartering, and other acts of contract.

And distributive justice, the justice of an arbitrator—that is to say, the act of defining what is just. Wherein, being trusted by them that make him arbitrator, if he perform his trust, he is said to distribute to every man his own; and this is indeed just distribution, and may be called, though improperly, distributive justice, but more properly equity, which also is a law of nature, as shall be shown in due place.

As justice depends on antecedent covenant, so does GRATITUDE depend on antecedent grace—that is to say, antecedent free gift—and is the fourth law of nature, which may be conceived in this form: *that a man which receives benefit from another of mere grace endeavor that he which gives it have no reasonable cause to repent him of his good will.* For no man gives but with intention of good to himself, because gift is voluntary, and of all voluntary acts the object is to every man his own good; of which if men see they shall be frustrated, there will be no beginning of benevolence or trust nor consequently of mutual help nor of reconciliation of one man to another; and therefore they are to remain still in the condition of *war,* which is contrary to the first and fundamental law of nature, which commands men to *seek peace.* The breach of this law is called *ingratitude,* and has the same relation to grace that injustice has to obligation by covenant.

A fifth law of nature is COMPLAISANCE—that is to say, *that every man strive to accommodate himself to the rest.* For the understanding whereof we may consider that there is in men's aptness to society a diversity of nature rising from their diversity of affections not unlike to that we see in stones brought together for building of an edifice. For as that stone which by the asperity and irregularity of figure takes more room from others than itself fills, and for the hardness cannot be easily made plain and thereby hinders the building, is by the builders cast away as unprofitable and troublesome, so also a man that by asperity of nature will strive to retain those things which to himself are superfluous and to others necessary, and for the stubbornness of his passions cannot be corrected, is to be left or cast out of society as cumbersome thereunto. For seeing every man, not only by right but also by necessity of nature, is supposed to endeavor all he can to obtain that which is necessary for his conservation, he that shall oppose himself against it for things superfluous is guilty of the war that thereupon is to follow, and therefore does that which is contrary to the fundamental law of nature, which commands *to seek peace.* The observers of this law may be called SOCIABLE (the Latins call them *commodi*), the contrary *stubborn, insociable, forward, intractable.*

A sixth law of nature is this: *that upon caution of the future time, a man ought to pardon the offenses past of them that, repenting, desire it.* For PARDON is nothing but granting of peace, which, though granted to them that persevere in their hostility, be not peace but fear, yet, not granted to them that give caution of the future time, is sign of an aversion to peace, and therefore contrary to the law of nature.

A seventh is *that in revenges*—that is, retribution of evil for evil—*men look not at the greatness of the evil past, but the greatness of the good to follow.* Whereby we are forbidden to inflict punishment with any other design than for correction of the offender or direction of others. For this law is consequent to the next before it that commands pardon upon security of the future time. Besides, revenge without respect to the example and profit to come is a triumph or glorying in the hurt of another, tending to no end; for the end is always somewhat to come, and glorying to no end is vainglory and contrary to reason; and to hurt without reason tends to the introduction of war, which is against the law of nature and is commonly styled by the name of *cruelty.*

And because all signs of hatred or contempt provoke to fight, insomuch as most men choose rather to hazard their life than not to be revenged, we may in the eighth place for a law of nature set down this precept: *that no man by deed, word, countenance, or gesture declare hatred or contempt of another.* The breach of which law is commonly called *contumely.*

The question who is the better man has no place in the condition of mere nature, where, as has been shown before, all men are equal. The inequality that now is has been introduced by the laws civil. I know that Aristotle in the first book of his *Politics*, for a foundation of his doctrine, makes men by nature some more worthy to command, meaning the wiser sort such as he thought himself to be for his philosophy, others to serve, meaning those that had strong bodies but were not philosophers as he; as if master and servant were not introduced by consent of men but by difference of wit, which is not only against reason but also against experience. For there are very few so foolish that had not rather govern themselves than be governed by others; nor when the wise in their own conceit contend by force with them who distrust their own wisdom, do they always, or often, or almost at any time, get the victory. If nature therefore have made men equal, that equality is to be acknowledged; or if nature have made men unequal, yet because men that think themselves equal will not enter into conditions of peace but upon equal terms, such equality must be admitted. And therefore for the ninth law of nature, I put this: *that every man acknowledge another for his equal by nature.* The breach of this precept is *pride.*

On this law depends another: *that at the entrance into conditions of peace, no man require to reserve to himself any right which he is not content should be reserved to every one of the rest.* As it is necessary for all men that seek peace to lay down certain rights of nature—that is to say, not to have liberty to do all they list—so is it necessary for man's life to retain some, as right to govern their own bodies, enjoy air, water, motion, ways to go from place to place, and all things else without which a man cannot live or not live well. If in this case, at the making of peace, men require for themselves that which they would not have to be granted to others, they do contrary to the precedent law that commands the acknowledgment of natural equality and therefore also against the law of nature. The observers of this law are those we call *modest,* and the breakers *arrogant* men. The Greeks call the violation of this law πλεονεξία—that is, a desire of more than their share.

Also if *a man be trusted to judge between man and man,* it is a precept of the law of nature *that he deal equally between them.* For without that, the controversies of men cannot be determined but by war. He, therefore, that is partial in judgment does what in him lies to deter men from the use of judges and arbitrators, and consequently, against the fundamental law of nature, is the cause of war.

The observance of this law, from the equal distribution to each man of that which in reason belongs to him, is called EQUITY and, as I have said before, distributive justice; the violation, *acception of persons,* προσωποληψία.

And from this follows another law: *that such things as cannot be divided be enjoyed in common, if it can be; and if the quantity of the thing permit, without stint; otherwise proportionably to the number of them that have right.* For otherwise the distribution is unequal and contrary to equity.

But some things there be that can neither be divided nor enjoyed in common. Then the law of nature, which prescribes equity, requires *that the entire right, or else—making the use alternate— the first possession, be determined by lot.* For equal distribution is of the law of nature; and other means of equal distribution cannot be imagined.

Of *lots* there be two sorts: *arbitrary* and *natural.* Arbitrary is that which is agreed on by the competitors; natural is either *primogeniture* (which the Greek calls κληρονομία, which signifies *given by lot*) or *first seizure.*

And therefore those things which cannot be enjoyed in common, nor divided, ought to be adjudged to the first possessor; and in some cases to the first-born, as acquired by lot.

It is also a law of nature *that all men that mediate peace be allowed safe conduct.* For the law that commands peace, as the *end,* commands intercession, as the *means;* and to intercession the means is safe conduct.

And because, though men be never so willing to observe these laws, there may nevertheless arise questions concerning a man's action—first, whether it were done or not done; secondly, if done, whether against the law or not against the law; the former whereof is called a question *of fact,* the latter a question *of right*—therefore, unless the parties to the question covenant mutually to stand to the sentence of another, they are as far from peace as ever. This other to whose sentence they submit is called an ARBITRATOR. And therefore it is of the law of nature *that they that are at controversy submit their right to the judgment of an arbitrator.*

And seeing every man is presumed to do all things in order to his own benefit, no man is a fit arbitrator in his own cause; and if he were never so fit, yet, equity allowing to each party equal benefit, if one be admitted to be judge the other is to be admitted also; and so the controversy—that is, the cause of war—remains against the law of nature.

For the same reason no man in any cause ought to be received for arbitrator to whom greater profit or honor or pleasure apparently arises out of the victory of one party than of the other; for he has taken, though an unavoidable bribe, yet a bribe, and no man can be obliged to trust him. And thus also the controversy and the condition of war remains, contrary to the law of nature.

And in a controversy of *fact,* the judge being to give no more credit to one than to the other, if there be no other arguments, must give credit to a third, or to a third and fourth, no more; for else the question is undecided and left to force, contrary to the law of nature.

These are the laws of nature dictating peace for a means of the conservation of men in multitudes, and which only concern the doctrine of civil society. There be other things tending to the destruction of particular men—as drunkenness and all other parts of intemperance—which may therefore also be reckoned among those things which the law of nature has forbidden, but are not necessary to be mentioned nor are pertinent enough to this place.

And though this may seem too subtle a deduction of the laws of nature to be taken notice of by all men—whereof the most part are too busy in getting food and the rest too negligent to understand—yet to leave all men inexcusable they have been contracted into one easy sum, intelligible even to the meanest capacity, and that is *Do not that to another which you would not have done to yourself;* which shows him that he has no more to do in learning the laws of nature but, when weighing the actions of other men with his own they seem too heavy, to put them into the other part of the balance and his own into their place, that his own passions and self-love may add nothing to the weight, and then there is none of these laws of nature that will not appear unto him very reasonable.

The laws of nature oblige *in foro interno*[6]—that is to say, they bind to a desire they should take place—but *in foro externo*[7]—that is, to the putting them in act—not always. For he that should be modest and tractable and perform all he promises in such time and place where no man else should do so should but make himself a prey to others and procure his own certain ruin, contrary to the ground of all laws of nature, which tend to nature's preservation. And again, he that, having sufficient security that others shall observe the same laws toward him, observes them not himself, seeks not peace but war and consequently the destruction of his nature by violence.

And whatsoever laws bind *in foro interno* may be broken, not only by a fact contrary to the law, but also by a fact according to it, in case a man think it contrary. For though his action in this case be according to the law, yet his purpose was against the law, which, where the obligation is *in foro interno*, is a breach.

The laws of nature are immutable and eternal, for injustice, ingratitude, arrogance, pride, iniquity, acception of persons, and the rest can never be made lawful. For it can never be that war shall preserve life and peace destroy it.

The same laws, because they oblige only to a desire and endeavor—I mean an unfeigned and constant endeavor—are easy to be observed. For in that they require nothing but endeavor, he that endeavors their performance fulfills them; and he that fulfills the law is just.

And the science of them is the true and only moral philosophy. For moral philosophy is nothing else but the science of what is *good* and *evil* in the conversation and society of mankind. *Good* and *evil* are names that signify our appetites and aversions, which in different tempers, customs, and doctrines of men are different; and divers men differ not only in their judgment on the senses of what is pleasant and unpleasant to the taste, smell, hearing, touch, and sight but also of what is conformable or disagreeable to reason in the actions of common life. Nay, the same man in divers times differs from himself, and one time praises—that is, calls good—what another time he dispraises and calls evil; from whence arise disputes, controversies, and at last war. And therefore so long as a man is in the condition of mere nature, which is a condition of war, private appetite is the measure of good and evil; and consequently all men agree on this: that peace is good, and therefore also the way or means of peace, which, as I have showed before, are *justice, gratitude, modesty, equity, mercy,* and the rest of the laws of nature, are good—that is to say, *moral virtues*—and their contrary *vices* evil. Now the science of virtue and vice is moral philosophy; and therefore the true doctrine of the laws of nature is the true moral philosophy. But the writers of moral philosophy, though they acknowledge the same virtues and vices, yet, not seeing wherein consisted their goodness nor that they come to be praised as the means of peaceable, sociable, and comfortable living, place them in a mediocrity of passions; as if not the cause but the degree of daring made fortitude, or not the cause but the quantity of a gift made liberality.

These dictates of reason men used to call by the name of laws, but improperly, for they are but conclusions or theorems concerning what conduces to the conservation and defense of themselves, whereas law, properly, is the word of him that by right has command over others.

But yet if we consider the same theorems as delivered in the word of God, that by right commands all things, then are they properly called laws.

NOTES

1. [Matt. 7:12; Luke 6:31. The Latin expresses the same rule negatively: "What you would not have done to you, do not do to others."]
2. [Without legal basis.]
3. [Merit based on conformity and merit based on worthiness.]
4. [Pss. 14, 53.]
5. [Sir Edward Coke (1552–1634), English jurist, the first Lord Chief Justice of England. The first volume of his *Institutes* was a translation of, and commentary on, the *Treatise on Tenures* of Sir Thomas de Littleton (*c.* 1407–1481). It is commonly called *Coke on Littleton*.]
6. [In conscience.]
7. [In civil law.]

Justice as Fairness

JOHN RAWLS

John Rawls (1921–2002) is the author of the influential work *A Theory of Justice*. He taught for many years at Harvard University.

THE MAIN IDEA OF THE THEORY OF JUSTICE

My aim is to present a conception of justice which generalizes and carries to a higher level of abstraction the familiar theory of the social contract as found, say, in Locke, Rousseau, and Kant.[1] In order to do this we are not to think of the original contract as one to enter a particular society or to set up a particular form of government. Rather, the guiding idea is that the principles of justice for the basic structure of society are the object of the original agreement. They are the principles that free and rational persons concerned to further their own interests would accept in an initial position of equality as defining the fundamental terms of their association. These principles are to regulate all further agreements; they specify the kinds of social cooperation that can be entered into and the forms of government that can be established. This way of regarding the principles of justice I shall call justice as fairness.

Thus we are to imagine that those who engage in social cooperation choose together, in one joint act, the principles which are to assign basic rights and duties and to determine the division of social benefits. Men are to decide in advance how they are to regulate their claims against one another and what is to be the foundation charter of their society. Just as each person must decide by rational reflection what constitutes his good, that is, the system of ends which it is rational for him to pursue, so a group of persons must decide once and for all what is to count among them as just and unjust. The choice which rational men would make in this hypothetical situation of equal liberty, assuming for the present that this choice problem has a solution, determines the principles of justice.

In justice as fairness the original position of equality corresponds to the state of nature in the traditional theory of the social contract. This original position is not, of course, thought of as an actual historical state of affairs, much

Reprinted by permission of the publisher from *A Theory of Justice* by John Rawls, pp. 11–21, 60–63, 136–140, Cambridge, Mass.: The Belknap Press of the Harvard University Press, Copyright © 1971, 1999 by the President and Fellows of Harvard College.

less as a primitive condition of culture. It is understood as a purely hypothetical situation characterized so as to lead to a certain conception of justice.[2] Among the essential features of this situation is that no one knows his place in society, his class position or social status, nor does any one know his fortune in the distribution of natural assets and abilities, his intelligence, strength, and the like. I shall even assume that the parties do not know their conceptions of the good or their special psychological propensities. The principles of justice are chosen behind a veil of ignorance. This ensures that no one is advantaged or disadvantaged in the choice of principles by the outcome of natural chance or the contingency of social circumstances. Since all are similarly situated and no one is able to design principles to favor his particular condition, the principles of justice are the result of a fair agreement or bargain. For given the circumstances of the original position, the symmetry of everyone's relations to each other, this initial situation is fair between individuals as moral persons, that is, as rational beings with their own ends and capable, I shall assume, of a sense of justice. The original position is, one might say, the appropriate initial status quo, and thus the fundamental agreements reached in it are fair. This explains the propriety of the name "justice as fairness": it conveys the idea that the principles of justice are agreed to in an initial situation that is fair. The name does not mean that the concepts of justice and fairness are the same, any more than the phrase "poetry as metaphor" means that the concepts of poetry and metaphor are the same.

Justice as fairness begins, as I have said, with one of the most general of all choices which persons might make together, namely, with the choice of the first principles of a conception of justice which is to regulate all subsequent criticism and reform of institutions. Then, having chosen a conception of justice, we can suppose that they are to choose a constitution and a legislature to enact laws, and so on, all in accordance with the principles of justice initially agreed upon. Our social situation is just if it is such that by this sequence of hypothetical agreements we would have contracted into the general system of rules which defines it. Moreover, assuming that the

original position does determine a set of principles (that is, that a particular conception of justice would be chosen), it will then be true that whenever social institutions satisfy these principles those engaged in them can say to one another that they are cooperating on terms to which they would agree if they were free and equal persons whose relations with respect to one another were fair. They could all view their arrangements as meeting the stipulations which they would acknowledge in an initial situation that embodies widely accepted and reasonable constraints on the choice of principles. The general recognition of this fact would provide the basis for a public acceptance of the corresponding principles of justice. No society can, of course, be a scheme of cooperation which men enter voluntarily in a literal sense; each person finds himself placed at birth in some particular position in some particular society, and the nature of this position materially affects his life prospects. Yet a society satisfying the principles of justice as fairness comes as close as a society can to being a voluntary scheme, for it meets the principles which free and equal persons would assent to under circumstances that are fair. In this sense its members are autonomous and the obligations they recognize self-imposed.

One feature of justice as fairness is to think of the parties in the initial situation as rational and mutually disinterested. This does not mean that the parties are egoists, that is, individuals with only certain kinds of interests, say in wealth, prestige, and domination. But they are conceived as not taking an interest in one another's interests. They are to presume that even their spiritual aims may be opposed, in the way that the aims of those of different religions may be opposed. Moreover, the concept of rationality must be interpreted as far as possible in the narrow sense, standard in economic theory, of taking the most effective means to given ends. I shall modify this concept to some extent, but one must try to avoid introducing into it any controversial ethical elements. The initial situation must be characterized by stipulations that are widely accepted.

In working out the conception of justice as fairness one main task clearly is to determine which principles of justice would be chosen in the original position. To do this we must describe this situation in some detail and formulate with care the problem of choice which it presents. These matters I shall take up in the immediately succeeding chapters. It may be observed, however, that once the principles of justice are thought of as arising from an original agreement in a situation of equality, it is an open question whether the principle of utility would be acknowledged. Offhand it hardly seems likely that persons who view themselves as equals, entitled to press their claims upon one another, would agree to a principle which may require lesser life prospects for some simply for the sake of a greater sum of advantages enjoyed by others. Since each desires to protect his interests, his capacity to advance his conception of the good, no one has a reason to acquiesce in an enduring loss for himself in order to bring about a greater net balance of satisfaction. In the absence of strong and lasting benevolent impulses, a rational man would not accept a basic structure merely because it maximized the algebraic sum of advantages irrespective of its permanent effects on his own basic rights and interests. Thus it seems that the principle of utility is incompatible with the conception of social cooperation among equals for mutual advantage. It appears to be inconsistent with the idea of reciprocity implicit in the notion of a well-ordered society. Or, at any rate, so I shall argue.

I shall maintain instead that the persons in the initial situation would choose two rather different principles: the first requires equality in the assignment of basic rights and duties, while the second holds that social and economic inequalities, for example inequalities of wealth and authority, are just only if they result in compensating benefits for everyone, and in particular for the least advantaged members of society. These principles rule out justifying institutions on the grounds that the hardships of some are offset by a greater good in the aggregate. It may be expedient but it is not just that some should have less in order that others may prosper. But there is no injustice in the greater benefits earned by a few provided that the situation of persons not so fortunate is thereby improved.

The intuitive idea is that since everyone's well-being depends upon a scheme of cooperation without which no one could have a satisfactory life, the division of advantages should be such as to draw forth the willing cooperation of everyone taking part in it, including those less well situated. Yet this can be expected only if reasonable terms are proposed. The two principles mentioned seem to be a fair agreement on the basis of which those better endowed, or more fortunate in their social position, neither of which we can be said to deserve, could expect the willing cooperation of others when some workable scheme is a necessary condition of the welfare of all. Once we decide to look for a conception of justice that nullifies the accidents of natural endowment and the contingencies of social circumstance as counters in quest for political and economic advantage, we are led to these principles. They express the result of leaving aside those aspects of the social world that seem arbitrary from a moral point of view.

The problem of the choice of principles, however, is extremely difficult. I do not expect the answer I shall suggest to be convincing to everyone. It is, therefore, worth noting from the outset that justice as fairness, like other contract views, consists of two parts: (1) an interpretation of the initial situation and of the problem of choice posed there, and (2) a set of principles which, it is argued, would be agreed to. One may accept the first part of the theory (or some variant thereof), but not the other, and conversely. The concept of the initial contractual situation may seem reasonable although the particular principles proposed are rejected. To be sure, I want to maintain that the most appropriate conception of this situation does lead to principles of justice contrary to utilitarianism and perfectionism, and therefore that the contract doctrine provides an alternative to these views. Still, one may dispute this contention even though one grants that the contractarian method is a useful way of studying ethical theories and of setting forth their underlying assumptions.

Justice as fairness is an example of what I have called a contract theory. Now there may be an objection to the term "contract" and related expressions, but I think it will serve reasonably well. Many words have misleading connotations which at first are likely to confuse. The terms "utility" and "utilitarianism" are surely no exception. They too have unfortunate suggestions which hostile critics have been willing to exploit; yet they are clear enough for those prepared to study utilitarian doctrine. The same should be true of the term "contract" applied to moral theories. As I have mentioned, to understand it one has to keep in mind that it implies a certain level of abstraction. In particular, the content of the relevant agreement is not to enter a given society or to adopt a given form of government, but to accept certain moral principles. Moreover, the undertakings referred to are purely hypothetical: a contract view holds that certain principles would be accepted in a well-defined initial situation.

The merit of the contract terminology is that it conveys the idea that principles of justice may be conceived as principles that would be chosen by rational persons, and that in this way conceptions of justice may be explained and justified. The theory of justice is a part, perhaps the most significant part, of the theory of rational choice. Furthermore, principles of justice deal with conflicting claims upon the advantages won by social cooperation; they apply to the relations among several persons or groups. The word "contract" suggests this plurality as well as the condition that the appropriate division of advantages must be in accordance with principles acceptable to all parties. The condition of publicity for principles of justice is also connoted by the contract phraseology. Thus, if these principles are the outcome of an agreement, citizens have a knowledge of the principles that others follow. It is characteristic of contract theories to stress the public nature of political principles. Finally there is the long tradition of the contract doctrine. Expressing the tie with this line of thought helps to define ideas and accords with natural piety. There are then several advantages in the use of the term "contract." With due precautions taken, it should not be misleading.

A final remark. Justice as fairness is not a complete contract theory. For it is clear that the contractarian idea can be extended to the choice of more or less an entire ethical system, that is, to a system including principles for all the virtues and not only for justice. Now for the most part I shall consider only principles of justice and others closely related to them; I make no attempt to discuss the virtues in a systematic way. Obviously if justice as fairness succeeds reasonably well, a next step would be to study the more general view suggested by the name "rightness as fairness." But even this wider theory fails to embrace all moral relationships, since it would seem to include only our relations with other persons and to leave out of account how we are to conduct ourselves toward animals and the rest of nature. I do not contend that the contract notion offers a way to approach these questions which are certainly of the first importance; and I shall have to put them aside. We must recognize the limited scope of justice as fairness and of the general type of view that it exemplifies. How far its conclusions must be revised once these other matters are understood cannot be decided in advance.

THE ORIGINAL POSITION AND JUSTIFICATION

I have said that the original position is the appropriate initial status quo which insures that the fundamental agreements reached in it are fair. This fact yields the name "justice as fairness." It is clear, then, that I want to say that one conception of justice is more reasonable than another, or justifiable with respect to it, if rational persons in the initial situation would choose its principles over those of the other for the role of justice. Conceptions of justice are to be ranked by their acceptability to persons so circumstanced. Understood in this way the question of justification is settled by working out a problem of deliberation: we have to ascertain which principles it would be rational to adopt given the contractual situation. This connects the theory of justice with the theory of rational choice.

If this view of the problem of justification is to succeed, we must, of course, describe in some detail the nature of this choice problem. A problem of rational decision has a definite answer only if we know the beliefs and interests of the parties, their relations with respect to one another, the alternatives between which they are to choose, the procedure whereby they make up their minds, and so on. As the circumstances are presented in different ways, correspondingly different principles are accepted. The concept of the original position, as I shall refer to it, is that of the most philosophically favored interpretation of this initial choice situation for the purposes of a theory of justice.

But how are we to decide what is the most favored interpretation? I assume, for one thing, that there is a broad measure of agreement that principles of justice should be chosen under certain conditions. To justify a particular description of the initial situation one shows that it incorporates these commonly shared presumptions. One argues from widely accepted but weak premises to more specific conclusions. Each of the presumptions should by itself be natural and plausible; some of them may seem innocuous or even trivial. The aim of the contract approach is to establish that taken together they impose significant bounds on acceptable principles of justice. The ideal outcome would be that these conditions determine a unique set of principles; but I shall be satisfied if they suffice to rank the main traditional conceptions of social justice.

One should not be misled, then, by the somewhat unusual conditions which characterize the original position. The idea here is simply to make vivid to ourselves the restrictions that it seems reasonable to impose on arguments for principles of justice, and therefore on these principles themselves. Thus it seems reasonable and generally acceptable that no one should be advantaged or disadvantaged by natural fortune or social circumstances in the choice of principles. It also seems widely agreed that it should be impossible to tailor principles to the circumstances of one's own case. We should insure further that particular inclinations and aspirations, and persons' conceptions of their good do not affect the principles adopted. The aim is to rule out those principles that it would be rational to propose for acceptance, however little the chance of success, only if one knew certain things that are irrelevant from the standpoint of justice. For example, if a man knew that he was wealthy,

he might find it rational to advance the principle that various taxes for welfare measures be counted unjust; if he knew that he was poor, he would most likely propose the contrary principle. To represent the desired restrictions one imagines a situation in which everyone is deprived of this sort of information. One excludes the knowledge of those contingencies which sets men at odds and allows them to be guided by their prejudices. In this manner the veil of ignorance is arrived at in a natural way. This concept should cause no difficulty if we keep in mind the constraints on arguments that it is meant to express. At any time we can enter the original position, so to speak, simply by following a certain procedure, namely, by arguing for principles of justice in accordance with these restrictions.

It seems reasonable to suppose that the parties in the original position are equal. That is, all have the same rights in the procedure for choosing principles; each can make proposals, submit reasons for their acceptance, and so on. Obviously the purpose of these conditions is to represent equality between human beings as moral persons, as creatures having a conception of their good and capable of a sense of justice. The basis of equality is taken to be similarity in these two respects. Systems of ends are not ranked in value; and each man is presumed to have the requisite ability to understand and to act upon whatever principles are adopted. Together with the veil of ignorance, these conditions define the principles of justice as those which rational persons concerned to advance their interests would consent to as equals when none are known to be advantaged or disadvantaged by social and natural contingencies.

There is, however, another side to justifying a particular description of the original position. This is to see if the principles which would be chosen match our considered convictions of justice or extend them in an acceptable way. We can note whether applying these principles would lead us to make the same judgments about the basic structure of society which we now make intuitively and in which we have the greatest confidence; or whether, in cases where our present judgments are in doubt and given with hesitation, these principles offer a resolution which we can affirm on reflection. There are questions which we feel sure must be answered in a certain way. For example, we are confident that religious intolerance and racial discrimination are unjust. We think that we have examined these things with care and have reached what we believe is an impartial judgment not likely to be distorted by an excessive attention to our own interests. These convictions are provisional fixed points which we presume any conception of justice must fit. But we have much less assurance as to what is the correct distribution of wealth and authority. Here we may be looking for a way to remove our doubts. We can check an interpretation of the initial situation, then, by the capacity of its principles to accommodate our firmest convictions and to provide guidance where guidance is needed.

In searching for the most favored description of this situation we work from both ends. We begin by describing it so that it represents generally shared and preferably weak conditions. We then see if these conditions are strong enough to yield a significant set of principles. If not, we look for further premises equally reasonable. But if so, and these principles match our considered convictions of justice, then so far well and good. But presumably there will be discrepancies. In this case we have a choice. We can either modify the account of the initial situation or we can revise our existing judgments, for even the judgments we take provisionally as fixed points are liable to revision. By going back and forth, sometimes altering the conditions of the contractual circumstances, at others withdrawing our judgments and conforming them to principle, I assume that eventually we shall find a description of the initial situation that both expresses reasonable conditions and yields principles which match our considered judgments duly pruned and adjusted. This state of affairs I refer to as reflective equilibrium.[3] It is an equilibrium because at last our principles and judgments coincide; and it is reflective since we know to what principles our judgments conform and the premises of their derivation. At the moment everything is in order. But this equilibrium is not necessarily stable. It is liable to be upset by further examination of the conditions which should be imposed on the

contractual situation and by particular cases which may lead us to revise our judgments. Yet for the time being we have done what we can to render coherent and to justify our convictions of social justice. We have reached a conception of the original position.

I shall not, of course, actually work through this process. Still, we may think of the interpretation of the original position that I shall present as the result of such a hypothetical course of reflection. It represents the attempt to accommodate within one scheme both reasonable philosophical conditions on principles as well as our considered judgments of justice. In arriving at the favored interpretation of the initial situation there is no point at which an appeal is made to self-evidence in the traditional sense either of general conceptions or particular convictions. I do not claim for the principles of justice proposed that they are necessary truths or derivable from such truths. A conception of justice cannot be deduced from self-evident premises or conditions on principles; instead, its justification is a matter of the mutual support of many considerations, of everything fitting together into one coherent view.

A final comment. We shall want to say that certain principles of justice are justified because they would be agreed to in an initial situation of equality. I have emphasized that this original position is purely hypothetical. It is natural to ask why, if this agreement is never actually entered into, we should take any interest in these principles, moral or otherwise. The answer is that the conditions embodied in the description of the original position are ones that we do in fact accept. Or if we do not, then perhaps we can be persuaded to do so by philosophical reflection. Each aspect of the contractual situation can be given supporting grounds. Thus what we shall do is to collect together into one conception a number of conditions on principles that we are ready upon due consideration to recognize as reasonable. These constraints express what we are prepared to regard as limits on fair terms of social cooperation. One way to look at the idea of the original position, therefore, is to see it as an expository device which sums up the meaning of these conditions and helps us to extract their consequences. On the other hand, this conception is also an intuitive notion that suggests its own elaboration, so that led on by it we are drawn to define more clearly the standpoint from which we can best interpret moral relationships. We need a conception that enables us to envision our objective from afar: the intuitive notion of the original position is to do this for us. . . .

TWO PRINCIPLES OF JUSTICE

I shall now state in a provisional form the two principles of justice that I believe would be chosen in the original position. In this section I wish to make only the most general comments, and therefore the first formulation of these principles is tentative. As we go on I shall run through several formulations and approximate step by step the final statement to be given much later. I believe that doing this allows the exposition to proceed in a natural way.

The first statement of the two principles reads as follows.

First: each person is to have an equal right to the most extensive basic liberty compatible with a similar liberty for others.

Second: social and economic inequalities are to be arranged so that they are both (a) reasonably expected to be to everyone's advantage, and (b) attached to positions and offices open to all. . . .

By way of general comment, these principles primarily apply, as I have said, to the basic structure of society. They are to govern the assignment of rights and duties and to regulate the distribution of social and economic advantages. As their formulation suggests, these principles presuppose that the social structure can be divided into two more or less distinct parts, the first principle applying to the one, the second to the other. They distinguish between those aspects of the social system that define and secure the equal liberties of citizenship and those that specify and establish social and economic inequalities. The basic liberties of citizens are, roughly speaking, political liberty (the right to vote and to be eligible for public office) together with freedom of speech and assembly; liberty of conscience and freedom of thought; freedom of the person along with the right to hold (personal) property;

and freedom from arbitrary arrest and seizure as defined by the concept of the rule of law. These liberties are all required to be equal by the first principle, since citizens of a just society are to have the same basic rights.

The second principle applies, in the first approximation, to the distribution of income and wealth and to the design of organizations that make use of differences in authority and responsibility, or chains of command. While the distribution of wealth and income need not be equal, it must be to everyone's advantage, and at the same time, positions of authority and offices of command must be accessible to all. One applies the second principle by holding positions open, and then, subject to this constraint, arranges social and economic inequalities so that everyone benefits.

These principles are to be arranged in a serial order with the first principle prior to the second. This ordering means that a departure from the institutions of equal liberty required by the first principle cannot be justified by, or compensated for, by greater social and economic advantages. The distribution of wealth and income, and the hierarchies of authority, must be consistent with both the liberties of equal citizenship and equality of opportunity.

It is clear that these principles are rather specific in their content, and their acceptance rests on certain assumptions that I must eventually try to explain and justify. A theory of justice depends upon a theory of society in ways that will become evident as we proceed. For the present, it should be observed that the two principles (and this holds for all formulations) are a special case of a more general conception of justice that can be expressed as follows.

[All social values—liberty and opportunity, income and wealth, and the bases of self-respect—are to be distributed equally unless an unequal distribution of any, or all, of these values is to everyone's advantage.]

Injustice, then, is simply inequalities that are not to the benefit of all. Of course, this conception is extremely vague and requires interpretation.

As a first step, suppose that the basic structure of society distributes certain primary goods, that is, things that every rational man is presumed to want. These goods normally have a use whatever a person's rational plan of life. For simplicity, assume that the chief primary goods at the disposition of society are rights and liberties, powers and opportunities, income and wealth.... [the primary good of self-respect has a central place.] These are the social primary goods. Other primary goods such as health and vigor, intelligence and imagination, are natural goods; although their possession is influenced by the basic structure, they are not so directly under its control. Imagine, then, a hypothetical initial arrangement in which all the social primary goods are equally distributed: everyone has similar rights and duties, and income and wealth are evenly shared. This state of affairs provides a benchmark for judging improvements. If certain inequalities of wealth and organizational powers would make everyone better off than in this hypothetical starting situation, then they accord with the general conception.

Now it is possible, at least theoretically, that by giving up some of their fundamental liberties men are sufficiently compensated by the resulting social and economic gains. [The general conception of justice imposes no restrictions on what sort of inequalities are permissible; it only requires that everyone's position be improved.] We need not suppose anything so drastic as consenting to a condition of slavery. Imagine instead that men forego certain political rights when the economic returns are significant and their capacity to influence the course of policy by the exercise of these rights would be marginal in any case. It is this kind of exchange which the two principles as stated rule out; being arranged in serial order they do not permit exchanges between basic liberties and economic and social gains. The serial ordering of principles expresses an underlying preference among primary social goods. When this preference is rational so likewise is the choice of these principles in this order....

THE VEIL OF IGNORANCE

The idea of the original position is to set up a fair procedure so that any principles agreed to will be just. The aim is to use the notion of pure procedural justice as a basis of theory. Somehow we must nullify the effects of specific contingencies which put men at odds and tempt them to exploit social and natural circumstances to their own advantage. Now in order to do this I assume that the parties are situated behind a veil of ignorance. They do not know how the various alternatives will affect their own particular case and they are obliged to evaluate principles solely on the basis of general considerations.

It is assumed, then, that the parties do not know certain kinds of particular facts. First of all, no one knows his place in society, his class position or social status; nor does he know his fortune in the distribution of natural assets and abilities, his intelligence and strength, and the like. Nor, again, does anyone know his conception of the good, the particulars of his rational plan of life, or even the special features of his psychology such as his aversion to risk or liability to optimism or pessimism. More than this, I assume that the parties do not know the particular circumstances of their own society. That is, they do not know its economic or political situation, or the level of civilization and culture it has been able to achieve. The persons in the original position have no information as to which generation they belong. These broader restrictions on knowledge are appropriate in part because questions of social justice arise between generations as well as within them, for example, the question of the appropriate rate of capital saving and of the conservation of natural resources and the environment of nature. There is also, theoretically anyway, the question of a reasonable genetic policy. In these cases too, in order to carry through the idea of the original position, the parties must not know the contingencies that set them in opposition. They must choose principles the consequences of which they are prepared to live with whatever generation they turn out to belong to.

As far as possible, then, the only particular facts which the parties know is that their society is subject to the circumstances of justice and whatever this implies. It is taken for granted, however, that they know the general facts about human society. They understand political affairs and the principles of economic theory; they know the basis of social organization and the laws of human psychology. Indeed, the parties are presumed to know whatever general facts affect the choice of the principles of justice. There are no limitations on general information, that is, on general laws and theories, since conceptions of justice must be adjusted to the characteristics of the systems of social cooperation which they are to regulate, and there is no reason to rule out these facts. It is, for example, a consideration against a conception of justice that in view of the laws of moral psychology, men would not acquire a desire to act upon it even when the institutions of their society satisfied it. For in this case there would be difficulty in securing the stability of social cooperation. It is an important feature of a conception of justice that it should generate its own support. That is, its principles should be such that when they are embodied in the basic structure of society men tend to acquire the corresponding sense of justice. Given the principles of moral learning, men develop a desire to act in accordance with its principles. In this case a conception of justice is stable. This kind of general information is admissible in the original position.

The notion of the veil of ignorance raises several difficulties. Some may object that the exclusion of nearly all particular information makes it difficult to grasp what is meant by the original position. Thus it may be helpful to observe that one or more persons can at any time enter this position, or perhaps, better, simulate the deliberations of this hypothetical situation, simply by reasoning in accordance with the appropriate restrictions. In arguing for a conception of justice we must be sure that it is among the permitted alternatives and satisfies the stipulated formal constraints. No considerations can be advanced in its favor unless they would be rational ones for us to urge were we to lack the kind of knowledge that is excluded. The evaluation of principles must proceed in terms of the general consequences of their public recognition and universal application, it being assumed that they will be complied with by everyone. To say that a certain conception of justice would be chosen in the original position is equivalent to saying that rational deliberation satisfying certain conditions and restrictions would reach a certain conclusion. If

necessary, the argument to this result could be set out more formally. I shall, however, speak throughout in terms of the notion of the original position. It is more economical and suggestive, and brings out certain essential features that otherwise one might easily overlook.

These remarks show that the original position is not to be thought of as a general assembly which includes at one moment everyone who will live at some time; or, much less, as an assembly of everyone who could live at some time. It is not a gathering of all actual or possible persons. To conceive of the original position in either of these ways is to stretch fantasy too far; the conception would cease to be a natural guide to intuition. In any case, it is important that the original position be interpreted so that one can at any time adopt its perspective. It must make no difference when one takes up this viewpoint, or who does so: the restrictions must be such that the same principles are always chosen. The veil of ignorance is a key condition in meeting this requirement. It insures not only that the information available is relevant, but that it is at all times the same.

It may be protested that the condition of the veil of ignorance is irrational. Surely, some may object, principles should be chosen in the light of all the knowledge available. There are various replies to this contention. Here I shall sketch those which emphasize the simplifications that need to be made if one is to have any theory at all.... To begin with, it is clear that since the differences among the parties are unknown to them, and everyone is equally rational and similarly situated, each is convinced by the same arguments. Therefore, we can view the choice in the original position from the standpoint of one person selected at random. If anyone after due reflection prefers a conception of justice to another, then they all do, and a unanimous agreement can be reached. We can, to make the circumstances more vivid, imagine that the parties are required to communicate with each other through a referee as intermediary, and that he is to announce which alternatives have been suggested and the reasons offered in their support. He forbids the attempt to form coalitions, and he informs the parties when they have come to an understanding. But such a referee is actually superfluous, assuming that the deliberations of the parties must be similar.

Thus there follows the very important consequence that the parties have no basis for bargaining in the usual sense. No one knows his situation in society nor his natural assets, and therefore no one is in a position to tailor principles to his advantage. We might imagine that one of the contractees threatens to hold out unless the others agree to principles favorable to him. But how does he know which principles are especially in his interests? The same holds for the formation of coalitions: if a group were to decide to band together to the disadvantage of the others, they would not know how to favor themselves in the choice of principles. Even if they could get everyone to agree to their proposal, they would have no assurance that it was to their advantage, since they cannot identify themselves either by name or description. The one case where this conclusion fails is that of saving. Since the persons in the original position know that they are contemporaries (taking the present time of entry interpretation), they can favor their generation by refusing to make any sacrifices at all for their successors; they simply acknowledge the principle that no one has a duty to save for posterity. Previous generations have saved or they have not; there is nothing the parties can now do to affect that. So in this instance the veil of ignorance fails to secure the desired result. Therefore I resolve the question of justice between generations in a different way by altering the motivation assumption. But with this adjustment no one is able to formulate principles especially designed to advance his own cause. Whatever his temporal position, each is forced to choose for everyone.

The restrictions on particular information in the original position are, then, of fundamental importance. Without them we would not be able to work out any definite theory of justice at all. We would have to be content with a vague formula stating that justice is what would be agreed to without being able to say much, if anything, about the substance of the agreement itself. The formal constraints of the concept of right, those applying to principles directly, are

not sufficient for our purpose. The veil of ignorance makes possible a unanimous choice of a particular conception of justice.

Without these limitations on knowledge the bargaining problem of the original position would be hopelessly complicated. Even if theoretically a solution were to exist, we would not, at present anyway, be able to determine it. . . .

A final comment. For the most part I shall suppose that the parties possess all general information. No general facts are closed to them. I do this mainly to avoid complications. Nevertheless a conception of justice is to be the public basis of the terms of social cooperation. Since common understanding necessitates certain bounds on the complexity of principles, there may likewise be limits on the use of theoretical knowledge in the original position. Now clearly it would be very difficult to classify and to grade for complexity the various sorts of general facts. I shall make no attempt to do this. We do however recognize an intricate theoretical construction when we meet one. Thus it seems reasonable to say that other things equal one conception of justice is to be preferred to another when it is founded upon markedly simpler general facts, and its choice does not depend upon elaborate calculations in the light of a vast array of theoretically defined possibilities. It is desirable that the grounds for a public conception of justice should be evident to everyone when circumstances permit. This consideration favors, I believe, the two principles of justice over the criterion of utility.

NOTES

1. As the text suggests, I shall regard Locke's *Second Treatise of Government,* Rousseau's The *Social Contract,* and Kant's ethical works beginning with *The Foundations of the Metaphysics of Morals* as definitive of the contract tradition. For all of its greatness, Hobbes's *Leviathan* raises special problems. A general historical survey is provided by J. W. Gough, The *Social Contract,* 2nd ed. (Oxford The Clarendon Press, 1957), and Otto Gierke, *Natural Law and the Theory of Society,* trans. with an introduction by Ernest Barker (Cambridge The University Press, 1934). A presentation of the contract view as primarily an ethical theory is to be found in G. R. Grice, *The*

Grounds of Moral Judgment (Cambridge, The University Press, 1967). See also §19, note 30.

2. Kant is clear that the original agreement is hypothetical. See *The Metaphysics of Morals,* pt. I (*Rechtslehre*), especially §§47, 52; and pt. II of the essay "Concerning the Common Saying: This May Be True in Theory but It Does Not Apply in Practice," in *Kant's Political Writings,* ed. Hans Reiss and trans. by H. B. Nisbet (Cambridge, The University Press, 1970), pp. 73–87. See Georges Vlachos, *La Pensée politique de Kant* (Paris, Presses Universitaires de France,

1962), pp. 326–335; and J. G. Murphy, *Kant: The Philosophy of Right* (London, Macmillan, 1970), pp. 109–112, 133–136, for a further discussion.

3. The process of mutual adjustment of principles and considered judgments is not peculiar to moral philosophy. See Nelson Goodman, *Fact, Fiction, and Forecast* (Cambridge, Mass., Harvard University Press, 1955), pp. 65–68, for parallel remarks concerning the justification of the principles of deductive and inductive inference.

God and Morality

PHILIP L. QUINN

Philip Quinn (1940–2004) taught at the University of Notre Dame. He wrote primarily in the areas of philosophy of science and philosophy of religion.

Many people in our society learn ethics in a religious context. A lot of parents combine ethical and religious education of children in the home, and ethical instruction is a major activity of religious institutions. So it is not surprising that many people think there is a close connection between religion and ethics. Monotheists, religious people who believe in one God, can find in their traditions support for the idea that there is such a connection. Judaism, Christianity, and Islam, which are the major forms of monotheism, all share the view that the Hebrew Bible, which Christians call the Old Testament, has religious authority. Its stories paint a picture in which ethics depends on God. Both Exodus 20:1–17 and Deuteronomy 5:6–21, which recount the revelation of the Ten Commandments, also known as the Decalogue, portray God as communicating with the human persons with whom a covenant is being established about how they ought to live their lives by issuing commands to them. It thus is natural enough to suppose that the ethical authority of the

Decalogue depends on the fact that it is divinely commanded or, more precisely, on the fact that its commands express God's will.

This supposition is reinforced in the Christian New Testament. It is a striking feature of its ethics of love that love is the subject of a command. In Matthew's Gospel, Jesus of Nazareth states the command in response to a lawyer who asks which commandment is the greatest. Jesus replies: "You shall love the Lord your God with your whole heart, with your whole soul, and with all your mind. This is the greatest and the first commandment. The second is like it: You shall love your neighbor as yourself" (Matthew 22:37–39). Mark 12:29–31 tells of Jesus giving essentially the same answer to a scribe, and Luke 10:27–28 speaks of a lawyer giving this answer to a question from Jesus and being told by Jesus that it is correct. And in his last discourse to them, reported in John's Gospel, Jesus tells his followers that "the command I give you is this, that you love one another" (John 15:17). So the authors of these narratives of the

This work was commissioned by the editors for the 11th edition of this anthology.

life of Jesus agree that the Christian ethics of love for one another takes the form of a command. If Jesus is God the Son, as traditional Christians believe, this command has its source in and expresses the will of God.

It is therefore clear that monotheists in general, and Christians in particular, can discover deep in their sacred scriptures the roots of the philosophical position known as theological voluntarism, which is the view that ethics depends on God's will. However, as people grow up, they normally question the ethical lore they have picked up from their parents or in the synagogue, the church, or the mosque. Theological voluntarism raises many questions in modern societies, in part because such societies are becoming increasingly secular in their public culture. Must ethics have religious foundations? In Dostoyevsky's novel *The Brothers Karamazov*, the character Ivan proclaims that everything is permitted if there is no God. Ivan's view seems to be just what one would expect someone who thinks ethics depends on religion to hold. But it is alarming. It suggests that a decline in religious belief would bring with it catastrophic consequences for ethics. Can ethics have religious foundations? Perhaps ethics can only be securely anchored in a scientific culture if grounded or based on scientific knowledge. But this too is an alarming suggestion. Popularizations of evolutionary theory seem to tell us that evolution selects for selfish behavior and selects against unselfish behavior, except when it is directed toward close biological kin or others who are likely to reciprocate. Philosophy can help us to think clearly and rigorously about questions concerning the relations between ethics and religion. Some of those questions are the topic of this essay. Let me try to clarify the exact questions to be considered.

Up to this point in the discussion, I have spoken mainly of relations between ethics and religion. However, this way of framing the issues is too broad for a couple of reasons, one having to do with religion and the other with ethics. The concept of religion applies to many different phenomena. In advaita Hinduism, for example, the ultimate religious reality, Brahman, is an impersonal ground of being rather than a personal deity. Brahman has no will and issues no commands. Of course advaita Hinduism has a great deal to say about how people should live their lives and how, in particular, they should be related to Brahman. But its ethical teachings, though they are religious, make no appeals to divine commands. Similarly, Theravada Buddhism does not acknowledge a personal deity. It has a lot to say about how people should live in order to reach eventually the good of religious liberation, but these ethical doctrines make no reference to God's will. Theological voluntarism is not a live option within these two religious traditions. It is important to be sensitive to the variety of ethical views within the major religions of the world, but it would be impossible to do justice to all such views within the confines of a single essay. So I must focus more narrowly. My choice is to restrict my attention to the monotheistic religions, chiefly because they are the ones I know best, and to emphasize Christianity, because it is my own tradition. It should therefore be kept in mind that what I have to say simply does not apply to religious traditions that are not monotheistic.

Nor will it be possible for me to range over the whole territory of ethics. The subject matter of ethics is how people should live their lives, and it has many different parts. For example, people need certain character traits in order to live well, and so a complete ethics will contain an account of virtues and vices. A complete ethics will also address questions about the contribution of emotions to living well. Some people think that living well involves eliminating painful feelings from one's life if one can do so; others argue that someone who felt no painful sorrow upon encountering a suffering child could not be sufficiently responsive to the true nature of suffering to be living well. Among the parts of ethics, one concerns duties, actions, or refrainings from action that seem to be required from us or demanded of us. Some philosophers refer to this subdomain within ethics as morality. Thus understood, morality concerns what we must do or must not do, and so it is natural to think of ourselves as living under one or more moral laws. In order to keep the size of this essay within manageable bounds, I shall confine my attention to morality. Hence I do not aspire to present a fully general treatment of ethics and religion; instead I plan to concentrate on the connection between morality and monotheism. The theory about that connection to be investigated is theological voluntarism restricted to the moral subdomain of ethics. Following the majority of recent philosophers who have written on this topic, I shall formulate the version of theological voluntarism under consideration in terms of God's commands. So the essay's specific topic is divine command morality.

It is worth mentioning that, though divine command morality has been an important part of the history of Christian moral thought, it has competitors. In the Roman Catholic tradition, natural law morality is a prominent example. According to natural law theory, moral law is natural in the sense that it can be known by human reason apart from any revelation from God. Natural lawyers, as proponents of this view are often called, therefore think that people who are not monotheists can have genuine moral knowledge of natural law. St. Thomas Aquinas makes this clear when he says that all people know "the common principles of the natural law" (*Summa Theologiae* I–II, 93, 2). However, Aquinas also holds that natural law is not independent of God. He tells us that "participation of the eternal law in a rational creature is called natural law" (*Summa Theologiae* I–II, 91, 2), and the eternal law is law of which God is the author. Hence, on his view, while people who are not monotheists can know the principles of natural law, they will be unaware of the ultimate source of those principles. Like divine command theory, natural law theory works with a picture of God as a legislator. Both theories are thoroughly theological in their accounts of the deepest source of morality. Because I believe that the strengths and weaknesses of theological theories of morality stand out most clearly in the case of divine command theory, I shall focus on it rather than natural law theory or other rivals within monotheistic traditions.

Having now finished explaining what lies behind my decision to include only divine command theories in this essay's treatment of God and morality, I can bring my preliminary remarks

to a close. The remainder of the essay is divided into three parts. In the first, I spell out in more detail a divine command theory of morality. In the second, I mobilize some reasons monotheists can offer for accepting a theory of this kind, and in the third, I develop and try to reply to some serious objections.

I. WHAT DOES A DIVINE COMMAND THEORY CLAIM?

As it is usually understood, morality works with three main concepts; they are rightness, wrongness, and obligation. Any attempt to define all three of them in terms of the others would obvious lead to circularity. So it is best to proceed by first explaining one of them without attempting to give a definition and then defining the other two in terms of it. I begin with rightness. Morally right actions are morally permissible; they are actions that, from the moral point of view, it is all right to perform. Using the concept of rightness, it is easy to define wrongness. Actions are morally wrong if and only if they are not morally right. Morally wrong actions may be thought of as actions that morality forbids or prohibits. Moral rightness and moral wrongness are mutually exclusive categories; no action is both right and wrong. They are also collectively exhaustive categories; every action is either right or wrong. Using the concept of wrongness thus defined, a definition of obligation is simple to state. Actions are morally obligatory if and only if not performing them is morally wrong or, alternatively, not performing them is not morally right. Morally obligatory actions may be thought of as actions that morality demands or requires. Moral obligation is commonly supposed to be a subcategory of moral rightness; some actions are right but not obligatory while others are both right and obligatory. Thus, for example, when I get up in the morning, it is morally right, that is, morally permissible, for me to put my right shoe on before my left shoe. But since it is not wrong for me to put my shoes on the other way around, it is not obligatory for me to put my right shoe on before my left shoe. By contrast, when I make a serious promise and nothing weighty interferes with my keeping it, it is morally right for me to keep my promise. However, because it is wrong for me not to keep my promise, it is also morally obligatory for me to keep it. Moral obligation and moral wrongness are matters of duty. Doing one's moral duty consists of performing obligatory actions and not performing wrong actions. In effect, then, morality is a system of requirements, permissions, and prohibitions governing actions. This much is common ground for competing theories of morality.

Different theories of morality contain different principles of requirement, permission, and prohibition. According to an act utilitarian principle of prohibition, for instance, actions are morally wrong if and only if the consequences of performing them yield less utility than the consequences of performing other actions the agent could have performed instead. The principles of a divine command theory of morality can be formulated in the following way:

(1) An action is morally right if and only if (i) God does not command that it not be performed, and (ii) if it is morally right, what makes it morally right is its not being the case that God commands that it not be performed;

(2) An action is morally wrong if and only if (i) God commands that it not be performed, and (ii) if it is morally wrong, what makes it morally wrong is God's commanding that it not be performed; and

(3) An action is morally obligatory if and only if (i) God commands that it be performed, and (ii) if it is morally obligatory, what makes it morally obligatory is God's commanding that it be performed.

These three principles make precise the idea that morality depends upon divine commands and, hence, on the underlying state of God's will that such commands express.

The radical nature of this dependency becomes apparent once it is realized that the proclamation attributed to Ivan Karamazov above is a straightforward consequence of these moral principles. According to (2), an action is morally wrong only if God commands that it not be performed. But if there is no God, there are no divine commands, and so no action is such that God commands that it not be performed. Hence, if there is no God, no action is morally wrong. However, every action is either morally right or morally wrong. Thus, if there is no God, every action is morally right in the sense of being morally permissible. Similarly, nothing is morally obligatory if there is no God. For according to (3), an action is morally obligatory only if God commands that it be performed. But, again, if there is no God, there are no divine commands, and so no action is such that God commands that it be performed. Hence, if there is no God, no action is morally obligatory. In short, according to a divine command morality, if there is no God, no action is either morally wrong or morally obligatory. In other words, on such a view, if there is no God, there are no moral duties.

Does this alarming cluster of conclusions that follow directly from the principles of a divine command theory by itself provide a sufficient reason to reject those principles? I shall address this question when I respond to objections in the third part of the essay. Before I turn to that task, however, I am going to discuss some of the reasons monotheists can offer in favor of a divine command theory of morality.

II. WHY SHOULD A MONOTHEIST ACCEPT A DIVINE COMMAND THEORY?

As far as I can tell, there is no deductive argument that would count, even for monotheists, as a conclusive proof for the principles of divine command morality. However, there seems to be no such proof for any other moral theory. So perhaps the best that can be done to recommend any set of moral principles is to support them with a cumulative case argument. In such an argument, a conclusion is supported by several considerations, none of which alone is decisive but each of which helps to build the case. In this essay I shall present a cumulative case argument with four parts. They support divine command theory in a way analogous to that in which the legs of a chair support the weight of a seated person. No one leg supports all the weight, but each leg makes a contribution to supporting the weight. Three of the four parts of my cumulative case appeal to Christian traditions; the fourth draws on general considerations from philosophical theology that are shared by the major monotheisms. The point of setting forth the cumulative case is to show why adopting a divine command theory should be regarded as an attractive choice for people who are already Christians and a live option for other monotheists. The point is not to persuade people who are not already monotheists to become divine command theorists. If convincing people who are not monotheists to adopt divine command morality were my aim, I would have to start by trying to argue for the existence of God, and I do not have space in this essay for that project. Hence all I hope to get people who are not monotheists to see is why divine command morality would be a plausible option for them if they were monotheists. I begin with the part of the cumulative case that focuses on the morality promulgated by Jesus.

Leg 1: Commanded Christian Love.

As noted above, the New Testament makes love of the neighbor the subject of a command. Is there a reason for this? I think so. It is that the love of neighbor of which Jesus speaks is very difficult for us in our present circumstances; it does not spontaneously engage our affections. If it were merely permissible, we would not love our neighbors in the way the Gospels teach. It is therefore no accident that Jesus commands love of the neighbor and thereby makes it a matter of obligation or duty.

Søren Kierkegaard has seen very clearly just how radical the demands of love of the neighbor are. In *Works of Love,* he draws a sharp distinction between erotic love and friendship, on the one hand, and Christian love of neighbor, on the other. Erotic love and friendship play favorites; Christian love of neighbor is completely impartial. Kierkegaard insists: "The object of both erotic love and friendship has therefore also the favorite's name, *the beloved, the friend,* who is loved in distinction from the rest of the world. On the other hand, the Christian teaching is to love one's neighbor, to love all mankind, all men, even enemies, and not to make exceptions, neither in favoritism nor in aversion."[1] His shocking idea is that the command to love the

neighbor places absolutely everyone, including one's beloved, one's friend, and one's very self, on the same footing as one's worst enemy or people with whom one has had no contact. Perhaps it is easy to imagine God loving all humans in this undiscriminating fashion. It is hard to imagine that we would do so unless doing so were obligatory for us, for we would surely not do so spontaneously. Therefore the impartiality of Christian love of the neighbor makes that love the appropriate object of a divine command that imposes obligations on us.

According to Kierkegaard, there is another way in which love of the neighbor differs from erotic love and friendship. The latter two depend on characteristics of the beloved and the friend that can and often do change. If the beloved loses the traits that made him or her erotically attractive, erotic love withers and dies. If the friend who was prized for having a virtuous character turns vicious, the friendship will be (or at least should be) broken off. Love of the neighbor, however, is supposed to be invulnerable to such changes in its objects. Kierkegaard puts the point this way: "No change, however, can take your neighbor from you, for it is not your neighbor who holds you fast—it is your love which holds your neighbor fast. If your love for your neighbor remains unchanged, then your neighbor also remains unchanged just by being."[2] If there is to be such a love that alters not where it alteration finds, it cannot depend on changeable features of the neighbor and ways in which they engage our natural feelings and preferences. For Kierkegaard, it can have the independence it needs from such feelings and preferences only if it is obligatory, for only then can it be motivated by a stable sense of duty rather than by changeable affections.

Kierkegaard thus has at least two powerful reasons for thinking that Christian love of the neighbor must be a matter of obligation. The first is that only a love which is obligatory can be extensive enough in scope to embrace absolutely anyone without distinction. Erotic love and friendship are always discriminating and exclusive. The second reason is that only a love which is obligatory can be invulnerable to changes in its objects. Erotic love and friendship naturally and properly change in response to changes in the valued features of their objects. These reasons support the view that Christian love of the neighbor has to be a commanded love.

I think that this commanded love is foundational for Christian morality and is what sets it apart from secular rivals. The stringency of the obligation to love is apt to give offense, as Kierkegaard himself recognizes. He tries to get us to see just how demanding the obligation really is and yet to accept it as binding upon us. "Only acknowledge it," he exhorts his readers, "or if it is disturbing to you to have it put in this way, I will admit that many times it has thrust me back and that I am yet very far from the illusion that I fulfill this command, which to flesh and blood is offense, and to wisdom foolishness."[3] I agree with Kierkegaard about the importance of highlighting rather than downplaying the stringency of the Christian obligation to love the neighbor even if, as a result of doing so, some people are thrust back or offended. But it seems to me that Christians who take the Gospels seriously are in no position to deny that they teach us that God has commanded us to love the neighbor or that this command places us under an obligation to do so. Hence I see in what is most distinctive of the Christian morality of love, the fact that it is commanded, a reason for Christians to favor a divine command theory of moral obligation.

Leg 2: Religious Practice.

According to an old saying, the law of prayer is the law of belief (*lex orandi, lex credendi*). We should probably regard this old saying as a rule of thumb rather than an exceptionless generalization, since popular devotion sometimes contains elements that are superstitious or even, as in the case of some cults, wicked. Yet often enough in Christianity, what is professed in religious practice is a good guide to what ought to be affirmed in sound theological theory. It is clear that the practice of Christian spirituality strongly emphasizes the theme of conforming one's own will to the will of God.

Janine M. Idziak has assembled numerous examples of this theme from Christian devotional sources.[4] It is found in traditional hymns such as the following: "Father, who didst fashion man/

Godlike in thy loving plan/ Fill us with that love divine/ And conform our wills to thine." It is also found in books of worship such as the Presbyterian *Daily Prayer:* "Eternal God, send your Holy Spirit into our hearts, to direct and rule us according to your will...", and "God of love, as you have given your life to us, so may we live according to your holy will revealed in Jesus Christ..." These examples, and others like them, indicate that conformity with God's will is an idea deeply embedded in Christian religious practice. Divine command principles reflect this theme at the level of moral theory. There seems to be nothing superstitious or otherwise amiss with this aspect of Christian devotional practice. Hence I think it provides some support for divine command theory in accord with the rule of *lex orandi, lex credendi*. In other words, the fact that conformity with the will of God is an important theme in Christian liturgical practices is a reason for Christians to adopt a moral theory in which divine commands that express God's will are the source of moral obligations.

I am not an expert on the religious practices of Judaism and Islam. However, I do know that traditional Judaism stresses obedience to the commands of Yahweh expressed in the Hebrew Bible. And I am also aware that Islam insists on submission to the will of Allah; indeed, the word "Islam" itself means submission (to Allah's will). So I think it safe to conjecture that Jews and Muslims have available to them arguments parallel to the argument I have just given for the case of Christianity. If this conjecture is correct, arguments of this sort will have some appeal not just for Christians but also for adherents of the other two major monotheisms.

Leg 3: The Immoralities of the Patriarchs.

A Christian tradition of interpreting some stories in the Hebrew Bible serves as the basis for an argument to the conclusion that the moral status of actions depends on divine commands. These stories recount the incidents sometimes described as the immoralities of the patriarchs. They are cases in which God commands something that appears to be wicked and, indeed, to violate a prohibition laid down in the Decalogue. Three such cases come up over and over again in Christian traditions of biblical commentary. The first is the case known as the *akedah,* the binding of Isaac, which involved a divine command to Abraham, recorded at Genesis 22:1–2, to offer his son Isaac as a sacrifice. The second is the divine command reported at Exodus 11:2, which was taken to be a command that the Israelites plunder the Egyptians. And the third is the divine command to the prophet Hosea, stated first at Hosea 1:2 and then repeated at Hosea 3:1, to have sexual relations with an adulteress. According to these stories, then, God has apparently commanded homicide, theft, and adultery (or at least fornication) in particular cases. What are we to make of these biblical tales?

The tradition of scriptural interpretation I am going to discuss takes the stories to be literally true; it supposes that God actually did issue the commands reported in the stories. It also assumes that these commands were binding on those to whom they were addressed. In his *City of God,* St. Augustine uses the *akedah* to make the point that the divine law prohibiting killing allows exceptions, "when God authorizes killing by a general law or when He gives an explicit commission to an individual for a limited time." Abraham, he says, "was not only free from the guilt of criminal cruelty, but even commended for his piety, when he consented to sacrifice his son, not, indeed, with criminal intent but in obedience to God" (*City of God* 1, 21). Augustine thinks God explicitly commissioned Abraham to kill Isaac and then revoked the commission just before the killing was to have taken place. It is clear that Augustine believes Abraham acted as he should in consenting to kill Isaac precisely because the killing had been commanded by God. He also believes that Abraham's consent, which would have been wrong in the absence of the command, was not wrong given its presence. In other words, the divine command alone determined the moral status of Abraham's consent.

St. Thomas Aquinas shares this view. He treats the three famous cases in the following passage:

> Consequently when the children of Israel, by God's command, took away the spoils of the Egyptians, this was not theft; since it was due to them by the sentence of God.—Likewise when Abraham consented to slay his son, he did not consent to murder, because his son was due to be slain by the command of God, Who is Lord of life and death; for He it is Who inflicts the punishment of death on all men, both godly and ungodly, on account of the sin of our first parent, and if a man be the executor of that sentence by Divine authority, he will be no murderer any more than God would be.—Again, Osee, by taking unto himself a wife of fornications, or an adulterous woman, was not guilty either of adultery or of fornication: because he took unto himself one who was his by command of God, Who is the author of the institution of marriage. (*Summa Theologiae* I–II, 100, 8)

In this passage, Aquinas reasons in the following way. Because God commanded the Israelites to plunder the Egyptians, what the Israelites took on their exit from Egypt was due to them. Since theft involves taking what is not one's due, the plunder of the Egyptians was not theft. Similarly, because God, who is lord of life and death, commanded Abraham to slay Isaac, Isaac was due to receive the punishment of death all humans deserve in consequence of Adam's original sin. Since murder involves slaying someone who is not due to be slain, Abraham's consent to the slaying of Isaac was not consent to murder. And because God, who is the author of marriage, commanded Hosea to take the adulteress as his wife, she was his wife, and so he was guilty of neither adultery nor fornication in having intercourse with her. For Aquinas, therefore, the action of the Israelites was, as a result of the divine command, not really theft and so was not wrong. Similarly, because of the divine command, Abraham's consent was not consent to murder and thus was not wrong. And, on account of the divine command, Hosea's sexual intercourse was neither adultery nor fornication and hence was not wrong. In all three cases, the divine commands determined the moral status of actions; they transformed actions that otherwise would have been wrong into actions that were not wrong.

It should be emphasized that learning from Augustine and Aquinas need not be restricted to Christians who share their belief that the divine commands recounted in the biblical stories actually occurred. Some Christians may treat one or more of these cases as hypothetical rather than actual but agree with the two saints that divine commands would, if they were issued, make precisely the moral difference the saints say they actually did make. I think there would be enough agreement among Christians about these and other actual and hypothetical cases to make it reasonable to claim that Christian moral intuitions support the conclusion that God's commands determine the moral status of actions in particular cases. It also seems to me reasonable to generalize inductively from such particular cases. Hence I conclude that moral intuitions underlying the tradition of biblical interpretation to which the two saints belong provide some support for the view that the moral status of any human action or omission depends on whether it is divinely commanded or not.

I cannot speak with authority about how the traditions of interpretation in Judaism and Islam consider it best to treat the incidents in the Hebrew Bible known as the immoralities of the patriarchs. It does seem to me, however, that Jews and Muslims could, if they wished to do so, employ the strategy of interpretation used by Augustine and Aquinas. If they do so, they will be in a position to use biblical cases to support the conclusion that the commands of Yahweh or Allah determine moral status.

Leg 4: Divine Sovereignty.

According to the doctrine of divine sovereignty, God is sovereign lord of the universe in the sense that things other than God depend on and are under the control of God. There are several reasons why monotheists of all stripes—Jews, Christians, and Muslims alike—would want to include a strong doctrine of divine sovereignty in their philosophical theology. Two of the most important pertain to creation and providence. Monotheists customarily wish to insist on a sharp distinction between God and the created world. Traditional accounts of divine creation and conservation assert that each contingent thing, which is to say each thing that might not have existed, depends on God's

power for its existence whenever it exists. God, by contrast, depends on nothing outside God-self for existence. So God has complete sovereignty over the realm of contingent existence. Monotheists also usually wish to maintain that we can trust God's promises about the future and our salvation without any reservations. Even if God does not control the finest details of history because of a prior decision to create a world in which there is real indeterminism at the quantum level or libertarian free will, God has the power to ensure that the created universe will serve divine purposes for it and all its inhabitants in the long run. So God also has extensive providential sovereignty over the realm of contingent events. Our philosophical theology will have greater theoretical unity if we extend divine sovereignty from the realm of contingent existence and events to the domain of morality. Doing so will also yield a philosophical theology that is simple. Because theoretical unity and simplicity are important virtues in any theory, we want them in our philosophical theology if we can manage to get them. Adopting divine command morality would extend divine sovereignty to cover the whole domain of morality; it would give us the theoretical unity and simplicity we seek. Hence we should adopt divine command morality because doing so increases the theoretical unity and simplicity of our philosophical theology.

I think the strength of the cumulative case for divine command theory I have outlined derives in part from the diversity of sources to which it appeals. The moral demands set forth by Jesus in the Gospels, considerations drawn from sound religious practice, commentary by two saints on incidents portrayed in the Hebrew Bible, and theoretical virtues from philosophical theology all converge in supporting the adoption of divine command theory. No doubt there are other considerations within the traditions of the major monotheisms that could be added to my cumulative case, but I cannot discuss them within the limits of this essay. So I must be content to hope that the four legs of my cumulative case support its conclusion to the same extent the four legs of my office chair support my weight.

III. HOW CAN A DIVINE COMMAND THEORY BE DEFENDED?

There are many objections to divine command theory. In this respect, it is neither in better shape nor in worse shape than any other moral theory. The important question for any moral theory is how well it can be defended against the objections to it. I do not have space in this essay to consider all the objections to divine command theory, and so I must confine my discussion to the objections that my experience leads me believe many people find particularly troublesome. Since I have presented four arguments in support of divine command theory, it seems only fair for me to respond to an equal number of objections that are meant to undermine it. I shall argue that divine command morality can be successfully defended against all four of the objections I raise. Think of each of the objections as an arrow intended to deliver a mortal wound to divine command morality. I shall try to show that none of them is a killing shot and that, taken together, they fall short of being lethal.

Arrow 1: The Karamazov Objection.

I return now to a worry I had earlier set aside. According to the theory I have formulated, if there is no God, no actions are wrong and none are obligatory. Ivan Karamazov's claim that everything is permitted or, better, is permissible is, therefore, a consequence of the theory. But why exactly is that objectionable? Perhaps it is supposed to be because Ivan's claim can be used as a premise in the following argument:

(4) If there is no God, everything is permissible.
(5) There is no God.
(6) So everything is permissible.

It is obvious that this argument is logically valid; its conclusion follows from its premises by *modus ponens*. One would hope that all decent people, whether they are monotheists or atheists, will reject its conclusion. Surely, they will insist, torturing innocent children just for one's own amusement is not morally permissible. So let us assume monotheists and atheists agree that (6) is false. Having rejected (6), they must then reject at least one of the argument's premises in order to remain consistent. Because atheists think that (5) is true, they will reject (4) and the principles of divine command theory of which it is a consequence. But monotheists can consistently accept (4) while rejecting (6) because they think (5) is false. In other words, given that (6) is false, the issue boils down to whether (5) is true and (4) is false, as the atheist holds, or (5) is false and (4) is true, as the monotheist who is a divine command theorist maintains. Without a proof of the existence of God, the divine command theorist is not in a position to show conclusively that (5) is false and the atheist is mistaken. But, equally, without a proof of the nonexistence of God, the atheist is not in a position to show conclusively that (5) is true and the divine command theorist is mistaken. It is generally agreed that none of the known arguments for or against the existence of God amounts to a proof. That being so, not being backed up by a proof of the nonexistence of God, this objection by itself does not yield a refutation of divine command theory.

Arrow 2: The Moral Skepticism Objection.

It is sometimes thought that divine command theory implies moral skepticism. An argument for this view might take the following form. According to divine command theory, we can come to know what is morally obligatory or wrong only by first coming to know what God has commanded. Hence only people who have religious knowledge can have moral knowledge. But no one actually has religious knowledge of what God has commanded. As Eric D'Arcy notes, "if immoral actions are immoral merely because God so wills it, merely because God legislates against them, it would be sheer coincidence if someone who knew nothing of God or his law happened to adopt the same views about particular actions as God did."[5] Mere coincidence of our views with God's views, however, would not give us religious knowledge of God's views, though it would yield true beliefs about them, because true beliefs are not sufficient for knowledge. Thus we could not derive moral knowledge from such true beliefs about God's views. And the best we can hope for when the subject is God's views is true beliefs. Even if some religious people have them, this is a matter of faith rather than knowledge. In sum, for divine command theory, the only route we have to moral knowledge is through religious knowledge of God's commands, and this route is blocked because our only access to God's commands is through faith which, while it may yield true beliefs about divine commands, is bound to fall short of producing knowledge.

One way the divine command theorist can reply to this objection is simply to assert that scripture, religious traditions, and personal religious experience can be sources of knowledge about what God commands. Though I tend to think this is true, I do not find it a convincing response. The objector can easily cast doubt on it by pointing to the sharp disagreement among religious people themselves about what those sources deliver. They quarrel about how to interpret scripture, which of the competing religious traditions preserves genuine revelation from God, and whose religious experiences are veridical.* Can such sources yield knowledge when they give rise to controversy of this sort? There is, however, a better response available to the divine command theorist. The theory asserts that God's commands make it the case that certain actions are morally obligatory and others are wrong. It makes no epistemological claims, and, in particular, it makes no claims about how we might come to know what God has commanded. It does not imply that we can come to know what is morally obligatory or wrong only by first coming to know what God commands. In other words, the subject matter of divine command theory is a certain kind of metaphysical dependency of morality on God's commands. But the order of epistemological access to things can be the reverse of the order of metaphysical dependency. Causation provides an example from ordinary life. Though effects are metaphysically dependent on their causes, we often come to know causes by first coming to know their effects. So it is not a consequence of divine command theory that only people who

have religious knowledge can have moral knowledge; the divine command theorist can consistently deny that our only route to moral knowledge is through religious knowledge. Therefore, the objection fails.

Indeed, the divine command theorist could consistently hold that we can only come to know what God's commands are by first coming to know what is morally obligatory or wrong. Jeremy Bentham, who was a utilitarian, once expressed a view of this kind. He said: "We may be perfectly sure, indeed, that whatever is right is conformable to the will of God: but so far is that from answering the purpose of showing us what is right, that it is necessary to know first whether a thing is right, in order to know from thence whether it be conformable to the will of God."[6] As this remark suggests, Bentham apparently thought that a moral theory would be useless unless it answered to the purpose of showing us what is right. It must be granted to Bentham that divine command theory does not answer to the purpose of showing us what is morally obligatory, permissible, and wrong if we can only come to know what God's commands are by first coming to know what is morally obligatory, permissible, and wrong. In that case, divine command theory would not provide us with a decision procedure for morality, a way of deciding or determining the moral status of an action. But so what? It is not obvious that failure to provide a decision procedure is a fatal flaw in a moral theory. Presumably it would be of theoretical interest to learn that what is morally obligatory, permissible, and wrong depends on God's commands, even if this knowledge were by itself of no practical use. In fact, it seems to be the case that Bentham's own utilitarianism runs into a similar difficulty. No one is in a position to calculate and assign numeral utility values to all the consequences of all the alternative actions open to the agent in many circumstances in which moral decisions must be made. When this is pointed out to utilitarians, some of them respond that it would be of theoretical interest to learn that utilitarianism is true, even if applying it to get solutions to urgent moral problems is often not a practical possibility. It would hardly be fair for utilitarians who use this response to

---

*[i.e., accurately conveying the truth]

defend their theory to object if divine command theorists say similar things in defense of their theory.

Arrow 3: The Divisiveness Objection.

Another objection to divine command theory is that it is bound to be a divisive position. William K. Frankena develops the idea this way:

> However deep and sincere one's own religious beliefs may be, if one reviews the religious scene, one cannot help but wonder if there is any rational and objective method of establishing any religious belief against the proponents of other religions or of irreligion. But then one is impelled to wonder also if there is anything to be gained by insisting that all ethical principles are or must be logically grounded on religious beliefs. For to insist on this is to introduce into the foundation of any morality whatsoever all of the difficulties involved in the adjudication of religious controversies, and to do so is hardly to encourage hope that mankind can reach, by peaceful and rational means, some desirable kind of agreement on moral and political principles.[7]

Though Frankena is in these remarks discussing views in which the relation between religion and morality is supposed to be a matter of logic, presumably he would have a similar worry about our divine command theory in which the relation is metaphysical. And, of course, Frankena is quite correct in pointing out that religious disagreement has in the past given rise to sharp moral disagreement and continues to do so in our own times. Still, there are three things worth saying in response to his worry.

First, religious disagreement does not inevitably lead to disagreement about moral principles. A divine command theorist can agree with a Kantian moral theorist who is not religious on the principle that torturing the innocent is always morally wrong. They will, to be sure, disagree about why torture of the innocent is always wrong. A divine command theorist will say that it is wrong because God has commanded that no one ever torture an innocent person. A secular Kantian may say that it is wrong because, involving as it does a failure to treat humanity in another person as an end in itself, it violates the categorical imperative. Disagreement at the deepest level of moral theory is therefore consistent with agreement at the level of moral principles. So despite religious disagreement, there are grounds for hope that we can reach, by peaceful and rational means, an overlapping consensus on at least some moral and political principles.

Second, not all moral disagreement is divisive. A Kierkegaardian Christian may think that Mother Teresa was only doing her duty toward her neighbor as specified by the Love Commandment in the Gospels, when she devoted herself to caring for wretched people in India, and regret the failure of the rest of us to satisfy her high standard of duty. One of her secular admirers may believe that much of the good she did was supererogatory, that is, above and beyond the call of duty. But if they agree that she did a great deal of good for others and that the earth would be better off if it had on it more people like her in this respect, their disagreement about whether some of her good works were obligatory or supererogatory is not apt to be especially divisive.

Yet, third, in spite of the fact that disagreement about religion is likely to lead to less moral disagreement than one might initially have imagined, it seems utterly unrealistic to expect agreement on all matters of moral and political principle as long as disagreement in moral theory persists. However, as Robert M. Adams has pointed out, nothing in the history of modern secular moral theory gives us reason to expect that general agreement on a single comprehensive moral theory will ever be achieved or that, if achieved, it would long endure in a climate of free inquiry. As any student who has taken a course in moral philosophy can testify, it is a subject chock full of combat between rival moral theories. The conclusion Adams draws, with which I agree, is that "the development and advocacy of a religious ethical theory, therefore, does not destroy a realistic possibility of agreement that would otherwise exist."[8] In other words, if those who accept divine command theory advocate it, they will not make the situation of disagreement worse. Moreover, if they refrain from advocating it, they will forfeit an opportunity to make the situation better. For if divine command theory is not advocated, it will not be subject to testing by public critical scrutiny in the marketplace of ideas. And if it is not tested in such debates, we will never discover whether there are reasons for rejecting it or grounds for accepting it above and beyond those we already have. So if divine command theory is not advocated, we will never get any closer than we are now to knowing whether or not it is true. But if it is advocated, there is at least a chance that we will, as a result of public debate, come closer to knowing whether or not it is true. Hence if those who accept divine command theory advocate it, we will not be made intellectually worse off and we may become intellectually better off. Therefore, even if it is granted, as I think it should be, that divine command theory is, to some extent, a divisive point of view, there are still good reasons of a practical sort to favor its advocacy and development. And it is worth noting that, despite his worry about the divisiveness of linking morality to religion, Frankena himself acknowledges that if the view that morality is dependent on religion rests on good grounds, we must accept it.[9]

Arrow 4: The Euthyphro Objection.

The most powerful objection to divine command theory is often traced back to classical antiquity. In the dialogue *Euthyphro,* Plato has Socrates ask Euthyphro to consider the following question. "Is what is pious loved by the gods because it is pious, or is it pious because it is loved" (*Euthyphro* 10a)? Some of the discussion in the dialogue turns on special features of the polytheism of Greek popular religion. For example, Socrates suggests that the gods might disagree about piety, some of them loving it while others hate it, and he persuades Euthyphro that perhaps in that case there would be things that are both pious and impious. What Socrates suggests does seem to be a real possibility for the quarrelsome gods portrayed in the epic poetry of Homer, but it obviously is not a possibility for monotheists. So the question needs to be rephrased if it is to be addressed to monotheists.

A question monotheists who believe that God does issue commands must confront is this: Are actions commanded by God because they are obligatory, or are actions obligatory because they are commanded by God? And there is, of course,

a similar question about wrongness and being contrary to the commands of God. Such questions seem to impale divine command theorists on the horns of a dilemma. On the one hand, if actions are commanded by God because they are obligatory, then such actions are obligatory prior to and independent of being divinely commanded. But divine command theorists cannot accept the view that actions are obligatory independent of being divinely commanded. It is not consistent with their view that divine commands make actions obligatory; actions that are made obligatory by divine commands are not obligatory independent of those commands. It also undercuts one of the legs in the cumulative case for divine command theory, since actions that are obligatory independent of God's commands are not actions over whose moral status God has sovereignty. On the other hand, however, if actions are obligatory because they are commanded by God, then it at any rate seems that obligation is completely arbitrary, because God could, just by commanding it, make any action whatsoever obligatory and, hence, no matter how horrendous an action might be, it would be obligatory if God were to command it. In the seventeenth century, Ralph Cudworth pressed this objection to divine command morality in particularly vivid and forceful language. He wrote:

> divers Modern Theologers do not only seriously, but zealously contend..., That there is nothing Absolutely, Intrinsically, and Naturally Good and Evil, Just and Unjust, antecedently to any positive command of God; but that the Arbitrary Will and Pleasure of God, (that is, an Omnipotent Being devoid of all Essential and Natural Justice) by its Commands and Prohibitions, is the first and only Rule and Measure thereof. Whence it follows unavoidably that nothing can be imagined so grossly wicked, or so foully unjust or dishonest, but if it were supposed to be commanded by this Omnipotent Deity, must needs upon that Hypothesis forthwith become Holy, Just and Righteous.[10]

Does the divine command theorist have anything to say in response to Cudworth's stinging indictment?

In order to address this question, I must introduce a new idea into the discussion. Up to this point, I have been working exclusively with the moral categories of rightness, wrongness, and obligation, but now I want to bring onto the scene another pair of ethical categories, goodness and badness. Monotheists have traditionally held that God is perfectly good. Putting this point in a way Plato might find congenial, God is the Good itself, and creatures are good only in virtue of resembling God in some respect. In the account of creation in Genesis 1, humans are said to have been made in the image and likeness of God. Monotheists might generalize from this story and say that creatures resemble God by bearing the relation of imaging to God. It is worth noting that this view does not make goodness independent of God and thus does not compromise the doctrine of divine sovereignty. After all, if God does not exist, then, on this view, the Good itself, the paradigm of goodness, does not exist either, and so nothing other than God is good because nothing bears the relation of imaging to a paradigm that does not exist. The divine command theorist can use this view of divine goodness as the basis of a reply to Cudworth.

Consider some state of affairs we are certain is foully unjust, say, an innocent child being tortured to death. Cudworth's complaint is that divine command theory has as a consequence the following conditional or hypothetical statement:

(7) If God commands someone to torture an innocent child to death, then it is morally obligatory for that person to torture the child to death.

And Cudworth is correct about this point because (7) does follow from (3). However, a refutation of divine command theory can be derived from this point only if it can be shown that (7) is false, and the divine command theorist is in a position to argue that (7) is, in fact, true. Since God is the Good itself, divine goodness constrains what God commands or, indeed, even could command. God never commands anyone to torture an innocent child to death, and so the antecedent of (7) is false. But according to elementary logic books, conditionals with false antecedents are themselves true. Hence, by the divine command theorist's lights, (7) is true. In short, God's commands are not arbitrary. So

the fact that (7) follows from divine command theory is not really a problem because it is open to the divine command theorists to grant that (7) is true.

Can this reply to Cudworth be generalized from the example of torturing an innocent child to death, and others like it, to cover all cases? Maybe not. Monotheists typically hold that God is a transcendent being. God's infinite goodness is not exactly the same as finite human goodness; they are, it is sometimes said, only analogous. God's goodness is therefore, at least to some extent, beyond our ken; we cannot completely grasp it; it is bound to remain, in some ways, incomprehensible to us. This does not mean that we could or should be prepared to accept as good a set of alleged divine commands that is totally contrary to our human ideas of goodness. It does, however, leave room for the possibility that there are a few divine commands that violate our assumptions about goodness. In order to face up to this possibility, let us return to the biblical story of the *akedah*.

In order to get a grip on what this story might mean for us, Robert M. Adams asks us to imagine a modern Abraham who at first finds overwhelmingly plausible all three of the following claims:

(8) If God commands me to do something, it is not morally wrong for me to do it.
(9) God commands me to kill my son.
(10) It is morally wrong for me to kill my son.[11]

Since the negation of (10) follows by *modus ponens* from (8) and (9), these claims are inconsistent, and Adams stipulates that his Abraham recognizes their mutual inconsistency. The question then becomes which of (8)–(10) it would be best for Abraham to reject. It would not be easy for a divine command theorist to endorse rejecting (8). By (3), if God commands Abraham to kill his son, it is obligatory for him to do it. Given the supposition, mentioned above, that obligation is a subdomain of rightness, if it is obligatory for Abraham to kill his son, it is right and hence not wrong for him to do it. And so, by the logical law known as the transitivity of implication, if God commands Abraham to kill his son, it is not wrong for him to do it. Thus Abraham's choice boils down to rejecting (9) or rejecting (10). Confronted with this choice, Abraham gets conflicting advice from two great modern philosophers.

Kant's advice is to reject (9), and Adams favors this option. In a famous passage in *The Conflict of the Faculties,* he tells Abraham precisely what he ought to do. Kant writes: "Abraham should have replied to this supposedly divine voice: 'That I ought not to kill my good son is quite certain. But that you, this apparition, are God—of that I am not certain, and never can be, not even if this voice rings down to me from (visible) heaven.' "[12] Perhaps the plausibility of Kant's position can be made clearer with the help of a thought experiment. Imagine you have just moved into a new house and, looking out the kitchen window, you spot your next door neighbor building a stone altar in his back yard. When you ask what it is for, he tells you he has been commanded by God to sacrifice his son, and he cordially invites you to drop by in the morning and take part in the ceremony. Surely your first reaction would be to think that your new neighbor ought to be in a mental hospital. Yet, though I acknowledge the force of such considerations, I do not believe they are decisive. If I did, my earlier argument that incidents resembling the *akedah* can be part of a cumulative case for divine command theory would be seriously undermined. But I do not believe that it is undermined, because I think Kant's claim that Abraham could never be certain that God had commanded him to kill his son can be successfully challenged. According to monotheists, God is, as Cudworth mentioned, omnipotent. It is therefore within God's power to give Abraham a sign that would make him certain that he has been commanded to kill his son. Suppose, for example, that one night, in the twinkling of an eye, the stars in the sky are rearranged to spell out the sentence "ABRAHAM, SACRIFICE ISAAC!" Abraham observes this transformation of the heavens. Observers all over the world, some of whom do not even know English, testify that they now see this pattern in the night sky, and Abraham learns of this testimony and uses it to rule out the possibility that he is hallucinating. Being a modern person, he reasons that

the stellar rearrangement he observed could not have occurred without many of the stars achieving velocities in excess of the speed of light and thereby miraculously violating a law of physics. In such circumstances, it seems to me, Abraham would be crazy not to believe that he had been divinely commanded to kill his son and would be certain if he believed it.

In a case of this sort, I think Abraham's best bet would be to reject (10) and to suppose that what Kierkegaard calls a teleological suspension of the ethical occurs. In *Fear and Trembling,* which he published under the pseudonym of Johannes de Silentio, Kierkegaard concludes that "the story of Abraham contains therefore a teleological suspension of the ethical."[13] It is a suspension of the ethical or, in the idiom of this essay, a suspension of the moral because God exempts Abraham from a moral principle that would otherwise be binding on him. In the circumstances, therefore, it is not wrong for Abraham to kill his son. The suspension is teleological because God suspends the moral in order to achieve a special goal (*telos*). According to Kierkegaard, God's goal in the *akedah* is to subject Abraham to a severe test of the depths of his faith, a test which Abraham passes. It is worth pointing out that the teleological suspension of the ethical plays the same role in Kierkegaard's thought about Abraham that the notion of a commission from God to an individual for a limited time plays in Augustine's thought and that the concept of being an executor of a death sentence by divine authority plays in Aquinas' thought. In all three cases, the general idea is that God can, in particular instances, create exceptions to or exemptions from moral principles that would otherwise be in force. I think divine command theorists ought to allow for the possibility of such divinely mandated exceptions or exemptions. If they do, they will be in a position to use the immoralities of the patriarchs as part of a cumulative case for divine command theory.

It does not follow from this view that divine command theorists must concede to Cudworth or, more generally, to the Euthyphro objection that God's commands are or could be completely arbitrary. So a divine command theorist can respond to the charge of arbitrariness by saying that actions are obligatory because God commands them and yet God's commands are not and could not be completely arbitrary because they are constrained by God's goodness. What must be conceded is that God's commands need not always conform to our ideas of goodness. I reckon that it is safe enough for monotheists to make this concession. To demand that God conform to our ideas would be to make our ideas rather than their transcendent object an absolute, and monotheists will rightly fear that absolutizing anything finite, including our ideas, would be a form of idolatry.

But divine command theorists must concede something to Cudworth. According to his complaint, divine command theory has among its consequences another conditional or hypothetical statement that is every bit as unattractive as (7). It is this:

(11) If God commands Abraham to kill his son, then it is morally obligatory for Abraham to kill his son.

And Cudworth is right on this point too because (11) does follow from (3). If divine command theorists do not imitate Kant in rejecting (9), they will be committed to holding that the antecedent of (11) is true. According to the logic books, however, the only way for (11) as a whole to be true, as the divine command theorists must insist that it is, when its antecedent is true, is for its consequent also to be true. So a Kierkegaardian divine command theorist is committed to holding that it is morally obligatory for Abraham to kill his son. Having rejected (10), the Kierkegaardian divine command theorist can consistently maintain that it is morally obligatory, and hence morally right and so not morally wrong, for Abraham to kill his son. People like Cudworth are sure to think such claims outrageously false. At this point, the Kierkegaardian divine command theorist has no choice except to bite the bullet and disagree with such people. It seems to me there is nothing amiss if the Kierkegaardian divine command theorist insists that they are true.

Having shown that divine command theory is not refuted by any one of the four objections

I have considered, let me conclude by asking whether, taken together, they add up to much of a cumulative case against it. In other words, given that none of the individual arrows directed against divine command theory delivers a mortal wound, how badly is it wounded, if at all, by all of them together? In my opinion, the second and third arrows simply miss the mark. Because the divine command theory I have formulated makes no epistemological claims, it has no epistemological consequences, and so it cannot be faulted for having false or unwarranted epistemic implications. And one cannot view the fact that there will be disagreement about it as a good reason to reject it unless one is also prepared in fairness to regard disagreement as a good reason to reject all known philosophical theories in morality, in ethics more generally and in politics, not to mention all known theories in a host of other areas of philosophy. However, I do admit that the first and fourth arrows hit their target, though I do not think that, either separately or together, they do lethal damage. The existence of evil, after all, does count to some extent, but not decisively, as evidence against monotheism, and so, for those who deny that everything is permissible, it provides a reason, though not, it seems to me, a conclusive reason, for accepting the antecedent of (4) and hence rejecting (4) and the principles of divine command theory of which it is a consequence. And while I think a teleological suspension of the ethical is possible and may even have occurred on a few occasions, I recognize that many people will find the claim that Abraham is or even could be under a moral obligation to kill his son, and similar claims in other cases, intuitively very implausible. So I am certainly prepared to allow that there is a cumulative case against divine command theory that has some real force.

After being examined, then, divine command theory winds up with both pluses and minuses on its score card. Monotheists can support it with a cumulative case argument, but there are also considerations adding up to a cumulative case argument that goes some way toward undermining it. Neither argument comes anywhere close to being a definitive proof of the sort one discovers in logic books. In this respect, divine command theory is just like all the other moral theories currently debated in philosophy. Each of them is such that there is no knock-down, drag-out argument for it and also no such argument against it. In a way, this is a frustrating situation; in another way, it is challenging. There is still an opportunity, which will excite people who enjoy doing philosophy, to join the search for arguments for or against moral theories that are stronger and more conclusive than any yet known to us. Perhaps this essay will stimulate some of its readers to take advantage of that opportunity.[14]

NOTES

1. Søren Kierkegaard, *Works of Love*. Trans. H. V. Hong and E. H. Hong (New York: Harper, 1964), p. 36.

2. *Ibid.*, p. 76.

3. *Ibid.*, p. 71.

4. Janine M. Idziak, "Divine Command Ethics," *A Companion to Philosophy of Religion*. Ed. P. L. Quinn and C. Taliaferro (Oxford: Blackwell, 1997), pp. 453–459. The two examples I quote come from p. 457.

5. Eric D'Arcy, "Worthy of Worship: A Catholic Contribution," *Religion and Morality*. Ed. G. Outka and J. P. Reeder, Jr. (Garden City, NY: Anchor, 1973), p. 194.

6. Jeremy Bentham, *An Introduction to the Principles of Morals and Legislation* (New York: Hafner, 1948), p. 22.

7. William K. Frankena, "Is Morality Logically Dependent on Religion?" *Religion and Morality*. Ed. G. Outka and J. P. Reeder, Jr. (Garden City, NY: Anchor, 1973), p. 313.

8. Robert M. Adams, "Religious Ethics in a Pluralistic Society," *Prospects for a Common Morality*. Ed. G. Outka and J. P. Reeder, Jr. (Princeton, NJ: Princeton University Press, 1993), p. 91.

9. Frankena, *op. cit.*, p. 314.

10. Ralph Cudworth, *A Treatise Concerning Eternal and Immutable Morality* (New York: Garland, 1976), pp. 9–10.

11. Robert M. Adams, *Finite and Infinite Goods: A Framework for Ethics* (New York and Oxford: Oxford University Press, 1999), p. 280. I have renumbered Adams' sentences.

12. Immanuel Kant, *The Conflict of the Faculties*. Trans. M. J. Gregor and R. Anchor, in Kant, *Religion and Rational Theology*, ed. A. W. Wood and G. di Giovanni (Cambridge: Cambridge University Press, 1996), p. 283.

13. Søren Kierkegaard, *Fear and Trembling*, in Kierkegaard, *Fear and Trembling and the Sickness unto Death*. Trans. W. Lowrie (Princeton, NJ: Princeton University Press, 1968), p. 77.

14. Some of the material in this essay is discussed in greater technical detail in Philip L. Quinn, "Divine Command Theory," *The Blackwell Guide to Ethical Theory*. Ed. H. LaFollette (Oxford: Blackwell, 2000), pp. 53–73.

The Good Will & The Categorical Imperative

IMMANUEL KANT

Immanuel Kant (1724–1804) was the greatest of the German philosophers. He spent his entire career at the University of Konigsburg.

THE GOOD WILL

It is impossible to think of anything at all in the world, or indeed even beyond it, that could be considered good without limitation except a **good will.** Understanding, wit, judgment and the like, whatever such *talents* of mind may be called, or courage, resolution, and perseverance

From *Groundwork of the Metaphysics of Morals* by Immanuel Kant; translated and edited by Mary Gregor, New York: Cambridge University Press, 1998, pp. 7–16, 25–39. Reprinted by permission of Cambridge University Press.

in one's plans, as qualities of *temperament,* are undoubtedly good and desirable for many purposes, but they can also be extremely evil and harmful if the will which is to make use of these gifts of nature, and whose distinctive constitution is therefore called *character,* is not good. It is the same with *gifts of fortune.* Power, riches, honor, even health and that complete well-being and satisfaction with one's condition called *happiness,* produce boldness and thereby often arrogance as well unless a good will is present which corrects the influence of these on the mind and, in so doing, also corrects the whole principle of action and brings it into conformity with universal ends—not to mention that an impartial rational spectator can take no delight in seeing the uninterrupted prosperity of a being graced with no feature of a pure and good will, so that a good will seems to constitute the indispensable condition even of worthiness to be happy.

Some qualities are even conducive to this good will itself and can make its work much easier; despite this, however, they have no inner unconditional worth but always presuppose a good will, which limits the esteem one otherwise rightly has for them and does not permit their being taken as absolutely good. Moderation in affects and passions, self-control, and calm reflection are not only good for all sorts of purposes but even seem to constitute a part of the *inner* worth of a person; but they lack much that would be required to declare them good without limitation (however unconditionally they were praised by the ancients); for, without the basic principles of a good will they can become extremely evil, and the coolness of a scoundrel makes him not only far more dangerous but also immediately more abominable in our eyes than we would have taken him to be without it.

A good will is not good because of what it effects or accomplishes, because of its fitness to attain some proposed end, but only because of its volition, that is, it is good in itself and, regarded for itself, is to be valued incomparably higher than all that could merely be brought about by it in favor of some inclination and indeed, if you will, of the sum of all inclinations. Even if, by a special disfavor of fortune or by the niggardly provision of a stepmotherly nature, this will should wholly lack the capacity to carry out its purpose—if with its greatest efforts it should yet achieve nothing and only the good will were left (not, of course, as a mere wish but as the summoning of all means insofar as they are in our control)—then, like a jewel, it would still shine by itself, as something that has its full worth in itself. Usefulness or fruitlessness can neither add anything to this worth nor take anything away from it. Its usefulness would be, as it were, only the setting to enable us to handle it more conveniently in ordinary commerce or to attract to it the attention of those who are not yet expert enough, but not to recommend it to experts or to determine its worth.

There is, however, something so strange in this idea of the absolute worth of a mere will, in the estimation of which no allowance is made for any usefulness, that, despite all the agreement even of common understanding with this idea, a suspicion must yet arise that its covert basis is perhaps mere high-flown fantasy and that we may have misunderstood the purpose of nature in assigning reason to our will as its governor. Hence we shall put this idea to the test from this point of view.

In the natural constitution of an organized being, that is, one constituted purposively for life, we assume as a principle that there will be found in it no instrument for some end other than what is also most appropriate to that end and best adapted to it. Now in a being that has reason and a will, if the proper end of nature were its *preservation,* its *welfare,* in a word its *happiness,* then nature would have hit upon a very bad arrangement in selecting the reason of the creature to carry out this purpose. For all the actions that the creature has to perform for this purpose, and the whole rule of its conduct, would be marked out for it far more accurately by instinct, and that end would have thereby been attained much more surely than it ever can be by reason; and if reason should have been given, over and above, to this favored creature, it must have served it only to contemplate the fortunate constitution of its nature, to admire this, to delight in it, and to be grateful for it to the beneficent cause, but not to submit its faculty of desire to that weak and deceptive guidance and meddle with nature's purpose. In a word, nature would have taken care that reason should not break forth into *practical use* and have the presumption, with its weak insight, to think out for itself a plan for happiness and for the means of attaining it. Nature would have taken upon itself the choice not only of ends but also of means and, with wise foresight, would have entrusted them both simply to instinct.

And, in fact, we find that the more a cultivated reason purposely occupies itself with the enjoyment of life and with happiness, so much the further does one get away from true satisfaction; and from this there arises in many, and indeed in those who have experimented most with this use of reason, if only they are candid enough to admit it, a certain degree of *misology*, that is, hatred of reason; for, after calculating all the advantages they draw—I do not say from the invention of all the arts of common luxury, but even from the sciences (which seem to them to be, at bottom, only a luxury of the understanding)—they find that they have in fact only brought more trouble upon themselves instead of gaining in happiness; and because of this they finally envy rather than despise the more common run of people, who are closer to the guidance of mere natural instinct and do not allow their reason much influence on their behavior. And to this extent we must admit that the judgment of those who greatly moderate, and even reduce below zero, eulogies extolling the advantages that reason is supposed to procure for us with regard to the happiness and satisfaction of life is by no means surly or ungrateful to the goodness of the government of the world; we must admit, instead, that these judgments have as their covert basis the idea of another and far worthier purpose of one's existence, to which therefore, and not to happiness, reason is properly destined, and to which, as supreme condition, the private purpose of the human being must for the most part defer.

Since reason is not sufficiently competent to guide the will surely with regard to its objects and the satisfaction of all our needs (which it to some extent even multiplies)—an end to which an implanted natural instinct would have led much more certainly; and since reason is

nevertheless given to us as a practical faculty, that is, as one that is to influence the *will;* then, where nature has everywhere else gone to work purposively in distributing its capacities, the true vocation of reason must be to produce a will that is good, not perhaps *as a means* to other purposes, but *good in itself,* for which reason was absolutely necessary. This will need not, because of this, be the sole and complete good, but it must still be the highest good and the condition of every other, even of all demands for happiness. In this case it is entirely consistent with the wisdom of nature if we perceive that the cultivation of reason, which is requisite to the first and unconditional purpose, limits in many ways—at least in this life—the attainment of the second, namely happiness, which is always conditional; indeed it may reduce it below zero without nature proceeding unpurposively in the matter, because reason, which cognizes its highest practical vocation in the establishment of a good will, in attaining this purpose is capable only of its own kind of satisfaction, namely from fulfilling an end which in turn only reason determines, even if this should be combined with many infringements upon the ends of inclination.

We have, then, to explicate the concept of a will that is to be esteemed in itself and that is good apart from any further purpose, as it already dwells in natural sound understanding and needs not so much to be taught as only to be clarified—this concept that always takes first place in estimating the total worth of our actions and constitutes the condition of all the rest. In order to do so, we shall set before ourselves the concept of **duty,** which contains that of a good will though under certain subjective limitations and hindrances, which, however, far from concealing it and making it unrecognizable, rather bring it out by contrast and make it shine forth all the more brightly.

I here pass over all actions that are already recognized as contrary to duty, even though they may be useful for this or that purpose; for in their case the question whether they might have been done *from duty* never arises, since they even conflict with it. I also set aside actions that are really in conformity with duty but to which human beings have *no inclination* immediately and which they still perform because they are impelled to do so through another inclination. For in this case it is easy to distinguish whether an action in conformity with duty is done *from duty* or from a selfseeking purpose. It is much more difficult to note this distinction when an action conforms with duty and the subject has, besides, an *immediate* inclination to it. For example, it certainly conforms with duty that a shopkeeper not overcharge an inexperienced customer, and where there is a good deal of trade a prudent merchant does not overcharge but keeps a fixed general price for everyone, so that a child can buy from him as well as everyone else. People are thus served *honestly;* but this is not nearly enough for us to believe that the merchant acted in this way from duty and basic principles of honesty; his advantage required it; it cannot be assumed here that he had, besides, an immediate inclination toward his customers, so as from love, as it were, to give no one preference over another in the matter of price. Thus the action was done neither from duty nor from immediate inclination but merely for purposes of self-interest.

On the other hand, to preserve one's life is a duty, and besides everyone has an immediate inclination to do so. But on this account the often anxious care that most people take of it still has no inner worth and their maxim has no moral content. They look after their lives *in conformity with duty* but not *from duty.* On the other hand, if adversity and hopeless grief have quite taken away the taste for life; if an unfortunate man, strong of soul and more indignant about his fate than despondent or dejected, wishes for death and yet preserves his life without loving it, not from inclination or fear but from duty, then his maxim has moral content.

To be beneficent where one can is a duty, and besides there are many souls so sympathetically attuned that, without any other motive of vanity or self-interest they find an inner satisfaction in spreading joy around them and can take delight in the satisfaction of others so far as it is their own work. But I assert that in such a case an action of this kind, however it may conform with duty and however amiable it may be, has nevertheless no true moral worth but is on the same footing with other inclinations, for example, the inclination to honor, which, if it fortunately lights upon what is in fact in the common interest and in conformity with duty and hence honorable, deserves praise and encouragement but not esteem; for the maxim lacks moral content, namely that of doing such actions not from inclination but *from duty.* Suppose, then, that the mind of this philanthropist were overclouded by his own grief, which extinguished all sympathy with the fate of others, and that while he still had the means to benefit others in distress their troubles did not move him because he had enough to do with his own; and suppose that now, when no longer incited to it by any inclination, he nevertheless tears himself out of this deadly insensibility and does the action without any inclination, simply from duty; then the action first has its genuine moral worth. Still further: if nature had put little sympathy in the heart of this or that man; if (in other respects an honest man) he is by temperament cold and indifferent to the sufferings of others, perhaps because he himself is provided with the special gift of patience and endurance toward his own sufferings and presupposes the same in every other or even requires it; if nature had not properly fashioned such a man (who would in truth not be its worst product) for a philanthropist, would he not still find within himself a source from which to give himself a far higher worth than what a mere good-natured temperament might have? By all means! It is just then that the worth of character comes out, which is moral and incomparably the highest, namely that he is beneficent not from inclination but from duty.

To assure one's own happiness is a duty (at least indirectly); for, want of satisfaction with one's condition, under pressure from many anxieties and amid unsatisfied needs, could easily become a great *temptation to transgression of duty.* But in addition, without looking to duty here, all people have already, of themselves, the strongest and deepest inclination to happiness because it is just in this idea that all inclinations unite in one sum. However, the precept of happiness is often so constituted that it greatly infringes upon some inclinations, and yet one can form no determinate and sure concept of the sum of satisfaction of all inclinations under the name of happiness. Hence it is not to be wondered at that a single inclination, determinate both as to what it promises and as to the time within which it can be satisfied, can often outweigh a fluctuating idea, and that a man—for example, one suffering from gout—can choose to enjoy what he likes and put up with what he can since, according to his calculations, on this occasion at least he has not sacrificed the enjoyment of the present moment to the perhaps groundless expectation of a happiness that is supposed to lie in health. But even in this case, when the general inclination to happiness did not determine his will; when health, at least for him, did not enter as so necessary into this calculation, there is still left over here, as in all other cases, a law, namely to promote his happiness not from inclination but from duty; and it is then that his conduct first has properly moral worth.

It is undoubtedly in this way, again, that we are to understand the passages from scripture in which we are commanded to love our neighbor, even our enemy. For, love as an inclination cannot be commanded, but beneficence from duty—even though no inclination impels us to it and, indeed, natural and unconquerable aversion opposes it—is *practical* and not *pathological* love, which lies in the will and not in the propensity of feeling, in principles of action and not in melting sympathy; and it alone can be commanded.

Thus the moral worth of an action does not lie in the effect expected from it and so too does not lie in any principle of action that needs to borrow its motive from this expected effect. For, all these effects (agreeableness of one's condition, indeed even promotion of others' happiness) could have been also brought about by other causes, so that there would have been no need, for this, of the will of a rational being, in which, however, the highest and unconditional good alone can be found. Hence nothing other than the *representation of the law* in itself, *which can of course occur only in a rational being,* insofar as it and not the hoped-for effect is the determining ground of the will, can constitute the preeminent good we call moral, which is already present

in the person himself who acts in accordance with this representation and need not wait upon the effect of his action.*

But what kind of law can that be, the representation of which must determine the will, even without regard for the effect expected from it, in order for the will to be called good absolutely and without limitation? Since I have deprived the will of every impulse that could arise for it from obeying some law, nothing is left but the conformity of actions as such with universal law, which alone is to serve the will as its principle, that is, *I ought never to act except in such a way that I could also will that my maxim should become a universal law.* Here mere conformity to law as such, without having as its basis some law determined for certain actions, is what serves the will as its principle, and must so serve it, if duty is not to be everywhere an empty delusion and a chimerical concept. Common human reason also agrees completely with this in its practical appraisals and always has this principle before its eyes. Let the question be, for example: may I, when hard

---

*It could be objected that I only seek refuge, behind the word *respect,* in an obscure feeling, instead of distinctly resolving the question by means of a concept of reason. But though respect is a feeling, it is not one *received* by means of influence; it is, instead, a feeling *self-wrought* by means of a rational concept and therefore specifically different from all feelings of the first kind, which can be reduced to inclination or fear. What I cognize immediately as a law for me I cognize with respect, which signifies merely consciousness of the *subordination* of my will to a law without the mediation of other influences on my sense. Immediate determination of the will by means of the law and consciousness of this is called *respect,* so that this is regarded as the *effect* of the law on the subject, and not as the *cause* of the law. Respect is properly the representation of a worth that infringes upon my self-love. Hence there is something that is regarded as an object neither of inclination nor of fear, though it has something analogous to both. The *object* of respect is therefore simply the *law,* and indeed the law that we impose upon *ourselves* and yet as necessary in itself. As a law we are subject to it without consulting self-love; as imposed upon us by ourselves it is nevertheless a result of our will; and in the first respect it has an analogy with fear, in the second with inclination. Any respect for a person is properly only respect for the law (of integrity and so forth) of which he gives us an example. Because we also regard enlarging our talents as a duty, we represent a person of talents also as, so to speak, an *example of the law* (to become like him in this by practice), and this is what constitutes our respect. All socalled moral *interest* consists simply in *respect* for the law.

pressed, make a promise with the intention not to keep it? Here I easily distinguish two significations the question can have: whether it is prudent or whether it is in conformity with duty to make a false promise. The first can undoubtedly often be the case. I see very well that it is not enough to get out of a present difficulty by means of this subterfuge but that I must reflect carefully whether this lie may later give rise to much greater inconvenience for me than that from which I now extricate myself; and since, with all my supposed *cunning*, the results cannot be so easily foreseen but that once confidence in me is lost this could be far more prejudicial to me than all the troubles I now think to avoid, I must reflect whether the matter might be handled *more prudently* by proceeding on a general maxim and making it a habit to promise nothing except with the intention of keeping it. But it is soon clear to me that such a maxim will still be based only on results feared. To be truthful from duty, however, is something entirely different from being truthful from anxiety about detrimental results, since in the first case the concept of the action in itself already contains a law for me while in the second I must first look about elsewhere to see what effects on me might be combined with it. For, if I deviate from the principle of duty this is quite certainly evil; but if I am unfaithful to my maxim of prudence this can sometimes be very advantageous to me, although it is certainly safer to abide by it. However, to inform myself in the shortest and yet infallible way about the answer to this problem, whether a lying promise is in conformity with duty, I ask myself: would I indeed be content that my maxim (to get myself out of difficulties by a false promise) should hold as a universal law (for myself as well as for others)? and could I indeed say to myself that every one may make a false promise when he finds himself in a difficulty he can get out of in no other way? Then I soon become aware that I could indeed will the lie, but by no means a universal law to lie; for in accordance with such a law there would properly be no promises at all, since it would be futile to avow my will with regard to my future actions to others who would not believe this avowal or, if they rashly did so, would pay me back in like coin;

and thus my maxim, as soon as it were made a universal law, would have to destroy itself.

I do not, therefore, need any penetrating acuteness to see what I have to do in order that my volition be morally good. Inexperienced in the course of the world, incapable of being prepared for whatever might come to pass in it, I ask myself only: can you also will that your maxim become a universal law? If not, then it is to be repudiated, and that not because of a disadvantage to you or even to others forthcoming from it but because it cannot fit as a principle into a possible giving of universal law, for which lawgiving reason, however, forces from me immediate respect. Although I do not yet *see* what this respect is based upon (this the philosopher may investigate), I at least understand this much: that it is an estimation of a worth that far outweighs any worth of what is recommended by inclination, and that the necessity of my action from *pure* respect for the practical law is what constitutes duty, to which every other motive must give way because it is the condition of a will good *in itself,* the worth of which surpasses all else.

Thus, then, we have arrived, within the moral cognition of common human reason, at its principle, which it admittedly does not think so abstractly in a universal form but which it actually has always before its eyes and uses as the norm for its appraisals. Here it would be easy to show how common human reason, with this compass in hand, knows very well how to distinguish in every case that comes up what is good and what is evil, what is in conformity with duty or contrary to duty, if, without in the least teaching it anything new, we only, as did Socrates, make it attentive to its own principle; and that there is, accordingly, no need of science and philosophy to know what one has to do in order to be honest and good, and even wise and virtuous. We might even have assumed in advance that cognizance of what it is incumbent upon everyone to do, and so also to know, would be the affair of every human being, even the most common. Yet we cannot consider without admiration how great an advantage the practical faculty of appraising has over the theoretical in common human understanding. In the latter, if common reason ventures to depart from laws of experience and perceptions of the senses it falls into sheer incomprehensibilities and self-contradictions, at least into a chaos of uncertainty, obscurity, and instability. But in practical matters, it is just when common understanding excludes all sensible incentives from practical laws that its faculty of appraising first begins to show itself to advantage. It then becomes even subtle, whether in quibbling tricks with its own conscience or with other claims regarding what is to be called right, or in sincerely wanting to determine the worth of actions for its own instruction; and, what is most admirable, in the latter case it can even have as good a hope of hitting the mark as any philosopher can promise himself; indeed, it is almost more sure in this matter, because a philosopher, though he cannot have any other principle than that of common understanding, can easily confuse his judgment by a mass of considerations foreign and irrelevant to the matter and deflect it from the straight course. Would it not therefore be more advisable in moral matters to leave the judgment of common reason as it is and, at most, call in philosophy only to present the system of morals all the more completely and apprehensibly and to present its rules in a form more convenient for use (still more for disputation), but not to lead common human understanding, even in practical matters, away from its fortunate simplicity and to put it, by means of philosophy, on a new path of investigation and instruction?

There is something splendid about innocence; but what is bad about it, in turn, is that it cannot protect itself very well and is easily seduced. Because of this, even wisdom—which otherwise consists more in conduct than in knowledge—still needs science, not in order to learn from it but in order to provide access and durability for its precepts. The human being feels within himself a powerful counterweight to all the commands of duty, which reason represents to him as so deserving of the highest respect—the counterweight of his needs and inclinations, the entire satisfaction of which he sums up under the name happiness. Now reason issues its precepts unremittingly, without thereby promising anything to the inclinations, and so, as it were, with disregard and contempt for those claims, which are so impetuous and besides so apparently equitable (and refuse to be neutralized

by any command). But from this there arises a *natural dialectic,* that is, a propensity to rationalize against those strict laws....

THE CATEGORICAL IMPERATIVE

Now, all imperatives command either *hypothetically* or *categorically.* The former represent the practical necessity of a possible action as a means to achieving something else that one wills (or that it is at least possible for one to will). The categorical imperative would be that which represented an action as objectively necessary of itself, without reference to another end.

Since every practical law represents a possible action as good and thus as necessary for a subject practically determinable by reason, all imperatives are formulae for the determination of action that is necessary in accordance with the principle of a will which is good in some way. Now, if the action would be good merely as a means *to something else* the imperative is *hypothetical;* if the action is represented as *in itself* good, hence as necessary in a will in itself conforming to reason, as its principle, *then it is categorical.*

The imperative thus says which action possible by me would be good, and represents a practical rule in relation to a will that does not straightaway do an action just because it is good, partly because the subject does not always know that it is good, partly because, even if he knows this, his maxims could still be opposed to the objective principles of a practical reason.

Hence the hypothetical imperative says only that the action is good for some *possible* or *actual* purpose. In the first case it is a **problematically** practical principle, in the second an **assertorically** practical principle. The categorical imperative, which declares the action to be of itself objectively necessary without reference to some purpose, that is, even apart from any other end, holds as an **apodictically** practical principle.

One can think of what is possible only through the powers of some rational being as also a possible purpose of some will; accordingly, principles of action, insofar as this is represented as necessary for attaining some possible purpose to be brought about by it, are in fact innumerable. All sciences have some practical part, consisting of problems [which suppose] that some end is possible for us and of imperatives as to how it can be attained. These can therefore be called, in general, imperatives of **skill.** Whether the end is rational and good is not at all the question here, but only what one must do in order to attain it. The precepts for a physician to make his man healthy in a well-grounded way, and for a poisoner to be sure of killing his, are of equal worth insofar as each serves perfectly to bring about his purpose. Since in early youth it is not known what ends might occur to us in the course of life, parents seek above all to have their children learn *a great many things* and to provide for *skill* in the use of means to all sorts of *discretionary* ends, about none of which can they determine whether it might in the future actually become their pupil's purpose, though it is always *possible* that he might at some time have it; and this concern is so great that they commonly neglect to form and correct their children's judgment about the worth of the things that they might make their ends.

There is, however, *one* end that can be presupposed as actual in the case of all rational beings (insofar as imperatives apply to them, namely as dependent beings), and therefore one purpose that they not merely *could* have but that we can safely presuppose they all actually *do have* by a natural necessity, and that purpose is *happiness.* The hypothetical imperative that represents the practical necessity of an action as a means to the promotion of happiness is **assertoric.** It may be set forth not merely as necessary to some uncertain, merely possible purpose but to a purpose that can be presupposed surely and a priori in the case of every human being, because it belongs to his essence. Now, skill in the choice of means to one's own greatest well-being can be called *prudence** in the narrowest sense. Hence the imperative that

refers to the choice of means to one's own happiness, that is, the precept of prudence, is still always *hypothetical;* the action is not commanded absolutely but only as a means to another purpose.

Finally there is one imperative that, without being based upon and having as its condition any other purpose to be attained by certain conduct, commands this conduct immediately. This imperative is **categorical.** It has to do not with the matter of the action and what is to result from it, but with the form and the principle from which the action itself follows; and the essentially good in the action consists in the disposition, let the result be what it may. This imperative may be called the imperative **of morality.**

Volition in accordance with these three kinds of principles is also clearly distinguished by *dissimilarity* in the necessitation of the will. In order to make this dissimilarity evident, I think they would be most suitably named in their order by being said to be either *rules* of skill, or *counsels* of prudence, or *commands* (*laws*) of morality. For, only law brings with it the concept of an *unconditional* and objective and hence universally valid *necessity,* and commands are laws that must be obeyed, that is, must be followed even against inclination. *Giving counsel* does involve necessity, which, however, can hold only under a subjective and contingent condition, whether this or that man counts this or that in his happiness; the categorical imperative, on the contrary, is limited by no condition and, as absolutely although practically necessary, can be called quite strictly a command. The first imperative could also be called *technical* (belonging to art), the second pragmatic[†] (belonging to welfare), the third moral (belonging to free conduct as such, that is, to morals).

Now the question arises: how are all these imperatives possible? This question does not

---

*The word "prudence" is taken in two senses: in the one it may bear the name of "knowledge of the world," in the other that of "private prudence." The first is a human being's skill in influencing others so as to use them for his own purposes. The second is the insight to unite all these purposes to his own enduring advantage. The latter is properly that to which the worth even of the former is reduced, and if someone is prudent in the first sense but not in the second, we might better say of him that he is clever and cunning but, on the whole, nevertheless imprudent.

[†]It seems to me that the proper meaning of the word *pragmatic* can be most accurately determined in this way. For *sanctions* are called "pragmatic" that do not flow strictly from the right of *states* as necessary laws but from *provision* for the general welfare. A *history* is composed pragmatically when it makes us *prudent*, that is, instructs the world how it can look after its advantage better than, or at least as well as, the world of earlier times.

inquire how the performance of the action that the imperative commands can be thought, but only how the necessitation of the will, which the imperative expresses in the problem, can be thought. How an imperative of skill is possible requires no special discussion. Whoever wills the end also wills (insofar as reason has decisive influence on his actions) the indispensably necessary means to it that are within his power. This proposition is, as regards the volition, analytic; for in the volition of an object as my effect, my causality as acting cause, that is, the use of means, is already thought, and the imperative extracts the concept of actions necessary to this end merely from the concept of a volition of this end (synthetic propositions no doubt belong to determining the means themselves to a purpose intended, but they do not have to do with the ground for actualizing the act of will but for actualizing the object). That in order to divide a line into two equal parts on a sure principle I must make two intersecting arcs from its ends, mathematics admittedly teaches only by synthetic propositions; but when I know that only by such an action can the proposed effect take place, then it is an analytic proposition that if I fully will the effect I also will the action requisite to it; for, it is one and the same thing to represent something as an effect possible by me in a certain way and to represent myself as acting in this way with respect to it.

If only it were as easy to give a determinate concept of happiness, imperatives of prudence would agree entirely with those of skill and would be just as analytic. For it could be said, here just as there: who wills the end also wills (necessarily in conformity with reason) the sole means to it that are within his control. But it is a misfortune that the concept of happiness is such an indeterminate concept that, although every human being wishes to attain this, he can still never say determinately and consistently with himself what he really wishes and wills. The cause of this is that all the elements that belong to the concept of happiness are without exception empirical, that is, they must be borrowed from experience, and that nevertheless for the idea of happiness there is required an absolute whole, a maximum of well-being in

my present condition and in every future condition. Now, it is impossible for the most insightful and at the same time most powerful but still finite being to frame for himself a determinate concept of what he really wills here. If he wills riches, how much anxiety, envy and intrigue might he not bring upon himself in this way! If he wills a great deal of cognition and insight, that might become only an eye all the more acute to show him, as all the more dreadful, ills that are now concealed from him and that cannot be avoided, or to burden his desires, which already give him enough to do, with still more needs. If he wills a long life, who will guarantee him that it would not be a long misery? If he at least wills health, how often has not bodily discomfort kept someone from excesses into which unlimited health would have let him fall, and so forth. In short, he is not capable of any principle by which to determine with complete certainty what would make him truly happy, because for this omniscience would be required. One cannot therefore act on determinate principles for the sake of being happy, but only on empirical counsels, for example, of a regimen, frugality, courtesy, reserve and so forth, which experience teaches are most conducive to well-being on the average. From this it follows that imperatives of prudence cannot, to speak precisely, command at all, that is, present actions objectively as practically *necessary;* that they are to be taken as counsels (*consilia*) rather than as commands (*praecepta*) of reason; that the problem of determining surely and universally which action would promote the happiness of a rational being is completely insoluble, so that there can be no imperative with respect to it that would, in the strict sense, command him to do what would make him happy; for happiness is not an ideal of reason but of imagination, resting merely upon empirical grounds, which it is futile to expect should determine an action by which the totality of a series of results in fact infinite would be attained. This imperative of prudence would, nevertheless, be an analytic practical proposition if it is supposed that the means to happiness can be assigned with certainty; for it is distinguished from the imperative of skill only in this: that in the case of the latter the end is merely possible, whereas in the former it is given; but since both merely command the means to what it is presupposed one wills as an end, the imperative that commands volition of the means for him who wills the end is in both cases analytic. Hence there is also no difficulty with respect to the possibility of such an imperative.

On the other hand, the question of how the imperative of *morality* is possible is undoubtedly the only one needing a solution, since it is in no way hypothetical and the objectively represented necessity can therefore not be based on any presupposition, as in the case of hypothetical imperatives. Only we must never leave out of account, here, that it cannot be made out *by means of any example,* and so empirically, whether there is any such imperative at all, but it is rather to be feared that all imperatives which seem to be categorical may yet in some hidden way be hypothetical. For example, when it is said "you ought not to promise anything deceitfully," and one assumes that the necessity of this omission is not giving counsel for avoiding some other ill—in which case what is said would be "you ought not to make a lying promise lest if it comes to light you destroy your credit"—but that an action of this kind must be regarded as in itself evil and that the imperative of prohibition is therefore categorical: one still cannot show with certainty in any example that the will is here determined merely through the law, without another incentive, although it seems to be so; for it is always possible that covert fear of disgrace, perhaps also obscure apprehension of other dangers, may have had an influence on the will. Who can prove by experience the nonexistence of a cause when all that experience teaches is that we do not perceive it? In such a case, however, the so-called moral imperative, which as such appears to be categorical and unconditional, would in fact be only a pragmatic precept that makes us attentive to our advantage and merely teaches us to take this into consideration.

We shall thus have to investigate entirely a priori the possibility of a *categorical* imperative, since we do not here have the advantage of its reality being given in experience, so that the possibility would be necessary not to establish it but merely to explain it. In the meantime, however, we can see this much: that the categorical imperative alone has the tenor of a practical **law;** all the others can indeed be called *principles* of the will but not laws, since what it is necessary to do merely for achieving a discretionary purpose can be regarded as in itself contingent and we can always be released from the precept if we give up the purpose; on the contrary, the unconditional command leaves the will no discretion with respect to the opposite, so that it alone brings with it that necessity which we require of a law.

Second, in the case of this categorical imperative or law of morality the ground of the difficulty (of insight into its possibility) is also very great. It is an a priori synthetic practical proposition; and since it is so difficult to see the possibility of this kind of proposition in theoretical cognition, it can be readily gathered that the difficulty will be no less in practical cognition.

In this task we want first to inquire whether the mere concept of a categorical imperative may not also provide its formula containing the proposition which alone can be a categorical imperative. For, how such an absolute command is possible, even if we know its tenor, will still require special and difficult toil, which, however, we postpone to the last section.

When I think of a *hypothetical* imperative in general I do not know beforehand what it will contain; I do not know this until I am given the condition. But when I think of a *categorical* imperative I know at once what it contains. For, since the imperative contains, beyond the law, only the necessity that the maxim* be in conformity with this law, while the law contains no condition to which it would be limited, nothing is left with which the maxim of action is to conform but the universality of a law as such; and this

---

*A *maxim* is the subjective principle of acting, and must be distinguished from the *objective* principle, namely the practical law. The former contains the practical rule determined by reason conformably with the conditions of the subject (often his ignorance or also his inclinations), and is therefore the principle in accordance with which the subject *acts;* but the law is the objective principle valid for every rational being, and the principle in accordance with which he *ought to act,* i.e., an imperative.

conformity alone is what the imperative properly represents as necessary.

There is, therefore, only a single categorical imperative and it is this: *act only in accordance with that maxim through which you can at the same time will that it become a universal law.*

Now, if all imperatives of duty can be derived from this single imperative as from their principle, then, even though we leave it undecided whether what is called duty is not as such an empty concept, we shall at least be able to show what we think by it and what the concept wants to say.

Since the universality of law in accordance with which effects take place constitutes what is properly called *nature* in the most general sense (as regards its form)—that is, the existence of things insofar as it is determined in accordance with universal laws—the universal imperative of duty can also go as follows: *act as if the maxim of your action were to become by your will a* **universal law of nature.**

We shall now enumerate a few duties in accordance with the usual division of them into duties to ourselves and to other human beings and into perfect and imperfect duties.*

1) Someone feels sick of life because of a series of troubles that has grown to the point of despair, but is still so far in possession of his reason that he can ask himself whether it would not be contrary to his duty to himself to take his own life. Now he inquires whether the maxim of his action could indeed become a universal law of nature. His maxim, however, is: from self-love I make it my principle to shorten my life when its longer duration threatens more troubles than it promises agreeableness. The only further questoin is whether this principle of self-love could become a universal law of nature. It is then seen at once that a nature whose law it

would be to destroy life itself by means of the same feeling whose destination is to impel toward the furtherance of life would contradict itself and would therefore not subsist as nature; thus that maxim could not possibly be a law of nature and, accordingly, altogether opposes the supreme principle of all duty.

2) Another finds himself urged by need to borrow money. He well knows that he will not be able to repay it but sees also that nothing will be lent him unless he promises firmly to repay it within a determinate time. He would like to make such a promise, but he still has enough conscience to ask himself: is it not forbidden and contrary to duty to help oneself out of need in such a way? Supposing that he still decided to do so, his maxim of action would go as follows: when I believe myself to be in need of money I shall borrow money and promise to repay it, even though I know that this will never happen. Now this principle of self-love or personal advantage is perhaps quite consistent with my whole future welfare, but the question now is whether it is right. I therefore turn the demand of self-love into a universal law and put the question as follows: how would it be if my maxim became a universal law? I then see at once that it could never hold as a universal law of nature and be consistent with itself, but must necessarily contradict itself. For, the universality of a law that everyone, when he believes himself to be in need, could promise whatever he pleases with the intention of not keeping it would make the promise and the end one might have in it itself impossible, since no one would believe what was promised him but would laugh at all such expressions as vain pretenses.

3) A third finds in himself a talent that by means of some cultivation could make him a human being useful for all sorts of purposes. However, he finds himself in comfortable circumstances and prefers to give himself up to pleasure than to trouble himself with enlarging and improving his fortunate natural predispositions. But he still asks himself whether his maxim of neglecting his natural gifts, besides being consistent with his propensity to amusement, is also consistent with what one calls duty. He now sees that a nature could indeed

---

*It must be noted here that I reserve the division of duties entirely for a future *Metaphysics of Morals,* so that the division here stands only as one adopted at my discretion (for the sake of arranging my examples). For the rest, I understand here by a perfect duty one that admits no exception in favor of inclination, and then I have not merely external but also internal *perfect duties;* although this is contrary to the use of the word adopted in the schools, I do not intend to justify it here, since for my purpose it makes no difference whether or not it is granted me.

always subsist with such a universal law, although (as with the South Sea Islanders) the human being should let his talents rust and be concerned with devoting his life merely to idleness, amusement, procreation—in a word, to enjoyment; only he cannot possibly **will** that this become a universal law or be put in us as such by means of natural instinct. For, as a rational being he necessarily wills that all the capacities in him be developed, since they serve him and are given to him for all sorts of possible purposes.

Yet a *fourth,* for whom things are going well while he sees that others (whom he could very well help) have to contend with great hardships, thinks: what is it to me? let each be as happy as heaven wills or as he can make himself; I shall take nothing from him nor even envy him; only I do not care to contribute anything to his welfare or to his assistance in need! Now, if such a way of thinking were to become a universal law the human race could admittedly very well subsist, no doubt even better than when everyone prates about sympathy and benevolence and even exerts himself to practice them occasionally, but on the other hand also cheats where he can, sells the right of human beings or otherwise infringes upon it. But although it is possible that a universal law of nature could very well subsist in accordance with such a maxim, it is still impossible to **will** that such a principle hold everywhere as a law of nature. For, a will that decided this would conflict with itself, since many cases could occur in which one would need the love and sympathy of others and in which, by such a law of nature arisen from his own will, he would rob himself of all hope of the assistance he wishes for himself.

These are a few of the many actual duties, or at least of what we take to be such, whose derivation from the one principle cited above is clear. We must *be able to will* that a maxim of our action become a universal law: this is the canon of moral appraisal of action in general. Some actions are so constituted that their maxim cannot even be *thought* without contradiction as a universal law of nature, far less could one *will* that it *should* become such. In the case of others that inner impossibility is indeed not to be found, but it is still impossible to *will* that their maxim be raised

to the universality of a law of nature because such a will would contradict itself. It is easy to see that the first is opposed to strict or narrower (unremitting) duty, the second only to wide (meritorious) duty; and so all duties, as far as the kind of obligation (not the object of their action) is concerned, have by these examples been set out completely in their dependence upon the one principle.

If we now attend to ourselves in any transgression of a duty, we find that we do not really will that our maxim should become a universal law, since that is impossible for us, but that the opposite of our maxim should instead remain a universal law, only we take the liberty of making an *exception* to it for ourselves (or just for this once) to the advantage of our inclination. Consequently, if we weighed all cases from one and the same point of view, namely that of reason, we would find a contradiction in our own will, namely that a certain principle be objectively necessary as a universal law and yet subjectively not hold universally but allow exceptions. Since, however, we at one time regard our action from the point of view of a will wholly conformed with reason but then regard the very same action from the point of view of a will affected by inclination, there is really no contradiction here but instead a resistance of inclination to the precept of reason (*antagonismus*), through which the universality of the principle (*universalitas*) is changed into mere generality (*generalitas*) and the practical rational principle is to meet the maxim half way. Now, even though this cannot be justified in our own impartially rendered judgment, it still shows that we really acknowledge the validity of the categorical imperative and permit ourselves (with all respect for it) only a few exceptions that, as it seems to us, are inconsiderable and wrung from us.

We have therefore shown at least this much: that if duty is a concept that is to contain significance and real lawgiving for our actions it can be expressed only in categorical imperatives and by no means in hypothetical ones; we have also—and this is already a great deal—set forth distinctly and as determined for every use the content of the categorical imperative, which must contain the principle of all duty (if there is such a thing at all). But we have not yet advanced so far as to prove a priori that there really is such an imperative, that there is a practical law, which commands absolutely of itself and without any incentives, and that the observance of this law is duty.

For the purpose of achieving this it is of the utmost importance to take warning that we must not let ourselves think of wanting to derive the reality of this principle from the *special property of human nature*. For, duty is to be practical unconditional necessity of action and it must therefore hold for all rational beings (to which alone an imperative can apply at all) and *only because of this* be also a law for all human wills. On the other hand, what is derived from the special natural constitution of humanity—what is derived from certain feelings and propensities and even, if possible, from a special tendency that would be peculiar to human reason and would not have to hold necessarily for the will of every rational being—that can indeed yield a maxim for us but not a law; it can yield a subjective principle on which we might act if we have the propensity and inclination, but not an objective principle on which we would be *directed* to act even though every propensity, inclination, and natural tendency of ours were against it—so much so that the sublimity and inner dignity of the command in a duty is all the more manifest the fewer are the subjective causes in favor of it and the more there are against it, without thereby weakening in the least the necessitation by the law or taking anything away from its validity.

Here, then, we see philosophy put in fact in a precarious position, which is to be firm even though there is nothing in heaven or on earth from which it depends or on which it is based. Here philosophy is to manifest its purity as sustainer of its own laws, not as herald of laws that an implanted sense or who knows what tutelary nature whispers to it, all of which—though they may always be better than nothing at all—can still never yield basic principles that reason dictates and that must have their source entirely and completely a priori and, at the same time, must have their commanding authority from this: that they expect nothing from the inclination of human beings but everything from the supremacy of the law and the respect owed it or, failing this, condemn the human being to contempt for himself and inner abhorrence.

Hence everything empirical, as an addition to the principle of morality, is not only quite inept for this; it is also highly prejudicial to the purity of morals, where the proper worth of an absolutely good will—a worth raised above all price—consists just in the principle of action being free from all influences of contingent grounds, which only experience can furnish. One cannot give too many or too frequent warnings against this laxity, or even mean cast of mind, which seeks its principle among empirical motives and laws; for, human reason in its weariness gladly rests on this pillow and in a dream of sweet illusions (which allow it to embrace a cloud instead of Juno) it substitutes for morality a bastard patched up from limbs of quite diverse ancestry, which looks like whatever one wants to see in it but not like virtue for him who has once seen virtue in her true form.*

The question is therefore this: is it a necessary law *for all rational beings* always to appraise their actions in accordance with such maxims as they themselves could will to serve as universal laws? If there is such a law, then it must already be connected (completely a priori) with the concept of the will of a rational being as such. But in order to discover this connection we must, however reluctantly, step forth, namely into metaphysics, although into a domain of it that is distinct from speculative philosophy, namely into metaphysics of morals. In a practical philosophy, where we have to do not with assuming grounds for what *happens* but rather laws for what *ought to happen* even if it never does, that is, objective practical laws, we do not need to undertake an investigation into the grounds on account of which something pleases or displeases; how the satisfaction of mere sensation differs from taste,

---

*To behold virtue in her proper form is nothing other than to present morality stripped of any admixture of the sensible and of any spurious adornments of reward or self-love. By means of the least effort of his reason everyone can easily become aware of how much virtue then eclipses everything else that appears charming to the inclinations, provided his reason is not altogether spoiled for abstraction.

and whether the latter differs from a general satisfaction of reason; upon what the feeling of pleasure or displeasure rests, and how from it desires and inclinations arise, and from them, with the cooperation of reason, maxims; for all that belongs to an empirical doctrine of the soul, which would constitute the second part of the doctrine of nature when this is regarded as *philosophy of nature* insofar as it is based *on empirical laws*. Here, however, it is a question of objective practical laws and hence of the relation of a will to itself insofar as it determines itself only by reason; for then everything that has reference to the empirical falls away of itself, since if reason entirely by itself determines conduct (and the possibility of this is just what we want now to investigate), it must necessarily do so a priori.

The will is thought as a capacity to determine itself to acting in conformity with the *representation of certain laws*. And such a capacity can be found only in rational beings. Now, what serves the will as the objective ground of its self-determination is an end, and this, if it is given by reason alone, must hold equally for all rational beings. What, on the other hand, contains merely the ground of the possibility of an action the effect of which is an end is called a *means*. The subjective ground of desire is an *incentive;* the objective ground of volition is a *motive;* hence the distinction between subjective ends, which rest on incentives, and objective ends, which depend on motives, which hold for every rational being. Practical principles are *formal* if they abstract from all subjective ends, whereas they are *material* if they have put these, and consequently certain incentives, at their basis. The ends that a rational being proposes at his discretion as *effects* of his actions (material ends) are all only relative; for only their mere relation to a specially constituted faculty of desire on the part of the subject gives them their worth, which can therefore furnish no universal principles, no principles valid and necessary for all rational beings and also for every volition, that is, no practical laws. Hence all these relative ends are only the ground of hypothetical imperatives.

But suppose there were something the *existence of which in itself* has an absolute worth, something which as *an end in itself* could be a ground of determinate laws; then in it, and in it alone, would lie the ground of a possible categorical imperative, that is, of a practical law.

Now I say that the human being and in general every rational being *exists* as an end in itself, *not merely as a means* to be used by this or that will at its discretion; instead he must in all his actions, whether directed to himself or also to other rational beings, always be regarded *at the same time as an end*. All objects of the inclinations have only a conditional worth; for, if there were not inclinations and the needs based on them, their object would be without worth. But the inclinations themselves, as sources of needs, are so far from having an absolute worth, so as to make one wish to have them, that it must instead be the universal wish of every rational being to be altogether free from them. Thus the worth of any object *to be acquired* by our action is always conditional. Beings the existence of which rests not on our will but on nature, if they are beings without reason, still have only a relative worth, as means, and are therefore called *things*, whereas rational beings are called *persons* because their nature already marks them out as an end in itself, that is, as something that may not be used merely as a means, and hence so far limits all choice (and is an object of respect). These, therefore, are not merely subjective ends, the existence of which as an effect of our action has a worth *for us*, but rather *objective ends*, that is, beings the existence of which is in itself an end, and indeed one such that no other end, to which they would serve *merely* as means, can be put in its place, since without it nothing of *absolute worth* would be found anywhere; but if all worth were conditional and therefore contingent, then no supreme practical principle for reason could be found anywhere.

If, then, there is to be a supreme practical principle and, with respect to the human will, a categorical imperative, it must be one such that, from the representation of what is necessarily an end for everyone because it is an *end in itself*, it constitutes an *objective* principle of the will and thus can serve as a universal practical law. The ground of this principle is: *rational nature exists as an end in itself*. The human being necessarily represents his own existence in this way; so far it is thus a *subjective* principle of human actions. But every other rational being also represents his existence in this way consequent on just the same rational ground that also holds for me; thus it is at the same time an *objective* principle from which, as a supreme practical ground, it must be possible to derive all laws of the will. The practical imperative will therefore be the following: *So act that you use humanity, whether in your own person or in the person of any other, always at the same time as an end, never merely as a means.* We shall see whether this can be carried out.

To keep to the preceding examples:

First, as regards the concept of necessary duty to oneself, someone who has suicide in mind will ask himself whether his action can be consistent with the idea of humanity *as an end in itself.* If he destroys himself in order to escape from a trying condition he makes use of a person *merely as a means* to maintain a tolerable condition up to the end of life. A human being, however, is not a thing and hence not something that can be used *merely* as a means, but must in all his actions always be regarded as an end in itself. I cannot, therefore, dispose of a human being in my own person by maiming, damaging or killing him. (I must here pass over a closer determination of this principle that would prevent any misinterpretation, e.g., as to having limbs amputated in order to preserve myself, or putting my life in danger in order to preserve my life, and so forth; that belongs to morals proper.)

Second, as regards necessary duty to others or duty owed them, he who has it in mind to make a false promise to others sees at once that he wants to make use of another human being *merely as a means,* without the other at the same time containing in himself the end. For, he whom I want to use for my purposes by such a promise cannot possibly agree to my way of behaving toward him, and so himself contain the end of this action. This conflict with the principle of other human beings is seen more distinctly if examples of assaults on the freedom and property of others are brought forward. For then it is obvious that he who transgresses the rights of human beings intends to make use of the person of others merely as means, without taking into consideration that, as rational beings, they are always to be valued at the same time as ends, that is, only as beings who must also be able to contain in themselves the end of the very same action.

Third, with respect to contingent (meritorious) duty to oneself, it is not enough that the action does not conflict with humanity in our person as an end in itself; it must also *harmonize with it.* Now there are in humanity predispositions to greater perfection, which belong to the end of nature with respect to humanity in our subject; to neglect these might admittedly be consistent with the *preservation* of humanity as an end in itself but not with the *furtherance* of this end.

Fourth, concerning meritorious duty to others, the natural end that all human beings have is their own happiness. Now, humanity might indeed subsist if no one contributed to the happiness of others but yet did not intentionally withdraw anything from it; but there is still only a negative and not a positive agreement with *humanity as an end in itself* unless everyone also tries, as far as he can, to further the ends of others. For, the ends of a subject who is an end in itself must as far as possible be also *my* ends, if that representation is to have its *full* effect in me.

This principle of humanity, and in general of every rational nature, *as an end in itself* (which is the supreme limiting condition of the freedom of action of every human being) is not borrowed from experience; first because of its universality, since it applies to all rational beings as such and no experience is sufficient to determine anything about them; second because in it humanity is represented not as an end of human beings (subjectively), that is, not as an object that we of ourselves actually make our end, but as an objective end that, whatever ends we may have, ought as law to constitute the supreme limiting condition of all subjective ends, so that the principle must arise from pure reason. That is to say, the ground of all practical lawgiving lies (in accordance with the first principle) *objectively in the rule* and the form of universality which makes it fit to be a law (possibly a law of nature); *subjectively,* however, it lies in the *end;* but the subject of all ends is every rational being as an end in itself (in accordance with the second principle); from this there follows now the third practical principle of the will, as supreme condition of its harmony with universal practical reason, the idea *of the will of every rational being as a will giving universal law.*

Utilitarianism

JOHN STUART MILL

John Stuart Mill (1806–1873) was one of the leading British moral philosophers of the nineteenth century. He also wrote important works on logic, economics, education, and feminism, and served for a time as a Member of Parliament.

1. GENERAL REMARKS

There are few circumstances, among those which make up the present condition of human knowledge, more unlike what might have been expected, or more significant of the backward state in which speculation on the most important subjects still lingers, than the little progress which has been made in the decision of the controversy respecting the criterion of right and wrong. From the dawn of philosophy, the question concerning the *summum bonum* or, what is the same thing, concerning the foundation of morality, has been accounted the main problem in speculative thought, has occupied the most gifted intellects and divided them into sects and schools, carrying on a vigorous warfare against one another. And, after more than two thousand years, the same discussions continue, philosophers are still ranged under the same contending banners, and neither thinkers nor mankind at large seem nearer to being unanimous on the subject than when the youth Socrates listened to the old Protagoras, and asserted (if Plato's dialogue be grounded on a real conversation) the theory of utilitarianism against the popular morality of the so-called Sophist.

It is true that similar confusion and uncertainty, and in some cases similar discordance, exist respecting the first principles of all the sciences, not excepting that which is deemed the most certain of them—mathematics—without much impairing, generally indeed without impairing at all, the trustworthiness of the conclusions of those sciences. An apparent anomaly, the explanation of which is that the detailed doctrines of a science are not usually deduced from, nor depend for their evidence upon, what are called its first principles. Were it not so, there would be no science more precarious, or whose conclusions were more insufficiently made out, than algebra, which derives none of its certainty from what are commonly taught to learners as its elements, since these, as laid down by some of its most eminent teachers, are as full of fictions as English law, and of mysteries as theology. The truths which are ultimately accepted as the first principles of a science are really the last results of metaphysical analysis practiced on the elementary notions with which the science is conversant, and their relation to the science is not that of foundations to an edifice, but of roots to a tree, which may perform their office equally well though they be never dug down to and exposed to light. But though, in science the particular truths precede the general theory, the contrary might be expected to be the case with a practical art, such as morals or legislation. All action is for

From J. S. Mill, *Utilitarianism*, Chaps. 1 and 2. First published in 1863.

the sake of some end; and rules of action, it seems natural to suppose, must take their whole character and color from the end to which they are subservient. When we engage in a pursuit, a clear and precise conception of what we are pursuing would seem to be the first thing we need, instead of the last we are to look forward to. A test of right and wrong must be the means, one would think, of ascertaining what is right or wrong, and not a consequence of having already ascertained it.

The difficulty is not avoided by having recourse to the popular theory of a natural faculty, a sense or instinct, informing us of right and wrong. For, besides that the existence of such a moral instinct is itself one of the matters in dispute, those believers in it who have any pretensions to philosophy have been obliged to abandon the idea that it discerns what is right or wrong in the particular case in hand, as our other senses discern the sight or sound actually present. Our moral faculty, according to all those of its interpreters who are entitled to the name of thinkers, supplies us only with the general principles of moral judgments; it is a branch of our reason, not of our sensitive faculty, and must be looked to for the abstract doctrines of morality, not for perception of it in the concrete. The intuitive, no less than what may be termed the inductive, school of ethics, insists on the necessity of general laws. They both agree that the morality of an individual action is not a question of direct perception, but of the application of a law to an individual case. They recognize also, to a great extent, the same moral laws, but differ as to their evidence, and the source from which they derive their authority. According to the one opinion, the principles of morals are evident *a priori*, requiring nothing to command assent, except that the meaning of the terms be understood. According to the other doctrine, right and wrong, as well as truth and falsehood, are questions of observation and experience. But both hold equally that morality must be deduced from principles, and the intuitive school affirm, as strongly as the inductive, that there is a science of morals. Yet they seldom attempt to make out a list of the *a priori* principles which are to serve as the premises of the science; still more rarely do they make any effort to reduce those various principles to one first principle, or common ground of obligation. They either assume the ordinary precepts of morals as of *a priori* authority, or they lay down as the common groundwork of those maxims some generality much less obviously authoritative than the maxims themselves, and which has never succeeded in gaining popular acceptance. Yet, to support their pretensions, there ought either to be some one fundamental principle or law at the root of all morality, or, if there be several, there should be a determinate order of precedence among them, and the one principle, or the rule for deciding between the various principles when they conflict, ought to be self-evident.

To inquire how far the bad effects of this deficiency have been mitigated in practice, or to what extent the moral beliefs of mankind have been vitiated or made uncertain by the absence of any distinct recognition of an ultimate standard, would imply a complete survey and criticism of past and present ethical doctrine. It would, however, be easy to show that whatever steadiness or consistency these moral beliefs have attained has been mainly due to the tacit influence of a standard not recognized. Although the nonexistence of an acknowledged first principle has made ethics not so much a guide as a consecration of men's actual sentiments, still, as men's sentiments, both of favor and of aversion, are greatly influenced by what they suppose to be the effects of things upon their happiness, the principle of utility, or, as Bentham latterly called it, the greatest-happiness principle, has had a large share in forming the moral doctrines even of those who most scornfully reject its authority. Nor is there any school of thought which refuses to admit that the influence of actions on happiness is a most material and even predominant consideration in many of the details of morals, however unwilling to acknowledge it as the fundamental principle of morality and the source of moral obligation. I might go much further, and say that, to all those *a priori* moralists who deem it necessary to argue at all, utilitarian arguments are indispensable. It is not my present purpose to criticize these thinkers, but I cannot help referring, for illustration, to a systematic treatise by one of the most illustrious of them—the *Metaphysics of Ethics,* by Kant. This remarkable man, whose system of thought will long remain one of the landmarks in the history of philosophical speculation, does, in the treatise in question, lay down a universal first principle as the origin and ground of moral obligation. It is this: "So act, that the rule on which thou actest would admit of being adopted as a law by all rational beings." But when he begins to deduce from this precept any of the actual duties of morality, he fails, almost grotesquely, to show that there would be any contradiction, any logical (not to say physical) impossibility, in the adoption by all rational beings of the most outrageously immoral rules of conduct. All he shows is that the *consequences* of their universal adoption would be such as no one would choose to incur.

On the present occasion, I shall, without further discussion of the other theories, attempt to contribute something towards the understanding and appreciation of the Utilitarian or Happiness theory and towards such proof as it is susceptible of. It is evident that this cannot be proof in the ordinary and popular meaning of the term. Questions of ultimate ends are not amenable to direct proof. Whatever can be proved to be good, must be so by being shown to be a means to something admitted to be good without proof. The medical art is proved to be good by its conducing to health, but how is it possible to prove that health is good? The art of music is good, for the reason, among others, that it produces pleasure, but what proof is it possible to give that pleasure is good? If, then, it is asserted that there is a comprehensive formula, including all things which are in themselves good, and that whatever else is good is not so as an end, but as a mean, the formula may be accepted or rejected, but is not a subject of what is commonly understood by proof. We are not, however, to infer that its acceptance or rejection must depend on blind impulse or arbitrary choice. There is a larger meaning of the word "proof," in which this question is as amenable to it as any other of the disputed questions of philosophy. The subject is within the cognizance of the rational faculty, and neither does that faculty deal with it solely in the way of intuition. Considerations may be presented capable of de-

termining the intellect either to give or withhold its assent to the doctrine, and this is equivalent to proof.

We shall examine presently of what nature are these considerations, in what manner they apply to the case, and what rational grounds, therefore, can be given for accepting or rejecting the utilitarian formula. But it is a preliminary condition of rational acceptance or rejection that the formula should be correctly understood. I believe that the very imperfect notion ordinarily formed of its meaning is the chief obstacle which impedes its reception, and that, could it be cleared even from only the grosser misconceptions, the question would be greatly simplified, and a large proportion of its difficulties removed. Before, therefore, I attempt to enter into the philosophical grounds which can be given for assenting to the utilitarian standard, I shall offer some illustrations of the doctrine itself, with the view of showing more clearly what it is, distinguishing it from what it is not, and disposing of such of the practical objections to it as either originate in, or are closely connected with, mistaken interpretations of its meaning. Having thus prepared the ground, I shall afterwards endeavor to throw such light as I can upon the question, considered as one of philosophical theory.

2. WHAT UTILITARIANISM IS

A passing remark is all that needs be given to the ignorant blunder of supposing that those who stand up for utility, as the test of right and wrong, use the term in that restricted and merely colloquial sense in which utility is opposed to pleasure. An apology is due to the philosophical opponents of utilitarianism for even the momentary appearance of confounding them with any one capable of so absurd a misconception, which is the more extraordinary, inasmuch as the contrary accusation, of referring every thing to pleasure, and that, too, in its grossest form, is another of the common charges against utilitarianism, and, as has been pointedly remarked by an able writer, the same sort of persons, and often the very same persons, denounce the theory "as impracticably dry when the word 'utility' precedes the word 'pleasure,' and as too practicably voluptuous when the word 'pleasure' precedes the word 'utility.'" Those who know any thing about the matter are aware that every writer from Epicurus to Bentham who maintained the theory of utility meant by it, not something to be contradistinguished from pleasure, but pleasure itself, together with exemption from pain, and, instead of opposing the useful to the agreeable or the ornamental, have always declared that the useful means these, among other things. Yet the common herd, including the herd of writers, not only in newspapers and periodicals, but in books of weight and pretension, are perpetually falling into this shallow mistake. Having caught up the word "utilitarian," while knowing nothing whatever about it but its sound, they habitually express by it the rejection or the neglect of pleasure in some of its forms, of beauty, of ornament, or of amusement. Nor is the term thus ignorantly misapplied solely in disparagement, but occasionally in compliment, as though it implied superiority to frivolity and the mere pleasures of the moment. And this perverted use is the only one in which the word is popularly known, and the one from which the new generation are acquiring their sole notion of its meaning. Those who introduced the word, but who had for many years discontinued it as a distinctive appellation, may well feel themselves called upon to resume it, if by doing so they can hope to contribute any thing towards rescuing it from this utter degradation.

The creed which accepts as the foundation of morals Utility, or the Greatest-happiness Principle, holds that actions are right in proportion as they tend to promote happiness, wrong as they tend to produce the reverse of happiness. By happiness is intended pleasure and the absence of pain, by unhappiness, pain and the privation of pleasure. To give a clear view of the moral standard set up by the theory, much more requires to be said, in particular, what things it includes in the ideas of pain and pleasure, and to what extent this is left an open question. But these supplementary explanations do not affect the theory of life on which this theory of morality is grounded—namely, that pleasure and freedom from pain are the only things desirable as ends, and that all desirable things (which are as numerous in the utilitarian as in any other scheme) are desirable either for the pleasure inherent in themselves, or as means to the promotion of pleasure and the prevention of pain.

Now, such a theory of life excites in many minds, and among them in some of the most estimable in feeling and purpose, inveterate dislike. To suppose that life has (as they express it) no higher end than pleasure—no better and nobler object of desire and pursuit—they designate as utterly mean and groveling, as a doctrine worthy only of swine, to whom the followers of Epicurus were, at a very early period, contemptuously likened; and modern holders of the doctrine are occasionally made the subject of equally polite comparisons by its German, French, and English assailants.

When thus attacked, the Epicureans have always answered, that it is not they, but their accusers, who represent human nature in a degrading light, since the accusation supposes human beings to be capable of no pleasures except those of which swine are capable. If this supposition were true, the charge could not be gainsaid but would then be no longer an imputation; for, if the sources of pleasure were precisely the same to human beings and to swine, the rule of life which is good enough for the one would be good enough for the other. The comparison of the Epicurean life to that of beasts is felt as degrading, precisely because a beast's pleasures do not satisfy a human being's conceptions of happiness. Human beings have faculties more elevated than the animal appetites, and, when once made conscious of them, do not regard any thing as happiness which does not include their gratification. I do not, indeed, consider the Epicureans to have been by any means faultless in drawing out their scheme of consequences from the utilitarian principle. To do this in any sufficient manner, many Stoic as well as Christian elements require to be included. But there is no known Epicurean theory of life which does not assign to the pleasures of the intellect, of the feelings and imagination, and of the moral sentiments, a much higher value as pleasures than to those of mere sensation. It must be admitted, however, that utilitarian writers in general have placed the superiority of mental over bodily pleasures chiefly in the greater permanency, safety, uncostliness, etc., of the former—that is, in their circumstantial advantages rather than in their intrinsic nature. And, on all these points, utilitarians have fully proved their case, but they might have taken the other, and, as it may be called, higher ground, with entire consistency. It is quite compatible with the principle of utility to recognize the fact that some *kinds* of pleasure are more desirable and more valuable than others. It would be absurd that while, in estimating all other things, quality is considered as well as quantity, the estimation of pleasures should be supposed to depend on quantity alone.

If I am asked what I mean by difference of quality in pleasures, or what makes one pleasure more valuable than another, merely as a pleasure, except its being greater in amount, there is but one possible answer. Of two pleasures, if there be one to which all or almost all who have experience of both give a decided preference, irrespective of any feeling of moral obligation to prefer it, that is the more desirable pleasure. If one of the two is, by those who are competently acquainted with both, placed so far above the other that they prefer it, even though knowing it to be attended with a greater amount of discontent, and would not resign it for any quantity of the other pleasure which their nature is capable of, we are justified in ascribing to the preferred enjoyment a superiority in quality so far outweighing quantity, as to render it, in comparison, of small account.

Now, it is an unquestionable fact, that those who are equally acquainted with and equally capable of appreciating and enjoying both do give a most marked preference to the manner of existence which employs their higher faculties. Few human creatures would consent to be changed into any of the lower animals for a promise of the fullest allowance of a beast's pleasures; no intelligent human being would consent to be a fool, no instructed person would be an ignoramus, no person of feeling and conscience would be selfish and base, even though they should be persuaded that the fool, the dunce, or the rascal is better satisfied with his lot than they are with theirs. They would not resign what they possess more than he for the most complete satisfaction of all the desires which they have in common

with him. If they ever fancy they would, it is only in cases of unhappiness so extreme that, to escape from it, they would exchange their lot for almost any other, however undesirable in their own eyes. A being of higher faculties requires more to make him happy, is capable probably of more acute suffering, and certainly accessible to it at more points, than one of an inferior type, but, in spite of these liabilities, he can never really wish to sink into what he feels to be a lower grade of existence. We may give what explanation we please of this unwillingness: we may attribute it to pride, a name which is given indiscriminately to some of the most and to some of the least estimable feelings of which mankind are capable; we may refer it to the love of liberty and personal independence—an appeal to which was with the Stoics one of the most effective means for the inculcation of it; to the love of power, or to the love of excitement, both of which do really enter into and contribute to it; but its most appropriate appellation is a sense of dignity, which all human beings possess in one form or other, and in some, though by no means in exact, proportion to their higher faculties, and which is so essential a part of the happiness of those in whom it is strong, that nothing which conflicts with it could be, otherwise than momentarily, an object of desire to them. Whoever supposes that this preference takes place at a sacrifice of happiness, that the superior being, in any thing like equal circumstances, is not happier than the inferior—confounds the two very different ideas of happiness and content. It is indisputable that the being whose capacities of enjoyment are low has the greatest chance of having them fully satisfied, and a highly endowed being will always feel that any happiness which he can look for, as the world is constituted, is imperfect. But he can learn to bear its imperfections, if they are at all bearable, and they will not make him envy the being who is indeed unconscious of the imperfections, but only because he feels not at all the good which those imperfections qualify. It is better to be a human being dissatisfied than a pig satisfied, better to be Socrates dissatisfied than a fool satisfied. And if the fool or the pig are of a different opinion, it is because they only know their own side of the question. The other party to the comparison knows both sides.

It may be objected that many who are capable of the higher pleasures occasionally, under the influence of temptation, postpone them to the lower. But this is quite compatible with a full appreciation of the intrinsic superiority of the higher. Men often, from infirmity of character, make their election for the nearer good, though they know it to be the less valuable, and this no less when the choice is between two bodily pleasures than when it is between bodily and mental. They pursue sensual indulgences to the injury of health, though perfectly aware that health is the greater good. It may be further objected, that many who begin with youthful enthusiasm for everything noble, as they advance in years sink into indolence and selfishness. But I do not believe that those who undergo this very common change voluntarily choose the lower description of pleasures in preference to the higher. I believe that, before they devote themselves exclusively to the one, they have already become incapable of the other. Capacity for the nobler feelings is in most natures a very tender plant, easily killed, not only by hostile influences but by mere want of sustenance, and, in the majority of young persons, it speedily dies away if the occupations to which their position in life has devoted them, and the society into which it has thrown them, are not favorable to keeping that higher capacity in exercise. Men lose their high aspirations as they lose their intellectual tastes, because they have not time or opportunity for indulging them, and they addict themselves to inferior pleasures, not because they deliberately prefer them, but because they are either the only ones to which they have access or the only ones which they are any longer capable of enjoying. It may be questioned whether any one who has remained equally susceptible to both classes of pleasures ever knowingly and calmly preferred the lower, though many in all ages have broken down in an ineffectual attempt to combine both.

From this verdict of the only competent judges, I apprehend there can be no appeal. On a question which is the best worth having of two pleasures, or which of two modes of existence is the most grateful to the feelings, apart from its moral attributes and from its consequences, the judgment of those who are qualified by knowledge of both, or, if they differ, that of the majority among them, must be admitted as final. And there needs be the less hesitation to accept this judgment respecting the quality of pleasures, since there is no other tribunal to be referred to even on the question of quantity. What means are there of determining which is the acutest of two pains, or the intensest of two pleasurable sensations, except the general suffrage of those who are familiar with both? Neither pains nor pleasures are homogeneous, and pain is always heterogeneous with pleasure. What is there to decide whether a particular pleasure is worth purchasing at the cost of a particular pain, except the feelings and judgment of the experienced? When, therefore, those feelings and judgment declare the pleasures derived from the higher faculties to be preferable *in kind,* apart from the question of intensity, to those of which the animal nature disjoined from the higher faculties is susceptible, they are entitled on this subject to the same regard.

I have dwelt on this point, as being a necessary part of a perfectly just conception of Utility or Happiness, considered as the directive rule of human conduct. But it is by no means an indispensable condition to the acceptance of the utilitarian standard, for that standard is not the agent's own greatest happiness, but the greatest amount of happiness altogether; and if it may possibly be doubted whether a noble character is always the happier for its nobleness, there can be no doubt that it makes other people happier, and that the world in general is immensely a gainer by it. Utilitarianism, therefore, could only attain its end by the general cultivation of nobleness of character, even if each individual were only benefited by the nobleness of others, and his own, so far as happiness is concerned, were a sheer deduction from the benefit. But the bare enunciation of such an absurdity as this last renders refutation superfluous.

According to the Greatest-happiness Principle, as above explained, the ultimate end with reference to and for the sake of which all other things are desirable (whether we are considering our own good or that of other people) is an existence exempt as far as possible from pain, and as rich as possible in enjoyments, both in point of quantity and quality; the test of quality, and the rule for measuring it against quantity, being the preference felt by those who in their opportunities of experience, to which must be added their habits of self-consciousness and self-observation, are best furnished with the means of comparison. This being, according to the utilitarian opinion, the end of human action is necessarily also the standard of morality; which may accordingly be defined, the rules and precepts for human conduct by the observance of which an existence such as has been described might be, to the greatest extent possible, secured to all mankind, and not to them only but, so far as the nature of things admits, to the whole sentient creation.

Against this doctrine, however, arises another class of objectors who say that happiness, in any form, cannot be the rational purpose of human life and action, because, in the first place, it is unattainable; and they contemptuously ask, What right hast thou to be happy? a question which Mr. Carlyle clinches by the addition, What right, a short time ago, hadst thou even *to be?* Next they say that men can do *without* happiness, that all noble human beings have felt this, and could not have become noble but by learning the lesson of *Entsagen* or renunciation, which lesson, thoroughly learned and submitted to, they affirm to be the beginning and necessary condition of all virtue.

The first of these objections would go to the root of the matter, were it well founded; for, if no happiness is to be had at all by human beings, the attainment of it cannot be the end of morality, or of any rational conduct. Though, even in that case, something might still be said for the utilitarian theory, since utility includes not solely the pursuit of happiness, but the prevention or mitigation of unhappiness; and, if the former aim be chimerical, there will be all the greater scope and more imperative need for the latter, so long at least as mankind think fit to live, and do not take refuge in the simultaneous act of suicide recommended under certain conditions by Novalis. When, however, it is thus positively asserted to be impossible that human life should be happy, the assertion, if not something like a verbal quibble, is at least an exaggeration. If by happiness be meant a continuity of highly pleasurable excitement, it is evident enough that this is impossible. A state of exalted pleasure lasts only moments, or in some cases, and with some intermissions, hours or days, and is the occasional brilliant flash of enjoyment, not its permanent and steady flame. Of this the philosophers who have taught that happiness is the end of life were as fully aware as those who taunt them. The happiness which they meant was not a life of rapture, but moments of such, in an existence made up of few and transitory pains, many and various pleasures, with a decided predominance of the active over the passive, and having, as the foundation of the whole, not to expect more from life than it is capable of bestowing. A life thus composed, to those who have been fortunate enough to obtain it, has always appeared worthy of the name of "happiness." And such an existence is even now the lot of many, during some considerable portion of their lives. The present wretched education and wretched social arrangements are the only real hindrance to its being attainable by almost all.

The objectors, perhaps, may doubt whether human beings, if taught to consider happiness as the end of life, would be satisfied with such a moderate share of it. But great numbers of mankind have been satisfied with much less. The main constituents of a satisfied life appear to be two, either of which by itself is often found sufficient for the purpose—tranquillity and excitement. With much tranquillity, many find that they can be content with very little pleasure; with much excitement, many can reconcile themselves to a considerable quantity of pain. There is assuredly no inherent impossibility in enabling even the mass of mankind to unite both, since the two are so far from being incompatible, that they are in natural alliance, the prolongation of either being a preparation for, and exciting a wish for, the other. It is only those in whom indolence amounts to a vice that do not desire excitement after an interval of repose; it is only those in whom the need of excitement is a disease, that feel the tranquillity which follows excitement dull and insipid, instead of pleasurable in direct proportion to the excitement which preceded it.

When people who are tolerably fortunate in their outward lot do not find in life sufficient enjoyment to make it valuable to them, the cause generally is caring for nobody but themselves. To those who have neither public nor private affections, the excitements of life are much curtailed and, in any case, dwindle in value as the time approaches when all selfish interests must be terminated by death; while those who leave after them objects of personal affection, and especially those who have also cultivated a fellow feeling with the collective interests of mankind, retain as lively an interest in life on the eve of death as in the vigor of youth and health. Next to selfishness, the principal cause which makes life unsatisfactory is want of mental cultivation. A cultivated mind—I do not mean that of a philosopher, but any mind to which the fountains of knowledge have been opened, and which has been taught, in any tolerable degree, to exercise its faculties—finds sources of inexhaustible interest in all that surrounds it, in the objects of nature, the achievements of art, the imaginations of poetry, the incidents of history, the ways of mankind past and present, and their prospects in the future. It is possible, indeed, to become indifferent to all this, and that, too, without having exhausted a thousandth part of it, but only when one has had from the beginning no moral or human interest in these things, and has sought in them only the gratification of curiosity.

Now, there is absolutely no reason in the nature of things why an amount of mental culture sufficient to give an intelligent interest in these objects of contemplation should not be the inheritance of every one born in a civilized country. As little is there an inherent necessity that any human being should be a selfish egotist, devoid of every feeling or care but those which center in his own miserable individuality. Something far superior to this is sufficiently common even now to give ample earnest of what the human species may be made. Genuine private affections and a sincere interest in the public good are possible, though in unequal degrees, to every rightly brought up human being. In a world in which there is so much to interest, so much to enjoy, and so much also to correct and improve, every one who has this moderate amount of moral and intellectual requisites is capable of an existence which may be called enviable; and unless such a person, through bad laws or subjection to the will of others, is denied the liberty to use the sources of happiness within his reach, he will not fail to find this enviable existence, if he escape the positive evils of life, the great sources of physical and mental suffering—such as indigence, disease, and the unkindness, worthlessness, or premature loss, of objects of affection. The main stress of the problem lies, therefore, in the contest with these calamities, from which it is a rare good fortune entirely to escape, which, as things now are, cannot be obviated, and often cannot be in any material degree mitigated. Yet no one whose opinion deserves a moment's consideration can doubt that most of the great positive evils of the world are in themselves removable, and will, if human affairs continue to improve, be in the end reduced within narrow limits. Poverty, in any sense implying suffering, may be completely extinguished by the wisdom of society, combined with the good sense and providence of individuals. Even that most intractable of enemies, disease, may be indefinitely reduced in dimensions by good physical and moral education, and proper control of noxious influence, while the progress of science holds out a promise for the future of still more direct conquests over this detestable foe. And every advance in that direction relieves us from some, not only of the chances which cut short our own lives but, what concerns us still more, which deprive us of those in whom our happiness is wrapped up. As for vicissitudes of fortune and other disappointments connected with worldly circumstances, these are principally the effect either of gross imprudence, of ill-regulated desires, or of bad or imperfect social institutions. All the grand sources, in short, of human suffering are in a great degree, many of them almost entirely, conquerable by human care and effort; and though their removal is grievously slow, though a long succession of generations will perish in the breach before the conquest is completed, and this world becomes all that, if will and knowledge were not wanting, it might easily be made—yet every mind sufficiently intelligent and generous to bear a part, however small and unconspicuous, in the endeavor will draw a noble enjoyment from the contest itself, which he would not, for any bribe in the form of selfish indulgence, consent to be without.

And this leads to the true estimation of what is said by the objectors concerning the possibility and the obligation of learning to do without happiness. Unquestionably, it is possible to do without happiness; it is done involuntarily by nineteentwentieths of mankind, even in those parts of our present world which are least deep in barbarism, and it often has to be done voluntarily by the hero or the martyr, for the sake of something which he prizes more than his individual happiness. But this something—what is it, unless the happiness of others, or some of the requisites of happiness? It is noble to be capable of resigning entirely one's own portion of happiness, or chances of it; but, after all, this self-sacrifice must be for some end; it is not its own end, and if we are told that its end is not happiness but virtue, which is better than happiness, I ask, Would the sacrifice be made if the hero or martyr did not believe that it would earn for others immunity from similar sacrifices? Would it be made if he thought that his renunciation of happiness for himself would produce no fruit for any of his fellow-creatures but to make their lot like his, and place them also in the condition of persons who have renounced happiness? All honor to those who can abnegate for themselves the personal enjoyment of life, when by such renunciation they contribute worthily to increase the amount of happiness in the world, but he who does it, or professes to do it, for any other purpose is no more deserving of admiration than the ascetic mounted on his pillar. He may be an inspiriting proof of what men *can* do, but assuredly not an example of what they *should*.

Though it is only in a very imperfect state of the world's arrangements that any one can best serve the happiness of others by the absolute sacrifice of his own, yet, so long as the world is in that imperfect state, I fully acknowledge that the readiness to make such a sacrifice is the highest virtue which can be found in man. I will add that in this condition of the world, paradoxical as the assertion may be, the conscious ability to do without happiness gives the best prospect of realizing such happiness as is attainable. For nothing except that consciousness can raise a person above the chances of life, by making him feel that, let fate and fortune do their worst, they have not power to subdue him; which, once felt, frees him from excess of anxiety concerning the evils of life, and enables him, like many a Stoic in the worst times of the Roman Empire, to cultivate in tranquillity the sources of satisfaction accessible to him, without concerning himself about the uncertainty of their duration, any more than about their inevitable end.

Meanwhile, let utilitarians never cease to claim the morality of self-devotion as a possession which belongs by as good a right to them as either to the Stoic or to the Transcendentalist. The utilitarian morality does recognize in human beings the power of sacrificing their own greatest good for the good of others. It only refuses to admit that the sacrifice is itself a good. A sacrifice which does not increase, or tend to increase, the sum total of happiness, it considers as wasted. The only selfrenunciation which it applauds is devotion to the happiness, or to some of the means of happiness, of others, either of mankind collectively, or of individuals within the limits imposed by the collective interests of mankind.

I must again repeat what the assailants of utilitarianism seldom have the justice to acknowledge, that the happiness which forms the utilitarian standard of what is right in conduct is not the agent's own happiness but that of all concerned. As between his own happiness and that of others, utilitarianism requires him to be as strictly impartial as a disinterested and benevolent spectator. In the golden rule of Jesus of Nazareth, we read the complete spirit of the ethics of utility. To do as you would be done by, and to love your neighbor as yourself, constitute the ideal perfection of utilitarian morality. As the means of making the nearest approach to this ideal, utility would enjoin, first, that laws and social arrangements should place the happiness or (as, speaking practically, it may be called) the interest of every individual as nearly as possible in harmony with the interest of the whole; and secondly, that education and opinion, which have so vast a power over human character, should so use that power as to establish in the mind of every individual an indissoluble association between his own happiness and the good of the whole—especially between his own happiness, and the practice of such modes of conduct, negative and positive, as regard for the universal happiness prescribes—so that not only he may be unable to conceive the possibility of happiness to himself consistently with conduct opposed to the general good, but also that a direct impulse to promote the general good may be in every individual one of the habitual motives of action, and the sentiments connected therewith may fill a large and prominent place in every human being's sentient existence. If the impugners of the utilitarian morality represented it to their own minds in this its true character, I know not what recommendation possessed by any other morality they could possibly affirm to be wanting to it, what more beautiful or more exalted developments of human nature any other ethical system can be supposed to foster, or what springs of action, not accessible to the utilitarian, such systems rely on for giving effect to their mandates.

The objectors to utilitarianism cannot always be charged with representing it in a discreditable light. On the contrary, those among them who entertain any thing like a just idea of its disinterested character sometimes find fault with its standard as being too high for humanity. They say it is exacting too much to require that people shall always act from the inducement of promoting the general interests of society. But this is to mistake the very meaning of a standard of morals, and confound the rule of action with the motive of it. It is the business of ethics to tell us what are our duties or by what test we may know them, but no system of ethics requires that the sole motive of all we do shall be a feeling of duty; on the contrary, ninetynine hundredths of all our actions are done from other motives, and rightly so done, if the rule of duty does not condemn them. It is the more unjust to utilitarianism that this particular misapprehension should be made a ground of objection to it, inasmuch as utilitarian moralists have gone beyond almost all others in affirming that the motive has nothing to do with the morality of the action though much with the worth of the agent. He who saves a fellow creature from drowning does what is morally right, whether his motive be duty or the hope of being paid for his trouble; he who betrays the friend that trusts him is guilty of a crime, even if his object be to serve another friend to whom he is under greater obligations. But to speak only of actions done from the motive of duty, and in direct obedience to principle: it is a misapprehension of the utilitarian mode of thought to conceive it as implying that people should fix their minds upon so wide a generality as the world or society at large. The great majority of good actions are intended, not for the benefit of the world but for that of individuals, of which the good of the world is made up; and the thoughts of the most virtuous man need not on these occasions travel beyond the particular persons concerned, except so far as is necessary to assure himself that, in benefiting them, he is not violating the rights—that is, the legitimate and authorized expectations—of any one else. The multiplication of happiness is, according to the utilitarian ethics, the object of virtue; the occasions on which any person (except one in a thousand) has it in his power to do this on an extended scale—in other words, to be a public benefactor—are but exceptional, and on these occasions alone is he called on to consider public utility; in every other case, private utility, the interest or happiness of some few persons, is all he has to attend to. Those alone, the influence of whose actions extends to society in general, need concern themselves habitually about so large an object. In the case of abstinences indeed—of things which people forbear to do from moral considerations, though the consequences in the particular case might be beneficial—it would be unworthy of an intelligent agent not to be consciously aware that the action is of a class which, if practised generally, would be generally injurious, and that this is the ground of the obligation to abstain from it. The amount of regard for the public interest implied in this recognition is no greater than is demanded by every system of morals, for they all enjoin to abstain from whatever is manifestly pernicious to society.

The same considerations dispose of another reproach against the doctrine of utility, founded on a still grosser misconception of the purpose of a standard of morality, and of the very meaning of the words "right" and "wrong." It is often affirmed that utilitarianism renders men cold and unsympathizing, that it chills their moral feelings towards individuals, that it makes them regard only the dry and hard consideration of the consequences of actions, not taking into their moral estimate the qualities from which those actions emanate. If the assertion means that they do not allow their judgment respecting the rightness or wrongness of an action to be influenced by their opinion of the qualities of the person who does it, this is a complaint, not against utilitarianism but against having any standard of morality at all; for certainly no known ethical standard decides an action to be good or bad because it is done by a good or bad man, still less because done by an amiable, a brave, or a benevolent man, or the contrary. These considerations are relevant, not to the estimation of actions, but of persons, and there is nothing in the utilitarian theory inconsistent with the fact that there are other things which interest us in persons besides the rightness and wrongness of their actions. The Stoics indeed, with the paradoxical misuse of language which was part of their system and by which they strove to raise themselves above all concern about any thing but virtue, were fond of saying that he who has that has everything, that he, and one he, is rich, is beautiful, is a king. But no claim of this description is made for the virtuous man by the utilitarian doctrine. Utilitarians are quite aware that there are other desirable possessions and qualities besides virtue, and are perfectly willing to allow to all of them their full worth. They are also aware that a right action does not necessarily indicate a virtuous character, and that actions which are blamable often proceed from qualities entitled to praise. When this is apparent in any particular case, it modifies their estimation, not certainly of the act but of the agent. I grant that they are notwithstanding of opinion that, in the long run, the best proof of a good character is good actions, and resolutely refuse to consider any mental disposition as good, of which the predominant tendency is to produce bad conduct. This makes them unpopular with many people; but it is an unpopularity which they must share with every one who regards the distinction between right and wrong in a serious light, and the reproach is not one which a conscientious utilitarian need be anxious to repel.

If no more be meant by the objection than that many utilitarians look on the morality of actions, as measured by the utilitarian standards, with too exclusive a regard, and do not lay sufficient stress upon the other beauties of character which go towards making a human being lovable or admirable, this may be admitted. Utilitarians who have cultivated their moral feelings but not their sympathies nor their artistic perceptions, do fall into this mistake, and so do all other moralists under the same conditions. What can be said in excuse for other moralists is equally available for them, namely that, if there is to be any error, it is better that it should be on that side. As a matter of fact, we may affirm that among utilitarians, as among adherents of other systems, there is every imaginable degree of rigidity and of laxity in the application of their standard; some are even puritanically rigorous, while others are as indulgent as can possibly be desired by sinner or by sentimentalist. But on the whole, a doctrine which brings prominently forward the interest that mankind have in the repression and prevention of conduct which violates the moral law, is likely to be inferior to no other in turning the sanctions of opinion against such violations. It is true, the question, What does violate the moral law? is one on which those who recognize different standards of morality are likely now and then to differ. But difference of opinion on moral questions was not first introduced into the world by utilitarianism, while that doctrine does supply, if not always an easy, at all events a tangible and intelligible mode of deciding such differences.

It may not be superfluous to notice a few more of the common misapprehensions of utilitarian ethics, even those which are so obvious and gross that it might appear impossible for any person of candor and intelligence to fall into them, since persons even of considerable mental endowments often give themselves so little trouble to understand the bearings of any opinion against which they entertain a prejudice, and men are in general so little conscious of this voluntary ignorance as a defect, that the vulgarest misunderstandings of ethical doctrines are continually met with the deliberate writings of persons of the greatest pretensions both to high principle and to philosophy. We not uncommonly hear the doctrine of utility inveighed against as a *godless* doctrine. If it be necessary to say any thing at all against so mere an assumption, we may say that the question depends upon what idea we have formed of the moral character of the Deity. If it be a true belief that God desires, above all things, the happiness of his creatures, and that this was his purpose in their creation, utility is not only not a godless doctrine but more profoundly religious than any other. If it be meant that utilitarianism does not recognize the revealed will of God as the supreme law of morals, I answer that an utilitarian, who believes in the perfect goodness and wisdom of God, necessarily believes that whatever God has thought fit to reveal on the subject of morals must fulfil the requirements of utility in a supreme degree. But others besides utilitarians have been of opinion that the Christian revelation was intended, and is fitted, to inform the hearts and minds of mankind with a spirit which should enable them to find for themselves what is right and incline them to do it when found, rather than to tell them, except in a very general way, what it is, and that we need a doctrine of ethics, carefully followed out, to *interpret* to us the will of God. Whether this opinion is correct or not, it is superfluous here to discuss, since whatever aid religion, either natural or revealed, can afford to ethical investigation, is as open to the utilitarian moralist as to any other. He can use it as the testimony of God to the usefulness or hurtfulness of any given course of action, by as good a right as others can use it for the indication of a transcendental law, having no connection with usefulness or with happiness.

Again: Utility is often summarily stigmatized as an immoral doctrine by giving it the name of Expediency and, taking advantage of the popular use of that term, to contrast it with Principle. But the Expedient, in the sense in which it is opposed to the Right, generally means that which is expedient for the particular interest of the agent himself, as when a minister sacrifices the interests of his country to keep himself in place. When it means any thing better than this, it means that which is expedient for some immediate object, some temporary purpose, but which violates a rule whose observance is expedient in a much higher degree. The Expedient, in this sense, instead of being the same thing with the useful, is a branch of the hurtful. Thus it would often be expedient, for the purpose of getting over some momentary embarrassment or attaining some object immediately useful to ourselves or others, to tell a lie. But inasmuch as the cultivation in ourselves of a sensitive feeling on the subject of veracity is one of the most useful, and the enfeeblement of that feeling one of those most hurtful, things to which our conduct can be instrumental, and inasmuch as any, even unintentional, deviation from truth does that much towards weakening the trustworthiness of human assertion, which is not only the principal support of all present social well-being, but the insufficiency of which does more than any one thing that can be named to keep back civilization, virtue, every thing on which human happiness on the largest scale depends—we feel that the violation, for a present advantage, of a rule of such transcendent expediency is not expedient, and that he who, for the sake of a convenience to himself or to some other individual, does what depends on him to deprive mankind of the good, and inflict upon them the evil, involved in the greater or less reliance which they can place in each other's word, acts the part of one of their worst enemies. Yet that even this rule, sacred as it is, admits of possible exceptions is acknowledged by all moralists, the chief of which is, when the withholding of some fact (as of information from a malefactor, or of bad news from a person dangerously ill) would save an individual (especially an individual other than one's self) from great and unmerited evil and when the withholding can only be effected by denial. But in order that the exception may not extend itself beyond the need and may have the least possible effect in weakening reliance on veracity, it ought to be recognized and, if possible, its limits defined, and, if the principle of utility is good for any thing, it must be good for weighing these conflicting utilities against one another, and marking out the region within which one or the other preponderates.

Again: defenders of utility often find themselves called upon to reply to such objections as this—that there is not time, previous to action, for calculating and weighing the effects of any line of conduct on the general happiness. This is exactly as if any one were to say that it is impossible to guide our conduct by Christianity, because there is not time, on every occasion on which any thing has to be done, to read through the Old and New Testaments. The answer to the objection is that there has been ample time, namely, the whole past duration of the human species. During all that time, mankind have been learning by experience the tendencies of actions, on which experience all the prudence as well as all the morality of life are dependent. People talk as if the commencement of this course of experience had hitherto been put off and as if, at the moment when some man feels tempted to meddle with the property or life of another, he had to begin considering for the first time whether murder and theft are injurious to human happiness. Even then, I do not think that he would find the question very puzzling, but at all events the matter is now done to his hand. It is truly a whimsical supposition that, if mankind were agreed in considering utility to be the test of morality, they would remain without any agreement as to what *is* useful, and would take no measures for having their notions on the subject taught to the young and enforced by law and opinion. There is no difficulty in proving any ethical standard whatever to work ill, if we suppose universal idiocy to be conjoined with it; but on any hypothesis short of that, mankind must by this time have acquired positive beliefs as to the effects of some actions on their happiness, and the beliefs which have thus come down are the rules of morality for the multitude, and for the philosopher, until he has succeeded in finding better. That philosophers might easily do this, even now, on many subjects, that the received code of ethics is by no means of divine right, and that mankind have still much to learn as to the effects of actions on the general happiness—I admit or, rather, earnestly maintain. The corollaries from the principle of utility, like the precepts of every practical art, admit of indefinite improvement and, in a progressive state of the human mind, their improvement is perpetually going on. But to consider the rules of morality as improvable is one thing; to pass over the intermediate generalizations entirely, and endeavor to test each individual action directly by the first principle, is another. It is a strange notion, that the acknowledgment of a first principle is inconsistent with the admission of secondary ones. To inform a traveler respecting the place of his ultimate destination is not to forbid the use of landmarks and direction posts on the way. The proposition that happiness is the end and aim of morality does not mean that no road ought to be laid down to that goal, or that persons going thither should not be advised to take one direction rather than another. Men really ought to leave off talking a kind of nonsense on this subject which they would neither talk nor listen to on other matters of practical concernment. Nobody argues that the art of navigation is not founded on astronomy, because sailors cannot wait to calculate the "Nautical Almanac." Being rational creatures, they go to sea with it ready calculated, and all rational creatures go out upon the sea of life with their minds made up on the common questions of right and wrong, as well as on many of the far more difficult questions of wise and foolish. And this, as long as foresight is a human quality, it is to be presumed they will continue to do. Whatever we adopt as the fundamental principle of morality, we require subordinate principles to apply it by; the impossibility of doing without them, being common to all systems, can afford no argument against any one in particular; but gravely to argue as if no such secondary principles could be had, and as if mankind had remained till now and always must remain without drawing any general conclusions from the experience of human life, is as high a pitch, I think, as absurdity has ever reached in philosophical controversy.

The remainder of the stock arguments against utilitarianism mostly consist in laying to its charge the common infirmities of human nature, and the general difficulties which embarrass conscientious persons in shaping their course through life. We are told that an utilitarian will be apt to make his own particular case an exception to moral rules and, when under temptation, will see an utility in the breach of a rule greater than he will see in its observance. But is utility the only creed which is able to furnish us with excuses for evil-doing, and means of cheating our own conscience? They are afforded in abundance by all doctrines which recognize as a fact in morals the existence of conflicting considerations, which all doctrines do that have been believed by sane persons. It is not the fault of any creed, but of the complicated nature of human affairs, that rules of conduct cannot be so framed as to require no exceptions, and that hardly any kind of action can safely be laid down as either always obligatory or always condemnable. There is no ethical creed which does not temper the rigidity of its laws by giving a certain latitude, under the moral responsibility of the agent, for accommodation to peculiarities of circumstances and, under every creed, at the opening thus made, self-deception and dishonest casuistry get in. There exists no moral system under which there do not arise unequivocal cases of conflicting obligation. These are the real difficulties, the knotty points both in the theory of ethics and in the conscientious guidance of personal conduct. They are overcome practically with greater or with less success according to the intellect and virtue of the individual, but it can hardly be pretended that any one will be the less qualified for dealing with them, from possessing an ultimate standard to which conflicting rights and duties can be referred. If utility is the ultimate source of moral obligations, utility may be invoked to decide between them when their demands are incompatible. Though the application of the standard may be difficult, it is better than none at all; while in other systems, the moral laws all claiming independent authority, there is no common umpire entitled to interfere between them, their claims to precedence one over another rest on little better than sophistry, and unless determined, as they generally are, by the unacknowledged influence of considerations of utility, afford a free scope for the action of personal desires and partialities. We must remember that only in these cases of conflict between secondary principles is it requisite that first principles should be appealed to. There is no case of moral obligation in which some secondary principle is not involved and, if only one, there can seldom be any real doubt which one it is, in the mind of any person by whom the principle itself is recognized.

What Makes Right Acts Right?

W. D. ROSS

W. D. Ross (1877–1967) was a British classical scholar and influential moral philosopher who spent his career at Oxford.

...The point at issue is that to which we now pass, viz. whether there is any general character which makes right acts right, and if so, what it is. Among the main historical attempts to state a single characteristic of all right actions which is the foundation of their rightness are those made by egoism and utilitarianism. But I do not propose to discuss these, not because the subject is unimportant, but because it has been dealt with so often and so well already, and because there has come to be so much agreement among moral philosophers that neither of these theories is satisfactory. A much more attractive theory has been put forward by Professor Moore: that what makes actions right is that they are productive of more *good* than could

From W. D. Ross, *The Right and the Good* (Oxford University Press, 2003), pp. 16–24, 28–41. Reprinted by permission of Oxford University Press.

have been produced by any other action open to the agent.

This theory is in fact the culmination of all the attempts to base rightness on productivity of some sort of result. The first form this attempt takes is the attempt to base rightness on conduciveness to the advantage or pleasure of the agent. This theory comes to grief over the fact, which stares us in the face, that a great part of duty consists in an observance of the rights and a furtherance of the interests of others, whatever the cost to ourselves may be. Plato and others may be right in holding that a regard for the rights of others never in the long run involves a loss of happiness for the agent, that "the just life profits a man." But this, even if true, is irrelevant to the rightness of the act. As soon as a man does an action *because* he thinks he will promote his own interests thereby, he is acting not from a sense of its rightness but from self-interest.

To the egoistic theory hedonistic utilitarianism supplies a much-needed amendment. It points out correctly that the fact that a certain pleasure will be enjoyed by the agent is no reason why he *ought* to bring it into being rather than an equal or greater pleasure to be enjoyed by another, though, human nature being what it is, it makes it not unlikely that he *will* try to bring it into being. But hedonistic utilitarianism in its turn needs a correction. On reflection it seems clear that pleasure is not the only thing in life that we think good in itself, that for instance we think the possession of a good character, or an intelligent understanding of the world, as good or better. A great advance is made by the substitution of "productive of the greatest good" for "productive of the greatest pleasure."

Not only is this theory more attractive than hedonistic utilitarianism, but its logical relation to that theory is such that the latter could not be true unless *it* were true, while it might be true though hedonistic utilitarianism were not. It is in fact one of the logical bases of hedonistic utilitarianism. For the view that what produces the maximum pleasure is right has for its bases the views (1) that what produces the maximum good is right, and (2) that pleasure is the only thing good in itself.... If, therefore, it can be

shown that productivity of the maximum good is not what makes all right actions right, we shall *a fortiori* have refuted hedonistic utilitarianism.

When a plain man fulfils a promise because he thinks he ought to do so, it seems clear that he does so with no thought of its total consequences, still less with any opinion that these are likely to be the best possible. He thinks in fact much more of the past than of the future. What makes him think it right to act in a certain way is the fact that he has promised to do so—that and, usually, nothing more. That his act will produce the best possible consequences is not his reason for calling it right. What lends colour to the theory we are examining, then, is not the actions (which form probably a great majority of our actions) in which some such reflection as "I have promised" is the only reason we give ourselves for thinking a certain action right, but the exceptional cases in which the consequences of fulfilling a promise (for instance) would be so disastrous to others that we judge it right not to do so. It must of course be admitted that such cases exist. If I have promised to meet a friend at a particular time for some trivial purpose, I should certainly think myself justified in breaking my engagement if by doing so I could prevent a serious accident or bring relief to the victims of one. And the supporters of the view we are examining hold that my thinking so is due to my thinking that I shall bring more good into existence by the one action than by the other. A different account may, however, be given of the mater, an account which will, I believe, show itself to be the true one. It may be said that besides the duty of fulfilling promises I have and recognize a duty of relieving distress, and that when I think it right to do the latter at the cost of not doing the former, it is not because I think I shall produce more good thereby but because I think it the duty which is in the circumstances more of a duty. This account surely corresponds much more closely with what we really think in such a situation. If, so far as I can see, I could bring equal amounts of good into being by fulfilling my promise and by helping some one to whom I had made no promise, I should not hesitate to regard the former as my duty.

Yet on the view that what is right is right because it is productive of the most good I should not so regard it.

There are two theories, each in its way simple, that offer a solution of such cases of conscience. One is the view of Kant, that there are certain duties of perfect obligation, such as those of fulfilling promises, of paying debts, of telling the truth, which admit of no exception whatever in favour of duties of imperfect obligation, such as that of relieving distress. The other is the view of, for instance, Professor Moore and Dr. Rashdall, that there is only the duty of producing good, and that all "conflicts of duties" should be resolved by asking "by which action will most good be produced?" But it is more important that our theory fit the facts than that it be simple, and the account we have given above corresponds (it seems to me) better than either of the simpler theories with what we really think, viz. that normally promise-keeping, for example, should come before benevolence, but that when and only when the good to be produced by the benevolent act is very great and the promise comparatively trivial, the act of benevolence becomes our duty.

In fact the theory of "ideal utilitarianism," if I may for brevity refer so to the theory of Professor Moore, seems to simplify unduly our relations to our fellows. It says, in effect, that the only morally significant relation in which my neighbours stand to me is that of being possible beneficiaries by my action.[1] They do stand in this relation to me, and this relation is morally significant. But they may also stand to me in the relation of promisee to promiser, of creditor to debtor, of wife to husband, of child to parent, of friend to friend, of fellow countryman to fellow countryman, and the like; and each of these relations is the foundation of a *prima facie* duty, which is more or less incumbent on me according to the circumstances of the case. When I am in a situation, as perhaps I always am, in which more than one of these *prima facie* duties is incumbent on me, what I have to do is to study the situation as fully as I can until I form the considered opinon (it is never more) that in the circumstances one of them is more incumbent than any other; then I am bound to think that to do this *prima facie* duty is my duty *sans phrase* in the situation.

I suggest "*prima facie* duty" or "conditional duty" as a brief way of referring to the characteristic (quite distinct from that of being a duty proper) which an act has, in virtue of being of a certain kind (e.g. the keeping of a promise), of being an act which would be a duty proper if it were not at the same time of another kind which is morally significant. Whether an act is a duty proper or actual duty depends on *all* the morally significant kinds it is an instance of....

There is nothing arbitrary about these *prima facie* duties. Each rests on a definite circumstance which cannot seriously be held to be without moral significance. Of *prima facie* duties I suggest, without claiming completeness or finality for it, the following division.[2]

(1) Some duties rest on previous acts of my own. These duties seem to include two kinds, (a) those resting on a promise or what may fairly be called an implicit promise, such as the implicit undertaking not to tell lies which seems to be implied in the act of entering into conversation (at any rate by civilized men), or of writing books that purport to be history and not fiction. These may be called the duties of fidelity. (b) Those resting on a previous wrongful act. These may be called the duties of reparation. (2) Some rest on previous acts of other men, i.e. services done by them to me. These may be loosely described as the duties of gratitude. (3) Some rest on the fact or possibility of a distribution of pleasure or happiness (or of the means thereto) which is not in accordance with the merit of the persons concerned; in such cases there arises a duty to upset or prevent such a distribution. These are the duties of justice. (4) Some rest on the mere fact that there are other beings in the world whose condition we can make better in respect of virtue, or of intelligence, or of pleasure. These are the duties of beneficence. (5) Some rest on the fact that we can improve our own condition in respect of virtue or of intelligence. These are the duties of self-improvement. (6) I think that we should distinguish from (4) the duties that may be summed up under the title of "not injuring others." No doubt to injure others is incidentally to fail to

do them good; but it seems to me clear that non-maleficence is apprehended as a duty distinct from that of beneficence, and as a duty of a more stringent character. It will be noticed that this alone among the types of duty has been stated in a negative way. An attempt might no doubt be made to state this duty, like the others, in a positive way. It might be said that it is really the duty to prevent ourselves from acting either from an inclination to harm others or from an inclination to seek our own pleasure, in doing which we should incidentally harm them. But on reflection it seems clear that the primary duty here is the duty not to harm others, this being a duty whether or not we have an inclination that if followed would lead to our harming them; and that when we have such an inclination the primary duty not to harm others gives rise to a consequential duty to resist the inclination. The recognition of this duty of non-maleficence is the first step on the way to the recognition of the duty of beneficence; and that accounts for the prominence of the commands "thou shalt not kill," "thou shalt not commit adultery," "thou shalt not steal," "thou shalt not bear false witness," in so early a code as the Decalogue. But even when we have come to recognize the duty of beneficence, it appears to me that the duty of non-maleficence is recognized as a distinct one, and as *prima facie* more binding. We should not in general consider it justifiable to kill one person in order to keep another alive, or to steal from one in order to give alms to another.

The essential defect of the "ideal utilitarian" theory is that it ignores, or at least does not do full justice to, the highly personal character of duty. If the only duty is to produce the maximum of good, the question who is to have the good—whether it is myself, or my benefactor, or a person to whom I have made a promise to confer that good on him, or a mere fellow man to whom I stand in no such special relation—should make no difference to my having a duty to produce that good. But we are all in fact sure that it makes a vast difference....

If the objection be made, that this catalogue of the main types of duty is an unsystematic one resting on no logical principle, it may be replied, first, that it makes no claim to being ultimate. It is

a *prima facie* classification of the duties which reflection on our moral convictions seems actually to reveal. And if these convictions are, as I would claim that they are, of the nature of knowledge, and if I have not misstated them, the list will be a list of authentic conditional duties, correct as far as it goes though not necessarily complete. The list of *goods* put forward by the rival theory is reached by exactly the same method—the only sound one in the circumstances—viz. that of direct reflection on what we really think. Loyalty to the facts is worth more than a symmetrical architectonic or a hastily reached simplicity. If further reflection discovers a perfect logical basis for this or for a better classification, so much the better.

It may, again, be objected that our theory that there are these various and often conflicting types of *prima facie* duty leaves us with no principle upon which to discern what is our actual duty in particular circumstances. But this objection is not one of which the rival theory is in a position to bring forward. For when we have to choose between the production of two heterogeneous goods, say knowledge and pleasure, the "ideal utilitarian" theory can only fall back on an opinion, for which no logical basis can be offered, that one of the goods is the greater; and this is no better than a similar opinion that one of two duties is the more urgent. And again, when we consider the infinite variety of the effects of our actions in the way of pleasure, it must surely be admitted that the claim which *hedonism* sometimes makes, that it offers a readily applicable criterion of right conduct, is quite illusory.

I am unwilling, however, to content myself with an *argumentum ad hominem,* and I would contend that in principle there is no reason to anticipate that every act that is our duty is so for one and the same reason. Why should two sets of circumstances, or one set of circumstances, *not* possess different characteristics, any one of which makes a certain act our *prima facie* duty? When I ask what it is that makes me in certain cases sure that I have a *prima facie* duty to do so and so, I find that it lies in the fact that I have made a promise; when I ask the same question in another case, I find the answer lies in the fact that I have done a wrong. And if on reflection I find (as I think I do) that neither of these reasons is reducible to the other, I must not on any *a priori* ground assume that such a reduction is possible. . . .

It is necessary to say something by way of clearing up the relation between *prima facie* duties and the actual or absolute duty to do one particular act in particular circumstances. If, as almost all moralists except Kant are agreed, and as most plain men think, it is sometimes right to tell a lie or to break a promise, it must be maintained that there is a difference between *prima facie* duty and actual or absolute duty. When we think ourselves justified in breaking, and indeed morally obliged to break, a promise in order to relieve some one's distress, we do not for a moment cease to recognize a *prima facie* duty to keep our promise, and this leads us to feel, not indeed shame or repentance, but certainly compunction, for behaving as we do; we recognize, further, that it is our duty to make up somehow to the promisee for the breaking of the promise. We have to distinguish from the characteristic of being our duty that of tending to be our duty. Any act that we do contains various elements in virtue of which it falls under various categories. In virtue of being the breaking of a promise, for instance, it tends to be wrong; in virtue of being an instance of relieving distress it tends to be right. Tendency to be one's duty may be called a parti-resultant attribute, i.e. one which belongs to an act in virtue of some one component in its nature. *Being* one's duty is a toti-resultant attribute, one which belongs to an act in virtue of its whole nature and of nothing less than this. . . .

Another instance of the same distinction may be found in the operation of natural laws. *Qua* subject to the force of gravitation towards some other body, each body tends to move in a particular direction with a particular velocity; but its actual movement depends on *all* the forces to which it is subject. It is only by recognising this distinction that we can preserve the absoluteness of laws of nature, and only by recognising a corresponding distinction that we can preserve the absoluteness of the general principles of morality. But an important difference between the two

cases must be pointed out. When we say that in virtue of gravitation a body tends to move in a certain way, we are referring to a casual influence actually exercised on it by another body or other bodies. When we say that in virtue of being deliberately untrue a certain remark tends to be wrong, we are referring to no causal relation, to no relation that involves succession in time, but to such a relation as connects the various attributes of a mathematical figure. And if the word "tendency" is thought to suggest too much a causal relation, it is better to talk of certain types of act as being *prima facie* right or wrong (or of different persons as having different and possibly conflicting claims upon us), than of their tending to be right or wrong.

Something should be said of the relation between our apprehension of the *prima facie* rightness of certain types of act and our mental attitude towards particular acts. It is proper to use the word "apprehension" in the former case and not in the latter. That an act, *qua* fulfilling a promise, or *qua* effecting a just distribution of good, or *qua* returning services rendered, or *qua* promoting the good of others, or *qua* promoting the virtue or insight of the agent, is *prima facie* right, is self-evident; not in the sense that it is evident from the beginning of our lives, or as soon as we attend to the proposition for the first time, but in the sense that when we have reached sufficient mental maturity and have given sufficient attention to the proposition it is evident without any need of proof, or of evidence beyond itself. It is self-evident just as a mathematical axiom, or the validity of a form of inference, is evident. The moral order expressed in these propositions is just as much part of the fundamental nature of the universe (and, we may add, of any possible universe in which there were moral agents at all) as is the spatial or numerical structure expressed in the axioms of geometry or arithmetic. In our confidence that these propositions are true there is involved the same trust in our reason that is involved in our confidence in mathematics; and we should have no justification for trusting it in the latter sphere and distrusting it in the former. In both cases we are dealing with propositions that cannot be proved, but that just as certainly need no proof. . . .

Our judgements about our actual duty in concrete situations have none of the certainty that attaches to our recognition of the general principles of duty. A statement is certain, i.e., is an expression of knowledge, only in one or other of two cases: when it is either self-evident, or a valid conclusion from self-evident premises. And our judgements about our particular duties have neither of these characters. (1) They are not self-evident. Where a possible act is seen to have two characteristics, in virtue of one of which it is *prima facie* right, and in virtue of the other *prima facie* wrong, we are (I think) well aware that we are not certain whether we ought or ought not to do it; that whether we do it or not, we are taking a moral risk. We come in the long run, after consideration, to think one duty more pressing than the other, but we do not feel certain that it is so. And though we do not always recognize that a possible act has two such characteristics, and though there *may* be cases in which it has not, we are never certain that any particular possible act has not, and therefore never certain that it is right, nor certain that it is wrong. For, to go no further in the analysis, it is enough to point out that any particular act will in all probability in the course of time contribute to the bringing about of good or of evil for many human beings, and thus have a *prima facie* rightness or wrongness of which we know nothing. (2) Again, our judgements about our particular duties are not logical conclusions from self-evident premises. The only possible premises would be the general principles stating their *prima facie* rightness or wrongness *qua* having the different characteristics they do have; and even if we could (as we cannot) apprehend the extent to which an act will tend on the one hand, for example, to bring about advantages for our benefactors, and on the other hand to bring about disadvantages for fellow men who are not our benefactors, there is no principle by which we can draw the conclusion that it is on the whole right or on the whole wrong. In this respect the judgement as to the rightness of a particular act is just like the judgement as to the beauty of a particular natural object or work of art. A poem is, for instance, in respect of certain qualities beautiful and in respect of certain others

not beautiful; and our judgement as to the degree of beauty it possesses on the whole is never reached by logical reasoning from the apprehension of its particular beauties or particular defects. Both in this and in the moral case we have more or less probable opinions which are not logically justified conclusions from the general principles that are recognized as self-evident.

There is therefore much truth in the description of the right act as a fortunate act. If we cannot be certain that it is right, it is our good fortune if the act we do is the right act. This consideration does not, however, make the doing of our duty a mere matter of chance. There is a parallel here between the doing of duty and the doing of what will be to our personal advantage. We never *know* what act will in the long run be to our advantage. Yet it is certain that we are more likely in general to secure our advantage if we estimate to the best of our ability the probable tendencies of our actions in this respect, than if we act on caprice. And similarly we are more likely to do our duty if we reflect to the best of our ability on the *prima facie* rightness or wrongness of various possible acts in virtue of the characteristics we perceive them to have, than if we act without reflection. With this greater likelihood we must be content.

Many people would be inclined to say that the right act for me is not that whose general nature I have been describing, viz. that which if I were omniscient I should see to be my duty, but that which on all the evidence available to me I should think to be my duty. But suppose that from the state of partial knowledge in which I think act *A* to be my duty, I could pass to a state of perfect knowledge in which I saw act *B* to be my duty, should I not say "act *B* was the right act for me to do"? I should no doubt add "though I am not to be blamed for doing act *A*." But in adding this, am I not passing from the question "what is right" to the question "what is morally good"? At the same time I am not making the *full* passage from the one notion to the other, for in order that the act should be morally good, or an act I am not to be blamed for doing, it must not merely be the act which it is reasonable for me to think my duty; it must also be done for that reason, or from some other morally good motive. Thus the conception of the right act as the act which it is reasonable for me to think my duty is an unsatisfactory compromise between the true notion of the right act and the notion of the morally good action.

The general principles of duty are obviously not self-evident from the beginning of our lives. How do they come to be so? The answer is, that they come to be self-evident to us just as mathematical axioms do. We find by experience that this couple of matches and that couple make four matches, that this couple of balls on a wire and that couple make four balls; and by reflection on these and similar discoveries we come to see that it is of the nature of two and two to make four. In a precisely similar way, we see the *prima facie* rightness of an act which would be the fulfilment of a particular promise, and of another which would be the fulfilment of another promise, and when we have reached sufficient maturity to think in general terms, we apprehend *prima facie* rightness to belong to the nature of any fulfilment of promise. What comes first in time is the apprehension of the self-evident *prima facie* rightness of an individual act of a particular type. From this we come by reflection to apprehend the self-evident general principle of *prima facie* duty. From this, too, perhaps along with the apprehension of the self-evident *prima facie* rightness of the same act in virtue of its having another characteristic as well, and perhaps in spite of the apprehension of its *prima facie* wrongness in virtue of its having some third characteristic, we come to believe something not self-evident at all, but an object of probable opinion, viz. that this particular act is (not *prima facie* but) actually right. . . .

Supposing it to be agreed, as I think on reflection it must, that no one *means* by "right" just "productive of the best possible consequences," or "optimific," the attributes "right" and "optimific" might stand in either of two kinds of relation to each other. (1) They might be so related that we could apprehend *a priori*, either immediately or deductively, that any act that is optimific is right and any act that is right is optimific, as we can apprehend that any triangle that is equilateral is equiangular and *vice versa*.

Professor Moore's view is, I think, that the coextensiveness of "right" and "optimific" is apprehended immediately. He rejects the possibility of any proof of it. Or (2) the two attributes might be such that the question whether they are invariably connected had to be answered by means of an inductive inquiry. Now at first sight it might seem as if the constant connexion of the two attributes could be immediately apprehended. It might seem absurd to suggest that it could be right for any one to do an act which would produce consequences less good than those which would be produced by some other act in his power. Yet a little thought will convince us that this is not absurd. The type of case in which it is easiest to see that this is so is, perhaps, that in which one has made a promise. In such a case we all think that *prima facie* it is our duty to fulfil the promise irrespective of the precise goodness of the total consequences. And though we do not think it is necessarily our actual or absolute duty to do so, we are far from thinking that any, even the slightest, gain in the value of the total consequences will necessarily justify us in doing something else instead. Suppose, to simplify the case by abstraction, that the fulfilment of a promise to A would produce 1,000 units of good[3] for him, but that by doing some other act I could produce 1,001 units of good for B, to whom I have made no promise, the other consequences of the two acts being of equal value; should we really think it self-evident that it was our duty to do the second act and not the first? I think not. We should, I fancy, hold that only a much greater disparity of value between the total consequences would justify us in failing to discharge our *prima facie* duty to A. After all, a promise is a promise, and is not to be treated so lightly as the theory we are examining would imply. What, exactly, a promise is, is not so easy to determine, but we are surely agreed that it constitutes a serious moral limitation to our freedom of action. To produce the 1,001 units of good for B rather than fulfil our promise to A would be to take, not perhaps our duty as philanthropists too seriously, but certainly our duty as makers of promises too lightly. . . .

Such instances—and they might easily be added to—make it clear that there is no self-evident connexion between the attributes "right" and "optimific." The theory we are examining has a certain attractiveness when applied to our decision that a particular act is our duty (though I have tried to show that it does not agree with our actual moral judgements even here). But it is not even plausible when applied to our recognition of *prima facie* duty. For if it were self-evident that the right coincides with the optimific, it should be self-evident that what is *prima facie* right is *prima facie* optimific. But whereas we are certain that keeping a promise is *prima facie* right, we are not certain that it is *prima facie* optimific (though we are perhaps certain that it is *prima facie* bonific). Our certainty that it is *prima facie* right depends not on its consequences but on its being the fulfilment of a promise. The theory we are examining involves too much difference between the evident ground of our conviction about *prima facie* duty and the alleged ground of our conviction about actual duty....

I conclude that the attributes "right" and "optimific" are not identical, and that we do not know either by intuition, by deduction, or by induction that they coincide in their application, still less that the latter is the foundation of the former. It must be added, however, that if we are ever under no special obligation such as that of fidelity to a promisee or of gratitude to a benefactor, we ought to do what will produce most good; and that even when we are under a special obligation the tendency of acts to promote general good is one of the main factors in determining whether they are right.

In what has preceded, a good deal of use has been made of "what we really think" about moral questions; a certain theory has been rejected because it does not agree with what we really think. It might be said that this is in principle wrong; that we should not be content to expound what our present moral consciousness tells us but should aim at a criticism of our existing moral consciousness in the light of theory. Now I do not doubt that the moral consciousness of men has in detail undergone a good deal of modifications as regards the things we think right, at the hands of moral theory. But if we are told, for instance, that we should give up our view that there is a special obligatoriness

attaching to the keeping of promises because it is self-evident that the only duty is to produce as much good as possible, we have to ask ourselves whether we really, when we reflect, *are* convinced that this is self-evident, and whether we really *can* get rid of our view that promise-keeping has a bindingness independent of productiveness of maximum good. In my own experience I find that I cannot, in spite of a very genuine attempt to do so; and I venture to think that most people will find the same, and that just because they cannot lose the sense of special obligation, they cannot accept as self-evident, or even as true, the theory which would require them to do so. In fact it seems, on reflection, self-evident that a promise, simply as such, is something that *prima facie* ought to be kept, and it does *not,* on reflection, seem self-evident that production of maximum good is the only thing that makes an act obligatory. And to ask us to give up at the bidding of a theory our actual apprehension of what is right and what is wrong seems like asking people to repudiate their actual experience of beauty, at the bidding of a theory which says" only that which satisfies such and such conditions can be beautiful." If what I have called our actual apprehension is (as I would maintain that it is) truly an apprehension, i.e. an instance of knowledge, the request is nothing less than absurd.

I would maintain, in fact, that what we are apt to describe as "what we think" about moral questions contains a considerable amount that we do not think but know, and that this forms the standard by reference to which the truth of any moral theory has to be tested, instead of having itself to be tested by reference to any theory. I hope that I have in what precedes indicated what in my view these elements of knowledge are that are involved in our ordinary moral consciousness.

It would be a mistake to found a natural science on "what we really think," i.e. on what reasonably thoughtful and well-educated people think about the subjects of the science before they have studied them scientifically. For such opinions are interpretations, and often misinterpretations, of sense-experience; and the man of science must appeal from these to sense-experience itself, which furnishes his real data. In ethics no such appeal is possible. We have no more direct way of access to the facts about rightness and goodness and about what things are right or good, than by thinking about them; the moral convictions of thoughtful and well-educated people are the data of ethics just as sense-perceptions are the data of a natural science. Just as some of the latter have to be rejected as illusory, so have some of the former; but as the latter are rejected only when they are in conflict with other more accurate sense-perceptions, the former are rejected only when they are in conflict with other convictions which stand better the test of reflection. The existing body of moral convictions of the best people is the cumulative product of the moral reflection of many generations, which has developed an extremely delicate power of appreciation of moral distinctions; and this the theorist cannot afford to treat with anything other than the greatest respect. The verdicts of the moral consciousness of the best people are the foundation on which he must build; though he must first compare them with one another and eliminate any contradictions they may contain.

NOTES

1. Some will think it, apart from other considerations, a sufficient refutation of this view to point out that I also stand in that relation to myself, so that for this view the distinction of oneself from others is morally insignificant.

2. I should make it plain at this state that I am *assuming* the correctness of some of our main convictions as to *prima facie* duties, or, more strictly, am claiming that we *know* them to be true. To me it seems as self-evident as anything could be, that to make a promise, for instance, is to create a moral claim on us in someone else. Many readers will perhaps say that they do *not* know this to be true. If so, I certainly cannot prove it to them; I can only ask them to reflect again, in the hope that they will ultimately agree that they also know it to be true. The main moral convictions of the plain man seem to me to be, not opinions which it is for philosophy to prove or disprove, but knowledge from the start; and in my own case I seem to find little difficulty in distinguishing these essential convictions from other moral convictions which I also have, which are merely fallible opinions based on an imperfect study of the working for good or evil of certain institutions or types of action.

3. I am assuming that good is objectively quantitative, but not that we can accurately assign an exact quantitative measure to it. Since it is of a definite amount, we can make the *supposition* that its amount is so-and-so, though we cannot with any confidence *assert* that it is.

ETHICAL PROBLEMS

Crito

PLATO

Socrates. Why have you come so early, Crito? Or is it not still early?

 Crito. It certainly is.

 Socrates. How early?

 Crito. Early dawn.

 Socrates. I am surprised that the warder was willing to listen to you.

 Crito. He is quite friendly to me by now, Socrates I have been here often and I have given him something.

From Plato, *Five Dialogues*, 2/e, trans. G. M. A. Grube, revised by John Cooper (Hackett Publishing Company 2002). Reprinted by permission of Hackett Publishing Company, Inc. All rights reserved.

Socrates. Have you just come, or have you been here for some time?

Crito. A fair time.

Socrates. Then why did you not wake me right away but sit there in silence?

Crito. By Zeus no, Socrates, I would not myself want to be in distress and awake so long. I have been surprised to see you so peacefully asleep. It was on purpose that I did not wake you, so that you should spend your time most agreeably. Often in the past throughout my life, I have considered the way you live happy, and especially so now that you bear your present misfortune so easily and lightly.

Socrates. It would not be fitting at my age to resent the fact that I must die now.

Crito. Other men of your age are caught in such misfortunes, but their age does not prevent them resenting their fate.

Socrates. That is so. Why have you come so early?

Crito. I bring bad news, Socrates, not for you, apparently, but for me and all your friends the news is bad and hard to bear. Indeed, I would count it among the hardest.

Socrates. What is it? Or has the ship arrived from Delos, at the arrival of which I must die?

Crito. It has not arrived yet, but it will, I believe, arrive today, according to a message some men brought from Sunium, where they left it. This makes it obvious that it will come today, and that your life must end tomorrow.

Socrates. May it be for the best. If it so please the gods, so be it. However, I do not think it will arrive today.

Crito. What indication have you of this?

Socrates. I will tell you. I must die the day after the ship arrives.

Crito. That is what those in authority say.

Socrates. Then I do not think it will arrive on this coming day, but on the next. I take to witness of this a dream I had a little earlier during this night. It looks as if it was the right time for you not to wake me.

Crito. What was your dream?

Socrates. I thought that a beautiful and comely woman dressed in white approached me. She called me and said: "Socrates, may you arrive at fertile Phthia[1] on the third day."

Crito. A strange dream, Socrates.

Socrates. But it seems clear enough to me, Crito.

Crito. Too clear it seems, my dear Socrates, but listen to me even now and be saved. If you die, it will not be a single misfortune for me. Not only will I be deprived of a friend, the like of whom I shall never find again, but many people who do not know you or me very well will think that I could have saved you if I were willing to spend money, but that I did not care to do so. Surely there can be no worse reputation than to be thought to value money more highly than one's friends, for the majority will not believe that you yourself were not willing to leave prison while we were eager for you to do so.

Socrates. My good Crito, why should we care so much for what the majority think? The most reasonable people, to whom one should pay more attention, will believe that things were done as they were done.

Crito. You see, Socrates, that one must also pay attention to the opinion of the majority. Your present situation makes clear that the majority can inflict not the least but pretty well the greatest evils if one is slandered among them.

Socrates. Would that the majority could inflict the greatest evils, for they would then be capable of the greatest good, and that would be fine, but now they cannot do either. They cannot make a man either wise or foolish, but they inflict things haphazardly.

Crito. That may be so. But tell me this, Socrates, are you anticipating that I and your other friends would have trouble with the informers if you escape from here, as having stolen you away, and that we should be compelled to lose all our property or pay heavy fines and suffer other punishment besides? If you have any such fear, forget it. We would be justified in running this risk to save you, and worse, if necessary. Do follow my advice, and do not act differently.

Socrates. I do have these things in mind, Crito, and also many others.

Crito. Have no such fear. It is not much money that some people require to save you and get you out of here. Further, do you not see that those informers are cheap, and that not much money would be needed to deal with them? My money is available and is, I think, sufficient. If, because of your affection for me, you feel you should not spend any of mine, there are those strangers here ready to spend money. One of them, Simmias the Theban, has brought enough for this very purpose. Cebes, too, and a good many others. So, as I say, do not let this fear make you hesitate to save yourself, nor let what you said in court trouble you, that you would not know what to do with yourself if you left Athens, for you would be welcomed in many places to which you might go. If you want to go to Thessaly, I have friends there who will greatly appreciate you and keep you safe, so that no one in Thessaly will harm you.

Besides, Socrates, I do not think that what you are doing is just, to give up your life when you can save it, and to hasten your fate as your enemies would hasten it, and indeed have hastened it in their wish to destroy you. Moreover, I think you are betraying your sons by going away and leaving them, when you could bring them up and educate them. You thus show no concern for what their fate may be. They will probably have the usual fate of orphans. Either one should not have children, or one should share with them to the end the toil of upbringing and education. You seem to me to choose the easiest path, whereas one should choose the path a good and courageous man would choose, particularly when one claims throughout one's life to care for virtue.

I feel ashamed on your behalf and on behalf of us, your friends, lest all that has happened to you be thought due to cowardice on our part: the fact that your trial came to court when it need not have done so, the handling of the trial itself, and now this absurd ending which will be thought to have got beyond our control through some cowardice and unmanliness on our part, since we did not save you, or you save yourself, when it was possible and could be done if we had been of the slightest use. Consider, Socrates, whether this is not only evil, but shameful, both for you and for us. Take counsel with yourself, or rather the time for counsel is past and the decision should have been taken, and there is no further opportunity, for this whole business must be ended tonight. If we delay now, then it will no longer be possible; it will be too late. Let

me persuade you on every count, Socrates, and do not act otherwise.

Socrates. My dear Crito, your eagerness is worth much if it should have some right aim; if not, then the greater your keenness the more difficult it is to deal with. We must therefore examine whether we should act in this way or not, as not only now but at all times I am the kind of man who listens to nothing within me but the argument that on reflection seems best to me. I cannot, now that this fate has come upon me, discard the arguments I used; they seem to me much the same. I value and respect the same principles as before, and if we have no better arguments to bring up at this moment, be sure that I shall not agree with you, not even if the power of the majority were to frighten us with more bogeys, as if we were children, with threats of incarcerations and executions and confiscation of property. How should we examine this matter most reasonably? Would it be by taking up first your argument about the opinions of men, whether it is sound in every case that one should pay attention to some opinions, but not to others? Or was that well-spoken before the necessity to die came upon me, but now it is clear that this was said in vain for the sake of argument, that it was in truth play and nonsense? I am eager to examine together with you, Crito, whether this argument will appear in any way different to me in my present circumstances, or whether it remains the same, whether we are to abandon it or believe it. It was said on every occasion by those who thought they were speaking sensibly, as I have just now been speaking, that one should greatly value some people's opinions, but not others. Does that seem to you a sound statement?

You, as far as a human being can tell, are exempt from the likelihood of dying tomorrow, so the present misfortune is not likely to lead you astray. Consider then, do you not think it a sound statement that one must not value all the opinions of men, but some and not others, nor the opinions of all men, but those of some and not of others? What do you say? Is this not well said?

Crito. It is.

Socrates. One should value the good opinions, and not the bad ones?

Crito. Yes.

Socrates. The good opinions are those of wise men, the bad ones those of foolish men?

Crito. Of course.

Socrates. Come then, what of statements such as this: Should a man professionally engaged in physical training pay attention to the praise and blame and opinion of any man, or to those of one man only, namely a doctor or trainer?

Crito. To those of one only.

Socrates. He should therefore fear the blame and welcome the praise of that one man, and not those of the many?

Crito. Obviously.

Socrates. He must then act and exercise, eat and drink in the way the one, the trainer and the one who knows, thinks right, not all the others?

Crito. That is so.

Socrates. Very well. And if he disobeys the one, disregards his opinion and his praises while valuing those of the many who have no knowledge, will he not suffer harm?

Crito. Of course.

Socrates. What is that harm, where does it tend, and what part of the man who disobeys does it affect?

Crito. Obviously the harm is to his body, which it ruins.

Socrates. Well said. So with other matters, not to enumerate them all, and certainly with actions just and unjust, shameful and beautiful, good and bad, about which we are now deliberating, should we follow the opinion of the many and fear it, or that of the one, if there is one who has knowledge of these things and before whom we feel fear and shame more than before all the others? If we do not follow his directions, we shall harm and corrupt that part of ourselves that is improved by just actions and destroyed by unjust actions. Or is there nothing in this?

Crito. I think there certainly is, Socrates.

Socrates. Come now, if we ruin that which is improved by health and corrupted by disease by not following the opinions of those who know, is life worth living for us when that is ruined? And that is the body, is it not?

Crito. Yes.

Socrates. And is life worth living with a body that is corrupted and in bad condition?

Crito. In no way.

Socrates. And is life worth living for us with that part of us corrupted that unjust action harms and just action benefits? Or do we think that part of us, whatever it is, that is concerned with justice and injustice, is inferior to the body?

Crito. Not at all.

Socrates. It is more valuable?

Crito. Much more.

Socrates. We should not then think so much of what the majority will way about us, but what he will say who understands justice and injustice, the one, that is, and the truth itself. So that, in the first place, you were wrong to believe that we should care for the opinion of the many about what is just, beautiful, good, and their opposites. "But," someone might say, "the many are able to put us to death."

Crito. That too is obvious, Socrates, and someone might well say so.

Socrates. And, my admirable friend, that argument that we have gone through remains, I think, as before. Examine the following statement in turn as to whether it stays the same or not, that the most important thing is not life, but the good life.

Crito. It stays the same.

Socrates. And that the good life, the beautiful life, and the just life are the same; does that still hold, or not?

Crito. It does hold.

Socrates. As we have agreed so far, we must examine next whether it is just for me to try to get out of here when the Athenians have not acquitted me. If it is seen to be just, we will try to do so; if it is not, we will abandon the idea. As for those questions you raise about money, reputation, the upbringing of children, Crito, those considerations in truth belong to those people who easily put men to death and would bring them to life again if they could, without thinking; I mean the majority of men. For us, however, since our argument leads to this, the only valid consideration, as we were saying just now, is whether we should be acting rightly in giving money and gratitude to those who will lead me out of here, and ourselves helping with the escape, or whether in truth we shall do wrong in doing all this. If it appears that we shall be acting unjustly, then we have no need at all to take into account whether we shall have to die if we stay here and keep quiet, or suffer in another way, rather than do wrong.

Crito. I think you put that beautifully, Socrates, but see what we should do.

Socrates. Let us examine the question together, my dear friend, and if you can make any objection while I am speaking, make it and I will listen to you, but if you have no objection to make, my dear Crito, then stop now from saying the same thing so often, that I must leave here against the will of the Athenians. I think it important to persuade you before I act, and not to act against your wishes. See whether the start of our inquiry is adequately stated, and try to answer what I ask you in the way you think best.

Crito. I shall try.

Socrates. Do we say that one must never in any way do wrong willingly, or must one do wrong in one way and not in another? Is to do wrong never good or admirable, as we have agreed in the past, or have all these former agreements been washed out during the last few days? Have we at our age failed to notice for some time that in our serious discussions we were no different from children? Above all, is the truth such as we used to say it was, whether the majority agree or not, and whether we must still suffer worse things than we do now, or will be treated more gently, that, nonetheless, wrongdoing or injustice is in every way harmful and shameful to the wrongdoer? Do we say so or not?

Crito. We do.

Socrates. So one must never do wrong.

Crito. Certainly no.

Socrates. Nor must one, when wronged, inflict wrong in return, as the majority believe, since one must never do wrong.

Crito. That seems to be the case.

Socrates. Come now, should one mistreat anyone or not, Crito?

Crito. One must never do so.

Socrates. Well then, if one is oneself mistreated, is it right, as the majority say, to mistreat in return, or is it not?

Crito. It is never right.

Socrates. Mistreating people is no different from wrongdoing.

Crito. That is true.

Socrates. One should never do wrong in return, nor mistreat any man, no matter how one has been mistreated by him, And Crito, see that you do not agree to this, contrary to your belief. For I know that only a few people hold this view or will hold it, and there is no common ground between those who hold this view and those who do not, but they inevitably despise each other's views. So then consider very carefully whether we have this view in common, and whether you agree, and let this be the basis of our deliberation, that neither to do wrong nor to return a wrong is ever right, nor is bad treatment in return for bad treatment. Or do you disagree and do not share this view as a basis for discussion? I have held it for a long time and still hold it now, but if you think otherwise, tell me now. If, however, you stick to our former opinion, then listen to the next point.

Crito. I stick to it and agree with you. So say on.

Socrates. Then I state the next point, or rather I ask you: when one has come to an agreement that is just with someone, should one fulfill it or cheat on it?

Crito. One should fulfill it.

Socrates. See what follows from this: if we leave here without the city's permission, are we mistreating people whom we should least mistreat? And are we sticking to a just agreement, or not?

Crito. I cannot answer your question, Socrates. I do not know.

Socrates. Look at it this way. If, as we were planning to run away from here, or whatever one should call it, the laws and the state came and confronted us and asked: "Tell me, Socrates, what are you intending to do? Do you not by this action you are attempting intend to destroy us, the laws, and indeed the whole city, as far as you are concerned? Or do you think it possible for a city not to be destroyed if the verdicts of its courts have no force but are nullified and set at naught by private individuals?" What shall we answer to this and other such arguments? For many things could be said, especially by an orator on behalf of this law we are destroying, which orders that the judgments of the courts shall be carried out. Shall we say in answer, "The city wronged me, and its decision was not right." Shall we say that, or what?

Crito. Yes, by Zeus, Socrates, that is our answer.

Socrates. Then what if the laws said: "Was that the agreement between us, Socrates, or was it to respect the judgments that the city came to?" And if we wondered at their words, they would perhaps add: "Socrates, do not wonder at what we say but answer, since you are accustomed to proceed by question and answer. Come now, what accusation do you bring against us and the city, that you should try to destroy us? Did we not, first bring you to birth, and was it not through us that, your father married your mother and begat you? Tell us, do you find anything to criticize in those of us who are concerned with marriage?" And I would say that I do not criticize them. "Or in those of us concerned with the nurture of babies and the education that you too received? Were those assigned to that subject not right to instruct your father to educate you in the arts and in physical culture?" And I would say that they were right. "Very well," they would continue, "and after you were born and nurtured and educated, could you, in the first place, deny that you are our offspring and servant, both you and your forefathers? If that is so, do you think that we are on an equal footing as regards the right, and that whatever we do to you it is right for you to do to us? You were not on an equal footing with your father as regards the right, nor with your master if you had one, so as to retaliate for anything they did to you, to revile them if they reviled you, to beat them if they beat you, and so with many other things. Do you think you have this right to retaliation against your country and its laws? That if we undertake to destroy you and think it right to do so, you can undertake to destroy us, as far as you can, in return? And will you say that you are right to do so, you who truly care for virtue? Is your wisdom such as not to realize that your country is to be honored more than your mother, your father, and all your ancestors, that it is more to be revered and

more sacred, and that it counts for more among the gods and sensible men, that you must worship it, yield to it, and placate its anger more than your father's? You must either persuade it or obey its orders, and endure in silence whatever it instructs you to endure, whether blows or bonds, and if it leads you into war to be wounded or killed, you must obey. To do so is right, and one must not give way or retreat or leave one's post, but both in war and in courts and everywhere else, one must obey the commands of one's city and country, or persuade it as to the nature of justice. It is impious to bring violence to bear against your mother or father, it is much more so to use it against your country." What shall we say in reply, Crito, that the laws speak the truth, or not?

Crito. I think they do.

Socrates. "Reflect now, Socrates," the laws might say, "that if what we say is true, you are not treating us rightly by planning to do what you are planning. We have given you birth, nurtured you, educated you; we have given you and all other citizens a share of all the good things we could. Even so, by giving every Athenian the opportunity, once arrived at voting age and having observed the affairs of the city and us the laws, we proclaim that if we do not please him, he can take his possessions and go wherever he pleases. Not one of our laws raises any obstacle or forbids him, if he is not satisfied with us or the city, if one of you wants to go and live in a colony or wants to go anywhere else, and keep his property. We say, however, that whoever of you remains, when he sees how we conduct our trials and manage the city in other ways, has in fact come to an agreement with us to obey our instructions. We say that the one who disobeys does wrong in three ways, first because in us he disobeys his parents, also those who brought him up, and because, in spite of his agreement, he neither obeys us nor, if we do something wrong, does he try to persuade us to do better. Yet we only propose things, we do not issue savage commands to do whatever we order; we give two alternatives, either to persuade us or to do what we say. He does neither. We do say that you too, Socrates, are open to those charges if you do what you have in mind; you would be among, not the least, but the most guilty of the Athenians." And if I should say "Why so?" they might well be right to upbraid me and say that I am among the Athenians who most definitely came to that agreement with them. They might well say: "Socrates, we have convincing proofs that we and the city were congenial to you. You would not have dwelt here most consistently of all the Athenians if the city had not been exceedingly pleasing to you. You have never left the city, even to see a festival, nor for any other reason except military service; you have never gone to stay in any other city, as people do; you have had no desire to know another city or other laws; we and our city satisfied you.

"So decisively did you choose us and agree to be a citizen under us. Also, you have had children in this city, thus showing that it was congenial to you. Then at your trial you could have assessed your penalty at exile if you wished, and you are now attempting to do against the city's wishes what you could then have done with her consent. Then you prided yourself that you did not resent death, but you chose, as you said, death in preference to exile. Now, however, those words do not make you ashamed, and you pay no heed to us, the laws, as you plan to destroy us, and you act like the meanest type of slave by trying to run away, contrary to your commitments and your agreement to live as a citizen under us. First then, answer us on this very point, whether we speak the truth when we say that you agreed, not only in words but by your deeds, to live in accordance with us." What are we to say to that, Crito? Must we not agree?

Crito. We must, Socrates.

Socrates. "Surely," they might say, "you are breaking the commitments and agreements that you made with us without compulsion or deceit, and under no pressure of time for deliberation. You have had seventy years during which you could have gone away if you did not like us, and if you thought our agreements unjust. You did not choose to go to Sparta or to Crete, which you are always saying are well governed, nor to any other city, Greek or foreign. You have been away from Athens less than the lame or the blind or other handicapped people. It is clear that the city has been outstandingly more

congenial to you than to other Athenians, and so have we, the laws, for what city can please without laws? Will you then not now stick to our agreements? You will, Socrates, if we can persuade you, and not make yourself a laughingstock by leaving the city.

"For consider what good you will do yourself or your friends by breaking our agreements and committing such a wrong. It is pretty obvious that your friends will themselves be in danger of exile, disfranchisement, and loss of property. As for yourself, if you go to one of the nearby cities—Thebes or Megara, both are well governed—you will arrive as an enemy to their government, all who care for their city will look on you with suspicion, as a destroyer of the laws. You will also strengthen the conviction of the jury that they passed the right sentence on you, for anyone who destroys the laws could easily be thought to corrupt the young and the ignorant. Or will you avoid cities that are well governed and men who are civilized? If you do this, will your life be worth living? Will you have social intercourse with them and not be ashamed to talk to them? And what will you say? The same as you did here, that virtue and justice are man's most precious possession, along with lawful behavior and the laws? Do you not think that Socrates would appear to be an unseemly kind of person? One must think so. Or will you leave those places and go to Crito's friends in Thessaly? There you will find the greatest license and disorder, and they may enjoy hearing from you how absurdly you escaped from prison in some disguise, in a leather jerkin or some other things in which escapees wrap themselves, thus altering your appearance. Will there be no one to say that you, likely to live but a short time more, were so greedy for life that you transgressed the most important laws? Possibly, Socrates, if you do not annoy anyone, but if you do, many disgraceful things will be said about you.

"You will spend your time ingratiating yourself with all men, and be at their beck and call. What will you do in Thessaly but feast, as if you had gone to a banquet in Thessaly? As for those conversations of yours about justice and the rest of virtue, where will they be? You say you want to live for the sake of your children, that you may bring them up and educate them. How so? Will you bring them up and educate them by taking them to Thessaly and making strangers of them, that they may enjoy that too? Or not so, but they will be better brought up and educated here, while you are alive, though absent? Yes your friends will look after them. Will they look after them if you go and live in Thessaly, but not if you go away to the underworld? If those who profess themselves your friends are any good at all, one must assume that they will.

"Be persuaded by us who have brought you up, Socrates. Do not value either your children or your life or anything else more than goodness, in order that when you arrive in Hades you may have all this as your defense before the rulers there. If you do this deed, you will not think it better or more just or more pious here, nor will any one of your friends, nor will it be better for you when you arrive yonder. As it is, you depart, if you depart, after being wronged not by us, the laws, but by men; but if you depart after shamefully returning wrong for wrong and mistreatment for mistreatment, after breaking your agreements and commitments with us, after mistreating those you should mistreat least—yourself, your friends, your country, and us—we shall be angry with you while you are still alive, and our brothers, the laws of the underworld, will not receive you kindly, knowing that you tried to destroy us as far as you could. Do not let Crito persuade you, rather than us, to do what he says."

Crito, my dear friends, be assured that these are the words I seem to hear, as the Corybants seem to hear the music of their flutes, and the echo of these words resounds in me, and makes it impossible for me to hear anything else. As far as my present beliefs go, if you speak in opposition to them, you will speak in vain. However, if you think you can accomplish anything, speak.

Crito. I have nothing to say, Socrates.

Socrates. Let it be then, Crito, and let us act in this way, since this is the way the god is leading us.

NOTE

1. A quotation from the ninth book of the *Iliad* (363). Achilles has rejected all the presents of Agamemnon for him to return to the battle and threatens to go home. He says his ships will sail in the morning, and with good weather he might arrive on the third day "in fertile Phthia" (which is his home). Socrates takes the dream to mean that he will die, and his soul will find its home, on the third day. As always, counting the first member of a series, the third day is the day after tomorrow.

Judging Other Cultures: The Case of Genital Mutilation

MARTHA NUSSBAUM

Martha Nussbaum is Ernst Freund Distinguished Service Professor of Law and Ethics at the University of Chicago. She has written important work in many areas, including ancient philosophy, ethics, and the theory of emotions.

In June 1997, the Board of Immigration Appeals of the United States Immigration and Naturalization Service (INS) granted political asylum to a nineteen-year-old woman from Togo who had fled her home to escape the practice of genital mutilation. Fauziya Kassindja is the daughter of Muhammed Kassindja, a successful owner of a small trucking business in Kpalimé. Her father opposed the ritual practice: He remembered his sister's screams during the rite and her suffering from a tetanus infection she developed afterwards. Hajia, his wife, recalled the death of her older sister from an infection associated with the rite; this tragedy led Hajia's family to exempt her from cutting, and she, too, opposed the practice for her children. During his lifetime, Muhammed, being wealthy, was able to defy the tribal customs of the Tchamba-Kunsuntu, to which he belonged. Both illiterate themselves, the Kassindjas sent Fauziya to a boarding school in Ghana, so that she could learn English and help her father in his business. Meanwhile, her four older sisters married men of their own choice, genitals intact.

Fauziya's family was thus an anomaly in the region. Rakia Idrissou, the local genital exciser, told a reporter that girls usually have the procedure between the ages of four and seven. If weak, they are held down by four women; if stronger, they require five women, one to sit on their chests and one for each arm and leg. They must be kept still, she said, because if they jerk suddenly the razor blade used for the surgery can cut too deep.

When Fauziya was fifteen, however, her father died. Her mother was summarily turned out of the house by hostile relatives, and an aunt took control of the household, ending Fauziya's education. "We don't want girls to go to school too much," this aunt told a reporter from *The New York Times*. The family patriarch then arranged for Fauziya to become the fourth wife of an electrician; her prospective husband insisted that she have the genital operation first. To avoid the marriage and the mutilation that would have preceded it, Fauziya decided to leave home; her mother gave her $3,000 of the $3,500 inheritance that was her only sustenance. On her wedding day, Fauziya left her aunt's house, flagged down a taxi, and, with nothing but the clothes on her back, asked the driver to take her across the border into Ghana, some twenty miles away. Once in Ghana, she got on a flight to Germany; with help from people who

befriended her there, she got a flight to the United States.

On landing in Newark she confessed that her documents were false and asked for political asylum. After weeks of detention in an unsanitary and oppressive immigration prison, she got legal assistance—again with the help of her mother, who contacted a nephew who was working as a janitor in the Washington area. Scraping together $500, the nephew hired a law student at American University, Ms. Miller Bashir, to handle Fauziya's case. At first, Bashir was unsuccessful, and a Philadelphia immigration judge denied Fauziya's request for asylum. Through the determined efforts of activists, journalists, and law faculty at American University, she successfully appealed the denial. The appellate ruling stated that the practice of genital mutilation constitutes persecution and concluded. "It remains particularly true that women have little legal recourse and may face threats to their freedom, threats or acts of physical violence, or social ostracization for refusing to undergo this harmful traditional practice, or attempting to protect their female children."

In recent years, the practice of female genital mutilation has been increasingly in the news, generating a complex debate about cultural norms and the worth of sexual functioning. This chapter attempts to describe and to sort out some aspects of this controversy. First, however, a word about nomenclature. Although discussions sometimes use the terms "female circumcision" and "clitoridectomy," female genital mutilation" (FGM) is the standard generic term for all these procedures in the medical literature. "Clitoridectomy" standardly designates a subcategory, described shortly. The term "female circumcision" has been rejected by international medical practitioners because it suggests the fallacious analogy to male circumcision, which is generally believed to have either no effect or a positive effect on physical health and sexual functioning. Anatomically, the degree of cutting in the female operations described here is far more extensive. (The male equivalent of the clitoridectomy would be the amputation of most of the penis. The male equivalent of infibulation would be "removal of the entire penis, its roots of soft tissue, and part of the scrotal skin."[1]) This discussion is confined to cases that involve substantial removal of tissue and/or functional impairment; I make no comment on purely symbolic procedures that involve no removal of tissue, and these are not included under the rubric "female genital mutilation" by international agencies that study the prevalence of the procedure.

Three types of genital cutting are commonly practiced: (1) In *clitoridectomy,* a part or the whole of the clitoris is amputated and the bleeding is stopped by pressure or a stitch. (2) In *excision,* both the clitoris and the inner lips are amputated. Bleeding is usually stopped by stitching, but the vagina is not covered. (3) In *infibulation,* the clitoris is removed, some or all of the labia minora are cut off, and incisions are made in the labia majora to create raw surface. These surfaces are either stitched together or held in contact until they heal as a hood of skin that covers the urethra and most of the vagina. Approximately 85% of women who undergo FGM have type 1 or type 2; infibulation, which accounts for only 15% of the total, nonetheless accounts for 80 to 90% of all operations in certain countries, for example, the Sudan, Somalia, and Djibouti.

The practice of female genital mutilation remains extremely common in Africa, although it is illegal, and widely resisted, in most of the countries where it occurs. The World Health Organization estimates that overall, in today's world between 85 and 115 million women have had such operations. In terms of percentages, for example, 93% of women in Mali have undergone genital cutting, 98% in Somalia, 89% of women in the Sudan, 43% in the Central African Republic, 43% in the Ivory Coast, and 12% in Togo. Smaller numbers of operations are now reported from countries such as Australia, Belgium, France, the United Kingdom, and the United States.

Female genital mutilation is linked to extensive and in some cases lifelong health problems. These include infection, hemorrhage, and abscess at the time of the operation; later difficulties in urination and menstruation; stones in the urethra and bladder due to repeated infections; excessive growth of scar tissue at the site, which may become disfiguring; pain during intercourse; infertility (with devastating implications for a woman's other life chances); obstructed labor and damaging rips and tears during childbirth. Complications from infibulation are more severe than those from clitoridectomy and incision; nonetheless, the false perception that clitoridectomy is "safe" frequently leads to the ignoring of complications.

Both in the implicated nations and outside, feminists have organized to demand the abolition of this practice, citing its health risks, its impact on sexual functioning, and the violations of dignity and choice associated with its compulsory and nonconsensual nature. These opponents have been joined by many authorities in their respective nations, both religious and secular. In Egypt, for example, both the Health Minister, Ismail Sallem, and the new head of Al Azhar, the nation's leading Islamic institution, support a ban on the practice. The World Health Organization has advised health professionals not to participate in the practice since 1982 and repeated its strong opposition in 1994; the practice has also been condemned by the U.N. Commission on Human Rights, UNICEF, the World Medication Organization, Minority Rights Group International, and Amnesty International.

At the same time, however, other writers have begun to protest that the criticism of genital mutilation is inappropriate and "ethnocentric," a demonizing of another culture when we have many reasons to find fault with our own. They have also charged that the focus on this problem involves a Western glamorization of sexual pleasure that is inappropriate, especially when we judge other cultures with different moral norms. To encounter such positions we do not need to turn to scholarly debates. We find them in our undergraduate students, who are inclined to be ethical relativists on such matters, at least initially, hesitant to make any negative judgment of a culture other than their own. Because it seems important for anyone interested in political change in this area to understand these views in their popular and nonacademic form, I shall illustrate them from student writings I have encountered both in my own teaching and in my research for a book on liberal education, adding some points from the academic debate.

Many students, like some participants in the academic debate, are general cultural relativists, holding that it is always inappropriate to criticize the practices of another culture, and that cultures can appropriately be judged only by their own internal norms. That general position would indeed imply that it is wrong for Westerners to criticize female genital mutilation, but not for any reasons interestingly specific to genital mutilation itself. For that reason, and because I have already considered that family of views in chapter 1,* discussing the views of relativists in anthropology and development policy, I shall focus here on four criticisms that, while influenced by relativism, stop short of the general relativist thesis:

(1) It is morally wrong to criticize the practices of another culture unless one is prepared to be similarly critical of comparable practices when they occur in one's own culture. (Thus, a typical student reaction is to criticize the "ethnocentrism" of a stance that holds that one's own culture is the benchmark for "the principles and practices that are appropriate for all people.")[2]

(2) It is morally wrong to criticize the practices of another culture unless one's own culture has eradicated all evils of a comparable kind. (Thus, a typical undergraduate paper comments that criticism of genital mutilation is unacceptable "when one considers the domestic problems we are faced with in our own cultures.")

(3) Female genital mutilation is morally on a par with practices of dieting and body shaping in American culture. (I observed quite a few courses in which this comparison played a central role, and the comparison has often been suggested by my own students. In a similar vein, philosopher Yael Tamir writes that "Western conceptions of female beauty encourage women to undergo a wide range of painful, medically unnecessary, and potentially damaging processes."[3]

(4) Female genital mutilation involves the loss of a capacity that may not be especially central to the lives in question, and one to which Westerners attach disproportionate significance. Thus "references to clitoridectomy commonly reveal a patronizing attitude toward women, suggesting that they are primarily sexual beings."[4]

These are significant charges, which should be confronted. Feminist argument should not be condescending to women in developing countries who have their own views of what is good. Such condescension is all the more damaging when it comes from women who are reluctant to criticize the flaws in their own culture, for then it is reminiscent of the worst smugness of "white man's burden" colonialism. Our students are surely right to think that withholding one's own judgment until one has listened carefully to the experiences of members of the culture in question is a crucial part of intelligent deliberation. On the other hand, the prevalence of a practice, and the fact that even today many women endorse and perpetuate it, should not be taken as the final word, given that there also many women in African cultures who struggle against it, and given that those who do perpetuate it may do so in background conditions of intimidation and economic and political inequality. How, then, should we respond to these very common charges?

The first thesis is true, and it is useful to be reminded of it. Americans have all too often criticized other cultures without examining their own cultural shortcomings. It is less clear, however, that lack of self-criticism is a grave problem for Americans on such issues. We find no shortage of criticism of the ideal female body image, or of practices of dieting intended to produce it. Indeed, American feminists would appear to have devoted considerably more attention to these American problems than to genital mutilation, to judge from the success of books such as Naomi Wolf's *The Beauty Myth* and Susan Bordo's *Unbearable Weight*. Indeed, a review of the recent feminist literature suggests the problem may lie in exactly the opposite direction, in an excessive focusing on our own failings. We indulge in moral narcissim when we flagellate ourselves for our own errors while neglecting to attend to the needs of those who ask our help from a distance.

The second thesis is surely false. It is wrong to insist on cleaning up one's own house before

*[An earlier essay in the collection (*Sex and Social Justice*) from which the present article was excerpted—Eds.]

responding to urgent calls from outside. Should we have said "Hands off Apartheid," on the grounds that racism persists in the United States? Or, during the Second World War, "Hands off the rescue of the Jews," on the grounds that in the 1930s and 1940s every nation that contained Jews was implicated in anti-Semitic practices? It is and should be difficult to decide how to allocate one's moral effort between local and distant abuses. To work against both is urgently important, and individuals will legitimately make different decisions about their priorities. But the fact that a needy human being happens to live in Togo rather than Idaho does not make her less my fellow, less deserving of my moral commitment. And to fail to recognize the plight of a fellow human being because we are busy moving our own culture to greater moral heights seems the very height of moral obtuseness and parochialism.

We could add that FGM is not as such the practice of a single culture or group of cultures. As recently as in the 1940s, related operations were performed by U.S. and British doctors to treat female "problems" such as masturbation and lesbianism. Nor is there any cultural or religious group in which the practice is universal. As Nahid Toubia puts it, "FGM is an issue that concerns women and men who believe in equality, dignity and fairness to all human beings, regardless of gender, race, religion or ethnic identity.... It represents a human tragedy and must not be used to set Africans against non-Africans, one religious groups against another, or even women against men."[5]

If the third thesis were true, it might support a decision to give priority to the local in our political action (though not necessarily speech and writing): If two abuses are morally the same and we have better local information about one and are better placed politically to do something about it, that one seems to be a sensible choice to focus on in our actions here and now. But is the third thesis true? Surely not. Let us enumerate the differences.

1. Female genital mutilation is carried out by force, whereas dieting in response to culturally constructed images of beauty is a matter of choice, however seductive the persuasion. Few mothers restrict their children's dietary intake to unhealthy levels in order to make them slim; indeed most mothers of anorexic girls are horrified and deeply grieved by their daughters' condition. By contrast, during FGM small girls, frequently as young as four or five, are held down by force, often, as in Togo, by a group of adult women, and have no chance to select an alternative. The choices involved in dieting are often not fully autonomous: They may be the product of misinformation and strong social forces that put pressure on women to make choices, sometimes dangerous ones, that they would not make otherwise. We should criticize these pressures and the absence of full autonomy created by them. And yet the distinction between social pressure and physical force should also remain salient, both morally and legally. (Similarly, the line between seduction and rape is difficult to draw; frequently it turns on the elusive distinction between a threat and an offer, and on equally difficult questions about what threatened harms remove consent.) Nonetheless, we should make the distinction as best we can, and recognize that there remain relevant differences between genital mutilation and dieting, as usually practiced in America.

2. Female genital mutilation is irreversible, whereas dieting is, famously, far from irreversible.

3. Female genital mutilation is usually performed in conditions that in and of themselves are dangerous and unsanitary, conditions to which no child should be exposed; dieting is not.

4. Female genital mutilation is linked to extensive and in some cases lifelong health problems, even death. (In Kassindja's region, deaths are rationalized by the folk wisdom that profuse bleeding is a sign that a girl is not a virgin.) Dieting is linked to problems of this gravity only in the extreme cases of anorexia and bulimia, which, even then, are reversible.

5. Female genital mutilation is usually performed on children far too young to consent even were consent solicited; dieting involves, above all, adolescents and young adults. Even when children are older, consent is not solicited. Typical is the statement of an Ivory Coast father of a twelve-year-old girl about to be cut. "She

has no choice," he stated. "I decide. Her viewpoint is not important." His wife, who personally opposes the practice, concurs: "It is up to my husband," she states. "The man makes the decisions about the children."[6]

6. In the United State, as many women as men complete primary education, and more women than men complete secondary education; adult literacy is 99% for both females and males. In Togo, adult female literacy is 32.9% (52% that of men); in the Sudan, 30.6% (56% that of men); in the Ivory Coast, 26.1% (56%); in Burkina Faso, 8% (29%). Illiteracy is an impediment to independence; other impediments are supplied by economic dependency and lack of employment opportunities. These facts suggest limits to the notions of consent and choice, even as applied to the mothers or relatives who perform the operation, who may not be aware of the extent of resistance to the practice in their own and relevantly similar societies. To these limits we may add those imposed by political powerlessness, malnutrition, and intimidation. The wife of the patriarch in Fauziya Kassindja's clan told a reporter that she is opposed to the practice and would have run away like Fauziya had she been able—but nonetheless, she will allow the operation for her infant daughter. "I have to do what my husband says," she concludes. "It is not for women to give an order. I feel what happened to my body. I remember my suffering. But I cannot prevent it for my daughter."

7. Female genital mutilation means the irreversible loss of the capability for a type of sexual functioning that many women value highly, usually at an age when they are far too young to know what value it has or does not have in their own life. In the rare case in which a woman can make the comparison, she usually reports profound regret. Mariam Razak, a neighbor of the Kassindjas, was fifteen when she was cut, with five adult women holding her down. She had had sex with the man who is now her husband prior to that time and found it satisfying. Now, they both say, things are difficult. Mariam compares the loss to having a terminal illness that lasts a lifetime. "Now," her husband says, "something was lost in that place.... I try to make her feel pleasure, but it doesn't work very well."[7]

8. Female genital mutilation is unambiguously linked to customs of male domination. Even its official rationales, in terms of purity and propriety, point to aspects of sex hierarchy. Typical is the statement of Egyptian farmer Said Ibrahim, upset about the government ban: "Am I supposed to stand around while my daughter chases men?" To which Mohammed Ali, age seventeen, added, "Banning it would make women wild like those in America." Sex relations constructed by the practice are relations in which intercourse becomes a vehicle for one-sided male pleasure rather than for mutuality of pleasure.

By contrast, the ideal female body image purveyed in the American media has multiple and complex resonances, including those of male domination, but also including those of physical fitness, independence, and boyish nonmaternity.

These differences help explain why there is no serious campaign to make ads for diet programs, or the pictures of emaciated women in *Vogue,* illegal whereas FGM is illegal in most of the countries in which it occurs. (In the Sudan, the practice is punishable by up to two years' imprisonment.) Such laws are not well enforced, but their existence is evidence of a widespread movement against the practice in the countries implicated. Women in local regions where the practice is traditional give evidence of acquiescing, insofar as they do, out of intimidation and lack of options; women in adjacent regions where the practice is not traditional typically deplore it, citing health risks, loss of pleasure, and unnecessary suffering.

These differences also explain why Fauziya Kassindja was able to win political asylum. We shall not see similar arguments for political asylum for American women who have been pressured by the culture to be thin—however much it remains appropriate to criticize the norms of female beauty displayed in *Vogue* (as some advertisers have begun to do), the practices of some mothers, and the many covert pressures that combine to produce eating disorders in our society. Similarly, whereas the prospect of footbinding of the traditional Chinese type (in which the bones of the feet were repeatedly broken and the flesh of the foot became rotten) would, in my view, give grounds for political asylum; the presence of advertisements for high-heeled shoes surely would not, however many problems may be associated with the fashion. Even the publication of articles urging women to undergo FGM should be seen as altogether different from forcing a woman to undergo the procedure.

How, then, is FGM traditionally justified, when it is? In social terms, it is highly likely that FGM emerged as the functional equivalent to the seclusion of women. African women, unlike their counterparts in India, Pakistan, and elsewhere, are major agricultural producers. There is no barrier to women's work outside the home, and indeed the entire organization of agriculture in Africa traditionally rests on the centrality of female labor. In India, women's purity is traditionally guaranteed by seclusion; in Africa, this guarantee was absent, and another form of control emerged. But this functional history clearly does not justify the practice. What arguments are currently available?

It is now generally agreed that there is no religious requirement to perform FGM. The prophet Mohammed's most cited statement about the practice (from a reply to a question during a speech) makes the process nonessential, and the force of his statement seems to have been to discourage extensive cutting in favor of a more symbolic type of operation. The one reference to the operation in the *hadith* classifies it as a *makrama,* or nonessential practice. FGM is not practiced at all in many Islamic countries, including Pakistan, Algeria, Tunisia, Saudia Arabia, Iran, and Iraq. Defenses appealing to morality (FGM keeps women from extramarital sex) have resonance because they connect with the practice's likely original rationale, but they presuppose an unacceptable picture of women as whorish and childish. However sincerely such arguments are addressed, they should not be accepted by people with an interest in women's dignity. Defenses in terms of physical beauty are trickier, because we know how much cultures differ in what they regard as beautiful, but even perceptions of beauty (also at issue in Chinese footbinding) should yield before evidence of impairment of health and sexual functioning. Arguments claiming that without the practice

women will not be acceptable to men may state something true in local circumstances (as was also the case with footbinding) and may therefore provide a rationale for individual families to defer to custom as the best of a bad business (although this is less true now than formerly, given the widespread resistance to the practice in most areas where it occurs). Such arguments, however, clearly cannot justify the practice in moral or legal terms; similarly, arguments advising slaves to behave themselves if they do not want to be beaten may give good advice but cannot justify the institution of slavery.

The strongest argument in favor of the practice is an argument that appeals to cultural continuity. Jomo Kenyatta and others have stressed the constitutive role played by such initiation rites in the formation of a community and the disintegrative effect of interference. For this reason, Kenyatta opposed criminalization of the surgery and recommended a more gradual process of education and persuasion. Although one must have some sympathy with these concerns, it is still important to remember that a community is not a mysterious organic unity but a plurality of people standing in different relations of power to one another. It is not obvious that the type of cohesion that is effected by subordination and functional impairment is something we ought to perpetuate. Moreover, sixty years after Kenyatta's ambivalent defense, we see widespread evidence of resistance from within each culture, and there is reason to think that the practice is kept alive above all by the excisers themselves, paramedical workers who enjoy both high income and high prestige in the community from their occupation. These women frequently have the status of priestesses and have great influence over social perceptions. Countries that move against the practice should certainly make provision for the economic security of these women, but this does not mean taking them as unbiased interpreters of cultural tradition. To the extent that an initiation ritual is still held to be a valuable source of cultural solidarity, such rituals can surely be practiced (as they already are in some places) using a merely symbolic operation that does not remove any tissue.

Let me now turn to the fourth thesis. A secondary theme in recent feminist debates about

FGM is skepticism about the human value of sexual functioning. Philosopher Yael Tamir, for example, argues that hedonistic American feminists have ascribed too much value to pleasure. She suggests that it is men, above all, whose interests are being served by this, because female sexual enjoyment in our society is "seen as a measure of the sexual power and achievements of men," and because men find women who do not enjoy sex more intimidating than those who do.

I am prepared to agree with Tamir to this extent: The attention given FGM seems to me somewhat disproportionate, among the many gross abuses the world practices against women: unequal nutrition and health care, lack of the right to assemble and to walk in public, lack of equality under the law, lack of equal access to education, sex-selective infanticide and feticide, domestic violence, marital rape, rape in police custody, and many more. Unlike Tamir, I believe that the primary reason for this focus is not a fascination with sex but the relative tractability of FGM as a practical problem, given the fact that it is already widely resisted and indeed illegal, and given that it is not supported by any religion. How much harder to grapple with women's legal inequality before Islamic courts, their pervasive hunger, their illiteracy, their subjection to battery and violence. But surely Tamir is right that we should not focus on this one abuse while relaxing our determination to make structural changes that will bring women closer to full equality worldwide. And she may also be right to suggest that the fascination with FGM contains at least an element of the sensational or even the prurient.

Tamir, however, does not simply criticize the disproportionate focus of FGM. She offers a more general denigration of the importance of sexual pleasure as an element in human flourishing. This part of her argument is flawed by the failure to make a crucial distinction: that between a function and the capacity to choose that function. Criticizing her opponents for their alleged belief that the capacity for sexual pleasure is a central human good, she writes:

> Nuns take an oath of celibacy, but we do not usually condemn the church for preventing its clergy from enjoying an active sex life. Moreover, most of us do not think that Mother Teresa is leading a worse life than Chichulina, though the latter claims to have experienced an extensive number of orgasms. It is true that nuns are offered spiritual life in exchange for earthly goods, but in the societies where clitoridectomy is performed, the fulfilling life of motherhood and child bearing are offered in exchange. Some may rightly claim that one can function as a wife and a mother while still experiencing sexual pleasures. Others believe that full devotion to God does not require an oath of celibacy. Yet these views are, after all, a matter of convention.[8]

There are a number of oddities in this argument. (It is hard, for example, to know what to make of the assertion that the possibility of combining sexual pleasure with motherhood is a mere "matter of convention.") More centrally, however, Tamir mischaracterizes the debate. No feminist opponent of FGM is saying or implying that celibacy is bad, that nuns all have a starved life, that orgasms the be-all and end-all of existence. I know of no opponent who would not agree with Tamir's statement that women are not merely sexual agents, that their ability to lead rich and rewarding lives does not depend solely on the nature of their sex life. "But there is a great difference between fasting and starving just so, there is also a great difference between a vow of celibacy and FGM. Celibacy involves the choice not to exercise a capability to which nuns, insofar as they are orthodox Roman Catholics, ascribe considerable human value. Its active exercise is thought good for all but a few of those humans, and even for them it is the choice not to use a capacity one has (as in the case of fasting) that is deemed morally valuable. (A Catholic should hold that a survivor of FGM cannot achieve the Christian good of celibacy.) FGM, by contrast, involves forgoing altogether the very possibility of sexual functioning—and, as I said, well before one is of an age to make such a choice. We all know that people who are blind or unable to walk can lead rich and meaningful lives; nonetheless, we would all deplore practices that deliberately disabled people in those respects, nor would we think that critics of those practices are giving walking or seeing undue importance in human life.

Can even the mothers of these girls make an informed choice as to the value of female sexual pleasure? They have been immersed in traditional beliefs about women's impurity; lacking literacy and education, as a large proportion do, they have difficulty seeking out alternative paradigms. As the immigration report points out, their situation is made more difficult by fear and powerlessness. Equally important, their own experience of sexual life cannot have contained orgasmic pleasure if they themselves encountered FGM as girls; even if they did not, they are highly likely to have experienced marriage and sexual life as a series of insults of their dignity, given the ubiquity of domestic violence and marital rape. Should they believe that FGM is a bad thing for their daughters—as a remarkable proportion of the women interviewed in the recent stories clearly do—they have no power to make their choices effective and many incentives to conceal the views they hold. Such facts do not show that women who have had a more fortunate experience of marriage and sexuality are making a mistake when they hold that the capacity for sexual pleasure should be preserved for those who may choose to exercise it. There is certainly something wrong with any social situation in which women are viewed only or primarily as sex objects; but criticizing such perceptions has nothing to do with defending FGM.

Nor does Tamir give us any reason to suppose that the importance of women's sexual pleasure is a mythic construct of the male ego. Many women have reported enjoying sex a good deal, and there is no reason to think them all victims of false consciousness. It is probably true that some men find women who do not enjoy sex more intimidating than those who do, but it would be more than a little perverse to deny oneself pleasure simply in order to intimidate men. Moreover, in the situation we are contemplating in the case of FGM, the operative male fear is surely that of women's sexual agency, which is a sign that the woman is not simply a possession and might even experience pleasure with someone other than her owner. It would be highly implausible to suggest that African women can gain power and intimidate men by undergoing FGM. The attack on FGM is part and parcel of a more general attempt by women to gain control of their sexual capacities; it is thus a relative of attacks on rape, marital rape, sexual harassment,

and domestic violence. It is precisely this challenge to traditional male control that many men find threatening.

In the concluding section of her discussion of FGM, Yael Tamir imagines a country called Libidia, where women with unnaturally enlarged clitorises find they cannot do anything else but have sex and therefore seek to remove the clitoris in order to have better lives. In this way she suggests that sexual pleasure undermines other valuable human function—so one might plausibly deem its removal a helpful thing, rather like a trip to the dentist to get rid of a diseased tooth. She here expresses a Platonic idea about the relation between continence and intellectual creativity that may be true for some individuals at some times but is surely not a universal datum of human experience. Plato did indeed hold in the *Phaedo* that mental life would be much better if the bodily appetites could be put to one side insofar as possible—though even he did not maintain this position with absolute consistency, nor did he suggest genital mutilation as a remedy. Aristotle, on the other hand, held that someone who has insensible to the full range of the bodily pleasures would be "far from being a human being." We do not need to decide which thinker is right—or indeed for which people each of them is right—to decide sensibly that FGM is not like an appendectomy—that it involves the removal of a capability for whose value history and experience have had a great deal to say. Individuals may then choose whether and how to exercise it, just as we also choose whether and how to use our athletic and musical capacities.

Internal criticism is slowly changing the situation in the nations in which FGM has traditionally been practiced. The eighteen-year-old son of the patriarch of the Kassindja family told reporters that he wanted to marry a women who had not been cut, because teachers in his high school had influenced his thinking. The patriarch himself now favors making the practice optional, to discourage more runaways who give the family a bad name. The very fact that the age of cutting in Togo has been moving steadily down (from twelve to four), in order (the exciser says) to discourage runaways, gives evidence of mounting resistance to the practice. But many of the women and men in the relevant nations who are struggling against this practice are impoverished or unequal under the law or illiterate or powerless or in fear—and often all of these. There is no doubt that they wish outside aid. There is also no doubt that they encounter local opposition—as is always the case when one moves to change a deeply entrenched custom connected with the structures of power. (As I have suggested, some of the people involved have strong personal economic and status interests in the status quo.) Suzanne Aho, director of Togo's Office for the Protection and Promotion of the Family, explains that she tries to counsel men about women's rights of choice, but she encounters the dead weight of custom. Of the Kassindja patriarch she says: "'You cannot force her,' I told him. He understood, but he said it is a tradition."

These upholders of tradition are eager, often, to brand their internal opponents as Westernizers, colonialists, and any other bad thing that may carry pubic sentiment. Even so, Fauziya's father was accused of "trying to act like a white man." But this way of deflecting internal criticism should not intimidate outsiders who have reasoned the matter out, at the same time listening to the narratives of women who have been involved in the reality of FGM. The charge of "colonialism" presumably means that the norms of an oppressor group are being unthinkingly assimilated, usually to curry favor with that group. That is not at all what is happening in the case of FGM. In the United Nations, in Human Rights Watch, in many organizations throughout the world, and in countless local villages the issue has been debated. Even the not very progressive Immigration and Naturalization Service (INS) has been swayed by the data it collected. The vigor of internal resistance should give confidence to those outside who work to oppose the practice. Frequently external pressure can assist a relatively powerless internal group that is struggling to achieve change.

In short, international and national officials who have been culpably slow to recognize gender-specific abuses as human rights violations are beginning to get the idea that women's rights are human rights, and that freedom from FGM is among them. Without abandoning a broader concern for the whole list of abuses women suffer at the hands of unjust customs and individuals, we should continue to keep FGM on the list of unacceptable practices that violate women's human rights, and we should be ashamed to ourselves if we do not use whatever privilege and power has come our way to make it disappear forever.

NOTES

1. Nahid Toubia, *Female Genital Mutilation: A Call for Global Action* (hereafter *FGM*) (New York: UNICEF, 1995), 5. Toubia was the first woman surgeon in the Sudan. She is an advisor to the World Health Organization, vice chair of the Women's Rights Project of Human Rights Watch, and director of the Global Action against FGM Project at the Columbia University School of Public Health. Other medical discussions include Toubia, "Female Circumcision as a Public Health Issue," *New England Journal of Medicine* 331 (1994), 712 ff. Amy O. Tsui, Judith N. Wasserheit, and John G. Haaga, eds., *Reproductive Health in Developing Countries: Expanding Dimensions, Building Solutions* (Washington, DC: National Academy Press, 1997), 32–3 with bibliography; N. El-Saadawi, "Circumcision of Girls," and R. H. Dualeh and M. Fara-Warsame, "Female Circumcision in Somalia," in *Traditional Practices Affecting the Health of Women and Children*, ed. T. Baasher, R. H. Bannerman; H. Rushwan, and I. Sharif (Alexandria, Egypt: the World Health Organization, 1982); C. P. Howson et al., eds., *In Her Lifetime: Female Morbidity and Mortality in Sub-Saharan Africa* (Washington, DC: National Academy Press, 1996); World Health Organization, "WHO Leads Action Against Female Genital Mutilation," *World Health Forum* 15 (1994), 416 ff; L. Heise, "Gender-based Violence and Women's Reproductive Health," *International Journal of Gynecology and Obstetrics* 46 (1994); 221–9.

2. Quotations from student writing are from a course on practices of control and shaping of the female body at St. Lawrence University.

3. Tamir, "Hands Off Clitoridectomy," *The Boston Review* 21 (3/4) (1996), 21. Compare Obiora, "Bridges and Barricades: Rethinking Polemic's and Intransigence in the Campaign Against Female Circumcision," *Case Western Reserve Law Review* 47 (1997); 318–20.

4. Tamir, 21.
5. *FGM*, 7.
6. Celia W. Dugges, "African Ritual Pain: Genital Cutting," *New York Times,* October 5, 1996.
7. Toubia has encountered rare cases in which women who have undergone clitoridectomy and even intermediate infibulation convince her that they have experienced orgasm. She attributes this to unusual psychological resourcefulness, together with the capacities of secondary sources of sexual stimulation.
8. Tamir, 21.

Famine, Affluence, and Morality

PETER SINGER

Peter Singer, author of the best-selling *Animal Liberation,* teaches moral philosophy at Princeton University.

As I write this, in November 1971, people are dying in East Bengal from lack of food, shelter, and medical care. The suffering and death that are occurring there now are not inevitable, not unavoidable in any fatalistic sense of the term. Constant poverty, a cyclone, and a civil war have turned at least nine million people into destitute refugees; nevertheless, it is not beyond the capacity of the richer nations to give enough assistance to reduce any further suffering to very small proportions. The decisions and actions of human beings can prevent this kind of suffering. Unfortunately, human beings have not made the necessary decisions. At the individual level, people have, with very few exceptions, not responded to the situation in any significant way. Generally speaking, people have not given large sums to relief funds; they have not written to their parliamentary representatives demanding increased government assistance; they have not demonstrated in the streets, held symbolic fasts, or done anything else directed toward providing the refugees with the means to satisfy their essential needs. At the government level, no government has given the sort of massive aid that would enable the refugees to survive for more than a few days. Britain, for instance, has given rather more than most countries. It has, to date, given £14,750,000. For comparative purposes, Britain's share of the nonrecoverable development costs of the Anglo-French Concorde project is already in excess of £275,000,000, and on present estimates will reach £440,000,000. The implication is that the British government values a supersonic transport more than thirty times as highly as it values the lives of the nine million refugees. Australia is another country which, on a per capita basis, is well up in the "aid to Bengal" table. Australia's aid, however, amounts to less than one-twelfth of the cost of Sydney's new opera house. The total amount given, from all sources, now stands at about £65,000,000. The estimated cost of keeping the refugees alive for one year is £464,000,000. Most of the refugees have now been in the camps for more than six months. The World Bank has said that India needs a minimum of £300,000,000 in assistance from other countries before the end of the year. It seems obvious that assistance on this scale will not be forthcoming. India will be forced to choose between letting the refugees starve or diverting funds from her own development program, which will mean that more of her own people will starve in the future.[1]

Peter Singer, "Famine, Affluence, and Morality," *Philosophy & Public Affairs.* Vol. 1, No. 3 (Spring 1972), pp. 229–243. Copyright © 1972 by Princeton University Press. Reprinted with permission of Princeton University Press.

These are the essential facts about the present situation in Bengal. So far as it concerns us here, there is nothing unique about this situation except its magnitude. The Bengal emergency is just the latest and most acute of a series of major emergencies in various parts of the world, arising both from natural and from man-made causes. There are also many parts of the world in which people die from malnutrition and lack of food independent of any special emergency. I take Bengal as my example only because it is the present concern, and because the size of the problem has ensured that it has been given adequate publicity. Neither individuals nor governments can claim to be unaware of what is happening there.

What are the moral implications of a situation like this? In what follows, I shall argue that the way people in relatively affluent countries react to a situation like that in Bengal cannot be justified; indeed, the whole way we look at moral issues—our moral conceptual scheme—needs to be altered, and with it, the way of life that has come to be taken for granted in our society.

In arguing for this conclusion I will not, of course, claim to be morally neutral. I shall, however, try to argue for the moral position that I take, so that anyone who accepts certain assumptions, to be made explicit, will, I hope, accept my conclusion.

I begin with the assumption that suffering and death from lack of food, shelter, and medical care are bad. I think most people will agree about this, although one may reach the same view by different routes. I shall not argue for this view. People can hold all sorts of eccentric positions, and perhaps from some of them it would not follow that death by starvation is in itself bad. It is difficult, perhaps impossible, to refute such positions, and so for brevity I will henceforth take this assumption as accepted. Those who disagree need read no further.

My next point is this: if it is in our power to prevent something bad from happening, without thereby sacrificing anything of comparable moral importance, we ought, morally, to do it. By "without sacrificing anything of comparable moral importance" I mean without causing anything else comparably bad to happen, or doing something that is wrong in itself, or failing to promote some moral good, comparable in significance to the bad thing that we can prevent. This principle seems almost as uncontroversial as the last one. It requires us only to prevent what is bad, and not to promote what is good, and it requires this of us only when we can do it without sacrificing anything that is, from the moral point of view, comparably important. I could even, as far as the application of my argument to the Bengal emergency is concerned, qualify the point so as to make it: if it is in our power to prevent something very bad from happening, without thereby sacrificing anything morally significant, we ought, morally, to do it. An application of this principle would be as follows: if I am walking past a shallow pond and see a child drowning in it, I ought to wade in and pull the child out. This will mean getting my clothes muddy, but this is insignificant, while the death of the child would presumably be a very bad thing.

The uncontroversial appearance of the principle just stated is deceptive. If it were acted upon, even in its qualified form, our lives, our society, and our world would be fundamentally changed. For the principle takes, firstly, no account of proximity or distance. It makes no moral difference whether the person I can help is a neighbor's child ten yards from me or a Bengali whose name I shall never know, ten thousand miles away. Secondly, the principle makes no distinction between cases in which I am the only person who could possibly do anything and cases in which I am just one among millions in the same position.

I do not think I need to say much in defense of the refusal to take proximity and distance into account. The fact that a person is physically near to us, so that we have personal contact with him, may make it more likely that we *shall* assist him, but this does not show that we *ought* to help him rather than another who happens to be further away. If we accept any principle of impartiality, universalizability, equality, or whatever, we cannot discriminate against someone merely because he is far away from us (or we are far away from him). Admittedly, it is possible that we are in a better position to judge what needs to be done to help a person near to us than one far away, and perhaps also to provide the assistance we judge to be necessary. If this were the case, it would be a reason for helping those near to us first. This may once have been a justification for being more concerned with the poor in one's own town than with the famine victims in India. Unfortunately for those who like to keep their moral responsibilities limited, instant communication and swift transportation have changed the situation. From the moral point of view, the development of the world into a "global village" has made an important, though still unrecognized, difference to our moral situation. Expert observers and supervisors, sent out by famine relief organizations or permanently stationed in famine-prone areas, can direct our aid to a refugee in Bengal almost as effectively as we could get it to someone in our own block. There would seem, therefore, to be no possible justification for discriminating on geographical grounds.

There may be a greater need to defend the second implication of my principle—that the fact that there are millions of other people in the same position, in respect to the Bengali refugees, as I am, does not make the situation significantly different from a situation in which I am the only person who can prevent something very bad from occurring. Again, of course, I admit that there is a psychological difference between the cases; one feels less guilty about doing nothing if one can point to others, similarly placed, who have also done nothing. Yet this can make no real difference to our moral obligations.[2] Should I consider that I am less obliged to pull the drowning child out of the pond if on looking around I see other people, no further away than I am, who have also noticed the child but are doing nothing? One has only to ask this question to see the absurdity of the view that numbers lessen obligation. It is a view that is an ideal excuse for inactivity; unfortunately most of the major evils—poverty, overpopulation, pollution—are problems in which everyone is almost equally involved.

The view that numbers do make a difference can be made plausible if stated in this way: if everyone in circumstances like mine gave £5 to the Bengal Relief Fund, there would be enough to provide food, shelter, and medical care for the refugees; there is no reason why I should give more than anyone else in the same circumstances as I am; therefore I have no obligation to give more than £5. Each premise in this argument is true, and the argument looks sound. It may convince us, unless we notice that it is based on a hypothetical premise, although the conclusion is not stated hypothetically. The argument would be sound if the conclusion were: if everyone in circumstances like mine were to give £5, I would have no obligation to give more than £5. If the conclusion were so stated, however, it would be obvious that the argument has no bearing on a situation in which it is not the case that everyone else gives £5. This, of course, is the actual situation. It is more or less certain that not everyone in circumstances like mine will give £5. So there will not be enough to provide the needed food, shelter, and medical care. Therefore by giving more than £5 I will prevent more suffering than I would if I gave just £5.

It might be thought that this argument has an absurd consequence. Since the situation appears to be that very few people are likely to give substantial amounts, it follows that I and everyone else in similar circumstances ought to give as much as possible, that is, at least up to the point at which by giving more one would begin to cause serious suffering for oneself and one's dependents—perhaps even beyond this point to the point of marginal utility, at which by giving more one would cause oneself and one's dependents as much suffering as one would prevent in Bengal. If everyone does this, however, there will be more than can be used for the benefit of the refugees, and some of the sacrifice will have been unnecessary. Thus, if everyone does what he ought to do, the result will not be as good as it would be if everyone did a little less than he ought to do, or if only some do all that they ought to do.

The paradox here arises only if we assume that the actions in question—sending money to the relief funds—are performed more or less simultaneously, and are also unexpected. For if it is to be expected that everyone is going to contribute something, then clearly each is not obliged to give as much as he would have been obliged to had others not been giving too. And if everyone is not acting more or less simultaneously, then those giving later will know how much more is needed, and will have no obligation to give more than is necessary to reach this amount. To say this is not to deny the principle that people in the same circumstances have the same obligations, but to point out that the fact that others have given, or may be expected to give, is a relevant circumstance: those giving after it has become known that many others are giving and those giving before are not in the same circumstances. So the seemingly absurd consequence of the principle I have put forward can occur only if people are in error about the actual circumstances—that is, if they think they are giving when others are not, but in fact they are giving when others are. The result of everyone doing what he really ought to do cannot be worse than the result of everyone doing less than he ought to do, although the result of everyone doing what he reasonably believes he ought to do could be.

If my argument so far has been sound, neither our distance from a preventable evil nor the number of other people who, in respect to that evil, are in the same situation as we are, lessens our obligation to mitigate or prevent that evil. I shall therefore take as established the principle I asserted earlier. As I have already said, I need to assert it only in its qualified form: if it is in our power to prevent something very bad from happening, without thereby sacrificing anything else morally significant, we ought, morally, to do it.

The outcome of this argument is that our traditional moral categories are upset. The traditional distinction between duty and charity cannot be drawn, or at least, not in the place we normally draw it. Giving money to the Bengal Relief Fund is regarded as an act of charity in our society. The bodies which collect money are known as "charities." These organizations see themselves in this way—if you send them a check, you will be thanked for your "generosity." Because giving money is regarded as an act of charity, it is not thought that there is anything wrong with not giving. The charitable man may be praised, but the man who is not charitable is not condemned. People do not feel in any way ashamed or guilty about spending money on new clothes or a new car instead of giving it to famine relief. (Indeed, the alternative does not occur to them.) This way of looking at the matter cannot be justified. When we buy new clothes not to keep ourselves warm but to look "well-dressed" we are not providing for any important need. We would not be sacrificing anything significant if we were to continue to wear our old clothes, and give the money to famine relief. By doing so, we would be preventing another person from starving. It follows from what I have said earlier that we ought to give money away, rather than spend it on clothes which we do not need to keep us warm. To do so is not charitable, or generous. Nor is it the kind of act which philosophers and theologians have called "supererogatory"—an act which it would be good to do, but not wrong not to do. On the contrary, we ought to give the money away, and it is wrong not to do so.

I am not maintaining that there are no acts which are charitable, or that there are no acts which it would be good to do but not wrong not to do. It may be possible to redraw the distinction between duty and charity in some other place. All I am arguing here is that the present way of drawing the distinction, which makes it an act of charity for a man living at the level of affluence which most people in the "developed nations" enjoy to give money to save someone else from starvation, cannot be supported. It is beyond the scope of my argument to consider whether the distinction should be redrawn or abolished altogether. There would be many other possible ways of drawing the distinction— for instance, one might decide that it is good to make other people as happy as possible, but not wrong not to do so.

Despite the limited nature of the revision in our moral conceptual scheme which I am proposing, the revision would, given the extent of both affluence and famine in the world today, have radical implications. These implications may lead to further objections, distinct from those I have already considered. I shall discuss two of these.

One objection to the position I have taken might be simply that it is too drastic a revision of our moral scheme. People do not ordinarily judge in the way I have suggested they should. Most people reserve their moral condemnation for those who violate some moral norm, such as the norm against taking another person's property. They do not condemn those who indulge in luxury instead of giving to famine relief. But given that I did not set out to present a morally neutral description of the way people make moral judgments, the way people do in fact judge has nothing to do with the validity of my conclusion. My conclusion follows from the principle which I advanced earlier, and unless that principle is rejected, or the arguments shown to be unsound, I think the conclusion must stand, however strange it appears.

It might, nevertheless, be interesting to consider why our society, and most other societies, do judge differently from the way I have suggested they should. In a well-known article, J. O. Urmson suggests that the imperatives of duty, which tell us what we must do, as distinct from what it would be good to do but not wrong not to do, function so as to prohibit behavior that is intolerable if men are to live together in society.[3] This may explain the origin and continued existence of the present division between acts of duty and acts of charity. Moral attitudes are shaped by the needs of society, and no doubt society needs people who will observe the rules that make social existence tolerable. From the point of view of a particular society, it is essential to prevent violations of norms against killing, stealing, and so on. It is quite inessential, however, to help people outside one's own society.

If this is an explanation of our common distinction between duty and supererogation, however, it is not a justification of it. The moral point of view requires us to look beyond the interests of our own society. Previously, as I have already mentioned, this may hardly have been feasible, but it is quite feasible now. From the moral point of view, the prevention of the starvation of millions of people outside our society must be considered at least as pressing as the upholding of property norms within our society.

It has been argued by some writers, among them Sidgwick and Urmson, that we need to have a basic moral code which is not too far beyond the capacities of the ordinary man, for otherwise there will be a general breakdown of compliance with the moral code. Crudely stated, this argument suggests that if we tell people that they ought to refrain from murder and give everything they do not really need to famine relief, they will do neither, whereas if we tell them that they ought to refrain from murder and that it is good to give to famine relief but not wrong not to do so, they will at least refrain from murder. The issue here is: Where should we draw the line between conduct that is required and conduct that is good although not required, so as to get the best possible result? This would seem to be an empirical question, although a very difficult one. One objection to the Sidgwick-Urmson line of argument is that it takes insufficient account of the effect that moral standards can have on the decisions we make. Given a society in which a wealthy man who gives five percent of his income to famine relief is regarded as most generous, it is not surprising that a proposal that we all ought to give away half our incomes will be thought to be absurdly unrealistic. In a society which held that no man should have more than enough while others have less than they need, such a proposal might seem narrow-minded. What it is possible for a man to do and what he is likely to do are both, I think, very greatly influenced by what people around him are doing and expecting him to do. In any case, the possibility that by spreading the idea that we ought to be doing very much more than we are to relieve famine we shall bring about a general breakdown of moral behavior seems remote. If the stakes are an end to widespread starvation, it is worth the risk. Finally, it should be emphasized that these considerations are relevant only to the issue of what we should require from others, and not to what we ourselves ought to do.

The second objection to my attack on the present distinction between duty and charity is one which has from time to time been made against utilitarianism. It follows from some forms of utilitarian theory that we all ought, morally, to be working full time to increase the balance of happiness over misery. The position I have taken here would not lead to this conclusion in all circumstances, for if there were no bad occurrences that we could prevent without sacrificing something of comparable moral importance, my argument would have no application. Given the present conditions in many parts of the world, however, it does follow from my argument that we ought, morally, to be working full time to relieve great suffering of the sort that occurs as a result of famine or other disasters. Of course, mitigating circumstances can be adduced—for instance, that if we wear ourselves out through overwork, we shall be less effective than we would otherwise have been. Nevertheless, when all considerations of this sort have been taken into account, the conclusion remains: we ought to be preventing as much suffering as we can without sacrificing something else of comparable moral importance. This conclusion is one which we may be reluctant to face. I cannot see, though, why it should be regarded as a criticism of the position for which I have argued, rather than a criticism of our ordinary standards of behavior. Since most people are self-interested to some degree, very few of us are likely to do everything that we ought to do. It would, however, hardly be honest to take this as evidence that it is not the case that we ought to do it.

It may still be thought that my conclusions are so wildly out of line with what everyone else thinks and has always thought that there must be something wrong with the argument somewhere. In order to show that my conclusions, while certainly contrary to contemporary Western moral standards, would not have seemed so extraordinary at other times and in other places, I would like to quote a passage from a writer not normally thought of as a way-out radical, Thomas Aquinas.

> Now, according to the natural order instituted by divine providence, material goods are provided for the satisfaction of human needs. Therefore the division and appropriation of property, which proceeds from human law, must not hinder the satisfaction of man's necessity from such goods. Equally, whatever a man has in super-abundance is owed, of natural right, to the poor for their sustenance. So Ambrosius says, and it is also to be found in the *Decretum Gratiani:* "The bread which you withhold belongs to the hungry; the clothing you shut away, to the naked; and the money you bury in the earth is the redemption and freedom of the penniless."[4]

I now want to consider a number of points, more practical than philosophical, which are relevant to the application of the moral conclusion we have reached. These points challenge not the idea that we ought to be doing all we can to prevent starvation, but the idea that giving away a great deal of money is the best means to this end.

It is sometimes said that overseas aid should be a government responsibility, and that therefore one ought not to give to privately run charities. Giving privately, it is said, allows the government and the noncontributing members of society to escape their responsibilities.

This argument seems to assume that the more people there are who give to privately organized famine relief funds, the less likely it is that the government will take over full responsibility for such aid. This assumption is unsupported, and does not strike me as at all plausible. The opposite view—that if no one gives voluntarily, a government will assume that its citizens are uninterested in famine relief and would not wish to be forced into giving aid—seems more plausible. In any case, unless there were a definite probability that by refusing to give one would be helping to bring about massive government assistance, people who do refuse to make voluntary contributions are refusing to prevent a certain amount of suffering without being able to point to any tangible beneficial consequence of their refusal. So the onus of showing how their refusal will bring about government action is on those who refuse to give.

I do not, of course, want to dispute the contention that governments of affluent nations should be giving many times the amount of genuine, nostrings-attached aid that they are giving now. I agree, too, that giving privately is not enough, and that we ought to be campaigning actively for entirely new standards for both public and private contributions to famine relief. Indeed, I would sympathize with someone who thought that campaigning was more important than giving oneself, although I doubt whether preaching what one does not practice would be very effective. Unfortunately, for many people the idea that "it's the government's responsibility" is a reason for not giving which does not appear to entail any political action either.

Another, more serious reason for not giving to famine relief funds is that until there is effective population control, relieving famine merely postpones starvation. If we save the Bengal refugees now, others, perhaps the children of these refugees, will face starvation in a few years' time. In support of this, one may cite the now well-known facts about the population explosion and the relatively limited scope for expanded production.

This point, like the previous one, is an argument against relieving suffering that is happening now, because of a belief about what might happen in the future; it is unlike the previous point in that very good evidence can be adduced in support of this belief about the future. I will not go into the evidence here. I accept that the earth cannot support indefinitely a population rising at the present rate. This certainly poses a problem for anyone who thinks it important to prevent famine. Again, however, one could accept the argument without drawing the conclusion that it absolves one from any obligation to do anything to prevent famine. The conclusion that should be drawn is that the best means of preventing famine, in the long run, is population control. It would then follow from the position reached earlier that one ought to be doing all one can to promote population control (unless one held that all forms of population control were wrong in themselves, or would have significantly bad consequences). Since there are organizations working specifically for population control, one would then support them rather than more orthodox methods of preventing famine.

A third point raised by the conclusion reached earlier relates to the question of just how much we all ought to be giving away. One possibility, which has already been mentioned, is that we ought to give until we reach the level of marginal utility—that is, the level at which, by giving more, I would cause as much suffering to myself or my dependents as I would relieve by my gift. This would mean, of course, that one would reduce

oneself to very nearly the material circumstances of a Bengali refugee. It will be recalled that earlier I put forward both a strong and a moderate version of the principle of preventing bad occurrences. The strong version, which required us to prevent bad things from happening unless in doing so we would be sacrificing something of comparable moral significance, does seem to require reducing ourselves to the level of marginal utility. I should also say that the strong version seems to me to be the correct one. I proposed the more moderate version—that we should prevent bad occurrences unless, to do so, we had to sacrifice something morally significant—only in order to show that even on this surely undeniable principle a great change in our way of life is required. On the more moderate principle, it may not follow that we ought to reduce ourselves to the level of marginal utility, for one might hold that to reduce oneself and one's family to this level is to cause something significantly bad to happen. Whether this is so I shall not discuss, since, as I have said, I can see no good reason for holding the moderate version of the principle rather than the strong version. Even if we accepted the principle only in its moderate form, however, it should be clear that we would have to give away enough to ensure that the consumer society, dependent as it is on people spending on trivia rather than giving to famine relief, would slow down and perhaps disappear entirely. There are several reasons why this would be desirable in itself. The value and necessity of economic growth are now being questioned not only by conservationists, but by economists as well.[5] There is no doubt, too, that the consumer society has had a distorting effect on the goals and purposes of its members. Yet looking at the matter purely from the point of view of overseas aid, there must be a limit to the extent to which we should deliberately slow down our economy; for it might be the case that if we gave away, say, forty percent of our Gross National Product, we would slow down the economy so much that in absolute terms we would be giving less than if we gave twenty-five percent of the much larger GNP that we would have if we limited our contribution to this smaller percentage.

I mention this only as an indication of the sort of factor that one would have to take into account in working out an ideal. Since Western societies generally consider one percent of the GNP an acceptable level for overseas aid, the matter is entirely academic. Nor does it affect the question of how much an individual should give in a society in which very few are giving substantial amounts.

It is sometimes said, though less often now than it used to be, that philosophers have no special role to play in public affairs, since most public issues depend primarily on an assessment of facts. On questions of fact, it is said, philosophers as such have no special expertise, and so it has been possible to engage in philosophy without committing oneself to any position on major public issues. No doubt there are some issues of social policy and foreign policy about which it can truly be said that a really expert assessment of the facts is required before taking sides or acting, but the issue of famine is surely not one of these. The facts about the existence of suffering are beyond dispute. Nor, I think, is it disputed that we can do something about it, either through orthodox methods of famine relief or through population control or both. This is therefore an issue on which philosophers are competent to take a position. The issue is one which faces everyone who has more money than he needs to support himself and his dependents, or who is in a position to take some sort of political action. These categories must include practically every teacher and student of philosophy in the universities of the Western world. If philosophy is to deal with matters that are relevant to both teachers and students, this is an issue that philosophers should discuss.

Discussion, though, is not enough. What is the point of relating philosophy to public (and personal) affairs if we do not take our conclusions seriously? In this instance, taking our conclusion seriously means acting upon it. The philosopher will not find it any easier than anyone else to alter his attitudes and way of life to the extent that, if I am right, is involved in doing everything that we ought to be doing. At the very least, though, one can make a start. The philosopher who does so will have to sacrifice some of the benefits of the consumer society, but he can find compensation in the satisfaction of a way of life in which theory and practice, if not yet in harmony, are at least coming together.

NOTES

1. There was also a third possibility: that India would go to war to enable the refugees to return to their lands. Since I wrote this paper, India has taken this way out. The situation is no longer that described above, but this does not affect my argument, as the next paragraph indicates.

2. In view of the special sense philosophers often give to the term, I should say that I use "obligation" simply as the abstract noun derived from "ought," so that "I have an obligation to" means no more, and no less, than "I ought to." This usage is in accordance with the definition of "ought" given by the *Shorter Oxford English Dictionary:* "the general verb to express duty or obligation." I do not think any issue of substance hangs on the way the term is used; sentences in which I use "obligation" could all be rewritten, although somewhat clumsily, as sentences in which a clause containing "ought" replaces the term "obligation."

3. J. O. Urmson, "Saints and Heroes," in *Essays in Moral Philosophy,* ed. Abraham I. Melden (Seattle and London, 1958), p. 214 (included in this anthology, pp. 541–548). For a related but significantly different view see also Henry Sidgwick, *The Methods of Ethics,* 7th edn. (London, 1907), pp. 220–221, 492–493.

4. *Summa Theologica,* II-II, Question 66, Article 7, in *Aquinas, Selected Political Writings,* ed. A. P. d'Entreves, trans. J. G. Dawson (Oxford, 1948), p. 171.

5. See, for instance, John Kenneth Galbraith, *The New Industrial State* (Boston, 1967); and E. J. Mishan, *The Costs of Economic Growth* (London, 1967).

Kantian Approaches to Some Famine Problems

ONORA O'NEILL

Onora O'Neill is Principal of Newnham College, Cambridge. Her works include *Acting on Principle* and *Faces of Hunger*.

A SIMPLIFIED ACCOUNT OF KANT'S ETHICS

Kant's moral theory has acquired the reputation of being forbiddingly difficult to understand and, once understood, excessively demanding in its requirements. I don't believe that this reputation has been wholly earned, and I am going to try to undermine it. I shall try to reduce some of the difficulties, and try to show the implications of a Kantian moral theory for action toward those who do or may suffer famine. Finally, I shall compare Kantian and utilitarian approaches and assess their strengths and weaknesses.

The main method by which I propose to avoid some of the difficulties of Kant's moral theory is by explaining only one part of the theory. This does not seem to me to be an irresponsible approach in this case. One of the things that makes Kant's moral theory hard to understand is that he gives a number of different versions of the principle that he calls the Supreme Principle of Morality, and these different versions don't look at all like one another. They also don't look at all like the utilitarians' Greatest Happiness Principle. But the Kantian principle is supposed to play a similar role in arguments about what to do.

Kant calls his Supreme Principle the *Categorical Imperative;* its various versions also have sonorous names. One is called the Formula of Universal Law; another is the Formula of the Kingdom of Ends. The one on which I shall concentrate is known as the *Formula of the End in Itself.* To understand why Kant thinks that these picturesquely named principles are equivalent to one another takes quite a lot of close and detailed analysis of Kant's philosophy. I shall avoid this and concentrate on showing the implications of this version of the Categorical Imperative.

THE FORMULA OF THE END IN ITSELF

Kant states the Formula of the End in Itself as follows:

> Act in such a way that you always treat humanity, whether in your own person or in the person of any other, never simply as a means but always at the same time as an end.

To understand this we need to know what it is to treat a person as a means or as an end. According to Kant, each of our acts reflects one or more *maxims.* The maxim of the act is the principle on which one sees oneself as acting. A maxim expresses a person's policy, or if he or she has no settled policy, the principle underlying the particular intention or decision on which he or she acts. Thus, a person who decides "This year I'll give 10 percent of my income to famine relief" has as a maxim the principle of tithing his or her income for famine relief. In practice, the difference between intentions and maxims is of little importance, for given any intention, we can formulate the corresponding maxim by deleting references to particular times, places, and persons. In what follows I shall take the terms "maxim" and "intention" as equivalent.

Whenever we act intentionally, we have at least one maxim and can, if we reflect, state what it is. (There is of course room for self-deception here—"I'm only keeping the wolf from the door" we may claim as we wolf down enough to keep ourselves overweight, or, more to the point, enough to feed someone else who hasn't enough food.)

When we want to work out whether an act we propose to do is right or wrong, according to Kant, we should look at our maxims and not at how much misery or happiness the act is likely to produce, and whether it does better at increasing happiness than other available acts. We just have to check that the act we have in mind will not use anyone as a mere means, and, if possible, that it will treat other persons as ends in themselves.

USING PERSONS AS MERE MEANS

To use someone as a *mere means* is to involve them in a scheme of action *to which they could not in principle consent*. Kant does not say that there is anything wrong about using someone as a means. Evidently we have to do so in any cooperative scheme of action. If I cash a check I use the teller as a means, without whom I could not lay my hands on the cash; the teller in turn uses me as a means to earn his or her living. But in this case, each party consents to her or his part in the transaction. Kant would say that though they use one another as means, they do not use one another as *mere* means. Each person assumes that the other has maxims of his or her own and is not just a thing or a prop to be manipulated.

But there are other situations where one person uses another in a way to which the other could not in principle consent. For example, one person may make a promise to another with every intention of breaking it. If the promise is accepted, then the person to whom it was given must be ignorant of what the promisor's intention (maxim) really is. If one knew that the promisor did not intend to do what he or she was promising, one would, after all, not accept or rely on the promise. It would be as though there had been no promise made. Successful false promising depends on deceiving the person to whom the promise is made about what one's real maxim is. And since

the person who is deceived doesn't know that real maxim, he or she can't in principle consent to his or her part in the proposed scheme of action. The person who is deceived is, as it were, a prop or a tool—a mere means—in the false promisor's scheme. A person who promises falsely treats the acceptor of the promise as a prop or a thing and not as a person. In Kant's view, it is this that makes false promising wrong.

One standard way of using others as mere means is by deceiving them. By getting someone involved in a business scheme or a criminal activity on false pretenses, or by giving a misleading account of what one is about, or by making a false promise or a fraudulent contract, one involves another in something to which he or she in principle cannot consent, since the scheme requires that he or she doesn't know what is going on. Another standard way of using others as mere means is by coercing them. If a rich or powerful person threatens a debtor with bankruptcy unless he or she joins in some scheme, then the creditor's intention is to coerce; and the debtor, if coerced, cannot consent to his or her part in the creditor's scheme. To make the example more specific: If a moneylender in an Indian village threatens not to renew a vital loan unless he is given the debtor's land, then he uses the debtor as a mere means. He coerces the debtor, who cannot truly consent to this "offer he can't refuse." (Of course the outward form of such transactions may look like ordinary commercial dealings, but we know very well that some offers and demands couched in that form are coercive.)

In Kant's view, acts that are done on maxims that require deception or coercion of others, and so cannot have the consent of those others (for consent precludes both deception and coercion), are wrong. When we act on such maxims, we treat others as mere means, as things rather than as ends in themselves. If we act on such maxims, our acts are not only wrong but unjust; such acts wrong the particular others who are deceived or coerced.

TREATING PERSONS AS ENDS IN THEMSELVES

Duties of justice are, in Kant's view (as in many others'), the most important of our duties. When we fail in these duties, we have used some other or others as mere means. But there are also cases where, though we do not use others as mere means, still we fail to use them as ends in themselves in the fullest possible way. To treat someone as an end in him or herself requires in the first place that one not use him or her as mere means, that one respect each as a rational person with his or her own maxims. But beyond that, one may also seek to foster others' plans and maxims by sharing some of their ends. To act beneficently is to seek others' happiness, therefore to intend to achieve some of the things that those others aim at with their maxims. If I want to make others happy, I will adopt maxims that not merely do not manipulate them but that foster some of their plans and activities. Beneficent acts try to achieve what others want. However, we cannot seek everything that others want; their wants are too numerous and diverse, and, of course, sometimes incompatible. It follows that beneficence has to be selective.

There is then quite a sharp distinction between the requirements of justice and of beneficence in Kantian ethics. Justice requires that we act on *no* maxims that use others as mere means. Beneficence requires that we act on *some* maxims that foster others' ends, though it is a matter for judgment and discretion which of their ends we foster. Some maxims no doubt ought not to be fostered because it would be unjust to do so. Kantians are not committed to working interminably through a list of happiness-producing and misery-reducing acts; but there are some acts whose obligatoriness utilitarians may need to debate as they try to compare total outcomes of different choices, to which Kantians are stringently bound. Kantians will claim that they have done nothing wrong if none of their acts is unjust, and that their duty is complete if in addition their life plans have in the circumstances been reasonably beneficent.

In making sure that they meet all the demands of justice, Kantians do not try to compare all available acts and see which has the best effects. They consider only the proposals for action that occur to them and check that these proposals use no other as mere means. If they do not, the act is permissible; if omitting the act would use another as mere means, the act is obligatory. Kant's theory has less scope than utilitarianism. Kantians do

not claim to discover whether acts whose maxims they don't know fully are just. They may be reluctant to judge others' acts or policies that cannot be regarded as the maxim of any person or institution. They cannot rank acts in order of merit. Yet, the theory offers more precision than utilitarianism when data are scarce. One can usually tell whether one's act would use others as mere means, even when its impact on human happiness is thoroughly obscure.

KANTIAN DELIBERATIONS ON FAMINE PROBLEMS

The theory I have just sketched may seem to have little to say about famine problems. For it is a theory that forbids us to use others as mere means but does not require us to direct our benevolence first to those who suffer most. A conscientious Kantian, it seems, has only to avoid being unjust to those who suffer famine and can then be beneficent to those nearer home. He or she would not be obliged to help the starving, even if no others were equally distressed.

Kant's moral theory does make less massive demands on moral agents than utilitarian moral theory. On the other hand, it is somewhat clearer just what the more stringent demands are, and they are not negligible. We have here a contrast between a theory that makes massive but often indeterminate demands and a theory that makes fewer but less unambiguous demands and leaves other questions, in particular the allocation of beneficence, unresolved. We have also a contrast between a theory whose scope is comprehensive and one that is applicable only to persons acting intentionally and to those institutions that adopt policies, and so maxims. Kantian ethics is silent about the moral status of unintentional action; utilitarians seek to assess all consequences regardless of the intentions that led to them.

KANTIAN DUTIES OF JUSTICE IN TIMES OF FAMINE

In famine situations, Kantian moral theory requires unambiguously that we do no injustice. We should not act on any maxim that uses another as mere means, so we should neither deceive nor coerce others. Such a requirement can become quite exacting when the means of life are scarce, when persons can more easily be coerced, and when the advantage of gaining more than what is justly due to one is great. I shall give a list of acts that on Kantian principles it would be unjust to do, but that one might be strongly tempted to do in famine conditions.

I will begin with a list of acts that one might be tempted to do as a member of a famine-stricken population. First, where there is a rationing scheme, one ought not to cheat and seek to get more than one's share—any scheme of cheating will use someone as mere means. Nor may one take advantage of others' desperation to profiteer or divert goods onto the black market or to accumulate a fortune out of others' misfortunes. Transactions that are outwardly sales and purchases can be coercive when one party is desperate. All the forms of corruption that deceive or put pressure on others are also wrong: hoarding unallocated food, diverting relief supplies for private use, corruptly using one's influence to others' disadvantage. Such requirements are far from trivial and frequently violated in hard times. In severe famines, refraining from coercing and deceiving may risk one's own life and require the greatest courage.

Second, justice requires that in famine situations one still try to fulfill one's duties to particular others. For example, even in times of famine, a person has duties to try to provide for dependents. These duties may, tragically, be unfulfillable. If they are, Kantian ethical theory would not judge wrong the acts of a person who had done her or his best. There have no doubt been times in human history where there was nothing to be done except abandon the weak and old or to leave children to fend for themselves as best they might. But providing the supporter of dependents acts on maxims of attempting to meet their claims, he or she uses no others as mere means to his or her own survival and is not unjust. A conscientious attempt to meet the particular obligations one has undertaken may also require of one many further maxims of self-restraint and of endeavor—for example, it may require a conscientious attempt to avoid having (further) children; it may require contributing one's time and effort to programs of economic development. Where there is no other means to fulfill particular obligations, Kantian principles may require a generation of sacrifice. They will not, however, require one to seek to maximize the happiness of later generations but only to establish the modest security and prosperity needed for meeting present obligations.

The obligations of those who live with or near famine are undoubtedly stringent and exacting; for those who live further off it is rather harder to see what a Kantian moral theory demands. Might it not, for example, be permissible to do nothing at all about those suffering famine? Might one not ensure that one does nothing unjust to the victims of famine by adopting no maxims whatsoever that mention them? To do so would, at the least, require one to refrain from certain deceptive and coercive practices frequently employed during the European exploration and economic penetration of the now underdeveloped world and still not unknown. For example, it would be unjust to "purchase" valuable lands and resources from persons who don't understand commercial transactions or exclusive property rights or mineral rights, so do not understand that their acceptance of trinkets destroys their traditional economic pattern and way of life. The old adage "trade follows the flag" reminds us to how great an extent the economic pentration of the less-developed countries involved elements of coercion and deception, so was on Kantian principles unjust (regardless of whether or not the net effect has benefited the citizens of those countries).

Few persons in the developed world today find themselves faced with the possibility of adopting on a grand scale maxims of deceiving or coercing persons living in poverty. But at least some people find that their jobs require them to make decisions about investment and aid policies that enormously affect the lives of those nearest to famine. What does a commitment to Kantian moral theory demand of such persons?

It has become common in writings in ethics and social policy to distinguish between one's *personal responsibilities* and one's *role responsibilities*. So a person may say, "As an individual I sympathize, but in my official capacity I can do nothing"; or we may excuse persons' acts of coercion because they are acting in some particular capacity—e.g., as a soldier or a jailer. On the other hand, this distinction isn't made or accepted by everyone. At the Nuremberg trials of war criminals, the defense "I was only doing my job" was disallowed, at least for those whose command position meant that they had some discretion in what they did. Kantians generally would play down any distinction between a person's own responsibilities and his or her role responsibilities. They would not deny that in any capacity one is accountable for certain things for which as a private person one is not accountable. For example, the treasurer of an organization is accountable to the board and has to present periodic reports and to keep specified records. But if she fails to do one of these things for which she is held accountable she will be held responsible for that failure—it will be imputable to her as an individual. When we take on positions, we *add* to our responsibilities those that the job requires; but we do not lose those that are already required of us. Our social role or job gives us, on Kant's view, no license to use others as mere means; even business executives and aid officials and social revolutionaries will act unjustly, so wrongly, if they deceive or coerce—however benevolent their motives.

If persons are responsible for all their acts, it follows that it would be unjust for aid officials to coerce persons into accepting sterilization, wrong for them to use coercive power to achieve political advantages (such as military bases) or commercial advantages (such as trade agreements that will harm the other country). It would be wrong for the executives of large corporations to extort too high a price for continued operation employment and normal trading. Where a less-developed country is pushed to exempt a multinational corporation from tax laws, or to construct out of its meager tax revenues the infrastructure of roads, harbors, or airports (not to mention executive mansions) that the corporation—but perhaps not the country—needs, then one suspects that some coercion has been involved.

The problem with such judgments—and it is an immense problem—is that it is hard to identify coercion and deception in complicated institutional settings. It is not hard to understand what is coercive about one person threatening another with serious injury if he won't comply with the first person's suggestion. But it is not at all easy to tell where the outward forms of political and commercial negotiation—which often involve an element of threat—have become coercive. I can't here explore this fascinating question. But I think it is at least fairly clear that the preservation of the outward forms of negotiation, bargaining, and voluntary consent do *not* demonstrate that there is no coercion, especially when one party is vastly more powerful or the other in dire need. Just as our judiciary has a long tradition of voiding contracts and agreements on grounds of duress or incompetence of one of the parties, so one can imagine a tribunal of an analogous sort rejecting at least some treaties and agreements as coercive, despite the fact that they were negotiated between "sovereign" powers or their representatives. In particular, where such agreements were negotiated with some of the cruder deceptions and coercion of the early days of European economic expansion or the subtler coercions and deceptions of contemporary superpowers, it seems doubtful that the justice of the agreement could be sustained.

Justice, of course, is not everything, even for Kantians. But its demands are ones that they can reasonably strive to fulfill. They may have some uncertain moments—for example, does advocating cheap raw materials mean advocating an international trade system in which the less developed will continue to suffer the pressures of the developed world—or is it a benevolent policy that will maximize world trade and benefit all parties, while doing no one an injustice? But for Kantians, the important moral choices are above all those in which one acts directly, not those in which one decides which patterns of actions to encourage in others or in those institutions that one can influence. And such moral decisions include decisions about the benevolent acts that one will or will not do.

KANTIAN DUTIES OF BENEFICENCE IN TIMES OF FAMINE

The grounds of duties of beneficence are that such acts not merely don't use others as mere means but are acts that develop or promote others' ends and that, in particular, foster others' capacities to pursue ends, to be autonomous beings.

Clearly there are many opportunities for beneficence. But one area in which the *primary* task of developing others' capacity to pursue their own ends is particularly needed is in the parts of the world where extreme poverty and hunger leave people unable to pursue *any* of their other ends. Beneficence directed at putting people in a position to pursue whatever ends they may have has, for Kant, a stronger claim on us than beneficence directed at sharing ends with those who are already in a position to pursue varieties of ends. It would be nice if I bought a tennis racquet to play with my friend who is tennis mad and never has enough partners; but it is more important to make people able to plan their own lives to a minimal extent. It is nice to walk a second mile with someone who requests one's company; better to share a cloak with someone who may otherwise be too cold to make any journey. Though these suggestions are not a detailed set of instructions for the allocation of beneficence by Kantians, they show that relief of famine must stand very high among duties of beneficence.

THE LIMITS OF KANTIAN ETHICS: INTENTIONS AND RESULTS

Kantian ethics differs from utilitarian ethics both in its scope and in the precision with which it guides action. Every action, whether of a person or of an agency, can be assessed by utilitarian methods, provided only that information is available about all the consequences of the act. The theory has unlimited scope, but, owing to a lack of data, often lacks precision. Kantian ethics has a more restricted scope. Since it assesses actions by looking at the maxims of agents, it can only assess intentional acts. This means that it is most at home in assessing individuals' acts; but it can be extended to assess acts of agencies that (like corporations and governments and student unions) have decision-making procedures. It can do nothing to assess patterns of action that reflect no intention or policy, hence it cannot assess the acts of groups lacking decision-making procedures, such as the student movement, the women's movement, or the consumer movement.

It may seem a great limitation of Kantian ethics that it concentrates on intentions to the neglect of results. It might seem that all conscientious Kantians have to do is to make sure that they never intend to use others as mere means, and that they sometimes intend to foster others' ends. And, as we all know, good intentions sometimes lead to bad results, and correspondingly, bad intentions sometimes do no harm, or even produce good. If Hardin is right, the good intentions of those who feed the starving lead to dreadful results in the long run. If some traditional arguments in favor of capitalism are right, the greed and selfishness of the profit motive have produced unparalleled prosperity for many.

But such discrepancies between intentions and results are the exception and not the rule. For we cannot just *claim* that our intentions are good and do what we will. Our intentions reflect what we expect the immediate results of our action to be. Nobody credits the "intentions" of a couple who practice neither celibacy nor contraception but still insist "we never meant to have (more) children." Conception is likely (and known to be likely) in such cases. Where people's expressed intentions ignore the normal and predictable results of what they do, we infer that (if they are not amazingly ignorant) their words do not express their true intentions. The Formula of the End in Itself applies to the intentions on which one acts—not to some prettified version that one may avow. Provided this intention—the agent's real intention—uses no other as mere means, he or she does nothing unjust. If some of his or her intentions foster others' ends, then he or she is sometimes beneficent. It is therefore possible for people to test their proposals by Kantian arguments even when they lack the comprehensive causal knowledge that utilitarianism requires. Conscientious Kantians can work out whether they will be doing wrong by some act even though they know that their foresight is limited and that they may cause some harm or fail to cause some benefit. But they will not cause harms that they can foresee without this being reflected in their intentions.

The Survival Lottery

JOHN HARRIS

John Harris works mainly in ethics and political philosophy. He teaches at the University of Manchester.

Let us suppose that organ transplant procedures have been perfected; in such circumstances if two dying patients could be saved by organ transplants then, if surgeons have the requisite organs in stock and no other needy patients, but nevertheless allow their patients to die, we would be inclined to say, and be justified in saying, that the patients died because the doctors refused to save them. But if there are no spare organs in stock and none otherwise available, the doctors have no choice, they cannot save their patients and so must let them die. In this case we would be disinclined to say that the doctors are in any sense the cause of their patients' deaths. But let us further suppose that the two dying patients, Y and Z, are not happy about being left to die. They might argue that it is not strictly true that there are no organs which could be used to save them. Y needs a new heart and Z new lungs. They point out that if just one healthy person were to be killed his organs could be removed and both of them be saved. We and the doctors would probably be alike in thinking that such a step, while technically possible, would be out of the question. We would not say that the doctors were killing their patients if they refused to prey upon the healthy to save the sick. And because this sort of surgical Robin Hoodery is out of the question we can tell Y and Z that they cannot be saved, and that when they die they will have died of natural causes and not of the neglect of their doctors. Y and Z do not however agree, they insist that if the doctors fail to kill a healthy man and use his organs to save them, then the doctors will be responsible for their deaths.

Many philosophers have for various reasons believed that we must not kill even if by doing so we could save life. They believe that there is a moral difference between killing and letting die. On this view, to kill A so that Y and Z might live is ruled out because we have a strict obligation not to kill but a duty of some lesser kind to save life. A. H. Clough's dictum "Thou shalt not kill but need'st not strive officiously to keep alive" expresses bluntly this point of view. The dying Y and Z may be excused for not being much impressed by Clough's dictum. They agree that it is wrong to kill the innocent and are prepared to agree to an absolute prohibition against so doing. They do not agree, however, that A is more innocent than they are. Y and Z might go on to point out that the currently acknowledged right of the innocent not to be killed, even where their deaths might give life to others, is just a decision to prefer the lives of the fortunate to those of the unfortunate. A is innocent in the sense that he has done nothing to deserve death, but Y and Z are also innocent in this sense. Why should they be the ones to die simply because

From John Harris, "The Survival Lottery," *Philosophy,* 1975, pp. 81–87. Reprinted by permission of Cambridge University Press.

they are so unlucky as to have diseased organs? Why, they might argue, should their living or dying be left to chance when in so many other areas of human life we believe that we have an obligation to ensure the survival of the maximum number of lives possible?

Y and Z argue that if a doctor refuses to treat a patient, with the result that the patient dies, he has killed that patient as sure as shooting, and that, in exactly the same way, if the doctors refuse Y and Z the transplants that they need, then their refusal will kill Y and Z, again as sure as shooting. The doctors, and indeed the society which supports their inaction, cannot defend themselves by arguing that they are neither expected, nor required by law or convention, to kill so that lives may be saved (indeed, quite the reverse) since this is just an appeal to custom or authority. A man who does his own moral thinking must decide whether, in these circumstances, he ought to save two lives at the cost of one, or one life at the cost of two. The fact that so called "third parties" have never before been brought into such calculations, have never before been thought of as being involved, is not an argument against their now becoming so. There are of course, good arguments against allowing doctors simply to haul passers-by off the streets whenever they have a couple of patients in need of new organs. And the harmful side-effects of such a practice in terms of terror and distress to the victims, the witnesses and society generally, would give us further reasons for dismissing the idea. Y and Z realize this and have a proposal, which they will shortly produce, which would largely meet objections to placing such power in the hands of doctors and eliminate at least some of the harmful side-effects.

In the unlikely event of their feeling obliged to reply to the reproaches of Y and Z, the doctors might offer the following argument: they might maintain that a man is only responsible for the death of someone whose life he might have saved, if, in all the circumstances of the case, he ought to have saved the man by the means available. This is why a doctor might be a murderer if he simply refused or neglected to treat a patient who would die without treatment, but not if he could only save the patient by doing something

he ought in no circumstances to do—kill the innocent. Y and Z readily agree that a man ought not to do what he ought not to do, but they point out that if the doctors, and for that matter society at large, ought on balance to kill one man if two can thereby be saved, then failure to do so will involve responsibility for the consequent deaths. The fact that Y's and Z's proposal involves killing the innocent cannot be a reason for refusing to consider their proposal, for this would just be a refusal to face the question at issue and so avoid having to make a decision as to what ought to be done in circumstances like these. It is Y's and Z's claim that failure to adopt their plan will also involve killing the innocent, rather more of the innocent than the proposed alternative.

To back up this last point, to remove the arbitrariness of permitting doctors to select their donors from among the chance passers-by outside hospitals, and the tremendous power this would place in doctors' hands, to mitigate worries about side-effects and lastly to appease those who wonder why poor old A should be singled out for sacrifice, Y and Z put forward the following scheme: they propose that everyone be given a sort of lottery number. Whenever doctors have two or more dying patients who could be saved by transplants, and no suitable organs have come to hand through "natural" deaths, they can ask a central computer to supply a suitable donor. The computer will then pick the number of a suitable donor at random and he will be killed so that the lives of two or more others may be saved. No doubt if the scheme were ever to be implemented a suitable euphemism for "killed" would be employed. Perhaps we would begin to talk about citizens being called upon to "give life" to others. With the refinement of transplant procedures such a scheme could offer the chance of saving large numbers of lives that are now lost. Indeed, even taking into account the loss of the lives of donors, the numbers of untimely deaths each year might be dramatically reduced, so much so that everyone's chance of living to a ripe old age might be increased. If this were to be the consequence of the adoption of such a scheme, and it might well be, it could not be dismissed lightly. It might of course be objected that it is likely that more old people will need transplants to prolong their lives than will the young, and so the scheme would inevitably lead to a society dominated by the old. But if such a society is thought objectionable, there is no reason to suppose that a program could not be designed for the computer that would ensure the maintenance of whatever is considered to be an optimum age distribution throughout the population.

Suppose that inter-planetary travel revealed a world of people like ourselves, but who organized their society according to this scheme. No one was considered to have an absolute right to life or freedom from interference, but everything was always done to ensure that as many people as possible would enjoy long and happy lives. In such a world a man who attempted to escape when his number was up or who resisted on the grounds that no one had a right to take his life, might well be regarded as a murderer. We might or might not prefer to live in such a world, but the morality of its inhabitants would surely be one that we could respect. It would not be obviously more barbaric or cruel or immoral than our own.

Y and Z are willing to concede one exception to the universal application of their scheme. They realize that it would be unfair to allow people who have brought their misfortune on themselves to benefit from the lottery. There would clearly be something unjust about killing the abstemious B so that W (whose heavy smoking has given him lung cancer) and X (whose drinking has destroyed his liver) should be preserved to over-indulge again.

What objections could be made to the lottery scheme? A first straw to clutch at would be the desire for security. Under such a scheme we would never know when we would hear *them* knocking at the door. Every post might bring a sentence of death, every sound in the night might be the sound of boots on the stairs. But, as we have seen, the chances of actually being called upon to make the ultimate sacrifice might be slimmer than is the present risk of being killed on the roads, and most of us do not lie trembling a-bed, appalled at the prospect of being dispatched on the morrow. The truth is that lives might well be more secure under such a scheme.

If we respect individuality and see every human being as unique in his own way, we might want to reject a society in which it appeared that individuals were seen merely as interchangeable units in a structure, the value of which lies in its having as many healthy units as possible. But of course Y and Z would want to know why A's individuality was more worthy of respect than theirs.

Another plausible objection is the natural reluctance to play God with men's lives, the feeling that it is wrong to make any attempt to re-allot the life opportunities that fate has determined, that the deaths of Y and Z would be "natural," whereas the death of anyone killed to save them would have been perpetrated by men. But if we are able to change things, then to elect not to do so is also to determine what will happen in the world.

Neither does the alleged moral differences between killing and letting die afford a respectable way of rejecting the claims of Y and Z. For if we really want to counter proponents of the lottery, if we really want to answer Y and Z and not just put them off, we cannot do so by saying that the lottery involves killing and object to it for that reason, because to do so would, as we have seen, just beg the question as to whether the failure to save as many people as possible might not also amount to killing.

To opt for the society which Y and Z propose would be then to adopt a society in which saintliness would be mandatory. Each of us would have to recognize a binding obligation to give up his own life for others when called upon to do so. In such a society anyone who reneged upon this duty would be a murderer. The most promising objection to such a society, and indeed to any principle which required us to kill A in order to save Y and Z, is, I suspect, that we are committed to the right of self-defence. If I can kill A to save Y and Z then he can kill me to save P and Q, and it is only if I am prepared to agree to this that I will opt for the lottery or be prepared to agree to a man's being killed if doing so would save the lives of more than one other man. Of course there is something paradoxical about basing objections to the lottery scheme on the right of self-defence since, *ex hyposthesi,* each person would have a better chance of living to a ripe old age if the lottery scheme were to be implemented. None the less, the feeling that no man should be required to lay down his life for others makes many people shy away from such a scheme, even though it might be rational to accept it on prudential grounds, and perhaps even mandatory on utilitarian grounds. Again, Y and Z would reply that the right of self-defence must extend to them as much as to anyone else; and while it is true that they can only live if another man is killed, they would claim that it is also true that if they are left to die, then someone who lives on does so over their dead bodies.

It might be argued that the institution of the survival lottery has not gone far to mitigate the harmful side-effects in terms of terror and distress to victims, witnesses and society generally, that would be occasioned by doctors simply snatching passers-by off the streets and disorganizing them for the benefit of the unfortunate. Donors would after all still have to be procured, and this process, however it was carried out, would still be likely to prove distressing to all concerned. The lottery scheme would eliminate the arbitrariness of leaving the life and death decisions to the doctors, and remove the possibility of such terrible power falling into the hands of any individuals, but the terror and distress would remain. The effect of having to apprehend presumably unwilling victims would give us pause. Perhaps only a long period of education or propaganda could remove our abhorrence. What this abhorrence reveals about the rights and wrongs of the situation is however more difficult to assess. We might be inclined to say that only monsters could ignore the promptings of conscience so far as to operate the lottery scheme. But the promptings of conscience are not necessarily the most reliable guide. In the present case Y and Z would argue that such promptings are mere squeamishness, an over-nice self-indulgence that costs lives. Death, Y and Z would remind us, is a distressing experience whenever and to whomever it occurs, so the less it occurs the better. Fewer victims and witnesses will be distressed as part of the side-effects of the lottery scheme than would suffer as part of the side-effects of not instituting it.

Lastly, a more limited objection might be made, not to the idea of killing to save lives, but to the involvement of "third parties." Why, so the objection goes, should we not give X's heart to Y or Y's lungs to X, the same number of lives being thereby preserved and no one else's life set at risk? Y's and Z's reply to this objection differs from their previous line of argument. To amend their plan so that the involvement of so called "third parties" is ruled out would, Y and Z claim, violate their right to equal concern and respect with the rest of society. They argue that such a proposal would amount to treating the unfortunate who need new organs as a class within society whose lives are considered to be of less value than those of its more fortunate members. What possible justification could there be for singling out one group of people whom we would be justified in using as donors but not another? The idea in the mind of those who would propose such a step must be something like the following: since Y and Z cannot survive, since they are going to die in any event, there is no harm in putting their names into the lottery, for the chances of their dying cannot thereby be increased and will in fact almost certainly be reduced. But this is just to ignore everything that Y and Z have been saying. For if their lottery scheme is adopted they are not going to die anyway—their chances of dying are no greater and no less than those of any other participant in the lottery whose number may come up. This ground for confining selection of donors to the unfortunate therefore disappears. Any other ground must discriminate against Y and Z as members of a class whose lives are less worthy of respect than those of the rest of society.

It might more plausibly be argued that the dying who cannot themselves be saved by transplants, or by any other means at all, should be the priority selection group for the computer programme. But how far off must death be for a man to be classified as "dying"? Those so classified might argue that their last few days or weeks of life are as valuable to them (if not more valuable) than the possibly longer span remaining to others. The problem of narrowing down the class of possible donors without discriminating unfairly against some sub-class of society is, I suspect, insoluble.

Such is the case for the survival lottery. Utilitarians ought to be in favour of it, and absolutists cannot object to it on the ground that it involves killing the innocent, for it is Y's and Z's case that any alternative must also involve killing the innocent. If the absolutist wishes to maintain his objection he must point to some morally relevant difference between positive and negative killing. This challenge opens the door to a large topic with a whole library of literature, but Y and Z are dying and do not have time to explore it exhaustively. In their own case the most likely candidate for some feature which might make this moral difference is the malevolent intent of Y and Z themselves. An absolutist might well argue that while no one intends the deaths of Y and Z, no one necessarily wishes them dead, or aims at their demise for any reason, they do mean to kill A (or have him killed). But Y and Z can reply that the death of A is no part of their plan, they merely wish to use a couple of his organs, and if he cannot live without them...*tant pis!* None would be more delighted than Y and Z if artificial organs would do as well, and so render the lottery scheme otiose.

One form of absolutist argument perhaps remains. This involves taking an Orwellian stand on some principle of common decency. The argument would then be that even to enter into the sort of "macabre" calculations that Y and Z propose displays a blunted sensibility, a corrupted and vitiated mind. Forms of this argument have recently been advanced by Noam Chomsky (*American Power and the New Mandarins*) and Stuart Hampshire (*Morality and Pessimism*). The indefatigable Y and Z would of course deny that their calculations are in any sense "macabre," and would present them as the most humane course available in the circumstances. Moreover they would claim that the Orwellian stand on decency is the product of a closed mind, and not susceptible to rational argument. Any reasoned defence of such a principle must appeal to notions like respect for human life, as Hampshire's argument in fact does, and

these Y and Z could make conformable to their own position.

Can Y and Z be answered? Perhaps only by relying on moral intuition, on the insistence that we do feel there is something wrong with the survival lottery and our confidence that this feeling is prompted by some morally relevant difference between our bringing about the death of A and our bringing about the deaths of Y and Z. Whether we could retain this confidence in our intuitions if we were to be confronted by a society in which the survival lottery operated, was accepted by all, and was seen to save many lives that would otherwise have been lost, it would be interesting to know.

There would of course be great practical difficulties in the way of implementing the lottery. In so many cases it would be agonizingly difficult to decide whether or not a person had brought his misfortune on himself. There are numerous ways in which a person may contribute to his predicament, and the task of deciding how far, or how decisively, a person is himself responsible for his fate would be formidable. And in those cases where we can be confident that a person is innocent of responsibility for his predicament, can we acquire this confidence in time to save him? The lottery scheme would be a powerful weapon in the hands of someone willing and able to misuse it. Could we ever feel certain the lottery was safe from unscrupulous computer programmers? Perhaps we should be thankful that such practical difficulties make the survival lottery an unlikely consequence of the perfection of transplants. Or perhaps we should be appalled.

It may be that we would want to tell Y and Z that the difficulties and dangers of their scheme would be too great a price to pay for its benefits. It is as well to be clear, however, that there is also a high, perhaps an even higher, price to be paid for the rejection of the scheme. That price is the lives of Y and Z and many like them, and we delude ourselves if we suppose that the reason why we reject their plan is that we accept the sixth commandment.

Active and Passive Euthanasia

JAMES RACHELS

The distinction between active and passive euthanasia is thought to be crucial for medical ethics. The idea is that it is permissible, at least in some cases, to withhold treatment and allow a patient to die, but it is never permissible to take any direct action designed to kill the patient. This doctrine seems to be accepted by most doctors, and it is endorsed in a statement adopted by the House of Delegates of the American Medical Association on December 4, 1973:

> The intentional termination of the life of one human being by another—mercy killing—is contrary to that for which the medical profession stands and is contrary to the policy of the American Medical Association.
>
> The cessation of the employment of extraordinary means to prolong the life of the body when there is irrefutable evidence that biological death is imminent is the decision of the patient and/or his immediate family. The advice and judgment of the physician should be freely available to the patient and/or his immediate family.

However, a strong case can be made against this doctrine. In what follows, I will set out some of the relevant arguments, and urge doctors to reconsider their views on this matter.

To begin with a familiar type of situation, a patient who is dying of incurable cancer of the throat is in terrible pain, which can no longer be satisfactorily alleviated. He is certain to die within a few days, even if present treatment is continued, but he does not want to go on living for those days since the pain is unbearable. So he asks the doctor for an end to it, and his family joins in the request.

Suppose the doctor agrees to withhold treatment, as the conventional doctrine says he may. The justification for his doing so is that the patient is in terrible agony, and since he is going to die anyway, it would be wrong to prolong his suffering needlessly. But now notice this. If one simply withholds treatment, it may take the patient longer to die, and so he may suffer more than he would if more direct action were taken and a lethal injection given. This fact provides strong reason for thinking that, once the initial decision not to prolong his agony has been made, active euthanasia is actually preferable to passive euthanasia, rather than the reverse. To say otherwise is to endorse the option that leads to more suffering rather than less, and is contrary to the humanitarian impulse that prompts the decision not to prolong his life in the first place.

Part of my point is that the process of being "allowed to die" can be relatively slow and painful, whereas being given a lethal injection is relatively quick and painless. Let me give a different sort of example. In the United States about one in 600 babies is born with Down's syndrome. Most of these babies are otherwise healthy—that is, with only the usual pediatric care, they will proceed to an otherwise normal infancy. Some, however, are born with congenital defects such as intestinal obstructions that require operations if they are to live. Sometimes, the parents and the doctor will decide not to operate, and let the infant die. Anthony Shaw describes what happens then:

> ...When surgery is denied [the doctor] must try to keep the infant from suffering while natural forces sap the baby's life away. As a surgeon whose natural inclination is to use the scalpel to fight off death, standing by and watching a salvageable baby die is the most emotionally exhausting experience I know. It is easy at a conference, in a theoretical discussion, to decide that such infants should be allowed to die. It is

altogether different to stand by in the nursery and watch as dehydration and infection wither a tiny being over hours and days. This is a terrible ordeal for me and the hospital staff—much more so than for the parents who never set foot in the nursery.[1]

I can understand why some people are opposed to all euthanasia, and insist that such infants must be allowed to live. I think I can also understand why other people favor destroying these babies quickly and painlessly. But why should anyone favor letting "dehydration and infection wither a tiny being over hours and days"? The doctrine that says that a baby may be allowed to dehydrate and wither, but may not be given an injection that would end its life without suffering, seems to patently cruel as to require no further refutation. The strong language is not intended to offend, but only to put the point in the clearest possible way.

My second argument is that the conventional doctrine leads to decisions concerning life and death made on irrelevant grounds.

Consider again the case of the infants with Down's syndrome who need operations for congenital defects unrelated to the syndrome to live. Sometimes, there is no operation, and the baby dies, but when there is no such defect, the baby lives on. Now, an operation such as that to remove an intestinal obstruction is not prohibitively difficult. The reason why such operations are not performed in these cases is, clearly, that the child has Down's syndrome and the parents and doctor judge that because of that fact it is better for the child to die.

But notice that this situation is absurd, no matter what view one takes of the lives and potentials of such babies. If the life of such an infant is worth preserving, what does it matter if it needs a simple operation? Or, if one thinks it better that such a baby should not live on, what difference does it make that it happens to have an unobstructed intestinal tract? In either case, the matter of life and death is being decided on irrelevant grounds. It is the Down's syndrome, and not the intestines, that is the issue. The matter should be decided, if at all, on that basis, and not be allowed to depend on the essentially irrelevant question of whether the intestinal tract is blocked.

What makes this situation possible, of course, is the idea that when there is an intestinal blockage, one can "let the baby die," but when there is no such defect there is nothing that can be done, for one must not "kill" it. The fact that this idea leads to such results as deciding life or death on irrelevant grounds is another good reason why the doctrine should be rejected.

One reason why so many people think that there is an important moral difference between active and passive euthanasia is that they think killing someone is morally worse than letting someone die. But is it? Is killing, in itself, worse than letting die? To investigate this issue, two cases may be considered that are exactly alike except that one involves killing whereas the other involves letting someone die. Then, it can be asked whether this difference makes any difference to the moral assessments. It is important that the cases be exactly alike, except for this one difference, since otherwise one cannot be confident that it is this difference and not some other that accounts for any variation in the assessments of the two cases. So, let us consider this pair of cases:

In the first, Smith stands to gain a large inheritance if anything should happen to his six-year-old cousin. One evening while the child is taking his bath, Smith sneaks into the bathroom and drowns the child, and then arranges things so that it will look like an accident.

In the second, Jones also stands to gain if anything should happen to his six-year-old cousin. Like Smith, Jones sneaks in planning to drown the child in his bath. However, just as he enters the bathroom Jones sees the child slip and hit his head, and fall face down in the water. Jones is delighted; he stands by, ready to push the child's head back under if it is necessary, but it is not necessary. With only a little thrashing about the child drowns all by himself, "accidentally," as Jones watches and does nothing.

Now Smith killed the child, whereas Jones "merely" let the child die. That is the only difference between them. Did either man behave better, from a moral point of view? If the difference between killing and letting die were in itself a morally important matter, one should say that Jones's behavior was less reprehensible than Smith's. But does one really want to say that? I think not. In the first place, both men acted from the same motive, personal gain, and both had exactly the same end in view when they acted. It may be inferred from Smith's conduct that he is a bad man, although that judgment may be withdrawn or modified if certain further facts are learned about him—for example, that he is mentally deranged. But would not the very same thing be inferred about Jones from his conduct? And would not the same further considerations also be relevant to any modification of this judgment? Moreover, suppose Jones pleaded, in his own defense, "After all, I didn't do anything except just stand there and watch the child drown. I didn't kill him; I only let him die." Again, if letting die were in itself less bad than killing, this defense should have at least some weight. But it does not. Such a "defense" can only be regarded as a grotesque perversion of moral reasoning. Morally speaking, it is no defense at all.

Now, it may be pointed out, quite properly, that the cases of euthanasia with which doctors are concerned are not like this at all. They do not involve personal gain or the destruction of normally healthy children. Doctors are concerned only with cases in which the patient's life is of no further use to him, or in which the patient's life has become or will soon become a terrible burden. However, the point is the same in these cases: the bare difference between killing and letting die does not, in itself, make a moral difference. If a doctor lets a patient die, for humane reasons, he is in the same moral position as if he had given the patient a lethal injection for humane reasons. If his decision was wrong—if, for example, the patient's illness was in fact curable—the decision would be equally regrettable no matter which method was used to carry it out. And if the doctor's decision was the right one, the method used is not in itself important.

The AMA policy statement isolates the crucial issue very well; the crucial issue is "the intentional termination of the life of one human being by another." But after identifying this issue, and forbidding "mercy killing," the statement goes on to deny that the cessation of treatment is the intentional termination of a life. This is where the mistake comes in, for what is the cessation of treatment, in these circumstances, if it is not "the intentional termination of the life of one human being by another?" Of course, it is exactly that, and if it were not, there would be no point to it.

Many people will find this judgment hard to accept. One reason, I think, is that it is very easy to conflate the question of whether killing is, in itself, worse than letting die, with the very different question of whether most actual cases of killing are more reprehensible than most actual cases of letting die. Most actual cases of killing are clearly terrible (think, for example, of all the murders reported in the newspapers), and one hears of such cases every day. On the other hand, one hardly ever hears of a case of letting die, except for the actions of doctors who are motivated by humanitarian reasons. So one learns to think of killing in a much worse light than of letting die. But this does not mean that there is something about killing that makes it in itself worse than letting die, for it is not the bare difference between killing and letting die that makes the difference in these cases. Rather, the other factors—the murderer's motive of personal gain, for example, contrasted with the doctor's humanitarian motivation—account for different reactions to the different cases.

I have argued that killing is not in itself any worse than letting die; if my contention is right, it follows that active euthanasia is not any worse than passive euthanasia. What arguments can be given on the other side? The most common, I believe, is the following:

"The important difference between active and passive euthanasia is that, in passive euthanasia, the doctor does not do anything to bring about the patient's death. The doctor does nothing, and the patient dies of whatever ills already afflict him. In active euthanasia, however, the doctor does something to bring about the patient's death: he kills him. The doctor who gives the patient with cancer a lethal injection has himself caused his patient's death; whereas if he merely ceases treatment, the cancer is the cause of the death."

A number of points need to be made here. The first is that it is not exactly correct to say that in passive euthanasia the doctor does nothing, for he does do one thing that is very important: he lets the patient die. "Letting someone die" is certainly different, in some respects, from other types of action—mainly in that it is a kind of action that one may perform by way of not performing certain other actions. For example, one may let a patient die by way of not giving medication, just as one may insult someone by way of not shaking his hand. But for any purpose of moral assessment, it is a type of action nonetheless. The decision to let a patient die is subject to moral appraisal in the same way that a decision to kill him would be subject to moral appraisal: it may be assessed as wise or unwise, compassionate or sadistic, right or wrong. If a doctor deliberately let a patient die who was suffering from a routinely curable illness, the doctor would certainly be to blame for what he had done, just as he would be to blame if he had needlessly killed the patient. Charges against him would then be appropriate. If so, it would be no defense at all for him to insist that he didn't "do anything." He would have done something very serious indeed, for he let his patient die.

Fixing the cause of death may be very important from a legal point of view, for it may determine whether criminal charges are brought against the doctor. But I do not think that this notion can be used to show a moral difference between active and passive euthanasia. The reason why it is considered bad to be the cause of someone's death is that death is regarded as a great evil—and so it is. However, if it has been decided that euthanasia—even passive euthanasia—is desirable in a given case, it has also been decided that in this instance death is no greater an evil than the patient's continued existence. And if this is true, the usual reason for not wanting to be the cause of someone's death simply does not apply.

Finally, doctors may think that all of this is only of academic interest—the sort of thing that philosophers may worry about but that has no practical bearing on their own work. After all, doctors must be concerned about the legal consequences of what they do, and active euthanasia is clearly forbidden by the law. But even so, doctors should also be concerned with the fact that the law is forcing upon them a moral doctrine that may well be indefensible, and has a considerable effect on their practices. Of course, most doctors are not now in the position of being coerced in this matter, for they do not regard themselves as merely going along with what the law requires. Rather, in statements such as the AMA policy statement that I have quoted, they are endorsing this doctrine as a central point of medical ethics. In that statement, active euthanasia is condemned not merely as illegal but as "contrary to that for which the medical profession stands," whereas passive euthanasia is approved. However, the preceding considerations suggest that there is really no moral difference between the two, considered in themselves (there may be important moral differences in some cases in their *consequences,* but, as I pointed out, these differences may make active euthanasia, and not passive euthanasia, the morally preferable option). So, whereas doctors may have to discriminate between active and passive euthanasia to satisfy the law, they should not do any more than that. In particular, they should not give the distinction any added authority and weight by writing it into official statements of medical ethics.

NOTE

1. A. Shaw: "Doctor, Do We Have a Choice?" *The New York Times Magazine,* Jan. 30, 1972, p. 54.

All Animals Are Equal...
or why the ethical principle on which human equality rests requires us to extend equal consideration to animals too

PETER SINGER

Peter Singer teaches at Princeton University.

"Animal Liberation" may sound more like a parody of other liberation movements than a serious objective. The idea of "The Rights of Animals" actually was once used to parody the case for women's rights. When Mary Wollstonecraft, a forerunner of today's feminists, published her *Vindication of the Rights of Woman* in 1792, her views were widely regarded as absurd, and before long an anonymous publication appeared entitled *A Vindication of the Rights of Brutes.* The author of this satirical work (now known to have been Thomas Taylor, a distinguished Cambridge philosopher) tried to refute Mary Wollstonecraft's arguments by showing that they could be carried one stage further. If the argument for equality was sound when applied to women, why should it not be applied to dogs, cats, and horses? The reasoning seemed to hold for these "brutes" too; yet to hold that brutes had rights was manifestly absurd. Therefore the reasoning by which this conclusion had been reached must be unsound, and if unsound when applied to brutes, it must also be unsound when applied to women, since the very same arguments had been used in each case.

In order to explain the basis of the case for the equality of animals, it will be helpful to start with an examination of the case for the equality of women. Let us assume that we wish to defend the case for women's rights against the attack by Thomas Taylor. How should we reply?

One way in which we might reply is by saying that the case for equality between men and women cannot validly be extended to nonhuman animals. Women have a right to vote, for instance, because they are just as capable of making rational decisions about the future as men are; dogs, on the other hand, are incapable of understanding the significance of voting, so they cannot have the right to vote. There are many other obvious ways in which men and women resemble each other closely, while humans and animals differ greatly. So, it might be said, men and women are similar beings and should have similar rights, while humans and nonhumans are different and should not have equal rights.

The reasoning behind this reply to Taylor's analogy is correct up to a point, but it does not go far enough. There are obviously important differences between humans and other animals, and these differences must give rise to some differences in the rights that each have. Recognizing this evident fact, however, is no barrier to the case for extending the basic principle of equality to nonhuman animals. The differences that exist between men and women are equally undeniable, and the supporters of Women's Liberation are aware that these differences may give rise to different rights. Many feminists hold that women have the right to an abortion on request. It does not follow that since these same feminists are campaigning for equality between men and women they must support the right of men to have abortions too. Since a man cannot have an abortion, it is meaningless to talk of his right to have one. Since dogs can't vote, it is meaningless

From *Animal Liberation,* first published 1975, 2nd ed., 1990 (Ecco, New York), pp. 1–23. Reprinted by permission of the author.

to talk of their right to vote. There is no reason why either Women's Liberation or Animal Liberation should get involved in such nonsense. The extension of the basic principle of equality from one group to another does not imply that we must treat both groups in exactly the same way, or grant exactly the same rights to both groups. Whether we should do so will depend on the nature of the members of the two groups. The basic principle of equality does not require equal or identical *treatment;* it requires equal consideration. Equal consideration for different beings may lead to different treatment and different rights.

So there is a different way of replying to Taylor's attempt to parody the case for women's rights, a way that does not deny the obvious differences between human beings and nonhumans but goes more deeply into the question of equality and concludes by finding nothing absurd in the idea that the basic principle of equality applies to so-called brutes. At this point such a conclusion may appear odd; but if we examine more deeply the basis on which our opposition to discrimination on grounds of race or sex ultimately rests, we will see that we would be on shaky ground if we were to demand equality for blacks, women, and other groups of oppressed humans while denying equal consideration to nonhumans. To make this clear we need to see, first, exactly why racism and sexism are wrong. When we say that all human beings, whatever their race, creed, or sex, are equal, what is it that we are asserting? Those who wish to defend hierarchical, inegalitarian societies have often pointed out that by whatever test we choose it simply is not true that all humans are equal. Like it or not we must face the fact that humans come in different shapes and sizes; they come with different moral capacities, different intellectual abilities, different amounts of benevolent feeling and sensitivity to the needs of others, different abilities to communicate effectively, and different capacities to experience pleasure and pain. In short, if the demand for equality were based on the actual equality of all human beings, we would have to stop demanding equality.

Still, one might cling to the view that the demand for equality among human beings is based on the actual equality of the different races and sexes. Although, it may be said, humans differ as individuals, there are no differences between the races and sexes as such. From the mere fact that a person is black or a woman we cannot infer anything about that person's intellectual or moral capacities. This, it may be said, is why racism and sexism are wrong. The white racist claims that whites are superior to blacks, but this is false; although there are differences among individuals, some blacks are superior to some whites in all of the capacities and abilities that could conceivably be relevant. The opponent of sexism would say the same: a person's sex is no guide to his or her abilities, and this is why it is unjustifiable to discriminate on the basis of sex.

The existence of individual variations that cut across the lines of race or sex, however, provides us with no defense at all against a more sophisticated opponent of equality, one who proposes that, say, the interests of all those with IQ scores below 100 be given less consideration than the interests of those with ratings over 100. Perhaps those scoring below the mark would, in this society, be made the slaves of those scoring higher. Would a hierarchical society of this sort really be so much better than one based on race or sex? I think not. But if we tie the moral principle of equality to the factual equality of the different races or sexes, taken as a whole, our opposition to racism and sexism does not provide us with any basis for objecting to this kind of inegalitarianism.

There is a second important reason why we ought not to base our opposition to racism and sexism on any kind of factual equality, even the limited kind that asserts that variations in capacities and abilities are spread evenly among the different races and between the sexes: we can have no absolute guarantee that these capacities and abilities really are distributed evenly, without regard to race or sex, among human beings. So far as actual abilities are concerned there do seem to be certain measurable differences both among races and between sexes. These differences do not, of course, appear in every case, but only when averages are taken. More important still, we do not yet know how many of these differences are really due to the different genetic endowments of the different races and sexes, and how many are due to poor schools, poor housing, and other factors that are the result of past and continuing discrimination. Perhaps all of the important differences will eventually prove to be environmental rather than genetic. Anyone opposed to racism and sexism will certainly hope that this will be so, for it will make the task of ending discrimination a lot easier; nevertheless, it would be dangerous to rest the case against racism and sexism on the belief that all significant differences are environmental in origin. The opponent of, say, racism who takes this line will be unable to avoid conceding that if differences in ability did after all prove to have some genetic connection with race, racism would in some way be defensible.

Fortunately there is no need to pin the case for equality to one particular outcome of a scientific investigation. The appropriate response to those who claim to have found evidence of genetically based differences in ability among the races or between the sexes is not to stick to the belief that the genetic explanation must be wrong, whatever evidence to the contrary may turn up; instead we should make it quite clear that the claim to equality does not depend on intelligence, moral capacity, physical strength, or similar matters of fact. Equality is a moral idea, not an assertion of fact. There is no logically compelling reason for assuming that a factual difference in ability between two people justifies any difference in the amount of consideration we give to their needs and interests. *The principle of the equality of human beings is not a description of an alleged actual equality among humans: it is a prescription of how we should treat human beings.*

Jeremy Bentham, the founder of the reforming utilitarian school of moral philosophy, incorporated the essential basis of moral equality into his system of ethics by means of the formula: "Each to count for one and none for more than one." In other words, the interests of every being affected by an action are to be taken into account and given the same weight as the like interests of any other being. A later utilitarian, Henry Sidgwick, put the point in this way: "The good of any one individual is of no more importance, from the point of view (if I may say so) of the Universe, than the good of any

other." More recently the leading figures in contemporary moral philosophy have shown a great deal of agreement in specifying as a fundamental presupposition of their moral theories some similar requirement that works to give everyone's interests equal consideration—although these writers generally cannot agree on how this requirement is best formulated.[1]

It is an implication of this principle of equality that our concern for others and our readiness to consider their interests ought not to depend on what they are like or on what abilities they may possess. Precisely what our concern or consideration requires us to do may vary according to the characteristics of those affected by what we do: concern for the well-being of children growing up in America would require that we teach them to read; concern for the well-being of pigs may require no more than that we leave them with other pigs in a place where there is adequate food and room to run freely. But the basic element—the taking into account of the interests of the being, whatever those interests may be—must, according to the principle of equality, be extended to all beings, black or white, masculine or feminine, human or nonhuman.

Thomas Jefferson, who was responsible for writing the principle of the equality of men into the American Declaration of Independence, saw this point. It led him to oppose slavery even though he was unable to free himself fully from his slaveholding background. He wrote in a letter to the author of a book that emphasized the notable intellectual achievements of Negroes in order to refute the then common view that they had limited intellectual capacities:

> Be assured that no person living wishes more sincerely than I do, to see a complete refutation of the doubts I myself have entertained and expressed on the grade of understanding allotted to them by nature, and to find that they are on a par with ourselves... but whatever be their degree of talent it is no measure of their rights. Because Sir Isaac Newton was superior to others in understanding, he was not therefore lord of the property or persons of others.[2]

Similarly, when in the 1850s the call for women's rights was raised in the United States, a remarkable black feminist named Sojourner

Truth made the same point in more robust terms at a feminist convention:

> They talk about this thing in the head; what do they call it? ["Intellect," whispered someone nearby.] That's it. What's that got to do with women's rights or Negroes' rights? If my cup won't hold but a pint and yours holds a quart, wouldn't you be mean not to let me have my little half-measure full?[3]

It is on this basis that the case against racism and the case against sexism must both ultimately rest; and it is in accordance with this principle that the attitude that we may call "speciesism," by analogy with racism, must also be condemned. Speciesism—the word is not an attractive one, but I can think of no better term—is a prejudice or attitude of bias in favor of the interests of members of one's own species and against those of members of other species. It should be obvious that the fundamental objections to racism and sexism made by Thomas Jefferson and Sojourner Truth apply equally to speciesism. If possessing a higher degree of intelligence does not entitle one human to use another for his or her own ends, how can it entitle humans to exploit nonhumans for the same purpose?[4]

Many philosophers and other writers have proposed the principle of equal consideration of interests, in some form or other, as a basic moral principle; but not many of them have recognized that this principle applies to members of other species as well as to our own. Jeremy Bentham was one of the few who did realize this. In a forwardlooking passage written at a time when black slaves had been freed by the French but in the British dominions were still being treated in the way we now treat animals, Bentham wrote:

> The day *may* come when the rest of the animal creation may acquire those rights which never could have been withholden from them but by the hand of tyranny. The French have already discovered that the blackness of the skin is no reason why a human being should be abandoned without redress to the caprice of a tormentor. It may one day come to be recognized that the number of the legs, the villosity of the skin, or the termination of the *os sacrum*

are reasons equally insufficient for abandoning a sensitive being to the same fate. What else is it that should trace the insuperable line? Is it the faculty of reason, or perhaps the faculty of discourse? But a full-grown horse or dog is beyond comparison a more rational, as well as a more conversable animal, than an infant of a day or a week or even a month, old. But suppose they were otherwise, what would it avail? The question is not, Can they *reason?* nor Can they *talk?* but, Can they *suffer?*[5]

In this passage Bentham points to the capacity for suffering as the vital characteristic that gives a being the right to equal consideration. The capacity for suffering—or more strictly, for suffering and/or enjoyment or happiness—is not just another characteristic like the capacity for language or higher mathematics. Bentham is not saying that those who try to mark "the insuperable line" that determines whether the interests of a being should be considered happen to have chosen the wrong characteristic. By saying that we must consider the interests of all beings with the capacity for suffering or enjoyment Bentham does not arbitrarily exclude from consideration any interests at all—as those who draw the line with reference to the possession of reason or language do. The capacity for suffering and enjoyment is a *prerequisite for having interests at all*, a condition that must be satisfied before we can speak of interests in a meaningful way. It would be nonsense to say that it was not in the interests of a stone to be kicked along the road by a schoolboy. A stone does not have interests because it cannot suffer. Nothing that we can do to it could possibly make any difference to its welfare. The capacity for suffering and enjoyment is, however, not only necessary, but also sufficient for us to say that a being has interests—at an absolute minimum, an interest in not suffering. A mouse, for example, does have an interest in not being kicked along the road, because it will suffer if it is.

Although Bentham speaks of "rights" in the passage I have quoted, the argument is really about equality rather than about rights. Indeed, in a different passage, Bentham famously described "natural rights" as "nonsense" and "natural and imprescriptible rights" as "nonsense upon stilts." He talked of moral rights as a shorthand way of referring to protections that people and animals morally ought to have; but the real weight of the moral argument does not rest on the assertion of the existence of the right, for this in turn has to be justified on the basis of the possibilities for suffering and happiness. In this way we can argue for equality for animals without getting embroiled in philosophical controversies about the ultimate nature of rights.

In misguided attempts to refute the arguments of this book, some philosophers have gone to much trouble developing arguments to show that animals do not have rights.[6] They have claimed that to have rights a being must be autonomous, or must be a member of a community, or must have the ability to respect the rights of others, or must possess a sense of justice. These claims are irrelevant to the case for Animal Liberation. The language of rights is a convenient political shorthand. It is even more valuable in the era of thirty-second TV news clips than it was in Bentham's day; but in the argument for a radical change in our attitude to animals, it is in no way necessary.

If a being suffers there can be no moral justification for refusing to take that suffering into consideration. No matter what the nature of the being, the principle of equality requires that its suffering be counted equally with the like suffering—insofar as rough comparisons can be made—of any other being. If a being is not capable of suffering, or of experiencing enjoyment or happiness, there is nothing to be taken into account. So the limit of sentience (using the term as a convenient if not strictly accurate shorthand for the capacity to suffer and/or experience enjoyment) is the only defensible boundary of concern for the interests of others. To mark this boundary by some other characteristic like intelligence or rationality would be to mark it in an arbitrary manner. Why not choose some other characteristic, like skin color?

Racists violate the principle of equality by giving greater weight to the interests of members of their own race when there is a clash between their interests and the interests of those of another race. Sexists violate the principle of equality by favoring the interests of their own sex. Similarly, speciesists allow the interests of their own species to override the greater interests of members of other species. The pattern is identical in each case.

Most human beings are speciesists. The following chapters show that ordinary human beings—not a few exceptionally cruel or heartless humans, but the overwhelming majority of humans—take an active part in, acquiesce in, and allow their taxes to pay for practices that require the sacrifice of the most important interests of members of other species in order to promote the most trivial interests of our own species.

There is, however, one general defense of the practices to be described in the next two chapters that needs to be disposed of before we discuss the practices themselves. It is a defense which, if true, would allow us to do anything at all to nonhumans for the slightest reason, or for no reason at all, without incurring any justifiable reproach. This defense claims that we are never guilty of neglecting the interests of other animals for one breathtakingly simple reason: they have no interests. Nonhuman animals have no interests, according to this view, because they are not capable of suffering. By this is not meant merely that they are not capable of suffering in all the ways that human beings are—for instance, that a calf is not capable of suffering from the knowledge that it will be killed in six months time. That modest claim is, no doubt, true; but it does not clear humans of the charge of speciesism, since it allows that animals may suffer in other ways—for instance, by being given electric shocks, or being kept in small, cramped cages. The defense I am about to discuss is the much more sweeping, although correspondingly less plausible, claim that animals are incapable of suffering in any way at all; that they are, in fact, unconscious automata, possessing neither thoughts nor feelings nor a mental life of any kind.

Although, as we shall see in a later chapter, the view that animals are automata was proposed by the seventeenth-century French philosopher René Descartes, to most people, then and now, it is obvious that if, for example, we stick a sharp knife into the stomach of an unanesthetized dog, the dog will feel pain. That this is so is assumed by the laws in most civilized countries that prohibit wanton cruelty to animals. Readers whose common sense tells them that animals do suffer may prefer to skip the remainder of this section, moving straight on to the next section, since the pages in between do nothing but refute a position that they do not hold. Implausible as it is, though, for the sake of completeness this skeptical position must be discussed.

Do animals other than humans feel pain? How do we know? Well, how do we know if anyone, human or nonhuman, feels pain? We know that we ourselves can feel pain. We know this from the direct experience of pain that we have when, for instance, somebody presses a lighted cigarette against the back of our hand. But how do we know that anyone else feels pain? We cannot directly experience anyone else's pain, whether that "anyone" is our best friend or a stray dog. Pain is a state of consciousness, a "mental event," and as such it can never be observed. Behavior like writhing, screaming, or drawing one's hand away from the lighted cigarette is not pain itself; nor are the recordings a neurologist might make of activity within the brain observations of pain itself. Pain is something that we feel, and we can only infer that others are feeling it from various external indications.

In theory, we *could* always be mistaken when we assume that other human beings feel pain. It is conceivable that one of our close friends is really a cleverly constructed robot, controlled by a brilliant scientist so as to give all the signs of feeling pain, but really no more sensitive than any other machine. We can never know, with absolute certainty, that this is not the case. But while this might present a puzzle for philosophers, none of us has the slightest real doubt that our close friends feel pain just as we do. This is an inference, but a perfectly reasonable one, based on observations of their behavior in situations in which we would feel pain, and on the fact that we have every reason to assume that our friends are beings like us, with nervous systems like ours that can be assumed to function as ours do and to produce similar feelings in similar circumstances.

If it is justifiable to assume that other human beings feel pain as we do, is there any reason why a similar inference should be unjustifiable in the case of other animals?

Nearly all the external signs that lead us to infer pain in other humans can be seen in other species, especially the species most closely related to us—the species of mammals and birds. The behavioral signs include writhing, facial contortions, moaning, yelping or other forms of calling, attempts to avoid the source of pain, appearance of fear at the prospect of its repetition, and so on. In addition, we know that these animals have nervous systems very like ours, which respond physiologically as ours do when the animal is in circumstances in which we would feel pain: an initial rise of blood pressure, dilated pupils, perspiration, an increased pulse rate, and, if the stimulus continues, a fall in blood pressure. Although human beings have a more developed cerebral cortex than other animals, this part of the brain is concerned with thinking functions rather than with basic impulses, emotions, and feelings. These impulses, emotions, and feelings are located in the diencephalon, which is well developed in many other species of animals, especially mammals and birds.[7]

We also know that the nervous systems of other animals were not artificially constructed—as a robot might be artificially constructed—to mimic the pain behavior of humans. The nervous systems of animals evolved as our own did, and in fact the evolutionary history of human beings and other animals, especially mammals, did not diverge until the central features of our nervous systems were already in existence. A capacity to feel pain obviously enhances a species' prospects of survival, since it causes members of the species to avoid sources of injury. It is surely unreasonable to suppose that nervous systems that are virtually identical physiologically, have a common origin and a common evolutionary function, and result in similar forms of behavior in similar circumstances should actually operate in an entirely different manner on the level of subjective feelings.

It has long been accepted as sound policy in science to search for the simplest possible explanation of whatever it is we are trying to explain. Occasionally it has been claimed that it is for this reason "unscientific" to explain the behavior of animals by theories that refer to the animal's conscious feelings, desires, and so on—the idea being that if the behavior in question can be explained without invoking consciousness or feelings, that will be the simpler theory. Yet we can now see that such explanations, when assessed with respect to the actual behavior of both human and nonhuman animals, are actually far more complex than rival explanations. For we know from our own experience that explanations of our own behavior that did not refer to consciousness and the feeling of pain would be incomplete; and it is simpler to assume that the similar behavior of animals with similar nervous systems is to be explained in the same way than to try to invent some other explanation for the behavior of nonhuman animals as well as an explanation for the divergence between humans and nonhumans in this respect.

The overwhelming majority of scientists who have addressed themselves to this question agree. Lord Brain, one of the most eminent neurologists of our time, has said:

> I personally can see no reason for conceding mind to my fellow men and denying it to animals.... I at least cannot doubt that the interests and activities of animals are correlated with awareness and feeling in the same way as my own, and which may be, for aught I know, just as vivid.[8]

The author of a book on pain writes:

> Every particle of factual evidence supports the contention that the higher mammalian vertebrates experience pain sensations at least as acute as our own. To say that they feel less because they are lower animals is an absurdity; it can easily be shown that many of their senses are far more acute than ours—visual acuity in certain birds, hearing in most wild animals, and touch in others; these animals depend more than we do today on the sharpest possible awareness of a hostile environment. Apart from the complexity of the cerebral cortex (which does not directly perceive pain) their nervous systems are almost identical to ours and their reactions to pain remarkably similar, though lacking (so far as we know) the philosophical and moral overtones. The emotional element is all too evident, mainly in the form of fear and anger.[9]

In Britain, three separate expert government committees on matters relating to animals have accepted the conclusion that animals feel pain. After noting the obvious behavioral evidence for this view, the members of the Committee on Cruelty to Wild Animals, set up in 1951, said:

> ...we believe that the physiological, and more particularly the anatomical, evidence fully justifies and reinforces the commonsense belief that animals feel pain.

And after discussing the evolutionary value of pain the committee's report concluded that pain is "of clear-cut biological usefulness" and this is "a third type of evidence that animals feel pain." The committee members then went on to consider forms of suffering other than mere physical pain and added that they were "satisfied that animals do suffer from acute fear and terror." Subsequent reports by British government committees on experiments on animals and on the welfare of animals under intensive farming methods agreed with this view, concluding that animals are capable of suffering both from straightforward physical injuries and from fear, anxiety, stress, and so on.[10] Finally, within the last decade, the publication of scientific studies with titles such as *Animal Thought*, *Animal Thinking*, and *Animal Suffering: The Science of Animal Welfare* have made it plain that conscious awareness in nonhuman animals is now generally accepted as a serious subject for investigation.[11]

That might well be thought enough to settle the matter; but one more objection needs to be considered. Human beings in pain, after all, have one behavioral sign that nonhuman animals do not have: a developed language. Other animals may communicate with each other, but not, it seems, in the complicated way we do. Some philosophers, including Descartes, have thought it important that while humans can tell each other about their experience of pain in great detail, other animals cannot. (Interestingly, this once neat dividing line between humans and other species has now been threatened by the discovery that chimpanzees can be taught a language.[12]) But as Bentham pointed out long ago, the ability to use language is not relevant to the question of how a being ought to be treated—unless that ability can be linked to the capacity to suffer, so that the absence of a language casts doubt on the existence of this capacity.

This link may be attempted in two ways. First, there is a hazy line of philosophical thought, deriving perhaps from some doctrines associated with the influential philosopher Ludwig Wittgenstein, which maintains that we cannot meaningfully attribute states of consciousness to beings without language. This position seems to me very implausible. Language may be necessary for abstract thought, at some level anyway; but states like pain are more primitive, and have nothing to do with language.

The second and more easily understood way of linking language and the existence of pain is to say that the best evidence we can have that other creatures are in pain is that they tell us that they are. This is a distinct line of argument, for it is denying not that non-language-users conceivably *could* suffer, but only that we could ever have sufficient reason to *believe* that they are suffering. Still, this line of argument fails too. As Jane Goodall has pointed out in her study of chimpanzees, *In the Shadow of Man,* when it comes to the expression of feelings and emotions language is less important than nonlinguistic modes of communication such as a cheering pat on the back, an exuberant embrace, a clasp of the hands, and so on. The basic signals we use to convey pain, fear, anger, love, joy, surprise, sexual arousal, and many other emotional states are not specific to our own species.[13] The statement "I am in pain" may be one piece of evidence for the conclusion that the speaker is in pain, but it is not the only possible evidence, and since people sometimes tell lies, not even the best possible evidence.

Even if there were stronger grounds for refusing to attribute pain to those who do not have a language, the consequences of this refusal might lead us to reject the conclusion. Human infants and young children are unable to use language. Are we to deny that a year-old child can suffer? If not, language cannot be crucial. Of course, most parents understand the responses of their children better than they understand the responses of other animals; but this is just a fact about the relatively greater knowledge that we have of our own species and the greater contact we have with infants as compared to animals. Those who have studied the behavior of other animals and those who have animals as companions soon learn to understand their responses as well as we understand those of an infant, and sometimes better.

So to conclude: there are no good reasons, scientific or philosophical, for denying that animals feel pain. If we do not doubt that other humans feel pain we should not doubt that other animals do so too.

Animals can feel pain. As we saw earlier, there can be no moral justification for regarding the pain (or pleasure) that animals feel as less important than the same amount of pain (or pleasure) felt by humans. But what practical consequences follow from this conclusion? To prevent misunderstanding I shall spell out what I mean a little more fully.

If I give a horse a hard slap across its rump with my open hand, the horse may start, but it presumably feels little pain. Its skin is thick enough to protect it against a mere slap. If I slap a baby in the same way, however, the baby will cry and presumably feel pain, for its skin is more sensitive. So it is worse to slap a baby than a horse, if both slaps are administered with equal force. But there must be some kind of blow—I don't know exactly what it would be, but perhaps a blow with a heavy stick—would cause the horse as much pain as we cause a baby by slapping it with our hand. That is what I mean by "the same amount of pain," and if we consider it wrong to inflict that much pain on a baby for no good reason then we must, unless we are speciesists, consider it equally wrong to inflict the same amount of pain on a horse for no good reason.

Other differences between humans and animals cause other complications. Normal adult human beings have mental capacities that will, in certain circumstances, lead them to suffer more than animals would in the same circumstances. If, for instance, we decided to perform extremely painful or lethal scientific experiments on normal adult humans, kidnapped at random from public parks for this purpose, adults who enjoy strolling in parks would become fearful that they would be kidnapped. The resultant terror would be a form of suffering additional to the pain of the experiment. The same experiments performed on nonhuman animals would cause less suffering since the animals would not have the anticipatory dread of being kidnapped and experimented upon. This does not mean, of course, that it would be *right* to perform the experiment on animals, but only that there is a reason, which is *not* speciesist, for preferring to use animals rather than normal adult human beings, if the experiment is to be done at all. It should be noted, however, that this same argument gives us a reason for preferring to use human infants—orphans perhaps—or severely retarded human beings for experiments, rather than adults, since infants and retarded humans would also have no idea of what was going to happen to them. So far as this argument is concerned nonhuman animals and infants and retarded humans are in the same category; and if we use this argument to justify experiments on nonhuman animals we have to ask ourselves whether we are also prepared to allow experiments on human infants and retarded adults; and if we make a distinction between animals and these humans, on what basis can we do it, other than a bare-faced—and morally indefensible—preference for members of our own species?

There are many matters in which the superior mental powers of normal adult humans make a difference: anticipation, more detailed memory, greater knowledge of what is happening, and so on. Yet these differences do not all point to greater suffering on the part of the normal human being. Sometimes animals may suffer more because of their more limited understanding. If, for instance, we are taking prisoners in wartime we can explain to them that although they must submit to capture, search, and confinement, they will not otherwise be harmed and will be set free at the conclusion of hostilities. If we capture wild animals, however, we cannot explain that we are not threatening their lives. A wild animal cannot distinguish an attempt to overpower and confine from an attempt to kill; the one causes as much terror as the other.

It may be objected that comparisons of the sufferings of different species are impossible to make and that for this reason when the interests of animals and humans clash the principle of equality gives no guidance. It is probably true that comparisons of suffering between members of different species cannot be made precisely, but precision is not essential. Even if we were to prevent the infliction of suffering on animals only when it is quite certain that the interests of humans will not be affected to anything like the extent that animals are affected, we would be forced to make radical changes in our treatment of animals that would involve our diet, the farming methods we use, experimental procedures in many fields of science, our approach to wildlife and to hunting, trapping and the wearing of furs, and areas of entertainment like circuses, rodeos, and zoos. As a result, a vast amount of suffering would be avoided.

So far I have said a lot about inflicting suffering on animals, but nothing about killing them. This omission has been deliberate. The application of the principle of equality to the infliction of suffering is, in theory at least, fairly straightforward. Pain and suffering are in themselves bad and should be prevented or minimized, irrespective of the race, sex, or species of the being that suffers. How bad a pain is depends on how intense it is and how long it lasts, but pains of the same intensity and duration are equally bad, whether felt by humans or animals.

The wrongness of killing a being is more complicated. I have kept, and shall continue to keep, the question of killing in the background because in the present state of human tyranny over other species the more simple, straightforward principle of equal consideration of pain or pleasure is a sufficient basis for identifying and protesting against all the major abuses of animals that human beings practice. Nevertheless, it is necessary to say something about killing.

Just as most human beings are speciesists in their readiness to cause pain to animals when they would not cause a similar pain to humans for the same reason, so most human beings are speciesists in their readiness to kill other animals when they would not kill human beings. We need to proceed more cautiously here, however, because people hold widely differing views about when it is legitimate to kill humans, as the continuing debates over abortion and euthanasia attest. Nor have moral philosophers been able to agree on exactly what it is that makes it wrong to kill human beings, and under what circumstances killing a human being may be justifiable.

Let us consider first the view that it is always wrong to take an innocent human life. We may call this the "sanctity of life" view. People who take this view oppose abortion and euthanasia. They do not usually, however, oppose the killing of nonhuman animals—so perhaps it would be more accurate to describe this view as the "sanctity of *human* life" view. The belief that human life, and only human life, is sacrosanct is a form of speciesism. To see this, consider the following example.

Assume that, as sometimes happens, an infant has been born with massive and irreparable brain damage. The damage is so severe that the infant can never be any more than a "human vegetable," unable to talk, recognize other people, act independently of others, or develop a sense of self-awareness. The parents of the infant, realizing that they cannot hope for any improvement in their child's condition and being in any case unwilling to spend, or ask the state to spend, the thousands of dollars that would be needed annually for proper care of the infant, ask the doctor to kill the infant painlessly.

Should the doctor do what the parents ask? Legally, the doctor should not, and in this respect the law reflects the sanctity of life view. The life of every human being is sacred. Yet people who would say this about the infant do not object to the killing of nonhuman animals. How can they justify their different judgments? Adult chimpanzees, dogs, pigs, and members of many other species far surpass the brain-damaged infant in their ability to relate to others, act independently, be self-aware, and any other capacity that could reasonably be said to give value to life. With the most intensive care possible, some severely retarded infants can never achieve the intelligence level of a dog. Nor can we appeal to the concern of the infant's parents, since they themselves, in this imaginary example (and in some actual cases) do not want the infant kept alive. The only thing that distinguishes the infant from the animal, in the eyes of those

who claim it has a "right to life," is that it is, biologically, a member of the species Homo sapiens, whereas chimpanzees, dogs, and pigs are not. But to use *this* difference as the basis for granting a right to life to the infant and not to the other animals is, of course, pure speciesism.[14] It is exactly the kind of arbitrary difference that the most crude and overt kind of racist uses in attempting to justify racial discrimination.

This does not mean that to avoid speciesism we must hold that it is as wrong to kill a dog as it is to kill a human being in full possession of his or her faculties. The only position that is irredeemably speciesist is the one that tries to make the boundary of the right to life run exactly parallel to the boundary of our own species. Those who hold the sanctity of life view do this, because while distinguishing sharply between human beings and other animals they allow no distinctions to be made within our own species, objecting to the killing of the severely retarded and the hopelessly senile as strongly as they object to the killing of normal adults.

To avoid speciesism we must allow that beings who are similar in all relevant respects have a similar right to life—and mere membership in our own biological species cannot be a morally relevant criterion for this right. Within these limits we could still hold, for instance, that it is worse to kill a normal adult human, with a capacity for self-awareness and the ability to plan for the future and have meaningful relations with others, than it is to kill a mouse, which presumably does not share all of these characteristics; or we might appeal to the close family and other personal ties that humans have but mice do not have to the same degree; or we might think that it is the consequences for other humans, who will be put in fear for their own lives, that makes the crucial difference; or we might think it is some combination of these factors, or other factors altogether.

Whatever criteria we choose, however, we will have to admit that they do not follow precisely the boundary of our own species. We may legitimately hold that there are some features of certain beings that make their lives more valuable than those of other beings; but there will surely be some nonhuman animals whose lives, by any standards, are more valuable than the lives of some humans. A chimpanzee, dog, or pig, for instance, will have a higher degree of self-awareness and a greater capacity for meaningful relations with others than a severely retarded infant or someone in a state of advanced senility. So if we base the right to life on these characteristics we must grant these animals a right to life as good as, or better than, such retarded or senile humans.

This argument cuts both ways. It could be taken as showing that chimpanzees, dogs, and pigs, along with some other species, have a right to life and we commit a grave moral offense whenever we kill them, even when they are old and suffering and our intention is to put them out of their misery. Alternatively one could take the argument as showing that the severely retarded and hopelessly senile have no right to life and may be killed for quite trivial reasons, as we now kill animals.

Since the main concern of this book is with ethical questions having to do with animals and not with the morality of euthanasia I shall not attempt to settle this issue finally.[15] I think it is reasonably clear, though, that while both of the positions just described avoid speciesism, neither is satisfactory. What we need is some middle position that would avoid speciesism but would not make the lives of the retarded and senile as cheap as the lives of pigs and dogs now are, or make the lives of pigs and dogs so sacrosanct that we think it wrong to put them out of hopeless misery. What we must do is bring nonhuman animals within our sphere of moral concern and cease to treat their lives as expendable for whatever trivial purposes we may have. At the same time, once we realize that the fact that a being is a member of our own species is not in itself enough to make it always wrong to kill that being, we may come to reconsider our policy of preserving human lives at all costs, even when there is no prospect of a meaningful life or of existence without terrible pain.

I conclude, then, that a rejection of speciesism does not imply that all lives are of equal worth. While self-awareness, the capacity to think ahead and have hopes and aspirations for the future, the capacity for meaningful relations with others and so on are not relevant to the question of inflicting pain—since pain is pain, whatever other capacities, beyond the capacity to feel pain, the being may have—these capacities are relevant to the question of taking life. It is not arbitrary to hold that the life of a self-aware being, capable of abstract thought, of planning for the future, of complex acts of communication, and so on, is more valuable than the life of a being without these capacities. To see the difference between the issues of inflicting pain and taking life, consider how we would choose within our own species. If we had to choose to save the life of a normal human being or an intellectually disabled human being, we would probably choose to save the life of a normal human being; but if we had to choose between preventing pain in the normal human being or the intellectually disabled one—imagine that both have received painful but superficial injuries, and we only have enough painkiller for one of them—it is not nearly so clear how we ought to choose. The same is true when we consider other species. The evil of pain is, in itself, unaffected by the other characteristics of the being who feels the pain; the value of life is affected by these other characteristics. To give just one reason for this difference, to take the life of a being who has been hoping, planning, and working for some future goal is to deprive that being of the fulfillment of all those efforts; to take the life of a being with a mental capacity below the level needed to grasp that one is a being with a future—much less make plans for the future—cannot involve this particular kind of loss.[16]

Normally this will mean that if we have to choose between the life of a human being and the life of another animal we should choose to save the life of the human; but there may be special cases in which the reverse holds true, because the human being in question does not have the capacities of a normal human being. So this view is not speciesist, although it may appear to be at first glance. The preference, in normal cases, for saving a human life over the life of an animal when a choice *has* to be made is a preference based on the characteristics that normal humans have, and not on the mere fact that they are members of our own species. This is why when we consider members of our own species who lack the characteristics of normal humans we can no longer say that their lives are always to be preferred to those of other animals. This issue comes up in a practical way in the following chapter. In general, though, the question of when it is wrong to kill (painlessly) an animal is one to which we need give no precise answer. As long as we remember that we should give the same respect to the lives of animals as we give to the lives of those humans at a similar mental level, we shall not go far wrong.[17]

In any case, the conclusions that are argued for in this book flow from the principle of minimizing suffering alone. The idea that it is also wrong to kill animals painlessly gives some of these conclusions additional support that is welcome but strictly unnecessary. Interestingly enough, this is true even of the conclusion that we ought to become vegetarians, a conclusion that in the popular mind is generally based on some kind of absolute prohibition on killing.

NOTES

1. For Bentham's moral philosophy, see his *Introduction to the Principles of Morals and Legislation,* and for Sidgwick's see *The Methods of Ethics,* 1907 (the passage is quoted from the seventh edition; reprint, London: Macmillan, 1963), p. 382. As examples of leading contemporary moral philosophers who incorporate a requirement of equal consideration of interests, see R. M. Hare, *Freedom and Reason* (New York: Oxford University Press, 1963), and John Rawls, *A Theory of Justice* (Cambridge: Harvard University Press, Belknap Press, 1972). For a brief account of the essential agreement on this issue between these and other positions, see R. M. Hare, "Rules of War and Moral Reasoning," *Philosophy and Public Affairs* 1 (2) (1972).

2. Letter to Henry Gregoire, February 25, 1809.

3. Reminiscences by Francis D. Gage, from Susan B. Anthony, *The History of Woman Suffrage,* vol. 1; the passage is to be found in the extract in Leslie Tanner, ed., *Voices From Women's Liberation* (New York: Signet, 1970).

4. I owe the term "speciesism" to Richard Ryder. It has become accepted in general use since the first edition of this book, and now appears in *The Oxford English Dictionary,* second edition (Oxford: Clarendon Press, 1989).

5. *Introduction to the Principles of Morals and Legislation,* chapter 17.

6. See M. Levin, "Animal Rights Evaluated," *Humanist* 37: 14–15 (July/August 1977); M. A. Fox, "Animal Liberation: A Critique," *Ethics* 88: 134–138 (1978); C. Perry and G. E. Jones, "On Animal Rights," *International Journal of Applied Philosophy* 1: 39–57 (1982).

7. Lord Brain, "Presidential Address," in C. A. Keele and R. Smith, eds., *The Assessment of Pain in Men and Animals* (London: Universities Federation for Animal Welfare, 1962).

8. Lord Brain, "Presidential Address," p. 11.

9. Richard Serjeant, *The Spectrum of Pain* (London: Hart Davis, 1969), p. 72.

10. See the reports of the Committee on Cruelty to Wild Animals (Command Paper 8266, 1951), paragraphs 36–42; the Departmental Committee on Experiments on Animals (Command Paper 2641, 1965), paragraphs 179–182; and the Technical Committee to Enquire into the Welfare of Animals Kept under Intensive Livestock Husbandry Systems (Command Paper 2836, 1965), paragraphs 26–28 (London: Her Majesty's Stationery Office).

11. See Stephen Walker, *Animal Thoughts* (London: Routledge and Kegan Paul, 1983); Donald Griffin, *Animal Thinking* (Cambridge: Harvard University Press, 1984); and Marian Stamp Dawkins, *Animal Suffering: The Science of Animal Welfare* (London: Chapman and Hall, 1980).

12. See Eugene Linden, *Apes, Men and Language* (New York: Penguin, 1976); for popular accounts of some more recent work, see Erik Eckholm, "Pygmy Chimp Readily Learns Language Skill," *The New York Times,* June 24, 1985; and "The Wisdom of Animals," *Newsweek,* May 23, 1988.

13. *In the Shadow of Man* (Boston: Houghton Mifflin, 1971), p. 225. Michael Peters makes a similar point in "Nature and Culture," in Stanley and Roslind Godlovitch and John Harris, eds., *Animals, Men and Morals* (New York: Taplinger, 1972). For examples of some of the inconsistencies in denials that creatures without language can feel pain, see Bernard Rollin, *The Unheeded Cry: Animal Consciousness, Animal Pain, and Science* (Oxford: Oxford University Press, 1989).

14. I am here putting aside religious views, for example the doctrine that all and only human beings have immortal souls, or are made in the image of God. Historically these have been very important, and no doubt are partly responsible for the idea that human life has a special sanctity. (For further

historical discussion see Chapter 5.) Logically, however, these religious views are unsatisfactory, since they do not offer a reasoned explanation of why it should be that all humans and no nonhumans have immortal souls. This belief too, therefore, comes under suspicion as a form of speciesism. In any case, defenders of the "sanctity of life" view are generally reluctant to base their position on purely religious doctrines, since these doctrines are no longer as widely accepted as they once were.

15. For a general discussion of these questions, see my *Practical Ethics* (Cambridge: Cambridge University Press, 1979), and for a more detailed discussion of the treatment of handicapped infants, see Helga Kuhse and Peter Singer, *Should the Baby Live?* (Oxford: Oxford University Press, 1985).

16. For a development of this theme, see my essay, "Life's Uncertain Voyage," in P. Pettit, R. Sylvan and J. Norman, eds., *Metaphysics and Morality* (Oxford: Blackwell, 1987), pp. 154–172.

17. The preceding discussion, which has been changed only slightly since the first edition, has often been overlooked by critics of the Animal Liberation movement. It is a common tactic to seek to ridicule the Animal Liberation position by maintaining that, as an animal experimenter put it recently, "Some of these people believe that every insect, every mouse, has as much right to life as a human." (Dr. Irving Weissman, as quoted in Katherine Bishop, "From Shop to Lab to Farm, Animal Rights Battle is Felt," *The New York Times,* January 14, 1989.) It would be interesting to see Dr. Weissman name some prominent Animal Liberationists who hold this view. Certainly (assuming only that he was referring to the right to life of a human being with mental capacities very different from those of the insect and the mouse) the position described is not mine. I doubt that it is held by many—if any—in the Animal Liberation movement.

Italic terms within the definition are defined in the glossary.

Academics Members of Plato's school of philosophy.

Active euthanasia Mercy killing that involves the intention, on the part of the doctor, to terminate the life of the patient for the patient's own good.

Ad hoc (Latin, "for a specific purpose.") An hypothesis is ad hoc if it is adopted purely to save a theory from a difficulty without an independent motivation of its own.

Ad infinitum Into infinity; endlessly.

Aesthetic Belonging to the appreciation of beauty.

Aesthetics Pertaining to the appreciation of beauty and other values of pictorial art, music, poetry, fiction, and drama.

A fortiori (Latin, "from the stronger.") This means "and even more so" or "all the more." For example, John owns horses of all ages; a fortiori he owns young horses.

Agnoiology The theory of ignorance.

Agnosticism The view that something is not known, and perhaps cannot be known. In theology, the view that the existence or nonexistence of God is not known. Neither *theism* nor *atheism* can be justified.

Akrasia (Greek, for "weakness of the will.") Not being able to make yourself do what you think it would be best for you to do.

Altruism Any act that seeks to advance the good of others for their own sake and not for the sake of advancing the self-interest of the agent. (See *ethical altruism*.)

Analytical behaviorism See *behaviorism, logical*.

Analytic statement Originally introduced by Kant, an analytic statement is one where the concept of the predicate is contained within the concept of the subject. For example, the statement that all bachelors are unmarried is analytic. The concept "unmarried" is contained within the concept "bachelor." Frege generalized the notion to cover more than just subject-predicate statements. For Frege, an analytic statement is true solely in virtue of the meanings of the words in which it is expressed. Also known as a "tautology." (See *synthetic statement*.)

Antecedent What comes before. In a statement of the form, "If *A* then *B*," *A* is the antecedent, and *B* is the consequent.

Anthropomorphism Attributing human characteristics, such as human form or human thoughts and intentions, to something that is not human. For example, attributing intentions to rocks to explain why they move or attributing a human appearance to God.

A posteriori Knowledge that is not a priori. A posteriori knowledge, though it may involve the use of reason, depends upon evidence from experience.

A priori Knowledge that is based on reason, independently of experience. The *ontological argument* is an example of an a priori argument.

Arbitrary Providing no better reason to adopt one position rather than another.

Argument A series of one or more statements called *premises* that are meant to support another statement called *conclusion*. (See also *valid* and *sound*.)

Argument from design See *teleological argument*.

Argumentum ad hominem An argument that attacks the character of an opponent and not the content of the opponent's position or argument. For example, arguing that because John is a jerk or John is uneducated that he cannot be correct.

Artificial intelligence (AI), strong The view that an appropriately programmed computer can have "intelligence," or, more generally, that such a computer can have a whole variety of cognitive states such as believing, wanting, intending, understanding, and so on.

Artificial intelligence (AI), weak The view that computers give us a useful research tool for investigating the mind, but they do not have and cannot be programmed to have true cognitive states in the sense that humans have such states.

Atheism The view that God does not exist.

Automaton A self-moving mechanical being capable of simulating the behavior of a conscious agent, but itself not a conscious agent.

Autonomy The capacity, right, or actual condition of self-government, or the determination of one's own actions.

Bayes's theorem A statistical theorem describing how, given an observed outcome, the conditional probability of each of a set of possible causes can be computed from knowledge of the probability of each cause and the conditional probability of the outcome, given each cause.

Begging the question The logical fallacy of assuming in the premises of an argument the very conclusion which is to be proved. For example, to argue that God exists because the Bible says so, and the Bible is reliable because it is the word of God, is to assume the very proposition one set out to prove in the process of its own proof. Also called "petitio principii." (See *circular reasoning.*)

Behaviorism, logical A view about the meaning of mental state terms. The view claims that mental terms such as "pain," "belief," or "desire" are equivalent in meaning to behavioral terms. This is supposed to show that mental states are dispositions to behave in certain ways. (Also called analytical behaviorism.)

Behaviorism, radical The methodological claim that psychology should study only regularities exhibited in behavior—such as principles connecting stimuli and responses. (Also called methodological behaviorism.)

Benevolence Desire or disposition to be good to others, kindly and charitable.

Bourgeois A member of the middle class in a market economy, with its characteristic tastes and ideas. Originally, the term referred to the class of capitalists in a market economy who owned the means of production.

Brute fact A fact for which there can be no explanation.

Cartesian Of, pertaining to, or related to Descartes or his philosophy.

Capitalism An economic system in which trade and industry are controlled by private owners. The owners provide the capital with which to produce goods and employ workers.

Catastrophism The geological doctrine, prevalent well into the 18th century, that the geological features of the surface of the Earth are the result of violent cataclysms. The doctrine assumed that the Earth is only a few thousand years old, and was congenial to theological accounts of the origin and history of the Earth.

Categorical imperative A moral directive from reason that is binding without condition; a command that applies to all rational beings, no matter what. Kant formulated the categorical imperative as: "Act only according to that maxim by which you can at the same time will that it should become a universal law."

Causal theory of perception The theory that material objects are the causes of the ideas, appearances, or sense data we have of them. The material substance itself is distinct from its own qualities (including its *primary qualities*) and, not being directly perceivable, must simply be posited as an unknowable *substratum* for its powers and properties.

Causally possible Consistent with the causal laws of nature. A statement is causally possible if it is true in at least one physically *possible world.*

Causation The relationship between two events, one as cause, the other as effect. If the first event occurs, the second produces or necessitates the second.

Causa sui the cause of itself

Ceteris paribus other things being equal

Christolatry The worship of Christ as divine.

Circular reasoning When the conclusion is concealed within the premises of an argument. (See *begging the question.*)

Civil disobedience A nonviolent, conscientious, public form of protest contrary to the law that is done with the aim of bringing about a change in the law or policies of the government.

Cogito ergo sum This means "I think, therefore I am." This inference played a central role in Descartes's argument for the distinction between the mental and the physical and in his response to *skepticism.*

Cognitive process Mental operations such as reasoning, inferring, deliberating, planning, and perceiving.

Cognitive science The interdisciplinary study of cognitive processes in human beings, animals and machines. The core disciplines are psychology, computer science, linguistics, neuroscience, and philosophy.

Compatibilism See *determinism, soft.*

Computational theory of mind The view that mental states and processes are identical to computational states and processes. On this view, the mind is a (suitably programmed) computer.

Conclusion In an *argument,* the statement that is being argued for and that the *premises* are meant to jointly establish.

Consequentialism A type of moral theory stating that to act morally we must base our actions on their probable results or consequences, rather than acting out of duty, in cases where duty and promoting good consequences come into conflict. It can be contrasted with *deontology.* Examples of consequentialism are *ethical egoism, utilitarianism,* and *ethical altruism.*

Contiguity Contact or proximity; the state of being close together.

Contingent being A being whose existence depends on something else and therefore might not have come to exist. For example, your existence was contingent on your mother having conceived. (See also *necessary being.*)

Contractarianism The theory that the correct way to derive a principle of justice is to decide whether it would be chosen over any alternative principle of justice that could be proposed to a group of normally self-interested, rational persons.

Contradiction Occurs when a statement is alleged to be both true and false.

Conventionalism The doctrine that the truth of a proposition, or a class of propositions, is determined not by fact but by social agreement or usage. Conventionalism is opposed to versions of realism, which hold that the truth of a proposition, or a class of propositions, is determined by objective facts of nature.

Corollary A proposition that is incidentally proved in proving another proposition.

Corporeal Bodily.

Corporeal substances Bodily substances.

Cosmogony (From the Greek word "kosmogonia" for creation of the world) Theory of the origin and development of the *cosmos.*

Cosmological argument Argument for the existence of God that holds (1) every being is either a *dependent being* or a *self-existent being;* (2) not every being can be a dependent being; (3) therefore, there exists a self-existent being, who is God.

Cosmos (From the Greek for "order") The whole universe conceived as ordered and law-governed.

Counterfactuals Statements describing what would have been true if something else were true. The interesting property of such statements for philosophical purposes is that they can be true even when the conditions described are not actually met. For instance, the statement that this wine glass would shatter if thrown to the ground could be true of only an unshattered glass—one that has never met the conditional part of the counterfactual. Counterfactuals are thus a good way of expressing dispositions, tendencies, and other scientifically interesting regularities.

Creationism The theory in the philosophy of biology that God intervenes into the natural order to create new species and to create people.

Criterion A standard of judgment that is either a sufficient condition for something being the case, or a condition that provides good evidence for something being the case.

Culpable Deserving blame.

Cultural relativism The view that morality is relative to a given culture; what is right in one culture may be wrong in another. For example, cannibalism might be wrong for Greeks but right for Callations. Cultural relativism goes beyond merely stating the fact that different cultures have different beliefs; it asserts that for each society, its beliefs are really right (not just believed to be right by its members). (See *moral relativism.*)

Darwinism Acceptance of the theory of *evolution* by natural selection developed originally by Charles Darwin (1809–1882).

Decision theory The theory of rational choices aimed at achieving an optimal outcome where the amount of information available to the agent is limited. The agent has only incomplete information about the true state of affairs and the possible consequences of each possible action.

Deductive argument An argument whose *conclusion* must be true if the *premises* are all true, as long as the argument is valid.

Deicide The killing of God.

De novo anew

Deontology A type of moral theory stating that morality consists in doing one's duty, rather than in considering the probable consequences of one's actions, in cases where duty and the promotion of good consequences come into conflict. Can be contrasted to *consequentialism.* An example of a deontological theory is Kantian ethics.

Dependent being A being whose existence is causally dependent on and explained by other things.

Determinism The theory that all events, including human actions and choices, are, without exception, totally determined.

Determinism, hard A kind of determinist view that rejects the compatibility of determinism and free will.

Determinism, soft The view that holds that *determinism* is true and that determinism is compatible with free will and responsibility.

Deus ex machina "God from a machine." An artificial or improbable device introduced to resolve an entanglement in a plot or argument. A person invokes a *deus ex machina* when introducing some contrivance to save a theory from some large problem.

Diallelus A vicious circle in a proof.

Diarchal Pertaining to a joint mode of government by two independent authorities.

Dilemma An argument that presents a choice between two alternatives.

Divine command theory The view that actions are right in virtue of being commanded by God.

Doxastic (From the Greek word, "doxa," for "belief.") Theories of justification that are doxastic are those that hold that a belief can be justified only by another belief.

Dualism Generally, the view that there are two kinds of stuff. More specifically, "dualism" is associated with the doctrine that mental states, events, or processes are distinct from physical or material states, events, or processes.

Dualistic interactionism The view that mental states, events, and processes can causally affect physical states, events, and processes.

Efficient cause The physical or mechanical cause of an effect or thing. Efficient causes are one of the four types of causes of Aristotle. Consider a table. For Aristotle, the "material" cause of the table is the material or stuff that the table is made of. The "formal" cause is the blueprint or shape that determines the form of the table. The "final" cause is the reason or purpose for which the table was built. The "efficient cause" is the actual agency or mechanical production of the table by the builder out of material. Efficient causation is often contrasted with "teleological" causation, causation that is the result of purposes or ends (Aristotelian "final" causes).

Egalitarianism A theory asserting equality among all people, usually political or economic.

Egoistic hedonism The theory that, in deciding how to act, a person ought to choose (among those acts open) the act that is likely to cause the greatest net balance of pleasure over pain for oneself.

Elective freedom The freedom to do, or to forebear from doing, one's duty. (See also *rational freedom*.)

Eliminative materialism The view that mental states and processes as we ordinarily conceive of them simply do not exist, in the same way as witches and phlogiston do not exist.

Empirical generalization A statement of the form: All *F*s are *G*s. For example, "All the coins in my pockets are pennies." Such generalizations need not express a tendency, disposition, or natural law.

Empirical hypothesis A kind of *synthetic statement* whose function is to sum up past experience and enable us to successfully predict or anticipate future experience.

Empiricism The theory that all our ideas come from experience and that no proposition about any matter of fact can be known independently of experience.

Epicureanism From the views of the Greek philosopher Epicurus, 341–270 B.C. Epicureans advocated the pursuit of certain pleasures that bring tranquillity and freedom from mental anxiety in order to achieve happiness. In metaphysics, Epicurus was an atomist who attempted to avoid *determinism* by allowing for chance events due to the unpredictable "swerving" of atoms.

Epiphenomenalism The view that there is only one form of interaction between the mental and the physical, that in which the physical affects the mental. In this view, the mental can never affect the physical. The mind is not itself a material thing; rather, it is a distinct but causally impotent by-product (*epiphenomenon*) of the world of physics. This is a kind of *dualism*.

Epiphenomenon A mere by-product of a process that has no real effect on the process itself.

Epistemic Relating to knowledge.

Epistemology The theory of knowledge. The study of the origin, nature, and limits of knowledge, including especially the study of the nature of epistemic justification.

Equivocation A *fallacy of argument* whereby one uses an ambiguous word in more than one way.

Ergo therefore

Eros sexual longing or desire; love

Eschatology The development of theories relating to the end of life, as in Christian theology, or to the ultimate end of the *cosmos*.

Esoteric Intended only for people with special knowledge or interest. The opposite of "exoteric" (opinions or ideas suitable for the uninitiated).

Ethical altruism The theory that morality requires us to forget our own interests and selflessly devote ourselves to the interests of others.

Ethical egoism The view that to act morally, individuals should act solely so as to promote their own best interests. Ethical egoism is a moral view; it states a thesis about how humans ought to act. In this it differs from *psychological egoism*, which states a thesis about how humans always do act.

An ethical egoist holds that people do not always act to promote their own well-being, even though they should.

Ethical naturalism The theory which claims that, despite appearances, moral facts really are natural, scientific facts.

Ethical nonnaturalism The theory which claims that there are no true naturalistic analyses of moral terms.

Ethical relativism See *moral relativism*.

Ethical skepticism The view that no moral knowledge is possible.

Ethical subjectivism See *meta-ethical subjectivism* and *normative subjectivism*.

Evolution The process by which something develops gradually from a different form. In biology, evolution is the origin and transformations of biological populations through time due to genetic variation and interaction with the environment, and not by special creation.

Ex hypothesi by hypothesis

Existentialism A loose-knit philosophical viewpoint connecting a rejection of determinism with a focus on the responsibility of the agent for making his or her own character out of his or her freely chosen actions. Existentialism rejects the rationalistic view of the universe as planned and comprehensible and consequently faces life with a feeling of dread and a sense of the absurdity of life. Major existentialists are Kierkegaard and Sartre.

Ex nihilo out of nothing

Expected utility (EU) The utility of an uncertain outcome multiplied by its probability.

Fallacy A logical mistake in reasoning, especially one which often gives the appearance of being sound.

Falsifiable Refutable by experience. For example, if a theory predicts that an eclipse will occur on a certain day, then experience will refute the theory if the eclipse does not occur. *Freudianism* and *Creationism* are often criticized as being unfalsifiable.

Fatalism The theory that all events are fated to happen; they would have happened no matter what the person involved might have done to avoid it. This is a stronger view than *determinism*.

Fideist A theist whose belief is based on faith rather than argument or reason.

Final cause The end, purpose, or goal for which something is working or moving; one of Aristotle's four causes. (See *efficient cause*.)

Freudianism Relating to the views of Sigmund Freud, 1856–1939. Freud developed an elaborate psychological theory focusing on sexual desires and the subconscious. For Freud, the ego is the conscious self. The ego stands between the Id, which demands that basic sexual and physical desires be satisfied, and the superego, which represses the desires of the Id. Freud hypothesized that there exist a variety of repressive mechanisms responsible for neurotic behavior. Freud developed the therapeutic technique of psychoanalysis.

Functional equivalence Two systems are functionally equivalent when they do the same tasks or when they have the same capacities. (See *strong equivalence*.)

Functionalism Generally, the view that concepts should be defined according to their function. In cognitive theory, the view that mental states, events, and processes are "functional" states of the brain (or other *hardware*). Functional states of a device are those that are defined in terms of their relations to the device's input, its internal transitions, and its output. According to the functionalist, these causal relations and dispositions are what constitute the mental.

Gestalt A conception of organization based on the idea that a perceived whole is not just the sum of its parts. The parts are organized into structures and derive their character from the structure of the whole. Gestalt psychology denies the atomistic theory of perception whereby perceptions of patterns or wholes arrive from constructing the whole out of its independently existing parts.

Good will For Kant, a good will determines to act in accordance with universal moral law, regardless of the effects of the act in the world, selfish or otherwise.

Greatest happiness principle The utilitarian principle, put forth by John Stuart Mill, stating that actions are right in proportion as they promote happiness (pleasure) and wrong in proportion as they promote pain. (See *utilitarianism*.)

Hardware The physical apparatus that executes the software in programming a computer. The analog for an organism is its brain (often called its "wetware"). (See also *software*.)

Hedonism The view that pleasure is the ultimate good for humans.

Hedonism, universalistic The theory that in deciding how to act, I ought to choose (among those acts open to me) the act that is likely to cause the greatest net balance of pleasure over pain, counting my own interests as no less and no more important than everyone else's. The theory is universalistic because it considers everyone equally and hedonistic because it tells us to choose the act that will create the most pleasure.

Heuristics Rules of thumb which are useful generalizations for problem-solving tasks, such as "get your queen out early" in chess.

Hierophany Pertaining to the official expounding of sacred mysteries or ceremonies or the interpretation of *esoteric* principles.

Humanism Generally, any view in which human interests and welfare play a central role. More specifically, the theory that emphasizes reason, scientific inquiry, and human welfare, often rejecting the importance of belief in God.

Humanitarian theory of punishment The theory that the goal of punishment should be to mend or "cure" the offender, rather than to punish because he or she deserves it.

Hypothetical imperative An action that you should do if you want to promote some goal or end you already have. For example, if you want a good grade, you have a hypothetical imperative to study; if you want some chocolate ice cream, you have a hypothetical imperative to go to the store and buy some. Can be contrasted to a *categorical imperative*, which says that you should perform an action regardless of your ends.

Ideal morality Standards of moral excellence that a moral tradition or community sets up as models to aspire to and admire. Praise, honor, and respect are the rewards of those who live according to the standards of ideal morality. However, people are not in general blamed for failing to live up to the standards of ideal morality, or even for not aiming at them. (See *practice morality*.)

Idealism The theory that there are only immaterial minds and their mental "contents." The body itself is nothing but a collection of actual or possible sense-data—sights, sounds, touches, and smells. By holding that there is only mind and no matter, idealism avoids the problems of causal interaction between radically different kinds of substances.

Idealism, subjective The theory that matter is merely the projection of a finite mind and has no external, independent existence.

Identity theory A kind of *materialism* stating that mental events are simply identical to brain processes, the same way that lightning flashes are "identical" to electrical discharges. The mental event (a thought, desire, or sensation) *is* a brain process.

Ideology Any set of general ideas or system of beliefs that form the basis of an economic or political theory. The term is used pejoratively to characterize a person's set of beliefs as both false and as adopted to disguise or ignore the economic or political realities of the status quo.

Ignoratio elenchi The *fallacy* of irrelevance, that is, of proving a *conclusion* that is not relevant to the matter at hand.

Immaterialist One who believes that reality is not material. (See *idealism*.)

Immoralist One who rejects conventional morality, arguing that it is in his or her, or even our, best interests, and therefore rational, to act against the dictates of conventional morality.

Immutable Unchangeable.

Imperative Command. (See also *categorical imperative; hypothetical imperative*.)

Imperfect duty A duty that is not owed to any particular person or persons. For example, I have an imperfect duty to help alleviate poverty, but I do not owe it to any particular poor person to feed her, nor to each individual poor person. (See *perfect duty*.)

Impersonal evil Evil that is natural and not caused by human action—for example, natural disasters and disease. Even if humans were morally perfect, there would still be impersonal evil. (Also called nonmoral evil.)

Incompatibilism See *determinism, hard*.

Indeterminate Not fixed in extent or character. The truth value of a statement is indeterminate when the relevant facts fail to determine whether the statement is true or false.

Indeterminism The view that some events are not determined.

Indeterminism, simple The theory that human action is not determined; rather, it is caused by inner *volition*.

Indubitable Incapable of being doubted; beyond all doubt. Descartes, for example, searched for indubitable truths to combat *skepticism*.

Inductive argument An argument whose *premises* establish a probability (rather than a certainty) that its conclusion is true; for example, if no one has ever seen a green flamingo, then there probably are no green flamingos. The argument from design is an example of an inductive argument.

Inductive inference An *inference* from evidence to hypothesis, where the evidence does not entail or necessitate that the hypothesis is true, but it is nevertheless reasonable to suppose that the hypothesis is true.

Inference The movement from *premises* to a *conclusion*. Inferences can be *deductive* or *inductive*.

In infinitum into infinity; endlessly

Innate idea An idea that we are born with inherited dispositions to have. *Rationalism* argues that human minds have the disposition to acquire concepts such as being, substance, duration, and even God, once a certain amount of experience is added.

Intentionality The property that some mental states have of being about something. Thus, one belief might be about Caesar's crossing the Rubicon, and another might be about the first person to orbit the Earth. By contrast, a mental state such as a free-floating anxiety need not be about anything in particular and thus not have intentionality.

Interactionism See *dualistic interactionism.*

Intertheoretic reduction See *reduction.*

Intrinsic good Something that is good in and of itself.

Intuition Direct knowledge or awareness of a truth or fact, independent of any reasoning process.

Intuitionism Any theory in which *intuition* is appealed to as the basis of knowledge.

Ipso facto by that very fact

Justification In *epistemology,* knowledge is traditionally defined as justified true belief. To know *p* you must not only believe *p, p* must be true and your belief that *p* is true must be justified. Epistemologists disagree about the nature of justification. Some think that a belief is justified if it is caused in the right way or if it is based on another belief that counts as knowledge or if the agent can give reasons in defense of why she holds the belief, and so forth.

Kin altruism The disposition to favor the interests of one's near relatives (as distinct from one's own interests) over the interests of complete strangers. Such a disposition may have evolutionary advantages by increasing the probability that those who share many of the individual's genes will survive and reproduce.

Lamarckism In the philosophy of biology, the view that offspring may inherit the characteristics that their parents acquired during their adult lives. This view is no longer held to be credible.

Lexical order In John Rawls's theory of justice, the ordering of principles that requires us to satisfy the first principle before going on to consider the second principle; once the first principle is satisfied, we can go on to attempt to satisfy the second principle. (Also called serial order.)

Libertarianism In metaphysics, the theory that we possess free will and that our free will is neither determined nor the result of random chance, but instead the result of rational agency. In politics and economics, the theory that emphasizes the importance of personal liberty as opposed to state interference. Political libertarians often oppose taxation for social welfare programs as unjust intrusions into personal freedom.

Liberum arbitrium indifferentiae The freedom of indifference; the ability of the will to choose independently of *antecedent* determination.

Liturgy A fixed form of public worship used in churches.

Logically impossible Not *logically possible.*

Logically possible Consistent with the laws of logic. A statement is logically possible if it is true in at least one logically *possible world:* for example, that the next President of the United States is a woman. A statement is logically impossible if it is inconsistent with the laws of logic. A logically impossible statement is, or entails, a contradiction. For example, that some squares are round. Since squares are, by definition, not round, it is a contradiction to say that some squares are round.

Manslaughter The act of killing a person unlawfully but not intentionally or by negligence.

Marxism From the views of the German philosopher Karl Marx (1818–1883), on which communism is putatively based. Marxism rejects *capitalism* and predicts the development of society beyond capitalism through a revolution by the working class. Inherent to all forms of Marxism is the rejection of the exploitation of labor due to the private control of the means of production.

Materialism The view that everything—every object, state, event, and process—is a material object, state, event, or process and nothing else. According to materialists, there is no immaterial mind or soul and thus no problem of interaction between radically different kinds of substances. (Also called *physicalism.*)

Maxim A principle or rule of conduct.

Maximin strategy A principle of decision theory for choice under uncertainty. The strategy ranks the best decision as that which is superior to the worst outcomes of other possible decisions. The strategy "maximizes" the "minimum" outcome.

Mediately perceivable Perceivable indirectly, by means of something else.

Mendelian genetics The theory developed by Gregor Mendel (1822–1884) that the inheritance of any particular characteristic is controlled by the inheritance of *genes,* which occur in pairs and separate independently of each other in meiosis, a stage of cell division.

Mens rea The accompanying intention to commit a crime or pursue a wrongful aim which makes the act a crime.

Mentalism Originally, the term referred to idealistic doctrines such as Berkeley's, which held that only minds and their subjective states exist. In contemporary philosophy of mind, mentalism is the view that *cognitive processes* can be explained only by postulating a set of internal mental representations and rules that operate on the representations. (See *artificial intelligence* and *computational theory of mind*.)

Meta-ethical subjectivism The view that ethical judgments are neither true nor false, they are simply expressions of commands, preferences, or emotions, and as such are not eligible candidates for truth.

Meta-ethical theory A theory that focuses on whether normative theories can be justified or true.

Metaphysics The study of the ultimate nature of reality. Common metaphysical views are *materialism*, *idealism*, and *dualism*.

Methodicide The death or killing of method or methodology.

Methodist Epistemologists who first answer the question, How are we to decide whether we know? What are the *criteria* of knowledge? and then use their answer to go on to answer the question, What do we know? What is the extent of our knowledge? A methodist is the opposite of a *particularist*.

Methodological behaviorism See *behaviorism, radical*.

Modus ponens In logic, an argument of the following form: If P then Q.

>P.

>Therefore Q.

Modus tolens In logic, an argument of the following form: If P then Q.

>Not-Q.

>Therefore Not-P.

Monism The view that reality is ultimately made up of only one kind of thing. *Idealism* and *materialism* are two different monistic theories. Can be contrasted to *dualism*, which holds that there are two kinds of things: mind and body.

Monotheism Belief in one, and only one, God.

Moral equivalence The idea that everyone's ultimate moral views are as plausible as everyone else's.

Moral evil Evil that is caused by human action, rather than natural causes such as earthquakes. If humans were as morally perfect as God, there would be no moral evil.

Morally infallible Unable to make mistakes in moral matters.

Moral relativism The view that the "truth" of moral judgments is always relative to a given system of beliefs that itself cannot be proven correct.

Mutation Change or alteration in form.

The Myth of Gyges The story in Plato's *Republic* that is meant to show that injustice is in our self-interest; Gyges found a ring of invisibility that allowed him to act unjustly and reap the benefits. Plato argues against the *immoralist*'s challenge presented by the Myth of Gyges in the rest of the *Republic*.

Naïve realism See *realism, naïve*.

Narcissism A tendency to self-worship. An excessive or erotic interest in one's own personal features.

Naturalism (1) The view that the universe is self-existent, self-explanatory, and self-operating, requiring no supernatural or spiritual cause or explanation. (2) The view that nature does not require a *teleological* explanation; scientific laws are adequate to cover all phenomena.

Necessary being A being whose existence depends on nothing else and who necessarily has to exist. Some people have argued that God is such a being. (See also *contingent being*.)

Necessary condition If *A* is a necessary condition for *B*, then *B* cannot be true unless *A* is true. For instance, being alive is a necessary condition for going golfing. If you are dead, you cannot golf. (See *sufficient condition*.)

Negligence Lack of proper care or attention; carelessness.

Nonmaleficence Not injuring others.

Nonmoral evil See *impersonal evil*.

Normative Having to do with norms or standards; regulative. In ethics, norms are standards for right conduct.

Normative subjectivism The view that ethical judgments can be true or false, but that their truth depends entirely on whether they accurately report the sentiments of those who issue the judgments.

Normative theory A theory that attempts to specify conditions under which an action is morally right or wrong.

Objective Something that is objective has a particular nature that is not dependent on us or our judgments of it. For example, those who hold that there are objective moral truths believe that such truths are there for us to discover and hold regardless of any of our beliefs or judgments.

Occasionalism A kind of *dualism* stating that mind and body do not really interact. Being kicked does not *cause* my pain; rather, it is the occasion for God, whose infinite nature somehow encompasses both mind and matter, to cause me to feel pain. Similarly, my mental states are occasion for God to cause my body to act.

Omnipotent All-powerful; able to do anything.

Omniscient All-knowing.

Ontological argument An *a priori* argument for the existence of God stating that the very concept or definition of God automatically entails that God exists; because of the special nature of the concept, there is no way that God could fail to exist.

Ontology The theory of being, or of existence. From the Greek *ontos* (being) and *logos* (theory, account).

Ontophany The appearance of being; the manifestation of existence.

Original contract In *social contract theories,* the hypothetical contract that establishes the fundamental principles of justice and/or structure of society, to which all rational, normally self-interested persons would agree in entering society.

Original position In John Rawls's contractarian theory of justice (*contractarianism*), the original position is the hypothetical gathering of people in a condition of equal power and ignorance for the purpose of determining fair principles of justice for society. (See *veil of ignorance.*)

Orthodox Beliefs that are declared by a group to be true and normative. Heresy is a departure from and relative to a given orthodoxy. Of or holding correct or conventional or currently accepted beliefs, especially in religion.

Paradox of hedonism This paradox is that the single-minded pursuit of happiness is necessarily self-defeating, for the way to get happiness is to forget it; then it may come to you. If you aim exclusively at pleasure itself, with no concern for the things that bring pleasure, then pleasure will never come. One must first desire something other than satisfaction to achieve satisfaction.

Paradox of omnipotence Can an *omnipotent* being make things which he subsequently cannot control, or make rules which bind himself? For example, can God create a rock so heavy that even He cannot lift it? On the one hand, it seems as though he should be able to, since he is, by definition, able to do anything. But if he did make a rule that bound himself—which he could not violate—it seems as though he would not still be all-powerful.

Parallelism A kind of *dualism* stating that mind and body only appear to interact because of a kind of "preestablished harmony" between them, like two clocks independently striking at the same moment. Thus, because of this harmony, when I kick the table, I also feel pain; the kicking does not cause the pain.

Particular A specific example of a class of things, rather than the class itself or that which defines the class. An individual rather than a *universal.*

Particularist Epistemologists who first answer the question, What do we know? What is the extent of our knowledge? and then use their answer to go on to answer the question, How are we to decide whether we know? What are the *criteria* of knowledge? A particularist is the opposite of a *methodist.*

Pascal's wager Blaise Pascal's argument that we should believe in (or "bet on") God because the stakes are infinitely high on the side of God. The rewards for believing correctly and the penalties for wrongly not believing are high, and the costs of believing mistakenly are low. (Also called a wager argument.)

Passive euthanasia Mercy killing that involves the medical staff's decision, in conjunction with the patient, to allow the patient to die.

Paternalism Governing as though a benevolent parent-figure.

Patriarchy The domination or government of a social structure or institution by the fathers or male elders.

Pedagogy The art of teaching.

Perceptron A device designed by Frank Rosenblatt in the 1950s to understand perceptual recognition tasks. A perceptron consists of three layers of connected units—an input layer, an associative layer, and an output layer. Additional layers of units can be added to further complicate the device.

Perfect duty A duty that is owed to a particular person or persons. For example, I have a perfect duty to my banker to repay my loan and to every person not to lie to them. (See *imperfect duty.*)

Personal identity The problem of explaining what constitutes both the identity of a person at a time and the identity of a person through time.

Petitio principii See *begging the question* and *circular reasoning.*

Phenomenalism The theory that our only knowledge of reality is mind-dependent; the phenomena we experience are the only objects of knowledge. Phenomenalists may affirm or deny the existence of a reality of things-in-themselves behind the phenomena.

Phenomenology A descriptive study of subjective processes such as consciousness, feelings, emotions, and so on. The study of "what it is like" to be in a certain mental state. (See *qualia.*)

Physicalism (1) *Materialism.* (2) The theory that every object, state, event, or process can be completely described and explained by the physical sciences. And we are to understand that some things in the physical sciences are *not* material—for instance, gravitational fields and electromagnetic radiation. According to this use of the term, one could believe that physicalism is true but *materialism* is false.

Physicalism, token A version of *physicalism* that contends that being in a mental state (process, etc.)

always involves being in a physical state (process, etc.). This allows for the possibility that there might be different physical states for different thinking beings. For instance, adding 2 + 2, for a human being might involve certain electrical activity in neurons located in certain areas of the brain; but adding 2 + 2 for a computer, might involve electrical activity in silicon chips.

Physicalism, type A version of *physicalism* that denies that it is possible for different thinkers to have the same kind of mental state without being in the same kind of physical state. Thus, in this view, a person and a computer could both be said to be adding 2 + 2 only if there were some physical process that they were both in at the same time.

Platonism The philosophy of Plato stating that the *particular,* individual things we see are merely imperfect "copies" of perfect, unchanging, universal forms.

Polytheism Belief in more than one God.

Posit To assume that something is true without argument, either because it is a self-evident truth or merely as an arbitrary assumption.

Possible world A complete state of affairs, and so the actual world is itself a possible world. Complete states of affairs distinct from the actual world are ways the actual world might have been. Complete states of affairs that are consistent with the laws of logic are logically possible worlds. Complete states of affairs that are consistent with both the laws of logic and the laws of nature are physically or causally possible worlds.

Postulate A self-evident truth or fundamental principle.

Practice morality The standards of conduct actually expected of, and generally practiced by, persons living within a given moral tradition or community. The part of morality concerned with requirements, those standards for which people are blamed, criticized, or punished for failing to live up to. See *ideal morality* and *supererogation.*

Pragmatic Of or pertaining to practical considerations.

Pragmatism The theory that the meaning or value of concepts should be understood in terms of their practical consequences.

Predicate That which is said of a subject.

Predominant egoism The claim that as a matter of fact the egoistic or self-interested motivations of human behavior tend to override their altruistic or other-regarding motivations until they have achieved a satisfactory level of security and well being. (See *altruism* and *psychological egoism.*)

Premise In an *argument,* the reasons that are given to support the *conclusion.*

Prima facie at first appearance

Prima facie duty A self-evident duty, such as promise keeping, which we are required to act upon if no other, more weighty, duty intervenes.

Primary qualities Intrinsic characteristics of a physical object itself, such as solidity, extension in space (size), figure (shape), motion or rest, and number. Primary qualities are ones that objects would continue to possess even if there were no perceiving beings in the world, for they are inseparable from the material object and found in every part of it. (See also *secondary qualities.*)

Principle of sufficient reason (PSR) For everything that happens there must be a sufficient reason for its happening and not some other thing.

Privation The condition of a substance that lacks a certain quality which it is capable of possessing and normally does possess. Loss or lack of something.

Problem of evil Problem posed for theists: If God is all-good, *omnipotent,* and *omniscient,* how can his existence be compatible with the existence of evil?

Program A sequence of instructions, in some computer language, that causes a physical apparatus (*hardware*) to perform some task or sequence of operations.

Projectible property When past instances of a property are a guide to predictions about future instances of a property. For example, if every raven I have seen is black, then it is reasonable to predict that future ravens will be black. But if every raven I have seen is alive in the twentieth century, it does not follow that it is reasonable to predict that future ravens will be alive in the twentieth century. Being black is a projectible property of ravens; being alive in the twentieth century is not.

Propositional calculus (logic) Systems of logic that concern themselves with how statements can be combined—using such connectives as "and," "or," "if then," and "not"—into more complex statements and with the logical properties possessed by such statements.

Prudential reasonableness When an act conforms to the norms of rationality that govern the selection and performance of actions.

Psychological egoism A theory about the psychology of humans stating that the only thing anyone is capable of desiring or pursuing ultimately (as an end in itself) is one's own self-interest. According to psychological egoism, people always act selfishly. If someone appears to act altruistically, that person is doing it only because taking the interests of other people is the means to promoting his or her own good; genuinely disinterested acts of benevolence do not exist. (See also *ethical egoism.*)

Psychological egoistic hedonism A common form of *psychological egoism* stating that our only kind of ultimate desire is to prolong our own pleasure and reduce our own pains.

Punitive Inflicting or intending to inflict punishment.

QED which has been demonstrated

Qua As; in the character or capacity of. For example, your duties *qua* student are different from your duties *qua* friend.

Qualia The qualitative feels of mental experiences: the hurt of pain, the color of red, the taste of wine, the scent of a rose, the longing of love, the ecstasy of an orgasm. The qualitative character of an experience is "what it is like" to have that experience. (See *phenomenology.*)

Ratiocination The process of logical reasoning.

Rational freedom The freedom that a person has to the degree that her will is led by moral principles. (See also *elective freedom.*)

Rationalism The theory that there are *innate ideas* and that certain general propositions (usually called necessary, or *a priori,* propositions) can be known to be true in advance of or in the absence of empirical verification.

Rawls, John, (1921–2002) American moral and political philosopher, author of *A Theory of Justice,* 1971.

Realism The theory that the objects of our knowledge have an independent existence rather than being mind-dependent.

Realism, naïve The theory that *primary* and *secondary qualities* are both strictly part of physical objects and that both can exist quite independently of perceiving minds.

Realism, representative The theory that our ideas are faithful representations of the real, external world.

Realism, sophisticated The theory that physical substances and their *primary qualities* can exist independently of perceiving beings and only the *secondary qualities* are mind-dependent.

Reciprocity A relation of mutual exchange.

Reductio ad absurdum A method of demonstrating that a proposition is false by showing that its truth, along with other accepted propositions, would entail a logical contradiction.

Reduction One theory (T_1) reduces to another theory (T_2) when the propositions and principles of the first are entailed by the second, then apply to the same cases, but the second theory does not contain some items (such as "light" or "belief") from the first. These items in T_1 have been reduced to something else in T_2. (Also called intertheoretic reduction.)

Reify To treat a concept or idea as a thing. Reification is the philosophical mistake of treating a concept, abstraction, convention, or artificial construct as if it were a real natural thing.

Relativism In general, the doctrine that truth is relative to the standpoint of the individual or of the community or culture.

Relativism, cultural Relativism about values stems from the fact that the values or ethical principles of individuals vary widely. Cultural relativism holds that most disagreements about values or ethical principles stem from enculturation in different ethical traditions. Cultural relativism need not entail *moral relativism.*

Relativism, moral The view that the truth of moral judgments is relative to the judging subject or community. We ought to do that, and only that, which we think we ought to do. The having of an opinion about what we ought to do, individually or collectively, makes it true that that is what we ought to do.

Repentance The feeling of regret about what one has done or failed to do.

Res cogitans (Latin, "thinking thing") Used by Descartes to refer to the mind.

Result theories of punishment See *utilitarian theories of punishment.*

Retributive theory The theory of punishment stating that the primary justification of punishment is the fact that a committed offense deserves punishment, rather than any advantage gained through punishment.

Rule utilitarianism The view that the standards of conduct should be those which, if widely adopted, would lead to the greatest overall utility.

Secondary qualities Those qualities of an object (such as color, taste, smell, sound, warmth, and cold) that exist (according to some theories) only when actually sensed and then only "in the mind" of the one who senses them. (See also *primary qualities.*)

Self-existent being A being whose existence is not dependent on other things, but rather is accounted for by its own nature.

Self-presenting That which is directly evident to an agent. Thoughts are self-presenting if to have them is to think that you have them. So if I believe that Socrates is mortal, then if my belief is self-presenting it will be the case by that very fact that it is evident to me that I believe that Socrates is mortal.

Semantics The study of the meanings of words.

Serial order See *lexical order.*

Skepticism The position that denies the possibility of knowledge. A skeptic might hold that no